NEW OLD-STOCK
BREITLING

Here's your chance to
"turn back the hands of time."
Genuine old factory stock production through 1972 complete with original Breitling labels.

Visit our web site for additional models and information. www.oldworldjewelers.com

809.4 Cosmonaut **$2,195**

815.4 Long Playing **$1,295**

2114 Chrono-matic **$1,995**

8808.3 Chronomat Auto **$3,195**

7101 Pupitre **$1,995**

2105.3 Superocean **$1,495**

2734.3 Football **$1,195**

7104.3 Long Playing **$895**

2034.3 Datora **$895**

7808 Chronomat Manual **$2,895**

2016 Sprint **$750**

7103.3 Long Playing Date **$895**

AVAILABLE EXCLUSIVELY AT **OLD WORLD JEWELERS**

1301 West 22nd St. Suite 308, Oak Brook, IL 60523 630-990-0100 **1-800-322-3871** www.oldworldjewelers.com

COOKSEY SHUGART

TOM ENGLE

RICHARD E. GILBERT

The *Complete Price Guide To Watches*, published by Shugart Publications, authored by Cooksey Shugart with co-authors Tom Engle and Richard E. Gilbert. All three have been active horologists since the early 1960's and members of the National Association of Watch and Clock Collectors since the early 1970's. They have searched for fine timepieces all over the world and are the foremost experts in the field of antique horology.

They each have traveled extensively to auctions throughout the United States and Europe, to regional and national conventions, meets and shows, and keep an up-to-date pulse of the watch market. They continually expand their horological reference library and their extensive selection of watch photographs. Because of the unique knowledge of the market these co-authors possess, this volume should be considered one of the most authoritative watch references on the market today. Each edition contains updated and revised information and prices, and has become the accepted standard reference work of the watch market. ''We see this book as an extension of the information we have been gathering for years and take great pride in sharing it with other collectors who have a deep and abiding interest in watches,'' the authors stated.

Mr. Shugart resides in Cleveland, Tenn., Mr. Engle resides in Louisville, KY. and Mr. Gilbert resides in Sarasota, FL.

COMPLETE
PRICE GUIDE TO
WATCHES

COOKSEY SHUGART
TOM ENGLE • RICHARD E. GILBERT

EDITED BY MARTHA SHUGART

Important Notice. All of the information, including valuations, in this book has been compiled from the most reliable sources, and every effort has been made to eliminate errors and questionable data. Nevertheless, the possibility of error, in a work of such immense scope, always exists. The publisher or authors will not be held responsible for losses which may occur in the purchase, sale, statements of its advertisers or other transaction of items, because of information contained herein. Readers who feel they have discovered errors are invited to write and inform us, so they may be corrected in subsequent editions.

The Complete Price Guide To Watches is published independently and is not associated with any watch manufacturer.

* This book endeavors to be a <u>Guide</u> or helpful manual and offers a wealth of material and information to be used as a tool not as a absolute document. The Complete Price Guide To Watches is like some *watches*, the worst may be better than none at all, but at best cannot be expected to be 100% accurate. I will respect & appreciate positive sound reliable comments, corrections, improvements or remarks but reserve the right to accept the statement or keep my own observations & views. (*Cooksey*)

The Complete Price Guide to Watches goal is to stimulate the orderly exchange of <u>Watches</u> between *"buyers"* and *"sellers"*.

Copyright 2004 by Cooksey G. Shugart

Published by: **COOKSEY SHUGART PUBLICATIONS**
P. O. BOX 3147
CLEVELAND, TN. 37320-3147
TEL. (423) 479 – 4813

Distributed by: **COLLECTOR BOOKS**
P. O. BOX 3009
5801 KENTUCKY DAM ROAD
PADUCAH, KY. 42002-3009
TEL. 1 - 800 - 626 - 5420

TWENTY FOURTH EDITION: JAN., 2004

Manufactured in the United States of America

TABLE OF CONTENTS

CONTENTS OF ESCAPEMENTS

4

ACKNOWLEDGMENTS

I am especially appreciative of **Bob Overstreet**, author of The Overstreet Comic Book Price Guide, for his encouragement and without his assistance this book would have been impossible.
To my wife **Martha**, for her complete understanding and assistance in compiling this book.
To best friend **TOM ENGLE** whose help is invaluable a very special thanks.
A special thanks to **Henry B. Fried**, Dr. Adolphe Chapiro, Derek Pratt, Joe Cerullo, Philippe Dufour, Dr. George Daniels, Christophe Claret and Dan Crawley.
To the NAWCC Museum, Hamilton Watch Co., and Bowman Technical School, for allowing us to photograph their watches. Also Lindell V. Riddle and NAWCC Chapter 185.
To Christie's, Osvaldo Patrizzi, Dr. H. Crott, J. Wachsmann of Pieces of Time and Gisbert A. Joseph of Joseph Auctions for photographs of watches.

And to the following people whose help was invaluable and will be long remembered: Frank Irick, John Cubbins, Harold Harris, Paul Gibson, Robert L. Ravel, M.D., William C. Heilman Jr., M.D., Thomas McEntyre, Paul Morgan, Bill Selover, Oscar Laube, Ed Kieft, Charles Wallace, Bob Walters, Jack Warren, Howard Schroeder, Edward M. McGinnis, James Gardner, Paul Zuercher, Irving E. Roth, Don Bass, Stephen Polednak, Dick Stacy, Ernest J. Lewis, Herbert McDonald, David Steiger, Fred Favour, Ralph Warner, Estus Harris, Norman Howard, Charles Cleves, Tom McIntyre, Ralph Ferone, Arnold C. Varey, Jeffrey Ollswang, Tom Rohr, Leon Beard, Glenn Smith, Kenneth Vergin, Thomas Rumpf, Frank Diggs, Tom Thacker, Bob Lavoie, Constantin Tanasecu, Rod Minter, Ernest Luffman, John Amneus, Lawrence D. Harnden, Mike Kirkpatrick, Clint B. Geller, Art W. Rontree, and a special thanks to Peter Kushnir, Dr. J. Mauss, Robert D. Gruen, Jeff Hess, Col. R. A. Mulholland, Dick Ziebell, Jack Warren, Dick Flaute, Ralph Vinge, Edward Fletcher, Richard Walker, Alex Wolanguk, Carl Goetz, Miles Sandler, Dave Mycko, Martin & Patrick Cullen, Benjy Rook, Phillip Welsh, Paul Craft, Fred Fox, Fred Andrus, Ellis Gifford, Steve Berger, Bruce Ellison, Lawrence D. Harnden, Geoff White, Bob & Pat Wingate, David Searles, Ray R. Tyulty Jr., Don Levison, Robert M. Toborowsky M.D., Dr. John R. Dimar, Jonathan Snellenburg, Kent L. Singer, Tom Reindl, Paul A. Duggan, Gregory A. Hill, Don & Sandy Robbins, Bernie Kraus, Veron Willams, Fred Hansen, Drew Schmidt, Norman M. Tallan, Harry Blair, Jack Kurdzionak, Robert Schussel, Douglas L. Conner, Ira P. Mish, Dan Anderson, Seth Finkelstein, R.H.(Dick) Hanewald, Bill Campbell, Ted Hake, Don Barrett, Darold Hanson, John Grass, Lyle & Donna Stratton, Joe DeMesy, Pete Lamb, Caleb Stephenson, Mike Spine, M. Meyer, Lindell V. Riddle, NAWCC Chapter 185, Steve Campbell.

Special Consultant & Advisors

JIM WOLF   **PAUL DUGGAN**   **MILES SANDLER**
Associate Editor

Darold Hanson   **Steve Campbell**   **Harry Blair**

Send only corrections, additions, deletions and comments to
COOKSEY SHUGART, P. O. BOX 3147, CLEVELAND, TN. 37320-3147.
When *corresponding*, please send a ⊟ *self-addressed, stamped envelope.*

INTRODUCTION

This book is dedicated to all watch collectors who we hope will find it an enjoyable and valuable reference to carry on buying trips or to trace the lost history of that priceless family heirloom.

Understanding the VALUE of watches. Study this book it should repay its cost to you many times over. Be informed"Buy the book before the watch." You can't have too much knowledge. Collecting without regards to cost and value can be expensive. This Price Guide will be helpful for several reasons, it will teach you about market value, identification, desirability, how to determine the age and much more. Important: you must <u>READ</u> the first 100 pages and study to gain insight, examine, search into and understand and master the subject of watch collecting. *Be an informed buyer and seller.* Please remember your job is to determine many factors that will define the watches true value and this book is designed to help you.

Watches are unique collectibles and since the beginning of civilization man has held a fascination for time. When man scooped up a handful of sand and created the hourglass, portable timepieces have been in demand for the wealthy and poor alike. Man has sought constantly to improve his time-measuring instruments and has made them with the finest metals and jewels. The pocket watch, in particular, became an ornamentation and a source of pride, and this accounts for its value among families for generation after generation.

The watch has become precious and senti-mental to so many because it is one of the true personal companions of the individual night and day. Mahatma Gandhi, the father of India and one of the rare people in history who was able to renounce worldly possessions, was obsessed with the proper use of his time. Each minute, he held, was to be used in the service of his fellow man. His own days were ordered by one of his few personal possessions, a sixteen-year-old, eight-shilling Ingersoll pocket watch that was always tied to his waist with a piece of string.

Another factor that has made watches unique collectibles is the intricate artisanship with which they are put together. Many of the watches of yesteryear, which were assembled with extreme accuracy and fine workmanship, continue to be reliable timepieces today. They stand out as unique because that type of watch is no longer hand made. In today's world of mass production, the watch with individual craftsmanship containing precious jewels and metals can rarely be found—and, if found, it is rarely affordable.

The well-made watch is a tribute to man's skills, artisanship and craftsmanship at their finest level. That is why the watch holds a special place in the collectible field. In America, there are more than 240,000 avid watch collectors and millions own several watches, also an untold number possess at least one or more of these precious heirlooms.

The word <u>Complete</u> in the title of this book, a watch listed is **COMPLETE** with case and movement and with out any of the parts missing. (Complete)
⊕ **The Complete Price Guide to Watches goal is to stimulate the orderly exchange of <u>Watches</u> between *"buyers"* and *"sellers"*.**

The Complete Price Guide to Watches does not attempt to establish or fix values or selling prices in the watch trade market.

It does, however, reflect the trends of buying and selling in the collector market. Prices listed in this volume are based on data collected and analyzed from dealers and shops all over the country. These prices should serve the collector as a guide only. The price you pay for any watch will be determined by the value it has to you. The intrinsic value of any particular watch can be measured only by you, the collector, and a fair price can be derived only after mutual agreement between both the buyer and the seller.

Keep in mind the fair market values at the **Trade Show** level (as outlined in this price guide) and buying wisely, but don't hesitate, as the better and scarce pieces are quickly sold.

It is our hope that this volume can help make your watch collecting venture both pleasurable and profitable. Hopefully, everyone interested in horology will research the watch and add to his library on the subject.

Information contained herein may not necessarily apply to every situation. Data is still being found, which may alter statements made in this book. These changes, however, will be reflected in future editions.

COLLECTAMANIA
Hobby — Business — Pastime — Entertainment

Just name it. More than likely someone will want to buy or sell it: books, coins, stamps, bottles, beer cans, gold, glassware, baseball cards, guns, clocks, watches, comics, art, cars, and the list goes on and on.

Most Americans seem to be caught up in collectamania . More and more Americans are spending hour after hour searching through antique shops, auctions, flea markets and yard sales for those rare treasures of delight that have been lying tucked away for generations just waiting to be found.

This sudden boom in the field of collecting may have been influenced by fears of inflation or disenchantment with other types of investments. But more people are coming into the field because they gain some degree of nostalgic satisfaction from these new tangible ties with yesteryear. Collecting provides great fun and excitement. The tales of collecting and the resultant "fabulous finds" could fill volumes and inspire even the non-collector to embark upon a treasure hunt.

Collecting for the primary purpose of investment may prove to have many pitfalls for the amateur. The lack of sufficient knowledge is the main cause of disappointment. The inability to spot fakes or flawed merchandise can turn excitement into disappointment. And, in many fields, high-class forgers are at work, doing good and faithful reproductions in large quantities that can sometimes fool even the experts the first time they see them.

Collecting for fun and profit can be just that if you observe a fair amount of caution. Always remember, amidst your enthusiasm, that an object may not be what it would first appear. Next are a few guidelines that may be helpful.

LEARN - FOCUS - CONDITION - TRUST

"LOOK UNDER THE HOOD"
"If it is worth FAKING **it will be**."

1. **Gain all the knowledge you can** and **LEARN** all about the objects you collect. The more knowledge you have the more successful you will be in finding valuable, quality pieces. The best way to predict the future is to study the past. Amassing the knowledge required to be a good collector is easier if you have narrowed your scope of interest. Otherwise, it may take years to become an ''expert.'' Don't try to learn everything there is to know about a variety of fields. This will end in frustration and disappointment. Specialize and **learn** NAWCC trade show fair market **values** (Used in this BOOK).

2. **Make up your mind** and **FOCUS** on what you want to collect and concentrate in this area. Your field of collecting should be one that you have a genuine liking for, and it helps if you can use the objects. It may also help to narrow your field even further, for instance, in collecting watches, to choose only one company or one type or style and have a method of collecting.

3. **Buy the best CONDITION you can afford**, assuming the prices are fair. The advanced collector may want only mint articles; but the novice collector may be willing to accept something far less than mint condition due to caution and economics. Collectible items in better condition continue to rise in value at a steady rate.

4. **Deal with reputable dealers** whom you can **TRUST**. Talk with the dealer; get to know the seller; get a business card; know where you can contact the dealer if you have problems, or if you want the dealer to help you find something else you may be looking for.

FAIR MARKET PRICE: Fair price may be defined as a fair **reasonable** range of prices usually paid for a watch or a watch of **good value** as used in this book (*at the* **Trade Show LEVEL**). This market level includes a particular time frame, desirability, condition and quality. A guide to fair purchase prices is subject to sales and transactions between a large number of buyers and sellers who are informed, up to date on all normal market influences (while keeping in mind the difference between compulsiveness and acceptable buying), and buy and sell on a large scale from coast to coast. A willing buyer and a willing seller acting carefully and judiciously in their own best interest while, doing business in a normal and fair manner and preferable with payment immediately.

The **Complete Price Guide to Watches goal is to stimulate the orderly exchange of WATCHES between buyers and sellers**.

Keep in mind the **Trade Show fair market values** as outlined in this price guide and buying wisely, but don't *hesitate*, as the better and scarce watches are *quickly* sold. ***The best way to predict the future is study the past.***

🕑 Pricing in this Guide are fair market price for **COMPLETE** watches which are reflected from the "**NAWCC**" National and regional shows.

HOW TO USE THIS BOOK

The Complete Price Guide to Watches is a simple reference, with clear and carefully selected information. The first part of the book is devoted to history, general information, and a how-to section. The second part of the guide consists mainly of a listing of watch manufacturers, identification guides, and prices. This is a unique book because it is designed to be taken along as a handy reference for identifying and pricing watches. With the aid of this book, the collector should be able to make on-the-spot judgments as to identification, age, quality, and value. This **Complete Price Guide to Watches**, money, a folding pocket knife case opener, and pocket magnifying glass or watchmakers loupe will be good to take on your buying trips.

Right: Folding pocket case opener. **Middle**: A Magnification glass. **Left**: Watchmakers **Loupe**.

Watch collecting is fast growing as a hobby and business. Many people collect for the enjoyment and profit. The popularity of watches continues to rise because watches are a part of history. The American railroad brought about the greatest watch of that time, the railroad pocket watch. Since that time America has produced some of the best quality pocket watches that money could buy. The gold-filled cases made in America have never been surpassed in quality or price in the foreign market. With the quality of movement and cases being made with guaranteed high standards as well as beauty, the American pocket watch became very desirable. Because they are no longer being made in the U. S. A., pocket watches continue to rise in value. The watch is collected for its beauty, quality in movement and case, and the value of metal content. Solid gold and platinum are the top of the line; silver is also very desirable. (Consider that some watches in the early 1900's sold between $700 and $1,000. This is equal to or greater than the price of a good car of the same period.) As with limited edition prints, a watch of supreme excellence is also limited and will increase in value. There is universal appeal and excitement in owning a piece of history, and your heirloom is just that. At one time pocket watches were a status symbol. Everyone competed for beauty and quality in the movement and case. Solid gold cases were adorned with elaborate engraving's, diamonds, and other precious jewels. The movements were beautiful and of high quality. Manufacturers went to great lengths to provide movements that were both accurate and lovely. Fancy damaskeening on the back plates of nickel with gold lettering, 26 jewels in gold settings, and a solid gold train (gears) were features of some of the more elaborate timepieces. The jewels were red rubies, or diamond-end stones, or sapphires for the pallet stones. There were gold timing screws, and more. The enamel double-sunk dials were made by the best artisans of the day, hand-painted and with fancy hands.

HOW TO DETERMINE MANUFACTURER

When identifying a watch, look on the face or dial for the name of the company and then refer to the alphabetical list of watch companies in this book. If the face or dial does not reveal the company name you will have to seek information from the movement's back plate. **First** determine from what **country** the watch originated. The company name or the town where it was manufactured will likely be inscribed there. The name engraved on the back plate is referred to as the "signature." After locating the place of manufacture, see what companies manufactured in that town. This may require reading the histories of several companies to find the exact one. Use the process of elimination to narrow the list. Note: Some of the hard-to-identify watches are extremely collectible and valuable. Therefore, it is important to learn to identify them.

In order to establish the true manufacturer of the movement, one must **study** the construction, taking note of the **SIZE**, number of jewels, shape, location of parts, plate layout (is it full or 3/4), shape of the balance cock and the regulator, location of jewels, location of screws, etc. Compare and match your watch movement with every photograph or drawing from each watch company in this volume until the manufacturer is located.

Important Note: Generic or Nameless = (Unmarked grades), for watch movements are listed under the Company name or initials of the Company, etc. by **size, jewel count and description**. Such as American Watch Co. or Amn Watch Co. or A.W.W.Co., Elgin W. Co. or Elgin National W. Co., Hampden W.Co. or Duber W.Co., Illinois W. Co.or I.W.Co., Rockford or R.W.Co., South Bend, etc..

Compare & match your watch to a illustration in this book.

HOW TO DETERMINE AGE

After establishing the name of the manufacturer, you may be interested in the age of the watch (where production tables are listed). This information can be obtained by using the serial number inscribed on the back movement plate and referring to the production table. It is often difficult to establish the exact age, but this method will put you within a two or three-year period of the date of the manufacture.

To establish the age of a pre-1850 watch there are many points to be considered. The dial, hands, pillars, balance cock and pendant, for example, contain important clues in determining the age of your watch. However, no one part alone should be considered sufficient evidence to draw a definite conclusion as to age. The watch as a whole must be considered. First determine from what country the case originated and from what country did the movement originate for example, an English-made silver-cased watch will have a hallmark inside the case. It is quite simple to refer to the London Hallmark Table for hallmarks after 1697. The hallmark will reveal the age of the case only. This does not fix the age of the movement. Many movements are housed in cases made years before or after the movement was produced.

The **case** that houses the movement is **not** necessarily a good clue to the origin of the movement and the case serial number is of **no** help. It was a common practice for manufacturers to ship the movements to the jewelers and watchmakers uncased. The customer then married the movement and case. That explains why an expensive movement can be found in a cheaper case or vice versa.

If the "manufacturer's" name and location are no help, the inscription could possibly be that of a jeweler and his location. Then it becomes obvious there is no quick and easy way to identify some American made watches. However, the following steps may be helpful. Some watches can be identified by comparing the models of each company until the correct model is found. Start by sizing the watch and then comparing the varied plate shapes and styles. The cock or bridge for the balance may also be a clue. The general arrangement of the movement as to jeweling, whether it is an open face or hunting case, and style of regulators may help to find the correct identification of the manufacturer of the movement.

Numbers on a watch case should not be considered as clues to the age of the movement because cases were both American and foreign made, and many of the good watches were re-cased through the years.

APPRAISING WATCHES

Watch collecting is still young when compared to fields of the standard collectibles: coins and stamps. The watch collecting field is growing but information is still scarce, fragmented, and sometimes unreliable. To be knowledgeable in any field, one must spend the time required to study it.

The value of any collectible is determined first by demand. Without demand there is no market. In the watch trade, the law of supply and demand is also true. The supply of the American watches has stopped and the demand among collectors continues to rise. There are many factors that make a watch desired or in demand. Only time and study will tell a collector just which pieces are most collectible. After the collector or investor finds out what is desirable, then a value must be placed on it before it is sold. If it is priced too high, the watch will not sell; but, on the other hand, if it is priced too low, it will be hard to replace at the selling price. The dealer must arrive at a fair market price that will move the watch. As with limited edition prints, a watch of supreme excellence is also limited and will increase in value. There is universal appeal and excitement in owning a piece of history, and your heirloom is just that. At one time pocket watches were a status symbol. Everyone competed for beauty and quality in the movement and case. Solid gold cases were adorned with elaborate engraving's, diamonds, and other precious jewels.

Note: The value of a watch may be $5,000.00 today, $1,000.00 or $50,000.00 five years from now.

The movements were beautiful and of high quality. Manufacturers went to great lengths to provide movements that were both accurate and lovely. Fancy damaskeening on the back plates of nickel with gold lettering, 26 jewels in gold settings, and a solid gold train (gears) were features of some of the more elaborate timepieces. The jewels were red rubies, or diamond-end stones, or sapphires for the pallet stones. There were gold timing screws, and more. The faces were made by the best artisans of the day. Hand-painted, jewel-studded, with fancy hands and double-sunk dials made of enamel and precious metals.

There are no two watches alike. This makes the appraising more difficult and often-times arbitrary. But there are certain guidelines one can follow to arrive at a fair market price. When watches were manufactured, most companies sold the movements to a jeweler, and the buyer had a choice of dials and cases. Some high-grade movements were placed in a low-grade case and vice versa. Some had hand-painted multi-colored dials; some were plain. The list of contrasts goes on. Conditions of watches will vary greatly, and this is a big factor in the value. The best movement in the best original case will bring the top price for any type of watch. (*The IRON law; supply and demand rule.*)

Prices are constantly changing in the watch field. Gold and silver markets affect the price of the cases. Scarcity and age also affect the value. These prices will fluctuate regularly. (*The IRON law; supply and demand rule.*)

APPRAISING GUIDELINES

Demand, supply, **desirability**, condition, and value must be the prime factors in appraising a watch. Demand maybe the most important element. Demand can be determined by the **number** of buyers for the particular item. The watch may be rare (one or a few) but the *number* of collectors may be even more rare & the collector just as hard to find. A simple but true axiom is that value is determined by the price someone is willing to pay. (*What is it worth to you?*)

In order to obtain a better knowledge in appraising and judging watches, the following guidelines are most useful. Consider all these factors before placing a value on the watch. (There is no rank or priority to the considerations listed.)

1. Demand: **Interest** high or low? (**very important desirability**)
   How many collectors **want** your **rare** watch.
2. Supply & Availability: How *rare* or *scarce* is the watch?
   How many of the total production remain? (Survival rate)
3. **Condition** of both the case and movement (very important) .
4. Low serial numbers: The first one made would be more
   valuable than later models.
5. Type of **escapement** also technical design of movement. (**Unique**)
6. Historical value.   7. Age, how old is the Watch.

8. Is it in its **original** case? (very important).
9. Is it an early handmade watch?
10. Complications: Repeaters, for example.
11. Value of metal content, style or type of case, beauty and eye appeal.
12. Size, number of jewels, type of plates (3/4, full and bridge), type of balance, type of winding (key-wind, lever-set, etc.), number of adjustments, gold jeweled settings, damaskeening, gold train.
13. What grade of **condition** is it? Pristine, Mint, Extra Fine, Average, Fair, or Scrap? You must determine condition and value or price.
14. Identification ability.
15. Future potential as an **investment**.
16. Quality (high or low grade), or low cost production watches (dollar watch). How much will this watch scrap for?

GRADING WATCHES

Pricing in this book is based on the following grading system:

100% **PRISTINE MINT (G-10)**: _NEW OLD STOCK._ Absolutely factory new; **Unused** in factory box with wax paper still intact & all tags & papers etc.The pristine mint grade is not listed in this book & command significant **premiums**. (A select group of watches maybe assigned to a "rarity grade" which are historical or technically important also, early horological examples.)

MINT PLUS (G-9): 99% Still in factory box. (**Exceptional, Perfect**)

*MINT (G-8): 97% Same as factory new but with very little use; **no** faint scratches & **no** trace of a screwdriver mark; is original in every way crystal, hands, dial, case, movement; used briefly & stored away, may still be in box. (Dealers "Trade Show" price _after_ OVERHAUL)

NEAR MINT (G-7): 93% Completely original in every way; faint marks may be seen with a loupe only; expertly repaired; movement may have been cleaned and oiled. (Excellent)

*EXTRA FINE (G-6): 87% May or may not be in factory box; looks as though watch was used very little; original case, hands, dial, and movement. If watch has been repaired, all original replacement parts have been used. Faint case scratches are evident but hard to detect with the eye. No dents & no hairline on dial are detectable.

FINE (G-5): 80% May have new hands and new crystal, but original case, dial and movement; **faint** hairline & no chips on dial; no large scratches & no brass seen on case; slight stain on movement; movement must be sharp with only **minor** scratches.

*AVERAGE- GOOD (G-4): 75% Original case, dial & movement; movement may have had a part replaced, but part was near to original; no brass showing through on gold-filled case; no rust or chips in dial; may have hairlines in dial that are hard to see. Marks are hard to detect, but may be seen without a loupe. (What some dealer "MAY" pay = <u>Wholesale</u> price.)

FAIR (G-3): 60% Hairlines in dial and small chips; slight amount of brass can be seen through worn spots on gold-filled case; rust marks in movement; a small dent in case; wear in case, dial, and movement; well used; may not have original dial or case.

POOR (G-2): 30% Watch not working; needs new dial; case well worn, many dents; hands may be gone; replacement crystal may be needed.

SCRAP (G-1): 15% Movement not working; bad dial; rusty movement; brass showing badly; may not have case; some parts not original; no crystal or hands. Good for parts only.

🕐 Pricing in this Guide are fair market price for **COMPLETE** watches which are reflected from the "**NAWCC**" National and regional shows.

🕐 **The Complete Price Guide to Watches goal is to stimulate the orderly exchange of <u>Watches</u> between "*buyers*" and "*sellers*".**

Hamilton 992B

100%	G-10	$800
99%	G-9	$650
97%	**G-8**	**$575**
93%	G-7	$425
87%	**G-6**	**$335**
80%	G-5	$290
75%	**G-4**	**$275**
60%	G-3	$185
30%	G-2	$95
15%	G-1	$65

MINT
<u>G-8</u> = (Trade Show)

AVERAGE
<u>G-4</u>=(Dealers May Pay)

Above is an example of how the price is affected by the different grades of the same watch:

Note: The value of a watch may be $5,000.00 today, $1,000.00 or $50,000.00 five years from now.

The value of a watch can only be assessed after the watch has been carefully inspected and graded. It may be difficult to evaluate a watch honestly and objectively, especially in the rare or scarce models.

If the watch has any defects, such as a small scratch on it, it can not be Pristine. It is important to realize that older watches in grades of Extra Fine or above are extremely rare and may never be found.

Watches listed in this book are priced at the collectable **Trade Show level,** as **COMPLETE** watches having an original 14k gold-filled case and Key Wind with silver, an original white enamel single sunk dial, and with the entire original movement in good working order with no repairs needed.

Keep in mind the fair market values at **Trade Show level,** as outlined in this price guide and buying wisely, but don't *"hesitate"*, as the better and scarce watches are *quickly* sold.

🕐 The value of a watch may be $5,000.00 today, $1,000.00 or $50,000.00 five years from now.

COLLECTING ON A LIMITED BUDGET

Most collectors are always looking for that sleeper, which is out there waiting to be found. One story goes that the collector went into a pawn shop and asked the owner if he had any gold pocket watches for sale. The pawn broker replied, ''No, but I have a 23J silver cased pocket watch at a good price.'' Even though the pocket watch was in a cheaper case, the collector decided to further explore the movement. When he opened the back to look at the movement, there he saw engraved on the plates 24J Bunn Special and knew immediately he wanted to buy the pocket watch. The movement was running, and looked to be in first grade shape. The collector asked the price. The broker said he has been trying to get rid of the pocket watch, but had no luck and if he wanted it, he would sell it for $35. The collector took the pocket watch and replaced the bent-up silver case for a gold-filled J. Boss case, and sold it a month later for $400. He had a total of $100 invested when he sold it, netting a cool $300 profit.

Most collectors want a pocket watch that is in mint or near-mint condition and original in every way. But consider the railroad pocket watches such as the Bunn Special in a cheaper case. The railroad man was compelled to buy a watch with a quality movement, even though he may have only been able to afford a cheap case. The railroad man had to have a pocket watch that met certain standards set by the railroad company. A watch should always be judged on quality and performance and not just on its appearance. The American railroad pocket watch was unsurpassed in reliability. It was durable and accurate for its time, and that accounts for its continuing value today.

If you are a limited-budget collector, you would be well advised not to go beyond your means. But watch collecting can still be an interesting, adventurous, and profitable hobby. If you are to be successful in quadrupling your purchases that you believe to be sleepers, you must first be a hard worker, have perseverance and let shrewdness and skill of knowledge take the place of money. A good starting place is to get a working knowledge of how a pocket watch works. Learn the basic skills such as cleaning, mainspring and staff replacement. One does not have to be a watchmaker, but should learn the names of parts and what they do. If a watch that you are considering buying does not work, you should know how and what it takes to get it in good running order or pass it by. Stay away from pocket watches that do not wind and set. Also avoid ''odd'' movements that you hope to be able to find a case for.

Old watches with broken or missing parts are expensive and all but impossible to have repaired. Some parts must be made by hand. The odd and low-cost production watches are fun to get but hard to repair. Start out on the more common basic-jeweled lever pocket watches. The older the watch, the harder it is to get parts. Buy an inexpensive pocket watch movement that runs and play with it. Get the one that is newer and for which parts can be bought; and get a book on watch repairing.

You will need to know the *pricing history* and **demand** of a watch. Know what collectors are looking for in your area. If you cannot find a buyer, then, of course, someone else's unwanted stock has become yours.

JOIN THE NAWCC ®

The authors of this book Mr. Shugart, Mr. Richard Gilbert & Mr. Tom Engle recommend you join the NAWCC ® today and share a fascination for watches with other members.

The National Association of Watch and Clock Collectors (NAWCC ®) is a non-profit, scientific and educational corporation founded in 1943 and now serving the horological needs and interests of about 34,000 members (professional horologists and **amateurs**) in the United States and 40 others countries. Help to its members is only a telephone call away.

Participation in National & Regional *Conventions* also *Local Activities* and *Seminars*.

12 PUBLICATIONS Per Year
SIX per year The **NAWCC ® Mart**
SIX per year The **NAWCC ® Bulletin**

The **Bulletin** is an absorbing, abundantly illustrated articles on historic, artistic and technical aspects of time keeping, answers by experts to your questions in the "Answer Box" , concise reviews of horological books, members' opinions and comments in "VOX TEMPORIS", research findings and request, slide programs available to Chapters, news and announcements of local Chapters, Regional and National activities.

The **Mart** is a informal medium of exchange in which, for a nominal fee, you can list any horological item you may wish to **buy, sell or trade**... an absorbing and entertaining way to find items to fill out your collection or dispose of pieces you no-longer want. Announcements of Regional and National *Conventions & Seminars*.

TO JOIN THE NAWCC ® Call or Send for a FREE copy of their brochure with additional information on the NAWCC ®, membership and benefits.

NAWCC, INC.
514 Poplar Street
Columbia, PA   17512
(717) 684-8261

Recommended by member COOKSEY SHUGART membership number - **23,843.**
Also see AD in the ADVERTISING SECTION of this book.

THAT GREAT AMERICAN
RAILROAD POCKET WATCH

It was the late nineteenth century in America. The automobile had not yet been discovered. The personal Kodak camera was still not on the market. Women wore long dresses, and the rub board was still the most common way to wash clothes. Few homes had electricity, and certainly the radio had not yet invaded their lives. Benjamin Harrison was president. To be sure, those days of yesteryear were not quite as nostalgically simple as most reminiscing would have them be. They were slower, yes, because it took longer to get things done and longer to get from one place to another. The U.S. mail was the chief form of communication linking this country together, as America was inching toward the Twentieth Century.

The tremendous impact of the railroad on the country during this era should not be under estimated. Most of the progress since the 1830s had chugged along on the back of the black giant locomotives that belched steam and fire, up and down the countryside. In fact, the trains brought much life and hope to the people all across the country, delivering their goods and food, bringing people from one city to another, carrying the U.S. mail, and bringing the democratic process to the people by enabling candidates for the U.S. Presidency to meet and talk with people in every state.

Truly the train station held memories for most everyone and had a link with every family.

Above: **Allen A. Shugart** (my father) was photographed in the summer of 1981 at the Chattanooga Tenn. train station also called Chattanooga **Choo-Choo** Station.

Taking effect June 15, 1892, the Illinois Central Railroad inaugurated a watch inspection. Employees are now required to summit their watches for a quarterly examination & weekly comparison with standard time to the various local inspectors who have been appointed for the purpose. The minimum standard of excellence adopted by this company for watches is of a grade equal to what is known among American movements as 15 jewels, patent regulator, adjusted to temperature, the variation of which must not exceed 30 seconds per week.

TIME RECORD Note Variation in Seconds
R. D.—Run Down   St.—Stopped

| DATE COMPARED | SECONDS | | R-REG S-SET |
	FAST	SLOW	
4 9-6			O K. *Bowrin*

Above part of a Watch inspection card.
Carried by a Fireman on Erie Lackawanna R.R.Co.

The Great American Railroad Pocket Watch, unrivaled in quality and reliability. *"What is a railroad watch"*? There is not an easy answer to this question. With 500 to 1,000 American Railroads & each one used many different rules and specifications. Some railroads used requirements only and some listed only watch company grades that were acceptable. Also Railroad **rules & watches evolved** and changed from year to year. In the late **1860's** a movement was commissioned by Pennsylvania Railroad Co. & had "Pennsylvania Railroad Co." on the dial and "B.W. Raymond" on the movement. The movement made by Elgin was a 18 size, 15 jewels, key wind and set. In 1887 the American Railroad Companies had a meeting to interpret and specify requirements of standard time and watch inspection. In the spring of **1894**, American Waltham Watch Co. ad states

1916
Waltham
AD

The first watch constructed especially for railroad service was this CRESCENT ST., made in 1870.

"Systematic railroad watch inspection was first adopted during <u>recent years</u>". The ad also says "Waltham watch movements expressly designed for railroad use". The ad shows a 1892 model Vanguard grade with 17 jewels and double roller. In **Feb. of 1894,** The United States Watch Co. of Waltham introduced a watch & their ad states "Fellow Engineers & Railroad Men: The President, is a first quality nickel, 18 size, full plate, stem winding & lever setting, double roller escapement and adjusted to heat cold, isochronism & all positions. The Company guarantees the movement will-vary less than six seconds in a calendar month."

Note: A railroad watch is a watch that satisfies the requirements in effect at the time the watch was made. (Railroad rules evolved and changed from year to year.)

Prior to 1893, the definition of a railroad watch was optional with individual railroads. About 1893 the General Railroad Timepiece Standards Commission presented these new **guidelines** (below). **After** 1893, American watch manufacturers set out to meet these guidelines, later railroad lines used these standards as a guideline for <u>NEW</u> railway watches, but not **ALL**. Some Railroad Companies were vague about their regulations and some had none at all. Note: With over 500 American Railroad Companies and **each one** (No nation-wide rules) used similar but different rules and specifications. NOTE: 15 jewel watches were accepted by some Railroad Watch Inspectors as late as early 1900's.

Be open faced, size 18 or 16, have a minimum of 17 jewels, adjusted to at least five positions, keep time accurately to within a gain or loss of only **30 seconds a week** *, adjusted to temperatures of 34 to 100 degrees Fahrenheit, have a double roller, steel escape wheel, lever set, micrometric regulator, winding stem at 12 o'clock, grade on back plate, use plain Arabic numbers printed bold and black on a white dial, and have bold black hands.*

NOTE: By *about* 1900 the **above** <u>guidelines</u> were used by many Railroad Companies Inspectors.

The American watch industry was compelled to produce just such an instrument which it did. The railroad watch was a phenomenal timekeeper and durable in long life and service. It had the most minute adjustments, no small feat because watchmaking was rendered far more difficult than clock making, due to the fact that a clock is always in one position and powered by a constant force-it's weights,while watches must be accurate in several positions with a variable power source. After 1875-80 a RR employee had to buy his own watch.

After 1893 railroad pocket watch standards guidelines were adopted by some railroad lines for <u>new</u> watches. While <u>each</u> company had its **individual** standards guideline, many included the basic recommendations of the **commission**.

One of the figures in developing the railroad watch standards was Webb C. Ball of Cleveland, Ohio, the general time inspector for over 125,000 miles of railroad in the U.S., Mexico, and Canada. Ball was authorized by railroad officials to help to establish the timepiece inspection system. After Ball presented his guidelines, most American manufacturers set out to meet those standards and a list of the different manufacturers producing watches of the grade that would pass inspection, was soon available. <u>These standards changed from year to year.</u>

According to the regulations, if a watch fell behind or gained **30 seconds in 7 to 14 days**, it must be sent in for adjustment or repair. Small cards were given to the engineers and conductors the railroad timekeepers and a complete record of the watch's performance was written in ink. All repairs and adjustments were conducted by experienced and approved watchmakers; inspections were conducted by authorized **inspectors**.

Because this system was adopted the American watch manufacturers produced a superior railroad watch, the traveling public was assured of increased safety and indeed the number of railroad accidents occurring as a result of faulty timepieces was minimized.

Prior to the 1890s, some railroad companies had already initiated standards and were issuing lists of those watches approved for railroad use. Included were the Waltham 18s, 1883 model, Crescent Street Grade, and the B.W. Raymond, 18s, both in open & hunter cases with lever or pendant set.

By the mid 1890s hunter cases were being turned down as well as pendant set. Watches meeting approval then included Waltham, 18s, 1892 model; Elgin, 7th model; and Hamilton, 17j, open face, lever set.

Hamilton Grade 992, 16 size, 21 jewels, nickel 3/4 plate movement, lever set only, gold jewel settings, gold center wheel, steel escape wheel, micrometric regulator, double roller, compensating balance. Adjusted to temperature, isochronism and 5 positions. Marked *Elinvar* under balance wheel. Serial number 2584307 & listed as **992E** under the "Hamilton serial numbers and grades" section.

By 1900 the double roller, sapphire pallets and steel escape wheels with a minimum of five positions were required.

The early Ball Watch Co. movements, made by Howard, used initials of railroad labor organizations such as "B. of L.E. Standard" and "B. of L.F. Standard." Ball also used the trademark "999" and "Official Railroad Standard." Some watches may turn up that are marked as "loaners." These were issued by the railroad inspectors when a watch had to be kept for repairs.

By 1920 the 18 size watch had lost popularity with the railroad men and by 1950 most railroad companies were turning them down all together. In 1936 duty on Swiss watches were lowered by 50 percent, and by 1950 the Swiss imports had reached a level of five million a year. In 1969 the last American railroad pocket watch was sold by Hamilton Watch Co. a Grade 992B.

NOTE: Railroad Standards, Railroad Approved & Railroad Grade **terminology,** as defined and used in this *__BOOK__*. **RAILROAD STANDARDS** = A commission or board appointed by the railroad companies outlined a set of **requirements** to be accepted or approved by **each** railroad line. **RAILROAD APPROVED** = After 1875-80 a RR employee had to buy his own watch. A *__LIST__* of watches each railroad line would approve if purchased by their employee's. (this list changed through the years). **RAILROAD GRADE** = A watch made by manufactures to meet or exceed the railroad **standards**. Grades such as 992, Vanguard and B.W. Raymond, etc.
* NOTE: Some GRADES **exceeded** the R.R. standards or requirements, such as watches with 23 jewels, diamond end stone, gold train, raised gold jewel settings, double sunk dial and the list goes on. Examples: such as Veritas, Sangamo, 950 & Riverside Maximus and many others.
Note: A railroad watch is a watch that satisfies the requirements in effect at the time the watch was made. There were no rules or guidelines used NATION-WIDE, each railroad used their own rules and list of approved watches.

RAILROAD GRADE WATCH ADJUSTMENTS

The railroad watch, as well as other fine timepieces, had to compensate for several factors in order to be reliable and accurate at all times. These compensations, called adjustments, were for heat and cold, isochronism, and five to six different positions. These adjustments were perfected only after experimentation and a great deal of careful hand labor on each individual movement.

All railroad grade watches were adjusted to a closer rate to compensate for heat and cold. The compensation balance has screws in the rim of the balance wheel which can be regulated by the watchmaker. The movement was tested in an ice box and in an oven, and if it did not keep the same time in both temperature extremes, as well as under average conditions, the screws in the balance wheel was shifted or adjusted until accuracy was achieved.

The isochronism adjustment maintained accuracy of the watch both when the mainspring was fully wound up and when it was nearly run down. This was achieved by selecting a hairspring of exact proportions to cause the balance wheel to give the same length of arc of rotation regardless of the amount of the mainspring that had been spent.

Railroad watches were adjusted to be accurate whether they were laying on their face or back, or being carried on their edges with pendants up or down, or with the three up or the nine up. These adjustments were accomplished by having the jewels, in which the balance pivots rest, of proper thickness in proportion to the diameter of the pivot and, at the same time, equal to the surface on the end of the pivot which rests on the cap jewel. To be fully adjusted for positions, the balance wheel and the pallet and escape wheel must be perfectly poised. Perfect poise is achieved when the pivots can be supported on two knife-edged surfaces, perfectly smooth and polished and when the wheel is placed in any edge, it will remain exactly as it is placed. If it is not perfectly poised, the heaviest part of the wheel will always turn to the point immediately under the lines of support.

Example: Of a Bunn 16 size, 17 jewels, nickel 3/4 plate movement, lever set , gold jewel settings, gold center wheel, double roller, steel escape wheel, micrometric regulator, compensating balance. Adjusted to temperature, isochronism and 5 positions, artistically damaskeened.

⊕ NOTE: Railroad grade watches had a compensation balance made of brass and steel. Brass was used on the outside rim and steel on the inside. Brass is twice as sensitive to temperature changes and twice as thick as the steel balance (one-piece is welded to the steel balance wheel) and after finishing, the rim is cut at one end near the arm of the balance and at the same spot 180 across. In higher temperature, the dominant brass would "grow" longer but welded to the steel rim, it would curve inward, thus, in effect, placing the mass of the balance closer to the center of the balance wheel. This would cause the balance to go faster. However, the steel hairspring in rising temperature would also grow longer but more important would also lose some of its resilience. This would cause the watch to lose time. The balance, remember under the same condition, in effect became smaller and this action by the balance compensated for the loss of the hairsprings elasticity and lengthening. In cold temperatures, the opposite effect took place. This is why the balance is called a "compensation" balance. (It compensates for the temperature errors in the hairspring.)

NOTE: Movements marked *Adjusted* have a diversity or combination, of features. The best way to know for sure is to check the factory grade lists for specific adjustments. After about 1905 the movements were marked with the number of adjustments.

The micrometric regulator or the patent regulator is a device used on all railroad grade and higher grade watches for the purpose of assisting in the finer manipulation of the regulator. It is arranged so that the regulator can be moved the shortest possible distance without fear of moving it too far. There is always a fine graduated index attached which makes it possible to determine just how much the regulator has been moved.

E. Howard Watch Co. Railroad Chronometer, Series 11, 16 size, 21 jewels, designed for the railroad trade.

Uncommon **RADIAL**, note the Arabic numbers slant to the center of dial. Seen on many dials with Roman numerals.

The hairspring used on the so-called ordinary and medium-grade watches is known as the flat hairspring. The Breguet hairspring was an improvement over the flat hairspring and was used on railroad and high-grade watches. The inside coil of any hairspring is attached to a collet on the balance staff and the end of the outside coil of the hairspring is attached to a stud which is held firmly by a screw in the balance wheel bridge. Two small regulator pins are fastened to the regulator. These pins clasp the outer side of the hairspring a short distance from the hairspring stud. If the regulator index is moved toward the ''S,'' the regulator pins will move, allowing the hairspring to lengthen and the balance wheel to make a longer arc of rotation. This causes the watch to run slower because it requires a longer time for the wheel to perform the longer arc.

Bunn Special

1924 AD
Jewelers listed cost for movement only =**$24.00**
&
Jewelers selling price for movement only = **$45.00**

18 Size, 21 Jewels, Adjusted 6 Positions

21 ruby and sapphire jewels; gold settings; adjusted to temperature, SIX positions and isochronism; compensating balance; gold screws including timing screws; double roller; steel escape wheel; Breguet hairspring, patent micrometric screw regulator, safety screw center pinion, beautifully damaskeened with black enamel lettering, double sunk dial.

When the regulator is moved toward the "F" these regulator pins are moved from the stud which shortens the hairspring and makes shorter arcs of the balance wheel, thus causing the movement to run faster. Sometimes, after a heavy jolt, the coil next to the outside one will catch between these regulator pins and this will shorten the length of the hairspring just one round, causing a gaining rate of one hour per day. When this occurs, the hairspring can be easily released and will resume its former rate.

The Breguet <u>overcoil</u> hairspring, which is used on railroad grade movements, prevented the hairspring from catching on the regulator pins and protected against any lateral or side motion of the balance wheel ensuring equal expansion of the outside coil.

Railroad grade watches also used the patent or safety pinion which was developed to protect the train of gears from damage in the event of breakage of the mainspring. These pinions unscrewed in event of mainspring breakage, allowing the force to be harmlessly spent by the spinning barrel.

Some earlier railroad grade watches had non-magnetic movements. This was achieved by the use of non-magnetic metals for the balance wheel, hairspring, roller table and pallet. Two of the metals used were iridium and palladium, both very expensive.

Waltham, 18 size, unusual Railroad double sunk white porcelain dial is marked with uniquely placed minute numbers on the outer chapter and the hour chapter is in the center, the dial is also marked "Waltham Pat. Appl'd. For". This watch is a 1892 model & Appleton Tracy & Co. grade.

Ball Watch Co. Motto: "Carry a Ball and Time Them All." This case is made of base metal with a Ball's patented Stirrup Bow. With the simple easy to read dial, this watch was a favorite among railroad men. **WWII** Ball and cased for Railroad watches.

RAILROAD WATCH DIALS

Railroad watch dials are distinguished by their simplicity. A true railroad watch dial contained no fancy lettering or beautiful backgrounds. The watches were designed to be functional and in order to achieve that, the dials contained bold black Arabic numbers against a white background. This facilitated ease of reading the time under even the most adverse conditions.

True railroad watches had the winding stem at the 12 o'clock position. The so-called *side winder*, that winds at the 3 o'clock position, was not approved for railroad use. (The **side winder** is a watch movement designed for a hunter case but one that has been placed in an open-faced case.)

One railroad watch dial design was patented by a Mr. Ferguson. On this dial, the five minute numbers were much larger than the hour numbers which were on the inside. This dial never became very popular.

About 1904 the Montgomery dials began to appear on some RR watches. The distinguishing feature of the Montgomery dial is that each minute is numbered around the hour chapter. The five-minute divisions were in red, and the true Montgomery dial has the number "6" inside the minute register. These dials were favored by the railroad men.

The so-called Canadian dial had a 24-hour division inside the hour chapter.

The double time hands are also found on some railroad grade watches. One hour hand was in blue or black and the other was in red or gold, one hour apart, to compensate for passing from one time zone to another. About 1900 **"Double Time Hands"** began to appear on 18 & 16 size watches.

Rockford Watch Co., Enamel **Railroad** double sunk dial, with two hour hands for a second time zone the hour hand at 2 O'clock is **BLUE**, the hour hand at 3 O'clock is **RED or GOLD**.

This style **Illinois** railroad watch cases were fitted with movements, re-rated and timed in their specially designed case at the factory as complete watches in a gold filled case with a hinged bezel . Note: This Illinois 60 hour single sunk dial, 17 size & referred to as a 16 size by the trade.

RAILROAD WATCH CASES

Open face cases were the only ones approved for railroad use. Railroad men sought a case that was tough and durable; one that would provide a dust-free environment for the movement.

The swing-out case offered the best protection against dust, but the screw-on back and bezel were the most popular open-face cases.

The lever-set was a must for railroad-approved watches and some of the case manufacturers patented their own styles of cases, most with a heavy bow. One example is the Stirrup Bow by the Ball Watch Co. Hamilton used a bar above the crown to prevent the stem from being pulled out. Glass was most commonly used for the crystal because it was not as likely to scratch.

RAILROAD GRADE OR RAILROAD SERVICE

Note: Not all railroad GRADE watches were railroad **APPROVED**, to be approved each railroad line or company made a list of watch grades that they would approve for example, Southern Railway, Lake Shore Railroad & Santa Fe Railway System etc. Not all watches listed here are railroad approved, even though all are railroad grade. Below are some watches that were railroad grade but may not have been railroad APPROVED. (below not a complete list)

BALL All official R.R. standard with 19, 21, & 23J, Adj.5p, 18 &16S, open face.

COLUMBUS WATCH CO.
Columbus King, 21, 23, 25J; Railway King, 17-25J; Time King, 21-25J, 18S; Ruby Model, 16S.

ELGIN
1. "Pennsylvania Railroad Co." on dial, 18S, 15J & 17J, KW-KS, first model "B. W. Raymond."
2. "No. 349," 18S, seventh model, 17-21J.
3. Veritas, B. W. Raymond, or Father Time, 18S, 21-23J.
4. Grades 162, 270, 280, or 342 marked on back plate, 16S, 17-21J.
5. Veritas, Father Time, or Paillard Non-Magnetic, 16S, 19-23J.
6. 571, 21J or 572, 16S, 19J., also **All** wind indicator models.

HAMILTON
1. 18S= Grade 946= 23J, & 940, 942= 21J, & 944= 19J, & 924, 926, 934, 936, 938, 948 = 17J.
2. 16S = Grades 950, 950B, 950E= 23J, & 992, 992B, 992E, 954, 960, 970, 994, 990= 21J.
3. 16S = Grade 996= 19J & 972, 968, 964= 17J.

HAMPDEN
1. Special Railway, 17J, 21J, 23J; New Railway, 23J & 17J; North Am. Railroad, 21J;
   Wm. McKinley, 21J; John Hancock, 21J & 23J; John C. Duber, 21J, 18S.
2. 105, 21J; 104, 23J; John C. Duber, 21J; Wm. McKinley, 17, 21;
   New Railway, 21J; Railway, 19J; Special Railway, 23J, 16S.

E. HOWARD & CO.
1. **All** Howard models marked "Adjusted" or deer symbol.
2. Split plate models, 18S or N size; 16S or L size.

HOWARD WATCH CO.
All 16S with 19, 21, & 23J.

Above: Double Hour Time Zone Hands, available in, RED & BLUE or GOLD & BLACK.

ILLINOIS
1. Bunn 15J "Adjusted," & Stuart, 15J "Adjusted," 18S; Burlington,19J.DR.Adj. 16S;
2. Benjamin Franklin,17-26J; Bunn 17- 24J; Bunn Special,21-26J; Chesapeake & Ohio Sp.,21-24J;
   Interstate Chronometer, 23J;Lafayette, 24J; A. Lincoln, 21J; Paillard W. Co., 17-24J;
   Trainsmen, 23J; Pennsylvania Special 17-26J; The Railroader & Railroad King, 18S.
3. Benjamin Franklin,17-25J; Bunn,17-19J; Bunn Special,21-23J; Diamond Ruby Sapphire,21-23J;
   Interstate Chronometer,23J; Lafayette,23J; A.Lincoln,21J; Paillard Non-MagneticW.Co.,17-21J;
   Pennsylvania Special, 17, 21, & 23J; Santa Fe Special, 21J; Sangamo, 21-26J;
   Sangamo Special, 19-23J; grades 161, 161A=21J;163, 163A=23J & 187, and 189, 17J, 16S.

PEORIA WATCH CO.
15 & 17J with a patented regulator, 18S.

ROCKFORD
1. **All** 21 or more jewels, 16-18S, **All** and wind indicators.
2. Grades 900, 905, 910, 912, 918, 945, 200, 205, 18S.
3. Winnebago, 17-21J, 505, 515, 525, 535, 545, 555, 16S.

SETH THOMAS
Maiden Lane, 21-28J; Henry Molineux, 20J; G#260,18S.

SOUTH BEND
1. *The Studebaker* 329, 323, Grade Nos. 327, 21J, 18S.
2. *The Studebaker* 229, 223, G# 227, 293, 295, 21J,
   also Polaris,21J;16 size

UNITED STATES WATCH CO., MARION
United States, 18 size, 17-19J, gold train.

U. S. WATCH CO., WALTHAM
The President, 17-21J, 18 size, double roller.

WALTHAM
1. 1857 KW with Pennsylvania R.R. on dial, Appleton Tracy & Co. on movement.
2. Crescent Street, 17-23J; 1883 & 1892 Models; Appleton Tracy & Co., 1892 Model; Railroader,
   1892 Model; Pennsylvania Railroad; Special RR, Special RR King, Vanguard, 17 -23J, 1892
   Model; Grade 845, **All** wind indicators 18S.
3. American Watch Co., 17-21J, 1872 Models; American Watch Co., All wind indicators,
   ALL 17-23J Bridge Models; Crescent Street, 17-21J, 1899 & 1908 Models;
   Premier Maximus; Railroader; Riverside Maximus, 21-23J; Vanguard, 19-23J; 645 16S.

Note: A railroad watch is a watch that satisfies the requirements in effect at the time the watch was made. There were no rules or guidelines used NATION-WIDE, each railroad used their own rules and list of approved watches.

RAILROAD
MODEL
NO. 2

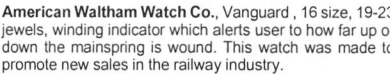

American Waltham Watch Co., Vanguard , 16 size, 19-23 jewels, winding indicator which alerts user to how far up or down the mainspring is wound. This watch was made to promote new sales in the railway industry.

Hamilton Watch Co., This was a favorite railroad style case by Hamilton model NO. 2 supplied in 10K or 14K gold filled. Note the Railroad style dial with red marginal figures as well as the bar-over-crown with "Hamilton Railroad" on crown.

CANADIAN PACIFIC SERVICE
RAILROAD APPROVED WATCHES 1899 to 1910

WALTHAM
Vanguard, 18-16S, 19-21-23 jewels
Crescent St., 18S, 19J; 18-16S, 21J
Appleton-Tracy 17J; also No. 845, 21J
Riverside 16S, 19J; Riverside Maximus, 16S, 23J;
No. 645, 16S, 21J, C. P. R. 18-16S, 17J; C.T. S. 18-16S, 17J
ELGIN
Veritas, 18-16S, 21-23J
B. W. R. 18-16S, 17-19-21J
Father Time 18-16S, 21J
Grade 349, 18S, 21J
HAMILTON
18S, 946, 23J; 940-942, 21J; 944, 19J; 936-938, 17J
16S, 950, 23J; 960-990-992, 21J; 952, 19J; 972, 17J
SOUTH BEND
18S, 327-329, 21J; 323, 17J
16S, 227-229, 21J; 223, 17J
BALL
All Balls 18S, 16S, 17-19-21-23J
ILLINOIS
Bunn Special, 18-16S, 21-23J; also Bunn 18-16S, 17-19J
A. Lincoln, 18-16S, 21J; Sangamo Special, 16S, 19-21-23J
SETH THOMAS
Maiden Lane, 18S, 25J; No. 260, 21J; No. 382, 17J
E. HOWARD WATCH CO.
16S Series, 0-23J, 5-19J, 2-17J, 10-21J; also No. 1, 21J
ROCKFORD
18S, Grade 918-905, 21J; Winnebago, 17J; also Grade 900, 24J
16S, Grades 545, 525, 515, 505, 21J; 655 W.I., 21J; and Grade 405, 17J
LONGINES
18S, Express Monarch, 17-19-21-23J
16S, Express Monarch, 17-19-21-23J
BRANDT-OMEGA
18S& 16S, D.D.R., 23J = very best, 18 gold settings; D.R., 19J = extra fine, 15 gold settings;
C.C.C.R., 23J = fine quality; 15 gold settings;   C.C.R., 19J = quality, 10 gold settings.
(This list changed from year to year.)

AMERICAN RAILROAD APPROVED WATCHES 1930

The following requirements for **NEW** railroad approved watches are outlined by Mr. R. D. Montgomery, General Watch Inspector of the Santa Fe Railway System:

"Regulation for **new** watches designated as of 1930 to be standard is described as follows:"

"16 size, American, lever-setting, 19 jewels or more, open face, winding at "12", double-roller escapement, steel escape wheel, adjusted to 5 positions, temperature and isochronism, which will rate within a variation not exceeding 6 seconds in 72 hour tests, pendant up, dial up and dial down, and be regulated to run within a variation not exceeding 30 seconds per week."

"The following listed makes and grades meet the requirements and comprise a complete list of watches acceptable. Watches bearing the name of jewelers or other names not standard trade marks or trade numbers will not be accepted:" (**This list changed from year to year.**)

AMERICAN WALTHAM W. CO.
(16 Size)
23J Premier Maximus
23J Riverside Maximus
23J Vanguard
    6 position
    winding indicator
23J Vanguard
    6 position
21J Crescent Street
21J No. 645
19J Vanguard
19J Riverside

BALL WATCH CO.
(16 Size)
23J Official R.R. Standard
21J Official R.R. Standard
19J Official R.R. Standard

ELGIN WATCH CO.
(16 Size)
23J Veritas
21J Veritas
21J B. W. Raymond
21J Father Time
21J No. 270

HAMILTON WATCH CO.
(16 Size)
23J No. 950
21J No. 990
21J No. 992
19J No. 952
19J No. 996

HAMPDEN WATCH CO.
(16 Size)
23J Special Railway
21J New Railway
19J Railway

HOWARD WATCH CO.
(16 Size)
All 23J
All 21J
All 19J

ILLINOIS WATCH CO.
(16 Size)
23J Sangamo Special
23J Sangamo
23J Bunn Special
21J Bunn Special
21J Sangamo
21J A. Lincoln
19J Bunn

SOUTH BEND WATCH CO.
(16 Size)
21J No. 227
21J No. 229
21J No. 295
19J No. 293

Union Pacific Railroad Time Inspectors , June, 1936

All new WATCHES must be **16 size** with double roller adjust to 5 positions & so stamped on plates, lever set, plain Arabic numbers , open-faced & wind at 12, maintain a rate of 30 seconds. The following will govern the NEW RAILROAD STANDARDS. **BALL**=21&23 jeweled "Official Railroad Standard"; **ELGIN**=21&23 jeweled "B.W. Raymond"; **HAMILTON**="950 & 992"; **ILLINOIS**=21&23 jeweled "Bunn Special"; **WALTHAM**=23 jeweled "Vanguard".

CP RAIL SERVICE AS OF FEBRUARY 1, 1957

WALTHAM (16 SIZE)
23J Vanguard S. # 29, 634, 001 and up

ELGIN (16 Size)
21J B.W.R.
21J No. 571

HAMILTON (16 SIZE)
23J No. 950B
21J No. 992B

BALL W. Co.(16 Size)
21J (Hamilton) No. 992B
21J No. 435C

ZENITH (16 Size)
21J Extra RR 56

APPROVED WRIST WATCHES IN
CP RAIL SERVICE

CYMA
17J RR 2852 M
25J RR 2872 A

GIRARD PERREGAUX
17J CP 307H.F.

LONGINES
17J RR 280

UNIVERSAL
19J RR 1205

ZENITH
18J RR 120 T

FERGUSON Patented RR Dial : Patent numbers on back. Hr.1-12 in red, Min. 5-60 in black, hr. hand red, min. hand black. Valued at ; BALL = **$1,000 to $1,550** and A.W.W.Co., Elgin, Hamilton, Illinois, etc. = **$500 to $900** for MINT dials.

ELGIN WATCH CO., Classic Montgomery RR Dial (note 6 inside seconds bit) with red marginal numbers at 5, 10, 15, 20, 25, 30, 35, 40, 45, 50, 55, & 60. Valued at **$75 to $135.** Montgomery RR Dials first used <u>about</u> 1904.

APPROVED WRIST WATCHES IN
CP RAIL SERVICE 1965
BATTERY POWERED

BULOVA ACCUTRON
17J 214
17J 218 Calendar

RODANIA
13J RR 2780 Calendar

WITTNAUER
13J RR 12 WT Calendar

APPROVED WRIST WATCHES SEMI-MECHANICAL
Q = QUARTZ ANALOG BATTERY POWERED
IN CP RAIL SERVICE AS OF 1978

CYMA
7J Calendar RR 9361 Q
6J Calendar RR 960 Q

BULOVA
7J Calendar RR 9362 Q
6J Calendar RR 960.111Q

RODANIA
6J Calendar 9952.111RR
7J Calendar RR 9361 Q

ROTARY
7J Calendar RR 9366 Q

WYLER
7J Calendar RR 9361 Q

WITTNAUER
7J Calendar RR 2 Q 115 C

ADJUSTMENTS

There are **nine** basic adjustments for watch movements. They are:

heat 1
cold 1
isochronism 1
positions 6
TOTAL 9

THE SIX POSITION ADJUSTMENTS ARE:

Stem UP
Stem Down
This position adjustment not required on railroad watches.
Stem Left
Stem Right
Dial Up
Dial Down

🕐 A watch marked as **5 positions** is equivalent to one marked *eight adjustments* (the most common found on RR watches) and will be listed in this book as: **"Adj.5P"** (adjusted to heat,cold, isochronism and 5 positions). A watch marked as **nine adjustments** is equivalent to one marked *6 positions* & listed as **"Adj.6P"** (adjusted to heat,cold, isochronism and 6 positions). A watch that is marked as *ADJUSTED* only is adjusted to isochronism & in poise in all temperatures & is listed as **"Adj."**.
* Later some manufactures used a variations of 8 adjustments, six to position, 1-isochronism, 1-temperature or as in the Elgin grade 571 two to temperature in about 1950.

🕐 Not all railroad GRADE watches were railroad **APPROVED**, to be approved each railroad line or company made a list of watch grades that they would **approve** for example, Southern Railway, Lake Shore Railroad, CP Rail Service & Santa Fe Railway System etc.

WRIST WATCHES POSITION ADJUSTMENTS

CROWN UP - CROWN DOWN- CROWN LEFT - CROWN RIGHT - DIAL DOWN - DIAL UP
Main vertical position: Wrist Watches = CROWN DOWN & Pocket Watches = PENDANT UP.

28

The total number of pocket watches made for the railroad industry was small in comparison to the total pocket watches produced. Generally, watches defined as "Railroad Watches" fall into five categories:

1. **Railroad Approved-** A list of Grades and Models approved by the railway companies.
2. **Railroad Grade-**Those advertised as being able to pass or exceed railroad inspection.
3. **Pre-Commission Watches-**Those used by the railroads before 1893.
4. **Company Watches-**Those with a railroad logo or company name on the dial.
5. **Train Watches-**Those with a locomotive painted on the dial or inscribed on the case.

1.Not all railroad employees were required to purchase or use approved watches, just the employees that were responsible for schedules. But many employees did buy the approved watches because they were the standard in reliability.
2. These were used primarily by those railroaders who were not required to submit their watches for inspection.
3. There were many watches made for railroad use prior to 1893. **Some of the key wind ones, especially, are good quality and highly collectible.**
4 & 5. Some manufacturers inscribed logos & terms such as railroader, special railroad, dispatcher, etc. on the dials & back plates of the movements.

NOTE: Railroad Standards, Railroad Approved & Railroad Grade **terminology,** as defined and used in this _**BOOK**_. **RAILROAD STANDARDS** = A commission or board appointed by the railroad companies outlined a set of **guidelines** or requirements to be approved by each railroad line. **RAILROAD APPROVED** = After 1875-80 a RR employee had to buy his own watch. A _**LIST**_ of watches each railroad line would approve if purchased by their employee's. **This list changed through the year**. **RAILROAD GRADE** = A watch made by manufactures to meet or exceed the railroad **standards**. Grades such as 992, Vanguard and B.W. Raymond, etc.
* Some GRADES **exceeded** the R.R. standards requirements such as 23 jewels, diamond end stone, gold train, raised gold jewel settings, double sunk dial and the list goes on. Examples: such as Veritas, Sangamo, 950 & Riverside Maximus and many others.

COLONIAL WATCHMAKERS (PRE—1850)

Early American _Colonial watchmakers_ came from Europe and **most** all the movements were made near _**Prescot Lancashire England;**_ these hand-fabricated watches were made largely from imported parts. It was common practice for a watchmaker to use rough castings made by several craftsmen. 99% of English watches were made by numerous tradesman's and each person made a separate portion of the watch before being completed. These were referred to as ebauche or"movements in the gray". The watchmaker finished the ebauche movements & parts, then assembled them to make a complete watch. He would then engrave his name on the finished timepiece. Some of the early American watchmakers designed the cases or other parts, but most imported what they needed. The Colonial watchmakers were also _clock makers._ The Colonial clock-watchmakers made the cases for the tall clocks and imported the clock movement. The demand was low and most made both clocks and watches. These early hand-made watches are hard to find; therefore, only the name of the watchmaker will be listed. This compilation comes from old ads in newspapers and journals and other sources. It is not considered to be complete. Because of the shortage and condition of these early Colonial watches, prices may vary widely from $400, $1,200 to $12,000.

As early as 1775 the first Swiss made watches came into the U.S.A. and made in the London style. In 1830, Vacheron & Constantin established a connection in New York through Jean Magnin. Later in the mid 1830's extending their trade to Philadelphia and New Orleans and by 1838 Agassiz and later Jurgensen. Early in the 1860's the Swiss Firms of Cortebert, E. Borel and Courvoisier made and **designed** watches to closely resemble the style of American watch case and movement. Examples: the Ohio Watch Co. was distributed by Leon Lesquereaux and son (Junior) of Columbus, Ohio. E. Borel & Co. produced American style watches and shipped them to Lucien Morel & Ed Droz in New York. These were followed later by the entire original designs of the Swiss watch manufactures.

George Bowen, Boston Mass., engraved on movement "Chronometer Maker", KW KS, Spring Detent., Ca. 1850.

Davis Watson & Co. Boston, Fusee with right angle escapement lever, serial No. 8028 Ca. 1850.

Example of watch paper placed inside a pair-cased watch by a watch maker. This was a form of advertisement placed in the watch after repair was made.

Ephraim Clark, 18 size, non-jeweled, made between 1780-1800; a good example of a colonial watch. These early watches usually included chain driven fusees, verge type escapements, hand pierced balance cock, key wind & set; note the circular shaped regulator above the balance Cock.

Effingham Clark, New York, on dial & movement, the inner with Roman hour chapter and a sweep second outer dial, diamond stone, serial No. 720, Ca. 1800.

E. EMBREE, NEW YORK engraved on movement, serial # 790, chain driven fusee, silver pair cased watch, ca. early 1800's.

B. F. S. Patten, Bangor, Maine, LEFT & RIGHT; left a 48mm, 6 jewels, <u>Cylinder</u> escapement bar style Ebauche movement which may have been manufactured by Japy Freres with branches in France, Switzerland & England. Right; showing the movement cover that reads four holes jeweled but 6 jewels exits, Ca.1855 to 1865.("Continental Watch")

GREENLEUF & OAKES, Hartford, Ca. 1805, Greenleuf & Oakes formed a partnership in 1804, verge, pierced cock.

MARQUAND & CO., New York, Ca. 1850s, gold case, right angle lever escapement, fusee, gold dial.

J. H. MULFORD, Albany, N. Y., produced watches from about 1835 to 1875, the two watch movements (A & B) are illustrated, A is about size 18, KWKS, gold jewel settings, compensated balance with gold screws. Movement B is 3 arm balance, diamond end stone. Note the J. H. Mulford patented verge style escapement patented # 2465, dated Feb. 21, 1842. illustrated to the far right.

EARLY AMERICAN WATCHMAKERS
(With Location and Approximate Date)

Adams, Nathan (Boston, MA, 1800)
Adams, William (Boston, MA, 1810)
Alden, & Eldridge (Bristol, Conn., 1820)
Aldrich, Jacob (Wilmington, DE, 1802)
Alrichs, Jonas (Wilmington, DE, 1880)
Allebach, Jacob (Phila., PA, 1825-1840)
Amant, Fester (Phila., PA, 1793)
Atherton, Nathan (Phila., PA, 1825)
Atkins & Allen (Bristol, Ct., 1820)
Atkinson, James (Boston, MA, 1745)
Austin, Isaac (Phila., PA, 1785)
Backhouse, John (Lancaster, PA, 1725)
Bagnall, Benjamin (Phila., PA, 1750)
Bailey, John (Boston, MA, 1810)
Bailey & Kitchen:(Phila,PA, 1832-46) name
changed to **Bailey, Banks & Biddle**
Bailey, William (Phila., PA, 1820)
Baker, Benjamin (Phila., PA, 1825)
Banks, Joseph (Phila., PA, 1790)
Banstein, John (Phila.,PA, 1790)
Barnes, Timothy (Litchfield, Conn. 1790)
Barnhill, Robert (Phila., PA, 1775)
Barrow, Samuel (Phila., PA, 1771)
Barry, Standish (Baltimore, MD, 1785)
Basset, John F. (Phila., PA, 1798)
Batterson, James (New York 1705-30)
Bayley, Simeon C., (Phila., PA 1795)
Beard, Duncan (Appoquinemonk, Del.1765)
Belk, William (Phila., PA 1796)
Belknap, William (Boston, MA, 1815)
Bell, William (Phila., PA, 1805)
Benedict, S. W. (New York, NY, 1835)
Bigger & Clarke (Baltimore, MD, 1783)
Billion, C. (Phila., PA, 1775-1800)
Billow, Charles & Co. (Phila., PA 1796)
Bingham & Bricerly (Phila., PA, 1778-1799)
Birge, Mallory & Co. (Bristol, Conn. 1830)
Birge, Peck & Co. (Bristol, Conn. 1830)
Birnie, Laurence (Phila., PA, 1774)
Blundy, Charles (Charleston, SC, 1750)
Blunt & Nichols (New York, NY, 1850)
Boardman, Chauncey (Bristol, Conn.1815)
Boardman, & Dunbar (Bristol, Conn. 1811)
Boardman, & Wells (Bristol, Conn. 1815)
Bode, William (Phila., Pa 1796)
Bogardus, Evarardus (New York, 1698)
Bond, William (Boston,MA, 1800-1810)
Bonnaud (Phila., PA, 1799)
Bower, Michael (Phila., PA, 1790-1800)
Bowman, Joseph (Lancaster, PA, 1821-44)
Boyd & Richards (Phila., PA, 1808)
Boyter, Daniel (Lancaster, PA, 1805)
Brands & Matthey (Phila., PA, 1799)
Brandt, Aime (Phila., PA, 1820)
Brant, Brown & Lewis (Phila., PA, 1795)
Brazier, Amable (Phila., PA, 1795)
Brearley, James (Phila., PA, 1790-1800)
Brewer, William (Phila., PA, 1785-1791)
Brewster, Abel (Norwich, CT) 1802
Brewster &Ingraham(Bristol,CT,1827-39)
Brown, Davis (Boston, 1800)
Brown, Garven (Boston, MA, 1767)
Brown, John (Lancaster, PA, 1840)
Brown, Samuel (New York, 1820-1850)
Brownell, A. P. (New Bedford, MA.1840-60)
Burkelow, Samuel (Phila., PA, 1791-1799)

Burnop, Daniel (E. Windsor, Conn., 1793)
Bush, George (Easton, PA, 1790-1800)
Cairns, John (Providence, 1785-1809)
Campbell, Charles (Phila., PA, 1796)
Campbell, William (Carlisle, PA, 1765)
Canby, Charles (Wilmington, Del., 1825)
Capper, Michael (Phila., PA, 1799)
Carey, James (Brunswick, ME, 1830)
Carrell, John (Phila., PA, 1791-1793)
Carter, Jacob (Phila., PA, 1805)
Carter, Thomas (Phila., PA, 1823)
Carver, Jacob (Phila., PA, 1790)
Carvill, James (New York, NY, 1803)
Chandlee, John(Wilmington,DE,1795-1810)
Chaudron, Co., (Phila., PA, 1799- 1815)
Chauncey & Joseph Ives (Bristol, CT, 1825)
Cheney, Martin (Windsor, VT, 1800)
Chick, M. M. (Concord, NH, 1845)
Clark,Benjamin(Wilmington,DE,1737-1750)
Clark, Charles (Phila., PA 1810)
Clark, Ephraim (Phila., PA, 1780-1820)
Clark, J.H. & Co. (Memphis Tenn, 1835)
Clark, John (New York, NY, 1770-1790)
Clark, John (Phila., PA, 1799)
Clark, Thomas (Boston, MA, 1764)
Claudon,John-George (Charleston SC,1773)
Cook, William (Boston, MA, 1810)
Crow, George (Wilmington, DE, 1740-1770)
Crow, John (Wilmington, DE, 1770-1798)
Crow, Thomas (Wilmington, DE, 1770-98)
Currier & Trott (Boston, MA, 1800)
Curtis, Solomon (Phila., PA, 1793-1795)
Dakin, James (Boston, MA, 1795)
Davis, Samuel (Boston, MA, 1820)
Davis,Watson & Co.(Boston, 1840-1850)
Delaplaine, James K.(New York, 1786-1800)
DeVacht, Joseph & Frances **(Gallipolis, OH, 1792)**
Dickinson, Thos. (Boston, 1810)
Dix, Joseph (Phila., PA, 1770)
Downes, Anson (Bristol, CT, 1830)
Downes, Arthur (Charleston, SC, 1765)
Downes, Ephriam (Bristol, CT, 1830)
Droz, Hannah (Phila., PA, 1840)
Droz, Humbert (Phila., PA, 1793-1799)
Duffield, Edward W. (Whiteland, PA, 1775)
Dunheim, Andrew (New York, NY, 1775)
Dupuy, John (Phila., PA, 1770)
Dupuy, Odran (Phila., PA, 1735)
Dutch, Stephen, Jr. (Boston, MA.1800-10)
Eberman, George (Lancaster, PA, 1800)
Eberman, John (Lancaster, PA, 1780-1820)
Ellicott, Joseph (Buckingham, PA, 1763)
Elsworth, David (Baltimore, MD.1780-1800)
Embree, Effingham (New York, NY, 1785)
Evans, David (Baltimore, MD, 1770-1773)
Fales, James (New Bedford, MA.1810-20)
Ferris, Tiba (Wilmington, DE, 1812-1850)
Fessler, John (Phila., PA, 1785-1820)
Feton, J. (Phila., PA, 1825-1840)
Filber, John (Lancaster, PA, 1810-1825)
Fister, Amon (Phila., PA, 1794)
Fix, Joseph (Reading, PA, 1820-1840)
Fowell, J & N (Boston, MA, 1800-1810)
Frances,Basil & Alexander Vuille(Baltimore,1766)
Galbraith, Patrick (Phila., PA, 1795)
Gibbons, Thomas (Phila., PA, 1750)

Goodfellow, William (Phila., PA,1793-1795)
Goodfellow & Son, William (Phila., PA,1796)
Gooding, Henry (Boston, MA, 1810-1820)
Green, John (Phila., PA, 1794)
Griffen, Henry (New York, 1790)
Groppengeiser, J. L. (Phila., PA, 1840)
Grotz, Issac (Easton, PA, 1810-1835)
Hall, Jonas (Boston, MA, 1848-1858)
Harland, Theodore (Norwich, CT,1750-90)
Harland, Thomas (New York, 1805)
Harland, Thomas (Norwich, CT, 1802)
Harrison, James (Shrewbury, MA, 1805)
Hawxhurst & Demilt (New York, 1800)
Hawxhurst, Nath. (New York, NY, 1784)
Heilig, Jacob (Phila., PA, 1770-1824)
Heilig, John (Germantown, PA, 1824-1830)
Hepton, Frederick (Phila., PA, 1785)
Hequembourg, C. (Paterson N.J. 1815-1830)
Heron, Isaac (New York, NY, 1770-1780)
Hill, D. (Reading, PA 1830)
Hodgson, William (Phila., PA, 1785)
Hoff, John (Lancaster, PA, 1800)
Hoffner, Henry (Phila., PA, 1791)
Howard, Thomas (Phila., PA, 1789-1791)
Howe, Jubal (Shrewbury, MA, 1800)
Huguenail, Charles (Phila., PA, 1799)
Hunt, Hiram (Robbinston, ME, 1800)
Hutchins, Abel (Concord, MA, 1785-1818)
Hutchins, Levi (Concord, MA, 1785-1815)
Hyde, John E. (New York, NY, 1805)
Hyde & Goodrich (New Orleans, LA, 1850)
Ingersoll, Daniel B. (Boston, MA, 1800-10)
Ingold, Pierre Frederick (NY, NY,1845-50)
Ives, Chauncy & Joseph (Bristol, CT, 1825)
Jacob, Charles & Claude (Annapolis, 1775)
Jackson, Joseph H. (Phila., PA, 1802-1810)
Jessop, Jonathan (Park Town, PA, 1790)
Jeunit, Joseph (Meadville, PA, 1763)
Johnson, Chauncy (AlbanyN.Y., (1825-1840)
Johnson, David (Boston, MA, 1690)
Johnson, John (Charleston, SC, 1763)
Jones, George (Wilmington, DE, 1815-35)
Jones, Low & Ball (Boston, MA, 1830)
Keith, William (Shrewbury, MA, 1810)
Kennedy, Patrick (Phila., PA, 1795-1799)
Kincaid, Thomas (Christiana Bridge, DE, Ca. 1775)
Kirkwood, John (Charleston, SC, 1761)
Kumble, Wm. (New York- 1776)
Launy, David F. (Boston & N. Y., 1800)
Leavenworth, Mark (Waterbury, CT, 1820)
Leavenworth, Wm. (Waterbury, CT, 1810)
Leslie & Co., Baltimore, MD, 1795)
Leslie & Price (Phila., PA, 1793-1799)
Leslie, Robert (Baltimore, MD, 1788-1791)
Levely, George (Phila., PA, 1774)
Levi, Michael & Issac (Baltimore,MD,1785)
Limeburner, John (Phila., PA, 1790)
Lind, John (Phila., PA, 1791-1799)
Lowens, David (Phila., PA, 1785)
Ludwig, John (Phila., PA, 1791)
Lufkins & Johnson (Boston, MA, 1800-10)
Lukins, Isaac (Phila., PA, 1825)
Macdowell, Robert (Phila., PA, 1798)
MacFarlane, John (Boston, MA, 1800-1810)
Mahve, Matthew (Phila., PA, 1761)
Manross, Elisha (Bristol, CT, 1827)
Martin, Patrick (Phila., PA, 1830)
Mathey, Louis (Phia., PA, 1800)

Maunroe & Whitney (Concord,MA,1800's)
Maus, Frederick (Phila., PA, 1785- 1793)
Maynard, George(New York,NY,1702-1730)
McCabe, John (Baltimore, MD, 1774)
McDowell, James (Phila., PA, 1795)
McGraw, Donald (Annapolis, MD, 1767)
Medley, Josia (Boston, 1732)
Mends, James (Phila., PA, 1795)
Merriman, Titus (Bristol, CT, 1830)
Merry, Charles F. (Phila., PA, 1799)
Meters, John(Fredricktown, MD,1795-1825)
Miller, Abraham (Easton, PA, 1810-1830)
Mitchell & Atkins (Bristol, CT, 1830)
Mitchell, Henry (N. Y., NY, 1787-1800)
Mohler, Jacob (Baltimore, MD, 1773)
Moir, J & W (Waterbury, CT, 1790)
Montandon, Julien (Shrewbury, CT, 1812)
Moollinger, Henry (Phila., PA, 1794)
Morgan, Thomas (Phila. & Balti., 1774-93)
Moris, William (Grafton, MA, 1765-1775)
Mulford, J. H. (Albany, NY, 1845)
Mulliken, Nathaniel (Boston, MA, 1765)
Munroe & Whitney (Concord, MA, 1820)
Narney, Joseph (Charleston, SC, 1753)
Neiser, Augustine (Phila., PA, 1739-1780)
Nicholls, George (New York, NY, 1728-50)
Nicollette, Mary (Phila., PA, 1793-1799)
O'Hara, Charles (Phila., PA, 1799)
Oliver, Griffith (Phila., PA, 1785-1793)
Ormsby, James (Baltimore, MD, 1771)
Palmer, John (Phila., PA, 1795)
Palmer, John Peter (Phila., PA, 1795)
Park, Seth (Parktown, PA, 1790)
Parke, Solomon (Phila., PA, 1791-1795)
Parke, Solomon & Co. (Phila., PA, 1799)
Parker, James (Cambridge, OH, 1790)
Parker, Thomas (Phila., PA, 1783)
Parry, John J. (Phila., PA, 1795-1800)
Patton, Abraham (Phila., PA, 1799)
Patton, David (Phila., PA, 1800)
Payne, Lawrence (New York, NY,1732-55)
Pearman, W. (Richmond, VA, 1834)
Perkins, Thomas (Phila., PA. 1785-1800)
Perry, Marvin (New York, NY, 1770-1780)
Perry, Thomas (New York, NY, 1750-1775)
Phillips, Joseph (New York, NY, 1713-35)
Pierret, Mathew (Phila., PA, 1795)
Pope, Joseph (Boston, MA, 1790)
Price, Philip (Phila., PA, 1825)
Proctor, Cardan (New York, NY.1747-75)
Proctor, William (New York,NY.1737-1760)
Proud, R. (Newport, RI, 1775)
Potter, J.O.&J.R. (Providence,R.I.1849-59)
Purse, Thomas (Baltimore, MD, 1805)
Quimby, Phineas & William (Belfast, ME, 1825)
Reily, John (Phila., PA, 1785-1795)
Rich, John (Bristol, CT, 1800)
Richardson, Francis (Phila., PA, 1736)
Ritchie, George (Phila., PA, 1785-1790)
Roberts, John (Phila., PA, 1799)
Roberts, S & E (Trenton, NJ, 1830)
Rode, William (Phila., PA, 1785)
Rodger, James (New York, NY, 1822-1878)
Rodgers,Samuel (Plymouth,MA, 1800's)
Russell, George (Phila., PA, 1840)
Saxton & Lukens (Phila., PA, 1828)
Schriner, Martin (Lancaster, PA.1790-1830)
Schriner, M & P (Lancaster, PA, 1830-40)

Seddinger, Margaret (Phila., PA, 1846)
Severberg, Christian (NY, NY, 1755-1775)
Sherman, Robert(Wilmington, DE.1760-70)
Sibley, O. E. (New York, NY, 1820)
Simpson, Saml. (Clarksville,Tenn - 1855)
Smith, J. L. (Middletown, CT, 1830)
Smith & Goodrich (Bristol, CT, 1827-1840)
Soloman, Henry (Boston, MA, 1820)
Souza, Sammuel (Phila., PA, 1820)
Sprogell, John (Phila., PA, 1791)
Spurck, Peter (Phila., PA, 1795-1799)
Stanton, Job (New York, NY, 1810)
Stein, Abraham (Phila., PA, 1799)
Stevens, E. (Boston, 1730)
Stever & Bryant (Wigville, CT, 1830)
Stillas, John (Phila., PA, 1785-1793)
Stinnett, John (Phila., PA, 1769)
Stokel, John (New York, NY, 1820-1840)
Store, Marmaduke (Phila., PA, 1742)
Strech, Thomas (Phila., PA, 1782)
Syderman, Philip (Phila., PA, 1785)
Taf, John James (Phila., PA, 1794)

Taylor, Samuel (Phila, PA, 1799)
Tonchure, Francis (Baltimore, MD, 1805)
Townsend, Charles (Phila., PA, 1799)
Townsend, David (Boston, MA, 1800)
Trott, Andrew (Boston, MA, 1800-1810)
Turrell, Samuel (Boston, MA, 1790)
Voight, Henry (Phila., PA, 1775-1793)
Voight, Sebastian (Phila., PA, 1775-1799)
Voight, Thomas (Henry's son) (Phila., PA, 1811-1835)
Vuille, Alexander (Baltimore, MD, 1766)
Warner, George T. (New York, NY, 1795)
Watson, Davis (Boston, 1840-50)
Weller, Francis (Phila., PA, 1780)
Wells, George & Co. (Boston, MA, 1825)
Wells, J.S. (Boston, MA, 1800)
Wetherell, Nathan (Phila., PA, 1830-1840)
Wheaton, Caleb (Providence, RI, 1800)
White, Sebastian (Phila., PA, 1795)
Whittaker, William (NY, NY, 1731-1755)
Wood, John (Phila., PA, 1770-1793)
Wright, John (New York, NY, 1712-1735)
Zahm, G.M. (Lancaster, PA, 1865)

Watch made by Andrew, Dunheim of New York in about 1775. Note the hand pierced case.

Louis Mathey, Philadelphia engraved on movement, about 18 size, very thin movement, **Virgule** escapement, key wind & set from back, Ca.1795-1805.

H. Mitchell, New York, 18 size, verge chain driven fusee; note the regulator below hand-pierced cock, Ca. 1790.

HOW TO DETERMINE SIZE

AMERICAN MOVEMENT SIZES
LANCASHIRE GAUGE

Size	Inches	Inches	mm	Lignes	Size	Inches	Inches	mm	Lignes
18/0	18/30	.600	15.24	6 3/4	2	1 7/30	1.233	31.32	13 7/8
17/0	19/30	.633	16.08	7 1/8	3	1 8/30	1.266	32.16	14 1/4
16/0	20/30	.666	16.92	7 1/2	4	1 9/30	1.300	33.02	14 7/8
15/0	21/30	.700	17.78	7 7/8	5	1 10/30	1.333	33.86	15 1/8
14/0	22/30	.733	18.62	8 1/4	6	1 11/30	1.366	34.70	15 3/8
13/0	23/30	.766	19.46	8 5/8	7	1 12/30	1.400	35.56	15 3/4
12/0	24/30	.800	20.32	9 1/8	8	1 13/30	1.433	36.40	16 1/8
11/0	25/30	.833	21.16	9 3/8	9	1 14/30	1.466	37.24	16 1/2
10/0	26/30	.866	22.00	9 3/4	10	1 15/30	1.500	38.10	16 7/8
9/0	27/30	.900	22.86	10 1/8	11	1 16/30	1.533	38.94	17 1/4
8/0	28/30	.933	23.70	10 1/2	12	1 17/30	1.566	39.78	17 5/8
7/0	29/30	.966	24.54	10 7/8	13	1 18/30	1.600	40.64	18 1/8
6/0	1	1.000	25.40	11 1/4	14	1 19/30	1.633	41.48	18 3/8
5/0	1 1/30	1.033	26.24	11 5/8	15	1 20/30	1.666	42.32	18 3/4
4/0	1 2/30	1.066	27.08	12 1/8	16	1 21/30	1.700	43.18	19 1/8
3/0	1 3/30	1.100	27.94	12 3/8	17	1 22/30	1.733	44.02	19 1/2
2/0	1 4/30	1.133	28.78	12 3/4	18	1 23/30	1.766	44.86	19 7/8
0	1 5/30	1.166	29.62	13 1/8	19	1 24/30	1.800	45.72	20 1/4
1	1 6/30	1.200	30.48	13 1/2	20	1 25/30	1.833	46.56	20 3/4

NOTE: There are many movements styles with many different sizes in **thickness** and **diameter**, making it **very difficult** trying to find a case to fit a movement. This it true in ALL sizes.

SWISS MOVEMENT SIZES
Lignes With Their Equivalents in Millimeters and Decimal Parts of an Inch

Lignes	Inches Decimals	Millimeters
7	.622	15.79
8	.710	18.05
9	.799	20.30
10	.888	22.56
11	.977	24.81
12	1.066	27.07
13	1.154	29.32
14	1.243	31.58
15	1.332	33.84
16	1.421	36.09
17	1.510	38.35
18	1.599	40.60
19	1.687	42.86
20	1.776	45.11
21	1.865	47.37
22	1.954	49.63

DIAL

PILLAR PLATE

GAUGES FOR MEASURING YOUR WATCH SIZE

The size of a watch is determined by measuring the outside diameter of the dial side of the lower pillar plate. The gauges below may be placed across the face of your watch to calculate its approximate size.

AMER. MOVEMENT SIZES

SWISS MOVEMENT SIZES
LIGNES

IMPORTANT NOTE: Have your watch case **TESTED** to make sure of gold quality or Karat.

SOLID GOLD MARKS

IMPORTANT NOTE: Have your watch case TESTED to make sure of gold quality or Karat.

The term **KARAT** is a word of definition in regards to the quality of gold, one 24th part (of pure gold). For example: Pure or fine gold is 24 karats; 18 Karat (abbreviated 18 K)consist of 18 parts of pure gold and mixed with 6 parts of other metal. The term **CARAT** is a unit of weight for gemstones, 200 milligrams equal 1 Carat. Karat = gold content & Carat = weight of GEMS.

GOLD-FILLED CASES

The first patent for gold-filled cases was given to J. Boss on **May 3, 1859.** Gold-filled cases are far more common than solid gold cases. Only about 5 percent of the cases were solid gold. In making the gold-filled case, the following process was used: two bars of gold, 12″ long, 2″ wide, and 1/2 ″ thick were placed on either side of a bar of base metal. The bar of base metal was 3/4″ thick and the same length and width as the gold bars. These three bars were soldered together under pressure at high temperature. The bars were sent through rolling mills under tremendous pressure; this rolling was repeated until the desired thickness was reached. The new sandwich-type gold was now in a sheet. Discs were punched out of the sheet and pressed in a die to form a dish-shaped cover. Finally the lip, or ridge, was added. The bezel, snap, and dust caps were added in the finishing room. Gold-filled cases are usually 10k or 14k gold. The cases were marked ten-year, fifteen-year, twenty-year, twenty-five-year, or thirty-year. The number of years indicated the duration of guarantee that the gold on the case would not wear through to the base metal. The higher the number of years indicates that more gold used and that a higher original price was paid.

In 1924 the government prohibited any further use of the guarantee terms of 5, 10, 15, 20, 25, or 30 years. After that, manufacturers marked their cases 10k or 14k Gold-Filled and 10k Rolled Gold Plate. Anytime you see the terms ''5, 10, 15, 20, 25 and 30-year,'' this immediately identifies the case as being gold-filled. The word ''guaranteed'' on the case also denotes gold-filled.

Rolled Gold

Rolled gold involved rolling gold into a micro thinness and, under extreme pressure, bonding it to each sheet of base metal. Rolled gold carried a five-year guarantee. The thickness of the gold sheet varied and had a direct bearing on value, as did the richness of the engraving.

Gold Gilding

Brass plates, wheels and cases are often gilded with gold. To do this, the parts are hung by a copper wire in a vessel or porous cell of a galvanic battery filled with a solution of ferro-cyanide of potassium, carbonate of soda, chloride of gold, and distilled water. An electric current deposits the gold evenly over the surface in about a six-minute period. One ounce of gold is enough for heavy gilding of six hundred watches. After gilding, the plates are polished with a soft buff using powdered rouge mixed with water and alcohol. The older method is fire-gilt which uses a gold and mercury solution. The metal is subjected to a high temperature so the mercury will evaporate and leave the gold plating. This is a very dangerous method, however, due to the harmful mercury vapor.

JAS. BOSS Railroad Model 10K Gold Filled cases sold for **$14.00** in 1927

GOLD-FILLED MARKS

The following gold-filled and rolled gold plate marks are not complete, but if you have any doubt that the case is solid gold, **pay** only the *gold-filled* price.

GOLD FILLED MARKS

☆ 10 K ROLLED GOLD PLATE

BEE HIVE

(14K. Filled.)

(Jas. Boss 10K. Filled. 20 Years.)

CROWN 14K. FILLED
(25 Years.)

(Keystone Extra, Substitute for All-Gold Case.)

CROWN 10K. FILLED
(20 Years.)

(Rolled Gold.)

(Jas. Boss 14K. Filled. 25 Years.)

EMPRESS
(Gold Filled, 10 Years.)

FORTUNE
(Gold Filled, 20 Years.)

(10 Years.)

PREMIER
(Gold Filled, 25 Years.)

(14K. Filled.)

XV.

THE BELL 14K.
(25 Years.)

XX.

CASHIER
(Gold Filled, 25 Years.)

(10K. Gold Filled.)

V.
(5 Years.)

(15 Years.)

(20 Years.)

(25 Years.)

THE COMET
(10 Years.)

SILVER CASE MARKS

A.W.W. CO. COIN.

(Discontinued.)

(Discontinued.)

NEWPORT COIN

(Coin Silver with Albata Cap)
(Discontinued.)

DUEBER COIN

(Coin Silver with Silver Cap)
(Discontinued.)

(Coin Silver, with Silver Caps, Gold Joints and Crowns.)

CHAMPION COIN.

STERLING 925/1000 FINE

(Sterling Silver.)

Sterling Silver

IMPORTANT NOTE: Have your watch case **TESTED** to make sure of gold quality or Karat. NICKEL SILVER is 66% Copper, 24% Zinc, and 10% Nickel (also known as **Silveroid** etc.)

SILVER CASE MARKS

(Sterling Silver.)

HUNTING CASES

A hunting case is identified by a cover over the face (concealed dial) of the watch. The case is opened by pressing the stem or the crown of the watch. The hunter style watch was used for protection of the watch and carried by men of status and used as a dress watch.

HOW TO HANDLE A HUNTING CASE WATCH

Hold the watch in your right hand with the bow or swing ring between the index finger and thumb. Press on the pendant-crown with the right thumb to release the cover exposing the face.

When closing, do not **SNAP** the cover. Press the crown to move the catch in, close the cover, then release the crown. This will prevent wear to the soft gold on the rim and catch.

Above: Example of a hunting case

Right: Example of a swing-out case

SWING-OUT MOVEMENT

On some pocket watches the movement swings out from the front. On these type watches the movement can be swung out by unscrewing the bezel and pulling the stem out to **release** the movement. **SEE EXAMPLE ABOVE.**

Above: Engine - Turned
Demi-Hunting Case

Example of a 14 Karat gold **TRUE Box Hinged** case, selling for $94.00 in 1890. Note to be a TRUE Box Hinged case the top will match the bottom.

Left: Example of a screw bezel and screw back case.

Note: The screw on bezel was invented by E. C. Fitch in 1886.

Above Right: Example of a reversible case to either hunting case or open face.
Also 2 illustrations of a Muckle reversible case markings stamped or engraved inside the case. (1.) Engraved on movement cover - E. A. Muckle, Pat'd April 3, 1883 or 1888 + 2 & case serial # 30002. (2.) Marked on the lid or cover of same case - ROCKFORD COIN + a shield with R and I interwoven also case serial # 30002. (E. A. Muckle case, patent dates, Aug. 3, 1883 also April 3, 1883 or 1888).

MOVEMENT IDENTIFICATION

1. Grade Number. 2. Nickel Motor Barrel Bridge. 3. Center Wheel (2nd Wheel). 4. Winding Wheel with Jewel Setting. 5. First Barrel Wheel. 6. Winding Click. 7. Case Screw. 8. Pendant Crown. 9. Pendant Bow or Swing Ring. 10. Crown Wheel with Screw. 11. Damaskeening-horizontal pattern. 12. Number of Jewels. 13. Center Wheel Jewel with Setting. 14. Adjusted to Heat, Cold, Isochronism & 5 Positions. 15. Patented Regulator with Index & Spring. 16. Balance End Stones (Diamonds, Rubies, & Sapphires were used). 17. Balance Screws. 18. Compensating Balance Wheel. 19. Hairspring. 20. Escapement Bridge. 21. Escapement Wheel Jewel with Setting (Diamonds, Rubies, & Sapphires were used). 22. Escapement Wheel. 23. Fourth Wheel Jewel with Setting. 24. Third Wheel. 25. Fourth Wheel. 26. Fourth Wheel Bridge. 27. Third Wheel Jewel with Setting. 28. Center & Third Wheel Bridge. 29. Bridge Screw. 30. Manufacturers Name & Location. 31. Jewel Setting Screw.

Lever

Many railroad company's required a watch to be lever set. Lever set means moving a lever allowing the crown (winding button) to engage with the hands to set them, to correct time. This was used to prevent accidentally changing the time while winding. The lever is located under the bezel that hold the crystal. On a open face watch, the lever is usually located between 6 minutes to 11 minutes, note the lever has a tab extending up. Remove the bezel to expose the lever, the bezel may be hinged, snap or screw off. Now that the bezel is off, with your thumbnail against the tab on lever move the lever outward, in the outward position turning the crown the hands may be set to correct time.

42

NOMENCLATURE
OF
WATCH PARTS

Ratchet Wheel

Crown or Main Wheel

Click Spring

Setting Cam

Bevel Pinion

Crown or Main
Screw Washer

Winding Arbor

Winding and
Setting Clutch

Setting
Lever

Setting Spring

Click

Setting
Spring Cam

Winding Sleeve

Clutch Lever

NOMENCLATURE
OF
WATCH PARTS

Barrel

Center Wheel

Third Wheel

Minute Wheel

Hour Wheel

Fourth Wheel

Escape Wheel

Center Arbor Washer

Third Pinion

Fourth Pinion

Center Staff

Center Pinion

Escape Pinion

Cannon Pinion

Balance Staff

Pallet Fork and Arbor

Combination Roller

Barrel Arbor

Regulator

Balance Wheel

BRASS

STEEL

EFFECT OF HEAT

EFFECT OF COLD

Overcoil Hairspring

MEAN TIME SCREWS

CASE PRICES

Case prices are for complete cases with bezel, crystal, stem, crown and bow. Hunting case style watches must have workable lift spring.

SILVEROID CASES

Size and Style	Avg	Ex-Fn	Mint
18S, OF, SW	$25	$35	$85
18S, OF, KW	45	50	100
18S, HC, SW	50	60	105
18S, HC, KW	60	70	135
16S, OF, SW	25	35	85
16S, HC	50	55	95
12S, OF	20	25	70
12S, HC	45	55	95
6S-0S, OF	15	20	65
6S-0S, HC	40	45	95

COIN-SILVER CASES

Size and Style	Avg	Ex-Fn	Mint
18S, OF, SW	$50	$65	$165
18S, OF, KW	60	75	190
18S, HC, SW	70	85	195
18S, HC, KW	80	125	240
16S, OF	40	55	140
16S, HC	55	75	175
12S, OF	20	35	90
12S, HC	35	50	125
6S & 0S, OF	15	25	85
6S & 0S, HC	35	50	100

Note: Fancy engraved Cases are Worth 20% to 50% MORE.
Mint or near mint silver cases hard to find & 4 oz 18-16 size add 50% to 100% more.

GOLD-FILLED CASES

Size and Style	Avg	Ex-Fn	Mint
18S, OF, Plain or Engine-Turned	$75	$110	$225
18S, OF, Fancy or **RR** or Ex-Heavy	125	185	325
18S, HC, Plain or Engine-Turned	100	160	275
18S, HC, BOX & Fancy or Ex-Heavy	200	285	475
18S, HC, MULTI-COLOR BOX & Fancy	350	425	700
16S, OF, Plain or Engine-Turned (**DISPLAY CASES**)	75	100	175
16S, OF, Fancy or **RR** or Ex-Heavy	100	175	275
16S, HC, Plain or Engine-Turned	100	160	225
16S, HC, BOX & Fancy or Ex-Heavy	225	285	450
16S, HC, MULTI-COLOR BOX & Fancy	250	395	675
12S, OF, Plain or Engine-Turned	30	55	95
12S, OF, Fancy or Ex-Heavy	35	65	125
12S, HC, Plain or Engine-Turned	55	95	200
12S, HC, Fancy or Ex-Heavy	60	100	225
6S & 0S, OF, Plain or Engine-Turned	25	45	100
6S & 0S, OF, Fancy or Ex-Heavy	30	50	125
6S & 0S, HC, Plain or Engine-Turned	35	50	125
6S & 0S, HC, BOX or Ex-Heavy	75	130	250
6S & 0S, HC, MULTI-color BOX	150	245	400

Note: Ladies size watches are used for jewelry so that decorative quality effect their value.

🕐 **Note:** Plain enamel single sunk dial bring $30 to $60.

Clue to a recased watch.

The screw mark <u>indicates</u> a recased watch.
Not original to the movement.

—movement

—case

The screw on left is a case screw, extra screw mark (⚖) on case <u>indicates</u> a recased watch.

14K SOLID GOLD CASES

Size and Style	Avg	Ex-Fn	Mint
18S, OF, Plain or Engine-Turned	$325	$400	$550
18S, OF, Fancy or RR or Ex-Heavy	375	450	650
18S, HC, Plain or Engine-Turned	400	500	675
18S, HC, Fancy or Ex-Heavy	450	575	875
18S, HC, BOX & Fancy	650	900	1,500
16S, OF, Plain or Engine-Turned	225	325	450
16S, OF, Fancy or RR or Ex-Heavy	325	400	575
16S, HC, Plain or Engine-Turned	375	500	725
16S, HC, Fancy or Ex-Heavy	375	495	735
16S, HC, BOX & Fancy	525	675	1,100
12S, OF, Plain or Engine-Turned	175	225	350
12S, OF, Fancy or Ex-Heavy	225	275	450
12S, HC, Plain or Engine-Turned	250	325	475
12S, HC, Fancy or Ex-Heavy	275	385	485
6S & 0S, OF,	135	185	285
6S & 0S, HC, Plain or Engine-Turned	165	200	335
6S & 0S, HC, BOX or Heavy	200	285	485

18K SOLID GOLD CASES

Size and Style	Avg	Ex-Fn	Mint
18S, OF, Plain or Engine-Turned	$500	$575	$775
18S, OF, Fancy or RR or Ex-Heavy	600	675	925
18S, HC, Plain or Engine-Turned	685	800	1,000
18S, HC, Fancy or Ex-Heavy	1,000	1,250	1,900
18S, HC, BOX & Heavy & Fancy	1,200	1,550	2,300
16S, OF, Plain or Engine-Turned	425	500	675
16S, OF, Fancy or RR or Ex-Heavy	475	625	900
16S, HC, Plain or Engine-Turned	525	625	985
16S, HC, Fancy or Ex-Heavy	550	650	1,000
16S, HC, BOX & Fancy	675	900	1,450
12S, OF, Plain or Engine-Turned	275	325	450
12S, OF, Fancy or Ex-Heavy	275	325	550
12S, HC, Plain or Engine-Turned	350	385	550
12S, HC, Fancy or Ex-Heavy	400	450	675
6S & 0S, OF,	175	225	350
6S & 0S, HC, Plain or Engine-Turned	225	300	500
6S & 0S, HC, BOX or Heavy	300	400	675

14K MULTI–COLOR SOLID GOLD CASES

Size and Style	Avg	Ex-Fn	Mint
18S, OF, Plain or Engine-Turned	$700	$825	$1,000
18S, OF, BOX or Ex-Heavy	1,100	1,350	1,800
18S, HC, Plain or Engine-Turned	1,000	1,200	1,600
18S, HC, BOX	1,600	2,500	3,600
18S, HC, BOX & Fancy or Ex-Heavy	2,500	3,800	5,200
16S, OF, Plain or Engine-Turned	600	700	950
16S, OF, BOX or Ex-Heavy	850	950	1,300
16S, HC, Plain or Engine-Turned	800	1,000	1,400
16S, HC, BOX	800	1,000	1,500
16S, HC, BOX & Fancy or Ex-Heavy	1,500	2,000	3,000
6S & 0S, OF,	350	425	525
6S & 0S, HC, Plain or Engine-Turned	425	500	625
6S & 0S, HC, BOX & Fancy or Ex-Heavy	450	600	785

* Note: ADD 25-35% for 18K Multi & Multi with box cases.

Note: Most 18 & 16 size movements were not cased by the factory. Between 1910 and 1925 marked the start of **advertised** factory cased movements. Most high grade 12 & 10 after 1915 were factory cased. 12 & 10 size Hamilton & Howard were all cased by the factory. All Hampden 12 size (thin) & most South Bend 12 & 10 size were factory cased. Some Illinois and Waltham were cased at factory. Brand names as Ariston, Santa Fe, Burlington and others using Illinois movements used their name. Dollar watches were factory cased. Early Walthams made their own cases, so were cased at factory. Most or many European movements were cased by the watchmaker.

INSPECTING OPEN-FACED WATCHES

For watches with a screw-on front and back, as in railroad models, hold the watch in the left hand and, with the right hand, turn the bezel counter clockwise. While removing the bezel, hold onto the stem and swing ring in order not to drop the watch. Lay the bezel down, check the dial for cracks and crazing, nicks, chips, etc. Look for lever and check to see that it will allow hands to be set. After close examination, **replace** the bezel and turn the watch over. Again, while holding the stem between the left thumb and index finger, remove the back cover. If it is a screw-on back cover, turn it counter clockwise. If it is a snap on cover, look for the lip on the back and use a watch opener to pry the back off.

Left: Example of **OPEN FACE** case.

16 Size, Bridge, Lever Set, New Thin Model, Hunting or Open Face.

Nickel, 17 extra fine, high colored ruby jewels, gold settings; accurately adjusted to temperature, six positions and isochronism, very carefully timed; compensation balance, gold screws, including four timing screws; gold beveled polished train; highly finished, hardened, beveled steel escape wheel, chamfered teeth; hand finished conical pivots on balance staff; counterpoised fork and pallet; best quality Swiss Breguet hairspring, Philippe coil; patent micrometric screw regulator; all steel parts highly polished; visible concaved winding wheel; best quality Swiss mainspring; double sunk glass enameled dial; damaskeened in new style bright rayed pattern, black enamel lettering. A strictly high-grade watch for exacting requirements.

No. 187 Bridge.................**$40 00**

1905 Illinois AD
"**damaskeened** in new style bright rayed pattern"

DAMASKEENING

A *special* American **factory** terminology used in **ALL** their advertisements. Damaskeening is a technique of embellishing movement plates by using small polishing wheels of ivory or boxwood with abrasive paste and is called DAMASKEENING (pronounced dam-a-skeen-ing). A Mr. F.Wilmot came from St. Imier Switzerland to **help develop** and teach this process first to U.S. Watch Co. of Marion, then to other USA factories. Damaskeening was first used in USA by U.S. Watch Co. of Marion in about **1868-69**. Am. Waltham Watch Co. first used Damaskeening about 1871 on the 16 size, model 1872 & Elgin started Damaskeening about mid 1870's. Damaskeening on watch plates became popular in the late 1870s by most manufactures. Howard, Illinois, Rockford, Seth Thomas and others competed fiercely for beauty of Damaskeening. Damaskeening can be in two colors (2 tone) of metal such as copper or gold on nickel or gilt. (not the gold, red or black lettering)

In Europe this decoration on watches, the terminology or expression is, Fausse Cotes, Cotes de Geneve or Geneva Stripes.

DISPLAY CASE WATCHES

Display case watches were used by salesmen and in jewelry stores to show the customer the movement. Both front and back had a glass crystal. These are not rare, but they are nice to have in a collection to show off a watch movement.

DISPLAY CASE with a bezel & glass crystal to view movement.

North American Watch Co. offered this Patented Railroad 16 size case for sale in 1925.

WATCH CASE PRODUCTION

Before the Civil War, watchmaking was being done on a very small scale, and most of the companies in business were making their own movements as well as their own cases. After the War, tradesmen set up shops specializing exclusively in cases, while other artisans were making the movements. The case factories, because of mass production, could supply watch manufacturers with cases more economically than the manufacturers could produce their own.

A patent granted to James Boss on May 3, 1859, were not the first gold-filled cases made from sandwich-type sheets of metal, but Boss did invent a new process that proved to be very successful, resulting in a more durable case that he sold with a 20-year money-back guarantee.

....Gold
Base Metal
Gold

The illustrations at left is a sandwiched type gold-filled case.

GOLD CASE WEIGHTS BY SIZE

Size & Style of Case	Ex. Heavy	Heavy	Medium	Light	Ex. Light
	Pennyweights (DWT)				
18 size Hunting Case	60 to 65	50 to 55	45 to 50	40 to 45	35
16 size Hunting Case	55 to 60	45 to 50	40 to 45	35 to 40	32
18 size Open Face Case		40 to 45	38	35	
16 size Open Face Case		40	36	30	
12 size Open Face Case		14 to 16			
6 size Hunting Case	24	22	20	18	
0 size Hunting Case		14 to 16			

An 18 size movement with a full plate weighs 50 DWT; a 16 size movement with a ¼ plate weighs 35 DWT. These weights do not include the case.

TROY WEIGHT = 24 grains=1dwt., 1 Grain= 0.0648 grams, 20dwt = 1 OZ., 12oz = 1 LB.
NOTE: Gold & Silver Standards Vary from Country to Country. U.S.A. Coin Gold =.900 or 21 3/5K, Silver Coin=.900.
Gold Standards: 24K=1,000%or 1.0, 23K=.958 1/3, 22K=.916 2/3, 21K=.875, 20K=.833 1/3, 19K=.791 2/3, 18K=.750,
17K=.708 1/3, 16K=.666 2/3, 15K=.625, 14K=.583 1/3, 13K=.541 2/3, 12K=.500, 11=.458 1/3, 10K=.416 2/3, 9K=. 375.
8K=.333 1/3, 7K=.291 2/3, 6K=.250, 5K=.208 1/3, 4K=.166 2/3, 3K=.125, 2K=.83 1/3, 1K=.41 2/3.

OPENING WATCH CASES

Most American watch factories made movements and not the cases; with only a few exceptions the watch factory movements were made to fit a standard size case. To buy a watch the buyer would go to a jeweler or a watchmaker decide on the maker of watch, model, size, and grade of a movement and next select a case style to fit the movement. Some time after the mid 1920's this changed and factories started to provide assembly for **complete** watches (case & movement). Complete factory cased watches could also be fitted with different models, size, and grade of a movement, as well as, choose from a variety of cases. Which brings us to how to open the case to see the movement.

It is important to open a case to see the works for inspection and to identify make, model, grade, quality & size of the movement. So first and foremost take care and do not force it open but open with normal amounts of effort or force.

A **hunting case** (HC) is identified by a front lid or cover over the face (concealed dial) of the watch. The front case lid is opened by pressing the stem or the crown of the watch. The hunter style watch was used for protection of the watch and carried by men of status and used as a dress watch. Hold the watch in your right hand with the bow or swing ring between the index finger and thumb. Press on the pendant-crown with the right thumb to release the cover also at the same time hold your left hand over the cover which will ease the lid without letting it snap open hard which may spring the lid. When closing, do not **Snap** the cover. Press the crown to move the catch in, close the cover, then release the crown. This will prevent wear to the soft gold on the rim and catch.

A hunting cased watch may have a **hinged** front lid, back lid & hinged Cuvette (dust cover) for a total of 3 hinges (front , back lid & cuvette). To open the back (to see movement) check to see if there is a slightly raised opening or **lip** on the back, next it is best to use your thumb-nail in the slot or slit and slide your nail around the edge of the case and with pressure it should open. **Snap** back use the same method as before insert the fingernail and with a circular motion snap the back open. Do not try to pry with your nail, it just may break your nail. For lifting or prying the front snap bezel or hinge back or bezel use a case opener. A dull knife for safety may be used with a cloth or mouse pad. Set the watch face down on your pad and with the edge of opener use moderate force by rotating the opener with the movement of your wrist in each direction till it snaps open. Warning: If your watch case does not want to open with a normal applied effort, do NOT force it open.

LEFT: Hunting Case (HC), note Lip, also Slot or Slit and Hinges. **Right**: Screw Bezel, (Watch in center) & Screw Back.

Screw Backs & Bezels (that holds glass crystal) watches have no hinges but can be recognized by a fine line or slit between the back or bezel and the center of the watch case (the part that the winding stem is attached). For watches with a screw-on front and back, as in railroad models, hold the watch in the left hand, and with the right hand, turn the bezel **counter** clockwise. While removing the bezel, hold onto the stem and swing ring in order not to drop the watch. After close examination, **replace** the bezel and turn the watch over. Again, while holding the stem between the left thumb and index finger, remove the back cover. To unscrew the back turn it **counter** clockwise.

Slit or fine line Center View

There are some **screw** back cases, English style, that may screw or turn clockwise. You may also use a rubber jar opener or a rubber sheet type household pad to assist you in opening the case. If it is hard to unscrew the back or bezel, check again to see that it is not a hinged style case. Try asking a watch collector friend or dealer for help. There is a useful WEB site: the National Association of Watch & Clock Collectors (NAWCC), **www.nawcc.org/home.htm**, click on **Message Board**. You may post a message on their board. Describe your **problem** and hopefully you will get your difficulty solved. This Board will NOT help with VALUES of timepieces, or accept Sale Ads.

 Swing out cases there is only one fine line or slit visible, which is for the screw off bezel. Screw off the bezel pull up on the crown as if to set the hands, the stem is now in a outer position. Note the grove opening just under the dial at 6 O'clock put your finger nail into the grove and lift up swing-ring and the movement upward away from the case. You may also have to rotate the crown.

GROVE

LEVER

 Many **railroad** company's required a watch to be lever set. Lever set means moving a lever allowing the crown (winding button) to engage with the hands to set them, to correct time. This was used to prevent accidentally changing the time while winding. The lever is located under the bezel that hold the crystal. On a open face watch, the lever is usually located between 6 minutes to 11 minutes, note the lever has a tab extending up. Remove the bezel to expose the lever, the bezel may be hinged, snap or screw off. Now that the bezel is off, with your thumbnail against the tab on lever move the lever outward, in the outward position turning the crown the hands may be set to correct time.

 Early American **Colonial** and **European** watches may have double, triple or as many as four cases. Most of these watches have a button on the rim or side of the case, also note that the case is hinged. Push the button and the cover or bezel will swing up and open the case. For the last case check to see if there is a slightly raised opening or lip on this bezel or back, also note this case is hinged, it is best to use your thumb-nail in the slot and slide your nail around the edge of the case and with pressure it should open to expose the dial. Now that you have it opened check at the bottom of the dial (at the 6 o'clock position) for a pin on top of the dial or a latch just under the dial, push the pin or latch toward the center of the dial and swing the dial and movement open. If the movement is not exposed it will have a dust cover over the movement. The dust cover has a crescent shaped slide spring catch, in the center find a pin and with your thumbnail slide the catch to the right or left. After you have moved the slide you can now lift the dust cover up to expose the movement.

PIN

 Triple Cased Watch   **Dust Cover**

 Wrist watches usually have **snap** on back or bezel or a screw on back. For the **snap** on back or bezel use a case opener or your thumbnail. Check to see if there is a slit and slightly raised opening or **lip** on the back, next in the slit type slot or lip apply pressure and the back or bezel should open. Some wrist watches are also hinged so you may use the same method to open the case as the snap on back case. The **water tight** style screw on back, wrist watches will have slots or notches on the back and require a **case wrench**.

Wrist Watch Case Wrench

Wrist Watch Snap on Back or Bezel

Fold Up Pocket Knife style Case opener

Ω OMEGA

CARE OF WATCHES

To some people a watch is just a device that keeps time. They do not know the history of its development nor how it operates. They have no appreciation for improvements made over the years. That the watch is a true miracle of mechanical genius and skill, is seldom more than a fleeting thought. The average person will know it must be wound to run, that it has a mainspring and possibly a hairspring. Some even realize there are wheels and gears and, by some strange method, these work in harmony to keep time. If for some reason the watch should stop, the owner will merely take it to a watch repair shop and await the verdict on damage and cost.

To be a good collector one must have some knowledge of the components of a watch and how they work and the history of the development of the watch. To buy a watch on blind faith is indeed risky, but many collectors do it every day because they have limited knowledge.

How does a watch measure time and perform so well? Within the case one can find the fulcrum, lever, gear, bearing, axle, wheel, screw, and the spring which overcomes nature's law of gravity. All these parts harmonize to provide an accurate reading minute by minute. A good collector will be able to identify all of them.

After acquiring a watch, you will want to take good care of it. A watch should be cleaned inside and out. Dirt will wear it out much faster, and gummy oil will restrict it and keep it from running all together. After the watch has been cleaned it should be stored in a dry place. Rust is the No. 1 enemy. A watch is a delicate instrument but, if it is given proper care, it will provide many years of quality service. A pocket watch should be wound at regular intervals about once every 24 hours, early each morning so the mainspring has its full power to withstand the abuse of daily use. Do not carry a watch in the same pocket with articles that will scratch or tarnish the case. A fully wound watch can withstand a jar easier than a watch that has been allowed to run down. Always wind a watch and leave it running when you ship it. If you are one who enjoys carrying a watch be sure to have it cleaned at least once every two years.

EXAMINATION AND INSPECTION OF A WATCH BEFORE PURCHASING

The examination & inspection of a watch before purchasing is of paramount importance. This is by no means a simple task for there are many steps involved in a complete inspection.

The first thing you should do is to listen to a watch and see how it sounds. Many times the trained ear can pick up problems in the escapement and balance. The discriminating buyer will know that sounds cannot be relied on entirely because each watch sounds different, but the sound test is worthwhile and is comparable to the doctor putting the stethoscope to a patient's heart as his first source of data.

—movement

—case

The screw on left is a case screw, **extra** screw mark (✻) on case <u>indicates</u> a recased watch.

Check the bow to see if it is securely fastened to the case and look at the case to see if correction is necessary at the joints. The case should close firmly at both the back and front. (If the case closes too firmly, rub the rim with beeswax which will ease the condition and prolong the life of the rim.) Take note of the dents, scratches, wear and other evidence of mis-use. Does the watch have a generally good appearance? Check the bezel for proper fit and the crystal to see if it is free of chips. Remove the bezel and check the dial for chips and hairline cracks. Look for stains and **discoloration**; and check to see if the dial is loose. It is important to note that a simple dial with only a single sunk dial is by nature a stronger unit due to the fact that a double sunk dial is constructed of three separate pieces. If it is a stem-winder, try winding and setting. Problems in this area can be hard to correct. Parts are hard to locate and may possibly have to be handmade. If it is a lever set, pull the lever out to see if it sets properly into gear. Also check to see that the hands have proper clearance.

Now that the external parts have been inspected, open the case to view the movement. Check to see that the screws hold the movement in place securely. Note any repair marks and any missing screws. Check for **extra** case screw marks on case, this indicates a **recased** watch. Check **all** the components for **discoloration** and similarity in **color** this will tell you if a part has been **recently** replaced. Make a visual check for rust and **discoloration**, dust, dirt and general appearance. If the movement needs cleaning and oiling, this should be deducted from the price of the watch, as well as any repair that will have to be made. Note the quality of the movement. Does it have raised gold jewel settings or a gold train (center wheel or all gears)? Are the jewels set in or pressed in? Does it have gold screws in the balance wheel? Diamond end stones? Jeweled motor barrel? How many adjustments does it have? Does it have overall beauty and eye appeal?

Examine the balance for truth. First look directly down upon the balance to detect error truth in the roundness. Then look at it from the side to detect error in the flat swing or rotation. It should be smooth in appearance. Examine the hairspring in the same manner to detect errors in truth. When a spring is true in the round, there will be no appearance of jumping when it is viewed from the upper side. The coils will appear to uniformly dilate and contract in perfect rhythm when the balance is in motion. Check the exposed portion of the train wheels for burred, bent, or broken teeth. Inspect pinions and pivots for wear. If a watch has complicated features such as a repeater, push the slides, plungers, and buttons to see that they are in good working order.

After the movement and case have been examined to your satisfaction and all the errors and faults are found, talk to the owner as to the history and his personal thoughts about the watch. Is the movement in the original case? Is the dial the original one? Just what has been replaced?

Has the watch been cleaned? Does it need any repairs? If so, can the seller recommend anyone to repair the watch? Finally, see if the seller makes any type of guarantee, and get an address and phone number. It may be valuable if problems arise, or if you want to buy another watch in the future.

HOW A WATCH WORKS

There are five basic components of a watch:
1. The mainspring, and its winding mechanism, which provides power.
2. The train which consists of gears, wheels & pinions that turn the hands.
3. The escapement consisting of the escape wheel and balance that regulates or controls.
4. The dial and hands that tell the time & setting mechanism.
5. The housing consisting of the case and plates that protect.

A watch is a machine with a power source that drives the escapement through a train of gears, and it has a subsidiary train to drive a hand. The motion of the balance serves the watch the same as a pendulum serves a clock. The balance wheel and roller oscillate in each direction moving the fork and lever by means of a roller jewel or pin. As the lever moves back and forth it allows the escape wheel to unlock at even intervals to insure equal time through the 24 hours and causes the train of gears to move in one direction under the power of the mainspring. Thus, the mainspring is allowed to be let down or unwind one pulse at a time. (The escape wheel moves in one direction similar to a turnstile.)

WATCH MOVEMENT PARTS

Mechanical watches are small engines powered by a main spring, which keeps the balance in motion. The **uniformity** of this motion relies on the balance and escapement; the **durability** rests on the quality of material and construction of the complete movement.

JOIN THE AWI

For those interested in Horology as a profession or a vocation the authors of this book recommend the **American Watchmakers-Clockmakers Institute**. This international non-profit corporation is dedicated to the advancement of the art and science of horology. The **AWI** publishes the *"Horological Times"* a monthly magazine. The AWI offers watch & clock repair programs of one-week and two-week classes in various phases of watch & clock repair techniques.

For a brochure & sample copy of *"Horological Times"* phone **(513) 367-9800** or write: **American Watchmakers-Clockmakers Institute**
701 Enterprise Drive
Harrison, OH 45030

1 Main Wheel.	26 **Fork or (Counter-poised lever)**
2 Main Wheel Washer.	27 Pallet.
3 Main Screw.	28 Pallet Stones.
4 Ratchet Wheel.	29 Roller Jewel Pin.
5 Ratchet Wheel Washer.	30 Safety Roller.
6 Jewel Setting.	31 Table Roller.
7 Barrel Arbor.	32 Banking Screws.
8 Barrel Arbor Hub.	33 Breg. Hair Spring.
9 Barrel Hub Screw.	34 Hair Spring Stud.
10 Barrel Hub.	35 Hair Spring Collet.
11 Barrel.	36 Balance Staff.
12 Main Spring Hooked.	37 Regulator.
13 Main Spring.	38 Balance.
14 Recoiling Click.	39 Index.
15 Click Screw.	40 Reg. Adj. Nut.
16 First Wheel.	41 Hour Hand.
17 Center Wheel.	42 Minute Hand.
18 Center Pinion.	43 Minute Wheel.
19 Third Pinion.	44 Hour Wheel.
20 Third Wheel.	45 Setting Wheel.
21 Fourth Wheel.	46 Winding Arbor.
22 Fourth Pinion.	47 Wind. & Set. Clutch.
23 Escape Pinion	48 Bevel Pinion.
24 Escape Wheel.	49 **Pendant Bar.**
25 Second Hand.	

First Wheel 78 Teeth, 1 Rev. in 6 Hours, 30 Minutes.
Center Pinion 12 Teeth, 1 Rev. in 1 Hour.
Center Wheel 80 Teeth, 1 Rev. in 1 Hour.
3rd Pinion 10 Teeth, 1 Rev. in 7½ Minutes.
3rd Wheel 75 Teeth, 1 Rev. in 7½ Minutes.
4th Pinion 10 Teeth, 1 Rev. in 1 Minute.
4th Wheel 80 Teeth, 1 Rev. in 1 Minute.
Escape Pinion 8 Teeth, 1 Rev. in 6 Seconds.
Escape Wheel 15 Teeth, 1 Rev. in 6 Seconds.
Balance Vibrates 30 times in 6 Seconds.
    300 times in 1 Minute.
    18,000 times in 1 Hour.
    432,000 times in 1 Day.
    157,680,000 times in 1 Year.

Note: Model is not the same defination as grade. A model may exist in many different grades & grade names (as Bunn, Riverside, Veritas) may be used in many different models (as model 1 18 size, model 1 in 16 size).

Dumbbell foliot style balance.

Early style watch with a stackfreed (tear shaped cam). Note the dumbbell shaped **foliot** balance & hog-bristle regulator.

Early Drum shaped portable time-piece, (1.) note the **foliot** balance with T-shaped end, iron plates, 3 or 4 wheel train, brass gut fusee on a steel great wheel, steel contrate wheel with brass teeth, (2.) hog-bristle regulator, about 34mm high. Examples of ball-shaped case with a loop on top allows the watch to be worn on a chain. Ca. 1530 - 1550.

THE MAINSPRING

Watches were developed from the early portable clocks. The coiled spring or mainspring provided the drive power. The first coiled springs were applied to clocks about 1450. For the small portable watch, coiled springs were first used about 1470. The power from a mainspring is not consistent and this irregular power was disastrous to the first watches.

The Germans' answer to irregular power was a device called a stackfreed. Another apparatus employed was the fusee. The fusee proved to be the best choice. At first catgut was used between the spring barrel and fusee. By around 1660 the catgut was replaced by a chain. Today, the fusee is still used in naval chronometers. One drawback to the fusee is the amount of space it takes up in the watch. Generally, the simplest devices are best.

The mainspring is made of a piece of hardened and tempered steel about 20 inches long and coiled in a closed barrel between the upper and lower plates of the movement. It is matched in degree of strength, width, and thickness most suitable for the watch's need or design. It is subject to differing conditions of temperature and tensions (the wound-up position having the greatest tension). The lack of uniformity in the mainspring affects the time keeping qualities.

The power assembly in a watch consists of the mainspring, mainspring barrel, arbor, and cap. The mainspring furnishes the power to run the watch. It is coiled around the arbor and is contained in the mainspring barrel, which is cylindrical and has a gear on it which serves as the first wheel of the train. The arbor is a cylindrical shaft with a hook for the mainspring in the center of the body. The cap is a flat disk which snaps into a recess in the barrel. A hook on the inside of the mainspring barrel is for attaching the mainspring to the barrel.

The mainspring is made of a long thin strip of steel, hardened to give the desired resiliency. Mainsprings vary in size but are similar in design; they have a hook on the outer end to attach to the mainspring barrel, and a hole in the inner end to fasten to the mainspring barrel arbor.

Power unit for modern watch showing the various parts. Mainspring Bridles showing a few different designs.

By turning the crown clockwise, the barrel arbor is rotated and the mainspring is wound around it. The mainspring barrel arbor is held stationary after winding by means of the ratchet wheel and click. As the mainspring uncoils, it causes the mainspring barrel to revolve. The barrel is meshed with the pinion on the center wheel, and as it revolves it sets the train wheels in motion. Pocket and wrist watches, in most cases, will run up to 40 hours on one winding.

Jeweled Motor Barrel Unit: 1. Barrel top jewel screw. 2. Barrel top jewel and setting. 3. Ratchet wheel. 4. Barrel bridge. 5. Barrel hub. 6. Barrel head. 7. Mainspring (in barrel). 8. Barrel. 9. Barrel arbor (riveted to barrel). 10. Barrel lower jewel and setting. 11. Pillar plate.

CLICKS

A click acts on the teeth of the ratchet wheel, so that the barrel-arbor can turn in one direction only, that of the winding. The click is made to mesh constantly with the ratchet teeth by the click spring. In older watches a device known as stop-work which restricted the two extremes of the mainspring was used. A modern watch uses the click-work which prevents the mainspring from being over wound by a certain amount of recoil.

Above a sketch of Huygen's spiral balance spring. Also note the balance staff with a pinion driven by a wheel on the arbor carrying the balance spring is called a **pirouette**.

Overcoil Hairspring

Flat Hairspring

BALANCE - SPRING or HAIRSPRING

In about 1675 a contest between Huygens and Hooke for priority in inventing the **spiral** balance spring. The balance-spring or **hairspring** is the brain of the watch and is kept in motion by the mainspring. The hairspring is the most delicate tension spring made. It is a piece of flat wire about 12 inches long, 1/100th of an inch wide, 0.05mm or 0.0019685 inches thick, and weighs only about 1/9,000th of a pound. Thousands of these hairsprings can be made from one pound of steel. The hairspring controls the action of the balance wheel. The hairspring steel is drawn through the diamond surfaces to a third the size of a human hair. There are two kinds of hairsprings in the watches of later times, the flat one and the Breguet. The Breguet (named for its French inventor) is an overcoil given to the spring. There are two methods for overcoil, the oldest is the way the spring is bent by hand; and with the other method the overcoil is bent or completed in a form at one end and at the same time is hardened and tempered in the form. The hairspring contracts and expands 432,000 times a day.

A (Am. Waltham Co.) **PATENTED regulator**. Note the triangular shaped hairspring stud which is located on the balance bridge between the screw and curb pin.

REGULATORS
Identification

Overcoil concentric to travel of regulator pins

Regulator pins

Curve of Hairspring overcoil

Hairspring stud

Hairspring stud screw

Regulator

Balance Cock

E. Howard & Co.

South Bend

AM. Waltham

Breguet

Ball Howard 18S

Ball Hamilton 18s

Ball Elgin 18s

Ball Hamilton 16s

Ball Illinois 16s

Ball Waltham 16s

Hampden

Marion

E.Howard & Co.

J.P. Stevens

F S

Agassiz

Waltham

Petek Philippe

swiss- 2 piece

Fasoldt

Hampden

U.S. Waltham

U.S. Waltham

AM. Waltham

Early Columbus

REGULATORS
Identification

Fredonia & Peoria

J. Jurgensen

Keystone

Keystone

AM.
Waltham

Otay

U.S. Waltham

Illinois

Elgin

Elgin COCK

Improved Swiss

Rockford

Columbus

Thomas Tompion
1638-1700

HOBT MOORE
FIRST MAINSPRING
1675

Hamilton

English & American 1800-1850

Undersprung

Nathaniel Barrow 1750

Grossman Glasshutte

Glashutte

Elevation of a **GEAR-TRAIN**
(a.) mainspring barrel, (b.) center wheel (carries minute hand), (c.) third wheel, (d.) fourth wheel (carries seconds hand),
(e.) escape wheel, 8 day watches use a intermediate (8 day wheel) placed between the barrel and the center wheel.

THE TRAIN

The gear-train which, transmits mainspring-barrel torque to the escape-wheel consists of a four-wheel multiplying train. The time train consists of the mainspring barrel, center wheel and pinion, third wheel and pinion, fourth wheel and pinion, and escape wheel which is part of the escapement. The function of the time train is to reduce the power of the mainspring and extend its time to 36 hours or more. The mainspring supplies energy in small units to the escapement, and the escapement delays the power from being spent too quickly. The Escapement is the turnstile of the watch, metering out a tiny unit of power for each tick and tock.

The long center wheel arbor projects through the pillar plate and above the dial to receive the cannon pinion and hour wheel. The cannon pinion receives the minute hand and the hour wheel the hour hand. As the mainspring drives the barrel, the center wheel is rotated once each hour.

Alignment of chain driven fusee with train. **Fusee** at right and main-spring barrel at left. Note chain between fusee and main-spring barrel. **F**= fusee **B**= barrel

The gear-train which "transmits" mainspring-barrel torque to the escape wheel consists of a four-wheel multiplying train. **B** = barrel, **C** = center wheel

Actual alignment of **Train Unit**

60

The second or center wheel of the watch turns once every hour. It is the second largest wheel in the watch, and the arbor or post of the center wheel carries the minute hand. The center wheel pinion is in mesh with the mainspring barrel (pinions follow and the wheel supplies the power). The center wheel is in mesh with the third wheel pinion (the third wheel makes eight turns to each turn of the center wheel). The third wheel is in mesh with the fourth wheel pinion, and the fourth wheel pinion is in mesh with the escape wheel pinion. The fourth wheel post carries the second hand and is in a 1:60 ratio to the center wheel (the center wheel turns once every hour and the fourth wheel turns 60 turns every hour). The escape wheel has 15 teeth (shaped like a flat foot) and works with two pallets on the lever. The two pallet jewels lock and unlock the escape wheel at intervals (1/5 sec.) allowing the train of gears to move in one direction under the influence of the mainspring. The lever (quick train) vibrates 18,000 times to one turn of the center wheel (every hour). The hour hand works from a motion train. The mainspring barrel generally makes about five turns every 36 hours.

SOLID GOLD TRAIN

Some watches have a gold train instead of brass wheels. These watches are more desirable. To identify gold wheels within the train, look at a Hamilton 992; in most of these watches, the **center** wheel is made of gold and the other wheels are made of brass. Why a gold train? Pure gold is soft, but it has a **smooth** surface and it molds easily. Therefore, the wheels have less friction and properly alloyed it is sturdy. These wheels do not move fast, and a smooth action is more important than a hard metal. Gold does not tarnish or rust and is non-magnetic. The arbors and pinions in these watches will be steel. Many watches have some gold in them, and the collector should learn to distinguish it.

Special note: Some wheels or gears are **gold gilded** on brass and not solid gold, the appearance is rough and not, as smooth as, solid gold gears or wheels.

Balance Wheel
Pallet
Verge
Pallet
Contrate Wheel
Crown or Escape Wheel

ABOVE: **Verge Escapement**

TYPES OF ESCAPEMENTS

The purpose of the escapement is to control or maintain the rate of speed which causes the train to move in tiny increments in one direction (a governor). The verge escapement is the earliest form of escapement. It was first used in clocks as far back as the early 1300s. The verge escapement consists of a crown escape wheel, a verge which has two flags called pallets, and a balance. Early German watches had a balance shaped like a dumbbell, called a "foliot." Later most other watches used a balance shaped like a wheel. The crude weights of the foliot could be adjusted closer to or farther from the center of the balance for better time keeping. In about 1675 a contest between Huygens and Hooke for priority in inventing the spiral balance spring.

The verge escapement was used by Luther Goddard in America as well as most of the Colonial watchmakers.

Movement of the common chain driven fusee & verge escapement.

A - is the **barrel** containing the mainspring. **B** - is the **fusee**, to which the key is applied in winding, and which is connected with the barrel by the chain **b**. **C** - is the **fusee-wheel**, called also the **first** or **great wheel**, which turns with the fusee, and works into the pinion **D**, called the **center-wheel pinion**. This pinion, with the **center-wheel**, or **second wheel**, **E**, turns once in an hour. The center-wheel E works into the **third-wheel** pinion **F**; and on the same arbor is **G**, the **third wheel**, which drives the **fourth** or **contrate-wheel pinion H**, and along with it the **contrate wheel I**. The teeth of this wheel are placed at right angles to its plane, and act in the pinion **K**, called the **balance-wheel pinion**, **L** being the **balance-wheel, escape-wheel**, or **crown-wheel**. The escape-wheel acts on the two **pallets, m** and **n**, attached to the **verge**, or arbor, of the balance **M**, which regulates the movement.

Note: Escapements may be classified into 2 categories Frictional & Detached. (1.) Frictional Escapements example: Verge, Virgule, Duplex and Cylinder. (2.) Detached or Free Escapements example Lever Escapements, Detent Escapements also combination of lever, detent and Rotating Escapement as Karrusel and Tourbillon. Frictional Escapements the escape wheel is in contact with the balance staff or a part of it during the whole oscillation of the balance. Detached or Free Escapements have an arrangement where the escape teeth wheel are arrested for unlocking & impulse & then made free. Thus the Balance can rotate an arc of an oscillation with complete freedom.

🕐 The isochronism test consists of reading your watch every two hours until the watch has run down. This will show how much the rate varies according to the time elapsed since winding.

Right: **Cylinder Escapement**   Left: **Breguet's** Hanging Ruby Cylinder Escapement

About 1695 the cylinder escapement was invented by Tompion & improved by George Graham, both Englishman. The cylinder escapement was a great improvement over the verge. Even so, the cylinder escapement was not popular until Abraham Louis Breguet adopted the idea in the late 1790s. **Thomas Mudge's** invention of the detached lever escapement in about 1759. (**Below**)

Thomas Mudge Escapement

Thomas Mudge Escapement

Below: Duplex Escapement

Balance Wheel

Impulse Pin

Short Impulse Tooth

Long Tooth

Escape Wheel

Illustrating and American form of the **Duplex Escapement** as first employed by the Waterbury Watch Co.

Balance Wheel

Impulse Pin

Long Tooth

Escape Wheel

Short Impulse Tooth

CYLINDER ESCAPEMENT

VIRGULE ESCAPEMENT

DOUBLE VIRGUGLE

Resilient Escapement

Escape wheel teeth: A,B,C

Spring detent

Passing spring

Locking pallet

PIVOTED DETENT

Escape wheel

Pallet #2

Pallet #1

Staff

SPRING DETENT (chronometer escapement)

64

The Escapement has many modifications, long and short lever, single and two roller table, right angle and straight line lever, pointed teeth and club-teeth escape wheel. Escapements (1) & (2) right angle lever and (3) & (4) straight line lever. (5) Chronometer Spring Detent Escapement. (A) Club-Tooth escape wheel, (B) Club-tooth escape wheel, (C) Pointed tooth escape wheel. (D) Double Roller made of 2 discs, upper disc with the impulse jewel is called the impulse roller and the lower disc is the safety roller. (E) Single Roller made of 1 disc with impulse jewel. (F)-(G)-(H) different style of table & safety rollers. (J)-(K) different style horns, safety fingers or guard pins. (6-7-8-9-) different style impulse jewels. (6) nearly elliptic. (7) semi-circular with convex base. (8) triangular with convex sides and radius corners. (9) triangular with one convex side.

The escape wheel is fixed on the last pinion of the train.

DeLONG Escapement

The Charles E. DeLong upright D shaped pallet escapement is similar to a Brocot escapement and maybe seen in front of the dial in some French clocks. The Delong pallets are slightly over half-cylinder shaped and are staked into a steel lever having **holes with spring action** and require no cement. The DeLong escapement can be found and listed in the Ball, Hamilton and Illinois section under the heading 16 size (pricing sections) as *DeLong upright D shaped pallet escapement*. Manhattan used their own version of upright D shaped pallet type of escapement as early 1883-84. Delong had patents No. 1,192,812 in July,1916 and No. 1,327,226 in 1920. He claimed watch to have strong draw and the recoil was extremely low and his escapement system was not interchangeable (different in many respects). Some of his escapement depthing could be adjusted by rotating the arbor which used a eccentric style pivot on the pallet arbor. In 1908 he was employed by McIntyre W. Co. and 1912 to 1919 by Illinois W. Co..

Above comparison of the standard lever escapement and the DeLong escapement.
(1.)- Receiving pallet action in standard escapement. The distance between arcs V & U show the distance the escape wheel must be turned back by stored energy in the balance during unlocking.
(2.)- With same center distance and same lift and lock the arrangement of the Delong D shaped pallet giving 27 degree lock instead of 12 degree as in Fig 1. The pallet R''' with rounded locking corner is a possible substitution of R''.
(3.)- Note: The R and D pallets are staked into spring friction holes in the lever.

The duplex escapement is accredited generally to Pierre LeRoy, a Frenchman, around 1750, but was never popular in France. This type of escapement was favored in England up to the mid 1850s. The New England Watch Co. of Waterbury, Conn., used the duplex from 1898 until 1910. The Waterbury Watch Company used it from 1880 to 1898. The roller and lever escapement was invented by Thomas Mudge in about 1750.

Rack and pinion lever escapement. **1.** Balance wheel pinion. **2.** Rack. **3.** Lever. **4.** Ratchet escape wheel.

Right Angle Lever used in earlier American made watches & **the Detached Escapement** which was used extensively in England. note: **P** = *pallet*.

The rack and pinion lever escapement was invented by Hautefeuille in 1722. The famous Breguet used the detached lever escapement early in the 1800s. By 1830 the English watchmakers had established the superiority of the lever escapement. In France and Switzerland the teeth of the lever escapement wheel were boot-shaped to provide a wider impulse plane. In England, pointed or ratchet teeth were preferred, and the right-angle lever was preferred over the straight line lever, also referred to as the Swiss lever. Pitkins and Custer both used the lever escapements. The right-angle lever was used in the early Am. Walthams, Elgin, Newark, Tremont, New York, Hampden, Illinois, Cornell, and other early American watches. The American factories settled on a Swiss style escapement (straight line lever & club tooth escape wheel) by the 1870s.

The escape wheel turns in one direction much as a **turnstile**.

Purpose of Escape Wheel

The purpose of the escapement is to control or maintain the rate of speed which causes the train to move in tiny increments in one direction (a governor). If a movement consisted only of the mainspring and a train of wheels, and the mainspring were wound up, the train would run at full speed resulting in the power being spent in a few moments. For this reason, the escapement has been arranged to check it (the brakes). The duty of the escapement is to allow each tooth of the escape wheel to pass at a regulated interval. The escapement is of no service alone and, therefore, must have some other arrangement to measure and regulate these intervals. This is accomplished by the balance assembly.

The escape wheel is in most cases made of steel and is staked on a pinion and arbor. It is the last wheel of the train and connects the train with the escapement. It is constructed so that the pallet jewels move in and out between its teeth, allowing but one tooth to escape at a time, turnstile fashion. The teeth are club-foot-shaped for additional impulse.

The pallet jewels are set at an angle to make their inside corners reach over three teeth and two spaces of the escape wheel. The outside corners of the jewels will reach over two teeth and three spaces of the escape wheel with a small amount of clearance. At the opposite end of the pallet, directly under the center of the fork slot, is a steel or brass pin called the guard pin. The fork is the connecting link to the balance assembly.

BALANCE AND HAIRSPRING

In earlier watches the hairspring was just that. Bristles from a wild boar was used to control the balance wheel. The **sprial** hair-spring was invented in about <u>1675</u>. The rotation of the balance wheel is controlled by the hairspring. The inner end of the hairspring is pinned to the collet, and the collet is held friction-tight on the staff above the balance wheel.

Left: example of **flat hairspring**.　　Center: Balance & Hairspring.　　Right: example of Breguet or **overcoil hairspring**.

The outer end of the hairspring is pinned to a stud which is held stationary on the balance cock by the stud screw. The roller jewel is cemented in the large roller assembly, which is mounted on the staff directly under the balance wheel. Under the first roller is a smaller one which acts as a safety roller. This is necessary because of the crescent cut out in the roller table which allows the guard pin of the escapement assembly to pass through.

The balance wheel rotates clockwise and counterclockwise on its axis by means of the impulse it receives from the escapement. The motion of the balance wheel is constant due to the coiling and uncoiling of the hairspring. The impulse, transmitted to the roller jewel by the swinging of the pallet fork to the left, causes the balance to rotate in a counterclockwise direction. The position of the fork allows the roller jewel to move out of the slot of the fork freely and in the same direction. The fork continues on until it reaches the banking pin. Meanwhile the balance continues in the same direction until the tension of the hairspring overcomes the momentum of the balance wheel. When this occurs the balance returns to its original position, which causes the roller jewel to again enter the slot of the fork.

The PALLET STONE
A. The LOCKING or RECEIVING CORNER.
B. The LIFTING or IMPULSE FACE.
C. The LET-OFF CORNER.

Modern or Swiss Lever Escapement

A. Lever
B. Entrance pallet
C. Exit pallet
D. Fork
E. Banking pins
F. Fork slot
G. Horns
H. Impulse roller jewel
K. Safety finger
L. Notch of small plate M
M. Safety roller
N. Roller table
P. Impulse plane of the teeth of the wheel
R. Escape wheel

The ESCAPE WHEEL TOOTH
A. The LOCKING CORNER OR HEEL.
B. The LET-OFF CORNER OR TOE.
C. The LIFTING FACE.

Pallet and Escape Tooth Action. The momentum that has been built up during the return of the balance, causes the roller pin to impart an impulse on the inside of the fork slot. This impulse is great enough to push the fork away from its position against the banking pin. As the fork is pushed away, it causes the pallet stone to slide on the toe of the escape wheel tooth. When the pallet stone has slid down to its edge, it frees the escape wheel tooth, thereby unlocking the escape wheel. The escape wheel, being impelled by the force of the mainspring, starts to rotate. As the escape wheel turns, the tooth glides along the impulse face of the pallet jewel, forcing it to move out of the way. The moving pallet carries the fork with it and imparts the impulse to the roller jewel. The right pallet stone intercepts a tooth of the escape wheel to lock it, as the fork moves toward the banking pin. Having a short "run" left to the banking pin, the pressure of the escape wheel tooth against the locking face of the pallet jewel draws the stone deeper into the escape wheel and, therefore, causes the fork to complete its run and holds it against the banking pin. Meanwhile the balance continues in a clockwise direction until the tension of the hairspring overcomes the momentum of the balance and returns it to its original position.

Rate of Escape Tooth Release. Through the motion of the escapement, the mainspring keeps the balance vibrating, and the balance regulates the train. The escape wheel has 15 teeth and is allowed to revolve 10 turns per minute. Thus, 150 teeth glide over each pallet stone in 1 minute. The gliding of the escape wheel teeth over the impulse faces of the pallet stones will cause the balance to vibrate 300 vibrations or beats per minute. These vibrations will continue until the force of the mainspring is spent.

  SCREWS

Screws used in watches are very small and precise. These screws measure 254 threads to the inch and 47,000 of them can be put into a thimble. The screws were hardened and tempered and polished to a cold hard brilliance. By looking at these screws through a magnifying glass one can see the uniformity.

EQUIDISTANT ESCAPEMENT

The term Equidistant Escapement is a form of lever escapement. The locking of each pallet takes place at the same distance from the pallet arbor. A similar form of escapement is the circular pallet with the circular form of escapement. The impulses are given at equal distance from the center line. The Swiss preferred the equidistant while the Americans preferred the circular. There is little difference in performance between these two types of escapement.

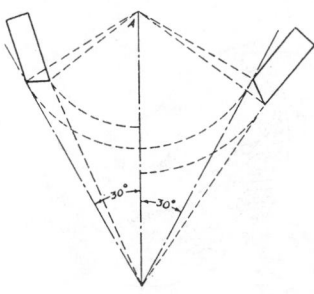

Equidistant form of Escapement

Circular form of Escapement

TRAIN
BRIDGE

ESCAPE BRIDGE

WATCH — TRAIN SIDE

PILLAR PLATE

PALLET
BRIDGE

BALANCE COCK

BARREL BRIDGE

The plates and bridges which hold all the parts in proper relation to each other.

THE PLATES

The movement of a watch has two plates and the works are sandwiched in between. The plates are called the top plate and the pillar plate. The top plate fully covers the movement. The 3/4 plate watch and the balance cock are flush and about 1/4 of a full plate is cut out to allow for the balance, thus the 3/4 plate. The bridge style watch has two or three fingers to hold the wheels in place and together are called a bridge. The term bridge (horologically) is one that is anchored at both ends. A cock is a wheel support that is attached at one end only. English balance cock for verge watches and lever watches have but one screw. French and Dutch verge watches have their balance bridges secured at both ends. The metal is generally brass, but on better grade watches, nickel is used. The full plate is held apart by four pillars. In older watches the pillars were very fancy, and the plates were pinned, not screwed, together. The plates can be gilded or engraved when using brass. Some of the nickel plates have damaskeening. There are a few watches with plates made of gold. The plates are also used to hold the jewels, settings, etc. Over 30 holes are drilled in each plate for pillars, pivots, and screws.

The pinion is the smaller of the two wheels that exist on the shaft or arbor. They are small steel gears and usually have six teeth called leaves. Steel is used wherever there is great strain, but where there is much friction, steel and brass are used together; one gear of brass, and a pinion of steel. After the leaves have been cut, the pinions are hardened, tempered, and polished.

LEFT = PILLAR PLATE   RIGHT = TOP PLATE -(3/4 plate)

THE FUSEE FIRST UTILIZED IN 1525
1. MAINSPRING BARREL   2. FUSEE CHAIN   3. FUSEE WHEEL

THE FUSEE

A mainspring gives less and less power as it lets down. To equalize the power a fusee was first used. Fusee leverage increases as the main spring lets down. A fusee is smaller at the top for a full mainspring. When the chain is at the bottom, the mainspring is almost spent, and the fusee has more leverage. Leonardo da Vinci is said to have invented the fusee.

When the mainspring is fully wound, it also pulls the hardest. At that time the chain is at the small end of the fusee. As the spring grows weaker, the chain descends to the larger part of the fusee. In shifting the tension, it equalizes the power.

On the American watch, the fusee was abandoned for the most part in 1850 and an adjustment is used on the hairspring and balance wheel to equalize the power through the 24 hours. When a watch is first wound the mainspring has more power than it does when it is nearly run down. With or without the fusee, the number of parts in a watch are about the same: close to 300.

NOTE: Most fusee style watches wind to left or counter-clock wise. Most non-fusse watches wind clock-wise.

The above is a HAMILTON MODEL 21 **FUSEE** used in a Ships **Chronometer**.
Note the sustaining spring which is also called maintaining spring, to avoid a watch from trying to stop while being wound, therefore maintaining the power to the escapement, this device was **introduced by Harrison.**

1. Illustration of pivot before 1700. 2. Pivot used in early 1700s. 3. Pivot used in late 1700s.

JEWELS AND PIVOTS

Before 1700, holes were drilled only part way into the plates and the pivot rested directly on the bottom of the hole, as in Illustration No. 1. The shoulder of the pivot was above the plate, however, reducing part of the function, as in Illustration No. 1A.

In the early 1700s, a French watchmaker, Sully, improved the pivot friction as seen in Illustration No. 2B. Illustration No. 3 shows a later improvement, perfected by Julien Le Roy.

N.F. de Duiller of Geneva, in conjunction with Peter and Jacob Debaufre, French immigrants living in London, developed a method of piercing jewels. This method was patented in 1704; however, it was not until around 1800 that holed jewels started to appear in watch movements and then only in high grade watches.

In the mid-1800s experiments were already being made for artificial rubies. In 1891 Fremy solved the problem and by the early 1900s the reconstructed ruby was popular.

Escape Wheel
2 cap jewels
2 hole jewels

Fourth Wheel
2 hole jewels

Lever Arbor
& Pallet
2 cap jewels
2 hole jewels
2 pallet jewels

Balance Staff
2 cap jewels
2 hole jewels
1 roller jewel

Third Wheel
2 hole jewels

Center Wheel
2 hole jewels

Mainspring
Barrel Arbor
2 hole jewels

Jewel Count and location for a 23 Jewel, 16 Size, Samago Special. (Ca.1913)

SHOCK ABSORBERS

When a watch is dropped or subjected to a hard shock, the balance and pivots usually suffer the most. A shock-resisting device was invented by Breguet in 1789; he called it a parachute. This device was a spring steel arm supporting the endstone. The parachute gives a cushioning effect to the balance staff. The American watch industry tried to find a device to protect pocket watch pivots, but it was the Swiss who perfected the device for wrist watches around 1933.

Left: Breguet's "parachute"

Above: A & E = **Parachute,** popular after 1800. (**F** for temperature)   Above **Right:** Incabloc 1st used about 1933.

Above: Illustrates Parachute shock absorbing system. Note end stone and spring in raised position giving a cushioning effect to the balance staff.

Location of jewels in balance

Above LEFT : Incabloc spring, cap-jewel, hole jewel, bearing block & balance-staff.

NOTE: Collectable watches with a higher jewel count usually demand a greater price, *when watches were produced the higher the jewel count the higher the cost*, however, lower production of some models this <u>collectable</u> **rule** does not apply. Example 7, 11 and 15 jewel Hamiltons will bring higher prices than a 17 jewel Hamilton, also a 19 jeweled "Sangamo Special" will bring a higher price than 21 jeweled "Sangamo Special". Most American made watches with 15 jewels and up are marked. (**Generally speaking it is accepted that good to medium quality watches have 15 to 17 jewels and are said to be "fully jeweled".**)
When counting **VISIBLE** jewels beware that some manufactures added <u>non-functional</u> jewels for eye appeal, disassembling the watch is the only way to get a true accurate count.

74

COUNTERPOISED LEVER

Left: Example of Counterpoised Lever used in some of **D. Gruen** Extra Precision watches. This style counterbalance lever is referred to as a **"Moustache"** lever. (may be GOLD)

Right: Example of Counterpoised Lever used in Elgin found in some early 12 size, grade 190. This style counterbalance lever is referred to as a **"Moustache"** lever.

TYPES OF JEWELS

Watch jewels are of four distinct types, each type having a particular function. (1) **HOLE JEWELS.** Hole jewels are used to form the bearing surface for wheel arbors and balance staff pivots. (2) **CAP JEWELS.** Cap jewels (also called end stones) are flat jewels. They are positioned at the ends of wheel staffs, outside the hole jewels, and limit the end thrust of the staff. (3) **ROLLER JEWELS.** The roller jewel (pin) is positioned on the roller table to receive the impulse for the balance from the fork. (4) **PALLET JEWELS.** The pallet jewels (stones) are the angular shaped jewels positioned in the pallet to engage the teeth of the escape wheel.

JEWEL COUNT (American)

Jewels are used as bearings to reduce metal-to-metal contacts which produce friction and wear. They improve the performance and accuracy of the watch, and materially prolong its usefulness. The materials used for making watch jewels are diamonds, sapphires, rubies, and garnets. The diamond is the hardest but is seldom used except for cap jewels. The sapphire is the next in hardness and is the most commonly used because of its fine texture. Garnets are softer than sapphires and rubies.

Number and Location of Jewels. Most **American** watches have either 7, 9, 11, 15, 17, 19, 21, or 23 jewels. The problem in jewel counting is that you can not see the jewels in the pillar plate. In most American watches, 9,11 and 13 jewel watches the **extra** jewels (the other half) are in the top plate not in the pillar plate. So do not assume all jewels are in pairs. The location of the jewels vary somewhat in different makes & grades, but the **general** practice is as follows:

7-JEWEL WATCHES. Seven-jewel watches have: two hole jewels-one at each end of the balance staff; two cap jewels-one at each end of the balance staff; one roller jewel; and two pallet jewels.

9-11-13-JEWEL WATCHES. These have the 7 jewels mentioned in 7 jewel watches. In most American watches, 9,11 and 13 jewel watches the **extra** jewels (the other half) are in the top plate not in the pillar plate. So 11 jewel watches look like **15** jewel watches.
* Do not assume all jewels are in pairs.

15-JEWEL WATCHES. These watches have the 11 jewels found in 11-jewel watches, with the addition of the following: two hole jewels-one at each end of the third-wheel; and two hole jewels-one at each end of the fourth-wheel staff. Note: There are some **16** jewel watches.

17-JEWEL WATCHES. The 15 jewels in 15-jewel watches are used with the addition of two hole jewels- one at each end of the center wheel staff.

To get a quick rough idea or approximation of the jewelling of American watches there are 7J. for the balance area, add 2 more for each visible gear that is jeweled. Also you can look at the jewels from the back & assume they are the same on both sides. You may also start at the center & go backwards. If center wheel is jeweled chances are it is 17J. if not, and the third wheel is, chances are it is 15J. Movements with 21J.- 23J. or more are usually marked.

Above: Cross section of a 17 jewel pocket watch showing upper and lower jewel location.

19-JEWEL WATCHES. In these watches, the jewels are distributed as in the 17-jewel watch, with the addition of two hole jewels-one for each pivot of the **barrel mainspring.**

21-JEWEL WATCHES. The jewels in these are distributed as in the 17-jeweled grade, with the addition of two **cap** jewels (USUALLY 2 at pallet arbor and 2 at escape wheel) a **few** have 2 jewels for the barrel.

Center Wheel — 2	Center Wheel— 2	Center Wheel— 2	Center Wheel— 2
Third Wheel — 2	Third Wheel — 2	Third Wheel — 2	Third Wheel — 2
Fourth Wheel — 2	Fourth Wheel— 2	Fourth Wheel— 2	Fourth Wheel— 2
Escape Wheel— 2	Escape Wheel—2	Escape Wheel—2+2	Escape Wheel— 2+2
Pallet & Arbor— 4	**Barrel Arbor** — 2	Pallet & Arbor—4+2	**Barrel Arbor** — 2
Balance Staff — 4	Pallet & Arbor— 4	Balance Staff — 4	Pallet & Arbor— 4+2
Roller jewel — 1	Balance Staff — 4	Roller jewel — 1	Balance Staff — 4
TOTAL — 17J	Roller jewel — 1	TOTAL—21J	Roller jewel — 1
	TOTAL — 19J		TOTAL— 23J

23-JEWEL WATCHES. The jewels are distributed as in the 21-jewel watch, with the addition of one for each pivot of the **barrel & mainspring.**

24J., 25J., and 26 JEWEL WATCHES. In all of these watches, the additional jewels were distributed as cap jewels. These were not very functional but were offered as **prestige** movements for the person who wanted more. **In many cases, these jewel arrangements varied according to manufacturer. All jeweled watches may <u>NOT</u> fit these descriptions.**

Collectable watches with a higher jewel count usually demand a greater price, *when watches were produced the higher the jewel count the higher the cost*, however, lower production of some models this collectable rule does not apply. Example 7, 11 and 15 jewel Hamiltons will bring higher prices than a 17 jewel Hamilton, also a 19 jeweled "Sangamo Special" will bring a higher price than 21 jeweled "Sangamo Special". Most American made watches with 15 jewels and up are marked. (**Generally speaking it is accepted that good to medium quality watches have 15 to 17 jewels and are said to be "fully jeweled".**)

When counting **VISIBLE** jewels beware that some manufactures added <u>non-functional</u> jewels for eye appeal, disassembling the watch is the only way to get a true accurate count. Note: When counting jewels from the movement back plate (with dial on) at the visible jewels a 11J. could appear to be a 15J. watch. A jewel which has a scribed circle around it plus two screws is a **mock** setting usually have one jewel for top jewel only & no lower jewel.

Left: Diamond faceted end stone.   **Center:** Cylindrical pivot.   **Right:** Conical pivot & Cap jewel.

WINDING AND SETTING

The simplest, but not the most practical method for winding up the mainspring of a pocket watch was to wind the barrel staff by means of a key, but then it is necessary to open up the watch case. The key method of winding proved unpopular, as oftentimes the key became lost.

Stem in for Winding

Stem out for Setting

WINDING & SETTING PARTS

1. Ratchet Wheel	6. Stem and Crown	10. Clutch Lever	14. Hour Wheel
2. Crown Wheel	7. Winding Pinion	11. Clutch Lever Spring	15. Minute Wheel
3. Crown Wheel Center	8. Clutch Wheel	12. Setting Wheel	16. Dial Washer
4. Click	9. Setting Lever	13. Yoke	17. Cannon Pinion
5. Click Spring			

WINDING MECHANISM. a-Winding and setting clutch. p-Winding pinion. b-Barrel. r-Ratchet wheel. c-Crown or main wheel. t- Winding arbor.

The modern principle of the winding of the mainspring and hand setting by pulling on the crown, dates back to 1842. We owe this combination to Adrian Philippe, associate of Patek, of Geneva.

The winding and setting mechanism consists of the stem, crown, winding pinion, clutch wheel, setting wheel, setting lever, clutch lever, clutch spring, crown wheel, and ratchet wheel. When the stem is pushed in, the clutch lever throws the clutch wheel to winding position. Then, when the stem is turned clockwise, it causes the winding pinion to turn the crown and ratchet wheels. The ratchet wheel is fitted on the square of the mainspring arbor and is held in place with a screw. When the stem and crown are turned, the ratchet wheel turns and revolves the arbor which winds the mainspring, thereby giving motive power to the train. Pulling the stem and crown outward pushes the setting lever against the clutch lever, engaging the clutch wheel with the setting wheel. The setting wheel is in constant mesh with the minute wheel; therefore, turning the stem and crown permits setting the hands to any desired time.

SETTING MECHANISM. Clutch a. meshes with m. and the minute works wheel b. The minute works wheel meshes with the cannon pinion h. The hour cannon d. bears the hour hand H. C. center wheel M. Minute hand.

The dial train consists of the cannon pinion, minute, and hour wheels. The cannon pinion is a hollow steel pinion which is mounted on the center wheel arbor. A stud which is secured in the pillar plate holds the minute wheel in mesh with the cannon pinion. A small pinion is attached to the minute wheel which is meshed with the hour wheel.

The center arbor revolves once per hour. A hand affixed to the cannon pinion on the center arbor would travel around the dial once per hour. This hand is used to denote minutes. The hour wheel has a pipe that allows the hour wheel to telescope over the cannon pinion. The hour wheel meshes with the minute wheel pinion. This completes the train of the cannon pinion, minute wheel, and hour wheel. The ratio between the cannon pinion and the hour wheel is 12 to 1; therefore, the hand affixed to the hour wheel is to denote the hours. With this arrangement, time is recorded and read.

A—PINION
B—CLUTCH WHEEL
C—SETTING WHEEL
D—MINUTE WHEEL
E—CANNON PINION
F—HOUR WHEEL
G—CLUTCH LEVER
H—SETTING SPRING
J—SETTING SPRING CAM

KENDRICK & DAVIS, WATCH KEY FACTORY was founded in 1876. They produced a dust-proof key which was looked upon as quite a wonderful patented watch key & sold world wide & also found with different foreign trade marks.

AUTOMATIC WINDING.

The self-winding watch uses the movements of the body in order to wind up the mainspring slowly and nearly continuously. The first pocket self-winding watches were executed by a watchmaker from Le Locle, Abraham-Louis Perrelet, around 1770. They were improved soon after by Abraham-Louis Breguet. In the case of the pocket watch, the movements causing the winding of the watch were essentially the result of walking. This system of winding was never widely adopted. The watch was a fancy model and not a really useful one. Herman von der Heydt was the only maker in America to work with the self-winding pocket watch. However, inventors always kept the idea of the self-winding watch in mind.

Early self wind pocket watch by Breguet.

ETERNA-MATIC AUTOMATIC WINDING MECHANISM. 1–Oscillating Weight. 2–Oscillating gear. 3–Upper wheel of auxiliary pawl-wheel. 4–Lower wheel of auxiliary pawl-wheel. 5–Pawl-wheel with pinion. 6–Lower wheel of pawl-wheel with pinion. 7–Transmission-wheel with pinion. 8–Crown-wheel yoke. 9–Winding pinion. 10–Crown-wheel. 11–Ratchet-wheel. 12–Barrel. 13–Driving runner for ratchet-wheel. 14–Winding stem. 15–Winding button.

In 1923, the British firm Harwood took up once again the solution of the problem of automatic winding, for wrist watches. This was the spark which rapidly resulted in research to improve and simplify this type of mechanism. A company was formed in London to manufacture Harwood's watch, and before long over 500 jewelers in the United Kingdom were selling his automatic watch. A second company was formed in France, and a third in the United States. The business flourished about two and one-half years. Then, in 1931, these companies were liquidated.

Illustration of Self Winding mechanism used by Harwood NOTE: The 2 BUFFER springs used on earlier movements.

This 1931 wrist watch made by Perpetual Self-Winding Watch Co. of America originally sold for $29.75.

THE BALANCE ARC OF VIBRATION

If the watch is to function with any degree of satisfaction, the proper arc of motion of a balance should be no less than 180 degrees in a single vibration direction. Wind up the watch, stop the balance; upon releasing the balance, carefully observe the extent of the swing or vibration. After 30 seconds it should have reached its maximum. If it takes longer, the full power of the mainspring is not being communicated strongly enough. With the watch fully wound, the balance should vibrate between 180 degrees and 315 degrees in a single vibration direction. 220 degrees is said to be perfect.

HIGH ARC   LOW ARC

JUDGING QUALITY

Judging the quality of a watch need not be difficult. While observing a watch movement there are two major determining factors to keep in mind. (1.) The quality or precious material. (2.) The amount of workmanship and time it takes to produce the parts for the movement. About **85% of the cost** of a _high-grade_ watch _movement_ is **labor**. The precious materials such as 18k or 14k gold, diamond or rubies, gold jewel settings or brass jewel settings. The amount of labor may be measured by the finished parts of the movement such as polishing, chamfered parts (removing sharp edges), & bluing of screws, also complications require more labor. The collector must learn to compare watches from the same time period because changes were made to improve the time keeping. To assist you the partial list below may be helpful in judging the quality of a watch.

LARGE CROWN for EASY WINDING
EXTRA HEAVY PENDANT
SAFETY RECOILING CLICK
CONCAVED AND POLISHED
WINDING WHEELS
SAFETY CENTER PINION
JEWELED MOTOR BARREL
19 TO 23 SELECTED RUBY AND
SAPPHIRE JEWELS
GOLD TRAIN WHEELS
BREGUET OVER COILED HAIRSPRING

NON PULL-OUT BOW
DUST PROOF CASE
RAISED SOLID GOLD JEWEL SETTINGS
9 ADJUSTMENTS = 6 POSITIONS - 1 HEAT
1 COLD AND 1 ISOCHRONISM
POSITIVE MICROMETRIC REGULATOR
SPRING TEMPERED COMPENSATING
BALANCE WITH SOLID GOLD SCREWS
DOUBLE ROLLER & ENTIRE
ESCAPEMENT IS CAP JEWELED
STEEL ESCAPE WHEEL

Escapement: detent, lever (with banking pins) or cylinder; **gold**, steel, gilded or brass escape wheel. _Balance wheel;_ number of platinum, gold or brass screws, mean-time screws are used in higher grade watches and two pair (4) of mean-time screws is higher than one pair (2), expansion full cut, 1/2 cut or uncut. In older movements gold or brass balance wheel. _Balance cock;_ diamond or ruby end stone, amount of engraving or hand pierced workmanship. _Regulator;_ free sprung, precision or simple. _Hair spring;_ helical, elinvar, overcoil or flat. _Adjustments;_ Isochronism, temperature, 6 to 3 positions, adjusted or unadjusted. _Note polished and quality finish under dial also under side of wheels and all parts._

The train of gears: Wolf tooth gearing, highly polished, **gold train,** gilded or brass gears; chamfered above & below, rounded, beveled or flat spokes.

Finish to the plates: Engraved, carved, skeletonized, damaskeened with lavished or conservative finish, highly finished or polished, solid or plated, nickel, brass, gold inlaid, gilt or frosted plates. Hardening of various parts.

Screws: Highly finished or polished, chamfered or beveled, oval or flat heads, blued or plain, also chamfered screw holes.

Jewels and settings: Number of jewels; diamond, sapphire, ruby, other semi-precious jewels as garnet, aquamarine. Size of raised gold jewel settings held by 3 or 2 screws, flush gold jewel settings held by 3 or 2 screws, composition or gilded settings, fake engraved settings or jewels pressed directly into plates. Roller with jeweled impulse pin. Entire escapement with capped jewels as lever, balance & escape wheel. Sapphire pallet jewels. **Jeweled mainspring barrel.**

Dials: _Enamel dial;_ enamel on gold or copper, triple sunk, double sunk, single sunk or unsunk. _Metal dial;_ gold or silver, hand carved or engraved, etched or plated; applied, raised, inlaid or hand painted numbers.

Cases: Platinum or white gold, 18k or 14k gold, multi-color gold, "Pinchbeck gold", silver or silveroid. Hand pierced, Repousse, porcelain or enamel, engraved or engine turned. Boxed hinged or reversible, Hunting & Demi-hunter, open face, _unusual shape,_ **heavy** or light weight, **thick,** thin. Raised applied ornamentation, diamonds or semi-precious jewels. Inter-dust cover, bow & crown made of gold or brass. Beware of _Pinchbeck_ gold which is **fake** gold.

Metals used in watches: Bell metal or bronze, Beryllium white colored alloyed with iron, cobalt, copper, etc.; Bi-metallic (brass fused to steel), Nickel, Brass, Carbon steel, Chromium, Chrome steel, Copper; Elinvar, German metal, gilding metal, Glucinum, Gold, Gold-filled, Gunmetal, Invar, Iron, Palladium, Platinum, White gold, Silver, Silver plated, Stainless steel, Steel, Tin and Zinc

NOTE: Top **first** quality watches are fully chamfered, polished and finished, above and below on all the parts, as lever, escape wheel and train wheels, etc. The next down from Top First quality only the top or **visible** side are camfered, polished and finished. Extra flat watches the thinner the watch - the higher the production cost and Extra flat watches was considered the Highest or Top of the line.

1903 AD

1907 AD
PRICE
$2.25

"Locomotice Special" $7 00
Guaranteed Good Timekeeper.
American manufacture, 18 size, elaborately damaskeened nickel and gilt movement, ruby jewels in raised settings, quick train, straight line escapement, exposed pallets, compensation balance, stem wind and set, hard enameled dial, locomotive on movement and dial and movement stamped "17 Jewels Adjusted." Has the appearance of $25.00 railroad movement. Hunting or open face.

Right: Min. Repeater with perpetual calendar.
(Complications + Extra Flat + Quality finish.)

Left: (1903 AD) **Cheap Imitation** Watch made by Trenton W. Co. also made in 23 jewels (GLASS jewels)

OFFER VERSUS APPRAISALS

When you want to sell your watches you need a offer, not an appraisal. An offer is the actual price someone will pay for your item at a given point in time. The price will be determined by several factors: Demand or collect-ability, rarity, condition, quality, grade, complications, appeal, size, age, metal content , style and the timing may be very critical in determining the price.

Jewelers and most appraisers use the insurance replacement cost, (an estimate of the retail replacement price). This type of appraisal is fine for contemporary watches and jewelry, but not for collectable watches and antique jewelry items. The fair market value at the NAWCC trade show level is a more realistic estimate of price. If done by an appraiser with "current market" knowledge, then a fair market appraisal will be the correct evaluation of the dollar level at that *time* for your items.

Selling your watches may be a new experience. The task requires experience in the sale of watches. There is a market for watches, but as in any area of sales, knowledge of your BUYER is important. Collectors may not advertise that they are willing buyers; Collectors may not have enough ready cash at the time. Sending watches to a prospective buyer is a judgment call-- is the buyer trustworthy? Will it be worth the time involved? As a seller, you must guarantee the watch to work, offer return privileges, and refunds. The task of selling requires a knowledge of repair, shipping, the cost of advertising, time to market the watch, and someone standing by to talk to the collector. This is a short list and almost imperative that the seller be in the business of selling watches to be successful at selling. The collector may pay a higher price than a dealer, but the collectors are hard to find and may not have the ready cash at that time.

Selling to dealers may be more pleasant. Dealers will have a qualified staff, including buyers and seller, ready to respond to ads, as well as, a cash reserve for purchases. When dealing with an established business, that can provide you with good references and has a trustworthy record. Each customer is handled in a professional manner by a competent staff member. A dealer understands that selling maybe a new experience and will take you through the process one step at a time. Summation: Considering the cost, time and attempting to find a willing collector, you may be ahead to sell your watches to a qualified dealer.

When selling your watches to collectors or dealers it may involve sending the watch from one place to another. To receive the best price it will be vital to see the watches before a offer is made, this is a common practice in the watch market. Suggestions for mailing your package to the buyer. Make a detailed list of the items you are sending. Keep a copy and send a copy also list your name, address and daytime phone number. The jewelry industry sends millions of dollars worth of jewelry by **REGISTERED** MAIL. The Post Office Service has close control of the registered mail. Each person who handles the package must sign for it and be responsible for it's safety. Your package will be kept in a secure area much like a bank vault. Your package may be insured up to $25,000.00. Your package must also be able to withstand the shipping stress. Before sealing the box make sure to add one or two inchs of padding between your watch and the sides, bottom and top of the box. Cushion these spaces with newspaper, tissue, cotton, bubble or foam padding. Seal the box securely then wrap the outside with gummed PAPER tape that can be written on.

When your package arrives at the dealer the mail staff will open and inspect your package, and log each item. One of the experts in charge will examine each item and call as soon as possible with the offer. If you accept the offer a check will be delivered to you. If the offer is turned down the items will be returned.

When buying watches for RESALE **know what the buyer will pay**. How many buyers are there for, prices above $1,000.00, $2,000.00, $5,000.00 $10,000.00 or as high as $50,000.00 to $100,000.00 and do they have ready cash. Can you find the collector that will pay more or pay your asking price. **The collector may be just as rare as your rare watch!** (SUPPLY & DEMAND)

"George Washington, New York", engraved on movement, patterned after the 1857 model by Waltham, (SWISS).

"The Nassau" on dial, "Hartford adjusted, jewels, heat & cold" on the movement. (<u>SWISS FAKE</u>)

COTTAGE INDUSTRY WATCHMAKING IN COLONIAL AMERICA

The cottage industry (pre-1700s to 1800s) consisted of organized, skilled craftsmen having separate divisions for the purpose of producing watches. The movements were handmade using manpowered tools. The parts generally were not given a final finish. The cottage industries were in most countries including France, England, Switzerland, Germany, and others, but not in America. Each skilled parts maker specialized in a specific part of the watch. There were fusee makers, wheel makers, plate and cock makers, spring makers, case makers and enamelers, to name a few. In the cottage industry each maker became an expert in his field. Expenses and overhead were less because fewer tools and less labor were required. Because all components were produced separately, a larger volume of watches resulted.

The enterprising colonial watchmaker in America would order all the parts and assemble them to complete a finished movement. This finisher, or watchmaker, would detail the parts, such as filing them to fit, polishing and gilding the parts, fitting the movement to a case, installing a dial, and adjusting the movement to perform. The finisher would then engrave his name and town of manufacture to the movement or dial. The finisher determined the time keeping quality of the completed watch, thus gaining a good reputation.

Most watchmakers used this system during this period; even, to some extent, Abraham L. Breguet. A colonial watchmaker or finisher could produce about 50 watches a year. There were few colonial watchmakers because only the wealthy could afford such a prized possession as a watch. Most colonial watchmakers struggled financially, and supplemented their businesses with repair work on European-made watches. Since most of them understood the verge escapement, and imported this type of part from England to produce watches, many colonial watches have the verge escapement. Few colonial watches survive today.

Side-view of 17th Century single-hand movement with fusee and catgut line to barrel. This three-wheel movement normally ran from 15 to 16 hours between windings. Also note the balance has no hairspring. Watch movements changed from 3 wheel to 4 wheels after about 1700.

English style 1/4 Hr. Repeater Ebauche, thought to be from Nicole, Nielsen for the Charles Frodsham work shop in London, no escape wheel, right angle lever, 30J., wolfs tooth winding, highly finished repeater steel works, Ca.1850-60.

Dial side of English style 1/4 Hr. Repeater Ebauche, thought to be from Nicole, Nielsen for the Charles Frodsham work shop in London, no escape wheel, right angle lever, 30J., wolfs tooth winding, highly finished repeater steel works.

EBAUCHES

The stamping out of plates and bridges began with Frederic Japy of Beaucourt, France, around 1770. First Ebauche in 1771-72, by 1795, 400 workers and 40,000 movements, 1813, 300,000 movements and in 1851, 500,000. At first, ebauches consisted of two plates with barrel and train bridges, the cock and fusee, pillars, and the clicks and assembly screws. The ebauches were stamped-out or rough movements. Japy invented machinery a common laborer could operate, including a circular saw to cut brass sheets into strips, a machine for cutting teeth in a wheel, a machine for making pillars, a press for the balance, and more. These machines were semi-automatic and hard to keep in alignment or register. But, with the aid of these new machines the principal parts of the movement could be produced in a short period of time with some precision. However, the parts of watches at this time were not interchangeable. These movements in the rough or "gray" were purchased by finishers. The finisher was responsible for fitting and polishing all parts and seeing to the freedom and depth of these wheels and working parts. He had to drill the holes to fit the dial and hands. The plates, cock and wheel, after being fitted and polished, were gilded. After the parts were gilded, the movement would be reassembled, regulated for good time keeping, and placed in a case. The finisher had to be a master watchmaker.

In England, during the early 1700s to late 1800s, Lancashire became the center of the ebauche movement trade. One of the better known English ebauche makers was Joseph Preston & Sons of Prescot. The movements were stamped J. P. Some Swiss ebauches would imitate or stylize the movement for the country in which they were to be sold, making it even harder to identify the origin.

As the watch industry progressed, the transformation of the ebauche to a more completed movement occurred. Automation eventually made possible the watch with interchangeable parts, standard sizing, and precision movements that did not need retouching. This automation began about 1850 (in America) with such talented mechanics as Pierre Fredric Ingold, the Pitkins Brothers, A. L. Dennison, G. A. Leschot with Vacheron and Constantin, Patek, Philippe, and Frederic Japy of Beaucourt. The pioneers in the 1850s who set the standards for modern watchmaking included the American Pitkin Brothers, Dennison, Howard, and Jacob Custer. By 1880 most other countries had begun to follow the lead of America in the manufacture of the complete pocket watch with interchangeable parts.

In Switzerland there are **four** major categories of watch producers :
1. Complete 2. Ebauche 3. Parts or **Specialized 4. Finishers.** *Complete* watch producers manufacture 75% to 100% on their own premises as Le Coultre. *Ebauche* produce rough movements or movements in the gray called ebauche or blank movements such as ETA in Grenchen. These are made in the valley of Joux and Val-de-Ruz regions, in and around the towns of Granges, Grenchen, La Chaux-de-Fonds, Le Locle and Solothurn, in the Bernese Jura, the valley of St. Imier, Val-de-Travers, at Preseux, in the Ticino, and elsewhere. *Specialized or Parts* are made more or less all over the Swiss regions. Balances more so in Valley of Sagne and at Les Ponts. Lever assortments as the escape wheel, fork, & roller in Jour Valley, at Bienne, in Bernese Jura and especially, at Le Locle. Hairsprings as *"Nivarox"* are made near La Chaux-de-Fonds, Geneva, Bienne and St. Imier. Mainspring, dial, hands, cases, jewels, pendant, bow, crowns, crystals, screws, pins, generally speaking are made throughout Switzerland. *Finishers* buy blank movements, parts, cases, etc. and finish the watch as a complete watch with their own name engraved on the watch as *Tiffany & Co., Ball W. Co.* and many more.

By mid 1950s' the high quality watches made under **"one roof"** by Am.Waltham, Elgin, Hamilton and Illinois could not compete with the Swiss division of manufacturing. This Swiss system of manufacturing encourages improvement within its own field. Each **specialist** company has experience and can improve quality while speeding up large production at a competitive price. This specialized system is still used today with most Swiss Watch Companies.

Swiss Ebauche Assembly Tray, cardboard production tray has 6 compartments with 4 raw movements and extra parts. Upper right of lid is a operation card and printed on the 1st line is *Ebauches No. Serie* = ebauches number series, 4th line *Demontagt* = dismantling, 5th line *Adoucissage* = smoothing, 7th line *Dorage* = gilding, also hand written notes. On cover of box St. Imier & a Coat of Arms.

English Ebauche by J. Wycherly of Prescot, Left 8 size, 3/4 plate movement, Right dial side & engraved on plate 8*04 JW. Mr. Wycherly started making raw movements in early 1867.

Ebauches   S.A.

Ebauches S.A. with its main office in Neuchatel, Switzerland, at one time the following 17 affiliated firms were part of Ebauche S.A. and in the year of 1968 they had produced ABOUT- 40,000,000 WATCHES. In 1932 Eterna divided into 2 companies Eterna and ETA.

A. Schild S.A., Grenchen

Fabrique d'Horlogerie de Fontainemelon, fontainemelon

Eta S.A., Fabrique d'Ebauches, Grenchen

Fabrique d'Horlogerie de Fontainemelon, Succursale du Landeron, Le Landeron

A. Michel S.A., Grenchen

Felsa S.A., Grenchen

Fabriques d'Ebauches Bernoises S.A., Etablissement Aurore, Villeret

Fabrique d'Ebauches Venus S.A., Moutier

Fabrique d'Ebauches Unitas S.A., Tramelan

Fabrique d'Ebauches de Fleurier S.A., Fleurier

Fabrique d' Ebauches de Peseux S.A., Peseux

Fabriques d'Ebauches Reunies Arogno S.A., Arogno

Fabriques d'Ebauches de bettlach, Bettlach

Fabrique d'Ebauches de Chezard S.A., Chezard

Derby S.A., La Chaux-de-Fonds

Nouvelle Fabrique S.A., Tavannes

Valjoux S.A., Les Bioux

FRENCH EBAUCHE

Examples of four ebauches: **Upper left:** Example of a Chinese duplex. **Lower left:** An ebauche circa 1900-1930. **Upper right:** A three-finger bridge movement, circa 1890-1910. **Lower right:** Bridge movement, circa 1885-1900.

WORM GEAR ESCAPEMENT

This oddity was advertised as, "The Watch With a Worm in It," Robert J. Clay of Jersey City was given a patent on October 16, 1886. Mr. Clay said, "The principal object of my invention is to provide a watch movement that is very simple and has but few parts." The worm gear or continuous screw was by no means simple. Mr. Clay and William Hanson of Brooklyn revamped the original worm gear and obtained another patent on January 18, 1887.

The first watch containing a worm gear escapement reached the market in 1887. However, the New York Standard Watch Co. soon converted to a more conventional lever escapement. About 12,000 watches with the worm gear were made, but few survived.

Enlarged **worm gear escapement**. Note endless screw was referred to by the New York Watch Co. as **"A watch with a worm in it."**

Movement with top plate removed.

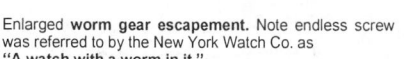

ENAMEL WATCH DIAL MAKING

In ALL American <u>watch</u> ads the words **enamel dial** was always used and never referred to as porcelain dials. Enamel may be described as the art of fusing melted glass on metal. Enamel should not be confused with paint or baking enamels. Enamel is made of silica (quartz), also may have borax, lead, and potash. The more lead and potash used the softer and more brilliant the enamel becomes. Enamel watch dials are basically hand produced. The base for enamel dials is a metal disc whose edge has been turned up holding the enamel in place. Next temporary feet are soldered on the disc. Enamel is ground to a very fine powder and sifted through a sieve upon the copper disc. It is then fired in a furnace at a high heat (about 1400 to 1800 degrees fahrenheit) which fuses the enamel and causes it to flow evenly over the copper disc. This process may be repeated 2 or 3 times. Next a steel plate with numbers engraved on it, the depressions are filled with a black enamel. A soft gelatin pad then comes in contact with the steel plate, the black enamel adhering to the rubber pad, is then transferred to the enameled dial. This operation is repeated in order to insure a good impression.

Note: Enamel dials can be glass enamel or hard enamel. <u>Glass</u> type uses a clear coat over the dial also called under glaze. <u>Hard</u> type **no** clear seal on top of dial. Glass enamel dials have a higher gloss. Hard dial enamel does not shine as much. Hard enamel dials, the numbers are raised or standing proud.

Note: American **hand-painted** dials were declining by 1880's.

Next the dial with the new applied numbers is placed in a furnace at a lower heat than the original process. Next the dial is laid on a template for drilling the center hole, the turned-up edge that held the enamel in place is now ground off and at the same time is reduced to the required diameter. Subdials or double-sunk dials are formed by stamping these parts out separately, treating them the same as the main part of the dial already described and then soldering these dial pieces carefully together. So that a double sunk dial is really a combination of three separate dials.

Note: Due to numbers being fired at a lower heat, a enamel dial can not be fired again at a higher heat (such as for repair purposes).

Minute Hand
Hour Hand   Second Hand

SINGLE SUNK = SECONDS DIAL

ABOVE: Single sunk dial .

CENTER DIAL

SECONDS DIAL

Minute Hand
Hour Hand   Second Hand

ABOVE: Side view showing different levels of a
double sunk dial.

ABOVE: **DOUBLE SUNK DIAL.**Top view of a Double sunk dial. Single sunk is one level below the hour ring. Double sunk is two levels below the hour ring.

Note: Some single sunk dials have inner marked circle made to look like double sunk dial.
Note: Due to numbers being fired at a lower heat, a enamel dial can not be fired again at a higher heat (such as for repair purposes).

CRAZING

The word "craze" means a minute crack in the glaze of the enamel. This is not a **crack** in the dial because the dial has a backing of copper. Crazing does little damage to the structure of the enamel, even though it may go all the way through to the copper.

FIRST DIALS

Thomas Gold was the first to make enamel dials in America in about 1838 in New York City. Thomas had a partner from 1846-51 named Thomas Reeves of Brooklyn. American Watch Co. (Waltham) made their own dials from the beginning by dial-makers John Todd & John T. Gold. Henry Foucy found employment in 1856 with the American Watch Co. he was from Geneva.

PIN LEVER ESCAPEMENT (DOLLAR WATCHES)

The pin lever escapement is sometimes erroneously referred to as "Roskopf escapement" and watches with pin lever escapements are sometimes referred to as "Roskopf watches."

The original Roskopf watch, which was publicly exhibited at the Paris Exposition in 1867, was a rugged "poor man's watch." The chief Roskopf patent, decreases the number of wheels by creating a large barrel whose diameter encroached upon the center of the watch. The loose cannon pinion and hour wheel were driven by a friction-clutch minute wheel mounted to the barrel cover and enmeshing with the loose cannon pinion and hour wheel. The cannon pinion rode loosely on a steel pin threaded to the center of the main plate. The true term, "Roskopf" applies to the barrel with its clutch fitted minute wheel driving the dial train. The Roskopf ebauches watch was made by **Cortebert** factory in La Chaux-de-Fonds, Switzerland. The first Roskopf watch was sold for 25 franc in January of 1870.

🕐NOTE: Some fakes use the name **"Rosskopf."**

PIN-LEVER ESCAPEMENT
(TOP AND SIDE VIEWS)

LOW COST PRODUCTION WATCHES
(DOLLAR WATCHES)

Jason R. Hopkins hoped to produce a watch that would sell for no more than 50 cents as early as the 1870s. He had a plan for which he received a patent (No. 161513) on July 20, 1875. It was a noble idea even though it was never fully realized. In 1876, Mr. Hopkins met a Mr. Fowle who bought an interest in the Hopkins watch. The movement was developed by the Auburndale Watch Co., and the Auburndale Rotary Watch was marketed in 1877. It cost $10, and 1,000 were made. The 20 size had two jewels and was open-face, pendant wind, lever set, and detent escapement. The 18 size had no jewels and was open-face.

In December, 1878, D. A. A. Buck introduced a new watch, at a record low price of $3.50, under the name of Benedict and Burnham Manufacturing Co. It was a rotary watch, open-face, with a skeleton dial which was covered with paper and celluloid. The movement turned around in the case, once every hour, and carried the minute hand with it. There were 58 parts and all of them were interchangeable. They had no jewels but did have a duplex style escapement. The teeth on the brass escape wheel were alternately long and short, and the short teeth were bent down to give the impulse. The Long main spring is laid on a plate on the bed of the case. The click was also fastened to the case. The extremely long mainspring took 120 to 140 full turns of the stem to be fully wound. It came to be known as the "long wind" Waterbury and was the source of many jokes, *Here, wind my Waterbury for awhile; when you get tired, I'll finish winding it.*

"Trail Blazer" by E. Ingraham Co. TOP view is the original Box, bottom. LEFT is Fob"Wings Over The Pole".
RIGHT: Watch has original green crystal. Note: engraving on the back of watch is same scene as depicted on box.

Waterbury long wind with duplex escapement & long mainspring. Right: 2 wheel train rather than the standard 4 wheel train.

The Waterbury Clock Co., Jumbo and the New Haven Clock Co. line of watches first appeared in about 1889. They were large backwind and set watches about 2 inches in size. In 1892, Ingersoll ordered 10,000 watches from Waterbury and offered them for sale for $12.00/dozen, they were sold retail at $1.50 per watch. In 1896, Ingersoll sold the first watch at $1.00, the *Yankee*. "The Watch that made the Dollar Famous" slogan was used by Ingersoll later. Typical wages in 1892 was about 8 cents an hour.

The E.N. Welch Manufacturing Co. sold a very large watch with a embossed commemorative back at the 1893 Columbia Exposition, but dropped production soon after. In 1895 the New York City Watch Co. introduced a watch with a unique pendant crank to wind the watch ("Lever Winder"). The Ansonia Watch Co. produced a large number of watches from 1896 to 1929. In 1899 came the Western Clock Mfg. Co., and later became the Westclox Corporation.

Also, among the low cost production watches were the ''comic character'' watches. They have become prime collectibles in recent years.

About 70 percent of the watches sold in the U. S. were Dollar type. These watches were characterized by the pin lever, non-jeweled (for the most part), and with a paper dial or other inexpensive material. These watches were difficult to repair and the repairs cost more than the price of a new one. Thus they were thrown away, and today it is hard to find one in good condition.

DOLLAR WATCH CHARACTERISTICS:

1. Sold at a price that everyone could afford.   **2.** Used pin lever or duplex escapement.
3. Stamped or pressed out fewer parts. **4.** Were non-jeweled but rugged and practical.
5. Dial made of paper or inexpensive material. **6.** Case and movement were sold as one unit.

PRODUCTION LEDGER FOR MOVEMENTS

The superintendent decided on what model and grade to produce and how many to each lot or batch. This lot of unassembled movement frames (100 to 1,000) were numbered, but were not all completed in one lot. Typically ten finished frames were stored in a wooden **assembly tray.**

Above: Ten numbered movement frames ready for the works. (All Hamilton plates & S# = 4C144XXX.)

The ten-compartment tray served many purposes. 1. Inventory control kept each **numbered** movement and it parts together during the manufacturing process. 2. Each lot of ten unassembled movements could be produced as **demand** required. 3. They were carried from one sub-assembly department to a another, such as balance wheel, hairspring and timing (16 or more). 4. Storage of movements, it required several months for parts & material to emerge as a finished movement. All the while the factory is producing all sizes, models & grades. (Watches not shipped in numeric order.)

Model is not the same definition as grade. A model may exist in many different grade names or number (as Bunn, 992, Riverside, Veritas) and grade names may be used in many different models (as model 1, 18 size, model 1 in 16 size and model 1 in 12 size, etc.). The model # is to identify the size, movement **layout** (full plate or 3/4 plate), location of jewels screws and gears (as model # 1892, or model 5, 18 size). The grade of a movement was to identify the **quality** of the finished movement such as gold jewel settings, 23 jewels and 5 to 6 adjustments high grade(Riverside Maximus) or as a low grade with 7 jewels (Sterling). The company assigned a grade name or number to a movement, however, they also may have changed with the quality upgraded or downgraded as the years passed on. Unassembled movements could be produced as demand required, a batch of movements could be side tracked, thus allowing a different grade for the **same** model to be made. Example A finished Rockford grade and *marked* **915** on movement (18 size,OF, 17J, **same** model 7) is listed in Rockford Company Production Ledger as a **920** grade (18 size,OF, 17J, **same** model 7) and in the Sales Ledger as 915. The greater cost of a finished movement was the labor factor. About 85% of the cost of a high-grade watch movement is labor. Some unfinished movements were destroyed. The destroyed movements were listed in production ledger but not in the sales ledger. This occurred in most American Watch Factories. The average **production** cost of a Waltham movement in 1913 was $3.75.

SALES LEDGER for FINISHED MOVEMENTS

The Sales Ledger reflects movements that were **finished** and sold. The sales ledger lists the serial number, date sold, price, buyers name and how many movements purchased. Example: The production ledger listed date Oct. 5th, 1924 + serial numbers 4,540,001 to 4,541,000 16 size, model 9, grade Bunn Special and description. Later (months or years) when a order came in, the movements were completed and a entry in the sales ledger was made with date shipped March 8th 1926, serial numbers of watches 4,540,075 to 4,541,080, grade Bunn, price $43.25 per movement, along with the buyers name (Smiths Jewelry). Smiths Jewelry later sells a customer a gold filled Boss 16 size case & 16 size, grade Bunn Special with serial # on movement 4,540,079 as a **complete** watch for $75.50 on June, 10th 1929.(Watches not shipped in numeric order.)

LEFT: Factories shipped some movements in a selling case. Note hang tag *"Bunn Special 21 jewels 4540079 Open Face 16 size"*.Thus a customer could view the movement, then was sold a **new** case of his choice to fit the movement. Jobber retained the selling case.

SPECIAL NAMED or PRIVATE LABEL MOVEMENTS

It was common practice for watch manufacturers to personalize watches for wholesalers, distributors, jobbers, firms, jewelers & individuals. This was done either by engraving a name on the movement or painting on the dial, such as Ball Watch Co., Sears, Montgomery Ward, and Burlington Watch Co..

Each manufacturer used its own serial number system even though there may have been a variety of names on the movement and/or dial. Knowledge of this will aid the collector in identifying watches as well as determining age.

Decorated Dials and Louis XIV Hands on all grades of Movements, $1.00 (list) extra.

Orders will be accepted for special named Elgin Movements in all grades. Full Plate requiring about one month and Three-quarter Plate about three months for Delivery.

A charge of 80 cents (list) each will be made for naming all 7 Jeweled Movements, and Orders for less than five, either Hunting or Open Face, of these will not be accepted. Other grades of Movements named Free of Charge. Special named Dials, no charge on any grade.

Orders accepted subject to prices ruling on date of delivery.

Note Above: **A 1903 Elgin AD for wholesale dealers only.** "Special named" all 7 jewel movements 80 cents charge. Other "Special named" grades **"5"** or more no extra charge.

To establish the true manufacturer of the **"Special Named"** movement, study the construction, taking note of the shape & plate layout (is it full or 3/4), shape of the balance cock and the regulator, location of jewels, location of screws, etc. Compare and match your watch movement with every photograph or **drawing** from each watch company until the manufacturer is located.

"Remington Watch Co."-marked on movement and case, made by N.Y. Standard Watch Co., NOTE: The CROWN wheel and RATCHET without a CLICK, these visible wheels are for show only, 16 size, 11 jewels.

"E.F. Randolph"-marked on movement,made by Illinois Watch Co., 23j, hunting, model No. 4. NOTE: The wavy ribbon damaskeening pattern

16 size, No. 390, made by New York Standard Watch Co. Same model as above.

Model 4, 16 size, made by Illinois Watch Co. Same model as above.

PRIVATE LABEL watch movement by ILLINOIS, engraved on movement & on dial B.A. BELL Chattanooga, Tenn., 18 size, adjusted, 15 jewels, OF.

MODEL 4, 18 size, open face, fine train, this matches the watch on the LEFT

PRIVATE LABEL watch movement by ROCKFORD. Engraved on movement. "W.G. Gane, Special Railway, 17j, Adj, serial No. 344551." To identify, see the Identification of Movement section of all watch companies, noting plate design & screw locations to determine that it is a ROCKFORD Model No. 8.

PRIVATE LABEL watch movement by HAMILTON. Engraved on movement, "Mayer, Chattanooga, Tenn., Adjusted, 21J., Grade 940, serial No. 254507." To identify, see the Identification of Movement section of all watch companies, noting plate design & screw locations to determine that it is an 18 size, open face HAMILTON model. Then by using the serial number, the grade can be determined.

Model 8, 18 size, Rockford, full plate, hunting, lever set. This illustration from the identification section matches the model above.

Grade 936, 18 size, Hamilton, open face. This matches the model above.

The basic **model** will have the key mechanical features and construction. The *decoration,* damaskeening and jewel count determine the *__grade.__* Basic models will have such things as, size, hunting or open face, key or stem wind, lever or stem set, and basic layout design. The 18 size may be Transition models and note the location of the cock to the barrel bridge. The 16 size consider the winding parts may not be seen or they could be exposed (crown & ratchet wheel).

Example: Washington Watch Co. 16 size, 17 jewel, Senate grade. Illinois Watch Co. made a custom watch for (Montgomery Ward) using the name Washington Watch Co. and altered the appearance of the movement, however, the basic model was not significantly changed. The mechanical function remain the same to allow the parts to fit the altered model.

Washington Watch Co. , SENATE, 16 size, 17J, Adj. 3P, HC, polished jewel settings, damaskeen finish, double sunk enamel dial, pendant set, serial # 2457094.

ALTERED drawing of Illinois W. Co., this matches the watch to the left. NOTE: The extra screw & cut out . This also is the same model as below (MODEL # 6).

BASIC Illinois Watch Co. **MODEL** 6 as shown in the Illinois W. Co. section. note this drawing is NOT altered.

Upper drawing is Example of a BASIC train bridge not cut out. Lower drawing is the same train bridge and cut out to give it a different appearance only. The lower train bridge is cut out to look like three separate bridges.

🕐 Generic, nameless, custom or private label watches or unmarked grades for watch movements are listed under the company name or initials of the company, etc. by size, jewel count and description.

After the correct manufacturer has been determined, the serial number can be used to determine the age. Taking the age, grade, size, and manufacturer into consideration, the approximate value can be determined by comparing similar watches from the parent company. If a jeweler's name and location are on the watch, this particular watch will command a higher price in that area.

The custom or **Special Named** watches are really just variations of a type or style of a grade and may show the serial number production dates. The production run may have called for 1,000 movements of a basic model and grade that may contain 700 with the Watch Co. name on movement and 300 of the custom or personalized watches with customers name on the watch. Therefore its difficult to determine how many of this type of custom made watches were produced. Usually the differences between the custom and basic grades can be seen with out a tear down of the movement. Unfortunately it may require a disassembling of the watch and you may want to have a watchmaker to help to make positive identification.

Compare and match the following list, it may aid you in the identification of your watches: first determine SIZE, then hunting or open face model, key or lever or pendant set, location of balance cock to winding barrel, location of jewels, location of screws, full, 3/4, 1/2, plate or bridge model. **Grade** differences may include: number of jewels (7-23J.), unadjusted - Adjusted to 3-5 positions, style of regulator & click, (some regulators and click were patented), style of decoration as damaskeening, *no name* or grade name. The grade without a name were the generic type or style of grade. Generic, nameless, private label, Jobber watches or unmarked grades for watch movements are listed under the company name or initials of the company, etc. by size, jewel count and description.

(A): ON MOVEMENT: J. P. STEVENS & BRO. 15 jewels, ON DIAL J.P. STEVENS & BRO. ATLANTA, GA. the size is 18 Size, hunting case model = a **Aurora new model**.

(B): ON DIAL *EAGLE* , On movement illustration of a *EAGLE* and serial number 512929, hunting case model, and is 18 size made by **Seth Thomas** model # 7.

Special Note on **FAKE** watches: Be a knowledgeable wise buyer. Do your homework before you buy. If it is worth faking it will be. If you are not sure of the difference between a fake and a true original and non-original case, dial and movement, find a expert that will know. If you can not determine a fake from a real one, no matter how bad or good the fake is, do not buy it.
Investing in watches is not "Risk Free".

FAKE 21 & 23 JEWEL WATCHES

MARKED: 21 jewels, adjusted, R. R. SPECIAL on movement, the watch has 21 fake jewels and is not adjusted also
the R. R. SPECIAL implies it is a railroad watch. Also a
Locomotive is depicted on movement. (Swiss movement)

Marked: "23 jewels adjusted, Locomotive Special Chicago
U.S.A." on 2-tone movement, 23 glass jewels & is not fully
adjusted, Locomotive on dial which implies it is a railroad
watch. Made by Trenton W. Co. M # 6, 18 size, OF, Ca.1903.

SWISS IMPORTED FAKES

Before 1871 a flood of pocket watches were made with names strikingly similar to many well-known American watches. These were made in foreign countries as well as in America and looked and sounded like high quality watches. But they were fakes, inferior in quality.

These key-wind imitations of American pocket watches are a fascinating and inexpensive watch type that would make a good collection. The watches closely resembled the ones they were intended to emulate. Names such as "Hampton Watch Company" might fool the casual buyer into thinking he had purchased a watch from Hampden. "Rockville Watch Co." could easily be mistaken for the American Rockford Watch Co. Initials were also used such as H. W. Co., R. W. Co., and W. W. Co., making it even harder to determine the true identity.

In 1871 Congress passed a law requiring all watches to be marked with the country of origin. The Swiss tried to get around this by printing "Swiss" so small on the movement that it was almost impossible to see. Also the word "Swiss" was printed on the top of the scroll or on a highly engraved area of the movement, making it difficult to spot.

By 1885 these Swiss imitations were of better quality and resembled even more closely what was popular in America. But the Swiss fakes did not succeed, and by 1900-10 they were no longer being sold here.

Boston.

Note: Right example similar to the authentic American Waltham W. Co. model 1857, many Swiss fake **are similar** to this.

Example of a Swiss imported fake. Note misspelled signature "P.S. Barrett." The authentic American Waltham watch is spelled "P.S. Bartlett."

Example of a NEW HAVEN WATCH CO. imported Swiss fake. Marked on movement New Haven Watch Co. New Haven Conn. Serial # 778883.

HOW TO IDENTIFY A SWISS FAKE

1. At first they were keywind and keyset; then they became stem wind, full plate, about 18 size, large jewels on the plate side, and used Roman numerals.

2. Most had American-sounding names so close to the original that it looks merely like a misspelling.

3. The material was often crudely finished with very light gilding.

4. The dial used two feet; American watches used three.

5. The balance wheel was made to look like a compensated balance, but it did not have the cut in the balance wheel.

6. The large flat capped jewels were blue in color.

These characteristics are not present with all imported fakes. Some or none of these factors may be present. The later the date, the more closely the fake resembled the American watch.

Ohio Watch Co. imported Swiss fake distributed by Leon Lesquereaux of Columbus Ohio. This style watch may have been made by E. Borel & Co. (Swiss) about 1860-75.

Brooklyn Watch Co. New York serial # 6423, note the similarity to E. Howard & Co. Boston watch movement.

CONDENSED PRICE LIST
HIGH GRADE MOVEMENTS.
MANUFACTURED BY THE
HAMPDEN WATCH COMPANY.

1898 AD

1906 AD

18 Size

No. 800 Hunting }
No. 900 Open Face }   **$60.00**

18 Size Movements.   O. F. and Htg.

Special Railway	23 Jewels, Nickel Adj.			$35.00
New Railway	23	"	"	"	28.00
John Hancock	21	"	"	"	23.00
Special Railway	17	"	"	"	30.00
New Railway	17	"	"	"	20.00
Anchor	17	"	"	"	16.00
No. 48 or 68	17	"	"	"	16 00
John C. Dueber Special	17	"	"	"	15.00
No. 47 or 67	17	"	"	"	15.00
John C. Dueber	17	"	"	"	12.00
No. 43 or 63	17	"	"	"	12.00
No. 80 or 81	17	"	"	"	10.00
No. 49 or 69	17	"	Gilt	"	9.50
Dueber	17	"	Nickel		8.00
The Dueber Watch Co.	15	"	"		6.50
No. 45 or 65	11	"	"		5.00
No. 46 or 66	11	"	Gilt,		4.75
Champion	7	"	"		3.00

John C. Dueber. No. 43 and 63, damaskeened in two colors when specially ordered.

24 extra fine ruby and sapphire jewels in gold settings, sapphire jewel pin, double roller escapement, steel escape wheel, sapphire exposed pallets, compensating balance in recess, adjusted to temperature, isochronism and five positions, mean time screws, Breguet hair spring, patent micrometric regulator, safety pinion, poised pallet and fork, handsomely damaskeened nickel plates, gold lettering, champfered steel parts, double sunk glass, enamel dial with red marginal figures, Roman or Arabic, elegantly finished throughout. Certificate of rating furnished upon application.

1926 AD

1926 AD

BUNN SPECIAL
9 Adjustments   21 Jewels
$45.00

SUGGESTED PRICES: Complete in any plain screw—
10K Filled Case, $55.00   14K Filled Case, $65.00
Fancy Cases and Fancy Dials Proportionately More.

21 ruby and sapphire jewels; gold settings; adjusted to SIX positions, heat, cold and isochronism; compensating balance; gold screws including timing screws; double roller; steel escape wheel; Breguet hairspring; patent micrometric screw regulator; safety screw center pinion; beautifully damaskeened with black enamel lettering; double sunk dial.

THE 60 HOUR 6 POSITION
BUNN SPECIAL
23 Jewels, $58.00 -:- 21 Jewels, $50.00
9 ADJUSTMENTS

SUGGESTED PRICES: Complete in any plain screw cases:
23J., 10K Filled Case, $65.00   14K Filled Case, $72.50
21J., 10K Filled Case, $57.50   14K Filled Case, $65.00
Special or Fancy Cases and Fancy Dials Proportionately More.

Ruby and sapphire jewels; raised gold settings; adjusted to SIX positions, heat, cold and isochronism; spring tempered compensating balance with gold screws including timing screws; double roller; steel escape wheel; gold train wheels; safety screw center pinion; Illinois superior motor barrel; patent micrometric screw regulator; recoiling safety click; concaved and polished winding wheels; double sunk dial.

The 23 jewel grade contains the Illinois Superior Jeweled Motor Barrel and two jewels in which barrel staff pivots operate.

No. 89
17 Jewels, Adjusted to Temperature
$22.50

SUGGESTED PRICES: Complete in any plain screw—
10K Filled Case, $32.50   14K Filled Case, $40.00
Fancy Cases and Fancy Dials Proportionately More.

17 jewels; polished settings; adjusted to temperature; compensating balance with timing screws; Breguet hairspring; patent regulator; safety screw center pinion; polished steel work; damaskeened in attractive pattern; double sunk dial.

THE 60 HOUR
BUNN
8 Adjustments   19 Jewels
$43.50

SUGGESTED PRICES: Complete in any plain screw—
10K Filled Case, $50.00   14K Filled Case, $57.50
Fancy Cases and Fancy Dials Proportionately More.

19 ruby and sapphire jewels; raised gold settings; adjusted to five positions, heat, cold and isochronism; special quality hardened and tempered compensating balance with gold screws, including mean time screws; gold train wheels; double roller escapement; steel escape wheel; Breguet hairspring; safety screw center pinion; Illinois superior mainspring; patent micrometric screw regulator; recoiling click; Illinois superior jeweled motor barrel; concaved and polished winding wheels; double sunk dial.

The average Manufactured cost of a Waltham movement in **1913 was $3.75** (case not included).

MARKET REPORT 2003
A $23,500 INVESTMENT IN 1975 NOW WORTH $157,000 !

	1975	2003
Am. Waltham, Premier Maximus, PW., 18K case OF	$2,000	$8,500
Ball 23 jewels, by Illinois, PW., gold filled case OF	$795	$1,800
Hamilton, **950** grade, PW., gold train, gold filled case OF	$375	$1,800
E. Howard & Co., nickel split plate, PW., 14K HC	$795	$3,800
Ingersoll, Mickey Mouse, (1933) Pocket Watch	$70	$650
New York City W. Co.., (Lever Winder) Pocket dollar watch, OF.	$135	$1,200
Rockford multi-color box hinged **14K**, PW., 18 size HC	$500	$4,000
Bovet, superior quality gold and enamel Chinese duplex, gold HC	$4,000	$20,000
Early Sun and Moon, verge escapement, PW., Ca. 1680-1700	$1,200	$8,000
Patek Philippe, minute repeater pocket watch, 18K OF	$2,000	$10,000
Pocket Watch Totals	**$11,870**	**$59,750**
Audemars Piguet, auto-wind, 18K wrist watch	$475	$2,200
Gruen, Duo Dial, gold filled wrist watch	$175	$1,600
Hamilton, Duo Dial, gold filled wrist watch	$155	$950
Illinois, **Ritz** model, gold filled wrist watch	$75	$800
Patek Philippe, chronograph 18K wrist watch, Ca. 1948	$2,500	$28,000
Patek Philippe, Calatrava (classic) 18K wrist watch	$800	$5,000
Rolex, Bubble Back, 18K gold wrist watch, Ca. 1940	$800	$4,500
Rolex, duo dial "Railway", 18K gold wrist watch, Ca. 1930	$1,200	$12,000
Rolex, Oyster, Moon phase + Calendar, **Star dial**, 18K WW., Ca. 1945	$5,000	$40,000
Universal, Tri Compax, moonphase, stainsteel wrist watch	$450	$2,200
Wrist Watch Totals	**$11,630**	**$97,250**
PW. & WW. Investment TOTALS	**$23,500**	**$157,000**

A World record was set for a dial **only**. (**$3,302.00**) It was a *Ferguson* enamel railroad dial, pristine mint new old stock and never on a movement, made for **Illinois Ball**, 16 size and on back of dial stamped (6192 patented USA 1908-Canada 1908-Mexico 1908-England 1909-France 1909-Spain 1909-Australia 1908-Switzerland 1908). Also a new old stock *Ferguson* 16 size RR dial never on a movement for a **Howard Waltham** with the above also stamped on back of dial and sold for **$1,802.77**. A Waltham **"Stone Movement"** with perfectly transparent 3/4-crystal plate movement **only** in a display case, serial # 16, 16 size, 16 jewels, gold train, Fogg's tadpole regulator, transparent crystal cock bridge and enamel dial not in good condition. This rare movement fetched a price of **$31,000.00**. A Edward Howard, 16 size, 23J., sapphire banking pins, wolf-tooth winding, Free Sprung, Adj.5P, DR, with original outer card and mahogany fitted box, extra mainspring, crystal and certificate, 18K Edward Howard case, sold for **$17,200.00**. A Rockford grade 950 winding indicator, 21 jewels, gold filled case, sold for **$6,900.00**. A Hamilton "Navigation Master", grade 3992B, base metal case sold for **$3,450.00**. A Hamilton "Spur" wrist watch 14K white gold case with original box and papers sold for **$8,995.00**. A Ball Official RR Standard by Hamilton, 16 size, 23 jewels, with C. E. DeLong's upright **D** shaped pallets, S# B606,764, gold filled case sold for **$9,200.00**.

C. E. DE LONG.
ESCAPEMENT FOR WATCHES.
APPLICATION FILED MAY 20, 1915.

1,192,812.

Patented July 25, 1916.

DeLong Pat.# 1,192,812. Note # 3 upright **D**-shaped pallets.
DeLong worked 1st for McIntire W. Co. then Illinois W. Co.

AMERICAN LISTINGS

Pricing At Collectable Fair Market Value At Trade Show Level
(As Complete Watches With Case & Movement)

Watches listed in this book are priced at the collectable fair market value at the **Trade Show** level (A collector should expect to pay modestly higher prices at **local shops**) and as *complete watches*, having an original 14k gold-filled case with an original white enamel single sunk dial. The entire original movement is in good working order with no repairs needed, unless otherwise noted. Watches listed as 14k and 18k are solid gold cases. Coin or silveroid-type and stainless steel cases will be listed as such. Key-wind and keyset watches are listed as having original coin silver cases. Dollar-type watches or low cost production watches are listed as having a base metal type case and a composition dial. Wrist watches are priced as having original gold-filled case with the movement being all original and in good working order, and the wrist watch band being made of leather except where bracelet is described.

Many of the watch manufacturers were commissioned to put jewelers' or jobbers' names on their movements in place of their own. Due to this practice, the true manufacturers of these movements are difficult to identify. These watch models are listed under the original manufacturer and can be identified by comparison with the model sections under each manufacturer. See "Personalized & CustomWatches" for more detailed information.

The watch manufacturers who personalized & custom made watches for jobbers or jewelry firms, with exclusive private signed or marked movements must first be found by using a illustration & matched to the manufacture shown in this book. After you identify the movement now the value can be determined. The valuable collectable watches are listed under the signed or marked movement. Other exclusive private signed or marked movements will have equivalent value are only slightly higher value & should be compared to Generic or Nameless movements. Railroad signed or marked (dials & movements) are usually more collectable & higher in value .

The prices shown were averaged from dealers' lists just prior to publication and are an indication of the collectable trade show level or what collectors will pay. Prices are provided in three categories: average condition, extra fine, and mint condition, and are shown in whole dollar amounts only. The values listed are a guide for the collectable trade show level and are provided for your information only. Dealers will not necessarily pay **full trade show price**. Prices listed are for watches with original cases and dials.

Important Notice. All of the information, including valuations, in this book has been compiled from the most reliable sources, and every effort has been made to eliminate errors and questionable data. Nevertheless, the possibility of error, in a work of such immense scope, always exists. The publisher or authors will not be held responsible for losses which may occur in the purchase, sale, statements of its advertisers, or other transaction of items, because of information contained herein. Readers who feel they have discovered errors are invited to write and inform us, so they may be corrected in subsequent editions.

☉ Descriptions and serial number ranges listed for early watches cannot be considered 100 percent accurate due to the manner in which records were kept by these companies.

☉ Watch terminology or communication in this book has evolved over the years, in search of better and more precise language with a effort to improve, purify, adjust itself and make it easier to understand.

ABBREVIATIONS USED IN
THE COMPLETE PRICE GUIDE TO WATCHES

🕐 — **Below a rating scale for rarity.**
(★ Star Rating) & **5 Stars = Rarest**
★★★★★ — **RARE**
★★★★— Scarce
★★★ — **VERY FEW**
★★— **SPARSE**
★— **UNCOMMON**
◨ — In Demand, technical or historical interest.
ADJ —Adjusted (to temperature or heat & cold,
   also isochronism). Adj.5P = Adjusted to 5
   positions, 3 positions or 4 positions etc
aux. sec.—auxiliary seconds
BASE—Base metal used in cases; e.g., silveroid
BB —Bubble Back (Rolex style case)
BRG—Bridge plate design movement
Ca. — Circa (about or approximate date)
Cal. —Calendar also Calibre (model)
C&B — Case and Band
Chrono.—Chronograph
Co.—Company
COIN—Coin silver
DES—Diamond end stones
DMK—Damaskeened
DSD—Double sunk dial
DR—Double roller
DWT—Penny weight: 1/20 Troy ounce
ETP—Estimated total production
ESC.—Escapement
EX—Extra nice; far above average
FULL—Full plate design movement
3/4—3/4 plate design movement
1F brg—One finger bridge design and a 3/4 plate
   (see Illinois 16s M#5)
2F brg—Two finger bridge design
3F brg—Three finger bridge design
GF—Gold filled
GJS—Gold jewel settings
G#—Grade number
GT—Gold train (gold gears)
GCW—Gold center wheel
GRO—Good running order
HC—Hunter case
id. — identification
(illo.) —Illustration of watches etc.
J—jewel (as 21J)
K—Karat (14k solid gold—not gold filled)

K(w) —WHITE GOLD as in 14k(w)
K(y) —YELLOW GOLD as in 14k(y)
KS—Key set
KW—Key wind
KW/SW— transition (Key wind/stem wind)
LS—Lever set
MCC—Multi-color case
MCD—Multi-color dial
M#—Model number
mm —Millimeter (over all case size)
mvt.— movement or movement only no case
NI—Nickel plates or frames
OF—Open face
P—as Adj.5P = Adjusted to 5 positions,
   3 positions or 4 positions etc.
PORC—Porcelain (porc. dial)
PS—Pendant set
PW — Pocket Watch
RF# —Reference Factory number
Reg.—Register on a chronograph
REP.—Repeater
RGJS—Raised gold jewel setting
RGP—Rolled gold plate
RR—Railroad
S—Size as 16S = 16 size
SBB—Screw back and bezel
SR—Single Roller
SRC—Swing ring case
SS—Stainless steel
SSD—Single Sunk Dial
SW—Stem wind
S#—Serial number
TEMP—Temperature
TP—Total production
2T—Two-tone (damaskeened in 2 colors)
WGF—White gold filled
W.I. also W. Ind. —Wind indicator or
   (up and down indicator)
/ = **WITH** as KW/SW or SW/LS
/ = **Also** as OF/HC
WW—Wrist watch
YGF—Yellow gold filled
@ = AT or About

MODEL = Size, open face or hunter, full or 3/4 plate, key or stem wind, **design** & layout of parts.
GRADE= 1st., 2nd., & 3rd., Quality etc. some manufactures used names or numbers (**Bunn** , 992).
  Note: Model is not the same defination as grade. A model may exist in many different grades or grade
names (as 992, Bunn, Riverside, Veritas) and may be used in many different models (as model **1**, 18
size, open or hunting case, model **1**, in 16 size open or hunting case, model **1** in 12 size) etc..
1. **Ebauche** = Manufacture movements in the rough.
2. **Manufacture** = 75% to 100% of movements Manufacture on premises.
3. **Watchmaker** & **Finisher** = Finished movement in the rough or used Special named movement.
4. **Jobber**, Distributor, Firms, Special named, Customized or Personalized movement = Retail only.

INFORMATION NEEDED: We are interested in any facts and information you might have that
should possibly be considered for future editions. I will respect and appreciate positive sound reliable
comments, corrections or remarks but reserve the right to accept the statement or keep my own
observations & views. Documented facts are needed, so please send photo or sources of information.
  Send to: Cooksey Shugart, P. O. BOX 3147, Cleveland, Tennessee 37320-3147.

  (When *Corresponding, Please Include A* 🖃 *Self-addressed, Stamped Envelope.*)

Railroad Standards, Railroad Approved & Railroad Grade "TERMINOLOGY"

NOTE: Railroad Standards, Railroad Approved & Railroad Grade **terminology,** as defined and used in this _**BOOK**_.

1. **RAILROAD STANDARDS** = A commission or board appointed by the railroad companies outlined a set of **guidelines** to be accepted or approved by each railroad line.

2. **RAILROAD APPROVED** = A _**LIST**_ of watches each railroad line would approve if purchased by their employee's. (this list changed through the years).

3. **RAILROAD GRADE** = A watch made by manufactures to meet or exceed the guidelines set by the railroad **standards**. Grades such as 992, Vanguard and B.W. Raymond, etc.

🕐 Some GRADES **exceeded** the R.R. standards such as 23 jewels, diamond end stone, gold train, raised gold jewel settings, double sunk dial and the list goes on. Examples: such as Veritas, Sangamo, 950 & Riverside Maximus and many others.

ABOVE: **GENERIC, NAMELESS OR UNMARKED MOVEMENTS**

Generic, Nameless or Unmarked grades for watch movements are listed under the Company name or initials of the Company, etc. by size, jewel count and description. Such as American Watch Co. or Amn Watch Co. or A.W.W.Co., Elgin W. Co. or Elgin National W. Co., Hampden W.Co. or Duber W.Co., Illinois W. Co.or I.W.Co., Rockford or R.W.Co., South Bend. **Example** name on movement Illinois Watch Co. and the watch is 18 size, 17 jewels, stem wind, adjusted, nickel, and damaskeened this watch can be found and will be listed under Illinois Watch Co. next look under the correct size (18 size) unmarked grade section as **Illinois Watch Co. or I.W.C., 15J, SW, ADJ, NI, DMK** these are Generic or unmarked grades. Movements with a grade **name** such as Bunn can be found and listed under **SIZE** then the name **Bunn** & jewels & etc..

MODEL = Size, open face or hunter, full or 3/4 plate, key or stem wind, design & layout of parts.
GRADE= 1st., 2nd., & 3rd., Quality etc. some manufactures used names or numbers (**Bunn , 992**).

🕐 **The Complete Price Guide to Watches goal is to stimulate the orderly exchange of Watches between "_buyers_" and "_sellers_".**

🕐 Watch terminology or communication in this book has evolved over the years, in search of better and more precise language with a effort to improve, purify, adjust itself and make it easier to understand.

ABBOTT'S STEM WIND

Henry Abbott first patented his stem wind attachment on June 30, 1876. The complete Abbott's stem wind mechanism is arranged in such a way as to convert key wind to stem wind. He also made a repeater-type slide mechanism for winding. On January 18, 1881, he received a patent for an improved stem wind attachment. Abbott sold over 50,000 wind attachments, and were fitted to Cornell, Elgin, Hampden, Illinois, N.Y. W. Co., Rockford, Tremont, U.S. Marion, Waltham 16-18-20 size and Howard above S# 30,000.

Abbott Stem Wind Attachment. LEFT: normal view of an Illinois watch movement with 'hidden' Abbott Stem Wind Attachment (pat. Jan., 18th, 1881). **RIGHT:** Same watch with dial removed exposing the Abbott Stem Wind Attachment.
NOTE: Most Abbott's stem wind levers move up and down, while most standard levers move up & out.

ABBOTT WATCH CO.
(MADE BY **HOWARD WATCH CO.**) 1908 - 1912

Abbott Sure Time Watches were made by the E. Howard Watch Co.(Keystone), and are similar to Howard Watch Co. 1905 model. These watches sold for $8.75 and had 17 jewels. Some of the open face watches are actually hunting case models without the second bits register.

Description		Avg	Ex-Fn	Mint
Abbott Sure Time, 16S, 17J, OF, GF Case ....★		$85	$175	$325
Abbott Sure Time, 16S, 17J, HC, GF Case		110	195	400
Abbott Sure Time, 16S, 17J, **14K Abbott HC** ....△		350	475	750

Abbott Watch Co., 16 size, 17 jewels, gold jeweled settings, hunting case. Note similarity to the Howard Watch Co. model 1905. Serial number 993932.

Abbott Watch Co., 16 size, 17 jewels, gold jeweled settings, open face. Note similarity to the Howard Watch Co. series 9.

ADAMS PERRY WATCH MANUFACTURING CO.

Lancaster, Pennsylvania (1874-1877)

This company, like so many others, did not have sufficient capital to stay in business for long. The first year was spent in setting up and becoming incorporated. The building was completed in mid-1875, and watches were being produced by September. The first watches were limited to three grades, and the escapement and balance were bought from other sources. The first movement was finished April 7, 1876, but in May of 1876, they closed. (*very few watches were sold from this factory*) The next year the company remained idle. In August 1877, the company was sold to the Lancaster Watch Company. In 1892 Hamilton acquired the assets. Seen: **Serial # 1,** movement marked **"Adams Perry & Co. Lancaster Pa., Perrys Patents, No.1,** (also next to the click marked with a **Z"**).

Description	Avg	Ex-Fn	Mint
19S, 20J, GJS, PS, SW, 2 GJS, **18K** original case .... ★★★	$2,800	$3,500	$6,200
19S, 20J, GJS, PS, SW, 2 GJS, gilt mvt, gold filled case......... ★★	1,200	1,900	3,500
19S, 20J, GJS, PS, SW, 2 GJS, DMK, **nickel mvt.,** GF case ★★★	1,600	2,300	3,900

Marked on movement **"Lancaster Watch Penna. 1681".** This basic model about 19 size, consists of 20 jewels, 2 gold jeweled settings screwed in place, stem wind and pendant set, Geneva stop-works, serial number 1681. The above is the so called **Adams Perry & Co.,** model.

J. H. ALLISON movement 16 jewels, gold train and escape wheel with a pivoted detent, key wind and key set, serial number 19.

J. H. ALLISON

Detroit, Michigan

1853 - 1890

The first watch J. H. Allison made was in 1853; it was a chronometer with full plate and a fusee with chain drive. The balance had time screws and sliding weights. In 1864, he made a 3/4 plate chronometer with gold wheels. He also damaskeened the nickel movement. He produced only about 25 watches, of which 20 were chronometers. By 1883 he was making 3/4 plate movements with a stem wind of his own design. Allison made most of his own parts and designed his own tools. He also altered some key wind watches to stem wind. Allison died in 1890.

Description	Avg	Ex-Fn	Mint
Full Plate & 3\4 Plate, GT, NI, DMK .... ★★★★	$11,000	$15,000	$21,000
Detent Chronometer Escapement, 16J, KW/KS, GT .... ★★★★	13,000	17,000	23,000

⊕ **The Complete Price Guide to Watches goal is to stimulate the orderly exchange of <u>Watches</u> between "*buyers*" and "*sellers*".**

AMERICAN REPEATING WATCH CO.

Elizabeth, New Jersey
1885 - 1892

Around 1675, a repeating mechanism was attached to a clock for the first time. The first repeating watch was made about 1687 by Thomas Tompion or Daniel Quare. Five-minute, quarter-hour and half-hour repeaters were popular by 1730. The minute repeater became common about 1830.

Fred Terstegen applied for a patent on August 21, 1882, for a repeating attachment that would work with any American key-wind or stem-wind watch. He was granted three patents: No. 311,270 on January 27, 1885; No. 421,844 on February 18, 1890; and No. 436,162 in September 1890. It is not known how many repeaters were made, but it is estimated to be about **500** to **1,000**. This repeating attachment fits most American **18 & 16** size movements. The Terstegen repeating attachments were made and sold as a **KIT** to fit different models of American watches.

18 SIZE, with REPEATER ATTACHMENT

Name — Description		Avg	Ex-Fn	Mint
HOWARD, w/ 5 min. repeater attachment, COIN	★★	$4,000	$5,000	$8,000
GOLD CASE	★★	7,000	8,000	12,000
Keystone,or Lancaster, w/ 5 min. rep. attachment, COIN	★★	3,500	4,000	7,000
GOLD CASE	★★	4,000	5,000	8,000
SETH THOMAS,w/ 5 min. repeater attachment, COIN	★★	3,500	4,000	7,000
GOLD CASE	★★	5,000	6,000	9,000

ABOVE: **American Repeating Attachment**. illustration at **LEFT** shows Terstegen's patented repeating attachment only. Illustration at **RIGHT** shows attachment as normally found on movement. The two outside circles on left illustration are wire gongs. The hammer can be seen at upper **LEFT** Illustration in the shape of a boot.

🕐 Watches listed in this book are priced at the collectable fair market value at the **Trade Show** level, as complete watches having an original 14k gold filled case, KEY WIND with silver, an original white enamel single sunk dial, and with the entire original movement in good working order with no repairs needed, unless otherwise noted.

🕐 Some grades are not included. Their values can be determined by comparing with **similar** age, size, metal content, style, models and grades listed.

16 SIZE, with REPEATER ATTACHMENT

Name — Description		Avg	Ex-Fn	Mint
COLUMBUS, w/ 5 min. rep. attachment, GF or COIN	★★	$3,500	$4,000	$7,000
GOLD CASE	★★	4,200	5,000	8,000
ELGIN, w/ 5 min. rep. attachment, GF or COIN	★★	3,500	4,000	7,000
GOLD CASE	★★	4,200	5,000	8,000
HAMPDEN, w/ 5 min. rep. attachment, GF or COIN	★★	3,000	3,600	6,000
GOLD CASE	★★	3,500	4,500	7,000
HOWARD, w/ 5 min. rep. attachment, GF or COIN	★★	5,500	6,500	9,000
GOLD CASE	★★	7,000	8,000	12,000
ILLINOIS, w/ 5 min. rep. attachment, GF or COIN	★★	3,500	4,500	7,500
GOLD CASE	★★	6,000	8,000	12,000
Non-magnetic (Paillard),w/ 5 min. rep. attachment, gold-filled	★★	2,200	3,200	5,700
GOLD CASE	★★	3,100	4,200	6,500

🕐 A collector should expect to pay modestly higher prices at local shops.

🕐 Watches listed in this book are priced at the **collectable fair market value** at the Trade Show level, as complete watches having an original 14k gold filled case, KEY WIND with silver, an original white enamel single sunk dial, and with the entire original movement in good working order with no repairs needed, unless otherwise noted.

🕐 Some grades are not included. Their values can be determined by comparing with **similar** age, size, metal content, style, models and grades listed.

🕐 **The Complete Price Guide to Watches goal is to stimulate the orderly exchange of <u>Watches</u> between "*buyers*" and "*sellers*".**

THE AMERICAN WALTHAM WATCH CO.
1851 - 1957 (Waltham Watch Co.)

To trace the roots of the Waltham family one must start with the year 1850 in Roxbury, Massachusetts, No. 34 Water Street. That fall David Davis, a Mr. Dennison, and Mr. Howard together formed a watch company. Howard and Dennison had a dream of producing watches with interchangeable parts that were less expensive and did not result in less quality.

American Watch Co., 18-20 size, serial # 50,100, thought to be a prototype model.

Vibrating hairspring stud, the hairspring is studded to a pivoted lever and movement is restricted by a regulating screw. Thus, the length of the hairspring remains constant.

Howard served an apprenticeship to Aaron Willard Jr. in about 1829. Several years later, in 1842, Howard formed a clock and balance scale manufacturing company with Davis. Howard and Dennison combined their ideas and, with financing provided by Samuel Curtis, the first of their watches was made in 1850. But they had problems. They were trying out ideas such as using jewels, making dials, and producing steel with mirror finishes. This required all new machinery and resulted in a great financial burden. They discovered, too, that although all watches were produced on the same machines and of the same style, each watch was individual with its own set of errors to be corrected. This they had not anticipated. It took months to adjust the watches to the point they were any better than any other timepieces on the market. The first watch was sold in 1853 the **Warren** model.

Example of a Warren model, about 18S, 15J., engraved on the movement *Warren N0 44 BOSTON,* plain dial, under sprung, steel balance, right angle lever, escape wheel has pointed teeth, KW & KS from front, Ca.1853. Note: This movement was made to fit an English size case and will not fit a standard 18S American case. (No.44 may be highest # known)

But Howard had perfected and patented many automatic watchmaking machines that produced precision watch parts. In 1851 the factory building was completed and the name **Warren Manufacturing Co.** and **not** *American Horologe Co.*. The first 17 watches were not placed on the market but went to officials of the company. It was not until late 1853 that the **first watches** were sold to the public, signed " **Warren Boston**", after a famed Revolutionary War hero. Watches numbered 18 through 110 were marked "**Warren Boston**" the next 800 were marked "**Samuel Curtis**" a few were marked "Fellows & Schell" and sold for $40. *Note: The first watches were marketed in 1853.*

The name was changed to the Boston Watch Company in September 1853, and a factory was built in Waltham, Massachusetts, in October 1854. The movements that were produced here carried serial numbers 1,001 to 5,000 and were marked "Dennison, Howard & Davis," "C. T. Parker," and "P. S. Bartlett." Boston Watch Company failed in 1857 and was sold at a sheriff's auction to Royal E. Robbins. In May 1857, it was reorganized as the Appleton, Tracy & Co., and the watches produced carried serial numbers 5,001 to 14,000, model 1857. The first movements were marked Appleton, Tracy & Co. The C. T. Parker was introduced as model 1857 and sold for $12.00, 399 of these models were made. In 1855 **brass clocks** were selling just over **$1.00.** Also 598 chronodrometers were produced and in January 1858 the P. S. Bartlett grade. In August of 1865 prices for movement only: Ellery-$13, P. S. Bartlett-$16, Bartlett Ladies-$30, Appleton Tracy & Co.-$38, A.T. & Co. Ladies-$40, and the American Watch Co. grade was $175.

Engraved on movement *SAMUEL CURTIS ROXBURY. NO 112,* 18 size, 15 jewels, under sprung, steel balance, Ca. 1853. This movement was made to fit in the typical English size case. (112 may be lowest # known)

Engraved on movement "*C.T. PARKER WALTHAM MASS. NO 1099*", 7 jewels, under sprung, steel balance, Ca. November 1857. Note: Balance cock not engraved.

In January 1859, the Waltham Improvement Co. and the Appleton, Tracy & Co. merged to form the American Watch Company. In 1860, as Lincoln was elected president and the country was in Civil War, the American Watch Co. was faced with serious problems. The next year, business came to a standstill. There seemed to be little hope of finding a market for watches, and bankruptcy again seemed close at hand. At this point it was decided to cut expenditures to the lowest possible figure and keep the factory in operation.

American horology owes much to members of the Waltham Watch group such as Bacon, Church, Dennison, Fogg, Howard, Marsh, Webster, and Woerd, who contributed much to its development and success. In early 1861, the name "J. Watson" appeared on model 1857 (first run: Nos. 23,601 to 24,300 total production 1,200).

The next model 1857 was the "R. E. Robbins" of which 2,800 were made. The William Ellery, marked "Wm. Ellery," (model 1857) was then introduced with the first serial number of 46,201. It was key wind and key set and had 7 to 15 jewels.

A size 10 woman's watch was made in July of 1861 with first serial numbers of 44,201. It was marked "Appleton, Tracy & Co." gold balance, key wind and key set, 3/4 plate, 13 to 15 jewels. Some were marked "P. S. Bartlett" and a 15 jewel was marked "Appleton, Tracy & Co." A special model, 10 size, serial numbers of 45,801 to 46,200, is extremely rare. The first stem wind, beginning with serial number 410,698, was produced in 1868. By 1880 all watches were quick-train. The last key wind was serial No. 22,577,000, about 1919, 18 size, 1883 model, 7J, sterling, produced for export.

🕒 **Abraham Lincoln** owned & carried a "William Ellery" model, silver-cased, key wind, 11 jewels, so stated Carl Sandburg in his biography of Lincoln. The watch was produced by American Watch Co. in Jan., of 1863 & was a 18 size, hunting case.

WALTHAM ESTIMATED SERIAL NUMBERS AND PRODUCTION DATES

DATE - SERIAL NO.	DATE - SERIAL NO.	DATE - SERIAL NO.
1852 – 50	1888 – 3,800,000	1924 – 24,550,000
1853 – 400	1889 – 4,200,000	1925 – 24,800,000
1854 – 1,000	1890 – 4,700,000	1926 – 25,200,000
1855 – 2,500	1891 – 5,200,000	1927 – 26,100,000
1856 – 4,000	1892 – 5,800,000	1928 – 26,400,000
1857 – 6,000	1893 – 6,300,000	1929 – 26,900,000
1858 – 10,000	1894 – 6,700,000	1930 – 27,100,000
1859 – 15,000	1895 – 7,100,000	1931 – 27,300,000
1860 – 20,000	1896 – 7,450,000	1932 – 27,550,000
1861 – 30,000	1897 – 8,100,000	1933 – 27,750,000
1862 – 45,000	1898 – 8,400,000	1934 – 28,100,000
1863 – 65,000	1899 – 9,000,000	1935 – 28,600,000
1864 – 110,000	1900 – 9,500,000	1936 – 29,100,000
1865 – 180,000	1901 – 10,200,000	1937 – 29,400,000
1866 – 260,000	1902 – 11,100,000	1938 – 29,750,000
1867 – 330,000	1903 – 12,100,000	1939 – 30,050,000
1868 – 410,000	1904 – 13,500,000	1940 – 30,250,000
1869 – 460,000	1905 – 14,300,000	1941 – 30,750,000
1870 – 500,000	1906 – 14,700,000	1942 – 31,050,000
1871 – 540,000	1907 – 15,500,000	1943 – 31,400,000
1872 – 590,000	1908 – 16,400,000	1944 – 31,700,000
1873 – 680,000	1909 – 17,600,000	1945 – 32,100,000
1874 – 730,000	1910 – 17,900,000	1946 – 32,350,000
1875 – 810,000	1911 – 18,100,000	1947 – 32,750,000
1876 – 910,000	1912 – 18,200,000	1948 – 33,100,000
1877 – 1,000,000	1913 – 18,900,000	1949 – 33,500,000
1878 – 1,150,000	1914 – 19,500,000	1950 – 33,560,000
1879 – 1,350,000	1915 – 20,000,000	1951 – 33,600,000
1880 – 1,500,000	1916 – 20,500,000	1952 – 33,700,000
1881 – 1,670,000	1917 – 20,900,000	1953 – 33,800,000
1882 – 1,835,000	1918 – 21,800,000	1954 – 34,100,000
1883 – 2,000,000	1919 – 22,500,000	1955 – 34,450,000
1884 – 2,350,000	1920 – 23,400,000	1956 – 34,700,000
1885 – 2,650,000	1921 – 23,900,000	1957 – 35,000,000
1886 – 3,000,000	1922 – 24,100,000	
1887 – 3,400,000	1923 – 24,300,000	

D.S. Marsh, No. 1852 engraved on
movement. (8 day watch)

🕐 The above list is provided for determining the **APPROXIMATE** age of your watch. Match serial number with date.
Watches were not necessarily *SOLD* and *DELIVERED* in the exact order of manufactured or production dates.

G. V. WOERD.
Compensation-Balance.
No. 203,976.   Patented May 21, 1878.

Witnesses.   Inventor

HOWARD, DAVIS & DENNISON: 20 Size, 15 Jewels, 8
day, two mainsprings and gilt movement. Serial # 1 - 17 were
made for the officials of the company, Ca. 1852.

Woerd's patented compensating balance the above illustration is a copy of the blue print of Mr. Woerd's patented
SAW TOOTH BALANCE. The Serrated Tooth Balance may
be found on some 16 size 1872 models. (**VERY RARE**)

🕐 A collector should expect to pay modestly higher prices at local shops.

🕐 Generic, nameless or unmarked grades for watch movements are listed under the Company
name or initials of the Company, etc. by size, jewel count and description.

20 SIZE
MODEL 1862 = 20 KW - (T. P. 3,500)

Grade or Name–Description		Avg	Ex -Fn	Mint
American Watch Co., 19J, KW, **18K, HC**, all original	★★★	$7,000	$9,500	$13,000
American Watch Co., 15 to19J, KW, KS,3/4, vibrating hair-spring stud, silver case	★★	2,000	3,400	7,000
American Watch Co., 15 to 19J, KW, KS, 3/4, vibrating hair-spring stud, **18K HC**, all original	★★★	3,700	6,000	10,000
American Watch Co., 15 & 17J, 3/4, KW, ADJ	★	400	950	1,600
American Watch Co., 19J, 3/4, KW, ADJ	★★	3,000	4,400	6,500
American Watch Co., 19J, 3/4, KW, ADJ, with Maltese cross stopwork, all original silver case	★★	4,000	5,500	8,000
American W. Co., Nashua S# under dial, (below 51,000)	★★★	5,000	7,800	13,000
Am'n W. Co., 7-11J, 3/4, KW	★	275	500	900
Am'n W. Co., 15J, KW,3/4, coin case	★	450	700	1,200
Appleton, Tracy & Co., 15J, 3/4, KW, with Maltese cross stopwork, all original	★	650	900	1,600
Appleton, Tracy & Co., 15-17J, 3/4, KW	★	450	800	1,200
Appleton, Tracy & Co., 15 & 17J, 3/4, KW, vibrating hair spring stud, silver case	★★	1,500	2,600	4,000
Appleton, Tracy & Co., 15 & 17J, 3/4, KW, vibrating hair spring stud, **18K HC**	★★★	3,000	5,000	9,000
Appleton Tracy & Co., 15J, KW, vibrating hairspring stud Straton barrel, Foggs Pat.	★★	1,000	1,900	3,000
Appleton Tracy & Co., 15J, KW, 3/4, **Mvt. only no case**		250	300	500
Appleton Tracy & Co., 19J, KW, 3/4	★★	500	800	1,500
Howard, Davis & Dennison, S#1-17, 8 day, Ca.1852	★★★★★	60,000	80,000	150,000

NOTE: **RARE in original gold cases add ($1,500.00 in 14K) & ($2,000.00 in 18K).**

American Watch Co., Model 1862, 20 size, 17-19 jewels, gold balance and escape wheel, gold jeweled settings, key wind, key set from back, serial number 80111.

Appleton Tracy & Co., Model 20KW, 20 size, 15 jewels, serial number 125004. Note vibrating hairspring stud.

Escape Wheel for the "Chronodrometer". ☞
Note: 8 tooth, solid brass, escape wheel.
Also it has a sweep second hand which makes one
circuit in 4 minutes. In the lower part of the dial
there is a second hand in the usual place, and it
makes one round in 4 seconds in beats of
1/4 second each as it is mounted on the escape
wheel arbor. In the upper portion of the dial is the
usual hour & minute hands in a small 12 hour circle.

American Watch Co., Model 18KW, 18 size, 15 jewels, serial number 36369. Reversible clutch center pinion, patented Nov. 30th, 1858. Note: Thin disk at the center of the center wheel.

Model 1857, 18 size, 15-16 jewels, "Chronodrometer" on dial, "Appleton Tracy & Co." or "P.S. Bartlett, key wind & set, 1/4 jump seconds, S.# 14,752 . Listed under "Appleton Tracy & Co. Chronodrometer", lst serial # 13,701. Note: Stop - start botton at 4 o'clock.

18 SIZE
MODELS 1857, (18 KW =1859), 1870, 1877, 1879, 1883, 1892

Grade or Name – Description	Avg	Ex-Fn	Mint
American Watch Co., 17J,3/4, M#1859 or M#**18KW** ...... ★★★★	$3,000	$4,700	$9,000
American Watch Co., 19J, 3/4, M#1859............................ ★★★★	5,500	8,000	13,000
American Watch Co., 15J, M#1859,3/4, Pat. Nov. 30, 1858, Reversible center pinion, original silver case .... ★★★	4,200	6,000	10,000
American Watch Co., 17J, M#1859,3/4, KW, Fitts Pat. Reversible center pinion, Originial **18K case** .... ★★★★	5,000	7,000	11,000
American Watch Co., 21J, M#1883, **Special**, ADJ, GJS ... ★★★★	1,000	1,800	3,300

☉ Generic, nameless or unmarked grades for watch movements are listed under the Company name or initials of the Company, etc. by size, jewel count and description.

	Avg	Ex-Fn	Mint
AM'n. Watch Co., 15J, M#1857, (*Waltham W. Co.*), KW, KS	$165	$275	$475
AM'n. Watch Co., 15J, M#1857, (*Waltham W. Co.*), SW / KS .....★	200	350	550
AM'n. Watch Co., 15J, M#1857, (*Waltham W. Co.*), SW / KW ....★	200	350	550
AM'n. Watch Co., 15-17J, M#1857, (*Waltham W. Co.),* SW / LS ...	175	250	450
AM'n. Watch Co., 17J, M#1857, KW, KS ....★	175	250	450
AM'n. Watch Co., **14K, HC, heavy box hinged, multi - 4 colors**	2,600	3,700	6,000
AM'n. Watch Co., 11J, thin model, KW, 3/4 plate ....★	125	250	550
AM'n Watch Co., 15J, M#1870, KW	125	250	550
AM'n. Watch Co., 17J, M#1870, KW, ADJ	150	300	600
AM'n. Watch Co., 17J, M#1892	125	185	350
AM'n. Watch Co., 21J, M#1892	200	325	550
AM'n. Watch Co., 7J, M#1877	95	135	250
AM'n. Watch Co., 11J, M#1877	95	135	250
AM'n. Watch Co., 7J, M#1883, SW/ KW	95	135	250
AM'n. Watch Co., 11-13J, M#1883, SW/ KW	95	135	250
AM'n. Watch Co., 15J, M#1883, SW/ KW	100	175	300
AM'n Watch Co., 16-17J, M#1883..	100	175	300
Appleton, Tracy & Co., 15J, M#1857, SW / LS	150	250	400
Appleton, Tracy & Co., 7-11J, KW, M#1857	150	250	400
Appleton, Tracy & Co., 11J, **thin model**, KW,3/4 ....★	225	375	650
Appleton, Tracy & Co., 15J, M#1857, KW	150	250	400
Appleton, Tracy & Co., 15-16J, M#1857, KW, serial # below 10,000...★	1,000	1,500	2,600

☉ Some watch manufacturers personalize watches for jobbers or jewelry firms, with exclusive private signed or marked movements. The valuable collectable watches are listed under the signed or marked movement. Other exclusive private signed or marked movements will have equivalent value or only slightly higher value and should be compared to Generic or Nameless movements. Railroad signed or marked (dials & movements) are usually more collectable & higher in value.

Grade or Name–Description	Avg	Ex-Fn	Mint
Appleton, Tracy & Co., 15J, M#1859, 3/4, reverse pinion, Pat. Nov. 30, 1858, orig. silver case .... ★★★	$2,000	$3,000	$5,000
Appleton, Tracy & Co., 11-15-16-17J, KW, 3/4, M# 1859 ....★	200	350	650
Appleton, Tracy & Co., 16J, M#1857, **Ist run** (5,001-5,100) Am.W. Co. (Eagle) silver HC .... ★★★★	1,600	2,800	4,500
Appleton, Tracy & Co., 15J, M#1857, KW, **18K HC**.....................	1,400	2,500	4,000
Appleton, Tracy & Co., 16J, M#1857, KW	250	350	700
Appleton, Tracy & Co., 15J, 3/4, KW, with vibrating hairspring stud, Stratton's Pat., Foggs Pat., orig. coin case .... ★★★	2,000	3,000	5,000
Appleton, Tracy & Co., 15J, 3/4, KW, with vibrating hairspring stud, Stratton's Pat., Foggs Pat., orig. **18K case** .... ★★★	2,800	4,000	7,500
Appleton,Tracy & Co., **Sporting, (Chronodrometer)**,M#1857, 15-16J, KW,KS, orig. case, with stop feature............... ★★★	2,900	4,000	7,500
Appleton, Tracy & Co., 15J, 3/4, M# 1859, KW......................★	225	325	550
Appleton, Tracy & Co., 11-15J, M#s 1877, 1879, SW	80	135	275
Appleton, Tracy & Co., 15J, M#1877, KW	80	135	275
Appleton, Tracy & Co., 15J, M#s 1877-1879, SW, OF	80	135	275
Appleton, Tracy & Co., 15J, M#s 1877-1879, SW, HC	100	185	300
Appleton, Tracy & Co., 15J, M#1883, SW, OF	75·	135	285
Appleton, Tracy & Co., 15J, M#1883, SW, **non- magnet,** OF	125	225	365
Appleton, Tracy & Co., 15-17J, M#1883, **gold plate** -Mvt.	175	275	500
Appleton, Tracy & Co., 15J, M#1883, SW, HC	95	155	300
Appleton, Tracy & Co., 15J, M#1892, SW, OF .... ★★	235	375	675
Appleton, Tracy & Co., 17J, M#1883, SW, HC	75	135	275
Appleton, Tracy & Co., 17J, M#1892, SW, Premiere	75	135	275
Appleton, Tracy & Co., 17J, M#1892, NI, SW, OF	75	135	275
Appleton, Tracy & Co., 17J, M#1883, OF	75	135	275
Appleton, Tracy & Co., 17J, M#1892, SW, HC	125	175	300
Appleton, Tracy & Co., 19J, M#1892, SW, OF	200	300	475
Appleton, Tracy & Co., 19J, M#1892, SW, HC	250	385	550
Appleton, Tracy & Co., 21J, M#1892, SW, OF	225	300	475
Appleton, Tracy & Co., 21J, M#1892, SW, HC ....★	275	400	600

Appleton, Tracy & Co. (20 size), 15-17 jewels, Fogg's safety pinion pat. Feb. 14, 1865, key wind & set from back, serial number 250107.

P. S. Bartlett, Model 18KW or 1859, 18 size, 11 jewels, key wind & set from back, serial number 41597.

⊕ A collector should expect to pay modestly higher prices at local shops.

⊕ **The Complete Price Guide to Watches goal is to stimulate the orderly exchange of <u>Watches</u> between "*buyers*" and "*sellers*".**

🕐 Generic, nameless or unmarked grades for watch movements are listed under the Company name or initials of the Company, etc. by size, jewel count and description.

Grade or Name – Description	Avg	Ex-Fn	Mint
A. W. W. Co., 7-9J, M#1883, **KW,** ....★	$200	$300	$550
A. W. W. Co., 7-9J, M#1883, SW	75	110	200
A. W. W. Co., 11-13J, LS, HC..	85	135	225
A. W. W. Co., 11-13J, M#1879, OF	75	110	200
A. W. W. Co., 11-13J, M#1883, SW, OF	75	110	200
A. W. W. Co., 15J, OF	75	110	200
A. W. W. Co., 15J, HC...	85	135	225
A. W. W. Co., 15J, **14K (5) multi-colors TRUE boxcase HC**	2,700	3,400	6,000
A. W. W. Co., 15J, **14K (4) multi-colors TRUE boxcase HC**......	2,500	2,900	5,000
A. W. W. Co., 15J, **14K (3) multi-colors boxcase HC**................	1,900	2,300	3,800
A. W. W. Co., 15J, M#1879, OF..	75	110	200
A. W. W. Co., 15J, M#1883	75	110	200
A. W. W. Co., 16 or 18J, OF..	75	110	200
A. W. W. Co., 16 or 18J, HC	100	135	225
A. W. W. Co., 17J, M#1857, gold bal. wheel, GJS, ...★	300	425	750
A. W. W. Co., 17J, "for R.R. Service" on dial ....★★	600	850	1,500
A. W. W. Co., 17J, M#1883, OF...	90	135	250
A. W. W. Co., 17J, M#1883, HC...	100	175	300
A. W. W. Co., 17J, M#1892, LS, OF....................................	75	110	200
A. W. W. Co., 17J, M#1892, PS, OF....................................	75	110	200
A. W. W. Co., 17J, M#1892, HC	100	165	275
A. W. W. Co., 19J, M#1892, OF...	165	250	500
A. W. W. Co., 21J, M#1892, OF...	250	395	700
A. W. W. Co., 23J, M#1892, OF...	325	500	850

P.S. Bartlett, 18 size, 15 jewels, Model 1857, Engraved on back "4 PR. Jewels." Serial number 13446.

Appleton, Tracy & Co. 18S, 15J, M # 1877, stem wind, quick train, S # 1,389,078. Note the **TRUE** Box Hinged Case.

Grade or Name – Description	Avg	Ex-Fn	Mint
P. S. Bartlett, 7J, M#1857, KW, **1st Run** (1,401-1,500)			
Am.W. Co. (Eagle) silver HC ....★★★★	$2,000	$3,500	$7,000
P. S. Bartlett, 15J, M#1857, KW, **2nd Run** (1,551-1,650)			
Am.W. Co. (Eagle) silver HC ....★★★	1,600	2,500	5,000
P. S. Bartlett, 11J, M#1857, KW, **3rd Run** ....★★	800	1,200	2,000
P. S. Bartlett, 15J, M#1857, KW, **3rd Run** ....★★	900	1,400	2,300
P. S. Bartlett, 7J, M#1857, KW	150	185	300
P. S. Bartlett, 11J, M#1857, KW.......................................	165	200	335
P. S. Bartlett, 15J, M#1857, KW	150	185	300
P. S. Bartlett, 15J, M#1857, KW , S# below <u>180,000</u> (Pre Civil War)	365	500	900
P. S. Bartlett, 11-15J, M#1857, KW, Eagle inside case lid	400	675	1,000
P. S. Bartlett, 15J, M#1857, SW / LS (**note let down screw**)	265	350	650
P. S. Bartlett, 7-11J, M#1859, KW/KS	165	225	350
P. S. Bartlett, 11-15J, M#1877, KW-SW, HC	100	165	285

Grade or Name – Description	Avg	Ex-Fn	Mint
P. S. Bartlett, 15J, M#1877, SW, marked **special**, HC	$125	$185	$325
P. S. Bartlett, 11-15J, M#1879, KW-SW, OF	100	175	235
P. S. Bartlett, 11J, M#1883, SW	70	100	200
P. S. Bartlett, 15J, M#1883, **KW** ★	200	325	525
P. S. Bartlett, 15J, M#1883, SW	75	100	200
P. S. Bartlett, 17J, M#1883, SW	75	100	200
P. S. Bartlett, 11J, M#1859, 3/4, thin model, KS from back	400	600	1,000
P. S. Bartlett, 15J, M#1859, 3/4, thin model, KS from back	500	700	1,100
P. S. Bartlett, 15J, **pinned plates**, M#1857, KW ★★	675	850	1,500
P. S. Bartlett, 15J, M#1892, SW ★	125	250	400
P. S. Bartlett, 17J, M#1892, SW, OF, LS	95	175	285
P. S. Bartlett, 17J, M#1892, SW, HC	125	200	350
P. S. Bartlett, 17J, M#1892, SW, OF, PS	95	150	300
P. S. Bartlett, 17J, M#1892, SW, **2-Tone**	165	285	450
P. S. Bartlett, 19J, M#1892, SW	150	275	400
P. S. Bartlett, 21J, M#1892, SW	225	300	450
P. S. Bartlett, 21J, M#1892, SW, **2-Tone**	275	400	650
Broadway, 7J, M#1857, KW, HC	95	170	350
Broadway, 11J, M#1857, KW, HC	100	185	375
Broadway, 7-11J, M#1877, KW, SW, NI, HC	85	150	350
Broadway, 7J, M#1883, KW, HC	85	150	350
Broadway, 11J, M#1883, KW, HC	85	150	350
Broadway, 11J, M#1883, SW, HC	80	135	275
Canadian Pacific R.R., 17J, M#1883 ★★	600	800	1,500
Canadian Pacific R.R., 17J, M#1892 ★★	750	1,000	2,000
Canadian Pacific R.R., 21J, M#1892, OF ★★	900	1,200	2,500
Canadian Pacific R.R., 21J, M#1892, HC ★★★	950	1,500	2,800
Canadian Railway Time Service, 17J, M#1883-1892, Adj.5P.. ★★	600	800	1,300
Central Park, 15J, M#1857, KW	200	275	400
Champion, 15J, M#1877, OF	60	85	175
Conklins Railroad Special, 21J, G#1892 ★★	600	700	1,000

Marked **Canadian Pacific Railway**, Model 1892 HC,18 size, 21 jewels, S# 10,082,662. Note beaver on shield.

Crescent Street, Model 1870, 18 size, 15 J., Key wind & set from back, serial number 552,526. This grade was the **first** American watch to be advertised as a railroad watch.

IMPORTANT NOTE: Railroad Standards, Railroad Approved & Railroad Grade **terminology,** as defined and used in this _**BOOK**_.

1. **RAILROAD STANDARDS** = A commission or board appointed by the railroad companies outlined a set of **guidelines** to be accepted or approved by each railroad line.

2. **RAILROAD APPROVED** = A _**LIST**_ of watches each railroad line would approve if purchased by their employee's. (this list changed through the years).

3. **RAILROAD GRADE** = A watch made by manufactures to meet or exceed the guidelines set by the railroad **standards**. Grades such as 992, Vanguard and B.W. Raymond, etc.

Some GRADES **exceeded** the R.R. standards such as 23 jewels, diamond end stone, gold train, raised gold jewel settings, double sunk dial and the list goes on. Examples: such as Veritas, Sangamo, 950 & Riverside Maximus and many others.

Grade or Name–Description	Avg	Ex-Fn	Mint
Crescent Street, 15J, M#1870, KW	$150	$250	$450
Crescent Street, 15J, M#1870, **pin or nail set**	185	275	550
Crescent Street, 17J, M#1870, KW/SW ★	185	275	550
Crescent Street, 15J, M#1870, SW	85	145	300
Crescent Street, 15J, M#1883, SW, non-magnetic, OF	85	145	300
Crescent Street, 15J, M#1883, SW, non-magnetic, HC	125	195	395
Crescent Street, 15J, M#1883, SW, 2-Tone	125	195	395
Crescent Street, 17J, M#1883, SW, OF	70	100	265
Crescent Street, 17J, M#1883, SW, HC	95	175	295
Crescent Street, 19J, M#1883 ★	200	325	550
Crescent Street, 17J, M#1892, SW, **GJS**	100	185	275
Crescent Street, 17J, M#1892, SW, OF	95	165	265
Crescent Street, 17J, M#1892, SW, HC	135	200	300
Crescent Street, 19J, M#1892, SW, Adj.5P, GJS ,OF	150	250	375
Crescent Street, 19J, M#1892, SW, Adj.5P, GJS ,HC	200	300	450
Crescent Street, 21J, M#1892, SW, Adj.5P, GJS, OF	200	325	550
Crescent Street, 21J, M#1892, SW, Adj.5P, GJS, **2 tone**, OF	275	400	650
Crescent Street, 21J, M#1892, SW, Adj.5P, GJS, HC	250	355	550
Crescent Street, 21J, M#1892, **Wind Indicator** ★	1,400	1,800	2,400
Cronometro Supremo, 21J, M#1892, Adj., GJS, OF ★★★	525	675	1,000
Cronometro Victoria, 17J, dial & mvt. marked Adjusted ★★★	600	750	1,100
Samuel Curtis, 11-15J, M#1857, KW, S# less than **200**, original 17S silver case ★★	2,900	4,000	7,000
Samuel Curtis, 11-15J, M#1857, KW, S# less than **400**, original 17S silver case ★★	2,400	3,500	6,000
Samuel Curtis, 11-15J, M#1857, KW, S# less than **600**, original 17S silver case ★★	2,200	2,800	5,000
Samuel Curtis, 11-15J, M#1857, KW, S# less than **1,000**, original 17S silver case	1,900	2,600	4,000
(Samuel Curtis **"not"** in original silver case, deduct $800 to $1,000 from value)			
Dennison, Howard, Davis, 7J, M#1857, KW, W/**original case**	1,200	2,000	3,400
Dennison, Howard, Davis, 11-13J, M#1857, KW, W/**original case**	1,400	2,200	3,800
Dennison, Howard, Davis, 15J, M#1857, KW, W/**original case**	1,600	2,400	4,400
Dennison, Howard, Davis, 15J, M#1857, KW, 1st. run **(1,002-1,100)** W/**original** case Am.W. Co. (**Eagle**)silver HC ★★★	1,900	2,800	4,700
Dennison, Howard, Davis, 15J, M#1857, KW, S# less than **2,000** W/**original** case Am.W. Co. (**Eagle**)silver HC ★	1,400	2,200	3,800

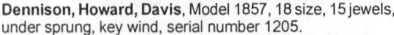

Dennison, Howard, Davis, Model 1857, 18 size, 15 jewels, under sprung, key wind, serial number 1205.

Howard & Rice, Model 1857, 18 size, 15 jewels, under sprung, serial number 6003.

🕐 Watches listed in this book are priced at the collectable Trade Show level, as **complete** watches having an original 14k gold-filled case and Key Wind with silver, an original white enamel single sunk dial, and with the entire original movement in good working order with no repairs needed.

Grade or Name –Description	Avg	Ex-Fn	Mint
D.& R.G. Special (Denver & Rio Grande), 17J, M#1892, GJS, Adj.5P ★★★	$2,600	$3,000	$6,800
D.& R.G. Special (Denver & Rio Grande), 21J, M#1892, GJS, Adj.5P ★★★	3,100	3,600	7,300
Dominion Railways, 15-17J, M#1883, OF, SW, train on dial ★★★	2,500	3,200	6,500
Wm. Ellery, 7-11J, M#1857, Boston, Mass. all original silver HC case with Am. Watch Co.& eagle, serial # below **46,600** ★★	400	600	1,000
Wm. Ellery, 7-11J, M#1857, Boston, Mass.	85	150	300
Wm. Ellery, 7-11J, M#KW, 3/4, M#1859	85	150	300
Wm. Ellery, 15J, KW, 3/4, M#1859 ★	200	275	495
Wm. Ellery, 7-11J, M#1859, KW-KS from back, **18K, HC**	1,500	1,900	3,600
Wm. Ellery, 7J, M#1857, KW, KS from back	200	300	550
Wm. Ellery, 15J, M#1857, **SW** / LS, (with let down screw) ★	225	350	600
Wm. Ellery, 7-15J, M#1877, M#1879, KW	100	185	300
Wm. Ellery, 11-15J, M#1877 & 1879, SW	100	185	300
Wm. Ellery, 7-13J, M#1883	100	185	300
Excelsior, 1-15J, M#1857, engraved on bal. cock (made only for Howard & Co. Fifth Avenue New York)	100	185	300
Excelsior, 11-15J, M#1877, KW	100	185	300
Export, 7-11J, M#1877	100	185	300
Export, 7-11J, M#1883, KW	100	185	300
Express Train, 15-17J, M# 1883, LS, OF ★★	400	600	900
Favorite, 15J, M#1877	85	175	275
Fellows & Schell, 15J, KW, KS, 1857 model ★★★	2,600	3,600	7,500
Franklin, 7J, M#1877, SW	125	185	350
Home Watch Co., 7-15J, M#1857-1883, KW	75	150	225
Home Watch Co., 7J, M#1877, KW	75	150	225
Home Watch Co., 7-11J, M#1879, SW	75	150	225
Howard & Rice, 15J, M#1857, KW, KS, **mvt. by Waltham,** (serial numbers range from 6,000 to 6,500) ★★★	2,600	3,500	5,600
E. Howard & Co., Boston (on dial & mvt.), English style escape wheel, upright pallets, 15J, M#1857, KW, KS, mvt. by Waltham, S#s about 6,400 to 6,500 ★★★★	3,100	5,000	8,000
Lehigh Valley Railroad 17J, M#1883, SW, Appleton, Tracy & Co. grade ★★	1,100	1,700	2,500
Lehigh Valley Railroad 17J, M#1883, SW, **2 tone mvt.** Appleton, Tracy & Co. grade ★★	1,600	2,200	3,200
Martyn Square, 7-15J, M#1857-77-79, KW, SW (exported) ★	200	275	400
Mermod, Jaccard & King Paragon Timekeeper, **23J,** M#1892, Vanguard, LS, GJS, HC ★★	500	650	900

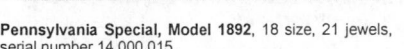

Pennsylvania Special, Model **1892**, 18 size, 21 jewels, serial number 14,000,015.

American Waltham Watch Co., Model 1883, 18 size, 15 jewels, serial number 3,093,425.

Grade or Name –Description	Avg	Ex-Fn	Mint
Non-Magnetic, 15J, M#1892, SW, LS..........	$95	$175	$275
Non-Magnetic, 17J, M#1892, SW, LS..............................	125	195	325
Paragon, 15J, M#1883, HC ....★	300	400	650
"Chas. T. Parker" marked, 11-15J, M#1857, KW, HC .... ★★	1,600	2,400	3,400
C. T. Parker, 7-11J, M#1857, KW, Am.W. Co. (Eagle) silver HC			
serial # below 1,200.. ★★	1,900	2,800	4,500
C. T. Parker, 7-11J, M#1857, KW, Am.W. Co. 18K, HC			
serial # below 1,200................. ★★	2,800	3,900	7,000
Pennsylvania R.R. on dial, Appleton, Tracy & Co. on Mvt.,			
KW, KS, M# 1857............................ ★★★★★	4,000	6,000	12,000
Pennsylvania Special, 21J, M#1892, HC .... ★★★	2,700	3,600	5,000
Pennsylvania Special, 21J, M#1892, OF .... ★★★	3,000	3,900	5,800
Pennsylvania Special, 21J, M#1892, HC			
GOLD DAMASKEENED, gold train.................. ★★★★★	8,000	12,000	18,000
Pennsylvania Special, 23J, M#1892, OF .... ★★★★	4,000	5,400	7,500
Pioneer, 7J, M#1883	70	85	150
Premier, 17J, M#1892, LS, OF	80	100	175
Railroader, 17J, M#1892, LS .... ★★★	1,800	2,200	3,600
Railroader, 21J, M#1892, LS, ... ★★★	2,000	2,500	4,500
Railroad Inspector, 21J, M#1892, LS,			
(loaner with # on case) .... ★★	650	800	1,700
Railroad King, 15J, M#1883, LS .... ★★	350	465	875
Railroad King, 15J, M#1883, 2-Tone..................... ★★	400	600	1,000
Railroad King, 17J, Special, M#1883, LS .... ★★	500	700	1,100
Railroad Standard, 19J, G#1892, OF .... ★★★	1,400	2,000	2,900
Railway TimeKeeper 15J, 1892 .... ★★	200	250	550
Riverside, 17J, M#1892...★	175	250	500
Roadmaster, 17J, M#1892, LS .... ★★	625	750	1,300
R. E. Robbins, 11-15J, M#1857, KW S# (25,101-25,200)........ ★★	1,400	1,600	3,000
R. E. Robbins, 13-15J, M#1877, KW	225	300	575
R. E. Robbins, 13J, M#1883...................................	125	150	300
Royal, 17J, M#1892, OF	95	150	250
Royal, 17J, M#1892, HC	150	175	325

Sidereal, model #1892, 17j, 24 hour dial used by astrono-mers. (marked Sidereal on dial above sub. seconds dial)

Vanguard, model 1892, 18S, 23J, diamond end stone, gold jewel settings, exposed winding gears, S# 10,533,465.

🕐 A collector should expect to pay modestly higher prices at local shops.

🕐 **The Complete Price Guide to Watches goal is to stimulate the orderly exchange of** <u>Watches</u> **between** *"buyers"* **and** *"sellers"*.

Grade or Name – Description		Avg	Ex-Fn	Mint
Santa Fe Route, 17J, M#1883-92, HC-OF	★★	$525	$800	$1,400
Santa Fe Route, 21J, M#1892, OF	★★	850	1,000	1,600
Santa Fe Route, 21J, M#1892, HC	★★★	1,000	1,500	2,200
Sidereal, M#1892, 19J, (marked **Sidereal** on dial) OF	★★★	1,600	2,500	3,800
M#1892, 17J, Astronomical (marked **Sidereal** on dial) OF..	★★★	1,600	2,500	3,800
Sol, 7-11J, M#1883, (with sun on dial), OF	★	150	275	500
Sol, 17J, OF		80	135	200
Special Railroad, 17J, M#1883, LS, OF	★★	425	600	1,000
Special R. R. King, 15-17J, M#1883	★★	475	650	1,100
Special R. R. King, 15-17J, M#1883, HC	★★	525	685	1,300
Sterling, 7J, M#1857, KW, **Silver** case		125	175	300
Sterling, 7-11J, M#1877, M#1879		65	115	200
Sterling, 7-11J, M#1883, **KW**	★	95	150	275
Sterling, 11-15J, M#1883, SW		65	125	200
Tourist, 11J, M#1877		65	125	200
Tourist, 7J, M#1877		65	125	200
Tracy, Baker & Co., 15J, **18K original A.W.W. Co.** case	★★★★★	10,000	18,000	32,000
Vanguard, 17J, M#1892, GJS, HC	★★	450	700	1,100
Vanguard, 17J, M#1892, LS, Adj.5P, DR, GJS, OF	★★	400	600	900
Vanguard, 17J, M#1892, **Wind Indicator**, Adj.5P, DR, GJS	★	1,600	2,400	3,200
Vanguard, 19J, M#1892, LS, Adj.5P, Diamond end stones		200	350	650
Vanguard, 19J, M#1892, LS, Adj.5P, DR, GJS, OF		200	350	650
Vanguard, 19J, M#1892, **Wind Ind.**, LS, Adj.5P, DR, GJS	★★	1,600	2,400	3,200
Vanguard, 19J, M#1892, Adj.5P, GJS, HC	★	325	475	750
Vanguard, 21J, M#1892, Adj.5P, PS		250	350	550
Vanguard, 21J, M#1892, GJS, Adj.5P, HC		325	425	650
Vanguard, 21J, M#1892, LS, Adj.5P, DR, GJS, OF		250	335	550
Vanguard, 21J, M#1892, LS, Adj.5P, Diamond end stone		250	335	550
Vanguard, 21J, M#1892, **Wind Indicator**, Adj.5P, GJS, OF...	★★	1,900	2,500	3,400
Vanguard, 23J, M#1892, LS, Adj.5P, DR, GJS, OF		300	395	600
Vanguard, 23J, M#1892, LS, Adj.5P, DR, GJS, HC	★	400	550	850
Vanguard, 23J, M#1892, LS, Adj.5P, DR, GJS, Diamond end stone		300	425	650
Vanguard, 23J, M#1892, PS, Adj.5P, DR, GJS, OF		300	400	600
Vanguard, 23J,M#1892, **Wind Indicator**, Adj.5P, OF.	★★	1,800	2,600	4,000
Vanguard, 23J, M#1892, **Wind Indicator**, Adj.5P, HC	★★★★	3,700	5,000	7,000
Waltham,17J, Adj., G#1892, (**non magnetic**), OF		200	275	400
Waltham Standard,17J, Adj., G#1892, (locomotive), OF	★★★	900	1,100	2,400
Waltham Standard,19J, Adj., G#1892, (locomotive), OF	★★★	1,500	2,100	3,200
Waltham Watch Co., 15J, **M#1857**, SW / LS, (W/let down screw)		225	325	525

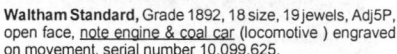

Waltham Standard, Grade 1892, 18 size, 19 jewels, Adj5P, open face, note engine & coal car (locomotive) engraved on movement, serial number 10,099,625.

Marked **845**, Model 1892, 18 size, 21 jewels, railroad grade, Adj.5P, serial number 15,097,475

Waltham Watch Co., 1857 model with factory stem wind, 18S, 15J, S# 778763, Fogg's Patent. This is not a Abbott's stem wind conversion. NOTE **let down screw.** Most Abbott's stem wind with lever set, the levers move up and down, while most stem winds the levers move up & out.

J. WATSON, Boston Mass engraved on movement, 18 size, 11 jewels, hunting case, key wind key set, serial number 28,635, Ca. April 1863.

Grade or Name – Description		Avg	Ex-Fn	Mint
Warren, 15J, M#1857, KW, KS, **S#18-29**, original 17S silver case	★ ★ ★ ★ ★	$25,000	$38,000	$75,000
Warren, 15J, M#1857, KW, KS, **S#30-60**, original 17S silver case	★ ★ ★ ★	20,000	28,000	55,000
Warren, 15J, M#1857, KW, KS, **S#61-90**, original 17S silver case	★ ★ ★ ★	18,000	25,000	50,000
Warren, 15J, M#1857, KW, KS, **S#91-110**, original 17S silver case	★ ★ ★ ★	15,000	20,000	45,000
(Warren not in original silver case, deduct $6,000 to $12,000)				
George Washington, M#1857, KW	★ ★	700	1,000	1,800
George Washington, M#1879, SW		300	500	800
J. Watson, 7J, M#1857, KW, marked"Boston" ★ S# (**28,201-28,270**)	★ ★ ★	1,100	1,800	3,300
J. Watson, 7-11J, M#1857, KW, marked"London" S# (**23,700-23,800**)	★ ★ ★	1,100	1,800	3,300
454, 21J, GT, 3/4,	★	200	300	550
820, 15J, OF		65	95	150
845, 21J, M#1892, OF		200	300	550
845, 21J, M#1892, HC		300	400	650
836, 17J, DR, Adj.4P, LS, OF		75	100	200

American Watch Co., Model 16KW or Model 1868, 16 size, key wind and set from back, Gold Train, serial number 501,561.

American Watch Co., Model 1888, 16 size, 19 jewels, gold jewel settings, gold train, high grade movement, serial number 5,000,297.

16 SIZE
MODELS 16KW =1860, 1868, 1872, 1888,
1899, 1908, BRIDGE MODEL

Grade or Name – Description	Avg	Ex-Fn	Mint
AM'n. Watch Co., 7-15J, M#1872, KW KS,			
sweep sec. with a **slide stop** button............... ★ ★ ★	$700	$1,000	$1,700
AM'n. Watch Co., 7-11J, M#1888, 3/4, SW	80	100	200
AM'n. Watch Co., 7-11J, M#1888-1899	80	100	200
AM'n. Watch Co., 11J, M#16KW or 1868, KW & KS from back,			
original silver case .... ★ ★	1,000	1,500	2,500
AM'n. Watch Co., 11J, M#1868, 3/4, KW	700	900	1,700
AM'n. Watch Co., 13J, M#1888-1899............................	95	135	250
AM'n. Watch Co., 15-17J, M#1868, 3/4, KW.............. ★	700	1,000	1,700
AM'n. Watch Co., 15J, M#1868-1872, 3/4, SW	300	500	1,000
AM'n. Watch Co., 15J, M#16KW, KW & KS from back .... ★ ★	500	700	1,500
AM'n. Watch Co., 15-16J, M#1888-1899, HC	80	150	325
AM'n. Watch Co., 15J, M#1888-1899, SW, HC.............	80	150	325
AM'n. Watch Co., 15J, M#1888-1899, SW, ...	65	110	225
AM'n. Watch Co., 16-17J, M#1872, 3/4, SW	200	375	650
AM'n. Watch Co., 17J, M#1888-1899............................	95	150	285
AM'n. Watch Co., 19J, M#1872, 3/4, SW............. ★ ★ ★	1,300	2,000	2,900
AM'n. Watch Co., 19J, M#1899	125	225	375

☺ Generic, nameless or unmarked grades for watch movements are listed under the Company name or initials of the Company, etc. by size, jewel count and description.

American Watch Co., Model 1888, 16 size, 21 jewels, gold train, note tadpole regulator.

American Watch Co., Bridge Model, 16 size, 23 jewels gold train, Adj.5P.

Grade or Name –Description	Avg	Ex-Fn	Mint
American Watch Co., 19J Maltese cross stopwork, gilt mvt.			
all original 1860 Model, **18K**case .... ★ ★	$2,000	$3,400	$5,200
American Watch Co., 17-19J, 3/4, KW & KS from back,			
vibrating hairspring stud, 1860 Model, **18K**case .... ★ ★ ★	2,100	3,600	4,800
American Watch Co., 19J, 3/4 , KW & KS from back, **nickel mvt.**			
1860 Model, original case, **18K** case .... ★ ★ ★ ★	5,500	7,500	11,000
American Watch Co., 15J, M#1868, 3/4, KW, Silver .... ★ ★ ★	1,100	1,800	2,900
American Watch Co., 17-18J, M#1872,3/4,SW,**HC,14K** .... ★	1,500	2,200	3,500
American Watch Co., 17J, M#1868, 3/4, KW, ADJ, Silver ..... ★ ★	1,000	1,500	2,400
American Watch Co., 17J, M#1899, Adj.5P, ... ★	395	500	750
American Watch Co., 18J, M#1868, SW, nickel mvt. .... ★	475	600	925
American Watch Co., 19J, M#1868, SW, nickel mvt.			
Silver case .... ★ ★ ★	5,000	6,300	8,300
American Watch Co., 19J, M#1888, SW, nickel mvt. .... ★ ★ ★	1,000	1,900	3,200
American Watch Co., 19J, M#1899, SW, nickel mvt. .... ★ ★	550	800	1,100

☺ Pricing in this Guide are fair market price for COMPLETE watches which are reflected from the **"NAWCC"** National and regional shows.

Grade or Name — Description	Avg	Ex-Fn	Mint
American Watch Co., 19-21J, M#**1872**, 3/4, SW .... ★★★	$2,200	$2,800	$5,200
American Watch Co., 19-21J, M#**1872**, 3/4, SW, **18k**......... ★★★	3,500	5,000	7,500
American Watch Co., 19-21J, M# 1872, GJS, **With sawtooth bal. (see illo. below)**			
marked *"Woerd's pat. compensating balance"*. ... ★★★★★	5,000	7,000	10,000
American Watch Co., 15-21J, M#1868-1872, 3/4, GJS,"**NO**" sawtooth bal.			
"Woerd's patents" under balance, square roller jewel..........★	1,500	2,000	3,500
American Watch Co., 19J, M#1888, **14K** .... ★★★	1,600	2,200	3,800
American Watch Co., 19J, M#1888 .... ★★★	800	1,200	2,200
American Watch Co., 21J, M#1888, NI, 3/4 .... ★★★	950	1,400	2,500
American Watch Co., 23J, M# 1899, Adj.5P, GT, GJS .... ★★	650	1,000	1,900
American Watch Co., 23J, BRG, Adj.5P, GT, GJS, **14K**			
original case... ★★	1,300	1,800	2,600
American Watch Co., 23J, BRG, Adj.5P, GT, GJS, **18K**			
original case... ★★	1,500	2,400	3,400
American Watch Co., 23J, BRG, Adj.5P, GT, GJS .... ★★	800	1,200	1,900
American Watch Co., 21J, BRG, Adj.5P, GT, GJS .... ★	450	700	1,100
American Watch Co., 19J, BRG, Adj.5P, GT, GJS .... ★	350	500	800
American Watch Co., 17J, BRG, Adj.5P, GT, GJS	250	350	650
Appleton, Tracy & Co., 15J, M#1860, 3/4, KW & KS from			
back, all original silver case	600	800	1,600
Appleton, Tracy & Co., 15-19J, M#1868, 3/4, KW	600	800	1,600
Appleton, Tracy & Co., 15-19J, 3/4, KW, with vibrating			
hairspring stud, all original, silver case .... ★★	1,100	1,700	2,800
Appleton, Tracy & Co., 15-19J, 3/4, KW, with vibrating			
hairspring stud, **18K**, original case .... ★★★	1,800	2,500	4,000

☉ Generic, nameless or unmarked grades for watch movements are listed under the Company name or initials of the Company, etc. by size, jewel count and description.

A. W. Co., 7J, M#1872, SW, HC...	$100	$150	$325
A. W. W. Co., 7J, SW, M#1888...	65	100	200
A. W. W. Co., 7J, SW, DMK..	65	100	200
A. W. Co., 9J, SW, ...	65	100	200
A. W. W. Co., 11-13J, SW	65	100	200
A. W. Co., 11J, M#1899, SW...	65	100	200
A. W. W. Co., 11-15J, M#1872, SW, HC..............................	125	225	350
A. W. W. Co., 13J, M#1888-99, OF	65	100	200

RIGHT: **Woerd's pat. compensating balance,** is engraved on movement, from a blue print of Mr. Woerd's patented <u>Saw Tooth Balance.</u> This balance **must** be in watch for **top prices**.

Appleton, Tracy & Co. (16 size), 15J, KW & KS from back, S# 140,030 Ca. 1864. *Stratton's Patent* engraved on movement = safety maintaining barrel. *Fogg's Pat. Feb.2,1864*, engraved on cock = vibrating hairspring stud.

Crescent Street, Model 16–S (CENTER SECONDS), 16 size, movement, 22J, Adj6p, lever set, Wind indicator.

Top Right: Fogg's Patented, vibrating hairspring stud.

Note: Vibrating hairspring stud, the hairspring is studded to a pivoted lever and movement is restricted by a regulating screw. Thus, the length of the hairspring remains constant. <u>Also</u> these style watches use of a maintaining spring barrel, the advantage was safety against damage due to breaking of mainspring in going barrel. (See Herman Von Der Heydt page)

🕐 Generic, nameless or unmarked grades for watch movements are listed under the Company name or initials of the Company, etc. by size, jewel count and description.

Grade or Name—Descripion	Avg	Ex-Fn	Mint
A. W. W. Co., 15J, M#1899, OF	$80	$125	$250
A. W. W. Co., 15J, M#1888, SW, HC	85	135	275
A. W. W. Co., 16-17J, M#1888, SW, OF	85	135	275
A. W. W. Co., 16J, M#1899, SW, DMK, HC	95	175	300
A. W.W. Co., 17J, M#1872, SW, DMK, GJS, DES, HC ★	300	475	850
A. W. W. Co., 17J, SW, OF	85	125	250
A.W.W.Co., 19J, Adj.5P, LS, OF	95	175	300
A.W.W.Co., 19J, Adj.5P, LS, HC	125	200	425
A.W.W.Co., 21J, Adj.5P, PS, OF	200	275	550
A.W.W.Co., 21J, Adj.5P, PS, HC	225	300	650
A.W.W.Co., 23J, Adj.5P, PS, OF	225	300	650
A.W.W.Co., 23J, Adj.5P, PS, HC	265	325	695
P. S. Bartlett, 17J, M#1899, OF	65	100	200
P. S. Bartlett, 17J, M#1899, HC	100	135	250
P. S. Bartlett, 17J, M#1908, OF	65	100	200
Bond St., 7J, M#1888	65	100	200
Bond St., 11J, M#1888	65	100	200
Bond St., 15J, M#1888	65	100	200
Bond St., 7J, M#1899	65	100	200
Canadian Pacific RR, M#s 1888, 1899, 1908 ★★★	650	1,100	1,900
Canadian Railway Time Service, M#1908 ★★	500	750	1,300
CHRONOGRAPH are listed as 14 SIZE SEE Chronograph under 14 size			
Crescent St., 19J, M#1899, Adj.5P, LS, OF	100	185	325
Crescent St., 19J, M#1899, Adj.5P, PS, OF	100	185	325
Crescent St., 19J, M#1899, Adj.5P,LS, HC	125	200	375
Crescent St., 21J, M#1899, Adj.5P, PS, OF	100	175	300
Crescent St., 21J, M#1899, Adj.5P, LS, OF	100	175	300
Crescent St., 21J, M#1899, Adj.5P, PS, **HC**	150	275	425
Crescent St., 19J, M#1908, Adj.5P, LS, OF	100	175	300
Crescent St., 19J, M#1908, Adj.5P, PS, OF	100	175	300
Crescent St., 21J, M#1908, Adj.5P, LS, OF	150	325	425
Crescent St., 21J, M#1908, Adj.5P, PS, OF	150	325	425
Crescent St., 21J, M#1908, Adj.6P, LS, OF	150	325	425
Crescent St., 21J, M#1908, Adj.5P, PS, HC	200	285	500
Crescent St., 21J, M#1908, Adj.5P, LS, **Wind Indicator** ★	725	950	1,400
Crescent St., 21J, M#1912, Adj.5P, LS, **Wind Indicator** ★	725	950	1,400
Crescent St., 22J, M#16–S, Adj.6P, **DECK WATCH**			
LS, center sec., **Wind Indicator.** ★★★	850	1,200	1,800
* Cronometro Supremo &Victoria, may have a **Sun logo**, ("EXPORT") to Spanish Countries.			
Cronometro Victoria, 15J, M#1899, OF ★★	250	350	650
Cronometro Victoria, 15J, M#1899, HC ★★	300	400	700
Cronometro Supremo, 21J, M#1899, LS, OF ★★	350	500	950
Cronometro Supremo, 21J, M#1899, LS, HC ★★	375	550	1,000
Cronometro Victoria, 21J, M#1899, HC ★★	350	450	950
Diamond Express, 17J, M#1888, PS, OF,			
Diamond End Stones ★★	750	1,000	2,000
Electric Railway, 17J, OF, LS, Adj.3P	150	225	500
Equity, 7-11J, PS, OF, 16 1/2 Size	55	85	150
Equity, 7-11J, PS, HC, 16 1/2 Size	55	85	150
Equity, 15-17J, PS, OF, 16 1/2 Size	55	85	150
Equity, 15-17J, PS, HC, 16 1/2 Size	55	85	150
Giant, 7-11J, PS, OF, 16 1/2 Size	55	85	150
Giant, 7-11J, PS, HC, 16 1/2 Size	55	85	150
Hillside, 7J, M#1868, ADJ	95	150	300
Hillside, 7J, M#1868-1872, **sweep sec. & STOP** ★★★	1,200	2,000	3,700
Marquis, 15J, M#1899, LS	65	95	185
Marquis, 15J, M#1908, LS	65	95	185
Non-Magnetic, 15J, NI, HC	95	175	285
Park Road, 11-13-15J, M#1872, PS	175	225	400
Park Road, 16J, M#1872, PS	175	225	400

Note: A true O'Hara dial is signed O'Hara Dial Company in a logo on back of the dial.

Premier Maximus, "Premier" on movement. "Maximus" on dial, 16 size, 23 jewels (two diamond end stones), open face, pendant set, serial number 17,000,014.

American Waltham Watch Co., 5 minute repeater, 16 size, 16 jewels, 3/4 plate, adj, 2 gongs, Note: The **slide** on side of case to activate repeater, Pat. June 1888, S# 3,793,502.

Grade or Name — Description	Avg	Ex-Fn	Mint
Premier, 9J, M#1908, PS, OF	$45	$75	$150
Premier, 11J, M#1908	65	100	185
Premier, 15J, M#1908, LS, OF	65	100	185
Premier, 17J, M#1908, PS, OF	65	100	185
Premier, 17J, M#1908, PS, OF, Silveroid	65	100	185
Premier, 21J, M#1908,	125	175	365
Premier, 22J, M#1908, LS, Adj.6P, **Stainless steel case**, OF	150	225	425
Premier, 23J, M#1908, LS, OF	200	300	465
Premier Maximus, 23J, GT, gold case, LS,GJS, Adj.6P, original WI, DR, **18K** Maximus case, **box & papers** ★★	9,500	10,500	15,500
Premier Maximus, 23J, GT, gold case, LS, GJS,Adj.6P, WI, DR, **original 14K or 18K** Maximus case, **NO box** .. ★★	7,000	7,500	11,500
Premier Maximus, 23J, GT, **RECASED**	1,800	2,200	3,500
Railroader, 17J, M#1888, LS, NI ★★★	600	950	1,700
Railroad Time, 15-17J, ADJ, OF ★	200	400	750

Note: The Waltham Serial number with description book list Two runs of **Repeaters** 1st run from 3,793,001 to 3,793,400 with **chronograph** = 400 and 2nd run from 3,793,401 to 3,794,200 = 800.

Grade or Name — Description	Avg	Ex-Fn	Mint
REPEATER, 16-17J, 5 min., original HC gold filled case ★★	$ 2,000	$3,000	$4,700
REPEATER, 16-17J, 5 min., original **HC coin** case ★★	2,300	3,500	5,200
REPEATER, 16-17J, 5 Min., original **HC 14K** case ★★★	3,200	3,800	6,200
REPEATER, 16-17J, 5 Min., original **HC 18K** case ★★★★	4,500	5,000	7,500
REPEATER, 16-17J, 5 Min., chronograph with register, **HC 18K** case, all original ★★★★	6,500	8,500	12,200
REPEATER, **1 minute**, moon phase, M# 1872, Perpetual Calendar, **HC 18K** case, all original ★★★★★	45,000	60,000	90,000

🕐 Watches listed in this book are priced at the collectable trade show level, as **complete** watches having an original 14k gold-filled case and *Key Wind* with silver, an original white enamel single sunk dial, and with the entire original movement in good working order with no repairs needed.

🕐 **The Complete Price Guide to Watches goal is to stimulate the orderly exchange of <u>Watches</u> between "*buyers*" and "*sellers*".**

🕐 A collector should expect to pay modestly higher prices at local shops.

Grade or Name — Description	Avg	Ex-Fn	Mint
Riverside, 15-16J, M#1872, NI, OF	$100	$175	$300
Riverside, 15-16J, M#1872, **gilded**, OF	100	175	300
Riverside, 16-17J, M#1888, NI, OF, **14K**	525	700	1,100
Riverside, 16-17J, M#1888, NI, OF	100	175	300
Riverside, 17J, M#1888, gilded, OF	100	175	300
Riverside, 15J, M#1888, gilded, OF	100	175	300
Riverside, 17J, M#1888, checker goldtone DMK, raised gold jewel settings, OF	100	175	300
Riverside, 17J, M#1899, LS, DR, OF	100	175	300
Riverside, 17J, M#1899, LS, DR, HC	100	175	300
Riverside, 19J, M#1899, LS, DR, OF	125	200	325
Riverside, 19J, M#1908, Adj.5P, PS, DR, HC ★	125	200	350
Riverside, 21J, M#1888-1899-1908, LS, DR, OF	200	250	425
Riverside, 21J, M#1888-1899-1908, LS, DR, HC	250	300	575
Note: **Riverside Maximus have Raised gold jewel settings, gold train, Diamond end stones, Adj. to positions**			
Riverside Maximus, 21J, M#1888, Adj., GJS, GT, DR, OF ★★	675	850	1,600
Riverside Maximus, 21J, M#1888, Adj., GJS, GT, DR, HC ★★	750	950	1,700
Riverside Maximus, 21J, M#1888, Adj., GJS, GT, DR, HC, **14K** ★★	1,200	1,500	2,200
Riverside Maximus, 21J, M#1899, Adj., GJS, GT, DR, OF ★	400	575	950
Riverside Maximus, 21J, M#1899, Adj., GJS, GT, DR, HC ★★	600	800	1,300
Riverside Maximus, 23J, M#1899, Adj., GJS, GT, DR, OF	400	575	950
Riverside Maximus, 23J, M#1899, Adj., GJS, GT, DR, **14K** OF	700	1,000	1,500
Riverside Maximus, 23J, M#1899, Adj., GJS, GT, DR, HC	600	850	1,400
Riverside Maximus, 23J, M#1899 Adj., GJS, GT, DR, **Wind Ind., OF** ★★★★	3,200	4,500	6,200
Riverside Maximus, 23J, M#1908, Adj., GJS, DR, OF	465	600	995
Riverside Maximus, 23J, M#1908, Adj., GJS, DR, **14K** OF	750	1,100	1,650
Riverside Maximus, 23J, M#1908, Adj., GJS, DR, HC ★★★	600	850	1,400
Riverside Maximus, 23J, M#1908, Adj., GJS, GT, DR, **14K HC** ★★★	1,000	1,400	1,900
Riverside Maximus, 23J, M#1908, Adj., GJS, GT, DR, **Wind Ind. OF** ★★★	3,200	4,500	6,200

American Watch Co., model 1872, 16 size, 16-17-21 jewels, gold train, serial number 871199.

Riverside Maximus, Model 1899, 16 size, 23 jewels, gold train, raised gold jewel settings, **4** diamond end stones, adjusted to 5 positions, hunting case, serial # 12,509,200.

🕐 Some grades are not included. Their values can be determined by comparing with similar age, size, metal content, style, models and grades listed.

🕐 A collector should expect to pay modestly higher prices at local shops.

Stone Movement, 16 size, 16-17 jewels, crystal plates, Model 1872, gold train, gold jeweled settings, Adj5p, S # 20.

Vanguard, 16 size, 23 jewels, Adj6p, note pressed-in jewels rather than gold jewel settings. c. 1945.

Grade or Name — Description	Avg	Ex-Fn	Mint
Roadmaster, 17J, M#1899, LS, OF GJS .... ★★	$475	$600	$1,000
Royal, 13-15J, M#1872	65	95	175
Royal, 17J, M#1888, PS, OF	65	95	175
Royal, 17J, M#1888, PS, HC	100	150	250
Royal, 17J, M#1899, Adj.3P, OF	65	95	175
Royal, 17J, M#1899-1908, Adj.5P, OF	65	95	175
Royal, 17J, M#1899-1908, Adj.5P,HC	90	150	250
Royal Special, 17J, M#1888	100	165	295
Santa Fe Route, M#s 1888, 1899, 1908 .... ★★★	750	1,100	1,700
Sol, 7J, M#1888	50	75	150
Sol, 7J, M#1908	50	75	150
Stone Movement, 16-17J, M#1872, GT, **Crystal plates** .. ★★★★	15,000	25,000	45,000
Supremo, 17J, M#1899....................................	65	95	175
SWISS made, 17-25J, ...	50	75	150
Traveler, 7J, M#1888, 1899, 1908 & 16 1/2 size(Equity).............	50	75	150
Tennyson,15J, M#1888, OF .... ★	150	250	425
Vanguard, 19J, M#1899, PS, LS, Adj.5P, GJS, DR, OF	175	250	425
Vanguard, 19J, M#1899, PS, LS, Adj.5P, GJS, DR, HC	225	275	475
Vanguard, 21J, M#1899, Adj.5P, OF .... ★★	250	325	575
Vanguard, 21J, M#1899, Adj.5P, **HC** .... ★★	300	375	625
Vanguard, 23J, M#1899, LS, Adj.5P, GJS, DR, OF	250	325	525
Vanguard, 23J, M#1899, PS, Adj.5P, GJS, DR, OF	250	325	525
Vanguard, 23J, M#1899, Adj.6P, OF......................	250	325	525
Vanguard, 23J, M#1899, Adj.5P, **HC**	275	375	675
Vanguard, 23J, M#1899, PS, **Wind Indicator,** Adj.5P, GJS, DR★	750	950	1,300

🕐 Watches listed in this book are priced at the collectable trade show level, as **complete** watches having an original 14k gold-filled case and *Key Wind* with silver, an original white enamel single sunk dial, and with the entire original movement in good working order with no repairs needed.

🕐 Some grades are not included. Their values can be determined by comparing with similar age, size, metal content, style, models and grades listed.

🕐 Watch **terminology or communication** in this book has evolved over the years, in search of better and more precise language with a effort to improve, purify, adjust itself and make it easier to understand.

🕐 **The Complete Price Guide to Watches goal is to stimulate the orderly exchange of <u>Watches</u> between "*buyers*" and "*sellers*".**

Grade or Name — Description	Avg	Ex-Fn	Mint
Vanguard, 19J, M#1908, LS & PS, Adj.5P, GJS, DR	$200	$250	$425
Vanguard, 21J, M#1908, Adj.5P, GJS, DR, PS, LS, OF .... ★ ★	275	350	575
Vanguard, 21J, M#1908, Adj.5P, **Sidereal, Wind Ind.**,OF ★ ★ ★	1,200	1,800	3,000
Vanguard, 21J, M#1908, Adj.5P, GJS, DR, PS, LS, HC .... ★ ★	325	425	625
Vanguard, 23J, M#1908, LS, Adj.5P, GJS, DR, OF	275	350	575
Vanguard, 23J, M#1908, LS, Adj.5P, GJS, DR, HC	325	450	625
Vanguard, 23J, M#1908, PS, Adj.5P, GJS, DR	275	350	595
Vanguard, 23J, M#1908, Adj.5P, **Wind Indicator**, GJS, DR	750	950	1,300
Vanguard, 23J, M#1908, Adj.5P, GJS, Diamond end stone	250	300	525
Vanguard, 23J, M#1908, Adj.5P, GJS, HC ....★	325	425	675
Vanguard, 23J, M#1908, OF, **14K**	700	950	1,300
Vanguard, 23J, M#1908, Adj.6P, **Wind Indicator**, GJS, DR	725	950	1,300
Vanguard, 23J, M#1908, Adj.5-6P, **Wind Ind.**, **Lossier**, GJS,DR	650	800	1,200
Vanguard, 23J, M#1912, **Press Jewels**	175	250	400
Vanguard, 23J, M#1912, PS, military (case), **Wind Indicator** ★	850	1,000	1,400
Vanguard, **24J**, & marked 9J., center sec. .... ★ ★ ★	700	900	1,500
Weems, 21J, Navigation watch, **Wind Indicator** .... ★ ★ ★	900	1,200	1,900
Weems, 23J, Navigation watch, **Wind Indicator** .... ★ ★ ★	1,000	1,400	2,500
M#1888, G #s 650, 640	50	75	150
M#1899, G #s 615, 618, 620, 625, 628, ...	50	75	150
M#1908, G #s 611, 613, 614, 618, 621, 623, 628, 630, 641, 642	50	75	150
G#637-640=3 pos., G#636=4pos., G#1617=2 pos., ALL=17J.	50	75	150
G#610=7-11J., **unadjusted** & 620=15J..	50	75	150
G#620-625-630-635=17J., Adj., OF	50	75	150
G#645, 21J, GCW, OF, LS	175	250	400
G#645, 21J, GCW, OF, LS, **wind indicator** .... ★ ★ ★	1,300	1,800	3,100
G#645, 19J, OF, LS	175	250	400
G#665, 19J, GJS, BRG, HC	600	700	1,000
G#16-A, 22J, Adj.3P, 24 hr. dial	200	275	400
G#16-A, & G#1024, 17J, Adj.5P	80	100	200
G#1617, 17J, adj.	80	100	200
G#1621, 21J, Adj.5P	150	200	375
G#1622, 22J, Adj.5P	175	250	425
G#1623, 23J, Adj.5P	250	350	575

Weems Navigation watch, 21j, Weems pat. seconds dial, pusher for seconds scale setting, ca. 1942.

Vanguard, Model 1908, 16 size, 23 jewels, diamond end stone, gold jewel settings, exposed winding gears, serial number 11,012,533.

14 SIZE
MODELS 14KW FULL PLATE, 1874,
1884, 1895, 1897, COLONIAL-A

Grade or Name — Description	Avg	Ex-Fn	Mint
Adams Street, 7J, M#14KW, full plate, KW, Coin	$60	$150	$265
Adams Street, 11J, M#14KW, full plate, KW, Coin	80	175	350
Adams Street, 15J, M#14KW, full plate, KW	100	200	400
� Generic, nameless or unmarked grades for watch movements are listed under the Company name or initials of the Company, etc. by size, jewel count and description.			
A. W. Co., 7-11J, M#14KW, full plate, **KW**	50	80	175
A. W. W. Co., 7-11J, M#1874, SW, LS, HC	65	100	225
A. W. Co., 7-11J, M#s FP, 1884, & 1895	50	80	175
A. W. Co., 13J, M#1884	50	80	175
A. W. Co., 15-16J, M#1874, SW	50	80	175
A. W. Co., 17J, SW, OF	60	95	200
A.W.Co., 19J, GJS, GCW	75	125	250
Am. Watch Co., 7-11J	50	80	175
Am. Watch Co., 13J, M#1874-84, SW	50	80	175
Am. Watch Co., 15J, M#1874-84,	50	80	175
Am. Watch Co., 16J, M#1874, SW	65	110	225
Am. Watch Co., 7-11J, M#14KW, **Full Plate, KW**	75	150	275
Am. Watch Co., 16J, M#1884, SW	75	150	275
Am. Watch Co., 15J, M#1897, SW	50	80	175
Bond St., 7-11J, M#1895, SW	50	80	175
Bond St., 9-11J, M#1884, **KW**	80	100	250
Bond St., 7J, M#1884, SW, PS	50	80	175
Beacon, 15J, M#1897, SW	50	80	175
Chronograph, 13J, 1874, **14K**, OF, **Am. W. Co. case**	1,000	1,400	2,200
Chronograph, 13J, 1874, **14K**, OF, W/ register, Am. W. Co. case ★	1,300	1,600	2,500
Chronograph, 13J, 1874, **14K, HC**, W/ register, Am. W. Co. case ★	1,600	2,200	3,700
Chronograph, 13J, 1874, **18K**, HC, W/ register, Am. W. Co. case ★	1,900	2,800	3,900
Chronograph, 13J, 1874, **SILVER HC, *Am. W. Co. case***	400	600	1,000
Chronograph, 16J, 1874, **double dial, "coin"**, Am. W. Co. case	2,200	3,200	5,200
Chronograph, 16J, 1874, **double dial, 18K**, Am. W. Co. case	3,500	4,400	7,400

Chronograph, Model 1874, split-second, 14 size. Note two split second hands on dial and two pushers at 2 & 4.

Hillside, 14 size, 13 jewels, M#1874, stem wind, hunting case, Woerds Pat., serial number 1,696,188, 18K.

⏰ This book endeavours to be a GUIDE or helpful manual and offers a wealth of material to be used as a tool not as an absolute document. Price Guides are like watches the worst may be better than none at all, but at best cannot be expected to be 100% accurate.

Grade or Name — Description	Avg	Ex-Fn	Mint
Chronograph, 13J, M# 1884 , OF	$200	$300	$625
Chronograph, 13J, M# 1884, HC	300	450	725
Chronograph, 13J, 1884, **14K**, HC, **Am. W. Co. case**	900	1,300	2,500
Chronograph, 13J, 1884, **18K**, HC, **Am. W. Co. case** ★	1,100	1,600	2,800
Chronograph, 15J, M# 1874-1884 , OF	200	275	550
Chronograph, 15J, M#1874-1884, HC	250	350	650
Chronograph, 17J, M#1874-1884 , OF	200	285	550
Chronograph, 17J, M#1874-1884, HC	250	365	650
Chronograph, 17J, split second, Am. W. Co. case ★★★	950	1,200	2,000
Chronograph, 15J, split sec., **14K,** HC ★★★	2,600	3,800	5,000
Chronograph, 15J, split second, **min. register, 14K**			
Am. W. Co. HC ★★★★	3,000	4,500	7,000
Church St., 7J, M#1884,	75	125	250
Crescent Garden, 7-11J, M#14KW	50	80	175
Crescent Garden, 7J, Full Plate, KW	50	80	175
Cronometro Victoria, 15J, M#1897, OF (may have sun logo) . ★★	400	550	800
Wm. Ellery, 7J, M#1874, SW	50	80	175
Gentleman, 7J, M#1884, SW	50	80	175
Hillside, 7-15J, M#1874, SW	50	80	175
Hillside, 7-11J, M#FP, SW	50	80	175
Hillside, 7-13J, M#1884, KW	50	80	175
Hillside, 9-11J, M#1884, KW	50	80	175
Hillside, 15J, M#1884, SW	50	80	175
Hillside, 16J, M#1874, (calendar date only on outside chapter)			
SW, GJS, OF,(calendar sets from back with lever) ★★★	650	900	1,600
Hillside, 7-13J, M#1895	50	80	175
Maximus, 21J, Colonial A, Adj.5P, GT, model 1912, OF ★	125	200	395
Maximus, 21J, Colonial A, Adj.5P, GT, model 1912, **14K OF** ... ★	350	500	750
Night Clock, 7J, M#1884, KW	100	150	250
Perfection, 15J, M#1897, OF ★	65	110	185
Perfection, 15J, M#1897, HC ★★	95	175	225

Chronograph, M# 1884-double dial, 14 size, 15 jewels, hunting case.

Chronograph, Model 1884-Split Second, 14 size, 15 jewels, open face, gold escape wheel, gold train, serial number 303,094.

🕐 Some watch manufacturers personalize watches for jobbers or jewelry firms, with exclusive private signed or marked movements. The valuable collectable watches are listed under the signed or marked movement. Other exclusive private signed or marked movements will have equivalent value or only slightly higher value and should be compared to Generic or Nameless movements. Railroad signed or marked (dials & movements) are usually more collectable & higher in value.

🕐 A collector should expect to pay modestly higher prices at local shops.

Five Minute Repeater, Model 1884, 14 size, 13-15 jewels, hunting case, slide activated, serial number 2,605,848. Note: estimated Total about 1,250 to 1,300.

Chronograph, 14 size, Model # 1874, Lugrin Pat., Sept. 28, 1880, serial # 3,162,800. Also Pat. date (Oct. 3,1876).

Grade or Name — Description	Avg	Ex-Fn	Mint
Repeater (5 min.), 16J, M#1884, SW, LS, **14K** ....★	$3,500	$4,500	$6,700
Repeater (5 min.), 16J, M#1884, SW, LS, **18K** ....★	3,800	4,800	7,400
Repeater (5 min.), 16J, M#1884, split second chronograph, **18K** case ....★★	5,000	7,500	12,000
Repeater (5 min.), 16J, M#1884, SW, LS, chronograph , with register, **14K** Am. W. Co. case	4,000	5,200	7,500
Repeater (5 min.), 16J, M#1884, SW, LS, chronograph , with register, **18K** Am. W. Co. case	4,500	6,800	9,500
Repeater (5 min.), 16J, M#1884, SW, LS, original **Coin** case........	2,800	3,500	5,000
Repeater (5 min.), 16J, M#1884, SW, LS, original **gold filled** case	2,200	2,600	3,800
Repeater (5 Min.), **18K**, HC ....★★	4,000	5,500	8,200
Repeater **(1 Min.), perpetual calendar, moon ph., 18K** ......★★★★★	32,000	55,000	95,000
Riverside, 11-15J, M#s 1874	95	150	275
Riverside, 15J, M#1884	50	80	175
Riverside, 15J, M#1895, nickel, OF......................................★★★	300	385	535
Riverside, 19J, Colonial A, Adj.5P, OF	95	150	250
Riverside, 21J, Colonial A, Adj.5P, OF ....★★	150	235	425
Royal, 11-13-15J, M#s 1874, 1884	50	80	175
Seaside, 7-11J, M#1884, SW	50	80	175
Sol, 7J, M#1897..	50	80	175
Special, 7J, M#1895, HC	50	80	175
Sterling, 7J, M#1884	50	80	175
Waltham, Mass., 7J, Full Plate, KW	95	150	250

12 SIZE
MODELS KW, 1894, BRIDGE, COLONIAL SERIES

Grade or Name — Description	Avg	Ex-Fn	Mint
A. W. W. Co., 7J, M#1894, **14K**, OF	$175	$235	$550
A. W. W. Co., 11J, M#1894, also Colonial model	50	80	175
A. W. W. Co., 15J, M#1894, also Colonial model	50	80	175
A. W. W. Co., 15J, M#1894, Colonial, **14K**, HC	275	350	600
A. W. W. Co., 17J, M#1894, also Colonial model	50	80	175
A. W. W. Co., 17J, M#1894, also Colonial, **14K** OF.....................	225	300	500
A. W. W. Co., 19J, OF..	50	80	175
A. W. W. Co., 21J, OF..	65	100	200
A. W. W. Co., 23J, OF..	150	225	350
P. S. Bartlett, 19J, M#1894, **14K**, HC	275	350	625
P. S. Bartlett, 19J, M#1894	50	80	175
Bond St., 7-13J, M#1894	50	80	175
Bridge Model, 21J, GJS, Adj.5P, GT, OF ....★★	200	285	400
Bridge Model, 21J, GJS, Adj.5P, GT, **14K**, HC ....★★	450	600	900
Bridge Model, 23J, GJS, Adj.5P, GT ....★★	250	350	650

Actual size illustration of a cushion style shaped watch depicting thinness with emphasis on style and beauty. This watch was popular in the 1930s.

Grade or Name — Description	Avg	Ex-Fn	Mint
Duke, 7-15J, M#1894	$50	$80	$150
Digital Hour & Second Window, 17J	75	125	250
Elite, 17J, OF	50	80	175
Ensign, 7J, OF	50	80	175
Equity, 7J,adj.	50	80	175
Martyn Square, 7-11J, M#KW	95	150	250
Maximus, 21J, GJS, GT	150	225	350
Premier, 17J, M#1894	50	80	175
Premier, 19J, M#1894	65	90	200
Premier, 21J, M#1894	125	195	300
Premier, 23J, M#1894, OF **14K**	225	350	600
Riverside, 17-19J, M#1894, Colonial	50	80	175
Riverside, 21J, M#1894, Colonial	150	225	385

A.W.W.Co., Model 1894, 12 size, 7-11 jewels, open face, serial number 7,565,004.

Riverside, Colonial series, 12 size, 19 jewels, open face or hunting, Adj5p, double roller.

Grade or Name – Description	Avg	Ex-Fn	Mint
Riverside, 19-21J, M#1894, also Colonial, **14K**, HC	$350	$450	$750
Riverside Maximus, 21J, M#1894, also Colonial, GT, GJS	200	285	500
Riverside Maximus, 23J, M#1894, also Colonial, GT, GJS ★	250	350	550
Riverside Maximus, 23J, M#1894, also Colonial, GT, GJS,**14K** ★	350	475	700
Royal, 17J, OF, PS, Adj, or Adj.3P	35	60	150
Royal, 19J, OF, PS, Adj.3P	55	85	150
Secometer, 17J, (revolving seconds dial only) OF	90	125	300
G# 210, 7J, G# 220, 15J	35	60	150
G# 225, 17J	55	95	175

THE OPERA WATCH
10-12 size case & a 6/0 size Jewel Series movement

Grade or Name – Description		Avg	Ex-Fn	Mint
12-6/0 size, 17-19J, Adj, **18K gold case**	★★	$475	$525	$950
12-6/0 size, 17-19J, Adj, **14K gold case**	★★	275	325	750
12-6/0 size, 17-19J, Adj, **Platinum case**	★★★	600	775	1,450
12-6/0 size, 17-19J, Adj, **gold filled case**	★	125	250	485

A unique designed Gents dress watch about 10-12 size case with a fancy framed 6/0 movement (Jewel Series).

10 SIZE
MODEL KW, 1861, 1865, 1874

Grade or Name – Description		Avg	Ex-Fn	Mint
Am. W. Co., 7-15J, M#1874-1878, KW, **14K**		$200	$335	$650
A. W. Co., 7-11J, SW , OF		50	85	175
A. W. Co.,15-17J, SW , OF		50	85	175
A. W. Co., 19-21J, SW , OF		85	150	250
American Watch Co., 11-15J, M#1874, **14K, HC**		250	350	550
Appleton, Tracy & Co., 7-11-15J, M#1861 or 1874, **14K**, KW		275	425	600
Appleton, Tracy & Co., 7-11-15J, M#1861, **KW** multi-color box case, **18K**		700	1,100	1,900
P. S. Bartlett, 7-11J, M#1861, KW, **14K**		350	500	800
P. S. Bartlett, 13J, M#KW, gold balance, 1st S# 45,801, last 46,200, Pat. Nov. 3, 1858, **14K,**	★★★	550	700	1,000
P. S. Bartlett, 13J, M#KW, gold balance, 1st S#45,801, last 46,200, Pat. Nov. 3, 1858, **18K**	★★★	700	850	1,200
P. S. Bartlett, 13J, M#1861 or 1865, KW, **14K**		300	450	625

Appleton Tracy & Co., Model 10KW, 10 size, 7-15 jewels,   P. S. Bartlett, 10 size, 7-15 jewels, serial # 181,602.
key wind and set from back, serial number 370,411.

NOTE: These watches (excluding Colonial) are usually found with solid gold cases, and are therefore priced accordingly. Without cases, these watches have very little value due to the fact that the cases are difficult to find. Many of the cases came in octagon, decagon, hexagon, cushion and triad shapes.

Grade or Name – Description	Avg	Ex-Fn	Mint
Crescent Garden, 7J, M#1861, KW, **14K**	$175	$285	$475
Colonial R, 9J, model 1945	50	80	175
Colonial R, 17J, Adj.5P, model 1945	50	80	175
Colonial R, 21J, Adj.5P, model 1945	75	125	200
Colonial R, 23J, Adj.5P, model 1945 ★★	100	185	325
Wm. Ellery, 7,11,15J, M#1861, KW, **14K**	175	275	425
Home W. Co., 7J, M#1874, KW, **14K**	175	275	425
Martyn Square, 7-11J, M#1861, **14K**	175	275	425
Maximus "A", 21J, model 1918, **14K** ★★★	250	385	600
Maximus "A", 23J, model 1918, **14K** ★	225	350	550
Riverside A, 19J, Adj.5P, model 1918, GF	75	125	200

8 SIZE
MODEL 1873

NOTE: Collectors usually want solid gold cases in small watches.

Grade or Name – Description	Avg	Ex-Fn	Mint
Am. W. Co., 15-17J, M#1873, **14K, Multi-Color Box Hinged case**	$550	$650	$1,200
Am. W. Co., 15-16J, M#1873	40	65	150
P. S. Bartlett, 15-16J, M#1873	40	65	150
Wm. Ellery, 7-11J, M#1873	40	65	150
Wm. Ellery, 7J, **14K, HC**	225	300	475
Riverside, 7-11J, M#1873, **18K, HC**	285	400	650
Riverside, 7-11J, M#1873	40	65	150
Royal, 7-16J, M#1873	40	65	150
Victoria, 11-15J, tu-tone movement, **18k HC** ★	250	325	600

VICTORIA, 8 size 1873 model, 11-15 jewels, tu-tone high grade movement, HC, S# 871256

6 size Ladies movement. This basic model came in the following grades: J=7 jewels, gilt; Y=7 jewels, nickel; N=15 jewels, gilded or nickel; X=15 jewels, nickel, gold jewel settings; K=16 jewels nickel, raised gold settings; RIVERSIDE=17 jewels, nickel, raised gold settings.

6 SIZE
MODEL 1873, 1889 , 1890

Grade or Name – Description	Avg	Ex-Fn	Mint
A,B,C,D,E,F,G,H,J,K	$40	$75	$150
A,B,C,D,E,F,G,H,J,K, **14K, HC**	150	250	400
A. W. W. Co., 19J, **18K, HC**	225	375	600
A. W. W. Co., 19J, **14K, Multi-Color gold case**	400	575	950
A. W. W. Co., 7J, M#1873	40	75	150

Grade or Name – Description	Avg	Ex-Fn	Mint
A. W. W. Co., 15J, **multi-color GF**, HC	$175	$275	$500
A. W. W. Co., 15J, **2 tone** mvt., HC	60	100	250
A. W. W. Co., 11J, HC	40	75	150
Am. W. Co., 7-11J, M#1889 -1890	40	75	150
American W. Co., 7J, KW & KS from back, **10K, HC**	175	250	425
Wm. Ellery, 7J, M#1873	40	75	150
Lady Waltham, 16J, M#1873, Demi, HC, **14K**	185	285	535
Lady Waltham, 16J, M#1873, **18K**	235	325	625
Riverside Maximus, 19J, GT, Adj., DR, HC ★★★	250	350	700
Riverside, 15-17J, PS	40	75	150
Seaside, 7-15J, M#1873	40	75	150
Royal, 16J, HC	45	85	175

American Watch Co., Model 1889, 6 size 7 jewels, serial number 4,700,246.

Stone Movement or Crystal clear see through Plates, size 4, 16 jewels, gold train, open face, serial number 28.

4 SIZE

Grade or Name – Description	Avg	Ex-Fn	Mint
Stone Movement or crystal movement, 4 size, 16-17 ruby jewels in gold settings, gold train, exposed pallets, compensation balance adjusted to temperature, isochronism & positions, Breguet hairspring, and crystal top plate, 14K case ★★★★	$5,000	$8,000	$15,000

1 SIZE & 0 SIZE
MODELS 1882, 1891, 1900, 1907

Grade or Name – Description	Avg	Ex-Fn	Mint
A.W.Co., 7-16J, OF	$30	$65	$150
A.W.Co., 7-16J, HC	50	85	225
A.W.Co., 7-15J, multi-color **14K HC**	325	450	700
A. W. Co., 7J, **14K, HC**	200	285	550
American Watch Co., 15J, SW, OF &HC	60	100	250
"B" grade = 13J., "F" & "G" grade = 9J., 1 size	50	85	165

Right: 1 size
"B" grade = 13J., "F" & "G" grade = 9J.

Lady Waltham, Model 1900, 0 size, 16 jewels, open face or hunting, adjusted, stem wind, pendant set.

American Watch Co., Model 1891, 0 size, 7 jewels, stem wind, originally sold for $13.00.

Grade or Name – Description	Avg	Ex-Fn	Mint
American Watch Co., 15J, S.W., **14K, HC**	$175	$285	$500
P. S. Bartlett, 11J, M#1891, OF, **14K**	150	185	300
P. S. Bartlett, 16J, **14K, HC**	200	285	475
Cronometro Victoria, 15J ★★	200	285	450
Lady Waltham, 15J, SW, **14K, HC**	255	300	475
Lady Waltham, 15-16J, SW, HC	65	100	250
Maximus, 19J, SW, HC ★	200	275	350
Riverside, 15J,16J,17J, SW, HC	95	165	250
Riverside, 15J,16J,17J, SW, **14K, HC**	200	275	400
Riverside Maximus, 19J, SW, HC	175	250	400
Riverside Maximus, 19J, **14K, HC** ★	350	500	700
Royal, 13-16J, SW, HC	50	85	175
Seaside, 15J, SW, **14K, HC**	125	200	350
Seaside, 11J, SW, OF, **multi-color dial, no chips**	150	250	400
Seaside, 11J, SW, HC	50	90	200
Seaside, 7J, HC	45	90	175
Seaside, 7J, **14K, HC**	150	250	465
Special, 11J, M#1891, **14K, OF**	135	225	425
G# 61, 7J, HC	40	75	150
G# 115, 15J, HC	50	85	175

Riverside, Jewel Series, 6/0 size, 17 ruby jewels, raised gold settings, gold center wheel.

Ruby, Jewel Series, 6/0 size, 15 jewels, adjusted to temperature, open face or hunting.

JEWEL SERIES or 6/0 SIZE

Grade or Name – Description	Avg	Ex -Fn	Mint
Diamond, 17J, gold train, diamond end stone, **14K, HC** ★	$175	$200	$425
Emerald, 21J, gold train, **14K, HC** ★	225	285	450
Maximus, 17J, gold train, diamond end stone, **14K HC** ★	235	300	535
Patrician, 15J, pin set, GJS, **18K, OF** ★	225	285	525
Riverside, 17J, Jewel Series, **14K, HC** ★	225	250	425
Ruby, 15-17J, Jewel Series, **14K, OF** ★	175	200	400
Sapphire, 15J, Jewel Series, **14K, OF** ★	175	200	400

RF # 1A
gold filled : $60 - $85 - $275
dial: $40 - $80 - $180

RF # 2B
gold filled : $60- $85 - $285
dial: $20 - $40 - $100

RF # 3C
gold plate: $50 - $75 - $185
dial: $10 - $25 - $50

RF # 4D
gold filled : $60 - $85 - $260
dial: $40 - $80 - $150

RF # 5E
gold filled : $80 - $150 - $400
dial: $40 - $80 - $160

RF # 6F
gold filled : $75 - $125 - $275
dial: $20 - $40 - $100

MONTGOMERY DIAL

RF # 7G
LOCOMOTIVE model
gold filled : $70 - $100 - $275
dial: $40 - $65 - $120

RF # 8H
Heavy-Duty
gold filled : $80 - $150 - $325
dial: $20 - $40 - $80

RF # 9L
gold filled : $50 - $85 - $225
dial: $20 - $40 - $80

NOTE: Factory Advertised as a **complete** watch and was fitted with a certain matched, timed and rated movement and sold in the factory designed case style as a **complete** watch. The factory also sold _uncased_ movements to **JOBBERS** such as Jewelry stores & they cased the movement in a case styles the **CUSTOMER requested.** All the factory advertised **complete** watches came with a enamel dial **SHOWN or CHOICE** of other Railroad dials.

137

AMERICAN WALTHAM WATCH CO.
IDENTIFICATION OF MOVEMENTS
BY MODEL NUMBER

How to Identify Your Watch Size & Model: Compare the movement of your watch with the illustrations in this section. While comparing, note the location of the balance, jewels, screws, gears, and type of back plate (Full, 3/4, Bridge) these will be clues in identifying the movement you have.

20 size, 1862 or KW 20 model. Note vibrating hairspring stud. 1st serial number 50,001

18 size, 1859 or KW 18 model. 1st serial number 28,821

Model 1857, KW, KS. 1st serial number 1,001

Model 1870, KW, KS from back 1st serial number 500,001

I will respect & appreciate positive sound reliable comments, corrections, improvements or remarks but reserve the right to accept the statement or keep my own observations & views. (*Cooksey*)

Model 1877, 18 size

Model 1879, 18 size

Model 1883, hunting
1st serial number 2,354,001

Model 1883, open face

Model 1892, open face

Model 1892, hunting.
1st serial number 6,026,001

Model is not the same defination as grade. A model may exist in different grade numbers or grade names (as Riverside-P.S.Bartlett) and may be used in many different models (as model **1892**, 18 size, open or hunting case, model **1899**, in 16 size open or hunting case, model **1894** in 12 size) etc..

16½ size, Equity open face

Model 1860=16KW or 1868
16 size

Model 1872, 16 size open face

Model 1872, 16 size hunting case

Model 1888, 16 size, hunting

Bridge Model, 16 size

1908 Model has lever setting at 11:00

ALSO MODEL 1912

Model 1899 or Model 1908, 16 size, open face

Model 1899 or Model 1908, 16 size, hunting

Model 1899 or Model 1908, 16 size, open face

Model 16-A, 16 size

Model 1622, Deck Watch 16 size, sweep second

Model 1874 & 1884, 14 size

Model 1874, 14 size, hunting

Model 1884, 14 size, open face

5 Minute Repeater, 14 size

14 SIZE FULL PLATE KW KS
1 st. SERIAL # 909,001

Model 1874, 14 size

Model 1884, 14 size

**Model 1895, 14 size,
open face**

Model 1897, 14 size

Colonial A Model, 14 size

Colonial Series, 14 size

Model 1924, The Colonial

Model 1894, 12 size

Model 1924, The Colonial

Model 1894, 12 size   Model 10KW, 10 size

Colonial A, 10 size   Model 1873, 8 size   Model 1873, 8&6 size

Model 1889, 6 size   Model 1890, 6 size   Model 1890, 6 size

Stone Movement,
4 size   Model 1882, 1 size   Model 1891, 0 size

Model 1900, 0 size   Model 1907, 0 size   Jewel Series

Model 1900, 0/3 size,   Model 1907, 0/3 size,   Model 1898 & 1912,
open face   hunting   0/6 size, hunting

Model 1898 & 1912,   10½ ligne   10 ligne
0/6 size, open face

⊕ Generic, nameless or unmarked grades for watch movements are listed under the Company name or initials of the Company, etc. by size, jewel count and description.

⊕ Some grades are not included. Their values can be determined by comparing with similar age, size, metal content, style, models and grades listed.

⊕ Watches listed in this book are priced at the collectable Trade Show level, as complete watches having an original 14k gold-filled case and Key Wind with silver, an original white enamel single sunk dial, and with the entire original movement in good working order with no repairs needed.

⊕ This book endeavours to be a GUIDE or helpful manual and offers a wealth of material to be used as a tool not as a absolute document. Price Guides are like watches the worst may be better than none at all, but at best cannot be expected to be 100% accurate.

⊕ Characteristics of watches differ for the same age of both case and movement, because these features vary it may not be accurate to date a watch by one single influence. Example: the second hand was not commonly found on watches before 1750, but common about 1800. The first second hand appeared in 1665 and another in 1690. Therefore statements are broad rather than accurate.

ANSONIA CLOCK CO.

Brooklyn, New York
1896 - 1929

The Ansonia Watch Co. was owned by the Ansonia Clock Company in Ansonia, Connecticut. Ansonia started making clocks in about 1850 and began manufacturing watches in 1896. They produced about 10,000,000 dollar- type watches. The company was sold to a Russian investor in 1930. "Patented April 17, 1888," is on the back plate of some Ansonia watches.

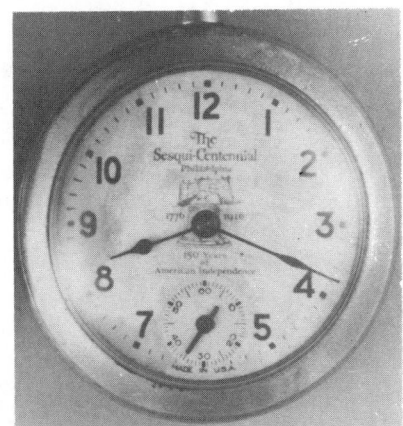

Ansonia Watch Company. Example of a basic movement, 16 size, stem wind.

Ansonia Watch Co., Sesqui-Centennial model.

Grade or Name–Description	Avg	Ex-Fn	Mint
Ansonia watch with a White Dial in Nickel case	$25	$65	$125
Ansonia watch with a Radium Dial in Nickel case	30	60	110
Ansonia watch with a Black Dial in Nickel case	40	65	115
Ascot	30	60	110
Bonnie Laddie Shoes	65	110	275
Dispatch	30	60	110
Faultless	40	65	115
Guide	40	65	115
Lenox	45	70	125
Mentor	35	60	110
Piccadilly	50	90	150
Rural	45	65	115
Sesqui-Centennial ★★★	250	375	495
Superior	45	65	115
The Auto	45	65	115
The Guide	45	65	115
Tutor	45	65	115

🕐 Some grades are not included. Their values can be determined by comparing with similar age, size, metal content, style, models and grades listed.

🕐 A collector should expect to pay modestly higher prices at local shops.

APPLETON WATCH CO.
(REMINGTON WATCH CO.)
Appleton, Wisconsin - 1901 - 1903

In 1901, O. E. Bell bought the machinery of the defunct Cheshire Watch Company and moved it to Appleton, Wisconsin, where he had organized the Remington Watch Company. The first watches were shipped from the factory in February 1902; production ceased in mid-1903 and the contents were sold off before the end of that year. Most movements made by this firm were modified Cheshire movements and were marked "Appleton Watch Company." Advertisements for the firm in 1903 stated that they made 16 and 18 size movements with 11, 15, or 17 jewels. Serial numbers range from 89,000 to 104,950. During the two years they were in business, the company produced about 2,000 to 3,000 watches.

Appleton Watch Co., 18 size, 7 jewels, "The Appleton Watch Co." on dial. Engraved on movement "Appleton Watch Co., Appleton, Wis." Note that the stem is attached to movement. Serial number 93,106.

Description		Avg	Ex-Fn	Mint
18S, 7J, OF, NI, 3/4, DMK, SW, PS, stem attached	★★	$400	$600	$1,100
18S, 7J, OF, NI, 3/4, DMK, SW, PS, Coin, OF	★★	400	600	1,100
18S, 15J, NI, LS, SW, 3/4, M#2	★★	500	700	1,300
16S, 7-11J, 3/4, **stem attached**	★★★	550	800	1,400

Note:With **ORIGINAL** APPLETON cases add **$300 to $400** more. This case is **difficult** to find.

AUBURNDALE WATCH CO.
Auburndale, Massachusetts
1876 - 1883

This company was the first to attempt an inexpensive watch. Jason Hopkins was issued two patents in 1875 covering the "rotary design." The rotary design eliminated the need of adjusting to various positions, resulting in a less expensive watch. The company was formed about 1876, and the first watches were known as the "Auburndale Rotary." In 1876, equipment was purchased from the Marion Watch Co., and the first rotary designed watches were placed on the market for $10 in 1877. Auburndale produced about 6,000 watches before closing in 1883. **Rotary** design as few as **500** made and **very few** known to exist. The Auburndale rotary watch, the movements whole assembly revolves once in 2 1/2 hours.

HORSE TIMERS—(only.)

In Nickel Cases.   Stem Wind.

No. 633. Auburndale Timer. Sweep Second Hand, Beats ¼ Seconds, Stop and Fly Back. (3 hands.)....$17 25

No. 634. Auburndale Timer. Split Sweep Seconds, Beats ¼ Seconds, Stop and Fly Back.......... 31 50

Auburndale Timer, 18 size, 7 jewels, stem wind, 10 minute, split seconds, fly back, 1/4 second jump timer.

Auburndale 10 min. Timer, 1/4 beat jump seconds, sweep second hand, stop & fly back, back wind.

Grade or Name – Description	Avg	Ex-Fn	Mint
Auburndale Rotary, 20S, 2-5J, SW, NI case, detent ...... ★★★★★	$2,200	$3,500	$6,000
Auburndale Rotary, 18S, 2-5J, SW, NI case, lever .... ★★★★	1,500	2,500	4,000
Bentley, 18S, 7J, LS, NI case, SW, 3/4............................. ★★★	850	1,600	3,000
Lincoln, 18S, 7J, LS, NI case, KW, 3/4................................ ★★★	850	1,600	3,000
Auburndale Timer, 18S, 5-7J, SW, NI case, 10 min. timer, 1/4 sec. jump second	350	485	800
Auburndale Timer, 18S, 5-7J, SW, NI case, 10 min. timer, 1/4 sec. jump seconds, with a 24 hour dial ....★	400	550	900
Auburndale Timer, 18S, 5-7J, KW, NI case, 10 min. timer, 1/4 sec. jump seconds, **with split seconds** ....★★	600	800	1,800
Auburndale Timer, 18S, marked "207", gold balance, OF	350	485	800

Bentley, 18 size, 7 jewels, 3/4 plate, stem wind, serial number 2.

Auburndale Rotary Mass, 16S, 2-5J., rotating once in about 2.5 hours, "*Patents, Mar. 30 1875, July 20 1875, June 20 1876, Jan. 30 1877*", S# 319. Note: **Extremely RARE.**

Right: **Auburndale Rotary** escapement, two different styles of levers used and two different styles for the escape wheel were used. Also note two banking pins in the right example.

AURORA WATCH CO.

Aurora, Illinois 1883 - 1892

Aurora Watch Co. was organized in mid-1883 with the goal of getting one jeweler in every town to handle Aurora watches. The first movements were 18S, full plate, and were first sold in the fall of 1884. There were several watches marked No. 1. About 95% were 18 size & 5% 6 size. For the most part Aurora produced medium to low grade(Note Waltham, Elgin, Illinois and others also made low grade watches; and at one time made about 100 movements per day. The Hamilton Watch Co. **purchased** the company on June 19, 1890.

AURORA WATCH CO.
Estimated Serial Nos. and Production Dates

1884 – 10,001	1888 – 200,000
1885 – 60,000	1889 – 215,000
1886 – 101,000	1891 – 230,901
1887 – 160,000	

Hurd's Pat. regulator first used in early 1886.

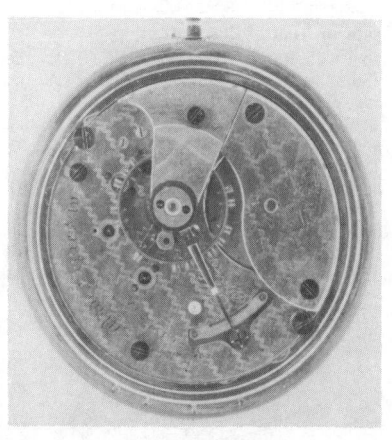

Aurora Watch Co., 18 size, 15 jewels, "NEW MODEL", serial number 142,060. Made for railroad service.

Aurora Watch Co., 18 size, 15 jewels, Adj, Hurd's Pat. regulator, engraved on movement "*Made expressly R.J.A.*" also note **5th pinion**, serial number 73,529.

Description	Avg	Ex-Fn	Mint
18S, 7J, KW, KS, Gilded, OF	$95	$175	$325
18S, 7J, KW, KS, Gilded, HC	150	225	450
18S, 7J, 5th pinion, Gilded, LS, SW, OF	95	175	325
18S, 7J, LS, SW, Gilded, new model, HC	150	225	450
18S, 11J, KW, KS, Gilded, HC	125	200	400
18S, 11J, KW, KS, Gilded, OF	125	200	400
18S, 11J, 5th pinion, LS, SW, Gilded, new model, OF	95	175	325
18S, 11J, 5th pinion, LS, SW, NI, OF.................................	125	200	400
18S, 11J, 5th pinion, LS, SW, NI, GJS, new model, OF	125	200	400
18S, 11J, LS, SW, Gilded, **made expressly for the guild**, HC.... ★	200	325	575
18S, 11J, 5th pinion, LS, SW, NI, OF			
made expressly for the guild............................ ★	250	375	625
18S, 15J, KW, KS, NI, GJS, DMK, OF or HC............................ ★	175	275	450
18S, 15J, 5th pinion, LS, SW, Gilded, OF..........................	125	200	400
18S, 15J, 5th pinion, LS, SW, NI, GJS, DMK, ADT, OF	125	200	400
18S, 15J, 5th pinion, LS, SW, NI, GJS, DMK, ADJ, new model, OF	150	200	450
18S, 15J, LS, SW, NI, GJS, DMK, ADJ, new model, HC	150	200	450
18S, 15J, LS, SW, NI, GJS, ADJ, marked **Ruby Jewels**.......... ★★	500	650	1,100
18S, 15J, LS, SW, NI, GJS, ADJ, 2 Tone DMK, checker-			
board or snowflake, **Ruby Jewels**, HC.............................. ★★	600	750	1,300
18S, 15J, LS, SW, NI, GJS, ADJ, 2 Tone DMK, checker-			
board or snowflake, 5th pinion, **Ruby Jewels**, OF....... ★★★	750	900	1,500

MARKED **"RUBY JEWELS"**, = Aurora's highest grade.

Size and Description		Avg	Ex-Fn	Mint
18S, marked **15 Ruby Jewels** but has 17J, 5th pinion, LS, SW, NI, GJS, 2 Tone, ADJ, OF	★★★	$750	$900	$1,500
18S, marked **15 Ruby Jewels**, only 15J, LS, SW, NI, GJS, 2 Tone DMK, ADJ, HC	★★★	700	850	1,400
18S, marked **15 Ruby Jewels**, only 15J, LS, SW, NI, GJS, ADJ, 2 Tone DMK, OF	★★★	700	850	1,400
18S, 15J, LS, SW, NI, GJS, DMK, ADJ, Railroad Time Service or Caufield Watch, new model, HC	★★	800	950	1,500
18S, 15J, Chronometer, LS, SW, NI, DMK, ADJ, new model HC	★★	625	800	1,300
18S, 15J, Chronometer, LS, SW, NI, GJS, DMK, ADJ, HC	★★	600	750	1,200
18S, 15J, LS, Gilded, "Eclipse, Chicago", new model, HC		300	475	700
18S, 15J, LS, SW, NI, DMK, made expressly for the guild, HC	★	275	400	650
18S, 15J, 5th pinion, LS, SW, Gilded, made expressly for the guild, OF	★	325	485	775
18S, 15J, LS, SW, Gilded, made expressly for the "RJA" (Retail Jeweler's Assoc.), HC	★	325	485	775

Right: Aurora, 6 Size.

6 SIZE

Size and Description	Avg	Ex-Fn	Mint
6S, 11-15J, LS, SW, Gilded, 3/4, HC ..	$90	$125	$250
6S, 11-15J, LS, SW, NI, GJS, DMK, 3/4, HC	100	150	300
6S, 11-15J, LS, SW, 3/4 plate, **14K, HC**	250	325	600

BALL WATCH CO.
Cleveland, Ohio
1879 - 1969

The Ball Watch Company did not manufacture watches but did help formulate the specifications of watches used for railroad service. Webb C. Ball of Cleveland, Ohio, was the general time inspector for over 125,000 miles of railroad in the U. S., Mexico, and Canada. In 1891 there was a collision between the Lake Shore and Michigan Southern Railways at Kipton, Ohio. The collision was reported to have occurred because an engineer's watch had stopped, for about four minutes, then started running again. The railroad officials commissioned Ball to establish the timepiece inspection system. Ball knew that the key to safe operations of the railroad was the manufacturing of sturdy, precision timepieces. He also knew they must be able to withstand hard use and still be accurate. Before this time, each railroad company had its own rules and standards. After Ball presented his guidelines, most American manufacturers set out to meet these standards and soon a list was made of the manufacturers that produced watches of the grade that would pass inspection. Each railroad employee had a card that he carried showing the record of how his watch performed on inspection. Ball was also instrumental in the formation of the Horological Institute of America. By 1908 Ball furnished over **100 different railroad** companies with watches.
* Webb C. Ball started selling RR grade watches in 1893, some marked Superior Grade.

ESTIMATED SERIAL NUMBERS AND PRODUCTION DATES
FOR RAILROAD GRADE WATCHES

(Hamilton) Date – Serial #	
1895 - 13,000	
1897 - 20,500	
1900 - 42,000	
1902 - 170,000	
1905 - 462,000	
1910 - 600,000	
1915 - 603,000	
1920 - 610,000	
1925 - 620,000	
1930 - 637,000	
1935 - 641,000	
1938 - 647,000	
1939 - 650,000	
1940 - 651,000	
1941 - 652,000	
1942 - 654,000	

(Am.Waltham)
Date – Serial #
1900 - 060,700
1905 - 202,000
1910 - 216,000
1915 - 250,000
1920 - 260,000
1925 - 270,000

(Illinois)
Date – Serial #
1929 - 800,000
1930 - 801,000
1931 - 803,000
1932 - 804,000
(Elgin)

1904-1906
S # range:
11,853,000 - 12,282,000

(E. Howard & C0.)
1893-1895
S # range:
226,000 - 308,000

(Hampden)
1890-1892
S # range:
626,750 - 657,960
759,720

The above list is provided for determining the **APPROXIMATE** age of your watch. Match serial number with date. Watches were not necessarily sold in the exact order of manufactured date.

🕐 NOTE: BALL WATCHES ARE PRICED AS HAVING A ORIGINAL BALL DIAL & CASE. Watches MARKED **"BALL & Co."** are more difficult to find than **BALL WATCH Co.**

BALL — AURORA
18 SIZE

Description		Avg	Ex-Fn	Mint
15-17J, marked Webb C. Ball, OF .... ★★★★		$3,000	$3,700	$5,500
15-17J, marked Ball, HC .... ★★★★		4,500	6,300	9,600

Ball-Elgin, Grade 333, 18 size, 17 jewels, rare hunting case model, serial number 11,958,002.

Ball-Elgin, Grade 333, 18 size, 17 jewels, open face model, serial number 11,856,801.

BALL — ELGIN 18 SIZE G. F. CASES

Description		Avg	Ex-Fn	Mint
16J, G#327, Commercial Standard, LS, OF	★	$300	$500	$900
17J, G#328, Commercial Standard, LS, HC	★	450	600	1,100

Note: 18 Size Ball watches in **hunting cases** are scarce.

🕐 **The Complete Price Guide to Watches goal is to stimulate the orderly exchange of Watches between "buyers" and "sellers".**

BALL — ELGIN (continued)   151

Description	Avg	Ex-Fn	Mint
17J, G#328, Coin, LS, HC ......★	$375	$450	$850
17J, G#329, NI, Adj.5P, LS, HC ......★★	1,200	1,400	2,500
16J, G#331, NI, Adj.5P, PS, Commercial Std, OF. ......★★	375	450	850
16J, G#331, NI, Adj.5P, PS, Commercial Std, HC ......★★★	400	475	950
17J, G#331, NI, Adj.5P, PS, OF	250	325	550
17J, G#332, Commercial Std, OF ......★	250	325	550
17J, G#333, NI, Adj.5P, LS, OF	250	325	550
17J, G#333, NI, Adj.5P, LS, HC ......★★★	1,500	2,200	3,300
21J, G#333, NI, Adj.5P, LS, OF ......★	700	900	1,500
21J, G#333, NI, Adj.5P, LS, HC ......★★	800	1,200	1,700
21J, G#330, LS, Official RR std., HC ......★★★★	2,000	2,900	5,300
21J, G#334, NI, Adj.5P, LS, OF	700	1,000	1,500

BALL — HAMILTON
18 SIZE G. F. CASES

Description	Avg	Ex-Fn	Mint
17J, M#936, **first trial run S# 601 to 625** single roller.....★★★★	$2,500	$3,500	$6,600
17J, M#936, single roller or double roller......★	1,000	1,400	2,100
17J, M#936, marked Superior, Adj. ......★★	1,200	1,800	2,900
17J, M#-937-939, Official RR std, LS, Adj., **HC**......★★	2,000	2,800	4,300
17J, M#938, NI, DR, OF ......★★★	700	900	1,300
17J, M#999, marked single roller......★	600	800	1,000
17J, M#999, Commercial Standard	300	450	850
17J, M#999, NI, Official RR std, Adj.5P, LS, OF, Coin......	300	450	850
17J, M#999, Official RR std, NI, Adj.5P, LS, OF......	300	450	850
17J, M#999, "A" model adj. OF ......★	350	500	900
17J, M#999, NI, Adj.5P, marked "**Loaner**" on case ......★	525	750	1,200
19J, M#999, Official RR std, NI, Adj.5P, LS, OF......	500	675	1,000
21J, M#999, Official RR std, NI, Adj.5P, LS, OF......	525	700	1,200
23J, M#999, NI, Adj.5P, LS, Gold Filled OF Case ......★★	4,000	4,800	7,200
23J, M#999, NI, Adj.5P, LS , OF, **14K case**......★★★	6,000	7,500	11,200
23J, M#999, NI, Adj.5P, LS, **HC,14K case** ......★★★★	7,000	9,500	13,500
Early Ball & Co., 16-17J, (low serial # 13,001 to 13,400), OF marked dial & mvt. *Railroad Watch Co.* (second run)★★★	1,500	2,000	3,300
Early Ball & Co., 16-17J, (low serial # 14,001 to 15,000), OF marked dial & mvt. *Railroad Watch Co.* (third run)......★★	1,200	1,700	3,100
Ball & Co., 16-17J, marked dial & mvt. *Railroad Watch Co* ..★★	1,100	1,500	2,900
Brotherhood of Locomotive Engineers, 17J, OF......★★	3,000	3,800	5,200
Brotherhood of Locomotive Engineers, 19J, OF......★★	3,200	4,500	6,200

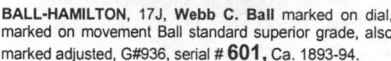

BALL-HAMILTON, 17J, **Webb C. Ball** marked on dial, marked on movement Ball standard superior grade, also marked adjusted, G#936, serial #**601,** Ca. 1893-94.

BALL-HAMILTON, Grade 999, 18 size, 17 jewels, marked *"Railroad Watch Co."*, Ca.June,1896, S# 20,793.

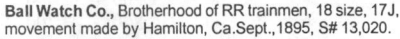

Ball Watch Co., Brotherhood of RR trainmen, 18 size, 17J, movement made by Hamilton, Ca.Sept.,1895, S# 13,020.

Ball Watch Co. (Hamilton). Grade 999, 18 size, 21-23 J., sun ray damaskeening, S# 548,157, Ca. Aug., 1907.

Description		Avg	Ex-Fn	Mint
Brotherhood of Locomotive Engineers, 21J, OF	★★	$3,500	$4,800	$6,700
Brotherhood of Locomotive Firemen, 17J, OF	★★	3,000	3,600	5,800
Brotherhood of Locomotive Firemen, 19J, OF	★★	3,200	4,500	6,200
Brotherhood of Locomotive Firemen, 21J, OF	★★	3,500	4,800	6,700
Brotherhood of Railroad Trainmen, 17J, OF	★★	3,000	3,500	5,700
Brotherhood of Railroad Trainmen, 19J, OF	★★	3,200	4,000	6,200
Brotherhood of Railroad Trainmen, 21J, OF	★★	3,500	4,700	6,700
Order of Railway Conductors, 17J, OF	★★	3,000	3,600	5,800
Order of Railway Conductors, 19J, OF	★★	3,200	4,500	6,200
Order of Railway Conductors, 21J, OF	★★★	3,500	4,600	6,500
Order of Railroad Telegraphers, 17J, OF	★★★★	4,000	5,200	7,500
Order of Railroad Telegraphers, 19J, OF	★★★★	4,200	5,200	7,500
Order of Railroad Telegraphers, 21J, OF	★★★★	5,000	6,400	8,500
Private Label or Jewelers name, 17J, Adj., OF	★★★	900	1,400	2,200

BALL WATCH Co. In line gear train, 19-21J., gold train, movement by Waltham, on dial "Ball Watch Co. Cleveland Ohio", rectangular 14K case. ($5,000 to $8,000)

BALL WATCH Co. DIAL (Order of Railway Conductors), ORC is intertwined, 18 size.

BALL– DeLONG ESCAPEMENT 16 SIZE

Description	Avg	Ex-Fn	Mint
21-23J, Adj.5P, upright **D** shaped pallets, **14K OF Case** .. ★★★★	$5,000	$6,000	$10,000
21-23J, Adj.5P, upright **D** shaped pallets, gold filled case. ★★★★	4,000	5,500	8,000

Ball-Hamilton, Model 998 Elinvar, 16 size, 23 jewels, with center bridge.

BALL W. CO. (HAMILTON),16 size, 21jewels, official RR standard, ADJ.5p, serial no.611429, Ca. 1908.

BALL — HAMILTON
16 SIZE G. F. CASES

Description	Avg	Ex-Fn	Mint
16J, M#976, 977, 999-HC, NI, OF, LS ....★	$350	$475	$950
17J, M#974, NI, OF, LS	200	275	575
17J, Official RR Standard, OF	250	325	625
19J, Official RR Standard, OF	250	325	625
19J, M#999, NI, Off. RR Stan., OF, LS..	250	325	625
21J, M#999, NI, Off. RR Stan., OF, LS..	500	600	950
21J, M#**999B-marked**, Off. RR Stan., OF, **marked-Adj.6P**	650	900	1,500
21J, M#999, Off. RR Stan., Coin case	450	600	900
21J, M#999 , Off. RR Stan., marked Loaner, coin case .... ★★	600	800	1,300
21J, M#992B, NI, marked **992B** & Off RR Stan. **Adj.6P**..... ★★★	1,000	1,700	3,200
23J, M#999, NI, Off. RR Stan., OF, LS..	800	1,200	2,300
23J, M#999B, Off. RR Stan., NI, OF, LS, **Adj.6P**.............. ★★★	900	1,500	2,400
23J, M#998 **marked-Elinvar**, Off. RR Stan., Adj.5P ....★	1,800	2,600	3,500
Brotherhood of Locomotive **Engineers**, OF............................ ★★	2,600	3,500	4,200
Brotherhood of Locomotive Firemen,(Enginmen), OF .... ★★	2,600	3,500	4,200
Brotherhood of Rairoad Trainmen, OF .... ★★	2,600	3,500	4,200
Order of Railway Conductors, OF .... ★★	2,600	3,500	4,200
17-19J, Brotherhood or Order, HUNTING CASE .... ★★★	2,200	2,800	5,300
Private Label or Jewelers name, 21J, Adj., OF............................★	625	850	1,500

BALL — HAMPDEN 18 SIZE

Description	Avg	Ex-Fn	Mint
15-17J, LS, SW, HC, marked Superior Grade ★★★	$2,500	$3,200	$4,600
15-17J, LS, SW, OF, marked **Superior Grade** .... ★★	1,800	2,400	3,100
15-17J, LS, SW, OF.. ★★	400	600	1,100
15-17J, LS, SW, HC .... ★★★	600	950	1,700

BALL- NEW YORK WATCH CO. 18 SIZE

Description	Avg	Ex-Fn	Mint
Whitcomb & Ball, E.W. Bond style 3/4 plate, 17-19J, NI, ★★★★	$2,600	$3,800	$7,200

Ball-Hampden, 18 size, 17 jewels, serial number 759,728.

BALL & CO. (E. HOWARD & CO.), Series VIII, 18 size, 17 jewels. (Order of Railway Conductors), serial number 307,488. Ca.1900.

BALL — E. HOWARD & CO.
18 SIZE

Description		Avg	Ex-Fn	Mint
VII, Ball, 17J, nickel, SW, GF, HC	★★★	$4,000	$5,200	$8,000
VII, Ball, 17J, nickel, SW, **14K** orig. HC	★★★	5,000	6,000	10,000
VII, Ball ,17J, nickel, **18K** orig. HC	★★★	8,000	10,000	14,000
VIII, Ball, 17J, nickel, SW, GF, OF	★★★	2,500	3,000	4,500
VIII, Ball, 17J, nickel, SW, **14K** orig. OF	★★★	3,500	4,000	6,000
VIII, Ball, 17J, 3/4, PS, GJS, *Brotherhood of Locomotive Engineers*, or *Order of Railway Conductors*, **gold filled** orig.OF,	★★★★	6,000	8,000	13,000
VIII, Ball, 17J, 3/4, PS, GJS, *Brotherhood of Locomotive Engineers, or Order of Railway Conductors*, **14K** orig.OF,	★★★★	7,000	9,000	16,000

A total of about 120=**B of LE** & about 70=**O of RC** made by E. Howard & Co., for Webb C. Ball.

BALL W. Co. (E. HOWARD WATCH CO.), 16 size, 21J. (KEYSTONE). This watch believed to be **one-of-a-kind** prototype, serial number 982,201.

Ball Watch Co., Illinois Model, 16 size, 23 jewels. Note: The CORRECT HANDS FOR BALL ILLINOIS WATCH.

⊕ BALL Watches are priced as having a **ORIGINAL BALL DIAL & CASE**.

BALL — E. HOWARD WATCH CO. (Keystone)
16 SIZE

Description	Avg	Ex-Fn	Mint
17J, Keystone Howard, GJS, OF... ★★★	$2,500	$3,000	$4,500
21J, Keystone Howard, Adj, GJS, OF .... ★★★★★	7,000	8,000	12,000

Ball Watch Co., Illinois Model # 11, 16 size, 23 jewels. To identify, note back plates that circle around balance wheel, serial number B801,758.

BALL regulator identification, note: styles and location of hairspring stud. "Pat.Dec.8.08" on some balance cocks.

BALL — ILLINOIS
18 & 16 SIZE

Description	Avg	Ex-Fn	Mint
18 size, 11-15J. or (Garland model), OF..	$200	$350	$600
16 size, 23J, 3/4, LS, Off. RR Stan., Adj. 5P, GJS, OF............ ★★	1,800	2,600	4,500

Top Left: Ball-Hamilton, 16 size, 23 jewels. Bottom left: Ball-Illinois, 16 size, 23 jewels. Above: Ball- AM. Waltham, 16 size, 21-23 jewels. These three movements are similar in appearance. To identify, note where the hair spring stud attaches to the balance bridge, which is slightly different on each movement.

BALL — SETH THOMAS   18 SIZE

Description	Avg	Ex-Fn	Mint
17J, M#3, LS, OF,3/4, GJS .... ★★★★	$6,000	$8,500	$14,500

BALL — AM. WALTHAM   18 SIZE

Description	Avg	Ex-Fn	Mint
1892, 17J, OF, LS, SW,			
marked Webb C. Ball, Cleveland.............................. ★★★★	$3,000	$4,500	$6,800

BALL — AM. WALTHAM   16 SIZE

Description	Avg	Ex-Fn	Mint
15J, Commercial Std.,3/4, **HC**, GCW... ★★	$300	$425	$750
15-16J, Commercial std., OF..	150	225	450
16J, Commercial std., HC...	225	335	650
17-19J, Commercial std., OF..	150	225	450
17-19J, Commercial std., HC..	225	335	650
17J, LS, 3/4, Adj.5P, Multi-color case, GF, OF	300	450	850
17J, LS, 3/4, Adj.5P, Off. RR Stan., OF......................................	225	335	650
17J,Official RR std., HC... ★★	800	1,000	1,500

Ball-Am. **Waltham**, 16 size, 19 jewels, ORC (Order of Railway Conductors), serial number B204,475.

Ball–Am. **Waltham**, 23 jewels, Official Railroad Standard, lever set, Adjusted to 5 positions, serial# B060,915.

Description	Avg	Ex-Fn	Mint
19J, LS, Off. RR Stan., Ball stirrup style case, OF	$275	$375	$750
19J, LS, Off. RR Stan., OF, Coin..	275	375	750
19J, LS, Off. RR Stan., **OF 14K** .... ★★	1,200	1,900	3,400
19J, Official RR std., LS, GCW,GJS, **HC**.............................. ★★	800	1,300	2,200
19J, LS, 3/4, Adj.5P, Off. RR Stan., OF, **Wind Ind.** .... ★★★★★	5,500	6,900	11,000
all the above, **Wind Ind., OF 14K Case**.............. ★★★★★	7,500	9,500	15,000
21J, Commercial std., LS, OF	200	275	650
21J, Official RR std., LS, GCW,GJS, OF......................................	450	550	900
21J, LS, 3/4, Adj.5P, Off. RR Stan., OF	450	550	900
21J, LS, OF, Adj.5P, Off. RR Stan., marked **Loaner,** OF ....★	500	700	1,200
23J, LS, Adj.5P, NI, GJS, Off. RR Stand., OF,			
very rare .... ★★★★★	6,000	8,000	12,500

Above Am. Waltham balance cock note shape of balance cock & triangular hairspring stud.

Description		Avg	Ex-Fn	Mint
17J, Brotherhood, marked ORC, BoFLE & *other etc. dials*, OF	★★	$2,500	$3,200	$4,200
19J, Brotherhood, marked ORC, BoFLE & *other etc. dials*, OF	★★	2,800	3,500	4,500
17-19J, Brotherhood, marked ORC, BoFLE & *other etc. dials*, HC	★★	4,000	5,400	7,300
21J, Brotherhood, marked ORC, BoFLE & *other etc. dials*, OF	★★	3,000	3,800	4,600
21J, Brotherhood, marked ORC, BoFLE & *other etc. dials*, HC.	★★★	4,000	5,500	7,700

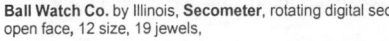

Ball Watch Co. by Illinois, **Secometer**, rotating digital sec, open face, 12 size, 19 jewels,

Record Watch Co. (BXC), 16 size, 21jewels, M# 435-B, Adj.6P, Swiss made Ca.1961.

12 SIZE (NOT Railroad Grade)

Description	Avg	Ex-Fn	Mint
19J, Illinois, OF, PS	$150	$225	$375
19J, Illinois, **14 K** OF	275	400	600
19J, Illinois, Secometer, rotating digital sec, OF ★	250	375	600
17J, Waltham, Commercial Standard, OF, PS, ★	150	225	350

0 SIZE (NOT Railroad Grade)

Description	Avg	Ex-Fn	Mint
17-19J, Waltham, OF, PS	$200	$285	$450
19J, HC, PS, ''Queen'' in Ball case	250	375	500

NO. 333
NO. 999

999
STANDARD

OFFICIAL RR STANDARD

OFFICIAL TIME SERVICE STANDARD

STANDARD   B OF RT

B OF LE

B OF LF

The B. of L. E. Standard Watch.
The B. of L. F. Standard Watch.
The B. of R. T. Standard Watch.
The O. of R. C. Standard Watch.
The Official R. R. Standard Watch.
The O. of R. T. Standard Watch.

O OF RC

SAFETY
FIRST

Ball-Audemars Piguet & Co., 14 size, 31 jewels, minute repeater, open face, serial number 4,220.

Ball-Vacheron & Constantin, 43mm, 18 jewels, hunting; note wolf-teeth winding.

BALL — SWISS   12-16 SIZE

Description	Avg	Ex-Fn	Mint
17J, "Garland"	$100	$135	$250
18-21J, Longines, OF	125	150	275
21J, Time Ball Special, OF (**Swiss Fake**)	85	100	175
21J, M#435, (B or C), LS, Adj.6P, Ball case, stirrup bow, OF	150	200	300
21J, M#477-B, Adj.6P (BXC-Record Watch Co.)	150	200	300
40mm Audemar Piguet, min. repeater, jeweled thru hammers, triple signed Webb C. Ball, **18K, OF** ★★	4,500	5,500	9,500
43-44mm Vacheron & Constantin, 18J, **HC, 18K** ★★	1,600	2,200	3,900
12 size, 17J, by Longines, marked "Made expressly for Webb C. Ball" Adj. temperature 2 pos. Ca. 1922 ★	200	275	350
12 size, marked *made especially for The Webb C. Ball Co. extra superior Swiss* 21J., 8 adjustments, **14K** Gold OF ★★★	350	450	600

PATENT SAFETY BOW

Above
The Webb C. Ball Co. 12 size.

20 th CENTURY CASE

18 size: 14K=$500 - $650 - $1,300
18 size: gold filled= $175 - $275 - $600
16 size: 14K = $400 -$550 - $1,100
16 size: gold filled= $125 - $225 - $500
16-18 size: silveroid=$100 - $200 - $400

Ball RR Dials

18 size: $40 - $80 - $150
16 size: $35 - $60 - $125

ANTIQUE BOW

18 size: 14K=$550 - $675 - $1,400
18 size: gold filled= $175 - $270 - $600
16 size: 14K= $450 -$550 - $1,200
16 size: gold filled= $125 - $225 - $500

BLE (Brotherhood dials)

18size: $300 - $400 - $900
16 size: $250 - $300 - $650

CATALOG CASE # 106
gold filled case $100 - $185 - $400

CATALOG CASE # 110
gold filled case $150 - $200 - $475

"BOX CAR" Dial;
found on Hamilton & Illinois made Ball

"CONVENTIONAL" Dial;
found on Waltham made Ball

CATALOG CASE # 114
gold filled case $150 - $185- $475

CATALOG CASE # 118
gold filled case $175 - $200 - $500

🕐 NOTE: A 1902 advertisement for Ball Watch Company read, "We do not sell movements or cases separately". BALL advertised as a **COMPLETE** watch with a choice of BALL dials and was fitted with a certain matched, timed and rated movement and sold in the BALL designed case style as a **COMPLETE** watch. **ALL THE ABOVE CASES ARE GOLD FILLED.**

Ca. 1913

CATALOG CASE # 122
gold filled case $175 - $200 - $475

CATALOG CASE # 126
gold filled case $125 - $165 - $400

OFFICIAL **RR** STANDARD. BALL Dial

CATALOG CASE # 130
gold filled case $150 - $175 - $400

CATALOG CASE # 134
gold filled case $175 - $200 - $425

🕐 NOTE: A 1902 advertisement for Ball Watch Company read, "We do not sell movements or cases separately". BALL advertised as a **COMPLETE** watch with a choice of BALL dials and was fitted with a certain matched, timed and rated movement and sold in the BALL designed case style as a **COMPLETE** watch. <u>**ALL THE ABOVE CASES ARE GOLD FILLED.**</u>

BANNATYNE WATCH CO.
1905 - 1911

Mr. Bannatyne had previously worked for Waterbury Clock Co., in charge of watch production. Bannatyne made non-jeweled watches that sold for about $1.50. Ingraham bought this company in 1912.

ESTIMATED SERIAL NUMBERS AND PRODUCTION DATES

Date	Serial No.	Date	Serial No.	Date	Serial No.
1906	40,000	1908	140,000	1910	250,000

Description		Avg	Ex-Fn	Mint
16-18S, OF, SW, NI- case	★★	$300	$400	$850
12-14S, OF, SW, NI- case	★★	200	275	450

Bannatyne Watch Co. (left), Ingraham Watch Co. (right). Note similarity of movements. Both patented Aug. 27th, 1907 & Sept. 3rd, 1907.

BENEDICT & BURNHAM MFG. CO.
Waterbury, Connecticut 1878 - 1880

The name **BENEDICT & BURNHAM MFG. CO**. will be found on back of movement on the large mainspring spring cover. D. A. A. Buck designed a **rotary** watch with 58 parts. The first "long wind" Waterbury watches made in 1878. These watches had skeletonized movements with open dials that made the works visible. They used 58 parts and were unique and attractive. The company was re-organized in March of 1880 as the Waterbury Watch Co. and in 1898 became the New England Watch Co.

Benedict & Burnham Mfg. Co. 18 size, long wind, 3 spoke skeletonized dial.
Benedict & Burnham Mfg. Co. will be found on back of movement on the large mainspring spring cover.

Benedict & Burnham Mfg. Co. dial & movement, 18 size, long wind, 3 spoke skeletonized dial.

Benedict & Burnham Mfg. Co. will be found on back of movement on the large mainspring spring cover.

Description	Avg	Ex-Fn	Mint
18S, duplex escapement, movement rotates as time advances, long wind			
3 spoke, Nickel OF case .... ★★★★	$900	$1,200	$1,800
4 spoke, Nickel OF case .... ★★★★★	1,200	1,500	2,000
6 spoke, Nickel OF case .... ★★★★	800	1,000	1,500

BOWMAN WATCH CO.   1879 - 1882

In March 1877, Ezra F. Bowman, a native of **Lancaster, Pa.**, opened a retail jewelry and watch business. He employed William H. Todd to supervise his watch manufacturing. Todd had previously been employed by the Elgin and Lancaster Watch companies. Bowman made a 17 Size, 3/4 plate, fully-jeweled movement. The escape wheel was a star tooth design, fully capped, similar to those made by Charles Frodsham, an English watch maker. They were stem wind with dials made by another company. Enough parts were made and bought for 300 watches, but only about 50 watches were completed and sold by Bowman. These watches performed very well. The company was sold to J. P. Stevens of Atlanta, Ga.

Description	Avg	Ex-Fn	Mint
*17S, 19-21J, 3/4, GJS, NI, LS, SW, made by (Bowman W. Co.)			
marked **E. F. Bowman** , (S# 1 to 50) .... ★★★★	$9,000	$11,000	$23,000
18S, 17J, by Hamilton G# 928, OF, marked E. F. Bowman .... ★★	600	750	1,400
16S, 21J, by Hamilton G# 960, OF, marked E. F. Bowman ..... ★★	550	700	1,300
16S, 21J, by Hamilton G# 961, HC, marked E. F. Bowman. ★★★	700	800	1,500

Bowman Watch Co., 16-18 size, 19-21 jewels, 3/4 plate, gold jewel settings, lever set, stem wind. Note free sprung balance. S# 17, Ca.1880. (made by *Bowman W. Co.*)

Bowman Watch Co., 16-18 size, 19-21 jewels, 3/4 plate, gold jewel settings, lever set, stem wind. Note free sprung balance. S# 19, Ca.1880. (made by *Bowman W. Co.*)

CALIFORNIA WATCH CO.

San Francisco - Berkeley, California
1876 - 1877

The Cornell Watch Co. was reorganized in early 1876 as the California Watch Co. The new company bought machinery to make watch cases of gold and silver. In a short time the company was in bad financial trouble and even paid its employees with watches. The business closed in the summer of 1876. Albert Troller bought the unfinished watches that were left. In about four months, he found a buyer in San Francisco. The factory was then closed and sold to the Independent Watch Co. Only about 5,000 watches were made by the California Watch Company.

Description		Avg	Ex-Fn	Mint
18S, 15J, FULL, KW, KS, "**Berkeley**"	★★★	$1,300	$1,800	$3,700
18S, 11-15J, FULL, KW, KS or SW	★	900	1,100	1,800
18S, 19J, FULL, KW, KS or SW	★★★	1,100	1,400	2,000

California Watch Co., 18 size, 15 jewels, full plate.   California Watch Co., 18 size, 7 jewels, full plate, serial number 29,029.

CHESHIRE WATCH CO.

Cheshire, Connecticut
1883 - 1890

In October 1883, the Cheshire Watch Company was formed by George J. Capewell with D. A. A. Buck (designer of the long-wind Waterbury) as superintendent. Their first movement was 18S, 3/4 gilt plate, stem wind, stem set, with the pendant attached to the movement. It fit into a nickel case which was also made at the Cheshire factory. The first watches were completed in April 1885. A new 18S nickel movement with a second hand was made to fit standard size American cases, and was introduced in 1887. By that date production was at about 200 watches per day.

Serial numbers range from 201 to 89,650. All Cheshire watches were sold through L. W. Sweet, general selling agent, in New York City. The factory closed in 1890, going into receivership. The receiver had 3,000 movements finished in 1892. In 1901 O. E. Bell bought the machinery and had it shipped to Appleton, Wisconsin, where he had formed the Remington Watch Company. The watches produced by Remington are marked "Appleton Watch Co." on the movements.

NOTE: George J. Capewell, inventor of the Capewell horse shoe nail.

Note stem attached → to movement.

Cheshire Watch Co., 20 size, 4 jewels, **model** number 1.
Note stem attached and will not fit standard size case, serial
number 201. NOTE: Closed top plate near balance. The
lowest serial number know to exist is **201**.

Cheshire Watch Co., 20 size, 4 jewels, **model** number 1.

Description	Avg	Ex-Fn	Mint
20S, 4-7J, FULL, OF, SW, NI case, stem attached, low serial #			
1st **model**, closed top plate (S # **201 to 300**) .... ★★★★	$500	$750	$1,300
20S, 4-7J, FULL, OF, SW, NI case, stem attached,			
1st **model**, closed top plate .... ★★	400	565	825
18S, 4-7J, 3/4, SW, OF, NI case, stem attached, 2nd model .... ★	275	325	450
18S, 4-7J, HC/ OF fits standard case, 3rd model .... ★	250	300	425
18S, 11J, HC/ OF, standard case, 3rd model .... ★	250	300	425
18S, 15J, HC/ OF, NI, ADJ, standard case, 3rd model .... ★	275	325	450
18S, **21J**, HC / OF, SW, Coin, standard case, 3rd model...... ★★★	400	500	675
6S, 3/4, HC/ OF, SW, NI case... ★	195	250	465

Cheshire Watch Co., 18 size, 4-7 jewels. This model
number 2 was manufactured with the stem attached and
requires a special case. NOTE: open top plate at Balance.

Cheshire Watch Co., 18 size, 4-7 jewels. This model fits
standard 18 size cases. Model number 3.

⏱ 1st & 2nd model Cheshire movements will not fit standard 18 size cases.
Model # 1, S# 201 to15,000 - Model # 2, S # 30,001 to 40,000 - Model # 3, S # 50,001 to 89,650.

CHICAGO WATCH CO.

Chicago, Illinois 1895 - 1903

The Chicago Watch Company's (ALL watches in ALL sizes) were made by **other manufacturing companies** and sold by Chicago Watch Co.

Description	Avg	Ex-Fn	Mint
18S, 7J, OF	$95	$165	$300
18S, 7-11J, HC or OF, Swiss	35	60	80
18S, 11J, KW	125	200	350
18S, 15J, OF, SW	125	200	350
18S, Made by Columbus, 15J, SW, NI, OF ★	150	200	375
18S, Made by Columbus, 15J, SW, NI, HC ★	200	265	400
18S, Made by New York Standard, marked 23J., (fake jewels) Locomotive on dial & movement ★★	100	150	225
18S, Made by Illinois, 11J, SW, NI ★	200	265	400
18S, Made by Waltham, 15J, SW ★	200	265	400
12S, 15J, OF	40	65	150
12S, 15J, YGF, HC	85	135	200

Chicago Watch Co., 18 size, 15 jewels, Hunting case, made by COLUMBUS Watch Co., nickel movement, lever set, serial # 209,145.

Columbia Watch Co., 0 size, 4 jewels, stem wind, open face and hunting, duplex escapement, the escape wheel teeth were milled to give better quality than the Waterbury movements.

COLUMBIA WATCH CO.

Waltham, Massachusetts
1896 - 1899

The Columbia Watch Company was organized in 1896 by Edward A. Locke, formerly General Manager of the Waterbury Watch Company. The firm began manufacturing an 0-size, 4-jewel gilt movement with duplex escapement in 1897. These movements were marked "Columbia Watch Co., Waltham, Mass." The firm also made movements marked "Hollers Watch Co., Brooklyn, NY," as well as nickeled movements marked "Cambridge Watch Co., New York."

Locke turned the business over to his son-in-law, Renton Whidden, in 1898, and the firm changed to an 0-size, 7-jewel nickel movement with lever escapement called the Suffolk. The firm name was not changed until early 1901.

Description	Avg	Ex-Fn	Mint
0S, 4J, SW, Duplex, gilded, HC	$40	$75	$150
0S, 4J, SW, Duplex, gilded, OF	35	65	135
0S, 7J, SW, lever escapement, OF	40	75	150

COLUMBUS WATCH CO.

Columbus, Ohio
1874 - 1903

Dietrich Gruen, born in Osthofen, Germany in 1847, started a business as the Columbus Watch Co. on Dec. 22, 1874 in Columbus, Ohio. At the age of 27, he received a U.S. patent for an improved safety pinion. The new company finished movements made from **Madretsch**, Switzerland, a suburb of Beil. The imported movements were made in a variety of sizes and were in nickel or gilt. The early watches usually had the initials C.W.CO. intertwined in script on the dial. The serial numbers generally ran up to around 20,000's a few examples are in the 70,000's.

D. Gruen and W.J. Savage decided in late 1882 to manufacture watches locally. By August of 1883 the first movements were being produced with a train consisting of 72 teeth on the barrel, 72 on the center wheel, 11 on the center pinion, 60 on the third wheel with a pinion of 9, 70 on the fourth wheel with a pinion of 9 with a 7 leaf escape pinion. The new manufacture primarily made 18 size movements but also pioneered the 16 size watch while reducing the size and thickness. Several new innovations were used into the design including a completely covered main spring barrel, a new micrometric regulator and the ability to change the main spring without removing the balance cock. By 1884 they were making their own dials, but no cases were ever manufactured.

The company went into receivership in 1894 with new management. That same year Frederick Gruen started again as D. Gruen & Son. They had PAUL ASSMANN to produce 18 size & 16 size movements with 18 & 21 jewels with the escapement designed by Moritz Grossman of Glasshute. Soon after this time movements were obtained from Switzerland and the new Gruen veri-thin movement was developed. In 1898 this company moved to Cincinnati, Ohio.

From 1894 through February 14, 1903 the Columbus Watch Co. produced watches both under the Columbus Watch Co. and the New Columbus Watch Co. name. The re-organized company produced the same models, but switched primarily to named grades such as Time King, Columbus King, etc. The higher grade watches were assigned a special block of serial numbers from 500,000 to 506,000 . In keeping with the industry several models with 25 jewels were produced in this block of serial numbers.

In 1903 the Columbus Watch Co. was sold to the Studebakers and the South Bend Watch Co. started. The machinery, unfinished movements, parts and approximately 3/4 of the 150 employees moved to South Bend, Indiana. Some marked Columbus Watch Co. movements were finished by the South Bend W. Co. Examples exist of dials made in the South Bend style and movements marked Columbus Watch Co.

COLUMBUS WATCH CO., Private Label, 19 Lignes or about 18-16 size, 16 jewels, gold jewel settings, marked Pat. pinion, OPEN FACE model. (Swiss contract)

Note: Regulator

COLUMBUS WATCH CO., 19 Lignes or about 18-16 size, 15 jewels, hunting case, engraved on movement *"1874"* .

COLUMBUS
ESTIMATED SERIAL NUMBERS AND PRODUCTION DATES

DATE - SERIAL NO.	DATE— SERIAL NO.	
1874—- 1	1888 – 97,000	21 jewels or more
1875– 1,000	1889 – 119,000	Columbus King,
1876– 3,000	1890 – 141,000	Railway King,
1877– 6,000	1891 – 163,000	Time King,
1878– 9,000	1892 – 185,000	and Ruby.
1879– 12,000	1893 – 207,000	
1880– 15,000	1894 – 229,000	SPECIAL BLOCK
1881– 18,000	1895 – 251,000	OF SERIAL NOS.
1882– 21,000	1896 – 273,000	DATE— SERIAL NO.
1883 – 25,000	1897 – 295,000	1894 – 500,001
1884 – 30,000	1898 – 317,000	1896 – 501,500
1885 – 40,000	1899 – 339,000	1898 – 503,000
1886 – 53,000	1900 – 361,000	1900 – 504,500
1887 – 75,000	1901 – 383,000	1902 – 506,000

The above list is provided for determining the **APPROXIMATE** age of your watch. Match serial number with date. Watches were not necessarily **SOLD** and **DELIVERED** in the exact order of manufactured or production dates.

SWISS, 3/4 PLATE, & MADE FROM 1874–1883

Most marked COL. WATCH CO. with single sunk dials and may be SW/KW Transitional, serial # up to about **20,000**.

Grade or Name — Description	Avg	Ex-Fn	Mint
18S, 7J, pressed J., nickel or gilded, OF/HC	$80	$100	$250
18S, 11, pressed J., nickel or gilded, OF/HC	100	150	300
18S, 15J, GJS or pressed J., nickel, Adj., OF/HC	150	200	350
18S, 16J, **raised** GJS, 2 tone or nickel, Adj., OF/HC	200	275	475
Grade or Name — Description	Avg	Ex-Fn	Mint
16S, 11J, pressed J., nickel, OF/HC	$150	$200	$400
16S, 15J, pressed J. or GJS, Adj., nickel, OF/HC	150	200	400
16S, 16J, **raised** GJS, Adj., nickel, OF/HC	165	225	450
Private Label, KW or SW, 11-15 jewels, OF/HC			
Grade or Name — Description	Avg	Ex-Fn	Mint
14S, 16J, GJS, nickel, Adj., OF/HC	$150	$200	$350
Grade or Name — Description	Avg	Ex-Fn	Mint
9S, 15J, GJS or pressed J., nickel, Adj., OF/HC	$95	$150	$295
Grade or Name — Description	Avg	Ex-Fn	Mint
8S, 11J, pressed J., nickel, OF/HC	$95	$150	$295
8S, 15J, pressed J., nickel, OF/HC	95	150	295

FOR ABOVE HUNTING CASED MODEL ADD **$35.00 to $65.00**
NOTE: These Odd size movements are difficult to case.

COLUMBUS WATCH CO., 19 Lignes or about 16 size, 15 jewels, exposed winding wheels, marked Gruen Patent, OPEN FACE model, serial # 1,661. (Swiss contract) The above finished by Columbus W. Co.

COLUMBUS WATCH CO., about 14 size, 16 jewels, gold jewel settings, nickel plates, marked Gruen's pat. pinion, HUNTING CASE model. (Swiss contract)

18 SIZE-KW, FULL PLATE, MODEL # 1 & TRANSITIONAL
Serial # up to 100,000, balance cock set flush to barrel bridge and may have pinned dial.
Marked Col. Watch Co., Ohio Columbus Watch Co.

Grade or Name — Description	Avg	Ex-Fn	Mint
11-13J, KW / KS, gilded, OF/HC	$250	$350	$650
13J, KW / KS, nickel, (marked 13 jewels), OF/HC ★★	350	450	700
15J, KW / KS, gilded, Adj., OF/HC	250	350	600
16J, KW / KS, gilded, OF/HC ★	325	425	700
Grade or Name — Description	**Avg**	**Ex-Fn**	**Mint**
11-13J, SW/ KW, gilded or nickel, OF/HC	$135	$165	$350
15J, SW/ KW, gilded or nickel, GJS, OF/HC	150	225	400
16J, SW/ KW, gilded or nickel, GJS, OF/HC	175	265	450

FOR ABOVE HUNTING CASED MODEL ADD $25.00 to $50.00

COLUMBUS WATCH CO., 18 size, marked 13J., pressed jewels, key wind & key set, nickel plates, marked on movement Col. Watch Co. Columbus Ohio Pat. pinion, on dial "*Ohio Columbus Watch Co.*", serial #40,198.

COLUMBUS WATCH CO., 18 size, 15 jewels, key wind key set, hunting case, on movement "Columbus Watch Co. Columbus, Ohio Pat. Pinion", serial # 66,577.

18 SIZE, FULL PLATE, PRE-1894
Marked "Columbus Watch Co. Columbus, Ohio", all marked Safety Pinion

Grade or Name — Description	Avg	Ex-Fn	Mint
7J, G#90, pressed J., OF	$55	$95	$200
7J, G#20, pressed J., HC	80	135	250
11J, G#92, pressed J., nickel, OF	65	95	200
11J, G#22, pressed J., nickel, HC	85	165	250
15J, G#64 / G#93, gilded, OF	65	95	200
15J, G#24 / G#32, gilded, HC	90	165	250
15J, G#63 / G#94, nickel, Adj., OF	80	125	200
15J, G#23 / G#33, nickel, Adj., HC	85	165	250
15J, G#95, nickel, Adj., D.S. dial, OF	75	125	250
15J, G#34, nickel, Adj., D.S. dial, HC	85	165	350
16J, G#97, GJS, nickel, Adj., D.S. dial, OF	95	165	250
16J, G#27, GJS, nickel, Adj., D.S. dial, HC	110	200	350
16J, G#98, raised GJS, 2 tone nickel, Adj., D.S. dial, OF	110	200	350
16J, G#28, raised GJS, 2 tone nickel, Adj., D.S. dial, HC	150	235	400
16J, G#99, raised GJS, 2 tone nickel, Adj., D.S. dial, OF	125	250	450
16J, G#18, raised GJS, 2 tone nickel, Adj., D.S. dial, HC	150	285	500

18 SIZE-FULL PLATE, POST-1894

Some Marked "New Columbus Watch Co. Columbus Ohio"

Grade or Name — Description	Avg	Ex-Fn	Mint
7J, G#10, pressed J., gilded, OF	$55	$95	$200
7J, G#9, pressed J., gilded, HC	75	135	275
11J, G#8, nickel, OF	65	95	200
11J, G#7, nickel, HC	90	150	300
16J, G#6, GJS, nickel, OF	80	95	200
16J, G#5, GJS, nickel, HC	95	150	295
16J, G#4, GJS, 2 tone nickel, Adj., D.S. dial, OF	150	200	350
16J, G#3, GJS, 2 tone nickel, Adj., D.S. dial, HC	175	250	400
17J, G#204, GJS, 2 tone nickel, Adj., D.S. dial, OF	175	250	400
17J, G#203, GJS, 2 tone nickel, Adj., D.S. dial, HC	200	300	450
17J, G#2, raised GJS, 2 tone nickel, Adj., D.S. dial, OF	200	300	450
17J, G#1, raised GJS, 2 tone nickel, Adj., D.S. dial, HC	250	350	475

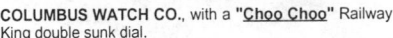

COLUMBUS WATCH CO., with a **"Choo Choo"** Railway King double sunk dial.

COLUMBUS WATCH CO., Railway King, 18 size, 17J, 2 tone, note **missing** screw on barrel bridge,S # 313,005.

18 SIZE FULL PLATE, NAMED GRADES

Marked Names, Double Sunk Dials

Grade or Name — Description	Avg	Ex-Fn	Mint
Am. Watch Club, 15J, 2 tone, Adj., D.S. dial, OF/HC ★	$300	$450	$625
Burlington Route C.B. & QR.R., 15J, nickel, Adj., D.S. dial, OF ★★★★★	2,500	3,500	5,200
Champion, 15J, gilded, Adj., D.S.dial, OF	60	125	250
Champion, 15J, gilded, Adj., D.S.dial, HC	85	165	300
Champion, 15J, Nickel, Adj., D.S.dial, OF	65	125	250
Champion, 15J, Nickel, Adj., D.S.dial, HC	85	165	300
Champion, 16J, Nickel, Adj., D.S.dial, OF	85	165	300
Champion, 16J, Nickel, Adj., D.S.dial, HC	125	235	350

🕐 Watches listed in this book are priced at the collectable trade show level, as **complete** watches having an original 14k gold-filled case & **KEYW IND** with silver case, an original white enamel single sunk dial, and with the entire original movement in good working order with no repairs needed.

170 / COLUMBUS WATCH CO. (continued)

Grade or Name — Description	Avg	Ex-Fn	Mint
Columbus King, 17J, raised GJS, nickel, Adj., D.S. dial, OF	$200	$300	$550
Columbus King, 17J, raised GJS, nickel, Adj., D.S. dial, HC	250	400	650
Columbus King, 17J, raised GJS, nickel, Adj., **choo choo** D.S. dial, 2 tone, OF............	500	800	1,400
Columbus King, 17J, raised GJS, nickel, Adj., **Angled** choo choo D.S. dial, OF............	500	800	1,400
Columbus King, 21J, raised GJS, nickel, Adj., D.S. dial, OF	450	550	950
Columbus King, 21J, raised GJS, nickel, Adj., D.S. dial, HC	400	500	875
Columbus King, 23J, raised GJS, nickel, Adj., D.S. dial, OF.......★	1,000	1,300	2,400
Columbus King, 23J, raised GJS, nickel, Adj., D.S. dial, HC .....★	1,000	1,300	2,400
Columbus King, 25J, raised GJS, nickel, Adj., D.S. dial, OF .... ★★★	3,200	3,800	5,600
Columbus King, 25J, raised GJS, nickel, Adj., D.S. dial, HC............ ★★★	2,800	3,300	5,100
F.C. & P.R.R., 17J, GJS, nickel, Adj., D.S. dial, OF .... ★★★	900	1,200	2,100
Jackson Park, 15J, 2 tone, Adj., D.S. dial, OF............★	450	550	950
Jay Gould, Railroad King, 15J, nickel,Adj., D.S. dial, OF .. ★★★	1,000	1,300	2,300
New York Susquehanna &Western R.R.,16J, GJS, SW/KW, gold flash, D.S. dial, OF .... ★★★★	2,500	3,000	4,600
Non-magnetic, 16J, raised GJS, 2 tone, Adj., OF/HC............	300	400	700
North Star, 11J, gilded, OF............	85	125	300
North Star, 11J, gilded, HC............	100	165	350
North Star, 11J, nickel, OF............	85	150	295
North Star, 11J, nickel, HC	100	165	350
North Star, 15J, nickel, OF............	100	165	350
North Star, 15J, nickel, HC	150	185	400
The President, 17J, GJS, Adj, 2 tone, D.S. dial, OF............★	400	500	850
Railroad Regulator, 15J, GJS, nickel, Adj., D.S. dial, OF ....★	450	550	950
Railroad Regulator, 16J, GJS, nickel, Adj., D.S. dial, OF ....★	450	500	950
Railway, 17J, GJS, 2 tone, Adj., D.S. dial, OF............★	300	400	675

Columbus King, 18 size, 25 jewels, **open face** serial number 503,094. Note **two screws** between balance cock & barrel bridge.

Railway King, 18 size, 23 jewels, adjusted, stem wind, **hunting case**, serial number 503,315. Note **one screw** between balance cock & barrel bridge.

🕐 Watches listed in this book are priced at the collectable Trade Show level, as **complete** watches having an original 14k gold-filled case & *KEYW IND* with silver case, an original white enamel single sunk dial, and with the entire original movement in good working order with no repairs needed.
🕐 **The Complete Price Guide to Watches goal is to stimulate the orderly exchange of <u>Watches</u> between "*buyers*" and "*sellers*".**

Grade or Name — Description	Avg	Ex-Fn	Mint
Railway King, 16J, GJS, 2 tone nickel, Adj., D.S. dial, OF............	$275	$350	$575
Railway King, 16J, GJS, 2 tone nickel, Adj., D.S. dial, HC...........	350	465	675
Railway King, 16J, GJS, 2 tone nickel, Adj., (black red blue) **choo choo** D.S. dial, OF.............................	400	575	1,100
Railway King, 16J, GJS, 2 tone nickel, Adj., (black red blue) **choo choo** D.S. dial, HC.............................	400	575	1,100
Railway King, 16J, GJS, 2 tone nickel, Adj., Angled **choo choo** dial, OF..	550	700	1,200
Railway King, 16J, GJS, 2 tone nickel, Adj., Angled **choo choo** dial, HC...	550	700	1,200
Railway King, 17J, raised GJS, nickel, Adj., D.S. dial, OF............	275	350	550
Railway King, 17J, raised GJS, nickel, Adj., D.S. dial, HC............	300	435	600
Railway King, 21J, raised GJS, nickel, Adj., D.S. dial, OF............	450	550	750
Railway King, 21J, raised GJS, nickel, Adj., D.S. dial, HC............	475	575	800
Railway King, 23J, raised GJS, nickel, Adj., Railway King D.S. dial, OF .... ★★★	1,000	1,300	2,100
Railway King, 23J, raised GJS, nickel, Adj., Railway King D.S. dial, HC .... ★★★	1,000	1,300	2,100
Railway King, 25J, raised GJS, nickel, Adj., Railway King D.S. dial, OF .... ★★★★	2,500	3,200	4,300
Railway King, 25J, raised GJS, nickel, Adj., Railway King D.S. dial, HC .... ★★★★	3,000	4,200	5,600
Railway King Special, 17J, GJS, nickel, Adj., D.S. dial, OF..........	300	435	625
Railway Monarch, 17J, GJS, nickel, Adj., D.S. dial, OF .... ★	300	435	625
Railway Monarch, 17J, GJS, nickel, Adj., D.S. dial, HC............. ★	300	435	625
Railway Time Service, 17J, GJS, nickel, Adj., D.S. dial, OF .... ★	375	485	825
The Regent, 15J, D.S. dial, OF...	150	225	425
R.W.K. Special, 15J, GJS, Adj., 2 tone, D.S. dial, OF..................	250	350	525
R.W.K. Special, 15J, GJS, Adj., 2 tone, D.S. dial, HC	250	350	525
R.W.K. Special, 16J, GJS, Adj., 2 tone, D.S. dial, OF..................	250	350	525
R.W.K. Special, 16J, GJS, Adj., 2 tone, D.S. dial, HC	300	400	575
Springfield Mo.W. Club, 16J, GJS, nickel, Adj., D.S. dial, HC ... ★	350	475	675
Special, 17J, GJS, nickel, D.S. dial, OF......................................	200	275	475
J.P. Stevens & Co. (see listing under J.P. Stevens & Co. **HEADING**)			
The New Menlo Park, 15J, HC .... ★★	200	325	525
The Railroader, 16J., LS, nickel, Adj., OF .... ★★	200	325	525
The Star, 11-15J, nickel, OF/HC..	175	225	425
Time King, 21J, raised GJS, 2 tone nickel, Adj., D.S. dial, OF	300	425	625
Time King, 21J, raised GJS, 2 tone nickel, Adj., D.S. dial, HC	325	450	650
U.S. Army, 15J, nickel, HC... ★	400	535	725

Catalog August 1, 1895

18 size **OPEN FACE** Model
NOTE: (2) SCREWS
Grade # **4**, 16J., Adjusted

18 size **HUNTING CASE** Model
NOTE: (1) SCREW
Grade # **5**, 16J.

NOTE: May not be true for KEY WIND or TRANSITIONAL MODELS

16 SIZE, 3/4 Plate

Marked "New Columbus Watch Co. Columbus Ohio"

Grade or Name — Description	Avg	Ex-Fn	Mint
7J, G#80 / G#20, gilded, OF..	$50	$95	$200
7J, G#40 / G#19, gilded, HC	75	135	225
11J, G#81, gilded, OF...	60	100	200
11J, G#41, gilded, HC	75	135	225
11J, G#83 / G#18, nickel, OF...	60	100	195
11J, G#43 / G#17, nickel, HC...	75	135	225
15J, G#84, Adj., gilded, OF...	60	100	200
15J, G#44, Adj., gilded, HC...	80	135	250
15J, G#86, GJS, Adj., nickel, D.S. dial, OF	70	100	225
15J, G#46, GJS, Adj., nickel, D.S. dial, HC......................	80	100	250
16J, G#87 / G#316, GJS, Adj., nickel, D.S. dial, OF	80	100	250
16J, G#47 / G#315, GJS, Adj., nickel, D.S. dial, HC..........	85	125	275
16J, G#14, GJS, Adj., 2 tone nickel, D.S. dial, OF	125	175	300
16J, G#13, GJS, Adj., 2 tone nickel, D.S. dial, HC	150	185	400
16J, G#88, raised GJS, Adj., 2 tone nickel, D.S. dial, OF..............	125	165	300
16J, G#48, raised GJS, Adj., 2 tone nickel, D.S. dial, HC	150	185	400
17J, G#12, raised GJS, Adj., 2 tone nickel, D.S. dial, OF..............	125	175	300
17J, G#11, raised GJS, Adj., 2 tone nickel, D.S. dial, HC	150	185	400
Ruby, 21J, raised GJS, Adj., 2 tone nickel, D.S. dial, OF .... ★ ★	350	550	950
Ruby, 21J, raised GJS, Adj., 2 tone nickel, D.S. dial, HC........ ★ ★	450	700	1,200

NEW Columbus Watch Co., 16 size, 16 jewels, gold train, 2-tone, serial number 341,339.

Columbus Watch Co., Ruby Model, 16 size, 21 jewels, three quarter plate, gold jewel settings, gold train, Adj.6p.

August 1, 1895 Catalog ☞

The following movements are all finely finished and very accurately adjusted, and will stand the most Critical Inspection of the Railway Watch Inspectors.

𝒲 E are putting all of our Movements in beautiful Brass Boxes, with glass top and bottom. These boxes are made so that the movement can be wound and set without removing them from the boxes, thus enabling retail jewelers to show these Movements to their customers without the annoyance of dust or finger marks.

We buy the outside box, with original label, from the retail jeweler of the following names and numbers, at the price below:

Time King · · · · · · . . Outside Box, $2 50	
Nos. 1 and 2	" " 1 50
" 203 and 204	" " 1 00
" 3 and 4	" " 1 00
Ruby	" " 3 00
Nos. 11 and 12	" " 2 00
" 13 and 14	" " 1 00
" 100	" " 1 00

You have only to send the boxes to us, charges prepaid, and we will send you the cash. No waiting until you have sold the movements.

The New Columbus Watch Co.

Note: The following movements are all finely finished and very accurately adjusted, and will stand the most Critical Inspection of the **Railway Watch Inspectors**. Also note shipping movements in brass boxes, with glass top & will buy them back.

6 SIZE

Grade or Name — Description	Avg	Ex-Fn	Mint
7J, G#102, gilded, OF	$60	$85	$200
7J, G#102, gilded, HC	75	100	225
11J, G#101 / G#51 / G#53, nickel or gilded, HC	75	100	225
13J, G#103, nickel, HC	75	100	225
15J, G#104 / G#55, GJS, nickel, D.S. dial, HC	100	150	250
16J, G#57, raised GJS, nickel, D.S. dial, OF/HC	100	150	250
16J, G#100, raised GJS, 2 tone, D.S. dial, (marked 16J.), OF	150	225	325
16J, G#100, raised GJS, 2 tone, D.S. dial, (marked 16J.), HC	150	225	325

Columbus Watch Co., 8-10 size, 13 jewels, 3/4 plate, stem wind, serial number 13,372. For price see 2nd page of Columbus W. Co. under Swiss, 3/4 plate (1874-1883).

New Columbus Watch Co. Example of a basic model for 6 size, 3/4 plate, 7-16 jewels, gilded and nickel.

4 SIZE

Grade or Name — Description	Avg	Ex-Fn	Mint
11J, nickel or gilded, OF/HC ★	$100	$175	$300
15J, nickel or gilded, OF/HC ★	125	200	325

18 Size, 21 Jewels.
NEW COLUMBUS TIME KING.

Hunting and Open Face.

Nickel, 21 Genuine Ruby Jewels, set in red, Solid Gold Raised Settings, Escapement Cap Jeweled, Adjusted to temperature, Positions and Isochronism, Breguet Hair Spring, Patent Center Pinion, Patent Regulator, Polished Dust Band and Stem Wind, Beveled Steel Work, Pearled Plates; fine, white, cut and beveled edge, hard enameled, double sunk, Red marginal figured Roman or Arabic Dial; handsomely damaskeened in Gold on Nickel $25 00

16 Size, Twenty-one Jewels.
NEW COLUMBUS RUBY.

Hunting and Open Face.

Nickel, 21 Genuine Ruby Jewels, set in red Solid Gold Raised Settings, Escapement Cap Jeweled, Adjusted to Temperature, Beveled Steel Work, Positions and Isochronism, Breguet Hair Spring, Patent Center Pinion, Patent Regulator, Polished Stem Wind, Beveled Edge Steel Work, Pearled Plates; fine, white, cut and beveled edge, hard enameled, double sunk, red marginal, figured Roman or Arabic Dial; handsomely Damaskeened in Gold on Nickel $30 00

CORNELL WATCH CO.
Chicago, Illinois
1870 - 1874
San Francisco, California
1875 - 1876

The Cornell Watch Co. bought the Newark Watch Co. and greatly improved the movements being produced. In the fall of 1874, the company moved to San Francisco, Calif., with about 60 of its employees. The movements made in California were virtually the same as those made in Chicago. The company wanted to employ Chinese who would work cheaper, but the skilled employees refused to go along and went on strike. The company stayed alive until 1875 and was sold to the California Watch Co. in January 1876. But death came a few months later.

C.L. Kidder from 1869 to 1872 worked with F.A. Jones in Switzerland to form the *International Watch Co.*. Mr. Kidder returned to U.S.A. and took on a position with Cornell.

The Chronology of the Development of Cornell Watch Co.
Newark Watch Co. 1864-1870; S#s 6901 to about 12,000.
Cornell Watch Co., Chicago, Ill. 1870-1874; S#s 12,001 to about 23,000 or up to 25,000.
Cornell Watch Co., San Francisco, Calif. 1874-Jan. 1876; S# s 23,001 to about 35,000.
California Watch Co., Jan. 1876-mid 1876.

1871 AD for the Cornell Watch Co. Factory

18 SIZE

Grade or Name — Description		Avg	Ex-Fn	Mint
J. C. Adams, 11J, KW	★	$250	$350	$700
C. T. Bowen, FULL, KW	★	300	400	850
C. M. Cady, 15J, **SW**	★	400	500	900
Cornell W. Co., 7J, San Francisco on mvt., KW	★	700	1,000	1,900
Cornell W. Co., 7J, San Francisco on mvt., **SW**	★	700	1,000	1,800
Cornell W. Co., 11J, KW	★	300	400	650
Cornell W. Co., 11J, San Francisco on mvt., KW	★★	900	1,300	2,100
Cornell W. Co., 15J, KW	★	325	475	850
Cornell W. Co., 15J, San Francisco on mvt., KW	★	900	1,300	2,200
Cornell W. Co., 15J, San Francisco on mvt., **SW**	★★	950	1,400	2,300
Cornell W. Co., 19-20J, San Francisco on mvt., GJS, ADJ., **SW**	★★★	2,200	2,800	4,200
Paul Cornell, 19-20J, GJS, ADJ, **SW**	★★★	2,200	3,000	4,500
John Evans, 15J, KW		250	375	700
Excelsior, 15J, FULL, KW, KS	★	275	400	750

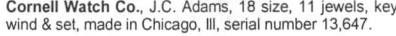

Cornell Watch Co., J.C. Adams, 18 size, 11 jewels, key wind & set, made in Chicago, Ill, serial number 13,647.

Cornell Watch Co., 18 size, 15 jewels, key wind & set, marked "John Evans," serial number 16,868.

Grade or Name — Description		Avg	Ex-Fn	Mint
H. N. Hibbard, 11J, KW, ADJ	★	$350	$475	$800
C.L. Kidder, 7J, KW,KS, OF	★	350	475	800
George F. Root, 15J, KW	★	400	550	900
George Waite, 7J, (Hyde Park), KW	★★	350	475	800
E. S. Williams, 7J, KW	★	250	385	700
Eugene Smith, 17J	★	450	600	900
Ladies Stemwind	★	200	300	500

JACOB D. CUSTER

Norristown, Pennsylvania   1840 - 1845

At the age of 19, Jacob Custer repaired his father's watch. He was then asked to repair all the watches within his community. Custer was basically self-taught and had very little formal education and little training in clocks and watches. He made all the parts except the hairspring and fusee chains. The watches were about 14 size, and only **12 to 15** watches were made. The 14S **fusee** watches had lever escapement, 3/4 plate and were sold in his **own gold cases**. He made a few chronometers, one with a helical spring.

J.D. Custer, 14-16 size, engraved on movement is **J.D. Custer, Norristown, Pa. Patented Feb. 4, 1843** Key-wind Key-set, Fusee.

Above: J.D. Custer patent No. 2,939, with his drawing, Note the key.

Description

	Avg	Ex-Fn	Mint
14S, OF, engraved on mvt. (*J. D. Custer, Patented Feb. 4, 1843*)			
very RARE watch, original gold case ★★★★★	$20,000	$30,000	$55,000

DUDLEY WATCH CO.

Lancaster, Pennsylvania
1920 - 1925

William Wallace Dudley became interested in watches and horology at the age of 13 and became an apprentice making ship chronometers in Canada. When he moved to America, he worked for the South Bend and Illinois Watch companies and the Trenton Watch Co. before going to Hamilton Watch Co. in Lancaster. He left Hamilton at age 69 to start his own watch company. In 1922 his first watches were produced; they were 14S, 19J, and used many Waltham Model 1894 – 1897, 14 size parts, including the train and escapement. The plates and winding mechanism were made at the Dudley plant. Dials and hands were made to Dudley's specifications in Switzerland. At first jewels were obtained from a manufacturer in Lancaster, but by 1925 they were Swiss supplied. The cases came from Wadsworth Keystone and the Star Watch Case Co. Dudley also made a 12S, 19J watch. By 1924, the company was heavily in debt, and on February 20, 1925, a petition for bankruptcy was filed. The Masonic Watch was his most unusual watch.

DUDLEY WATCHES			ESTIMATED TOTAL PRODUCTION
Dudley Watch Co.	1920-1925	Model No.1 = S#	500—1,900 = 1,400
P. W. Baker Co.	1925-1935	Model No.2 = S#	2,001—4,800 = 2,800
XL Watch Co., N.Y.	1935-1976	Model No.3 = S#	4,801—6,500 = 1,700
			TOTAL = 5,900

🕐 NOTE: Not all movements were finished and sold as complete watches.

Model No. 1, 14S, 19J, OF, can be distinguished by the "Holy Bible" engraved on the winding arbor plate, and a gilded pallet bridge matching the plates.

Model No. 2, 12S, 19J, used the 910 and 912 Hamilton wheels and escapement, has a flat silver-colored Bible.

Model No. 3, 12S, can be distinguished by the silver Bible which was riveted in place and was more three-dimensional. The 3rd wheel bridge was rounded off at one end.

Dudley Watch Co., Model 1, 14 size, 19J., open face, Masonic form plates, flip back, serial # 1232, Ca. 1924.

Dudley Watch Co., Model 2, 14 size, 19J., open face, with original paper. The watch also came with a keystone shaped box, Ca 1927.

12 SIZE - 14 SIZE
"MASONS" MODEL

Grade or Name — Description	Avg	Ex-Fn	Mint
14S, Dudley, 19J, 14K, flip open back, Serial #1 (made 5 experimental models with Serial #1) .... ★	$5,500	$8,000	$15,000
14S, M#1, 19J, OF, **14K** flip open back .... ★	2,800	3,200	4,600
14S, M#1, 19J, OF, **14K** flip open back, w/box & papers .... ★	3,100	3,600	5,200
12S, M#2, 19J, OF, flip open back, **GF** .... ★	1,800	2,300	3,500
12S, M#2, 19J, OF, **14K,** flip open back case .... ★	2,200	2,600	3,800
12S, M#2, 19J, OF, **14K** display case .... ★	2,000	2,400	3,400
12S, M#3, 19J, OF, display case, **GF** .... ★	1,500	2,000	3,100
12S, M#3, 19J, OF, **14K** flip open case .... ★	2,100	2,400	3,700

Dudley Watch Co., Model 2, 12 size, 19 jewels, open face, serial number 2,420.

Dudley Watch Co., Model 3, 12 size, 19 jewels, open face. NOTE: 3rd wheel bridge is rounded off at one end.

ELGIN WATCH CO.
(NATIONAL WATCH CO.)
Elgin, Illinois 1864 - 1964

Above: *B. W. Raymond*   *First wooden building in Jan. 1865.*(30X60)

This was the largest watch company in terms of production; in fact, Elgin produced half of the total number of pocket watches (dollar-type not included). Some of the organizers came from Waltham Watch Co., including P. S. Bartlett, D. G. Currier, Otis Hoyt, Charles H. Mason and others. The idea of beginning a large watch company for the mid-West was discussed by J. C. Adams, Bartlett and Blake. After a trip to Waltham, Adams went back to Chicago and approached Benjamin W. Raymond, a former mayor of Chicago, to put up the necessary capital to get the company started. Adams and Raymond succeeded in getting others to pledge their financial support. The National Watch Co. (Elgin) was formed in August 1864. The factory was completed in 1866, & the 1st. movement was a B. W. Raymond, 18 size.

Elgin 1st Movements

Movements	1st App.	1st S#	Movements	1st. App.	1st. S#
18S B. W. Raymond	April 1867	101	10S Lady Elgin	Jan. 1869	40,001
18S H. Z. Culver	July 1867	1,001	10S Frances Rubie	Aug. 1870	50,001
18S J. T. Ryerson	Oct. 1867	5,001	10S Gail Borden	Sept. 1871	185,001
18S H. H. Taylor	Nov. 1867	25,001	10S Dexter Street	Dec. 1871	201,001
18S G. M. Wheeler	Nov. 1867	6,001			
18S Matt Laflin	Jan. 1868	9,001	1st Stem Wind, H.Z.Culver June 1873		155,000
18S W.H. Ferry	No date	30,056	1st Nickel Movement	Aug.15, 1879	
18S J.V. Farwell	No date	30,296	Convertible	Fall 1878	
18S M.D. Ogden	No date	30,387	1st 16 Size watch	No date	600,001
18S Charles Fargo	No date	30,490	18 size with double roller	G# 214	8,400,001
18S Father Time	No date	2,300,001	16 size with double roller	G# 156	10,249,901
18S Overland	No date	6,653,401			
18S Veritas	No date	8,400,001			

B.W. Raymond retailed for $117.00 without case in 1867. First run of Advance, Age & Chief = 255,901- 256,000.

The first watch a **B.W. Raymond** was sold April 1, 1867, selling for about $115.00, and was a 18 size, KW and quick train serial # 101. This **First** Pocket Watch, Serial No. 101, **was once again sold for $12,000.00** in 1988 at a SALE in NEW YORK. The first stem wind model was an H. Z. Culver with serial No. 155,001, lever set and quick train made in June 1873. In 1874, the name was changed to the Elgin National Watch Co., and they produced watches into the 1950s. The first **WRIST WATCH** made by Elgin was sold in 1910.

Some Serial Nos. have the first two numbers replaced by a letter; i.e., 49,582,000 would be F 582,000.

X= 38 & 39	F= 49
C,E,T & Y= 42	S= 50
L= 43	R= 51
U= 44	P= 52
J= 45	K= 53
V= 46	I = 54
H= 47	
N= 48	

🕐 If the letters do not match the list above; the movement was produced after 1954.

Elgin National Watch Factory
ELGIN, U. S. A.

ELGIN ESTIMATED SERIAL NUMBERS AND PRODUCTION DATES

DATE – SERIAL #	DATE–SERIAL #	DATE–SERIAL #
1867 -101= April - 9,000 =Dec	1897 – 7,000,000 Oct.28th	1927 – 30,050,000
1868 — 25,001-Nov.20th	1898 – 7,494,001 May 14th	1928 – 31,599,001-Jan.11
1869 — 40,001-May 20th	1899 – 8,000,000 Jan.18th	1929 – 32,000,000
1870 — 50,001-Aug.24th	1900 – 9,000,000 Nov.14th	1930 – 32,599,001-July
1871 – 185,001-Sep. 8th	1901 – 9,300,000	1931 – 33,000,000
1872 – 201,001-Dec.20th	1902 – 9,600,000	1932 – 33,700,000
1873 – 325,001	1903 – 10,000,000 May 15th	1933 – 34,558,001-July 24th
1874 – 400,001-Aug.28th	1904 – 11,000,000 April 4th	1934 – 35,000,000
1875 – 430,000	1905 – 12,000,000 Oct.6th	1935 – 35,650,000
1876 – 480,000	1906 – 12,500,000	1936 – 36,200,000
1877 – 520,000	1907 – 13,000,000 April 4th	1937 – 36,978,001-July 24th
1878 – 570,000	1908 – 13,500,000	1938 – 37,900,000
1879 – 625,001-Feb.8th	1909 – 14,000,000 Feb.9th	1939 – 38,200,000
1880 – 750,000	1910 – 15,000,000 April 2nd	1940 – 39,100,000
1881 – 900,000	1911 – 16,000,000 July 11th	1941 – 40,200,000
1882 – 1,000,000- March,9th	1912 – 17,000,000 Nov.6th	1942 – 41,100,000
1883 – 1,250,000	1913 – 17,339,001- Apr.14th	1943 – 42,200,000
1884 – 1,500,000	1914 – 18,000,000	1944 – 42,600,000
1885 – 1,855,001-May 23rd	1915 – 18,587,001-Feb.11th	1945 – 43,200,000
1886 – 2,000,000- Aug. 4th	1916 – 19,000,000	1946 – 44,000,000
1887 – 2,500,000	1917 – 20,031,001-June 27th	1947 – 45,000,000
1888 – 3,000,000 June 20th	1918 – 21,000,000	1948 – 46,000,000
1889 – 3,500,000	1919 – 22,000,000	1949 – 47,000,000
1890 – 4,000,000 Aug.16th	1920 – 23,000,000	1950 – 48,000,000
1891 – 4,449,001-Mar.26th	1921 – 24,321,001-July 6th	1951 – 50,000,000-Sept. 7th
1892 – 4,600,000	1922 – 25,100,000	1952 – 52,000,000
1893 – 5,000,000 July 1st	1923 – 26,347,001-Dec.28th	1953 – 53,500,000
1894 – 5,500,000	1924 – 27,000,000	1954 -- 54,000,000
1895 – 6,000,000 Nov.26th	1925 – 28,421,001-July 14th	1955 – 54,500,000
1896 – 6,500,000	1926 – 29,100,000	1956 – 55,000,000

🕐The above list is provided for determining the **APPROXIMATE** age of your watch. Match serial number with date. Watches were not necessarily **SOLD** and **DELIVERED** in the exact order of manufactured or production dates.

It required several months for raw material to emerge as a finished movement. All the while the factory is producing all sizes, models and grades. The numbering system was basically *"consecutive"*, due to demand a batch of movements could be side tracked, thus allowing a different size and model to move ahead to meet this demand. Therefore, the dates some movements were <u>sold</u> and delivered to the trade, may not be *"consecutive"*.

There are 129 parts & 2,145 operations in the construction of a full-plate 18 size Elgin Watch.

NOTE: Egin starts to engrave **Adjusted to 5 Positions** about S# 15,158,001.

In 1950 the B. W. Raymond grade 571made the following three changes. First, friction jewels; second, a solid balance wheel; third, a "DuraPower" mainspring. This was also the 47th model made by the Elgin Watch Co.. This model conformed with all railroad specifications as 16 size, 21 jewels and (8) eight adjustments; the movement is lever-set has a white enamel dial & black numbers.

* * Important note most production DATES for this section of Elgin are from a photograph of a 4 1/2 foot display made by Elgin with **83 movements** and arranged in chronological order. For each production model and under each movement is a inscription listing model, size, serial number & date. Example of inscription: (18 Size, 6th Model, Number 1,855,001, Made May 23, 1885.)

Some collectors seek out low serial numbers and will usually pay a premium for them. The lower the number, the more desirable the watch. The table shown below lists the first serial number of each size watch made by Elgin.

Size	1st Serial Nos.		Size	1st Serial Nos.
18	101		10	40,001
17	356,001		6	570,001
16	600,001		0	2,889,001
14	351,001			

B.W. Raymond, 18 size, 15 jewels, model # 1, key wind & set, 1st. run in April of 1867, **serial number 101**.

Father Time, 18 size, 21 jewels, model #8 with wind indicator, free sprung model, serial number 22,888,020

18 SIZE

Grade or Name — Description	Avg	Ex-Fn	Mint
Advance, 11J, gilded, KW, FULL, HC ....★	$100	$185	$325
Age, 7J, gilded, KW, FULL, OF/HC ....★	100	185	325
Atlas Watch Co., 7J, , LS, FULL, HC (1st 7,090,001)...................	75	100	195
California Watch, 15J, gilded, KW, KS, FULL, HC......................	175	285	475
Chief, 7J, gilded, KW, FULL, HC ....★	100	225	375
Convertible, 7J= G#98, 11J=G#99, gilded, 3/4, M#6	125	175	375
Convertible, 15J=G#100, gilded, 3/4, M#6..................................	150	250	425
H.Z.Culver (Howard Z. Culver)			
H.Z.Culver, 15J, gilded, KW, KS, FULL, **ADJ**, HC, low S#	200	300	550
H.Z. Culver, 15J, gilded, KW, KS, FULL, **ADJ**, HC	150	225	400
H.Z. Culver, 15J, KW, KS, **14K, HC**	700	900	1,500
H.Z. Culver, 15J, gilded, KW, KS, FULL, HC	125	250	375
H.Z. Culver, 15J, gilded, SW, FULL, HC	70	125	225
H.Z. Culver, 15J, gilded, KW, FULL, LS, HC	100	185	300

⊕ **Generic, nameless or unmarked** grades for watch movements are listed under the Company name or initials of the Company, etc. by size, jewel count and description.

Grade or Name — Description	Avg	Ex-Fn	Mint
Elgin N. W. Co., 7J, OF, SW	$70	$100	$200
Elgin N. W. Co., 7J, KW, gilded, HC	70	100	200
Elgin N. W. Co., 11J, SW/KW, LS	70	100	200
Elgin N. W. Co., 11J, LS, SW, **HC, 9K-10K**	250	350	575
Elgin N. W. Co., 11J, LS, SW, HC, Silveroid	60	95	175
Elgin N. W. Co., 11J, LS,KW/ SW, OF	60	95	175
Elgin N. W. Co., 13J, KW/SW, PS/LS, OF	60	95	175
Elgin N. W. Co., 13J, KW/SW, PS/LS, HC	70	100	200
Elgin N. W. Co., 15J, SW, LS, OF...................................	70	100	200
Elgin N. W. Co., 15J, KW, LS, HC	125	175	300
Elgin N. W. Co., 15J, KW/SW, LS, HC	70	100	200
Elgin N. W. Co., 15J, KW, **hidden key, COIN silver case**	250	325	600

Elgin W. Co., engraved on movement California Watch, 18 size, 15 jewels, gilded, key wind & set, serial # 200,700.

Convertible, 18 size, 15 jewels, converts to either hunting or open face, Gilded, G#100, S#2,226,720.

Grade or Name — Description	Avg	Ex-Fn	Mint
Elgin N. W. Co., 15-17J, KW/SW, LS, **box–hinge YGF, HC**	$300	$400	$700
Elgin N. W. Co., 15-17J, KW/SW, LS, **box–hinge 14K, HC**	1,400	2,000	3,300
Elgin N. W. Co., 15-17, KW/SW, LS, **Multi-color box YGF, HC**	600	800	1,100
Elgin N. W. Co., 15-17J, KW/SW, **14K case, OF**	400	600	1,000
Elgin N. W. Co., 15-17J, KW/SW, **14K case, HC**	450	700	900
Elgin N. W. Co., 15-17J, KW/SW, **18K case, HC**	600	800	1,400
Elgin N. W. Co., 15-17J,KW/ SW, **Multi-color, 14K, HC**	2,000	3,000	5,200
Elgin N. W. Co., 15-17J, KW/SW, LS, **COIN Silver** 6 oz, OF	300	450	750
Elgin N. W. Co., 15-17J, KW/SW, LS, **COIN Silver**, OF	95	150	250
Elgin N. W. Co., 17J, KW/SW, LS, OF	90	135	225
Elgin N. W. Co., 17J, SW, LS or PS, HC	125	200	350
Elgin N. W. Co., 21J, SW, LS or PS, OF	200	275	550
Elgin N. W. Co., 21J, SW, LS, **box case, GF,OF**	300	375	700
Elgin N. W. Co., 21J, LS, **HC, 14K**	700	900	1,400
Elgin N. W. Co., 21J, SW, LS, Silveroid	200	275	475
Elgin N. W. Co., 21J, SW, LS, HC	300	375	625
Elgin N. W. Co., 21J, **Wind Indicator**	1,700	2,300	3,200
Elgin N. W. Co., 21J, **Wind Indicator, free sprung**	1,900	2,700	3,600
Elgin N. W. Co., 23J, SW, LS, OF	250	375	625
Elgin N. W. Co., 23J, SW, LS, HC ★	350	450	725

C.S. Moseley & G. Hunter
Micro. Regulator
Pat. Nov. 17, 1874

Above example of the *nameless* or unmarked **grades.** MARKED on movement "**Elgin W. Co. 17 jewels**", and listed under the Company name or initials (Elgin W. Co.) etc. as 18 Size, Elgin W. Co., 17J., & Description (KW, OF. etc.)

Above example of MARKED on movement "**Elgin W. Co. No. 349, 21 jewels Adjusted**", and is a 18 size movement and is listed under the 18 size, grade 349, 21J, Adj., etc.

Nameless or unmarked **grades** for watch movements which are listed under the Company name or **initials** of the Company, (Elgin W. Co.) etc. by Size, Jewel count & Description.

Pennsylvania Railroad Co. on dial. B.W. Raymond on movement. One of the first railroad watches commissioned by Penn. RR Co., 18 size, 15 jewels, key wind and set, serial number 123,245, Ca. 1871. (See foot note below)

Grade or Name — Description	Avg	Ex-Fn	Mint
Charles Fargo, 7J, gilded, KW, HC	$150	$250	$425
J. V. Farwell, 11J, gilded, KW, HC ★★	185	325	575
Father Time, 17J, NI, FULL, OF	125	200	400
Father Time, 17J, SW, OF, Silveroid	125	175	400
Father Time, 17J, SW, HC	200	285	500
Father Time, **20J**, NI, FULL, HC or OF ★	300	400	675
Father Time, 21J, NI, SW, FULL, GJS, OF	200	300	575
Father Time, 21J, NI, SW, 3/4, GJS, DMK, HC	300	400	625
Father Time, 21J, NI, SW, 3/4, GJS, OF	200	295	525
Father Time, 21J, GJT, ADJ.5P, DES, **free sprung**, OF ★	550	750	1,000
Father Time, 21J, GJT, ADJ.5P, Diamond end stone, OF	200	275	500
Father Time, 21J, NI, SW, 3/4, OF, GJS, **wind indicator**	1,800	2,000	2,600
Father Time, 21J, SW, 3/4, GJS, **wind indicator, HC** ★★★	3,000	4,000	6,200
Father Time, G# 367, 21J, SW, 3/4, GJS, military style **wind indicator**, free sprung, sterling case	4,000	5,000	7,500
Father Time, G# 367, 21J, SW, 3/4, GJS, military style **wind indicator**, free sprung, **35 size with gimbals & box**	2,000	2,600	3,700
85 size, Model# 600, 14J, **free sprung**, helical hair spring, dent escapement, **wind indicator, 85 size** with Gimbals & Box ★★	3,000	4,000	6,400
W. H. Ferry, 11J, gilded, KW, HC	95	150	225
W. H. Ferry, 15J, gilded, KW, HC	125	185	275
Mat Laflin, 7J, gilded, KW, HC	125	185	275
National W. Co., 7J, KW, KS	95	150	225
National W. Co., 11J, KW, KS	95	150	225
National W. Co., 15J, KW, KS	95	150	225
M. D. Ogden, 15J, KW, HC	125	185	275
M. D. Ogden, 11J, gilded, KW, HC	125	185	275
Order of Railway Conductors, 17J, LS, OF ★★★	1,500	2,000	3,200
Overland, 17J, NI, KW, HC	150	225	400
Overland, 17J, NI, SW, OF	150	225	400
Pennsylvania Railroad Co. on dial, B. W. Raymond on mvt., **must be ALL original,** 15J, KW, KS, (1st RR watches) ★★★	2,200	3,400	6,200

* Below from a 1870, Elgin AD: *

PENN'A R.R. Co.. Gen,l Supt.'s Office, Altoona, *Jan. 19th, 1870*.
T.M. Avery, Esq. Pres't National Watch Co., Chicago.

Dear Sir: This Company has purchased and put in the hands of its enginemen **eighty** " Raymond movements," which have given excellent satisfaction and proved to be very reliable time-keepers. In addition to these, quite a number of Elgin Watches have been purchased by officers and employees of this Company, all of whom have been well pleased with the efficiency and regularity of the movements manufactured by the National Watch Company.
Respectfully, Edward H. Williams, Gen'l Sup't.

B.W. Raymond, 18 size, 19 jewels, wind indicator. Note small winding indicator gear next to crown wheel.

H.H. Taylor, 18 size, 15 jewels, key wind & set, S# 288,797. note the S# **288797,** 88 larger than digits 2 & 797 (??)

Grade or Name — Description	Avg	Ex-Fn	Mint
Railway Timer, 15J, FULL, HC.......................................★	$400	$550	$850
B. W. Raymond, 15-17J, KW, low S# **under 200**	850	1,200	1,800
B. W. Raymond, 15-17J, KW, low S# **201 to 500**	600	750	1,300
B. W. Raymond, 15-17J, KW, low S# **501 to 1,000**	400	550	900
B. W. Raymond, 15J, gilded, KW, FULL, HC....................	150	225	350
B. W. Raymond, 15J, SW, HC.......................................	100	175	300
B. W. Raymond, 15J, **box case 14K**.............................	1,100	1,600	2,500
B. W. Raymond, 17J, gilded, KW, FULL, HC..................	150	225	350
B. W. Raymond, 17J, NI, FULL, HC.............................	165	235	400
B. W. Raymond, 17J, all G#s, NI, FULL, OF	100	175	300
B. W. Raymond, 17J, gilded, or NI, SW, FULL, **ADJ**, OF	125	185	325
B. W. Raymond, 17J, **Wind Indicator**.........................	1,400	1,700	2,200
B. W. Raymond, 19J, NI, 3/4, SW, OF, GJS, G#240, GT	200	285	425
B. W. Raymond, 19J, 3/4, GJS, **jeweled barrel, Wind Indicator**	1,300	1,600	2,100
B. W. Raymond, 19J, 3/4, GJS, GT, Diamond end stone	200	285	425
B. W. Raymond, 21J, 3/4, GJS, GT, Diamond end stone, OF	200	285	475
B. W. Raymond, 21J, SW, Silveroid.................................	150	210	300
B. W. Raymond, 21J, SW, GJS, GT, G#274, HC ....★★	350	425	750
B. W. Raymond, 21J, NI, 3/4, SW, GJS, G#389 & 390, GT, OF	225	300	500
B. W. Raymond, 21J, NI, 3/4, SW, GJS, **Wind Indicator**, DMK ..	1,500	1,900	3,000
J. T. Ryerson, 7J, gilded, FULL, KW, HC.........................	150	235	400
R.W. Searson dial, 15J., R.W. Sears Special on movement,			
(Special order by Sears prior to Sears, Roebuck & Co.). ★★	225	300	525
Solar W. Co., 15J, **Multi-color dial**	165	250	475
Standard, 17J, OF, LS..	125	185	300
Sundial, 7J, SW, PS (1st 7,080,001)	75	110	250
H. H. Taylor, 15J, gilded, FULL, KW, HC	95	155	275
H. H. Taylor, 15J, NI, FULL, KW, DMK, HC.................	95	155	275
H. H. Taylor, 15J, NI, FULL, **SW**, HC, DMK, quick train	125	200	350
H. H. Taylor, 15J, SW, Silveroid	85	145	200
H. H. Taylor, 15J, SW, slow train................................	85	145	200

IMPORTANT NOTE: Railroad Standards, Railroad Approved & Railroad Grade **terminology,** as defined and used in this ***BOOK***.
1. **RAILROAD STANDARDS** = A commission or board appointed by the railroad companies outlined a set of **guidelines** to be accepted or approved by each railroad line.
2. **RAILROAD APPROVED** = A ***LIST*** of watches each railroad line would approve if purchased by their employee's. (this list changed through the years).
3. **RAILROAD GRADE** = A watch made by manufactures to meet or exceed the guidelines set by the railroad **standards.** Grades such as 992, Vanguard and B.W. Raymond, etc.
* Some GRADES **exceeded** the R.R. standards such as 23 jewels, diamond end stone, gold train, raised gold jewel settings, double sunk dial and the list goes on. Examples: such as Veritas, Sangamo, 950 & Riverside Maximus and many others.

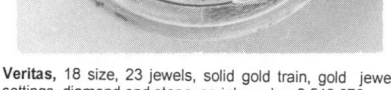

Veritas, 18 size, 23 jewels, solid gold train, gold jewel settings, diamond end stone, serial number 9,542,678.

G.M. Wheeler, Grade 369, 18 size, 17 jewels, open face, gold jewel settings, serial number 14,788,315

The word VERITAS translated is "TRUTH".

Grade or Name — Description	Avg	Ex-Fn	Mint
Veritas, 21J, 3/4, NI, GJS, DMK, GT, G#239, OF	$265	$350	$600
Veritas, 21J, 3/4, GJS, GT, Diamond end stones	285	350	625
Veritas, 21J, SW, PS, GJS, GT, HC	300	375	675
Veritas, 21J, SW, LS, GJS, GT, HC	300	375	675
Veritas, 21J, 3/4, GJS, GT, Diamond end stones, G#274, HC	325	400	700
Veritas, 21J, 3/4, NI, GJS, Wind Indicator, DMK, G#239, OF	1,900	2,400	3,200
Veritas, 21J, 3/4, NI, GJS, Wind Indicator, DMK, G#274,HC★★	3,500	4,500	7,000
Veritas, 23J, 3/4, NI, GJS, OF, DMK, GT	350	475	800
Veritas, 23J, 3/4, NI, GJS, OF, DMK, GT, Diamond end stone	350	475	800
Veritas, 23J, G#214, 3/4, NI, GJS, Wind Indicator, OF	1,900	2,400	3,200
Veritas, 23J, G#494, Wind Indicator, "Free Sprung", OF.. ★★★	2,500	3,000	4,200
Veritas, 23J, G#214, SW, OF	350	475	800
Veritas, 23J, 3/4, SW, NI, GJS, GT, LS, HC ★★★	500	650	1,000
Veritas, 23J, SW, OF, 14K	650	875	1,300
Wabash, 21J, G # 349, Adj.5P, LS, OF ★	300	500	900
G. M. Wheeler, 11J, gilded, KW, HC	85	135	200
G. M. Wheeler, 13-15J, gilded, FULL, KW, SW	85	135	200
G. M. Wheeler, 15J, NI, FULL, KW, DMK, HC	100	150	250
G. M. Wheeler, 15J, SW, NI, FULL, DMK, OF	85	135	200
G. M. Wheeler, 17J, KW, NI, FULL, DMK, OF	100	150	250
G. M. Wheeler, 17J, SW, NI, DMK, OF	85	135	200

MOVEMENTS WITH NO NAME

Grade or Name — Description	Avg	Ex-Fn	Mint
No. 5 & No. 17, 7J, gilded, FULL, HC	$75	$125	$200
No. 23 & No. 18, 11J, gilded, FULL, HC	85	135	200
No. 69, 15J, M#1, KW, quick train, HC	85	135	200
No. 150, 20-21J, full plate, GJS, LS	200	250	475
No. 155, 17J, GJS, Adj.5P, HC	125	195	285
No. 274, 21J., marked 274, GT, Adj.5p, diamond end stone	250	375	625
No. 316, 15J, NI, FULL, DMK, HC	85	135	200
No. 317, 15J, NI, FULL, ADJ, DMK, OF	85	135	200

Ⓛ Generic, nameless or unmarked grades for watch movements are listed under the Company name or initials of the Company, etc. by size, jewel count and description.

Ⓛ Watches listed in this book are priced at the collectable Trade Show level, as complete watches having an original 14k gold-filled case and Key Wind with silver, an original white enamel single sunk dial, and with the entire original movement in good working order with no repairs needed.

🕐 Generic, nameless or unmarked grades for watch movements are listed under the Company name or initials of the Company, etc. by size, jewel count and description.

Grade or Name — Description	Avg	Ex-Fn	Mint
No. 326, 15J, OF	$85	$125	$200
No. 327, 15J, HC	100	135	250
No. 331, **16J**, M# 11, NI, OF ★	125	150	265
No. 335, 17J, HC	110	135	250
No. 336, 17J, NI, FULL, DMK, OF	85	125	200
No. 348, 21J, NI, FULL, GJS, DMK, HC	300	435	625
No. 349, 21J, , LS, OF	250	300	450
No. 349, 21J, , LS, **MARKED LOANER**, OF ★	350	475	750
No. 378, 17-19J, NI, FULL, DMK, HC	125	185	325
No. 379, 17-19J, OF	125	185	300
No. 411, 21J, PS, **2-tone**, NI, OF ★★★	375	500	900

Elgin Watch Co., Leader, 17 size, 11 jewels, made for English market, serial number 418,220.

Elgin Watch Co., 17 size, 7 jewels, key wind & set, serial number 499,076. Made for Kennedy & Co.

17 SIZE

Grade or Name — Description	Avg	Ex-Fn	Mint
Avery, 7J, gilded, KW, FULL, HC (1st 400,001)	$95	$185	$300
Inter-Ocean, 7J, KWKS, HC ★★★	400	550	950
Leader, 7J, gilded, KW, FULL, HC (1st 356,001)	85	150	250
Leader, 11J, gilded, KW, FULL, HC,	75	125	250
Sunshine, 15J, M# 1, **KW & KS from back** ★	150	200	275
grade11, 14, 15, 51, 59, 7J, gilded, KW, FULL, HC	95	135	250
17 Size, KW, Silveroid	65	95	185

Note model # 1, 17 size is key-wind key-set both from the back.

16 SIZE

Grade or Name — Description	Avg	Ex-Fn	Mint
Braille or Blind Man's Watch, 9-17J, HC	$125	$175	$350
Convertible Model, 7J=G#47 & 11J=G#93, 13J=G#48, 3/4, gilded	75	110	210
Convertible Model, 13J=G#90, 3F BRG	125	175	275
Convertible Model, 15J=G#49, 3/4, gilded	100	175	275
Convertible Model, 15J=G#50, 3/4, NI, ADJ,	125	185	295
Convertible Model, 15J=G#50, 3/4, NI, ADJ, **14K, HC**	900	1,000	1,600
Convertible Model, 15J=G#85, 3F BRG, gilded	175	225	375
Convertible Model, 15J=G#86, 3F BRG, NI	175	225	375
Convertible Model, 21J=G#72, 3/4, NI, ADJ, GJS ★★	1,500	2,000	3,200
Convertible Model, 21J=G#72, 3/4, NI, ADJ, GJS, **14K** ★★★	2,200	2,800	4,000
Convertible Model, 21J=G#91, 3F BRG, NI ★★★	1,600	2,000	3,200
Convertible Model, 21J, G#91, 3F BRG,NI, **14K** ★★★	2,200	2,800	4,000

NOTE: **Convertible** = Same **movement** can be changed to either a hunting or open face case.

🕐 A collector should expect to pay modestly higher prices at local shops.

Elgin Watch Co., 16 size, 21J, 3/4, Convertible Model GRADE # 72, S#607,061. Convertible movement s= Can be converted to a hunting or open face case.

Elgin W. Co., Convertible Model, 16 size, 15 jewels, three-fingered bridge model, G # 86, adjusted, S # 4,907,178. Convertible = Can be converted to a HC or OF case.

Grade or Name — Description	Avg	Ex-Fn	Mint
Doctors Watch, 13J, 4th Model, NI, GT, sweep second hand, G#89 gilded, GF	$300	$475	$800
Doctors Watch, 15J, 4th Model, NI, GT, sweep second hand, G# 83 gilded & G#84 nickel, GF case	300	475	800
Doctors Watch, 15J, 4th Model, gilded, sweep second hand, coin silver case	350	500	850
Doctors Watch, 15J, 4th Model, sweep second hand, **14K, OF**	900	1,000	1,900
Elgin N. W. Co., Locomotive + **diamond** on lantern on case, **multi-color gold, 14K HC**	2,500	3,500	5,500

Elgin Watch Co., 16 size, Multi- Color Gold hunting case, the locomotive has a diamond in the lantern, the case has white, yellow, rose flowers & green leaf designs, Ca.1880.

Doctors Watch, 16 size, 15 jewels, fourth model, gold jewel settings, gold train, sweep second hand, serial number 926,458.

🕐 **The Complete Price Guide to Watches goal is to stimulate the orderly exchange of <u>Watches</u> between "*buyers*" and "*sellers*".**

🕐 **Generic, nameless or unmarked** grades for watch movements are listed under the Company name or initials of the Company, etc. by size, jewel count and description.

Grade or Name — Description	Avg	Ex-Fn	Mint
Elgin N. W. Co., 7-9J, OF	$40	$75	$150
Elgin N. W. Co., 7-9J, HC	40	75	175
Elgin N. W. Co., 11J, OF	40	75	150
Elgin N. W. Co., 11J, HC	60	100	180
Elgin N. W. Co., 13J, OF	40	75	150
Elgin N. W. Co., 13J, OF, Silveroid	40	75	150
Elgin N. W. Co., 13J, HC	65	100	175
Elgin N. W. Co., 15J, HC	75	135	200
Elgin N. W. Co., 15J, OF	65	100	150
Elgin N. W. Co., 15J, OF **14K case**	350	475	750
Elgin N. W. Co., 15J, HC, **14K**	450	600	950
Elgin N. W. Co., 15J, **multi-color gold +diamond, HC, 14K**	1,700	2,300	4,000
Elgin N. W. Co., 16J, OF	85	150	225
Elgin N. W. Co., 16J, **Chronograph,** M # 4, LS, OF ★★★★★	3,000	4,000	6,500
Elgin N. W. Co., 17J, OF	75	125	200
Elgin N. W. Co., 17J, LS, **multi-color HC, YGF**	250	350	675
Elgin N. W. Co., 17J, **multi-color HC, 14K**	1,000	1,500	2,600
Elgin N. W. Co., 17J, **14K, HC**	400	500	900
Elgin N. W. Co., 17J, HC	95	175	300
Elgin N. W. Co., 19J, OF	100	185	310
Elgin N. W. Co., 21J, HC	175	300	500
Elgin N. W. Co., 21J, OF, **Silveroid**	95	175	300
Elgin N. W. Co., 21J, OF	150	225	375
Elgin N. W. Co., 23J, OF	250	335	550
3F Bridge Model, 15J, NI, DMK,, OF	95	185	300
3F Bridge Model, 15J, NI, DMK, HC	150	225	350
3F Bridge Model, 17J, NI, DMK, OF	95	165	295
3F Bridge Model, 17J, Adj., NI, DMK, GJS, HC ★★	200	275	475
3F Bridge Model, 17J, **Adj.5P,** NI, DMK, GJS, GT, OF ★★★	300	400	600
3F Bridge Model, 21J, Adj.5P, NI, DMK, GJS, GT, OF	550	700	900
3F Bridge Model, 21J, Adj.5P, NI, DMK, GJS, GT, **18K**	1,300	1,800	2,800
Father Time, 21J, 3/4, NI, GJS, DR, DMK, ADJ.5P, HC	225	300	500
Father Time, 21J, 3/4, NI, GJS, DR, **Wind Indicator,** OF	900	1,100	1,600
Father Time, 21J, 3/4, NI, GJS, DR, **pendant set,** ADJ.5P, OF ★	200	275	500
Father Time, 21J, NI, GJS, DR, ADJ.5P, GT, OF	200	275	500
Lord Elgin, 21J, GJS, DR, Adj.5P, 3F BRG, **14K, OF** ★★	1,600	2,000	2,600
Lord Elgin, 21J, GJS, DR, Adj.5P, 3F BRG, **14K, HC** ★★	1,900	2,200	3,000
Lord Elgin, 23J, GJS, DR, Adj.5P, 3/4, **14K, OF** ★★	1,900	2,200	3,000
Lord Elgin, 23J, GJS, DR, Adj.5P, 3/4, Gold filled OF ★★	1,200	1,500	2,000

ELGIN W. Co., Chronograph, 16 size, 16 jewels, model # 4, lever set. (Very rare may one of a **Kind**)

Father Time, 16 size, 21 jewels, gold train; Note model 19 up and down wind indicator movement does not show the differential wheel as does the 18 size, S# 18,106,465.

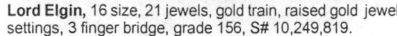

Lord Elgin, 16 size, 21 jewels, gold train, raised gold jewel settings, 3 finger bridge, grade 156, S# 10,249,819.

B.W. Raymond, 16 size, 19 jewels, gold jewel settings, Grade 350, serial number 17,822,991.

Grade or Name — Description	Avg	Ex-Fn	Mint
B. W. Raymond, 17J, 3/4, GJS, **14K, OF**	$400	$550	$900
B. W. Raymond, 17J, 3/4, GJS, SW, HC	200	335	500
B. W. Raymond, 17J, 3F BRG ★★	400	550	800
B. W. Raymond, 17J, LS, NI, **Wind Indicator** ★★	900	1,100	1,600
B. W. Raymond, 17J, GJS, SW, Adj., ALL G#s, OF	150	225	350
B. W. Raymond, 17J, 3/4, GJS, DR, Adj.5P, DMK	150	225	350
B. W. Raymond, 19J, 3/4, GJS, DR, Adj.5P, DMK, OF	175	265	400
B. W. Raymond, 19J, (Elgin **The Railroader** on dial) Adj.5P, OF	400	575	950
B. W. Raymond, 19J, OF, **14K, 30 DWT**	400	600	950
B. W. Raymond, 19J, 3/4, GJS, DR, Adj.5P, DMK, **Wind Indicator**	800	1,000	1,300
B. W. Raymond, 19J, M#8, G# 372, 455, Adj.5P, OF	175	225	400
B. W. Raymond, 19J, GJS, G#371, 401,Adj.5P, HC	200	275	450
B. W. Raymond, 21J, **14K, OF**	450	600	900
B. W. Raymond, 21J, G#472, 478, 506, 571, 581, 590, Adj.5P, OF	200	275	450
B. W. Raymond, 21J, 3/4, GJS, DR, Adj.5P, HC	300	400	600
B. W. Raymond, 21J, G# 391, 3/4, GJS, DR, Adj.5P, DMK, OF	200	275	450
B. W. Raymond, 21J, **gold flashed movement**, OF	275	375	500
B. W. Raymond, 21J, 3/4, GJS, DR, Adj.5P, DMK,**Wind Indicator**	800	950	1,400
B. W. Raymond, 21J, 3/4, GJS, DR, **Adj.6P**, DMK,**Wind Indicator**	800	950	1,400
B. W. Raymond, 22J, WWII Model, sweep second hand	250	400	550
B. W. Raymond, 23J, 3/4, GJS, DR, Adj.5P, G#376, 494, 540	350	475	650
B. W. Raymond, 23J, 3/4, GJS, DR, Adj.5P, DMK, **Wind Indicator**	1,100	1,500	2,200
B. W. Raymond, 23J, 3/4, GJS, DR, **Adj.6P**, DMK, **Wind Indicator**	1,100	1,500	2,200
B. W. Raymond, 23J, 3/4, GJS, DR, Adj.5P, DMK,**Wind Indicator** military style	1,000	1,400	2,000

Veritas, 16 size, 23 jewels, (Veritas = "TRUTH"), solid gold train, gold jeweled settings, S # 16,678,681.

Elgin Watch Co., LORD ELGIN, Grade 351, 16 size, 23 J., gold train, gold jewel settings, S # 12,718,340. NOTE: This watch came from the first run of **G # 351**, 23J. Lord Elgins.

Grade or Name — Description	Avg	Ex-Fn	Mint
Veritas, 19J, G# 401, GJS, Adj. 5P., HC ....★	$400	$575	$800
Veritas, 21J, GJS, DR, Adj.5P, DMK, 3/4, **Wind Indicator**	1,400	1,800	2,500
Veritas, 21J, 3F brg, GJS, G#360..............................★	375	450	725
Veritas, 21J, GJS, DR, Adj.5P, DMK, 3/4, G#401, HC..................	425	525	825
Veritas, 21J, GJS, SW, Grade 360 ....★	375	450	725
Veritas, 21J, GJS, SW, Adj.5P, OF, Grade 270 & 375	300	425	675
Veritas, 23J, GJS, Adj.5P, **14K, OF**	600	775	1,100
Veritas, 23J, GJS, Adj.5P, **HC**	500	600	900
Veritas, 23J, GJS, DR, Adj.5P, 3/4, G# 375- 376- 453, OF...........	375	450	700
Veritas, 23J, GJS, DR, Adj.5P, DMK, 3/4, Diamond end stone, Grade 350 ....★	375	450	725
Veritas, 23J, GJS, DR, Adj.5P, Grade 453 & 376 DMK, 3/4, **Wind Indicator**	1,500	2,000	3,000
G. M. Wheeler, 17J, DR, Adj.3P, DMK, 3/4................................	65	100	200
G. M. Wheeler, 17J, 3F BRG	80	150	250
G. M. Wheeler, 17J, **HC, 14K**	350	500	800
WWII Model, 17J, OF...	100	175	300
WWII Model, 21J, OF...	175	275	450
M#13, 9J, HC...	65	110	200
M#48, 13J, HC..	65	110	200

(Add $50 to $75 to hunting case models listed as open face)

MODELS WITH NO NAMES

Grade or Name — Description	Avg	Ex-Fn	Mint
Grade #155-160, 17J, GT, GJS, HC..............................	$100	$175	$250
Grade #156, 21J, 3/4, NI, DR, DMK, GT, GJS, HC .... ★	350	475	700
Grade #156, 21J, 3/4, NI, DR, DMK, GT, GJS, HC, **14K** .... ★	600	800	1,100
Grade #161, **17J**, SW, PS, NI, GJS, GT, OF .... ★★	300	450	700
Grade #162, 21J, SW, PS, NI, GJS, GT, OF	225	300	450
Grade #270, 21J, 3F BRG, GJS, **marked** 270 on mvt.	275	350	525
Grade #280, 17J, 3F BRG, **marked** 280 on mvt, OF.....................	175	245	425
Grade #290 HC& #291 , **7J**, 3/4, NI, DMK, OF	65	95	150

A watch marked as **5 positions** is <u>equivalent</u> to one marked *eight adjustments* (the most common found on RR watches) and will be listed in this book as: **"Adj.5P"** (adjusted to heat,cold, isochronism and 5 positions). A watch marked as **nine adjustments** is <u>equivalent</u> to one marked *6 positions* & listed as **"Adj.6P"** (adjusted to heat,cold, isochronism and <u>6 positions</u>). A watch that is marked as *ADJUSTED* only is adjusted to isochronism & in poise in all temperatures & is listed as **"Adj."**.
  * Later some manufactures used a variations of **8 adjustments, six to position, 1-isochronism, 1-temperature** or as in the Elgin grade 571 two to temperature in about 1950.

Grade or Name — Description	Avg	Ex-Fn	Mint
Grade #291, 7J, 3/4, HC, **14K**	$300	$450	$650
Grade #312 & #313, 15J, 3/4, NI, DR, DMK, OF	75	100	200
Grade # 340, 17J, 3 finger bridge, OF	75	100	200
Grade #372, 19J, M#15, LS, OF, Adj.5P	200	250	350
Grade #374, 21J, M#15, LS, OF, Adj.5P	250	335	450
Grade #381 & #382, 17J, 3/4, NI, DR, DMK, OF	100	165	300
Grade#401, 19J, M#17, LS, HC	200	275	425
Grade #540, **23J**, Adj.5P, OF	275	385	550
Grade #572, 19J, Adj.5P, OF	135	225	350
Grade #573, 17J, Adj.5P, OF	125	175	275
Grade #575, 15J, Adj.3P, OF	100	150	250
Grade #581, 21J, Adj.5P, **center sec, hacking, Army,** OF	200	275	400
Grade # 845, 23J, Adj., (by **Buren** W. Co.) **Swiss**	65	90	175

14 SIZE

Grade or Name — Description	Avg	Ex-Fn	Mint
Lord Elgin, 15J, G# 357, OF	$65	$95	$175
Lord Elgin, 17J, G# 358-359 OF	70	100	200
7J, M#1, gilded, KW, **14K, HC**	250	350	575
7J, M#1, gilded, KW, YGF, HC	40	70	125
11J, M#1, gilded, KW, YGF, HC	40	70	125
11J, M#1, gilded, KW, YGF, OF	40	70	125
13J, M#1, gilded, KW, OF	40	70	125
15J, M#1, gilded, KW, OF	40	70	125
7J, M#2, SW, OF	40	70	125
15J, M#2, SW, OF	40	70	125
15J, M#2, SW, **14K, HC**	200	285	450
15J, M#1, grade # 46, KW, 3/4, HC	75	100	200

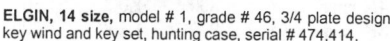

ELGIN, **14 size,** model # 1, grade # 46, 3/4 plate design, key wind and key set, hunting case, serial # 474,414.

ELGIN EIGHT DAY, **12 size,** 21 jewels, wind indicator, bridge movement, open face, serial number 12,345,678.

12 SIZE

Grade or Name — Description		Avg	Ex -Fn	Mint
Eight Day, 21J, 8-Day Wind Indicator, BRG	★ ★ ★ ★ ★	$2,700	$3,300	$5,500
24 hour dial in one revolution	★	900	1,200	2,200
Elgin N. W. Co., Aux. dial for date of month & day of week	★	900	1,200	2,200

🕑 Generic, nameless or unmarked grades for watch movements are listed under the Company name or initials of the Company, etc. by size, jewel count and description.

C. H. Hulburd, 19J, thin BRG model (12 /14 size), 8 Adj. Ca. 1920-1925. Advertised as **ALL** in a **Unique case**. Mr. Charles H. Hulburd became president of Elgin in 1898.

ELGIN W. Co., 12 size, G# 190, 23J, GJS, Adj.5P, NI, DMK, GT, M# 2, <u>Mustache lever</u>, HC, (**Hi-grade**) S# 7412238. Note the illustration of counterpoised <u>Mustache lever</u>.

Grade or Name — Description	Avg	Ex-Fn	Mint
Elgin N. W. Co. # 30, 7J, gilded, **KW**, OF	$85	$145	$250
Elgin N. W. Co. # 89, 19J, HC	75	110	200
Elgin N. W. Co. # 190, 23J, GJS, Adj.5P, NI, DMK, GT, M# 2, *(Hi-grade)* **Mustache or Standard lever, Gold Filled, HC**	225	300	500
Elgin N. W. Co. # 190, 23J, GJS, Adj.5P, NI, DMK, GT, M# 2, *(Hi-grade)* **Mustache lever, 18K, HC** ★	1,200	1,400	1,700
Elgin N. W. Co. # 194, 23J, GJS, Adj.5P, NI, DMK, GT, OF	175	225	350
Elgin N. W. Co. # 236, 21J, GJS, Adj.5P, NI, DMK, GT, HC ★	150	200	275
Elgin N. W. Co. # 237 or 273, 21J, GJS, Adj.5P, NI, GT, OF ★	125	175	250
Elgin N. W. Co. # 301 7J, HC	50	85	150
Elgin N. W. Co. # 314, 15J, HC	90	145	250
Elgin N. W. Co. # 384, 17J, OF	60	95	175
Elgin N. W. Co., 7-15J, **14K, Multi-color**	1,000	1,200	1,600
Elgin N. W. Co., 7-15J, OF, GF	60	85	150
Elgin N. W. Co., 7-15J, **HC, 14K**	250	350	575
Elgin N. W. Co., 17J, OF,GF	60	95	175
Elgin N. W. Co., 19J, OF, gold filled	75	110	200
Elgin N. W. Co., 19J, HC, gold filled	75	110	200
Elgin N. W. Co., 19J, **HC, 14K**	250	350	625
Elgin N. W. Co., 19J, **14K, OF**	175	275	475
Elgin N. W. Co., 21J, OF, gold filled case	100	185	310
12 size movements, Model 2 & 3 were spread or made to fit a "16 size CASE"			
Elgin N. W. Co., 15-17J, Model 3, 12 size **spread** to 16 size, OF ..	$75	$100	$150
Elgin N. W. Co., 15-17J, Model 2, 12 size **spread** to 16 size, HC..	85	125	200
Elgin N. W. Co., 19-21J, Model 3, 12 size **spread** to 16 size, OF ..	85	125	200
Elgin N. W. Co., 19-21J, Model 2, 12 size **spread** to 16 size, HC..	100	175	250
STANDARD 12 SIZE (continued)			
Elete, 17J, GJS, Adj.4P, OF	$40	$75	$135
C. H. Hulburd, 19J, thin BRG model (12 /14 size) **14K case** ★	800	1,000	1,500
C. H. Hulburd, 19J, thin BRG model (12 /14 size) **18K case** ★	900	1,200	1,700
C. H. Hulburd, 19J, thin BRG model (12 /14 size) **Platinum** ★	1,300	1,600	2,100
Lord Elgin, 17J, OF	60	95	150
Lord Elgin, 17, HC	75	110	200
Lord Elgin ,19 , ADJ, OF	75	110	200
Lord Elgin, 19J, ADJ, HC	125	185	250
Lord Elgin, 21, GJS, DR, Adj.5P, DMK, NI, OF	125	185	250
Lord Elgin, 21J,GJS, DR, Adj.5P, DMK, NI, **14K, OF**	200	285	500
Lord Elgin, 21J, GJS, DR, Adj.5P, DMK, NI, HC	150	200	350
Lord Elgin ,23, G# 194, GJS, DR, Adj.5P, DMK, NI, OF ★ ★ ★	150	200	350
Lord Elgin, 23J,G# 190, GJS, DR, Adj.5P, DMK, NI, HC.. ★ ★ ★	225	300	400
Lord Elgin, 23J, GJS, DR, Adj.5P, DMK, NI, **14K,** HC ★ ★ ★	300	450	650

Lord Elgin, 12 size, 23 jewels, gold jewel settings, Adj.5p, originally sold for $110.00.

G.M. Wheeler, 12 size, 17 jewels, Adj3p, originally sold for $27.00.

Grade or Name — Description	Avg	Ex-Fn	Mint
Masonic dial, 15-17J, (**with original Masonic dial**), OF	$200	$275	$500
Pierce Arrow, 17J, (**with original dial**), OF	325	450	850
B. W. Raymond, 19J, G# 189, GJS, Adj.5P, DR, DMK, NI, HC	80	135	275
B. W. Raymond, 19J, G# 193, GJS, Adj.5P, DR, DMK, NI, OF	50	75	200
B. W. Raymond, 19J, G# 448, GJS, Adj.5P, DR, DMK, NI, OF	50	75	200
Transit, 17J., **2 tone**, OF..	80	135	275
G. M. Wheeler, 17J, DR, Adj.5P, DMK, NI, OF	30	50	125
G. M. Wheeler, 17J, DR, Adj.5P, DMK, NI, HC	40	70	150

Frances Rubie, Grade 23, 10 size, 15 jewels, key wind & set.

Gail Borden, Grade 22, 10 size, 11 jewels, key wind & set, serial number 947,696.

10 SIZE
(HC)

Grade or Name — Description	Avg	Ex-Fn	Mint
Elgin, **multi-color case, gold filled**, HC	$225	$350	$550
Elgin, 15J, Silveroid, HC...	40	60	100
Elgin, 15J, YGF, HC...	65	85	150
Dexter St., 7J, KW, HC, **14K**...	225	350	525
Dexter St., 7J, KW, HC, **18K**...	250	385	625
Dexter St., 7J, gilded, KW, HC, gold filled	75	95	150
Frances Rubie, 15J, gilded, KW, HC, **14K**...............................★	500	635	825
Frances Rubie, 15J, KW, HC, **18K**.. ★★	600	750	950

🕐 Watches listed in this book are priced at the collectable Trade Show level, as **complete** watches having an original 14k gold-filled case and *Key Wind* with silver, an original white enamel single sunk dial, and with the entire original movement in good working order with no repairs needed.

Grade or Name — Description	Avg	Ex-Fn	Mint
Gail Borden, 11J, gilded, KW, HC, **14K**	$225	$350	$575
Gail Borden, 11J, KW, HC, gold filled	65	100	150
Gail Borden, 11J, KW, HC, **18K**	300	400	675
Lady Elgin, 15J, gilded, KW, HC, **14K**	225	300	525
Lady Elgin, 15J, KW, HC, **18K**	300	400	675
Grade # 21 or 28, 7J, gilded, KW, HC, gold filled	65	100	175

Elgin W. Co., Grade 121, 6 size, 15 jewels, hunting, serial number 4,500,445.

Elgin W. Co., 6 size, ENGRAVED movement, enamel & gold case, fancy dial, G# 94, S# 1,886,804.

6 SIZE
(HC Only)

Grade or Name — Description	Avg	Ex-Fn	Mint
Atlas, 7J, HC	$40	$65	$150
Elgin N. W. Co. #286, 7J, HC, DMK, NI	40	65	150
Elgin N. W. Co. #295, 15J, HC, DMK, NI	40	65	150
Elgin N. W. Co. #168, **16J**, nickel, HC	100	165	275
Elgin N. W. Co., 7J, HC, **14K**	150	250	450
Elgin N. W. Co., 11J, HC, **14K**	150	250	450
Elgin N. W. Co., ENGRAVED movement, **enamel & gold case, fancy dial, G# 94, 14K** HC	700	900	1,400
Elgin N. W. Co., 15J, YGF, HC	60	85	175
Elgin N. W. Co., 15J, YGF demi-HC	60	85	175
Elgin N. W. Co., 15J, HC, **YGF** multi-color case	200	250	575
Elgin N. W. Co., 15J, HC, **10K**	175	250	400
Elgin N. W. Co., 15J, HC, **14K**	225	285	475
Elgin N. W. Co., 15J, **14K, Multi-color HC**	500	700	1,200
Elgin N. W. Co., 15J, HC, **18K**	400	500	675
Elgin N. W. Co., 15J, SW, HC, **Enamel case, 18K**	500	800	1,300
Elgin N. W. Co., **16J**, G# 230, gilded or nickel, HC	95	135	265

🕐 A collector should expect to pay modestly higher prices at local shops.

🕐 **Generic, nameless or unmarked** grades for watch movements are listed under the Company name or initials of the Company, etc. by size, jewel count and description.

🕐 Pricing in this Guide are fair market price for COMPLETE watches which are reflected from the **"NAWCC"** National and regional shows.

Elgin W. Co., 6 size, 15 jewels

Elgin W. Co., Grade 201-HC, 205-OF, 0 size, 19 jewels, gold train.

0 SIZE

Lady Raymond, 5/0 size. 15J.

Grade or Name — Description	Avg	Ex-Fn	Mint
Atlas W. Co., 7J, HC	$40	$100	$200
Elgin N. W. Co., 7J, NI, DR, DMK, OF	35	55	150
Elgin N. W. Co., 15J, NI, DR, DMK, OF	35	55	150
Elgin N. W. Co., 15J, NI, DR, DMK, HC	50	90	225
Elgin N. W. Co., 17J, NI, DR, DMK, ADJ, OF	50	90	175
Elgin N. W. Co., 19J, NI, DR, DMK, GJS, ADJ, OF	35	55	150
Elgin N. W. Co., 15J, OF, **14K**	150	250	450
Elgin N. W. Co., 15J, HC, **14K**	200	275	550
Elgin N. W. Co., 15J, HC, **multi-color GF**	150	250	400
Elgin N. W. Co., 15J, OF, **multi-color dial**	150	250	400
Elgin N. W. Co., 15J, HC, **10K**	150	200	300
Elgin N. W. Co., 15J, **14K, Multi-color case**	375	500	900
Elgin N. W. Co., 15J, **14K, Multi-color case + diamond**	500	700	1,100
Frances Rubie, 19J, HC ★★	250	375	625

3/0 and 5/0 SIZE (HC ONLY)

Grade or Name — Description	Avg	Ex-Fn	Mint
Lady Elgin, 15J, PS, HC	$40	$75	$175
Lady Elgin, 15J, **14K**, HC	135	250	425
Lady Raymond, 15J, PS, HC	40	75	175
Elgin N. W. Co., 7J, HC	40	55	125

Style: 3056
Center: Ca. 1950s Diamond Bar Bezel
gold filled: $90 - $125 - $225
DIAL: $30 - $50 - $95

Ca. 1950s Plain Bezel
gold filled: $90 - $125 - $195
DIAL: $30 - $50 - $95

Style: 3055 - Streamline
Ca. 1950s **Tear Drop** Plain Bezel
gold filled: $90 - $125 - $225
DIAL: $30 - $50 - $95
Above Right: **Tear Drop** bezel came with a Diamond Bar Bezel.

STYLE NO. 40
gold filled : $90 - $125 - $300
DIAL: $20 - $30 - $50

STYLE NO. 39, Ca.1923
gold filled : $95- $110 - $275
DIAL: $20 - $30 - $50

STYLE NO. 38
gold filled : $95- $110 - $265
DIAL: $ 20 - $30 - $50

STYLE NO. 19
gold filled : $95 - $125 - $300
wind-ind.-DIAL: $40 - $80 - $225

STYLE NO. 18
CHROME: $25 - $40 - $90
DIAL: $15 - $20 - $40

STYLE NO. 25
gold filled : $95- $125 - $275
wind-ind.-DIAL: $40 - $80 - $225

STYLE NO. 26
gold filled : $90 - $125 - $200
wind-ind.-DIAL: $40 - $80 - $225

ANTIQUE BOW
gold filled : $95- $125 - $250
DIAL: $30 - $50 - $95

RIGID BOW
gold filled : $95- $125 - $290
DIAL: $30 - $40 - $60

🕐 NOTE: Factory Advertised as a **complete** watch and was fitted with a certain matched, timed and rated movement and sold in the factory designed case style as a **complete** watch. The factory also sold *uncased* movements to **JOBBERS** such as Jewelry stores & they cased the movement in a case style the **CUSTOMER requested.** All the factory advertised **complete** watches came with a enamel dial **SHOWN or CHOICE** of other **Railroad** dials.

ELGIN NATIONAL WATCH CO.

GRADES OF MOVEMENTS
WITH
CLASSIFICATION AND DESCRIPTION
AS ORIGINALLY MADE

Grade.	Class.	Size.		Style.		Model.	Sett.	Train.	Jewels.
Advance	5	18	F. Pl.	Htg.	Gilded	1st to 4th	Key or Lever	Slow	11
Age	5	"	"	"	"	"	"	"	7
Avery	15	17	"	"	"	1st	Key	"	7
Chief	5	18	"	"	"	1st to 4th	Key or Lever	"	7
Culver	2	"	"	"	"	"	"	Quick	15
Dexter St	48	10	¾ Pl.	"	"	1st	Key	"	7
Father Time	1	18	F. Pl.	"	Nickel	2d to 4th	Lever	"	20-21
Father Time	1	"	"	"	"	"	"	"	17
Father Time	7	"	"	O. F.	"	5th	Pend.	"	20-21
Father Time	7	"	"	"	"	"	"	"	17
Father Time	65	"	"	"	"	7th	Lever	"	17-21
Father Time	90	"	¾ Pl.	"	"	8th	"	"	21
Father Time	99	"	"	Htg.	"	9th	"	"	21
Father Time	134	"	"	O. F.	"	8th	"	"	21
Father Time	98	16	"	"	"	15th	"	"	21
Father Time	126	"	"	Htg.	"	14th	"	"	21
Father Time	126	"	"	"	"	17th	"	"	21
Fargo	5	18	F. Pl.	"	Gilded	1st	Key	Slow	7
Farwell	5	"	"	"	"	"	"	"	11
Ferry	4	"	"	"	"	"	"	"	15
Frances Rubie	46	10	¾ Pl.	"	"	"	"	Quick	15
Frances Rubie	76	0	"	"	Nickel	2d	Pend.	"	19
Frances Rubie	80	"	"	O. F.	"	3d	"	"	19
Gail Borden	48	10	"	Htg.	Gilded	1st	Key	"	11
Lady Elgin	47	"	"	"	"	"	"	"	15
Lady Elgin	133	5/0	"	"	Nickel	"	Pend.	"	15
Lady Elgin	96	10/0	"	O. F.	"	"	"	"	17
Lady Elgin	97	"	"	"	"	"	"	"	15
Lady Raymond	133	5/0	"	Htg.	"	"	"	"	15
Lady Raymond	136	"	"	O. F.	"	2d	"	"	15
Laflin	4	18	F. Pl.	Htg.	Gilded	1st to 4th	Key or Lever	Slow	7
Leader	15	17	"	"	"	1st to 2d	"	"	7
Lord Elgin	36	16	¾ Pl.	Htg. Br.	Nickel	6th	Pend.	Quick	21
Lord Elgin	41	"	"	O. F. Br.	"	7th	"	"	21
Lord Elgin	41	"	"	O. F.	"	"	"	"	23
Lord Elgin	67	12	"	Htg.	"	2d	"	"	23
Lord Elgin	71	"	"	O. F.	"	3d	"	"	23
Lord Elgin	135	"	"	"	"	4th	"	"	17
Lord Elgin	135	"	"	"	"	"	"	"	21
Ogden	5	18	F. Pl.	Htg.	Gilded	1st to 4th	Key or Lever	Slow	11
Overland	3	"	"	"	Nickel	2d to 4th	Lever	Quick	17
Overland	4	"	"	"	"	"	"	"	17
Overland	8	"	"	O. F.	"	5th	Pend.	"	17
Overland	9	"	"	"	"	"	"	"	17
Overland	66	"	"	"	"	7th	Lever	"	17
Overland	123	"	"	Htg.	"	2d to 4th	"	"	17
Overland	124	"	"	O. F.	"	7th	"	"	17
Raymond	1	"	"	Htg.	Gilded or Nickel	1st to 4th	Key or Lever	"	15-17
Raymond	7	"	"	O. F.	"	5th	Pend.	"	15-17
Raymond	65	"	"	"	Nickel	7th	Lever	"	17
Raymond	91	"	¾ Pl.	"	"	8th	"	"	19
Raymond	91	"	"	"	"	"	"	"	21
Raymond	99	"	"	Htg.	"	9th	"	"	21
Raymond	134	"	"	O. F.	"	8th	"	"	17
Raymond	98	16	"	"	"	15th	"	"	19
Raymond	98	"	"	"	"	"	"	"	21
Raymond	102	"	"	O. F. Br.	"	9th	"	"	17
Raymond	102	"	"	O. F.	"	13th	"	"	17
Raymond	102	"	"	"	"	15th	"	"	17
Raymond	125	"	"	Htg. Br.	"	8th	"	"	19
Raymond	126	"	"	Htg.	"	14th	"	"	19
Raymond	126	"	"	"	"	17th	"	"	19
Raymond	68	12	"	"	"	2d	Pend.	"	19
Raymond	72	"	"	O. F.	"	3d	"	"	19
Ryerson	4	18	F. Pl.	Htg.	Gilded	1st	Key	Slow	7
Taylor	3	"	"	"	"	2d to 4th	Lever	"	15
Taylor	3	"	"	"	Gilded or Nickel	1st to 4th	Key or Lever	Quick	15
Taylor	8	"	"	O. F.	Gilded	5th	Pend.	"	15
Veritas	89	"	¾ Pl.	"	Nickel	8th	Lever	"	23
Veritas	90	"	"	"	"	"	"	"	21
Veritas	99	"	"	Htg.	"	9th	"	"	21
Veritas	98	16	"	O. F. Br.	"	"	"	"	21
Veritas	98	"	"	O. F.	"	13th	"	"	21
Veritas	98	"	"	"	"	"	"	"	23
Veritas	98	"	"	"	"	15th	"	"	21
Veritas	132	"	"	"	"	"	"	"	23
Wheeler	4	18	F. Pl.	Htg.	Gilded	1st to 4th	Key or Lever	Slow	15
Wheeler	4	"	"	"	Gilded or Nickel	"	Lever	Quick	13-15
Wheeler	4	"	"	"	"	2d to 4th	"	"	15-17
Wheeler	9	"	"	O. F.	"	5th	Pend.	"	15-17

ELGIN NATIONAL WATCH CO.

Grades of Movements with Classification and Description as Originally Made

Grade.	Class.	Size.		Style.		Model.	Sett.	Train.	Jewels.
Wheeler	122	18	F. Pl.	O. F.	Nickel	7th	Lever	Quick	17
Wheeler	123	"	"	Htg.	"	2d to 4th	"	"	17
Wheeler	124	"	"	O. F.	"	7th	"	"	17
Wheeler	130	"	¾ Pl.	Htg.	"	9th	"	"	17
Wheeler	131	"	"	O. F.	"	8th	"	"	17
Wheeler	33	16	"	Htg. Br.	"	6th	Pend.	"	17
Wheeler	38	"	"	O. F. Br.	"	7th	"	"	17
Wheeler	127	"	"	"	"	9th	Lever	"	17
Wheeler	111	12	"	Htg.	"	2d	Pend.	"	17
Wheeler	112	"	"	O. F.	"	3d	"	"	17
No. 1	25	16	"	Htg.	Gilded	"	Lever	"	7
No. 2	25	"	"	"	"	"	"	"	13-15
No. 3	24	"	"	"	"	"	"	"	15
No. 4	24	"	"	"	Nickel	"	"	"	15
No. 5	5	18	F. Pl.	"	"	2d to 4th	"	Q. or S.	11
No. 6	6	"	"	"	Gilded	"	"	Slow	7
No. 7	6	"	"	"	"	1st	Key	"	7
No. 8	5	"	"	"	"	2d to 4th	Lever	"	7
No. 9	5	"	"	"	"	"	"	"	7
No. 10	5	"	"	"	"	"	"	Q. or S.	11
No. 11	15	17	"	"	"	2d	"	Slow	7
No. 12	5	18	"	"	"	1st	Key	"	7
No. 13	5	"	"	"	"	"	"	"	11
No. 14	15	17	"	"	"	"	"	"	7
No. 15	15	"	"	"	"	"	"	"	11
No. 16	4	18	"	"	"	"	"	"	7
No. 17	4	"	"	"	"	"	"	"	11
No. 18	5	"	"	"	"	"	"	"	11
No. 19	5	"	"	"	"	2d to 4th	Lever	"	11
No. 20	3	"	"	"	"	"	"	"	15
No. 21	48	10	¾ Pl.	"	"	1st	Key	Quick	7
No. 22	48	"	"	"	"	"	"	"	11
No. 23	47	"	"	"	"	"	"	"	15
No. 24	45	12	"	"	"	"	"	"	11
No. 25	45	"	"	"	"	"	"	"	15
No. 26	44	"	"	"	"	"	"	"	11
No. 27	1	18	F. Pl.	"	Nickel	2d to 4th	Lever	"	15-17
No. 28	48	10	¾ Pl.	"	Gilded	1st	Key	"	7
No. 29	47	"	"	"	"	"	"	"	11
No. 30	45	12	"	"	"	"	"	"	7
No. 31	45	"	"	"	"	1st	"	"	7
No. 32	44	"	"	"	"	"	"	"	11
No. 33	3	18	F. Pl.	"	Nickel	2d to 4th	Lever	"	15
No. 34	43	14	¾ Pl.	"	Gilded	1st	Key	"	7
No. 35	43	"	"	"	"	"	"	"	7
No. 36	43	"	"	"	"	"	"	"	11
No. 37	42	"	"	"	"	"	"	"	15
No. 38	3	18	F. Pl.	"	"	"	"	Slow	15
No. 39	43	14	¾ Pl.	"	"	"	"	Quick	13
No. 40	43	"	"	"	"	"	"	"	7
No. 41	42	"	"	"	"	"	"	"	13
No. 42	42	"	"	"	"	"	"	"	15
No. 43	10	18	F. Pl.	O. F.	Nickel	5th	Pend.	"	11
No. 44	9	"	"	"	"	"	"	"	15
No. 45	51	6	¾ Pl.	Htg.	"	1st	Lever	"	13
No. 46	42	14	"	"	"	"	Key	"	15
No. 47	19	16	"	Htg. and O.F.	Gilded	"	Lever	"	7
No. 48	18	"	"	"	"	"	"	"	13
No. 49	17	"	"	"	"	"	"	"	15
No. 50	17	"	"	"	Nickel	"	"	"	15
No. 51	15	17	F. Pl.	Htg.	Gilded	1st	Key	Slow	7
No. 52	15	"	"	"	"	"	"	"	11
No. 53	48	10	¾ Pl.	"	"	"	"	Quick	7
No. 54	48	"	"	"	"	"	"	"	13
No. 55	5	18	F. Pl.	"	"	"	"	Slow	7
No. 56	4	"	"	"	"	"	"	"	11
No. 57	4	"	"	"	"	"	"	"	13
No. 58	3	"	"	"	"	"	"	"	15
No. 59	15	17	"	"	"	"	"	"	7
No. 60	5	18	"	"	"	"	"	"	7
No. 61	2	"	"	"	"	2d to 4th	Lever	Quick	15
No. 62	2	"	"	"	"	1st	Key	"	15
No. 63	4	"	"	"	"	2d to 4th	Lever	Slow	13
No. 64	51	6	¾ Pl.	"	"	1st	"	Quick	7
No. 65	51	"	"	"	"	"	"	"	13
No. 66	50	"	"	"	"	"	"	"	15
No. 67	50	"	"	"	Nickel	"	"	"	15
No. 68	5	18	F. Pl.	"	Gilded	2d to 4th	"	Slow	15
No. 69	1	"	"	"	"	1st	Key	Quick	15
No. 70	1	"	"	"	"	2d to 4th	Lever	"	15-17
No. 71	49	6	¾ Pl.	"	Nickel	1st	"	"	17
No. 72	16	16	"	Htg. and O.F.	"	"	"	"	21
No. 73	11	18	F. Pl.	O. F.	Gilded	5th	Pend.	"	7
No. 74	10	"	"	"	"	"	"	"	11
No. 75	9	"	"	"	"	"	"	"	15
No. 76	8	"	"	"	"	"	"	"	15
No. 77	7	"	"	"	"	"	"	"	15-17
No. 78	5	"	"	Htg.	Nickel	1st	Key	Q. or S.	11
No. 79	3	"	"	"	Gilded	"	"	Quick	15

ELGIN NATIONAL WATCH CO.

Grades of Movement with Classification and Description as Originally Made.

Grade.	Class.	Size.	Style.			Model.	Sett.	Train.	Jewels.
No. 80	3	18	F. Pl.	Htg.	Gilded	2d to 4th	Lever	Quick	15
No. 81	4	"	"	"	"	1st	Key	"	13–15
No. 82	4	"	"	"	"	2d to 4th	Lever	"	13–15
No. 83	27	16	¾ Pl.	S. Sec.	"	4th	"	"	15
No. 84	27	"	"	"	Nickel	"	"	"	15
No. 85	22	"	"	Htg. and O.F.	Gilded	2d	"	"	15
No. 86	22	"	"	"	Nickel	"	"	"	15
No. 87	5	18	F. Pl.	Htg.	"	1st	Key	"	11
No. 88	5	"	"	"	"	2d to 4th	Lever	"	11
No. 89	28	16	¾ Pl.	S. Sec.	Gilded	4th	"	"	13
No. 90	23	"	"	Htg. and O.F.	"	2d	"	"	13
No. 91	21	"	"	"	Nickel	"	"	"	21
No. 92	26	"	"	Htg.	Gilded	3d	"	"	11
No. 93	20	"	"	Htg. and O.F.	"	1st	"	"	11
No. 94	52	6	"	Htg.	"	"	"	"	11
No. 95	52	"	"	"	"	"	"	"	7
No. 96	6	18	F. Pl.	"	"	2d to 4th	"	"	7
No. 97	6	"	"	"	"	1st	Key	"	7
No. 98	14	"	¾ Pl.	Htg. and O.F.	"	6th	Pend.	"	7
No. 99	13	"	"	"	"	"	"	"	11
No. 100	12	"	"	"	"	"	"	"	15
No. 101	52	6	"	Htg.	Nickel	1st	Lever	"	11
No. 102	5	18	F. Pl.	"	"	2d to 4th	"	"	11
No. 103	4	"	"	"	"	"	"	"	15
No. 104	31	16	¾ Pl.	O. F.	Gilded	5th	Pend.	"	7
No. 105	31	"	"	"	"	"	"	"	11
No. 106	30	"	"	"	"	"	"	"	13–15
No. 107	29	"	"	"	"	"	"	"	15
No. 108	29	"	"	"	Nickel	"	"	"	15
No. 109	60	0	"	Htg.	Gilded	1st	"	"	7
No. 110	60	"	"	"	Nickel	"	"	"	11
No. 111	58	"	"	"	"	"	"	"	15
No. 112	57	"	"	"	"	"	"	"	17
No. 113	60	"	"	"	Gilded	"	"	"	11
No. 114	26	16	"	"	"	3d	"	"	7
No. 115	59	0	"	"	Nickel	1st	"	"	13
No. 116	7	18	F. Pl.	O. F.	"	5th	"	"	15–17
No. 117	56	6	¾ Pl.	Htg.	Gilded	2d	"	"	7
No. 118	56	"	"	"	"	"	"	"	11
No. 119	56	"	"	"	Nickel	"	"	"	11
No. 120	55	"	"	"	"	"	"	"	13
No. 121	54	"	"	"	"	"	"	"	15
No. 122	53	"	"	"	"	"	"	"	17
No. 123	9	18	F. Pl.	O. F.	Gilded	5th	"	"	15
No. 124	9	"	"	"	Nickel	"	"	"	15
No. 125	4	"	"	Htg.	Gilded	2d to 4th	Lever	"	15
No. 126	4	"	"	"	Nickel	"	"	"	15
No. 127	26	16	¾ Pl.	"	"	3d	"	"	11
No. 128	31	"	"	O. F.	"	5th	Pend.	"	11
No. 129	60	0	"	Htg.	Gilded	1st	"	"	15
No. 130	60	"	"	"	Nickel	"	"	"	15
No. 131	58	"	"	"	"	"	"	"	15
No. 132	56	6	"	"	Gilded	2d	"	"	15
No. 133	56	"	"	"	Nickel	"	"	"	15
No. 134	54	"	"	"	"	"	"	"	15
No. 135	26	16	"	"	Gilded	3d	Lever	"	15
No. 136	26	"	"	"	Nickel	"	"	"	15
No. 137	25	"	"	"	Gilded	"	"	"	13–15
No. 138	31	"	"	O. F.	"	5th	Pend.	"	15
No. 139	31	"	"	"	Nickel	"	"	"	15
No. 140	30	"	"	"	Gilded	"	"	"	13–15
No. 141	5	18	F. Pl.	Htg.	"	2d to 4th	Lever	"	15
No. 142	5	"	"	"	Nickel	"	"	"	15
No. 143	4	"	"	"	Gilded	"	"	"	15–17
No. 144	4	"	"	"	Nickel	"	"	"	15–17
No. 145	10	"	"	O. F.	Gilded	5th	Pend.	"	15
No. 146	10	"	"	"	Nickel	"	"	"	15
No. 147	9	"	"	"	Gilded	"	"	"	15–17
No. 148	9	"	"	"	Nickel	"	"	"	15–17
No. 149	1	"	"	Htg.	"	2d to 4th	Lever	"	20–21
No. 150	7	"	"	O. F.	"	5th	Pend.	"	20–21
No. 151	35	16	¾ Pl.	Htg.	Gilded	6th	"	"	7
No. 152	35	"	"	"	Nickel	"	"	"	15
No. 153	34	"	"	"	"	"	"	"	17
No. 154	33	"	"	"	"	"	"	"	17
No. 155	32	"	"	"	"	"	"	"	17
No. 156	36	"	"	Htg. Br.	"	"	"	"	21
No. 157	40	"	"	O. F.	Gilded	7th	"	"	7
No. 158	40	"	"	"	Nickel	"	"	"	15
No. 159	39	"	"	"	"	"	"	"	17
No. 160	38	"	"	"	"	"	"	"	17
No. 161	37	"	"	"	"	"	"	"	17
No. 162	41	"	"	O. F. Br.	"	"	"	"	21
No. 163	3	18	F. Pl.	Htg.	"	2d to 4th	Lever	"	17
No. 164	1	"	"	"	"	"	"	"	17
No. 165	8	"	"	O. F.	"	5th	Pend.	"	17
No. 166	7	"	"	"	"	"	"	"	17
No. 167	58	0	¾ Pl.	Htg.	"	1st	"	"	16
No. 168	54	6	"	"	"	2d	"	"	16

ELGIN NATIONAL WATCH CO.

Grades of Movements with Classification and Description as Originally Made.

Grade.	Class.	Size.	Style.		Model.	Sett.	Train.	Jewels.
No. 169	5	18	F. Pl.	Htg.	Nickel	2d to 4th	Lever	Quick	15
No. 170	10	"	"	O. F.	"	5th	Pend.	"	15
No. 171	6	"	"	Htg.	"	2d to 4th	Lever	"	7
No. 172	11	"	"	O. F.	"	5th	Pend.	"	7
No. 173	60	0	¾ Pl.	Htg.	"	1st	"	"	7
No. 174	57	"	"	"	"	"	"	"	17
No. 175	56	6	"	"	"	2d	"	"	7
No. 176	53	"	"	"	"	"	"	"	17
No. 177	..	"	"	"	..	"	"	"	7
No. 178	..	18	F. Pl.	"	..	2d to 4th	Lever	"	7
No. 179	..	"	"	O. F.	..	5th	Pend.	"	7
No. 180	65	"	"	"	Nickel	7th	Lever	"	17
No. 181	65	"	"	"	"	"	"	"	21
No. 182	31	16	¾ Pl.	"	Gilded	5th	Pend.	"	7
No. 183	1	18	F. Pl.	Htg.	Nickel	2d to 4th	Lever	"	17
No. 184	7	"	"	O. F.	"	5th	Pend.	"	17
No. 185	35	16	¾ Pl.	Htg.	Gilded	6th	"	"	15
No. 186	40	"	"	O. F.	"	7th	"	"	15
No. 187	70	12	"	Htg.	Nickel	2d	"	"	15
No. 188	69	"	"	"	"	"	"	"	17
No. 189	68	"	"	"	"	"	"	"	19
No. 190	67	"	"	"	"	"	"	"	23
No. 191	74	"	"	O. F.	"	3d	"	"	15
No. 192	73	"	"	"	"	"	"	"	17
No. 193	72	"	"	"	"	"	"	"	19
No. 194	71	"	"	"	"	"	"	"	23
No. 195	31	16	"	"	Gilded	5th	"	"	15
No. 196	70	12	"	Htg.	Nickel	2d	"	"	7
No. 197	74	"	"	O. F.	"	3d	"	"	7
No. 198	79	0	"	Htg.	"	2d	"	"	7
No. 199	78	"	"	"	"	"	"	"	15
No. 200	77	"	"	"	"	"	"	"	17
No. 201	76	"	"	"	"	"	"	"	19
No. 202	83	"	"	O. F.	"	3d	"	"	7
No. 203	82	"	"	"	"	"	"	"	15
No. 204	81	"	"	"	"	"	"	"	17
No. 205	80	"	"	"	"	"	"	"	19
No. 206	75	6	"	Htg.	"	2d	"	"	7
No. 207	61	18	F. Pl.	"	"	2d to 4th	Lever	"	7
No. 208	63	"	"	O. F.	"	5th	Pend.	"	7
No. 209	75	6	¾ Pl.	Htg.	Gilded	2d	"	"	7
No. 210	92	16	"	"	Nickel	6th	"	"	7
No. 211	94	"	"	O. F.	"	7th	"	"	7
No. 212	92	"	"	Htg.	Gilded	6th	"	"	7
No. 213	94	"	"	O. F.	"	7th	"	"	7
No. 214	89	18	"	"	Nickel	8th	Lever	"	23
No. 215	63	"	F. Pl.	"	Gilded	5th	Pend.	"	7
No. 216	75	6	¾ Pl.	Htg.	Nickel	2d	"	"	15
No. 217	61	18	F. Pl.	Htg.	"	2d to 4th	Lever	"	15
No. 218	63	"	"	O. F.	"	5th	Pend.	"	15
No. 219	84	0	¾ Pl.	Htg.	Gilded	1st	"	"	7
No. 220	92	16	"	"	Nickel	6th	"	"	15
No. 221	94	"	"	O. F.	"	7th	"	"	15
No. 222	84	0	"	Htg.	"	1st	"	"	7
No. 223	84	"	"	"	"	"	"	"	15
No. 224	85	"	"	"	"	2d	"	"	11
No. 225	86	"	"	O. F.	"	3d	"	"	11
No. 226	5	18	F. Pl.	Htg.	Gilded	2d to 4th	Lever	"	17
No. 227	10	"	"	O. F.	"	5th	Pend.	"	17
No. 228	5	"	"	Htg.	Nickel	2d to 4th	Lever	"	17
No. 229	10	"	"	O. F.	"	5th	Pend.	"	17
No. 230	56	6	¾ Pl.	Htg.	Gilded	2d	"	"	16
No. 231	56	"	"	"	Nickel	"	"	"	16
No. 232	87	12	"	"	"	"	"	"	7
No. 233	87	"	"	"	"	"	"	"	15
No. 234	88	"	"	O. F.	"	3d	"	"	7
No. 235	88	"	"	"	"	"	"	"	15
No. 236	68	"	"	Htg.	"	2d	"	"	21
No. 237	72	"	"	O. F.	"	3d	"	"	21
No. 238	61	18	F. Pl.	Htg.	Gilded	1st	Key	"	7
No. 239	90	"	¾ Pl.	O. F.	Nickel	8th	Lever	"	21
No. 240	91	"	"	"	"	"	"	"	19
No. 241	33	16	"	Htg. Br.	"	6th	Pend.	"	17
No. 242	33	"	"	"	"	"	"	"	17
No. 243	32	"	"	"	"	"	"	"	17
No. 244	38	"	"	O. F. Br.	"	7th	"	"	17
No. 245	38	"	"	"	"	"	"	"	17
No. 246	37	"	"	"	"	"	"	"	17
No. 247	93	"	"	Htg. Br.	"	6th	"	"	15
No. 248	95	"	"	O. F. Br.	"	7th	"	"	15
No. 249	62	18	F. Pl.	Htg.	Gilded	2d to 4th	Lever	"	17
No. 250	64	"	"	O. F.	"	5th	Pend.	"	17
No. 251	61	"	"	Htg.	"	2d to 4th	Lever	"	7
No. 252	65	"	"	O. F.	Nickel	7th	"	"	21
No. 253	87	12	¾ Pl.	Htg.	Gilded	2d	Pend.	"	7
No. 254	88	"	"	O. F.	"	3d	"	"	7
No. 255	97	10/0	"	"	Nickel	1st	"	"	15
No. 256	96	"	"	"	"	"	"	"	17
No. 257	92	16	"	Htg.	"	6th	"	"	15

ELGIN NATIONAL WATCH CO.

Grades of Movements with Classification and Description as Originally Made.

Grade.	Class.	Size.	Style.		Model.	Sett.	Train.	Jewels.
No. 258	94	16	¾ Pl.	O. F.	Nickel	7th	Pend.	Quick	15
No. 259	87	12	"	Htg.	"	2d	"	"	15
No. 260	88	"	"	O. F.	"	3d	"	"	15
No. 261	61	18	F. Pl.	Htg.	"	2d to 4th	Lever	"	15
No. 262	63	"	"	O. F.	"	5th	Pend.	"	15
No. 263	77	0	¾ Pl.	Htg.	"	2d	"	"	17
No. 264	81	"	"	O. F.	"	3d	"	"	17
No. 265	66	18	F. Pl.	"	"	7th	Lever	"	17
No. 266	65	"	"	"	"	"	"	"	17–21
No. 267	85	0	¾ Pl.	Htg.	"	2d	Pend.	"	15
No. 268	86	"	"	O. F.	"	3d	"	"	15
No. 269	85	"	"	Htg.	"	2d	"	"	7
No. 270	98	16	"	O. F. Br.	"	9th	Lever	"	21
No. 271	60	0	"	Htg.	"	1st	Pend.	"	16
No. 272	56	6	"	"	"	2d	"	"	16
No. 273	65	18	F. Pl.	O. F.	"	7th	Lever	"	17
No. 274	99	"	¾ Pl.	Htg.	"	9th	"	"	21
No. 275	100	12	"	"	"	2d	Pend.	"	17
No. 276	101	"	"	O. F.	"	3d	"	"	17
No. 277	65	18	F. Pl.	"	"	7th	Lever	"	21
No. 278	4	"	"	Htg.	"	2d to 4th	"	"	17
No. 279	9	"	"	O. F.	"	5th	Pend.	"	17
No. 280	102	16	¾ Pl.	O. F. Br.	"	9th	Lever	"	17
No. 281	85	0	"	Htg.	"	2d	Pend.	"	11
No. 282	86	"	"	O. F.	"	3d	"	"	7
No. 283	66	18	F. Pl.	"	"	7th	Lever	"	17
No. 284	75	6	¾ Pl.	Htg.	Gilded	2d	Pend.	"	15
No. 285	63	18	F. Pl.	O. F.	"	5th	"	"	15
No. 286	115	6	¾ Pl.	Htg.	Nickel	2d	"	"	7
No. 287	105	18	F. Pl.	"	"	2d to 4th	Lever	"	7
No. 288	106	"	"	O. F.	"	5th	Pend.	"	7
No. 289	115	6	¾ Pl.	Htg.	Gilded	2d	"	"	7
No. 290	109	16	"	O. F.	Nickel	6th	"	"	7
No. 291	110	"	"	O. F.	"	7th	"	"	7
No. 292	109	"	"	Htg.	Gilded	6th	"	"	7
No. 293	110	"	"	O. F.	"	7th	"	"	7
No. 294	106	18	F. Pl.	"	"	5th	"	"	7
No. 295	115	6	¾ Pl.	Htg.	Nickel	2d	"	"	15
No. 296	105	18	F. Pl.	"	"	2d to 4th	Lever	"	15
No. 297	106	"	"	O. F.	"	5th	Pend.	"	15
No. 298	116	0	¾ Pl.	Htg.	Gilded	2d	"	"	7
No. 299	109	16	"	"	Nickel	6th	"	"	15
No. 300	110	"	"	O. F.	"	7th	"	"	15
No. 301	113	12	"	Htg.	"	2d	"	"	7
No. 302	113	"	"	"	"	"	"	"	15
No. 303	114	"	"	O. F.	"	3d	"	"	7
No. 304	114	"	"	"	"	"	"	"	15
No. 305	107	16	"	Htg. Br.	"	6th	"	"	15
No. 306	108	"	"	O. F. Br.	"	7th	"	"	15
No. 307	103	18	F. Pl.	Htg.	Gilded	2d to 4th	Lever	"	17
No. 308	104	"	"	O. F.	"	5th	Pend.	"	17
No. 309	105	"	"	Htg.	"	2d to 4th	Lever	"	7
No. 310	113	12	¾ Pl.	"	"	2d	Pend.	"	7
No. 311	114	"	"	O. F.	"	3d	"	"	7
No. 312	109	16	"	Htg.	Nickel	6th	"	"	15
No. 313	110	"	"	O. F.	"	7th	"	"	15
No. 314	113	12	"	Htg.	"	2d	"	"	15
No. 315	114	"	"	O. F.	"	3d	"	"	15
No. 316	105	18	F. Pl.	Htg.	"	2d to 4th	Lever	"	15
No. 317	106	"	"	O. F.	"	5th	Pend.	"	15
No. 318	116	0	¾ Pl.	Htg.	"	2d	"	"	15
No. 319	117	"	"	O. F.	"	3d	"	"	15
No. 320	116	"	"	Htg.	"	2d	"	"	15
No. 321	111	12	"	"	"	"	"	"	7
No. 322	112	"	"	O. F.	"	3d	"	"	17
No. 323	116	0	"	Htg.	"	2d	"	"	11
No. 324	117	"	"	O. F.	"	3d	"	"	7
No. 325	115	6	"	Htg.	Gilded	2d	"	"	15
No. 326	106	18	F. Pl.	O. F.	"	5th	"	"	15
No. 327	118	"	"	Htg.	Nickel	10th	Lever	"	16
No. 328	118	"	"	"	"	"	"	"	17
No. 329	119	"	"	"	"	"	"	"	17
No. 330	119	"	"	"	"	"	"	"	21
No. 331	120	"	"	O. F.	"	11th	Pend.	"	16
No. 332	120	"	"	"	"	"	"	"	17
No. 333	121	"	"	"	"	"	Lever	"	17
No. 334	121	"	"	"	"	"	"	"	21
No. 335	105	"	"	Htg.	"	4th	"	"	17
No. 336	106	"	"	O. F.	"	5th	Pend.	"	17
No. 337	33	16	¾ Pl.	Htg. Br.	"	6th	"	"	17
No. 338	38	"	"	O. F. Br.	"	7th	"	"	17
No. 339	107	"	"	Htg. Br.	"	6th	"	"	17
No. 340	108	"	"	O. F. Br.	"	7th	"	"	17
No. 341	125	"	"	Htg. Br.	"	8th	Lever	"	17
No. 342	127	"	"	O. F. Br.	"	9th	"	"	17
No. 343	122	18	F. Pl.	O. F.	"	7th	"	"	17
No. 344	113	12	¾ Pl.	Htg.	"	2d	Pend.	"	17
No. 345	114	"	"	O. F.	"	3d	"	"	17
No. 346	111	"	"	Htg.	"	2d	"	"	17

ELGIN NATIONAL WATCH CO.

Grades of Movements with Classification and Description as Originally Made.

Grade.	Class.	Size.		Style.		Model.	Sett.	Train.	Jewels.
No. 347	112	12	¾ Pl.	O. F.	Nickel	3d	Pend.	Quick	17
No. 348	1	18	F. Pl.	Htg.	"	2d to 4th	Lever	"	21
No. 349	65	"	"	O. F.	"	7th	"	"	21
No. 350	98	16	¾ Pl.	"	"	13th	"	"	23
No. 351	41	"	"	"	"	7th	Pend.	"	23
No. 352	123	18	F. Pl.	Htg.	"	2d to 4th	Lever	"	17
No. 353	124	"	"	O. F.	"	7th	"	"	17
No. 354	116	0	¾ Pl.	Htg.	"	2d	Pend.	"	15
No. 355	117	"	"	O. F.	"	3d	"	"	15
No. 356	128	14	"	"	"	2d	"	"	7
No. 357	128	"	"	"	"	"	"	"	15
No. 358	128	"	"	"	"	"	"	"	17
No. 359	129	"	"	"	"	"	"	"	17
No. 360	98	16	"	"	"	13th	Lever	"	21
No. 361	102	"	"	"	"	"	"	"	17
No. 363	113	12	"	Htg.	Gilded	2d	Pend.	"	15
No. 364	114	"	"	O. F.	"	3d	"	"	15
No. 365	109	16	"	Htg.	"	6th	"	"	15
No. 366	110	"	"	O. F.	"	7th	"	"	15
No. 367	90	18	"	"	Nickel	8th	Lever	"	21
No. 368	130	"	"	Htg.	"	9th	"	"	17
No. 369	131	"	"	O. F.	"	8th	"	"	17
No. 370	102	16	"	"	"	15th	"	"	17
No. 371	126	"	"	Htg.	"	14th	"	"	19
No. 372	98	"	"	O. F.	"	15th	"	"	19
No. 373	126	"	"	Htg.	"	14th	"	"	21
No. 374	98	"	"	O. F.	"	15th	"	"	21
No. 375	98	"	"	"	"	"	"	"	21
No. 376	132	"	"	"	"	"	"	"	23
No. 377	116	0	"	Htg.	Gilded	2d	Pend.	"	15
No. 378	105	18	F. Pl.	"	Nickel	2d to 4th	Lever	"	17
No. 379	106	"	"	O. F.	"	5th	Pend.	"	17
No. 380	133	5/0	¾ Pl.	Htg.	"	1st	"	"	15
No. 381	107	16	"	Htg. Br.	"	6th	"	"	17
No. 382	108	"	"	O. F. Br.	"	7th	"	"	17
No. 383	113	12	"	Htg.	"	2d	"	"	17
No. 384	114	"	"	O. F.	"	3d	"	"	17
No. 385	134	18	"	"	"	8th	Lever	"	17
No. 386	109	16	"	Htg.	"	6th	Pend.	"	17
No. 387	110	"	"	O. F.	"	7th	"	"	17
No. 388	98	"	"	"	"	15th	Lever	"	21
No. 389	134	18	"	"	"	8th	"	"	21
No. 390	91	"	"	"	"	"	"	"	21
No. 391	98	16	"	"	"	15th	"	"	21
No. 392	135	12	"	"	"	4th	Pend.	"	17
No. 393	113	"	"	Htg.	Gilded	2d	"	"	7
No. 394	114	"	"	O. F.	"	3d	"	"	7
No. 395	113	"	"	Htg.	"	2d	"	"	15
No. 396	114	"	"	O. F.	"	3d	"	"	15
No. 397	33	16	"	Htg. Br.	Nickel	6th	"	"	17
No. 398	38	"	"	O. F. Br.	"	7th	"	"	17
No. 399	136	5/0	"	O. F.	"	2d	"	"	15
No. 400	131	18	"	"	"	8th	Lever	"	17
No. 401	126	16	"	Htg.	"	17th	"	"	19
No. 402	126	"	"	"	"	"	"	"	21
No. 403	133	5/0	"	"	"	1st	Pend.	"	7
No. 404	97	10/0	"	O. F.	"	"	"	"	15
No. 405	96	"	"	"	"	"	"	"	17
No. 406	116	0	"	Htg.	Gilded	2d	"	"	13
No. 407	135	12	"	O. F.	Nickel	4th	"	"	21
No. 408	133	5/0	"	Htg.	"	1st	"	"	15
No. 409	117	0	"	O. F.	Gilded	3d	"	"	7
No. 410	117	"	"	"	"	"	"	"	15
No. 411	106	18	F. Pl.	"	Nickel	5th	"	"	21
No. 412	91	"	¾ Pl.	"	"	8th	Lever	"	21
No. 413	116	3/0	"	Htg.	"	2d	Pend.	"	7
No. 414	117	"	"	O. F.	"	3d	"	"	7
No. 415	116	"	"	Htg.	"	2d	"	"	15
No. 416	117	"	"	O. F.	"	3d	"	"	15

Left Dial: 18 & 16 size=$30-$50-$100   Center: wind-ind.18 size=$55-$85-$275   Right: 24 Hr. 18 size=$35-$55-$125
Left Dial: 12 size=$25-$35-$60   Center: wind-ind.16 size=$55-$85-$275   Right: 24 Hr. 16 size=$35-$55-$125
Left Dial: 6 & 0 size=$15-$2-$45   Right: 24 Hr. 12 size=$30-$45-$100

ELGIN NATIONAL WATCH CO.
IDENTIFICATION OF MOVEMENTS
BY MODEL NUMBER

How to Identify Your Watch Size & Model: Compare the movement of your watch with the illustrations in this section. While comparing, note the location of the balance, jewels, screws, gears, and type of back plate (Full, 3/4, Bridge) these will be clues in identifying the movement you have.

Model 2
S# 1,001
July, 1867
Model 3
S# 6,001
Aug., 1867
Model 4
S# 25,001
Nov., 1868

Model 1, 18 size, full plate, hunting, key wind & set, first serial number 101, Apr., 1867.

Model 2-4, 18 size, full plate, hunting, lever set,

Model 6
S# 1,855,001
May, 1885

Model 5, 18 size, full plate, open face, pendant set, first serial number, 2,110,001, Grade 43, Dec., 1885.

Model 6, 18 size, three-quarter plate, hunting, open face, pendant set.

I will respect & appreciate positive sound reliable comments, corrections, improvements or remarks but reserve the right to accept the statement or keep my own observations & views. (*Cooksey*)

Model 7, 18 size, fu" plate, open face, lever set, first serial number 6,563,821, Grade 265, Apr., 1897.

Model 8, 18 size, three-quarter plate, open face, lever set, first serial number 8,400,001, Grade 214, Dec., 1900.

Model 8, 18 size, three-quarter plate, open face, lever set with winding indicator.

Model 9, 18 size, three-quarter plate, hunting, lever set, first serial number 9,625,001, Grade 274, May, 1904.

Model 9, 18 size, three-quarter plate, hunting, lever set with winding indicator.

Model 1
S# 400,001
Aug., 1874

Model 1, 17 size, full plate, hunting, Key wind and set **from the back**.

Note: Model is not the same defination as grade. A model may exist in many different grades or grade names (asB.W. Raymond) and may be used in many different models (as model **1**, 18 size, open or hunting case, model **1**, in 16 size open or hunting case, model **1** in 12 size) etc..

Model 2, 17 size, full plate, hunting, lever set.

16 size
Model 1
S# 603,001

Model 1, 16 size, three-quarter plate, hunting & open face, lever set.

Model 2, 16 size, three-quarter plate, bridge, hunting & open face, lever set.

Model 3, 16 size, three-quarter plate, hunting, lever set, first serial number 625,001, Grade 1, Feb., 1879.

Model 4, 16 size, three-quarter plate, sweep second, hunting & open face, lever set.

Model 5, 16 size, three-quarter plate, open face, pendant set.

Model 5, 16 size, three-quarter plate, open face, pendant set, first serial number 2,811,001, Grade 105, Oct., 1887.

Model 6, 16 size, three-quarter plate, hunting, pendant set, first serial number 6,458,001, Grade 151, Aug., 1895.

Model 6, 16 size, three-quarter plate, bridge, hunting, pendant set, first serial number 6,463,001, Grade 156, May, 1896.

Model 7, 16 size, three-quarter plate, open face, pendant set, first serial number 6,464,001. Grade 157, Sept., 1895.

Model 7, 16 size, three-quarter plate, bridge, open face, pendant set, first serial number 6,469,001, Grade 162, Apr., 1896.

Model 8, 16 size, three-quarter plate, bridge, hunting, lever set, serial number 12,283,001, Grade 341, Jan., 1907.

Model 9, 16 size, three-quarter plate, bridge, open face, lever set, first serial number 9,250,001, Grade 270, July, 1902.

Model 13, 16 size, three-quarter plate, open face, lever set, first serial number 12,717,001, Grade 350, June, 1908.

Model 14, 16 size, three-quarter plate, hunting, lever set.

Model 15, 16 size, three-quarter plate, open face, lever set.

Model 17, 16 size, three-quarter plate, hunting, lever set.

Model 19, 16 size, three-quarter plate, open face, lever set with winding indicator.

Model 20, 16 size, three-quarter plate, open face, Grades 571, 572, 573, 574, 575, 616.

Model 1, 14 size, three-quarter plate, hunting, key wind and set.

Model 2, 14 size, three-quarter plate, open face, pendant set.

Model 1, 12 size, three-quarter plate, hunting, key wind and set.

Model 2, 12 size, three-quarter plate, hunting, pendant set, first serial #7,410,001, Grade 188, Dec., 1897.

Model 2, 12 size, three-quarter plate, spread to 16 size, hunting, pendant set.

Model 3, 12 size, three-quarter plate, open face, pendant set, serial number 7,423,001, Grade 192, May 1898.

Model 3, 12 size, three-quarter plate, spread to 16 size, open face, pendant set.

Model 4, 12 size, three-quarter plate, open face, pendant set, serial number 16,311,001, Grade 392, July, 1912.

Model 1, 10 size, three-quarter plate, style 1, hunting, key wind and set.

Model 2, 10 size, three-quarter plate, hunting, key wind and set.

Model 3, 10 size, three-quarter plate, hunting.

Model 4, 10 size, three-quarter plate, hunting.

Model 5 & 6, 10 size, three-quarter plate.

Model 1, 6 size, three-quarter plate, hunting.

Model 1, 6 size, three-quarter plate, hunting.

Model 2, 6 size, three-quarter plate, hunting.

Model 1, 0 size, three-quarter plate, hunting.

Model 2, 0 size, three-quarter plate, hunting.

Model 2, 0 size, three-quarter plate, hunting.

Model 3, 0 size, three-quarter plate, open face.

Model 3, 0 size, three-quarter plate, open face.

Model 2, 3-0 size, three-quarter plate, hunting.

Charles Fasoldt's coaxial escape wheel with odd shaped lever. The escape wheels were designed to eliminate the use of oil on the chronometer escapement & prevent over-banking.

Charles Fasoldt, 18-20 size, 16 jewels, coaxial double escape wheel, key wind & set, bar gilded movement, Serial # 132, note patented regulator (not gold), series II.

CHARLES FASOLDT WATCH CO.
Rome, New York   1849 - 1861
Albany, New York   1861 - 1878

Charles Fasoldt came from Dresden, Germany to Rome, New York in 1848. In 1861 he moved to Albany, New York where he set up a factory to make watches and clocks and other instruments. One of his first watches, Serial No. 27, was for General Armstrong and was an eight-day movement. At about that same time, he made several large regulators and a few pocket chronometers. He displayed some of his work at fairs in Utica and Syracuse and received four First-Class Premiums and two diplomas. In 1850, he patented a micrometric regulator (generally called the Howard Regulator because Howard bought the patent). He also patented a **chronometer** escapement with a coaxial double escape wheel in 1859 & 1865, a watch regulator in 1864, and a hairspring stud in 1877.

The reliability of his coaxial double escape wheel was demonstrated when Mr. Fasoldt **strapped** one of his watches (serial # 6), along with some other brand watches, to the **drive-rod** of the Empire Express locomotive. This round trip run from Albany to New York proved his point; all the other manufacturer's watches stopped about a minute after the train started. Mr. Fasoldt's watch, serial # 6, made the entire trip running, and was within a few minutes of the correct time.

Mr. Fasoldt's coaxial double escape wheel was designed to eliminate the use of oil at the escapement and prevent over-banking. Each watch he made has minor changes making no two watches alike and these masterpieces sold for about $300.00 dollars. Mr. Fasoldt was also known for his tower clocks, for which he received many awards and medals. He made **less than 400 watches in Albany N.Y.** and **about 50 watches in Rome N.Y..** Serial numbers **200 to 299** have not been seen. Note a few movements were made **with no serial numbers.**

Charles Fasoldt, 18-20 size, 16 jewels, stem wind, key set, bar movement, note: the barrel ratchet wheel only having wolf tooth form, note: Single Winding Bridge, series III.

Charles Fasoldt, 18-20 size, 16 jewels, stem wind, key set, bar movement, note: the barrel ratchet wheel only having wolf tooth form, note: Double Winding Bridge, series III.

Estimated serial numbers & Production Dates
For Albany, New York MODELS (ONLY)

Year	Model	Style	Serial # Range
1861-1863	Series I	KW/KS, 1/2 plate	5-40
1864-1866	Series II	KW/KS, Bar	41-99
1867-1868	Series II	KW/KS, Bar	100-199
1868-1869	Series II	KW/KS, Bar	300-399
1869-1871	Series III	SW/KS, Bar	400-499
1872-1875	Series III	SW/KS, Bar	500-540

Serial numbers _200_ to _299_ have **not** been seen.

Serial # reported = 3, 5, 6, 27, 46, 59, 61, 64, 66, 87, 88, 90, 112, 113, 122, 124, 132, 135, 161, 166, 174, 335, 338, 349, 350, 384, 385, 388, 390, 395, 400, 402, 415, 418, 421, 424, 436, 437, 438, 439, 456, 457, 481, 484, 485, 496, 500, 504, 508, 510, 512 = 12 size, 540.

Grade or Name — Description	Avg	Ex-Fn	Mint
18 - 20 Size, 22J, chronograph,Wind Ind., dual mainsprings & dual train, GJS, KW or SW, **18K case**.......................★ ★ ★ ★	$17,000	$28,000	$45,000
18 - 20 Size, 16J, GJS, **KW/ KS**, coaxial double escape wheel, **18K case** ....★ ★ ★	12,000	20,000	35,000
* All of the above and below with a **REMONTOIRE**.. ★ ★ ★ ★ ★	14,000	30,000	40,000
18 - 20 Size, 16J, GJS, **SW/ KS**, coaxial double escape wheel, **18K case** ....★ ★ ★	12,000	20,000	35,000
18 - 20 S, 16J, **pivoted dentent**, SW/KS, **recased** 18K ★ ★ ★ ★ ★	6,000	7,000	12,000
18 - 20 Size, 16J, GJS, double escape wheel, **movement & dial**....	4,000	6,000	9,000
10 - 12 Size, 16J, by C. Fasoldt,GJS, KW & SW, KS, **14K**..........	3,500	5,200	8,500
by **Otto H. Fasoldt**, _18S,_ 15J, SW, Swiss made or American	375	450	975

Charles Fasoldt, 18-20 size, 16 jewels, key wind, key set, half plate, coaxial double escape wheel, S. # 6, series I.

Charles Fasoldt, 18-20 size, 16 jewels, stem wind, key set, patented **chronometer** escapement with a coaxial double escape wheel, **gold regulator**, Serial No. 438, series III.

Remontoire: The constant force device is placed on the third wheel which bears two coaxial independent wheels kept in traction between themselves by a linear spring. Similar to **maintaining power** used on a fusee & clocks.

Fasoldt, 18-20 size, pivoted dentent, S# 315, micrometric regulator, on dial & mvt. A.M.Edwards Buffalo,N.Y.

FASOLDT, CO-AXIAL DOUBLE ESCAPE WHEEL WITH ODD SHAPED LEVER

Mr. Fasoldt's coaxial double escape wheel was designed to eliminate the use of oil at the escapement and prevent over-banking. The impulse jewel **E** on its return has just unlocked pallet **D** and the smaller escape wheel is beginning impulse on **K**. At **K'** and **K''** the impulse is continuing. At **K'''** the impulse is finished and the large escape wheel locks on **R'''**. The impulse jewel having made its excursion to the right will unlock **D''''** and with some recoil in unlocking the escape wheel tooth, will begin impulse on **K''''** and continue as at **K**.

FITCHBURG WATCH CO.

Fitchburg, Massachusetts
1875 - 1878

In 1875, S. Sawyer decided to manufacture watches. He hired personnel from the U. S. Watch Company to build the machinery, but by 1878 the company had failed. It is not known how many, if any, watches were made. The equipment was sold to Cornell and other watch companies.

E. H. FLINT

Cincinnati, Ohio
1877 - 1879

The Flint watch was patented September 18, 1877, and about 100 watches were made. The serial number is found under the dial.

Grade or Name — Description		Avg	Ex-Fn	Mint
18 Size, 4–7J, KW, Full Plate, OF, Coin	★★★★	$4,200	$5,700	$10,000
18 Size, 4–7J, KW, Full Plate, **14K**, HC	★★★★	6,000	8,500	12,000

E.H. Flint dial and movement, 18 size, 4-7 jewels, open face, key wind & set, "Lancaster Pa." on dial, "Patented Sept. 18th,1877" on movement.

FREDONIA WATCH CO.
Fredonia, New York
1881 - 1885

This company sold the finished movements acquired from the Independent Watch Co. These movements had been made by other companies. The Fredonia Watch Company was sold to the Peoria Watch Co. in 1885, after having produced approximately 20,000 watches. Fredonia makes a official Announcement that read as Follows:

Chronology of the Development of Fredonia:

Independent Watch Co. 1875 –1881
Fredonia Watch Co.   1881 –1885
Peoria Watch Co.   1885 –1889

212

*"Born at 2 o'clock p. m., Wednesday, Feb. 1st (1882), the **"Mark Twain"** gilt key winding movement. The child is vigorous and healthy, and there seems to be a large and increasing number of him. His parents are proud of him, and he already promises to become as universal a favorite as his illustrious namesake."*

Fredonia, "Mark Twain", 18S, 11J, KW, KS, dial signed "Independent Watch Co.", S# 202,263, Ca 1883

Fredonia Watch Co., 18 size, 15 jewels, signature on movement "Cyrus N. Gibbs, Mass.," key wind & set, serial number 4403.

Fredonia Watch Co., 18 size, 15 jewels, adjusted, serial number 8,368. NOTE: FREDONIA Regulator disc will have teeth all around the disc.

Fredonia Watch Co., with a reversible case; changes to either hunting or open face.

Grade or Name — Description	Avg	Ex-Fn	Mint
18S, 7J, SW, OF	$175	$250	$425
18S, 7J, SW, HC	225	335	475
18S, 9J, SW, OF	175	250	425
18S, 9J, SW, HC	225	335	475
18S, 11J, SW, OF	175	250	425
18S, 11J, KW, KS, HC, Coin	225	335	475
18S, 15J, SW, Multi-color, **14K, HC**	1,600	2,200	3,700
18S, KW, **Silver Reversible case**	600	800	1,200
18S, 15J, SW, LS, **Gilt**, OF	225	335	475
18S, 15J, straight line escapement, NI, marked **Adjusted**	300	450	650
18S, 15J, SW, LS, **Gold Plated**, OF	300	450	650
18S, 15J, HC, **low serial number**	350	585	800
18S, 15J, personalized mvt.	250	345	550
18S, 15J, KW, HC, marked **Lakeshore W. Co.**	250	345	550
18S, 15J, Anti-Magnetic, OF	300	450	625
18S, 15J, Anti-Magnetic, HC	335	475	675
18S, 15J, Anti-Magnetic, Special, OF ★	335	450	650
18S, 15J, Anti-Magnetic, Special, HC ★	365	500	700
18S, 15J, Anti-Magnetic, Special Superior Quality, OF ★★	475	700	1,000
18S, 15J, Anti-Magnetic, Special Superior Quality, HC ★★	500	775	1,200
18S, Mark Twain, 11J, KW, KS ★★★	1,100	1,600	2,800

NOTE: Some of the above watches were marked **Quick Beat**.

FREEPORT WATCH CO.
Freeport, Illinois
1874 - 1875

Probably less than 20 nickel watches made by Freeport have survived. Their machinery was purchased from Mozart Co., and a Mr. Hoyt was engaged as superintendent. The building erected was destroyed by fire on Oct. 27, 1875. A safe taken from the ruins contained 300 completed brass movements which were said to be ruined.

Grade or Name — Description	Avg	Ex-Fn	Mint
18S, 19J, KW, SW, gold train, raised gold jewel settings 18K case ★★★★	$9,000	$12,000	$29,000
18S, 15J, KW, KS, gold train, friction jewels 18K case ★★★★	$8,000	$11,000	$21,000
Geo. P. Rose, Dubuque, Iowa, 18S, 15J, KW, KS, gold train, friction jewels, 18K case ★★★★	$6,000	$8,000	$12,500

Freeport Watch Co., Example of a basic movement, 18 size, 15 jewels, key wind & set, pressed jewels, gold train, high grade movement, serial number 11.

Freeport Watch Co., 15 jewels, gold train, damaskeened, large over coiled hairspring with a floating stud, steel lever & escape wheel with single roller.

SMITH D. FRENCH

Wabash, Indiana
1866 - 1878

On August 21, 1866, Mr. French was issued a patent for an improved escapement for watches. The escape wheel has triangular shaped pins and the lever has two hook-shaped pallets. The pin wheel escapement was probably first used by Robert Robin, about 1795, for pocket watches. Antoine Tavan also used this style escape wheel around 1800. Mr. French's improved pin wheel and hook shaped lever (about 70 total production) can be seen through a cutout in the plates of his watches.

Illustration from the patent office, patent number 57,310, patented Aug. 21, 1866. Note pin wheel escapement with adjustable hook shaped lever.

Grade or Name — Description	Avg	Ex-Fn	Mint
18S, 15J, 3/4, KW, KS, gilt, pin wheel escapement, Silver case................................. ★★★★	$9,000	$13,000	$20,000
18S, 15J, 3/4, KW, KS, gilt, pin wheel escapement, 18K case................................. ★★★★	12,000	16,000	25,000

S.D. French, about 18 size, 15J., gilt 3/4 movement, key wind & set, with pin wheel escapement, engraved on movement "S.D. French, Wabash Ind., Aug. 21, 1866, No. 24."

L. Goddard, 55mm, 7 jewels, full plate movement with solid cock, chain driven fusee, flat steel balance, serial number 235, ca. 1809-1817.

LUTHER GODDARD

Shrewsbury, Massachusetts

1809 - 1825

The first significant attempt to produce watches in America was made by Luther Goddard. William H. Keith, who became president of Waltham Watch Co. (1861 -1866) and was once apprenticed to Goddard, said that the *hands, dials, round and dovetail brass, steel wire, mainsprings and hairsprings, balance, verge, chains, and pinions were all imported.* The plates, wheels, and brass parts were cast at the Goddard shop, however. He also made the cases for his movements which were of the usual style open faced, double case-and somewhat in advance of the prevalent style of thick bull's eye watches of the day. About 400+ watches were made. They were of good quality and more expensive than the imported type. The first watch was produced about 1809 and was sold to the father of ex-governor Lincoln of Worcester, Massachusetts. In 1820 his watches sold for about $60.00.

Goddard built a shop one story high with a hip roof about 18' square; it had a lean-to at the back for casting. The building was for making clocks, but a need for watches developed. He earned the distinction of establishing the first watch factory in America. He was also one of the first to use a rack and pinion lever escapement and going barrel. A Luther Goddard & James Hamilton ad Nov.16, 1803 in NAWCC Bulletin No. 338.

Watches **imported** from England were signed Worcester, & watches signed, Shrewsbury used brass parts (plates & wheels) & were cast at the Goddard **shop** & steel parts were all **imported** (hands, dials, mainsprings, hairsprings, balance, verge, chains, and pinions).

Frank A. Knowlton purchased the company and operated it until 1933.

Chronology of the Development of Luther Goddard:

Luther Goddard, L. Goddard, L. Goddard & Son	1809-1825
P.& D. Goddard	1825-1842
D. Goddard & Son	1842-1850
Luther D. Goddard	1850-1857
Goddard & Co.	1857-1860
D. Goddard & Co., & Benj'n Goddard	1860-1872

D. Goddard, 18-20, 15 jewels," Worcester, Mass."on movement, key wind & set, solid balance, under sprung, serial number 8.

L. Goddard & Co.,16-18 size, pair case, open face-thick bulls-eye type, and of high quality for the time.

NOTE: Watches listed below are with original silver cases.

Grade or Name — Description		Avg	Ex-Fn	Mint
Benj'n Goddard...	⊠★★★	$2,100	$2,700	$4,200
Luther Goddard, S#1-35 with **eagle** balance bridge ...	⊠★★★★★	10,000	14,000	21,000
Luther Goddard without eagle on cock	⊠★★★	6,300	8,600	16,000
Luther Goddard,L.Goddard, Luther Goddard & Son	⊠★★★	5,500	7,600	13,000
L. Goddard & Co., D. Goddard & Son	⊠★★★	4,400	6,500	10,000
Luther D. Goddard, Goddard & Co., D. Goddard & Co. ..	⊠★★★	4,000	6,100	8,500
P. Goddard, with eagle on cock....................................	⊠★★★	5,600	7,200	11,000
P & D Goddard, 7J., (Worcester), fusee, KWKS, OF	⊠★★★	2,000	2,700	5,700

* Note: See other Goddard **illustrations** on previous page and also on next page.

L. Goddard & Son. Example of basic movement, about 18 size, open face, pair case, S# 351, CA.1818. Note: Brass parts were made at the Goddard shop but steel parts were imported.

L. Goddard & Son, about 18 size, pair case, verge escapement, engraved on movement "L. Goddard & Son, Shrewsbury," serial number 460.

JONAS G. HALL
Montpelier, Vermont 1850 - 1870
Millwood Park, Roxbury, Vermont 1870 - 1890

Jonas G. Hall was born in 1822 in Calais, Vermont. He opened a shop in Montpelier where he sold watches, jewelry, silverware, and fancy goods. While at this location, he produced more than 60 full plate, lever style watches. Hall, later established a business in Roxbury, where he manufactured watch staking tools and other watchmaking tools. At Roxbury, he made at least one watch which was a three-quarter plate model. He also produced a few chronometers, about 20-size with a fusee and detent escapement and a wind indicator on the dial.

Hall was employed by the American Waltham Watch Co. for a short time and helped design the first lady's model. He also worked for Tremont Watch Co., E. Howard & Co., and the United States Watch Co. of Marion, New Jersey.

Style or Name–Description		Avg	Ex-Fn	Mint
18S, 15J, Full plate, KW KS	★ ★ ★	$4,000	$6,000	$10,000
18S, 15J, 3/4 plate, gilded, KW KS	★ ★ ★	5,000	7,000	11,000
20S, 15J, Detent Chronometer, KW KS	★ ★ ★ ★	6,000	9,000	16,000

J.G. Hall, 18 size, 15 jewels, full plate, key wind & set, engraved on movement "J.G. Hall, Montpelier, VT.," serial number 25, ca. 1857.

J.G. Hall, 18 size, 15 jewels, 3/4 plate, key wind and set, engraved on movement "J.G. Hall, Millwood Park, Roxbury, VT," no serial number, ca. 1880.

HAMILTON WATCH CO.
Lancaster, Pennsylvania
December 14, 1892 - Present

Hamilton's roots go back to the Adams & Perry Watch Manufacturing Co. On Sept. 26, 1874, E. F. Bowman made a model watch, and the first movement was produced on April 7, 1876. It was larger than an 18S, or about a 19S. They decided to start making the watches a standard size of 18, and no more than 1,000 of the large-size watches were made. Work had commenced on Sept. 1, 1877, at the Lancaster Watch Co. The watches were designed to sell at a cheaper price than normal. It had a one-piece top 3/4 plate and a pillar plate that was fully ruby-jeweled (4 1/2 pairs). It had a gilt or nickel movement and a new stem-wind device designed by Mosely & Todd. By mid-1878, the Lancaster Watch Co. had made 150 movements. Four grades of watches were produced: Keystone, Fulton, Franklin, and Melrose. In September 1879 the company had manufactured 334 movements. In 1880 some 1,250 movements had been made. In mid-1882, about 17,000 movements had been assembled.

HAMILTON
No. 950 MOVEMENT

Without an equal among fine timekeepers

THE

Hamilton Watch

Phenomenally accurate and dependable

A most accurate and dependable movement designed by Hamilton to meet the most exacting standards of timekeeping.

No. 950 OPEN FACE—white gold finish, bridge movement, pendant or lever set, 23 extra fine ruby and sapphire jewels in gold settings, patent motor barrel, gold train, escapement cap jeweled, steel escape wheel, double roller escapement, sapphire pallets, Breguet hairspring, micrometric regulator, compensation balance, double sunk dial, adjusted to temperature, isochronism, and five positions.

RAIL ROAD TIMEKEEPER
OF AMERICA.
LANCASTER, PA.

ABOVE: AD 1910

GRADE 992 ELINVAR MOVEMENT

16 size, nickel, 3/4 plate, lever set, 21 extra fine ruby and sapphire jewels, double roller escapement, sapphire pallets, gold center wheel, steel escape wheel, micrometric regulator, ELINVAR hairspring, monometallic balance, friction set roller jewel, double sunk dial, two piece friction fit balance staff, beautifully damaskeened. Adjusted to five positions and automatically regulated to temperature. Sold cased only.

Note: Automatically regulated to temperature (1933 AD)

ABOVE: AD 1924
(TIME BOOK)
Note: "white gold finish"

Grade 936, 18 size, 17 jewels, Note: **serial number 1.**   Grade 936, 18 size, 17 jewels, serial number 2, c. 1893.

The first Hamilton movement to be sold was No. 15 to W. C. Davis on January 31, 1893. The No. 1 movement was finished on April 25, 1896, and was never sold. The No. 2 was finished on April 25, 1893, and was shipped to Smythe & Ashe of Rochester, N. Y. serial Nos. 1 & 2 are at the N.A.W.C.C. museum.

Chronology of the Development of Hamilton:

Adams & Perry Watch Co. .... Sept. 1874 - May 1876
Lancaster Penna.Watch .... Aug. 1877 - May 1879
Lancaster Watch Co. .... May 1883 - 1886
Keystone Standard Watch Co. 1886-1890
Hamilton Watch Co. .... Dec. 14, 1892 - Present

In 1893 the first watch was produced by Hamilton. The watches became very popular with railroad men and by 1923 some 53 percent of Hamilton's production were railroad watches. The 940 model watch was discontinued in 1910. Most Hamilton watches are fitted with a 42-hour mainspring.

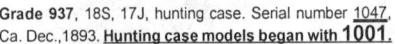

Grade 937, 18S, 17J, hunting case. Serial number 1047,   Hamilton Watch Co., 18 size, 7 jewels, serial number 2934.
Ca. Dec.,1893. **Hunting case models began with 1001.**   Ca. 1894. NOTE: Gilded plates.

The 950B was introduced in 1940 and by this time a total of about 25,000 grade (950) had been sold. The 992 watch sold for about $60.00 in 1929, the price remained the same $60.00 until 1940. Hamilton discontinued manufacturing pocket watches in December of 1969, the last railroad-grade watch to to be made was a 992B 21-jewel Railway Special, and sale would be discontinued when supplies were exhausted.

The Elinvar hairspring was patented in 1931 and used in all movements thereafter. Elinvar, taking its name from the words " Elasticity Invariable". On October 15, 1940, Hamilton introduced the 992B, also the Elinvar **extra** hairspring, all watches were fitted with the new hairspring. Elinvar and Invar are trade names and are the same 36 percent nickel steel. Although the Hamilton Watch Co. is still in busines today, they last produced American made watches in about 1969.

HAMILTON ESTIMATED SERIAL NUMBERS
AND PRODUCTION DATES

Date–Serial No.	Date–Serial No.	Date–Serial No.	Date–Serial No.	
1893 -1 to 2,000	1906 — 500,000	1919—1,600,000	1932—2,440,000	NOTE: THE
1894 — 5,000	1907 — 580,000	1920—1,700,000	1933—2,480,000	serial numbers
1895 — 11,500	1908 — 680,000	1921—1,800,000	1934—2,520,000	BELOW were
1896 — 16,000	1909— 750,000	1922—1,900,000	1935—2,560,000	**NOT USED**
1897 — 27,000	1910— 790,000	1923—2,000,000	1936—2,600,000	S# 2,655,301 TO
1898 — 50,000	1911— 860,000	1924—2,050,000	1937—2,900,000	S# 2,900,000
1899 — 74,000	1912— 940,000	1925—2,100,000	1938—3,200,000	
1900—104,000	1913—1,000,000	1926—2,150,000	1939—3,400,000	also **not used**
1901—143,000	1914—1,100,000	1927—2,200,000	1940—4,000,000	S# 3,460,901 TO
1902—196,000	1915—1,200,000	1928—2,250,000	1941—4,250,000	S# 4,000,000
1903—260,000	1916—1,300,000	1929—2,300,000	1942—4,500,000	
1904—340,000	1917—1,400,000	1930—2,350,000		
1905—435,000	1918—1,500,000	1931—2,400,000		

The **ABOVE** list is provided for determining the APPROXIMATE age of your watch. Match serial number with date. Watches were not necessarily **SOLD** in the exact order of manufactured date.

Some serial numbers have the first numbers replaced by a (date) letter such as A, B, C, E, F, G, H, J, L, M, N, R, S, T, V, W, X, Y, CY, HW. These letters were used from late 30's to about late 60's. The date letter "2B + Ser.#" found on 950B, the date letter "C + Ser.#" found on 992B, the date letter "S + Ser.#" found on 950B and **HA = SWISS**.

992B with first letter of C + serial no.	950B with first letter of 2B + serial no.	4992B with first letter of 4C + serial no.
1940= C001	1941=2B001	1941=4CXXXX
1941= C40,000	1942=2B400	
1942= C60,000	1943=2B800	1942=4C40,000
1943= C90,000		
1944=C120,000	950B with first letter of S + serial no.	1944=4C90,000
1946=C170,000	1941=S001	
1947=C215,000	1944=S1,500	1950=4C120,000
1948=C255,000	1945=S2,800	
1950=C350,000	1946=S4,000	1960=4C135,000
1951=C390,000	1947=S4,500	
1954=C420,000	1948=S6,500	1968=4C145,000
1956=C455,000	1949=S7,500	
1959=C500,000	1951=S10,000	
1964=C520,000	1955=S25,000	3992B-made from about1943 to 1945
1969=C529,200	1962=S28,000	
	1965=S30,000	

NOTE: *It required several months for raw material to emerge as a finished movement. All the while the factory is producing all sizes, models and grades. The numbering system was basically "consecutive", due to demand a batch of movements could be side tracked, thus allowing a different size and model to move ahead to meet this demand. Therefore, the dates some movements were **sold** and delivered to the trade, the serial numbers may not be "consecutive".*

The Hamilton Masterpiece

The adjoining illustration shows the Hamilton Masterpiece. The dial is sterling silver with raised gold numbers and solid gold hands. This watch sold for $685.00 in 1930. All 922 **MP** Models included the following: 12 size, 23 jewels, were adjusted to heat, cold, isochronism, and five positions, with a motor barrel, solid gold train, steel escape wheel, double roller, sapphire pallets and a micrometric regulator.

HAMILTON SERIAL NUMBERS AND GRADES

To help determine the size and grade of your watch, the following serial number list is provided. Serial numbers 30,001 through 32,000, which are omitted from the list, were not listed by Hamilton. To identify your watch, simply look up its serial number which will identify the grade. After determining the grade, your watch can be easily located in the pricing section.

Note: Some of the early watches were re-numbered, S# 07 re-numbered as 30,007, S# 12 re-numbered as 30,012, S# 1006 re-numbered as 31006, S# 1016 re-numbered as 31016, The above list is just a few examples also some returned and renumbered.

Serial	Grade	Serial	Grade	Serial	Grade	Serial	Grade
1-20	936	27001-28000	929	56801-900	974	73001-200	975
21-30	932	28001-29000	999	56901-57000	976	73201-300	973
31-60	936	29001-800	927	57001-300	977	73301-74000	977
61-400	932	29801-30000	935	57301-500	975	74001-400	974
401-1000	936	32001-300	926	57501-600	973	74401-600	972
1001-20	937	32301-700	930	57601-800	975	74601-75000	976
1021-30	933	32701-33000	934	57801-58000	977	75001-76799	HWW*
1031-60	937	33001-500	931	58001-100	972	76002-76800	HWW*
1061-1100	933	33501-800	927	58101-200	974	77001-100	969
1101-300	937	33801-34000	935	58201-300	972	77101-300	973
1301-600	933	34001-500	928	58301-400	966	77301-500	975
1601-2000	937	34501-700	930	58401-500	976	77501-600	971
2001-3000	7J	34701-800	926	58501-600	972	77601-700	973
3001-100	931	34801-35000	934	58601-800	974	77701-900	975
3101-500	935	35001-800	931	58801-59000	976	77901-78000	977
3501-600	931	35801-36000	935	59001-300	973	78001-500	970
3601-900	935	36001-37000	928	59301-500	967	78501-700	972
3901-4000	931	37001-38000	929	59501-700	975	78701-900	974
4001-300	930	38001-500	926	59701-60000	977	78901-79000	976
4301-5100	934	38501-600	930	60001-500	976	79001-100	973
5101-400	926	38601-900	934	60501-700	974	79101-300	975
5401-600	934	38901-39000	926	60701-61000	976	79301-700	977
5601-6000	930	39001-200	931	61001-200	975	79701-900	975
6001-600	936	39201-500	935	61201-500	977	79901-80000	973
6601-700	938	39501-700	927	61501-600	973	80001-200	972
6701-800	936	39701-900	935	61601-800	975	80201-400	974
6801-7000	932	39901-40000	931	61801-62000	977	80401-600	970
7001-10	17J	40001-200	930	62001-100	972	80601-700	972
7011-600	937	40201-500	934	62101-300	974	80701-900	974
7601-700	939	40501-41000	926	62301-500	976	80901-81000	976
7701-800	937	41001-500	929	62501-700	974	81001-300	961
7801-8000	933	41501-42000	927	62701-900	972	81301-500	965
8001-700	936	42001-43000	999	62901-63000	974	81501-82000	961
8701-800	938	43001-300	941	63001-500	977	82001-300	972
8801-9000	936	43301-500	943	63501-600	975	82301-500	974
9001-300	937	43501-700	937	63601-800	977	82501-600	970
9301-600	939	43701-900	941	63801-900	975	82601-700	972
9601-800	937	43901-44000	943	63901-64000	973	82701-800	974
9801-900	933	44001-02	21J	64001-100	976	82801-900	968
9901-10000	939	44003-400	938	64101-200	972	82901-83000	976
10001-200	938	44401-500	942	64201-300	974	83001-400	977
10201-400	936	44501-45000	936	64301-600	972	83401-500	971
10401-50	932	45001-46000	929	64601-700	976	83501-700	975
10451-500	936	46001-500	926	64701-900	974	83701-800	973
10501-700	938	46501-800	934	64901-65000	976	83801-900	975
10701-900	936	46801-47000	930	65001-200	973	83901-84000	969
10901-11000	938	47001-500	927	65201-300	977	84001-400	974
11001-12000	936	47501-700	935	65301-400	975	84401-500	970
12001-200	939	47701-48000	931	65401-500	973	84501-700	972
12201-13000	937	48001-05	942	65501-700	977	84701-800	968
13001-400	999	48006-300	940	65701-900	975	84801-85000	976
13401-14000	938	48301-500	942	65901-66000	977	85001-200	937
14001-15000	999	48501-900	940	66001-200	974	85201-900	941
15001-300	939	48901-49000	942	66201-300	974	85901-86000	943
15301-15401	21J	49001-400	927	66301-500	972	86001-87000	928
15302-700	937	49401-900	925	66501-600	976	87001-88000	929
15701-16000	939	49901-50	11J	66601-700	974	88001-500	926
16001-100	931	50071-500	962	66701-800	972	88501-89000	930
16101-200	930	50501-750	960	66801-67000	974	89001-500	941
16201-300	927	50751-50850	964	67001-100	977	89501-90000	937
16301-400	931	50851-51000	960	67101-300	975	90001-100	926
16401-600	927	51001-51300	16s	67301-600	973	90101-950	999
16601-17000	931	51301-400	963	67601-800	977	91001-92000	925
17001-500	929	51401-650	961	67801-68000	977	92001-200	940
17501-18000	931	51651-750	965	68001-800	960	92201-93000	936
18001-200	928	51751-52000	961	68801-69000	964	93001-94000	927
18201-300	926	52001-300	16s	69001-100	977	94001-003	934
18301-500	928	52301-500	976	69101-200	975	94004-95000	928
18501-19500	930	52501-700	974	69201-400	973	95001-96000	923
19501-700	926	52701-800	966	69401-600	975	96001-100	942
19701-20000	930	52801-53000	976	69601-70000	977	96101-700	940
20001-300	934	53001-53070	16s	70001-200	976	96701-97000	936
20301-500	926	53071-53530	977	70201-400	970	97001-900	929
20501-21000	999	53501-900	975	70401-600	968	97901-98000	927
21001-300	935	53901-54000	967	70601-900	972	98001-99000	924
21301-500	927	54001-200	972	70901-71000	974	99001-100000	925
21501-800	935	54201-300	974	71001-200	975	100001-101000	924
21801-22500	927	54301-500	976	71201-500	971	101001-102000	925
22501-800	931	54501-700	974	71501-700	975	102001-103000	922
22801-23000	935	54701-800	968	71701-90	973	103001-104000	927
23001-200	928	54801-55000	976	71791-800	969	104001-105000	940
23201-500	7J	55001-300	973	71801-900	977	105001-500	925
24001-500	926	55301-600	977	71901-72000	975	105501-106000	927
24501-25000	934	55601-700	969	72001-100	974	106001-107000	940
25001-100	11J	55701-800	977	72101-300	976	107001-400	941
25101-400	927	55801-56000	975	72301-600	974	107401-500	943
25401-800	931	56001-300	974	72601-700	968	107501-800	941
25801-26000	935	56301-500	976	72701-900	976	107801-108000	943
26001-500	930	56501-600	966	72901-73000	972	108001-200	928
26501-27000	928	56601-800	972				

Serial	No.	Serial	No.	Serial	No.	Serial	No.
108201-109000	926	186001-187000	942	275202-460	HWW*	322001-323000	974
109001-500	927	187001-188000	927	275462-500	HWW*	323001-700	975
109501-110000	925	188001-189000	924	276001-277000	940	323701-324000	973
110001-900	940	189001-190000	925	277001-278000	941	324001-325000	960
110901-111000	942	190001-191000	926	278001-279000	940	325001-100	965
111001-500	937	191001-192000	927	279001-280000	925	325101-326000	961
111501-112000	941	192001-193000	924	280001-281000	936	326001-327000	974
112001-200	928	193001-194000	925	281001-282000	927	327001-300	971
112201-113000	928	194001-195000	926	282001-283000	926	327301-500	973
113001-114000	925	195001-500	935	283001-284000	925	327501-328000	975
114001-003	940	195501-196000	927	284001-500	934	328001-300	992
114004-115000	936	196001-197000	926	284501-900	924	328301-500	990
115001-116000	927	197001-198000	937	284901-285000	999	328501-329000	992
116001-117000	940	198001-199000	936	285001-286000	925	329001-330000	975
117001-118000	925	199001-200000	925	286001-287000	940	330001-100	992
118001-119000	999	200001-201000	926	287001-288000	927	330101-500	990
119001-120000	925	201001-202000	925	288001-289000	940	330501-331000	992
120001-121000	924	202001-500	926	289001-290000	927	331001-200	973
121001-500	941	202501-203000	934	290001-800	936	331201-400	975
121501-122000	943	203001-204000	927	290801-291000	938	331401-500	969
122001-300	940	204001-100	934	291001-292000	925	331501-700	971
122301-400	942	204101-500	926	292001-500	940	331701-800	973
122401-123000	940	204501-205000	934	292501-293000	942	331801-332000	975
123001-124000	941	205001-206000	941	293001-294000	925	332001-200	992
124001-100	942	206001-207000	940	294001-295000	926	332201-800	972
124101-800	940	207001-208000	927	295001-296000	927	332801-333000	974
124801-125000	942	208001-900	999	296001-297000	940	333001-500	975
125001-126000	927	208901-209000	940	297001-298000	927	333501-700	971
126001-127000	924	209001-210000	925	298001-299000	940	333701-900	973
127001-128000	941	210001-211000	940	299001-300000	925	333901-334000	975
128001-129000	936	211001-212000	927	300001-300	972	334001-200	972
129001-130000	925	212001-213000	940	300301-800	970	334201-800	992
130001-500	924	213001-500	941	300801-900	974	334801-335000	990
130501-131000	926	213501-600	937	300901-301000	968	335001-600	975
131001-132000	925	213601-214000	925	301001-400	975	335601-800	971
132001-100	926	214001-215000	924	301401-500	971	335801-900	973
132101-200	934	215001-216000	927	301501-302000	973	335901-336000	975
132201-500	926	216001-217000	940	302001-100	990	336001-200	972
132501-133000	924	217001-218000	927	302101-200	992	336201-337000	974
133001-134000	937	218001-219000	940	302201-300	990	337001-338000	975
134001-135000	924	219001-220000	925	302301-900	992	338001-200	974
135001-136000	925	220001-221000	924	302901-303000	990	338201-900	992
136001-137000	926	221001-222000	927	303001-100	973	338901-339000	990
137001-100	11J	222001-223000	926	303101-300	971	339001-300	971
137101-138000	927	223001-02	927	303301-800	975	339301-500	973
138001-139000	940	223003-04	941	303801-304000	973	339501-340000	975
139001-140000	937	223005	937	304001-100	970	340001-200	974
140001-300	938	223006-224000	927	304101-400	972	340201-300	972
140301-141000	942	224001-225000	924	304401-305000	974	340301-600	970
141001-142000	941	225001-226000	927	305001-100	973	340601-341000	974
142001-143000	940	226001-227000	940	305201-300	969	341001-200	973
143001-100	927	227001-228000	925	305301-900	975	341201-342000	975
143101-144000	925	228001-229000	924	305901-306000	973	342001-300	990
144001-145000	924	229001-230000	925	306001-400	972	342301-343000	992
145001-146000	925	230001-500	926	306401-307000	974	343001-344000	975
146001-400	934	230501-231000	924	307001-100	975	344001-200	970
146401-147000	924	231001-565	937	307101-300	971	344201-400	972
147001-148000	927	231566-232000	927	307301-400	975	344401-345000	970
148001-149000	940	232001-233000	940	307401-500	973	345001-346000	975
149001-150000	925	233001-234000	941	307501-600	975	346001-300	992
150001-151000	924	234001-235000	940	307601-700	971	346301-347000	974
151001-400	927	235001-236000	941	307701-900	975	347001-180	993
151401-500	935	236001-237000	936	307901-308000	969	347181-200	991
151501-152000	927	237001-238000	941	308001-700	990	347201-300	975
152001-153000	936	238001-239000	926	308701-309000	992	347301-400	973
153001-154000	941	239001-500	943	309001-100	971	347401-700	993
154001-155000	936	239501-240000	941	309101-400	973	347701-900	991
155001-156000	927	240001-241000	940	309401-310000	975	347901-348000	973
156001-157000	940	241001-242000	941	310001-400	970	348001-200	970
157001-158000	925	242001-243000	940	310401-311000	974	348201-800	974
158001-159000	940	243001-244000	927	311001-700	975	348801-349000	972
159001-160000	941	244001-245000	936	311701-312000	973	349001-350000	975
160001-161000	940	245001-246000	925	312001-200	970	350001-300	990
161001-162000	941	246001-247000	940	312201-500	972	350301-400	974
162001-163000	926	247001-248000	927	312501-600	968	350401-600	990
163001-164000	943	248001-249000	940	312601-313000	974	350601-351000	992
164001-165000	940	249001-250000	927	313001-100	973	351001-352000	975
165001-166000	925	250001-251000	926	313101-400	971	352001-100	968
166001-167000	924	251001-252000	927	313401-600	969	352101-353000	974
167001-168000	927	252001-253000	924	313601-314000	975	353001-354000	975
168001-169000	940	253001-254000	925	314001-600	974	354001-400	992
169001-400	935	254001-255000	940	314601-900	972	354401-355000	974
168401-170000	927	255001-256000	925	314901-315000	970	355001-800	975
170001-171000	999	256001-257000	926	315001-100	971	355801-900	973
171001-172000	925	257001-258000	941	315101-400	973	355901-356000	993
172001-100	934	258001-259000	924	315401-316000	975	356001-500	990
172101-173000	926	259001-260000	941	316001-200	992	356501-357000	974
173001-174000	925	260001-261000	940	316201-300	972	357001-358000	975
174001-175000	924	261001-262000	927	316301-500	992	358001-359000	974
175002-176000	HWW*	262001-263000	926	316501-317000	972	359001-360000	975
175001-699	HWW*	263001-264000	925	317001-600	975	360001-550	960
176001-177000	940	264001-265000	940	317601-700	969	360801-361000	960
177001-178000	927	265001-266000	927	317701-318000	973	361001-100	993
178001-179000	942	266001-267000	940	318001-100	972	361101-300	991
179001-500	935	267001-268000	925	318101-900	974	361301-400	993
179501-180000	927	268001-269000	940	318901-319000	970	361401-700	975
180001-181000	940	269001-270000	927	319001-100	971	361701-20	973
181001-182000	941	270001-271000	940	319101-320000	975	361721-362000	975
182001-300	926	271001-272000	925	320001-300	972	362001-900	974
182301-400	934	272001-273000	926	320301-400	968	362901-363000	990
182401-183000	926	273001-274000	941	320401-321000	974	363001-364000	975
183001-184000	941	274001-275000	924	321001-200	973	364001-365000	974
184001-185000	940	275002-100	HWW*	321201-322000	975	365001-100	975
185001-186000	925	275102-200	HWW*			365101-300	973

Serial Numbers	No.
365301-366000	975
366001-367000	974
367001-500	975
367501-368000	993
368001-369000	974
369001-370000	992
370001-100	990
370101-400	992
370401-500	974
370501-800	990
370801-371400	992
371401-500	972
371501-373500	974
373501-700	990
373701-374000	992
374001-200	974
374201-700	990
374701-375000	974
375001-100	993
375101-500	991
375501-376000	975
376001-200	972
376201-500	974
376501-377000	992
377001-200	973
377201-378000	975
378001-379000	974
379001-380800	992
380801-381000	990
381001-382000	992
382001-100	990
382101-383000	974
383001-300	992
383301-700	990
383701-384000	972
384001-700	974
384701-980	972
384901-385000	974
385001-600	972
385601-800	974
385801-386000	990
386001-800	974
386801-900	992
386901-387000	972
387001-100	990
387101-900	992
387901-388000	972
388001-400	990
388401-389000	992
389001-391000	974
391001-300	972
391301-392000	974
392001-800	992
392801-393000	990
393001-400	975
393401-600	973
393601-394000	993
394001-200	972
394201-395000	974
395001-100	993
395101-900	991
395901-396000	993
396001-397000	992
397001-200	990
397201-398000	992
398001-200	972
398201-399000	992
399001-600	993
399601-400000	975
400001-401000	924
401001-402000	940
402001-404000	924
404001-405000	926
405001-406000	924
406001-407000	940
407001-408000	926
408001-416000	940
416001-417000	926
417001-418000	940
418001-419000	926
419001-420000	941
420001-421000	940
421001-422000	926
422001-423000	924
423001-425000	926
425001-426000	924
426001-500	936
426501-427000	944
427001-428000	924
428001-429000	926
429001-430000	925
430001-431000	924
431001-432000	925
432001-433000	940
433001-434000	924
434001-500	940
434501-600	942
434601-435000	946
435001-436000	924
436001-438500	940
438501-800	946
438801-900	942
438901-440000	946
440001-441000	924
441001-442000	940
442001-400	946
442401-500	942
442501-443000	946
443001-444000	926
444001-445000	924
445001-446000	927
446001-447000	924
447001-448000	925
448001-449000	926
449001-450000	924
450001-451000	926
451001-452000	925
452001-453000	940
453001-454000	924
454001-456000	940
456001-457000	999
457001-458000	940
458001-459000	999
459001-110	946
459111-118	942
459119-200	946
459201-700	942
459701-460000	946
460001-461900	940
461901-462000	940
462001-463000	999
463001-500	940
463501-464000	940
464001-466000	926
466001-467000	924
467001-468000	924
468001-469000	940
469001-470000	924
470001-471000	926
471001-472000	946
472001-473000	924
473001-474000	940
474001-475000	924
475001-476000	940
476001-477000	924
477001-478000	940
478001-479000	926
479001-480000	944
480001-481000	926
481001-482000	927
482001-483000	924
483001-484000	926
484001-485000	940
485001-486000	925
486001-487000	999
487001-488000	924
488001-489000	999
489001-492000	924
492001-493000	940
493001-494000	946
494001-495000	946
495001-496000	940
496001-497000	925
497001-498000	999
498001-499000	936
499001-501000	940
501001-900	925
501901-502000	934
502001-503000	926
503001-504000	999
504001-507000	940
507001-508000	999
508001-509900	940
509901-510000	942
510001-511500	940
511501-700	942
511701-517000	940
517001-519000	924
519001-521000	925
521001-523000	944
523001-524000	946
524001-531000	940
531001-532000	926
532001-10	934
532011-533000	926
533001-535500	999
535501-536000	940
536001-537000	936
537001-538000	924
538001-543000	940
543001-544000	927
544001-200	934
544201-545000	926
545001-546000	925
546001-547000	924
547001-548000	926
548001-549000	999
549001-551000	946
551001-553000	944
553001-555000	940
555001-556000	936
556001-558000	924
558001-560000	924
560001-561000	999
561001-562000	926
562001-564000	924
564001-565000	926
565001-568000	940
568001-569000	936
569001-571000	924
571001-576000	940
576001-200	942
576201-578000	940
578001-580000	924
580001-582000	926
582001-584000	925
584001-585000	927
585001-587000	999
587001-592000	940
592001-593000	926
593001-594000	924
594001-601000	940
B600001-601000	999 Ball
601001-601800	926
B601001-601800	999 Ball
601801-602000	934
B601801-602000	999 Ball
602001-603000	926
B602001-603000	999 Ball
603001-604000	926
B603001-604000	999 Ball
604001-605000	926
B604001-605000	999 Ball
605001-606000	925
B605001-606000	999 Ball
606001-607000	925
B606001-607000	999 Ball
607001-608000	925
B607001-608000	999 Ball
608001-613000	924
B608001-613000	999 Ball
613001-614000	925
B613001-614000	999 Ball
614001-616500	924
B614001-616500	999 Ball
616501-617000	934
B616501-617000	999 Ball
617001-619000	926
B617001-619000	999 Ball
619001-620000	927
B619001-620000	999 Ball
620001-622700	940
B620001-622700	999 Ball
622701-623000	942
B622701-623000	999 Ball
623001-624000	941
B623001-624000	999 Ball
624001-625000	936
B624001-625000	999 Ball
625001-626000	925
B625001-626000	999 Ball
626001-627000	926
B626001-627000	999 Ball
627001-628000	924
B627001-628000	999 Ball
628001-630800	925
B628001-630800	999 Ball
631001-636000	940
B631001-636000	999 Ball
636001-637000	941
B636001-637000	999 Ball
637001-638000	936
B637001-638000	999 Ball
638001-639000	926
B638001-639000	999 Ball
639001-640000	925
B639001-640000	999 Ball
640001-642000	924
B640001-644400	999 Ball
644401-645000	940
645001-645500	927
B645001-645500	999 Ball
645501-646000	925
B645501-646000	999 Ball
646001-647000	926
B646001-647000	999 Ball
647001-648000	940
B647001-648000	999 Ball
648001-649000	940
B648001-649000	998 Ball
649001-650000	998
B649001-650000	998 Ball
650001-651000	999
B650001-651000	999 Ball
651001-652000	940
B651001-652000	998 Ball
652001-652700	924
B652001-652700	998 Ball
652701-652800	924
652801-652900	927
652901-653000	937
653001-655000	940
B653001-655000	999 Ball
655001-655200	924
B655001-655200	999 Ball
655201-656000	924
B655201-656000	999 Ball
656001-657000	926
657001-659000	927
659001-660000	925
660001-661000	927
661001-662000	924
662001-664000	940
664001-666000	924
666001-667000	940
667001-668000	941
668001-669000	926
669001-670000	999
670001-100	937
670501-673000	925
673001-675000	926
675001-677000	940
677001-678000	924
678001-679200	927
679201-680000	926
680001-685000	940
685001-687000	940
687001-688000	925
688001-689000	946
689001-694000	940
694001-696000	924
696001-697000	941
697001-700000	924
700001-702000	974
702001-703800	992
703801-704000	990
704001-400	992
704401-705000	990
705001-700	972
705701-706000	974
706001-707000	990
707001-800	972
707801-708000	990
708001-709500	975
709501-710000	973
710001-800	993
710801-711000	991
711001-300	973
711301-712000	975
712001-600	993
712601-713000	991
713001-714900	975
714901-715000	991
715001-716000	993
716001-100	972
716101-717000	974
717001-200	991
717201-718000	975L
718001-721500	974
721501-722000	992
722001-724000	974
724001-725000	972
725001-726000	974
726001-727000	992
727001-728000	974
728001-729000	992
729001-730000	975
730001-731000	992
731001-732000	975
732001-734000	992
734001-735000	975
735001-736000	940
736001-738000	975
738001-739000	974
739001-740000	975
740001-100	974
740101-200	972
740201-900	974
740901-741000	975
741001-742000	992
742001-743000	974
743001-300	975
743301-400	993
743401-744000	975
744001-500	992
744501-747000	974
747001-700	974
747701-748000	992
748001-749500	992
749501-750000	974
750001-100	961
750101-200	961
750201-700	950
750701-751000	952
751001-752000	960
752001-500	952
752501-753000	950
753001-500	950
753501-754000	950
754001-100	960
754101-500	952
754501-755000	960
755001-400	992
755401-500	974
755501-700	972
755701-900	974
755901-756000	972
756001-757000	974
757001-300	975
757301-500	993
757501-758000	975
758001-100	972
758101-759000	992
759001-760000	975
760001-400	992
760401-600	972
760601-800	974
760801-761000	992

Serial Range	Grade
761001-400	975
761401-600	993
761601-762000	975
762001-200	992
762201-300	972
762301-763000	974
763001-300	993
763301-600	973
763601-764000	975
764001-300	992
764301-400	972
764401-765000	974
765001-300	992
765301-767000	974
767001-600	992
767601-800	972
767801-768000	974
768001-769000	975
769001-700	992
769701-770000	972
770001-100	974
770101-771200	992
771201-400	972
771401-772000	974
772001-773000	975
773001-800	992
773801-774000	972
774001-775000	975
775001-500	952
775501-776000	950
776001-300	973
776301-700	993
776701-777000	975
777001-300	972
777301-778300	974
778301-800	992
778801-900	972
778901-779300	974
779301-780100	992
780101-300	972
780301-781300	992
781301-400	972
781401-500	974
781501-782000	992
782001-783000	975
783001-600	992
783601-784000	974
784001-785000	992
785001-500	952
785501-786000	950
786001-787000	992
787001-400	974
787401-788000	972
788001-791300	992
791301-792600	974
792601-900	972
792901-793700	992
793701-900	990
793901-794000	992
794001-200	972
794201-795000	974
795001-796400	992
796401-800	972
796801-797200	974
797201-500	974
797501-798000	954
798001-500	990
798501-800	972
798801-799000	974
799001-200	954
799201-600	992
799601-800000	954
800001-802000	974
802001-200	954
802201-2	972
802203-300	954
802301-500	972
802501-803700	974
803701-804200	954
804201-806000	974
806001-807000	975
807001-500	993
807501-808800	975
808801-809000	993
809001-500	974
809501-600	972
809601-810000	974
810001-300	990
810301-812000	974
812001-700	992
812701-813000	974
813001-814000	974P
814001-800	974L
814801-815900	992
815901-816000	974L
816001-817000	974P
817001-819000	974L
819001-820000	974P
820001-821500	974L
821501-822000	990L
822001-700	992L
822701-823000	974L
823001-824000	974P
824001-826000	975P
826001-500	975L
826501-827000	993
827001-828000	975P
828001-829000	974L
829001-830000	974P
830001-500	990L
830501-831000	992L
831001-100	954P
831101-200	972P
831201-500	954P
831501-832000	974P
832001-400	974L
832401-833000	992L
833001-834000	990L
834001-600	974P
834601-800	974L
834801-835000	974P
835001-600	992L
835601-800	990L
835801-836000	974L
836001-500	974P
836501-900	954P
836901-837000	974P
837001-838000	975P
838001-839000	975L
839001-400	974L
839401-700	992L
839701-840000	990L
840001-400	952L
840401-900	950L
840901-841000	952L
841001-842000	975P
842001-843000	974L
843001-844000	974P
844001-200	993
844201-845000	975
845001-200	992
845201-400	972
845401-700	954
845701-846000	972
846001-500	952
846501-847000	950
847001-200	972
847201-849000	974
849001-850000	975
850001-300	992
850301-800	990
850801-851000	972
851001-400	993
851401-852000	975
852001-853000	992
853001-854000	974
854001-600	950
854601-900	952
854901-855100	960L
855101-856000	950L
856001-857840	975
857841-858000	975L
858001-500	974
858501-859000	972
859001-860000	974
860001-862300	992
862301-400	954
862401-500	972
862501-600	954
862601-800	972
862801-863000	974
863001-864000	992
864001-865000	975
865001-866000	992
866001-600	974
866601-700	954
866701-867000	972
867001-868000	975
868001-869000	992
869001-870000	975
870001-872000	992
872001-200	992
872201-874000	993
874001-800	974
874801-875000	975
875001-300	952
875301-876000	975
876001-600	992
876601-877000	975
877001-400	992
877401-700	975
877701-878000	993
878001-879400	975
880001-600	992
880601-882400	974
882401-883400	992
883401-884100	974
884101-885300	992
885301-886000	974
886001-887000	992
887001-300	974
887301-890300	992
890301-891000	974
891001-600	992
891601-892200	978
892201-896200	992
896201-897800	974
897801-898000	972
898001-899100	992
899101-500	978
899501-900000	974
900001-902000	940
902001-904000	926
904001-906000	924
906001-914000	940
914001-916000	926
916001-917000	927
917001-919000	925
919001-921000	940
921001-923000	924
923001-500	999
923501-924000	925
924001-926000	940
926001-100	927
927001-929000	926
929001-933000	924
933001-935000	925
935001-937000	926
937001-939000	940
939001-941000	924
941001-944000	940
944001-949000	926
949001-952000	925
952001-958000	924
958001-960000	926
960001-968000	940
968001-970000	926
970001-971700	924
971701-972000	948
972001-973000	924
973001-974000	936
974001-975400	924
975401-25 Spec.	926
975426-976000	924
976001-979000	940
979001-100	942
979101-981000	940
981001-982000	948
982001-984000	924
984001-986000	940
986001-987000	946
987001-988000	936
988001-992000	940
992001-996000	924
996001-999998	940
999999-1000000	947
1000001-1000300	972
1000301-1003000	992
1003001-1004000	974
1004001-900	992
1004901-1007100	974
1007101-1008300	992
1008301-1009500	974
1009501-1010700	992
1010701-1011200	972
1011201-1012700	974
1012701-1013000	992
1013001-1015000	978
1015001-300	974
1015301-1016000	992
1016001-300	975
1016301-600	973
1016601-1018000	993
1018001-1020000	992
1020001-1022600	950
1022601-1023000	952
1023001-700	992
1023701-1024500	974
1024501-600	974
1024601-1025000	972
1025001-1027000	975
1027001-400	993
1027401-1029600	975
1029601-1030000	973
1030001-1032000	992
1032001-1033000	974
1033001-200	972
1033201-800	954
1033801-1035300	974
1035301-600	972
1035601-1036000	972
1036001-300	992
1036301-800	954
1036801-1037000	992L
1037001-1038000	974
1038001-1039000	992
1039001-200	972
1039201-500	978
1039501-1040300	974
1040301-1041000	992
1041001-1042000	974
1042001-700	992
1042701-1043000	972
1043001-700	978
1043701-1044000	992
1044001-1045000	974
1045001-1046000	992
1046001-1047000	975
1047001-1048000	974L
1048001-1049000	992
1049001-500	990
1049501-1051000	992
1051001-200	975
1051201-1052000	993
1052001-500	972P
1052501-900	954
1052901-1053000	974
1053001-1054000	992
1054001-1056000	974
1056001-1057000	975
1057001-1061300	992
1061301-1062300	972
1062301-1068000	992
1068001-1069000	975
1069001-1070000	974
1070001-1071000	992L
1071001-1073000	975P
1073001-1075000	992
1075001-1076200	974L
1076201-700	972L
1076701-1077000	978L
1077001-1079000	974P
1079001-1080000	992L
1080001-100	952L
1080101-200	960L
1080201-400	994L
1080401-1081000	950L
1081001-1082000	978L
1082001-400	993L
1082401-1083000	973L
1083001-1084000	990L
1084001-1085000	992L
1085001-1086000	992L
1086001-1088000	974P
1088001-1091000	992L
1091001-200	978L
1091201-1092000	974L
1092001-1093000	992L
1093001-1095000	974P
1095001-1096000	992P
1096001-400	974L
1096401-1097000	974P
1097001-1098000	992L
1098001-400	975P
1098401-1099000	975L
1099001-600	993L
1099601-1100000	975P
1100001-1104000	992L
1104001-1105000	974P
1105001-1106000	992L
1106001-500	978L
1106501-1107000	972L
1107001-1109000	992L
1109001-1111000	972L
1111001-1112000	974L
1112001-1113000	974P
1113001-1116000	992L
1116001-900	974P
1116901-1117000	974L
1117001-1119000	992L
1119001-1120000	978L
1120001-1122000	992L
1122001-1123000	974P
1123001-500	972P
1123501-1125000	974P
1125001-1127000	992L
1127001-1128000	972L
1128001-1129000	974L
1129001-1130500	974P
1130501-1131000	956P
1131001-1132000	992L
1132001-1133000	990L
1133001-1134000	978L
1134001-1135000	972L
1135001-1137000	992L
1137001-1138000	956P
1138001-1139000	956P
1139001-1140000	978L
1140001-1141000	972L
1141001-1142000	956P
1142001-500	974P
1142501-1145000	974L
1145001-1146000	975P
1146001-500	956P
1146501-1149000	974P
1149001-1150000	974L
1150001-600	950L
1150601-1151800	952L
1151801-1152000	952P
1152001-900	950P
1152901-1153200	952P
1153201-300	
1153301-500	994P
1153501-800	994L
1153801-1154000	960L
1154001-500	950L
1154501-1155000	950P
1155001-200	994P
1155201-500	994L
1156001-1158000	996L
1158001-1160000	974P
1160001-1162000	992L
1162001-500	993L
1162501-1164000	992L
1164001-1166000	974P

Serial Numbers	Grade	Serial Numbers	Grade
1166001-1167000	974L	1394001-1396000	992L
1167001-1168000	956P	1396001-500	972L
1168001-1169000	975P	1396501-1398000	974L
1169001-1170000	974P	1398001-400	974P
1170001-1174000	956P	1398401-1399000	956P
1174001-1176000	974P	1399001-1400000	992L
1176001-1177000	992L	1400001-1401000	936
1177001-1178000	956P	1401001-1403000	924
1178001-1179000	974P	1403001-1409000	940
1179001-1181000	996L	1409001-500	946
1181001-1182000	992L	1409501-1410000	940
1182001-1183000	996L	1410001-1414000	924
1183001-1184400	974P	1414001-300	941
1184401-1185400	956P	1414501-1415000	925
1185401-1186000	974P	1415001-1417000	924
1186001-1187000	992L	1417001-1419000	940
1187001-1188000	996L	1419001-1420000	924
1188001-1189000	992L	1420001-1421000	940
1189001-1190000	974P	1421001-1422000	924
1190001-1192000	996L	1422001-1424000	940
1192001-1193000	975P	1424001-1428000	924
1193001-1194000	974P	1428001-1430000	940
1194001-1195000	956P	1430001-200	924
1195001-1196000	974P	1430201-400	948
1196001-1199000	992L	1430401-1431000	924
1199001-1201000	974P	1431001-1433000	940
1201001-1202000	975P	1433001-1438000	924
1202001-1203000	992L	1438001-500	926
1203001-1204000	992L	1438501-1439500	924
1204001-500	956P	1439501-1440000	926
1204501-1206000	974P	1440001-1441000	940
1206001-1207000	992L	1441001-1442000	924
1207001-1210000	974P	1442001-500	926
1210001-1212000	992L	1442501-1444000	924
1212001-1213000	974P	1444001-1445000	940
1213001-500	996L	1445001-1447000	924
1213501-1214000	992L	1447001-1448200	940
1214001-1214600	993L	1449001-1450500	924
1214601-1215000	975P	1500001-600	974P
1215001-1216000	974L	1500601-1501200	956P
1216001-1219000	992L	1501201-1502000	974P
1219001-1220000	974P	1502001-1503000	993L
1220001-1221000	992L	1503001-1504000	996L
1221001-1223500	974P	1504001-500	974L
1223501-1224000	956P	1504501-1505200	972L
1224001-1227000	992L	1505201-700	978L
1227001-1228000	972L	1505701-1506000	974L
1228001-700	992L	1506001-1507000	975P
1228701-1229000	990L	1507001-1508000	992L
1229001-500	956P	1508001-400	974P
1229501-1230000	974P	1508401-1509000	956P
1230001-1231000	974L	1509001-1510000	992L
1231001-1232000	992L	1510001-1511000	974L
1232001-1233000	974P	1511001-1512000	975P
1233001-1236000	992L	1512001-1513200	992L
1236001-500	974P	1513201-600	992P
1236501-1237000	956P	1513601-1514000	992L
1237001-500	996L	1514001-200	956P
1237501-1238000	992L	1514201-1515000	974P
1238001-1239000	956P	1515001-1516000	992L
1239001-1241000	992L	1516001-1517000	974P
1241001-1242000	975P	1517001-1520000	992L
1242001-400	974L	1520001-1521200	974L
1242401-1243000	972L	1521201-1522000	978L
1243001-500	996L	1522001-600	974P
1243501-1244000	992L	1522601-1525000	956P
1244001-1245000	974P	1525001-1527000	996L
1245001-1246000	992L	1527001-1528000	992L
1246001-300	974P	1528001-1531000	974P
1246301-800	956P	1531001-1533000	992L
1246801-1247000	974L	1533001-600	974P
1247001-1248000	992L	1533601-1534000	956P
1248001-1249700	974P	1534001-100	975P
1249701-1250000	956P	1535101-200	975P
1250001-1252000	983	1535201-600	975P
1252001-1253000	985	1535601-1536000	993L
1253001-1257000	983	1536001-1537000	972L
1257001-900	985	1537001-1538000	992L
1260001-970	Chro.*	1538001-800	956P
1260971-1265000		1538801-1539000	974P
1265001-1266000	956P	1539001-1540000	992L
1266001-1267000	974P	1540001-500	992P
1267001-1268200	978L	1540501-1541000	992L
1268201-1269000	978L	1541001-1542200	974P
1269001-600	992L	1542201-800	956P
1269601-1270000	992L	1542801-1543000	974P
1270001-1271700	956P	1543001-1544000	996L
1271701-1272000	974P	1544001-1545000	992L
1272001-1274000	996L	1545001-400	978L
1274001-500	993L	1545401-1546000	974L
1274501-700	992L	1546001-1548000	992L
1274701-1275000	992L	1548001-600	974L
1275001-1276000	972L	1548601-1549000	972L
1276001-1277000	974L	1549001-1550000	974P
1277001-1278000	992L	1550001-500	972P
1278001-1279000	975P	1550501-1552000	974P
1279001-1280000	974P	1552001-1555000	992L
1280001-1281000	992L	1555001-1557000	993P
1281001-800	974P	1557001-800	972L
1281801-1282000	956P	1557801-1558000	974L
1282001-1284000	996L	1558001-500	956
1284001-1285000	992L	1558501-1559700	956P
1285001-1286000	956P	1559701-1560000	974P
1286001-1288000	978L	1560001-1561000	975P
1288001-500	993L	1561001-1563000	992L
1288501-1289100	992L	1563001-1565000	978L
1289101-700	990L	1565001-1567000	992L
1289701-1290000	992L	1567001-1568000	974L
1290001-1291500	974P	1568001-1569000	992L
1291501-1292000	992P	1569001-1571000	972L
1292001-1297000	992L	1571001-1572000	974P
1297001-1298000	974P	1572001-1573000	975P
1298001-1299000	992L	1573001-1575000	974P
1299001-1300000	975P	1575001-400	950L
1300001-1301000	974P	1575401-1576000	950P
1301001-1302000	974L	1576001-1577000	950L
1302001-500	992L	1577001-1578000	975P
1302501-1303000	990L	1578001-1580000	992L
1303001-500	972L	1580001-1581200	974L
1303501-1304000	972P	1581201-1582000	956P
1304001-1305000	978L	1582001-1583000	974P
1305001-1306000	956P	1583001-1584000	992L
1306001-1307000	974P	1584001-1585000	978L
1307001-1308500	992L	1585001-1586000	972L
1308501-1309000	993L	1586001-1587000	992L
1309001-1310000	974L	1587001-500	992P
1310001-1311000	972L	1587501-1589000	992L
1311001-1312000	992L	1589001-500	956P
1312001-800	974P	1589501-1590000	974P
1312801-1313000	956P	1590001-1591000	974L
1313001-1317000	992L	1591001-1592000	992L
1317001-1318000	956P	1592001-1593000	974P
1318001-1321000	992L	1593001-1595000	992L
1321001-300	990L	1595001-200	974P
1321301-1322000	992L	1595201-900	956P
1322001-700	974L	1595901-1596000	974P
1322701-1323000	972L	1596001-1611000	992L
1323001-1324000	992L	1611001-1612100	974P
1324001-1325000	996L	1612101-1613000	956P
1325001-1326500	975P	1613001-600	996L
1326501-1327000	993L	1614001-900	956P
1327001-300	956P	1614901-1615000	974P
1327301-1329000	974P	1615001-1625000	992L
1329001-1330000	992L	1625001-200	950L
1330001-1331300	974L	1625201-1626000	952L
1331301-800	972L	1626001-1627000	974P
1331801-1332000	978L	1627001-1633000	992L
1332001-1334000	992L	1633001-1635000	950L
1334001-400	974P	1635001-1636000	992L
1334401-1335000	956P	1636001-1637000	956P
1335001-300	978L	1637001-1638000	974P
1335301-1336000	972L	1638001-1642800	992L
1336001-1337000	992L	1642801-1643000	992P
1337001-1338200	996L	1643001-1644000	992L
1338201-1339000	996L	1644001-1646000	974L
1339001-1340000	956P	1646001-1648000	972L
1340001-1341000	992L	1648001-1649000	992L
1341001-300	972L	1649001-1652000	974P
1341301-500	974L	1652001-1653000	950L
1341501-1342000	978L	1653001-1654000	956P
1342001-1343000	992L	1654001-1657000	974P
1343001-400	956P	1657001-1660000	992L
1343401-1344000	974P	1660001-1661000	978L
1344001-1345000	992L	1661001-1663000	974P
1345001-600	974L	1663001-1664000	974L
1345601-1346000	972L	1664001-1665000	950L
1346001-1348000	975P	1665001-1666000	974P
1348001-1349000	974P	1666001-1667000	956P
1349001-1350000	992L	1667001-1669000	974P
1350001-600	972L	1669001-1670000	978L
1350601-1351000	974L	1670001-1671000	974P
1351001-1352000	993L	1671001-300	900
1352001-1352300	974L	1671301-900	992P
1352301-800	978L	1671901-1672000	992L
1352801-1353000	974L	1672001-1676000	974P
1353001-500	972P	1676001-1678000	992L
1353501-1354200	956P	1678001-1679000	974P
1354201-700	992P	1679001-1681000	974L
1354701-1355000	974P	1681001-1682000	974P
1355001-1356000	992L	1682001-1683000	956P
1356001-1357000	974P	1683001-1685000	974P
1357001-1359000	992L	1685001-1686000	992L
1359001-1361000	996L	1686001-1688000	974P
1361001-1362000	992L	1688001-500	978L
1362001-600	974P	1689001-600	975P
1362601-1363000	956P	1690001-1691000	956
1363001-1364000	992L	1691001-1693000	992L
1364001-1365000	975P	1693001-1696000	956P
1365001-800	956P	1696001-1699000	992L
1365801-1367000	974P	1699001-1703000	974P
1367001-1369400	992L	1703001-1704000	992L
1369401-1370000	996L	1704001-1705000	950P
1370001-1371000	974L	1705001-1706000	974P
1371001-600	996L	1706001-1707100	992L
1371601-1373000	992L	1707101-1714000	992L
1373001-1374000	975P	1714001-1715000	974P
1374001-1375000	992L	1715001-1717000	992L
1375001-1376000	950L	1717001-800	956
1376001-1377000	992L	1718001-1750000	992L
1377001-1378300	974P	1750001-1761000	900
1378301-1379000	956P	1761001-1765000	914
1379001-1380200	972L	1765001-1767000	920
1380201-1381000	978L	1767001-1768000	914
1381001-500	956P	1768001-1769000	900
1381501-1383000	974P	1769001-1770000	920
1383001-1384000	992L	1770001-1778200	914
1384001-1386100	974P	1778201-1779000	910
1386101-1387000	956P	1779001-1780000	920
1387001-1388000	992L	1780001-1782000	910
1388001-400	978L	1782001-500	920
1388401-1389000	978L	1782501-1783000	900
1389001-300	956P	1783001-1808000	910
1389301-1390000	956P	1808001-1810000	914
1390001-1391000	992L	1810001-1811000	910
1391001-500	956P	1811001-1813000	900
1391501-1392000	974P	1813001-1818000	910
1392001-1393000	992L	1818001-1819000	914
1393001-1394000	974P	1819001-1821000	910

Serial	Grade	Serial	Grade	Serial	Grade
1821001-1822000	914	1989001-400	914	2475001-2476000	992L
1822001-1827000	910	2000001-2001700	988	2476001-2477000	974P
1827001-600	914	2001701-2002400	986	2477001-2490000	992L
1827601-1829100	910	2002401-800	988	2490001-2492000	974L
1829101-500	914	2002801-2003100	986	2492001-2504000	992L
1829501-1830000	910	2004001-2035000	986	2504001-2505000	950L
1830001-1831000	900	2035001-2037200	981	2505001-300	950L
1831001-1832000	920	2040001-2064900	986	2506001-2526000	992L
1832001-700	910	2100001-2191300	986A	2526001-2528000	974P
1832701-1833300	914	2200001-2248000	987	2528001-2533000	992L
1833301-1834500	910	2248001-2300000	987F	2533001-2534000	974P
1834501-1835400	914	2300001-2311000	992L	2534001-2535000	992L
1835401-1836900	910	2311001-2312000	974L	2535001-2536000	974P
1836901-1837400	914	2312001-2321700	992L	2536001-2537000	974L
1837401-1839000	910	2321701-2323000	974L	2537001-2538000	974P
1839001-500	914	2323001-2326000	992L	2538001-2539000	974L
1839501-1844700	910	2326001-2327000	974P	2539001-2542000	974P
1844701-1845700	914	2327001-2333000	992L	2542001-2543000	992L
1845701-1848300	910	2333001-2336000	974P	2543001-2545000	974P
1848301-1849500	914	2336001-2338000	992L	2545001-2547000	992L
1849501-1851900	910	2338001-2339000	974P	2547001-2548400	974P
1851901-1853100	914	2339001-2340000	974L	2548401-2548600	974L
1853101-1856800	910	2340001-2341000	974P	2548601-2548700	974L
1856801-1857900	914	2341001-2346000	992L	2548701-2550000	974L
1857901-1860300	910	2346001-2347000	974P	2550001-2551000	992L
1860301-1861000	914	2347001-2356000	992L	2551001-2552000	974L
1861001-1863000	900	2356001-2358000	974P	2552001-2555000	992L
1863001-700	920	2358001-2364000	992L	2555001-2555600	974L
1863701-1864300	910	2364001-2365000	974P	2555701-2557000	974L
1864301-1865000	920	2365001-2374000	992L	2558001-2560000	992L
1865001-500	914	2374001-2375000	974P	2560001-2561000	974L
1865501-1870300	910	2375001-2378000	992L	2561001-2563000	992L
1870301-1871500	914	2378001-2380000	974L	2563001-2564000	974L
1871501-1875100	910	2380001-2383000	992L	2564001-2566000	992L
1875101-600	914	2383001-2384000	950L	2566001-2566000	974L
1875601-1876500	910	2384001-2385000	992L	2567001-2581000	992L
1876501-1877500	914	2385001-2396000	974P	2581001-2583900	992E
1877501-1878700	910	2386001-2390000	992L	2583901-2584300	992E
1878701-1880000	914	2390001-2391000	974P	2584301-2596000	992E
1880001-300	920	2391001-2393000	992L	2596001-2597000	974L
1880301-1881500	900	2393301-2395000	974P	2597001-2608000	992E
1881501-700	920	2395001-2397000	992L	2608001-2608800	974L
1881701-900	900	2397001-2398000	974L	2609001-2611000	974L
1881901-1882900	910	2398001-2401000	992L	2611001-2611400	950L
1882901-1885000	900	2401001-2402000	974P	2611401-2613000	950E
1885001-1887400	910	2402001-2407000	992L	2613001-2618000	992E
1887401-1888600	914	2407001-2409000	974P	2618001-2619000	950E
1888601-1891000	910	2409001-2413000	992L	2619001-2631000	992E
1891001-1892200	914	2413001-2414000	974P	2631001-2631600	950E
1892201-1894600	910	2414001-2415000	974L	2631801-2632000	950E
1894601-1895800	914	2415001-2418000	992L	2632001-2639000	992E
1895801-1899000	910	2418001-2420000	974P	2639001-2641000	950E
1899001-300	900	2420001-2422000	992L	2641001-2649000	992E
1899301-1900000	920	2422001-2423000	974P	2649001-2650600	950E
1900001-400	910	2423001-2432000	992L	2651001-2855300	992E
1900401-1902100	914	2432001-2433000	974P	2900001-2911500	979
1902101-1907000	910	2433001-2434000	992L	2911601-2931900	979F
1907001-1909000	914	2434001-2435000	974P	3000001-3002300	922
1909001-1910000	910	2435001-2437000	992L	3002301-3002500	922 M.P.
1910001-500	920	2437001-2438000	974P	3002501-3003800	922
1910501-1911000	900	2438001-2442000	992L	3003801-3004000	922 M.P.
1911001-1913000	920	2442001-2445000	974P	3004001-3006100	922
1913001-1914000	900	2445001-2451000	992L	3006101-3006300	922 M.P.
1914001-1920000	910	2451001-2453000	974P	3006301-3008000	922
1920001-1922000	920	2453001-2455000	992L	3008001-3008600	922 M.P.
1922001-1924000	910	2455001-2456000	974P	3008601-3010000	922
1924001-1925000	900	2456001-2457000	992L	3010001-3010500	922
1925001-1936000	910	2457001-2458000	950L	3010501-3010700	922 M.P.
1936001-1937000	920	2458001-2459000	974L	3010701-3011900	922
1937001-900	900	2459001-2461000	992L	3011901-3012500	922 M.P.
1940001-1941000	914	2461001-2462000	974L	3012501-3013100	922
1941001-1949000	910	2462001-2464000	992L	3013101-3013700	922 M.P.
1949001-1950000	914	2464001-2466000	974P	3013701-3015700	922
1950001-1962000	910	2466001-2468000	992L	3050001-3054800	902
1962001-1963000	914	2468001-2469000	974P	3054801-3056000	922
1963001-1975000	910	2469001-2472000	992L	3056001-3060800	902
1975001-1976000	914	2472001-2473000	974P	3061001-3065100	904
1976001-1980000	910	2473001-2474000	992L	3100001-3133800	916
1980001-1981000	914	2474001-2475000	974P	3135001-3152700	918
1981001-1988500	910			3200001-3460900	912
				4000001-4447201	987F
		*Hamilton 36 size chronometer watch		4447301-4523000	987E

Model	Grade
A-001 to A-8900	980B
1B-001 to 1B-25300	999B
2B-001 to 2B-700	999B
2B-701 to 2B-800	950B
C-001 to C-396300	992B
E-001 to E-114000	989
E-114001 to E-140400	
	989E
F-101 to F-57600	995
F-57601 to F-59850	995A
F-59851 to F-62000	995
F-62001 to F-63000	995A
F-63001 to F-63800	995
F-63801 to F-286200	995A
G-001 to G-13600	980
G-13601 to G-14600	
	980 & 980A
G-14601 to G-44500	980
G-44501 to G-45000	980A
G-45001 to G-47400	980
G-47401 to G-48400	980A
G-48401 to G-58200	980
G-58201 to G-58700	980A
G-58701 to G-61600	980
G-61601 to G-62500	980A
G-62501 to G-67500	980
G-67501 to G-68600	980A
G-68601- to G-651700	980
H-001 to H-1000	921
H-1001 to H-1800	
	400 & 921
H-1801 to H-2000	921
H-2001 to H-2800	
	400 & 921
H-2801 to H-3500	400
H-3501 to H-51700	921
H-50001 to H-57500	401
J-001 to J-6'0600	982
L-001 to L-165000	997
M-001 to M-201900	982M
N-001 to N-532200	721
O-1 to O-486300	987A
R-001 to R-3800	023
S-001 to S-18700	950B
SS-001 to SS-87400	987S
T-001 to T-783000	911
V-001 to V-127200	911M
X-001 to X-197600	917
Y-001 to Y-396200	747
CY-001 to CY-176700	748
O-01A to 622700-A	750
O-01C to 126000-C	751
001E to 47400E	752
001F to 63700F	753
001H to 26800H	754

NOTE: THE
serial numbers
BELOW were
NOT USED
S# 2,655,301 TO
S# 2,900,000

also not used
S# 3,460,901 TO
S# 4,000,000

* Hayden W. Wheeler model

NOTE: The above serial number and grade listing is an actual Hamilton factory list and is accurate in most cases. However, it has been brought to our attention that in rare cases the serial number and grade number do not match the list. One example is the Hayden W. Wheeler model.

Grade 936 single roller before S# 426,001, double roller after S# 426,000.
Grade 937 single roller before S# 652,901, double roller after S# 652,900.
Grade 940 single roller before S# 512,201, double roller after S# 512,200.
Grade 941 single roller before S# 419,101, double roller after S# 419,100.
Grade 972 single roller before S# 748,001, double roller after S# 748,000.
Grade 973 single roller before S# 711,301, double roller after S# 711,300.
Grade 992 single roller before S# 377,001, double roller after S# 379,000.
Grade 993 single roller before S# 367,801, double roller after S# 367,800.
Grade 956,964,965,968,969,975,976, & 977 single roller before S# 2,477,001, double roller after S# 2,477,000.
Grade 974 & 978 single roller before S# 2,490,001, double roller after S# 2,490,000.

Grade 925, 18 size, 17 jewels, hunting case, serial number 101,495.

Grade 932, 18 size, 16 jewels, open face, serial number 6,888. Ca. 1894.

HAMILTON 18 SIZE

Grade or Name — Description	Avg	Ex-Fn	Mint
7J, LS, FULL, OF (total production, **1,100**) .... ★★	$1,600	$1,900	$2,500
11J, LS, FULL, HC (total production, **63**) .... ★★★★	2,200	2,400	3,600
11J, LS, FULL, OF (total production, **328**) .... ★★★	1,700	2,500	3,200
922, 15J, OF.. ★★	400	600	1,000
923, 15J, HC .... ★★	550	800	1,100
924, 17J, NI, OF, DMK...	125	225	400
925, 17J, NI, HC, DMK...	125	225	400
926, 17J, NI, OF, DMK, ADJ..	125	225	400
927, 17J, NI, HC, DMK, ADJ..	125	225	400
928, 15J, NI, OF..	200	300	500
929, 15J, NI, HC, **14K** orig. case	650	900	1,500
929, 15J, NI, HC	200	300	600
930, 16J, NI, OF..	200	300	600
931, 16J, NI, HC	250	350	700
932, 16J, **S#21-30 1st run** , OF......................... ★★★★	3,000	3,500	4,500
932, 16J, NI, OF **(S#s less than 400)**	800	1,100	1,600
932, 16J, NI, OF.. ★★	400	575	1,100
933, 16J, NI, HC .... ★★	500	700	1,200
933, 16J, NI, HC *((Serial #s started at 1021-30))*	600	900	1,600
934, 17J, NI, DMK, ADJ, OF	125	250	450
934, 17J, NI, ADJ, Coin, OF	100	200	400
934 & 935 & 937, 17J, MARKED (**Main Line**)................ ★	350	500	900
935, 17J, NI, DMK, ADJ, HC....................................... ★	275	400	600
936, 17J, **S# 1-20, 1st run**, OF....................................	4,000	5,800	8,000
936, 17J, NI, DMK, SR & DR, OF	100	225	400
937, 17J, NI, MARKED on Mvt.(**Official Standard**), HC .... ★	750	1,000	1,700
937, 17J, NI, DMK, SR & DR, HC...............................	200	275	500
937, 17J, serial # 1001 to 1020 = **1st run** HC .... ★★	1,200	1,600	2,600
937, 17J, serial # 1031 to 1060 = **2nd run** HC........ ★★	600	900	1,700

FIRST Hunting Case serial # was **1001.**
Grade 937 *(Serial #s started at 1001)*

Note: Some of the early watches were re-numbered, S# 07 re-numbered as 30,007, S# 12 re-numbered as 30,012, S# 1006 re-numbered as 31,006, S# 1016 re-numbered as 31,016, The above list is just a few examples also some returned and re-numbered.

🕐 Watches listed in this book are priced at the collectable Trade Show level, as **Complete** watches having an original 14k gold-filled case for Stem Wind and *Key Wind* with silver case, an original white enamel single sunk dial, and with the entire original movement in good working order with no repairs needed.

Grade or Name — Description		Avg	Ex-Fn	Mint
938, 17J, NI, DMK, DR, OF	★★	$650	$775	$1,100
939, 17J, NI, DMK, DR, HC	★★	700	850	1,200
940, 21J, NI, Mermod Jaccards St. Louis Paragon , OF				
Time Keeper & a hour glass on mvt.	★	635	800	1,100
940, 21J, NI, DMK, SR & DR, Adj.5P, GJS, OF		225	275	450
940, 21J, NI, GF or Coin, OF		225	275	450
940, 21J, NI, SR & DR, **2-Tone**, OF	★	325	400	775
940, 21J, NI, DR, Marked **Extra**, OF	★	500	650	1,000
940, 21J, NI, DR, Marked **Special**, OF	★	500	650	1,000
940, 21J, NI, DR, Marked **Special for R R Service**, OF	★★★	2,500	3,000	4,000
940, 21J, NI, DR, Marked **Pennsylvania Special**, OF	★★	3,000	3,500	5,000
941, 21J, NI, SR, GJS, HC		275	350	550
941, 21J, NI, DR, GJS, Marked **Special**, HC	★	475	600	900
941, 21J, NI, DMK, DR, **Adj.5P**, GJS, HC		300	400	650
942, 21J, NI, DMK, DR, Adj.5P, GJS, OF		250	350	550
942, 21J, NI, DMK, DR, Adj.5P, GJS				
Marked **For Railroad Service**. OF	★★	2,500	3,000	5,000
943, 21J, NI, DMK, DR, Adj.5P, GJS, HC	★	300	425	750
943, 21J, Marked Burlington Special	★★	2,600	3,200	4,500
944, 19J, NI, DMK, DR, Adj.5P, GJS, OF		300	435	700
946, Anderson, (jobber name on movement), **14K**		1,200	1,700	2,700
946, 23J, Marked **Extra**, GJS, OF	★	1,000	1,400	2,400
946, 23J, Marked ''Loaner'' on case	★	800	1,000	1,800
946, 23J, NI, DMK, DR, Adj.5P, GJS, OF		650	800	1,300
946, 23J, NI, DMK, Adj.5P, GJS, unmarked, OF		650	800	1,300
947, 23J, NI, DMK, DR, Adj.5P, GJS, **14K, HC,**				
NOT MARKED ''947''	★★★	3,800	5,000	8,000
947, 23J, NI, DMK, DR, Adj.5P, GJS, **14K,** HC,				
MARKED ''947''	★★★	4,500	6,000	9,000
947, 23J, NI, DMK, DR, Adj.5P, GJS, **14K,** HC,				
MARKED ''947'' EXTRA	★★★★	5,500	7,000	10,000

* NOTE: **947 grade** is a up-jeweled version of the **943 - 21J. grade**. (check serial numbers list)

MOVEMENTS WITH ODD GRADE NUMBERS ARE HUNTING CASE example **947**.
MOVEMENTS WITH EVEN GRADE NUMBERS ARE OPEN FACE example **946**.
Note: Some 18 size movements are **marked** with grade numbers, some are not. Collectors prefer **MARKED** movement.

Grade **947 (marked)**, 18 size, 23 jewels, gold jewel settings, HC, Adj5p, S# **163,219**. (From 943 run 163,001-164,000) 947 grade is a up-jeweled version of the **943 - 21J. grade**.

Burlington Special, 18 size, 21 jewels, Grade 943, Hunting Case, serial number 121,614.

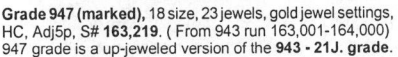

⏁ **The Complete Price Guide to Watches goal is to stimulate the orderly exchange of** <u>Watches</u> **between** *"buyers"* **and** *"sellers"*.

Grade or Name — Description		Avg	Ex-Fn	Mint
948, 17J, NI, DMK, DR, Adj.5P, GJS, OF	★	$350	$450	$875
948, 17J, NI, DMK, DR, Adj.5P, GJS, Coin, OF	★	350	450	875
The Banner, 928, 15J, NI, OF		175	250	450
The Banner, 940, 21J, NI, OF		275	350	550
The Banner, 940 special, 21J, NI, OF		375	500	900
The Banner, 941, 21J, NI, HC		325	400	650
The Banner, 17J, M#927, HC, ADJ		150	200	350
Burlington Special, 17J, Adj.5P, OF	★★	1,000	1,400	2,200
Burlington Special, 17J, Adj.5P, HC	★★	1,100	1,500	2,300
Burlington Special, 21J, Adj.5P, OF	★★	1,200	1,600	2,400
Burlington Special, 21J, Adj.5P, HC	★★	1,400	1,800	3,000
Chesapeake & Ohio, Special, (936)	★★★	2,500	3,200	5,000
Chesapeake & Ohio, Railway Special, (936)	★★★	2,500	3,200	5,000
Chesapeake & Ohio, Railway Special, (937)	★★★	2,500	3,200	5,000
Imperial Canada, GRADE 922, OF	★★	550	700	1,100
Imperial Canada, GRADE 923, HC	★★	600	800	1,300
Inspectors Standard, 21J, OF	★★	700	900	1,600
The Union, 17J, G# 924		175	225	450
The Union Special, 17J		175	225	450
The Union, 17J, G#925, HC		225	275	550

Grade 950, 16S, 23J, pendant set, gold train, gold jewel settings, white gold finish movement, OF, S# 1,020,650.

Grade 961, 16 size, 21 jewels, gold train, gold jewel settings, HC, serial number 81,848. CA. Feb, 1906.

16 SIZE

Grade or Name — Description		Avg	Ex-Fn	Mint
950, 23J, LS, BRG, DR, GT, 14K not Hamilton case OF	★★	$1,600	$2,200	$3,200
950, 23J, DR, BRG, GJS, Adj.5P, NI, GCW, OF		800	950	1,700
950, 23J, DR, GJS, BRG, Adj.5P, NI, Gold Train, OF		900	1,000	1,800
950B, 23J, LS, Adj.6P, NI, DR, BRG, OF	☑	900	950	1,700
950B, 23J, LS, Adj.6P, NI, DR, BRG, Gold Train, OF	☑	950	1,100	1,900
950B, 23J, LS, Adj.6P, NI, DR, BRG, OF, In Hamilton original two factory boxes with matching serial numbers	☑★★	1,500	2,000	3,000
950E, 23J, LS, Adj.6P, NI, DR, BRG, marked Elinvar, OF	☑	1,100	1,400	2,200
*951, 23J, LS, BRG, Adj.5P, NI, GT, GJS, DR, HC	★★★★	4,500	6,000	8,000
*951, 23J, PS, BRG, Adj.5P, NI, GT, GJS, DR, HC,14K	★★★★	5,000	6,500	8,500
952, 19J, LS or PS, BRG, Adj.5P, NI, GJS, DR, OF	★	300	350	550
952, 19J, LS or PS, BRG, Adj.5P, OF, 14K	★	500	700	1,000

* NOTE: **951** movements were made from the **961 runs.** (check serial numbers list)
The last made American Pocket Watch was Hamiltons 992B, in 1969.

🕐 Watches listed in this book are priced at the collectable Trade Show level, as **Complete** watches having an original 14k gold-filled case for Stem Wind and Key Wind with silver case, an original white enamel single sunk dial, and with the entire original movement in good working order with no repairs needed.

Grade or Name — Description	Avg	Ex-Fn	Mint
954, 17J, LS or PS, 3/4, DR, Adj., OF	$125	$200	$400
956, 17J, PS, 3/4, DR, Adj., OF	100	185	350
960, 21J, PS, BRG, GJS, GT, DR, Adj.5P, OF ★	400	500	850
960, 21J, LS, BRG, GJS, GT, DR, Adj.5P, OF ★	400	500	850
961, 21J, PS & LS, BRG, GJS, GT, DR, Adj.5P, HC ★★	450	585	950
962, 17J, PS, BRG, OF ★★	475	600	1,100
963, 17J, PS, BRG, HC ★★★	475	600	1,100
964, 17J, PS, BRG, OF ★★★	500	675	1,200
965, 17J, PS, BRG, HC ★★★	500	675	1,200
966, 17J, PS, 3/4, OF ★★★	500	675	1,200
967, 17J, PS, 3/4, HC ★★★	600	775	1,300
968, 17J, PS, 3/4, OF ★	400	500	800
969, 17J, PS, 3/4, HC ★	450	550	850
970, 21J, PS, 3/4, OF	200	300	525
971, 23J, Adj.5P, **SWISS MADE**	75	100	175
971, 21J, PS, 3/4, HC ★	200	335	550
972, 17J, PS & LS, OF, 3/4, NI, DR, GJS, Adj.5P, DMK, OF	125	200	375
973, 17J, PS & LS, 3/4, NI, DR, Adj.5P, HC	150	225	450
974, 17J, PS or LS, 3/4, NI, single roller, Adj.3P, OF	100	165	325
974, 17J, PS or LS, 3/4, NI, double roller, Adj.3P, OF	125	185	375
974 **special**, 17J, marked Special, double roller, Adj.3P, OF	125	185	375
974 **special**, 17J, Electric Railway, Electric Interurban, or Trolly Car, Adj.3P, OF	175	250	450
974, 17J, Adj.3P, 2-tone, OF	175	200	450
2974B, 17J, Adj.3P, **hacking, U.S. GOV.,** OF.	275	325	550
975, 17J, PS & LS, 3/4, NI, Adj.3P, HC	125	185	325
976, 16J, PS, 3/4, OF	125	185	325
977, 16J, PS, 3/4, HC	125	185	325
978, 17J, LS, 3/4, NI, DMK, OF	125	185	325
990, 21J, LS, GJS, DR, Adj.5P, DMK, NI, 3/4, GT, OF	175	275	500
991, 21J, LS, 3/4, DR, GJS, Adj.5P, DMK, NI, GT, HC ★	225	325	600

EARLY 16 size only made **670** - used a larger dial plate

	Avg	Ex-Fn	Mint
EARLY 16 size, 17J., ADJ, 1st run = 51,001 to 51,300 ★★★	$600	$675	$875
EARLY 16 size, 17J., ADJ, 2nd run = 52,001 to 52,300 ★★★	500	550	775
EARLY 16 size, 17J., ADJ, 3rd run = 53,001 to 53,070 ★★★	400	450	625

NOTE: For above see serial numbers and grades list. NO GRADE # **ASSIGNED**.

16 size NO GRADE # **ASSIGNED**, OF, PS, S# 52,135.
From 2nd run, Ca. 1897.

Grade 4992B, 16 size, 22 jewels, Adj.6p.
Note Extra wheel for center seconds hand.

Note: Prefix before serial no. was Hamilton's method of I.D.,(C & serial no.= 992B railroad watch),
(2B & serial no. = 950B railroad watch also **S**), (3C & serial #. = 3992B G.T.C. British & Canada),
(4C & serial no.= 4992B for U.S.A. Gov't), (2K & serial no.= 2974B used for comparing watch).

🕐 A collector should expect to pay modestly higher prices at local shops.

Grade 992E, 21jewels, gold center wheel (✿), gold jewel settings, Adj.5P, marked Elinvar under balance wheel, Note the wide striped style Damaskeening, serial #2,595,787.

Grade 3992B, 22J, Adj.6P, "Navigation Master", note outside chapter on dial 1–10, 5-60 in red with red minute hand. Ca. 1942. (NATO dial)

Grade or Name — Description	Avg	Ex-Fn	Mint
992, 21J, 3/4, Adj.5P, SR & DR, NI, OF	$200	$275	$425
992, 21J, 3/4, **gold center wheel**,GJS, Adj.5P, SR & DR, NI, OF..	225	300	475
992, 21J, 3/4, GJS, Adj.5P, DR, NI, DMK, **Mvt. 2 -Tone,** OF	265	385	625
992, 21J, **Extra**, 3/4, GJS, Adj.5P, DR, NI, DMK, OF ★	425	550	900
992, 21J, 3/4, DR, NI, **marked 8 Adj. for RR, Gold Flashed,** OF ★	550	750	1,300
992, 21J, marked **Special**, 3/4, PS & LS, GJS, Adj.5P, DR, **2-tone** NI, DMK, marked **Adj. for RR Service** on dial, OF... ★★★	1,300	1,700	2,600
992E, 21J, marked Elinvar, **NO** gold center wheel, 3/4, GJS, Adj.5P	275	325	650
992E, 21J, marked **Elinvar, gold center wheel**, 3/4, GJS, Adj.5P ..★	325	425	750
992B, 21J, LS, Adj.6P, 3/4, OF	275	335	575
992B, 21J, Adj.6P, **2-Tone case** ◹	300	385	675
992B, 21J, Adj.6P, 3/4, **Military** silver case, OF	325	425	675
3992B, 22J, Adj.6P, 12 hr. dial, (Canadian), Chrome case ... ★★★	300	400	750
3992B, 22J, Adj.6P, "Navigation Master", Chrome case .... ★★	500	600	850
4992B, 22J, LS, 3/4, 24-hr. dial, Greenwich Civil Time, silveroid .	250	350	550
4992B, 22J, LS, 3/4, 24-hr. dial, **Military** Silver case, OF...... ◹ ★	350	450	750
993, 21J, GJS, Adj.5P, DR, NI, DMK, HC .... ★	300	400	550
993, 21J, marked **Special, tu-tone**, GJS, Adj.5P, DMK, DR, HC ★	400	585	750
993, 21J, LS, GJS, Adj.5P, DMK, DR, NI, **14K**, HC ....★	600	750	1,000
993, 21J, LS, GJS, Adj.5P, DMK, DR, (**GF multi color case**) HC ★	400	550	800

ADMIRAL,16 size, 16 jewels, Damaskeened on nickel 3/4 plate, HC, grade 977, Ca. Sept, 1898, serial no. 57821.

Chronograph, Grade 23, 16 size, 19 jewels, start-stop-reset to 0. Chronograph Grade 23 starts in 1943 ends in 1956 & total production = 23,146.

Grade or Name — Description	Avg	Ex-Fn	Mint
994, 21J, BRG, GJS, GT, DR, Adj.5P, DMK, PS, OF .... ★★	$800	$900	$1,200
994, 21J, BRG, GJS, GT, DR, Adj.5P, DMK, LS, OF .... ★★	900	1,000	1,300
996, 19J, LS, 3/4 GJS, DR, Adj.5P, DMK, OF	200	250	450
Admiral, 16J., 3/4 plate, OF, ...	125	175	350
Admiral,16J, 3/4, NI, ADJ., DMK, HC ....★	250	325	450
DeLong Escapement, 21J., upright **D** shaped pallets .... ★★★★	4,000	5,500	8,000
Hayden W. Wheeler, 17J, OF...★	400	450	650
Hayden W. Wheeler, 17J, HC ....★	450	500	750
Hayden W. Wheeler, 21J...★	450	500	750
Hayden W. Wheeler, 21J, **14K & H.W.W**. on case......................★	800	950	1,200
Limited, 17J, G#974	200	250	350
Official Standard, 17J, OF...	250	375	600
Union Special, 17J	150	225	450
Swiss Mfg., 17J, Adj.2P, G#669, OF, GF case	75	100	150
Swiss Mfg., 17J, Adj.2P, G#670, **HC**, GF case	100	135	200
Swiss Mfg., 23J, Adj.3P, (by Buren W. Co. G# 971), Ca. 1969-70s	125	150	250

CHRONOGRAPH
Grade 23

Grade or Name — Description	Avg	Ex-Fn	Mint
16S, 19J, chronograph with start-stop-reset to zero	$350	$450	$600

12 SIZE

(Some cases were octagon, decagon, cushion, etc.)

Grade or Name — Description	Avg	Ex-Fn	Mint
900, 19J, BRG, DR, Adj.5P, GJS, OF, **14K** ....★	$250	$350	$525
900, 19J, BRG, DR, Adj.5P, GJS, OF	100	175	325
902, 19J, BRG, DR, Adj.5P, GJS, OF	100	175	325
902, 19J, BRG, DR, Adj.5P, GJS, **14K** ....★	250	375	525

Grade **918**, 12 size, 19 jewels, Adj3p, serial number 3,136,257.

Grade **920**, 12 size, 23 jewels, gold train, gold jewel settings, serial number 1,863,381.

🕐 A collector should expect to pay modestly higher prices at local shops.

🕐 Watches listed in this book are priced at the collectableTrade Show level, as **Complete** watches having an original 14k gold-filled case for Stem Wind and *Key Wind* with silver case, an original white enamel single sunk dial, and with the entire original movement in good working order with no repairs needed.

MOVEMENTS WITH ODD GRADE NUMBERS ARE HUNTING CASE example 951.
MOVEMENTS WITH EVEN GRADE NUMBERS ARE OPEN FACE example 950.

Grade or Name — Description	Avg	Ex-Fn	Mint
904, 21J, BRG, DR, Adj.5P, GJS, GT ....★	$150	$250	$475
910, 17J, 3/4, DR, ADJ..	50	100	175
912, 17J, **Digital model, rotating seconds**, OF	200	300	525
912, 17J, 3/4, DR, ADJ..	50	100	175
914, 17J, 3/4, DR, Adj.3P, GJS	50	100	175
914, 17J, 3/4, DR, Adj.3P, GJS, **14K**......................................	200	300	400
916, 17J, 3/4, DR, Adj.3P...	50	100	175
916, 17J, Adj.3P, silver case	50	100	175
918, 19J, Adj.3P, WGF...	100	135	275
918, 19J, 3/4, DR, Adj.3P, GJS, OF...	100	135	275
920, 23J, BRG, DR, Adj.5P, GJS, GT, OF	225	300	475
920, 23J, BRG, DR, Adj.5P, GJS, GT, **14K**.............................	425	500	700
922, 23J, BRG, DR, Adj.5P, GJS, GT, **14K**	425	500	700
922, 23J, BRG, DR, Adj.5P, GJS, GT, OF.................................	225	300	475
922 MP, 23J, marked (MASTERPIECE), 18K case ....★	700	900	1,500
922 MP, 23J, marked (MASTERPIECE), Iridium Platinum ....★	800	1,100	1,800
922 MP, **Gold Filled, Hamilton case**......................................	325	450	650
400, 21J, (Illinois 13 size M#2, 5 tooth click), the Tycoon Series,			
Hamilton on dial & case, **18K**, OF ....★	450	600	800

Grade 922MP, 12 size, 23 jewels, **marked** "masterpiece" serial number 3,013,390, c. 1930.

Grade 914, 10-12 size, 17J, gold jewel settings, double roller, open face, S # 1,767,782.

10 SIZE

Grade or Name — Description	Avg	Ex-Fn	Mint
917, 17J, 3/4, DR, Adj.3P...	$50	$75	$150
917, 17J, 3/4, DR, Adj.3P, **14K**	200	285	425
921, 21J, BRG, DR, Adj.5P..	125	200	325
923, 23J, BRG, DR, Adj.5P, **G.F.**..	150	225	375
923, 23J, BRG, DR, Adj.5P, (**spread** to fit a 12 size CASE),**14K** ..	225	300	500
923, 23J, **18K, and box**..	400	600	900
923, 23J, BRG, DR, Adj.5P, **Iridium Platinum**.........................★	600	750	1,100
945, 23J, Adj.5P, Masterpiece on DIAL....................................	100	185	325
945, 23J, Adj.5P, spread to **12 size**	100	185	325

🕐 A collector should expect to pay modestly higher prices at local shops.

🕐 **The Complete Price Guide to Watches goal is to stimulate the orderly exchange of <u>Watches</u> between "*buyers*" and "*sellers*".**

0 SIZE

Grade or Name — Description	Avg	Ex-Fn	Mint
981, 17J, 3/4, Adj.3P, DR, **18K, HC**	$200	$300	$575
982, 17-19J, same as 981 & 983 HC but no seconds bit	75	125	200
983, 17J, Adj.3P, DR, GJS, **18K, HC**	200	300	525
985, 19J, BRG, Adj.3P, DR, GJS, GT, **18K, HC**	200	300	550
Lady Hamilton, **14K** case, OF	200	250	400
Lady Hamilton, 23J, GJS, **gold filled OF**	150	185	300

Model 22, 21 jewels, 35 Size or 70mm, wind indicator, adjusted to 6 positions, base metal case.

Chronometer Model 22, 21 jewels, 35 Size or 70mm, wind indicator, 54 hour mainspring, adjusted to 6 positions.

Above: 36 size, Sterling silver case, wind indicator.
Right: Chronometer in gimbals and box, wind indicator.

CHRONOMETER

Grade or Name — Description	Avg	Ex-Fn	Mint
35S, M#22, 21J, Wind Indicator, **Adj.6P**, in gimbals and box, lever	$1,000	$1,400	$2,000
35S, M#22, 21J, Wind Indicator, **Adj.6P**, in a large base metal OF case	500	700	1,000
36S, M#36, 21J, **Adj.5P**, Wind Indicator, in gimbals and box	1,300	1,700	2,500
36S, M#36, 21J, 56 hr.W. Ind.,"SID" (sidereal), chrome case ..... ★	1,500	1,900	3,000
36S, M#36, 21J, Wind Indicator, in Hamilton sterling pocket watch case with bow (s# 1,260,001 to 1,260,970) .... ★★★	1,700	2,000	3,300
37S, 21J, 940 movement S# range= 420,001 to 421,000, ONLY 220 made for U.S. Navy, true 24 hour black dial .... ★★★	1,500	1,800	3,000
85S, M#21, 14J, KW, KS, **Fusee, Detent Escapement** with helical hairspring, gimbals and box, (all original)	1,500	1,800	3,000

Baton Hands Ca.1940

CASE MODEL # A
gold filled : $95 - $150 - $350
Dial:(23J RR)$30 - $50 - $100
Note: Baton Style hands Ca.1940

BOC = Bar Over Crown
CASE MODEL # 2,Ca.1926
gold filled : $95- $150 - $350
14K Gold : $500 - $600 - $1,000
2 TONE case GF:$150-$250-$550
Dial: RR,$20 - $40 - $100

CASE MODEL # 3 Ca.May 1926
gold filled : $125 - $200 - $375
Dial: $20 - $30 - $60
M#2 & M#3 first seen
Ca. May, 1926

Rigid Bow CASE MODEL # 4
gold filled : $125 - $200 - $375
Dial: $20 - $30 - $60
First seen Ca. Oct.,1927

CASE MODEL #5
gold filled : $100 - $150 - $275
Montgomery Dial: $30 - $45 - $100
First seen Ca. July, 1928

CASE MODEL # 6
gold filled : $125- $200 - $350
Dial: $25 - $35 - $65
First seen Ca. Sept., 1929

CASE MODEL # 7
White gold filled : $125 - $210 - $325
Montgomery Dial: $30 - $45 - $95
First seen Ca. May, 1930

CASE MODEL # 8
gold filled : $135- $225 - $400
Dial: $20 - $30 - $60
First seen Ca. Sept., 1931

CASE MODEL # 10
gold filled : $125- $210 - $350
Montgomery Dial: $35 - $50 - $95
First seen Ca. May 1936

Model "A" was advertised in a Gold-filled Case & advertised with a grade 950 movement. Models 2 & 17 came in 14K solid GOLD or gold-filled, model 2 advertised with 992 or 950. Models 3, 4, 5, 6, (7 white G.F.), 8, 10, 11, Cross Bar, & Traffic Special II all gold-filled. Model "16" gold plate and Model "15" & Traffic Special I was stainless steel case.

🕐 NOTE: Factory Advertised as a **complete** watch and was fitted with a certain matched, timed and rated movement and sold in the factory designed case style as a complete watch. The factory also sold _uncased_ movements to **JOBBERS** such as Jewelry stores & they cased the movement in a case styles the **CUSTOMER** requested. All the factory advertised complete watches came with the dial **SHOWN or CHOICE** of other **Railroad** dials.

CASE MODEL # 11
gold filled : $95 - $150 - $325
Dial: $20 - $40 - $80

CASE MODEL # 14
Nickel : $75- $100 - $175
Dial: $20 - $40 - $80

CASE MODEL # 15 Ca. 1945
S. Steel : $35- $50 - $100
Dial: $20 - $40 - $80

CASE MODEL # 16
gold filled : $80 - $95 - $225
M # 12 chrome:$40 - $50 - $100
Montgomery Dial: $45 - $65 - $125

CASE MODEL # 17
gold filled : $125- $195 - $375
14KGold : $450 - $600 - $1,000
Dial: $30 - $50 - $100

CASE MODEL Cross Bar
gold filled : $150- $300 - $500
Dial: $20 - $35 - $70
first seen in Nov. 1924

TRAFFIC SPECIAL I & #3
S. Steel : $35- $45 - $100
Montgomery Dial: $35 - $55 - $90

TRAFFIC SPECIAL II &#4
gold plated : $45- $55 - $100
Dial: $20 - $30 - $85

Baton
Hands
Ca.1940

The MAINLINER
gold filled : $100 - $165 - $325
Dial: $30 - $45 - $80
first seen Ca 1937

* Railway Specials were packed & shipped in a plastic ivory cigarette style box & came in 12 or more different colors. **THESE PLASTIC IVORY CIGARETTE STYLE BOX** sell for **$100 - $200 - $350 +.**

Model "A" was advertised in a Gold-filled Case & advertised with a grade 950 movement.
Models 2 & 17 came in 14K solid GOLD or gold-filled, model 2 advertised with 992 or 950.
Models 3, 4, 5, 6, 8, 10, 11, & Cross Bar gold-filled.
Model "16" gold plate and Model "15" & Traffic Special I was stainless steel case.
Case Model 14 = Nickel-Chrome.

HAMILTON W. CO. IDENTIFICATION OF MOVEMENTS

How To Identify Your Watch: Compare the movement with the illustration in this section. While comparing, note the location of the balance, jewels, screws, gears, and back plate (Full, 3/4, Bridge) these will be clues in identifying the movement you have. Having determined the size, the **GRADE** can also be found by looking up the serial number of your watch in the Hamilton Serial Number & Grades List. Illustrations of selected grades of the different size movements are shown to assist you in identifying movements. Hamilton movements that do not have grade numbers engraved on them <u>do</u> carry serial numbers which can be checked against the serial number list to secure the *grade number.*

S # 2

Grade 936, 18 SIZE, **Full Plate, OPEN FACE** SHOWN. Also grades 922, 924, 926, 928, 930, 932, 934, 938, 940, 942, 944, 946, & 948 All look SIMILAR to the above.

Grade 925, 18 SIZE, **Full Plate, Hunting Case** SHOWN. Also grades 923, 927, 929, 931, 933, 935, 937, 939, 941, 943, 945, and 947 All look SIMILAR to the above.

NOTE: 18 Size Grades 924, 925, 926, 927, 928, 929, 930, 931, 932, 933, 934, & 935 use 90% same parts but not plates. 18 Size Grades 936, 937, 938, 939, & 948 use 90% same parts but not plates. Grades 940, 941, 942, & 943 use 90% same parts but not plates. 18 Size Grades 944 & 946 use 90% same parts.

Grade 971, 16 SIZE, **Hunting Case,** 3/4 Plate, 21 jewels, Shown. Note Crown Wheel with 2 Screws this movement uses a 4 Footed Dial. Also grades 969, 973, 975, 991, & 993 all look SIMILAR to the above. Note location of the larger ratchet wheel next to balance cock.

Grade 992, 16 SIZE, **Open Face,** 3/4 Plate, 21 jewels, **1st. model** Shown. Note Crown Wheel with 2 Screws this movement uses a 4 Footed Dial. Also grades 954, 968, 970, 972, 974, & 990 all look SIMILAR to the above. Note location of the smaller Crown wheel next to balance cock. 1st. model.

NOTE: 16 Size Grades 950, 952, & 996 use 90% same parts. 16 Size Grades 954, 962, 963, 966, 967, 972, & 973 use 90% same parts but not plates. 16 Size Grades 956, 964, 965, 968, 969, 974, 975, 976, 977, & 978 use 90% same parts. 16 Size Grades 960, 961, 970, 971, 990,991, 992, 993, & 994 use 90% same parts but not plates. Grades 950E & 950B differ from grade 950. Grades 992E & 992B differ from grade 992.

Grade 992 Note: with narrow stripes, 16 size, 3/4 plate, 21 jewels, 5 positions, **2nd model** Shown. Note: Crown Wheel with 1 Screw. 2nd. model.

Grade 992 E = wide stripes Damaskeening with ELINVAR under balance wheel. 16 size, 3/4 plate, 21J., 5 positions, **3rd. model** Shown.

Grade 992 B, 16 size, 3/4 plate, 21J., **6 POSITIONS.** last model, model # 4.

Grade 950 16 size, BRIDGE, 23J., 5 positions. Note: with narrow stripes,

Grade 950 E = wide stripes Damaskeening with ELINVAR under balance wheel. 16 size, BRIDGE, 23J., 5 positions.

Grade 950 B, 16 size, BRIDGE, 23J., **6 POSITIONS.**

I will respect & appreciate positive sound reliable comments, corrections, improvements or remarks but reserve the right to accept the statement or keep my own observations & views. (*Cooksey*)

Grade 960, 16 SIZE, BRIDGE, OPEN FACE SHOWN. Also GRADES 950, 952, 962, 964, 994 all look SIMILAR to the above. Note location of the smaller Crown wheel next to balance cock.

Grade 961, 16 SIZE, BRIDGE, Hunting Case SHOWN. Also GRADES 951, 963, 965 all look SIMILAR to the above. Note location of the larger ratchet wheel next to balance cock.

SWISS MADE, 16 size, open face, 17 to 23 jewels, 3/4 plate.

Grade 902, 12 size
Open face, bridge movt., 19 jewels, double roller

Grade 912, 12 size
Open face, ¾ plate movt., 17 jewels, double roller

Grade 918, 12 size
Open face, ¾ plate movt., 19 jewels, double roller

Grade 922, 12 size
Open face, bridge movt., 23 jewels, double roller

Grade 917, 10 size
Open face, ¾ plate movt., 17 jewels, double roller

Grade 921, 10 size
Open face, bridge movt., 21 jewels, double roller

Grade 923, 10 size
Open face, bridge movt., 23 jewels, double roller

Grade 983, 0 size
Hunting, bridge movt., 17 jewels, double roller

Grade 979,6/0 size
Hunting, ¾ plate movt., 19 jewels, double roller

Grade 986, 6/0 size
Open face, ¾ plate movt., 17 jewels, double roller

IMPORTANT NOTE: Railroad Standards, Railroad Approved & Railroad Grade **terminology,** as defined and used in this ***BOOK***.
1. **RAILROAD STANDARDS** = A commission or board appointed by the railroad companies outlined a set of **guidelines** to be accepted or approved by each railroad line.
2. **RAILROAD APPROVED** = A **LIST** of watches each railroad line would approve if purchased by their employee's. (this list changed through the years).
3. **RAILROAD GRADE** = A watch made by manufactures to meet or exceed the guidelines set by the railroad **standards**. Grades such as 992, Vanguard and B.W. Raymond, etc.
🕑 Some GRADES **exceeded** the R.R. standards such as 23 jewels, diamond end stone, gold train, raised gold jewel settings, double sunk dial and the list goes on. Examples: such as Veritas, Sangamo, 950 & Riverside Maximus and many others.

HAMPDEN WATCH CO.
(DUEBER WATCH CO.)
Springfield, Massachusetts later Canton, Ohio
1877 - 1930

The New York Watch Co. preceded Hampden, and before that Don J. Mozart (1864) produced his three-wheel watch. Mozart was assisted by George Samuel Rice of New York and, as a result of their joint efforts, the New York Watch Co. was formed in 1866 in Providence, Rhode Island. It was moved in 1867 to Springfield, Massachusetts. Two grades of watches were decided on, and the company started with a 18S, 3/4 plate engraved "Springfield." They were sold for $60 to $75. The 18S, 3/4 plate were standard production, and the highest grade was a "George Walker" that sold for about $200 and a 16S, 3/4 plate "State Street" which had steel parts and exposed balance and escape wheels that were gold plated.

John C. Dueber started manufacturing watch cases in 1864 and bought a controlling interest in a company in 1886. At about this time a disagreement arose between Elgin, Waltham, and the Illinois Watch companies. Also, at this time, an anti-trust law was passed, and the watch case manufacturers formed a boycott against Dueber. Dueber was faced with a major decision, whether to stay in business, surrender to the watch case companies or buy a watch company. He decided to buy the Hampden Watch Co. of Springfield, Mass. By 1889 the operation had moved to Canton, Ohio. By the end of the year the company was turning out 600 watches a day. The first 16 size watch was produced in 1890 (serial number 800,xxx). In 1891 Hampden introduced the **first 23J** (16 size) movement made in America. Hampden assigned serial numbers at random to the New York Watch Co. movements for years after they purchased the N.Y.W.Co.Hampden W. Co. serial numbers start at about 58,000.

HAMPDEN ESTIMATED SERIAL NUMBER
AND PRODUCTION DATES

DATE-SERIAL NO.	DATE-SERIAL NO.	DATE-SERIAL NO.	DATE-SERIAL NO.
1877 — 59,000	1890 — 740,000	1903 — 1,768,000	1916 — 3,100,000
1878 — 70,000	1891 — 805,000	1904 — 1,896,000	1917 — 3,240,000
1879 — 100,000	1892 — 835,000	1905 — 2,024,000	1918 — 3,390,000
1880 — 140,000	1893 — 865,000	1906 — 2,152,000	1919 — 3,500,000
1881 — 180,000	1894 — 900,000	1907 — 2,280,000	1920 — 3,600,000
1882 — 215,000	1895 — 930,000	1908 — 2,400,000	1921 — 3,700,000
1883 — 250,000	1896 — 970,000	1909 — 2,520,000	1922 — 3,750,000
1884 — 300,000	1897 — 1,000,000	1910 — 2,650,000	1923 — 3,800,000
1885 — 350,000	1898 — 1,120,000	1911 — 2,700,000	1924 — 3,850,000
1886 — 400,000	1899 — 1,255,000	1912 — 2,760,000	1925 — 3,900,000
1887 — 480,000	1900 — 1,384,000	1913 — 2,850,000	1926 — 3,950,000
1888 — 560,000	1901 — 1,512,000	1914 — 2,920,000	1927 — 3,980,000
1889 — 640,000	1902 — 1,642,000	1915 — 3,000,000	

The above list is provided for determining the **APPROXIMATE** age of your watch. Match serial number with date. Watches were not necessarily sold in the exact order of manufactured date.

** In 1891 Hampden introduced the first "23Jewel" (16 size) watch made in America.

Left: **Teske's** patent round regulator, Ca.1875 Right: **Tucker's** patent square regulator both were applied by **watchmakers**. Can be found on 18 size movements such as Hampden Springfield, Waltham, Elgin, Rockford and others.

Chronology of the Development of Hampden Watch Co.:
The Mozart Watch Co., Providence, R. I. (1864-1866)
New York Watch Co., Providence, R. I. (1866-1867)
New York Watch Co., Springfield, Mass. (1867-1875)
New York Watch Mfg. Co., Springfield, Mass. (1875-1876)
Hampden Watch Co., Springfield, Mass. (1877-1886)
Hampden-Dueber Watch Co., Springfield, Mass. (1886-1888)
Hampden Watch Co., Canton, Ohio. (1888–1923)
Dueber Watch Co., Canton, Ohio. (1889–1923)
Dueber-Hampden Watch Co., Canton, Ohio. (1923–1931)
Amtorg, U.S.S.R (1930)

Issued 1890

Issued 1892

Issued 1895

NR inside flag = New Railway and SR inside flag = Special Railway
D & ★ D & anchor inside flag = Dueber and H inside flag = Hampden

Dueber Watch Co., 18 size, 15 jewels, nickel movement. Model 3, hunting case.

Canadian Pacific R.W., 17J, 18 size, Adj., Teske's patented regulator, M# 4, S# 761671, OF

HAMPDEN 18 SIZE

Grade or Name — Description	Avg	Ex-Fn	Mint
Anchor (inside flag), 17J, ADJ, GJS, DMK	$85	$110	$225
"3 Ball", 17J, ADJ, NI, (3 Ball-damaskeening pattern)	90	135	275
Boston W. Co. 11J, KW/SW	75	100	185
Canadian Pacific R.W., 17J, Adj., M# 4, OF ★★	1,200	1,600	2,100
Canadian Pacific RR, 17J, OF ★★	1,000	1,400	2,000
Canadian Pacific RR, 21J, OF ★★	1,400	1,900	2,500
Champion, 7-11J, ADJ, FULL, gilded, or, NI, OF	65	95	175
Champion, 7-11J, ADJ, FULL, gilded, or, NI, HC	85	125	200
Correct Time, 15J, HC ★	100	175	325
Dueber Chronometer, 16-19-21J, **detent escapement**, (Swiss)			
Helical hairspring, LS, NI, Adj.3P, GJS, HC ★★	500	650	1,000
Dueber, 11J, gilded, DMK	55	85	125
Dueber, 15J, gilded, DMK	65	95	175
Dueber, 16J, gilded, DMK	75	125	200
Dueber, 17J, gilded, DMK	65	100	175
Dueber Grand, 17J, OF	75	125	200
Dueber Grand, 17J, ADJ, HC	100	150	250
Dueber Grand, 21J, ADJ, DMK, NI, OF	125	255	375
Dueber Grand, 21J, ADJ, DMK, NI, HC	150	285	450
John C. Dueber, 15J, gilded, DMK, OF	65	85	175
John C. Dueber, 15J, gilded, DMK, HC	80	125	225
John C. Dueber, 17J, gilded, DMK, OF	65	95	175
John C. Dueber, 17J, NI, ADJ, DMK, OF	65	95	175
John C. Dueber, 17J, NI, ADJ, DMK, HC	95	150	250
John C. Dueber, Special, 17J, ADJ, DMK, OF	75	125	200
John C. Dueber, Special, 17J, ADJ, DMK, HC	100	185	325
John C. Dueber, 21J, HC	200	300	500

Chronometer "Dueber", 16-19-21J, detent escapement, **Helical hairspring**, LS, NI, Adj.3P, GJS, S# 50706, HC. **Swiss**

John C. Dueber Special, 18 size, 17 jewels, serial number 949,097.

Oriental, 18 size, 15 jewels, open face, serial number 117,825.

Grade or Name — Description	Avg	Ex-Fn	Mint
Dueber W. Co.,7-11J, OF	$50	$75	$125
Dueber W. Co., 15J, DMK, OF	60	85	150
Dueber W. Co., 15J, DMK, HC	85	110	200
Dueber W. Co., 16J, OF	65	95	150
Dueber W. Co., 16J, HC	85	125	200
Dueber W. Co., 17J, DMK, ADJ, OF	60	95	150
Dueber W. Co., 17J, Gilded	50	85	145
Dueber W. Co., 17J, DMK, ADJ, HC	85	100	200
Dueber W. Co., 19J, ADJ, GJS, HC ★	400	475	600
Dueber W. Co., 21J, Adj.5P, GJS, OF	150	225	325
Dueber W. Co., 21J, GJS, Adj.5P, HC	200	300	500
Forest City, 15J, KW	95	135	250
Gladiator, 7-9J, KW, OF	75	100	200
Gladiator, 9-11J, NI, DMK, OF	85	125	285
Gulf Stream Sp., 21J, R.R. grade, LS, OF ★★	750	900	1,600
Homer Foot, gilded, KW, OF (Early)	200	300	500

🕐 Generic, nameless or unmarked grades for watch movements are listed under the Company name or initials of the Company, etc. by size, jewel count and description.

	Avg	Ex-Fn	Mint
Hampden W. Co., 7J, KW, KS, <u>coin silver</u> OF	$90	$135	$275
Hampden W. Co., 7J, SW, OF	50	75	150
Hampden W. Co., 11J, KW, OF	50	80	155
Hampden W. Co., 11J, KW, HC,	60	95	175
Hampden W. Co., 11J, SW, OF	50	75	150
Hampden W. Co., 11J, SW, HC	75	110	200
Hampden W. Co., 15J, KW, OF	65	100	175
Hampden W. Co., 15J, KW, HC	75	110	200
Hampden W. Co., 15J, SW, HC	75	110	200
Hampden W. Co., 15J, SW, Gilded, OF	60	95	175
Hampden W. Co., 15J, SW, NI, OF	60	95	175
Hampden W. Co., 15J, **Multi-color, 14K, HC**	2,000	2,800	4,200
Hampden W. Co., 16J, OF	80	125	225
Hampden W. Co., 17J, SW, Gilded	80	125	225
Hampden W. Co., 17J, SW, NI, OF	80	125	225
Hampden W. Co., 17J, SW, HC	80	125	225
Hampden W. Co., 17J, LS, HC, **14K**	500	650	900
Hampden W. Co., 17J, LS, HC, **10K**	275	385	550
Hampden W. Co., 21J, SW, OF	175	250	400
Hampden W. Co., 21J, SW, HC	225	250	500

NR inside flag = New Railway and SR inside flag = Special Railway
D & ★ D & anchor inside flag = Dueber and H inside flag = Hampden

Menlo Park, 18 size, 17 jewels, serial number 1,184,116.

New Railway, 18 size, 23 jewels, open face only, gold jewel settings, originally sold for $50.00, Model 2.

Grade or Name — Description	Avg	Ex-Fn	Mint
John Hancock, 17J, GJS, Adj., OF	$75	$110	$200
John Hancock, 17J, GJS, Adj., HC	95	150	275
John Hancock, 21J, GJS, Adj.5P, OF	175	250	400
John Hancock, 23J, GJS, Adj.5P, OF	300	375	500
Hayward, 11J, SW	80	135	200
Hayward, 15J, KW	125	200	350
Lafayette, 11J, NI, HC	125	225	375
Lafayette, 15J, NI, **KW** ★	200	285	475
Lafayette, 15J, NI, HC	125	225	375
Lakeside, 15J, NI, SW, HC	135	175	350
M. J. & Co. Railroad Watch Co., 15J, HC ★★	400	600	950
Menlo Park, 11-15J,	125	150	200
Menlo Park, 17J, NI, ADJ, OF	135	175	300
Menlo Park, 17J, gilded, ADJ, HC	150	225	400
Mermod, Jaccard & Co., 15J, KW, HC	150	225	400
Metropolis, 15J, NI, SW, OF	95	150	300
Wm. McKinley, 17J, Adj.3P, OF	75	110	200
Wm. McKinley, 17J, Adj.3P, HC	80	125	225
Wm. McKinley, 21J, GJS, Adj.5P	135	200	375
New Railway, 17J, GJS, Adj.5P, OF	125	175	365
New Railway, 19J, GJS, Adj.5P, OF	175	225	425
New Railway, 19J, GJS, Adj.5P, HC	200	300	550

Railway, 18 size, 15-17 jewels, key wind & set, S# 115,143, early railroad watch, Ca. 1880.

Special Railway, 18 size, 23 jewels, Adj5p, serial number 3,357,284.

Grade or Name — Description	Avg	Ex-Fn	Mint
New Railway, 21J, GJS, Adj.5P, OF	$175	$250	$450
New Railway, 21J, GJS, Adj.5P, HC	200	275	525
New Railway, 23J, GJS, Adj.5P	250	350	600
New Railway, 23J, GJS, Adj.5P, **14K**, OF	500	700	1,000
North Am. RW, 21J, GJS, Adj.5P, OF	225	300	500
North Am. RW, 21J, GJS, Adj, HC	250	350	600
Order of Railroad Conductors, 17J, ADJ, OF ★★★	1,800	2,200	3,100
Oriental, 15 jewels, OF	85	135	200
Pennsylvania Special, 17J, GJS, Adj.5P, DR, NI ★★★	1,900	2,500	3,500
J. C. Perry, 15J, KW, gilded, HC	95	175	300
J. C. Perry, 15J, NI, SW, OF	75	110	200
J. C. Perry, 15J, gilded, SW, OF	75	110	200
Railway, 11J, gilded, OF	100	175	300
Railway, 15-17J, NI, OF	125	200	400
Railway, 15-17J, **KW**, marked on mvt., HC ★★	700	1,000	1,600
* **Railroad with R.R. names on dial and movement:**			
Private Label R.R. 17J, OF ★★	650	850	1,200
Special Railway, 17J, GJS, Adj.5P, NI, DR, OF	95	165	300
Special Railway, 21J, GJS, Adj.5P, NI, DR, OF	200	275	425
Special Railway, 21J, GJS, Adj.5P, NI, DR, **2-Tone**, OF	250	325	600
Special Railway, 21J, GJS, Adj.5P, NI, DR, HC	225	300	525
Special Railway, 23J, GJS, Adj.5P, NI, DR, OF	300	350	550
Special Railway, 23J, GJS, Adj.5P, NI, DR, **2-Tone**, OF	350	400	700
Special Railway, 23J, GJS, Adj.5P, NI, DR, HC	350	400	700
Special Railway, 23J, **14K, HC**	650	850	1,300
Springfield, 7-11J, KW, gilded, HC	95	175	300
Springfield, 7-11J, SW, NI, HC	95	175	300
Standard, 15J, gilded, HC	95	175	300
Train Service Standard, 17J, LS, M# 2, NI, HC ★	450	550	850
Theo. Studley, 9-15J, KW, KS, HC	95	175	300
Tramway Special, 17J, NI	150	225	375
Wisconsin Central R W, 17J, LS, OF ★	650	850	1,600
Woolworth, 11-15J, KW	90	150	275
Grade 30,31,45,46,54,57,65,66,70,71, **ALL =11J**	90	150	200
Grade 32,33,34,35,36,40,41,42,49,55,56,58,59,60,62, All =15J	90	150	200
Grade, 43,44,47,48,49,63,64,67,68,69,80,81, **ALL =16-17J**	100	165	250
Grade 85, **19J**, GJS, 2-Tone, HC ★★	500	700	1,100
Grade 95, **21J**, GJS, OF	175	250	450
Grade 125, **21J**, Adj.3P, OF	175	250	450

** In 1891 Hampden introduced the first "23Jewel" (16 size) watch made in America.

16 SIZE

Grade or Name — Description	Avg	Ex-Fn	Mint
Beacon, 7J, OF	$75	$110	$200
E.W. Bond & State Street models see New York W. Co. Springfield			
Champion, 7J, NI, 3/4, gilded, **coin**, OF	60	85	185
Champion, 7J, NI, 3/4, gilded, OF	60	85	185
Champion, 7J, NI, 3/4, gilded, HC	90	135	275
Chronometer, 21J, NI, Adj.3P, GJS, (lever Escap.), OF ★	500	650	850
Chronometer, 21J, NI, Adj.3P, GJS, (lever Escap.), HC ★	650	750	985
John C. Dueber, 17J, GJS, NI, Adj.5P, 3/4, LS, OF	75	110	200
John C. Dueber, 21J, GJS, NI, Adj.5P, 3/4	125	195	300
John C. Dueber, 21J, GJS, NI, Adj.5P, DR, BRG	150	225	325
Dueber Watch Co., 15-17J, ADJ, 3/4	70	110	200

NOTE: Railroad Standards, Railroad Approved & Railroad Grade terminology, as defined and used in this **BOOK**.
1. **RAILROAD STANDARDS** = A commission or board appointed by the railroad companies outlined a set of **guidelines** to be accepted or approved by each railroad line.
2. **RAILROAD APPROVED** = A **LIST** of watches each railroad line would approve if purchased by their employee's. (this list changed through the years).
3. **RAILROAD GRADE** = A watch made by manufactures to meet or exceed the guidelines set by the railroad **standards**. Grades such as 992, Vanguard and B.W. Raymond, etc.

🕐 Some GRADES **exceeded** the R.R. standards such as 23 J,. diamond end stone, gold train, raised gold jewel settings, double sunk dial and the list goes on. Examples: such as Veritas, Sangamo, 950 & Riverside Maximus and many others.

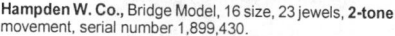

Hampden W. Co., Bridge Model, 16 size, 23 jewels, 2-tone movement, serial number 1,899,430.

Hampden W. Co., 16 size, 17 jewels, gold jewel settings, serial number 3,075,235.

🕐 Generic, nameless or unmarked grades for watch movements are listed under the Company name or initials of the Company, etc. by size, jewel count and description.

Grade or Name — Description	Av	Ex-Fn	Mint
Hampden W. Co., 7J, SW, OF	$45	$70	$135
Hampden W. Co., 7J, SW, HC	55	85	175
Hampden W. Co., 11J, SW, OF	50	75	150
Hampden W. Co., 11J, SW, HC	65	85	200
Hampden W. Co., 15J, SW, OF	60	85	175
Hampden W. Co., 15J, SW, HC	65	90	200
Hampden W. Co., 17J, SW, OF	70	85	225
Hampden W. Co., 17J, **14K, Multi-color**, HC	1,600	2,100	3,600
Hampden W. Co., 17J, SW, HC	90	135	275
Hampden W. Co., 21J, SW, HC	150	250	475
Hampden W. Co., 21J, SW, OF	150	225	425
Hampden W. Co., 23J, Adj.5P, GJS, 3/4	300	450	625
Hampden W. Co., 23J, Adj.5P, GJS, bridge model, **2-tone**	325	475	675
Hampden W. Co., 23J, Series 2, **Freesprung**, GJS GT, HC ★★★	700	950	1,600
Masonic Dial, 23J, GJS, 2-Tone **enamel dial**	700	950	1,600

Hampden W. Co., Series 1, 16 size, 15 jewels, stem wind open face.

Railway, 16 size, 17 jewels, Adj.5P, gold jewel settings, serial number 2,271,866.

NR inside flag = New Railway and SR inside flag = Special Railway
D & ★ D & anchor inside flag = Dueber and H inside flag = Hampden

🕐 Pricing in this Guide are fair market price for **COMPLETE** watches which are reflected from the "<u>**NAWCC**</u>" National and regional shows.

🕐 Generic, nameless or unmarked grades for watch movements are listed under the Company name or initials of the Company, etc. by size, jewel count and description.

Grade 104, 16 size, 23 jewels, gold jewel settings, gold train, Adj5p, open face, serial number 2,801,184.

Hampden style watch produced in Russia with the machinery purchased from Hampden W. Co. by the Russian factory. This watch is a 16 size 7 jewel movement Ca. 1935 engrave on Mvt. 7 KAMMEA 4-8, 28229 HKM MOCKER.

Grade or Name — Description	Avg	Ex-Fn	Mint
Wm. McKinley, 17J, GJS, Adj., NI, DR, 3/4	$75	$110	$200
Wm. McKinley, 21J, GJS, Adj.5P, NI, DR, OF	150	250	400
Wm. McKinley, 21J, GJS, Adj.5P, NI, DR, 3/4, **Coin**	150	250	400
Wm. McKinley, 21J, GJS, Adj.5P, NI, DR, HC	200	300	525
New Railway, 17J, GJS, LS, **NR** (in flag) ★★★	225	325	550
New Railway, 21J, GJS, Adj.5P	175	250	400
New Railway, 23J, GJS, Adj.5P, LS, HC	225	350	600
Ohioan, 21J, Adj., GJS, 3/4, OF & HC	150	250	500
Railway, 17-19J, GJS, Adj.5P, BRG, DR, OF	125	200	350
Special Railway, 17J, Adj, NI, BRG, DR, OF	125	200	350
Special Railway, 17J, Adj, NI, BRG, DR, HC	95	150	300
Special Railway, 23J, Adj.5P, NI, BRG, DR	300	425	675
Russian made model, 7-17J, 16 size, 3/4 plate ★★	175	235	400
Garfield, 21J., Adj.5P, OF	150	225	375
Gen'l Stark, 15J, DMK, BRG	75	110	200
Gen'l Stark, 17J, DMK, BRG	75	110	200
76, 21J, LS, Adj.3P	125	175	300
94-95, 21J, **marked "94 or 95"**, GJS, Adj.5P,	225	285	500
97 HC, 98 HC, 107 OF, 108 OF, **17J**, Adj.3P, NI, 3/4	75	120	250
97, 17J., **marked 97**, Adj., HC	200	275	350
99, 15J, 3/4, HC	75	120	250
103, 23J, GJS, Adj., NI,3/4, DR, free sprung, 2-tone, HC ★★★	700	900	1,600
104, 17J, NI, Adj., **2-tone**	250	375	600
104, 23J, GJS, Adj.5P, NI, 3\4 or BRG, DR, **marked**, OF	300	400	700
104, 23J, GJS, Adj.5P, NI, 3\4 or BRG, DR, **2-tone**, OF	350	450	800
104, 23J, GJS, Adj.5P, NI, BRG, DR, **marked**, HC	350	450	800
105, 21J, GJS, Adj.5P, NI, 3/4, DR, **marked**,OF	225	285	475
105, 23J, GJS, Adj.5P, NI, 3/4, DR, HC	275	385	650
106, 107 OF, & 108, **17J**, SW, NI, **marked**,	75	110	200
107, 17J, NI, Adj., **2-tone**	250	350	600
109, 15J, 3/4, **marked**, OF	75	100	200
110, 11J, 3/4	50	75	150
115, 21J, SW, NI, **marked**, OF	225	285	475
120, 21J, SW, NI, OF, **marked Chronometer on dial** ★	300	400	650
125, **marked**, 21J, DR, Adj.3p	200	275	375
340, 17J, SW, NI	85	125	225
440, 15J, 2-tone	85	125	225
555, 21J, GT, GJS, **marked 555, Chronometer on dial & mvt.** ★	600	775	1,100
555, 21J, GT, GJS, **marked 555, Chronometer on dial ONLY** ★	375	450	650
600, 17J, SW, NI, **marked, 600**	75	110	200

Dueber Grand, 12 size, 17 jewels, gold jewel settings, hunting case, serial number 1,737,354.

John Hancock, 21 jewels, Adj. 5P, lever set, came in HC & OF, Movement above is Hunting Case.

12 SIZE Standard Model

Grade or Name — Description	Avg	Ex-Fn	Mint
Aviator, 17J, Adj.4P, OF .... ★★	$90	$135	$275
Aviator, 19J, Adj.4P, OF	75	100	200
Beacon, 17J, OF (only seen in ads)............................ ★★★★	200	325	550
Biltmore, 17J, OF..★	75	100	200
Dueber Grand, 17J, BRG, OF	75	100	200
Dueber Grand, 17J, BRG, HC	100	150	275
Dueber Grand, 17J, 3/4 plate, **pin** set, OF	75	100	200
Dueber Grand, 17J, 3/4 plate, lever set, OF .... ★★	100	145	250
Dueber Grand, 17J, 3/4 plate, pendant set, OF .... ★	100	145	250
Dueber Grand, 17J, 3/4 plate, HC	100	145	250
Dueber Grand, 17J, BRG, lever set, HC	100	145	250
Dueber Grand, 17J, BRG, lever or pendant set, OF	75	100	200
Dueber W. Co. 17J, Adj., 3/4, pendant set, OF	75	100	200
Dueber W. Co. 17J, Adj., 3/4, pendant set, HC ....★	85	135	225
Duquesne, 19J, Adj., OF .... ★★	95	150	275
Gen'l Stark, 15J, M# 3 LS, HC	75	100	200
Gen'l Stark, 15J, M# 3 **PIN** or pendant set OF	65	95	150
Gen'l Stark, 15J, M# 3 lever set, OF............................★	100	135	250
Gen'l Stark, 15J, M# 4 lever set, HC, ...	75	100	200
Gen'l Stark, 15J,M# 4 pendant set OF	65	95	150
Gen'l Stark, 15J, M# 4 lever set OF ....★	60	90	150
Hampden W. Co., 17J, **14K, Multi-color, HC**	675	950	1,600
John Hancock, 21J, 3/4, **PIN** set, Adj.5P, GJS, OF .... ★★	125	175	250
John Hancock, 21J, 3/4, lever set, Adj.5P, GJS, HC ....★	150	200	300
John Hancock, 21J, BRG, pendant or lever set, Adj.5P, GJS, OF ★★	150	200	300
John Hancock, 21J, BRG, lever set, Adj.5P, GJS, HC ....★	150	200	300
Minute Man, 17J., (standard size), OF........................	85	135	250
Ohioan, 21J, Adj.3P, GJS, 3/4, OF ....★	125	175	275
Ohioan, 21J, Adj.3P, GJS, 3/4, HC .... ★★★	175	250	375
Viking, 17J, Adj, OF...★	75	110	200
No. 10, 7J, OF..	40	60	100
300, 7J, M# 3 LS, M# 5 stem set, HC........................	40	60	100
300, 7J, M# 5 lever set, HC....................................... ★★	50	75	135
302, 7J., M# 3 LS, M# 5 stem set, OF	40	60	100
302, 7J, M#5 lever set, OF ....★	50	75	135
304, 15J, HC	75	95	150
305, 17J, HC ....★	75	95	200
306, 15J, OF...	60	85	125
307, 17J, Adj, OF..	75	100	165
308, 17J, Adj, HC	85	135	200
310, 17J, Adj, OF..	65	95	150
310, 17J, Adj, **marked, 14K** OF case	175	250	425
312, **marked,** 21J, 3/4, Adj.5P, DMK, HC .... ★★	150	200	300
314, **marked,** 21J, DR, Adj. 5P, DMK, OF ....★	125	175	265
320, **marked,** 17J, DR, Adj., ... ★★	100	165	250
366, 17J., OF .... ★★	85	100	170
500, 17J, **marked,** OF ....★	85	100	170
500, 17, HC .... ★★★	125	165	225
603, 17J, OF..★	85	100	170
700, 15J, **marked,** OF	60	80	150
17 Jewel Special marked on Dial & Mvt., **2 tone,** OF .... ★★	95	125	195

Example of Hampden Watch Co.'s THIN MODEL showing dial and movement, 12 size, 17-19 jewels, Adj3-5p.

12 SIZE (THIN MODEL)

Grade or Name — Description		Avg	Ex-Fn	Mint
Nathan Hale, 15J	★	$75	$95	$250
Minute Man, 17J	★	85	125	275
Relgis, 15J, OF	★ ★	75	100	200
Relgis, 17J, OF	★ ★ ★	125	150	250
Paul Revere, 17J, OF, **14K**	★	225	275	600
Paul Revere, 17J	★	95	125	275
Paul Revere, 19J	★	125	150	325

Hampden 12 size (thin model) case are **not** interchangeable with other American 12 style cases.

6 SIZE

Grade or Name — Description	Avg	Ex-Fn	Mint
200, 7J (add $25 for HC)	$40	$65	$150
206, 11J (add $25 for HC)	40	65	150
213, 15J (add $25 for HC)	40	65	150
215, 16J, (add $25 for HC)	40	65	150
220, 17J (add $25 for HC)	40	65	150
Hampden W. Co., 15J, **multi-color Gold Filled, HC**	225	275	475
Hampden W. Co., 15J, **multi-color, 14K, HC**	400	500	925

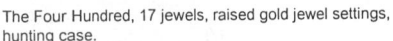

The Four Hundred, 17 jewels, raised gold jewel settings, hunting case.

Molly Stark, 000 size, 7 jewels, hunting or open face, and originally sold for $12.00.

000 SIZE

Grade or Name — Description		Avg	Ex-Fn	Mint
Diadem, 11-15J, **14K**, OF		$125	$175	$350
Diadem, 11-15J, **14K**, HC		225	275	475
Diadem, 11-15J, **Gold Filled**, HC		75	175	250
Molly Stark, 7J, **Gold Filled**, HC		75	175	250
Molly Stark, 7J, **14K**, HC		225	275	475
Molly Stark, 7J, Pin Set, OF		75	125	200
No.400, 16-17j, 14K **solid gold plates** & bridges, 14KHC	★ ★ ★	500	700	1,000
The Four Hundred, 17J, raised gold jewel settings, HC		100	150	275
14K Multi-color, HC		400	500	900

HAMPDEN WATCH CO.
IDENTIFICATION OF MOVEMENTS

How to Identify Your Watch Size & Model: Compare the movement of your watch with the illustrations in this section. While comparing, note the location of the balance, jewels, screws, gears, and type of back plate (Full, 3/4, Bridge) these will be clues in identifying the movement you have.

Series I, 18 size
Hunting or open face, key wind & set

Series II, 18 size
Hunting, stem wind, pendant or lever set

Series III, 18 size
Hunting, stem wind, pendant or lever set

Series IV, 18 size
Open face, stem wind, lever set

000 SIZE

No. 400 14 karat solid gold movement.
All plates and bridges made of 14k gold.
1897 ad priced at $65.00 case extra.

Series 1, 16 size
Open face, stem wind, pendant or lever set

Series II, 16 size
Hunting, stem wind, pendant or lever set

Series III, 16 size
Open face, stem wind, pendant set

Series IV, 16 size
Hunting, stem wind, pendant or lever set

Series V, 16 size
Open face, stem wind, pendant or lever set

Series VI, 16 size
Hunting, stem wind, pendant set

I will respect and appreciate positive sound reliable comments, corrections, improvements or remarks but reserve the right to accept the statement or keep my own observations & views. (*Cooksey*)

Series VII, 16 size
Open face, stem wind, pendant set

Series III, 12 size
Open face, stem wind, pendant set

Series I, 12 size
Hunting, stem wind, lever set

Series II, 12 size
Open face, stem wind, lever set

Series IV, 12 size
Open face, stem wind, pendant

Series V, 12 size
Open face, stem wind, pendant set

Series I, 6 size
Hunting, stem wind

Series I, 3/0 size
Hunting, stem wind

Series II, 3/0 size
Open face, stem wind, pendant

Series III, 3/0 size
Hunting, lever or pendant

Series IV, 3/0 size
Hunting, stem wind, pendant

No. 104

16 Size

Open Face and Hunting

Lever Setting

1908 AD
1922 PRICE
LIST

Nickel, bridge model, 23 extra fine Ruby and Sapphire jewels in solid gold settings, *Sapphire Roller Jewels* and *Pallet Stones, Steel Escape Wheel*, round arm polished train wheels, *Patent Safety Barrel No. 711476 with Main Wheel Arbor Pivots Revolving in Jewels*, patent center pinion, escape pinion and pallet arbor with conical pivots cap jeweled, patent microm. regulator, Breguet hairspring, New Model stud, compensation balance with gold screws and meantime screws, accurately *Adjusted to Temperature, Isochronism* and *5 Positions*, double sunk glass enameled dial with red marginal figures, beveled head gilt screws, elegantly engraved and damaskeened, gold lettering, highly polished steel work, first quality *"Hampden"* mainspring for patent barrel, and *Double Roller Escapement*.

1908 AD
1922 PRICE
LIST

Special Railway

18 Size   ☞

Open Face and Hunting

Lever Setting

Nickel, 23 extra fine Ruby and Sapphire jewels in solid gold settings, barrel arbor and center staff jeweled with the finest of Sapphires, escapement cap jeweled, conical pivots, finely graduated microm. regulator, compensating balance, gold screws, *Steel Escape Wheel*, Breguet hairspring, meantime screws, New Model stud, accurately *Adjusted to Temperature, Isochronism* and *5 Positions*, patent center pinion, beveled head gilt screws, highly polished steel work, fine double sunk glass enameled dial in Arabic or Roman figures, elegantly engraved and damaskeened in two colors, gold lettering.
The handsomest, most finely finished and closely timed Movement made in America.

HAMPDEN WATCH MOVEMENTS

18 SIZE

Special Railway	21J. OF	$24.70
Dueber Watch Co.	21J. OF	20.50
No. 64	17J. OF	9.35

16 SIZE

Special Railway	23J. OF only	$35.80
No. 104	23J. OF only	35.80
New Railway	21J. OF only	28.70
No. 105	21J. OF only	28.70
Wm. McKinley	21J. OF only	28.70
Railway	19J. OF only	24.85
Wm. McKinley	17J. Htg.-OF	12.25
No. 98—No. 108	17J. Htg.-OF	11.35
No. 99—No. 109	15J. Htg.-OF	9.05

12 SIZE

No. 305—No. 307	17J. Htg.-OF	$12.60
No. 304—No. 306	15J. Htg.-OF	10.65

Fancy solid silver dials fitted on 12 and 16 size movements — extra $2.50

BRACELET HEADS

We make a complete line of the various popular shapes and sizes of bracelet heads in white, green and regular solid gold and gold-filled cases.

WATCH CASES

Our line of watch cases includes the same high quality of solid gold, 25-year and 20-year gold-filled and silverine cases in all standard models, including white, green and regular colored gold-filled cases.

HERMAN VON DER HEYDT
CHICAGO SELF–WINDING WATCH CO.
Chicago, Illinois 1883- 1895

Herman von der Heydt patented a self-winding watch on Feb. 19, 1884. A total of about **35** watches were hand-made by von der Heydt. The watches were 18S, full plate, lever escapement and fully-jeweled. The wind mechanism was a gravity type made of heavy steel and shaped like a crescent. The body motion let the heavy crescent move, as it was connected to a ratchet on the winding arbor, resulting in self-winding. About **Five** movements were nickel and sold for about $90; the gilded model sold for about $75.

Grade or Name — Description		Avg	Ex-Fn	Mint
18S, 19J, FULL, NI	★★★★★	$12,000	$17,000	$23,000
18S, 19J, FULL, gilded	★★★★★	10,000	15,000	20,000

Herman Von Der Heydt, 18 size **self winding watch,** "Chicago S. W. Co." on dial. H. VON DER HEYDT, PATENTED, FEB.19, 84 on auxiliary dial.

Herman Von Der Heydt, 18 size, 19 jewels; America's only self winding pocket watch. Note crescent shaped winding weight, serial number 19.

Maintaining Power

Maintaining Power is a device for driving a watch during the operation of winding. Harrison introduced the Maintaining Spring device and was used in all fusee watches. The intermediate disc carried the pawl to engage the fusee ratchet and drove the main wheel by a small curved spring. The intermediate wheel did not turn during winding, being toothed on its outer edge and resist by a pawl set between the plates of the movement. The fusee was abandoned for American pocket watches and the going barrel employed. On some early Howards & Walthams maintaining power was used. The advantage was safety against damage due to breaking of mainsprings. G.P. Reed worked for Dennison, Howard & Davis and patented on April 14, 1857 a maintaining spring barrel. This device was used by Howard up to about S# 30,000 and American Waltham W. Co. used Stratton's, Pat. Feb. 2,1864.

Above: Harrison's Maintaining Spring. Fig.1 end of fusee & Fig. 2 ratchet placed next to fusee, a pin passes through the ball end of the spring Fig.3, & enters a slot in wheel Fig.4.

Above: Howard's Maintaining Spring in going barrel set into the pillar plate. **A** turned with the arbor & collet, **B** carried the pawl on its top side & maintaining spring **B** on its under side, driving the main wheel during winding.

E. HOWARD & CO.
Boston (Roxbury), Massachusetts
December 11, 1858 - 1903

After the failure of the Boston Watch Company (1853-57), Edward Howard decided to personally attempt the successful production of watches using the interchangeable machine-made parts system. He and Charles Rice, his financial backer, were unable to buy out the defunct watch company in Waltham, however, they did remove (per a prior claim) the watches in progress, the tools and the machinery to Howard and Davis' Roxbury factory (first watch factory in America), in late 1857. During their first year, the machinery was retooled for the production of a revolutionary new watch of Howard's design. Also, the remaining Boston Watch Co. movements were completed (E. Howard & Co. dials, Howard & Rice on the movement). By the summer of 1858, Edward Howard had produced his first watch. On December 11, 1858 the firm of E. Howard & Co. was formed for the manufacture of high-grade watches. Howard's first model was entirely different from any watch previously made. It introduced the more accurate "quick beat" train to American watchmaking. The top plate was in two sections and had six pillars instead of the usual four pillars in a full plate. The balance was gold or steel at first, then later it was a compensation balance loaded with gold screws. Reed's patented barrel was used for the first time. The size, based on the Dennison system, was a little larger than the regular 18 size. In 1861, a 3/4 plate model was put on the market. Most movements were being stamped with "N" to designate Howard's 18 size. On February 4, 1868 Howard patented a new steel motor barrel which was to supersede the Reed's, but not before some 28,000 had been produced. Also, in 1868 Howard introduced the stemwinding movement and was probably the first company to market such a watch in the U. S. By 1869, Howard was producing their "L" or 16 size as well as their first nickel movements. In 1870, G. P. Reed's micrometer regulator was patented for use by E. Howard & Co. The Reed style "whiplash" regulator has been used in more pocket watches, worldwide, than any other type. In 1878, the manufacturing of keywind movements was discontinued. Mr. Howard retired in 1882, but the company continued to sell watch movements of the grade and style set by him until 1903 and beyond. This company was the first to adjust to all six positions. Their dials were always a hard enamel and always bore the name "E. Howard & Co., Boston." In 1902, the company transferred all rights to use the name "Edward Howard," in conjunction with the production of watches, to the Keystone Watch Case Co. Most of their models were stamped "Howard" on the dial and "E. Howard Watch Co., Boston. U.S.A." on the movement. Edward Howard's company never produced its own watch cases, the great majority of which were solid gold or silver. Keystone, however, produced complete watches, many of which were gold filled.

CHRONOLOGICAL DEVELOPMENT OF E. HOWARD & CO.:

Warren Manufacturing Company, Roxbury, Mass., (1851-53)
Boston Watch Co., Roxbury, Mass., (1853-54) & Waltham, Mass., (1854-57)
Howard & Rice, Roxbury, Mass., (1857-58) with (E. Howard & Co. on dials)
E. Howard & Co., Roxbury, Mass., (1858-1903)
Keystone Watch Case Co. (Howard line), Jersey City, N. J., (1902-30)

Below: Lever with upright pallets.

Note: All E. Howards were adjusted to Isochronism.
LEFT: Balance cock unmarked =UNADJUSTED
CENTER: Balance cock marked heat &cold =adjusted to TEMPERATURE
RIGHT: Balance cock on movement marked adjusted =FULLY ADJUSTED

A list of initials for **most** of the Solid Gold Watch **Case** companies used by E. Howard & Co.

A.W.C. Co.=American Watch Case Co.
B & T = Booz & Thomas
B.W.C. Co.=Brooklyn Watch Case Co.
C & M =Crosby & Mathewson
C.E.H. & Co. = C.E. Hale & Co.
C.W. Mfg. Co. = Courvoisier Wilcox Mfg. Co.
D T W & Co.= D.T. Warren & Co.
F & Co. = Fellows & Co.
F & S = Fellows & Shell
J M H = J.M. Harper
J S (intertwined)= Jeannot & Shiebler

K (inside) U = Keller & Untermeyer
K E & F. Co.= Keller, Ettinger & Fink N.Y.
M B = Margot Bros.
M & B = Mathey Bros.
N.Y.G.W.C.Co =New York Gold Watch Case Co.
P & B = Peters & Boss
S & D = Serex & Desmaison
S & M B = Serex Maitre Bros.
S & R = Serex & Robert
W & S = Warren & Spadone
W P & Co = Wheeler Parsons & Co.
W W C Mfg. Co =Western Watch Case Co.

Crescent Watch Case Co.
Dueber Watch Case Co.
Keystone Watch Case Co.

Ladd Watch Case Co.
Marsh= Marsh Watch Case Co.
Muhr Watch Case Co.
Roy = Roy Watch Case Co.

NOTE: The "E.H.& Co." marking seen on cases, was put on cases by numerous different case makers, at the request of the Howard sales offices.

    NOTE: E. Howard & Co. movements will not fit standard cases properly.

E. HOWARD & CO., Series I, helical hair-spring, detent escapement, KW KS, N (18)size, serial # 1120

E. HOWARD & CO., N (18) size, 15 jewels, chronometer escapement engraved on balance cock, Robin's escapement, serial # 3126.

E. HOWARD & CO. III, 18 size, KW KS, note compensating balance above center wheel, serial # 3363.

E. HOWARD & CO., I (10) size, KW KS, **note** solid balance, unique escape wheel & pallet fork, serial # 3406.

E. HOWARD & CO.
APPROXIMATE DATES, SERIAL NOS., AND TOTAL PRODUCTION

Serial No.	Date	Series	Total Prod.
113-1,900—	1858-1860	I (18S)—	1,800
1,901-3,000—	1860-1861	II (18S)—	1,200
3,001-3,100—	1861-1862	K (14S)—	100
3,101-3,300—reserved for helicals & experimentals			
3,301-3,400—	1861-1863	III (18S)—	100
3,401-3,500—	1861-1863	i (10S)—	100
3,501-28,000—	1861-1871	III (18S)—	24,500
30,001-50,000—	1868-1883	IV (18S)—	20,000
50,001-71,500—	1869-1899	V (16S)—	21,500
100,001-105,500—	1874-1878	VI (6S)—	5,500
200,001-227,000—	1883-1899	VII (18S)—27,000	
*228,001-231,000—	1893-1894	VII (18S)—	3,000
300,001-309,000—	1884-1899	VIII (18S)—	9,000
*309,001-310,000—	1895-1903	VIII (18S)—	1,000
400,001-405,000—	1890-1895	IX (18S)—	5,000
500,001-501,500—	1892-1899	X (12S)—	1,500
*600,001-601,500—	1895-1903	XI (16S)—	1,500
*700,001-701,500—	1896-1904	XII (16S)—	1,500

(*) = 3/4 Split Plates & 17 J.   **Possible Total - 118,500**

The above list is provided for determining the age & help identify the Series of your watch. Match serial number with date & Series.

E. HOWARD & CO. WATCH SIZES

Letter	Inches	Approx. Size
N	1 13/16	18
L	1 11/16	16
K	1 10/16	14
J	1 9/16	12
I	1 8/16	10
H	1 7/16	8
G	1 6/16	6
F	1 5/16	4
E	1 4/16	2
D	1 3/16	0

Below: Mershon's Patent center wheel rack regulator (April 26, 1859).

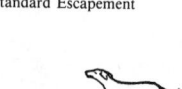

Coles Escapement
Resilient Escapement

Standard Escapement

Deer
Adjusted to
HcI6P

Horse
Adjusted to
HCI-No
positions

Hound
Unadjusted

Howard used a maintaining power device up to serial # 30,000.
1st NICKEL movement Ca. 1871.

All E. Howards were adjusted to Isochronism..

14 or K size, 15 jewels, right angle lever escapement, experimental model, serial number 3,022.

10 or I size, 15 jewels; note cut-out to view escape wheel, experimental model, serial number 3,472.

E. HOWARD & CO.
N SIZE (18)   (In Original Cases)

Series or Name — Description		Avg	Ex-Fn	Mint
I, II or III, 15J, gilded, KW, helical hairspring	★★★★	$14,000	$21,000	$30,000
I, 15J, marked "Howard & Rice"	★★★★	5,000	6,500	9,000

FOR, E. Howard & Co. on dial and movement, 15-16J, **1857 Model,**
See American Waltham Watch Co. section for 1857 Model for prices

Series 1, 18 size, 17 jewels, note the compensating balance on this early movement, **low** serial number 133.

Series II, 18 size, 15 jewels, key wind & set, serial number
2,477.

Series or Name — Description		Avg	Ex-Fn	Mint
I, 15J, with serial # below 125	★★★★★	$8,500	$10,000	$16,000
I, 15J, with serial # below 200	★★★★	5,300	5,900	8,200
I, 15J, with serial # below 300	★★★★	4,800	5,500	7,500
I, 15J, gilded, KW, **18K**, HC, OF, upright or horizontal pallets	★★	5,500	6,500	9,500
I, 15J, gilded, KW, silver HC	★★	2,800	3,300	5,200
I, 15J, (movement only)	★★	900	1,000	2,600
I, 17J, with unusual plate cut (movement only)	★★★	5,000	6,800	10,000
II, 15J, gilded, KW, **18K**, HC or OF	★★	2,500	3,500	6,200
II, 15J, gilded, KW, silver HC	★★	1,500	2,200	5,000
II, 15J, (movement only)	★★	800	1,000	2,200
II, 17J, with screw down jewel settings (movement only).	★★★★★	3,000	4,000	7,000
III, 15J, gilded, KW, **18K**, HC		1,200	1,700	3,500
III, 15J, gilded, KW, silver case		550	900	1,800
III, 15J, **nickel**, KW, silver case	★★★★	2,000	2,800	4,000
III, 15J, gilded, KW, Mershon's Patent		1,200	1,700	3,500
III, 15J, gilded, KW, Coles Resilient Escapement, **18K**,	★★	1,600	2,400	4,000
III, 15J, gilded, KW, Coles Resilient Escapement, (movement only)		300	400	600
III, 15J, nickel Coles Movement, **18K**	★★★★	3,500	4,700	7,000
III, 15J, Gold flashed DMK, Coles Movement, **18K**	★★★★	2,200	3,500	6,000
III, 15J, NI, Private label		800	1,300	2,000
III, 15J , gold flash ray DMK screw down settings (movement only)		950	1,400	2,200
III, 15J, with RAY & nickel DMK (movement only)		500	1,000	2,000
III, 15J, SW, 4 OZ. hand engraved **18K CASE**		2,500	3,100	5,100

Series III, 18 size, 15 jewels, note **Mershon's Patent** center
wheel rack regulator (April 26, 1859), serial # 22,693.

Series III, 18 size, 15J., note high balance wheel over
center wheel, S# number 4453. Note: Maintaining spring
barrel found on earlier Howard watches, advantage was
safety against damage due to breaking of mainspring in
going barrel. (protecting the train)

Series IV, 18 size, 15 jewels, key wind and set, serial number 37,893, Moustache Lever.

Series VII, 18 size, 15 jewels, nickel movement, note running deer on movement, "adjusted" on bridge, serial number 219,304.

Series or Name — Description	Avg	Ex-Fn	Mint
IV, 15J, gilded, KW, **18K,** HC	$1,000	$1,800	$3,000
IV, 15J, **nickel,** KW, **18K,** HC ★★★	2,400	3,000	4,000
IV, 15J, gilded, SW, **18K,** HC	1,000	1,200	2,500
IV, 15J, nickel, SW, **18K,** HC	1,000	1,500	2,600
IV, personalized with jobber's name, silver ★★	450	850	1,500
IV, SW, with Transitional dial, OF **14K**	1,400	2,000	3,200
IV, 15J (movement only)	100	200	500
VII, 15J, gilded or nickel, SW, **14K,** HC	650	1,000	2,000
VII, 15J, unusual **Moorhouse** dial, **14K**	1,100	1,800	3,000
VII, 15J, complex DMK (movement only)	150	300	500
VII, 15J (movement only)	125	200	450
VII, 17J, nickel, split plate, SW, **14K,** HC ★★★	1,500	2,000	3,600
VII, 17J, nickel, split plate, SW, silver, HC ★★★	700	1,200	2,400
VII, 19J, nickel, SW, **14K,** HC ★★★	2,500	3,500	6,000
VII, 21J, 3/4 plate (movement only) ★★★★	1,600	2,500	4,500
VIII, 15J, gilded or nickel, SW, **14K,** OF	700	950	2,000
VIII, 15J, nickel, Complex DMD (movement only)	150	300	600
VIII, 15J, unusual **Moorhouse** dial ★★★	1,100	1,800	3,000
VIII, 15J (movement only)	125	300	500
VIII, 17J, nickel, split plate, SW, **14K,** OF ★★★	1,800	2,400	3,800
VIII, 17J, nickel, split plate, SW, **silver,** OF ★★★	700	1,000	2,200
VIII, 17J, nickel or gilded, with RR on the side of balance cock, silver, OF	1,000	1,300	3,000

BALL - HOWARDS SEE **BALL W. Co.**.

Series VII, 18 size, 17J, nickel, split plate, adjusted, Stem Wind, serial number 228,055.

Series VIII, 18 size, 15 jewels, serial number 308,455.

Series VIII, 18 size, 17 jewels, split plate model, gold jewel settings, serial number 309,904.

Series IX, 18 size, 15 jewels, hunting. This series is gilded only and hound grade exclusively, S # 402,873.

Series or Name — Description	Avg	Ex-Fn	Mint
IX, 15J, gilded, SW, **14K**, HC	$900	$1,200	$2,500
IX, 15J, gilded, SW, **silver**, HC	450	700	1,500
IX, 15J, gilded, SW, unusual **Moorhouse** dial	1,100	1,800	3,000
IX, 15J (movement only)	100	200	500

L SIZE (16)
(In Original Cases)

Series or Name — Description	Avg	Ex-Fn	Mint
V, 15J, gilded, KW, **18K**, HC	$1,100	$1,800	$2,800
V, 15J, gilded, KW, **18K, Coles Escapement** ★★	1,300	2,000	3,200
V, 15J, nickel, **18K, Coles Escapement** ★★★★	3,000	4,400	6,000
V, 15J, gilded or nickel, SW, **14K**, HC	800	1,200	2,000
V, 15J, gilded, SW, **14K, Coles Escapement** ★★	1,000	1,500	2,400
V, 15J, SW, **14K** OF, with transitional dial ★★	1,300	1,900	2,800
V, 15J, SW, **14K** OF, with **Moorhouse** dial ★★	1,500	2,300	4,000
V, 15J, SW, **14K**, 24 Hr. dial (red/black) ★★★	1,300	1,900	3,000
V, 15J, nickel KW, (movement only)	400	600	1,000
V, 15J, gilded (movement only)	100	200	400
V, **Prescott**, 15J., gilded, LS, SW, NOTE: original case may show evidence of filled key holes on dust cover ★★★	2,500	3,200	8,000
V, Prescott, 15J., gilded, SW, (Series V **movement** only) ★★★	1,000	1,500	4,000

Series V, 16 or L size, Prescott Model, 15J., HC, S# 50,434. NOTE: Original case may show evidence of **filled key holes on dust cover**. When watches were returned to factory & converted from KW Coles movement to stem wind & lever set.

Series XI, 16 size, 17 jewels, split plate model, nickel movement, gold jewel settings, serial number 600,021.

Series XII, L-16 size, 21 jewels, split plate model, nickel movement, gold lettering, gold jewel settings, serial number 700,899.

Series or Name — Description		Avg	Ex-Fn	Mint
XI, 17J, nickel, split plate, SW, **14K,** HC	★★★	$1,100	$1,500	$3,200
XI, 17J, nickel, split plate, SW, **silver,** HC	★★★	600	1,000	2,400
XI, 17J (movement only)......................		300	500	1,200
XII, 17J, nickel, split plate, SW, **14K,** OF	★★★	1,000	1,300	3,000
XII, 17J, nickel, split plate, SW, **silver,** OF	★★★	500	800	2,200
XII, 17J (movement only)		100	300	600
XII, 21J, nickel, split plate, SW, **14K,** OF	★★★★	4,000	6,500	9,000

K SIZE (14)
(In Original Cases)

Series or Name — Description		Avg	Ex-Fn	Mint
K, 15J, gilded, KW, **Original case 18K,** HC	★★★★★	$9,000	$16,000	$25,000
K, 15J, gilded, (movement only)..........★★★★		6,000	7,000	9,500

Series K, 14 or K size, 15 jewels, key wind & set, serial number 3,004.

Example of Moorhouse style dial. Signed J. Moorhouse on back side of dial. Also note Mulberry style at 15 - 30 - 45 - 60 minuets.

J SIZE (12) (In Original Cases)

Series or Name – Description	Avg	Ex-Fn	Mint
X, 15J, nickel, hound, SW, **14K**, OF ....★	$750	$1,000	$1,700
X, 15J, nickel, hound, SW, fancy Moorhouse dial, **14K**, OF.........	950	1,500	2,200
X, 15J, nickel, horse, SW, **14K**, OF...★	850	1,100	1,800
X, 15J, nickel, deer, SW, **14K**, OF...★	950	1,200	1,900
X, 15J, hound (movement only)...★	250	300	650

Series X, 15J, J size or 12 size, nickel, hound, SW, serial # 500,003.

I size (10 size), 15 jewels, gilded, key wind, serial number 3,464.

I SIZE (10) (In Original Cases)

Series or Name — Description	Avg	Ex-Fn	Mint
I size (10 size), 15J, gilded, KW, **18K** HC ....★★★★	$4,000	$5,200	$9,300
I size (10 size), 15 jewels, gilded, key wind, with **unique escape wheel & pallet fork, 18K** case	7,000	9,000	12,500

G SIZE (6) (In Original Cases)

Series or Name — Description	Avg	Ex-Fn	Mint
VI, 15J, gilded, **KW, 18K,** HC ....★★★	$2,000	$2,800	$5,000
VI, 15J, gilded or nickel, **SW, 18K,** HC..	1,100	1,200	1,700
VI, 15J, gilded or nickel, Moorhouse dial, **14K**	1,100	1,200	1,700
VI, 15J, (movement only)	175	275	500
VI, 15J, (movement only) **adjusted**	300	500	900

I size (10 size), 15 jewels, gilded, key wind, with **unique escape wheel & pallet fork,** note special opening to view escapement, S# 3406

Series VI, 6 or G size, 15 jewels, stem wind, serial number 104,520.

Below 1888 AD

HOWARD WATCHES.

PRICE LIST OF

6 and 18 Size Stem Wind and Stem Set Howard Movements

MANUFACTURED BY

THE E. HOWARD WATCH AND CLOCK CO., BOSTON, MASS.

All Howard Movements are Full Ruby Jeweled and Chronometer Balance.

6 Size.

6 Size. **GILDED MOVEMENT.**
Plain Regulator $60 00
6 Size. **GILDED MOVEMENT.**
Patent Regulator $66 00
6 Size. **NICKEL MOVEMENT.**
Patent Regulator $90 00

GILDED MOVEMENT.
Patent Regulator $66 00

NICKEL MOVEMENT.
Patent Regulator $90 00

Open Face, Patent Regulator.

Hunting, Patent Regulator.

GILDED MOVEMENT.
Patent Regulator, adjusted to heat and cold............$82 00

NICKEL MOVEMENT.
Patent Regulator, adjusted to heat and cold............$106 00

Open Face, Patent Regulator, adjusted to heat and cold.

Hunting, Patent Regulator, adjusted to heat and cold.

GILDED MOVEMENT.
Patent Regulator, adjusted to heat, cold and position $122 00

NICKEL MOVEMENT.
Patent Regulator, adjusted to heat, cold and position $150 00

Open Face, Patent Regulator, adjusted to heat, cold and position.

Hunting, Patent Regulator, adjusted to heat, cold and position.

We have in stock a complete line of above Movements, also 14 and 18 karat gold cases for same, in plain and engine turned (Juergensen Style), top and bottom engraved, and Louis XIV. plain and border engraved, both Open Face and Hunting   Other styles engraved to order at short notice; also a full line of Boss Gold Filled and Silver Howard Cases always in stock. For gold cases to fit Howard Movements see page 31.

Note: A FULL line of Boss Gold Filled Cases And Silver Howard Cases always in stock.

I will respect and appreciate positive sound reliable comments, corrections, improvements or remarks but reserve the right to accept the statement or keep my own observations & views. (**Cooksey**)

E. HOWARD WATCH CO. (KEYSTONE)
Waltham, Massachusetts
1902 - 1930

The watches are <u>marked</u> **"E. Howard Watch Co. Boston, U. S. A."** The Howard name was purchased by the Keystone Watch Case Co. in 1902. There were no patent rights transferred, just the Howard name. The Edward Howard chronometer was the highest grade, 16 size, & was introduced in 1912 for $350 (about 300 made). All watches cased & timed at factory as a **complete** watch only.

Keystone Howard also gained control of U. S. Watch Co. of Waltham and New York Standard Watch Company.

ESTIMATED SERIAL NUMBERS AND PRODUCTION DATES

Date	Serial No.
1902—	850,000
1903—	900,000
1909—	980,000
1912—	1,100,000
1915—	1,285,000
1917—	1,340,000
1921—	1,400,000
1930—	1,500,000

Adjusted to Temperature & Isochronism. The arrows denote number of jewels and adjustments in each grade.

Cross =23 jewel, 5 positions

Star =21 jewel, Adj.5P, & 19J with V under star

Triangle =19 jewel, 5 positions

Circle =17 jewel, 3 positions

Model 1905, Series 7, 16 size, 17J., open face. This 3/4 model can be identified by the slant parallel damaskeening. This represents the 3/4 **top** grade, raised gold jewel settings, double roller, Adj.5P and sold for $115.00 in 1910. The above movement (ebauche) MADE by Hamilton??

1907 Bridge Model, Series 5, 19 jewels, **open face,** Serial # 953,733. **NOTE:** The escape wheel bridge & the fourth wheel bridge is <u>not</u> notched out.

Model 1905, Series 9, 16 size, 17 jewels, open face. This 3/4 model can be identified by the checkerboard damaskeening. This represents the 3/4 **mid** grade, GJS, double roller, Adj.3 & 5P and sold for $105.00 in 1910.

Model 1905, Series 3, 16 size, 17 jewels open face. This 3/4 model can be identified by the circular damaskeening. This represents the 3/4 **lowest** grade of the three with single roller, Adj.3P and sold for $100.00 in 1910.

E. Howard Watch Co., Model 1907, marked Series 0, 16 size, 23 jewels, in original E. Howard Watch Co. swing-out movement Keystone Extra gold filled Open Face case.

E. HOWARD WATCH CO. Model 1907, Series 0 (not marked), 16S, 23J., Hunting Case. Under balance wheel "Special Adjusted Five Positions, Temperature".

🕐 Model 1907= **bridge** OF & HC and Series or No., 0, 1, 2, 5 & 10 , see above illustrations, 1907 = Series or No. 0=23J, Series or No.1&10=21J, Series2=17J, Series5 or No.5 =19J.
Model 1905 = **3/4 plate** OF & HC and Series 3,7,9 = 17J.

E. HOWARD WATCH CO. (KEYSTONE)
16 SIZE

Series or Name — Description	Avg	Ex-Fn	Mint
No. 0, & 1907, 23J, BRG, Adj.5P, DR, OF	$400	$500	$825
1907 model & No.0, 23J, BRG, Adj.5P, DR, HC	425	600	850
Unmarked, 23J, BRG, Adj.5P, DR, OF	350	500	750
Series 0, 23J, BRG, Adj.5P, DR, **Ruby banking pins**	700	900	1,400
Series 0, 23J, BRG, Adj.5P, DR, **jeweled barrel**	700	900	1,400
Series 0, 23J, BRG, Adj.5P, DR, **OF, 14K**	900	1,100	1,600
Series 0, 23J, BRG, Adj.5P, DR, **HC, 14K**	1,000	1,400	2,000
No. 1, 21J, BRG, Adj.5P, DR ★	350	485	800
Series 1, 21J, BRG, Adj.5P, DR	300	450	625
Series 2, 17J, BRG, Adj.5P, DR, HC ★	200	300	450
Series 2, 17J, BRG, Adj.5P, DR, OF ★	175	250	400

Series II, marked *Railroad Chronometer*, 16 size, 21 jewels, Adj5p, serial number 1,217,534.

Edward Howard Model, 16 size, 23 blue sapphire jewels, frosted gold bridge, wolfteeth wind, serial # 77.

🕐 Pricing in this Guide are fair market price for **COMPLETE** watches which are reflected from the "<u>NAWCC</u>" National and regional shows.

Above: Note illustrations #1 & #2 = Howard regulators with the 2 jewel screws vertical or upright and #1 has a **square** hairspring stud also note #2 has a **sliding** stud & a bean shaped cover. Howard-**Waltham** regulators (#3) the 2 jewel screws are horizontal and **triangular** hairspring stud.

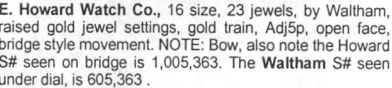

E. Howard Watch Co., 16 size, 23 jewels, by Waltham, raised gold jewel settings, gold train, Adj5p, open face, bridge style movement. NOTE: Bow, also note the Howard S# seen on bridge is 1,005,363. The **Waltham** S# seen under dial, is 605,363 .

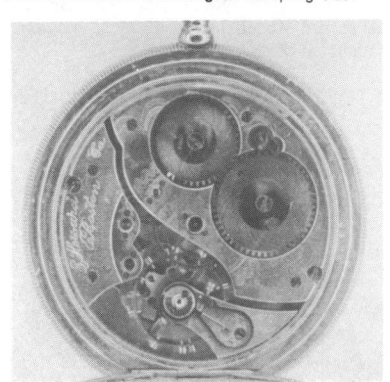

E. Howard Watch Co., 16S., 19J., by **Waltham**, **Equity** Model, Adj3p, 3/4 plate, gold center wheel.

Series or Name — Description	Avg	Ex-Fn	Mint
Series 3, 17J, 3/4, Adj.3P, circular DMK	$100	$175	$325
Series 3, 17J, Adj.3P, circular DMK, **14K** OF,	375	500	700
No. 5, 19J, BRG, GJS, HC ★	250	325	625
Series 5, 19J, BRG, Adj.5P, DR, **14K**	500	600	900
Series 5, 19J, BRG, Adj.5P, DR, 1907 Model	200	300	500
Series 7, 17J, 3/4, Adj.5P, DR, RGJS, slant parallel DMK, OF	100	175	325
Series 7, 17J, 3/4, Adj.5P, DR, RGJS, slant parallel DMK, HC	125	200	400
Series 9, 17J, 3/4, Adj.3P, LS, checkerboard DMK, OF	100	185	350
Series 9, 17J, 3/4, Adj.5P, DR, checkerboard DMK, RR grade,**14K**	500	600	900
Series 10, 21J, BRG, Adj.5P, DR, **Marked Non–Magnetic ★★★**	600	900	1,600
Series 10, 21J, BRG, Adj.5P, DR	325	450	800
No. 10, 21J, BRG, Adj.5P, DR	325	450	800
Series 11, 21J, **R.R. Chrono.**, Adj.5P, DR	325	450	800
Edward Howard, 23 blue sapphire pressed J, Free Sprung, Adj.5P, DR, **without** box, **18K** Edward Howard case ★★	5,500	7,500	12,000
Edward Howard, 23J., sapphire banking pins, Adj.5P, DR, wolf-tooth winding, Free Sprung, with original outer card and mahogany fitted box, extra mainspring, crystal and certificate, **18K** Edward Howard case ★★★	8,000	10,000	16,000
Climax,7J., (made for export), gilded, OF	75	135	250
23J, E. Howard W. Co. (mfg. by Waltham), **14K**, Brg model . ★★	1,200	1,400	2,200
23J, E. Howard W. Co. (mfg. by Waltham), gold filled, OF,	500	700	1,300
23J, E. Howard W. Co. (mfg. by Waltham), gold filled, HC	700	900	1,600
21J, E. Howard W. Co. (mfg. by Waltham), Bridge model, HC	350	500	1,000
21J, E. Howard W. Co. (mfg. by Waltham), 3/4, OF	200	275	500
19J, E. Howard W. Co. (mfg. by Waltham), Bridge model, HC	225	300	550
19J, E. Howard W. Co. (mfg. by Waltham), 3/4, OF	200	275	450
17J, E. Howard W. Co. (mfg. by Waltham), Bridge model, HC	200	300	500
17J, E. Howard W. Co. (mfg. by Waltham), **Equity model**, 3/4, OF .	175	250	400

12 SIZE - 1908 Model

Series or Name — Description	Avg	Ex-Fn	Mint
Series 6, 19J, BRG, DR, Adj.5P, 1908 Model, **14K**, HC	$300	$360	$650
Series 6, 19J, BRG, DR, Adj.5P, **14K**, OF	200	300	500
Series 6, 19J, BRG, DR, Adj.5P, OF	70	100	200
Series 7, 17J, BRG, DR, Adj.3P, **14K**, OF	200	300	500
Series 7, 17J, BRG, DR, Adj.3P, OF	75	100	200
Series 8, 21J, BRG, DR, Adj.5P, OF	100	185	325
Series 8, 23J, BRG, DR, Adj.5P, **14K**, OF	250	350	600
Series 8, 23J, BRG, DR, Adj.5P, OF	150	225	450
Series 8, 23J, BRG, DR, Adj.5P, **14K**, HC................................	450	600	800
21J, Waltham Model, BRG, HC.................................... ★ ★ ★	200	325	550
21J, Waltham Model, BRG, OF .... ★ ★ ★	250	350	650
19J, Waltham Model, gold center wheel, BRG, HC.......... ★ ★ ★	200	325	550
19J, Waltham Model, gold center wheel, BRG, OF .... ★ ★ ★	250	350	650
17J, Waltham Model, 3/4, HC.................................... ★ ★ ★	100	170	285
17J, Waltham Model, 3/4, OF .... ★ ★ ★	90	125	250

NOTE: First Serial # for 12 size with 17J.=977,001; 19J.=977,451; 21J.=1,055,851.

Series 8, 12 size, 21 jewels, open face, stop works, extra thin. **1908 MODEL** with 21 jewels, engraved under balance, "five positions and temperature".

E. Howard Watch Co., 10 size, 21J, Adj.,5p. **(Serial # started at about 1,001 on this model.)**

21 Jewels 5 Positions »—Ⓖ—►
19 Jewels 5 Positions »—Ⓐ—►
17 Jewels 3 Positions »—◯—►

10 SIZE (Ca. 1921)

NOTE: 10 Size Serial numbers start at about 1,001 on this model and used their own serial numbers list.

Series or Name — Description	Avg	Ex-Fn	Mint
Thin Model, 21J, Adj.5P, **14K** case, OF..	$200	$250	$425
Thin Model, 21J, Adj.5P, Gold filled, OF	75	100	200
Thin Model, 19J, Adj.5P, **14K** case, OF..	200	250	400
Thin Model, 19J, Adj.5P, Gold filled, OF	65	95	175
Thin Model, 17J, Adj.3P, **14K** case, OF..	175	200	400
Thin Model, 17J, Adj.3P, Gold filled, OF	65	95	175

🕒 A collector should expect to pay modestly higher prices at local shops.

🕒 Watches listed in this book are priced at the collectable Trade Show level, as **complete** watches having an original 14k gold-filled case and *Key Wind* with silver, an original white enamel single sunk dial, and with the entire original movement in good working order with no repairs needed.

STYLE R.R. Chronometer
gold filled: $150 - $250 - $500
Dial: $35 - $55 - $100

STYLE R.R. Plain swing out
gold filled: $95 - $150 - $325
Dial: $25 - $40 - $80

STYLE R.R. Antique Bow
gold filled: $95 - $165 - $375
Dial: $25 - $40 - $80

STYLE R.R. Engine, Turned swing out
gold filled: $95- $150 - $325
Dial: $25 - $40 - $80

STYLE R.R., SWING OUT
gold filled: $95 - $125 - $345
14K GOLD: $325 - $400 - $650
Montgomery Dial: $50 - $70 - $125

🕐 NOTE: Factory Advertised as a **complete** watch and was fitted with a certain matched, timed and rated movement and sold in the factory designed case style as a **complete** watch. The factory advertised as *"Howard movements and cases are not sold separately"*. All the factory advertised **complete** watches came with a enamel dial **SHOWN** or **CHOICE** of other **Railroad** dials.

Howard Railroad Watches

16s. SERIES No. 0 R.R. STANDARD
⚖ 23 J. Adj. 5 POS.

	Retail Price
	Keystone List $204.00
	$170.

14K Gold O. F.

35	–14K P.P.—Cap.	130.

Keystone Extra O. F.

55	–P.P.—Cap.	156.00	130.
65	–E.T.—Cap.	156.00	130.
95W	–White Screw Butler.	150.00	125.
95G	–Green Screw—P.P. or But.	150.00	125.

16s. SERIES No. 10 R.R. STANDARD
⚖ 21 J. Adj. 5 POS.

14K Gold O. F.

1035	–P.P.—Cap.	162.00	135.

Keystone Extra O. F.

1055	–P.P.—Cap.	114.00	95.
1065	–E.T.—Cap.	114.00	95.
1095W	–White Screw Butler.	108.00	90.
1095G	–Green Screw P.P. or But.	108.00	90.

16s. SERIES No. 11 R.R. CHRONOMETER
⚖ 21 J. Adj. 5 POS.

Keystone Extra O. F.

1195W	–White Screw Butler.	96.00	80.
1195G	–Green Screw—P.P. or But.	96.00	80.
1195	–Yellow Screw—P.P.	96.00	80.

Montgomery Dials supplied on Railroad Watches without extra charge.

July 1, 1926 Howard Watch Co. Price List.

ILLINOIS WATCH CO.
Springfield, Illinois
1869 - 1927

The Illinois Watch Company was organized mainly through the efforts of J. C. Adams. The first directors were J. T. Stuart, W. B. Miller, John Williams, John W. Bunn, George Black and George Passfield. In 1879 the company changed all its watches to a quick train movement by changing the number of teeth in the fourth wheel. The first nickel movement was made in 1879. The first mainspring made by the company was used in 1882. The next year soft enamel dials were used.

The Illinois Watch Co. used more names on its movements than any other watch manufacturer. To identify all of them requires extensive knowledge by the collector plus a good working knowledge of watch mechanics. Engraved on some early movements, for example, are "S. W. Co." or "I. W. Co., Springfield, Ill." To the novice these abbreviations might be hard to understand, thus making Illinois watches difficult to identify. But one saving clue is that the location "Springfield, Illinois" appears on most of these watches. It is important to learn how to identify these type watches because some of them are extremely collectible. Examples of some of the more valuable of these are: the Benjamin Franklin (size 18 or 16, 25 or 26 jewels), Paillard's Non-Magnetic, Pennsylvania Special, C & O, and B & O railroad models.

The earliest movements made by the Illinois Watch Co. are listed below. They made the first watch in early 1872, but the company really didn't get off the ground until 1875. Going by the serial number, the first watch made was the Stuart. Next was the Mason, followed by the Bunn, the Miller, and finally the Currier. The first stem-wind was made in 1875.

STUART, FIRST Run was serial numbers	1 to 100.
MASON, FIRST Run was serial numbers	101 to 200.
BUNN, FIRST Run was serial numbers	201 to 300.
MILLER, FIRST Run was serial numbers	301 to 400.
CURRIER, FIRST Run was serial numbers	401 to 500.

The Illinois Watch Company was sold to Hamilton Watch Co. in 1927. The Illinois factory continued to produce Illinois watches under the new management until 1932. After 1933 Hamilton produced watches bearing the Illinois name in their own factory until 1939.

CHRONOLOGY OF THE DEVELOPMENT OF ILLINOIS WATCH CO.:

Illinois Springfield Watch Co.	1869-1879
Springfield Illinois Watch Co.	1879-1885
Illinois Watch Co.	1885-1927
Illinois Watch Co. sold to Hamilton Watch Co.	1927

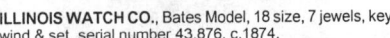

ILLINOIS WATCH CO., Bates Model, 18 size, 7 jewels, key wind & set, serial number 43,876, c.1874.

BUNN, 18 size, 16 jewels, hunting case, NOTE: Chalmer patented regulator, serial number 1,185,809.

🕐 NOTE: Numerous model 2 & 3 movements have key-wind style barrel arbors and stem wind *capabilities* they are referred to as **transition** Models. When model 2 & 3 were introduced the factory must have had a large supply of key-wind style barrel arbors so being frugal they were used.

ILLINOIS ESTIMATED SERIAL NUMBERS AND PRODUCTION DATES

DATE – SERIAL NO.	DATE – SERIAL NO.	DATE – SERIAL NO.
1872 – 5,000	1893 – 1,120,000	1914 – 2,600,000
1873 – 20,000	1894 – 1,160,000	1915 – 2,700,000
1874 – 50,000	1895 – 1,220,000	1916 – 2,800,000
1875 – 75,000	1896 – 1,250,000	1917 – 3,000,000
1876 – 100,000	1897 – 1,290,000	1918 – 3,200,000
1877 – 145,000	1898 – 1,330,000	1919 – 3,400,000
1878 – 210,000	1899 – 1,370,000	1920 – 3,600,000
1879 – 250,000	1900 – 1,410,000	1921 – 3,750,000
1880 – 300,000	1901 – 1,450,000	1922 – 3,900,000
1881 – 350,000	1902 – 1,500,000	1923 – 4,000,000
1882 – 400,000	1903 – 1,650,000	1924 – 4,500,000
1883 – 450,000	1904 – 1,700,000	1925 – 4,700,000
1884 – 500,000	1905 – 1,800,000	1926 – 4,800,000
1885 – 550,000	1906 – 1,840,000	1927 – 5,000,000
1886 – 600,000	1907 – 1,900,000	(Sold to Hamilton)
1887 – 700,000	1908 – 2,100,000	1928 – 5,100,000
1888 – 800,000	1909 – 2,150,000	1929 – 5,200,000
1889 – 900,000	1910 – 2,200,000	1931 – 5,400,000
1890 – 1,000,000	1911 – 2,300,000	1934 – 5,500,000
1891 – 1,040,000	1912 – 2,400,000	1948 – 5,600,000
1892 – 1,080,000	1913 – 2,500,000	

The above list is provided for determining the **APPROXIMATE** age of your watch. Match serial number with date. Watches were not necessarily sold in the exact order of manufactured date.

NOTE: It required several months for raw material to emerge as a finished movement. All the while the factory is producing all sizes, models and grades. The numbering system was basically "consecutive", due to demand a batch of movements could be side tracked, thus allowing a different size and model to move ahead to meet this demand. Therefore, the dates some movements were sold and delivered to the trade, may not be "consecutive".

(See Illinois Identification of Movements section located at the end of the Illinois price section to identify the movement, size and model number of your watch.)

ILLINOIS
18 SIZE (ALL FULL PLATE)

Grade or Name — Description	Avg	Ex-Fn	Mint
Alleghany, 11J, KW, gilded, OF	$80	$145	$250
Alleghany, 11J, M#1, NI, KW	80	145	250
Alleghany, 11J, M#2, NI, Transition	80	145	250
America, 7J, M#3, Silveroid ★	80	145	250
America, 7J, M#1-2, KW ★	100	175	325
America Special, 7J, M#1-2, KW ★	175	250	400
Army & Navy, 19J, GJS, Adj.5P, OF	200	300	500
Army & Navy, 19J, GJS, Adj.5P, HC	225	325	550
Army & Navy, 21J, GJS, Adj.5P, OF	200	300	500
Army & Navy, 21J, GJS, Adj.5P, HC	250	350	625
Baltimore & Ohio R.R. Special, 17J, GJS, ADJ ★★★	1,300	1,700	2,800
Baltimore & Ohio R.R. Special, 21J, GJS, NI, ADJ ★★★	1,500	1,900	3,000
Baltimore & Ohio R.R. Standard, 24J, GJS, ADJ ★★★	2,200	2,900	4,000
Bates, 7J, M#1-2, KW	175	275	525

🕑 Watches listed in this book are priced at the **collectable fair market value** at the **Trade Show** level, as **complete** watches having an original 14k gold filled case, *KEY WIND* with silver, an original white enamel single sunk dial, and with the entire original movement in good working order with no repairs needed, unless otherwise noted.

🕑 GENERIC, NAMELESS OR **UNMARKED GRADES** FOR WATCH MOVEMENTS ARE LISTED UNDER THE COMPANY NAME OR INITIALS OF THE COMPANY, ETC. BY SIZE, JEWEL COUNT AND DESCRIPTION.

🕑 Some watch manufacturers personalize watches for jobbers or jewelry firms, with exclusive private signed or marked movements. The valuable collectable watches are listed under the signed or marked movement. Other exclusive private signed or marked movements will have equivalent value or only slightly higher value and should be compared to Generic or Nameless movements. Railroad signed or marked (dials & movements) are usually more collectable & higher in value.

Illinois Watch Co., 18 size, railroad watch with a Ferguson dial with the numbers **1 through 12 in red.**
Illinois Ferguson = **18S**, Dial: $250 - $500 - $1,000

Army and Navy, 18 size, 19 jewels, engraved on movement "Washington Watch Co.," serial number 1,606,612.

Grade or Name — Description		Avg	Ex-Fn	Mint
Benjamin Franklin U.S.A., 17J, ADJ, NI	★	$425	$600	$ 1,000
Benjamin Franklin U.S.A., 21J, GJS, **Adj.6P**, NI	★	950	1,300	1,600
Benjamin Franklin U.S.A., 21J, GJS, Adj.5P, NI	★	950	1,300	1,600
Benjamin Franklin U.S.A., 24J, GJS, Adj.6P, NI	★	2,000	2,800	4,500
Benjamin Franklin U.S.A., 25J, GJS, Adj.6P, NI	★★★★	3,800	5,500	9,500
Benjamin Franklin U.S.A., 26J, GJS, Adj.6P, NI,	★★★★	4,800	6,500	11,000
Bunn, 15J, M#1, KW, KS, **1st. run S# 201 to 300**	★★★★	2,100	2,800	4,500
Bunn, 15J, M#1, KW, KS, **2nd. run S# 2,001 to 2,500**	★★	1,800	2,500	3,400
Bunn, 15J, M#1, KW, KS, OF	★	450	600	1,000
Bunn, 15J, M#1, KW, KS, **"ADJUSTED"**,	★	500	650	1,100
Bunn, 15J, KW/SW transition		250	425	850
Bunn, 15J, M#1, KW, Coin		375	475	900
Bunn, 15J, KW, M#1, HC		375	475	900
Bunn, 15J, SW, M#2, HC		375	475	900
Bunn, 16J, KW, (not marked 16J.), OF	★	400	485	900
Bunn, 16J, KW, (not marked 16J.), HC	★	400	485	900
Bunn, 16J, SW, (not marked 16J.), HC		350	450	825
Bunn, 16J, SW, **ADJ**, (not marked **16J.**), HC		375	475	875
Bunn, 17J, SW, NI, Coin		200	285	400
Bunn, 17J, SW, M#3, **5th pinion**, gilded, OF		300	385	625
Bunn, 17J, M#4, SW, NI, OF		150	250	500
Bunn, 17J, M#5, SW, NI, HC		200	350	600
Bunn, 17J, SW, M#5, **"Ruby Jewels"**, NI, Adj., HC	★	500	650	1,100
Bunn, 17J, M#6, SW, NI, OF		150	250	500
Bunn, 18J, SW, NI, **ADJ.**, (not marked **18J.**), OF	★★	500	650	900
Bunn, 19J, SW, NI, DR, LS, GJS, Adj.5P, **J. barrel**, OF		200	350	500
Bunn, 19J, SW, **Adj.6P**, DR, **J. barrel**, OF		285	385	600
Bunn, 19J, SW, GJS, DR, Adj.5P, **J. barrel, HC**	★	375	500	800

IMPORTANT NOTE: Railroad Standards, Railroad Approved & Railroad Grade **terminology,** as defined and used in this ***BOOK***.
1. **RAILROAD STANDARDS** = A commission or board appointed by the railroad companies outlined a set of **guidelines** to be accepted or approved by each railroad line.
2. **RAILROAD APPROVED** = A LIST of watches each railroad line would approve if purchased by their employee's. (this list changed through the years).
3. **RAILROAD GRADE** = A watch made by manufactures to meet or exceed the guidelines set by the railroad **standards**. Grades such as 992, Vanguard and B.W. Raymond, etc.
☉ Some GRADES **exceeded** the R.R. standards such as 23 jewels, diamond end stone, gold train, raised gold jewel settings, double sunk dial and the list goes on. Examples: such as Veritas, Sangamo, 950 & Riverside Maximus and many others.

Bunn Special, 18 size, 24 Ruby Jewels, adjusted, serial number 1,413,435

Bunn Special, 18 size, 26 Ruby jewels, "J. Home & Co." on dial, adjusted to six positions, gold jewel settings, serial number 2,019,415.

Grade or Name — Description	Avg	Ex-Fn	Mint
Bunn Special, 21J, SW, **Coin**	$200	$325	$600
Bunn Special, 21J, GJS, ADJ, HC	450	500	800
Bunn Special, 21J, GJS, ADJ, DR, OF	250	335	475
Bunn Special, 21J, GJS, DR, Adj.5P, OF	250	335	475
Bunn Special, 21J, GJS, DR, Adj.**6P**, OF	300	400	600
Bunn Special, 21J, GJS, Adj.5P, **HC, 14K**	700	900	1,500
Bunn Special, 21J, GJS, ADJ, **2-Tone**	325	400	700
Bunn Special, 21J, GJS, Adj.5P, DR	275	350	500
Bunn Special, 21J," **EXTRA**", GJS ★★	1,000	1,400	2,200
Bunn Special, 23J, GJS, ADJ, DR, OF	600	750	1,000
Bunn Special, 23J, GJS, Adj.6P, OF	650	750	1,000
Bunn Special, 23J, GJS, Adj.6P, DR, 2-Tone, OF ★★	700	800	1,200
Bunn Special, 23J, GJS, ADJ, DR, HC ★★★	2,000	2,600	4,800
Bunn Special, 24J, GJS, ADJ, DR, HC	1,000	1,300	1,900
Bunn Special, 24J, GJS, ADJ, DR, **14K, HC**	1,900	2,200	3,200
Bunn Special, 24J, GJS, ADJ, DR, OF	950	1,200	1,800
Bunn Special, 24J, GJS, **Adj.6P**, DR, OF	950	1,200	1,800
Bunn Special, 24J, GJS, **Adj.6P**, DR, HC	950	1,200	1,800
Bunn Special, 25J, GJS, **Adj.6P**, DR ★★★	5,000	6,200	9,200
Bunn Special, 26J, GJS, **Adj.6P**, DR ★★★	4,000	5,200	8,500
Central Truck Railroad, 15J, KW, KS ★★	700	1,000	1,800
Chesapeake & Ohio, 17J, ADJ, OF ★★	1,000	1,500	2,600
Chesapeake & Ohio Special, 21J, GJS, **2-Tone** ★★	1,400	2,000	3,500
Chesapeake & Ohio Special, 24J, NI, ADJ, GJS ★★	2,400	3,000	5,600
Chronometer, 11-15J, KW, OF ★	250	350	600
Chronometer, 15J, M#2, HC ★	285	400	700
Columbia, 11J, M#3, 5th Pinion	95	175	300
Columbia, 11J, M#1 & 2, KW	95	175	300
Columbia, 11J, M#1 & 2, Silveroid	80	150	250
Columbia Special, 11J, M#1-2-3, KW	80	150	250
Columbia Special, 11J, M#1-2-3, KW/SW, transition	95	175	300
Comet, 11J, M#3, OF, LS, SW	65	110	200
Commodore Perry, 15-16J, HC	150	235	350
Criterion, 11-15J, HC	95	175	300

⊕ Some watch manufacturers personalize watches for jobbers or jewelry firms, with exclusive private signed or marked movements. The valuable collectable watches are listed under the signed or marked movement. Other exclusive private signed or marked movements will have equivalent value or only slightly higher value and should be compared to Generic or Nameless movements. Railroad signed or marked (dials & movements) are usually more collectable & higher in value.

Chesapeake & Ohio Special, 21 Ruby Jewels, Adjusted Temperature 6 Positions Isochronsim, OF, S# 1785680.

Diurnal, 18 size, 7 jewels, key wind & set, only one run, total production 2,000, serial number 86,757.

Grade or Name — Description	Avg	Ex-Fn	Mint
Currier, 11-12J, KW, OF	$70	$145	$300
Currier, 11-12J, KW, HC	95	175	350
Currier, 11-12J, **1st run S# 401 to 500** ★★★	400	600	1,100
Currier, 11-12J, KW/SW, transition, OF	75	110	200
Currier, 13–15J, M#3, OF	75	110	200
Currier, 13–15J, M#3, HC	90	145	250
Dauntless, 11J	90	145	250
Dean, 15J, M#1, KW, HC ★★	300	450	900
Diurnal, 7J, KW, KS, HC, **Coin** ★	250	375	600
Dominion Railway, with train on dial ★★★	1,800	2,400	3,800
Eastlake, 11J, SW, KW, Transition	150	235	400
Emperor, 21J, M#6, LS, SW, ADJ	175	275	425
Enterprise, M#2, ADJ	125	185	250
Eureka, 11J	100	175	250
Favorite, 16J, LS, OF	100	175	250
Forest City, 7–11J, SW, LS, HC	100	175	250
Forest City, 17J, KW/SW, gilted,	110	185	275
General Grant or General Lee, 11J, M#1, KW ★	300	385	625
Hoyt, 7-9-11J, M#1-2, KW	75	110	200

🕐 **Generic, nameless,** Personalized Jobber Watches or unmarked grades for watch movements are listed under the Company name or initials of the Company, etc. by size, jewel count and description.

	Avg	Ex-Fn	Mint
Illinois Watch Co., 7-9J, M#1-2, KW	$75	$110	$200
Illinois Watch Co., 7-9J, M#2-6, SW	75	110	200
Illinois Watch Co., 11J, M#1-2, KW	75	110	200
Illinois Watch Co., 11J, M#3, SW	60	80	150
Illinois Watch Co., 12-13J, M#1-2, KW	75	110	200
Illinois Watch Co., 15J, M#1-2, KW	75	110	200
Illinois Watch Co., 15J, KW, ADJ, NI	95	125	235
Illinois Watch Co., 15J, SW, ADJ, DMK, NI	95	125	235
Illinois Watch Co., 15J, transition	50	70	150
Illinois Watch Co., 15J, SW, **Silveroid**	50	70	150
Illinois Watch Co., 15J, SW, **9K, HC**	225	350	525
Illinois Watch Co., 16J, SW, ADJ, DMK, NI	50	70	150
Illinois Watch Co., 16J, SW, ADJ, DMK, NI, marked **ADJ**	95	150	300
Illinois Watch Co., 17J, SW, **Silveroid**	50	70	150
Illinois Watch Co., 17J, KW/SW, transition	75	110	200
Illinois Watch Co., 17J, M#3, **5th Pinion**	95	150	300
Illinois Watch Co., 17J, SW, ADJ	75	110	200

🕐 Pricing in this Guide are fair market price for **COMPLETE** watches which are reflected from the "**NAWCC**" National and regional shows.

III. W. Co., 18 size, 17 jewels, adjusted, **2-tone movement,** serial number 1,404,442.

18 size, Note the 5th pinion which changed hunting case to open face.

🕐 **Generic, nameless,** Personalized Jobber Watches or unmarked grades for watch movements are listed under the Company name or initials of the Company, etc. by size, jewel count and description.

Grade or Name — Description	Avg	Ex-Fn	Mint
Illinois Watch Co., 17J, SW, **2 tone movement**	$125	$185	$300
Illinois Watch Co., 17J, SW, "**EXTRA**", Adj.4P ★	275	375	725
Illinois Watch Co., 19J, ADJ. **J. Barrel**, OF	150	250	450
Illinois Watch Co., 21J, Adj.3P, OF	195	275	475
Illinois Watch Co., 21J, ADJ5-6P,	300	375	575
Illinois Watch Co., 23J, ADJ6P, OF ★★★★	1,500	1,800	3,000
Illinois Watch Co., 24J, ADJ,	500	800	1,200
Inspector Special, 17J, LS, OF ★	300	450	750
Interior, 7J, KW & SW, OF	60	90	150
Interstate Chronometer, 17J, HC, (sold by Sears) ★★★	400	500	725
Interstate Chronometer, 17J, OF ★★	300	450	650
Interstate Chronometer, 23J, Adj.5P, GJS, NI, OF ★	1,000	1,200	2,000
Interstate Chronometer, 23J, Adj.5P, GJS, NI, HC ★★	1,200	1,400	2,200
Iowa W. Co., 7-11J, M#1-2, KW,	150	200	350
King of the Road, 16 &17J, NI, OF & HC, LS, ADJ ★	400	550	900
King Special, 17J, 2-tone, OF	150	200	500
King Philip Sp., 17J, (RR spur line) ★★★	350	450	900
Lafayette, 24J, GJS, Adj.6P, NI, SW, OF ★	1,000	1,200	1,700
Lafayette, 24J, GJS, Adj.6P, NI, SW, HC ★★	1,300	1,800	2,500
Lakeshore, 17J, OF, LS, NI, SW	125	175	300
Landis W. Co., 15-17J	100	150	250
Liberty Bell, 17J, LS, NI, SW, OF	100	150	250
Liberty Bell, 17J, LS, NI, SW, HC	125	175	300
Lightning Express, 11-13J, KWKS ★	200	285	500
A. Lincoln, 21J, Adj.5P, NI, DR, GJS, HC	400	500	800
A. Lincoln, 21J, Adj.5P, NI, DR, GJS,OF	250	300	500
Lincoln Park, 15-17J, LS, OF	75	110	200
Majestic Special, 17J, **2-tone movement**, OF	125	185	300
Locomotive, 11J, M# 2 grade 4, Locomotive engraved on Mvt.	225	325	550
Maiden Lane, 16-17J, 5th Pinion	300	450	650
Manhattan, 11-13J, NI, KW, LS, HC or OF	100	200	300
Manhattan, 15–17J, NI, KW, LS,HC or OF	125	225	350
Mason, 7J, KW, KS, HC	100	200	300
Mason, 7J, KW, KS, HC, **1st run S# 101 to 200** ★★	450	585	875
Miller, 15J,**1st run S# 301 to 400** ★★	400	550	850
Miller, 15J, M#1, HC, KW	95	135	275
Miller, 15J, M#1, HC, KW, ADJ	125	175	300
Miller, 15J, KW, OF	95	135	275
Miller, 17J, 5th Pinion, ADJ	150	185	375
Monarch W. Co., 17J, NI, ADJ, SW	125	175	325

Paillard Non-Magnetic W. Co., 18 size, 24 jewels, gold jewel settings, serial number 1,397,812.

Pennsylvania Special, 18 size, 26 Ruby Jewels, Adj6p, 2-tone movement, serial number 1,742,913.

Grade or Name — Description	Avg	Ex-Fn	Mint
Montgomery Ward, 15-17J, GJS, OF	$125	$200	$350
Montgomery Ward, 19J, GJS, OF	150	250	400
Montgomery Ward, 21J, OF	200	300	500
Montgomery Ward Timer, 21J, OF ★	200	285	475
Montgomery Ward, 24J, OF	900	1,200	1,700
Montgomery Ward, 24J, HC ★	1,100	1,400	2,000
Montgomery Ward, 24J, marked double roller, HC ★	1,100	1,400	2,000
Muscatine W. Co., 15J, LS, NI, HC	135	225	400
The National, 11J, SW, LS, OF	75	110	225
(Paillard Non-Magnetic W. Co. SEE Non-Magnetic W. Co.)			
Pennsylvania Special, 17J, GJS, ADJ ★★	900	1,100	1,600
Pennsylvania Special, 21J, DR, Adj.5P ★★	2,000	2,700	3,600
Pennsylvania Special, 24J, DR, GJS, ADJ ★★	3,000	3,700	4,600
Pennsylvania Special, 25J, DR, GJS, ADJ, NI ★★★	4,500	5,300	8,200
Pennsylvania Special, 26J, DR, GJS, ADJ, NI ★★★	5,500	6,800	9,400
Pierce Arrow, 17J, "automaker logo" ★	375	500	800
Plymouth W. Co., 15-17J, SW, (sold by Sears)	75	110	200
Potomac, 17J, ADJ, NI, OF	150	200	375
Potomac, 17J, ADJ, NI, HC ★	225	300	500
The President, 15J, NI, OF	100	200	400
The President, 17J, DMK, **14K gold case**	500	700	1,100
Rail Road Construction, 17J, OF	225	285	525
Rail Road Dispatcher Extra or Special, 15-17J, OF ★	250	325	600
Rail Road Dispatcher Extra, 15-17J, HC ★	250	325	600
Rail Road Employee's Special, 17J, NI, LS, HC ★	250	325	600
Rail Road King, 15J, NI, ADJ, OF ★	225	325	500
Rail Road King, 15J, NI, ADJ, HC ★	300	400	550
Rail Road King, 16J, NI, ADJ, OF ★	300	400	550
Rail Road King, 16J, NI, ADJ, HC ★	325	425	575
Rail Road King, 17J, NI, ADJ, OF ★	300	400	550
Rail Road King, 17J, NI, ADJ, HC ★	350	450	575
Rail Road King, 19J, NI, ADJ, **2 tone**, OF ★	350	465	600
4 Railroader, 11J, (Locomotive engraved on movement) ★	250	325	550

"4 Railroader"

Rail Road Timer Extra, 17-21J, (Montgomery Ward), OF ★	225	325	500
Railway , 11J, KW, KS, gilt ★	150	225	425
Railway Engineer, 15J ★	275	350	625
Railway Regulator, 11-15J, LS, (R.W.Sears Watch Co.) ★★	450	550	975
Remington W.Co. 17J, OF	200	275	450
Remington W.Co. 17J, HC	225	285	500
Remington Special, 21J, Adj.6P, OF	250	325	575

The President, 18 size, 17 jewels, Chalmer regulator Pat. Dec. 19, 1882, serial number 1,240,909.

Railroad King, 18 size, 17 jewels, Fifth Pinion Model, adjusted. Note Chalmer patented regulator, S# 1,160,836.

Grade or Name — Description	Avg	Ex-Fn	Mint
Standard W. Co., 15J, several models..★	$125	$200	$300
S. W. Co., 15J, M#1, KW, HC..	110	185	300
R.W. Sears Watch Co. Chicago,"Defiance" model, HC........... ★★	650	850	1,600
Sears & Roebuck Special, 15-17J, GJS, NI, DMK, Adj	150	200	350
Senate, 17J, NI, DMK, Washington W. Co.	150	200	350
Southern R.R. Special, 21J, LS, ADJ, OF .... ★★	1,400	1,900	2,900
Southern R.R. Special, 21J, M#5, LS, Adj., HC .... ★★	1,600	2,200	3,200
Star Light, 17J, 5th pinion, Chalmers Reg. OF............................	150	235	450
Stewart Special, 11J	60	95	150
Stewart Special, 15J, Adj.	75	110	200
Stewart Special, 17J, Adj...	95	165	250
Stewart Special, 21J, Adj.	150	200	300
Stuart, 15J, M#1, KW, KS...	300	450	950
Stuart, 15J, M#1, KW/SW, transition	250	400	850
Stuart, 15J, M#1, KW, KS, marked Adj. ....★	275	350	750
Stuart, 15J, ADJ, KW, Abbotts Conversion, 18K, HC ....★	1,200	1,600	2,300
Stuart, 15J, M#1, KW, KS, Coin ....★	500	650	1,100
Stuart, 15J, M#1, KW, KS, 1st run S# 1 to 10" .... ★★★★	4,200	6,500	11,000
Stuart, 15J, M#1, KW, KS, 1st run S# 11 to 100" .... ★★★	2,400	3,000	7,000
Stuart, 17J, M#3, 5th Pinion .... ★★	225	325	500
Stuart, 17J, M#3, 5th Pinion, Adj. .... ★★	250	385	600

Sears & Roebuck Special, 18 size, 17 jewels, serial number 1,481,879.

Washington W. Co., Lafayette model, 18 size, 24 Ruby jewels, gold jewel settings, adjusted, serial # 3,392,897.

Grade or Name — Description	Avg	Ex-Fn	Mint
Transition Models, 17J, KW/SW, OF	$75	$100	$200
Train Dispatcher Special, 17J, (Montgomery Ward), Adj, OF ..... ★	275	350	625
Time King, 17J, OF, LS, NI	100	150	300
Time King, 21J, OF, LS,	165	250	475
Union Pacific Sp., 17J, OF ★★	450	650	1,200
Vault Time Lock for Mosler, 15J, 72 hr.	100	175	300
Ward's Special, 15J, NI, FULL, LS,	70	135	200
George Washington,11J, HC ★★★	250	300	550
Washington, 11j, also (U.S.A) sold by **Montgomery Ward,**	100	135	200
Washington, 17J, also (U.S.A) sold by **Montgomery Ward,**	125	185	275
☉ **Washington W. Co.** (See Army & Navy, Liberty Bell, Lafayette, Senate)			
Wathiers Railway Watch, 15-17J, Adj., NI ★	450	625	1,200
N0. 5, 11J, KW KS, (**marked** No.5), HC	150	235	400
65, 15J, HC, LS, M#2	60	90	175
89, 17J, nickel, ADJ, OF	75	110	200
89, 21J, nickel, ADJ, HC	150	235	425
101, 11J, SW, KW, OF	60	90	175
101, 11J, SW, KW, Silveroid	60	90	175
101, 11J, SW, KW, HC	75	110	200
102, 13J, SW, KW, Silveroid	60	90	175
102, 13J, SW, KW, OF	75	110	200
102, 13J, SW, KW, HC	90	135	275
103, 15-16J, ADJ	80	120	250
104, 15J, M#2, HC ★★★	300	450	900
104, 17J, M#3, **early high grade** for RR, Ca. 1885, OF... ★★★★	375	575	1,000
105, 17J, M#3, **early high grade** for RR, Ca. 1885, OF... ★★★★	600	825	1,500
105, 15J, M#2, GJS, ADJ, KW, KS, HC ★★★	375	575	1,000
106, 15-17J, ADJ, KW, KS ★	250	350	600
107, 15-17J, NI, ADJ. ★	285	450	800
108, 15-17J, (if it is in the "Stuart" run it is 108) ★★★	1,000	1,300	1,800
1908 Special, 21J, NI, Adj.5P,(**marked** 1908 special), OF	325	475	750

STUART, 17 jewels, Model #3, 5th Pinion, Transition Model.

First Model in 14K white or green gold
filled Wadsworth case, showing
Montgomery numerical dial.

☉ A collector should expect to pay modestly higher prices at local shops.

☉ Pricing in this Guide are fair market price for **COMPLETE** watches which are reflected from
the "**NAWCC**" National and regional shows.

ILLINOIS 16 SIZE

Grade or Name — Description	Avg	Ex-Fx	Mint
Adams Street, 17J, 3/4, SW, NI, DMK	$200	$285	$550
Adams Street, 17J, 3/4, 2-tone, checkboard DMK, HC	250	385	700
Adams Street, 21J, 3F brg, NI, DMK ★	250	385	700
Ak-Sar-Ben (Nebraska backward), 17J, OF, GCW	150	225	350
Ariston, 11J, OF & HC	65	100	200
Ariston, 15J, OF & HC	65	100	200
Ariston, 17J, Adj, HC	125	225	400
Ariston, 17J, Adj, OF	100	185	350
Ariston, 19J, Adj.5P, OF	150	250	400
Ariston, 21J, GJS, Adj.6P, OF	200	365	600
Ariston, 21J, GJS, Adj.6P, HC	250	400	700
Ariston, 23J, GJS, Adj.6P, OF	500	675	950
Ariston, 23J, GJS, Adj.6P, HC ★★	700	900	1,200
Arlington Special, 17J, OF	100	150	275
Arlington Special, 17J, OF, Silveroid	85	135	245
Army & Navy, 19J, GJS, Adj.3P, NI, 1F brg, OF	150	250	400
Army & Navy, 19J, GJS, Adj.3P, NI, 1F brg, HC	200	300	500
Army & Navy, 21J, GJS, Adj.3P, 1F brg, OF	250	385	525
Army & Navy, 21J, GJS, Adj.3P, 1F brg, HC	350	485	600
B & M Special, 17J, BRG, Adj.4P (Boston & Maine) ★	450	600	1,000
B & O Standard, 21J ★★	1,100	1,600	2,300
Benjamin Franklin, 17J, ADJ, DMK, OF	300	385	700
Benjamin Franklin, 17J, ADJ, DMK, HC ★	400	500	800
Benjamin Franklin, 21J, GJS, Adj.5P, DR, GT, OF ★	700	950	1,300
Benjamin Franklin, 21J, GJS, Adj.5P, DR, GT, HC ★★	800	1,100	1,600
Benjamin Franklin, 25J, GJS, Adj.6P, DR, GT, OF ★★★	3,000	3,600	5,500
Benjamin Franklin, 25J, GJS, Adj.6P, DR, GT, HC ★★★	4,000	5,000	7,500

Ben Franklin, 16 size, 25 jewels, gold jewel settings, gold train, **OF Getty Model,** serial number 2,242,138.

Bunn Special, Model 163, 16 size, 23J., gold jewel settings, gold train, 60 hour movement, serial # 5,421,504.

Note: Bunn Special original cases were marked Bunn Special made and cased by Hamilton. Also GRADES 161 & 163 were made by Hamilton W. Co.

Special note: Some wheels or gears are **gold gilded** on brass and not solid gold, the appearance is rough and not, as smooth as, solid gold gears or wheels.

☾ Generic, nameless or **unmarked grades** for watch movements are listed under the Company name or initials of the Company, etc. by size, jewel count and description.

☾ Watches listed in this book are priced at the **collectable fair market** <u>value</u> at the Trade Show level, as complete watches having an original 14k gold filled case, KEY WIND with silver, an original white enamel single sunk dial, and with the entire original movement in good working order with no repairs needed, unless otherwise noted.

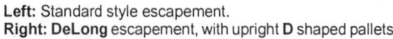

Left: Standard style escapement.
Right: DeLong escapement, with upright **D** shaped pallets.

Illinois Watch Co., 16 size, 25J., 3 fingered bridge Getty Model, gold train, note click near balance cock = HC model, serial number S731,870.

Grade or Name — Description	Avg	Ex-Fn	Mint
Bunn, 17J, LS, NI, 3/4, GJS, Adj.5P, OF	$175	$250	$450
Bunn, 17J, LS, NI, 3/4, Adj.5P, HC ★★★	650	800	1,400
Bunn, 19J, LS, NI, 3/4, GJS, Adj.5P, OF	200	300	500
Bunn, 19J, LS, NI, 3/4, Adj.5P, HC ★★★	800	1,000	1,500
Bunn, 19J, LS, NI, 3/4, GJS, Adj.5P, **60** hour, OF	400	550	800
Bunn, 19J, **marked Jeweled Barrel,** OF	300	385	600
Bunn Special, 19J, LS, NI, 3/4, Adj.6P, GT, OF	200	285	400
Bunn Special, 19J, LS, NI, 3/4, Adj.5P, GT, **60** hour , OF	400	575	950
Bunn Special, 21J, NI, Adj.6P, GT, HC ★★	575	700	1,100
Bunn Special, 21J, LS, NI, 3/4, GJS, Adj.6P, GT, OF	250	350	525
Bunn Special, 21J, LS, GJS, Adj.6P, GT, **gold plated Mvt.** ★★	575	700	1,100
Bunn Special, 21J, LS, NI, 3/4, GJS, Adj.6P, GT, **60** hour, OF	400	500	900
Bunn Special, 21J, LS, NI, 3/4, GJS, Adj.6P, GT, **60** hr. , OF			
marked Elinvar	700	900	1,500
Bunn Special, 21J, 60 hr., **Bunn Special case , OF 14K** ★	1,000	1,450	2,200
Bunn Special, 23J, LS, NI, 3/4, GJS, Adj.6P, GT, OF	500	650	1,100
Bunn Special, 23J, LS, NI, 3/4, GJS, Adj.6P, GT, **60** hour, OF	700	850	1,600
Bunn Special, 23J, LS, NI, 3/4, GJS, Adj.6P, GT, , OF			
with **23J, 60-hour on dial**	1,300	1,600	2,500
Bunn Special, 23J, LS, NI, GJS, GT, Adj.6P, HC ★★★★	2,500	3,200	5,200
161 Bunn Special, 21J, 3/4, Adj.6P, **60** hour, OF	700	1,000	1,700
161 Bunn Special, 21J, 3/4, Adj.6P, **60** hour on dial & movement			
in Illinois original factory box with Bunn papers ★★★★	1,800	2,500	3,800
161 Elinvar Bunn Special, 21J, 3/4, Adj.6P, **60** hour			
(**Elinvar** signed at edge of bridge)	1,000	1,300	2,000
161A Bunn Special, 21J, 3/4, Adj.6P, **60** hour (**Elinvar**			
signed under balance or on top plate)	900	1,200	1,900
161B, Bunn Special, 21J, **60** hour, pressed jewels , OF ★★★★	4,500	6,500	11,000
163 Bunn Special, 23J, GJS, Adj.6P, 3/4, **60** hour	1,600	2,000	2,800
163 Elinvar Bunn Special, 23J, GJS, Adj.6P, **60** hour, OF			
(**Elinvar** signed at bottom of cock, uncut balance) ★	1,800	2,300	3,000
163A Elinvar Bunn Special, 23J, GJS, Adj.6P, 3/4, **60** hour, OF			
(**Elinvar** signed under balance) ◪	1,900	2,500	3,200
163A Elinvar Bunn Special, 23J, Adj.6P, 3/4, **60** hour, OF			
(**Elinvar** signed on train bridge) ◪	2,000	2,600	3,500

🕐 Some grades are not included. Their values can be determined by comparing with **similar** age, size, metal content, style, models and grades listed.

Grade or Name — Description	Avg	Ex-Fn	Mint
Burlington W. Co., 11-15J, OF	$100	$165	$300
BurlingtonW. Co., 11- 15J, HC	125	185	365
BurlingtonW. Co., 17J, OF	95	160	300
Burlington W. Co., 17J, HC	125	185	365
Burlington W. Co., 19J, 3/4, NI, Adj.3P	95	165	300
Burlington W. Co., 19J, BRG, NI, Adj.3P	95	165	300
Burlington W. Co., 19J, 3/4, HC	95	165	300
Burlington W. Co., 19J, 3F brg, NI, Adj.3P	90	135	275
Burlington W. Co., 21J, 3/4, NI, Adj.3P	125	185	375
Burlington W. Co., 21J, Adj.6P, GJS, Getty, 2-tone	150	225	425
Burlington, Bull Dog- on dial, 21J, SW, LS, GJS, GT	275	385	750
C & O Special, 21J, 3/4, NI, ADJ ★★	900	1,200	1,700
Capitol, 17J, OF, BRG., NI., Adj., OF	95	145	250
Capitol, 19J, OF, G# 604, 3/4, NI, Adj.3P, OF ★	100	175	300
Central, 17J, SW, PS, OF	75	135	200
Commodore Perry Special, 21J, Adj.6P, GT, OF ★	250	350	700
Craftsman, 21J, Adj.3P, OF ★★★	500	600	800
D. & R. G. Special, 21J, GJS, GT, Adj.5P, (Denver & Rio Grand RR), OF ★★★★	3,100	3,800	5,500
DeLong Escapement, 21J, GJS, (Bunn Sp. or A. Lincoln) upright D shaped pallets, Adj.6P, 14K OF ★★★★	4,000	5,500	8,000
Dependon, 17J, (J.V.Farwell)	150	250	400
Dependon, 21J, (J.V.Farwell)	200	300	525
Diamond, Ruby, Sapphire, 21J, GJS, GT, Adj.6P, BRG, OF ★★★	1,600	2,100	3,200
Diamond, Ruby, Sapphire, 23J, GJS, GT, Adj.6P, BRG, OF ★★★	3,000	3,600	5,100
Diamond, Ruby, Sapphire, 23J, GJS, GT, Adj.6P, grade # 310, tall Arabic numbers on dial, BRG, DR, HC ★★★★	4,000	5,200	9,000
Diamond, Ruby, Sapphire, 23J, GJS, GT, Adj.6P, BRG, OF also marked Greenwich (Washington W.Co.) ★★★	3,000	3,600	6,000
Diamond, Ruby, Sapphire, 23J, GJS, GT, Adj.6P, 3/4 plate, OF ★★★	1,800	2,300	3,500
Dispatcher, 19J, Adj.3P	150	265	400
Fifth Ave.,19J, Adj.3P,GT,OF	100	175	300
Fifth Ave., 21J, Adj.3P,GT,OF	125	225	350
Franklin Street, 15J, 3/4, NI, ADJ	100	175	300
Grant, 17J, ADJ, LS, Getty Model, OF	150	250	400
Getty Model # 4 &5, 17J	100	175	300
Getty Model # 4 &5, 21J	200	285	475

Interstate Chronometer, 16 size, 23 jewels, one-fingered bridge, OF, **Getty Model**, serial number 2,327,614.

A. Lincoln, 16 size, 21 jewels, gold jewel settings, gold train, Adj5p, OF, **Getty Model**, serial number 2,237,406.

🕑 Pricing in this Guide are fair market price for COMPLETE watches which are reflected from the "NAWCC" National and regional shows.

Grade or Name — Description	Avg	Ex-Fn	Mint
Great Northern Special, 17J, BRG, ADJ	$200	$285	$500
Great Northern Special, 19J, BRG, ADJ	200	285	500
Great Northern Special, 21J, BRG, ADJ, Adj.3P	250	385	650
Illinois Central, 17-21J, 2-Tone, Adj.3P, GT	225	335	575
⊕ GENERIC, NAMELESS OR UNMARKED GRADES FOR WATCH MOVEMENTS ARE LISTED UNDER THE COMPANY NAME OR INITIALS OF THE COMPANY, ETC. BY SIZE, JEWEL COUNT AND DESCRIPTION.			
Illinois Watch Co., 7-9J, M#1-2-3	$45	$65	$150
Illinois Watch Co., 11J., OF	45	65	150
Illinois Watch Co., 13J, 3/4, OF	45	65	150
Illinois Watch Co., 11-13J, M#7, 3/4, OF	45	65	150
Illinois Watch Co., 11-13, M#6, 3/4, HC	85	100	200
Illinois Watch Co., 15J, M#2, OF	50	75	165
Illinois Watch Co., 15J, M#1, HC	90	145	265
Illinois Watch Co., 15J, M#3, OF	50	80	150
Illinois Watch Co., 15J, 3/4, ADJ	50	80	150
Illinois Watch Co., 15J, 3F brg, GJS	50	80	150
Illinois Watch Co., 16-17J, **14K, HC**	375	485	850
Illinois Watch Co., 16-17J, Adj.3P, OF	85	100	200
Illinois Watch Co., 16-17J, M#2-3, SW, OF	85	100	200
Illinois Watch Co., 17J, M#4-6, SW, HC	90	145	250
Illinois Watch Co., 17J, M#7, OF	85	100	200
Illinois Watch Co., 17J, M#5, 3/4, ADJ, HC	85	100	200
Illinois Watch Co., 17J, M#4, 3F brg, GJS, Adj.5P, HC	150	235	400
Illinois Watch Co., 19J, 3/4, GJS, Adj.5P , **jeweled barrel**	165	265	450
Illinois Watch Co., 19J, 3/4, BRG, Adj.3-4P	95	155	225
Illinois Watch Co., 21J, Adj.3P, OF	200	250	350
Illinois Watch Co., 21J, ADJ, OF	225	285	400
Illinois Watch Co., 21J, GJS, HC	235	300	475
Illinois Watch Co., 21J, 3/4, GJS, Adj.5P	225	285	400
Illinois Watch Co., 21J, 3F brg, GJS, Adj.4P	200	275	400
Illinois Watch Co., 21J, 3F brg, GJS, Adj.5P	225	285	450
Illinois Watch Co., 23J, GJS, Adj.5P, OF ★★	400	575	950
Illinois Watch Co., 23J, GJS, Adj.5P, HC ★★	500	650	1,000
Illinois Watch Co., 25J, 4th model,3F brg, GJS, Adj.5P, HC ★★★	3,500	4,300	6,300
Imperial Sp., 17J, SW, LS, Adj.4P, OF	125	175	375
Interstate Chronometer, 17J, GCW, Adj.3P, HC, (sold by Sears)	300	385	725
Interstate Chronometer, 17J, GCW, Adj.3P, OF	250	365	625
Interstate Chronometer, 23J, 1F brg, ADJ, OF ★	800	1,100	1,600
Interstate Chronometer, 23J, 1F brg, ADJ, HC ★★	1,200	1,500	2,200
Lafayette, 23J, Washington W.Co., GJS, Adj.5P, GT, OF ... ★★★	1,000	1,300	2,000
Lafayette, 23J, Washington W.Co., GJS, Adj.5P, GT, HC ... ★★★	1,400	1,800	2,700
Lakeshore, 17J, OF	75	110	200
Lakeshore, 17J, HC	125	200	350
⌐ ndis W. Co., 15-17J	75	100	200
Liberty Bell, 15-17J, OF	85	135	225
Liberty Bell, 15-17J, HC ★	300	385	675
A. Lincoln, 21J,3/4, GJS, Adj.5P, OF	225	300	500
A. Lincoln, 21J,3/4, GJS, Adj.5P, HC	400	500	800
The Lincoln, 15J, 3F brg,	125	185	300
Logan, 15J, OF	60	95	175
Marvel, 19J, GT, GJS, Adj.3P, Of	75	110	200
Marine Special, 21J, 3/4, Adj.3P	150	200	375
Monarch W. Co., 17J, NI, ADJ, SW	125	175	300
Monroe, 17J, NI,3/4, OF (Washington W. Co.)	85	135	200
Monroe, 15J, 3/4, OF (Washington W. Co.)	75	100	185
Montgomery Ward, 17J, LS, Thin Model , OF	100	175	275
Montgomery Ward, 21J, "Extra RR Timer", **2 tone**, G# 179 ★★	1,000	1,200	1,700
Our No. 1, 15J, HC, M#1	100	165	300
Overland Special, 19J, Adj., OF	100	165	300

⊕ Pricing in this Guide are fair market price for **COMPLETE** watches which are reflected from the "**NAWCC**" National and regional shows.

Sangamo, 16 size, 23 jewels, Adj.6p, gold jewel settings, gold train, OF Getty Model, serial number 2,307,867.

Sangamo Special, 17S, 23J., model 13, marked motor barrel, Adj.6p, Serial # 4,628,066, Ca. 1926. NOTE: This is 60 hour movement tested and runs from 60 to 65 hours.

Grade or Name Description	Avg	Ex-Fn	Mint
Pennsylvania Special, 17J, Adj.3P, HC ★	$450	$600	$1,100
Pennsylvania Special, 17J, Adj., **2 tone**, G# 176, HC ★	800	950	1,300
Pennsylvania Special, 19J, OF ★	600	750	1,200
Pennsylvania Special, 21J, Getty model, **2-tone**, Adj., OF ★	1,000	1,300	1,700
Pennsylvania Special, 21J, **2-tone**, (Finely Adj.), HC ★★★	2,000	2,500	3,200
Pennsylvania Special, 23J, 3/4, GJS, Adj.5P ★	1,400	1,900	2,700
Plymouth W. Co., 15-17J, OF (Add $50 for HC), (sold by Sears)	100	185	300
Precise, 21J, OF, LS, Adj.3P	100	175	275
Quincy Street, 17J, 3/4, NI, DMK, ADJ	95	135	275
Railroad Dispatcher, 11-17J, DMK, 3/4	175	250	425
Railroad Dispatcher Extra or Special, 15-17J, DMK, 3/4 ★	225	335	550
Railroad Employee's, 17J,	175	285	425
Railroad King, 16-17J, M#2 or 5-Getty model, NI, PS, OF	275	325	550
Railroad Official, 23J, 3 Finger bridge ★★★★★	2,000	2,400	3,200
Railway King, 17J, OF	175	235	425
Remington W.Co. 11-15J, OF	100	150	200
Remington W.Co. 17J, OF	125	185	265
Remington W.Co. 17J, HC	200	265	350
Rockland, 17-19J, GJS, GT, 7th model, grade 305, OF	75	110	200
Sangamo, 19J, model # 4, GJS, GT, ADJ., HC ★★★	4,000	5,500	8,400
Sangamo, 21J, GJS, Adj.6P, HC	250	350	650
Sangamo, 21J, GJS, Adj., OF	225	325	550
Sangamo, 21J, 3/4, GJS, DR, Adj.6P, OF	225	300	600
Sangamo, 21J, GJS, Adj.6P, <u>EXTRA or SPECIAL,</u> (Getty), HC ★	525	700	1,200
Sangamo, 21J, GJS, Adj.6P, <u>EXTRA or SPECIAL,</u> (Getty), OF ★	475	600	1,100
Sangamo, 21J, GJS, Adj., <u>marked SPECIAL</u> **2-tone Mvt.**, (**straight ribbon** - not wavy ribbon pattern), (Getty), OF ★	475	600	950
Sangamo, 23J, GJS, Adj., <u>marked SPECIAL</u> **2-tone Mvt.**, Adj.6P, (**straight ribbon** - not wavy ribbon pattern), (Getty), OF ★	625	775	1,200
Sangamo, 23J,3/4, GJS, DR, Adj.6P, OF	350	500	900
Sangamo, 23J, 3/4, GJS, DR, Adj.6P, HC	400	600	1,100
Sangamo, 25J, M#5, 3/4, GJS, DR, Adj.6P ★★★★	4,000	5,400	9,300
Sangamo, 26J, M#5, 3/4, GJS, DR, Adj.6P ★★★★	5,000	6,500	8,300
Sangamo Special, 19J, BRG, GJS, GT, Adj.6P, OF	350	450	750
Sangamo Special, 19J, BRG, GJS, GT, Adj.6P, HC ★★★	1,400	1,800	2,700
Sangamo, **Extra**, 21J, Adj.6P, gold train, Of ★★	425	525	950
Sangamo Special, 21J, M#8, BRG, HC ★★★	1,500	2,100	3,100
Sangamo Special, 21J, M#9, BRG, GJS, GT, Adj.6P, OF	400	550	900
Sangamo Special, 21J, BRG, GJS, GT, Diamond end cap	400	550	900

Grade or Name — Description	Avg	Ex-Fn	Mint
Sangamo Special, 23J, M#9-10, BRG, GJS, GT, Adj.6P, Sangamo Special **HINGED** case	$850	$1,200	$2,000
Sangamo Special, 23J, BRG, GJS, GT, Adj.6P, Diamond end stone, **screw back,** Sangamo Special case	750	950	1,500
Sangamo Special, 23J, M#8, GJS, GT, Adj.6P, **HC** ★★★	1,600	2,000	3,400
Sangamo Special, 23J, BRG, GJS, GT, Adj.6P, **not marked** 60 hour, rigid bow, Sangamo Special case	900	1,200	1,800
Sangamo Special, 23J, BRG, GJS, GT, Adj.6P, **marked 60 hour,** Sangamo Special case ★★★	1,600	2,500	3,800
Sangamo Special, 23J, BRG, GJS, GT, 60 hour, rigid bow, Sangamo Special case **14K gold case** ★	1,800	2,600	3,600
Santa Fe Special, 17J, BRG, Adj., (Triple Signed), OF	225	350	650
Santa Fe Special, 21J, 3/4, Adj., (Triple Signed), OF	450	550	800
Santa Fe Special, 21J, 3/4, Adj., (Triple Signed), **HC**	500	650	950
Sears, Roebuck & Co. Special, 15-17J, ADJ	85	125	225
Senate, 17J, (Washington W. Co.), **gilt escape wheel,** NI, 3/4, Adj.	95	135	250
Standard, 15J	75	110	200
Sterling, 17J, SW, PS, Adj.3P, OF	75	110	200
Sterling, 19-21J, SW, PS, Adj.3P, OF	125	175	250
Stewart, 17J	75	125	185
Stewart Special, 21J, Adj.,	125	175	250
Stewart Special, 19J, Adj.3P	75	110	200
Stewart Special, 15-17J,	60	85	165
The General, 15J, OF	75	110	200
Time King, 17J, OF	65	95	150
Time King, 19J, Adj.3P, OF	95	125	225
Time King, 21J, Adj, OF	150	200	325
Trainmen's Special, 17J, HC ★	150	225	475
Union Pacific,17J, Adj.,DR, 2-tone, DMK, OF ★★	500	650	1,100
Victor, 21J, 3/4, Adj.	150	200	350

⊕ **Washington W. Co.** (See Army & Navy, Liberty Bell, Lafayette, Senate)

Grade 163, 16 size, 23 jewels, adjusted to 6 positions, motor barrel, 60 hour model, serial number 5,421,504.

SENATE, 17J, 16S, Washington W.CO., Adj., **gilt escape wheel & train,** HC, S# 2,457,094 (M# 6 with <u>extra</u> cut out.)

161 through 163A —See Bunn Special

Grade or Name — Description	Avg	Ex-Fn	Mint
167, 17J, marked	$100	$135	$250
169, 19J, Adj.3P, OF	75	125	225
174, 17J, LS, GJS, Adj., OF	60	95	185
174, 211, LS, GJS, Adj., OF	165	200	325
174, 23J, LS, GJS, Adj., OF, **marked 174** ★★	500	650	925
175, 17J, RR grade & a (RR inspectors name on dial &mvt.) .. ★★	500	700	1,100
176, 17J, Getty model, LS, Adj.4P, 2-tone, HC ★	125	200	325
177, 17J, Getty model, Ruby Jewels, Adj.5P, HC-OF ★★	300	450	725

Grade or Name — Description	Avg	Ex-Fn	Mint
179, 21J, 3/4, GJS, GT, Adj.6P, Getty model, **marked** Ruby Jewels			
Getty model, HC or OF ★★	$300	$450	$725
181, 21J., ADJ, GJS, marked 21 ruby jewels ★★★★	600	800	1,200
184, 17-19J, 3F brg, LS, OF	95	150	250
184, 23J, 3F brg, LS, OF	500	650	1,100
186, 23J, 3F brg, LS, OF	500	650	1,100
186, 17J, 3F brg, Adj.4P, 2 tone, **marked** 186, HC	200	325	525
187, 17J, 3F brg, Adj.5P, GJS, GT, **marked** 187, HC	250	375	625
189, 21J, 3F brg, Adj.6P, GJS, DR, GT, **marked Ruby Jewels & Adjusted.**,			
Getty model, HC or OF ★	300	475	750
555, 17J, 3/4,	100	185	350
777, 17J, 3/4, ADJ ★	150	275	450
805, 17J, BRG, GJS, GT, DR, OF	75	110	200
809, 23J, Adj.6P, GT, **marked 809** ★★★	500	700	1,100
900, 19J, LS, Adj.3P	125	185	300

Grade 189, 21J, OF, 3Finger bridge, GJS, DR, GT, **marked** *"Ruby Jewels"* & **Adjusted.**, gold balance screws including 4 timing screws, gold beveled polished train, counterpoised fork & pallet, Getty model, advertised at a cost of 20% higher than a 23J., Sangamo, Ca.1903.

Illinois Watch Co., 14 size, 21J., adjusted, nickel movement, gold jewel settings, serial number 1,029,204.

ILLINOIS   14 SIZE

Grade or Name — Description	Avg	Ex-Fn	Mint
Illinois Watch Co., 7J, M#1, **GRADE 120, KW,** OF ★	$95	$135	$275
Illinois Watch Co., 7J, M#1-2-3, SW, OF	40	65	120
Illinois Watch Co., 11J, M#1-2-3, SW, OF	45	75	125
Illinois Watch Co., 15J, M#1-2-3, SW, OF	50	85	145
Illinois Watch Co., 16J, M#1-2-3, SW, OF	70	110	165
Illinois Watch Co., 21J, M#1-2-3, SW, OF ★	125	185	325
Illinois Watch Co., 22J, ★	150	250	425
NOTE: Add $35 for above watches in hunting case.			

ILLINOIS   12 SIZE and 13 SIZE

Grade or Name — Description	Avg	Ex-Fn	Mint
Accurate, 21J, GJS, OF	$75	$110	$200
Aristocrat, 17J, OF	55	85	150
Aristocrat, 19J, OF	60	95	175
Ariston, 11-17J, OF	60	80	165
Ariston, 17J, Adj.3P, BRG, OF	75	110	200
Ariston, 17J, Adj.3P, G# 506, 14 size dial & 12 size mvt., HC ★★★★	225	350	600
Ariston, 19J, OF	80	135	250
Ariston, 21J, Adj.5P, OF	100	185	375
Ariston, 21J, Adj.5P, HC ★★	225	350	600
Ariston, 23J, Adj.5P, OF ★	225	300	450
Ariston, 23J, Adj.5P, HC ★★	250	335	550
Ariston, 23J, Adj.6P, OF **18K** ★★★	400	600	925

Ben Franklin, 12 size, 17J., grade 273, open face, signed on movement Benjamin Franklin USA, S # 2,386,286.

Maiden America, 12 size, 17J, serial number 2,820,499.

Grade or Name — Description	Avg	Ex-Fn	Mint
Aluminum Watch, 17J, model #3, movement plates made of aluminum			
G#525, S# 3,869,251 to S# 3,869,300 .... ★★★★★	$2,000	$2,600	$3,700
Autocrat, 17J, Adj.3P..	60	85	150
Autocrat, 19J, Adj.3P..	65	95	175
Banker, 17J, Adj.3P, OF..	60	85	150
Banker, 21J, Adj.3P, OF..	75	110	200
Benjamin Franklin, 17J, OF	150	235	475
Benjamin Franklin, 21J, OF	200	285	575
Benjamin Franklin, 21J, G# 299, HC..	235	325	600
Bunn Special, 21J, Adj 3P, (by Hamilton), OF .... ★★	400	500	825
Burlington Special, 19J, GT, OF..	75	110	200
Burlington Special, 19J, GT, HC...	100	175	250
Burlington W. Co., 21J, GT, OF	75	110	200
Burlington W. Co., 21J, GT, HC	100	175	250
Central, 17J, OF, 2-Tone	50	90	125
Chronos, 21J., G# 299, GT, GJS, marked 21 Ruby Jewels.......... ★	250	375	600
Commodore Perry Special, 17J., adj.3P..★	100	150	250
Criterion, 21J, OF	75	110	200
Dependon, 17, (J.V.Farwell), HC,..	70	100	185
Elite, 19J, OF	75	110	200
Garland, 17J, Adj.,GT, OF	60	85	150
Gold Metal, 17J, OF	45	65	100

Example of Illinois Thin Model, 12 size, 17 jewels, adjusted to 3 positions.

Illini, 12-13 size, 21 jewels, bridge model, serial number 3,650,129. Note five tooth pinion click & jeweled barrel.

Santa Fe Special, 12 size, 21 jewels, three-quarter plate, serial number 3,414,422.

NOTE: The "**Illini**" 5 tooth click movement is a 13 size but advertised as 12 size.

Grade or Name — Description	Avg	Ex-Fn	Mint
Illini, 13 Size, 21J, Adj.5P, jeweled barrel, **5 tooth click**, (Hi-grade), OF, **14K** ★★	$250	$350	$600
Illini **Extra**, 13 S., 21J, Adj.5P, jeweled barrel, (Hi-grade) **5 tooth click**, OF, **14K** ★★★	350	450	750
Illini, 12 Size, 23J, Adj.6P, BRG, OF ★★★	175	225	450
Illini, 12 Size, 23J, Adj.6P, BRG, OF **14K** ★★★	250	350	585
Illinois Watch Co., 7-11-15J	40	60	100
Illinois Watch Co., 16-17J, OF, **14K**	200	275	475
Illinois Watch Co., 16-17J,GF, OF,	60	90	150
Illinois Watch Co., 17J, GF, HC	80	110	200
Illinois Watch Co., 19J	80	110	200
Illinois Watch Co., 21J, OF	100	125	225
Illinois Watch Co., 21J, marked (**21 SPECIAL**), OF	110	150	265
Illinois Watch Co., 21J, HC	125	175	250
Illinois Watch Co., 23J, OF	200	250	350
Illinois Watch Co., 19J, EXTRA THIN MODEL, **14K**, OF ★★	200	275	475
Illinois Watch Co., 21J, EXTRA THIN MODEL, **14K**, OF ★★	225	300	525
Illinois Watch Co., 21J, **Marked EXTRA**, extra thin model, **14K**, OF ★★★	250	325	575
Interstate Chronometer, 17J, OF, (sold by Sears) ★★★	95	135	275
Interstate Chronometer, 21J, GJS, OF ★★★	175	225	375
Interstate Chronometer, 21J, GJS, HC ★★★	225	275	475
Governor, 17J, OF	60	90	150
A. Lincoln, 19J, Adj.5P, GJS, DR, OF	95	135	275
A. Lincoln, 21J, Adj.5P, DR, GJS, OF	100	175	285
A. Lincoln, 21J, Adj.5P, DR, GJS, HC ★	150	235	385
Maiden America, 17J, ADJ	60	85	125
Marquis Autocrat, 17J, OF	60	85	125
Master, 21J, GT, GJS, OF	75	100	185
Masterpiece, 19J, Adj.3P, OF	65	95	175
A. Norton, 21J, OF	100	150	250
Penn Special, 17J, Adj.3P, G# 405, OF	100	125	225
Plymouth Watch Co., 15-17J, HC, (sold by Sears)	65	100	165
Railroad Dispatch , 11-15J,	55	85	150
Railroad Dispatch , 17-19J, SW, GT	75	110	175
Rockland, 17J,	50	75	125
Roosevelt, 17J, G#405, Adj.3P, OF	50	65	125
Roosevelt, 19-21J, G# 406, Adj.6P, OF	200	275	450
Santa Fe Special, 21J	200	275	450
Secometer, 19J., G# 407, OF **14K** ★★	225	300	475
Sterling, 17J, OF	40	60	95
Sterling, 19-21J, OF	60	95	175
Stewart Special, 17J, SW, Adj.3P	40	60	95
Stewart Special, 19J, SW, OF, GT	50	70	125

Grade or Name — Description	Avg	Ex-Fn	Mint
Time King, 19J, SW, Adj.3P	$50	$75	$150
Time King, 21J, SW, Adj.3P	60	95	175
Transit, 19J, OF, PS	50	65	150
Vim, 17J, ADJ, BRG, GJS, DR, OF	35	60	100
Washington W. Co., **Army & Navy,** 19J ★★	95	150	275
Washington W. Co., **Army & Navy,** 21J., G# 273, OF ★★★	125	185	325
Washington W. Co., **Monroe,** 11J, sold by Montgomery Ward	75	110	200
Washington W. Co., **Senate,** 17J, M#2, PS, ★★	60	95	175
121, 21J, Adj.3P	65	110	200
127, 17J, ADJ, (by Hamilton)	35	60	100
129, 19J, Adj.3P	45	85	150
219, 11J, M#1	30	50	85
299, 21J, Adj.5P, OF ★	75	95	185
299, 23J, Adj.5P, HC ★★★	300	400	650
299, 23J, Adj.6P, HC ★★★★	350	450	750
403, 15J, BRG	35	50	90
405, 17J, BRG, ADJ, OF	40	60	125
409, 21J, BRG, Adj.5P, GJS, OF ★	225	325	525
409, 21J, BRG, Adj.5P, GJS, HC ★★	250	385	625
410, 23J, BRG, GJS, Adj.6P, DR, OF ★	200	300	500
410, 23J, BRG, GJS, Adj.6P, DR, HC ★	250	350	600
509, 21J, BRG, Adj.5P, GJS, (**spread** to 14 size)	75	110	200
510, 23J, BRG, GJS, Adj.6P, DR, (**spread** to14 size) ★★	100	150	250

ILLINOIS 8 SIZE

Grade or Name — Description	Avg	Ex-Fn	Mint
Arlington, 7J, ★	$150	$185	$300
Rose LeLand, 13J, ★★	225	285	400
Stanley, 7J, ★★	195	275	450
Mary Stuart, 15J, ★★	225	285	500
Sunnyside, 11J, ★	40	75	125
151-152-155, 7-11J, 3/4	30	50	85
Illinois W. Co. , 11-15J, (nameless unmarked grades)	45	75	125
Illinois W. Co. , 16-17J, (nameless unmarked grades)	45	75	125

Illinois Watch Co., 8 size, 7 jewels

Grade 144, 6 size, 15 jewels, serial number 5,902,290.

ILLINOIS 6 SIZE

Grade or Name — Description	Avg	Ex-Fn	Mint
Illinois W. Co., 7J, LS, HC, **14K**	$200	$275	$400
Illinois W. Co., 7J, HC	45	55	125
Illinois W. Co., 7J, OF, Coin	30	45	95
Illinois W. Co., 11-12-13J, OF, HC	55	75	125
Illinois W. Co., 15J, OF, HC, **14K**	200	285	450
Illinois W. Co., 17J, OF, HC	55	65	125
Illinois W. Co., 19J, OF, HC	60	75	150
Plymouth Watch Co., 17J, OF, HC, (sold by Sears)	40	60	135
Sears & Roebuck Special, 15J, HC	55	75	110
Washington W. Co., 15J, Liberty Bell, HC	75	125	225
Washington W. Co., 11J, Martha Washington, HC ★	100	185	375

ILLINOIS
4 SIZE

Grade or Name — Description	Avg	Ex-Fn	Mint
Illinois W. Co., 7J, LS, HC	$45	$75	$125
Illinois W. Co., 11J, LS, HC	55	90	150
Illinois W. Co., 15-16J, LS, HC	55	90	150

ILLINOIS
0 SIZE

Grade or Name — Description	Avg	Ex-Fn	Mint
Accuratus, 17J, OF	$60	$85	$175
Ariste, 11-15-17J, OF & HC	95	155	225
Burlington Special, 15-17J, 3/4, OF	100	165	250
Illinois W. Co., 7 to 17J, LS, HC, **14K**	200	285	425
201, 11J, BRG, NI	40	65	125
203, 15J, BRG, NI	50	75	135
204, 17J, BRG, NI	55	85	150
Interstate Chronometer, 15J, HC, SW	125	200	400
Interstate Chronometer, 17J, HC, SW	125	200	400
Lady Franklin, 15-17J, HC	65	110	200
Plymouth Watch Co., 15-17J, HC, (sold by Sears)	75	90	125
Santa Fe Special, 15-17J	★	200	250	400
Washington W. Co., Liberty Bell, 15J, ADJ	60	95	185
Washington W. Co., Mt. Vernon, 17J, ADJ	70	110	225

Washington W. Co., Mt. Vernon, 0 size, 17J, hunting case.

Grade 203, 0 size, 15 jewels, originally sold for $10.40

Grade 204, 0 size, 17 jewels, originally sold for $12.83.

ILLINOIS
CAPRICE

Grade or Name — Description	Avg	Ex-Fn	Mint
Caprice, 17J, handbag, pocket or desk watch, snake or ostrich	$100	$185	$375

Ca. 1929 AD

The CAPRICE
Just the watch for the handbag, pocket or desk; for sports wear or dress. It's an entirely practical timekeeper, too. In genuine coverings of snake or ostrich. 17 jewels, 14K gold filled inner case **$50**

AD for 1921 - 1924
NET PRICE LIST TO JEWELERS
Illinois-Springfield Watches

18 SIZE, Open Face and Hunting

Bunn Special, 21 Jewels Adjusted 6 Positions - -	$24.00
No. 89, 17 Jewels Adj., Gilt Damsk., D. S. Dial -	10.00

16 SIZE

SANGAMO SPECIAL, Open Face Only
23 Jewels, Adj. 6 Positions, Illinois Motor Barrel

Fitted in 25 year, 14K. filled extra weight screw back and hinged bezel case, Complete - -	50.00
Fitted in 14K. extra weight, solid gold, jointed, inside cap case, Complete - - - -	92.50

16 SIZE, Open Face and Hunting

Bunn Special, 23J. Adj. 6 Pos., Illinois Motor Barrel	32.75
Bunn Special, 21 Jewels, Adjusted 6 Positions -	28.00
A. Lincoln, 21 Jewels, Adjusted 5 Positions - -	26.00
Bunn, 19 Jewels, Adj. 5 Pos., Illinois Motor Barrel -	24.00
Bunn, 17 Jewels, Adjusted 5 Positions - - -	20.00
(Special, 19 Jewels, Adjusted 3 Positions) Made on Special Order Only - -	
No. 706, 17 Jewels Adjusted 4 Positions, D. S. D. -	15.00
No. 305, 17 Jewels Adj., D. R., Steel escape, D.S.D.	13.25

12 SIZE, Open Face and Hunting

No. 410, 23 Jewels, Adjusted 6 Positions - -	37.50
A. Lincoln, 21 Jewels, Adjusted 5 Positions - -	26.50
(Special, 19 Jewels, Adjusted 3 Positions) Made on Special Order Only - -	
No. 405, 17 Jewels, Adj., D. R., Steel escape wheel -	13.50

6-0 Size or 11 Ligne Movements
Only delivered fitted in cases supplied by the Jobbers.

No. 907, 19 Jewels, double roller, steel escape wheel	20.00
No. 903, 15 Jewels, double roller - - - -	14.50

6-0 size full open and 3-4 open face dial movements have seconds hand.
Hunting and skylight dial movements do not have seconds hand.

RETAIL PRICE LIST
The ILLINOIS WATCH
SEPTEMBER 1, 1929

	Retailer	Consumer
FACTORY CASED RAILROAD GRADES		
Sangamo Special, 23 Jewels.		
60 Hour, 6 Position, Motor Barrel, 16 Size		
14K white, green or natural solid gold hinged case, with inside cap	$92.50	$150.00
14K white, green or natural gold filled case, hinged inside cap, also screw bezel and back, plain or eng. back	50.00	90.00
Bunn Special, 23 Jewels.		
60 Hour, 6 Position, Motor Barrel, 16 Size		
Model 28, 14K white, green or comb. gold filled case	40.75	75.00
Model 28, 10K natural gold filled case	37.25	70.00
Cases with Engraved backs, extra	.75	2.00
Bunn Special, 21 Jewels.		
60 Hour, 6 Position, Motor Barrel, 16 Size		
First Model, 14K white or green gold filled case	36.00	65.00
First Model, 10K natural gold filled case	32.50	60.00
Model 29, 14K white or green gold filled case	36.00	65.00
Model 29, 10K natural gold filled case	32.50	60.00
Model 181, 14K white gold filled	36.00	65.00
Model 181, 10K natural gold filled	32.50	60.00
Cases with Engraved backs, extra	.75	2.00
DISPATCHER, 16 Size, 19 Jewels, Adj. Temp. & 3 Pos. Pend. or Lever Set.		
14K white gold filled case	21.35	45.00
10K natural gold filled case	19.85	40.00
Cases with Engraved back, extra	.50	—
16 SIZE UNCASED WATCHES, Open Face		
Lever or Pendant Setting		
No. 167, (old No. 305) 17 J., Adj., S. S. Dial	12.60	24.00
No. 169, (old No. 707) Special, 19 J. Adj., 3 pos.	16.50	32.50
12 SIZE UNCASED WATCHES, Open Face		
No. 127, (old No. 405) 17 Jewels, Adj.	12.25	24.00
No. 129, (old No. 407) 19 J., Adj. 3 pos.	16.90	32.50
No. 121, (old No. 279) 21 J., Adj. 3 pos.	20.50	40.00
3/0 SIZE UNCASED WATCH.		
No. 307, (old No. 24) 17 Jewels Pat. Reg. luminous or printed dial	15.00	50.00

ILLINOIS, SPRINGFIELD MOVEMENTS,
NAMED AS FOLLOWS:

Full Plate, 18 Size.				Key Wind.	Stem-Wind
"STUART,"	15	Jew. Exp. Bal. Ad.		$44 00	$52 00
"BUNN,"	15	"	"	29 00	36 00
"MILLER,"	15	"	"	21 25	27 00
"MILLER,"	15	"	"	18 25	24 00
"CURRIER"	11	"	"	13 33	18 50
"HOYT,"	9	"	"	12 50	17 50
"DEAN,"	15	"	" half-cut	14 50	19 50
"MASON,"	7	"	" "	10 50	15 00
"BATES,"	7	" Exp. Chapo, Steel Bal.		10 00	14 50
"COLUMBIA,"	11 Jew. Cut Exp. Bal.			9 05	11 80
"AMERICA,"	7	"	" "	7 55	10 25

NAMELESS MOVEMENTS.

No. 25,	15	Jewels, Exp. Bal. Adj.		$21 25	$27 00
28,	15	"		18 25	24 00
30,	11	"	"	13 33	18 50
33,	9	"	"	12 50	17 50
35,	15	" Half Cut Bal.		14 50	19 50
34,	7	" Exp. Bal.		10 50	15 00
40,	7	" Im. Exp. Bal.		10 00	14 50
1,		Cut "		7 75	10 25
2,		" "		9 05	11 80

ABOVE: December 2, **1878** Price List AD to Jewelers.

Rigid bow 60 HR. MODEL
gold filled: $175 - $225 - $425
14K gold: $400 - $500 - $1,100
Dial: $35 - $50 - $95

Antique bow MODEL
gold filled: $100 - $125 - $285
14K gold: $375 - $450 - $700
Dial: $35 - $50 - $95

FIRST MODEL
gold filled: $110 - $135 - $375

Stiff bow 60 HR. MODEL
gold filled: $200 - $250 - $425
14K gold: $450 - $600 - $1,100
Dial: $40 - $60 - $95

Pyramid bow MODEL
gold filled: $95 - $150 - $325
14K gold: $400 - $500 - $775
Montgomery Dial: $40 - $60 - $125

MODEL 29
gold filled: $110 - $150 - $350
Montgomery Dial: $40 - $60 - $125

MODEL 28
gold filled: $135 - $180 - $450
gold filled **2 tone**: $180 - $275 - $600
Bunn Special Dial: $60 - $100 - $225

MODEL 107
gold filled: $110 - $150 - $350
Dial: $30 - $40 - $80

🕐 NOTE: April 1925 Factory Advertised as a **complete** watch and was fitted with a certain matched, timed and rated movement and sold in the factory designed case style as a **complete** watch. The factory also sold _uncased_ movements to **JOBBERS** such as Jewelry stores & they cased the movement in a case style the **CUSTOMER requested.** All the factory advertised **complete** watches came with the dial **SHOWN or CHOICE** of other **Railroad** dials.

MODEL 128
gold **plated**: $60 - $75 - $175
Dial: $35 - $50 - $95

MODEL 108
gold filled: $110 - $140 - $325
Bunn Special Dial: $40 - $65 - $175

MODEL 173
gold filled: $110 - $150 - $400
gold filled **2 tone**: $175 - $250 - $500
Bunn Special Montgomery Dial: $70 - $125 - $285

MODEL 181
gold filled: $110 - $150 - $400
Dial: $35 - $50 - $80

MODEL 193
gold filled: $110 - $150 - $400
Dial: $40 - $60 - $95

MODEL 206
gold filled: $95 - $150 - $325
gold filled **2 tone**: $140 - $195 - $500
Dial: $35 - $50 - $80

MODEL 118, Ca.1932
gold filled: $95 - $125 - $175
Dial: $35 - $50 - $80

BUNN SPECIALS were packed & shipped
in a ALUMINUM cigarette style box.
$90 — $150 — $275

🕐 NOTE: April 1925 Factory Advertised as a **complete** watch and was fitted with a certain matched, timed and rated movement and sold in the factory designed case style as a **complete** watch. The factory also sold _uncased_ movements to **JOBBERS** such as Jewelry stores & they cased the movement in a case style the **CUSTOMER requested**. All the factory advertised **complete** watches came with the dial **SHOWN or CHOICE** of other **Railroad** dials.

ILLINOIS SPRINGFIELD WATCH CO.
IDENTIFICATION OF MOVEMENTS
BY MODEL NUMBER

How to Identify Your Watch Size & Model: Compare the movement of your watch with the illustrations in this section. While comparing, note the location of the balance, jewels, screws, gears, and type of back plate (Full, 3/4, Bridge) these will be clues in identifying the movement you have.

THE ILLINOIS WATCH CO. MODEL CHART
By Size-Model and **started with first serial number.**

★ ★

Size	Model	Plate Design	Setting	Hunting or Open Face	Type Barrel	Started w/ Serial No.	Remarks
18	1	Full	Key	Htg	Reg	1	Course train
	2	Full	Lever	Htg	Reg	38,901	Course train
	3	Full	Lever	OF	Reg	46,201	Course train, 5th pinion
	4	Full	Pendant	OF	Reg	1,050,001	Fast train
	5	Full	Lever	Htg	Reg	1,256,101	Fast train, RR Grade
	6	Full	Lever	OF	Reg	1,144,401	Fast train, RR Grade
16	1	Full	Lever	Htg	Reg	1,030,001	Thick model
	2	Full	Pendant	OF	Reg	1,037,001	Thick model
	3	Full	Lever	OF	Reg	1,038,001	Thick model
	4	¼ & brg	Lever	Htg	Reg	1,300,001	Getty model
	5	¼ & brg	Lever	OF	Reg	1,300,601	Getty model
	6	¼ & brg	Pendant	Htg	Reg	2,160,111	DR & Improved RR model
	7	¼ & brg	Pendant	OF	Reg	2,160,011	DR & Improved RR model
	8	¼ & brg	Lever	Htg	Reg	2,523,101	DR & Improved RR model
	9	¼ & brg	Lever	OF	Reg	2,522,001	DR & Improved model
	10	Cent brg	Lever	OF	Motor	3,178,901	Also 17S Ex Thin RR gr 48 hr
	11	¼	Lever & Pen	OF	Motor	4,001,001	RR grade 48 hr
	12	¼	Lever & Pen	Htg	Motor	4,002,001	RR grade 48 hr
	13	Cent brg	Lever	OF	Motor	4,166,801	Also 17S RR grade 60 hr
	14	¼	Lever	OF	Motor	4,492,501	RR grade 60 hr
	15	¼	Lever	OF	Motor	5,488,301	RR grade 60 hr Elinvar
14	1	Full	Lever	Htg	Reg	1,009,501	Thick model
	2	Full	Pendant	OF	Reg	1,000,001	Thick model
	3	Full	Lever	OF	Reg	1,001,001	Thick model
13	1	brg	Pendant	OF	Motor		Ex Thin gr 538 & 539
12	1	¼	Pendant	OF	Reg	1,685,001	
Thin	2	¼	Pendant	Htg	Reg	1,748,751	
	3	Cent brg	Pendant	OF	Reg	2,337,011	Center bridge
	4	Cent brg	Pendant	Htg	Reg	2,337,001	Center bridge
	5	Cent brg	Pendant	OF	Motor	3,742,201	Center bridge
	6	Cent brg	Pendant	Htg	Motor	4,395,301	Center bridge
12T	1	True Ctr brg	Pendant	OF	Motor	3,700,001	1 tooth click, Also 13S
	2	True Ctr brg	Pendant	OF	Motor	3,869,301	5 tooth click
	3	¼	Pendant	OF	Motor	3,869,201	2 tooth click
8	1	Full	Key or lever	Htg	Reg	100,001	Plate not recessed
	2	Full	Lever	Htg	Reg	100,101	Plate is recessed
6	1	¼	Lever	Htg	Reg	552,001	
4	1	¼	Lever	Htg	Reg	551,501	
0	1	¼	Pendant	OF	Reg	1,815,901	
	2	¼	Pendant	Htg	Reg	1,749,801	
	3	Cent brg	Pendant	OF	Reg	2,644,001	
	4	Cent brg	Pendant	Htg	Reg	2,637,001	

I will respect and appreciate positive sound reliable comments, corrections, improvements or remarks but reserve the right to accept the statement or keep my own observations & views. (*Cooksey*)

Wheelers Pat. 6, 22, 80
LEFT (patented regulator)

BELOW
Chalmers Pat. 12, 19, 82 (patented regulator)

Model 1, 18 size, hunting, key wind & set.

Model 2, 18 size, hunting, lever set, coarse train.

5th pinion

Model 3, 18 size, open face, lever set, coarse train, with fifth pinion.

Model 4, 18 size, open face, pendant set, fine train.

Model 5, 18 size, hunting, lever set, fine train.

Model 6, 18 size, open face, lever set, fine train.

Model 1, 16 size, hunting, lever set.

Model 2, 16 size, open face, pendant set.

Model 3, 16 size, open face, lever set

Model 4, 16 size, three-quarter plate, hunting, lever set.

Model 4, 16 size, three-quarter plate, bridge, hunting, lever set.

Model 5, 16 size, three-quarter plate, open face, lever set.

Model 5, 16 size, three-quarter plate, bridge, open face, lever set.

Model 6, 16 size - Pendant set
Model 8, 16 size - Lever set
hunting, three-quarter plate

Model 6, 16 size - Pendant set
Model 8, 16 size - Lever set
hunting, bridge model

Model 7, 16 size - Pendant set
Model 9, 16 size - Lever set
open face, three-quarter plate

Model 7, 16 size - Pendant set
Model 9, 16 size - Lever set
open face, bridge model

Model 10, 16 size, bridge, extra thin, open face, lever set, motor barrel.

Note: Model is not the same defination as grade. A model may exist in many different grades or grade names (as Bunn, A.Lincoln) and may be used in many different models (as model **1**, 18 size, open or hunting case, model **1**, in 16 size open or hunting case, model **1** in 12 size) etc..

Model 11, 16 size, three-quarter plate, open face, pendant set, motor barrel.

Model 12, 16 size, three-quarter plate, hunting, pendant set, motor barrel.

Model 13, 17 size, bridge, open face, lever set, motor barrel.(no red border on bal. cock)

Model 14, 16 size, three-quarter plate, open face, lever set, 60-hour motor barrel.

Model 15, 60 Hr. Elinvar.

Model B, 16 size, hunting case.

Model C, 16 size, open face

Model D, 16 size, open face

Model 1, 14 size, hunting, lever set.

Model 2, 14 size, open face, pendant set.

Model 3, 14 size, open face, lever set.

Note five tooth pinion click & jeweled barrel.

Model 1, 13 size, bridge, extra thin, open face, pendant set, motor barrel.

Model 1, 12 size, three-quarter plate, open face, pendant set.

Model 1, 12 size, three-quarter plate, bridge, open face, pendant set.

Model 2, 12 size, three-quarter plate, hunting, pendant set.

Model 2, 12 size, three-quarter plate, bridge, hunting, pendant set.

Model 3, 12 size, **Model 4**, 12 & 14 size, bridge, open face, pendant set.

Model 4, 12 size, bridge, hunting, pendant set.

Model 5, 12 size, bridge, open face, pendant set, motor barrel.

Model 1, 12 size, extra thin, bridge, open face, pendant set, motor barrel.

Model 2, 12 size, extra thin, bridge, open face, pendant set, motor barrel.

Model 3, 12 size, extra thin, three-quarter plate, open face, pendant set, motor barrel.

Model A, 12 size, bridge, open face.

Model 1, 8 size, hunting, key or lever set.

Model 2, 8 size, hunting, lever set.

Model 1, 6 size, hunting, lever set.

Model 1, 4 size, hunting, lever set.

Model 1, 0 size, three-quarter plate, open face, pendant set.

Model 2, 0 size, three-quarter plate, hunting, pendant set.

Model 3, 0 size, bridge, open face, pendant set.

Model 4, 0 size, bridge, hunting, pendant set.

Model 3, 3/0 size, bridge, open face, pendant set.

Model 4, 3/0 size, bridge, hunting, pendant set.

Model 1, 6/0 size, three-quarter plate, open face, pendant set.

Model 2, 6/0 size, bridge, open face, pendant set.

No. 5277–269-D

18, 16, 12 Sizes S. S. & D. S.

Spread 12, 8, 6, 4, 0 & 3/0 Sizes S. S. Only

INDEPENDENT WATCH CO.
Fredonia, New York
1875 - 1881

The California Watch Company was idle for two years before it was purchased by brothers E. W. Howard and C. M. Howard. They had been selling watches by mail for sometime and started engraving the Howard Bros. name on them and using American-made watches. Their chief supply came from Hampden Watch Co., Illinois W. Co., U. S. Watch Co. of Marion. The brothers formed the Independent Watch Co. in 1880, but it was not a watch factory in the true sense. They had other manufacturers engrave the Independent Watch Co. name on the top plates and on the dials of their watches. These watches were sold by mail order and sent to the buyer C. O. D. The names used on the movements were "Howard Bros.," "Independent Watch Co.," "Fredonia Watch Co.," "Lakeshore Watch Co., Fredonia, N. Y." and "Empire Watch Co. Fredonia"

The company later decided to manufacture watches and used the name Fredonia Watch Co., but they found that selling watches two different ways was not very good. The business survived until 1881 at which time the owners decided to move the plant to a new location at Peoria, Illinois. Approximately180,000 watches were made that sold for $16.00.

CHRONOLOGY OF THE DEVELOPMENT OF INDEPENDENT WATCH CO.

Independent Watch Co. 1875–1881
Fredonia Watch Co. 1881–1885
Peoria Watch Co. 1885–1889

18 SIZE

Grade or Name — Description	Avg	Ex-Fn	Mint
18S, 7J, KW, KS, OF, made by U.S. W. Co. **Marion**, with expanded butterfly cutout .... ★★	$350	$450	$700
18S, 11J, KW, KS, by Hampden.................................	175	275	400
18S, 11J, KW, KS, Coin.......................................	175	275	400
18S, 11J, KW, KS..	175	275	400
18S, 15J, KW, KS..	175	275	400
18S, Empire Watch Co. Fredonia, 11-15J, KWS .... ★★★★	575	775	1,100
18S, Howard Bros., 11J, KW, KS.............................	300	400	650
18S, Independent W. Co., 11J, by Illinois W. Co.......................★	200	300	450
18S, Independent W. Co., 15J, transition model by Illinois ....★	225	350	500
18S, Lakeshore W. Co., 15J, KW, HC, by N.Y. W. Co. ....★	300	385	550

Independent Watch Co. on movement, on dial Howard Bros. Fredonia N.Y., 18 size, 11 jewels, key wind & stem wind, improved April 10,1879, serial number 126,319.

Independent Watch Co., 18 size, 15 jewels, key wind, made by U.S. Watch Co. **Marion**, note expanded butterfly cutout, serial number 192,661.

🕐 Watches listed in this book are priced at the **collectable fair market value** at the Trade Show level, as complete watches having an original 14k gold filled case, KEY WIND with silver, an original white enamel single sunk dial, and with the entire original movement in good working order with no repairs needed, unless otherwise noted.

ROBERT H. INGERSOLL & BROS.

New York, New York

1892 - 1922

In 1892 Ingersoll ordered 10,000 watches from Waterbury Clock Co. to sell in their mail order catalog. The first 1,000 said "the Universal Watch" on the dial. The remainder had R.H. Ingersoll & Bro. on the dial. In 1893, they sold about 85,000 embossed watches at the Columbian Exposition. In 1896 they introduced the "Yankee" that sold for $1.00. By 1899 their output was 8,000 per day, and in 1901 Ingersoll advertised that their watches were sold by 10,000 dealers at $1.00 in U.S.A. and Canada. Ingersoll bought the Trenton W. Co. in 1908 and the New England W. Co. in 1914. Their slogan became "The Watch that Made the Dollar Famous". In 1917 they introduced the "Reliance" which had jewels. Waterbury Clock Co. took over the Ingersoll name in 1922. In 1944 U. S. Time Corp. acquired the Waterbury Co. and continued the Ingersoll name.

ESTIMATED SERIAL NUMBERS
AND PRODUCTION DATES

DATE—SERIAL NO.	DATE—SERIAL NO.	DATE—SERIAL NO.	DATE—SERIAL NO.
1892 – 150,000	1902 – 7,200,000	1912 – 38,500,000	1922 – 60,500,000
1893 – 310,000	1903 – 7,900,000	1913 – 40,000,000	1923 – 62,000,000
1894 – 650,000	1904 – 8,100,000	1914 – 41,500,000	1924 – 65,000,000
1895 – 1,000,000	1905 –10,000,000	1915 – 42,500,000	1925 – 67,500,000
1896 – 2,000,000	1906 –12,500,000	1916 – 45,500,000	1926 – 69,000,000
1897 – 2,900,000	1907 –15,000,000	1917 – 47,000,000	1927 – 70,500,000
1898 – 3,500,000	1908 –17,500,000	1918 – 47,500,000	1928 – 71,500,000
1899 – 3,750,000	1909 –20,000,000	1919 – 50,000,000	1929 – 73,500,000
1900 – 6,000,000	1910 –25,000,000	1920 – 55,000,000	1930 – 75,000,000
1901 – 6,700,000	1911 –30,000,000	1921 – 58,000,000	1944 – 95,000,000

The above list is provided for determining the APPROXIMATE age of your watch. Match serial number with date. Watches were not necessarily sold in the exact order of manufactured date.

Ingersoll Back Wind & Set, patent date Dec. 23, 1890 and Jan. 13, 1891, c. late 1890s.

Ingersoll, engraved movement also pin set..

Ingersoll, Celluloid Case in Black or White.

Ingersoll, Blind Man's Watch.

INGERSOLL DOLLAR TYPE

NOTE: Prices are for complete watch in **good running order**. In some specialty markets, the comic character watches may bring higher prices in top condition.

Grade or Name — Description	Avg	Ex-Fn	Mint
Ingersoll Early **Back Wind** Models, (with cover plate)	$50	$75	$150
Ingersoll **Back Wind** Models	50	75	150
Ingersoll, Pin set or **Rim set** & Fancy **engraved** movement	75	95	200
Admiral Dewey, "Flagship Olympia" on back of case .... ★★★	600	850	1,250
Advance, (revolving seconds)	40	55	85
American Pride	75	95	150
Are U My Neighbor	40	55	75
B. B. H. Special, Backwind	65	75	120
Blind Man Pocket Watch	55	85	150
Boer War, on dial **Souvenir of South African War 1900** .... ★★★	900	1,300	2,000
Buck	40	55	85
Calendar (on moveable calendar on back of case)	75	85	135
Celluloid Case in Black or White	100	135	200
Champion (many models)	50	75	135
Chancery	50	75	135
Chicago Expo. 1933 ★★	300	450	850
Climax	50	65	120
Cloverine	40	55	95
Colby	35	45	75
Columbus (3 ships on back of case), back wind, 1893 .... ★★★	500	785	1,200
Connecticut W. Co.	40	55	75
Cord	40	55	85
Crown	40	55	75
Dan Dee	40	55	75
Defiance	40	55	75
Delaware W. Co.	40	55	75
Devon Mfg. Co.	40	55	75
Eclipse (many models)	40	55	75
Eclipse, back wind & set, engraved ★★	75	95	200
Eclipse Radiolite	45	65	85
Endura	40	55	75
Ensign	40	55	75
Escort	40	55	75

Scout watch (Be prepared)   Yankee watch with bicycle on dial.

NOTE : ADD $25 to $100 for original BOX and PAPERS

🕒 Pricing in this Guide are fair market price for **COMPLETE** watches which are reflected from the "**NAWCC**" National and regional shows.

Ingersoll Premium, early back wind & set.

Ingersoll Triumph, note slide-pin for rim setting.

Grade or Name — Description	Avg	Ex-Fn	Mint
Fancy Dials (unfaded to be mint)	$125	$200	$400
Freedom	40	55	75
Gotham	70	85	150
Graceline	45	55	75
Gregg	40	55	75
Junior (several models)	40	55	75
Junior Radiolite	40	55	75
Kelton	40	55	75
Lapel Watches	30	55	75
Leader	30	55	75
Leeds	30	55	75
Liberty U.S.A., backwind	75	125	250
Liberty Watch Co.	50	75	175
Limited, LEVER SET ON CASE RIM OF WATCH	50	75	175
Major	40	55	75
Maple Leaf	40	55	75
Master Craft	40	55	75
Mexicana	40	55	75
Midget (several models)	40	55	75
Midget , 6 size, "patd. Jan. 29 -01," Damaskeened, fancy case	40	75	175
Monarch	40	55	75
New West	40	55	75
New York World's Fair, 1939 ★★	275	400	725
Overland	40	55	75
Pan American Expo., Buffalo, 1901 ★★★	300	400	775
Paris World Expo., 1900 ★★★★	600	850	1,250
Patrol	40	55	75
Perfection	40	55	75
Pilgram	40	55	75

NOTE : ADD $25 to $75 for original BOX and PAPERS

⊕ Pricing in this Guide are fair market price for **COMPLETE** watches which are reflected from the "**NAWCC**" National and regional shows.

Left: Ingersoll Back Wind, c. 1895.   **Right:** Yankee Back Wind, c. 1893.

Grade or Name — Description	Avg	Ex-Fn	Mint
Premier, back wind, **eagle** on back, c. 1894 .... ★★★	$150	$250	$425
Premium Back Wind and Set	125	225	300
Progress, 1933 World's Fair Chicago .... ★★	250	300	600
Puritan	60	85	125
Quaker	60	85	125
Radiolite	45	70	85
Reliance, 7J	60	80	100
Remington W. Co. USA	60	80	100
Rotary International, c. 1920	50	70	100
Royal	45	55	75
St. Louis World's Fair (two models).......................... ★★	300	500	800
The Saturday Post...	70	135	250
Senator..	40	55	75
Senior	40	55	75
Sir Leeds	35	45	65
Solar	35	45	65
Souvenir Special	50	80	120
Sterling	35	45	65
Ten Hune...	60	80	125
Traveler with Bed Side Stand..	35	50	75
Triumph, 35 Size..	150	200	300
Triumph Pin set or rim set, large crown, engine turned case			
(early model) with engraved barrel or movement	200	275	400
True Test	35	45	65
Trump	35	45	65
USA (two models)	50	80	100
Universal, 1st model .... ★★★	250	350	500
Uncle Sam...	50	75	100
George Washington	150	175	325

Waterbury Watches & 35 size Duke or Duchess model see Waterbury W. Co. (Big Watch).

NOTE : ADD $35 to $150 for original BOX and PAPERS

🕐 A collector should expect to pay modestly higher prices at local shops.

🕐 Pricing in this Guide are fair market price for **COMPLETE** watches which are reflected from the "**NAWCC**" National and regional shows.

Grade or Name — Description	Avg	Ex-Fn	Mint
Winner	$40	$55	$75
Winner , with Screw Back & Bezel.	65	80	125
Yankee Backwind	85	100	200
Yankee Bicycle Watch (sold for $1.00 in 1896) ★★	200	265	400
Yankee Radiolite.	55	70	100
Yankee Radiolite with Screw Back & Bezel.	75	100	150
Yankee Special (many models)	75	100	150
Yankee, Perpetual calendar on back of case	100	135	200

Ingersoll moveable calendar for years 1929-1951 located on back of case.

Ingersoll movement made in Great Britain.

INGERSOLL LTD.
(GREAT BRITAIN)

Grade or Name — Description	Avg	Ex-Fn	Mint
Ingersoll Ltd. (many models)	$65	$80	$100
Coronation, Elizabeth II on watch ★	175	225	475
Coronation, June 2, 1953 on dial ★	175	225	450
16S, 7J, 3F Brg	55	70	95
16S, 15J, 3F Brg	90	100	135
16S, 17J, 3F Brg, ADJ	125	150	175
16S, 19J, 3F Brg, Adj5P	150	185	275
12S, 4J	45	65	85

E. INGRAHAM CO.
Bristol, Connecticut 1912 - 1968

The E. Ingraham Co. purchased the Bannatyne Co. in 1912. They produced their first pocket watch in 1913. A total of about 65 million pocket watches and over 12 million wrist watches were produced before they started to import watches in 1968.

Grade or Name — Description	Avg	Ex-Fn	Mint
Ingraham W. Co. (many models)	$30	$40	$65
Allure	30	40	65
Aristocrat Railroad Special	50	65	100
Autocrat	30	45	75
Basketball & Football Timer	50	65	100
Beacon	30	40	65
Biltmore	30	40	75
Biltmore Radium dial	50	65	100
Bristol	30	40	65
Clipper	30	40	65
Co-Ed	30	40	65
Comet	50	65	100
Companion, sweep second hand	50	65	100
Cub	25	30	55
Dale	30	40	65
Demi–hunter style cover	65	75	150
Digital seconds dial, (no second hand but a digital seconds on dial)	60	70	100
Dixie	35	45	70
Dot	35	45	60
Endura	35	45	60
Everbrite (all models)	40	55	75
Graceline,	30	45	65
Ingraham USA	30	45	65
Jockey	30	45	65
Laddie	25	30	50
Laddie Athlete	40	45	65
Lady's Purse Watch, with fancy bezel	50	65	100
Lendix Extra	30	45	60
Master	25	30	50
Master Craft	30	45	60
Miss Ingraham	25	30	50
New York to Paris(with box for mint) ★★	250	325	725
Overland	45	55	80
The Pal	30	45	65

INGRAHAM, Seven Seas, shows standard time, & Nautical time.

New York to Paris, with airplane model on dial, engraved bezel, commemorating Lindbergh's famous flight.

🕐 Prices are for complete watch in **good running order**. In some specialty markets, the comic character watches may bring higher prices in top condition.

NOTE : ADD $25 to $75 for original BOX and PAPERS

Pastor Stop Watch, Sterling W. Co. printed on dial, with start stop & fly back to zero function. The Sterling Watch Company, Inc.Waterbury, Conn. U.S.A. on movement

Grade or Name — Description	Avg	Ex-Fn	Mint
Pastor Stop Watch, (Sterling W. Co), fly back to zero ★	$125	$200	$350
Pastor on dial & E.Ingraham on movement, fly back to zero, ★	125	200	350
Pathfinder, compass on pendant (14 size)	95	150	250

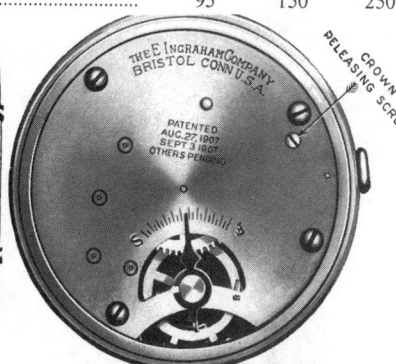

Path Finder showing compass in crown.

E. Ingraham Co. on movement, **14 SIZE**.

Grade or Name — Description	Avg	Ex-Fn	Mint
Patriot	$125	$165	$275
Peerless	30	40	60
Pilot	40	45	75
Pocket Pal	30	40	60
Pony	30	40	60
Pride	30	40	60
Princess	30	40	60
Prince	30	40	60
Professional	30	40	60
Pup	30	40	60
Reliance	40	45	75
Rex	30	40	60
Rite Time	30	40	60
St. Regis	30	40	60
Secometer	40	45	75
Sentinel, Sentinel Click	30	40	60
Sentinel Fold Up Travel	50	65	100
Sentry	30	40	60
Seven Seas, 24 hr. dial & nautical dial	55	85	150
Silver Star	30	40	60
Sturdy	30	40	60

Grade or Name — Description	Avg	Ex-Fn	Mint
Target	$30	$40	$60
The Best, The Pal	30	40	60
Time Ball	40	50	80
Time & Time	30	40	60
Tommy Ticker	30	40	60
Top Flight	30	40	60
Top Notch	30	40	60
Tower	30	40	60

Trail Blazer, Commemorating Byrd's Antarctic Expedition.

Showing back side of **Trail Blazer,** also depicted on box.

FOB

ABOVE, BOX - Same as depicted on BACK of watch.

Grade or Name — Description	Avg	Ex-Fn	Mint
Trail Blazer, Commemorating BYRD'S Antarctic Expedition ..... ★	$250	$325	$700
Trail Blazer, Commemorating BYRD'S Antarctic Expedition, *all original* **watch**, with **fob** (wings over the pole), + **box** .... ★★★	600	700	1,500
Treasure	15	20	35
Unbreakable Crystal	40	50	75
Uncle Sam (all models)	50	75	125
Uncle Sam Backwind & Set	125	150	265
United	30	35	55
Viceroy	30	40	60
Victory	30	40	60
Vogue about 14 size	30	40	60
Wings	40	50	75

Example of a basic **International Watch Co.** movement
with patent dates of Aug. 19, 1902, Jan. 27, 1903 & Aug. 11,
1903.

International Watch Co., "Highland" on dial.

INTERNATIONAL WATCH CO.

Newark City, New Jersey
1902 - 1907

This company produced only non-jeweled or low-cost production type watches that were inexpensive and nickel plated. Names on their watches include: Berkshire, Madison, and Mascot.

Grade or Name — Description	Avg	Ex-Fn	Mint
18 Size, **skeletonized, pinlever escape., first model**............ ★★	$200	$250	$425
Berkshire, OF .... ★	80	110	225
Highland .... ★	80	110	225
Madison, 18S, OF .... ★	80	110	225
Mascot, OF .... ★	80	110	225

KANKAKEE WATCH CO.

Kankakee, Illinois
1900

This company reportedly became the McIntyre Watch Co. Little or no information is available.

Grade or Name — Description	Avg	Ex-Fn	Mint
16S, BRG, NI .... ★★★★	$6,500	$7,500	$12,300

🕐 Watches listed in this book are priced at the **collectable fair market value** at the Trade Show level, as complete watches having an original 14k gold filled case, KEY WIND with silver, an original white enamel single sunk dial, and with the entire original movement in good working order with no repairs needed, unless otherwise noted.

KELLY WATCH CO.

Chicago, Illinois
c. 1900

Grade or Name — Description		Avg	Ex-Fn	Mint
16S, **aluminum** movement and OF case .... ★ ★ ★ ★ ★		$400	$500	$800

Very Rare (About **10**)

Kelly Watch Co., 16 size, **aluminum** movement, straight line lever, quick train, porcelain dial, stem set, reversible ratchet stem wind, originally sold for $2.20, Ca. 1900.

KEYSTONE STANDARD WATCH CO.

Lancaster, Pennsylvania
1886 - 1891

Abram Bitner agreed to buy a large number of stockholders' shares of the Lancaster Watch Co. at 10 cents on the dollar; he ended up with 5,625 shares out of the 8,000 that were available. Some 8,900 movements had been completed but not sold at the time of the shares purchase. The company Bitner formed assumed the name of Keystone Standard Watch Co. as the trademark but in reality existed as the Lancaster Watch Co. The business was sold to **Hamilton Watch Co.** in 1891.

Grade or Name — Description	Avg	Ex-Fn	Mint
18S, 7-15J, OF, **KW**	$100	$155	$275
18S, 7-15J, OF, SW, 3/4, LS	70	125	175
18S, 15J, dust proof, ADJ	100	165	275
18S, 11-15J, dust proof, OF	85	135	200
18S, 11-15J, dust proof, HC	125	175	275
18S, 17J, dust proof, HC	150	185	285
18S, 20J, dust proof, HC ★★	350	450	775
18S, West End, 15J, HC	100	135	200
8S, 11J, dust proof	100	135	200
6S, 7-10J, HC ★	100	165	275

Keystone Watch Co., dust proof model, 18 size, 15 jewels, serial number 352,766.

Knickerbocker movement, 16-18 size, 7 jewels, duplex escapement.

KNICKERBOCKER WATCH CO.

New York, New York
1890 - 1930

This company imported and sold Swiss and low-cost production American watches by New England Watch Co.

Grade or Name — Description	Avg	Ex-Fn	Mint
18S, 7J, OF, PS, NI, duplex escapement	$50	$70	$145
16S, 7J	35	45	85
12S, 7J, OF	40	55	95
10S, Barkley "8 Day" ★★★	125	185	275
6S, Duplex	35	45	85

🕐 Some grades are not included. Their values can be determined by comparing with **similar** age, size, metal content, style, models and grades listed.

🕐 Watches listed in this book are priced at the collectable fair market value at the Trade Show level, as complete watches having an original 14k gold filled case, KEY WIND with silver, an original white enamel single sunk dial, and with the entire original movement in good working order with no repairs needed, unless otherwise noted.

🕐 Pricing in this Guide are fair market price for **COMPLETE** watches which are reflected from the "**NAWCC**" National and regional shows.

LANCASTER WATCH CO.

Lancaster, Pennsylvania
1879 - 1886

Work commenced on Sept. 1, 1877, at the Lancaster Watch Co. The watches produced there were designed to sell at a cheaper price than normal. They had a solid top, 3/4 plate, and a pillar plate that was fully ruby-jeweled (4 pairs). They had a gilt and nickel movement and a new stem-wind device, modeled by Mosly & Todd. By mid-1878 the Lancaster Watch Co. had produced 150 movements. Four grades of watches were made: Keystone, Fulton, Franklin, and Melrose. In September 1879 the company had made 334 movements. In 1880 the total was up to 1,250 movements, and by mid-1882 about 17,000 movements had been produced. About 200,000 watch movements were made.

CHRONOLOGY OF THE DEVELOPMENT OF THE LANCASTER WATCH CO.

Adams and Perry Watch Mfg. Co. 1874-1876
Lancaster Penna. Watch Co. 1877-1879
Lancaster Watch Co. 1879-1886
Keystone Standard Co. 1886-1891
Hamilton Watch Co. .... 1892 to present

LANCASTER
18 SIZE
(All 3/4 Plate)

Grade or Name — Description	Avg	Ex-Fn	Mint
Chester, 7-11J, KW, dust proof, gilded...	$125	$175	$350
Comet, 7J, NI	125	175	350
Delaware, 20J, ADJ, SW, dust proof, gilded ....★	300	350	500
Denver, 7J, dust proof, gilded	80	125	250
Denver, 7J, gilded, dust proof, Silveroid	80	125	250
Elberon, 7J, dust proof..	125	175	350
Ben Franklin, 7J, KW, gilded..	150	225	500
Ben Franklin, 11J, KW, gilded..	175	275	550
Fulton, 7J, ADJ, KW, gilded	90	125	300
Fulton, 11J, ADJ, KW, gilded	90	125	300
Girard, 15J, ADJ, dust proof, gilded	90	125	300
Hoosac, 11J, OF...	80	150	350
Keystone, 15J, ADJ, gilded, GJS, dust proof.............	95	150	350
Keystone, 15J, ADJ, gilded, GJS, Silveroid	75	100	200
Lancaster, 7J, SW	70	95	200
Lancaster, 15J, SW, Silveroid	50	75	150
Lancaster, 15J, OF	60	110	225
Lancaster Pa., 20J, Adj. nickel, LS, OF ....★★★	325	400	700

"LANCASTER Watch PENNA.", 20J, ADJ, GJS, 19 size, low serial No.
   Referred to as (Adams Perry model), **for pricing see Adams Perry W. Co.** section.

🕐 Some grades are not included. Their values can be determined by comparing with similar age, size, metal content, style, models and grades listed.

🕐 A collector should expect to pay modestly higher prices at local shops.

🕐 Pricing in this Guide are fair market price for **COMPLETE** watches which are reflected from the "**NAWCC**" National and regional shows.

Lancaster Watch PENNA., 19 size, 20 jewels, gold jeweled
settings. Referred to as **Adams Perry model** S# 1747.

Stevens Model, 18 size, 15 jewels, adjusted, **dust proof**
model, swing-out movement, S# 153044, Ca.1886.

Above watch is *Lancaster Watch PENNA.*, 20J, ADJ, GJS, about 19 size, low serial No.
Referred to as (Adams Perry model), **for pricing see Adams Perry W. Co.** section.

Grade or Name — Description	Avg	Ex–Fn	Mint
Malvern, 7J, dust proof, gilded	$80	$125	$200
Melrose, 15J, NI, ADJ, GJS	100	150	250
Nation Standard American Watch Co., 7J, HC	200	250	450
New Era, 7J, gilded, KW, HC	90	150	200
New Era, 7J, gilded, KW, Silveroid	80	125	175
Paoli, 7J, NI, dust proof,	70	95	225
Wm. Penn, 20J, ADJ, NI, dust proof ★★	400	600	1,000
Radnor, 7J, dust proof, gilded	70	120	225
Record, 7J, dust proof, Silveroid	70	120	225
Record, 15J, NI	70	120	225

West End, 18 size, 15 jewels, key wind & set, serial number
158,080, c. 1878.

Lancaster movement, 8-10 size, 15 jewels, serial number
317,812.

🕐 A collector should expect to pay modestly higher prices at local shops.

🕐 Pricing in this Guide are fair market price for **COMPLETE** watches
which are reflected from the "**NAWCC**" National and regional shows.

Grade or Name — Description	Avg	Ex-Fn	Mint
Ruby, 7-16J, NI	$100	$150	$275
Sidney, 15J, NI, dust proof,	125	185	285
Stevens, 15J, ADJ, NI, dust proof	150	200	325
West End, 19J, HC, **KW**, gilded	450	550	700
West End, 15J, HC, **KW**, KS	125	185	325
West End, 15J, SW	100	150	275
West End, 15J, SW, Silveroid	90	125	200

8 SIZE

Grade or Name — Description	Avg	Ex-Fn	Mint
Cricket, 11J	$40	$60	$100
Diamond, 15J	40	60	100
Echo, 11J	40	60	100
Flora, 7-11J, gilded	40	60	100
Iris, 13J	40	60	100
Lady Penn, 20J, GJS, ADJ, NI ★★	300	400	650
Lancaster W. Co., 7J	40	60	100
Pearl, 7J	40	60	100
Red Rose, of Lancaster, 15J	40	60	100
Ruby, 15J	40	60	100

MANHATTAN WATCH CO.

New York, New York   1883 - 1891

The Manhattan Watch Co. made mainly low cost production watches. A complete and full line of watches was made, and most were cased and styled to be sold as a **complete** watch. The watches were generally 16S with full plate movements. The patented winding mechanism was different. These watches were both in hunter and open-face cases and later had a sweep second hand. Total production was 160,000 or more watches.

Manhattan Watch Co., stop watch, 16 size, note the escapement uses upright "D"—shaped pallets (steel), serial number 117,480.

Manhattan Watch Co., 16 size, stop watch. Note the two buttons on top; the right (at 2 o'clock) one sets the hands, the left (at 10 o'clock) starts and stops the watch.

Right: **Manhattan Watch Co.** escapement uses **upright "D"**—shaped pallets (steel).

16 SIZE

Grade or Name — Description	Avg	Ex-Fn	Mint
OF, with back wind, base metal case .... ★	$150	$250	$450
OF, 2 button stop watch, screw back & bezel, **enamel dial, gold-filled case** .... ★★★	275	400	800
OF, 2 button stop watch, snap back & bezel, paper dial, base metal case .... ★	150	250	550
HC, 2 button stop watch, snap back & bezel, paper dial, base metal case .... ★★	200	325	625
OF, 1 button, sweep sec., base metal case , paper dial .... ★	125	200	300
HC, 1 button, sweep sec., base metal case, paper dial .... ★	175	285	400
Ship's Bell Time Dial, OF or HC .... ★★★★	325	485	800
Twenty-Four Hour Dial, OF or HC .... ★★★★	325	485	800
Stallcup, 7J, OF .... ★	100	185	350

12 SIZE

Grade or Name — Description	Avg	Ex-Fn	Mint
12S .... ★	$80	$150	$350

Manhattan Watch Co., **16 size,** time only watch & note no second hand, the button at Right sets the hands.

Manhattan Watch Co., **16 size,** time only with Sweep-Second hand, the button at Right sets the hands.

Manhattan Watch Co., **16 size,** Ship's Bell Time **DIAL** for NAUTICAL USES & sweep second hand, Hunting Case.

Manhattan Watch Co., **16 size,** with a 24-HOUR DIAL.& sweep second hand, Hunting Case.

MANISTEE WATCH CO.
Manistee, Michigan
1908 - 1912

The Manistee watches, first marketed in 1909, were designed to compete with the low-cost production watches. Dials, jewels, and hairsprings were not produced at the factory. The first movement was 18S, 7J, and sold for about $5. Manistee also made 5J, 15J, 17J, and 21J watches in cheap cases in sizes 16 and 12. Estimated total production was 60,000. Most were sold by Star Watch Case Co.

18 SIZE

Grade or Name —Description		Avg	Ex-Fn	Mint
18S, 7J, 3/4, LS, HC	★	$300	$375	$500
18S, 7J, 3/4, LS, OF	★	200	275	400
18S, 7J, 3/4, LS, OF, **gold train**	★★★	375	450	700
18S, 7J, **cut out** movement	★★	200	275	400

16 TO 12 SIZE

Grade or Name —Description		Avg	Ex-Fn	Mint
16S, 7J, OF	★	$200	$250	$325
16S, 15J, OF	★	225	275	400
16S, 15J, HC	★	250	285	425
16S, 17J, OF	★	225	275	400
16S, 19J, HC	★	300	350	525
16S, 21J, OF	★	350	400	600
12S, 15J	★	150	185	300

Manistee movement, 18 size, 7 jewels, 3/4 plate, open face, serial number 0000919.

Manistee movement, 16 size, 17 jewels, three-quarter plate, open face, serial number 39,052.

Manistee cut out movement, 18 size, 7 jewels, open face, serial number 0006094.

McINTYRE WATCH CO.

Kankakee, Illinois
1908 - 1911

This company probably bought the factory from Kankakee Watch Co. In 1908 Charles DeLong was made master watchmaker, and he designed and improved the railroad watches. Only a few watches were made, estimated total production being about **eight watches.**

Grade or Name — Description		Avg	Ex-Fn	Mint
16S, 21J, BRG, NI, WI.. ★★★★★		$4,500	$6,000	$12,500
16S, 25J, BRG, **WI**, Adj.5P, equidistant escapement .... ★★★★★		5,500	7,000	15,000
12S, 19J, BRG.. ★★★★★		2,000	2,800	5,500

McIntyre Watch Co., 16 size, 25 jewels, adjusted to 5 positions with wind indicator, with equidistant escapement, manufactured about 1909. Above illustration taken from a blue print.

* * * * *

EXAMPLE OF A BREGUET STYLE DIAL   EXAMPLE OF A BOX CAR STYLE DIAL

MELROSE WATCH CO.
Melrose, Massachusetts (1866 - 1868)

In late 1866 the Tremont Watch Co. moved from Boston, Mass., and changed its name to Melrose Watch Co., and started making the complete watch movements, movement engraved "Melrose Watch Co". and dials marked Tremont W. Co. About 3,000 were produced. Serial # range 30,000 and higher. In about 1870 sold to the English and used the name Anglo-American Watch Co.

Factory at Melrose, Mass. General Agents, Messrs. WHEELER, PARSONS & CO., New York, Messrs. BIGELOW BROS. & KENNARD, Boston, and for sale by the trade generally. Every movement warranted.

The TREMONT WATCH CO. manufacture the only DUST-PROOF Watch movement in this country. They have a branch establishment in Switzerland, under the personal superintendence of Mr. A. L. DENNISON, (the ORIGINATOR of the American system of watch-making), where they produce their Balances and Escapements of a superior quality. The cheap skilled labor of Europe, working thus on the AMERICAN SYSTEM, enables them to offer a superior article at a low rate.

Melrose Watch Co. movement, 18 size, 15 jewels, key wind & set. Melrose W. Co. serial # range 30,000 and higher.

Above: **1867** ADVERTISEMENT

Grade or Name — Description		Avg	Ex-Fn	Mint
18S, 7J, KW, KS	★★	$250	$350	$525
18S, 11J, KW, KS, OF	★★	250	350	525
18S, 15J, KW, KS	★★	300	425	600
18S, 15J, KW, KS, Silveroid	★★	250	325	485

MOZART WATCH CO.
Providence, Rhode Island to Ann Arbor, Michigan (1864 - 1870)

In 1864 Don J. Mozart started out to produce a less expensive three-wheel watch in Providence, R. I. Despite his best efforts, the venture was declared a failure by 1866. Mozart left Providence and moved to Ann Arbor, Mich. There, again, he started on a **three-wheel** watch and succeeded in producing thirty. The three-wheel watch was not a new idea except to American manufacturers. Three-wheel watches were made many decades before Mozart's first effort, but credit for the first American-made three-wheel watch must go to him. The size was about 18 and could be called a 3/4 or full plate movement. The balance bridge was screwed on the top plate, as was customary. The round bridge partially covered the opening in the top plate and was just large enough for the balance to oscillate. The balance was compensated and somewhat smaller in diameter than usual. Mozart called it a chrono-lever, and it was to function so perfectly it would be free from friction, but no way was this true.

Mozart **Chrono-lever**; The escape wheel has 30 teeth and receives its impulse directly from the roller on the staff, while the escape tooth locked on the intermediate lever pallet. The escape pinion had a long pivot that carries the second hand, which made a circuit of the seconds dial, once in 12 seconds. The balance wheel has sliding weights, instead of screws.

The watch is about 18 size with a train that had a main wheel with the usual number of teeth and a ten-leaf center pinion, but it had a large center wheel of 108 teeth and a third wheel of 90 teeth, with a six-leaf third (escape)pinion. The escape wheel had 30 teeth and received its impulse directly from the roller on the staff, while the escape tooth locked on the intermediate lever pallet. The escape pinion had a long pivot that carried the second hand, which made a circuit of the dial, once in 12 seconds. The total number of Mozart watches produced was about 165 and only a few were ever finished.

Grade or Name — Description	Avg	Ex-Fn	Mint
18S, 3/4, KW & KS from back, 3-wheel ...... ★★★★★	$19,000	$28,000	$60,000

Mozart Watch Co. movement, 18 size,three-quarter plate, key wind & set, **three-wheel train,** "Patent Dec. 24th, 1868" & Patent # 72,528. Note sliding weights on balance wheel.

J. H. Mulford, 18 size, about 10 jewels, key wind, and is marked, "J. H. Mulford, patent, Albany, N.Y. S# 25".

J. H. MULFORD
Albany, New York (1842 - 1876)

John Mulford started out as a jeweler and by about 1842 was listed as a watchmaker. Mulford was granted a patent on Feb. 21, 1842 (no. 2465) for his style escapement. It appears that the basic movement was imported. Most were 18 size, key wind & set with a going barrel, and he used gold jewel screwed down settings. The verge style escapement and on the balance staff instead of pallets, he used two cylindrical jewels, and each jewel had a notch.

Grade or Name — Description	Avg	Ex-Fn	Mint
18S, 10-12J., 3/4, KW, KS .... ★★★★	$9,000	$12,000	$20,000

J. H. Mulford, drawing of his patented escapement. (Pat. # 2465 date Feb. 21, 1842) On the balance staff, instead of flag style pallets, there are two cylindrical jewels "J" each jewel has a notch similar to the notch of a duplex escapement. When the tip of the escape wheel tooth drops on the jewel it imparts a impulse against the side of the notched jewel.

NASHUA WATCH CO.
Nashua, New Hampshire
1859 - 1862

One of the most important contributions to the American Watch industry was made by the Nashua Watch Co. of Nashua, New Hampshire. Founded in 1859 by B. D. Bingham, the company hired some of the most innovative and creative watchmakers in America and produced an extremely high grade American pocket watch.

Since almost all the production material made by Nashua from 1859 until its incorporation into the American Watch Co. in 1862 was unfinished by Nashua, only about four examples of the 20-size keywind keyset from the back signed Nashua Watch Co. are known to exist.

NASHUA WATCH CO. (marked), 20 size, 19 jewels, gold jewel settings, key wind & set from back, stop work, serial number 1,219.

20-size keywind keyset from the back signed Nashua Watch Co.

Grade or Name — Description		Avg	Ex-Fn	Mint
Nashua (marked), 19J, KW, KS, 3/4, 18K	★★★★★	$19,000	$26,000	$36,000
Nashua (marked), 15J, KW, KS, 3/4, silver case	★★★★	14,000	20,000	30,000

NEWARK WATCH CO.
Newark, New Jersey
1864 - 1870

Arthur Wadsworth, one of the designers for Newark Watch Co., patented an 18 Size full plate movement. The first movements reached the market in 1867. This company produced only about 8,000 watches before it was sold to the Cornell Watch Co.

CHRONOLOGY OF THE DEVELOPMENT OF NEWARK WATCH CO.
Newark Watch Co. 1864-1870; S#s 4,301 to 12,000;
Cornell Watch Co.,Chicago, Ill. 1870-1874; S#s 12,001 to 25,000;
Cornell Watch Co., San Francisco, Calif. 1874-Jan. 1876; S#s 25,001 to 35,000;
California Watch Co., Jan. 1876-mid 1876.

🕐 A collector should expect to pay modestly higher prices at local shops.

🕐 **The Complete Price Guide to Watches goal is to stimulate the orderly exchange of <u>Watches</u> between "*buyers*" and "*sellers*".**

Newark Watch Co. Robert Fellows grade movement, 18 size, 15 jewels, key wind & set, serial number 12, 044.

Grade or Name — Description		Avg	Ex-Fn	Mint
18S, 15J, KW, KS, **HC**	★★	$325	$385	$550
18S, 15J, KW, KS, OF	★★	300	375	500
18S, 7J, KW, KS	★★	250	300	400
J. C. Adams, 11J, KW, KS	★★	300	375	500
J. C. Adams, 11J, KW, KS, Coin	★★	325	400	550
Edward Biven, 11-15J, KW, KS	★★	350	425	625
Robert Fellows, KW, KS	★★★	400	500	800
Keyless Watch Co., 15J, LS, SW	★★★	400	675	1,000
Newark Watch Co., 7-15J, KW, KS	★★	300	385	550
Arthur Wadsworth, SW	★★★	600	800	1,400
Arthur Wadsworth, 18S, 15J, 18K, HC, "*Arthur Wadsworth, New York*" on dial; "*Keyless Watch, Patent # 3655, June 19, 1866*" engraved on movement	★★★	1,500	2,000	3,300

NEW ENGLAND WATCH CO.
Waterbury, Connecticut   1898 - 1914

    The New England Watch Co., formerly the Waterbury Watch Co., made a watch with a duplex escapement, gilt, 16S, open faced. Watches with the skeletonized movement are very desirable. The company later became Timex Watch Co.

Grade or Name — Description		Avg	Ex-Fn	Mint
16S, OF, duplex, **SKELETON,** good running order	★	$300	$350	$600
12S, 16S, 18S, OF, pictures on dial: ladies, dogs, horses, trains, flags, ships, cards, etc.		150	250	525
12S, 16S, 18S, OF, duplex escapement, good running order		65	80	125
12S, 16S, 18S, OF, pin lever escapement, good running order		45	60	100

Above: Pictures on dial: ladies, dogs, horses, trains, flags, ships, cards, etc

Front & back view of a **skeletonized** New England Watch Co. movement. This watch is fitted with a glass display back and front, making the entire movement and wheels visible, 4 jewels, silver hands, black numbers, originally sold for $10-13.

Grade or Name — Description	Avg	Ex-Fn	Mint
6S, duplex	$40	$50	$75
6S, duplex, **SKELETON** model, OF	300	375	500
0 S, 15-17 J, lever escapement	55	80	125
Addison, (all sizes)	55	80	125
Alden, (all sizes)	35	55	85
Ambassador, 12S, duplex	35	55	85
Americus, duplex escapement	40	60	95
Berkshire, duplex escapement, **GF**	55	80	125

New England Watch Co., 16 size, 7 jewels, open face, double roller, Dan Patch stop watch.

New England Watch Co., Scout, about 16 size, 4 jewels, duplex escapement, New England base metal case.

🕐 A collector should expect to pay modestly higher prices at local shops.

🕐 Pricing in this Guide are fair market price for **COMPLETE** watches which are reflected from the "**NAWCC**" National and regional shows.

Addison, Duplex Escapement.

New England Watch Co., multi-colored paper dials, showing poker style playing cards. Watches complete with these type dials bring **$425 - $675 - $1,400.**

New England Watch Co., **Lady Mary**, 0 size, 17 jewels, lever escapement, serial # 1,000,283.

Grade or Name — Description	Avg	Ex-Fn	Mint
Cadish, duplex escapement	$35	$55	$85
Cavour, duplex escapement	35	55	85
Columbian	40	60	95
Chronograph, 7J, Start, Stop & Reset	125	175	300
Cruiser, duplex	40	60	85
Dan Patch, Chronograph, 7J, Start, Stop & Reset ★	275	375	550
Dominion, **0 size**	35	50	75
Elf, **series SS**, duplex	45	55	85
Excelsior, 7J	60	80	125
Enamel, full enamel cased watches back and bezel, blue, red, green, sizes from 6 size to 0 size	100	175	350
Embossed, base metal cases with duplex escapement	75	100	200
Fancy , **"unfaded dial"**	125	185	300
Fire Fly, about 8 size	40	55	85
Gabour	60	80	125
General	35	55	85
Hale, 7J	35	55	85
Jockey, duplex escapement	60	80	125
Lady Mary	60	80	125
Oxford	35	55	85
Padishah also Pilgram, both duplex escapement	60	80	125
Putnam	40	60	95
Queen Mab, duplex escapement - **0 size,** 4J	35	55	85
Rugby, stop watch	65	85	125
Scout, 12 Size, duplex escapement, HC	35	55	85
Senator, duplex escapement	35	55	85
Standish, about 12 size	35	55	85
Trump, duplex escapement	35	55	85
Tuxedo	35	55	85
Tuxedo, duplex escapement	60	80	125

🕐 Some grades are not included. Their values can be determined by comparing with **similar** age, size, metal content, style, models and grades listed.

NEW HAVEN CLOCK AND WATCH CO.

New Haven, Connecticut 1853 - 1956

The company started making Marine clock movements with a balance wheel in about 1875, and a used similar smaller movement to make watches in early 1880. The company soon reached a production of about 200 watches per day, making a total of some 40 million watches.

NEW HAVEN Clock & Watch Co., Angelus, with rotating dials, patented Jan 23, 1900.

NEW HAVEN, Ships Time, Ben Franklin style dial. Note this watch uses only one hand.

Grade or Name – Description	Avg	Ex-Fn	Mint
Always Right	$35	$55	$85
The Angelus, 2 rotating dials ★	135	225	365
Beardsley Radiant	55	75	115
Buddy	35	50	75
Bull Dog	30	45	70
Compensated	35	50	75
Captain Scout	75	100	160
Celluloid case (bold colors)	100	135	200
Chronometer	60	85	175
Earl	35	50	75
Elite	35	50	75
Elm City	35	50	75
Fancy dials, no fading	100	150	325
Football Timer ★	75	100	200
Ford Special	60	75	95
Hamilton	40	55	75
Handy Andy	65	85	165
Jerome USA	40	55	75

Traveler, with travel case.

Example of Kaiser Wilhelm.

Sport Timer + RED BOX and White Letters.

Grade or Name – Description	Avg	Ex-Fn	Mint
Kaiser Wilhelm .... ★★★	$475	$625	$1,000
Kermit	35	45	65
Laddie.........................	25	30	50
Leonard Watch Co.	30	40	60
Leonard	35	50	75
Mastercraft Rayolite	50	70	95
Miracle	35	50	75
Motor.........................	30	40	60
Nehi..........................	50	70	95
New Haven, pin lever, SW	60	75	125
New Haven, back wind.............	100	145	200
Panama Official Souvenir, 1915 ...... ★★★	350	450	850
Paul Pry, 14 size with a Locomotive on back of case ...	40	50	75
Pedometer, 14 size, OF............	40	50	75
Pentagon-shaped case	40	50	75
Playing cards on dial.............. ★★	400	575	975
Service........................	25	30	50
Ships Time, Franklin style dial (one hand)........... ★	75	100	175
Sports **Timer**...................	65	75	150
Sports **Timer** + **Box**	75	100	185
Surity.........................	35	50	75
Teller	30	45	70
Tip Top........................	20	30	60
Tip Top Jr......................	20	30	60
The American...................	40	55	85
The JAP 12 size	35	40	65
The Midget about 4 size	25	30	50
The Lady Clare 6 size.............	30	35	50
Tommy Ticker	30	35	50
Tourist........................	40	50	75
Traveler, with travel case	55	65	100
True Time......................	30	45	70
United........................	25	30	50
USA..........................	30	40	60
Victor.........................	25	30	50

NOTE : ADD $25 to $70 for original BOX and PAPERS

🕐 Pricing in this Guide are fair market price for **COMPLETE** watches which are reflected from the "**NAWCC**" National and regional shows.

NEW HAVEN WATCH CO.

New Haven, Connecticut
1883 - 1887

This company was organized October 16, 1883 with the intention of producing W. E. Doolittle's patented watch; however, this plan was soon abandoned. They did produce a "Model A" watch, the first was marketed in the spring of 1884. Estimated total production is **200.** The original capital became absorbed by Trenton W. Co.

"The New Haven Watch Co. Alpha, 149, Pat. Dec. 27-81," engraved on movement, lever escapement, open face, extremely rare watch.

Grade or Name – Description	Avg	Ex-Fn	Mint
"A" Model, about 18S, pat. Dec. 27, '81 .... ★★★★★	$625	$850	$1,200
Alpha Model, pat. Dec. 27, '81 .... ★★★★★	625	850	1,200

NEW YORK CITY WATCH CO.

New York, New York
1890 - 1897

This company manufactured the Dollar-type watches, which had a pendant-type crank. The watch is wound by **cranking the pendant,** and has a pin lever escapement. The hands are set from the back of the watch movement. The" **patent number 526,871",** is engraved on movement, patent is dated October 1894, and was held by S. Schisgall. The New York City Watch Co., 20 size watch has the words "Lever Winder" printed on the paper dial.

🕐 A collector should expect to pay modestly higher prices at local shops.

🕐 Watches listed in this book are priced at the collectable fair market value at the Trade Show level, as complete watches having an original 14k gold filled case, KEY WIND with silver, an original white enamel single sunk dial, and with the entire original movement in good working order with no repairs needed, unless otherwise noted.

Grade or Name – Description	Avg	Ex-Fn	Mint
18-20S, no jewels, "**Lever Winder**" on dial .... ★★★★	$625	$850	$1,200
18-20S, no jewels, "**SUN DIAL**" on dial .... ★★★★	$625	$850	$1,200

New York City Watch Co., about 18-20 size, "**Lever Winder**" printed on paper dial. This watch is <u>**WOUND**</u> **by cranking the pendant back and forth** , pin lever escapement, also **back set,** & *"New York City Watch Co., patent No. 526,871"* engraved on movement.

NEW YORK CHRONOGRAPH WATCH CO.

NEW YORK, NEW YORK

1883 -1885

This company sold about 800 watches marked "New York Chronograph Watch Co." The 18 size stop watch was manufactured by Manhattan Watch Co. 16 size made by ?

Grade or Name –Description	Avg	Ex-Fn	Mint
18S, 7J, stop watch, HC ....★	$125	$175	$275
18S, 7J, stop watch, OF ....★	100	125	200
16S, 7J, SW, time only, OF ....★	150	175	275
16S, 9-11J, SW, time only, OF..★	150	175	275
16S, 7-11J, SW, time only with sweep sec. hand, OF ....★	175	225	300
16S, 11J, SW, **true CHRONOGRAPH**, OF .... ★★★★★	400	700	1,500

N.Y. Chronograph Watch Co., dial and movement, 16 size, 11 jewels, open face, chronograph.

New York Chronograph Watch Co. dial and movement, 7 jewels, open face, buttons at the top of case set hands and stop watch.

No. 30

Hunting also seen Key Wind & Set   **Open Face**

NEW YORK STANDARD WATCH CO.
(CROWN WATCH CO.)
Jersey City, New Jersey 1885 - 1929

The first watch reached the market in early 1888 and was a 18S. The most interesting feature was a straight line lever with a "worm gear escapement." This was patented by R. J. Clay. All watches were quick train and open-faced. The company also made its own cases and sold a complete watch. Total production maybe, as high as, 30,000,000. A prefix number was added to some serial numbers.

New York Standard, Chronograph, 18 size, 7 jewels, stem wind, second hand start-stop and fly back, 3/4 plate.

New York Standard, converts to a hunting case movement or a open face movement, serial number 502,619.

N. Y. STANDARD 16 AND 18 SIZE

Grade or Name – Description	Avg	Ex-Fn	Mint
18S, 7J, N. Y. Standard, **KW, KS** .... ★★★	$250	$350	$500
18S, 7J, N. Y. Standard, SW	50	65	85
18S, 15J, N. Y. Standard, SW, LS, HC	100	125	175
Chicago, U.S.A. **17-23 fake jewels**, with a **Locomotive** on movement & Dial.	100	150	235
Chronograph, 7-11J, 3/4, NI, DMK, SW, fly back hand	150	225	400
Chronograph, 10J, (marked 10J), fly back hand ....★	185	265	425
Chronograph, 13J, sweep sec., stop & fly back hand	150	225	400
Chronograph, 15J, 3/4, NI, DMK, SW,fly back hand, ...	150	225	400
Convertible,15J.,16 size, can be changed to HC or OF .... ★★★★	300	450	850
Crown W. Co., 7J, OF or HC	45	55	75
Crown W. Co., 15J, HC	60	75	95
Dan Patch, 7J, stop watch (pat. DEC. 22 '08) ....★	250	365	575
Dan Patch, 17J, stop watch (pat. DEC. 22 '08) .... ★★	375	450	675
Edgemere, 7J, OF & HC	45	55	85
Excelsior, 7J, OF or HC	45	55	85

New York Standard, with WORM GEAR (located under cutout star), 18 size, OF, 5-7 jewels, there was 2 or 3 runs of the worm-drive model, 52,000 made, S# 31,138.

Remington W. Co. (marked on movement & case), 16 size, 11 jewels, 2-tone damaskeening, NOTE crown wheel & ratchet (no click), serial # CC021,331.

Grade or Name – Description	Avg	Ex-Fn	Mint
Harvard W. Co., 7–11J., ...	$40	$50	$75
Hi Grade	50	60	85
Ideal	50	60	85
Jefferson, 7J., ...	50	60	85
La Salle, 7J., ...	35	45	65
New Era, 7J., skeletonized (Poor Man's Dudley) OF- HC	250	325	550
New Era,7–11J.	40	50	75
New York Standard W. Co., 11J, 3/4	60	75	100
New York Standard, 7J, 3/4	60	75	100
New York Standard, 15J, BRG	75	85	125
N. Y. Standard, with (**" WORM GEAR"**), OF ....★	400	675	1,200
N. Y. Standard, with (**" WORM GEAR"**) multi-color dial .....★	600	875	1,500
N. Y. Standard, with (**" WORM GEAR"**), HC .... ★★★	950	1,400	2,250

Also **Watch Co.** names also signed **USA** as: Bay State, Chicago, Crown, Eldridge, Excelsior, Gloria, Hamlet, Hercules, Highgrade, Jefferson, LaSalle, New Era, Pacific, Remington, Rosemere, Solar, Tribune, Waldemar, Washington, & Wilmington Special etc.. $60 $75 $100

⊕ Note: Some styles, models and grades are not included. Their values can be determined by comparing with **similar** styles, size, age, models and grades listed.

⊕ A collector should expect to pay modestly higher prices at local shops.

Grade or Name – Description	Avg	Ex-Fn	Mint
Pan- America, 7J, OF	$60	$85	$150
Perfection, 7J, OF or HC	45	60	75
Perfection, 15J, OF or HC, NI	55	75	95
Remington W. Co., 11J, marked mvt. & case	75	100	160
Solar W. Co., 7J	50	65	85
Special USA, 7J	45	55	65
18S Tribune USA, **23J**, HC or OF, Pat. Reg. Adj. ★	150	185	300
Washington, 7-11J	50	65	85
William Penn, 7-11J	50	65	85
Wilmington, 7-11J	45	55	65

For watches with **O'Hara Multi-Color Dials,** add $75 -$100 to value in **mint condition**; add $40-$60 for Hunting Cases.

12 SIZE

Grade or Name – Description	Avg	Ex-Fn	Mint
N. Y. Standard, 7J-11J, OF	$25	$30	$45
N. Y. Standard, 7J-11J, HC	40	50	65
N. Y. Standard, 7J, **Multi-Color dial**	75	125	250
N. Y. Standard, 15J, OF	35	40	55
N. Y. Standard, 15J, HC	45	55	75
Columbia, 7J	50	65	85
Crown W. Co., 7J, OF or HC	30	40	55

New York Standard W. Co., 12 size, 7J., open face, S# 1,021,224. Note similarity to Keystone Howard Railroad Chronometer.

New York Standard W.Co., 6 size G# 144, Hunting Case.

6 SIZE - 0 SIZE - 3/0 SIZE

Grade or Name – Description	Avg	Ex-Fn	Mint
Alton, 7-15J	$35	$40	$55
American,7J	35	40	55
Empire State W. Co., 7J	45	55	80
Excelsior, 7J, HC	40	50	65
6S, Columbia, 7J, HC	55	65	85
Crown W. Co., 7J, 6 size & 0 size, OF or HC	40	50	65
Standard USA, 7J	35	40	55
6S, N. Y. Standard, 7J, HC	60	70	85
6S, Orient, SW	30	40	60
Tribune, 11J., (some spread or oversized)	50	65	100
6S, Progress, 7J	40	50	65
0S, Ideal, 7J, HC	55	65	85
0S, N. Y. Standard, 7J, HC	55	65	85

⊕ Pricing in this Guide are fair market price for **COMPLETE** watches which are reflected from the "**NAWCC**" National and regional shows.

NEW YORK STANDARD WATCH CO.
IDENTIFICATION OF MOVEMENTS

How to Identify Your Watch Size & Model: Compare the movement of your watch with the illustrations in this section. While comparing, note the location of the balance, jewels, screws, gears, and type of back plate (Full, 3/4, Bridge) these will be clues in identifying the movement you have.

18 size, 5th model, hunting

18 size, 6th model, open face

18 size, No. 80 OF

18 size, No. 64 HC

OF   18 size, No. 360

18 size, No. 60 OF

Note: Also In 18 & 6 size

HC No. 90

16 SIZE

18 size, No. 165 OF

18 size, 4th Model OF

16 size, No. 94
OF

16 size, No. 91

16 size, 1st Model,
converts to open
or hunting

CROWN

16 size, No. 1516 HC

16 size, No. 390 HC

12 size, No. 170 HC

12 size, No. 1570 HC

12 size, hunting

CROWN

12 size, No. 1512 HC

12 size, No. 370 OF

6 size, No. 146 OF

6 size, No. 44 HC

0 size, No. 300 OF

3/0 size, No. 730
HC

10/0 size, No. 1015
OF

NEW YORK SPRINGFIELD WATCH CO.

Springfield, Massachusetts

1866 - 1876

The New York Watch Co. had a rather difficult time getting started. The name of the company was changed from the Mozart Watch Co. to the New York Watch Co., and it was located in Rhode Island. Before any watches had been sold, they moved to Springfield, Mass., in 1867. A factory was built there, but only about 100 watches were produced before a fire occurred on April 23, 1870. Shortly after the fire, in 1870, a newly-designed watch was introduced. The first movements reached the market in 1871, and the first grade was a fully-jeweled adjusted movement called "Frederick Billings." The standard 18S and the Swiss Ligne systems were both used in gauging the size of these watches. The New York Watch Co. used full signatures on its movements. The doors closed in the summer of 1876. In January 1877, the Hampden Watch Co. was organized and commenced active operation in June 1877.

CHRONOLOGY OF THE DEVELOPMENT OF NEW YORK WATCH CO.

The Mozart Watch Co., Providence, R. I. 1864-1866
New York Watch Co., Providence, R. I. 1866-1867
New York Watch Co., Springfield, Mass. 1867-1875
New York Watch Mfg. Co., Springfield, Mass. 1875-1876
Hampden Watch Co., Springfield, Mass. 1877-1886
Hampden-Dueber Watch Co., Springfield, Mass. 1886-1888
Hampden Watch Co. Works, Canton, Ohio 1888-1923
Dueber-Hampden Watch Co., Canton, Ohio 1923-1930
Amtorg, U.S.S.R. 1930

NEW YORK WATCH CO.SPRINGFIELD

ESTIMATED SERIAL NUMBERS

AND PRODUCTION DATES

DATE – SERIAL NO.	DATE – SERIAL NO.
1866 – 1,000	1871 – 20,000
1867 – 3,000	1872 – 30,000
1868 – 5,000	1873 – 40,000
1869 – 7,000	1874 – 50,000
1870 – 10,000	1875 – 60,000

The above list is provided for determining the APPROXIMATE age of your watch. Match serial number with date. Watches were not necessarily sold in the exact order of manufactured date.

N. Y. W. SPRINGFIELD

SPRINGFIELD

18 TO 20 SIZE

Grade or Name – Description		Avg	Ex-Fn	Mint
Aaron Bagg, 7J, KW, KS .... ★		$225	$300	$550
Frederick Billings, 15J, KW, KS.................... ★		225	300	575
E. W. Bond, 15-17J, 3/4 .... ★★★		500	600	1,000
E. W. Bond, 18J, Adj., GJS, 3/4................ ★★★		600	775	1,200
J. A. Briggs, 11J, KW, KS, from back............ ★★		300	435	775

🕑 Some grades are not included. Their values can be determined by comparing with **similar** age, size, metal content, style, models and grades listed.

🕑 Watches listed in this book are priced at the collectable trade show level, as **complete** watches having an original 14k gold-filled case and *Key Wind* with silver, an original white enamel single sunk dial, and with the entire original movement in good working order with no repairs needed.

🕑 Pricing in this Guide are fair market price for **COMPLETE** watches which are reflected from the "**NAWCC**" National and regional shows.

E.W. **Bond** movement, 18 size, 15 jewels, three-quarter plate.

Chas. E. Hayward, 18 size, 15 jewels, key wind & set, note the **hidden key,** serial number 18,733.

Grade or Name – Description	Avg	Ex-Fn	Mint
Albert Clark, 11-15J, KW, KS, from back, 3/4 .... ★★	$300	$385	$550
Homer Foot, 11-15J, KW, KS, from back, 3/4 .... ★	225	300	475
Herman Gerz, 11J, KW, KS .... ★	225	300	475
John Hancock, 7J, KW, KS	100	175	300
John Hancock, 7J, KW, KS, Silveroid	85	145	250
John Hancock, 7J, KW, KS, Coin	100	175	300
Chas. E. Hayward, 11-15J, KW, KS, long balance cock................	175	225	350
Chas. E. Hayward, 11-15J, KW, KS, Coin	175	225	350
J. L. King, 15-17J, KW, KS, from back, 3/4 .... ★	400	500	900
New York Watch Co., 7 11J, KW, KS... ★	200	275	450
New York Watch Co., 15-19J, KW, KS, **Wolf's Teeth winding,**			
(**Serial #s below 75**) (20 lignes) .... ★★★★★	1,200	1,600	2,400
New York Watch Co., 15-19J, KW, KS, **Wolf's Teeth winding,**			
all original (20 lignes)... ★★★★	850	1,000	1,600
H. G. Norton, 15J, KW, KS, from back, 3/4 .... ★	165	225	400
H. G. Norton, 17J, KW, KS, from back, 3/4 .... ★	165	225	400
H. G. Norton, 19J, KW, KS, from back, 3/4 .... ★★★	475	575	825

H.G. Norton, 18 size, 15 jewels, three-quarter plate, gold escape wheel, serial number 6592.

SPRINGFIELD, (20 lignes), 15-19 jewels, stem wind, hunting case, note **wolf teeth winding**, serial number 978.

State Street movement, 18 size, 15 jewels, three-quarter plate.

Theo E. Studley movement, 18 size, 15 jewels, key wind & set, full plate.

Grade or Name – Description	Avg	Ex-Fn	Mint
J. C. Perry, 15J ....★	$100	$175	$350
J. C. Perry, 15J, Silveroid ....★	100	150	250
Railway, 15J, KW, FULL, Coin .... ★★★	700	900	1,600
Railway, 15J, KW, KS, FULL .... ★★★	600	800	1,500
William Romp,15J,KW,KS from back,3/4 .... ★★	300	450	775
Geo. Sam Rice, 7J, KW, KS...................................★	150	235	400
Springfield, 15J, KW, KS, from back, ADJ, **Wolf teeth winding,** serial Nos. below 1,000, (20 lignes) .... ★★★	800	1,000	1,550
Springfield, 19J, KW, KS, from back, ADJ, **Wolf teeth winding,** serial Nos. below 1,000, (20 lignes) .... ★★★	900	1,200	1,800
State Street, 11J, 3/4, SW .... ★★	200	325	525
State Street, 15J, 3/4, SW .... ★★	250	365	650
Theo E. Studley, 15J, KW, Coin	125	175	300
Theo E. Studley, 15J, KW, KS...	125	175	300
George Walker, 17J, KW, 3/4, ADJ....................................★	275	350	550
Chester Woolworth, 15J, KW, KS	125	175	300
Chester Woolworth, 11J, KW, KS	100	150	250
Chester Woolworth, 11J, KW, KS, Silveroid	95	125	200
Chester Woolworth, 11J, KW, KS, ADJ.............................	110	150	275
#4, 15J, ADJ, KW, KS	110	150	275
#5, 15J, KW, KS	100	135	200
#6, 11J, KW, KS	100	135	200
#6, 11J, KW, KS, Silveroid	75	110	175

🕐 Some KW, KS watches made by the New York Watch Co. have a hidden key.If you unscrew the crown, and the crown comes out as a key, add $100 to the listed value.

🕐 Watches listed in this book are priced at the collectable trade show level, as **complete** watches having an original 14k gold-filled case and *Key Wind* with silver, an original white enamel single sunk dial, and with the entire original movement in good working order with no repairs needed.

🕐 This book endeavours to be a GUIDE or helpful manual and offers a wealth of material to be used as a tool not as a absolute document. Price Guides are like watches the worst may be better than none at all, but at best cannot be expected to be 100% accurate.

🕐 Characteristics of watches differ for the same age of both case and movement, because these features vary it may not be accurate to date a watch by one single influence. Example: the second hand was not commonly found on watches before 1750, but common about 1800. The first second hand appeared in 1665 and another in 1690. Therefore statements are broad rather than accurate.

🕐 A collector should expect to pay modestly higher prices at local shops.

NON-MAGNETIC WATCH CO.

Geneva and America
1887 - 1905

The Non-Magnetic Watch Co. sold and imported watches from the Swiss as well as contracted watches made in America. Geneva Non-Magnetic marked watches appear to be the oldest type of movement. This company sold a full line of watches, high grade to low grade, as well as repeaters and ladies watches. An advertisement appeared in the monthly journal of "Locomotive Engineers" in 1887. The ad states that the "Paillard's patent non-magnetic watches are uninfluenced by magnetism of electricity." Each watch contains the Paillard's patent non-magnetic, inoxidizable compensation balance and hairspring. An ad in 1888 shows prices for 16 size Swiss style watches as low as $15 for 7 jewels and as high as $135 for 20 jewels.

18 SIZE
(must be marked Paillard's Patent)

Grade or Name – Description	Avg	Ex-Fn	Mint
Elgin, 17J, FULL, SW, LS, OF	$95	$135	$200
Elgin, 17J, FULL, SW, LS, HC	125	200	300
Elgin, 15J, FULL, SW, LS, OF	85	125	200
Elgin, 15J, FULL, SW, LS, HC	125	185	300
Illinois, 24J, GJS, NI, Adj.5P, OF	750	950	1,800
Illinois, 24J, GJS, NI, Adj.5P, HC ★★	900	1,300	2,000
Illinois, 23J, GJS, NI, Adj.5P, OF	650	750	1,100
Illinois, 23J, GJS, NI, Adj.5P, HC ★★★	1,600	1,900	2,500
Illinois, 21J, GJS, NI, Adj.5P, OF	250	350	600
Illinois, 21J, GJS, NI, Adj.5P, HC	300	400	700
Illinois, 17J, NI, ADJ, OF	125	175	250
Illinois, 17J, NI, ADJ, HC	175	245	350
Illinois, 15J, NI, OF	95	135	200
Illinois, 15J, NI, HC	125	175	250
Illinois, 11J, OF	60	85	185
Illinois, 11J, HC	85	125	225

Non-Magnetic Watch Co., 18 size, 15 jewels, gold jewel settings, Adj.5p, Hunting Case, by Peoria Watch Co.

Non-Magnetic Watch Co., 18 size, 21 Ruby jewels, Adj.5p, open face, note "Paillard" engraved on movement, made by Illinois Watch Co.

🕐 Watches listed in this book are priced at the collectable trade show level, as **complete** watches having an original 14k gold-filled case and *Key Wind* with silver, an original white enamel single sunk dial, and with the entire original movement in good working order with no repairs needed.

Non-Magnetic Watch Co., 18 size, min repeater, jewelled through to the hammers, S # 6,870.

Non-Magnetic Watch Co., 18 size, 16 jewels, Bar bridge model, example of a Swiss Ebauche.

Grade or Name – Description	Avg	Ex-Fn	Mint
Peoria, 17J, FULL, SW, LS, Adj., OF	$175	$275	$475
Peoria, 15J, FULL, SW, LS, Adj., OF	150	235	375
Peoria, 15J, FULL, SW, LS, Adj., HC	250	335	500
Peoria, 11J, FULL, SW, LS, OF	110	200	300
Peoria, 11J, FULL, SW, LS, HC	175	250	350
Swiss, 16J, 3/4 plate, SW, LS, Adj., OF	65	85	175
Swiss, 16J, 3/4 plate, SW, LS, Adj., HC	85	125	200
Swiss, 15-16J, bar bridge, SW, LS, Adj., OF	65	85	185
Swiss, 15-16J, bar bridge, SW, LS, Adj., HC	75	110	200
Swiss, 11J, 3/4 plate, SW, LS, OF, HC	70	85	175
Swiss, 11J, bar bridge, SW, LS, OF, HC	70	85	175
Swiss, **min repeater**, jewelled through to the hammers	2,000	2,600	3,500

Non-Magnetic Watch Co., 18 size, 17 Ruby jewels, HC, adjusted, made by Elgin Watch Co.

Non-Magnetic Watch Co., 16 size, 21 Ruby jewels, OF, adjusted, made by Illinois Watch Co. Model 5, G# 179.

🕐 Watches listed in this book are priced at the collectable fair market value at the Trade Show level, as complete watches having an original 14k gold filled case, KEY WIND with silver, an original white enamel single sunk dial, and with the entire original movement in good working order with no repairs needed, unless otherwise noted.

🕐 Pricing in this Guide are fair market price for **COMPLETE** watches which are reflected from the "<u>NAWCC</u>" National and regional shows.

Non-Magnetic Watch Co., 16 size, 3/4 plate, 16 jewels, lever set, gilded, hunting case, adjusted, "Paillard's Patent, Balance And Spring" engraved on movement, S# 251568. Swiss made.

Non-Magnetic Watch Co., 16 size, 1/2 plate, 15-20 jewels, note "Paillard's Patent, HC, Balance And Spring" engraved on movement. Swiss made.

16 SIZE
(must be marked Paillard's Patent)

Grade or Name – Description	Avg	Ex-Fn	Mint
Elgin, 21J, ADJ 5P, OF	$125	$185	$325
Elgin, 21J, ADJ 5P, HC	200	300	500
Elgin, 17J, ADJ 5P, OF	75	135	250
Elgin, 17J, ADJ 5P, HC	100	185	350
Illinois, 21J, GJS, 3/4, DR, Adj.6P, OF	200	275	500
Illinois, 21J, GJS, 3/4, DR, Adj.6P, HC	300	400	700
Illinois, 17J, 3/4, DR, ADJ, OF	75	150	275
Illinois, 17J, 3/4, DR, ADJ, HC	125	200	350
Illinois, 15J, HC	95	135	200
Illinois, 15J, OF	60	95	175
Illinois, 11J, OF	55	80	150
Illinois, 11J, HC	70	125	150
Swiss, 20J, GJS, DR, Adj.6P, NI, 1/2 ,OF	80	150	225
Swiss, 20J, GJS, DR, Adj.6P, NI, 1/2, HC	80	135	200
Swiss, 18J, GJS, DR, Adj.6P, NI, 1/2, OF	100	150	250
Swiss, 18J, GJS, DR, Adj.6P, NI, 1/2, HC	150	175	285
Swiss, 16J, GJS, DR, Adj.6P, NI, 1/2, OF	70	90	175
Swiss, 16J, GJS, DR, Adj.6P, NI, 1/2, HC	90	125	200
Swiss, 16J, DR, adjusted, gilded, 3/4, OF	50	90	150
Swiss, 16J, DR, adjusted, gilded, 3/4, HC	70	125	175
Swiss, 7-11J, gilded, 3/4, OF	40	60	95
Swiss, 7-11J, gilded, 3/4, HC	70	95	175

Non-Magnetic Watch Co., 16 size, 17J., Three finger bridge design, HC, by Elgin W. Co.

Non-Magnetic Watch Co., 16 size, 17J., 3/4 Plate design, HC, by Elgin W. Co.

OTAY WATCH CO.

Otay, California
1889 - 1894

This company produced about 1,000 watches with a serial number range of 1,000 to 1,500 and 30,000 to 31,000. The company was purchased by a Japanese manufacturer in 1894. Names on Otay movements include: Golden Gate, F. A. Kimball, Native Sun, Overland Mail, R. D. Perry, and P. H. Wheeler. Machinery sold to Osaka of Japan. Only a few watches were made. Osaka watches look about the same as Otay watches.

Otay Watch Co. Dial; note hunting case style and lever for setting hands.

Otay Watch Co., F.A. Kimball, 18 size, 15 jewels, lever set, hunting, serial number 1,264.

18 SIZE

Grade or Name – Description		Avg	Ex-Fn	Mint
California, 15J., LS, NI, HC	★★★	$2,000	$2,500	$3,500
Golden Gate, 15J, LS, NI, HC	★★★	2,200	3,000	4,500
F. A. Kimball, 15J, LS, Gilt, HC	★★	1,500	2,000	2,600
Native Son, 15J, LS, NI, HC	★★	3,000	3,500	4,500
Native Son, 15J, LS, NI, **2-tone** movement, HC	★★★★	3,500	4,000	5,000
Overland Mail, 15J, LS, NI, HC	★★★	2,600	3,000	4,600
R. D. Perry, 15J, LS, Gilt, HC	★★	1,500	2,000	2,600
P. H. Wheeler, 15J, LS, Gilt, HC	★★	1,500	2,000	2,600
Sunset, 7J, Gilt, HC	★★	1,800	2,400	3,000
Osaka W. Co., 15J, NI, or gilt, (made in Japan)	★★★★	3,200	3,800	4,900

D. D. PALMER WATCH CO.

Waltham, Massachusetts
1864 - 1875

In 1858, at age 20, Mr. Palmer opened a small jewelry store in Waltham, Mass. Here he became interested in pocket chronometers. At first he bought the balance and jewels from Swiss manufacturers. In 1864 he took a position with the American Watch Co. and made the chronometers in his spare time (only about 25 produced). They were, 18S, 3/4 plate, gilded, key wind, and some were nickel. At first they were fusee driven, but he mainly used going barrels. About 1870, Palmer started making lever watches and by 1875 he left the American Watch Co. and started making a 10S keywind, gilded movement, and a 16S, 3/4 plate, gilt and nickel, and a stem wind of his own invention (a vibrating crown wheel). In all he made about 1,500 watches. The signature appearing on the watches was "Palmer W. Co. Wal., Mass".

He basically had three grades of watches: Fine-Solid Nickel; Medium-Nickel Plated; and Medium-Gold Gilt. They were made in open-face and hunter cases.

D. D. Palmer Watch Co., 18 size, 15 jewels, Palmer's Pat. Stem Winder on movement, serial number 1,098.

Grade or name – Description	Avg	Ex-Fn	Mint
10-16S, 15-17J, 3/4 plate, spring detent chronometer .... ★★★★	$4,000	$5,500	$8,200
16-18S, 15-17J, NI, OF, **18K** .... ★★★	2,600	3,500	5,500

PEORIA WATCH CO.

Peoria, Illinois

1885 - 1895

The roots of this company began with the Independent Watch Co. (1875 - 1881). The watches marked Mark Twain were made by the Fredonia Watch Co. (1881 - 1885). Peoria Watch Co. opened Dec. 19, 1885, and made one model of railroad watches in about 1887.

Peoria watches were 18S, quick train, 15 jewel, and all stem wind. These watches are hard to find, as only about 3,000 were made. Peoria also made railroad watches for A. C. Smith's Non-Magnetic Watch Co. of America, from 1884-1888. The 18 size watches were full plate, adjusted, and had a whiplash regulator.

The Peoria Watch Co. closed in 1889, having produced about 47,000 watches.

Peoria Watch Co., 18 size, 15 jewels, nickel damaskeening plates, hunting, note patented regulator, serial number 11,532.

Grade or Name – Description	Avg	Ex-Fn	Mint
18S, 9-11J, SW, OF	$150	$250	$400
18S, 15J, SW, personalized name	250	365	500
18S, Peoria W. Co., 15J, SW, OF	185	285	450
18S, Peoria W. Co., 15J, SW, HC	250	325	525
18S, Peoria W. Co., 15J, SW, low S# ★	450	575	900
18S, Anti-Magnetic, 15J, OF	185	285	450
18S, Anti-Magnetic, 15J, HC	285	375	550
18S, Anti-Magnetic, 15J, For Railway Service, OF ★	385	500	800
18S, Anti-Magnetic, 15J, For Railway Service, HC ★	475	600	900
18S, Superior Quality Anti-Magnetic, 15J, NI, SW, GJS, Adj.5P, OF ★★	500	650	950
18S, Superior Quality Anti-Magnetic, 15J, NI, SW, GJS, Adj.5P, HC ★★★	550	700	975
18S, For Railway Service, 15J, NI, GJS, Adj.5P, OF ★	385	500	825
18S, For Railway Service, 15J, NI, GJS, Adj.5P, HC ★	450	600	900

PHILADELPHIA WATCH CO.

Philadelphia, Pennsylvania
1868 - 1886

Eugene Paulus organized the Philadelphia Watch Co. about 1868. Most all the parts were made in Switzerland, and finished and cased in this country. The International Watch Co. is believed to have manufactured the movements for Philadelphia Watch Co. Estimated total production of the company is 12,000 watches.

Issued by the U. S. Patent Office, August 25, and November 3, 1868.

Philadelphia Watch Co., 16 size, 15 jewels, gold jewel settings, hunting case model. "Paulus' Patents 1868. Aug. 25th, Nov. 3rd" on movement, serial number 5,751.

NOV. 1871 advertising 15,16,19, & 21 size watches for sale at their New York City and Philadelphia offices.

Grade or Name – Description	Avg	Ex-Fn	Mint
18S, 15J, SW, HC ★	$225	$335	$500
18S, 15J, KW, KS ★	225	335	500
18S, 15J, SW, OF ★	200	265	450
18S, HC, KW, KS, **18K** original case marked Philadelphia Watch Co. ★★	1,000	1,200	1,700
18S, 11J, KW, KS ★	100	135	200
16S, 15J, KW, KS ★	150	185	250
16S, 19J, KW, KS, GJS ★	300	425	700
8S-6S, 11J, HC ★	100	135	200
8S-6S, 15J, HC ★	125	175	225
8S-6S, Paulus, 19J, KW, KS ★	200	265	400
000/S, 7J, HC, PS ★	125	210	300

JAMES & HENRY PITKIN

Hartford, Connecticut
New York, New York
1838 - 1852

Henry Pitkin was the first to attempt to manufacture watches by machinery. The machines were of Pitkin's own design and very crude, but he had some brilliant ideas. His first four workers were paid $30 a year plus their board. After much hardship, the first watches were produced in the fall of 1838. The watches had going barrels, not the fusee and chain, and the American flag was engraved on the plates to denote they were American made and to exemplify the true spirit of American independence in watchmaking.

The first 50 watches were stamped with the name "Henry Pitkin." Others bore the firm name "H. & J. F. Pitkin." The movements were about 16S and 3/4 plate. The plates were rolled brass and stamped out with dies. The pinions were lantern style with eight leaves. The movement had a slow train of 14,400 beats per hour. Pitkin's first plan was to make the ends of the pinions conical and let them run in the ends of hardened steel screws, similar to the Marine clock balances. A large brass setting was put in the plates and extended above the surface. Three screws, with small jewels set in their ends, were inserted so that they closed about the pivot with very small end shake. This proved to be too expensive and was used in only a few movements. Next, he tried to make standard type movements extend above the plates with the end shake controlled by means of a screw running down into the end of the pivots, reducing friction. This "capped jewel train" was used for a while before he adopted the standard ways of jeweling. The escape wheels were the star type, English style. The balance was made of gold and steel. These movements were fire gilded and not interchangeable. The dials, hands, mainsprings and hairsprings were imported. The rounded pallets were manufactured by Pitkin, and the cases for his watches were made on the premises. As many as 900 watches could have been made by Pitkin.

Grade or Name – Description		Avg	Ex-Fn	Mint
Henry Pitkin S#1-50	★★★★★	$25,000	$40,000	$85,000
H. & J. F. Pitkin, S#51-377	★★★★	15,000	22,000	45,000
Pitkin & Co., **New York**, S#378-900	★★★★	6,000	9,000	18,000
W. Pitkin, Hartford, Conn., S# approx. 40,000, fusee lever, KW, Coin	★★	1,400	1,900	2,700

H. & J. F. Pitkin, about 16 size, engraved on movement
"H. & J. F. PITKIN DETACHED LEVER", key wind & set.

Movements marked with **New York** are English made. (Imports)

ALBERT H. POTTER WATCH CO.

New York, New York 1855 - 1875

Albert Potter started his apprenticeship in 1852. When this was completed he moved to New York to take up watchmaking on his own. He made about **35 to 40 watches in USA** that sold for $225 to $350. Some were chronometers, some were lever escapements, key wind, gilded movements, some were fusee driven, both bridge and 3/4 plate. Potter was a contemporary of Charles Fasoldt and John Mulford, both horological inventors from Albany, N. Y. Potter moved to Cuba in 1861 but returned to New York in 1868. In 1872 he worked in Chicago and formed the Potter Brothers Company with his brother William. He moved to Geneva in about 1876 to make his high grade Swiss timepieces and about 600 of these watches were made.(For futher information on Potter **Geneva** timepieces, **SEE European Section**)

Below U.S. mfg.

Grade or Name – Description	Avg	Ex-Fn	Mint
18S, BRG lever, Chronometer, signed A. H. Potter,			
NewYork, 18K Potter case, **U.S. mfg.** .... ★★★★★	$12,000	$17,000	$28,000
18S, BRG lever with wind indicator, **18K** Potter case .... ★★★	7,000	10,000	18,000
18S-20S, **Tourbillon**, signed A. H. Potter, **Boston**, gilded,			
18K Potter case, **U.S. mfg.** .... ★★★★★	35,000	50,000	75,000

below GENEVA Mfg. (Dollar Watch)

Grade or Name – Description	Avg	Ex-Fn	Mint
16S, "Charmilles," 3/4 plate, Geneva, (Dollar Watch).............. ★★	$325	$435	$850

(Note: For futher information on Potter **Geneva** timepieces, **SEE European Section**)

A.H. Potter Watch Co., BOSTON, 18 size, S#5, about 6J., detent escapement. note similarity to E. Howard & Co. (early ebauche?), not a typical A.H. Potter movement.

"Charmilles Geneva" on dial, made in Charmilles Switzerland by J.J.Badollet Co factory, 16S, 7-1J., 3/4 plate, Gun-Metal case, (dollar Watch), Ca. 1890-95.

THE "CHARMILLES" MOVEMENT

is made of solid nickel, handsomely damaskeened. The center of the case is a part of the movement, thus insuring greater strength and reducing cost. It is 16 size ¾ plate, Open Face, Stemwinding and Pendant Hand Setting; Straight line Lever Escapement; Seven Jewels; Non-Magnetic Balance, Hair Spring and Escapement; is non-magnetic and non-oxidizable. The wheels and pinions as well as all parts are better finished than in higher priced movements, *and guaranteed perfect timekeepers.*

"Charmilles" **AD Ca. 1896**. In Marshall Field & Co. sales catalog prices from $8.00 to $15.00.

GEORGE P. REED

Boston, Massachusetts 1865 - 1885

In 1854, George P. Reed entered the employment of Dennison, Howard and Davis, in Roxbury, Mass., and moved with the company to Waltham, Mass. Here he was placed in charge of the pinion finishing room. While there he invented and received a patent for the mainspring barrel and maintiming power combination. This patent was dated February 18, 1857. Reed returned to Roxbury with Howard who purchased his patented barrel. He stayed with the Howard factory as foreman and adjuster until 1865, when he left for Boston to start his own business.

He obtained a patent on April 7, 1868, for an improved chronometer escapement which featured simplified construction. He made about 100 chronometers with his improved escapement, to which he added a stem-wind device. His company turned out about 100 watches the first three years. Many of his watches run for two days and have up and down indicators. They are both 18S and 16S, 3/4 plate, nickel, and are artistically designed. Reed experimented with various combinations of lever and chronometer escapements. In all, about **350** watches were made.

Grade or Name – Description		Avg	Ex-Fn	Mint
18S, 15J, **pivoted detent** escapement, **18K case** .... ★★★★		$12,000	$20,000	$40,000
16S, 15J, LS, OF or HC, **with** chronometer, **18K case** ...... ★★★		8,000	12,000	20,000
16S, 15J, LS, OF or HC, not chronometer, **18K case** .... ★★★		7,000	10,000	15,000
16S, 15J, LS, OF, 31 day calendar, "Monitor", **18K case** ... ★★★		8,000	11,000	16,000
16S, 15-17J, Wind Indicator, "Monitor", **14K, OF** .... ★★★		7,000	10,000	15,000

George P. Reed, 18 size, 15 jewels, key & stem wind, key & lever set, lever escapement, 48 hour up and down wind indicator, serial number 262.

George P. Reed, 18 size, 15 jewels, key & stem wind, key & lever set, Chronometer escapement, serial number 5. Note: This escapement was used on maybe 20 watches.

George P. Reed, Reeds' Two Days, Monitor, No. 335, engraved on movement, 31 calendar, 18-16 Size.

George P. Reed Boston, Monitor, 18-16 size, 15 jewels, wind indicator, serial # 322.

ROCKFORD WATCH CO.
Rockford, Illinois
1873 - 1915

The Rockford Watch Company's equipment was bought from the Cornell Watch Co., and two of Cornell's employees, C. W. Parker and P. H. Wheeler, went to work for Rockford. The factory was located 93 miles from Chicago on the Rock River. The first watch was placed on the market on May 1, 1876. They were key wind, 18S, full plate expansion balance & dials made by outside contract. By 1877 the company was making 3/4 plate nickel movements that fit standard size cases. Three railroads came through Rockford, and the company always advertised to the railroad and the demand was very popular with them. The company had some problems in 1896, and the name changed to Rockford Watch Co. Ltd. It closed in 1915.

ROCKFORD ESTIMATED SERIAL NUMBERS & PRODUCTION DATES

DATE–SERIAL #	DATE–SERIAL #	DATE–SERIAL #	DATE–SERIAL #
1876 – 1,200	1886 – 267,100	1896 – 470,000	1906 – 670,000
1877 – 22,600	1887 – 287,200	1897 – 490,000	1907 – 690,000
1878 – 43,000	1888 – 308,300	1898 – 510,000	1908 – 734,000
1879 – 64,000	1889 – 328,400	1899 – 530,000	1909 – 790,000
1880 – 95,000	1890 – 349,500	1900 – 550,000	1910 – 824,000
1881 – 136,000	1891 – 369,600	1901 – 570,000	1911 – 880,000
1882 – 167,000	1892 – 390,700	1902 – 590,000	1912 – 936,000
1883 – 208,000	1893 – 410,800	1903 – 610,000	1913 – 958,000
1884 – 229,000	1894 – 430,900	1904 – 630,000	1914 – 980,000
1885 – 240,000	1895 – 450,000	1905 – 650,000	1915-1,000,000

The above list is provided for determining the APPROXIMATE age of your watch. Match serial number with date. Watches were not necessarily sold in the exact order of manufactured date.

ABOVE:
Early Rockford, note **RUBY JEWELS** made in both nickel & gilt, stem-wind only, Ca. 1876

From Rockford Catalog
Early 18 Size Regulators

ROCKFORD   18 SIZE

Grade or Name – Description	Avg	Ex-Fn	Mint
Belmont USA, 21J, LS, OF, NI, M#7	$250	$350	$500
Chronometer, 17J, ADJ, OF, G925.................................★	400	575	850
Dome Model, 9J, brass plates.......................................★	150	225	425

Rockford Watch Co., Enamel **Railroad** double sunk dial, with two hour hands for a second time zone the hour hand at 2 O'clock is **BLUE**, the hour hand at 3 O'clock is **RED**.

16-SIZE ROCKFORD

OUR SPECIAL No. 1000 21 JEWELS

Hunting or Open Face, nickel, 21 ruby and sapphire jewels in settings, **adjusted to heat and cold.** Compensating balance, Breguet hair spring, safety pinion, patent micrometric regulator, gold lettering, handsomely damaskeened, double sunk glass enameled dial, **pendant set.**

Above: 1913 AD

Note: S # 825,020, about the same as grade 645.

Rockford Watch Co., 18 size, 11 jewels, hunting, Model number 6, exposed escapement, serial number 190,564.

Special Railway, 18 size, 17 jewels, hunting, Model number 8, serial number 344,551.

Grade or Name – Description	Avg	Ex-Fn	Mint
King Edward, 21J, **Plymouth W. Co., 14K HC**	$675	$900	$1,400
King Edward, 21J, (Sears), Plymouth W. Co. GJS, ADJ, NI, OF.	300	400	600
King Edward, 21J, (Sears), Plymouth W. Co.GJS, ADJ, NI, HC .	350	475	800
Nacirema is American backward, on dial Nacirema Watch Co.	125	185	300
Paxton's, 21J, (**Special on dial**), OF	350	475	725
Pennsylvania Special, 17J, LS, Adj., OF ★★★	2,000	2,500	3,600
Pennsylvania Special, 25J, LS, Adj.6P, tu-tone, OF ★★★★	6,000	8,000	13,000
Railway King, 21J, OF ★	425	625	1,100
The Ramsey Watch, 11J, NI, KW or SW	125	200	300
The Ramsey Watch, 15J, NI, KW or SW	125	200	300
The Ramsey Watch, M#7, 21J, OF, NI, ADJ	350	475	700

🕐 Generic, **nameless** or **unmarked** grades for watch movements are listed under the Company name or initials of the Company, etc. by size, jewel count and description.

	Avg	Ex-Fn	Mint
Rockford Early KW-KS, M#1-2, with low Serial #s less than 500 ★★	$800	$1,000	$1,700
Rockford Early KW-KS, M#1-2, with low Serial #s from 500-1,000 ★	425	575	950
Rockford Early KW-KS, M#1-2, with **reversible case**	500	600	1,000
Rockford, 7J, KW, FULL, OF	75	145	250
Rockford, 7J, KW, FULL, Silveroid	75	145	250
Rockford, 9J, SW, FULL, HC	95	175	275
Rockford, M#1, 9J, KW, FULL, HC	95	175	275
Rockford, 11J, KW, Coin HC	150	225	325
Rockford, 11J, SW, FULL, OF	95	135	225
Rockford, 13J, HC	125	150	225
Rockford, 11-13J, M#6, exposed escape wheel, FULL, HC ★	250	350	650
Rockford, M#1-2, 11J, KW, FULL	150	225	350
Rockford, M#1-2, 11J, transition case, FULL	95	175	250
Rockford, 9J,SW/ KW, **M#5, 3/4 Plate,** HC Coin	250	385	550
Rockford, 11J, SW/KW, **M#5, 3/4 Plate,** HC Coin	275	450	600
Rockford, 15J, SW/KW, **M#5, 3/4 Plate,** HC Coin	350	475	650
Rockford, 15J, SW, FULL	95	165	200
Rockford, 15J, KW, FULL, **multi-color dial**	400	585	1,100
Rockford, 15J, SW, 2-Tone movement	150	235	400
Rockford, 15J, KW, FULL, marked- **ADJ**	150	225	375
Rockford, 15J, KW/SW	95	175	275
Rockford, 15J, KW/SW, Silveroid	95	135	225

Rockford movement, 18 size, 7 jewels, model 5, hunting, lever set, three-quarter plate.

Grade 900, 18 size, 24J., gold jewel settings, Adj5p. OF. Warning: 24J. fakes have been made from 21J. movements. The fakes are missing the eliptical jewel setting on the barrel bridge.

Grade or Name – Description	Avg	Ex-Fn	Mint
Rockford, 15J, M#6, exposed escapement wheel, FULL, HC, LS, nickel mvt. ....★	$300	$400	$600
Rockford, 15J, M#6, exposed escapement wheel, FULL, HC, LS, gilded mvt. ....★	225	300	500
Rockford, 15J, M#6, exposed wheel, nickel mvt., Coin	175	265	400
Rockford, M#1, 15J, KW, FULL............	100	150	250
Rockford, 16J, GJS, NI, DMK, SW............	100	150	250
Rockford, 16J, GJS, NI, DMK, SW, Silveroid	100	135	225
Rockford, 16J, GJS, NI, DMK, SW, Coin	100	135	225
Rockford, 17J, NI, DMK, SW, OF............	100	135	225
Rockford, 17J, GJS, NI, DMK, SW, Adj.5P	110	175	275
Rockford, 17J, GJS, NI, SW, 2-Tone, OF	200	285	425
Rockford Early,19J, SW-KS, M#1-2, nickel, marked Ruby Jewels, ADJ, Serial # less than 100 ....★★★★	2,600	3,200	5,200
Rockford, M#1-2, 19J, KS, gilt, marked Ruby Jewels, ADJ, HC ....★★	1,800	2,100	2,800
Rockford, 21J, SW, Silveroid............	225	325	500
Rockford, 21J, GJS, OF, Adj.5P, wind indicator ....★★★	3,000	4,000	5,600
Rockford, 21J, SW, DMK, ADJ, HC............	400	500	700
Rockford, 21J, NI, DMK, ADJ, OF	300	400	600
Rockford, 21J, GJS, NI, DMK, Adj.5P, marked "RG" OF	400	450	650
Rockford, ("22J", marked,) GJS, Adj.5P, 2 tone, HC ....★★★	1,450	1,800	2,600
Rockford, ("22J", marked,) Adj, NI, SW,"RG," OF.......★★★	800	1,100	1,700
Rockford, 25J, G#25, GJS, SW, LS, Adj.5P, NI, DMK ....★★★★	4,000	5,500	8,500
Rockford, 26J, G#25, GJS, SW, LS, Adj.5P, NI, DMK ★★★★★	9,000	12,000	21,000

🕐 Generic, nameless or unmarked grades for watch movements are listed under the Company name or initials of the Company, etc. by size, jewel count and description.

	Avg	Ex-Fn	Mint
R.W. Co., 7-9-11J, NI or Gilded	$60	$85	$145
R.W. Co., 15J, NI or Gilded, OF............	70	110	200
R.W. Co., 15J, NI or Gilded, HC	100	145	225
R.W. Co., 15J, SW, multi-color box hinged, 14K, HC	2,000	2,800	4,000
R.W. Co., 16-17J, Adj, NI, OF............	100	145	225
R.W. Co., 16-17J, Adj, NI, HC	125	175	265
R.W. Co., 21J, Adj, NI, SW, OF	175	275	400
R.W. Co., 21J, Adj, NI, SW, HC............	250	350	500

Note: Model is not the same defination as grade. A model may exist in many different grades or grade names (as Winnebago) and may be used in many different models (as model 1, 18 size, open or hunting case, model 1, in 16 size open or hunting case, model 1 in 12 size) etc..

LS/PS
SWITCH

Rockford Watch Co., 18 size, 15 jewels, model # 5, 3/4 plate, key & stem wind.

Rockford Watch Co., 18S, 11-15J., M# 7 & 8, SW, Note: LS/PS screw switch, G#68-69-85 HC & G#66-67-89 OF.

Grade or Name – Description	Avg	Ex-Fn	Mint
Special Railway, 17J, ADJ, 2-tone, SW, HC ★	$425	$575	$825
The Syndicate Watch Co., M#7, 15J, LS, NI, HC	175	265	400
Winnebago, 17J, LS, GJS, Adj.5P, DR, NI, DMK, HC	300	400	650
Winnebago, 17J, LS, GJS, Adj.5P, DR, NI, DMK, OF	200	350	500
24 Hour Dial, 15J, SW or KW ★★	250	385	750
40, 15J, M#3, HC ★★	275	400	650
43, 15J, M#3, HC, **2-Tone**	135	175	325
60, 7J., **2-tone**	125	150	275
66 & 67=11J, 89=15J., M#7, **LS/PS screw switch**, OF	70	100	225
66, 11J, M#7, HC, Silveroid	70	85	200
68=11J, 69-85=15J., M#8, **LS/PS screw switch**, HC	85	135	275
72, 15J, KW-SW, **exposed escapement**, HC ★	600	775	1,200
81, 9J, M#3, Gilt, HC	95	145	250
82, **Special**, 21J, SW ★★★	700	900	1,500
83, 15J, M#8, **2-Tone**, HC	150	200	370
93, 9J, M#8, Gilt, HC	90	135	250
94, 9J, M#7, OF	70	125	225
200, 17J, M#9, NI, LS, HC	95	175	250
205, 17J, M#9, NI, LS, OF	95	135	225
800, **24J**, GJS, DR, Adj.5P, DMK, HC ★	1,200	1,500	2,200
805, 21J, GJS, Adj.5P, NI, DMK, marked "**RG**" HC	425	550	800
810, 21J, NI, DMK, ADJ, HC	400	500	700
820, 17J, SW, HC ★★	300	400	600
825, 17J, FULL, HC,	75	125	225
830, 17J, FULL, HC	75	125	225
835, 17J, FULL, HC ★	125	175	300
845, 21J, GJS, FULL, HC ★	425	550	800
870, 7J, FULL, HC	70	125	225

IMPORTANT NOTE: Railroad Standards, Railroad Approved & Railroad Grade **terminology,** as defined and used in this ***BOOK***.
1. **RAILROAD STANDARDS** = A commission or board appointed by the railroad companies outlined a set of **guidelines** to be accepted or approved by each railroad line.
2. **RAILROAD APPROVED** = A **LIST** of watches each railroad line would approve if purchased by their employee's. (this list changed through the years).
3. **RAILROAD GRADE** = A watch made by manufactures to meet or exceed the guidelines set by the railroad **standards**. Grades such as 992, Vanguard and B.W. Raymond, etc.

🕐 Some GRADES **exceeded** the R.R. standards such as 23 jewels, diamond end stone, gold train, raised gold jewel settings, double sunk dial and the list goes on. Examples: such as Veritas, Sangamo, 950 & Riverside Maximus and many others.

Grade or Name – Description	Avg.	Ex-Fn	Mint
890, **24J**, GJS, DR, Adj.5P, NI, DMK, **HC** ★★	$1,500	$1,900	$2,500
900, **24J**, GJS, DR, Adj.5P, NI, DMK, OF ★★	1,000	1,300	1,800
900, **24J**, GJS, DR, Adj.5P, **14K**, OF case ★★	1,500	1,900	2,500
905, 21J, GJS, DR, Adj.5P, NI, DMK, OF ★	300	400	600
910, 21J, NI, DMK, ADJ, OF	200	250	400
912, 21J, Adj. 5P, LS, OF ★★	485	650	850
915, 17J, M# 7, SW, OF	175	250	350
915, 17J, M# **9**, SW, OF ★★★	700	900	1, 400
918, **24J**, GJS, DR, Adj.5P, NI, DMK, OF ★★	1,200	1,500	2,100
918, 21J, NI, GJS, Adj.5P, DR, OF	300	375	500
918, 21J, NI, GJS, Adj.5P, DR, , OF Coin	275	350	450
920 & 930, 17J, OF	175	250	350
925 & 935, 17J, OF	100	150	200
945, 21J, M#9, SW, OF	225	300	425
950-marked, 21J, GJS, Adj.5P, DR, OF, **Wind Indicator** .. ★★★	2,600	3,600	4,900
970, 7J, OF	75	100	175
970, 7J, OF Silveroid case	65	85	135

16 SIZE
(most HC grade numbers end with 0 & most OF grade numbers end with 5

Grade or Name – Description	Avg	Ex-Fn	Mint
Commodore Perry, 21J, GJS, GT, marked "RG", OF ★	$300	$385	$625
Commodore Perry, 15-17J, ADJ	125	175	275
Cosmos, 17J, OF, GJS, LS, DMK, marked dial & mvt.	250	350	500
Cosmos, 17J, **HC**, GJS, LS, DMK, marked dial & mvt.	300	385	625
Doll Watch Co., 17J, marked dial & mvt., OF ★★★	850	1,300	2,000
Doll Watch Co., 21J, marked dial & mvt., OF ★★★	1,000	1,500	2,200
Doll Watch Co., 23J, marked dial & mvt., OF ★★★	1,500	1,800	2,700
Doll Watch Co., 23J, (G#504-M# 4), triple signed, HC ★★★★	1,700	2,000	3,200
Dome Model, 15J	75	110	200
Dome Model, 17J	85	125	225
Dome Model, 17J, **2-tone**, HC	150	250	450
Herald Square, 7J, 3/4, OF	100	135	225
Iroquois, 17J, G# 630, DR, **14K, HC**	550	700	1,000
Iroquois, 17J, G# 635, DR, OF	200	275	400
Peerless, 17J, OF, NI, LS, DMK ★	150	285	400
Pocahontas, 17J, GJS, Adj.5P, DR, OF ★	200	300	550
Pocahontas, 17J, GJS, Adj.5P, DR, HC ★	275	400	700
Pocahontas, 21J, GJS, Adj.5P, DR, OF ★	300	475	750
Pocahontas, 21J, GJS, Adj.5P, DR, HC ★★	500	700	975
Prince of Wales (Sears), 21J, Plymouth W. Co., OF ★★	300	400	700
Prince of Wales (Sears), 21J, Plymouth W. Co., HC ★★	375	475	800

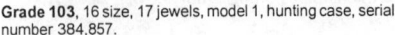

Grade 103, 16 size, 17 jewels, model 1, hunting case, serial number 384,857.

Cosmos movement, 16 size, 17 jewels, open face, gold jewel settings, grade 565, model 2.

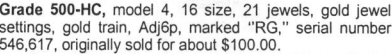

Grade 500-HC, model 4, 16 size, 21 jewels, gold jewel settings, gold train, Adj6p, marked "RG," serial number 546,617, originally sold for about $100.00.

Grade 505-OF, model 5, 16 size, 21 jewels, gold jewel settings, gold train, Adj6p, marked "RG," serial number 593,929, originally sold for about $100.00.

🕐 **Generic, nameless** or **unmarked** grades for watch movements are listed under the Company name or initials of the Company, etc. by size, jewel count and description.

Grade or Name – Description	Avg	Ex-Fn	Mint
Rockford, 7J, 3/4, HC	$75	$100	$200
Rockford, 9J, 3/4, SW, OF	65	95	185
Rockford, 9J, SW, Silveroid	65	85	165
Rockford, 9J, SW, HC	85	125	225
Rockford, 11J, SW, Silveroid	65	95	175
Rockford, 11J, 3/4, HC	75	125	250
Rockford, 15J, 3/4, ADJ, OF	70	110	200
Rockford, 15J, 3/4, ADJ, Silveroid	65	95	175
Rockford, 15J, 3/4, ADJ, HC	75	125	250
Rockford, 16J, 3/4, SW, Silveroid	65	85	165
Rockford, 16J, 3/4, ADJ, NI, DMK	65	95	175
Rockford, 17J, 3/4	65	95	175
Rockford, 17J, 3/4, **2-Tone**, marked "RG" ★	250	350	550
Rockford, 17J, BRG, Adj.3P, DR	125	175	250
Rockford, 17J, BRG, Silveroid	70	110	175
Rockford, 17J, 3/4, Silveroid	70	100	170
Rockford, 21J, 3/4, SW, Silveroid	250	300	400
Rockford, 21J, BRG, SW, Silveroid	250	300	400
Rockford, 21J, 3/4, GJS, Adj.5P	300	385	550
Rockford, 21J, BRG, GJS, Adj.5P, GT, DR	325	400	600
Winnebago, 17J, G#400, BRG, GJS, Adj.5P, NI, HC ★	250	350	650
Winnebago, 17J, G#405, BRG, GJS, Adj.5P, NI, OF	200	275	400
Winnebago, 21J, BRG, GJS, Adj.5P, NI ★	325	450	700
100, 16-17J, M#1, 3/4, **2-Tone**, HC	250	300	450
100S, 21J, **Special**, 3/4, LS, OF	300	385	575
102, 15J, M#1, HC ★	150	200	300
103, 15-17J, M#1, HC ★★	275	350	450
104, 11J, M#1, HC	75	100	175
110, 17J, **2 tone dome** style mvt., HC ★	325	385	600
115-125, 17J, **Special**, HC ★★★	525	700	1,000
120-130, 17J, HC ★★★	425	550	875

🕐 **Generic, nameless** or **unmarked** grades for watch movements are listed under the Company name or initials of the Company, etc. by size, jewel count and description.

🕐 Pricing in this Guide are fair market price for **COMPLETE** watches which are reflected from the "**NAWCC**" National and regional shows.

Rockford Watch Co., Pocahontas, 21 jewels., hunting case, bridge model, Adj.5P, serial # 670,203

Rockford Watch Co., 21j., Wind indicator, **marked 655,** adjusted to 5 positions, gold jewel settings, gold center wheel, double roller, Serial # 830,591.

Grade or Name – Description	Avg	Ex-Fn	Mint
400, 17J, NI, Adj.5P, GJS, DR, BRG, HC..	$125	$175	$275
405, 17J, NI, Adj.5P, GJS, DR, BRG, OF	100	135	250
440, 17J, GJS, HC..	125	175	275
445, 19J, GJS, OF .... ★★	900	1,000	1,300
500-501, 21J, BRG, NI, GJS, Adj.5P, GT, HC .... ★★★	500	650	975
505, 21J, BRG, NI, GJS, Adj.5P, GT, OF .... ★★★	500	650	975
510, 21J, BRG, NI, GJS, Adj.5P, GT, HC........................... ★★★	500	650	975
515 - 525 -545, 21J, 3/4, OF...	350	450	725
520, 21J, 3/4, HC	350	450	700
520 - 540, 21J, BRG, NI, GJS, Adj.5P, HC............................	450	575	800
525, 21J. M#5, GT, Adj.5P, OF ....★	350	450	625
530, 21J, GJS, Adj.5P, marked **"RG"**, HC ....★	375	500	800
535, 21J, 3/4, OF..★	300	400	600
537, 21J, OF, GJS, Adj.5P... ★★★	1,000	1,200	1,900
540, 21J,GT, BRG, Adj.5P, HC ....★	275	350	575
545, 21J,GT, BRG, Adj.5P, OF..	275	350	550
561, 17J, BRG, HC	150	200	400
566, 17J, BRG, OF	150	200	325
572, 17J, BRG, NI, HC...	150	200	350
573-575, 17J, 3/4 & BRG, NI, OF	150	200	325
578-579, 17J, PS, GJS .... ★★	300	400	600
584 15J, 3/4 NI, HC..	65	95	175
585, 15J, 3/4, NI, OF	65	85	150
620, 21J, 3/4, HC...★	325	450	650
625, 21J, 3/4, OF...★	300	400	600
640, 21J, GT, 3/4, Adj.5P, HC ....★	275	350	525
645, 21J, GT, 3/4, Adj.5P, OF..	275	350	525
655, 21J, **Wind Indicator**, Adj.5P, **marked 655**, OF .... ★★	1,200	1,600	2,400
665, 17J, **Wind Indicator**, Adj, 5P, OF ....★	1,000	1,200	2,000
700, 21J, Adj., BRG, HC	275	350	550
705, 21J, Adj., BRG, OF	250	335	475
810, 21J, 3/4, Adj. heat & cold, OF	275	375	500
1000, 21J, 3/4, Adj. heat & cold, OF .... ★★	325	485	750

🕐 Watches listed in this book are priced at the collectable Trade Show level, as **complete** watches having an original 14k gold-filled case and *Key Wind* with silver, an original white enamel single sunk dial, and with the entire original movement in good working order with no repairs needed.

Rockford Watch Co., 12 size, 15 jewels, model 1, hunting, pendant set.

Rockford Watch Co., 12 size, 15 jewels, model 2, open face, pendant set.

12 SIZE
All 3/4 Bridge

Grade or Name – Description		Avg	Ex-Fn	Mint
Doll Watch Co., 21J, marked on dial & movement, OF .... ★★		$275	$385	$700
Iroquois, 17J, BRG, DR, ADJ		100	185	350
Pocahontas, 21J, GJS, Adj.5P, BRG, DR		200	275	475
Rockford, 15J, BRG		45	75	150
Rockford, 17J, BRG, NI, DR, ADJ................		45	75	150
Rockford, 21J, BRG, NI, DR, ADJ................		100	175	300
Rockford, 21J, BRG, NI, DR, ADJ, Silveroid..................		75	95	200
300, 23J, 3/4, GJS, Adj.5P, HC .... ★★★		300	400	600
305, 23J, BRG, NI, GJS, Adj.5P, GT, OF .... ★★★		300	400	600
310(HC)-315(OF), 21J, BRG, NI, GJS, Adj.5P .... ★★		125	175	300
320(HC)-325(OF), 17J, BRG, NI, ADJ, DR		60	75	125
330, 17J, BRG, NI, DR, HC		70	85	150
335, 17J, BRG, NI, DR, OF		60	75	125
340(HC)-345(OF), 21J, M#1........................★		225	275	400
350, 17J, OF................		60	75	125
355, 17J, HC		65	85	150

Note: Add $10 to $25 to above watches with hunting case.

0 - Size movement in 12 - Size Case ("Xtremethin")

Grade or Name – Description	Avg	Ex-Fn	Mint
0 - Size movement in 12 - Size Case, 15J., Plain GF case	$65	$85	$150
0 - Size movement in 12 - Size Case, 15J., GF case & ENAMELED	125	175	250

8 SIZE

Grade or Name – Description	Avg	Ex-Fn	Mint
15J, 3/4, HC, LS, **14K, 40 DWT**	$400	$500	$700
9–15J, 3/4, KW or SW, LS, OF or HC, ...	70	100	175

🕑 A collector should expect to pay modestly higher prices at local shops.

🕑 Pricing in this Guide are fair market price for **COMPLETE** watches which are reflected from the "<u>**NAWCC**</u>" National and regional shows.

0 Size
Pendant Set

1906 AD

$37.00

No. 140

Rockford movement, 6 size, 17 jewels, quick train, straight line escapement, compensating balance, adjusted to temperature, micrometric regulator, 3/4 damaskeened plates.

Hunting, Nickel, 17 ruby jewels adjusted to temperature and position, gold round center wheel, steel escape wheel, double roller escapment, compensating balance, Breguet hair spring, micrometric regulator, gold lettering, handsomely damaskeened, sunk second glass enamel dial.

6 SIZE

Grade or Name – Description	Avg	Ex-Fn	Mint
9J, NI, **HC**	$90	$125	$225
15J, 3/4, NI	75	100	200
16J, 3/4, NI	75	100	200
17J, 3/4, ADJ, NI	75	100	200

0 SIZE

Grade or Name – Description	Avg	Ex-Fn	Mint
Iroquois, 17J., HC	$125	$200	$350
Plymouth Watch Co., 15-17J, HC	200	250	375
Winona, 15J., HC	125	200	350
7J, BRG, NI, DR, HC	75	100	200
11J, BRG, NI, DR, HC	75	100	200
15J, BRG, NI, DR, HC	85	125	250
17J, BRG, NI, DR, HC	85	125	250

**ROCKFORD
1906 AD**

16 Size

No. 500 Hunting }
No. 505 Open Face } Bridge $100.00

Nickel, 21 high colored ruby jewels, gold settings, accurately adjusted to temperature, all positions and isochronism. Closely rated in pocket position. Compensating balance with gold screws. also mean time screws,gold beveled polished train, double roller escapement, sapphire jewel pin, steel escape wheel ground and highly polished on all frictional surfaces. Red ruby pallet stone, patent micrometric regulator, positive action. Breguet hair spring of best quality. Beveled and rayed winding wheels, all steel work elegantly polished and cornered. First quality mainspring, double sunk glass, enamel dial, bronzed hands, gold lettering and artistically damaskeened.

WINNEBAGO 16 Size

Hunting }
Open Face } Bridge $37.50

Nickel, 17 Ruby and Sapphire jewels in gold settings, accurately adjusted to temperature, isochronism and five positions. Compensating balance with gold screws, also mean time screws. Red beveled train, double roller escapement, sapphire pallet stone, steel escape wheel, ground and polished on all acting surfaces, patent micrometric regulator. Breguet hair spring, beveled winding wheel, steel work highly polished and cornered. Double sunk glass enamel dial, gold lettering, attractively damaskeened. A 17 jewel watch elegantly finished and equipped with all modern improvements. Certificate of Rating furnished on application.

The Rockford Watch Company, Ltd.

JANUARY 1907
NUMBER AND GRADE

WITH

DESCRIPTION OF MOVEMENTS MANUFACTURED TO DATE

Number and Grade of Movement	GRADE	Size	Style (Description of Movement)	Jewels	Wind	Set	Model
1 to 114,000		18	Htg. F. Pl.		Key	Key	1
114,001 " 115,000		"	" ¾ Pl.		Stem	Lever	5
115,001 " 126,000		"	" F. Pl.		"	"	2
126,001 " 127,000		"	" ¾ Pl.		"	"	5
127,001 " 130,000		"	" F. Pl.		"	"	2
130,001 " 131,000		"	" ¾ Pl.		"	"	5
131,001 " 133,000		"	" F. Pl.		"	"	3
133,001 " 134,000		"	" ¾ Pl.		"	"	5
134,001 " 138,000		"	" F. Pl.		"	"	3
138,001 " 139,000		"	" ¾ Pl.		"	"	5
139,001 " 143,000		"	" F. Pl.		"	"	3
143,001 " 144,000		"	" ¾ Pl.		"	"	5
144,001 " 145,000		"	" F. Pl.		"	"	3
145,001 " 146,000		"	" ¾ Pl.		"	"	5
146,001 " 149,000		"	" F. Pl.		"	"	3
149,001 " 151,000		"	" ¾ Pl.		"	"	5
151,001 " 153,000		"	" F. Pl.		"	"	3
153,001 " 154,000		"	" ¾ Pl.		"	"	5
154,001 " 158,000		"	" F. Pl.		"	"	3
158,001 " 159,000		"	" ¾ Pl.		"	"	5
159,001 " 169,000		"	" F. Pl.		"	"	3
170,001 " 170,100		"	" ¾ Pl.	15	"	"	5
170,101 " 177,000		"	" F. Pl.		"	"	3
177,001 " 177,800		"	"		"	"	6
177,901 " 189,500		"	"		"	"	3
189,601 " 190,900		"	"		"	"	6
191,001 " 191,100		"	"		"	"	3
191,101 " 196,400		"	O. F.		"	"	4
196,501 " 197,000		"	Htg.		"	"	6
197,101 " 197,500		"	"		"	"	3
197,601 " 198,000		"	"		"	"	6
198,101 " 199,100		"	O. F.		"	"	4
199,201 " 199,500		"	Htg.		"	"	6
199,600 " 200,000		"	" ¾ Pl.		"	"	5
200,001 " 213,100		8	"		"	"	1
213,101 " 218,900		6	"		"	"	"
219,001 " 219,500		18	"		"	"	5
219,501 " 224,500		"	" F. Pl.		"	"	3
224,501 " 228,900		"	O. F.		"	"	4
229,001 " 232,000		"	Htg.		"	"	3
232,001 " 233,000		"	" ¾ Pl.		"	"	5
233,001 " 234,000	47	"	O. F. F. Pl. Nickel	15	"	"	4
234,001 " 235,000	45	"	" "		"	"	"
235,001 " 236,000	43	"	Htg. F. Pl. Gilt		"	"	3
236,001 " 237,000	44	"	" " Gilt		"	"	"
237,001 " 238,000	45	"	O. F. F. Pl. "		"	"	4
238,001 " 239,000		"	" " "	9	"	"	"
239,001 " 240,000	45	"	" " "	15	"	"	"
240,001 " 241,000	46	"	" " "	11	"	"	"
241,001 " 241,800	47	"	" " Nickel	15	"	"	"
241,801 " 242,000	40	"	Htg. " "		"	"	3
242,001 " 243,000	43	"	" " "		"	"	"
243,001 " 244,000	44	"	" " Gilt		"	"	"
244,001 " 244,300	49	"	" " Nickel		"	"	6
244,301 " 244,400	72	"	" " "		"	"	"
244,401 " 245,000	62	"	" " "	11	"	"	8
245,001 " 246,000	81	"	" " Gilt	9	"	"	3
246,001 " 247,000	44	"	" " "	15	"	"	"
247,001 " 248,000	64	"	O. F. " "	11	"	"	4
248,001 " 249,000	46	"	Htg. " "	15	"	"	6
249,001 " 250,000	49	"	" " Nickel		"	"	"
250,001 " 250,500	62	"	" " "	11	"	"	"
250,501 " 251,000	60	"	O. F. " "		"	"	7
251,001 " 252,000	66	"	" " "		"	"	"
252,001 " 253,000	67	"	" " Gilt		"	"	"
253,001 " 253,500	83	"	Htg. " Nickel	15	"	"	8
253,501 " 253,700	77	"	" " "		"	"	"
253,701 " 254,000	68	"	" " Gilt	11	"	"	"
254,001 " 254,600	86	"	O. F. " Nickel	15	"	"	7
254,601 " 254,800	76	"	" " "		"	"	"
254,801 " 255,000	78	"	" " Gilt		"	"	"
255,001 " 256,000	89	"	" " "		"	"	"
256,001 " 257,000	68	"	Htg. " "	11	"	"	8
257,001 " 258,000	93	"	" " "	9	"	"	"
258,001 " 259,000	69	"	" " Nickel	11	"	"	"

The Rockford Watch Company, Ltd.

Number and Grade of Movement	GRADE	Size			Style	Jewels	Wind	Sett	Model
259,001 to 260,000	66	18	O. F.	F. Pl.	Nickel	11	Stem	Lever	7
260,001 " 261,000	68	"	Htg.	"	Gilt	"	"	"	8
261,001 " 262,000	86	"	O. F.	"	Nickel	15	"	"	7
262,001 " 263,000	67	"	"	"	Gilt	11	"	"	"
263,001 " 264,000	83	"	Htg.	"	Nickel	15	"	"	8
264,001 " 265,000	69	"	"	"	"	"	"	"	"
265,001 " 266,000	68	"	"	"	Gilt	11	"	"	"
266,001 " 267,000	93	"	"	"	"	9	"	"	8
267,001 " 267,800	83	"	"	"	Nickel	15	"	"	"
267,801 " 268,000	77	"	"	"	"	"	"	"	"
268,001 " 269,000	68	"	"	"	Gilt	11	"	"	"
269,001 " 270,000	67	"	O. F.	"	"	11	"	"	7
270,001 " 270,800	85	"	Htg.	"	"	15	"	"	8
270,801 " 271,000	79	"	"	"	"	"	"	"	"
271,001 " 272,000	66	"	O. F.	"	Nickel	11	"	"	7
272,001 " 272,100	77	"	Htg.	"	"	15	"	"	8
272,101 " 272,200	83	"	"	"	"	"	"	"	"
272,201 " 272,300	77	"	"	"	"	"	"	"	"
272,301 " 272,600	83	"	"	"	"	"	"	"	"
272,601 " 272,700	77	"	"	"	"	"	"	"	"
272,701 " 272,900	83	"	"	"	"	"	"	"	"
272,901 " 273,000	77	"	"	"	"	"	"	"	"
273,001 " 274,000	69	"	"	"	"	"	"	"	"
274,001 " 275,000	83	"	"	"	"	"	"	"	"
275,001 " 276,000	69	"	"	"	"	11	"	"	"
276,001 " 277,000	83	"	"	"	"	15	"	"	"
277,001 " 278,000	85	"	"	"	Gilt	"	"	"	"
278,001 " 279,000	66	"	O. F.	"	Nickel	11	"	"	7
279,001 " 279,200	76	"	"	"	"	15	"	"	"
279,201 " 280,000	86	"	"	"	"	"	"	"	"
280,001 " 281,000	66	"	"	"	"	11	"	"	"
281,001 " 282,000	85	"	Htg.	"	Gilt	15	"	"	8
282,001 " 283,000	83	"	"	"	Nickel	"	"	"	"
283,001 " 284,000	93	"	"	"	Gilt	9	"	"	"
284,001 " 285,000	89	"	O. F.	"	"	15	"	"	7
285,001 " 286,000	69	"	Htg.	"	Hickel	11	"	"	8
286,001 " 286,200	83	"	"	"	Nick.& Gilt	15	"	"	"
286,201 " 286,500	84	"	"	"	"	"	"	"	"
286,501 " 287,000	83	"	"	"	Nickel	"	"	"	"
287,001 " 288,000	66	"	O. F.	"	"	11	"	"	7
288,001 " 289,000	67	"	"	"	Gilt	"	"	"	"
289,001 " 289,500	84	"	Htg.	"	Spot Gilt	15	"	"	8
289,501 " 291,000	83	"	"	"	Nickel	"	"	"	"
291,001 " 292,000	69	"	"	"	"	11	"	"	"
292,001 " 293,000	67	"	O. F.	"	Gilt	"	"	"	7
293,001 " 294,000	85	"	Htg.	"	"	15	"	"	8
294,001 " 295,000	93	"	"	"	"	9	"	"	"
295,001 " 296,000	66	"	O. F.	"	Nickel	11	"	"	7
296,001 " 297,000	89	"	"	"	Gilt	15	"	"	"
297,001 " 298,000	69	"	Htg.	"	Nickel	11	"	"	8
298,001 " 299,000	67	"	O. F.	"	Gilt	"	"	"	7
299,001 " 300,000	93	"	Htg.	"	"	9	"	"	8
300,001 " 300,500	84	"	"	"	Nick.& Gilt	15	"	"	"
300,501 " 300,700	83	"	"	"	Nickel	"	"	"	"
300,701 " 301,000	70	"	"	"	Nick.& Gilt	16	"	"	"
301,001 " 302,000	66	"	O. F.	"	Nickel	11	"	"	7
302,001 " 303,000	93	"	Htg.	"	Gilt	9	"	"	8
303,001 " 304,000	69	"	"	"	Nickel	11	"	"	"
304,001 " 304,500	84	"	"	"	Nick.& Gilt	15	"	"	"
304,501 " 305,000	83	"	"	"	Nickel	"	"	"	"
305,001 " 305,500	84	"	"	"	Nick.&Gilt	"	"	"	"
305,501 " 306,000	83	"	"	"	Nickel	"	"	"	"
306,001 " 307,000	66	"	O. F.	"	"	11	"	"	7
307,001 " 308,000	83	"	Htg.	"	"	15	"	"	8
308,001 " 309,000	93	"	"	"	Gilt	9	"	"	"
309,001 " 310,000	83	"	"	"	Nickel	15	"	"	"
310,001 " 310,500	87	"	O. F.	"	Nick.& Gilt	"	"	"	7
310,501 " 310,700	88	"	"	"	Nickel	16	"	"	"
310,701 " 311,000	86	"	"	"	"	15	"	"	"
311,001 " 312,000	69	"	Htg.	"	"	11	"	"	8
312,001 " 313,000	93	"	"	"	Gilt	9	"	"	"
313,001 " 314,000	83	"	"	"	Nickel	15	"	"	"
314,001 " 317,000	93	"	"	"	Gilt	9	"	"	"
317,001 " 318,000	85	"	"	"	"	15	"	"	"
318,001 " 319,000	93	"	"	"	"	9	"	"	"
319,001 " 320,000	85	"	"	"	"	15	"	"	"
320,001 " 321,000	84	"	"	"	Nick.& Gilt	"	"	"	"
321,001 " 322,000	83	"	"	"	Nickel	"	"	"	"
322,001 " 323,000	84	"	"	"	Nick.& Gilt	"	"	"	"
323,001 " 325,000	83	"	"	"	Nickel	"	"	"	"
325,001 " 326,000	85	"	"	"	Gilt	"	"	"	"
326,001 " 327,000	93	"	"	"	"	9	"	"	"
327,001 " 328,000	83	"	"	"	Nickel	15	"	"	"
328,001 " 329,000	89	"	O. F.	"	Gilt	"	"	"	7
329,001 " 329,100	84	"	Htg.	"	Nick.& Gilt	"	"	"	8
329,101 " 329,200	83	"	"	"	Special	.....	"	"	"
329,201 " 329,700	84	"	"	"	Nick.& Gilt	15	"	"	"
329,701 " 330,000	70	"	"	"	"	16	"	"	"
330,001 " 330,800	87	"	O. F.	"	Nickel	15	"	"	7

The Rockford Watch Company, Ltd.

Number and Grade of Movement	GRADE	Size	Style			Jewels	Wind	Sett	Model
330,801 to 331,000	88	18	O. F.	F. Pl.	Nick.& Gilt	16	Stem	Lever	7
331,001 " 332,000	68	"	Htg.	"	Gilt	11	"	"	8
332,001 " 333,000	86	"	O. F.	"	Nickel	15	"	"	7
333,001 " 334,000	69	"	Htg.	"	"	11	"	"	8
334,001 " 335,000	66	"	O. F.	"	"	"	"	"	7
335,001 " 336,000	94	"	"	"	Gilt	9	"	"	"
336,001 " 337,000	68	"	Htg.	"	"	11	"	"	8
337,001 " 338,000	94	"	O. F.	"	"	9	"	"	7
338,001 " 338,500	88	"	"	"	Nick.& Gilt	16	"	"	"
338,501 " 339,000	86	"	"	"	Nickel	15	"	"	"
339,001 " 339,500	70	"	Htg.	"	Nick.& Gilt	"	"	"	8
339,501 " 340,000	84	"	"	"	"	15	"	"	"
340,001 " 341,000	66	"	O. F.	"	Nickel	11	"	"	7
341,001 " 342,000	85	"	Htg.	"	Gilt	15	"	"	8
342,001 " 343,000	89	"	O. F.	"	"	"	"	"	7
343,001 " 344,000	94	"	"	"	"	9	"	"	"
344,001 " 345,000	84	"	Htg.	"	Nick.& Gilt	15	"	"	8
345,001 " 346,000	68	"	"	"	Gilt	11	"	"	"
346,001 " 347,000	87	"	O. F.	"	Nick.& Gilt	15	"	"	7
347,001 " 348,000	94	"	"	"	Gilt	9	"	"	"
348,001 " 348,300	88	"	"	"	Nick.& Gilt	16	"	"	"
348,301 " 348,500	87	"	"	"	"	15	"	"	"
348,501 " 349,000	86	"	"	"	Nickel	"	"	"	"
349,001 " 349,500	67	"	"	"	Gilt	11	"	"	"
349,501 " 350,000	89	"	"	"	"	15	"	"	"
350,001 " 350,500	70	"	Htg.	"	Nick.& Gilt	16	"	"	8
350,501 " 351,000	85	"	"	"	Gilt	15	"	"	"
351,001 " 352,000	87	"	O. F.	"	Nick & Gilt	"	"	"	7
352,001 " 352,500	88	"	"	"	"	16	"	"	"
352,501 " 353,000	67	"	"	"	Gilt	11	"	"	"
353,001 " 353,500	100	16	Htg.	¾ Pl.	Nick.& Gilt	16	"	"	1
353,501 " 353,800	101	"	"	"	Nickel	15	"	"	"
353,801 " 354,000	102	"	"	"	"	"	"	"	"
354,001 " 354,500	103	"	"	"	"	"	"	"	"
354,501 " 355,000	104	"	"	"	"	11	"	"	"
355,001 " 355,500	111	"	"	"	Gilt	15	"	"	"
355,501 " 356,000	112	"	"	"	"	"	"	"	"
356,001 " 356,500	113	"	"	"	"	11	"	"	"
356,501 " 357,000	114	"	"	"	"	9	"	"	"
357,001 " 358,500	68	18	"	F. Pl.	"	11	"	"	8
358,501 " 359,000	67	"	O. F.	"	"	"	"	"	7
359,001 " 359,500	87	"	"	"	Nick.& Gilt	15	"	"	"
359,501 " 360,000	86	"	"	"	Nickel	"	"	"	"
360,001 " 360,500	101	16	Htg.	¾ Pl.	Nick.& Gilt	"	"	"	1
360,501 " 361,000	102	"	"	"	Nickel	"	"	"	"
361,001 " 361,500	103	"	"	"	"	"	"	"	"
361,501 " 362,000	104	"	"	"	"	11	"	"	"
362,001 " 364,000	67	18	O. F.	F. Pl.	Gilt	"	"	"	7
364,001 " 365,000	112	16	Htg.	¾ Pl.	"	15	"	"	1
365,001 " 366,000	102	"	"	"	Nickel	"	"	"	"
366,001 " 367,000	103	"	"	"	"	"	"	"	"
367,001 " 368,000	67	18	O. F.	F. Pl.	Gilt	11	"	"	7
368,001 " 368,500	112	16	Htg.	¾ Pl.	"	15	"	"	1
368,501 " 369,000	101	"	"	"	Nick.& Gilt	"	"	"	"
369,001 " 370,000	104	"	"	"	Nickel	11	"	"	"
370,001 " 370,500	86	18	O. F.	F. Pl.	"	15	"	"	7
370,501 " 371,000	87	"	"	"	Nick.& Gilt	"	"	"	"
371,001 " 371,500	89	"	"	"	Gilt	"	"	"	"
371,501 " 372,000	94	"	"	"	"	9	"	"	"
372,001 " 372,500	113	16	Htg.	¾ Pl.	"	11	"	"	1
372,501 " 373,000	114	"	"	"	"	9	"	"	"
373,001 " 374,000	113	"	"	"	"	11	"	"	"
374,001 " 374,500	68	18	"	F. Pl.	"	"	"	"	8
374,501 " 375,000	94	"	O. F.	"	"	9	"	"	7
375,001 " 376,000	87	"	"	"	Nick.& Gilt	15	"	"	"
376,001 " 376,200	100	16	Htg.	¾ Pl.	"	16	"	"	1
376,201 " 376,700	101	"	"	"	"	15	"	"	"
376,701 " 377,000	102	"	"	"	Nickel	"	"	"	"
377,001 " 377,500	104	"	"	"	"	11	"	"	"
377,501 " 378,000	103	"	"	"	"	15	"	"	"
378,001 " 379,000	94	18	O. F.	F. Pl.	Gilt	9	"	'	7
379,001 " 379,500	86	"	"	"	Nickel	15	"	"	"
379,501 " 380,000	84	"	Htg.	"	Nick.& Gilt	"	"	"	8
380,001 " 380,500	101	16	"	¾ Pl.	"	"	"	"	1
380,501 " 381,000	104	"	"	"	Nickel	11	"	"	"
381,001 " 381,300	102	"	"	"	"	15	"	"	"
381,301 " 382,000	103	"	"	"	"	"	"	"	"
382,001 " 382,200	111	"	"	"	Gilt	"	"	"	"
382,201 " 383,000	112	"	"	"	"	"	"	"	"
383,001 " 383,500	113	"	"	"	"	11	"	"	"
383,501 " 384,000	114	"	"	"	"	9	"	"	"
384,001 " 384,500	100	"	"	"	Nick.& Gilt	16	"	"	"
384,501 " 385,000	103	"	"	"	Nickel	15	"	"	"
385,001 " 385,500	104	"	"	"	"	11	"	"	"
385,501 " 386,000	103	"	"	"	"	15	"	"	"
386,001 " 387,000	112	"	"	"	Gilt	"	"	"	"
387,001 " 387,500	93	18	"	F. Pl.	"	9	"	"	8
387,501 " 388,000	68	"	"	"	"	11	"	"	"

The Rockford Watch Company, Ltd.

Number and Grade of Movement	GRADE	Description of Movement				Jewels	Wind	Sett	Model
		Size		Style					
388,001 to 388,500	94	18	O. F.	F. Pl.	Gilt	9	Stem	Lever	7
388,501 " 389,000	89	"	"	"	"	15	"	"	"
389,001 " 389,100	76	"	"	"	Nickel	"	"	"	"
389,101 " 390,000	86	"	"	"	"	"	"	"	"
390,001 " 391,000	69	"	Htg.	"	"	11	"	"	8
391,001 " 391,400	162	6	"	¾ Pl.	Gilt	9	"	"	2
391,401 " 391,700	161	"	"	"	"	11	"	"	"
391,701 " 392,000	160	"	"	"	"	15	"	"	"
392,001 " 392,300	154	"	"	"	Nickel	9	"	"	"
392,301 " 392,500	153	"	"	"	"	11	"	"	"
392,501 " 392,700	152	"	"	"	"	15	"	"	"
392,701 " 392,900	151	"	"	"	Nick.& Gilt	"	"	"	"
392,901 " 393,000	150	"	"	"	"	16	"	"	"
393,001 " 393,500	154	"	"	"	Nickel	9	"	"	"
393,501 " 394,000	153	"	"	"	"	11	"	"	"
394,001 " 394,500	152	"	"	"	"	15	"	"	"
394,501 " 394,800	151	"	"	"	Nick.& Gilt	"	"	"	"
394,801 " 395,000	150	"	"	"	"	16	"	"	"
395,001 " 396,000	162	"	"	"	Gilt	9	"	"	"
396,001 " 396,500	161	"	"	"	"	11	"	"	"
396,501 " 397,000	160	"	"	"	"	15	"	"	"
397,001 " 397,800	162	"	"	"	"	9	"	"	"
397,801 " 398,600	161	"	"	"	"	11	"	"	"
398,601 " 399,000	160	"	"	"	"	15	"	"	"
399,001 " 400,200	153	"	"	"	Nickel	11	"	"	"
400,201 " 400,700	152	"	"	"	"	15	"	"	"
400,701 " 401,000	152	"	"	"	Nick.& Gilt	"	"	"	"
401,001 " 401,500	93	18	"	F. Pl.	Gilt	9	"	"	8
401,501 " 402,000	68	"	"	"	"	11	"	"	"
402,001 " 402,500	69	"	"	"	Nickel	"	"	"	"
402,501 " 403,000	85	"	"	"	Gilt	15	"	"	"
403,001 " 403,500	94	"	O. F.	"	"	9	"	"	7
403,501 " 404,000	86	"	"	"	Nickel	15	"	"	"
404,001 " 404,300	60	"	"	"	Nick.& Gilt	11	"	"	"
404,301 " 405,000	66	"	"	"	Nickel	17	"	"	"
405,001 " 405,500	86	"	"	"	"	15	"	"	"
405,501 " 406,000	83	"	Htg.	"	"	"	"	"	8
406,001 " 407,000	69	"	"	"	"	11	"	"	"
407,001 " 407,500	68	"	"	"	Gilt	"	"	"	"
407,501 " 408,000	85	"	"	"	"	15	"	"	"
408,001 " 408,500	93	"	"	"	"	9	"	"	"
408,501 " 409,000	94	"	O. F.	"	"	"	"	"	7
409,001 " 410,000	69	"	Htg.	"	Nickel	11	"	"	8
410,001 " 410,500	93	"	"	"	Gilt	9	"	"	"
410,501 " 411,000	68	"	"	"	"	11	"	"	"
411,001 " 411,500	94	"	O. F.	"	"	9	"	"	7
411,501 " 412,000	67	"	"	"	"	11	"	"	"
412,001 " 412,500	86	"	"	"	Nickel	15	"	"	"
412,501 " 413,000	69	"	Htg.	"	"	11	"	"	8
413,001 " 414,000	93	"	"	"	Gilt	9	"	"	"
414,001 " 415,000	94	"	O. F.	"	"	"	"	"	7
415,001 " 415,200	81	"	Htg.	"	Plain	17	"	"	8
415,201 " 415,500	83	"	"	"	Nickel	15	"	"	"
415,501 " 415,600	80	"	"	"	Spot Gilt	17	"	"	"
415,601 " 416,000	82	"	"	"	Plain	"	"	"	"
416,001 " 416,100	61	"	O. F.	"	....	"	"	"	7
416,101 " 416,500	86	"	"	"	Nickel	15	"	"	"
416,501 " 417,000	62	"	"	"	Plain	17	"	"	"
417,001 " 417,500	66	"	"	"	Nickel	11	"	"	"
417,501 " 418,000	83	"	Htg.	"	"	17	"	"	8
418,001 " 419,000	93	"	"	"	Gilt	9	"	"	"
419,001 " 419,500	94	"	"	"	"	"	"	"	"
419,501 " 420,500	153	6	"	¾ Pl.	Nickel	11	"	"	2
420,501 " 421,500	161	"	"	"	Gilt	"	"	"	"
421,501 " 422,500	162	"	"	"	"	9	"	"	"
422,501 " 423,000	66	18	O. F.	F. Pl.	Nickel	11	"	"	7
423,001 " 424,000	93	"	Htg.	"	Gilt	9	"	"	8
424,001 " 425,000	69	"	"	"	Nickel	11	"	"	"
425,001 " 425,500	94	"	O. F.	"	Gilt	9	"	"	7
425,501 " 426,000	66	"	"	"	Nickel	11	"	"	"
426,001 " 427,000	83	"	Htg.	"	"	15	"	"	8
427,001 " 428,000	69	"	"	"	"	11	"	"	"
428,001 " 429,000	66	"	O. F.	"	"	"	"	"	7
429,001 " 430,000	83	"	Htg.	"	"	15	"	"	8
430,001 " 431,000	68	"	"	"	Gilt	11	"	"	"
431,001 " 431,500	66	"	O. F.	"	Nickel	"	"	"	7
431,501 " 432,000	82	"	Htg.	"	Plain	17	"	"	8
432,001 " 433,000	67	"	O. F.	"	Gilt	11	"	"	7
433,001 " 433,100	83	"	Htg.	"	Nickel	15	"	"	8
433,101 " 433,140	82a	"	"	"	"	"	"	"	"
433,141 " 433,400	82	"	"	"	"	"	"	"	"
433,401 " 433,500	82	"	"	"	"	17	"	"	"
433,501 " 433,600	83	"	"	"	"	15	"	"	"
433,601 " 433,700	82	"	"	"	Plain	17	"	"	"
433,701 " 433,750	80	"	"	"	Spot Gilt	"	"	"	"
433,751 " 433,800	81	"	"	"	Plain	"	"	"	"
433,801 " 434,000	83	"	"	"	Nickel	15	"	"	"
434,001 " 434,500	69	"	"	"	"	"	"	"	"

The Rockford Watch Company, Ltd.

Number and Grade of Movement	GRADE	Size	Style		Jewels	Wind	Sett	Model
434,501 to 434,600	86	18	O.F.	F. Pl.	Nickel	15	Stem	Lever	7
434,601 " 434,700	62	"	.	"	Plain	17	"	"	"
434,701 " 435,000	86	"	O. F.	"	Nickel	15	"	"	"
435,001 " 435,500	85	"	Htg.	"	Gilt	"	"	"	8
435,501 " 436,000	94	"	O. F.	"	"	9	"	"	7
436,001 " 436,100	67	"	"	"	"	11	"	"	
436,101 " 436,200	89	"	"	"	"	15	"	"	
436,201 " 436,300	67	"	"	"	"	11	"	"	
436,301 " 437,000	89	"	"	"	"	"	"	"	
437,001 " 437,800	82	"	Htg.	"	Nickel	17	"	"	8
437,801 " 438,000	81	"	"	"	Plain	"	"	"	
438,001 " 438,500	83	"	"	"	"	15	"	"	
438,501 " 438,900	62	"	O. F.	"	"	17	"	"	7
438,901 " 439,000	86	"	"	"	Nickel	15	"	"	
439,001 " 439,500	82	"	Htg.	"	"	17	"	"	8
439,501 " 439,550	80	"	"	"	Nick.& Gilt	"	"	"	
439,551 " 439,650	82a	"	"	"	"	"	"	"	
439,651 " 439,700	81	"	"	"	Nickel	"	"	"	
439,701 " 439,750	62a	"	O. F.	"	"	"	"	"	7
439,751 " 439,850	62	"	"	"	"	"	"	"	
439,851 " 439,900	61	"	"	"	"	"	"	"	
439,901 " 439,950	86	"	"	"	"	15	"	"	
439,951 " 440,000	62a	"	"	"	"	17	"	"	
440,001 " 441,000	93	"	Htg.	"	Gilt	9	"	"	8
441,001 " 441,500	62	"	O. F.	"	Nickel	17	"	"	7
441,501 " 442,000	83	"	Htg.	"	Plain	15	"	"	8
442,001 " 442,050	80	"	"	"	Nick.& Gilt	17	"	"	
424,051 " 442,150	81	"	"	"	Plain	"	"	"	
442,151 " 442,500	82	"	"	"	Nickel	"	"	"	
500,001 " 500,054	930	"	O. F.	"	"	"	"	"	9
500,055	935	"	"	"	"	"	"	"	"
500,056 to 500,250	930	"	"	"	"	"	"	"	7
500,251 " 500,260	920	"	"	"	"	"	"	"	9
500,261 " 500,300	930	"	"	"	"	"	"	"	"
500,301 " 500,400	935	"	"	"	"	"	"	"	10
500,401 " 500,800	830	"	Htg.	"	"	"	"	"	"
500,801 " 500,900	835	"	"	"	"	"	"	"	"
500,901 " 501,100	830	"	"	"	"	"	"	"	"
501,101 " 501,900	835	"	"	"	"	"	"	"	"
501,901 " 502,400	830	"	"	"	"	"	"	"	"
502,401 " 502,481	930	"	O. F.	"	"	"	"	"	9
502,482 " 502,489	935	"	"	"	"	"	"	"	"
502,490 " 502 592	930	"	"	"	"	"	"	"	"
502,593	935	"	"	"	"	"	"	"	"
502,594 to 502,700	930	"	"	"	"	"	"	"	"
502,701 " 503,200	935	"	"	"	"	"	"	"	"
503,201 " 503,460	830	"	Htg.	"	"	"	"	"	10
503,461 " 503,470	820	"	"	"	"	"	"	"	8
503,471 " 503,483	830	"	"	"	"	"	"	"	10
503,484 " 503,489	820	"	"	"	"	"	"	"	8
503,490 " 503,520	830	"	"	"	"	"	"	"	10
503,521 " 503,531	830	"	"	"	"	"	"	"	8
503,532 " 503,536	830	"	"	"	"	"	"	"	10
503,537 " 503,540	820	"	"	"	"	"	"	"	8
503,541 " 503,550	825	"	"	"	"	"	"	"	10
503,551 " 503,610	830	"	"	"	"	"	"	"	"
503,611 " 503,620	820	"	"	"	"	"	"	"	8
503,621 " 503,700	830	"	"	"	"	"	"	"	10
503,701 " 504,000	835	"	"	"	"	"	"	"	"
504,001 " 504,100	830	"	"	"	"	"	"	"	"
504,101 " 505,150	835	"	"	"	"	"	"	"	"
505,151 " 505,200	830	"	"	"	"	"	"	"	"
505,201 " 505,300	835	"	"	"	"	"	"	"	"
505,301 " 505,350	830	"	"	"	"	"	"	"	"
505,351 " 505,360	835	"	"	"	"	"	"	"	"
505,361 " 505,370	830	"	"	"	"	"	"	"	"
505,371 " 505,398	835	"	"	"	"	"	"	"	"
505,399 " 505,400	830	"	"	"	"	"	"	"	"
505,401 " 505,700	835	"	"	"	"	"	"	"	"
505,701 " 506,000	830	"	"	"	"	"	"	"	"
506,001 " 506,800	935	"	O. F.	"	"	"	"	"	9
506,801 " 506,810	910	"	"	"	"	21	"	"	"
506,811 " 507,600	930	"	"	"	"	17	"	"	"
507,601 " 507,900	830	"	Htg.	"	"	"	"	"	10
507,901 " 508,500	835	"	"	"	"	"	"	"	"
508,501 " 509,000	830	"	"	"	"	"	"	"	"
509,001 " 509,100	820	"	"	"	"	"	"	"	8
509,101 " 509,700	925	"	O. F.	"	"	"	"	"	9
509,701 " 509,729	920	"	"	"	"	"	"	"	7
509,730	915	"	"	"	"	"	"	"	"
509,731 to 509,759	920	"	"	"	"	"	"	"	"
509,760	915	"	"	"	"	"	"	"	"
509,761 to 509,791	920	"	"	"	"	"	"	"	"
509,792	915	"	"	"	"	"	"	"	"
509,793 to 509,900	920	"	"	"	"	"	"	"	"
509,901 " 510,200	810	"	Htg.	"	"	21	"	"	10
510,201 " 510,700	825	"	"	"	"	17	"	"	"
510,701 " 511,300	830	"	"	"	"	"	"	"	"
511,301 " 511,600	835	"	"	"	"	"	"	"	"

The Rockford Watch Company, Ltd.

Number and Grade of Movement	GRADE	Size	Style			Jewels	Wind	Sett	Model
511,601 to 512,500	935	18	O. F.	F. Pl.	Nickel	17	Stem	Lever	9
512,501 " 512,600	910	"	"	"	"	21	"	"	"
512,601 " 512,700	920	"	"	"	"	17	"	"	7
512,701 " 512,800	930	"	"	"	"	"	"	"	9
512,801 " 512,850	920	"	"	"	"	"	"	"	7
512,851 " 512,872	830	"	Htg.	"	"	"	"	"	10
512,873	915	"	O. F.	"	"	"	"	"	7
512,874 to 512,875	920	"	"	"	"	"	"	"	7
512,876	915	"	"	"	"	"	"	"	"
512,877 to 512,900	920	"	"	"	"	"	"	"	"
512,901 " 513,101	830	"	Htg.	"	"	"	"	"	10
513,102 " 513,181	820	"	"	"	"	"	"	"	8
513,182	815	"	"	"	"	"	"	"	"
513,183 to 513,251	820	"	"	"	"	"	"	"	"
513,252 " 513,259	810	"	"	"	"	21	"	"	10
513,260 " 513,300	820	"	"	"	"	17	"	"	8
513,301 " 513,400	830	"	"	"	"	"	"	"	10
513,401 " 513,500	835	"	"	"	"	"	"	"	"
513,501 " 513,600	830	"	"	"	"	"	"	"	"
513,601 " 513,900	835	"	"	"	"	"	"	"	"
513,901 " 514,000	930	"	O. F.	"	"	"	"	"	9
514,001 " 514,100	935	"	"	"	"	"	"	"	"
514,101 " 514,150	825	"	Htg.	"	"	"	"	"	10
514,151 " 514,500	835	"	"	"	"	"	"	"	"
514,501 " 514,600	930	"	O. F.	"	"	"	"	"	9
514,601 " 514,900	935	"	"	"	"	"	"	"	"
514,901 " 515,100	835	"	Htg.	"	"	"	"	"	10
515,101 " 515,400	935	"	O. F.	"	"	"	"	"	9
515,401 " 515,500	810	"	Htg.	"	"	21	"	"	10
515,501 " 515,600	910	"	O. F.	"	"	"	"	"	9
515,601 " 516,000	935	"	"	"	"	17	"	"	"
516,001 " 516,300	925	"	"	"	"	"	"	"	"
516,301 " 516,400	935	"	"	"	"	"	"	"	"
516,401 " 516,500	925	"	"	"	"	"	"	"	"
516,501 " 517,200	825	"	Htg.	"	"	"	"	"	10
517,201 " 519,300	910	"	O. F.	"	"	21	"	"	9
519,301 " 519,400	900	"	"	"	"	24	"	"	"
519,401 " 519,500	800	"	Htg.	"	"	"	"	"	10
519,501 " 519,600	805	"	"	"	"	21	"	"	"
519,601 " 519,700	905	"	O. F.	"	"	"	"	"	9
519,701 " 520,000	835	"	Htg.	"	"	17	"	"	10
520,001 " 521,000	935	"	O. F.	"	"	"	"	"	9
521,001 " 522,000	870	"	Htg.	"	"	7	"	"	10
522,001 " 522,400	970	"	O. F.	"	"	"	"	"	9
522,401 " 523,500	870	"	Htg.	"	"	"	"	"	10
523,501 " 524,800	970	"	O. F.	"	"	"	"	"	9
524,801 " 525,000	935	"	"	"	"	17	"	"	"
525,001 " 525,100	900	"	"	"	"	24	"	"	"
525,101 " 525,400	935	"	"	"	"	17	"	"	"
525,401 " 525,900	925	"	"	"	"	"	"	"	"
525,901 " 526,700	825	"	Htg.	"	"	"	"	"	10
526,701 " 526,900	930	"	O. F.	"	"	"	"	"	9
526,901 " 527,900	935	"	"	"	"	"	"	"	"
527,901 " 528,800	930	"	"	"	"	"	"	"	"
528,801 " 529,800	935	"	"	"	"	"	"	"	"
529,801 " 530,800	925	"	"	"	"	"	"	"	"
530,801 " 531,800	835	"	Htg.	"	"	"	"	"	10
531,801 " 532,450	825	"	"	"	"	"	"	"	"
532,451 " 532,500	835	"	"	"	"	"	"	"	"
532,501 " 533,400	925	"	O. F.	"	"	"	"	"	9
533,401 " 534,000	935	"	"	"	"	"	"	"	"
534,001 " 534,012	920	"	"	"	"	"	"	"	7
534,013	915	"	"	"	"	"	"	"	"
534,014 to 534,035	920	"	"	"	"	"	"	"	"
534,036	915	"	"	"	"	"	"	"	"
534,037 to 534,039	920	"	"	"	"	"	"	"	"
534,040	915	"	"	"	"	"	"	"	"
534,041 to 534,064	920	"	"	"	"	"	"	"	"
534,065	915	"	"	"	"	"	"	"	"
534,066 to 534,112	920	"	"	"	"	"	"	"	"
534,113 " 534,115	915	"	"	"	"	"	"	"	"
534,116 " 534,119	920	"	"	"	"	"	"	"	"
534,120	915	"	"	"	"	"	"	"	"
534,121	920	"	"	"	"	"	"	"	"
534,122 to 534,123	915	"	"	"	"	"	"	"	"
534,124 " 534,127	920	"	"	"	"	"	"	"	"
534,128	915	"	"	"	"	"	"	"	"
534,129 to 534,130	920	"	"	"	"	"	"	"	"
534,131	915	"	"	"	"	"	"	"	"
534,132	920	"	"	"	"	"	"	"	"
534,133	915	"	"	"	"	"	"	"	"
534,134	920	"	"	"	"	"	"	"	"
534,135	915	"	"	"	"	"	"	"	"
534,136 to 534,138	920	"	"	"	"	"	"	"	"
534,139	915	"	"	"	"	"	"	"	"
534,140 to 534,144	920	"	"	"	"	"	"	"	"
534,145	915	"	"	"	"	"	"	"	"
534,146 to 534,147	920	"	"	"	"	"	"	"	"
534,148	915	"	"	"	"	"	"	"	"

The Rockford Watch Company, Ltd.

Number and Grade of Movement	GRADE	Size	Style			Jewels	Wind	Sett	Model
534,149....	920	18	O. F.	F. Pl.	Nickel	17	Stem	Lever	7
534,150....	915	"	"	"	"	"	"	"	"
534,151 to 534,155	920	"	"	"	"	"	"	"	"
534,156 " 534,157	915	"	"	"	"	"	"	"	"
534,158 " 534,163	920	"	"	"	"	"	"	"	"
534,164....	915	"	"	"	"	"	"	"	"
534,165 to 534,171	920	"	"	"	"	"	"	"	"
534,172....	915	"	"	"	"	"	"	"	"
534,173....	920	"	"	"	"	"	"	"	"
534,174....	915	"	"	"	"	"	"	"	"
534,175....	920	"	"	"	"	"	"	"	"
534,176 to 534,179	915	"	"	"	"	"	"	"	"
534,180 " 534,182	920	"	"	"	"	"	"	"	"
534,183....	915	"	"	"	"	"	"	"	"
534,184....	920	"	"	"	"	"	"	"	"
534,185....	915	"	"	"	"	"	"	"	"
534,186 to 534,188	920	"	"	"	"	"	"	"	"
534,189....	915	"	"	"	"	"	"	"	"
534,190 to 534,196	920	"	"	"	"	"	"	"	"
534,197....	915	"	"	"	"	"	"	"	"
534,198....	920	"	"	"	"	"	"	"	"
534,199....	915	"	"	"	"	"	"	"	"
534,200....	920	"	"	"	"	"	"	"	"
534,401 to 534,600	930	"	"	"	"	"	"	"	9
534,601 " 535,200	910	"	"	"	"	21	"	"	"
535,201 " 535,400	900	"	"	"	"	24	"	"	"
535,401 " 535,600	910	"	"	"	"	21	"	"	"
535,601 " 535,700	800	"	Htg.	"	"	24	"	"	10
535,701 " 535,800	805	"	"	"	"	21	"	"	"
535,801 " 536,300	910	"	O. F.	"	"	"	"	"	9
536,301 " 536,600	930	"	"	"	"	17	"	"	"
536,601 " 536,700	945	"	"	"	"	21	"	"	Special
536,701 " 537,400	910	"	"	"	"	"	"	"	9
537,401 " 539,400	935	"	"	"	"	17	"	"	"
539,401 " 540,400	910	"	"	"	"	21	"	"	"
540,401 " 541,400	935	"	"	"	"	17	"	"	"
541,401 " 541,500	905	"	"	"	"	21	"	"	"
541,501 " 542,000	835	"	Htg.	"	"	17	"	"	10
542,001 " 542,300	800	"	"	"	"	24	"	"	"
542,301 " 542,500	810	"	"	"	"	21	"	"	"
542,501 " 542,700	900	"	O. F.	"	"	24	"	"	9
542,701 " 542,800	905	"	"	"	"	21	"	"	"
542,801 " 543,300	805	"	Htg.	"	"	"	"	"	10
543,301 " 543,500	905	"	O. F.	"	"	"	"	"	9
543,501 " 544,000	835	"	Htg.	"	"	17	"	"	10
544,001 " 544,100	560	16	"	¾ Pl.	"	"	"	"	3
544,101 " 544,200	570	"	"	"	"	"	"	"	"
544,201 " 544,400	560	"	"	"	"	"	"	"	"
544,401 " 544,500	530	"	"	"	"	21	"	"	"
544,501 " 544,800	550	"	"	"	"	17	"	"	4
544,801 " 545,000	540	"	"	"	"	21	"	"	"
545,001 " 545,500	535	"	O. F.	"	"	"	"	"	2
545,501 " 546,500	570	"	Htg.	"	"	17	"	"	3
546,501 " 546,600	540	"	"	"	"	21	"	"	4
546,601 " 546,700	500	"	"	"	"	"	"	"	"
546,701 " 546,800	510	"	"	"	"	"	"	"	"
546,801 " 546,900	520	"	"	"	"	"	"	"	"
546,901 " 547,000	530	"	"	"	"	"	"	"	3
547,001 " 548,000	560	"	"	"	"	17	"	"	"
548,001 " 549,000	565	"	O. F.	"	"	"	"	"	2
549,001 " 550,000	575	"	"	"	"	"	"	"	"
550,001 " 550,500	560	"	Htg.	"	"	"	"	"	3
550,501 " 550,600	515	"	O. F.	"	"	21	"	"	5
550,601 " 550,700	525	"	"	"	"	"	"	"	"
550,701 " 550,900	545	"	"	"	"	"	"	"	"
550,901 " 551,200	555	"	"	"	"	17	"	"	"
551,201 " 551,700	530	"	Htg.	"	"	21	"	"	3
551,701 " 552,700	575	"	O. F.	"	"	17	"	"	2
552,701 " 553,200	565	"	"	"	"	"	"	"	"
553,201 " 554,200	570	"	Htg.	"	"	"	"	"	3
554,201 " 554,700	565	"	O. F.	"	"	"	"	"	2
554,701 " 554,900	555	"	"	"	"	21	"	"	5
554,901 " 554,920	535	"	"	"	"	"	"	"	2
554,921 " 554,927	570	"	Htg.	"	"	17	"	"	3
554,928 " 554,930	575	"	O. F.	"	"	"	"	"	2
554,931 " 554,940	560	"	Htg.	"	"	"	"	"	3
554,941 " 554,960	605	"	O. F.	"	"	11	"	Pend.	Special
554,961....		"	"	"	Gilt	"	"	"	"
554,962....		"	"	"	"	"	"	"	"
554,963....		"	"	"	"	"	"	"	"
554,964....		"	Htg.	"	Nickel	17	"	"	"
554,965....		"	"	"	Gilt	"	"	"	"
554,966....		"	"	"	"	"	"	"	"
554,967....		"	"	"	Nickel	"	"	"	"
554,968....		"	"	"	Gilt	15	"	"	"
554,699....		"	O. F.	"	....	"	"	"	"
554,970....		"	"	"	....	"	"	"	"
554,971....		"	Htg.	"	....	"	"	"	"
554,972....		"	"	"	....	"	"	"	"

The Rockford Watch Company, Ltd.

Number and Grade of Movement	GRADE	Size		Style		Jewels	Wind	Sett	Model
554,973		16	Htg.	¾ Pl.	Gilt	11	Stem	Pend.	Special
554,974	935	18	O. F.	F. Pl.	Nickel	17	"	Lever	9
554,975		16	Htg.	¾ Pl.	Nickel	11	"	Pend.	Special
554,976		"	"	"	....	"	"	"	"
554,977		"	"	"		"	"	"	"
554,978		"	O. F.	"	Nickel	17	"	"	"
554,979		"	"	"	"	"	"	"	"
554,981 to 554,992	25	18	"	F. Pl.	"	25	"	Lever	"
555,001 " 556 000	560	16	Htg.	¾ Pl.	"	17	"	"	3
556,001 " 558,000	575	"	O. F.	"	"	"	"	"	2
558,001 " 558,500	550	"	Htg.	"	"	"	"	"	4
558,501 " 559,000	540	"	"	"	"	21	"	"	"
559,001 " 560,000	560	"	"	"	"	17	"	"	3
560,001 " 560,500	545	"	O. F.	"	"	21	"	"	5
560,501 " 561,000	555	"	"	"	"	17	"	"	"
561,001 " 562,000	835	18	Htg.	F. Pl.	"	"	"	"	10
562,001 " 563,000	935	"	O. F.	"	"	"	"	"	9
563,001 " 565,000	570	16	Htg.	¾ Pl.	"	"	"	"	3
565,001 " 566,000	575	"	O. F.	"	"	"	"	"	2
566,001 " 566,500	918	18	"	F. Pl.	"	24	"	"	9
566,501 " 566,600	935	"	"	"	"	17	"	"	"
566,601 " 566,800	935	"	"	"	"	"	"	"	"
566,801 " 566,900	830	"	Htg.	"	"	"	"	"	10
566,901 " 566,940	500	16	"	¾ Pl.	"	21	"	"	4
566,941 " 567,000	501	"	"	"	"	"	"	"	"
567,001 " 568,000	575	"	O. F.	"	"	17	"	"	2
568,001 " 570,000	570	"	Htg.	"	"	"	"	"	3
570,001 " 571,000	575	"	O. F.	"	"	"	"	"	2
571,001 " 571,300	545	"	"	"	"	21	"	"	5
571,301 " 571,500	575	"	"	"	"	17	"	"	2
571,501 " 571,530	505	"	"	"	"	21	"	"	5
571,531 " 571,600	515	"	"	"	"	"	"	"	"
571,601 " 571,700	570	"	Htg.	"	"	17	"	"	3
571,701 " 571,900	575	"	O. F.	"	"	"	"	"	2
571,901 " 572,000	585	"	"	"	"	15	"	"	"
572,001 " 572,700	565	"	"	"	"	17	"	"	"
572,701 " 573,000	560	"	Htg.	"	"	"	"	"	3
573,001 " 573,500	810	18	"	F. Pl.	"	21	"	"	10
573,501 " 573,510	590	16	"	¾ Pl.	"	11	"	"	3
573,511 " 574,000	584	"	"	"	"	15	"	"	"
574,001 " 574,500	905	18	O. F.	F. Pl.	"	21	"	"	9
574,501 " 575,000	835	"	Htg.	"	"	17	"	"	10
575,001 " 577,000	570	16	"	¾ Pl.	"	"	"	"	3
577,001 " 577,500	584	"	"	"	"	15	"	"	"
577,501 " 577,800	565	"	O. F.	"	"	17	"	"	2
577,801 " 577,900	520	"	Htg.	"	"	21	"	"	4
577,901 " 578,000	525	"	O. F.	"	"	"	"	"	5
578,001 " 579,150	835	18	Htg.	F. Pl.	"	17	"	"	10
579,201 " 579,370	935	"	O. F.	"	"	"	"	"	9
579,401 " 579,500	570	16	Htg.	¾ Pl.	"	"	"	"	3
579,501 " 579,600	575	"	O. F.	"	"	"	"	"	2
579,601 " 579,700	560	"	Htg.	"	"	"	"	"	3
579,701 " 579,735	565	"	O. F.	"	"	"	"	:	2
579,801 " 579,900	830	18	Htg.	F. Pl.	"	"	"	"	10
579,901 " 580,000	930	"	O. F.	"	"	"	"	"	9
580,001 " 580,200	560	16	Htg.	¾ Pl.	"	"	"	"	3
580,201 " 580,300	565	"	O. F.	"	"	"	"	"	2
580,301 " 580,500	570	"	Htg.	"	"	"	"	"	3
580,501 " 580,600	575	"	O. F.	"	"	"	"	"	2
580,601 " 581,000	930	18	"	F. Pl.	"	"	"	"	9
581,001 " 582,000	585	16	"	¾ Pl.	"	15	"	"	2
582,001 " 583,000	584	"	Htg.	"	"	"	"	"	3
583,001 " 584,000	560	"	"	"	"	17	"	"	"
584,001 " 585,000	584	"	"	"	"	15	"	"	"
585,001 " 585,500	935	18	O. F.	F. Pl.	"	17	"	"	9
585,501 " 585,600	515	16	"	¾ Pl.	"	21	"	"	5
585,601 " 585,700	525	"	"	"	"	"	"	"	"
585,701 " 585,800	830	18	Htg.	F. Pl.	"	17	"	"	10
585,801 " 585,900	930	"	O. F.	"	"	"	"	"	9
585,901 " 586,000	835	"	Htg.	"	"	"	"	"	10
586,001 " 588,000	584	16	"	¾ Pl.	"	15	"	"	3
588,001 " 590,000	835	18	"	"	"	17	"	"	10
590,001 " 591,000	570	16	"	¾ Pl.	"	"	"	"	3
591,001 " 592,000	584	"	"	"	"	15	"	"	"
592,001 " 593,000	835	18	"	F. Pl.	"	17	"	"	10
593,001 " 593,100	560	16	"	¾ Pl.	"	"	"	"	3
593,101 " 593,200	570	"	"	"	"	"	"	"	"
593,201 " 593,300	100	"	"	"	"	21	"	Pend.	Special
593,301 " 593,400	101	"	O. F.	"	"	"	"	"	"
593,401 " 593,600	925	18	"	F. Pl.	"	17	"	Lever	9
593,601 " 593,700	835	"	Htg.	"	"	"	"	"	10
593,701 " 593,800	825	"	"	"	"	"	"	"	"
593,801 " 593,900	520	16	"	¾ Pl.	"	21	"	"	4
593,901 " 594,000	505	"	O. F.	"	"	"	"	"	5
594,001 " 596,000	590	"	Htg.	"	"	11	"	Pend.	3
596,001 " 597,000	595	"	O. F.	"	"	"	"	"	2
597,001 " 598,000	590	"	Htg.	"	"	"	"	"	3
598,001 " 599,000	586	"	"	"	"	15	"	"	5
599,001 " 599,500	587	"	O. F.	"	"	"	"	"	2

The Rockford Watch Company, Ltd.

Number and Grade of Movement	GRADE	Size	Style			Jewels	Wind	Sett	Model
			(case)	(plate)	(metal)				
599,501 to 599,502	575	16	O. F.	¾ Pl.	Nickel	17	Stem	Lever	2
599,503 " 599,504	565	"	"	"	"	"	"	"	"
599,505	575	"	"	"	"	"	"	Pend.	"
599,506 to 600,000	587	"	"	"	"	15	"	Pend.	"
600,001 " 601,000	935	18	"	F. Pl.	"	17	"	Lever	9
601,001 " 602,000	590	16	Htg.	¾ Pl.	"	11	"	Pend.	3
602,001 " 603,000	595	"	O. F.	"	"	"	"	"	2
603,001 " 605,000	561	"	Htg.	"	"	17	"	"	4
605,001 " 605,700	573	"	O. F.	"	"	"	"	"	5
605,701 " 605,850	845	18	Htg.	F. Pl.	"	21	"	Lever	Special
605,851 " 605,900	945	"	O. F.	"	"	"	"	"	"
605,901 " 605,950	540	16	Htg.	¾ Pl.	"	"	"	"	4
606,001 " 608,000	935	18	O. F.	F. Pl.	"	17	"	"	9
608,001 " 609,000	572	16	Htg.	¾ Pl.	"	"	"	Pend.	4
609,001 " 610,000	566	"	O. F.	"	"	"	"	"	5
610,001 " 613,000	605	"	"	"	"	11	"	"	2
613,001 " 614,000	587	"	"	"	"	15	"	"	"
614,001 " 615,000	600	"	Htg.	"	"	11	"	"	3
615,001 " 617,000	605	"	O. F.	"	"	"	"	"	2
617,001 " 617,500	586	"	Htg.	"	"	15	"	"	3
617,501 " 617,800	845	18	"	F. Pl.	"	21	"	Lever	Special
617,801 " 618,000	810	"	"	"	"	"	"	"	10
618,001 " 618,500	587	16	O. F.	¾ Pl.	"	15	"	Pend.	2
618,501 " 618,600	578	"	Htg.	"	"	17	"	"	3
618,601 " 618,700	579	"	O. F.	"	"	"	"	"	2
618,701 " 618,800	600	"	Htg.	"	"	11	"	"	3
618,801 " 618,900	586	"	"	"	"	15	"	"	"
618,901 " 618,950	120	"	"	"	"	17	"	"	Special
618,951 " 619,000	125	"	O. F.	"	"	"	"	"	"
619,001 " 619,300	525	"	"	"	"	21	"	Lever	5
619,301 " 619,700	600	"	Htg.	"	"	11	"	Pend.	3
619,701 " 619,900	565	"	O. F.	"	"	17	"	Lever	"
619,901 " 620,000	101	"	"	"	"	21	"	Pend.	Special
620,001 " 621,000	545	"	"	"	"	"	"	Lever	5
621,001 " 622,000	935	18	"	F. Pl.	"	17	"	"	9
622,001 " 622,300	160	0	Htg.	¾ Pl.	"	15	"	Pend.	1
622,301 " 622,350	140	"	"	"	"	17	"	"	"
622,351 " 622,500	150	"	"	"	"	"	"	"	"
622,501 " 623,000	160	"	"	"	"	15	"	"	"
623,001 " 623,100	200	18	O. F.	F. Pl.	"	17	"	Lever	10
623,101 " 623,500	605	16	"	¾ Pl.	"	11	"	Pend.	2
623,501 " 624,000	160	0	Htg.	"	"	15	"	"	1
624,001 " 624,200	205	18	O. F.	F. Pl.	"	17	"	Lever	10
624,201 " 624,300	945	"	"	"	"	21	"	"	Special
624,301 " 624,400	930	"	"	"	"	17	"	"	9
624,401 " 624,450	110	16	Htg.	¾ Pl.	"	"	"	Pend.	Special
624,451 " 624,500	115	"	O. F.	"	"	"	"	"	"
624,501 " 624,525	130	"	Htg.	"	"	"	"	"	"
624,526 " 624,550	135	"	O. F.	"	Gilt	"	"	"	"
624,601 " 624,800	540	"	Htg.	"	Nickel	21	"	Lever	4
625,001 " 625,400	400	"	"	"	"	17	"	Pend.	"
626,001 " 626,200	405	"	"	"	"	21	"	Lever	5
626,201 " 626,400	510	"	O. F.	"	"	"	"	"	4
626,401 " 626,600	515	"	Htg.	"	"	"	"	"	5
626,601 " 626,700	520	"	"	"	"	"	"	"	4
626,701 " 626,900	525	"	O. F.	"	"	"	"	"	5
626,901 " 627,000	845	18	Htg.	F. Pl.	"	"	"	"	Special
627,001 " 627,300	572	16	"	¾ Pl.	"	17	"	Pend.	4
628,001 " 628,100	500	"	"	"	"	21	"	Lever	"
628,101 " 628,300	520	"	"	"	"	"	"	"	5
628,301 " 628,500	515	"	O. F.	"	"	"	"	"	5
628,501 " 628,600	505	"	"	"	"	"	"	"	5
628,601 " 628,800	510	"	Htg.	"	"	"	"	"	4
628,801 " 628,950	100	"	"	"	"	"	"	Pend.	Special
628,951 " 629,000	101	"	O. F.	"	"	"	"	"	"
629,001 " 630,000	935	18	F. Pl.	"	"	17	"	Lever	9
630,001 " 630,600	835	"	Htg.	"	"	"	"	"	10
630,601 " 630,700	162	0	"	¾ Pl.	"	"	"	Pend.	1
630,701 " 630,800	150	"	"	"	"	"	"	"	"
630,801 " 631,000	160	"	"	"	"	15	"	"	"
631,001 " 632,000	586	16	"	"	"	"	"	"	3
632,001 " 632,500	825	18	"	F. Pl.	"	17	"	Lever	10
633,001 " 633,500	925	"	O. F.	"	"	"	"	"	9
634,001 " 635,000	587	16	"	¾ Pl.	"	15	"	Pend.	2
635,001 " 636,000	935	18	"	F. Pl.	"	17	"	Lever	9
636,001 " 636,500	160	0	Htg.	¾ Pl.	"	15	"	Pend.	1
636,501 " 636,600	160	"	"	"	"	17	"	"	"
636,601 " 638,000	150	"	"	"	"	15	"	"	"
638,001 " 639,000	160	"	"	"	"	15	"	"	"
639,001 " 640,000	600	16	"	"	"	11	"	"	3
640,001 " 641,000	160	0	"	"	"	15	"	Pend.	1
641,001 " 642,000	162	"	"	"	"	"	"	"	"
642,001 " 643,000	610	16	"	"	"	7	"	"	Special
643,001 " 644,000	615	"	O. F.	"	"	15	"	"	3
644,001 " 644,500	587	"	"	"	"	17	"	"	2
645,001 " 646,600	142	0	Htg.	"	"	15	"	"	"
646,001 " 647,000	162	"	"	"	"	"	"	"	1
647,001 " 648,000	610	16	"	"	"	7	"	"	Special
648,001 " 649,000	615	"	O. F.	"	"	15	"	"	3
649,001 " 650,000	160	0	Htg.	"	"	15	"	Pend.	1
	605	16	O. F.	"	"	11	"	"	2

The Rockford Watch Company, Ltd.

Number and Grade of Movement		GRADE	Size	Style		Jewels	Wind	Sett	Model
650,001 "	651,000	573	16	O. F.	¾ Pl.	Nickel	17	Stem	Pend.	5
651,001 to	656,000	160	0	Htg.	"	"	15	"	"	1
656,001 "	656,100	152	"	"	"	"	17	"	"	Special
657,001 "	657,200	182	"	"	"	"	7	"	"	"
658,001 "	659,000	600	16	"	"	"	11	"	"	3
659,001 "	659,200	930	18	O. F.	F. Pl.	"	17	"	Lever	9
660,001 "	660,100	910	"	"	"	"	21	"	"	9
661,101 "	661,200	810	"	Htg.	"	"	"	"	"	10
662,001 "	662,600	100	16	"	¾ Pl.	"	"	"	Pend.	Special
663,001 "	663,100	101	"	O. F.	"	"	"	"	"	"
664,001 "	664,100	845	18	Htg.	F. Pl.	"	"	"	Lever	"
665,001 "	665,100	830	"	"	"	"	17	"	"	10
666,001 "	666,100	900	"	O. F.	"	"	24	"	"	9
667,001 "	667,100	905	"	"	"	"	21	"	"	"
668,001 "	669,000	605	16	"	¾ Pl.	"	11	"	Pend.	2
669,001 "	669,100	912	18	"	F. Pl.	Spot Gilt	21	"	Lever	9
670,001 "	670,100	537	16	"	¾ Pl.	"	"	"	"	2
671,001 "	671,300	200	18	"	F. Pl.	Nickel	17	"	"	10
672,001 "	673,000	205	"	"	"	"	"	"	"	"
674,001 "	675,000	405	16	"	¾ Pl.	"	"	"	Pend.	5
675,001 "	675,500	525	"	"	"	"	21	"	Lever	"
676,001 "	677,000	566	"	"	"	"	17	"	Pend.	"
677,001 "	678,000	573	"	"	"	"	"	"	"	"
678,001 "	678,500	586	"	"	"	"	15	"	"	3
679,001 "	680,500	587	"	"	"	"	"	"	"	2
681,001 "	682,000	600	"	Htg.	"	"	11	"	"	3
682,001 "	686,000	605	"	O. F.	"	"	"	"	"	2
686,001 "	693,000	615	"	"	"	"	7	"	"	"
693,001 "	694,000	610	"	Htg.	"	"	"	"	"	3
694,001 "	694,500	935	18	O. F.	F. Pl.	"	17	"	Lever	9
695,001 "	695,500	945	"	"	"	"	21	"	"	Special

(More Serial Numbers and Grade of Movement next page.)

STYLE & NAMES OF U.S.A. HANDS

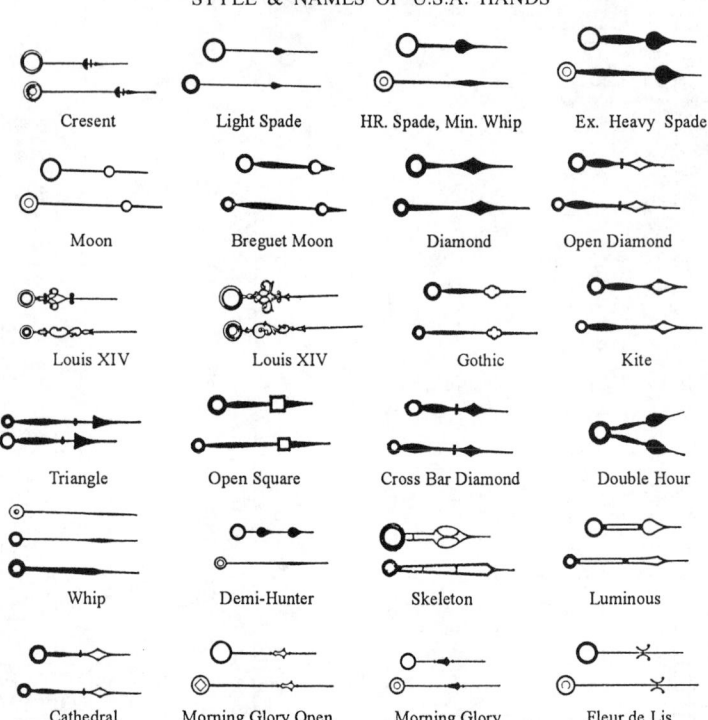

Cresent	Light Spade	HR. Spade, Min. Whip	Ex. Heavy Spade
Moon	Breguet Moon	Diamond	Open Diamond
Louis XIV	Louis XIV	Gothic	Kite
Triangle	Open Square	Cross Bar Diamond	Double Hour
Whip	Demi-Hunter	Skeleton	Luminous
Cathedral	Morning Glory Open	Morning Glory	Fleur de Lis

SERIAL NUMBER — Grade, Size, Style, Jewels, Model #

695501-696000=945,18S.O.F.21J,M#SP.
696001-697000=838,18S.H.C.17J.M#10
697001-698000=938,18S.O.F.17J.M# 9
698001-699000=150, 0S. H.C.17J.M# 1
699001-700000=140, 0S. H.C.17J.M# 1
700001-702100=180, 0S. H.C. 7J.M# 1
702101-703000=160, 0S. H.C.15J.M# 1
703001-703500=170, 0S. H.C.11J.M# 1
703501-704000=160, 0S. H.C.15J.M# 1
704001-704300=935,18S.O.F.17J.M# 9
704301-704400=930,18S.O.F.17J.M# 9
704401-704500=935,18S.O.F.17J.M# 9
704501-704600=930,18S.O.F.17J.M# 9
704601-705000=935,18S.O.F.17J.M# 9
705001-706000=572,16S.H.C.17J.M# 4
706001-707000=600,16S.H.C.11J.M# 3
707001-708000=918,18S.O.F.21J.M# 9
708001-709000=586,16S.O.F.15J.M# 4
709001-710000=587,16S.O.F.15J.M# 3
710001-710100=930,18S.O.F.17J.M# 9
710101-710600=935,18S.O.F.17J.M# 9
710601-710700=930,18S.O.F.17J.M# 9
710701-711000=935,18S.O.F.17J.M# 9
711001-711100=830,18S.H.C.17J.M# 9
711101-711500=835,18S.H.C.17J.M#10
711501-711600=830,18S.H.C.17J.M#10
711601-712000=835,18S.H.C.17J.M#10
712001-712700=573,16S.O.F.17J.M# 5
712701-713000=635,16S.O.F.17J.M# 5
713001-714000=610,16S.O.F. 7J.M#SP.
714001-715000=572,16S.H.C.17J.M# 4
715001-716000=586,16S.O.F.15J.M# 3
716001-717000=587,16S.O.F.15J.M# 2
717001-718000=600,16S.O.F.11J.M# 3
718001-719000=605,16S.O.F.11J.M# 2
719001-720000=615,16S.O.F. 7J.M# 3
720001-721000=610,16S.O.F. 7J.M#SP.
721001-721500=600,16S.H.C.11J.M# 3
721501-722000=586,16S.H.C.15J.M# 3
722501-722700=573,16S.O.F.17J.M# 5
722701-722800=635,16S.O.F.17J.M# 5
722801-722900=573,16S.O.F.17J.M# 5
722901-723000=635,16S.O.F.17J.M# 5
723001-724000=935,18S.O.F.17J.M#10
724001-725000=205,18S.O.F.17J.M# 9
725001-725100=930,18S.O.F.17J.M# 9
725101-726000=935,18S.O.F.17J.M# 9
726001-727000=405,16S.O.F.17J.M# 5
727001-728000=587,16S.O.F.15J.M# 2
728001-728500=573,16S.O.F.17J.M# 5
728501-728600=635,16S.O.F.17J.M# 5
728601-728800=573,16S.O.F.17J.M# 5
728801-729000=635,16S.O.F.17J.M# 5
729001-729800=600,16S.H.C.11J.M# 3
729801-730000=586,16S.O.F.15J.M# 3
730001-730700=610,16S.O.F. 7J.M#SP.
730701-731000=586,16S.O.F.15J.M# 3
731001-732000=615,16S.O.F. 7J.M# 3
732001-732500=162, 0S.H.C.17J.M# 1
732501-733000=150, 0S.H.C.17J.M# 1
733001-734000=572, 6S.H.C.17J.M# 4
734001-735000=586,16S.O.F.15J.M# 2
735001-735200=610,16S.H.C. 7J.M#SP.
735201-736000=586,16S.O.F.15J.M# 2
736001-738000=935,18S.O.F.17J.M# 9
738001-739000=938,18S.O.F.17J.M#10
739001-740000=925,18S.O.F.17J.M# 9
740001-740200=830,18S.H.C.17J.M#10
740201-741000=835,18S.H.C.17J.M#10
741001-741100=600,16S.H.C.11J.M# 3
741101-742000=586,16S.H.C.15J.M# 3
742001-742500=605,16S.O.F.11J.M# 2
742501-743000=587,16S,O,F.15J.M# 2
743001-745000=935,18S.O.F.17J.M# 9
745001-746000=930,18S.O.F.17J.M# 9
746001-747000=586,16S.O.F.15J.M# 2
747001-748000=935,18S.O.F.17J.M# 9
748001-749000=938,18S.O.F.17J.M#10
749001-749600=572,16S.H.C.17J.M# 4
749601-750000=630,16S.H.C.17J.M# 4
750001-750200=573,16S.O.F.17J.M# 5
750201-750600=635,16S.O.F.17J.M# 5
750601-751000=573,16S.O.F.17J.M# 5
751001-751200=605,16S.O.F.15J.M# 2
752001-752100=572,16S.H.C.17J.M# 4
752101-752200=630,16S.H.C.17J.M# 4
752201-753000=573,16S.O.F.17J.M# 4
753001-754000=573,16S.O.F.17J.M# 5
754001-755000=586,16S.H.C.15J.M# 3
755001-756000=587,16S.O.F.15J.M# 2
756001-757000=935,18S.O.F.17J.M# 9
757001-758000=925,18S.O.F.17J.M# 9
758001-759000=150, 0S.H.C.17J.M# 1
759001-759500=572,16S.H.C.17J.M# 4

FROM ROCKFORD PARTS CATALOG 1907 to 1910

SERIAL NUMBER — Grade, Size, Style, Jewels, Model #

759501-756000=620,16S.H.C.21J.M# 5
760001-760500=573,16S.O.F.17J.M# 5
760501-761000=625,16S.O.F.21J.M# 5
761001-762000=160, 0S.H.C.15J.M# 1
762001-762500=400,16S.H.C.17J.M# 4
762501-764000=405,16S.O.F.17J.M# 5
764001-765000=205,18S.O.F.17J.M#10
765001-765500=515,16S.O.F.21J.M# 5
765501-766000=545,16S.O.F.21J.M# 5
760010-767000=930,18S.O.F.17J.M# 9
767001-768000=572,16S.H.C.17J.M# 4
768001-769000=935,18S.O.F.17J.M# 9
769001-770000=918,18S.O.F.21J.M#10
770001-770500=938,18S.O.F.17J.M#10
770501-771000=835,18S.H.C.17J.M#10
771001-772000=586,16S.O.F.15J.M# 3
772001-772100=320,12S.H.C.17J.M# 1
772001-772200=330,12S.H.C.17J.M# 1
772201-772300=310,12S.H.C.17J.M# 1
772301-772400=300,12S.H.C.23J.M# 1
772401-772600=325,12S.O.F.17J.M# 2
772601-772800=335,12S.O.F.17J.M# 2
772801-772900=315,12S.O.F.21J.M# 2
772901-773000=305,12S.O.F.23J.M# 2
773001-773100=300,12S.H.C.23J.M# 1
773101-773200=310,12S.H.C.21J.M# 1
773201-773400=320,12S.H.C.17J.M# 1
773401-773500=305,12S.O.F.23J.M# 2
773501-773600=315,12S.O.F.21J.M# 2
773601-773800=325,12S.O.F.17J.M# 2
773801-774000=330,12S.H.C.17J.M# 1
774001-774500=335,12S.O.F.17J.M# 2
774501-774700=325,12S.O.F.17J.M# 2
774701-774000=330,12S.H.C.17J.M# 1
774901-775000=320,12S.H.C.17J.M# 1
775001-776000=587,16S.O.F.15J.M# 2
776001-777000=630,16S.H.C.17J.M# 5
777001-778000=635,16S.O.F.17J.M# 5
778001-779000=838,18S.H.C.17J.M#10
779001-779500=938,18S.H.C.17J.M#10
779501-780000=935,18S.O.F.17J.M# 9
780001-781000=835,18S.H.C.17J.M#10
781001-782000=545,16S.O.F.21J.M# 5
782001-783000=404,16S.O.F.17J.M# 5
783001-784000=561,16S.H.C.17J.M# 4
784001-785000=930,18S.O.F.17J.M# 9
785001-786000=205,18S.O.F.17J.M# 9
786001-787000=935,18S.O.F.17J.M# 9
787001-787200=310,12S.H.C.21J.M# 1
787201-788000=335,12S.O.F.17J.M# 2
788001-788100=315,12S.O.F.21J.M# 2
788101-789000=335,12S.O.F.17J.M# 2
789001-789100=330,12S.H.C.17J.M# 1
789001-789500=320,12S.H.C.17J.M# 1
789501-790000=330,12S.H.C.17J.M3 1
790001-791000=325,12S.O.F.17J.M# 2
791001-792000=330,12S.H.C.17J.M# 1
792001-792900=335,12S.O.F.17J.M# 2
722901-793000=355,12S.O.F.21J.M# 2
793001-796000=935,18S.O.F.17J.M# 9
796001-797000=930,18S.O.F.17J.M# 9
797001-798000=938,18S.O.F.17J.M# 9
798001-799000=830,18S.H.C.17J.M# 8
799001-800000=587,16S.O.F.15J.M# 2
800001-801000=572,16S.H.C.15J.M# 4
801001-802000=573,16S.O.F.17J.M# 5
802001-802500=573,16S.O.F.17J.M# 5
802501-803000=566,16S.O.F.17J.M# 5
803001-804000=573,16S.O.F.17J.M# 5
804001-805000=150, 0S.H.C.17J.M# 1
805001-806000=335,12S.O.F.17J.M# 2
806001-806100=300,12S.H.C.23J.M# 1
806101-807000=335,12S.O.F.17J.M# 2
807001-807100=305,12S.O.F.23J.M# 2
807101-808000=335,12S.O.F.17J.M# 2
808001-810000=573,16S.O.F.17J.M# 5
810001-811000=572,16S.H.C.17J.M# 4
811001-812000=160, 0S.H.C.15J.M# 1
812001-813000=330,12S.H.C.17J.M# 1
813001-814000=355,12S.O.F.17J.M# 2
814001-814500=350,12S.H.C.17J.M# 1
814501-814600=345,12S.O.F.21J.M# 2
814601-814700=340,12S.O.F.21J.M# 2
814701-815000=350,12S.H.C.17J.M# 1
815001-816000=335,12S.O.F.17J.M# 2
816001-817000=190, 0S.H.C.15J.M# 1
817001-818000=185 0S.H.C.17J.M# 1
818001-819000=335,12S.O.F.17J.M# 2
819001-820000=355,12S.O.F.17J.M# 2
820001-821000=190, 0S.H.C.15J.M# 1
821001-822000=335,12S.H.C.17J.M# 1
822001-823000=350,12S.H.C.17J.M# 1
823001-824000=330,12S.H.C.17J.M# 1

Model 1, 18 size, full plate, hunting, key wind & set.

Model 2, 18 size, full plate, hunting, lever set.

Model 3, 18 size, full plate, hunting, lever set.

Model 4, 18 size, full plate, open face, lever set.

Model 5, 18 size, three-quarter plate, hunting, lever set.

Model 6, 18 size, full plate, hunting, lever set, exposed escapement.

I will respect and appreciate positive sound reliable comments, corrections, improvements or remarks but reserve the right to accept the statement or keep my own observations & views. (*Cooksey*)

Model 7, 18 size, full plate, open face, lever set.

Model 8, 18 size, full plate, hunting, lever set.

Model 9, 18 size, full plate, open face, lever set.

Model 10, 18 size, full plate, hunting, lever set.

Model 1, 16 size, 3/4 plate hunting, lever set.

Model 2, 16 size, three-quarter plate, open face, pendant & lever set.

Model 3, 16 size, three-quarter plate, hunting, pendant & lever set.

Model 4, 16 size, three-quarter plate, bridge, hunting, pendant & lever set.

Model 4 "SPECIAL", 16 size, 3/4 plate, hunting, pendant set.

Model 5, 16 size, three-quarter plate, bridge, open face, pendant & lever set.

Model 1, 12 size, three-quarter plate bridge, hunting, pendant set.

Model 2, 12 size, three-quarter plate bridge, open face, pendant set.

Model 1, 6 & 8 size, three-quarter plate, hunting, lever set.

Model 2, 6 size, three-quarter plate, hunting, lever set.

Model 1, 0 size, three-quarter plate, bridge, hunting, pendant set.

Model 2, 0 size, three-quarter plate, bridge, open face, pendant set.

SAN JOSE WATCH CO.
California 1891

Very few watches were made by the San Jose Watch Co., and very little is known about them. The company purchased the Otay Watch Company and machinery and remaining watch movements. The San Jose Watch Co. produced a few dozen watches. Engraved on a San Jose Watch Co. movement S# 30,656 (First watch manufactured by San Jose Watch Co. November 1891). The San Jose W. Co was sold to Osaka, in Japan.

Grade or Name – Description		Avg	Ex-Fn	Mint
18S, 15J, LS, SW	★ ★ ★	$2,400	$3,200	$5,000

SAN JOSE WATCH CO. movement 18 size 15 jewels, Otay W. Co. material & machinery used to produce movement.

M.S. Smith & Co. movement Freeport style or Model, 18 size, 19 jewels, three-quarter plate, key wind & set.

M. S. SMITH & CO.
Detroit, Michigan 1870 - 1874

Eber B. Ward purchased the M. S. Smith & Co. which was a large jewelry firm. These watches carried the Smith name on them. A Mr. Hoyt was engaged to produce these watches and about 100 were produced before the Freeport Watch Co. purchased the firm. These watches are very similar to the "J.H.Allison" movements.

Grade or Name – Description		Avg	Ex-Fn	Mint
18S, 19J, 3/4, KW, KS, Freeport Model, **18K** case	★ ★ ★ ★	$3,000	$4,000	$7,000
18S, 19J, 3/4, KW, KS, Freeport Model	★ ★ ★ ★	2,000	2,800	5,000
18S, 15J, 3/4, wolf 's tooth -wind, **Swiss, 14K** HC	★	800	1,000	1,300
6S, 15J, KW, KS, HC **18K** case	★	500	700	1,000
6S, 15J, SW	★	200	335	500

M.S. Smith & Co., 18S, 15J, 3/4, wolf 's tooth -wind, **Swiss**, Ca. 1874.

M. S. Smith, 6-8 size, 15 jewels, KW KS, **Swiss**, 18K HC, Ca. 1870.

SOUTH BEND WATCH CO.
South Bend, Indiana - March 1902 - 1929

Brothers George, Clement & uncle John M. Studebaker, purchased the successful Columbus W. Co. The serial numbers started at 380,501 where the Columbus serial numbers stopped. Early South Bend full plate watches, some of which were actually assembled in Columbus, Ohio in 1902, they are re-worked Columbus designs. The Polaris, a 16 size, 21 jeweled watch came only in a solid gold case and *The Studebaker* 223 & 229 also grades 227, 292, 293, 294 and 295 were all Railroad grade watches, and the 18 size grades, *The Studebaker* 323, 328, and 329 as well as grade 327. The 12 size grade 431 is also a very high grade. Movement models are known by grade numbers 100 through 431. The **first** digit in the grade number as: 1 denotes 0 & 6 size, 2 denotes 16 size, 3 denotes 18 size and 4 denotes 12 size, the **last** digit denotes movement type, even # denotes hunting case (HC) & odd # denotes open face (OF). Example: Grade # 431 the first digit (4) denotes 12 size & the last digit (1) denotes open face (OF). They made over 850,000 watches in 71 grades, 5 sizes & 17 models.

SOUTH BEND ESTIMATED SERIAL NUMBERS AND PRODUCTION DATES

DATE – SERIAL NO.	DATE – SERIAL NO.	DATE – SERIAL NO.	DATE – SERIAL NO.
1903 – 380,501	1910 – 600,000	1917 – 860,000	1924 – 1,070,000
1904 – 390,000	1911 – 660,000	1918 – 880,000	1925 – 1,105,000
1905 – 405,000	1912 – 715,000	1919 – 905,000	1926 – 1,140,000
1906 – 425,000	1913 – 765,000	1920 – 935,000	1927 – 1,175,000
1907 – 460,000	1914 – 800,000	1921 – 975,000	1928 – 1,210,000
1908 – 500,000	1915 – 820,000	1922 – 1,000,000	1929 – 1,240,000
1909 – 550,000	1916 – 840,000	1923 – 1,035,000	

The above list is provided for determining the APPROXIMATE age of your watch. Match serial number with date. Watches were not necessarily sold in the exact order of manufactured date.

SOUTH BEND
18 SIZE (Lever set)

Grade or Name – Description	Avg	Ex-Fn	Mint
South Bend, 15J, OF	$85	$110	$175
South Bend, 15J, HC	125	175	250
South Bend, 17J, OF	100	125	200
South Bend, 17J, HC	135	185	265
South Bend, 21J, OF	325	400	600
South Bend, 21J, HC, **14K**	650	900	1,300
South Bend, 21J, OF, HC, Silveroid	300	365	500
South Bend, 21J, SW, HC	400	500	850
The Studebaker, G#323, 17J, GJS, NI, Adj.5P, OF	500	675	1,000
The Studebaker, G#328, 21J, GJS, NI, FULL, Adj.5P, HC ★★★	800	1,000	1,500
The Studebaker, G#329, 21J, GJS, NI, FULL, Adj.5P, OF	625	775	1,200

The **last** digit of Grade # denotes style of movement Even # = Hunting & Odd # = Open Face.

SOUTH BEND WATCH CO. PRICE LIST
FORM 78-5M-5-1-10

GRADE		MINIMUM PRICE	COST	JEWEL	SIZE
Hg.	O. F.				
100		$ 9.00		7	0
110		12.50		15	0
120		16.00		17	0
260	261	6.50		7	16
280	281	11.00		15	16
290	291	14.50		17 Adj.	16
298	299	20.00		17 Adj.	16
292	293	26.00		19 Adj.	16
294	295	35.00		21 Adj.	16
330	331	8.00		15	18
332	333	8.50		15	18
340	341	13.25		17 Adj.	18
344	313	14.00		17 Adj.	18
	345	20.00		17 Adj.	18
	323	26.00		17 Adj.	18
	329	35.00		21 Adj.	18
342	343	11.25		17	18
346	347	11.50		17	18

Above: South Bend Price List for movement only Ca. about **1910**

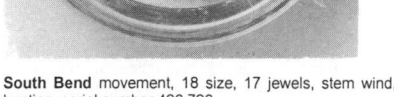

South Bend movement, 18 size, 17 jewels, stem wind, hunting, serial number 426,726.

The Studebaker in (in SCRIPT), 18 size, 21 jewels, gold jewel settings, marked 329, stem wind.

Grade or Name – Description		Avg	Ex-Fn	Mint
302, 15J, M# 1, HC, (not seen)	★★★★★	$225	$300	$500
304, 15J, HC		100	175	250
305, 15J, OF		90	110	150
305, 15J, Silveroid, OF		75	100	125
309, 17J, OF		100	135	225
312, 17J, NI, ADJ, HC	★★	110	175	250
313, 17J, NI, ADJ, **marked 313** OF	★	200	285	425
313, 17J, NI, ADJ, **Not** Marked, OF		125	200	325
315, 17J, NI, Adj.3P, OF		100	135	225
For - G#s 323, 328 & 329 see *"The Studebaker"*				
327, 21J, Adj.5P, marked 327, OF	★★★	350	425	700
330, 15J, M#1, LS, HC		100	165	250
331, 15J, M#1, LS, OF		90	125	200
332, 15J, HC		100	175	275
333, 15J, OF		90	125	200
337, 17J, OF		100	135	225
340, 17J, M#1, Adj.3P, NI, HC		125	185	285
341, 17J, M#1, ADJ, NI, Adj.3P, OF		100	135	225
342, 17J, M#1, LS		100	135	225
343, 17J, M#1, LS, OF		100	135	225
344, 17J, NI, Adj.3P, HC	★★	375	475	700
345, 17J, NI, Adj.3P, OF	★	325	385	650
346, 17J, NI, HC	★★	350	445	600
347, 17J, NI, OF		110	175	275

Grade # s are conveniently numbered if the starting digit is 1 it is for 0 & 6 sizes, starting digit 2=16 size, starting digit 3=18 size, starting digit 4=12 size. The **final** digit of the Grade # if it is Even it is a Hunting Case. if **final** digit is Odd it is Open Face. Example: G# 347, 3=18 size, 7=open faced.

Note: Gold Filled cases marked, South Bend or Pyramid - **30yr.**, =$60 - $100 - $250
　　　 Gold Filled cases marked, South Bend or Pilgrim - **25yr.**, =$50 - $80 - $180
　　　 Gold Filled cases marked, South Bend or Panama - **20yr.**, =$40 - $70 - $150

🕐 Generic, nameless or unmarked grades for watch movements are listed under the Company name or initials of the Company, etc. by size, jewel count and description.

🕐 A collector should expect to pay modestly higher prices at local shops.

🕐 Pricing in this Guide are fair market price for **COMPLETE** watches which are reflected from the "**NAWCC**" National and regional shows.

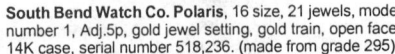

South Bend Watch Co. Polaris, 16 size, 21 jewels, model number 1, Adj.5p, gold jewel setting, gold train, open face, 14K case, serial number 518,236. (made from grade 295)

Grade marked 295, 16S, 21J., first model, gold jewel settings, Adj.5p, gold train, OF, S# 518,022. Example left & right came from same run(518,001-518,500)

Grade # s are conveniently numbered if the starting digit is 1 it is for 0 & 6 sizes, starting digit 2 = 16 size, starting digit 3 = 18 size, starting digit 4 = 12 size. The **final** digit of the Grade # if it is Even it is a Hunting Case. if **final** digit is Odd it is Open Face. Example: G# 347 =18 size, open faced.

16 SIZE

Grade or Name – Description	Avg	Ex-Fn	Mint
Polaris, 21J, M#1, Adj.5P, 3/4, NI, DR, GJS, GT,			
14K South Bend case marked **Polaris** on dial & Mvt. ...... ★★★★	$2,200	$3,300	$4,600
South Bend, 7J, OF	70	95	150
South Bend, 7J, HC	100	125	175
South Bend, 9J, OF	70	95	150
South Bend, 9J, HC	100	125	175
South Bend, 15J, OF	70	95	150
South Bend, 15J, HC	100	125	175
South Bend, 15J, OF, Silveroid	70	95	150
South Bend, 17J, OF	70	95	150
South Bend, 17J, HC, ADJ	125	150	200
South Bend, 17J, **14K HC**	450	550	850
South Bend, 21J, OF, Adj, 5P	300	350	500
South Bend, 21J, HC, ADJ	400	450	700
The Studebaker 223, 17J, M#2, 8Adj., GJS, DR, GT	600	700	1,200
The Studebaker 229, 21J, M#2, 8Adj., GJS, DR, GT	750	950	1,500
* Movements marked "Studebaker 8-adjustments" should not be confused with *The Studebaker*.			
Studebaker, 21J, PS, 8Adj, OF	235	285	435
203, 7J, 3/4, NI, OF	70	95	150
204, 15J, 3/4, NI, HC	90	125	200
207, 15J, PS	70	95	150
209, 9J, M#2, PS, OF	65	95	150
211, 17J, M#2, 3/4, NI, OF	75	95	175
212, 17J, M#2, LS, heat & cold, HC	125	165	250
215, 17J, M#2, LS, heat & cold, OF	70	95	150
217, 17J, M#2, NI, BRG, DR, GT, ADJ.3P, OF.	95	125	200
219 marked 219, 19J, DR, ADJ.4P, OF	150	200	350

A watch marked as **5 positions** is equivalent to one marked *eight adjustments* (the most common found on RR watches) and will be listed in this book as: **"Adj.5P"** (adjusted to heat, cold, isochronism and 5 positions). A watch marked as **nine adjustments** is equivalent to one marked *6 positions* & listed as **"Adj.6P"** (adjusted to heat,cold, isochronism and 6 positions). A watch that is marked as *ADJUSTED* only is adjusted to isochronism & in poise in all temperatures & is listed as **"Adj."**.
* Later some manufactures used a variations of **8 adjustments, six to position, 1-isochronism, 1-temperature** or as in the Elgin grade 571 two to temperature in about 1950.

Grade 211, 16 size, 17 jewels, three-quarter plate, marked 211, serial number 703,389.

Grade 227, 16 size, 21 jewels, RR approved, gold jewel settings, Adj5p, marked 227,serial number 1,222,843.

Grade or Name – Description	Avg	Ex-Fn	Mint
223, 17J, M#2, LS, ADJ.5P, OF	$75	$110	$200
227, 21J, M#2, 3/4, NI, LS, DR, ADJ.5P, marked 227, OF	225	300	500
260, 7J, M#1, HC	70	95	150
261, 7J, M#1, OF	70	95	150
280, 15J, M#1, HC	85	110	200
281, 15J, M#1, OF	70	95	150
290, 17J, M#1, LS, Adj..3P, HC	165	225	350
291, 17J, M#1, Adj.3P, OF	185	250	400
292, 19J, M#1, 3/4, GJS, NI, DR, Adj.5P, HC ★★	250	350	600
293, 19J, M#1, 3/4, GJS, NI, DR, Adj,5P, OF ★	200	285	500
294, 21J, M#1, ADJ.5P, GJS, GT, HC, marked 294, HC ★★	650	850	1,200
295, 21J, M#1, LS, ADJ.5P, GJS, GT, marked 295, OF ★★	600	750	1,000
298, 17J, M#1, ADJ.3P, HC ★	225	285	425
299, 17J, M#1, ADJ.3P, OF ★	175	235	375

12 SIZE Extra Thin
Chesterfield Series style cases (OF Only)

Grade or Name – Description	Avg	Ex-Fn	Mint
407, 15J, DR, Gold Filled case	$65	$70	$95
411, 17J, DR, GJS, Gold Filled case	70	85	110
415, 17J, ADJ to temp, Gold Filled case.	80	95	150
417 marked, 17J, DR, Adj.5p,GJS, South Bend G. F. OF ... ★★★	125	165	325
419, 17J, Adj.3P, Gold Filled Case ★	90	110	200
429, 19J, Adj.4P, DR, GJS, Gold Filled	100	150	235
14K case	185	250	400
429, South Bend **Digital**, 19J, BRG, NI, DR, GJS, ADJ.4P (marked 411 &429), 12 size ◪	225	300	450
431, 21J, Adj.5P, DR, GJS, Gold Filled Case	150	185	265
14K Case	225	285	450
18K Case ★★★	300	400	650
Studebaker, 21J, 8 Adj., OF ◪	175	250	450

* Movements marked "Studebaker 8-adjustments" should not be confused with *The Studebaker.*

🕀 Chesterfield Series (OF Only) comprises of a variety of case and dial combinations. Case styles such as Delmar, Carlton, Fairfax, Girard, Savoy, Senior, Tremont, Warwick, & Wellington. Chesterfield Series were cased and timed at the factory only as complete watches. Chesterfield Series case are **not** interchangeable with other American 12 standard style cases.

🕀 Pricing in this Guide are fair market price for **COMPLETE** watches which are reflected from the "<u>NAWCC</u>" National and regional shows.

Grade 411, 12 size, 17 jewels, open face, double roller.

Chesterfield, 12 size, 21 jewels, grade # 431, bridge, gold jewel settings, pendant set, double roller, Adj5p.

6 SIZE Hunting Case

Grade or Name – Description		Avg	Ex-Fn	Mint
South Bend, 11J, G#160, HC	★★	$75	$110	$185
South Bend, 15J, G#170, HC	★	90	125	200
South Bend, 17J, G#180, HC	★★★	100	165	265
South Bend, 17J, G#180, **14K,HC**	★★★★	250	300	500

ALL 6 size movements were re-worked Columbus movements.

South Bend, 6 size, grade # 170, 15 jewels.

Grade 120-HC, 121-OF, 0 size, 17 jewels, bridge, nickel, double roller, pendant set.

0 SIZE

Grade or Name – Description		Avg	Ex-Fn	Mint
South Bend, 7J, M# 1, PS, HC		$95	$125	$250
South Bend, 15J, M# 1, PS, HC	★★★	110	150	275
Grade 100 HC & 101 OF, 7J, PS		75	95	200
Grade 102 HC & 103 OF, 7J, BRG(some marked 102)	★★★	100	150	300
Grade 110 HC & 111 OF, 15J, 3F Brg, DR		90	125	200
Grade 120 HC & 121 OF, 17J, BRG, NI, DR, PS	★	90	150	250
Grade 150 HC & 151 OF, 17J, M# 3, BRG, NI, PS	★★	100	175	300

IDENTIFICATION OF MOVEMENTS BY MODEL NUMBER

How to Identify Your Watch: Compare the movement of your watch with the illustrations in this section. Upon matching the movement exactly, the model number and size can be determined. While comparing, note the location of the balance, jewels, screws, gears, and type of back plate (Full, 3/4, Bridge) these will be clues in identifying the movement you have. Having determined the size and model number, you can now find your watch in the main price listing by name or number (engraved on the movement).

Record of Serial and Grade Numbers of South Bend Watch Movements

1915

Serial Number	Grade	Size	Model	Jewels	Serial Number	Grade	Size	Model	Jewels
1000 to 4000...	Htg.	18	1	7	400001 to 401200...	331	18	1	15
4001 to 7000...	"	18	1	7	401201 to 403200...	330	18	1	15
7001 to 10000...	"	16	1	15	403201 to 407200...	341	18	1	17
10001 to 21000...	"	18	1	15	407201 to 408500...	340	18	1	17
21001 to 29500...	"	16	1	7	408501 to 408700...	342	18	1	17
29501 to 37000...	"	18	1	7	408901 to 409200...	342	18	1	17
37001 to 41000...	"	16	1	15	409201 to 412200...	330	18	1	15
41001 to 52000...	"	18	1	15	412201 to 413800...	290	16	1	17
52001 to 61000...	"	18	1	7	413801 to 414800...	342	18	1	17
61001 to 76000...	"	18	1	15	414801 to 415800...	291	16	1	17
76001 to 83000...	"	16	1	15	415801 to 417700...	331	18	1	17
83001 to 92000...	"	16	1	7	417701 to 418700...	342	18	1	17
92001 to 97000...	"	18	1	7	418701 to 419700...	343	18	1	17
97001 to 105000...	"	18	1	15	419701 to 420600...	290	16	1	17
105001 to 114000...	"	16	1	17	420601 to 421900...	291	16	1	17
114001 to 127000...	"	18	1	15	421901 to 422400...	281	16	1	15
127501 to 138000...	"	18	1	17	422401 to 423200...	280	16	1	15
138001 to 156000...	"	16	1	7	423201 to 423800...	343	18	1	17
156001 to 165000...	"	18	1	15	423801 to 425800...	261	16	1	7
165001 to 171000...	"	16	1	7	425801 to 426100...	281	16	1	15
171001 to 196000...	"	16	1	17	426101 to 428100...	342	18	1	17
196001 to 201000...	"	18	1	7	428101 to 431100...	260	16	1	7
201001 to 214000...	"	16	1	15	431101 to 431600...	280	16	1	15
214001 to 218000...	"	16	1	7	431601 to 432100...	281	16	1	15
218001 to 220000...	"	18	1	15	432101 to 433100...	342	18	1	17
220001 to 232000...	"	16	1	15	433101 to 435100...	340	18	1	17
232001 to 250000...	"	18	1	7	435101 to 436600...	280	16	1	15
250001 to 261000...	"	16	1	7	436601 to 437900...	281	16	1	15
261001 to 267000...	"	16	1	15	437901 to 438200...	280	16	1	15
267001 to 271000...	"	18	1	15	438201 to 438500...	290	16	1	17
271001 to 274000...	"	16	1	15	438501 to 439500...	293	16	1	19
274001 to 281000...	"	16	1	7	439501 to 440500...	280	16	1	15
281001 to 292000...	"	16	1	7	440501 to 441500...	290	16	1	17
292001 to 294000...	"	16	1	17	441501 to 441600...	260	16	1	7
294001 to 295500...	"	18	1	17	441601 to 441700...	261	16	1	7
295501 to 299100...	"	16	1	7	441701 to 441800...	290	16	1	17
299101 to 302000...	"	18	1	7	441801 to 441850...	293	16	1	17
302001 to 311000...	"	16	1	7	441901 to 445900...	280	16	1	15
311001 to 314000...	"	16	1	15	445901 to 446000...	Htg.	16	1	21
314001 to 321000...	"	18	1	15	446001 to 447000...	261	16	1	7
321001 to 329000...	"	16	1	7	447001 to 450000...	260	16	1	7
329001 to 334000...	"	18	1	7	450001 to 451000...	261	16	1	7
334001 to 341000...	"	16	1	15	451001 to 453000...	260	16	1	7
341001 to 347000...	"	16	1	7	453001 to 455000...	261	16	1	7
347001 to 349500...	"	16	1	17	455001 to 457000...	343	18	1	17
349501 to 354000...	"	16	1	15	457001 to 461000...	260	16	1	7
354001 to 361000...	"	18	1	7	461001 to 462500...	331	18	1	15
361001 to 366000...	"	16	1	7	462501 to 464000...	281	16	1	15
366001 to 368000...	"	18	1	17	464001 to 465300...	331	18	1	15
368001 to 371000...	"	16	1	15	465301 to 467300...	261	16	1	7
371001 to 374000...	"	18	1	15	467301 to 468800...	331	18	1	15
374001 to 376000...	"	16	1	17	468801 to 469300...	290	16	1	17
376001 to 377000...	"	16	1	15	469301 to 469800...	294	16	1	21
377001 to 378000...	"	18	1	17	469801 to 470100...	295	16	1	21
378001 to 379500...	"	18	1	15	*470101 to 470200...	295	16	1	21
379501 to 380500...	"	16	1	15	470201 to 470300...	295	16	1	21
380501 to 381000...	160	6	1	11	470301 to 471300...	281	16	1	15
381001 to 381500...	170	6	1	15	471301 to 472300...	250	16	1	15
381501 to 382500...	330	18	1	15	472301 to 473300...	281	16	1	15
382501 to 383000...	160	6	1	11	473301 to 474800...	330	18	1	15
383001 to 383500...	170	6	1	15	474801 to 475800...	331	18	1	15
383501 to 384000...	302	18	1	15	475801 to 476800...	290	16	1	17
384001 to 384500...	160	6	1	11	477001 to 478000...	261	16	1	7
384501 to 384900...	291	16	1	17	478001 to 479000...	330	18	1	15
384901 to 385200...	281	16	1	15	479001 to 480000...	261	16	1	7
385201 to 385500...	291	16	1	17	480001 to 480200...	295	16	1	21
385501 to 386400...	290	16	1	17	*480201 to 480500...	295	16	1	21
386401 to 386900...	280	16	1	15	480501 to 481500...	290	16	1	17
386901 to 387400...	170	6	1	15	481501 to 483500...	291	16	1	17
387401 to 387900...	330	18	1	15	483501 to 485000...	280	16	1	15
387901 to 388400...	331	18	1	15	485001 to 486000...	331	18	1	15
388401 to 389400...	160	6	1	17	486001 to 487000...	330	18	1	15
389401 to 389900...	170	6	1	15	487001 to 489000...	331	18	1	15
389901 to 390400...	341	18	1	17	489001 to 490500...	341	18	1	17
390401 to 390900...	331	18	1	15	*490001 to 490500...	294	16	1	21
390901 to 391200...	330	18	1	15	*490501 to 490800...	293	16	1	19
391201 to 391700...	341	18	1	17	*490801 to 490900...	293	16	1	19
391701 to 392600...	330	18	1	15	491001 to 492000...	281	16	1	15
392601 to 394100...	331	18	1	15	492001 to 493000...	330	18	1	15
394101 to 396000...	330	18	1	15	493001 to 494000...	340	18	1	17
396001 to 400000...	340	18	1	17					

Although grade numbers appear in this list some of the earlier watches did not have grade numbers stamped upon them. In all instances odd grade numbers indicate open face movement, even grade numbers indicate hunting movement.

*Watches with these serial numbers have double roller.

Serial Number	Grade	Size	Model	Jewels	Serial Number	Grade	Size	Model	Jewels
494001 to 495000...	290	16	1	17	570001 to 571000...	261	16	1	7
495001 to 497000...	331	18	1	15	*571001 to 572000...	313	18	2	17
497001 to 498000...	201	16	1	7	572001 to 573000...	280	16	1	15
498001 to 499000...	291	16	1	17	573001 to 574000...	347	18	2	17
499001 to 500000...	261	16	1	7	*574001 to 575000...	323	18	2	17
500001 to 501000...	281	16	1	15	*575001 to 576000...	217	16	2	17
501001 to 502000...	290	16	1	17	576001 to 577000...	333	18	2	15
502001 to 503000...	331	18	1	15	577001 to 578000...	281	16	1	15
503001 to 503500...	341	18	1	17	*578001 to 579000...	223	16	2	17
503501 to 504000...	343	18	1	17	*579001 to 580000...	329	18	2	21
504001 to 505000...	290	16	1	17	*580001 to 581000...	212	16	2	17
505001 to 505100...	293	16	1	19	*581001 to 582000...	333	18	2	15
*505101 to 505500...	293	16	1	19	582001 to 583000...	261	16	1	7
505501 to 506500...	261	16	1	7	*583001 to 584000...	227	16	2	21
506501 to 507500...	280	16	1	15	*584001 to 585000...	229	16	2	21
507501 to 508500...	261	16	1	7	585001 to 586000...	207	16	2	15
508501 to 509500...	280	16	1	15	586001 to 587000...	211	16	2	17
509501 to 510500...	281	16	1	15	*587001 to 588000...	215	16	2	17
510501 to 511400...	291	16	1	17	588001 to 589000...	260	16	1	7
511401 to 511500...	299	16	1	17	*589001 to 590000...	217	16	2	17
511501 to 511900...	292	16	1	19	590001 to 591000...	204	16	2	15
*511901 to 512000...	292	16	1	19	591001 to 592000...	203	16	2	7
512001 to 513000...	333	18	2	15	592001 to 593000...	207	16	2	15
513001 to 514000...	280	16	1	15	*593001 to 594000...	212	16	2	17
514001 to 515000...	261	16	1	7	594001 to 595000...	203	16	2	7
515001 to 516000...	260	16	1	7	595001 to 596000...	332	18	2	15
516001 to 516500...	298	16	1	17	*596001 to 597000...	215	16	2	17
*516501 to 516600...	298	16	1	17	*597001 to 598000...	223	16	2	17
516601 to 516800...	298	16	1	17	*598001 to 599000...	229	16	2	21
*516801 to 516900...	298	16	1	17	599001 to 600000...	260	16	1	7
516901 to 517000...	298	16	1	17	600001 to 601000...	211	16	2	17
517001 to 517700...	345	18	2	17	*601001 to 602000...	313	18	2	17
*517701 to 517800...	345	18	2	17	602001 to 603000...	203	16	2	7
*518001 to 518500...	295	16	1	21	603001 to 604000...	204	16	2	15
518501 to 519000...	294	16	1	21	604001 to 605000...	207	16	2	15
519001 to 520000...	347	18	2	17	605001 to 606000...	333	18	2	15
520001 to 521000...	332	18	2	15	606001 to 607000...	347	18	2	17
*521001 to 522000...	329	18	2	21	*607001 to 608000...	215	16	2	17
*522001 to 523000...	293	16	1	19	608001 to 609000...	211	16	2	17
523001 to 523400...	299	16	1	17	609001 to 610000...	203	16	2	7
*523401 to 524000...	299	16	1	17	*610001 to 611000...	215	16	2	17
524001 to 524300...	344	18	2	17	611001 to 612000...	207	16	2	15
*524301 to 524800...	344	18	2	17	612001 to 613000...	203	16	2	7
524801 to 525000...	344	18	2	17	*613001 to 614000...	212	16	2	17
525001 to 526000...	346	18	2	17	614001 to 615000...	305	18	2	15
526001 to 527000...	333	18	2	15	615001 to 616000...	204	16	2	15
527001 to 528000...	347	18	2	17	616001 to 617000...	207	16	2	15
*528001 to 529000...	345	18	2	17	617001 to 618000...	203	16	2	7
*529001 to 530000...	292	16	1	19	*618001 to 619000...	415	12	1	17
530001 to 531000...	260	16	1	7	*619001 to 620000...	431	12	1	21
531001 to 532000...	281	16	1	15	620001 to 621000...	211	16	2	17
532001 to 533000...	333	18	2	15	*621001 to 622000...	223	16	2	17
*533001 to 534000...	323	18	2	17	*622001 to 623000...	229	16	2	21
*534001 to 535000...	345	18	2	17	*623001 to 624000...	411	12	1	17
535001 to 536000...	347	18	2	17	*624001 to 625000...	215	16	2	17
536001 to 537000...	333	18	2	15	625001 to 626000...	203	16	2	7
537001 to 538000...	312	18	2	17	626001 to 627000...	305	18	2	15
538001 to 539000...	332	18	2	15	627001 to 628000...	207	16	2	15
*539001 to 539500...	298	16	1	17	*628001 to 629000...	419	12	1	17
539501 to 539700...	298	16	1	17	629001 to 630000...	260	16	1	7
*539701 to 540000...	298	16	1	17	*630001 to 631000...	407	12	1	16
*540001 to 540400...	299	16	1	17	*631001 to 632000...	217	16	2	17
540401 to 541000...	299	16	1	17	632001 to 633000...	204	16	2	15
*541001 to 542000...	328	18	2	21	633001 to 634000...	347	18	2	17
*542001 to 543000...	313	18	2	17	*634001 to 635000...	329	18	2	21
543001 to 544000...	261	16	1	7	635001 to 636000...	203	16	2	7
544001 to 545000...	260	16	1	7	*636001 to 637000...	217	16	2	17
545001 to 546000...	333	18	2	15	*637001 to 638000...	411	12	1	17
546001 to 547000...	332	18	2	15	638001 to 639000...	211	16	2	17
547001 to 548000...	333	18	2	15	*639001 to 640000...	212	16	2	17
548001 to 549000...	346	18	2	17	*640001 to 641000...	217	16	2	17
549001 to 550000...	261	16	1	7	*641001 to 642000...	415	12	1	17
550001 to 551000...	280	16	1	15	642001 to 643000...	203	16	2	7
551001 to 552000...	281	16	1	15	*643001 to 644000...	229	16	2	21
552001 to 553000...	347	18	2	17	644001 to 645000...	260	16	1	7
*553001 to 554000...	313	18	2	17	*645001 to 646000...	215	16	2	17
*554001 to 555000...	323	18	2	17	646001 to 647000...	207	16	2	15
*555001 to 556000...	327	18	2	21	*647001 to 648000...	407	12	1	15
*556001 to 557000...	298	16	1	17	*648001 to 649000...	419	12	1	17
*557001 to 558000...	299	16	1	17	649001 to 650000...	207	16	2	15
558001 to 559000...	347	18	2	17	650181 to 655200...	Htg.	0	1	17
559001 to 560000...	346	18	2	17	655201 to 656200...	"	0	1	15
*560001 to 561000...	313	18	2	17	656201 to 659700...	"	0	1	7
561001 to 562000...	333	18	2	15	659701 to 662400...	"	0	1	7
562001 to 563000...	332	18	2	15	662401 to 662500...	O.F.	0	2	7
563001 to 564000...	261	16	1	7	662501 to 665400...	Htg.	0	2	7
564001 to 565000...	347	18	2	17	665401 to 665500...	O.F.	0	2	7
565001 to 566000...	260	16	1	7	665501 to 666000...	Htg.	0	2	7
566001 to 567000...	211	16	2	17	666001 to 666500...	"	0	2	17
567001 to 569000...	333	18	2	15	666501 to 666600...	"	0	2	15
*569001 to 570000...	215	16	2	17	666601 to 666650...	O. F.	0	2	15

Although grade numbers appear in this list some of the earlier watches did not have grade numbers stamped upon them. In all instances odd grade numbers indicate open face movement, even grade numbers indicate hunting movement.
*Watches with these serial numbers have double roller.

Serial Number	Grade	Size	Model	Jewels	Serial Number	Grade	Size	Model	Jewels
666651 to 667500...	Htg.	0	2	15	*739001 to 740000...	217	16	2	17
667501 to 671500...	"	0	2	7	*740001 to 740200...	101	0	2	7
671501 to 671600...	O. F.	0	2	7	*740201 to 741000...	100	0	2	7
671601 to 672800...	Htg.	0	2	7	*741001 to 741200...	111	0	2	15
672801 to 672900...	O. F.	0	2	7	*741201 to 742000...	110	0	2	15
672901 to 673000...	Htg.	0	2	7	742001 to 743000...	207	16	2	15
673001 to 674000...	"	0	2	15	743001 to 744000...	203	16	2	7
674001 to 675000...	"	0	2	17	*744001 to 745000...	212	16	2	17
675001 to 676000...	"	0	2	7	*745001 to 746000...	227	16	2	21
676001 to 679400...	"	0	2	15	*746001 to 746100...	111	0	2	15
679401 to 679500...	O. F.	0	2	15	*746101 to 747000...	110	0	2	15
679501 to 680400...	Htg.	0	2	15	747001 to 748000...	305	18	2	15
680401 to 680500...	O. F.	0	2	15	748001 to 749600...	309	18	2	17
680501 to 681000...	Htg.	0	2	15	*749601 to 750000...	223	16	2	17
681001 to 682000...	"	0	2	17	750001 to 751000...	207	16	2	15
682001 to 682800...	"	0	2	15	*751001 to 751100...	101	0	2	7
682801 to 682900...	O. F.	0	2	15	*751101 to 752000...	100	0	2	7
682901 to 683000...	Htg.	0	2	15	752001 to 753000...	211	16	2	17
683001 to 684000...	"	0	2	17	*753001 to 754000...	229	16	2	21
684001 to 684600...	"	0	2	7	754001 to 755000...	203	16	2	7
684601 to 684700...	O. F.	0	2	7	*755001 to 756000...	215	16	2	17
684701 to 685000...	Htg.	0	2	7	*756001 to 757000...	313	18	2	17
685001 to 686000..	"	0	2	15	*757001 to 758000...	323	18	2	17
686001 to 686100...	101	0	2	7	758001 to 759000...	204	16	2	15
686101 to 687000...	100	0	2	7	*759001 to 759500...	Htg.	0	2	17
687001 to 687100...	111	0	2	15	759501 to 759510...	150	0	3	17
687101 to 688000...	110	0	2	15	759511 to 759520...	103	0	3	7
688001 to 688100...	101	0	2	7	759521 to 759530...	102	0	3	7
688101 to 689000...	100	0	2	7	759531 to 759540...	151	0	3	17
689001 to 689100...	111	0	2	15	759541 to 760000...	Htg.	0	2	17
689101 to 690000...	110	0	2	15	760001 to 761000...	305	18	2	15
690001 to 690100...	101	0	2	7	761001 to 762000...	207	16	2	15
690101 to 691000...	100	0	2	7	*762001 to 762100...	111	0	2	15
691001 to 691100...	101	0	2	7	762101 to 763000...	110	0	2	17
691101 to 692000...	100	0	2	7	763001 to 764000...	203	16	2	7
692001 to 692100...	111	0	2	15	*764001 to 765000...	215	16	2	17
692101 to 693000...	110	0	2	15	*765001 to 766000...	217	16	2	17
693001 to 693100...	101	0	2	7	766001 to 767000...	211	16	2	17
693101 to 694000...	100	0	2	7	*767001 to 768000...	217	16	2	17
*694001 to 695000...	217	16	2	17	*768001 to 769000...	212	16	2	17
695001 to 696000...	305	18	2	15	*769001 to 770000...	217	16	2	17
696001 to 696100...	111	0	2	15	*770001 to 771000...	151	0	3	17
696101 to 697000...	110	0	2	15	*771001 to 772000...	217	16	2	17
697001 to 697100...	101	0	2	7	*772001 to 773000...	150	0	3	17
697101 to 698000...	100	0	2	7	*773001 to 774000...	215	16	2	17
*698001 to 699000...	215	16	2	17	*774001 to 775000...	107	0	3	15
*699001 to 700000...	415	12	1	17	*775001 to 776000...	106	0	3	15
*700001 to 701000...	431	12	1	21	776001 to 777000...	207	16	2	15
*701001 to 702000...	313	18	2	17	*777001 to 778000...	102	0	3	7
702001 to 702100...	111	0	2	15	*778001 to 779000...	103	0	3	7
702101 to 703000...	110	0	2	15	779001 to 780000...	211	16	2	17
703001 to 704000...	211	16	2	17	780001 to 781000...	203	16	2	7
*704001 to 705000...	212	16	2	17	781001 to 782000...	305	18	2	15
705001 to 706000...	305	18	2	15	*782001 to 783000...	217	16	2	17
*706001 to 707000...	215	16	2	17	*783001 to 784000...	215	16	2	17
707001 to 708000...	203	16	2	7	784001 to 785000...	207	16	2	15
*708001 to 709000...	407	12	1	15	*785001 to 786000...	215	16	2	17
709001 to 710000...	204	16	2	15	*786001 to 787000...	227	16	2	21
710001 to 711000...	305	18	2	15	*787001 to 788000...	407	12	1	15
711001 to 712000...	260	16	1	7	*788001 to 789000...	217	16	2	17
712001 to 713000...	207	16	2	16	789001 to 790000...	211	16	2	17
*713001 to 713000...	111	0	2	15	*790001 to 791000...	215	16	2	17
*713101 to 714000...	110	0	2	15	*791001 to 792000...	217	16	2	17
*714001 to 715000...	227	16	2	21	*792001 to 793000...	407	12	1	15
715001 to 716000...	211	16	2	17	*793001 to 794000...	215	16	2	17
*716001 to 717000...	411	12	1	17	*794001 to 795000...	212	16	2	17
*717001 to 717100...	101	0	2	7	*795001 to 796000...	411	12	1	17
*717101 to 718000...	100	0	2	7	796001 to 797000...	203	16	2	7
*718001 to 719000...	215	16	2	17	*797001 to 798000...	407	12	1	15
719001 to 720000...	309	18	2	17	*798001 to 799000...	429	12	1	19
720001 to 721000...	203	16	2	7	*799001 to 800000...	411	12	1	17
*721001 to 722000...	227	16	2	21	*800001 to 801000...	219	16	2	19
722001 to 723000...	204	16	2	15	*801001 to 802000...	429	12	1	19
723001 to 724000...	207	16	2	15	*802001 to 804000...	219	16	2	19
724001 to 725000...	211	16	2	17	*804001 to 805000...	411	12	1	17
*725001 to 726000...	217	16	2	17	*805001 to 806000...	407	12	1	15
*726001 to 727000...	227	16	2	21	*806001 to 808000...	429	12	1	19
*727001 to 728000...	223	16	2	17	*808001 to 809000...	219	16	2	19
*728001 to 729000...	212	16	2	17	*809001 to 810000...	411	12	1	17
729001 to 730000...	305	18	2	15	*810001 to 811000...	429	12	1	19
730001 to 731000...	304	18	2	15	*811001 to 812000...	211	16	2	17
*731001 to 732000...	313	18	2	17	*812001 to 814000...	219	16	2	19
732001 to 733000...	309	18	2	17	*814001 to 815000...	429	12	1	19
733001 to 734000...	211	16	2	17	*815001 to 816000...	407	12	1	15
*734001 to 735000...	215	16	2	17	*816001 to 817000...	219	16	2	19
*735001 to 736000...	217	16	2	17	*817001 to 818000...	429	12	1	19
*736001 to 737000...		0	2	17	*818001 to 819000...	219	16	2	19
*737001 to 738000...	227	16	2	21	*819001 to 820000...	429	12	1	19
*738001 to 739000...	215	16	2	17					

Although grade numbers appear in this list some of the earlier watches did not have grade numbers stamped upon them. In all instances odd grade numbers indicate open face movement, even grade numbers indicate hunting movement.

*Watches with these serial numbers have double roller.

A-112

by -Lyle & Donna Stratton   (below all double roller)

SERIAL NUMBER-GRADE-SIZE-M#- Jewels
820001-821000 = 215 - 16 - 2 - 17j
821001-822000 = 415 - 12 - 1 - 17j
822001-823000 = 411 - 12 - 1 - 17j
823001-825000 = 429 - 12 - 1 - 19j
825001-826000 = 209 - 16 - 2 - 9j
826001-827000 = 207 - 16 - 2 - 15j
827001-828000 = 407 - 12 - 1 - 15j
828001-830000 = 429 - 12 - 1 - 19j
830001-831000 = 211 - 16 - 2 - 17j
831001-832000 = 407 - 12 - 1 - 15j
832001-833000 = 207 - 16 - 2 - 15j
833001-834000 = 429 - 12 - 1 - 19j
834001-835000 = 219 - 16 - 2 - 19j
835001-837000 = 429 - 12 - 1 - 19j
837001-838000 = 219 - 16 - 2 - 19j
838001-839000 = 209 - 16 - 2 - 9j
839001-840000 = 211 - 16 - 2 - 17j
840001-841000 = 219 - 16 - 2 - 19j
841001-842000 = 209 - 16 - 2 - 9j
842001-843000 = 207 - 16 - 2 - 15j
843001-844000 = 429 - 12 - 1 - 19j
844001-845000 = 411 - 12 - 1 - 17j
845001-846000 = 429 - 12 - 1 - 19j
846001-847000 = 209 - 16 - 2 - 9j
847001-848000 = 227 - 16 - 2 - 21j
848001-849000 = 429 - 12 - 1 - 19j
849001-850000 = 407 - 12 - 1 - 15j
850001-851000 = 211 - 16 - 2 - 17j
851001-852000 = 209 - 16 - 2 - 9j
852001-853000 = 429 - 12 - 1 - 19j
853001-854000 = 219 - 16 - 2 - 19j
854001-855000 = 429 - 12 - 1 - 19j
855001-856000 = 207 - 16 - 2 - 15j
856001-857000 = 209- -16 - 2 - 9j
857001-858000 = 407 - 12 - 1 - 15j
858001-859000 = 429 - 12 - 1 - 19j
859001-860000 = 204 - 16 - 2 - 15j
860001-861000 = 211 - 16 - 2 - 17j
861001-862000 = 411 - 12 - 1 - 17j
862001-863000 = 209 - 16 - 2 - 9j
863001-864000 = 429 - 12 - 1 - 19j
864001-865000 = 219 - 16 - 2 - 19j
865001-866000 = 209 - 16 - 2 - 9j
866001-867000 = 429 - 12 - 1 - 19j
867001-868000 = 411 - 12 - 1 - 17j
868001-869000 = 211 - 16 - 2 - 17j
869001-871000 = 227 - 16 - 2 - 21j
871001-872000 = 207 - 16 - 2 - 15j
872001-873000 = 209 - 16 - 2 - 9j
873001-874000 = 219 - 16 - 2 - 19j
874001-875000 = 407 - 12 - 1 - 15j
875001-876000 = 411 - 12 - 1 - 17j
876001-877000 = 429 - 12 - 1 - 19j
877001-878000 = 207 - 16 - 2 - 15j
878001-879000 = 211 - 16 - 2 - 17j
879001-880000 = 219 - 16 - 2 - 19j
880001-882000 = 407 - 12 - 1 - 15j
882001-883000 = 217 - 16 - 2 - 17j
883001-884000 = 209 - 16 - 2 - 9j
884001-885000 = 411 - 12 - 1 - 17j
885001-886000 = 229 - 16 - 2 - 21j
886001-887000 = 429 - 12 - 1 - 19j
887001-888000 = 209 - 16 - 2 - 9j
888001-889000 = 217 - 16 - 2 - 17j
889001-890000 = 219 - 16 - 2 - 19j
890001-891000 = 209 - 16 - 2 - 9j
891001-892000 = 207 - 16 - 2 - 15j
892001-893000 = 227 - 16 - 2 - 21j
893001-894000 = 315 - 18 - 2 - 17j
894001-895000 = 211 - 16 - 2 - 17j
895001-896000 = 204 - 16 - 2 - 15j
896001-897000 = 219 - 16 - 2 - 19j

SERIAL NUMBER-GRADE-SIZE-M#- Jewels
897001-898000 = 315 - 18 - 2 - 17j < last 18 size
898001-899000 = 207 - 16 - 2 - 15j
899001-900000 = 429 - 12 - 1 - 19j
900001-901000 = 227 - 16 - 2 - 21j
901001-902000 = 219 - 16 - 2 - 19j
902001-903000 = 211 - 16 - 2 - 17j
903001-904000 = 227 - 16 - 2 - 21j
904001-905000 = 411 - 12 - 1 - 17j
905001-906000 = 407 - 12 - 1 - 15j
906001-907000 = 429 - 12 - 1 - 19j
907001-908000 = 411 - 12 - 1 - 17j
908001-910000 = 209 - 12 - 1 - 9j
910001-911000 = 207 - 16 - 2 - 15j
911011-912000 = 219 - 16 - 2 - 19j
912001-913000 = 429 - 12 - 1 - 19j
913001-914000 = 207 - 16 - 2 - 15j
914001-915000 = 209 - 16 - 2 - 9j
915001-916000 = 219 - 16 - 2 - 19j
916001-917000 = 211 - 16 - 2 - 17j
917001-918000 = 207 - 16 - 2 - 15j
918001-919000 = 407 - 12 - 1 - 15j
919001-920000 = 219 - 16 - 2 - 19j
920001-921000 = 209 - 16 - 2 - 9j
921001-923000 = 429 - 12 - 1 - 19j
923001-924000 = 407 - 12 - 1 - 15j
924001-925000 = 227 - 16 - 2 - 21j
925001-926000 = 219 - 16 - 2 - 19j
926001-927000 = 429 - 12 - 1 - 19j
927001-928000 = 227 - 16 - 2 - 21j
928001-929000 = 204 - 16 - 2 - 15j
929001-930000 = 209 - 16 - 2 - 9j
930001-931000 = 217 - 16 - 2 - 17j
931001-932000 = 219 - 16 - 2 - 19j
932001-933000 = 407 - 12 - 1 - 15j
933001-934000 = 411 - 12 - 1 - 17j
934001-935000 = 211 - 16 - 2 - 17j
935001-937000 = 429 - 12 - 1 - 19j
937001-938000 = 207 - 16 - 2 - 15j
938001-939000 = 227 - 16 - 2 - 21j
939001-940000 = 407 - 12 - 1 - 15j
940001-941000 = 209 - 16 - 2 - 9j
941001-942000 = 211 - 16 - 2 - 17j
942001-943000 = 219 - 16 - 2 - 19j
943001-944000 = 209 - 16 - 2 - 9j
944001-946000 = 429 - 12 - 1 - 19j
946001-947000 = 219 - 16 - 2 - 19j
947001-948000 = 207 - 16 - 2 - 15j
948001-949000 = 411 - 12 - 1 - 17j
949001-950000 = 429 - 12 - 1 - 19j
950001-951000 = 407 - 12 - 1 - 15j
951001-952000 = 219 - 16 - 2 - 19j
952001-953000 = 211 - 16 - 2 - 17j
953001-954000 = 209 - 16 - 2 - 9j
954001-955000 = 227 - 16 - 2 - 21j
955001-956000 = 429 - 12 - 1 - 19j
956001-957000 = 209 - 16 - 2 - 9j
957001-958000 = 227 - 16 - 2 - 21j
958001-959000 = 407 - 12 - 1 - 15j
959001-960000 = 411 - 12 - 1 - 17j
960001-961000 = 429 - 12 - 1 - 19j
961001-962000 = 207 - 16 - 2 - 15j
962001-963000 = 211 - 16 - 2 - 17j
963001-964000 = 407 - 12 - 1 - 15j
964001-965000 = 429 - 12 - 1 - 19j
965001-966000 = 204 - 16 - 2 - 15j
966001-967000 = 219 - 16 - 2 - 19j
967001-968000 = 407 - 12 - 1 - 15j
968001-969000 = 209 - 16 - 2 - 9j
969001-970000 = 431 - 12 - 1 - 21j
970001-971000 = 227 - 16 - 2 - 21j
971001-972000 = 411 - 12 - 1 - 17j
972001-973000 = 219 - 16 - 2 - 19j

SERIAL NUMBER	GRADE-SIZE-M# -Jewels
973001-974000	= 207 - 16 - 2 - 15j
974001-975000	= 209 - 16 - 2 - 9j
975001-977000	= 429 - 12 - 1 - 19j
977001-978000	= 219 - 16 - 2 - 19j
978001-979000	= 211 - 16 - 2 - 17j
979001-980000	= 227 - 16 - 2 - 21j
980001-981000	= 429 - 12 - 1 - 19j
981001-982000	= 407 - 12 - 1 - 15j
982001-983000	= 209 - 16 - 2 - 9j
983001-984000	= 219 - 16 - 2 - 19j
984001-985000	= 207 - 16 - 2 - 15j
985001-986000	= 411 - 12 - 1 - 17j
986001-987000	= 429 - 12 - 1 - 19j
987001-988000	= 211 - 16 - 2 - 17j
988001-989000	= 219 - 16 - 2 - 19j
989001-990000	= 209 - 16 - 2 - 9j
990001-991000	= 207 - 16 - 2 - 15j
991001-992000	= 211 - 16 - 2 - 17j
992001-993000	= ? - ? - ? - ? - ?
993001-994000	= 411 - 12 - 1 - 17j
994001-995000	= 407 - 12 - 1 - 15j
995001-996000	= 219 - 16 - 2 - 19j
996001-999000	= 429 - 12 - 1 - 19j
999001-1001000	= 209 - 16 - 2 - 9j
1001001-1002000	= 411 - 12 - 1 - 17j
1002001-1003000	= 207 - 16 - 2 - 15j
1003001-1004000	= 211 - 16 - 2 - 17j
1004001-1005000	= 407 - 12 - 2 - 15j
1005001-1006000	= 204 - 16 - 2 - 15j
1006001-1007000	= 219 - 16 - 2 - 19j
1007001-1008000	= 227 - 16 - 2 - 21j
1008001-1009000	= 207 - 16 - 2 - 15j
1009001-1010000	= 209 - 16 - 2 - 9j
1010001-1011000	= 429 - 12 - 1 - 19j
1011001-1012000	= 209 - 16 - 2 - 9j
1012001-1014000	= 429 - 12 - 1 - 19j
1014001-1015000	= 407 - 12 - 1 - 15j
1015001-1016000	= 219 - 16 - 2 - 19j
1016001-1018000	= 429 - 12 - 1 - 19j
1018001-1019000	= 209 - 16 - 2 - 9j
1019001-1020000	= 227 - 16 - 2 - 21j
1020001-1021000	= 411 - 12 - 1 - 17j
1021001-1022000	= 211 - 16 - 2 - 17j
1022001-1023000	= 429 - 12 - 1 - 19j
1023001-1024000	= 411 - 12 - 1 - 17j
1024001-1025000	= 207 - 16 - 2 - 15j
1025001-1026000	= 227 - 16 - 2 - 21j
1026001-1027000	= 219 - 16 - 2 - 19j
1027001-1029000	= 429 - 12 - 1 - 19j
1029001-1030000	= 407 - 12 - 1 - 15j
1030001-1031000	= 204 - 16 - 2 - 15j
1031001-1032000	= 209 - 16 - 2 - 9j

SERIAL NUMBER	GRADE-SIZE-M# -Jewels
1032001-1033000	= 429 - 12 - 1 - 19j
1033001-1034000	= 227 - 16 - 2 - 21j
1034001-1036000	= 429 - 12 - 1 - 19j
1036001-1037000	= 411 - 12 - 1 - 17j
1037001-1038000	= 219 - 16 - 2 - 19j
1038001-1040000	= 429 - 12 - 1 - 19j
1040001-1041000	= 227 - 16 - 2 - 21j
1041001-1046000	= 429 - 12 - 1 - 19j
1046001-1047000	= 411 - 12 - 1 - 17j
1047001-1049000	= 429 - 12 - 1 - 19j
1049001-1050000	= 411 - 12 - 1 - 17j
1050001-1051000	= 429 - 12 - 1 - 19j
1051001-1052000	= 407 - 12 - 1 - 15j
1052001-1053000	= 429 - 12 - 1 - 19j
1053001-1054000	= 211 - 16 - 2 - 17j
1054001-1056000	= 429 - 12 - 1 - 19j
1056001-1062000	= 219 - 16 - 2 - 19j
1062001-1069000	= 211 - 16 - 2 - 17j
1069001-1072000	= 209 - 16 - 2 - 9j
1072001-1075000	=Studbebaker 12 -1 - 21j
1075001-1075100	=for directors 12 -1 - 19j
1075101-1076000	= 429 - 12 - 1 - 19j
1076001-1083000	=Studbebaker 12 -1 - 21j
1083001-1088000	= 411 - 12 - 1 - 17j
1088001-1093000	= 227 - 16 - 2 - 21j
1093001-1098000	=Studbebaker 12 -1 - 21j
1098001-1103000	= 429 - 12 - 1 - 19j
1103001-1108000	=Studbebaker 12 -1 - 21j
1108001-1113000	= 211 - 16 - 2 - 17j
1113001-1118000	= 411 - 12 - 1 - 17j
1118001-1128000	=Studbebaker 12 -1 - 21j
1128001-1133000	= 227 - 16 - 2 - 21j
1133001-1138000	= 429 - 12 - 1 - 19j
1138001-1143000	=Studbebaker 16 -2 - 21j
1143001-1153000	=Studbebaker 12 -1 - 21j
1153001-1158000	= 411 - 16 - 2 - 17j
1158001-1163000	=Studbebaker 16 -2 - 21j
1163001-1168000	=Studbebaker 12 -1 - 21j
1168001-1173000	=Studbebaker 16 -2 - 21j
1173001-1178000	= 429 - 12 - 1 - 19j
1178001-1183000	=Studbebaker 16 -2 - 21j
1183001-1188000	=Studbebaker 12 -1 - 21j
1188001-1193000	= 227 - 16 - 2 - 21j
1193001-1198000	=Studbebaker 12 -1 - 21j
1198001-1203000	=Studbebaker 16 -2 - 21j
1203001-1208000	= 211 - 16 - 2 - 17j
1208001-1213000	=Studbebaker 16 -2 - 21j
1213001-1218000	= 429 - 12 - 1 - 19j
1218001-1223000	= 227 - 16 - 2 - 21j
1223001-1228000	= 211 - 16 - 2 - 17j
1228001-1233000	= 411 - 12 - 1 - 17j
1233001-1238000	=Studbebaker 12 -1 - 21j
1238001-1241000	= 429 - 12 - 1 - 19j

The **last** digit of Grade # denotes style of movement Even # = Hunting & Odd # = Open Face.

For information about the South Bend W. Co. complete serial & grade BOOK contact:

Lyle and Donna Stratton
1314 N. Gay St.
Longmont, CO 80501
303-776-7531

The authors of "The Complete Price Guide to Watches" recommend this BOOK.

I will respect and appreciate positive sound reliable comments, corrections, improvements or remarks but reserve the right to accept the statement or keep my own observations & views. (*Cooksey*)

18 SIZE—MODEL 1
Open Face and Hunting Lever Set

No. 302—Hunting, 15 Jewels, Lever Set. (Factory listed but never seen)
No. 341—Open Face, 17 Jewels, Lever Set, Adjusted to Temperature & 3 Positions.
No. 340—Hunting, 17 Jewels, Lever Set, Adjusted to Temperature & 3 Positions.
No. 343—Open Face, 17 Jewels, Lever Set.
No. 342—Hunting, 17 Jewels, Lever Set.
No. 331—Open Face, 15 Jewels, Lever Set.
No. 330—Hunting, 15 Jewels, Lever Set.

Model 1, Full Plate, Open face.   Model 1 , Full Plate, Hunting

18 SIZE—MODEL 2
Open Face and Hunting, Lever Set

No. 329—21J, Open Face, "Studebaker," Adjusted to Temperature and 5 Positions.
No. 328—21J, Hunting, "Studebaker," Adjusted to Temperature and 5 Positions.
No. 327—21J, Open Face, Adjusted to Temperature and 5 Positions.
No. 323—17J, Open Face, "Studebaker," Adjusted to Temperature and 5 Positions.
No. 345—17J, Open Face, Adjusted to Temperature and 3 Positions.
No. 344—17J, Hunting, Adjusted to Temperature and 3 Positions.
No. 313—17J, Open Face, Adjusted to Temperature.
No. 312—17J, Hunting, Adjusted to Temperature.
Nos. 309, 337, 347—17J, Open Face.
No. 346—17J, Hunting.
Nos. 333, 305—15J, Open Face.
Nos. 332, 304—15J, Hunting.

Model 2, Full Plate, Open face.   Model 2, Full Plate, Hunting.

16 SIZE—MODEL 1 Open Face and Hunting, Lever Set

No. 295—Open Face, 21 Jewels, Adjusted to Temperature and 5 Positions.
No. 294—Hunting, 21 Jewels, Adjusted to Temperature and 5 Positions.
No. 293—Open Face, 19 Jewels, Adjusted to Temperature and 5 Positions.
No. 292—Hunting, 19 Jewels, Adjusted to Temperature and 5 Positions.
No. 299—Open Face, 17 Jewels, Adjusted to Temperature and 3 Positions.
No. 298—Hunting, 17 Jewels, Adjusted to Temperature and 3 Positions.
No. 291—Open Face, 17 Jewels, Adjusted to Temperature and 3 Positions.
No. 290—Hunting, 17 Jewels, Adjusted to Temperature and 3 Positions.
No. 281—Open Face, 15 Jewels, & No. 280—Hunting, 15 Jewels.
No. 261—Open Face, 7 Jewels, & No. 260—Hunting, 7 Jewels.

Model 1, 3/4 Plate, Open Face.   Model 1, 3/4 Plate, Hunting.

16 SIZE—MODEL 2 Open Face and Hunting, Pendant and Lever Set.

No. 229—21J, Open Face, Lever Set, "Studebaker," Adjust. to Temp. and 5 Positions.
No. 227—21J, Open Face, Lever Set, Adjusted to Temperature and 5 Positions.
No. 219—19J, Open Face, Pendant Set, Adjusted to Temperature and 4 Positions.
No. 223—17J, Open Face, Lever Set, "Studebaker," Adjust. to Temp. and 5 Positions.
No. 217—17J, Open Face, Lever Set, Adjusted to Temperature and 3 Positions.
No. 215—17J, Open Face, Pendant Set, Adjusted to Temperature.
No. 212—17J, Hunting, Lever Set, Adjusted to Temperature.
No. 211—17J, Open Face, Pendant Set
No. 207—15J, Open Face, Pendant Set, & **No. 204—15J, Hunting, Lever Set.**
No. 209—9J, Open Face, Pendant Set, & **No. 203—7J, Open Face, Pendant Set.**

Model 2, 3/4 Plate, HC.   Model 2, 3/4 Plate, OF.

Model 2, Bridges, Open Face.

12 SIZE—MODEL 1
Chesterfield Series and Grade 429 Special
Made in Pendant Set, Open Face Only

No. 431—21J, Adjusted to Temperature and 5 Positions.
No. 429—19J, Adjusted to Temperature and 4 Positions.
No. 419—17J, Adjusted to Temperature and 3 Positions.
No. 415—17J, Adjusted to Temperature.
No. 411—17J.
No. 407—15J.

Model 1, Bridges, Open Face.

Model 1, Lower Plate, Dial Side.

6 SIZE— MODEL 1
Hunting

Grade No. 180, 17 Jewels
Grade No. 170, 15 Jewels
Grade No. 160, 11 Jewels

Serial Number Range
380,501 to 389,900

Model 1, 3/4 Plate, 6 size

0 SIZE—MODEL 1
Open Face, No second hand, Hunting has second hand

Model numbers 1 & 2 serial numbers under 659,700. All open face and hunting, parts for this model except dial and fourth pinion are interchangeable.

Model 1, Open Face, 3/4 Plate, 7 jewels.

Model 1, Hunting, Bridges, 15-17 jewels.

0 SIZE—MODEL 2
Open Face, No second hand, Hunting has second hand

No. 100— 7 Jewels, Hunting, Bridge.
No. 101— 7 Jewels, Open Face, 3/4 Plate.
No. 110— 15 Jewels, Hunting, Bridge.
No. 111— 15 Jewels, Open Face, 3/4 Plate.
No. 120— 17 Jewels, Hunting, Bridge.
No. 121— 17 Jewels, Open Face, 3/4 Plate.

Model 2, Open Face, 3/4 Plate.   Model 2, Hunting, Bridge.

Model numbers 1 & 2 serial numbers under 659,700. All open face and hunting, parts for this model except dial and fourth pinion are interchangeable.

0 SIZE—MODEL 3
Both Open Face and Hunting have second hand

No. 151— 21J, Open Face, Bridge Model.
No. 150— 21J, Hunting, Bridge Model.
No. 121— 17J, Open Face, Bridge Model.
No. 120— 17J, Hunting, Bridge Model.

Model 3, Open Face, Bridges.   Model 3, Hunting, Bridges.

🕐 Pricing in this Guide are fair market price for **COMPLETE** watches which are reflected from the "<u>NAWCC</u>" National and regional shows.

J. P. STEVENS & CO.

J. P. STEVENS & BRO.
J. P. STEVENS WATCH CO.
Atlanta, Georgia
1882 - 1887

In mid-1881 J. P. Stevens bought part of the Springfield Watch Co. of Massachusetts; and some unfinished watch components from E. F. Bowman. He set up his watchmaking firm above his jewelry store in Atlanta, Ga., and started to produce the Bowman unfinished watches which were 16 size and 18 size, to which was added the "Stevens Patent Regulator." This regulator is best described as a simple disc attached to the plate which has an eccentric groove cut for the arm of the regulator to move in. This regulator is a prominent feature of the J. P. Stevens, and only the top is jeweled. These watches were 16S, 3/4 plate, stem wind and had a nickel plate with damaskeening. The pallets were equidistant locking and needed greater accuracy in manufacturing. About 50 of these watches were made. A line of gilt movements was added. The pallet and fork are made of one piece aluminum. The aluminum was combined with 1/10 copper and formed an exceedingly tough metal which will not rust or become magnetized. The lever of this watch is only one-third the weight of a steel lever. The aluminum lever affords the least possible resistance for overcoming inertia in transmitting power from the escape wheel to the balance. In 1884, the company was turning out about ten watches a day at a price of $20 to $100 each. In the spring of 1887 the company failed. Only 169 true Stevens watches were made, but other watches carried the J. P. Stevens name.

Original "J. P. Stevens Atlanta, Ga.", nickel movement, 16 size, 3/4 plate, lever set, gold jewel settings, note patented spiral grooved regulator, serial number 26.

J.P. Stevens Watch Co. movement by Columbus Watch Co., 18 size, 11-15 jewels.

16 TO 18 SIZE

Grade or Name – Description		Avg	Ex-Fn	Mint
Original Model, Serial Nos. 1 to 174, ALL original with J. P. Stevens dial & **18K** case	★★★★	$6,000	$7,500	$12,500
Original Model, Serial Nos. 1 to 174,(**recased**)	★★★	1,500	2,000	3,000
Aurora, 15-17J	★	400	500	950
Chronograph, 17J, Swiss made, fly back hand	★★	500	650	1,100
Columbus W. Co., 15-17J	★	400	550	900

🕐 A collector should expect to pay modestly higher prices at local shops.

🕐 Watches listed in this book are priced at the collectable Trade Show level, as **complete** watches having an original 14k gold-filled case and *Key Wind* with silver, an original white enamel single sunk dial, and with the entire original movement in good working order with no repairs needed.

J. P. Stevens & Bro., on movement & dial, made by Aurora, 18 size, 15 jewels, Hunting Case, S # 39806.

J.P. Stevens & Bro., Swiss chronograph movement, about 18 size, with fly back hand.

Grade or Name – Description	Avg	Ex-Fn	Mint
Elgin, 15-17J .... ★	$300	$375	$550
Hamilton, 17J .... ★	400	475	775
Hampden, 15-17J	300	375	550
Illinois, 15-17J .... ★	600	700	950
N. Y. W. Co., 17J, Full Plate, S#s range in 500s .... ★	700	900	1,400
N. Y. W. Co. "Bond" Model, S#s range in 500s .... ★★	900	1,200	1,800
Albert H. Potter, **14K case**, Swiss made .... ★★★★	3,000	3,800	6,400
Rockford, 15J, Full Plate, HC .... ★	450	585	950
18S Swiss, 15-17J, by "Vacheron & C.", wolf teeth winding	400	450	700
16S Swiss, 15-17J, Longines	175	225	350
16S Swiss, 15-17J, 3/4 plate	175	225	350
Waltham, 11-15-17J .... ★	425	525	800

J.P. Stevens & Bro., about 18 size, 17 jewels, Note: by "**Vacheron & Constantin**", wolf teeth winding, Ca. 1889.

J.P. Stevens Watch Co. movement by **Waltham**, 18 size, 11 jewels, serial number 1,240,058.

J.P. **Stevens** movement made by Hampden, 18 size, 17 jewels, note eccentric style regulator, serial # 515.

J.P. Stevens & Bro., movement made by Hampden, 18 size, 17 jewels, model 4, S#732,085.

6 SIZE

Grade or Name – Description	Avg	Ex-Fn	Mint
Ladies Model, 15J, LS, HC, **14K** .... ★	$475	$650	$900
Ladies Model, 15J, LS, GF case, HC	225	285	450
Ladies Model, 15J, LS, GF cases, OF	200	265	325
Ladies Model, 15J, LS, GF cases, Swiss made	145	185	275

J.P. **Stevens Watch Co.**, 16 size, 15 jewels, Adjusted to temperature & positions, serial number 21,814.

J.P. **Stevens Watch Co.**, 6 size, 11 jewels, exposed winding gears.

🕐 Generic, nameless or **unmarked** grades for watch movements are listed under the Company name or initials of the Company, etc. by size, jewel count and description.

🕐 Watches listed in this book are priced at the collectable Trade Show level, as **complete** watches having an original 14k gold-filled case and *Key Wind* with silver, an original white enamel single sunk dial, and with the entire original movement in good working order with no repairs needed.

🕐 Pricing in this Guide are fair market price for **COMPLETE** watches which are reflected from the "<u>**NAWCC**</u>" National and regional shows.

SUFFOLK WATCH CO.

Waltham, Massachusetts 1899 - 1901

The Suffolk Watch Company officially succeeded the Columbia Watch Company in March 1901. However, the Suffolk 0-size, 7-jewel nickel movement with lever escapement was being manufactured in the Columbia factory before the end of 1899. More than 25,000 movements were made. The factory was closed after it was purchased by the Keystone Watch Case Company on May 17, 1901. The machinery was moved to the nearby factory of the United States Watch Company (purchased by Keystone in April 1901), where it was used to make the United States Watch Company's 0-size movement,introduced in April 1902. Both the Columbia Watch Company and the Suffolk Watch Company made 0-size movements only.

Grade or Name – Description	Avg	Ex-Fn	Mint
0S, 7J, NI, HC .... ★	$75	$90	$165

Suffolk Watch Co., 0 Size, 7 jewels, serial number 216,841.   Seth Thomas, *Colonial U.S.A.* on movement, 18 size, 7 jewels, model # 11.

SETH THOMAS WATCH CO.

Thomaston, Connecticut

1883 - 1915

Seth Thomas was a very prominent clock manufacturer, and in early 1883, the company made a decision to manufacture watches. The watches were first placed on the market in 1885. They were 18S, open face, stem wind, 3/4 plate, and the escapement was between the plates. The compensating balance was set well below the normal. They were 11J, 16,000 beats per minute train, but soon went to 18,000 or quick train. In 1886, the company started to make higher grade watches and produced four grades: 7J, 11J, 15J, and 17J. That year the output was 100 watches a day.

SETH THOMAS ESTIMATED SERIAL NUMBERS AND PRODUCTION DATES

DATE – SERIAL NO.	DATE – SERIAL NO.	DATE–SERIAL NO.	DATE – SERIAL NO.
1885 – 5,000	1893 – 510,000	1901 – 1,230,000	1909 – 2,500,000
1886 – 20,000	1894 – 600,000	1902 – 1,320,000	1910 – 2,725,000
1887 – 40,000	1895 – 690,000	1903 – 1,410,000	1911 – 2,950,000
1888 – 80,000	1896 – 780,000	1904 – 1,500,000	1912 – 3,175,000
1889 – 150,000	1897 – 870,000	1905 – 1,700,000	1913 – 3,490,000
1890 – 235,000	1898 – 960,000	1906 – 1,900,000	1914 – 3,600,000
1891 – 330,000	1899 – 1,050,000	1907 – 2,100,000	
1892 – 420,000	1900 – 1,140,000	1908 – 2,300,000	

The above list is provided for determining the APPROXIMATE age of your watch. Match serial number with date. Watches were not necessarily sold in the exact order of manufactured date.

Seth Thomas movement, 18 size,17 jewels, Molineux model, 2 tone yellow gold, heavy damaskeening, H. C.

Seth Thomas 18 size,"Molineux" 17 J., 2 tone yellow gold gilt & nickel heavy damaskeening model #2 ,HC

18 SIZE

Grade or Name – Description	Avg	Ex-Fn	Mint
Century, 7J, OF	$65	$100	$175
Century, 7J, HC	95	125	200
Century, 15J, OF	75	110	185
Century, 15J, HC	100	150	225
Chautauqua, 15J, GJS, M#5 ★	150	250	450
Colonial U.S.A., 7J, model # 11	65	90	125
Cordnia Watch Co., 7J	65	90	125
Early model # 1, low serial # under **1,000** ★	300	450	800
Eagle Series, No. 36, 7J, OF	60	80	150
Eagle Series, No. 37, 7J, HC	100	135	200
Eagle Series, No. 106, 11J, OF	65	95	150
Eagle Series, No. 107, 11J, HC	100	135	200
Eagle Series, No. 206, 15J, OF	80	100	165

Liberty, Eagle Series,18 size, 7 jewels, hunting or open face, eagle on movement.

Seth Thomas, 18 size, **28** jewels, gold jewel settings, engraved dated =8,1,99. No serial number.(note regulator) Note: Cooksey Shugart & Tom Engle counted **28 jewels** with dial off. Just before this watch was photographed.

🕐 Pricing in this Guide are fair market price for **COMPLETE** watches which are reflected from the "**NAWCC**" National and regional shows.

Henry Molineux, 18 size, 17 jewels, "Corona W. Co. USA" on dial, open face, serial number 54,951.

Maiden Lane, 18 size, 25 jewels, 2-tone, gold jewel settings, DR., adj.5P, M# 5, S# 350872. A **Double Roller** grade is identified by a recessed area under balance wheel.

Grade or Name – Description	Avg	Ex-Fn	Mint
Eagle Series, No. 207, 15J, HC	$150	$185	$250
Eagle Series, 15J, M# 2, HC	125	175	225
Eagle Series, No. 210, 17J, OF	100	135	200
Eagle Series, No. 211, 17J, HC	150	185	325
Eagle Series, 17J, NI, 3/4, OF	100	135	200
Edgemere, 11J	50	75	150
Edgemere, 17J	60	85	175
Keywind M#2, 7J, 11J, & 15J, 3/4	165	250	400
Keywind M#4, 7J, 11J, & 15J, 3/4	165	250	400
Lakeshore, 17J, GJS, ADJ, NI	150	225	350
Liberty, 7J, 3/4, eagle on back plate	110	165	325
A **Double Roller** grade is identified by a recessed area under balance wheel.			
Maiden Lane, 17J, GJS, DR, Adj.6P, NI, marked, OF ★★★	1,200	1,500	2,200
Maiden Lane, 19J, GJS, DR, Adj.6P, NI, marked, OF ★★★	1,300	1,600	2,400
Maiden Lane, 21J, GJS, DR, Adj.6P, NI, marked, OF ★★★	1,400	1,700	2,500
Maiden Lane, 24J, GJS, DR, Adj.6P, marked, OF ★★★	1,600	1,800	2,600
Maiden Lane, 25J, GJS, DR, Adj.6P, NI, marked, OF ★★★	2,000	2,400	3,000
Maiden Lane, 25J, GJS, DR, Adj.6P, NI, **2 tone**, OF ★★★	2,200	2,600	3,400
Maiden Lane "grade", **28J**, GJS, DR, Adj.5P, NI, OF .. ★★★★★	15,000	22,000	35,000
Henry Molineux, M#3, 20-21J, 3/4, GJS, ADJ, OF ★★	575	700	900
Henry Molineux, M#2, 17-18J, GJS, ADJ, HC ★★	500	625	850
Henry Molineux, M#2, 19-21J, GJS, ADJ, HC ★★★	750	1,000	1,500
Monarch Watch Co., 7-15J, **2-tone**	125	185	285
R. R. Special USA, 7J, with a **locomotive** on dial	125	175	250
Republic USA, 7J, OF	50	65	125

☻ Generic, nameless or **unmarked** grades for watch movements are listed under the Company name or initials of the Company, etc. by size, jewel count and description.

S. Thomas, 7J, 3/4, **multi-color dial**	$175	$285	$650
S. Thomas, 7J, 3/4	55	70	135
S. Thomas, 11J, 3/4, HC	125	175	250
S. Thomas, 11J, 3/4, OF	60	80	150
S. Thomas, 15J, 3/4, HC	125	175	250
S. Thomas, 15J, 3/4, gilded, OF	70	85	150
S. Thomas, 15J, 3/4 , OF	75	90	150
S. Thomas, 16J, 3/4	75	95	175
S. Thomas, 17J, 3/4, OF, nickel	100	135	200

☻ A collector should expect to pay modestly higher prices at local shops.

☻ Pricing in this Guide are fair market price for **COMPLETE** watches which are reflected from the "__NAWCC__" National and regional shows.

Grade or Name – Description	Avg	Ex-Fn	Mint
S. Thomas, 17J, 3/4, **2-Tone**	$175	$250	$400
S. Thomas, 17J, 3/4, OF, gilded	60	85	175
S. Thomas, 17J, 3/4, HC	125	175	250
S. Thomas, 19J, GJS, DR, Adj.5P, OF ★★	700	850	1,150
S. Thomas, 21J, GJS, DR, Adj.5P	500	650	850
S. Thomas, **23**J, GJS, DR, Adj., OF ★★★	1,200	1,500	2,100
S. Thomas, G# 33, 7J, 3/4, gilded, OF	60	75	150
S. Thomas, G# 34, 7J, 3/4, gilded, HC	100	125	200
S. Thomas, G# 37, 7J, 3/4, NI, HC	100	125	200
S. Thomas, G# 44, 11J, 3/4, gilded, OF	60	75	150
S. Thomas, G# 47, 7J, gilded, FULL, OF	60	75	150
S. Thomas, G# 58, 11J, FULL, gilt, OF	60	75	150
S. Thomas, G# 70, 15J, 3/4, gilded, OF	60	75	150
S. Thomas, G# 71, 15J, 3/4, gilded, HC	110	150	225
S. Thomas, G# 80, 17J, 3/4, gilded, ADJ, HC	135	175	250
S. Thomas, G# 101, 15J, 3/4, gilded, ADJ, OF	60	75	150
S. Thomas, G# 149, 15J, gilded, FULL, OF	60	75	150
S. Thomas, G# 159, 15J, NI, FULL, OF	60	75	150
S. Thomas, G# 169, 17J, NI, FULL, OF	70	85	165
S. Thomas, G# 170, 15J, 3/4, NI, OF	60	75	150
S. Thomas, G# 171, 15J, 3/4, NI, HC	110	150	225
S. Thomas, G# 179, **16-18**J, 3/4, NI, ADJ, HC	175	200	300
S. Thomas, G# 180, 17J, 3/4, NI, HC	135	175	250
S. Thomas, G# 182, 17J, DR, NI, FULL, OF	100	125	175
S. Thomas, G# 201, 15J, 3/4, NI, ADJ, OF	95	125	150
S. Thomas, G# 202, 15J, 3/4, NI, ADJ, HC	100	150	200
S. Thomas, G# 245, 19J, GJS, **2-Tone**, HC ★★	1,000	1,200	1,700
S. Thomas, G# 248, 17-21J, FULL, DR, Adj.3P, OF, **2-tone**	250	300	400
S. Thomas, G# 260, 21J, DR, Adj.6P, NI, FULL, OF	400	550	800
S. Thomas, G# 281, 17J, FULL, DR, Adj.3P, OF, **2-tone**	250	300	400
S. Thomas, G# 282, 17J, FULL, DR, Adj.5P, OF	195	250	350
S. Thomas, G# 382, 17J, FULL, DR, Adj.5P, OF, **2-tone**	200	250	400
S. Thomas, G# 406-408, 17J, FULL, Adj., OF	200	250	350
S. Thomas, G# 408-508, 17J, FULL, Adj., HC	225	275	400
Special Motor Service,17J, LS, **2 tone**, OF ★★	400	500	750
Trainsmen Special, **fake "17-23"J Adj**, seen in model 10, 12, 13 .	75	125	250
20th Century (Wards), 11J	75	125	185
20th Century (Wards), 11J, **2-Tone**	125	250	275
Wyoming Watch Co., 7J, OF	95	125	250

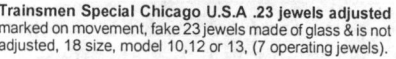

Trainsmen Special Chicago U.S.A .23 jewels adjusted marked on movement, fake 23 jewels made of glass & is not adjusted, 18 size, model 10,12 or 13, (7 operating jewels).

Grade 36, 16 size, 7 jewels, open face, three-quarter nickel plate.

16 SIZE
(OF Only)

Grade or Name – Description	Avg	Ex-Fn	Mint
Centennial, 7J, 3/4, NI, OF	$50	$70	$125
Locust, 7J, NI, 3/4, OF	50	70	125
Locust, 17J, NI, ADJ, 3/4, OF	60	80	150
Republic USA, 7J, OF	50	70	125

⊕ Generic, nameless or **unmarked** grades for watch movements are listed under the Company name or initials of the Company, etc. by size, jewel count and description.

	Avg	Ex-Fn	Mint
S. Thomas, G# 25, 7J, BRG, OF	$45	$60	$100
S. Thomas, G# 26, 15J, BRG, GJS, OF	50	70	125
S. Thomas, G# 27, 17J, BRG, GJS, OF	65	80	135
S. Thomas, G# 28, 17J, BRG, Adj.3P, GJS, OF	75	100	200
S. Thomas, G# 326, 7J, 3/4, NI, OF	45	60	100
S. Thomas, G# 328, 15J, 3/4, NI, OF	50	65	125
S. Thomas, G# 332, 7J, 3/4, NI, OF	45	60	100
S. Thomas, G# 334, 15J, NI, ADJ,3/4, DMK, OF	50	70	125
S. Thomas, G# 336, 17J, ADJ, 3/4, DMK, OF	75	100	150

Seth Thomas, 12 size, 7 jewels, open face, pendant set.

Seth Thomas, 12 size, 17 jewels, gold jewel settings, gold center wheel, open face, Adj3p.

12 SIZE
(OF Only)

Grade or Name – Description	Avg	Ex-Fn	Mint
Centennial, 7J	$35	$60	$100
Republic USA, 7J, OF	35	65	110
S. Thomas, G# 25, 7J, BRG, OF	35	60	100
S. Thomas, G# 26, 15J, BRG, GJS, OF	40	65	110
S. Thomas, G# 27, 17J, BRG, GJS, OF	45	75	125
S. Thomas, G# 28, 17J, OF, BRG, Adj.3P, GJS	50	85	150
S. Thomas, G# 326, 7J, OF, 3/4, NI	35	60	100
S. Thomas, G# 328, 15J, OF, 3/4, NI	40	65	120

⊕ Watches listed in this book are priced at the collectable Trade Show level, as complete watches having an original 14k gold-filled case and Key Wind with silver, an original white enamel single sunk dial, and with the entire original movement in good working order with no repairs needed.

⊕ Generic, nameless or unmarked grades for watch movements are listed under the Company name or initials of the Company, etc. by size, jewel count and description.

Seth Thomas movement, 6 size, 7 jewels, serial number 441,839. Sometimes appears in a 12 size case.

SETH THOMAS, 0 size, 15 jewels, pendant set, hunting case, serial number 200,449.

6 SIZE
(Some 6 Size were spread to fit 12 Size cases)

Grade or Name – Description	Avg	Ex-Fn	Mint
Century, 7J, NI, 3/4	$35	$60	$100
Countess Janet, 17J, Adj., HC	75	125	200
Eagle Series, 7J, No. 45, 3/4, NI, DMK, OF	50	65	100
Eagle Series, 7J, No. 205, 3/4, HC	60	125	150
Eagle Series, 15J, No. 35, 3/4, NI, DMK, OF	55	75	125
Eagle Series, 15J, No. 245, 3/4, HC	70	125	150
Edgemere, 7-11J,	55	75	125
Republic USA, 7J	50	65	100
Seth Thomas, 7J, 3/4, **14K, 26 DWT, HC**	300	400	600
Seth Thomas, 11J, 3/4, HC	70	80	150
Seth Thomas, 11J, 3/4, OF	55	75	125
S. Thomas, G# 35, 7J, NI, DMK,3/4, HC	75	135	165
S. Thomas, G# 119, 16J, GJS, NI, DMK, 3/4, HC	70	125	150
S. Thomas, G# 205, 15J, HC	70	125	150
S. Thomas, G# 320, 7J, NI, DMK, 3/4, OF	50	65	100
S. Thomas, G# 322, 15J, OF	55	70	110

NOTE: Add **$25** to **$50** for HC.

0 SIZE

Grade or Name – Description	Avg	Ex-Fn	Mint
Seth Thomas, 7J, No. 1, OF	$60	$75	$150
Seth Thomas, 7J, No. 1, HC	70	135	225
Seth Thomas, 15J, GJS, No. 3, OF	60	80	150
Seth Thomas, 15J, No. 3, HC	75	100	225
Seth Thomas, 17J, GJS, PS, No. 9, OF	60	80	150
Seth Thomas, 17J, GJS, PS, No. 9, HC	75	135	225

🕐 A collector should expect to pay modestly higher prices at local shops.

🕐 Pricing in this Guide are fair market price for **COMPLETE** watches which are reflected from the "**NAWCC**" National and regional shows.

Number	Model	Number	Model	Number	Model	Number	Model
1 to 10900	1	87601 " 87900	3	540001 " 541000	2	710601 " 712400	8
10901 " 25100	3	87901 " 89100	2	541001 " 542000	6	712401 " 713700	9
25101 " 25200	2	89101 " 89600	4	542001 " 544000	2	713701 " 715200	8
25201 " 25300	3	89601 " 90800	2	544001 " 547000	6	715201 to 715300	8
25301 " 25400	2	90801 " 90900	4	547001 " 549000	2	715301 " 715600	8
25401 " 28000	3	90901 " 91500	2	549001 " 551000	7	715601 " 717000	9
28001 " 29000	2	91501 " 92000	4	551001 " 556000	6	717001 " 718000	8
29001 " 34900	3	92001 " 94400	2	556001 " 558000	7	718001 " 718100	9
34901 " 35000	2	94401 " 94600	3	558001 " 559000	2	718101 " 718200	4
35001 " 36200	4	94601 " 95200	2	559001 " 562000	6	718201 " 721500	8
36201 " 40000	2	95201 " 95300	3	562001 " 568000	7	721501 " 722000	9
40001 " 41200	3	95301 " 95500	2	568001 " 569000	6	722001 " 722200	8
41201 " 41500	2	95501 " 95800	3	569001 " 570000	7	722201 " 722900	9
41501 " 42100	3	95801 " 96500	2	570001 " 571000	6	722901 " 725600	8
42101 " 44800	2	96501 " 97100	3	571001 " 575000	7	725601 " 725700	9
44801 " 46000	4	97101 " 98200	2	575001 " 577000	6	725701 " 727000	9
46001 " 47200	2	98201 " 98225	3	577001 " 579000	7	727001 " 728600	9
47201 " 47300	3	98226 " 98700	2	579001 to 581000	6	728601 " 729500	9
47301 " 48200	2	98701 " 99300	3	581001 " 582600	7	729501 " 730100	9
48201 " 48300	3	99301 " 100000	2	582601 " 582800	4	730101 " 730300	8
48301 " 48600	2	100001 " 128000	14	582801 " 584100	7	730301 " 730800	8
48601 " 49000	3	128001 " 137000	15	584101 " 585000	6	730801 " 731000	8
49001 " 50300	2	137001 " 138000	14	585001 " 585400	7	731001 " 731200	9
50301 " 50400	4	138001 " 139000	15	585401 " 585600	4	731201 " 734900	9
50401 " 51100	2	139001 " 141000	14	585601 " 586000	7	734901 " 735100	9
51101 " 52000	4	141001 " 142000	15	586001 " 590000	6	735101 " 736700	9
52001 " 53300	2	142001 " 144000	14	590001 " 591000	7	736701 " 737800	9
53301 " 54500	4	144001 " 160000	15	591001 " 592000	6	737801 " 738400	8
54501 " 54900	2	160001 " 165000	16	592001 " 592300	7	738401 " 738600	9
54901 " 55000	3	165001 " 166000	14	592301 " 592800	4	738601 " 740500	8
55001 " 55400	2	166001 " 200000	16	592801 " 593000	7	740501 " 741200	9
55401 " 55700	4	200001 " 400000	5	593001 " 607000	6	741201 " 743100	9
55701 " 56000	3	400001 " 420000	16	607001 " 608000	7	743101 " 744200	9
56601 " 57700	4	420001 " 500000	17	608001 " 610000	6	744201 " 747000	9
57701 " 58900	2	500001 " 500500	2	610001 " 612000	7	747001 " 747300	9
58901 " 59200	3	500501 " 502400	3	612001 " 615000	6	747301 " 747500	8
59201 " 59300	2	502401 " 503500	2	615001 " 616000	7	747501 " 747600	9
59301 " 60500	4	503501 to 505600	3	616001 " 617000	6	747601 " 747700	8
60501 " 60800	2	505501 " 506200	2	617001 " 618000	7	747701 " 747800	9
60801 " 61800	3	506201 " 507900	3	618001 " 620000	6	747801 " 748000	9
61801 " 62400	2	507901 " 508000	2	620001 " 621800	7	748001 " 748200	9
62401 " 63800	4	508001 " 509000	7	621801 " 622000	4	748201 " 749100	9
63801 " 64800	2	509001 " 509800	2	622001 " 632000	6	749101 " 749200	9
64801 " 65100	3	509801 " 510000	4	632001 " 633000	7	749201 " 750000	8
65101 " 65700	2	510001 " 512300	2	633001 " 640000	6	750001 " 752600	9
65701 " 65800	4	512301 " 513500	7	640001 " 640100	7	752601 " 753300	9
65801 " 66200	2	513501 " 514300	2	640101 " 640800	6	753301 " 754100	9
66201 " 67300	2	514301 " 514800	3	640801 " 641100	7	754101 " 758400	9
67301 " 68100	2	514801 " 515300	2	641101 " 641700	6	758401 " 758700	9
68101 " 68200	3	515301 " 516100	6	641701 " 642000	7	758701 " 759600	9
68201 " 68800	2	516101 " 516600	7	642001 " 642400	6	759601 " 760600	9
68801 " 69800	3	516601 " 516800	4	642401 " 642500	7	760601 " 761800	8
69801 " 70540	2	516801 " 517400	7	642501 " 647100	6	761801 " 762000	9
70541 " 70550	3	517401 " 517500	3	647101 " 647300	7	762001 " 769000	8
70551 " 71700	3	517501 " 518200	6	647301 " 647600	6	769001 " 769200	9
71701 " 71950	3	518201 " 519300	7	647601 " 647800	7	769201 " 770100	8
71951 " 72000	2	519301 " 519800	6	647801 " 700000	6	770101 " 770600	9
72001 to 73200	2	519801 " 521800	7	700001 " 700100	9	770601 " 777600	8
73201 " 73500	3	521801 " 523300	6	700101 " 700300	9	777601 " 778700	9
73501 " 74900	2	523301 " 523800	4	700301 " 700800	8	778701 " 778900	9
74901 " 75700	3	523801 " 523834	6	700801 " 700900	9	778901 " 784600	8
75701 " 77000	2	523835 " 528100	7	700901 " 701900	8	784601 " 784700	9
77001 " 78000	3	528101 " 528600	6	701901 " 702400	9	784701 " 785800	8
78001 " 79900	2	528601 " 528900	7	702401 " 702900	8	785801 " 786400	9
79901 " 80100	3	528901 " 529900	6	702901 " 703200	9	786401 " 786800	9
80101 " 80500	2	529901 " 530500	7	703201 " 703300	8	786801 " 786900	9
80501 " 81000	3	530501 " 530700	6	703301 " 703800	9	786901 to 788700	8
81001 " 82100	2	530701 " 530800	2	703801 " 703900	8	788701 " 790000	9
82101 " 82300	3	530801 " 531000	6	703901 " 704300	9	790001 " 795300	8
82301 " 84000	2	531001 " 531100	7	704301 " 705800	8	795301 " 795350	9
84001 " 84500	4	531101 " 532600	6	705801 " 706000	9		
84501 " 84900	2	532601 " 535000	7	706001 " 707400	8		
84901 " 85500	3	535001 " 536000	2	707401 " 708000	9		
85501 " 86000	4	536001 " 537000	7	708001 " 709100	8		
86001 " 87000	2	537001 " 538000	6	709101 " 709300	9		
87001 " 87500	4	538001 " 539000	7	709301 " 710200	8	900001 to 950000	17
87501 " 87600	2	539001 " 540000	6	710201 " 710600	9	950001 " 1000000	18

SETH THOMAS WATCH CO.
IDENTIFICATION OF MOVEMENTS
BY MODEL NUMBER

How to Identify Your Watch Size & Model: Compare the movement of your watch with the illustrations in this section. While comparing, note the location of the balance, jewels, screws, gears, and type of back plate (Full, 3/4, Bridge) these will be clues in identifying the movement you have.

Model 1, 18 size, Open Face

Model 2, 18 size, Hunting

Model 3, 18 size, Open Face

Model 4, 18 size, Key Wind

I will respect and appreciate positive sound reliable comments, corrections, improvements or remarks but reserve the right to except the statement or keep my own observations & views. (*Cooksey*)

Model 5, 18 size, Maiden Lane Series, Open Face.

Model 6, 18 Size, Open Face

Model 7 & 9, 18 size

Model 8, 18 size

Model 10, 18 size, Open Face

Model 11, 18 size, Hunting

Model 13, 18 size, Hunting

16 Size

16 Size, Open Face

12 Size, Open Face

6 Size, Open face

Model 14, 6 size

Model 16 & 17, 6 size

0 SIZE
No. 9=17 J.
No. 3=15 J.
No. 1=7 J.

TREMONT WATCH CO.

Boston, Massachusetts 1864 - 1866

In 1864 A. L. Dennison thought that if he could produce a good movement at a reasonable price, there would be a ready market for it. Dennison went to Switzerland to find a supplier of cheap parts, as arbors were too costly in America. He found a source for parts, mainly the train and escapement and the balance. About 600 sets were to be furnished. Dials were first made by Mr. Gold and Mr. Spear, then later by Mr. Hull and Mr. Carpenter. Tremont had hoped to produce 600 sets of trains per month. In May of 1865, the first movements were ready for the market. They were 18S, key wind, 7-15 jewels, and engraved "Tremont Watch Co." In the late 1866, the company moved to Melrose. The Melrose Watch Co. produced about 5,000 watches. Serial number range from 1 to about 10-11,000. (See Melrose W. Co.)

Tremont Watch Co., with "Washington Street Boston" engraved on movement, 18 size, 15 jewels, key wind and set, serial number 5,264.

Tremont movement, 18 size, 15 jewels, key wind & set, serial number 8,875.

Grade or Name – Description	Avg	Ex-Fn	Mint
18S, 7J, KW, KS	$250	$300	$425
18S, 11J, KW, KS	250	300	425
18S, 7-11-15J, KW, KS, gilded Silveroid	200	250	400
18S, 7-11-15J, KW, KS, gilded, marked LONDON	250	300	500
18S, 15J, KW, KS, gilded	250	300	450
18S, 15J, KW, KS, HC, **14K**	800	1,000	1,400
18S, 15J, KW, KS, gilded, Washington Street ★★	500	700	1,300
18S, 17J, KW, KS, gilded	300	375	500
18S, 7-15J, KW, **KS from back**, 3/4 plate,(English style) .. ★★★	1,800	2,500	3,500

Signed on movement Tremont Watch Co.,
18S, 3/4 plate,15J, KW, **KS from back**, (English style)

TRENTON WATCH CO.
Trenton, New Jersey
1885 - 1908

Trenton watches were marketed under the following labels: Trenton, Ingersoll, Fortuna, Illinois Watch Case Company, Calumet U.S.A., Locomotives Special, Marvel Watch Co., Reliance Watch Co.

Serial numbers started at 2,001 and ended at 4,100,000. Total production was about 1,934,000.

CHRONOLOGY OF THE DEVELOPMENT OF TRENTON WATCH CO.:
New Haven Watch Co., New Haven, Conn. 1883-1887
Trenton Watch Co., Trenton, N. J. 1887-1908
Sold to Ingersoll 1908-1922

TRENTON MODELS AND GRADES
With Years of Manufacture and Serial Numbers

Date	Numbers	Size	Model	Date	Numbers	Size	Model
1887-1889	2,001-61,000	18	1	1900-1903	2,000,001-2,075,000	6	2
1889-1891	64,001-135,000	18	2	1902-1905	2,075,001-2,160,000	6	3 LS
1891-1898 *1	135,001-201,000	18	3	"	"	12	2 LS
1899-1890	201,001-300,000	18	6	1905-1907	2,160,001-2,250,000	6	3 PS
1891-1900	300,001-500,000	18	4	"	"	12	2 PS
1892-1897	500,001-600,000	6	1	1899-1902	2,500,001-2,600,000	3/0	1
1894-1899	650,001-700,000	16	1	ca. 1906	2,800,001-2,850,000	6	3 PS
1898-1900	700,001-750,000	6	2	"	"	12	2 PS
1900-1904 * 2	750,001-800,000	18	4	1900-1904	3,000,001-3,139,000	16	2
1896-1900	850,001-900,000	12	1	1903-1907	3,139,001-3,238,000	16	3 OF
1898-1903	900,001-1,100,000	18	5	1903-1907	3,500,001-3,600,000	16	3 HC
1902-1907	1,300,001-1,400,000	18	6	1905-1907	4,000,001-4,100,000	0	1

1—7 jewel grades made only during 1891; 9 jewel chronograph Pat. Mar. 17, 1891, made 1891-1898.
2—A few examples are KWKS for export to England.

Trenton movement, 18 size, 4 jewels, model # 1, serial number 4,744. (New Haven STYLE.) Model #2 is similar.

Trenton movement, 18 size, 7 jewels, 4th model, serial number 788,313.

🕐 A collector should expect to pay modestly higher prices at local shops.

🕐 Pricing in this Guide are fair market price for **COMPLETE** watches which are reflected from the "**NAWCC**" National and regional shows.

18 SIZE

Grade or Name – Description	Avg	Ex-Fn	Mint
Trenton W. Co., M#1-2, gilded, OF................................★	$150	$185	$300
Trenton W Co., 7J, KW, KS...★	175	235	500
Trenton W. Co., M#3, 7J, 3/4...	60	80	125
Trenton W. Co., M#3, 9J, 3/4...	60	80	125
Trenton W. Co., M#4, 7J, FULL..	60	80	125
Trenton W. Co., M#4, 11J, FULL..	60	80	125
Trenton W. Co., M#4, 15J, FULL..	60	80	125
Trenton W. Co., M#4-5, FULL, OF, NI	60	80	125
Chronograph, 9J, start, stop, & fly back, **DMK** ....★★★★	275	400	750
Chronograph, 9J, start, stop, & fly back, **GILDED** ....★★★★	275	400	750
Locomotive Special, tu-tone, **marked 23J,** also 17J., 7 working jewels, a locomotive on dial & movement (fake jewels)..................★	100	175	275
Marvel W. Co. **Marked 23 jewels** (fake jewels) 7 working jewels	60	80	125
New Haven Watch Co. STYLE, M#1, 4J ....★★★	250	350	500

Note: Add $25 to value of above watches in hunting case.

Chronograph, **18** size, 9 jewels, **third model**; Gilded, start, stop & fly back, S# 135,069, pat.mar.17.91.

Trenton movement, 18 size, 7 jewels, model #3, serial number 148,945.

16 SIZE

Grade or Name – Description	Avg	Ex-Fn	Mint
Railroad Reliance, 17J, M# 5, OF ....★	$100	$125	$235
Trenton W. Co., M#1-2, 7J, 3/4, NI, OF	40	55	125
Trenton W. Co., M#3, 7J, 3F BRG	40	55	125
Trenton W. Co., M#3, 11J, 3F BRG	40	55	125
Trenton W. Co., M#3, 15J, 3F BRG	45	60	135
Trenton W. Co., 7,11,15J, 3F BRG, NI	45	60	135
Trenton W. Co., Grade #30 & 31, 7J	40	55	125
Trenton W. Co., Grade #35, 36 & 38, 11J	40	55	125
Trenton W. Co., Grade #45, 16J..	60	80	150
Trenton W. Co., Grade #125, 12J......................................	40	55	125
Trenton W. Co., 7J. **convertible model** converts .... to open face or hunting case ....★★★	150	235	365

🕐 Generic, nameless or **unmarked** grades for watch movements are listed under the Company name or initials of the Company, etc. by size, jewel count and description.

🕐 A collector should expect to pay modestly higher prices at local shops.

🕐 Watches listed in this book are priced at the collectable trade show level, as **complete** watches having an original 14k gold-filled case and *Key Wind* with silver, an original white enamel single sunk dial, and with the entire original movement in good working order with no repairs needed.

Ingersoll Trenton movement, 16 size, 19 jewels, three fingered bridge, adjusted, serial number 3,419,771.

Ingersoll Trenton movement, 16 size, 12 jewels; "Edgemere" engraved on movement.

Grade or Name – Description	Avg	Ex-Fn	Mint
Ingersoll Trenton, 7J, 3F BRG	$40	$60	$125
Ingersoll Trenton, 15J, 3F BRG, NI, ADJ	75	100	150
Ingersoll Trenton, 17J, 3F BRG, NI, ADJ	85	110	160
Ingersoll Trenton, 19J, 3F BRG, NI, Adj.5P, OF ★	150	225	350
Ingersoll Trenton, 19J, 3F BRG, NI, Adj.5P, HC ★★	175	250	400
Peerless, 7J, SW, LS	40	65	85
Reliance, 7J	40	65	85

Note: Add $25 to value of above watches in hunting case.

Locomotive Special Chicago U.S.A. 23 jewels adjusted Marked on movement, 18 size, OF, tu-tone, locomotive on dial & movement, model # 6, S# 1,366,044. This is a fake 23J., and is not adjusted, it implies it is a railroad watch.

Trenton movement, convertible model converts to open face or hunting case, 16 size, 7 J.

🕑 A collector should expect to pay modestly higher prices at local shops.

🕑 Pricing in this Guide are fair market price for **COMPLETE** watches which are reflected from the "**NAWCC**" National and regional shows.

10 - 12 SIZE

Grade or Name – Description	Avg	Ex-Fn	Mint
"Fortuna," 7J, 3 finger BRG	$35	$40	$65
Trenton W. Co., M#1, 7J, 3/4	35	40	65
Monogram, 7-15J, SW	35	40	65

Trenton Watch Co. movement, 12 size, *Fortuna*, 7 jewels, 3 finger BRG., quick train, cut expansion balance.

Trenton Watch Co. movement, 6 size, 7 jewels, open face & hunting, nickel damaskeened.

6 SIZE

Grade or Name – Description	Avg	Ex-Fn	Mint
Trenton W. Co., 7J, 3/4, NI	$25	$40	$55
Trenton W. Co., 7J, 3Finger BRG	25	40	55
Trenton W. Co., 15J, 3Finger BRG	35	50	90
"Fortuna," 7J, 3 Finger Bridge	30	40	55

Note: Add $25 to value of above watches in hunting case.

0 SIZE

Grade or Name – Description	Avg	Ex-Fn	Mint
Trenton W. Co., 7J, 3F BRG	$25	$45	$65
Trenton W. Co., 15J, 3F BRG	35	50	90

Note: Add $25 to value of above watches in hunting case.

Trenton Chronograph, 18 size, 9J, start, stop, & fly back, Model # 3, Ca. 1892-98.
The Trenton chronograph, basically the grade 40 or 41 with modifications of chronograph which was patented by Charles Schlatter on March 17, 1891(#448,549).

UNITED STATES WATCH CO.
Marion Watch Co.
Marion, New Jersey
1865 - 1877

The United States Watch Company was chartered in 1865, and the factory building was started in August 1865 and was completed in 1866. The first watch, called the "Frederic Atherton," was not put on the market until July 1867. It was America's first mass produced stem winding watch. This first grade was 18S, 19J, full plate and a gilt finish movement. A distinctive feature of the company's full plate movements was the butterfly shaped patented opening in the plate which allowed escapement inspection. That same year a second grade called the "Fayette Stratton" was introduced. It was also a gilt finish, full plate movement.

Most of these were 15J, but some of the very early examples have been noted in 17J. In 1868 the "George Channing," "Edwin Rollo," and "Marion Watch Co." grades were introduced. All were 18S, 15J, full plate movements in a gilt finish. In February 1869 the gilt version of the "United States Watch Co." grade was introduced. It was 18S, 19J, full plate and was the company's first entry into the prestige market. Later that year the company introduced their first nickel grade, a 19J, 18S, full plate movement called the "A. H. Wallis." About this same time, in December 1869, they introduced America's most expensive watch, the first nickel, 19J, 18S, full plate "United States Watch Co." grade. Depending on case weight, these prestige watches retailed between $500 and $600, more than the average man earned in a year at that time. The company also introduced damaskeening to the American market; first on gilt movements and later on the nickel grades. The damaskeening process was later improved by using **IVORY** disc in place of wooden disc. The United States and Wallis 19J prestige grades were beautifully finished with richly enameled engraving including a variety of unique designs on the balance cock. It is significant to note that no solid gold trains have been seen with these prestige items in the extant examples presently known.

Below butterfly cut-out.

pin set

FREDERIC ATHERTON & CO., 18 size, 19 J., gold jewel settings, key wind, also note the pin set on rim which will bring a HIGHER price. Note butterfly cut-out.

United States Watch Co. Marion,N.J.,1871 advertisement. Note the butterfly cut-out exposing the escapement.

In 1870 the company introduced their first watch for ladies, a 10S, 15J, plate, cock & bridge movement which was made to their specifications in Switzerland. This model was first introduced in two grades, the "R. F. Pratt" and "Chas. G. Knapp," both in a 15J, gilt finish movement. Later it was offered in a high grade, 19J "I. H. Wright" nickel finish movement. During 1870 and 1871 several other full plate grades in both gilt and nickel finish were introduced. In 1871 development on a new line of full plate, 3/4 plate, and plate & bridge was started but not introduced to the market until late in 1872 and early 1873. The 10S and 16S new grades in 3/4 plate and bridge were probably delayed well into 1873 and were not available long, just before the "Panic of 1873" started in September; this explains their relative scarcity.

By July 1874 the "Panic" had taken its toll and it was necessary for the company to reorganize as the Marion Watch Company, a name formerly used for one of their grades. At this time jewel count, finish standards, and prices were lowered on the full plate older grades, but this proved to be a mistake. That same year they introduced a cased watch called the "North Star", their cheapest watch at $15 retail.

The year of 1875 hit the watch industry the hardest; price cutting was predatory and the higher priced watches of the United States Watch Co. were particularly vulnerable. Further lowering of finish standards and prices did not help and in 1876 the company was once again reorganized into the Empire City Watch Co. and their products were displayed at the Centennial that year. The Centennial Exhibition was not enough to save the faltering company and they finally closed their doors in 1877. The Howard brothers of Fredonia, New York (Independent and Fredonia Watch Co.) purchased most of the remaining movements in stock and machinery. In the ten year period of movement production, current statistical studies indicate an estimated production of only some 60,000 watches, much smaller than the number deduced from the serial numbers assigned up to as high as 289,000.

NOTE: The above historical data and estimated production figures are based on data included in the new NAWCC book **MARION, A History of the United States Watch Company,** by William Muir and Bernard Kraus. This definitive work is available from NAWCC, Inc., 514 Poplar St., Columbia, PA. (Courtesy, Gene Fuller, MARION book editor.) This book is recommended for your library.

EMPIRE CITY W. CO. & EQUIVALENT U.S.W. CO. GRADES

Empire City W. Co.	United States W. Co.
W. S. Wyse	A. H. Wallis
L. W. Frost	Henry Randel
Cyrus H. Loutrel	Wm. Alexander
J. L. Ogden	S. M. Beard
E. F. C. Young	John W. Lewis
D. C. Wilcox	George Channing
Henry Harper	Asa Fuller
Jesse A. Dodd	Edwin Rollo
E. C. Hine	J. W. Deacon
New York Belle	A. J. Wood
The Champion	G. A. Read
Black Diamond	Young America

NOTE: Courtesy Gene Fuller, NAWCC "MARION" book editor.

Empire City W. Co., Henry Harper, note: movement does not have **Butterfly Cut-out.**

United States Watch Co. movement, 18 size, 19 jewels, gold jewel settings, key wind. Their highest grade watch.

United States Watch Co., Henry Randel, 15 jewels, KWKS, FROSTED plates, S.# 24,944

MARION
18 SIZE
(All with Butterfly Cut-out Except for 3/4 Plate)

Grade or Name – Description	Avg	Ex-Fn	Mint
Wm. Alexander, 15J, NI, KW, HC .... ★	$300	$400	$600
Wm. Alexander, 15J, NI, KW, OF .... ★	300	400	600
Wm. Alexander, 15J, NI, SW, OF .... ★	300	400	600
Frederic Atherton & Co., 15J, SW, gilded	275	350	500
Frederic Atherton & Co., 17J, KW, gilded, HC	350	400	600
Frederic Atherton & Co., 17J, KW, gilded, OF	285	350	535
Frederic Atherton & Co., 17J, SW, gilded, HC	300	375	550
Frederic Atherton & Co., 17J, SW, gilded, OF	285	350	535

U.S. Watch Co., dial and movement, 18 size, 20 jewels, hunting case, 3/4 plate, engraved on movement "N.D. Godfrey," serial number 72,042. Painted on the dial "New York 1873." The dial consists of day-date-month and moon phases.

NOTE: The **PIN** or **NAIL** set feature is considered more desirable & will bring a **HIGHER** price.

Grade or Name – Description	Avg	Ex-Fn	Mint
Frederic Atherton & Co., 19J, SW, gilded, ... ★ ★	$600	$800	$1,200
Frederic Atherton & Co., 19J, KW, gilded .... ★ ★	650	950	1,400
BC&M R.R., 11J, KW... ★ ★ ★ ★	2,000	2,600	4,200
BC&M R.R., 15J, gilded, KW .... ★ ★ ★ ★	2,000	2,600	4,200
S. M. Beard, 15J, KW, NI, OF .... ★	200	300	450
S. M. Beard, 15J, SW, NI, OF.. ★	200	300	450
S. M. Beard, 15J, SW or KW, HC .... ★	250	350	500
Centennial Phil., 11-15J, SW or KW, NI .... ★ ★ ★ ★	2,500	3,400	5,300
George Channing, 15J, KW, NI	200	300	450
George Channing, 15J, KW, gilded	200	300	450
George Channing, 15J, KW, NI, 3/4 Plate	250	350	500
George Channing, 17J, KW, NI	250	350	500
J. W. Deacon, 11-13J, KW, gilded................................	175	250	350
J. W. Deacon, 15J, KW, gilded	200	300	450
J. W. Deacon, 11-15J, KW, 3/4 Plate............................ ★	300	385	650
Empire City Watch Co., 11J, SW, **NO butterfly cut-out**. ★ ★ ★ ★	1,700	2,500	4,800
Empire Combination Timer, 11J, FULL, time & distance on dial.. ★ ★ ★	1,600	2,400	4,400
Empire Combination Timer, 15J, 3/4, time & distance on dial.. ★ ★ ★	1,500	2,200	4,200
Fellows, 15J, NI, KW .... ★	400	485	750
Benjamin Franklin, 15J, KW.. ★ ★	425	600	900
Asa Fuller, 7-11J, gilded, KW	200	275	400
Asa Fuller, 15J, gilded, KW...	200	275	400
Asa Fuller, 15J, gilded, KW, 3/4 Plate.................... ★ ★	275	350	500
N. D. Godfrey, 20J, NI, 3/4 plate, day date month, moon phases, c. 1873, HC, 18K .... ★ ★ ★ ★	5,200	7,000	14,000
John W. Lewis, 15J, NI, KW .... ★	200	275	400
John W. Lewis, 15J, NI, SW .... ★	250	375	500
John W. Lewis, 15J, NI, 3/4 Plate .... ★	250	375	500

Edwin Rollo, 18 size, 15 jewels, gilded, key wind & set, note butterfly cut-out, serial number 110,214.

Marion Watch Co. personalized Watch, 18 size, about 15J., pin set, note butterfly cut-out, serial # 106,761.

🕐 Watches listed in this book are priced at the collectable Trade Show level, as **complete** watches having an original 14k gold-filled case and *Key Wind* with silver, an original white enamel single sunk dial, and with the entire original movement in good working order with no repairs needed.

🕐 Pricing in this Guide are fair market price for **COMPLETE** watches which are reflected from the "**NAWCC**" National and regional shows.

🕐 A collector should expect to pay modestly higher prices at local shops.

Empire City Watch Co. on movement, U.S. Marion Watch Co. on dial, 18 size, 15 jewels, note **NO butterfly cut-out** on this model. **Second Quality**

United States Watch Co., 18 size, 19 jewels, gold jewel settings, key wind & pin set, serial number 24,054.

Grade or Name – Description	Avg	Ex-Fn	Mint
Marion Watch Co., 11J, KW, gilded.. ★	$175	$250	$375
Marion Watch Co., 15J, KW, gilded.. ★	200	275	400
Marion Watch Co., 15J, SW, gilded, 3/4 Plate .... ★ ★	300	400	600
Marion Watch Co., 17-19J, KW, gilded .... ★	400	500	750
N.J. R.R.&T. Co., 15J, gilded, KW............................... ★ ★ ★	1,300	1,700	2,800
Newspaper Special Order, 11-15J, gilded, SW or KW .... ★	500	650	1,100
North Star, 7J, KW, NI case.. ★	300	385	550
North Star, 7J, SW, KS.. ★	300	385	500
North Star, 7J, 3/4 Plate.. ★	375	450	600
Pennsylvania R.R., 15J, NI, KW, HC .... ★ ★ ★ ★	2,500	3,300	6,000
Personalized Watches, 7-11J, KW, 3/4 Plate............................ ★	250	335	500
Personalized Watches, 11J, KW, gilded .... ★	250	335	500
Personalized Watches, 15J, KW, gilded .... ★	250	335	500
Personalized Watches, 15J, KW, NI .... ★	250	335	500
Personalized Watches, 15J, KW, 3/4 Plate .... ★	250	335	500
Personalized Watches, 19J, KW, Full Plate.............................. ★	400	500	850
Henry Randel, 15J, KW, NI .... ★	225	300	450
Henry Randel, 15J, KW, **frosted plates** .... ★	300	375	575
Henry Randel, 15J, SW, NI.. ★	250	325	450
Henry Randel, 15J, 3/4 Plate .... ★	300	425	600
Henry Randel, 17J, KW, NI .... ★	300	375	600
G. A. Read, 7J, gilded, KW..	175	265	400
G. A. Read, 7J, 3/4 Plate	200	285	425
Edwin Rollo, 11J, KW, gilded...	150	200	400
Edwin Rollo, 15J, KW, gilded...	175	265	400
Edwin Rollo, 15J, SW, gilded	175	265	400
Edwin Rollo, 15J, 3/4 Plate .... ★	225	300	475
Royal Gold, 11J, KW.. ★	400	525	850
Royal Gold, 15J, KW.. ★	450	600	950
Royal Gold, 15J, 3/4 Plate .... ★ ★	500	700	1,300

🕐 A collector should expect to pay modestly higher prices at local shops.

🕐 Watches listed in this book are priced at the collectable Trade Show level, as **complete** watches having an original 14k gold-filled case and *Key Wind* with silver, an original white enamel single sunk dial, and with the entire original movement in good working order with no repairs needed.

A.H. Wallis on movement, Empire City Watch Co. on dial, 18 size, 19 jewels, three-quarter plate, hunting. This combination timer has listed on the dial, 16 cities showing the time of day and distance in comparison with New York City, serial number 54,409.

Grade or Name – Description		Avg	Ex-Fn	Mint
Rural New York, 15J, gilded	★	$400	$550	$800
Fayette Stratton, 11J, gilded	★	200	285	425
Fayette Stratton, 15J, KW, gilded	★	200	285	425
Fayette Stratton, 15J, SW, gilded	★	175	225	400
Fayette Stratton, 17J, KW, gilded	★	275	365	500
Fayette Stratton, 17J, SW, gilded	★	275	365	500
Union Pacific R.R., 15J, KW, gilded	★★★	2,200	2,800	4,600
United States Watch Co., 15J, NI, KW	★	750	900	1,200
United States Watch Co., 15J, NI, SW	★	800	950	1,300
United States Watch Co., 15J, 3/4 Plate, NI	★	800	950	1,300
United States Watch Co., 15J, 3/4 Plate, gilded	★	800	950	1,300
United States Watch Co., 19J, GJS, Adj.5P, **18K HC**, dial, mvt. & case all marked, Pin Set, SW	★★★	3,800	4,500	7,400
United States Watch Co., 19J, NI, KW	★★	1,300	1,800	2,500
United States Watch Co., 19J, NI, SW	★★	1,400	1,800	2,600
A. H. Wallis, 15J, KW, NI	★	200	250	400
A. H. Wallis, 15J, SW, NI	★	200	250	400
A. H. Wallis, 17J, KW, NI	★	200	250	450
A. H. Wallis, 17J, SW, NI	★	200	250	450
A. H. Wallis, 19J, KW, NI	★★★	450	550	900
A. H. Wallis, 19J, SW, NI	★★★	450	550	900
D. C. Wilcox, 15J, SW, **NO** butterfly cut-out	★	300	425	775
I. H. Wright, 11J, KW, gilded	★	200	250	400
I. H. Wright, 15J, KW, gilded	★	200	250	400

⊕ A collector should expect to pay modestly higher prices at local shops.

⊕ Watches listed in this book are priced at the collectable Trade Show level, as **complete** watches having an original 14k gold-filled case and *Key Wind* with silver, an original white enamel single sunk dial, and with the entire original movement in good working order with no repairs needed.

⊕ Some grades are not included. Their values can be determined by comparing with **similar** age, size, metal content, style, models and grades listed.

⊕ Pricing in this Guide are fair market price for **COMPLETE** watches which are reflected from the "**NAWCC**" National and regional shows.

16 SIZE
1/4 Plate

Grade or Name – Description		Avg	Ex-Fn	Mint
S. M. Beard, 15J, NI, KW,	★★★	$300	$385	$600
Marion Watch Co., 11-15J., KW	★★★	300	385	600
John W. Lewis, 15J, NI, KW	★★★	300	385	600
Personalized Watches, 15J, NI, SW	★★★	300	385	600
Edwin Rollo, 15J, KW	★★★	300	385	600
United States Watch Co., 15J, NI, SW	★★★	700	900	1,700
A. H. Wallis, 19J, NI, SW,	★★★	700	900	1,700

Note: 16S, 1/4 plate fewer % made of the U.S.W.Co.–Marion watches.

Asa Fuller, 16 size, 15 jewels, stem wind, one-quarter plate, serial number 280,018. Note: 3 screws on barrel bridge.

United States Watch Co., 14 size, 15 jewels, three-quarter plate, engraved on movement "Royal Gold American Watch, New York, Extra Jeweled."

14 SIZE
3/4 Plate

Grade or Name – Description		Avg	Ex-Fn	Mint
Centennial Phil., 11J, KW, gilded	★★★★	$900	$1,200	$2,200
J. W. Deacon, 11J,	★★	150	225	400
Asa Fuller, 15J,	★★	275	375	500
John W. Lewis, 15J, NI	★★	275	375	500
Marion Watch Co., 15J., KW	★	200	265	450
North Star, 15J,	★★	300	365	550
Personalized Watches, 7-11J,	★★	300	365	550
Edwin Rollo, 15J,	★	275	335	500
Royal Gold, 15J,	★	375	475	750
Young America, 7J, gilded	★	250	350	500

⊕ A collector should expect to pay modestly higher prices at local shops.

⊕ Watches listed in this book are priced at the collectable Trade Show level, as **complete** watches having an original 14k gold-filled case and *Key Wind* with silver, an original white enamel single sunk dial, and with the entire original movement in good working order with no repairs needed.

⊕ Some grades are not included. Their values can be determined by comparing with **similar** age, size, metal content, style, models and grades listed.

10 SIZE
1/4 Plate

Grade or Name – Description	Avg	Ex-Fn	Mint
Wm. Alexander, 15J, KW, NI	$135	$175	$375
S. M. Beard, 15J, KW, NI, 1/4 Plate	135	175	375
Empire City Watch Co., 15J, KW ★★★	500	625	1,100
Chas. G. Knapp, 15J, **Swiss**, 1/4 Plate, KW	100	145	275
Marion Watch Co., 11-15J., 1/4 Plate	125	175	350
Personalized Watches, 11-15J, 1/4 Plate	135	185	350
R. F. Pratt, 15J, **Swiss**, 1/4 Plate, KW	100	135	250
Edwin Rollo, 11-15J, 1/4 Plate	150	200	400
A. H. Wallis, 17-19J, KW, 1/4 Plate ★	185	275	450
A. J. Wood, 15J, 1/4 Plate, KW ★★	275	365	500
I. H. Wright, 19J, **Swiss**, NI, Plate, KW ★★	175	285	475

S. M. Beard, 10 size, 15 jewels, key wind, quarter plate, serial number 248,407. Note: 2 screws on barrel bridge.

Chas. G. Knapp, 10 size, 15 jewels, Swiss, quarter plate, key wind.

U. S. WATCH CO.
OF WALTHAM
Waltham, Massachusetts
1885 - 1905

The business was started as the Waltham Watch Tool Co. in 1879. It was organized as the United States Watch Co. in about 1885. The first watches were 16S, 3/4 plate pillar movement in three grades. They had a very wide mainspring barrel (the top was thinner than most) which was wedged up in the center to make room for the balance wheel. These watches are called dome watches and are hard to find. The fork was made of an aluminum alloy with a circular slot and a square ruby pin. The balance was gold at first, as was the movement which was a slow train, but the expansion balance was changed when they went to a quick train. The movement required a special case which proved unpopular. By 1887, some 3,000 watches had been made. A new model was then produced, a 16S movement that would fit a standard case. These movements were quick train expansion balance with standard type lever and 3/4 plate pillar movement. This company reached a top production of 10 watches a day for a **very short period.** The company was sold to the E. Howard Watch Co. (Keystone) in 1903. The United States Watch Co. produced watches with serial number as high as 890,000 so **possible** total is 890,000. Its top grade watch movement was the **"The President."**

⊕ Pricing in this Guide are fair market price for **COMPLETE** watches which are reflected from the "**NAWCC**" National and regional shows.

U.S. WATCH CO. OF WALTHAM
ESTIMATED SERIAL NUMBERS
AND PRODUCTION DATES

Date	Serial No.	Date	Serial No.
1887	3,000	1896	300,000
1888	6,500	1897	350,000
1889	10,000	1898	400,000
1890	30,000	1899	500,000
1891	60,000	1900	600,000
1892	90,000	1901	700,000
1893	150,000	1902	750,000
1894	200,000	1903	800,000
1895	250,000		

Acid Etched, 18 Size, 7-15J., HC

U.S. Watch Co. of Waltham, The President on dial & movement,18 size,17J, <u>hunting case</u>, marked Adjusted, serial # 150,020, produced in late 1893 or early 1894.

U.S. Watch Co. of Waltham, The President, 18 size, 17 jewels, <u>open face</u>, 2-tone, adj., note regulator, serial number 150,350. Note: A.C. Roebuck 17J. similar to President.

18 SIZE

Grade or Name – Description	Avg	Ex-Fn	Mint
A.C. Robuck 17J., Adjusted Special (similar to The President) ★★	$375	$450	$800
Acid Etched movement, 7-15J, (with good Finish)............... ★★	200	275	450
Express Train, 15J, ADJ, NI, OF .... ★	400	500	750
Express Train, 15J, ADJ, NI, HC... ★	625	750	975
The President, 17J, GJS, Adj.6P, DR, NI, DMK, HC .... ★★★	375	485	800
The President, 17J, GJS, Adj.6P, DR, NI, DMK, OF .... ★★	350	450	725
The President, 21J, GJS, Adj.6P, DR, NI, DMK, OF ... ★★★★★	800	1,000	1,500
The President, 21J, GJS, Adj.6P, DR, **14K** .... ★★★★★	1,200	1,400	2,000

Note: A Feb. 1st, **1894** ad states: The only 18 size **Double Roller**, Lever set movement on the market & guarantees that this (The **President**) movement will vary less than <u>Six-seconds</u> a Month.

Washington Square, 15J, HC... ★	$200	$250	$400

Generic, **nameless** or unmarked grades for watch movements are listed under the Company name or initials of the Company, etc. by size, jewel count and description.

U. S. Watch Co., 15J, OF, **2-tone, stem attached** .... ★	$300	$375	$575
U. S. Watch Co., 39 (HC) & 79 (OF), 17J, GJS, ADJ, NI, DMK, Adj.5P, BRG	100	135	200
U. S. Watch Co., 40 (HC) & 80 (OF), 17J, GJS.............................	100	135	200
U. S. Watch Co., 48 (HC) & 88 (OF), 7J, gilded, FULL	70	85	150
U. S. Watch Co., 48 (HC) & 88 (OF), 7J, gilded, FULL, Silveroid	60	75	125

🕐 Some grades are not included. Their values can be determined by comparing with **similar** age, size, metal content, style, models and grades listed.

Grade or Name – Description	Avg	Ex-Fn	Mint
U. S. Watch Co., 52 (HC)	$100	$135	$200
U. S. Watch Co., 92 (OF), 17J, Silveroid	65	85	150
U. S. Watch Co., 52 (HC) & 92 (OF), 17J	75	110	200
U. S. Watch Co., 53 (HC) & 93 (OF), 15J, NI, FULL, DMK	75	110	200
U. S. Watch Co., 54 (HC) & 94 (OF), 15J	75	110	200
U. S. Watch Co., 56 (HC) & 96 (OF), 11J	65	85	150
U. S. Watch Co., 57 (HC) & 97 (OF), 15J	75	110	200
U. S. Watch Co., 58 (HC) & 98 (OF), 11J, NI, FULL, DMK	65	85	150

U.S. Watch Co. of Waltham, 16 size, 7 jewels, gilded, note raised dome on center of movement, engraved on movement "Chas. V. Woerd's Patents," serial number 3,564.

U.S. Watch Co. of Waltham, 16 size, Hunting case, 7 jewels, "A New Watch Company At Waltham, Est'd 1885" on movement, serial number 770,771.

16 SIZE

Grade or Name – Description	Avg	Ex-Fn	Mint
Acid Etched , 7-15J, (with good Finish) ★★	$150	$200	$335
Dome plate style movement, 7J, gilded	100	175	325
U. S. Watch Co., 103, 17J, NI, 3/4, ADJ	65	85	150
U. S. Watch Co., 104, 17J, NI, 3/4	65	85	150
U. S. Watch Co., 104, 17J, NI, 3/4, Silveroid	65	85	150
U. S. Watch Co., 105, 15J, NI, 3/4, HC	75	100	225
U. S. Watch Co., 105, 15J, NI, 3/4, OF	65	85	150
U. S. Watch Co., 105, 15J, NI, 3/4, Silveroid	65	85	150
U. S. Watch Co., 106, 15J, gilded,3/4, Silveroid	65	85	150
U. S. Watch Co., 106, 15J, gilded,3/4	65	85	150
U. S. Watch Co., 108, 11J, gilded, 3/4	65	85	150
U. S. Watch Co., 109, 7J, NI, 3/4	65	85	150
U. S. Watch Co., 110, 7J, 3/4, HC	75	100	200
U. S. Watch Co., 110, 7J, 3/4, OF	65	85	150

Note: Add $25 - $50 to value of above watches in hunting case.

⊕ Generic, **nameless** or **unmarked** grades for watch movements are listed under the Company name or initials of the Company, etc. by size, jewel count and description.

⊕ Watches listed in this book are priced at the collectable Trade Show level, as complete watches having an original 14k gold-filled case and Key Wind with silver, an original white enamel single sunk dial, and with the entire original movement in good working order with no repairs needed.

⊕ Pricing in this Guide are fair market price for **COMPLETE** watches which are reflected from the "**NAWCC**" National and regional shows.

U.S. Watch Co., 16 size, 15 jewels, three-quarter plate. U.S. Watch Co.,16 size, Open Face, 7 jewels, S# 15761.

6 SIZE

Grade or Name – Description	Avg	Ex-Fn	Mint
U. S. Watch Co., 60, 17J, GJS, NI, 3/4, Adj.3P	$50	$65	$150
U. S. Watch Co., 60, 17J, GJS, NI, 3/4, Adj.3P, **HC, 14K**	250	300	575
U. S. Watch Co., 62, 15J, NI, 3/4	40	60	100
U. S. Watch Co., 63, 15J, gilded	40	60	100
U. S. Watch Co., 64, 11J, NI	40	60	100
U. S. Watch Co., 65, 11J, gilded	35	50	75
U. S. Watch Co., 66, 7J, gilded	35	50	75
U. S. Watch Co., 66, 7-11J, NI, 3/4	40	60	100
U. S. Watch Co., 68, 16J, GJS, NI, 3/4	45	75	125
U. S. Watch Co., 69, 7J, NI, HC	50	65	150
U. S. Watch Co., 69, 7J, NI, OF	40	60	100

Note: Add $25 - $50 to value of above watches in hunting case.

Grade 64, 6 size, 11 jewels

U.S. Watch Co. of Waltham, 0 size, 7 jewels, serial number 808,231. Engraved on movement United States Watch Co. New York U.S.A., 808,231.

0 SIZE

Grade or Name – Description	Avg	Ex-Fn	Mint
Betsy Ross, HC, GF case	$100	$150	$300
U. S. Watch Co., 15J, HC, GF case	90	125	200
U. S. Watch Co., 7-11J, HC, GF case	90	125	200

THE WASHINGTON WATCH CO.

Washington, D. C.   1872 - 1874

NOTE: **First** check your watch for a **grade** name as Liberty Bells, Potomac, Lafayette, Army & Navy, Senate, Monroe, and others which are listed under **Illinois section**. Washington Watch Co. was Montgomery Ward's private label and made by Illinois Watch Co.

J. P. Hopkins, though better known as the inventor of the Auburndale Rotary Watch, was also connected with the Washington Watch Co., they may have produced about 50 watches. They were 18S, key wind, 3/4 plate and had duplex escapements. Before Hopkins came to Washington Watch Co. he had handmade about six fine watches. The company had a total production of 45 movements with duplex escapements.

Grade or Name – Description		Avg	Ex-Fn	Mint
18S, 15J, 3/4, KW, KS	★★★★	$5,200	$6,500	$13,500

WATERBURY WATCH CO.

Waterbury, Connecticut

In 1880 Benedict & Burnham was renamed Waterbury W. Co.. D. A. A. Buck designed a **rotary** watch with 58 parts for Series A & 57 for B. The rotary **long wind** takes about **120** to **140** turns of the crown to fully wind. It had a two-wheel train rather than the standard four-wheel train. The Waterbury rotary long wind movement revolved once every hour & has a duplex escapement and paper dial, the watch was priced at $3.50 to $4.00 with case. In 1898 became the New England Watch Co.

in our new improved spring box, *satin lined.*

WATERBURY WATCH CO.

Waterbury, Conn., Nov. 1, 1881.

DW-1	Hour wheel	MSA	Mainspring arbor
DW-2	Fixed dial wheel	W-1	First wheel
PW-1	Pinion of 1st wheel	W-2	Second wheel
SW	Escape wheel	PW-2	Pinion of 2nd wheel
BS	Balance spring	PSW	Escape wheel pinion
BW	Balance wheel	P-1	Pillar
MSB	Mainspring barrel	TP	Top plate
MS	Mainspring	P-2	Pillar screw
L,L	Lugs		

Above: Waterbury **Rotary** movement.

SERIES B, REDUCED.

Above extracted at 100% from 2 small catalogs, Nov.1, 1881 Series **A** and Oct.1, 1882 for Series **B**

Waterbury Watch Co., skeletonized movement; so called a poor man's tourbillon due to the fact it rotated as a tourbillon does. Patented May 21, 1878 on top of crown. Note: The six spokes on dial and **CELLULOID** case.

Rotary long wind movement. Note **four** spokes on dial. For 3 & 4 spokes listing see *Benedict & Burnham* section.

18 TO 16 SIZES

Grade or Name – Description		Avg	Ex-Fn	Mint
Series A, **rotary long wind**, skeletonized, 6 spokes	★★	$300	$425	$700
Series A, **rotary long wind, skeletonized**, 6 spokes, celluloid case	★★★★	600	850	1,400
Series B, solid plates, **rotary long wind**	★★	150	250	400
Series C or E, solid plates, **rotary long wind**	★★	150	250	400
Series C or E, **rotary long wind,** advertising embossed on back Example Old Honesty,	★★	250	350	500
Series D, patented Feb. 5, 1884 engraved on Movement (4 times)	★★★★	400	600	1,000
Series F, Duplex escapement		150	235	400
Series G, 3/4 lever escapement	★	200	335	475
Series H, Columbian, Duplex	★★	200	335	475

Series E, note on back of watch (do'nt remove this cap unless you are a practical watch repairer).

Series L, Waterbury W. Co. 4 jewels, Duplex Escapement, about 8 size.

Series I, The Trump, about 18 size, 2 jewels, with Duplex escapement.   **Series T**, Oxford Duplex Escapement, about 18 size.

18 to 0 Size

Grade or Name – Description	Avg	Ex-Fn	Mint
Series I, 2J., Trump, Duplex, 18 size	$55	$75	$125
Series J, 4J., Americus,full plate, 18 size	55	75	125
Series J, 4J., Americus, Duplex, 3/4 plate, 18 size	75	100	150
Series K, 6J., Charles Benedict , 18 size ★	125	175	350
Series K, Addison, 18 size ★	125	175	250
Series L, 4J., gilt, Duplex 8 size	85	100	150
Series L, 4J., **aluminum** movement, Duplex, 8 size ★★	125	165	250
Series N, Addison, Duplex, 18 size ★	125	150	200
Series N, Addison, 4J., Duplex, gilt, 4 size	65	75	110
Series N, Addison, 4J., **aluminum** movement, 4 size ★★	125	165	225
Series P, 4 J., Rugby, Duplex, 10 size	60	75	150
Series R, 9J., Tuxedo, Duplex, 14 size	60	75	150
Series S, 6J., Elfin, 6/0 size	60	70	95
Series T, Oxford, Duplex	60	70	95
Series W, 6J., Addison, Duplex, 3/4 plate, 4 size	65	75	135
Series Z, Cavour	60	70	95

Waterbury Clock Co. 35 size Pat. Jan.15, 1878, May 6, '90, Dec.23,'90, Jan. 13,'91, on movement.

	Avg	Ex-Fn	Mint
Jumbo, (seconds bit at the 12:00 o'clock position) ... ★★★★	$300	$400	$650
Duke, 35 size back-wind and back-set	150	200	350
Duchess, same as duke with a fancier case	150	200	350

NOTE: Dollar -watches must be in **Running** condition to bring these prices.

Old Honesty, Series C, rotary longwind.   Waterbury Watch Co. **"ROTARY"** movement

E. N. WELCH MFG. CO.

Bristol, Connecticut
1834 - 1897

Elisha Welch founded this company about 1834. His company failed in 1897, and the Sessions Clock Co. took over the business in 1903. E. N. Welch Mfg. Co. produced the large watch which was displayed at the Chicago Exposition in 1893. This watch depicted the landing of Columbus on the back of the case.

E.N. Welch Mfg. Co., 36 size, back wind & set, made for the Chicago Exposition in 1893. Die debossed back depicting the landing of Columbus in America, Oct, 12th, 1492.

Grade or Name – Description		Avg	Ex-Fn	Mint
36S, Columbus Exhibition watch	★★	$425	$550	$850

WESTCLOX

United Clock Co. – Western Clock Mfg. Co.– General Time Corp.
Athens, Georgia
1899 - Present

The first Westclox pocket watch was made about 1899; however, the Westclox name did not appear on their watches until 1906. In 1903 they were making 100 watches a day, and in 1920 production was at 15,000 per day.

Grade or Name – Description	Avg	Ex-Fn	Mint
M#1, SW, push to set, GRO	$50	$75	$135
M#2, SW, back set, GRO	50	65	100
18S, Westclox M#4, OF, GRO	45	55	75
1910 Models to 1920, GRO	35	40	60
Anniversary	35	40	60
Antique	20	25	45
Boy Proof	50	55	90
Bingo	30	35	55
Bulls Eye (several models)	15	20	25
Campus	15	20	25
Celluloid case, 70mm	25	30	45
Coronado	15	20	25
Country Gentleman	35	45	70

Boy Proof Model, about 16 size, designed to be tamper proof.

Westclox movement, stem wind, back set.

Grade or Name – Description	Avg	Ex-Fn	Mint
Dax (many models)	$10	$15	$20
Dewey	10	15	30
Elite	25	30	40
Everbrite (several models)	30	45	65
Explorer ....★	200	325	500
Farm Bureau	55	65	95
Glo Ben	55	65	95
Glory Be	20	25	35
Johnny Zero (several models)	125	165	300
I Want You to Vote	55	65	95
Ideal	30	35	45
Lighted Dial	25	30	40
Magnetic	20	25	30
Major	25	30	40
Man Time	15	20	25
Mark IV	35	40	55
Mascot	20	25	30
Maxim	30	35	50

Zep, about 16 size with radiant numbers and hands, c. 1929.

Explorer, back of case and dial, "Wings Over The Pole, The Explorer" on back of case.

World's Fair watch & fob, (1982 -Knoxville Tn.){Wagner Time Inc.}, total production for watch 4,200 and 200 for the FOB, 16 size, dial in red,white & blue, sold for $30.00 in 1982.

Grade or Name – Description	Avg	Ex-Fn	Mint
Military Style, 24 hour	$65	$75	$100
Monitor	15	20	25
Mustang	35	40	60
NAWCC, total production = **1,000**, Ca.1968 ★	65	85	145
above wth box (25th. Anniversary) ★★	85	95	185
Panther	35	40	60
Pocket Ben (many models)	10	15	30
Ruby	25	30	45
Scepter	20	25	40
Scotty (several models)	15	20	30
Silogram	15	20	30
Smile	25	30	45
Solo	15	20	30
St. Regis	20	25	35
Sun Mark	30	35	40
Team Mate (various major league teams)	25	35	50
Tele Time	25	30	45
Texan	35	45	65
The Airplane	35	45	65
The American, **back SET**	50	80	195
The Conductor	45	55	85
Tiny Tim	150	175	300
Trail Blazer	60	100	265
Uncle Sam	40	45	60
Victor	80	95	130
Vote	25	30	45
Westclox	15	20	25
World's Fair (1982 -Knoxville Tn.){Wagner Time Inc.}	60	75	95
above wth box & (**FOB** total production =200) ★★★	95	150	325
Zep, (Zepplin) ★	225	350	500
Zodiak Time	35	40	55

🕐 Pricing in this Guide are fair market price for **COMPLETE** watches which are reflected from the "**NAWCC**" National and regional shows.

WESTERN WATCH CO.

Chicago, Illinois
1880

Albert Trotter purchased the unfinished watches from the California Watch Co. Mr. Trotter finished and sold those watches. Later he moved to Chicago, and with Paul Cornell and others, formed the Western Watch Company. Very few watches were completed by the Western Watch Co.

Grade or Name – Description		Avg	Ex-Fn	Mint
Western Watch Co., 18S, FULL ...... ★★★★		$2,000	$2,800	$4,700

Western Watch Co. movement, 18 size, 15 jewels, key wind & set.

WICHITA WATCH CO.

Wichita, Kansas
July, 1887 - 1888

This company completed construction of their factory in Wichita, Kansas in June 1st., 1888, maybe a half dozen watches were produced during the brief period the company was in operation. The president was J. R. Snively. These watches are 18S, 1/2 to 3/4 plate, adjusted, 15 jewels, Savage 2 pin **style** escapement.

Grade or Name – Description		Avg	Ex-Fn	Mint
18S, 15J, 3/4 plate, ADJ, Savage 2 pin style escapement .. ★★★★		$3,500	$4,700	$8,200

⊕ Watches listed in this book are priced at the collectable trade show level, as **complete** watches having an original 14k gold-filled case and *Key Wind* with silver, an original white enamel single sunk dial, and with the entire original movement in good working order with no repairs needed.

⊕ Pricing in this Guide are fair market price for **COMPLETE** watches which are reflected from the "**NAWCC**" National and regional shows.

⊕ A collector should expect to pay modestly higher prices at local shops.

COMIC AND CHARACTER WATCHES

When discussing the topic of watches and someone mentions Comic Character Watches, we immediately picture a watch with Mickey Mouse. Isn't Mickey Mouse the most famous of all watches in the world? Before Mickey appeared in the 1930's there were a handful of lesser known comic watches with characters like Skeezix, Smitty and Buster Brown, but it was the Mickey Mouse Watch that paved the way for all other comic character watches. As a collaboration between Walt Disney (the creator of Mickey Mouse) and Robert Ingersoll and his brother the founders of the Ingersoll-Waterbury Watch Company, the Mickey Mouse Watch was one of this century's greatest marketing concepts. In a two year period Ingersoll had sold nearly 2.5 million Mickey Mouse wrist and pocket watches. Throughout the 1930's they also introduced other watches with Disney characters such as Big Bad Wolf in 1934, as well as, the Donald Duck wrist watch. The Donald Duck pocket watch was produced several years later in 1939. The Mickey Lapel and Mickey Deluxe Wrist were produced in the late 1930's.

Ingersoll dominated the character watch market in the early 1930's due to the incredible popularity of the Disney characters, however by the mid 1930's other companies mainly Ingraham and New Haven secured the rights to other popular characters. Throughout the 1930's kids fell in love with these watches featuring their favorite comic character or hero, such as, Popeye, Superman, Buck Rogers, Orphan Annie, Dick Tracy and The Lone Ranger. There was also a couple of other well known characters, Betty Boop and Cowboy Tom Mix produced, but for some reason these watches did not become popular like all the others, so very small quantities were produced.

During World War II production of comic watches ceased, but after the war comic watches came back stronger than ever. Once again Disney was the overall leader. The Ingersoll name only appeared on some watches to keep the trade name still familiar, as Ingersoll was sold to U.S. Time Watch Co.

The late 1940's was very good to the character watch market and proof being the many character watches produced as the Twentieth Birthday Series for Mickey in 1948 that included with Mickey, Donald Duck, Pinocchio, Pluto, Bambi, Joe Carioca, Jiminy Cricket, Bongo Bear and Daisy Duck. Other watches from this time include Porky Pig, Puss-N-Boots, Joe Palooka, Gene Autry, Captain and Mary Marvel and others featuring characters of the comic and cartoons, space and western heroes.

The early to mid 1950's was also a vibrant time for character watch production with more Disney characters, western heroes and comic characters than ever before, but by 1958 manufacturing of character watches had almost completely stopped as manufacturing costs went up, popularity of some characters faded and many other circumstances led to a complete stop of any of these watches until the late 1960's. The watches were never the same again.

In the 1970's the Comic Character Watch once again made it's come back with the Bradley Watch Company (Elgin W. Co.) leading the way just as Ingersoll did in the first years of comic watches. Today there are hundreds of character watches to choose from, Disney Super Hero movie characters like E.T., and Roger Rabbit and a wealth of others, but today's fascination is not just with the new but with the old as we see in the re-issue of the original Mickey watches. There is a growing awareness and appreciation for all the originals. It is a very unusual attraction that draws people to love and collect the character watches of the past. Collectors appreciate the original boxes (that are fascinating works of art) and the face of the watch that features the character that we love. The manufacturing method of these simple pin lever movements were not the best of timekeepers, but were solidly constructed. All in all, when you put together the watches and boxes they are pieces of functional art and history that brings back memories of our youth. Something that no other kind of watch can do.

Tom Mix pocket watch on back "Always Find Time For A Good Deed / Tom Mix", & BOX inside color illo. of Tom on Tony.

Babe Ruth, by Exact Time, ca. 1948.

Betty Boop, by Ingraham, ca. 1934.

Style or Grade – Description	Avg	Ex-Fn	Mint	Mint +Box
Alice in Wonderland, WW, c. 1951, by U.S. Time	$50	$70	$150	$400
Alice, Red Riding Hood, & Marjory Daw, WW, c. 1953, by Bradley	50	75	150	400
Alice in Wonderland, WW, c. 1958, by Timex	40	60	100	300
Alice in Wonderland & Mad Hatter, WW, c. 1948, by New Haven	65	110	200	400
All * Stars, c.1965, autographed by Mickey Mantel, Rodger Maris, Willie Mays, Sandy Koufax, Swiss, GREEN DIAL	125	225	325	650
All * Stars, c.1965, autographed by Mickey Mantel, Rodger Maris, Willie Mays, Sandy Koufax, Swiss, BLACK DIAL	100	165	250	550
Annie Oakley, WW, (Action Gun) c. 1951, by New Haven	150	225	300	575
Archie, WW, c.1970s, Swiss,	50	65	100	275
Babe Ruth, WW, c. 1948, by Exact Time, box, baseball, pledge card	★ 200	350	775	2,000
Ballerina, WW, c.1955, Ingraham, Action legs,	40	50	65	100
Bambi, WW, c. 1949, by U.S. Time, Birthday series	100	200	350	600
Barbie, WW, c.1964, by Bradley, facing "3",	75	125	250	375
Barbie, WW, c.1970, by Bradley, action arms	75	125	250	375
Batman, WW, c. 1966 by Gilbert (band in shape of bat)	150	300	500	1,000
Batman, WW, c. 1978, by Timex	100	135	200	375
Betty Boop, PW, c. 1934, by Ingraham, (all original) (with diedebossed back)	★★★★450	850	2,000	4,000
Betty Boop, WW, c.1980s, with hearts on dial & band	40	50	65	100
Bert & Ernie, WW, c.1970s, swiss	40	50	65	100
Big Bad Wolf & 3 Pigs, PW, c. 1936, by Ingersoll	★ 400	650	1,300	2,300
Big Bad Wolf & 3 Pigs, WW, c. 1936, by Ingersoll	★ 500	775	1,400	2,900
Big Bird, WW, c.1970s, Swiss, action arms, (pop up box)	40	50	65	100
Blondie & Dagwood, WW, c.1950s, Swiss	150	200	275	500
Bongo Bear, WW, c.1946, Ingersoll, Birthday series	100	150	235	400
Boy Scout,PW, c.1937, by Ingersoll, be prepared hands	250	285	450	800
Boy Scout,WW, c.1938, by New Haven	75	95	150	300
Buck Rogers, PW, c.1935, Ingraham (lightning bolt hands)	350	650	1,200	2,200
Bud Man, WW, Swiss, c.1970s	40	50	65	100
Bugs Bunny, WW, c. 1951, Swiss, (carrot shaped hands)	100	200	350	625
Bugs Bunny, WW, c. 1951, Swiss, (without carrot hands)	75	110	195	350
Bugs Bunny, WW, c. 1970, Swiss, (standing bugs)	40	55	75	150

✪ NOTE: Beware (**COLOR COPY DIALS**) are being faked as Buck Rodgers, Babe Ruth, Hopalong Cassidy and others. *BUYER BEWARE*

The Complete Price Guide to Watches goal is to stimulate the orderly exchange of <u>Watches</u> between "*buyers*" and "*sellers*".

BIG BAD WOLF & 3 PIGS, + FOB INGERSOLL

BUSTER BROWN, INGERSOLL, Ca. 1925

BUGS BUNNY, EXACT TIME, Ca. 1949
3 styles of hands.

BUCK ROGERS, INGRAHAM, Ca. 1935

Ingersoll (1934)
BIG BAD WOLF & 3 PIGS

– DICK TRACY, NEW HAVEN, Ca.1948

– DICK TRACY, (six shooter action arm) Ca.1952

DIZZY DEAN, By Everbright W. Co.

DONALD, with mickey seconds hand, 3 grades.

Left: DONALD DUCK, by INGERSOLL, C. 1947.　　　Center; Snoopy, Ca.1968　　　DALE EVANS, INGRAHAM

DAN DARE, INGERSOLL made in England

FROM OUTER SPACE, INGERSOLL made in England

Style or Grade – Description	Avg	Ex-Fn	Mint	Mint +Box
Buster Brown, PW, c. 1928, by Ingersoll	$125	$185	$300	$675
Buster Brown, PW, c. 1928, by Ingersoll (Buster in circle)	135	200	400	725
Buster Brown, WW, c.1930, engraved case	125	150	250	500
Buzz Corey, WW, c. 1952, by U.S. Time	75	125	200	450
Buzzy the Crow, in red hat	40	50	70	125
Captain Liberty, WW, c. 1950, by U.S.Time, multi-color band	50	85	200	475
Captain Marvel, PW, c. 1945, by New Haven	200	275	550	1,000
Captain Marvel,WW, c.1948, New Haven (small w.w.)	85	125	300	700
Captain Marvel, WW, c.1948, by New Haven (larger size)	100	175	350	800
Captain Marvel, WW, c.1948, Swiss made	100	235	400	850
Captain Marvel **Jr.**, c. 1948, Swiss, small size	150	300	550	1,300
Captain Midnight, PW, c. 1948, by Ingraham	250	325	575	1,350
Casper, WW, c.1970s, Swiss, **Action arms**	45	55	75	150
Cat In The Hat, WW, c.1970s, Swiss, **Action arms**	40	50	65	125
Cinderella, WW, c. 1950, by U.S. Time (slipper box)	40	45	95	375
Cinderella, WW, c. 1955, by Timex (box with imitation cell)	40	50	95	375
Cinderella, WW, c. 1958, by Timex (box with plastic statue)	40	50	95	375
Cinderella, WW, c. 1958, by Timex (box & porcelain statue)	45	60	125	400
Coca Cola, PW, c. 1948, by Ingersoll	65	150	235	400
Cowboy, WW, c.1955, by Muros, Swiss, **Action Gun**	40	50	70	160
Cowgirl, WW, c.1951, by New Haven, **Action Gun**	40	50	70	160
Cub Scout, WW, by Timex	40	50	65	150
Daisy Duck, WW, c. 1947, by Ingersoll (tonneau style)	100	175	275	500
Daisy Duck, WW, c. 1948, by U.S. Time (fluted bezel, birthday series)	100	175	275	500
Daisy Duck, WW, c. 1949, by U.S. Time, (grooved bezel)	85	135	185	400
Dale Evans, WW, c.1949,by Ingraham,Dale standing, (tonneau)	80	125	175	400
Dale Evans, WW, c. 1950, by Bradley (western style leather band & necklace &lucky horseshoe), tonneau style case	75	100	165	400
Dale Evans, WW, c. 1960, by Bradley (round)	40	50	75	250
Dan Dare, PW, c. 1950, by *Ingersoll Ltd. England*, action arm	200	300	450	1,100
Davy Crockett, WW, c. 1951, by Bradley (round dial)	80	100	250	600
Davy Crockett, WW, c. 1954, Action gun, (round dial)	75	85	200	500
Davy Crockett, WW, c. 1954, Liberty , (round dial)	50	80	175	450
Davy Crockett, WW, c. 1955, by U.S. Time (& powder horn)	125	200	325	775
Davy Crockett, WW, c. 1956, by Bradley (barrel shaped dial)	50	80	200	450
Dennis the Menace, WW, c. 1970, by Bradley	45	55	80	150
Dick Tracy, PW, c. 1948, by Ingersoll	250	350	500	1,500
Dick Tracy, WW, c. 1948, by New Haven (round dial)	85	110	200	525
Dick Tracy, WW, c. 1948, by New Haven (small tonneau)	75	100	200	475
Dick Tracy, WW, c. 1935, by New Haven (large)	150	225	300	650
Dick Tracy, WW, c. 1951, by New Haven (6 shooter **action**)	200	275	350	800
Dizzy Dean, PW, c. 1935, by Ingersoll	★★ 200	325	500	1,200
Dizzy Dean, WW, c. 1938, by Everbright W.Co.	★★ 200	300	500	1,200

⊕ Note: To be mint condition, character watches must have **unfaded dials**, and boxes must have ALL inserts. (PW=Pocket Watch; WW=Wrist Watch)

COCA COLA, PW, Ca. 1948, by Ingersoll.

ADOLF HITLER, character wrist watch, Swiss movement "Roskopf" caliber, Ca. 1935.

Dizzy Dean, Ingersoll, ca. 1935   Donald Duck, Ingersoll, ca. 1940. Mickey on back of case.

Style or Grade – Description	Avg	Ex-Fn	Mint	Mint +Box
Donald Duck, PW, c. 1939, by Ingersoll (Mickey on back) .... ★★	$350	$500	$1,000	$2,200
Donald Duck, PW, Ward W. Co., c. 1954, Swiss made 75		150	265	600
Donald Duck, WW, c. 1935, by Ingersoll (Mickey on second hand) .... ★★ 500		800	1,200	2,600
Donald Duck, WW, c. 1942, by U.S. Time (tonneau style, silver tone) 100		150	400	900
Donald Duck, WW, c. 1948, by U.S. Time (tonneau style, gold tone) 150		200	450	950
Donald Duck, WW, c. 1948, by Ingersoll (fluted bezel, birthday series) with metal mickey bracelet 150		200	450	950
Donald Duck, WW, c. 1955, by U.S. Time, (plain bezel, pop-up in box) with leather band & Donald metal decal..... 75		100	285	625
Dopey, WW, c. 1948, by Ingersoll (fluted bezel, birthday series) 100		150	325	700
Dudley Do-Right, WW, 17J (Bullwinkle & Rocky) .... ★ 200		265	500	1,000
Elmer Fudd, WW, c.1970s, Swiss 55		100	150	375
Elvis, WW, c.1970s, Bradley 55		60	85	200
Flash Gordon, PW, c. 1939, by Ingersoll .... ★ 350		500	900	1,900
Flash Gordon,WW, c.1970, Precision 90		200	350	700
From Outer Space, PW, Ingersoll G.Britian, ... 75		150	225	500
Fred Flintstone, WW, (Fred on dial) 75		150	225	400
Garfield,WW, (The Cat Jumped Over The Moon) 40		55	95	200
Gene Autry, WW, c. 1939, by Ingersoll (Gene and Champion on dial) 100		175	350	850

Mickey, 32MM, Ca.1930.   – Gene Autry, (action gun), by Ingersoll, ca.1950. – Howdy with moving eyes Ca.1954.
Maybe HOAX ??

MICKEY MOUSE, by Ingersoll, original band, Ca.1933-34   MICKEY MOUSE, by Ingersoll, Ca. 1947

Mickey Mouse by Ingersoll, center lugs, Ca.1938.   Reproduction Box & Watch.   Mickey Mouse by Bradley, 1972-85.

MICKEY MOUSE, made in England by Ingersoll, Ca.1934   Who's afraid of the Big Bad Wolf.
Maybe "Proto Type"

Hopalong Cassidy, U.S. Time, ca. 1950s. Maybe HOAX??   Hopalong Cassidy, Ingersoll, ca. 1955.

Style or Grade – Description	Avg	Ex-Fn	Mint	Mint +Box
Gene Autry, WW, c. 1939, by Ingersoll	$100	$175	$325	$750
Gene Autry, WW, c. 1950, by New Haven, (action gun)	200	275	350	775
Gene Autry, WW, c.1956, Swiss made	65	95	225	450
Girl Scouts, WW, c.1955, by Timex	40	50	60	135
Goofy, WW, c. 1972, by Helbros, 17J (watch runs backward)	300	400	550	1,200
Hoky Poky, WW, c.1950, **action arm**	35	50	75	225
Hopalong Cassidy, WW, by U.S. Time (metal watch, box with saddle)	50	80	225	525
Hopalong Cassidy, WW, by U.S. Time (plastic watch, box with saddle)	50	80	225	525
Hopalong Cassidy, WW, by U.S. Time (small watch, leather Western band, flat rectangular box)	45	60	185	475
Hopalong Cassidy, WW, by U.S. Time (regular size watch, black leather cowboy strap), flat box	50	65	200	500
Hopalong Cassidy, PW, c. 1955, by U.S. Time (rawhide strap and fob)	125	225	300	725
Hot Wheels, WW, c.1971, Bradley -Swiss, checkered hands	45	55	75	175
Hot Wheels, WW, c.1971, Bradley -Swiss, rotating bezel	35	45	65	175
Hot Wheels, WW, c.1983, Swiss, LCD QUARTZ	25	35	45	100
Howdy Doody, WW, c. 1954, Swiss (with moving eyes)	100	200	400	875
Howdy Doody, WW, c. 1954, by Ingraham (with friends)	95	150	400	800
Jamboree, PW, c. 1951, by Ingersoll, Ltd.	75	110	250	500

Robin Hood, Ca.1958   —   BUD MAN Ca.1970s   —   Li'l Abner (waving flag)

LONE RANGER, New Haven, ca.1939

LONE RANGER, New Haven, ca.1939. 2 styles of backs

MICKEY MOUSE Ingersoll, ca.1933

MICKEY MOUSE Ingersoll, ca.1933

HOAX ??

LEFT: Mickey Mouse, Ingersoll, w/ Mickey seconds, ca.1938. **CENTER:** Mickey Mouse, 1947 Ingersoll dial in a 1938 Ingersoll case. **RIGHT:** Mickey Mouse, Ingersoll, grooved bezel NOT birthday series, ca.1948

Note: To be **mint** condition, character watches must have unfaded dials, and boxes must have all inserts. (PW=Pocket Watch; WW=Wrist Watch)

Style or Grade – Description	Avg	Ex-Fn	Mint	Mint +Box
James Bond 007, WW, c. 1972, by Gilbert	$90	$150	$250	$800
Jeff Arnold, PW, c. 1952, by Ingersoll (English watch with moving gun)	150	200	325	600
Jiminy Cricket, WW, c.1948, Ingersoll, Birthday series (fluted)	75	100	300	650
Jiminy Cricket, WW, c.1949, Ingersoll, Not Birthday (grooved)	75	100	300	650
Joe Carioca, WW, c. 1948, by U.S. Time (fluted bezel, birthday series)	75	85	285	525
Joe Palooka, WW, c. 1948, by New Haven	150	200	300	600
Li'l Abner, WW, c. 1948, by New Haven (waving flag)	150	200	275	625
Li'l Abner, WW, c. 1948, by New Haven (moving mule)	150	175	250	525
Li'l Abner, WW, c. 1955, all black dial	95	135	185	400
Little King, WW, c. 1968, by Timex	55	125	225	425
Little Pig Fiddler, WW, c.1947, by Ingersoll	125	200	300	625
Lone Ranger, PW, c. 1939, by New Haven (with fob) ★	150	250	400	1,000
Lone Ranger, WW, c. 1938, by New Haven (large)	100	185	350	650
Lone Ranger, WW, c. 1948, New Haven, (Fluted lugs)	75	125	250	500
Lone Ranger, WW, c. 1950's, round case	65	100	200	400
Louie, WW, c.1940s, by Ingersoll, (Donalds nephew)	95	150	250	475
Mary Marvel, WW, c. 1948, by U.S. Time (paper box)	65	85	175	500
Mary Marvel, WW, c. 1948, by U.S. Time (plastic box)	65	85	145	400
Mickey Mouse, PW, c.1933, by Ingersoll, #1&2 (tall stem)	285	400	650	1,100
Mickey Mouse, PW, c.1936, by Ingersoll, #3 & 4(short stem)	200	300	450	925
Mickey Mouse, PW, c. 1936, by Ingersoll, #4 lapel watch (short stem) with **rare FOB**	225	350	750	1,400
Mickey Mouse, PW, c. 1938, by Ingersoll (Mickey decal on back)	275	400	700	1,100
Mickey Mouse, PW, c. 1933, by Ingersoll Ltd. (English)	300	450	750	1,400
Mickey Mouse, PW, c. 1934, by Ingersoll (Foreign)	275	325	450	675
Mickey Mouse, PW, c.1976, by Bradley (bicentennial model)	40	50	110	300
Mickey Mouse, PW, c. 1974, by Bradley (no second hand)	40	50	60	110
Mickey Mouse, PW, c. 1974, by Bradley ("Bradley" printed at 6)	40	50	60	110
Mickey Mouse, small 32MM PW, Ingersoll, s. steel, Ca.1930s	85	125	250	425

MICKEY MOUSE, Ingersoll, model no.3 on the left.   Right: Model no.4 is called a lapel watch, Very RARE FOB.

NOTE: Beware (**COLOR COPY DIALS**) are being **FAKED** as Buck Rodgers, Babe Ruth, Hopalong Cassidy and others. *BUYER BEWARE*

The Complete Price Guide to Watches goal is to stimulate the orderly exchange of <u>Watches</u> between "*buyers*" and "*sellers*".

Style or Grade – Description	Avg	Ex-Fn	Mint	Mint +Box
Mickey Mouse, WW, c. 1933, by Ingersoll (metal band with 3 Mickeys' on seconds disc) $200		$300	$500	$1,200
Mickey Mouse, WW, c. 1933, by Ingersoll (English Mickey with 3 Mickeys' on seconds disc, 24 hr. outer dial).........200		300	475	1,100
Mickey Mouse, WW, c. 1938-9, by Ingersoll (one Mickey for second hand).....................................125		200	350	975
Mickey Mouse, WW, c. 1939, by Ingersoll, plain seconds..........85		125	250	525
Mickey Mouse, WW, c. 1938-9, by Ingersoll (girl's and boys style watch, 1 Mickey for second hand) 175		225	350	950
Mickey Mouse, WW, c. 1948, by Ingersoll (fluted Bezel, birthday series, 2 styles Mickey in a circle & no circle)..150		175	400	675
Mickey Mouse, WW, c. 1949, by Ingersoll, **grooved** bezel 125		150	250	450
Mickey Mouse, WW, c. 1946, by U.S. Time (10k gold plated) 95		125	225	450
Mickey Mouse, WW, c. 1946, **Kelton**...............................95		125	225	450
Mickey Mouse, WW, c. 1947, by U.S. Time (tonneau, plain, several styles) 75		100	175	425
Mickey Mouse, WW, c. 1947, by U.S. Time (same as above, gold tone)...85		100	185	450
Mickey Mouse, WW, c. 1950s, by U.S. Time (round style)........40		55	125	350
Mickey Mouse, WW, c. 1958, by U.S. Time (**statue** of Mickey in box) 75		100	225	525
Mickey Mouse, WW, c. 1965 to 1970, by Timex (Mickey Mouse electric) 95		125	235	450
Mickey Mouse, WW, c. 1965-70s, Timex (manual wind) 55		65	125	175
Mickey Mouse, WW, c. 1975, Elgin (**ELECTRIC MODEL**), **14K** GOLD CASE & leather band, 13 jewels ....★425		550	850	1,400
Mickey Mouse, WW, c. 1970s, by Bradley 40		50	60	100
Mickey Mouse, WW, c. 1980, by Bradley (colored min. chapter) 60		70	85	150
Mickey Mouse, WW, c. 1983, by Bradley (limited commemorative model).....................................60		75	100	175

Mickey Mouse, Bradley, ca. 1969.

Mickey Mouse, with wide bezel, Ingersoll, it is believed dealers have used a Wrist Watch dial in a Hopalong case, ca. 1955. **Maybe HOAX ??**

Note: To be **mint** condition, character watches must have unfaded dials, and boxes must have all inserts. (PW=Pocket Watch; WW=Wrist Watch)

Left: Captain Marvel, Ca. 1948. **Center:** Minnie Mouse, U.S.Time, Ca.1968. **Right:** Orphan Annie, New Haven, Ca.1939

ORPHAN ANNIE, New Haven, in 1940 sold for $5.95.   2 case styles of POPEYE & friends, New Haven, Ca. 1936

POPEYE, New Haven, (with friends), Ca. 1935   POPEYE, New Haven, Ca. 1936, (Wimpy only), originally sold for **.80** in 1936.

⏰ Note: To be **mint** condition, character watches must have unfaded dials, and boxes must have all inserts. (PW=Pocket Watch; WW=Wrist Watch)

LEFT: GOOFY watch runs backward. CENTER: Little Pig & fiddle. RIGHT: Porky Pig

Left: Pluto, Birthday Series, by Ingersoll. **Center:** Rocky Jones, Ca.1955. **Right:** Speedy Gonzales, Swiss

Ingraham tonneau-shaped movement Ca. 1934.

DONALD DUCK, Ward W. Co. made for the Austria market, Ca. 1940s.

Rare Dan Winslow watch front and back.

Style or Grade – Description	Avg	Ex-Fn	Mint	Mint +Box
Mickey Mouse, WW, c. 1985, by ETA (clear plastic bezel and band)	$40	$50	$65	$100
Mickey Mouse, WW, c.1980s, Bradley, (Tachometer dial)	45	50	60	85
Mighty Mouse, WW, c.1980s, Swiss, (Plastic case)	25	30	35	50
Minnie Mouse, WW, c. 1958, by U.S. Time (statue of Minnie in box)	50	65	200	475
Moon Mullins, PW, c. 1930, by Ingersoll	★ 200	300	500	1,100
Orphan Annie, WW, c. 1939, by New Haven (fluted bezel)	75	100	200	500
Orphan Annie, WW, c. 1935, by New Haven (large style)	65	90	185	475
Orphan Annie, WW, c. 1948, by New Haven smaller model)	50	65	150	325
Orphan Annie, WW, c. 1968, by Timex	45	55	75	150
Pee Wee Herman, WW, (Swiss), FLIP TOP	25	35	75	125
Peter Pan, PW, c. 1948, by Ingraham	150	200	300	725
Pinocchio, WW, c. 1948, by Ingersoll (fluted bezel, birthday series)	125	150	285	550
Pinocchio, WW, c. 1948, by U.S. Time (Happy Birthday cake box)	125	150	325	675
Pluto, WW, c. 1948, by U.S. Time(birthday series)	100	140	250	500
Popeye, PW, c. 1935, by New Haven (with friends on dial)	★ 275	450	650	1,200
Popeye, PW, c. 1936, by New Haven (plain dial)	225	375	550	1,100
Popeye, WW, c. 1936, by New Haven (tonneau style, with friends on dial)	★ 250	375	675	1,300
Popeye, WW, c. 1966, by Bradley (round style)	75	95	125	200
Popeye, WW, c. 1948, Swiss, Olive Oyl at 3	75	150	250	450
Porky Pig, WW, c. 1948, by Ingraham (tonneau)	100	175	250	525
Porky Pig, WW, c. 1949, by U.S. Time (round)	100	175	250	525
Punkin Head, WW, c.1946, Ingraham,	55	65	85	150
Puss-N-Boots, WW, c. 1959, by Bradley	95	175	250	400
Quarterback, WW, c.1965, Swiss, (Football action arm)	65	75	85	150
Red Ryder, WW, c.1949, Swiss, (with Little Beaver)	95	150	300	750
Robin, WW, c. 1978, by Timex	40	45	85	150
Robin Hood, WW, c. 1955, by Bradley (tonneau style)	100	175	275	525
Robin Hood, WW, c. 1958, by Viking (round)	85	135	275	500
Rocky Jones Space Ranger, WW, c. 1955, by Ingraham	125	235	350	775
Roy Rogers, PW, c. 1960, by Ingraham, (stop watch) rim set	150	350	650	1,200
Roy Rogers, WW, c. 1954, by Ingraham (Roy and rearing Trigger)	65	125	300	650

Joe Palooka, Ca.1948.   — Snow White U.S.Time. —   Roy Rogers, Ingraham, ca. 1954.

I will respect & appreciate positive sound reliable comments, corrections, improvements or remarks but reserve the right to except the statement or keep my own observations & views. (Cooksey)

ROY ROGERS, Ingraham,note rim set, Ca. 1960.

ROY ROGERS, Ingraham (large), Ca. 1951.

Left: ROY ROGERS, Note: This watch is a 1950's Ingraham dial in a 1938 Ingersoll case.

Center: Tom Corbett, Space Cadet, New Haven, Ca. 1935

Right: SKEEZIX, Ingraham, Ca. 1936.

Left: Smitty, New Haven, Ca.1936. Center: Superman, New Haven, Ca.1939. Right: Superman, New Haven, Ca.1939.

Style or Grade – Description	Avg	Ex-Fn	Mint	Mint +Box
Roy Rogers, WW, c. 1954, by Ingraham (Roy and Trigger)	$70	$135	$250	$650
Roy Rogers, WW, c. 1954, by Ingraham (expansion band).........	70	135	250	650
Roy Rogers, WW, c. 1956, by Ingraham (round dial).................	70	125	210	525
Rudolf the Red Nose Reindeer, c.1946, Ingraham	85	135	300	600
Rudy Nebb, PW, c. 1930, by Ingraham .... ★★	150	195	500	900
Shirley Temple, PW, c.1958, by Westclox .... ★★	275	375	450	800
Skeezix, PW, c. 1928, by Ingraham .... ★★	300	400	600	1,000
Sky King, WW, (action gun)..	75	85	150	425
Smitty, PW, c. 1928, by New Haven	225	275	350	700
Smitty, WW, c. 1936, by New Haven	150	200	300	600
Smokey Stover, WW, c. 1968, by Timex	75	85	150	300
Snoopy, WW, c. 1958 (tennis racket)	30	40	80	150
Snoopy, WW, c. 1958 (Woodstock)...	30	40	80	150
Snow White, WW, c. 1938, by Ingersoll (tonneau)....................	100	125	250	550
Snow White, WW, c. 1952, by U.S. Time (round).....................	45	50	65	185
Snow White, WW, c. 1956, by U.S. Time (statue in box)	40	45	80	400
Snow White, WW, c. 1962, by U.S. Time (plastic watch)...........	40	50	65	300
Space Explorer, c.1953, COMPASS watch	75	100	200	425
Speedy Gonzales, WW, Swiss	75	95	150	275
Spiro Agnew, WW,c.1970s, Swiss	60	80	150	275
Superman, PW, c. 1956, by Bradley (stop watch).....................	150	195	400	750
Superman, WW, c. 1938, by New Haven	195	250	400	875
Superman, WW, c.1946, by Ingraham(lightning bolt hands)....	150	185	285	575
Superman, WW, c. 1978, by Timex (large size).........................	50	65	85	175
Superman, WW, c. 1978, by Timex (small size).........................	45	50	75	150
Superman, WW, c.1975, Dabs & Co., yellow min. chapter.........	45	50	75	150
Superman, WW, c.1965, Swiss, rotating superman....................	55	75	150	300
Superman, WW, c.1976, Timex, sweep sec. hand......................	60	65	85	200
Texas Ranger, WW, c.1950, by New Haven, action gun	95	125	200	450
Three Little Pigs, PW, c. 1939, by Ingersoll................... ★★	400	600	1,000	1,800
Tom Corbett, WW, c. 1954, by New Haven........................ ★	195	295	600	1,200
Tom Mix, PW, c. 1934-5, by Ingersoll (with fob)....... ★★★	1,000	1,500	2,000	3,600
Tom Mix, WW, c. 1934-5, by Ingersoll........................ ★★★	400	600	900	3,200
Winnie the Pooh Bear, c.1970s, Swiss......................................	40	50	60	125
Wizard of Oz, c.1972, swiss..	40	55	70	150
Wonder Woman,WW, c.1975, stars at 1,2,4,5,7,8,10,11	65	70	150	225
Wonder Woman,WW, c.1975, Dabs & Co.	50	65	150	225
Woody Woodpecker, WW, c. 1948, by Ingersoll (tonneau)	100	135	250	725
Woody Woodpecker, WW, c. 1952, by Ingraham (round dial) ...	95	125	200	625
Yogi Bear, WW, c. 1964, by Bradley	50	55	75	200
Zorro, WW, c. 1956, by U.S. Time	60	75	175	425

Left: Tom Mix wrist watch, came with metal link band.

Center: Tom Mix, Ingersoll, ca. 1934-5. TOM MIX on TONY

Right: Woody Woodpecker, U.S. Time, ca. 1948.

Moon Mullins, by Ingersoll, ca. 1928
Reproductions seen

Rudy Nebb, by Ingersoll, ca. 1928

Shirley Temple, by Westclox, ca. 1958

1952 AD, by Ingersoll, Dan Dare Watch and Box.

CUB SCOUT by Timex   BOY SCOUT by New Haven   DAVY CROCKETT, by Ingraham

BELOW 4 ADVERTISEMENTS FROM THE 1930's

MICKEY MOUSE WRIST WATCH with metal or leather strap bearing Mickey's picture. The watch itself is smartly styled ... round and therefore entirely practical for a very little girl's wrist. Packed in Mickey Mouse display carton. Retails $2.75. List $3.90

MICKEY MOUSE WATCH AND FOB— a wonderful buy at $1.50 complete. Mickey on the dial of the watch pointing out the time—Mickey on the fob—three little Mickies on the second-circle chasing each other around. List $2.20

New Mickey Mouse Lapel Watch. A handsome lapel model with Mickey's hands telling time on small dial. Mickey on dial and back of a black glossy finished case with nickel trim. Black lapel cord and button. Each in a display box.

No. 1W61. Each.....................$2.10

LONE RANGER FOB WATCH

ABOVE: 20th Birthday series style case note **fluted** bezel. The Birthday series used different characters & sold for $6.95. The TEN CHARACTERS are: Mickey Mouse, Daisy Duck, Pluto, Bambi, Joe Carioca, Bongo, Donald Duck, Pinnochio, Dopey, and Jiminy Cricket.

New De Luxe Mickey Mouse Wrist Watch. A smarter thinner chromium plated rectangular case. Mickey appears in bright colors on the dial. Fitted with a perspiration proof leather band. Each in display box.

No. 11W440. Each.................$5.54

Above: From a 1938 ad

438

EARLY ANTIQUE WATCHES

Above:
Dumbbell foliot style balance.

Early German Alarm Iron movement, note Stackfreed with contoured cam, dumbbell foliot style balance, scroll cock, hand-form index arm with a bristle regulator, 70MM, made in Augsburg, Ca. 1570.

The early antique watches looked quite similar to small table clocks. The **mainspring** was introduced to clocks in about **1450**. These drum-shaped watches were about two inches in diameter and usually over one-half inch thick. The drum-shaped watch lost popularity in the late 1500s. The earliest portable timepieces did not carry the maker's name, but initials were common. The cases generally had a hinged lid which covered the dial. This lid was pierced with small holes to enable ready identification of the position of the hour hand. They also usually contained a bell. The dial often had the numbers "I" to "XII" engraved in Roman numerals and the numbers "13" to "24" in Arabic numbers with the "2" engraved in the form of a "Z." Even the earliest of timepieces incorporated striking. The oldest known watch with a date engraved on the case was made in 1548. A drum-shaped watch with the initials "C. W.," it was most likely produced by Casper Werner, a protege of Henlein.

Balance
Pallet
Verge
Pallet
Contrate Wheel
Crown or Escape Wheel

Early pocket watches were designed to run from 12 to 16 hours. The pinions usually bore five leaves, the great wheel 55 teeth, the second wheel 45 teeth, the third wheel 40 teeth, and the escape wheel 15 teeth. With one less pinion and wheel the escape wheel ran reverse to a standard four-wheel watch. During the 1500s, 1600s, and much of the 1700s, it was stylish to decorate not only the case and balance cock but all parts including the clicks, barrel, studs, springs, pillars, hands, and stackfreed.

The plates themselves were decorated with pierced and engraved metal scrolls, and in some instances the maker's name was engraved in a style to correspond with the general decoration of the movement. During these periods the most celebrated artists, designers, and engravers were employed. The early watches were decorated by famous artists such as Jean Vauquier 1670, Daniel Marot 1700, Gillis l'Egare 1650, Michel Labon 1630, Pierre Bourdon 1750, and D. Cochin 1750. Most of the artists were employed to design and execute pierced and repousse cases.

Alarm watch made by Bockel of London Ca. 1648.

THE MID-1700s

In the mid-1700s relatively minor changes are noticed. Decoration became less distinctive and less artistic. The newer escapements resulted in better time keeping, and a smaller balance cock was used. The table and foot became smaller. The foot grew more narrow, and as the century and the development of the watch advanced, the decoration on the balance cock became smaller and less elaborate. About 1720 the foot was becoming solid and flat. No longer was it hand pierced; however, some of the pierced ones were produced until about 1770. Thousands of these beautiful hand pierced watch cocks have been made into necklaces and brooches or framed. Sadly, many of the old movements were destroyed in a mad haste to cater to the buyers' fancy.

THE 1800s

As the 1800s approached the balance cocks became less artistic as the decoration on movements gradually diminished. Breguet and Berthoud spent very little time on the beauty or artistic design on their balance cocks or pillars. But the cases were often magnificent in design and beauty, made with enamels in many colors and laden with precious stones. During this period the movements were plain and possessed very little artistic character.

As early as 1820 three-quarter and one-half plate designs were being used with the balance cock lowered to the same level as the other wheels. The result was a slimmer watch. **Flat enamel** dials are being used in about 1810.

The DUST CAP Ca. 1685 to 1875
    Popular in England.
Note: To remove dust cap from
Movement, Slide crescent shaped
catch or latch **right or Left**.
Daniel Quare may have been
the first to use a Dust Cap.

WATCH-MAKER

The term watch-maker might originally denote the *maker* of *watches* from base material or one who manufactures watches. But as we shall see a watch-maker may better be described as the expert in charge of producing watches. One other note before we move on, a watch may be considered as a miniature spring driven clock, so early on many **clock-makers** were also *watch-makers.*

There are surviving artifacts that make it possible to make certain assumptions. Thomas Tompion (also a English clock-maker) born 1639, death 1713, used a production system for making watches. About 1675-80 Tompion divided and sub-divided laborers into various branches of manufacturing of watches. This meant each craftsman specialized in making single watch parts, thus the division of labor led to a faster rate of production, with higher quality and a lower cost to the ebauche movement. About 1775 John Elliott and John Arnold had much of their work done by other sub-divided workers. The quality of the employees work depends upon the watch-maker. Thus, the **PRICE depends** on the **reputation** of the master (watch-maker). The same holds true for todays prices, the reputation of the maker helps to determine the price they can fetch for the timepieces. The parts and materials are of little value in their original state, but the various pieces require such delicacy of manipulation and the management of production of watches, thus the responsibility for the action of the watch depends on the committee in the house of the maker. Prior to 1870 rough movements were **99%** produced in the **Prescot** area then finished in London, Liverpool, & etc.

In about 1760 to 1765 Lepine introduced the French or Lepine style calibre of ebauche movements. The Lepine style used separate bridges instead of the single top plate design. Frederic Japy (Japy Freres & Cie.) of Beaucourt, France, later manufactured ebauche Swiss bar style movements in the early 1770's. About 1776, Japy aids in setting up a factory in the LeLocle area and latter in England. Japy Freres & Co. were producing 30,000 movements each year by 1795, and over 60,000 ebauche style movements each year by 1860. Other "BAR" style Ebauche Companies: 1804-Sandoz & Trot of Geneva, 1840-G.A. Leschot with Vacheron & Constantin and about 1850- LeCoultre. These bar style ebauche movements were imported into the U.S.A. about 1850 and were used in the jewelry trade with the jewelers name on the case and dial until about 1875.

MOVEMENTS " IN THE GRAY "

Movements in an early stage of manufacture.

ABOUT MID 1600'S

ABOUT 1675-80

ABOUT 1790—1830
ENGLISH STYLE

EBAUCHE style movement with verge,
chain driven fusee, under sprung, KW,
ABOUT 1810 — 1860.

BAR STYLE movement, cylinder, **ABOUT 1840 t0 80.**

Le Locle style EBAUCHE **ABOUT 1870 to 1890.**

⌚ **Multi-color** cases became popular by 1800, 1st. used in 1760 & **Engine Turning** rarely found before early 1760s. **Tortoise Shell** 1st. used in 1620, but did not become popular till about 1780.

The ebauche makers and the cottage industry made different models designed to conform or answer the needs of each country to which they were trying to do business with such as French style, English style, Chinese style, etc. This makes it hard to determine the origin of the ebauche watch. The case may be made in England, the movement Swiss, and the dial French.

Below are some of the principle workmen employed in the sub-divided production of plain parts or ebauche simple watch movements (in the rough)from about 1800s. Some of these were small family specialist that formed a **cottage industry,** (some being females) they usually produced only one product.

1. Cock-maker (made brass blanks)
2. Pillar-maker (turn the pillars, etc.)
3. Frame-maker (full plates, bars, bridges, etc.)
4. Wheel-maker (small and large)
5. Wheel-cutter (cuts the teeth on the wheels)
6. Balance-makers (made of steel or brass)
7. Spring-maker(hair & main springs)

8. Fusee-maker
9. Verge-makers
10. Chain-makers
11. Pinion- maker
12. Escapement-maker
13. Hand-maker
14. Dial-maker

Below a list of craftsman making cases.
1. Case-maker (makes cupped lids for cases)
2. Side-maker (makes the side of the case)
3. Cap-maker (makes the lids of the case)
4. The joint-finisher (joints for cases)
5. Glass-maker (made crystals for bezels)
6. Bezel-makers & Pendant-maker

RIGHT: A English made movement, Ca. 1750s.

These blank movements, parts, dials and cases were bought, then shipped on to the final destination. The *watch-maker* or *finisher,* such as, the house of (CARTIER). The Finisher would often house or contract decorators to finish the cases. The Finisher completed, polished, engraved, timed, regulated and made all the adjustments to the movements. They added and fitted the case to the movement. They added and fitted the complications such as repeaters to the movements. The *finished* watch is now ready for sale.

This type of system of producing watches left time for the Master watch-makers or famous watch-makers to invent, design new and better ways to make watches, such as, Abraham Louis Breguet. In early 1800's Breguet firm received parts and Swiss ebauches from 18 different suppliers. Thus the more famous the maker the higher the price of the watch even though the watch-maker may not have **made** the smallest piece for the *finished* watch.

The cottage industry with its one man, one task system, make it difficult to establish who, when and where some watches were actually made. It is some what simpler to determine the origin or area, as Swiss, English, French or American, however it is rewarding with further research to unmask the disguise of watch-making. Close study, inspection and comparing movements over the years will prove helpful and may reveal the origin and age of your watch.

Most Swiss manufactures do not make the complete watch on their own premises. Some parts are supplied by specialized firms, such as; balance wheels, escape wheels, jewels, hairsprings, mainsprings, pendant bows and crowns, crystals, hands, cases, screws, pins and other small parts. There were a few factories in Le Locle, Switzerland that manufactured the Cylinder and escape wheel but most were made in the *Maiche district of **France**.* Brass plates were plated with RHODIUM for the most part in Swiss Industry. Ebauche or rough movements were made in the Valley of Joux and the Val-de-Ruz regions, in and around towns such as Granges, Bienne, Solothurn, La Chaux- de-Fonds also near by Le Locle, in the Bernese Jura, the Valley of St.Imier, and elsewhere.

CLUES TO DATING YOUR WATCH

To establish the age of a watch there are many points to be considered. The dial, hands, pillars, balance cock and pendant, for example, contain important clues in determining the age of your watch. However, no one part alone should be considered sufficient evidence to draw a definite conclusion as to age. The watch as a whole must be considered. For example, an English-made silver-cased watch will have a hallmark inside the case. It is quite simple to refer to the London Hallmark Table for hallmarks after 1697. The hallmark will reveal the age of the case only. This does not fix the age of the movement. Many movements are housed in cases made years before or after the movement was produced.

An informed collector will note that a watch with an **enamel dial**, for instance, could not have been made before 1635. **A pair of cases** indicates it could not have been made prior to 1640. A **dust cap** first appeared in 1680. The **minute hand** was introduced about 1680. The presence of a **cylinder escapement** would indicate it was made after 1710. **1750 the duplex escapement** was first used. *1776 Lepine* introduced the **thin** watch. **Flat enamel dial** being used in about 1810. **Keyless winding** came into being after 1820, but did not gain widespread popularity until *after* about 1860. All of these clues and more must be considered before accurately assessing the age of a watch. *Some watches were also updated such as minute hand added, enamel dial or new style escapement added.*

Example of an early pocket watch (Ca. 1548) with a stackfreed tear shaped cam design to equalize power much as a fusee does. Note dumbbell shaped foliot which served as a balance for verge escapement.

Thomas Tompion called the Father of English Watchmaking. Under his improvements, watches began to embody sound principles and accuracy. He introduced the division of labor, standardized parts, **spiral** balance spring, wide firm foot to the large balance cock and key actuated regulator for balance spring. The minute hand, the second wheel planted at center of movement, enamel dials, milled teeth for wheels and pinions and a general appearance in the steel finish. He started to number his watches in about **1680** and apparently the first watchmaker to do so, therefore there are no earlier serial numbers higher than the Tompion serial numbers listed below for **approximated** year produced.

T. Tompion (time only watch)
Year — Serial #
1682 — 400
1685 — 900
1690 — 1,600
1695 — 2,100
1700 — 2,800
1705 — 3,500
1710 — 4,000

G. Graham Continues
Year — Serial #
1715 — 4,600
1725 — 5,200
1735 — 5,600
1745 — 6,100
1750 — 6,400

IMPORTANT NOTE: **FORGED** Watches signed T. Tompion and G. Graham, watches were **forged** in their life-time. These watches are the same age, style, hallmarks and **difficult** to tell from the true authentic watches.

PILLARS

Pillars are of interest and should be considered as one of the elements in determining age. Through the years small watches used round pillars, and the larger watches generally used a square type engraved pillar.

(*Illus.* 1) This pillar is one of the earliest types and used in the 1800s as well. This particular pillar came from a watch which dates about 1550. It is known that this type pillar was used in 1675 by Gaspard Girod of France and also in 1835 by James Taylor of England.

(*Illus.* 2) This style pillar is called the tulip pattern. Some watchmakers preferred to omit the vertical divisions. This style was popular between 1660 and 1750 but may be found on later watches. It was common practice to use ornamentation on the tulip pillar.

(*Illus.* 3) The ornament shown was used by Daniel Quare of London from 1665 to 1725 and by the celebrated Tompion, as well as many others.

(*Illus.* 4) This type pillar is referred to as the Egyptian and dates from 1630 to the 1800s. The squared Egyptian pattern was introduced about 1630 and some may be found with a wider division with a head or bust inserted. This style was used by D. Bouquet of London about 1640 and by many other watchmakers.

(*Illus.* 1) (*Illus.* 2) (*Illus.* 3) (*Illus.* 4)

(*Illus.* 5) This pillar was used by Thomas Earnshaw of London about 1780. The plain style was prominent for close to two hundred years 1650 to 1825.

(*Illus.* 5) (Illus. 6) (Illus. 7) (Illus. 8)

(Illus. 6) This style was popular and was used by many craftsmen. Nathaniel Barrow of London put this in his watches about 1680.

(Illus. 7) This pillar may be seen in watches made by Pierre Combet of Lyons, France, about 1720. It was also used by many others.

(Illus. 8) This style pillar and the ornament were used by John Ellicott of England and other watchmakers from 1730 to 1770.

These illustrations represent just a few of the basic pillars that were used. Each watchmaker would design and change details to create his own individual identity. This sometimes makes it more difficult to readily determine the age of watches.

🕐 **Multi-color** cases became popular by 1800, 1st. used in 1760 & **Engine Turning** rarely found before early 1760s. **Tortoise Shell** 1st. used in 1620, but did not become popular till about 1780. **Flat enamel** dials are being used in about 1810.

Example of 2 Egyptian pillars left & right also a hand pierced ornament that is not a pillar. (Ca.1700)

BALANCE COCKS OR BRIDGES

The first balance cocks or bridges used to support the balance staff were a plain "S" shape. The cocks used on the old three-wheel watches were very elaborate; hand-pierced and engraved. At first no screws were used to hold the cock in place. It is noteworthy that on the three wheel watch the regulator was a ratchet and click and was used on these earlier movements to adjust the mainspring. About 1635 the balance cock was screwed to the plate and pinned on its underside, which helped steady the balance. The first cock illustrated is a beautifully decorated example made by Josias Jeubi of Paris about 1580. Note that it is pinned to a stud which passes through a square cut in the foot of the cock. Next is a balance cock made by Bouquet of London about 1640. The third balance cock is one made by Jean Rousseau and dates around 1650. The fourth one dates around 1655.

The next two bridges are supported on both sides of the balance bridge by means of screws or pins. They are strikingly different and usually cover much of the plate of the movement. This French & Swiss style of balance bridge was used around 1665 and was still seen as late as 1765.

The beautiful balance cock below at left, with the ornate foot, dates about 1660-70. The next illustrated balance cock with the heavy ornamentation was used from about 1675 to 1720 or longer. By 1720 a face was added to the design. The face shows up where the table terminates on most balance cocks.

Right:1660–1700 NOTE wavy edge to the foot & two ears on the table. **LEFT:** With **D** shaped foot & round table with two ears Ca. 1675-1720

1720 - 1760

1750–1780 NOTE the ballon shape table & "pierced" fan shaped foot on this cock.

1760–1830, NOTE solid foot

1810 - 1835

1810–1830

1810–1865, look for barrel bridge

1850 NOTE under-sprung

⏱ Characteristics of watches differ for the same age of both case and movement, because these features vary it may not be accurate to date a watch by one single influence. Example: the second hand was <u>not</u> commonly found on watches before 1750, but common about 1800. The first second hand appeared in 1665 and another in 1690. Therefore statements are **broad** rather than absolute.

Lepine style movement Ca. 1790 to 1820, with free standing barrel, also note the horse shoe shaped bridge, this denotes center seconds. (Virgule Escapement)

Lepine, or FRENCH style ebauche caliber, NOTE the step shaped and tapered bridges, also note the free standing barrel, Ca. 1800 to1825.

Lepine, or FRENCH style ebauche caliber, NOTE the step shaped and tapered bridges, also note the COVERED barrel bridge, this style movement was popular from Ca.1820 to 1840.

Lepine, or FRENCH style ebauche caliber, NOTE the step shaped and tapered bridges, also note the CURVED barrel bridge, this style movement was popular from Ca.1830 to 1845.

🕐 Characteristics of watches differ for the same age of both case and movement, because these features vary it may not be accurate to date a watch by one single influence. Example: the second hand was not commonly found on watches before 1750, but common about 1800. The first second hand appeared in 1665 and another in 1690. Therefore statements are **broad** rather than absolute.

Muti-colored cases became popular by 1800, 1st. used in 1760 & **Engine Turning** rarely found before early 1760s. **Tortoise Shell** 1st. used in 1620, but did not become popular till about 1780. An informed collector will note that a watch with an enamel dial, for instance, could not have been made before 1635. A pair of cases indicates it could not have been made prior to 1640. The minute hand was introduced in 1650. The presence of a cylinder escapement would indicate it was made after 1710. 1750 the duplex escapement was first used. A dust cap first appeared in 1774. 1776 Lepine introduced the thin watch. **Flat enamel** dials are being used in about 1785. Keyless winding came into being after 1820 but did not gain widespread popularity until after about 1860. All of these clues and more must be considered before accurately assessing the age of a watch. Some watches were also **updated** such as minute hand added or new style escapement added.

448

Bar (Le Coultre) SWISS style ebauche caliber, NOTE the flat straight bridges and parallel design, also the CURVED barrel bridge this movement was popular Ca.1830 to 1875.

Bar (Le Coultre) SWISS style ebauche caliber, NOTE the flat straight bridges and parallel design, also the STRAIGHT barrel bridge this movement was popular Ca.1840 to 1885.

JULES JURGENSEN Style Bar SWISS La Chaux de Fonds ebauche caliber, Ca.1870 to 1895.

SAVAGE, two pin.

Rack and lever escapement

Invented in 1722

ESCAPEMENTS

Virgule Escapement

Duplex escapement

Popular in 1750s

CHINESE DUPLEX
or CRAB LEG DUPLEX

The "Glucydur" Balance can be recognized by the **shape** of its spokes.

CHRONOLOGICAL LIST TO HELP ESTABLISH THE AGE OF YOUR WATCHES
DATES BELOW ARE WHEN COMPONENTS WERE FIRST INTRODUCED OR BECAME POPULAR.

1450 - Mainspring, also large watches made entirely of **IRON** & were round in shape.

1525 - Fusee by Jacob of Prague.

1530-1545 - Brass plates.

1550 - Screws & Oval shaped watches.

1564 - Swiss Watchmaking begins.

1570 - Hexagonal and octagonal shapes.

1590 - Rock Crystal & Form style watches.

1590 - Fusee CHAIN being used.

1590 - English Watchmaking.

1615 - **Glass** crystal to protect dials.

1620 - Tortoise shell covered cases & used till 1800.

1625 - Colored enamel cases and balance cock screwed to plate.

1635 - Enamel dial invented by Paul Viet, of Blois, France.

1640 - Pair cased watches.

1650 -80- Repousse Cases & Form watches.

1657 - Hair-spring. (Not Spiral)

1660 - Virgule escapement.

1675 - Large Bulb shaped or Oignon watches, shagreen cases being seen.

* 1675 - **Spiral** balance hair-spring. also Watchmaking in Scotland.

1677 - Subdivision of labor, cottage industry.

1680 - Minute hands & Serial numbers first appear on movements. Watches now run for about 24 hours. On English watches.

1685-90 - Repeating watches.

1690 to 1720 - All white Enamel watch dials now being used in ENGLAND.

1695-Cylinder escapement by Edward Booth, William Houghton and Thomas Tompion.

1700 - Pinchbeck "Gold" (Zink & Copper)

1704 - Watch JEWELS invented.

1715 - Repousse, dust band also seconds hand with tails.

1720 - Improved cylinder escapement by Graham, but not popular.

1722 - Rack lever escapement.(non-detached)

1724 - Duplex escapement invented.

1750 - Duplex escapement **popular.**

1759 - Detached Lever escapement by Mudge.

1760 - Engine Turning & multi- color gold found on cases.

1761 - John Harrison's chronometer # 4 went to sea for first trial.

1765 - Center seconds.

1766 - Compensation balance by Le Roy.

1767 - Virgule escapement.

1770 - Ebauche style watches by Japy.

1773-Detached escapement (Berthound)

1775 - Helical balance spring by Arnold.

1776 - Thin modern watches by Lepine.

1785 - Flat Enamel dials being used.

1780 - Overcoil balance spring.

1782 - Spring detent by Arnold & Earnshaw.

1790 - Musical works & Automaton style watches, 4 color gold dials.

1800 - Watches decorated with pearls.

1820 - Reproduction of **1600 Form** watches. Prest patent for winding only by pendant.

1825 - Single sunk Dial.

1830 - Club tooth escape wheel. Min repeater

1838-Louis Audemars 1st crown wind & set.

1835 - Chinese Duplex.

1844 - Heart shaped cam for chronograph.

1848 - Rocking bar keyless winding.

1867 - Roskopf (Dollar) watches.

1896 - Invar "Guillaume" balance.

1900 - Wrist Watches being used.

1924 - Auto-wind Wrist Watch.

1957 - 1st electric W. W. by Hamilton.

1960 - First Electronic Wrist Watch by Max Hetzel & by Bulova "Accutron".

1967 - Quartz crystal watch developed.

Jan. 1675 Isaac Thuret introduced a **model** of a escapement that had a regulatory **spiral hairspring**. Thomas Tompion made watches with a **Minute hand**, Ca. 1680 .

EARLY EUROPEAN WATCHMAKERS
NOTE ABBREVIATIONS USED
art = maker used this enamel case painter, enamel = enamel case painter or artist
pat. = patent or inventor, ca. = circa or about, since = founded to present
This list of EARLY EUROPEAN WATCHMAKERS is a small %.

Achard, J. Francois (Geneva, ca. 1750)
Addison, J. (London, 1760-1780)
Adamson, Gustave (Paris, 1775-1790)
Alfred, W. Humphreys (London, ca. 1905)
Alibut (Paris, ca. 1750s)
Alliez, Buchelard & Teron Co. (French, ca. 1830)
Amabric, Abraham (Geneva, ca. 1750-1800)
Amabric, Freres (Geneva, ca. 1760-1795)
Amon (Paris, 1913)
Andre, Jean (enamel) (Geneva, 1660-1705)
Anthony, Willams (London, 1785-1840)
Antram, J. (London, ca. 1700-1730)
Appleby, Edward (London, ca. 1675)
Appleby, Joshua (London, ca. 1720-1745)
Ardin, Coppet (ca. 1710)
Arlaud, Benjamin (London, c. 1680)
Arlaud, Louis (Geneva, ca. 1750)
Anord & Dent (London) ca. 1839
Arnold & Frodsham, Charles (London, 1845)
Arnold, Henery (London, ca. 1770-1780)
Arnold, John (London, ca. 1760-1790)
Arnold, John Roger, son of (London, ca. 1800-1830)
Arnold, Nicolas (ca. 1850)
Arnold & Lewis, Lote Simmons (Manchester, ca. 1860)
Arnold & Son (London, ca. 1787-1799)
Assman, Julius (Glasshutte, 1850-1885)
Auber, Daniel (London, ca. 1750)
Aubert, D. F. (Geneva, ca. 1825)
Aubert, Ferdinand (1810-1835)
Aubert & Co. (Geneva, ca. 1850)
Aubry, Irenee (Geneva, 1885-1910)
Audebert (Paris, 1810-1820)
Audemars, Freres (Swiss, 1810 until Co. splits in 1885)
Audemars, Louis-Benjamin (Swiss, 1811-1867)
Aureole (Swiss, 1921)
Auricoste, Jules (Paris, ca. 1910)
Bachhofen, Felix (Swiss, 1675-1690)
Badollet, Jean-Jacques (Geneva, 1779-1891)
Baillon, Jean-Hilaire (Paris, ca. 1727)
Baird, Wm. (London, 1815-1825)
Balsiger & Fils (ca. 1825)
Barberet, J. (Paris, ca. 1600)
Barbezat, Bole (Swiss, 1870)
Baronneau, Jean-Louis (France, 1675-1700)
Barnett, John (England) 1690
Barraud & Lunds (England) 1872
Barraud & Lunds (1812-1840)
Barraud, Paul-Philip (London, 1752-1820)
Barrow, Edward (London, ca. 1650-1710)
Barrow, Nathaniel (London, 1653-1689)
Barry, M. (French, ca. 1620)
Bartholomy, Abraham (Paris, 1750-1752)
Barton, J. (London, 1760-1780)
Barwise J.(London, 1800)
Bassereau, Jean-Hilaire (Paris, ca. 1800-1810)
Bautte, Jean-Francois (Geneva, 1800-1835)
Bautte & Moynier (Geneva, ca. 1825)
Beaumarchais, Caron (Paris, 1750-1795)
Beauvais, Simon (London, ca. 1690)
Beckman, Daniel (London, 1670-1685)
Beckner, Abraham (London, ca. 1640)
Beliard, Dominique (Paris, ca. 1750)
Bell, Benj. (London, 1650-1668)
Bennett, John (London, 1850-1895)
Benson, J. W. (London, 1825-1890)
Benson, J. W. (London, 1850-1900)
Bergstein, L. (London, ca. 1840)
Bernard, Nicholas (Paris, 1650-1690)

Bernoulli, Daniel (Paris, 1720-1780)
Berrollas, J. A. (Denmark, 1800-1830)
Berthoud, Augusta-Louis (Paris, ca. 1875)
Berthoud, Ferdinand (Paris, 1750-1805)
Beihler & Hartmann (Geneva, ca. 1875)
Blanc, Henri (Geneva, ends 1964)
Blanc, Jules (Geneva, 1929-1940)
Blanc & Fils (Geneva, 1770-1790)
Bock, Johann (German, 1700-1750)
Bockel (London, ca. 1650)
Bolslandon, Metz (ca. 1780)
Bolviller, Moise (Paris, 1840-1870)
Bommelt, Leonhart (Nuremburg, Ger., ca. 1690)
Bonney (London, ca. 1790)
Bonniksen, Bahne (England, 1890-1930) invented karrusel
Booth, Edward (name change to Barlow)
Bordier, Denis (France, ca. 1575)
Bordier, Freres (Geneva, 1787-1810)
Bordier, Jacques (enamel) (ca. 1670)
Bornand, A. (Geneva, 1895-1915)
Boubon (Paris, 1810-1820)
Bouquet, David (London, ca. 1630-1650)
Bovet (England) 1815 (used J.L.Richer Art)
Bovet, Edouard (Swiss, 1820-1918)
Bovier, G. (enamel painter) (Paris, c. 1750)
Brandt, Iacob (Swiss, ca. 1700)
Brandt, Robert & Co. (Geneva, ca. 1820)
Breitling, "Leon" (Swiss, since 1884)
Brookbank (London, 1776)
Brocke (London, ca. 1640)
Brodon, Nicolas (Paris, 1674-1682)
Bronikoff, a Wjatka (Russia, 1850 "watches of wood")
Bruguier, Charles A. (Geneva, 1800-1860)
Bull, Rainulph (one of the first British) (1590-1617)
Burgis, Eduardus (London, 1680-1710)
Burgis, G. (London, 1720-1740)
Burnet, Thomas (London, ca. 1800)
Busch, Abraham (Hamburg, Ger., ca. 1680)
Buz, Johannes (Augsburg, Bavaria, ca. 1625)
Cabrier, Charles (London, ca. 1690-1720)
Capt, Henry Daniel (Geneva, 1802-1880)
Caron, Augustus (Paris, ca. 1750-1760)
Caron, Francois-Modeste (Paris, 1770-1788)
Caron, Pierre (Paris, ca. 1700)
Caron, Pierre Augustin (pat. virgule escap.) (Paris,1750-1795)
Carpenter, William (London, 1750-1800)
Carte, John (England, 1680-1700)
Champod, P. Amedee (enamel) (Geneva, 1850-1910)
Chapeau, Peter (England) 1746
Chapponier, Jean (Geneva, 1780-1800)
Charlton, John (England) 1635
Charman (London, 1780-1800)
Charrot (Paris, 1775-1810)
Chartiere (enamel) (France, ca. 1635)
Chaunes (Paris, ca. 1580-1600)
Chauvel, J. (England) 1720-25
Chavanne & Pompejo (Vienna, 1785-1800)
Cheneviere, Louis (Geneva, 1710-1740)
Cheneviere, Urbain (Geneva, 1730-1760)
Cheriot or Cherioz, Daniel (ca. 1750-1790)
Cheuillard (Blois, France, ca. 1600)
Chevalier & Co. (Geneva, 1795-1810)
Cisin, Charles (Swiss, 1580-1610)
Clark, Geo. (London, 1750-1785)
Clay, Charles (England) 1750
Clerc (Swiss, ca. 1875)
Clouzier, Jacques (Paris, 1690-1750)
Cochin, D. (Paris, ca. 1800)

Cocque, Geo. (ca. 1610)
Cogniat (Paris, ca. 1675)
Coladon, Louis (Geneva, 1780-1850)
Cole, James Ferguson (London, 1820-1875)
Cole, Thomas (London, 1820-1864)
Collins, Clement (London, ca. 1705)
Collins, John (London, ca. 1720)
Collins, R. (London, ca. 1815)
Colondre & Schnee (ca. 1875)
Combret, Pierre (Lyons, France, ca. 1610-1625)
Cooper, T.F. (England) 1842-80 later "T.M."
Cotton, John (London, ca. 1695-1715)
Coulin, Jaques & Bry, Amy (Paris & Geneva, 1780-1790)
Court, Jean-Pierre (ca. 1790-1810)
Courvosier, Freres (Swiss, 1810-1852)
Courvoisier & Houriet (Geneva, ca. 1790)
Cox, James (London, 1760-1785)
Crofswell J.N. (London), ca. 1825
Csacher, C. (Prague, Aus., ca. 1725)
Cumming, Alexander (London, 1750-1800)
Cummins, Charles (London, 1820)
Cuper, Barthelemy (French, 1615-1635)
Curtis, John (London, ca. 1720)
Cusin, Charles (Geneva, ca. 1587)
Darling, William (British, ca. 1825)
Daniel, de St. Leu (England) 1815
De Baghyn, Adriaan (Amsterdam, ca. 1750)
Debaufre, Peter (French, 1690-1720) (Debaufre escap.)
Debaufre, Pierre (Paris, London, Geneva, 1675-1722)
De Bry, Theodore (German, 1585-1620)
De Charmes, Simon (London, France, 1690-1730)
De Choudens (Swiss & French, 1760-1790)
Decombaz, Gedeon (Geneva, 1780-1820)
Degeilh & Co. (ca. 1880-1900)
De Heca, Michel (Paris, ca. 1685)
De L Garde, Abraham (Paris, "Blois," ca. 1590)
Delynne, F. L. (Paris, ca. 1775)
"Dent", (Edward John)(London, 1815-1850)
Denham, Go. (London, 1750)
Derham, William (English, ca. 1677-1730)
Deroch, F. (Swiss, 1730-1770)
Des Arts & Co. (Geneva, 1790-1810)
Desquivillons & DeChoudens (Paris, ca. 1785)
Destouches, Jean-Francois-Albert (Holland, ca. 1760)
Devis, John (London, 1770-1785)
Dimier & Co. (Geneva, 1820-1925)
Dinglinger (enamel) (Dresden, Ger., ca. 1675)
Ditisheim & Co. "Maurice" (Swiss, 1894)
Ditisheim, Paul (Swiss, 1892)
Dobson, A. (London, 1660-1680)
Droz, Daniel (Chaux-de-Fonds, Sw., ca. 1760)
Droz, Henri (Chaux-de-Fonds, Sw., ca. 1775)
Droz, Pierre Jacquet (Chaux-de-Fonds, Sw., 1750-1775)
Droz, Pierre (Swiss, 1740-1770)
Droz & Co. (Swiss, ca. 1825)
Dubie (enamel) (Paris, ca. 1635)
Dubois & Fils (Paris, ca. 1810)
Duchene & Co. "Louis" (Geneva, 1790-1820)
Ducommun, Charles (Geneva, ca. 1750)
Duduict, Jacques (Blois, France, ca. 1600)
Dufalga, Philippe (Geneva, 1730-1790)
Dufalga, P. F. (Geneva, ca. 1750)
Dufour, Foll & Co. (Geneva, 1800-1830)
Dufour, J. E. & Co. (ca. 1890)
Dufour & Ceret (Ferney, Fr., ca. 1770-1785)
Dufour & Zentler (ca. 1870)
Duhamel, Pierre (Paris, ca. 1680)
Dunlop, Andrew (England) 1710
Dupin, Paul (London, 1730-1765)
Dupont (Geneva, ca. 1810-1830)
Dupont, Jean (enamel) (Geneva, 1800-1860)
Duru (Paris, ca. 1650)
Dutertre, Baptiste (ca. 1730) (pat. duplex escapement)
Dutton, William (London, 1760-1840)

Dyson, John & Sons (England) 1816
Earnshaw, Thomas (London, 1780-1825)
East, Edward (London, 1630-1670)
Edmonds, James (London to U.S.A., 1720-1766)
Edward, George & Son (London, ca. 1875)
Ekegren, Henri-Robert (Geneva, 1860)
Ellicott, John (London, 1728-1810)
Emanuel, E.& E (England) 1861
Emery, Josiah (Geneva, 1750-1800)
Etherington, George (England) 1700
Esquivillon & De Choudens (Paris, 1710-1780)
Ester, Jean Henry (Geneva, 1610-1665)
Etherington, George (London, 1680-1730)
Etienne Guyot & Co. (Geneva, ca. 1880)
Facio De Duillier, Nicholas (British, 1665-1710)
Fallery, Jacques (Geneva, ca. 1760)
Farmer, G. W. (wooden watches) (Germany, 1650-1675)
Fatio, Alfred (Geneva, 1920-1940)
Fatton, Frederick Louis (London, ca. 1822)
Favre Marius & Fils (Geneva, 1893)
Fenie, M. (ca. 1635)
Ferrero, J. (ca. 1854-1900)
Fiarce, Clement (Paris, ca. 1700)
Fitter, Joseph (London, ca. 1660)
Fontac (London, ca. 1775)
Forfaict, Nicolas (Paris, 1573-1619)
Fowles, Allen (Kilmarnock, Scot., ca. 1770)
French (London, 1810-1840)
Fureur (Swiss, 1910)
Gallopin "Henri Capt" (Geneva, 1875)
Gamod, G. (Paris, ca. 1640)
Garnier, Paul (Paris, 1825) (pat. Garnier escapement)
Garon, Peter (England) 1700
Garrault, Jacobus (Geneva, ca. 1650)
Garty & Constable (London, ca. 1750)
Gaudron, Antoine (Paris, 1675-1707)
Gaudron, Pierre (Paris, 1695-1740)
Geissheim, Smod (Augsburg, Ger., ca. 1625)
Gent, James & Son (London, 1875-1910)
Gerbeau, V. (Paris, 1900-1930)
Gerrard (British, 1790-1820)
Gibs, William (Rotterdam, ca. 1720)
Gibbons Joshua (London), ca. 1825
Gibson & Co., Ltd. (Ireland, ca. 1875-1920)
Gidon (Paris, ca. 1700)
Gillespey, Charles (Ireland, 1774-1171)
Girard, Perregaux (Swiss, 1856)
Girard, Theodore (Paris, 1623-1670)
Girardier, Charles (Geneva, 1780-1815)
Girod, B. (Paris, ca. 1810)
Girod, Gaspard (Paris, ca. 1670-1690)
Godod, E. (Paris, ca. 1790)
Godon, F. L. (Paris, ca. 1787)
Golay, A. Leresche & Fils (Geneva, 1844-1857)
Golay, H. (Swiss, 1969-1911)
Golay, Stahl & Fils (1878-1914)
Gollons (Paris, ca. 1663)
Gould, Christopher (England) 1650
Gounouilhou, P. S. (Geneva, 1815-1840)
Gout, Ralph (London, 1790-1830)
Graham, George (London, 1715-1750)
Grandjean, Henri (Swiss, 1825-1880)
Grandjean, L. C. (Swiss, 1890-1920)
Grant, John & Son (English, 1780-1867)
Grantham, William (London, ca. 1850-60)
Grasset, Isaac (Geneva, ca. 1896)
Gray & Constable (London, ca. 1750-90)
Grazioza (Swiss, ca. 1901)
Grebauval, Hierosme (ca. 1575)
Gregory, Jeremie (London, ca. 1652-1680)
Gregson, Jean P. (Paris, 1770-1790)
Grendon, Henry (England) 1645
Griblin, Nicolas (French, 1650-1716)
Griessenback, Johann G. (Bavaria, ca. 1660)

Grignion "family" (London, 1690-1825)
Grignion, Daniel & Thomas (London, 1780-1790)
Grinkin, Robert (England) 1625
Grosclaude, Ch. & Co. (Swiss, ca. 1865)
Grosjean, Henry (French, ca. 1865)
Gruber, Hans (Nurnberg, Ger., ca. 1520-1560)
Gruber, Michel (Nurnberg, Ger., ca. 1605)
Gruet (Geneva, Sw., ca. 1664)
Gubelin, E. (Lucern, Switzerland, ca. 1832)
Guillaume, Ch. (pat. Invar, Elinvar)
Haas Nevevx & Co. (founder B. J. Haas) (Swiss, 1828-1925)
Hagen, Johan (German, ca. 1750)
Haley, Charles (London, 1781-1825)
Hallewey (London, 1695-1720)
Hamilton & Co. (London, 1865-1920)
Hamilton G.(London), Ca.1800s
Harper, Henry (London, ca. 1665-1700)
Harrison, John (England, b.1693-1776) **Marine No.1-2-3-4**
Hasluck Brothers (London, ca. 1695)
Hautefeuille, Jean (Paris, 1670-1722)
Hautefeuille, John (Paris, 1660-1700)
Hawley, John (London, ca. 1850)
Hebert, Juliette (enamel) (Geneva, ca. 1890)
Helbros (Geneva, since 1918)
Hele or Henlein, Peter (Nurnberg, 1510-1540)
Heliger, J. (Zug, Sw., ca. 1575)
Henner, Johann (Wurtzburg, Ger., ca. 1730)
Henry, F. S. (Swiss, ca. 1850)
Hentschel, J. J. (French, ca. 1750)
Hess, L. (Zurich, Sw., ca. 1780)
Hessichti, Dionistus (ca. 1630)
Higgs & Evans (London, 1775-1825)
Hill, Ben. (London, 1640-1670)
Hindley, Henry (England) 1758
Hoddell, James, & Co. (England) 1869
Hoguet, Francois (Paris, ca. 1750)
Hooke, Robert (England, 1650-1700)
Hoseman, Stephen (London, ca. 1710-1740)
Houghton, James (England, ca. 1800-1820)
Houghton, Thomas (Chorley, England, ca. 1820-1840)
Houriet, Jacques Frederic (Paris 1810-1825)
Howells & Pennington (England) 1795
Huaud, Freres (enamel) (Geneva, ca. 1685)
Huber, Peter (German, ca. 1875)
Hubert, David (London, 1714-1747)
Hubert, James (England) 1760
Hubert, Oliver (London, ca. 1740)
Hubert, Etienne (French, 1650-1690)
Hues, Peter (Augsburg, Ger., ca. 1600)
Huguenin, David L. (Swiss, 1780-1835)
Humbert-Droz, David (Swiss, ca. 1790)
Hunt & Roskell (England) 1846
Huygens, Christian (Paris, 1657-1680)
Iaquier or Jacquier, Francois (Geneva, 1690-1720)
Ilbery, *William* (London, 1800-35) (used J.L. Richer art)
Ingold, Pierre-Frederic (Swiss, Paris, London, 1810-1870)
Invicta ("R. Picard") (Swiss, 1896)
Jaccard, E. H. & Co. (Swiss, ca. 1850)
Jacot, Charles-Edouard (Swiss, 1830-1860) (pat. Chinese duplex)
Jaeger, Edmond (Paris, 1875-1920)
Jaeger Le Coultre & Co. (Swiss, since 1833)
Jamison, Geo. (London, 1786-1810)
Janvier, Antide (Paris, 1771-1834)
Japy, Frederic & Sons "family" (French, Swiss, ca. 1776)
Jaquet, Pierre (Swiss, 1750-1790)
Jean Richard, Daniel (Swiss, 1685-1740)
Jean Richard, Edouard (Swiss, 1900-1930)
Jeannot, Paul (ca. 1890)
Jefferys & Gildert (London, 1790)
Jessop, Josias (London, 1780-1794)
Jeubi, Josias (Paris, ca. 1575)
Joly, Jacques (Paris, ca. 1625)
Jovat (London, ca. 1690)

Johnson Joseph. Liverpool (English), ca.1805-1855
Jones, Henry (London, ca. 1665-1690)
Jump, Joseph (English, ca. 1827-1850)
Junod, Freres (Geneva, ca. 1850)
Jurgensen, Urban & Jules (Copenhagen, Swiss,1745-1912)
Just & Son (London, 1790-1825)
Juvet, Edouard (Swiss, 1844-1880)
Juvet, Leo (Swiss, 1860-1890)
Keates, William (London, ca. 1780)
Keely, W. (London, ca. 1790)
Kendall, Larcum (London, ca. 1786)
Kendall, James (London, 1740-1780)
Kessels, H. J. (Holland, 1800-1845)
Kirkton, R. (London, ca. 1790)
Klein, Johann Heinr (Copenhagen, Den., ca. 1710)
Klentschi, C. F. (Swiss, 1790-1840)
Koehn, Edward (Geneva, 1860-1908)
Kreizer, Conard (German, 1595-1658)
Kuhn, Jan Hendrik (Amsterdam, 1775-1800)
Kullberg, Victor (Copenhagen to London, 1850-1890)
Lamy, Michel (Paris, 1767-1800)
Lang & Padoux (ca. 1860)
Larcay (Paris, ca. 1725)
Lardy, Francois (Geneva, ca. 1825)
Larpent, Isacc & Jurgensen (Copenhagen, 1748-1811)
Laurier, Francois (Paris, 1654-1675)
Le Baufre (Paris, ca. 1650)
Lebet (Geneva, ca. 1850)
Lebet & Fils (Swiss, 1830-1892)
Le Coultre, Ami (Geneva, ca. 1887)
Le Coultre, Eugene (Geneva, ca. 1850)
Leekey, C. (London, ca. 1750)
Leeky, Gabriel (London, ca. 1775-1820)
Lepaute, Jean-Andre (Paris, 1750-1774)
Lepine or L'Epine, Jean-Antoine (Paris, 1744-1814)
Le Prevost (Swiss), ca.1810
Le Puisne, Huand (enamel) (Blois, Fr., ca. 1635)
Leroux, John (England, 1758-1805)
Le Roy & Co. (Paris, ca. 1853)
Le Roy, Charles (Paris, 1733-1770)
Le Roy, Julien (Paris, 1705-1750)
Le Roy, Pierre (French, 1710-80) (improved duplex escap.)
Levy, Hermanos (Hong Kong, "Swiss," 1880-1890)
L'Hardy, Francois (Geneva, 1790-1825)
Lichtenauer (Wurzberg, Ger., ca. 1725)
Lindesay, G. (London, ca. 1740-1770)
Lindgren, Erik (England, 1735-1775) (pat. rack lever)
Litherland, Peter (English, 1780-1876)
Loehr, (Von) (Swiss, ca. 1880)
Long & Drew (enamel) (London, ca. 1790-1810)
Losada, Jose R. (London, 1835-1890)
Lowndes, Jonathan (London, ca. 1680-1700)
MacCabe, James (London, 1778-1830)
Maillardet & Co. (Swiss, ca. 1800)
Mairet, Sylvain (Swiss, 1825-1885) (London, 1830-1840)
Malignon, A. (Geneva, ca. 1835)
Marchand, Abraham (Geneva, 1690-1725)
Margetts, George (London, 1780-1800)
Markwick Markham, "Perigal" "Recordon"
(London, 1780-1825)
Marshall, John (London, ca. 1690)
Martin (Paris, ca. 1780)
Martin, Thomas (London, ca. 1870)
Martineau, Joseph (London, 1765-1790)
Martinot, "family" (Paris, 1570-1770)
Martinot, James (London, ca. 1780)
Mascarone, Gio Batt (London, ca. 1635)
Massey, Edward (England, 1800-1850)
Massey, Henry (London, 1692-1745)
E. Mathey-Tissot & Co. (Swiss, 1886-1896)
Matile, Henry (Swiss, ca. 1825)
Maurer, Johann (Fiessna, Ger., ca. 1640-1650)
May, George (English, 1750-1770)
Mayr, Johann Peter (Augsburg, Ger., ca. 1770)

McCabe, James (London, 1780-1710)
McDowall, Charles (London, ca. 1820-1860)
Meak, John (London, ca. 1825)
Mecke, Daniel (ca. 1760)
Melly, Freres (Geneva, Paris, 1791-1844)
Mercier, A. D. (Swiss, 1790-1820)
Mercier, Francois David (Paris, ca. 1700)
Meuron & Co. (Swiss, ca. 1784)
Meylan, C. H. "Meylan W. Co." (Swiss, ca. 1880)
Michel, Jean-Robert (Paris, ca. 1750)
Miller, Joseph (London, ca. 1728)
Milleret & Tissot (ca. 1835)
Miroir (London, ca. 1700-1725)
Mistral (Swiss, ca. 1902)
Mobilis (Swiss, ca. 1910)
Modernista (Swiss, ca. 1903)
Moillet, Jean-Jacques (Paris, 1776-1789)
Molina, Antonio (Madrid, Spain, ca. 1800)
Molinie (Swiss, ca. 1840)
Molyneux, Robert (London, ca. 1825-1850)
Montandon, Chs. Ad. (Swiss, 1800-1830)
Morand, Pierre (Paris, ca. 1790)
Moricand & Co. (Swiss, ca. 1780)
Moricand & Desgranges (Geneva, 1828-1835)
Moricand, Christ (Geneva, 1745-1790)
Morin, Pierre (English, French & Dutch style, ca. 1700)
Morliere (enamel) (Blois, Fr., ca. 1636-1650)
Moser, George Michael (London, ca. 1716-1730)
Motel, Jean Francois (French, 1800-1850)
Moulineux, Robert (London, 1800-1840)
Moulinier, Aine & Co. (Swiss, 1828-1851)
Moulinier, Freres & Co. (Swiss, ca. 1822)
Mudge, Thomas (London, 1740-1790)
Mulsund (enamel) (Paris, ca. 1700)
Munoz, Blas (Madrid, Spain, ca. 1806-1823)
Mussard, Jean (Geneva, 1699-1727)
Musy Padre & Figlo (Paris, 1710-1760)
Myrmecide (Paris, ca. 1525)
Nardin, Ulysse (Swiss, ca. 1846)
Nelson, W. (London, 1777-1818)
Nocturne (ca. 1920)
Noir, Jean-Baptiste (Paris, 1680-1710)
Norris, J. (Dutch, 1680-1700)
Norton (London), ca.1805
Nouwen, Michael (1st English, 1580-1600)
Noyean (ca. 1850)
Oldnburg, Johan (German, ca. 1648)
Oudin, Charles (Paris, 1807-1900)
Owen, John (English, ca. 1790)
Palmer, Samuel (London, ca. 1790-1810)
Panier, Iosue "Josue" (Paris, ca. 1790)
Papillon (ca. 1690)
Papillon, Francesco (Florence, ca. 1705)
Parr, Thomas (London, ca. 1735-1775)
Payne, H. & John (London, ca. 1735-1775)
Pellaton, Albert (Swiss, ca. 1873)
Pellaton, James (Swiss, 1903) (Tourbillon)
Pendleton, Richard (London, 1780-1805)
Pennington, Robert (English, 1780-1816)
Perigal, Francis (English, 1770-1790)
Pernetti, F. (Swiss, ca. 1850)
Perrelet, Abram (Swiss, 1780) (self wind)
Perret, Edouard (Swiss, 1850)
Perrin, Freres (Swiss, 1810)
Phillips, Edouard (Paris, ca. 1860)
Phleisot (Dijon, Fr., ca. 1540)
Piaget, George (Swiss, ca. 1881)
Picard, James (Geneva, ca. 1850)
Piguet & Capt (Geneva, 1802-1811)
Piguet & Meylan (Geneva, 1811-1828)
Piguet, Victorin-Emile (Geneva, 1870-1935)
Plairas, Solomon (Blois, Fr., ca. 1640)
Plumbe, David (ca. 1730)
Poitevin, B. (Paris, 1850-1935)

Poncet, J. F. (Dresden, 1750)
Poncet, Jean-Francois (Swiss, 1740-1800)
Potter, Harry (London, 1760-1800)
Pouzait, Jean-Moise (Geneva, 1780-1800)
Poy, Gottfrey (London, ca. 1725-1730)
Prest, Thomas (English, 1820-1855)
Prevost, Freres (ca. 1820)
Prior, Edward (London, 1825-1865)
Prior, George (London, 1800-1830) (used J.L. Richer art)
Pyke, John (English, 1750-1780)
Quare, Daniel (London, 1700-1724)
Quarella, Antonio (ca. 1790)
Racine, Cesar (Swiss, ca. 1902)
Racine, C. Frederic (la Chaux-de-Fonds, Swiss, ca.1810-32)
Raillard, Claude (Paris, 1662-1675)
Raiss (1890-1910) (enamel)
Rait, D. C. (German, ca. 1866)
Ramsay, David (Scotland, France, London, 1590-1654)
Ramuz, Humbert U. & Co. (Swiss, ca. 1882)
Ratel, Henri (Paris, 1850-1900)
Recordon, Louis (London, 1778-1824)
Redier, Antoine (Paris, 1835-1883)
Renierhes (London, ca. 1850)
Rey, Jn. Ante, & Fils (Paris, 1790-1810)
Reynaud, P. & Co. (1860)
Rich, John (Geneva, London, 1795-1825)
Richard, Daniel Jean (1685-1740)
Richer, J. L. (outstanding enamel artist) (Geneva, 1786-1840)
Rigaud, Pierre (Geneva, 1750-1800)
Rigot, Francois (Geneva, ca. 1825)
Robert & Courvoisier & Co. (Paris, 1781-1832)
Robin, Robert (Paris, 1765-1805)
Robinet, Charles (Paris, ca. 1640)
Robinson, Olivier & Fredmahn (Naples, 1727-1790)
Robinson William (Liverpool), ca.1850
Rogers, Isaac (London, 1770-1810)
Romilly, Sieur (Geneva, ca. 1750-1775)
Rooker, Richard (London, 1790-1810)
Rose, Joseph (London, 1752-1795)
Rosier, John (Geneva, ca. 1750)
Roskell, Robert (London, 1798-1830) (rack-lever)
Roskopf, G. (German to Swiss, 1835-1885)
Rosselet, Louis (Geneva, 1855-1900) (enamel)
Rousseau, Jean (Paris, 1580-1642)
Roux, Bordier & Co. (Geneva, ca. 1795)
Ruegger, Jacques (ca. 1800-1840)
Ruel, Samuel (Rotterdam, ca. 1750)
Rugendas, Nicholas (Augsburg, Ger., ca. 1700-1750)
Rundell & Bridge (London, ca. 1772-1825)
Russel, Thomas & Son (England) 1898
Sailler, Johann (Vienna, Aus., ca. 1575)
Sanchez, Cayetano (Madrid, Spain, c. 1790-1800)
Sandoz, Henri F. (Tavannes W. Co.) (ca. 1840)
Savage, George (London, 1808-1855) (Inv. pin lever)
Savage, William (London (1800-1850)
Savile, John (London, ca. 1656-1679)
Schatck, Johann Engel (Prague, ca. 1650)
Schultz, Michael (ca. 1600-1650)
Schuster, Caspar (Nunburg, ca. 1570)
Sermand, J. (Geneva, ca. 1640)
Sellar - Reading (England) 1854
Shepherd, Thomas (England) 1632
Sherman De Neilly (Belfort, ca. 1910)
Sherwood, J. (London, ca. 1750-1775)
Sidey, B. (England) 1770
Solson (London, 1750)
Soret (Geneva, ca. 1810)
Soret, Frederic II (1735-1806)
Soret, Isaac & Co. (1690-1760)
Sleightholm & Co. (England) 1800
Smith, C. (England) 1829
Smith, George (England) 1630
Smith, S, & Son (England) 1910
Snelling,J.50

Speakman, Edward (England) 1690
Spencer & Perkins (London, 1770-1808)
Stadlin, Francois (Swiss, 1680-1735)
Staples, James (1755-1795)
Stuffer, M. T. (Swiss, 1830-1855)
Stauffer "Stauffer Son & Co." (London, 1880)
Strasser & Rohde (Glashutte, 1875)
Sudek, J. (ca. 1850)
Sully, Henry (French, London, 1700-1725)
Swift, Thomas (London, ca. 1825-1865)
Tavan, Antoine (Geneva, 1775-1830)
Tavernier, Jean (Paris, 1744-1795)
Tempor Watch Co. (1930) (Masonic watch)
Terond, Allier & Bachelard (ca. 1805-1830)
Terrot & Fazy (ca. 1767-1775)
Terrot, Philippe (Geneva, ca. 1732)
Terroux (ca. 1776)
Theed & Pikett (ca. 1750)
Thierry, J. (London, ca. 1760)
Thierry, Niel (ca. 1810)
Thiout, Antoine (Paris, 1724-1760)
Tobias & Co. M.I. (England) 1805-68 (Michael Isac)
Tobias large family very active in exporting watches
Thomlinson, George (England) 1675
Thorne, Robert (London, 1850)
Thoroton, James (London, 1860)
Thuret, Jacques (Paris, ca. 1695)
Thomason J.N. (Edinburgh), ca.1830
Timing & Repeating W. Co. (Geneva, 1900)
Tompion, Thomas (English, 1671-1715)
Tonkin, Tho. (London, ca. 1760)
Torin, Daniel (England) 1750
Toutaia, Henri (French, 1650) (enamel)
Toutin, Jean (enamel) (Blois, Fr., ca. 1630)
Treffler, Sebastain (ca. 1750)
Tregent, J. (English, 1765-1800)
Truitte, Louis & Mourier (Geneva, ca. 1780)
Tupman (England) 1828
Tyrer, Thomas (London, ca. 1782)
Uhren Fabrik Union (Glashutte, 1893-1970)
Ullman, J. & Co. (Swiss, 1893)
Ulrich, Johann (London, 1820-1870)
Upjohn, W. J. (London, 1815-1824)
Vacheron, Abraham Girod (German, 1760-1843)
Valere (Paris, 1860)

Vallier, Jean (Lyons, Fr., ca. 1630)
Valove, James (London, ca. 1740)
Vanbroff, James (Germany, ca. 1600)
Van Ceule, J. (ca. 1799-1725)
Vandersteen (ca. 1725)
Vaucher, C. H. (Geneva, ca. 1835)
Vaucher, Daniel (Paris, 1767-1790)
Vaucher, Freres (Swiss, 1850)
Vauquer, Robert (French, ca. 1650) (enamel)
Veigneur, F. I. (ca. 1780)
Verdiere A. (Paris), ca.1810
Vernod, Henriette (Paris, ca. 1790)
Vigne, James (London, ca. 1770)
Viner (England) 1834
Vrard, L., & Co. (Pekin, 1860-1872)
Vulliamy, *Justin* (London, ca. 1830-1854)
Vully, Jaques (Swiss, ca. 1890-1900)
Vuolf (Swiss, ca. 1600)
Waldron, John (London, 1760)
Wales, Giles & Co. (Swiss, ca. 1870)
Walker, Allen (England) 1784
Waltrin (Paris, ca. 1820)
Webb, Benjamin (England) 1799
Weston, D. & Willis (enamel) (London, ca. 1800-1810)
Welldon, I. (England) 1731
Wichcote, Samuel (England) 1733
Widenham (England) 1824
Windmills,J. (England) 1710
Whitney, A. (Enniscorthy- S.of Dublin) Ca. 1810-1830
Whitthorne, James (Dublin, since 1725)
Willats, John (London, ca. 1860)
Williamson, Timothy (London, 1770-1790)
Wilter, John (London, ca. 1760)
Winckles, John (London, 1770-1790)
Winnerl, Joseph Thaddeus (Paris, 1829-1886)
Wiss, Freres & Menu (Swiss, ca. 1787-1810)
Wiss, G. (Geneva, ca. 1750)
Wood, William (England) 1860
Wright, Charles (London, 1760-1790)
Wright, Thomas (English, ca. 1770-1790)
Yates, Thomas (England) 1855
Young, Richard (London, 1765-1785)
Zech, Jacob (Prague, Aus. 1525-1540)
Zolling, Ferdinand (Frankfurt, Ger. ca. 1750)

Tambour style case, probably Nuremburg, Ca. 1575, hinged cover, pierced to revel engraved Roman chapter I-XII and Arabic 13-24 Center chapter, 60mm.

HALLMARKS OF ENGLAND

Hallmarks were used only on gold and silver **cases** made in England. These **case** marks, when interpreted, will help determine **age** of the **case** and location of the assay office. Hallmarks were used to denote information for the <u>**case only.**</u> The Maker's Mark (*W.C.Co.*) when interpreted is who made the **case only.**

The *London* date-marks (a single letter) used 20 letters, A-U, never using the letters W, X, Y, or Z. The letters J & I or U & V, because of their similarity in shape, were never used together within the same 20-year period.

A total of four marks maybe found on English **cases**, which are:

The **CASE MAKER'S MARK** with two or more letters was used to denote the manufacturer of the case <u>ONLY.</u>
The **STANDARD MARK** was used to denote a guarantee of the quality of the metal.
The **ASSAY OFFICE MARK** (also known as the town mark) was used to denote the location of the assay office.
The **DATE LETTER MARK** was a letter of the alphabet used to denote the year in which the article was stamped.
The stamp was used on gold and silver cases by the assay office.

Case Maker's Mark

The Standard Mark -22K -18K Silver-

The Assay Office Mark
1822 - UP
NO CROWN

 The Date Letter Mark
1478 to 1821

DUTY MARK
With George looking to the right
1786 to 1789 are uncommon.

     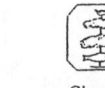

| Chester | Birmingham | Edinburgh | Dublin | Glasgow |

SWISS HALLMARKS

18k .750   14k .585   Platinum .950

Sterling Silver

Sterling Silver .925   Silver .800

Lucerne.   Neuchatel.
Poincons d'essai
de décembre 1852.

.800

German
silver mark

German
gold mark

FRENCH
.800

FRENCH
.950

FRENCH
Combination
Silver & Gold

TROY WEIGHT = 24 grains=1dwt., 1 Grain= 0.0648 grams, 20dwt = 1 OZ., 12oz = 1 LB.
NOTE: Gold & Silver Standards Vary from Country to Country. U.S.A. Coin Gold =.900 or 21 3/5K, Silver Coin=.900.
Gold Standards: 24K=1,000%or 1.0, 23K=.958 1/3, 22K=.916 2/3, 21K=.875, 20K=.833 1/3, 19K=.791 2/3, 18K=.750,
17K=.708 1/3, 16K=.666 2/3, 15K=.625, 14K=.583 1/3, 13K=.541 2/3, 12K=.500, 11=.458 1/3, 10K=.416 2/3, 9K=. 375.
8K=.333 1/3, 7K=.291 2/3, 6K=.250, 5K=.208 1/3, 4K=.166 2/3, 3K=.125, 2K=.83 1/3, 1K=.41 2/3.

LONDON DATE LETTER MARKS

Letter	Year	Letter	Year	Letter	Year	Letter	Year	Letter	Year	Letter	Year	Letter	Year	Letter	Year	Letter	Year
O	1551	M	1589	k	1627	J	1666	⌘	1709	r	1752	B	1797	f	1841	i	1884
P	1552	N	1590	l	1628	K	1667	S	1710	s	1753	C	1798	g	1842	k	1885
Q	1553	O	1591	m	1629	L	1668	T	1711	t	1754	D	1799	h	1843	l	1886
R	1554	P	1592	n	1630	M	1669	V	1712	u	1755	E	1800	i	1844	M	1887
S	1555	Q	1593	o	1631	N	1670	W	1713	a	1756	F	1801	k	1845	N	1888
T	1556	R	1594	p	1632	O	1671	X	1714	B	1757	G	1802	l	1846	O	1889
V	1557	S	1595	q	1633	P	1672	Y	1715	C	1758	H	1803	m	1847	P	1890
a	1558	T	1596	r	1634	Q	1673	A	1716	D	1759	I	1804	n	1848	Q	1891
b	1559	V	1597	s	1635	R	1674	B	1717	E	1760	K	1805	o	1849	R	1892
c	1560	W	1598	t	1636	S	1675	C	1718	F	1761	L	1806	p	1850	S	1893
d	1561	B	1599	u	1637	T	1676	D	1719	G	1762	M	1807	q	1851	T	1894
e	1562	C	1600	A	1638	U	1677	E	1720	H	1763	N	1808	r	1852	U	1895
f	1563	D	1601	B	1639	a	1678	F	1721	I	1764	O	1809	s	1853	a	1896
g	1564	E	1602	C	1640	b	1679	G	1722	k	1765	P	1810	t	1854	b	1897
h	1565	F	1603	D	1641	c	1680	H	1723	l	1766	Q	1811	u	1855	c	1898
i	1566	G	1604	E	1642	d	1681	I	1724	M	1767	R	1812	a	1856	d	1899
k	1567	h	1605	F	1643	e	1682	K	1725	n	1768	S	1813	b	1857	e	1900
l	1568	I	1606	G	1644	f	1683	L	1726	o	1769	T	1814	c	1858	f	1901
m	1569	K	1607	H	1645	g	1684	M	1727	p	1770	U	1815	d	1859	g	1902
n	1570	L	1608	I	1646	h	1685	N	1728	Q	1771	a	1816	e	1860	h	1903
o	1571	M	1609	K	1647	i	1686	O	1729	R	1772	b	1817	f	1861	i	1904
p	1572	N	1610	L	1648	k	1687	P	1730	S	1773	c	1818	g	1862	k	1905
q	1573	O	1611	M	1649	l	1688	Q	1731	T	1774	d	1819	h	1863	l	1906
r	1574	P	1612	N	1650	m	1689	R	1732	U	1775	e	1820	i	1864	m	1907
s	1575	Q	1613	O	1651	n	1690	S	1733	a	1776	f	1821	k	1865	n	1908
t	1576	R	1614	P	1652	o	1691	T	1734	b	1777	g	1822	l	1866	o	1909
U	1577	S	1615	Q	1653	p	1692	V	1735	c	1778	h	1823	m	1867	p	1910
A	1578	T	1616	R	1654	q	1693	a	1736	d	1779	i	1824	n	1868	q	1911
B	1579	V	1617	S	1655	r	1694	b	1737	e	1780	k	1825	o	1869	r	1912
C	1580	d	1618	T	1656	s	1695	c	1738	f	1781	l	1826	p	1870	s	1913
D	1581	b	1619	V	1657	t	1696	d	1739	g	1782	m	1827	q	1871	t	1914
E	1582	C	1620	a	1658	u	1697	d	1739	h	1783	n	1828	r	1872	u	1915
F	1583	d	1621	B	1659	v	1698	e	1740	i	1784	o	1829	s	1873	a	1916
G	1584	e	1622	C	1660	w	1699	f	1741	k	1785	p	1830	t	1874	b	1917
H	1585	f	1623	D	1661	x	1700	g	1742	l	1786	q	1831	u	1875	c	1918
I	1586	g	1624	E	1662	ff	1701	h	1743	m	1787	r	1832	A	1876	d	1919
K	1587	h	1625	F	1663	φ	1702	i	1744	n	1788	s	1833	B	1877	e	1920
L	1588	i	1626	G	1664	b	1703	k	1745	o	1789	t	1834	C	1878	f	1921
				H	1665	g	1704	l	1746	p	1790	u	1835	D	1879	g	1922
						k	1705	m	1747	q	1791	A	1836	E	1880	h	1923
						b	1706	n	1748	r	1792	B	1837	F	1881	i	1924
						V	1707	o	1749	s	1793	C	1838	G	1882	k	1925
						R	1708	p	1750	t	1794	D	1839	H	1883	l	1926
								q	1751	u	1795	e	1840				
										A	1796						

DATE LETTER MARKS FOR
BIRMINGHAM & CHESTER

BIRMINGHAM ASSAY OFFICE DATE LETTERS

Letter	Year	Letter	Year	Letter	Year	Letter	Year	Letter	Year
A	1773	a	1798	A	1824	A	1849	a	1875
B	1774	b	1799	B	1825	B	1850	b	1876
C	1775	c	1800	C	1826	C	1851	c	1877
D	1776	d	1801	D	1827	D	1852	d	1878
E	1777	e	1802	E	1828	E	1853	e	1879
F	1778	f	1803	F	1829	F	1854	f	1880
G	1779	g	1804	G	1830	G	1855	g	1881
H	1780	h	1805	H	1831	H	1856	h	1882
I	1781	i	1806	I	1832	I	1857	i	1883
K	1782	J	1807	K	1833	J	1858	k	1884
L	1783	k	1808	L	1834	K	1859	l	1885
M	1784	U	1809	M	1835	L	1860	m	1886
N	1785	m	1810	N	1836	M	1861	n	1887
O	1786	n	1811	O	1837	N	1862	o	1888
P	1787	o	1812	P	1838	O	1863	p	1889
Q	1788	p	1813	Q	1839	P	1864	q	1890
R	1789	q	1814	R	1840	Q	1865	r	1891
S	1790	r	1815	S	1841	R	1866	s	1892
T	1791	s	1816	T	1842	S	1867	t	1893
U	1792	t	1817	U	1843	T	1868	u	1894
V	1793	u	1818	W	1844	U	1869	v	1895
W	1794	v	1819	W	1845	V	1870	w	1896
X	1795	w	1820	X	1846	W	1871	x	1897
Y	1796	x	1821	Y	1847	X	1872	y	1898
Z	1797	y	1822	Z	1848	Y	1873	z	1899
		z	1823			Z	1874		

CHESTER ASSAY OFFICE DATE LETTERS

Letter	Year	Letter	Year	Letter	Year	Letter	Year	Letter	Year	Letter	Year	Letter	Year	Letter	Year
A	1701	A	1726	a	1751	a	1776	A	1797	A	1818	A	1839	a	1864
B	1702	B	1727	b	1752	b	1777	B	1798	B	1819	B	1840	b	1865
C	1703	C	1728	c	1753	c	1778	C	1799	C	1820	C	1841	c	1866
D	1704	D	1729	d	1754	d	1779	D	1800	D	1821	D	1842	d	1867
E	1705	E	1730	e	1755	e	1780	E	1801	E	1822	E	1843	e	1868
F	1706	F	1731	f	1756	f	1781	F	1802	F	1823	F	1844	f	1869
G	1707	G	1732	g	1757	g	1782	G	1803	G	1824	G	1845	g	1870
H	1708	H	1733	h	1758	h	1783	H	1804	H	1825	H	1846	h	1871
I	1709	I	1734	i	1759	i	1784	I	1805	H	1826	J	1847	i	1872
K	1710	K	1735	k	1760	k	1785	K	1806	I	1827	K	1848	k	1873
L	1711	L	1736	l	1761	l	1786	L	1807	K	1828	L	1849	l	1874
M	1712	M	1737	m	1762	m	1787	M	1808	L	1829	M	1850	m	1875
N	1713	N	1738	n	1763	n	1788	N	1809	M	1830	N	1851	n	1876
O	1714	O	1739	o	1764	o	1789	O	1810	N	1831	O	1852	o	1877
P	1715	P	1740	p	1765	p	1790	P	1811	O	1832	P	1853	p	1878
Q	1716	Q	1741	q	1766	q	1791	Q	1812	P	1833	Q	1854	q	1879
R	1717	R	1742	r	1767	r	1792	R	1813	Q	1834	R	1855	r	1880
S	1718	S	1743	s	1768	s	1793	S	1814	R	1835	S	1856	s	1881
T	1719	T	1744	t	1769	t	1794	T	1815	S	1836	T	1857	t	1882
U	1720	U	1745	u	1770	u	1795	U	1816	T	1837	U	1858	u	1883
V	1721	V	1746	u	1771	v	1796	V	1817	U	1838	V	1859	A	1884
W	1722	W	1747	v	1772							W	1860	B	1885
X	1723	X	1748	w	1773							X	1861	C	1886
Y	1724	Y	1749	x	1774							Y	1862	D	1887
Z	1725	Z	1750	y	1775							Z	1863	E	1888
														F	1889

The following will explain the French days of the week abbreviations, Sunday =**DIM** (Dimanche), Monday = **LUN** (Lundi), Tuesday = **MAR** (Mardi), Wednesday = **MER** (Mercedi), Thursday = **JEU** (Jeudi), Friday = **VEN** (Vendredi), Saturday = **SAM** (Samedi).

English Watch-Making Evolution

In about 1675-80 the watch trade divided into two segments. (1.) **99%** of Ebauche or rough movements were made at Prescot in Lancashire. (2.) These rough movements were then sold to finishers (watchmakers) in London, Liverpool, Coventry also to **America** and **Ireland**. This style of manufacturing of the movements, made the different components not inter-changeable. By 1780 they were producing about 200,000 rough movements per year. This type of system, the quality of the watch depends on the watchmaker thus his reputation helped to determine the price of the finished product.

By mid 1870s watchmaking changed to factory-made watches. Larger volumes of watches were made and to dispose of their product. There were wholesalers who dealt with the retail trade. It is common to find identical retail watches from such firms as English Watch Co. (1874-95), William Ehrhardt (1874-1924), Rotherham & Sons (1880-1930), P. & A. Guye (1880 - 1900), Nicole, Nielsen & Co. (1887 - 1914), Lancashire Watch Co. (1888 - 1910), Coventry Watch Movement Co. (1892-1914), J.W. Benson (1892-1941) and H.Williamson (1897-1931). Below are some of the trademarks for identification of the factory-maker. Most often found under dial.

English W. Co.	Ehrhardt	Ehrhardt	Lancashire	P. & A. Guye
Nicole, Nielsen	Coventry W. Co.	Coventry W. Co.	Rotherham	Williamson

In 1812 Edward Massey invented a form of detached escapement. The Massey styles of escapement became popular and widely used. They became known as Massey style or type levers 1, 2, 3, 4, & 5. Below are some illustrations of the right angle lever with different forms of the impulse pin.

Type I
in use from 1812-1820

Original **Massey** (type I) one tooth pinion (on balance staff) & the impulse slot at one end of lever.

II   III   IV   V

Left to Right: **Massey** rollers in use (II =1815-26), (III =1824-50), (IV =1820-40), (V =1825-30)

Note: Prior to 1870 English Watch-Making the rough movements were **99%** produced in the **Prescot** area then finished in London, Liverpool, & etc.

REPEATING WATCHES

Repeaters are those watches with an attachment added that will sound the time at the wish of the user. The repeating mechanism is operated by either a slide, plunger, or button in the case of the watch. There are basically five types of repeating mechanisms, some more common than others:

(1). **QUARTER REPEATERS**– The quarter repeater strikes the previous hour and quarter hour. In the older watches, usually verge, the striking is on a single bell attached to the inside of the case and the hour and quarter striking uses the same tone. There is first a series of hammer blows on the bell to indicate the hours, followed, after a short pause, by up to three twin strikes to denote the number of quarters elapsed. In later watches the striking is on wire gongs attached to the movement itself. The hours are struck on a single deep gong and the quarters on a higher-pitched gong followed by the deeper gong, producing a "ting-tang" sound.

(2). **HALF-QUARTER REPEATERS** -These strike the hours, followed by the quarters also an additional single blow to denote the passing of an additional **7 1/2** minutes. Half-quarter repeaters are mostly verge escapement and may be found on cylinder escapement watches. (uncommon)

(3). **FIVE-MINUTE REPEATERS**– These fall into two types. One system is similar to the half-quarter repeater but follows the 1/4 "ting-tang" by a single higher-pitched strike for each 5 minute interval elapsed since the last quarter. The other system strikes the hours on a deep gong and follows this with a single higher note for each 5 minute period after the hour, omitting a 1/4 striking.

(4).**MINUTE REPEATERS**– The most complicated of the repeater is similar to the 1/4 repeater with the addition of the minutes. The minute repeater strikes the last recorded hour, quarter and minutes. At 10:52; a minute repeater will strike 10 deep chimes for the hour, 3 double chimes (deep & high) producing a "ting-tang" for 3/4 hours & 7 high pitched chimes for 7 minutes (45+7=52).

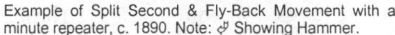

Example of Split Second & Fly-Back Movement with a minute repeater, c. 1890. Note: ♂ Showing Hammer.

Example of English Clock Watch, 20 size, jeweled through hammers, minute repeater.

(5). **CLOCK WATCHES**– The clock watch is essentially a repeater with the features of a striking clock. Where as the above-mentioned repeaters are all operated by a plunger or slide which winds the repeating function and runs down after the last strike, the clock watch is wound in the same way as the going train usually with a key and is operated by the touch of a button in the case. The repeat function can be operated many times before the watch needs to be rewound. The <u>CLOCK</u> part of the name comes from the watch also striking the hours &

sometimes the quarters or half hour in passing. The clock watch is easily recognizable by the two winding holes in either the case or the dial.

In addition to the five types described above, the features of striking are sometimes found with not only two but three and even four gongs, this producing a peal of notes. These repeaters are known as **"CARILLONS."**

At the other end of the scale from the carillon is the ''dumb'' repeater. This strikes on a block of metal in the case or on the movement and is felt rather than heard. It is said that the idea was to produce a watch that would not embarrass its owner when he wished to know when to slip away from boring company. Although the dumb repeater is less desirable for the average collector, it certainly should not be avoided– Breguet himself made dumb repeaters.

Grande Sonnerie and **Petite Sonnerie** have been used since early 1700's. The clock watch striking system at first was called *Dutch Striking* because it was used in clock making about 1665. The older system used striking on bells and struck the hours of the day. Then came the Dutch Striking which also struck the half-hour. This system later developed into a chiming function called **Grande Sonnerie** (grand strike or tone) which struck <u>both</u> the hour and quarter hours are struck ever 15 minutes (thus the hour is repeated every 15 minutes). The **Petite Sonnerie** limited to automatic strike of hours only.

L.Audemars 2 train Grande or Petite Sonnerie minute repeating clock watch. Note: Marked on bezel sonne & silence at 12 o'clock also Petite Sonnerie & Grande Sonnerie at 6 o'clock, Ca. 1870's.

L. Audemars 2 train Grande or Petite Sonnerie 1/4 repeating clock watch. Note: The push button in the pendant that activate the repeating gongs, Ca. 1850.

A BIT OF HISTORY

Now that we have seen what repeaters are supposed to do, it might be in order to look briefly at their origins. Before the days of electric light, it was a major project to tell the time at night, since striking a tinderbox was said to have taken up to fifteen minutes to accomplish. Clocks, of course, had striking mechanisms, but they tended to keep the occupants of the house awake listening for the next strike. The repeating addition to the clock meant that the master of the house could silence the passing strike at night and, at his whim, simply pull a cord over his bed to activate the striking in another part of the house and thus waking everyone. To silence those members of the household who did not appreciate a clock booming out in the early hours of the morning, the horologists of the day turned their thoughts to the idea of a repeating watch.

The first mention of repeating watches is in the contest between Daniel Quare (1649-1724) and the Rev. Edward Barlow (1639-1719) to miniaturize the repeating action of a clock. Barlow, who for some reason had changed his name from Booth, was a theoretical horologist of outstanding ability. Barlow's design made for him by Thomas Tompion and Quare's watch were both submitted to King James II and the Privy Council for a decision as to whom should be granted a patent. The King chose Quare's design because the repeating mechanism was operated by a single push-button, whereas Barlow's required two. Quare was granted a patent in 1687. Barlow had his share of fame earlier with the invention of rack-striking for clocks in 1676.

Quare went into production with his new repeater watches, but changed the design to replace the push-button in the case with a pendant that could be pushed in. The first of these watches showed a fault that is still found on the cheaper repeaters of this century – that is, if the pendant was not pushed fully in, then the incorrect hours were struck. To overcome this problem, he invented the so-called "all-or-nothing" piece. This is a mechanism whereby if the pendant was not pushed fully home, then the watch would not strike at all.

The half-quarter appeared shortly after the all-or-nothing piece, around 1710 the five-minute repeater was on the market. Some five years after this, a "deaf-piece" was often fitted to the watch. This was a slide or pin fitted to the case when activated, caused the hammers to be lifted away from the bell and had the same effect as a dumb repeater.

Sometime around 1730, Joseph Graham decided to dispense with the idea of a bell and arranged for the hammers to strike a dust-cover, thus making the watch slimmer and preventing dust from entering the pierced case.

About the middle of the century, the French master Le Roy carried the idea a stage further and dispensed with both bells and dust covers, and used a metal block which revolutionized the thickness of the repeating watch and introduced the dumb repeater. Breguet used wire gongs around 1789 and the pattern for the modern repeater was set. The minute repeater came into more common use after 1800, and earlier examples are definitely very rare, although it is known that Thomas Mudge made a complicated watch incorporating minute repeating for Ferdinand VI of Spain about 1750.

By the last quarter of the 1700s, Switzerland had gone for the repeater in a big way and the center of fine craftsmanship for complicated watches was in the Vallee de Joux. Here the principle of division of labor was highly refined and whole families were hard at work producing parts for repeating and musical watches. Since one person concentrated only on one part of the watch, it is hardly surprising that parts of excellent quality were turned out. The basic movements were then sold to watchmakers/finishers all over the Continent and even to England, where the principle of one man, one watch, among the stubborn majority eventually led to the downfall of what had once been the greatest watchmaking nation in history. Minute repeaters first appeared about 1830.

The greatest popularity of the repeater came, however, in the last quarter of the 1800s, when Switzerland turned them out in the tens of thousands. Although there were many different names on the dials of the watches, most seem to have been produced by the company "Le Phare" and only finished by the name on the dial. The production of repeaters in quantity seems to have ground to a finish around 1921 due to (a) the invention of luminous dials and universal electric or gas lighting, and (b) a lack of watchmakers willing to learn the highly demanding skills. The interest in horology over the past decade has, however, revived the idea of the repeater and several companies in Switzerland are now producing limited editions of expensive models.

BUYING A REPEATER

Since so many repeaters seem to have been repaired at some time in the past by incompetent watchmakers, it is often too expensive a purchase if the buyer does not know what he is doing. **Important: only SET hands clockwise.**

Rule One should be: if it does not work perfectly, avoid it like the plague unless a competent repairer first gives you an estimate which suits your pocket. All too often in the past the repairer was under the impression that metal grows with age and he has filed the teeth of a rack in order to get the full striking to work again. When it dawned on him that the problem was a worn bearing, the tooth was stretched with a punch and refiled, making it weak. It was then goodbye to a fine piece of craftsmanship. **Important only: SET hands clockwise.**

A better quality repeater is usually one which is ''jeweled to the hammers.'' This simply means that the hammers have jeweled bearings which can be seen by searching the movement for the hammers, locating the pivots around which they swing, and looking for the jeweled bearing in which they sit.

All repeaters have some system for regulating the speed of the repeating train. On the older fusee types, there was usually a rather primitive arrangement of a pinion in an eccentric bushing which could be turned to increase or decrease the depth of engagement of the pinion with the next wheel. Another system, a little better, uses an anchor and a toothed wheel as in an alarm clock. This system is usually located under the dial but can be detected by the buzzing sound it makes when the train is operated. The far superior system is the centrifugal governor that can be seen whizzing around in the top plate of the watch when the repeating action is operated. On the whole, the watch with the centrifugal governor is more desirable, although it must be mentioned that the Swiss turned out some inferior watches with this system.

Minute repeating movement by Dent of London. Minute repeating on two gongs and slide activated. Also note the watch has a split second chronograph, Ca. early 1900s.
IMPORTANT NOTE: If possible & it should be possible if you are investing a lot of money have a watchmaker check it.

Test the watch by operating the repeating train over a full hour, seeing that the quarters and minutes function correctly, then test each individual hour. Finally, set the hands to just before 1 o'clock (about 12:45) and test the striking. Any defect due to dirt or worn bearings will show up by the final blow(s), being either sluggish or not striking at all. If there is incorrect striking, have an expert look at it before you buy. **Important: only set hands clockwise.**

Try a partial operation of the slide or push-piece. If the watch has an all-or-nothing piece (as a reasonable grade movement should have), then the watch will not strike. Partial striking indicates either a low grade watch or a non-functioning all-or-nothing piece.

Note: Additional features such as chronograph functions, calendar, moon phase, etc., and will obviously affect the price of the watch.

Important note: Remember Rule One, if any function does not work, **BUYER BEWARE!**

🕐 The earth's orbit around the sun is 365 days, 5 hours, 48 minutes and 45.967685 seconds.

TOURBILLON

Breguet invented the tourbillon in 1795. A tourbillon is a device designed to reduce the position errors of a watch. This device has the escape wheel, lever and balance wheel all mounted in a **carriage** of light frameworks. The carriage turns 360 degrees at regular intervals (usually once per minute). The fourth wheel is **fixed** and is concentric with the carriage pinion and arbor. The escape wheel pinion meshes with the fourth wheel and will **rotate** around the fixed fourth wheel in the manner of a satellite. The escape wheel and lever are mounted on the carriage, and the third wheel drives the carriage pinion, turning the carriage once every minute. This rotation of the escapement will help reduce the position errors of a watch. One of the major objections is that the carriage and escapement weight mass must be stopped and started at each release of the escapement. The tourbillon design requires extreme skill to produce and is usually found on watches of high quality. Somewhat similar to the tourbillon is the *karrusel*, except it rotates about once per hour and the fourth wheel is **not** fixed. The escape pinion in a karrusel watch is driven in the normal manner by the fourth wheel.

Charles Frodsham, TOURBILLON escapement, minute repeating, split second chronograph, about 600 to 700 tourbillons are known to exist. About 85 % of the English tourbillon movements were made by Albert Pellaton, Favre and Nicole Nielson & Co. as in this watch. The TOURBILLON escapement, is located near the top of this movement.

Tourbillon

A. Fixed fourth wheel
B. Third wheel
C. Carriage (one revolution per minute)
D. Carriage pinion
E. Escape Wheel & pinion
F. Arbor for seconds hand
G. Escape cock
H. Lever & pallets

Right:
One minute Tourbillon
Chronometer Escapement
with Spring Detent

MUSICAL WATCHES
(Three basic types)

Stacked Tooth

Disc Type with individual teeth

Pinned Cylinder & Comb

Bonniksens' Karrusel

The *watch* has two *distinct* frames, one of which takes all parts but the escapement, the other taking the escapement. The *escapement frame* is made to *revolve* in the main frame at a uniform rate of about once per hour. The position of the escapement frame's bearing in the main frame is the same as that of the fourth wheel,—the axle of the escapement frame being large and having a hole through it of such a size that it admits the fourth pinion through freely, in order that the fourth wheel can run in its own jewelled holes without *interference*. The fourth wheel, c, will be seen inside the *escapement frame*, while the pinion of the fourth wheel A goes outside, so as to be *geared with* and *driven by* the 3rd wheel H.

F F B B is the *bed-plate* of the escapement frame : B B being its axle ; F F B B is turned out of *one piece* ; B B goes through a hole in the main frame, and to the end of B B is screwed the wheel D D, making this wheel *practically* one with F F B B.

Now as D D has teeth upon it and is just large enough to make a correct gearing with G, the third pinion, it follows that as the *third* pinion turns round it will take the wheel D D with it, and thus the *whole escapement* must go round for D D is fixed to the axle of the escapement frame.

All will now be plain on merely naming the parts in the illustration, which are as follows :—

P P is the pillar plate.

H and G are third wheel and pinion respectively.

M is the bar under dial.

L is the third wheel top cock.

D D is the wheel fixed to B B, and driven by G.

F F B B bed-plate of the escapement frame.

K is the fourth top cock which also takes bottom balance pivot.

S is the escape-cock, the escapement is left out of the illustration.

E the balance.

N the balance cock.

THE ¾ PLATE
REVOLVING ESCAPEMENT WATCH MOVEMENT

Above 1895-98 AD

The karrusel rotates slower than a tourbillon but the object is the same to average errors in the vertical position. A tourbillon uses a carriage which forms part of the train, in a karrusel the escapement is mounted on a revolving platform like a carousel, which is driven separately by the train. A tourbillon has a fixed fourth wheel and a karrusel does not have a fixed wheel. Other watch makers used ebauche movements made by Bonniksen. (Bonniksens' Karrusel invented in **1894**)

Where Watches Are Born

A trip to *"Where Watches Are Born,"* is recommended. In this area persists a strong cottage industry where in every small village and almost every street corner, a famous watch-maker or watch factory was born, and after this modern age of electronic and quartz watches still some survive. This area is the Jura Mountain chain which borders the French & Swiss countries.

A micro-techniques route may start at Montbeliard, France and go south to Geneva Switzerland. This micro-techniques route adjacent to the French & Swiss borders should include Factories, Museums, Workshops, and *Antique watch shops galore.* In Besancon, France its Fine Arts Museum with a collection that includes the LeRoy watch that has 25 indicators in addition to the time, also the Museum of Time. This is also home of the Lip watch factory. Next to Beaucourt, France to see the Frederic Japy Museum. Japy, a very productive maker which at one time produced 3,500 Ebauches a month. On to Valdahon and Morteau (Villers-le-Lac) and visit the Museum of Clock and Watch Making (Musee de Horlogerie du Haut-Doubs). Next LeLocle, Switzerland, home of Cyma, Ulysse Nardin, Tissot and Zenith also see the Watch Museum of the Chateau des Monts. Then La Chaux-de-Fonds home of Corum, Ebel, Girard-Perregaux and many more watch factories. Also visit the International Museum of Horology with a wealth of items also near by Antique Watch & Clock shops. In Neuchatel the Art Museum with the Jaquet Droz collection of mechanical dolls. Now go North to the area of Solothurn, Grenchen & Biel (Bienne) where the Rolex, Omega movement factory and many more as Mido, Urban Jurgensen, Swatch, Breitling, Movado and ETA factory. Further south the Vallee de Joux to see watch factories as Jaeger-LeCoultre, also smaller watchmakers as Daniel Roth & Philippe Dufour in LeSentier. Near by Le Brassus to see Audemars Piguet, Blancpain, and Breguet. On south to Geneva home of Patek Philippe, Rolex, Vacheron Constantin and many more also the see the Patek Philippe Museum in Geneva. You may wish to start in Geneva and reverse the above trip.

(Basel Watch Fair usually in the Spring.)

NOTE: **Nick Lerescu of Advantage Tours** has a Horological tour & seminar each year in late Spring or early Summer. *ADVANTAGE TOURS - P.O. BOX 401 - Glenwood, NJ 07418* or call Nick at 1-800-262-4284. Ask about the next trip for the **TIME TRIPPERS**." Hope to see you on a trip soon." *Cooksey*

EUROPEAN POCKET WATCH LISTINGS
Pricing at Collectable Fair Market Trade Show Level
(Complete Watches Only)

Unless otherwise noted, watches listed in this section are priced at the collectable fair market Trade Show level and as complete watches having an original 14k gold-filled case with an original white enamel single sunk dial, and the entire original movement in good working order with no repairs needed. Watches listed as 14k and 18k are solid gold cases. Coin or silveroid type and stainless steel cases will be listed as such. Keywind and keyset pocket watches are listed as having original coin silver cases. Dollar type watches, or low cost production watches, are listed as having composition metal type case & dial.

The prices shown were averaged from dealers' lists just prior to publication and are an indication of the Trade Show level or what collectors will pay. Prices are provided in three categories: average condition, extra fine, and mint condition, and are shown in whole dollar amounts only. The values listed are a guide for the *collectable* Trade Show level and are provided for your information only. Dealers will not necessarily pay FULL Trade Show PRICE. Prices listed are for watches with *original cases* and *dials*.

⊕ Descriptions and serial number ranges listed for early watches cannot be considered 100 percent accurate due to the manner in which records were kept by these companies. Watches were not necessarily sold in the exact order of manufactured date.

Important Notice. All of the information, including valuations, in this book has been compiled from the most reliable sources, and every effort has been made to eliminate errors and questionable data. Nevertheless, the possibility of error, in a work of such immense scope, always exists. The publisher or authors will not be held responsible for losses which may occur in the purchase, sale, statements of its advertisers, or other transaction of items, because of information contained herein. Readers who feel they have discovered errors are invited to write and inform us, so they may be corrected in subsequent editions.

The Complete Price Guide to Watches goal is to stimulate the orderly exchange of Watches between "*buyers*" and "*sellers*".

⊕ WATCH terminology or communication in this book has evolved over the years, in search of better and more precise language with a effort to improve, purify, adjust itself and make it easier to understand.

INFORMATION NEEDED

I will respect & appreciate positive sound reliable comments, corrections, improvements or remarks but reserve the right to accept the statement or keep my own observations & views. This price guide is interested in any facts and information you might have that should possibly be considered for future editions. Documented facts are needed. Please send photo or **sources** of information to: SEND INFORMATION TO:

COOKSEY SHUGART
P.O. BOX 3147
CLEVELAND, TENNESSEE
37320-3147

(WHEN CORRESPONDING, PLEASE INCLUDE A ✉
SELF-ADDRESSED, STAMPED ENVELOPE.)

AGASSIZ (Swiss)

Auguste Agassiz of Saint Imier & Geneva started manufacturing quality watches in 1832. They later became interested in making a flat style watch which proved to be very popular. The company was inherited by Ernest Francillion who built a factory called **Longines.**

Agassiz, 45mm or about 16 size, adjusted Ca. 1885.   Agassiz, 45mm or about 16 size, Ca. 1885.

TYPE – DESCRIPTION	Avg	Ex-Fn	Mint
Early, KW KS, Swiss bar Mvt., time only, Ca.1870, Silver case ...	$85	$100	$150
Time only, gold, 25-38mm, OF	175	250	350
HC	200	285	400
Time only, gold, 45- 50mm, OF	225	300	450
HC	250	345	500
Time only, gold & **enamel**, 45- 50mm, OF	400	650	1,000
HC	475	700	1,200
Cole's Resilient Escapement, 20J, gold, 45mm, Of	600	800	1,300
8 day, 21J, wind indicator, **18K gold,** 44mm, OF	800	1,100	1,700
14K gold, OF	600	800	1,300
S. S. case, OF	350	500	900

Agassiz, Time only, gold & **enamel**, 45- 50mm, OF   Agassiz, 40mm, 21 jewels, 8 day with wind indicator.

🕐 Watches listed in this book are priced at the collectable fair market **value** at the Trade Show level, as complete watches having an original case, an original white enamel dial, and with the entire original movement in good working order with no repairs needed, unless otherwise noted.

Agassiz, $20 gold 22 / 18K coin watch, Ca. 1950s.   **Agassiz**, 43mm, 17 jewels, World Time, 42 Cities, ca. 1940.

TYPE – DESCRIPTION	Avg	Ex-Fn	Mint
$20 gold 22 to **18K coin** watch, 34mm, Ca. 1950s.	$1,200	$1,800	$2,300
World Time, 42 Cities, gold, 43mm, OF	2,500	3,500	5,500
Chronograph, gold, 45-50mm, register, OF	475	550	700
HC	675	800	1,000
Split second chronograph, register, gold, OF	700	900	1,200
HC	850	1,200	1,500
1/4 hr. repeater, gold, 46-52mm, OF	850	1,200	1,500
HC	1,200	1,800	2,500
Minute repeater, gold, 46-52mm, OF	1,500	2,000	2,700
HC	2,000	2,600	3,500
Minute repeater, w/chrono., gold, 46-52mm, OF	2,200	2,800	3,800
HC	2,400	3,400	4,500
Minute repeater, Split sec. chrono & register, gold, 46-52mm, OF.	3,000	4,200	6,000
HC	4,000	5,500	8,000

ABOVE: Agassiz, 30mm or about 8 size, Ca. 1885.

COMPARISON OF WATCH CASE SIZES

U. S. A.	EUROPEAN
10-12 SIZE	40—44 MM
16 SIZE	45—49 MM
18 SIZE	50—55 MM

ASSMANN
Glasshute - Dresden

Julius Assmann began producing watches with the help of Adolf Lange in 1852. His watches are stylistically similar to those produced by Lange. Later on he adopted his own lever style. Assmann made highly decorative watches for the South American market that are highly regarded by some collectors.

Assmann, 50mm, 19 jewels, diamond cap jewels, gold jewel settings, gold lever escapement, serial number 3,086, BRIDGE MODEL, 1st Quality, Ca. 1875.

Assmann, 50mm, 19 jewels, diamond cap jewels, gold jewel settings, gold lever escapement, serial number 3,739, 1st Quality, Ca. 1877.

TYPE – DESCRIPTION	Avg	Ex-Fn	Mint
Time only, 45- 50mm, **1st Quality**, 18K OF	$2,500	$3,100	$4,000
18K HC	3,000	3,600	4,500
Time only, 45- 50mm, **2nd Quality**, 14K OF	2,000	2,600	3,500
14K HC	2,200	3,100	4,000
Chronograph, **1st Quality**, 55mm, 18K OF	4,000	5,700	8,500
18K HC	5,000	6,200	8,900
Split second chronograph, **1st Quality**, 57mm, 18K OF	5,500	7,200	10,000
18K HC	6,200	9,000	12,000
1/4 hr. repeater, gold, 50-55mm, OF	8,000	10,500	15,000
HC	8,500	11,500	16,000
Minute repeater, gold, 50-55mm, OF	10,000	12,500	18,000
HC	12,000	15,000	20,000
Perp. moonph. cal. w/min. repeater, gold, HC	50,000	70,000	100,000
Alpina, 15J., moustache lever, Glashutte, Gold, 52mm, OF	2,000	2,500	3,500

Assmann, OF, 52mm, 15 jewels, moustache lever, signed "H. Assmann Glashutte" case signed "J. Assmann Glashutte". The above movement is by ALPINA. In 1909 Alpina founded a company in Glashutte by the name "Pracisions Uhrenfabrik Alpina". Movements usefully high grade. Alpina also had factories in Geneva, Bienne, Besancon France, Glashutte.

AUDEMARS, PIGUET & CIE
Swiss

Audemars, Piguet & Cie was founded in 1875 by Jules Audemars and Edward Piguet, both successors to fine horological families. This company produced many fine high grade and complicated watches, predominantly in nickel and, with a few exceptions, fully jeweled. Their complicated watches are sought after more than the time only pocket and wrist watches.

Audemars Piguet, 40mm, about 10 size, 19 jewels, cabochon on winding stem, Platinum, OF.

Audemars Piguet, 50mm, hunting case, Grand, Petite & Silence Sonnerie, minute repeater on demand, split-second Chronograph, Perpetual Calendar, wind indicator & thermometer, taken from a French ad, ca. 1900.

TYPE – DESCRIPTION	Avg	Ex-Fn	Mint
Early, KW KS, Swiss bar Mvt., time only, Ca.1870, **Gold case**	$300	$425	$550
Time only, gold, 25-38mm, OF..	300	435	635
Time only, gold, 40-44mm, OF..	500	700	1,000
HC	750	900	1,200
Platinum, OF	800	1,100	1,800
Platinum, Diamond Dial & on hands, OF	1,300	1,800	2,500
Time only, gold, 45- 50mm, OF..	750	1,000	1,300
HC	1,000	1,400	2,000
Jumping hour w/ day-date-month, gold, 43mm., ca. 1925.	3,000	4,500	7,000
Rising Arms (Bras en L'Air), 44mm, one arm points to the hours & the other to the minute, 18K, OF	5,000	6,500	10,000
Chronograph, gold, 45-50mm, OF	1,500	2,000	3,000
HC	2,000	2,700	3,500
OF w/register..	2,000	2,700	3,500
HC w/register..	2,500	3,100	4,000

Audemars Piguet, (Bras en L'Air) a push-piece on rim of watch, lifts the arms of the bronze, one points to the hour and the other points to the minutes, 44mm, 18K, OF.

Audemars Piguet, Perpetual moon phase calendar, Astronomic watch showing the moon phases, and perpetual calendar showing day, date, & month, Ca.1920s.

AUDEMARS PIGUET, 46mm, 36 jewels, minute repeater, split-second chronograph, serial # 3853, Ca.1888.

AUDEMARS PIGUET, 46mm, Min. repeater, moon-phase, Chronograph, 18K, HC, Ca.1928.

TYPE – DESCRIPTION	Avg	Ex-Fn	Mint
Split second chronograph, gold, 45-52mm, OF	$4,000	$4,500	$6,000
HC	4,500	5,500	8,000
OF w/register	4,000	5,000	8,000
HC w/register	5,000	6,000	9,000
5 minute repeater, gold, 46-52mm, OF	3,500	4,000	5,000
HC	4,000	4,500	5,750
Minute repeater, gold, 46-52mm, OF	4,000	5,200	7,000
HC	5,000	6,500	9,000
OF w/chrono.	4,500	5,500	7,500
HC w/chrono.	5,500	7,000	9,000
OF w/chrono. & register	5,500	6,500	9,000
HC w/chrono. & register	6,000	7,500	10,000
OF w/split chrono. & register	7,000	10,000	15,000
HC w/split chrono. & register	8,000	15,000	20,000
Perpetual moonphase calendar, gold, OF	7,000	9,000	12,000
HC	8,000	11,000	15,000
Perp. moonphase cal. w/min.repeater, chronograph, gold, OF	30,000	38,000	50,000
HC	32,000	45,000	65,000
Grand & Petite Sonnerie, min. repeater, split-second Chron., Perp. Calendar, wind ind. & thermometer, 52-54mm, HC ★★★★	100,000	130,000	175,000

PRODUCTION TOTALS

Date- Serial #	Date- Serial #	Date- Serial #	Date- Serial #	Date- Serial #
1882 - 2,000	1905 - 9,500	1925 - 33,000	1945 - 48,000	1965 - 90,000
1890 - 4,000	1910-13,000	1930 - 40,000	1950 - 55,000	1970-115,000
1895 - 5,350	1915-17,000	1935 - 42,000	1955 - 65,000	1975-160,000
1900 - 6,500	1920-25,000	1940 - 44,000	1960 - 75,000	1980-225,000

REPEATER IDENTIFICATION

Calibre SMV

Calibre SMS

BARRAUD & LUNDS
LONDON (1750-1929)

The Barraud family (of which) there were several makers, one of them being Paul Philip Barraud. Paul was in the trade at 86 Cornhill from about 1796 to 1813. His sons John and James, traded at 41 Cornhill as Barraud & Sons from 1813 till 1838. After 1838 the firm became known as Barraud & Lunds. About 1885 their address was 49 Cornhill and 14 Bishopsgate about 1895. Advertised "machine-made" watches in about 1880 until 1929.

TYPE – DESCRIPTION	Avg	Ex-Fn	Mint
Time only, gold, 45- 50mm, OF	$450	$550	$700
HC	550	675	850
Time only, gold, 45- 50mm, **(wind indicator)**, OF	650	850	1,200
Chronograph, gold, 45-50mm, OF	800	1,000	1,400
HC	900	1,100	1,500
Split second chronograph, gold, 45-52mm, OF	1,500	1,900	2,500
HC	1,600	2,200	3,000
1/4 hr. repeater, gold, 46-52mm, OF	1,000	1,400	2,000
HC	1,200	1,600	2,200
Minute repeater, gold, 46-52mm, OF	1,800	2,200	3,000
HC	2,200	3,200	4,500
OF w/chrono.	2,600	3,500	4,500
HC w/chrono.	3,000	4,700	6,500
OF w/clock watch	8,000	11,000	15,000
HC w/clock watch	10,000	13,000	20,000

Barraud & Lunds, English lever and movement signed *"Barraud & Lunds 49 Cornhill London 3/3333"*, 3/4 plate with a fusee and chain, stem wind, Note: Engraved and raised barrel. With a white enamel signed *"Barraud & Lunds-Cornhill London 3/3333"*, with wind-indicator, Ca. 1886.

🕐 Some models and grades are not included. Their values can be determined by comparing with similar age, size, metal content, style, models and grades listed.

🕐 Watches listed in this book are priced at the collectable fair market **value** at the Trade Show level, as complete watches having an original case, an original white enamel dial, and with the entire original movement in good working order with no repairs needed, unless otherwise noted.

BARWISE
LONDON

John Barwise a leading watchmaker born 1790 died 1843. Dealer at 29 St.Martin's Lane, and with Weston Barwise from 1820 to 1842. John Barwise was also the chairman of British Watch Co., 1842 to 1843. The firm moved back to 29 St.Martin's Lane, 1845 to 1851, and 69 Piccadilly from 1856 to 1875.

TYPE – DESCRIPTION	Avg	Ex-Fn	Mint
Time only, gold, 45- 50mm, OF	$800	$1,000	$1,400
HC	1,000	1,300	1,800
Chronograph, gold, 45-50mm, OF	1,200	1,500	1,900
HC	1,400	1,600	2,000
7-1/2 Min. Repeater, gold, 46-52mm, **18K**, OF ★	4,800	5,300	7,000
1/4 hr. repeater, gold, 46-52mm, OF	2,000	2,600	3,500
HC	2,500	3,100	4,000
Minute repeater, gold, 46-52mm, OF	3,000	3,600	4,500
HC	3,500	4,600	6,000
Detent Chronometer, gold, 48-52mm, OF	5,000	6,200	8,000
HC	6,000	7,400	9,000

BARWISE, Rare 7-1/2 MINUTE REPEATER with ruby cylinder escapement, open face, key wind & key set, Signed BARWISE LONDON No. 5369, Ca. 1800.

COMPARISON OF WATCH CASE SIZES

U. S. A.	EUROPEAN
10-12 SIZE	40—44 MM
16 SIZE	45—49 MM
18 SIZE	50—55 MM

J. W. BENSON
London (1749)

The Benson signature is found on many medium to extremely high grade gilt movements. Factory English machine-made market circa 1870-1930. "Makers to the Admiralty" & "By Warrant to H.M. the Queen" can be found signed on the movements. Named models ("Bank", "Field", "Ludgate") 16 or 14 size.

TYPE – DESCRIPTION	Avg	Ex-Fn	Mint
KWKS, side lever, Silver hallmarked, 48-52mm, OF, C. 1875	$125	$150	$200
SW, 15-17J, side lever, ("Bank", "Field", "Ludgate")			
Silver, 49mm, C. 1870-1930	150	185	250
Gold, 49mm, C. 1870-1930	200	275	400
Fusee, lever escape., high grade, SW, **18K**, 54mm, OF, C.1875	500	685	800
Fusee **w/indicator**, KWKS, side lever, Silver, 54mm, OF, C.1870	450	575	750
Fusee, **w/indicator, free spring**, lever escape.,**18K**, 50mm, OF	750	1,000	1,500
Time only, gold, 45-48mm, OF	425	550	700
HC	550	750	1,000
Chronograph, gold, 45-52mm, OF	1,000	1,100	1,500
HC	1,200	1,400	1,800
Split second chronograph, gold, 45-52mm, OF	1,300	1,700	2,500
HC	1,500	2,000	3,000
Perpetual moonphase calendar, gold, OF......................................	8,000	10,000	14,000
HC	10,000	13,000	18,000
Minute repeater, gold, 46-52mm, OF...	3,000	3,700	5,000
HC	3,500	4,200	6,000
Minute, Clock Watch, OF	10,000	13,000	17,000
Minute, Clock Watch, HC	12,000	15,000	20,000
Minute, Perpetual, Clock Watch, OF	60,000	90,000	125,000
HC	90,000	110,000	150,000
Karrusel, gold, 48-55mm, OF...	4,000	5,500	8,000
Karrusel, silver, 48-55mm, OF...	3,000	3,600	4,500

J. W. Benson, 13-15 jewels, 3/4 plate, "The Field, Best London Make, By Warrant to H.M. the Queen" engraved on Movement. Serial Number C8764.

J. W. Benson, 45mm, Split Second Chronograph, 20 jewels, 3/4 plate, free sprung, hunting case, Ca. 1890.

COMPARISON OF WATCH CASE SIZES

U. S. A.	EUROPEAN
10-12 SIZE	40—44 MM
16 SIZE	45—49 MM
18 SIZE	50—55 MM

BOREL & COURVOISIER
NEUCHATEL, SWITZERLAND

Founded in 1859 by Jules Borel & first introduced into the United States in 1860. For some of their higher grade movements they used Girard - Perregaux.

BOREL & COURVOISIER, 15J, nickel movement with counterpoised lever, HC, Ca. 1889.

TYPE – DESCRIPTION	Avg	Ex-Fn	Mint
Time only, KW, **SILVER**, 45- 50mm, OF	$125	$150	$200
HC	150	175	235
Time only, KW, **Gold**, 45- 50mm, OF	250	335	475
HC	300	375	525
Time only, SW, nickel, **GF**, 45- 50mm, OF	175	200	275
HC	200	250	325
Time only, SW, nickel, **Gold**, 45- 50mm, OF	325	385	500
HC	350	400	550
Captains Watch, **SILVER**, 2 hour dials, 2 trains, Key Wind, center seconds, 50mm, OF	500	625	800
(SAME AS ABOVE) HC	525	650	850
Captains Watch, **GOLD**, 2 hour dials, 2 trains, Key Wind, center seconds, 50mm, OF	900	1,200	1,800
(SAME AS ABOVE) HC	1,000	1,400	2,000
1/4 hr. repeater, **SILVER**, 46-52mm, OF	600	750	1,000
1/4 hr. repeater, **GOLD**, 46-52mm, OF	900	1,100	1,600
Detent Chronometer, gold, 48-52mm, OF	1,800	2,000	2,500
HC	2,000	2,200	2,700

BOREL & COURVOISIER, both KW movements came in 15 - 21 lignes and four grades, extra, 1st, 2nd, and 3rd quality, Ca. 1860-75.

BOVET
FRENCH & SWISS

Edouard Bovet starts a company in the village of Fleurier Switzerland about 1818 and another firm in Besancon, France, in 1832. The Bovet firm specialized in watches for the chinese market. The Bovet Companies was purchased by Leuba Freres (Cesar & Charles). Bovet also signed watches "TEVOB" making his signature easily read by the Chinese. The new Bovet firm discontinued making watches for the Chinese market. The company was purchased by the Ullmann & Co. in 1918. **Fleurier** a village in Switzerland with **Superior Enamel** artist.

Above: *Superior* <u>FLEURIER</u> *quality* finely painted turquoise enamel watch set in pearls, 18K, 58mm, time only, Chinese Duplex Escapement, signed **BOVET - FLEURIER**, Ca. 1835.

TYPE – DESCRIPTION	Avg	Ex-Fn	Mint
Time only, LEVER escapement, KW, Silver, 58mm, OF	$200	$275	$375
HC	225	300	400
Time only, DUPLEX escapement, KW, Silver, 58mm, OF	225	300	400
HC	250	350	475
Time only, DUPLEX escapement, KW, GOLD, 58mm, OF	700	900	1,200
HC	800	1,000	1,300
Enamel, Time only, DUPLEX, KW, **Silver/gilded**, 58mm, OF	1,200	1,800	2,500
HC	1,500	2,200	3,000
(below ***SUPERIOR FLEURIER QUALITY*** **Gold & Enamel**, with <u>Chinese Duplex</u>)			
Gold &Enamel, Time only, Landscape or Floral, 55- 58mm, OF	8,000	10,000	15,000
HC	10,000	14,000	20,000

⊕ Some models and grades are not included. Their values can be determined by comparing with similar age, size, metal content, style, models and grades listed.

⊕ Watches listed in this book are priced at the collectable Trade Show level, as complete watches having an original case, an original dial, and with the entire original movement in good working order with no repairs needed.

The Complete Price Guide to Watches goal is to stimulate the orderly exchange of Watches between "buyers" and "sellers".

ABRAHAM-LOUIS BREGUET
BREGUET ET FILS
Paris

Abraham-Louis Breguet, one of the worlds
most celebrated watchmakers.　　　　　　Right: Breguet famous hands he called "a pomme".

Abraham-louis Breguet was born in Neuchatel Switzerland on Jan., 10, 1747. He was perhaps the greatest horologist of all time in terms of design, elegance, and innovation. He is responsible for the development of the tourbillon, the perpetual calendar, the shock-proof parachute suspension, the isochronal overcoil, and many other improvements. Abraham-Louis Breguet died on 17th day of September, 1823. It is difficult to include him in this section because of the complexity surrounding identification of his work which was frequently forged, and the fact that so many pieces produced by his shop were unique. Suffice it to say that the vast majority of watches one encounters bearing his name were either marketed only by his firm or are outright fakes made by others for the export market. Much study is required for proper identification. The first **Souscription** watch was sold in 1796. The Breguet firm continues today with the tradition started by Abraham-Louis. At first in the hands of his immediate successors and now under the guidance of the **"Swatch Group"**.

A short list of terms used by Breguet. A'tact=time by touch, a'toc=dumb repeater, parachute=shock protection, pull-twist piston=a plunger in the pendant first pull out & then twisted to engage lever to repeat, jump hour hand=hour hand used a 12 tooth star to jump forward the hour hand, Souscription=made by subscription or agreement, slotted teeth=slots drilled in the escape wheel teeth to assist with oil retention, Breguet balance spring= over-coiled balance spring.

Abraham-Louis Breguet, Production Totals

Date —	Serial #	Date —	Serial #
1795 —	250	1815 —	2700
1800 —	500	1820 —	3500
1805 —	1500	1825 —	4000
1810 —	2000	1830 —	4500

The year a watch was sold may differ
from the year it was **produced**.
　　Right: **Breguet's** Hanging Ruby Cyclinder Escapement.

Above: Reprints (Reduced) issued by the firm Breguet Ca. 1820s.

Above: Escapement by Breguet, Twenty tooth escape wheel with oil slots in each tooth, the lever **E** has circular locking and ruby pallets enclosed and pallet **R** is slightly convex and pallet **D** is concaved (see upper left), Ca. 1793.   (S' note oil slot)

Above: Escapement by Breguet, Twenty tooth escape wheel with oil pockets in every other tooth, A=oil pockets are also in the fork of the lever where it contacts the escape wheel roller table, Ca. 1811.

60 to 62mm. Example of Breguet **SOUSCRIPTION** style face and movement. Gilt movement with central winding arbor, balance with parachute suspension, HANGING ruby cylinder escapement. White enamel dial with secret signature at 12 o'clock. NOTE: Winds from center either front or back, also most had a silver case and gold bezel. Total production of **SOUSCRIPTION** style watches about 1,600. "**The above Example is actual size**". (illo.A)

TYPE – DESCRIPTION	Avg	Ex-Fn	Mint
Hanging ruby cylinder, parachute, KW, 18K, 49mm, OF, C.1800..	$3,000	$4,000	$6,000
Hanging ruby cylinder, enamel Souscription style dial, center wind, all original,18K, 60 to 62mm, OF, C. 1800,(illo.A)	8,000	12,000	18,000
1/4 repeater, **Hanging ruby cylinder**, jeweled parachute, 18K, 60-65mm, C.1795, C.1800 (illo.B)	8,500	13,000	20,000
1/4 Repeater Horologer De La Marine , silver dial, 2 gongs, Hanging ruby cylinder escapement, 18K OF, C.1800 (illo.C)	10,000	14,000	22,000
1/2-1/4 Repeater Horologer De La Marine , silver dial, **jump hour hand**, Hanging ruby cylinder escapement, 18K **HC**, C.1800	14,000	25,000	35,000
Montre'a tact, 6J ruby cylinder, pearl & enamel case, 18K, 36mm, C. 1790-1820, (illo.D)	15,000	19,000	25,000
Min. repeater, perpetual calendar chronograph, sector- wind indicator, 18K, 51mm, OF, C. 1932,(illo.E)	50,000	70,000	120,000
Min. repeater, split sec. chrono., min. register 18K, 2 tone case, 53mm, OF, C. 1945,(illo.F)	15,000	18,000	25,000

Note: Abraham Louis Breguet, made about **150 HUNTING CASE** watches.

Abraham Louis Breguet, repeating, ruby cylinder watch. Left: gilt movement with standing barrel. Note jeweled parachute suspension. Right: Dial side of movement, repeating train with exposed springs. (illo.B)

Important OF, 1/4 repeater Horologer De La Marine by Breguet. Left: Guilloche silver dial with roman numerals and typical Breguet hands. Right: Gilt brass movement with hanging ruby cylinder escapement and triple arm balance, parachute suspension, 2 gongs, open face. Note the pull and twist piston on pendant, to operate repeating train, Ca. 1800-25. (illo.C)

Breguet "montre a tact" or touch time watch, 36mm. Case embellished with 12 pearls for tactile hours (Braille style watch). The arrow on case revolves. Center: Key with a ratchet in its shaft to prevent turning the winding arbor the wrong way. Souscription movement with 6 jewels, central barrel, ruby cylinder escapement. (illo.D)

BREGUET, 51mm, chronograph with perpetual calendar and minute repeater. Note sector style wind indicator. (illo.E)

BREGUET, 53mm, minute repeating, split-second chronograph. Chronograph activated by crown and button on band. Repeater activated by slide. (illo.F)

Generic Breguet, 45-48mm, ruby cylinder, KW KS, Swiss bar Mvt., time only, Ca.1830, 18K case. (illo. G)

TYPE – DESCRIPTION	Avg	Ex-Fn	Mint
Jump hr.w/ aperture, revolving min.disc, 18K, 46mm, OF, C.1930	$6,500	$8,500	$13,000
Min. repeater, split sec. chronograph,			
two tone gold case, 53mm, C.1948	12,000	15,000	20,000
Perpetual calendar, thin digital watch, 18K case, 45mm	7,500	10,000	15,000
Small keyless watch, platinum balance, gold case, 18mm	12,000	15,000	20,000
Early, KW / KS, **generic Swiss bar Mvt.**, time only, Ca.1830,			
18K case, NOT TRUE BREGUET (illo. G)	200	325	550

BULOVA
U. S. A. & Swiss

Bulova was a leader in the mass production of quality wristwatches; however, their pocket watch output was small and limited to mostly basic time only varieties. The ultra thin "Phantom" was one of their limited production models.

Joseph Bulova started with a wholesale jewelry business in 1875. The first watches were marketed in the early 1920s. Bulova manufactured millions of movements in their own Swiss plant. The company cased these movements in the U.S.A. and imports all production today. The ACCUTRON was introduced in 1960 and sold about 5 million watches.

BULOVA Accutron, with date, gold filled hunting case, about 43mm, ca. 1970s.

TYPE – DESCRIPTION	Avg	Ex-Fn	Mint
GF, 17J, 42mm, OF, Ca. 1940	$50	$65	$95
Rose GF, art deco, 17J, 42mm, OF, Ca. 1930	75	100	145
14K, 17J, 42mm, OF, Ca. 1950	165	200	275
Platinum,"Phantom", ultra-thin, 18-21J., Adj.,43mm, OF, Ca.1920	400	500	650
Accutron, date, GF, 43mm, **pocket watch**, HC	135	150	200

HENRY CAPT
Geneva

Henry Daniel Capt of Geneva was an associate of Isaac Daniel Piguet for about 10 years from 1802 to 1812. Their firm produced quality watches and specialized in musicals, repeaters and chronometers. By 1844, his son was director of the firm and around 1880 the firm was sold to Gallopin.

TYPE – DESCRIPTION	Avg	Ex-Fn	Mint
Early, KW KS, Swiss bar Mvt., time only, Ca.1870, Silver case ...	$125	$150	$200
Early, KW KS, Swiss bar Mvt., time only, Ca.1870, Gold	300	385	550
Time only, gold, 45- 50mm, OF	400	475	600
HC	500	600	750
Chronograph, gold, 45-50mm, register, OF	700	850	1,000
HC	750	900	1,100
Split second chronograph, gold, 45-52mm, register, OF	1,000	1,300	1,700
HC	1,100	1,400	1,800
1/4 hr. repeater, gold, 46-52mm, OF	1,400	1,700	2,200
HC	1,500	1,800	2,500
Minute repeater, gold, 46-52mm, OF	2,000	2,800	3,500
HC	2,200	3,200	4,500
OF, w/split chrono.	5,000	6,000	8,000
HC, w/split chrono.	6,000	7,500	9,000
Minute repeater, w/ clock watch, OF	8,000	9,000	12,000
HC	10,000	12,000	15,000
Perpetual moonphase calendar, gold, OF	7,500	9,000	12,000
HC	8,000	10,000	14,000
Perp. moonphase cal., w/min.repeater, gold, OF	18,000	25,000	35,000
Perp. moonphase cal. ,w/min.repeater and chrono., gold, HC	20,000	35,000	45,000

HENRY CAPT, jeweled thru hammers, minute repeater, 53mm, Ca. 1900.

HENRY CAPT, 52mm, 32 jewels, minute repeater, serial number 34,711, ca. 1900.

CARTIER
Paris

CARTIER was a famous artisan from Paris who first made powder flasks. By the mid-1840s the family became known as the finest goldsmiths of Paris. Around the turn of the century the Cartier firm was designing watches and in 1904 the first wrist watches were being made.

Cartier, 52mm, 40 jewels, triple complicated-perpetual calendar, minute repeater, split-second chronograph.

Cartier, 45mm, 18 jewels, flat, astronomic with moon phases triple calendar, platinum watch, Ca. 1930s.

TYPE – DESCRIPTION	Avg	Ex-Fn	Mint
Time only, gold, 40- 44mm, signed E.W.C., OF	$1,400	$1,700	$2,500
HC	1,600	1,900	2,800
Time only, gold, 45- 50mm, signed E.W.C., OF	1,500	1,800	2,600
HC	1,700	2,200	3,000
Flat, astronomic w/ moon ph. triple calendar, signed E.W.C., platinum,OF	7,000	9,000	12,000
Chronograph, gold, 45-50mm, signed E.W.C., OF	2,500	3,200	4,500
5 minute repeater, gold, 46-52mm, signed E.W.C., OF	3,500	4,500	6,500
HC	4,000	5,000	7,000
Minute repeater, gold, 46-52mm, signed E.W.C., OF	7,500	9,500	12,000
HC	8,000	10,000	13,000
Triple complicated, astronomical moon ph. perpetual triple cal., signed E.W.C. min. repeater, split sec. chron. w/min. recorder, 18 K	70,000	95,000	125,000

Above: **Cartier**, 43mm, 18 jewels, dial has raised gold Arabic numbers, 18k, OF, Ca.1930s.

T. F. COOPER
Liverpool

The Cooper name is usually marked on inner dust covers which protect Swiss ebauche keywind bar movements. Numerous watches produced from 1850-1890 are found with this Liverpool name. The T.F. Cooper & later the T.W. Cooper firms supplied the U.S. market with low cost silver-cased keywinds.

TYPE – DESCRIPTION	Avg	Ex-Fn	Mint
KWKS, "full-jeweled" , Silver, 44-48mm, OF, Ca.1850-1875	$75	$100	$145
KWKS, 15J, Silver, 46-50mm, HC, Ca.1850-1870	85	125	185
KW, Fusee, lever, silver, 48mm, OF, C. 1870	135	165	225
KW, 15J, metal dust cover, gilt dial, 18K, OF, C. 1875	250	325	450
KW, 15J, Lady's , 18K, 44mm, fancy HC, C. 1875	300	385	550
KW, gold dial, bar movement w/side lever escap., parachute shock on balance, 18K, 50mm, OF, C. 1870	250	325	450
Captains double time, 15J, KWKS, silver, 48mm, OF, C.1865	400	550	800
18K, OF	600	900	1,500
18K, HC	800	1,200	2,000

T.F. Cooper, KW, bar movement with right angle lever escapement, parachute shock on balance, 18K, 50mm, OF, Ca. 1852.

Courvoisier, Freres, 37mm, cylinder escap. with wolf-tooth winding, front & back view, 18K & enamel HC, Ca.1880.

COURVOISIER, Freres
SWISS (La Chaux de Fonds)

Started as Courvoisier & Cie in 1810-11, by 1845 Henri-Louis and Philippe-Auguste became owners. In 1852 name changes to Courvoisier, Freres. The watches circa 1810 are signed with the older signature. They exported very ornate pieces for the Chinese market (Lepine bar caliber).

TYPE – DESCRIPTION	Avg	Ex-Fn	Mint
Time only, KW, SILVER, 45- 50mm, OF	$125	$150	$200
HC	135	175	235
Time only, KW, Gold, 45- 50mm, OF	200	325	450
HC	300	385	550
Time only, SW, Gold, 45- 50mm, OF	225	325	450
HC	300	385	550
Captains Watch, SILVER, 2 hour dials, 2 trains, Key Wind, center seconds, 50mm, OF	500	600	800
HC, (SAME AS ABOVE)	550	700	900
Captains Watch, GOLD, 2 hour dials, 2 trains, Key Wind, center seconds, 50mm, OF	900	1,300	2,000
HC, (SAME AS ABOVE)	1,000	1,400	2,200
1/4 hr. repeater, SILVER, 46-52mm, OF	600	750	1,000
1/4 hr. repeater, GOLD, 46-52mm, OF	850	1,000	1,500
Detent Chronometer, gold, 48-52mm, OF	1,800	2,000	2,500
HC	2,000	2,200	2,700

E. J. Dent
LONDON

Edward John Dent, born in 1790 died in 1853. Edward was in partnership with J.R.Arnold, at 84 Strand, from 1830-1840 and worked alone at 82 Strand from 1841 to 1849. Then moved to 61 Strand 1850 till 1853. The year before his death the Westminster Palace gave Dent the contract for making BIG BEN with a big bell weighing over 13 tons. The clock was built by Frederick Rippon Dent. E. Dent & Co. Ltd. was in business until about 1968 at 41 Pall Mall London.

DENT, PIVOTED Detent chronometer, about 15 jewels, fusee, gold, 48-52mm, Ca. 1870, open face. (illo.1A)

DENT, 1/4 hr. repeater, marked " Dent Watch Maker to the Queen 61 Strand London", S# 30077, note **early winding system** by Nicole Nilson, 46-52mm, OF, Ca. 1850. (illo. 2A)

TYPE – DESCRIPTION	Avg	Ex-Fn	Mint
Time only, gold, 45- 50mm, OF	$550	$675	$850
HC	650	800	1,100
Chronograph, gold, 45-50mm, OF	750	950	1,300
HC	800	1,100	1,600
Split second chronograph, gold, 45-52mm, OF	1,000	1,400	2,100
HC	1,100	1,600	2,500
Early stem wind, 1/4 hr. repeater, gold, 46-52mm, OF (illo. 2A)	2,000	2,800	4,200
1/4 hr. repeater, gold, 46-52mm, OF	1,800	2,300	3,100
HC	2,000	2,800	4,200
HC w/chrono., cal. & moonphase	5,800	7,200	10,000
Minute repeater, gold, OF	3,000	3,800	5,500
HC	3,200	4,200	6,500
OF w/chrono.	3,500	4,600	6,800
HC w/split chrono.	5,500	6,700	9,000
HC w/cal. & moonphase	8,000	12,000	20,000
Minute, w/clock watch	12,000	15,000	21,000
Pivoted Detent chronometer, fusee, gold, 48-52mm, OF (illo.1A)	3,500	4,500	6,000
Perpetual moonphase calendar, gold, OF	8,000	10,000	14,000
HC	9,000	11,000	15,000
Perp. moonphase cal. w/**min. repeater**, OF	22,000	28,000	35,000
HC	24,000	32,000	45,000
w/split sec., OF	40,000	55,000	75,000
w/split sec., HC	50,000	65,000	100,000

PAUL DITISHEIM
La Chaux de Fonds - Swiss

In 1892 Paul Ditisheim founded his own firm, which later became Vulcain. He made precision and novelty type watches. He gained many Prizes and awards also wrote many articles for improving watches. His research of new ideas were successful with oil and balances. Found on some watches, a balance, he called "**affix**". In about 1920 he formed the Solvil movement and later Titus .

TYPE – DESCRIPTION	Avg	Ex-Fn	Mint
Time only, gold, 40-44mm, OF	$300	$375	$550
HC	450	550	700
Time only, gold, 40-50mm, **Flat or Thin**, OF	450	550	700
Time only, gold, "**Affix**" balance, 45- 50mm, OF	600	650	875
HC	700	800	1,000
Time only, **platinum & diamond**, art deco, 41-42mm, OF	1,500	1,800	2,500
Chronograph, gold, 45-50mm, OF	700	900	1,200
HC	775	950	1,300
Split second chronograph, gold, 45-52mm, OF	900	1,100	1,600
HC	1,000	1,200	1,700
Deck chronometer w/box, detent chronometer, C. 1905	1,400	1,700	2,200
Pocket chronometer, **wind-indicato**r, 21J., GJS, OF, C.1920	1,200	1,400	1,800
Pocket chronometer, **pivoted detent,** gold, 57mm	3,000	3,600	5,700
Pocket chronometer, with **TOURBILLON**	25,000	34,000	47,000
1/4 hr. repeater, gold, 46-52mm, OF	1,800	2,200	2,800
HC	2,000	2,600	3,500
Minute repeater, gold, OF	3,000	3,900	5,500
HC	3,200	4,400	6,000

AFFIX Balance

Art Deco-style, 41mm, black onyx bezel and diamonds, Ca. 1920.

Pocket chronometer, Wind-Indicator, 21J., OF, C.1920

Solvil, 17J., with "**Affix**" balance, 49mm, OF, Ca. 1920s.

DUBOIS et FILS
Le Locle (SWISS)

Dubois a active merchant in the Le Locle region. In about 1761 Philippe Dubois began selling watches. They exported all over the world & specialized in repeater, automaton, skeleton watches also watches with false pendulums. They provided the Courvoisier Freres with movements. (Dew-bwah)

TYPE – DESCRIPTION	Avg	Ex-Fn	Mint
Verge, KW, pair case, silver, 48-52mm	$275	$325	$400
Verge, enamel w/scene & automata windmill, silver or gilt, 48-52mm..	1,100	1,600	2,500
Verge w/mock pendulum, chain & fusee, silver, OF, 48-52mm......	650	850	1,150
All above with **large** one second-beating balance wheel, **Pirouette** gearing			
and **double** escape wheel, Friction Rest Escapement..... ★★★★	4,000	6,000	9,000
Verge, KW, GOLD, OF, 50-54mm...................................	600	750	1,000
Verge, KW, GOLD w/enamel, OF,52mm	900	1,400	2,200
1/4 hr. repeater, SILVER, OF, 50-54mm......................	650	850	1,150
1/4 hr. repeater, GOLD, OF, 50-54mm.........................	900	1,100	1,400
1/4 hr. repeater w/automaton, **18K**, OF, 50-52mm........................	3,000	3,800	4,500
Minute **pump** repeater, gold, OF, 50-52mm .... ★★	8,000	10,000	15,000

Pirouette gearing

DuBois & Fils, Verge with mock pendulum, chain & fusee, silver, OF, enamel dial, 48-52mm, Ca. 1800. **Note:** This movement used a large seconds-beating balance wheel, with **pirouette** gearing and double escape wheel.

DuBois et Fils, Verge, enamel w/scene, silver or gilt, OF, painted enamel scene with windmill automata, 48-52mm. Ca. 1810.

Frictional rest escapement, Double escape wheel with 6 teeth on each escape wheel for a total of 12, also note the pinion to drive double escape wheel.

D = D-shaped **pallet**, inclined for impulse. B = Balance.
C = **Contrate** wheel. G= gear with 26 teeth at bottom.
W = counter **Weight**. P = false pendulum.

Note: Movement has a large seconds-beating balance wheel, **pirouette** gearing, double escape wheel & a single pallet. This DuBois **pirouette** is unlike most DeBaufre or Pauzait ect. where balance wheel was central to movement.

DUCHENE L., & Fils
GENEVA

Watchmaker, well known for their large and small pieces, including coach clocks, calendar watches and minute repeater watches. The firm was known also for decorative work with polychrome champleve enamel and painted enamel, and fantasy watches. The movements are classically-designed, with fusee & verge escapements. Cases are in "Empire-style", engraved or guilloche.

TYPE – DESCRIPTION	Avg	Ex-Fn	Mint
KW, cylinder, silver, 46mm, OF	$85	$125	$185
HC	100	150	225
KW, verge fusee, silver, 46-52mm, OF	275	325	450
KW, verge fusee, enamel case ,gilt, 52mm, OF	600	900	1,500
1/4 hr. repeater, silver, 54mm, OF	500	700	1,000
1/4 hr. repeater, gold, 52mm, OF	900	1,100	1,500
1/4 hr. repeater, w/automata, gold, 52mm, OF	3,000	4,000	5,500
Ball form, KWKS, cylinder, 29mm, 18K OF	450	600	900

Duchene L. & Fils, 1/4 Hour Repeater, fusee and cylinder escapement, repeats on gongs, 52mm, Ca. 1820.

Dunand, 1/4 hour repeater, about 15 jewels, repeater is slide activated, 49MM, OF, Ca. 1905

DUNAND
Swiss

The Dunand factory produced repeaters, timers & chronographs during the 1890-1930 time period.

TYPE – DESCRIPTION	Avg	Ex-Fn	Mint
Time only, gold, 45-50mm, OF	$185	$250	$325
HC	300	375	550
Chronograph, gold, 45-50mm,OF	400	475	650
HC	450	550	750
Split second chronograph, gold, 45-52mm, OF	800	950	1,200
HC	900	1,100	1,500
1/4 hr. repeater, gold, 46-52mm, OF	750	900	1,100
HC	800	950	1,200
OF w/chrono.	900	1,100	1,300
HC w/chrono.	1,100	1,300	1,500
Minute repeater, gold, 46-52mm, OF	1,500	1,900	2,500
HC	1,800	2,300	3,000

The Complete Price Guide to Watches goal is to stimulate the orderly exchange of **Watches** between *"buyers"* and *"sellers"*.

EARNSHAW, THOMAS
LONDON

Thomas Earnshaw born in 1749 died in 1829. In about 1781 he improves the spring detent. Earnshaw also contributed to the development of the chronometer. He pioneered the method of fusing brass and steel together to form a laminate of the compensation rims as in the modern method of today. Known for his chronometers he also made 1/4 and 1/2 hour repeaters with cylinder and duplex escapements.

THOMAS EARNSHAW, chronometer, KWKS, spring detent, Z or S balance with trapezoidal weights, helical hairspring, serial # 589, silver case, Ca.1810.

Signed: "T. EARNSHAW Invt et Fecit 665 London 9117" KW KS, spring detent chronometer, NOTE: compensation curb so called **"sugar-tongs"**, silver case, Ca.1803.

Right: Earnshaw spring detent escapement.

TYPE – DESCRIPTION	Avg	Ex-Fn	Mint
Time only, KW, **SILVER**, 45- 48mm, OF	$800	$1,000	$1,500
Time only, KW, **GOLD**, 45- 48mm, OF	1,500	2,000	3,200
1/4 hr. repeater, **GOLD**, 46-52mm, OF	4,000	5,000	6,500
Spring detent escapement, chronometer, gold, 48-54mm, OF	5,500	7,000	9,000
Spring detent escapement, chronometer, **(Sugar-Tongs)**, OF	7,500	9,000	12,000

H. R. EKEGREN
Copenhagen & Geneva

Henry Robert Ekegren, a Swiss maker of quality watches, started in business around 1870. The firm specialized in flat watches, chronometers and repeaters. Ekegren became associated with F. Koehn in 1891.

TYPE – DESCRIPTION	Avg	Ex-Fn	Mint
Time only, gold, 45- 50mm, register, OF	$550	$685	$950
HC	650	875	1,200
Chronograph, gold, 45-50mm, register, OF	800	1,100	1,600
HC	900	1,200	1,800
Split second chronograph, gold, 45-52mm, OF	1,200	1,500	1,900
HC	1,300	1,600	2,100
FIVE-Minute repeater, gold, 46-52mm, OF	1,800	2,100	2,800
HC	2,000	2,400	3,100

H.R. EKEGREN 46mm, minute repeater, slide activated, jeweled through hammers, open face, serial no. 78,268.

H.R. EKEGREN, 47mm, minute repeater, jeweled through hammers, hunting case.

TYPE – DESCRIPTION	Avg	Ex-Fn	Mint
Minute repeater, gold, 46-52mm, OF	$2,400	$2,900	$3,600
HC	2,800	3,500	5,000
OF w/chrono.	2,500	3,200	4,200
HC w/chrono.	3,000	3,600	5,000
OF w/split chrono.	4,000	4,600	7,000
HC w/split chrono.	4,500	6,500	10,000
Perpetual moonphase calendar, gold, OF	8,000	10,000	13,000
Perpetual moonphase cal. w/ min. repeater, OF	18,000	24,000	30,000
HC	20,000	26,000	35,000
Perp. moonphase cal. w/min. rep. and chrono., OF	22,000	25,000	32,000
HC	25,000	33,000	45,000
Karrusel, gold, 48-55mm, OF	8,000	10,000	13,000
Tourbillon, gold, 48-55mm, OF	40,000	50,000	75,000
Detent chronometer, gold, 48-52mm, OF	4,500	5,800	7,200
World time watch, gold, 48-52mm, OF	4,000	5,500	8,000

FAVRE–LEUBE
Le Locle & Geneva

Favre-Leube firm is still active and production has covered more than eight generations of watchmakers. The company has made watches since 1815.

FAVRE-LEUBE, 53mm, Minute repeater, 15 jewels, slide on rim activates the repeater mechanism, Ca.1895.

TYPE – DESCRIPTION	Avg	Ex-Fn	Mint
Early, KW KS, Swiss bar Mvt., time only, Ca.1870, Silver case ...	$100	$125	$195
KW, Gold w/enamel, 35-40mm, HC	700	800	1,000
KW, silver w/enamel, 45mm, HC	200	285	400
KW, Gold w/enamel, 45-48mm, OF	500	700	1,000
Chronograph, gold, 45-50mm, OF	500	600	800
HC	600	750	1,000
Split second chronograph, gold, 45-52mm, OF	700	850	1,100
HC	800	950	1,200
1/4 hr. repeater, gold, 46-52mm, OF	800	950	1,200
HC	950	1,100	1,400
Minute repeater, gold, 46-52mm, OF	1,200	1,400	1,800
HC	1,500	1,900	2,500

CHARLES FRODSHAM
London

Charles Frodsham followed in the footsteps of his father, William, whose father was close with Earnshaw. Charles became the most eminent of the family, producing very fine chronometers and some rare tourbillon and complicated watches. He died in 1871. After about 1850 his quality 3/4 plate movements endorse the letters A.D. FMSZ. **Arnold & Frodsham** signed watches and located at 84 Strand, London are from 1843-44 until 1857-58. He later moved to New Bond Street, London.

Arnold Chas. Frodsham 9139 *AD.FMSZ* on dial,
84 Strand, London on movement & dust cover, 16-18J.,
2 platinum balance screws, S# 9139, Ca.1856

Chas. Frodsham, 84 Strand London, 25 jewels, Fusee,
Freesprung, Diamond end stone, serial number 3520.

TYPE – DESCRIPTION	Avg	Ex-Fn	Mint
Time only, early mvt. **84 Strand**, silver, 45- 48mm, OF, C.1850 ...	$250	$350	$485
Time only, early mvt. **84 Strand, gold**, 45- 48mm, OF, C.1850	700	950	1,300
Time only, gold, 45- 50mm, OF	700	950	1,300
HC	900	1,100	1,500
Chronograph, gold, 45-50mm, OF	1,600	1,900	2,600
HC	1,800	2,400	3,200
Split second chronograph, gold, 45-52m, OF	2,800	3,900	6,000
HC	3,200	4,400	7,000

🕐 **The Complete Price Guide to Watches goal is to stimulate the orderly exchange of Watches between *"buyers"* and *"sellers"*.**

Frodsham, 46-50mm, jeweled through the center wheel, stem wind, 18K case, 84 Strand, S# 8132Ca. 1858.

Frodsham, 59mm, 60 minute Karrusel, 15J., stem wind, open face, S# 09050/ 56906,18K case, Ca. 1895.

TYPE – DESCRIPTION	Avg	Ex-Fn	Mint
Minute repeater, gold, 46-52mm,OF	$4,500	$5,700	$8,000
HC	5,000	6,500	9,000
OF w/split chrono.	12,000	16,000	22,000
HC w/split chrono.	15,000	19,000	25,000
Perpetual moonphase calendar, gold, OF	18,000	22,000	28,000
Perp. moonphase cal. w/min. repeater, OF	35,000	45,000	60,000
HC	40,000	55,000	75,000
Karrusel, 16J, (59 to 60 Min. Karrusel), 18K, C.1895	5,500	9,500	14,000
Tourbillon, gold, 48-55mm, OF	45,000	65,000	100,000
Marine chronometer, Parkinson-Frodsham, helical hairspring, w/ detent escape., 48 hr. WI, C. 1840, 97mm deck box	2,400	2,900	3,500
Detent chronometer, w/wind ind., silver, OF, KWKS, C. 1850	1,800	2,500	3,300
Box Chronometer, helical hair spring, with box	18,000	21,000	26,000
Clock Watch, Minute repeater, OF	10,000	16,000	25,000
HC	13,000	20,000	30,000

GIRARD-PERREGAUX
La Chaux-de-Fonds Switzerland

In 1856, The Constant Girard and Henry Perregaux families founded the Swiss firm of Girard-Perregaux. About 1860, the firm made a tourbillon with three golden bridges. A replica of this watch was made in 1982. Both were a supreme expression of horological craftsmanship. Girard-Perregaux **said** about 1880 the first wrist watches were made for the German Navy officers. In 1906, the company purchased the Hecht factory in Geneva. Girard-Perregaux has been recognized many times and still makes prestigious watches.

TYPE – DESCRIPTION	Avg	Ex-Fn	Mint
Skeletonized "Shell" (Shell Oil Co. advertising watch), 7J, Base metal display case, total production = 30,000 Ca.1940	$125	$165	$250

Skeletonized **"Shell Watch"** (Golden Shell Oil) advertising a watch filled with Shell car motor oil they wanted to prove even a watch would run on this top quality car motor oil. Most stopped with heavy car oil, so the oil was removed from some watches. Girard-Perregaux used a ebauche by A. Scheld calibre 1052, Base metal display case, only 7J, total production = 30,000, & sold for $5.00, Ca. June 5, 1940.

GIRARD-PERREGAUX, three golden bridges movement patented March 25th, 1884.

GIRARD-PERREGAUX, Chronometer, with pivoted dentent, gold train, 20 jewels, nickel movement, Ca. 1878.

Note: Watches with Gold embossed dial add $200.

TYPE – DESCRIPTION	Avg	Ex-Fn	Mint
Time only, gold 40-44mm, OF	$250	$325	$425
HC	350	475	625
Time only, gold 45- 50mm, OF	325	400	525
HC	475	585	775
3 gold bridges, with **silver** case, C. 1884,	3,500	4,700	6,500
with **gold** case	6,000	8,500	12,000
Chronometer, pivoted detent, 20J., gold train, 18K, C.1878	4,000	5,200	7,000
Chronograph, gold, 45-50mm, OF	800	1,000	1,300
HC	1,000	1,200	1,500
1/4 hr. repeater, gold, 45-52mm, OF	1,400	1,700	2,200
HC	1,600	2,100	2,800
HC w/chrono., cal. & moonphase	2,200	2,700	3,500
Minute repeater, gold, 46-52mm, OF	2,000	2,500	3,200
HC	2,700	3,100	3,800
OF w/chrono.	2,800	3,300	4,000
OF w/split chrono.	4,000	4,600	5,500
HC w/cal. & moonphase	4,800	6,000	7,500
Detent chronometer, gold, 48-54mm, OF	3,500	4,000	5,000
HC	4,500	5,000	6,000

🕐 Note: Some models and grades are not included. Their values can be determined by comparing with similar age, size, metal content, style, models and grades listed.

🕐 This book endeavors to be a GUIDE or helpful manual and offers a wealth of material to be used as a tool not as a absolute document. Price Guides are like watches the worst may be better than none at all, but at best cannot be expected to be 100% accurate.

COMPARISON OF WATCH CASE SIZES

U. S. A.	EUROPEAN
10-12 SIZE	40—44 MM
16 SIZE	45—49 MM
18 SIZE	50—55 MM

GOLAY A., LERESCHE & Fils
SWISS

Manufactured under the name Golay-Leresche from 1844-1857, then his son changed the name to Golay A., Leresche & Fils, he worked until the beginning of the 20th Century. Watches were primarily exported to U.S.A., he was well known for watches of all kinds and "grande complications".

TYPE – DESCRIPTION	Avg	Ex-Fn	Mint
Time only, gold, 45- 50mm, OF	$400	$475	$625
HC	500	575	725
Chronograph, gold, 45-50mm, OF	600	725	950
HC	700	835	1,100
Split second chronograph, gold, 45-52mm, OF	775	1,000	1,300
HC	900	1,100	1,500
1/4 hr. repeater, gold, 46-52mm, OF	1,400	1,800	2,300
HC	1,600	2,000	2,600
HC w/chrono., cal. & moonphase	4,000	5,200	6,500
Minute repeater, gold, OF	2,000	2,500	3,400
HC	2,200	2,800	3,600
OF w/chrono.	2,200	2,800	3,500
HC w/split chrono.	3,500	4,600	7,500
HC w/cal. & moonphase	6,000	7,200	9,500
Detent chronometer, gold, 48-52mm, OF	2,200	2,700	3,500
Perpetual moonphase calendar, gold, OF	8,000	9,500	12,500
HC	8,500	10,000	13,500
Perp. moonphase cal. w/min. repeater, OF	15,000	19,000	25,000
HC	18,000	22,000	28,000
Clock Watch, gold, 48-52mm, OF	6,000	7,500	10,000
HC	10,000	12,000	15,000

Golay A., Leresche & Fils, 1/4 hour repeater, 47mm, 41 jewels, key wind, Ca. 1855.

Golay A., Leresche & Fils, minute repeater, split seconds chronograph, moon phases, day date month, open face, Ca. 1896.

COMPARISON OF WATCH CASE SIZES

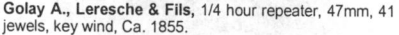

U. S. A.	EUROPEAN
10-12 SIZE	40—44 MM
16 SIZE	45—49 MM
18 SIZE	50—55 MM

H. GRANDJEAN

The son of David-Henri (1774-1845), this respected maker produced high quality complicated watches, chronometers and ornately decorated watches for the South American market. A Grandjean specialty was magnificent enamel and gem set ladies watches.

Note: Watches with Gold embossed dial add $300.

TYPE – DESCRIPTION	Avg	Ex-Fn	Mint
Time only, gold, 45- 50mm, OF	$500	$625	$850
HC	600	850	1,200
Chronograph, gold, 45-50mm, OF	650	785	1,000
HC	750	900	1,100
Split second chronograph, gold, 45-52mm, OF	1,100	1,400	1,800
HC	1,300	1,600	2,200
1/4 hr. repeater, gold, 46-52mm, OF	1,200	1,500	2,000
HC	1,600	1,800	2,300
HC w/chrono., cal. & moonphase	2,500	3,100	4,000
Minute repeater, gold, OF	2,200	2,700	3,500
HC	2,800	3,500	5,000
OF w/chrono.	2,400	2,800	3,500
HC w/split chrono.	3,800	4,800	6,000
HC w/cal. & moonphase	5,800	7,000	9,000
Detent chronometer, gold, 48-52mm, OF	3,000	3,600	4,500
Perpetual moonphase calendar, gold, OF	8,000	10,000	13,000
HC	8,500	11,000	15,000
Perp. moonphase cal. w/min. repeater, OF	20,000	27,000	35,000
HC	24,000	30,000	40,000
Grande & Petite Sonnerie repeating clock watch, 38J, fancy dial, 18k gold, 53mm, HC	10,000	14,000	20,000

H. GRANDJEAN, Grande & Petite Sonnerie repeating clock watch, 38Jewels, with tandem wind mechanism, fancy dial, 18k gold, 53mm, HC.

🕐 A collector should expect to pay modestly higher prices at local shops.

GRUEN WATCH CO.

Swiss & U. S. A. (1874 - 1953)

The early roots of the Gruen Company are found in Columbus, Ohio where Dietrich Gruen and W.J. Savage formed a partnership in 1876. The D. Gruen & Son legacy began in 1894 and flourished with the introduction of fine quality "Precision" movements. Curvex movements, ultra-thins and the prestigious 50th anniversary model are highlights of this prolific company.

D. Gruen & Son, OF, 44mm, 19-21J., by Assmann, plates are Argentan (silver & nickel), Adj.to HCIP on bal. bridge, gold moustache lever & escape wheel, S# 62,428, Ca.1895.

Gruen 50th Anniversary Watch, 10 size, 23J., 12K gold plates engraved, 600 made-1 for each month & marked all adjts 8 eight, 50 made later 1 for each year (S# 01-050).

TYPE – DESCRIPTION	Avg	Ex-Fn	Mint
17-21J, veri-thin or precision, 40-43mm, Grades, ... V1 - V2 - V3 - V4 - V5, C.1920-40, OF-**GF** case..................	$100	$150	$250
17-21J, veri-thin or precision, 40-43mm, Grades, ... V1 - V2 - V3 - V4 - V5, C.1920-40, OF-**14K** case................	250	350	500
Pentagon case ,17-21J, **GF**, 40-43mm, OF, C.1920-40	125	175	275
Pentagon case, 17-21J, precision, **14K**, 40-43mm, C.1920-40	300	400	700
23J., GJS, 47mm, wind indicator, micrometer regulator, **14K**	550	675	950
Madretsch Model, 21J., 16 size, **GF** OF ....★	250	365	500
21-23J, D. Gruen & Son, Swiss, **Gold**, 45-54mm, OF, C. 1900-20	275	385	650
21J, D. Gruen, (by **Assmann**), **14K**, OF, C. 1905........................	500	750	1,200
21J, D. Gruen, (by **Assmann**), **14K**, HC, C. 1905	750	1,200	1,800
50th anniversary , 12K gold movement, 21J + 2 diamonds = 23J, pentagon case, **18K**, 40mm, OF, C. 1924 ....★★	2,000	2,600	3,500

Gruen W. Co., Swiss made, 23 jewels in screwed settings, 47mm, wind indicator, micrometer regulator, Ca.1900's.

D. Gruen & Son, "Madretsch marked", 16 size, 21 jewels, open face, with end-less screw style regulator, Ca.1905.

No.-756, 17J.
Adjusted

No.-716 & 717, 15 J.
Adjusted

Verithin V7-17J.
Adjusted

Verithin Extra Precision
VE=21J., V1=21J.
V2=19J., V3=17J.

Verithin Precision
V1 1/2=21J., V2 1/2=19J.
V4=17J.

Ultra,VeriThin Precision
UV=17 jewels

No. 650, 17J.

Dietrich Gruen
Ultra Thin, UUT=19J.
Extra Precision

5648

5649

Above: hands for 650

No. 380 & 385=17J.,
No. 381 & 386=15J.

E. GUBELIN

Swiss

Jacques Edouard Gubelin joined the firm of Mourice Brithschmid in Lucerne around 1854. By 1919, Edouard Gubelin headed the firm. In 1921 they opened an office in New York & produced fine jewelry and watches for 5 generations.

E. GUBELIN, 50mm, 29J., min.repeater, chronograph, Perpetual day-date-month-moon phase, by Audemars, Piguet.

E. GUBELIN, 48mm, world time with 68 cities on outside bezel 24 hour on inter bezel, Gold Filled open face.

TYPE – DESCRIPTION	Avg	Ex-Fn	Mint
Time only, gold, 40- 44mm, OF	$300	$375	$500
HC	400	500	650
Time only, gold, 45- 50mm, OF	350	425	575
HC	550	675	800
Chronograph, gold, 45-50mm, OF	500	600	750
HC	600	725	900
Split second chronograph, gold, 45-52mm, OF	750	850	1,200
HC	900	1,100	1,500
1/4 hr. repeater, gold, 46-52mm, OF	1,200	1,600	2,200
HC	1,400	1,800	2,600
OF w/chrono.	1,300	1,700	2,300
HC w/chrono.	1,500	2,200	3,000
HC w/chrono., calendar & moonphase	3,200	3,800	4,500
5 minute repeater, gold, 46-52mm, OF	1,800	2,200	2,800
HC	2,000	2,500	3,200
Minute repeater, gold, 46-52mm, OF	2,200	2,800	3,500
OF w/chrono.	2,500	3,200	4,000
OF w/split chrono.	4,000	5,500	8,000
OF w/chrono., calendar & moonphase	4,800	6,000	9,000
World time watch, **Gold Filled,** 48-52mm, OF	500	675	900
World time watch, **18K Gold,** 48-52mm, OF	3,500	4,000	5,000
Perpetual moonphase calendar, gold, OF	8,500	10,000	12,500
Perp. moonphase cal. w/min. repeater, OF	24,000	28,000	35,000
Perp. moonphase cal. w/min.rep. and chrono., OF	26,000	32,000	40,000
Gold Clock Watch, OF	5,000	7,000	10,000
HC	7,000	9,000	12,000

The following will explain the French days of the week abbreviations, Sunday =**DIM** (Dimanche), Monday = **LUN** (Lundi), Tuesday = **MAR** (Mardi), Wednesday = **MER** (Mercedi), Thursday = **JEU** (Jeudi), Friday = **VEN** (Vendredi), Saturday = **SAM** (Samedi).

C. L. GUINAND & CO.

Swiss

Founded Ca. 1865 and became know for their Timers and Chronographs.

TYPE – DESCRIPTION	Avg	Ex-Fn	Mint
Timer, with register, base metal, OF, 46mm	$55	$60	$75
Timer, split second, register, base metal, OF, 46mm	65	70	90
Chronograph, 30 min. register,14K, 50mm, OF, C. 1910	400	550	850
HC	600	725	950
Split sec. chrono., 30 min. register, 14K, OF, 50mm, C. 1915	1,000	1,200	1,600
Minute repeater, **18K,** OF, 50mm, C. 1915	2,200	2,600	3,500
HC	3,000	3,400	4,000
Minute repeater, split sec. chrono., 18K, OF, 50mm, C. 1915	4,000	4,800	6,000

C.L. Guinand, 50mm, split-second chronograph, serial number 44,109.

Haas, Neveux & Co., 40mm, 31 jewels, minute repeater, 18k open face case, serial number 11,339.

HAAS, NEVEUX

Swiss

The Haas Neveux firm is one of the oldest in Switzerland, founded by Leopold & Benjamin Haas in 1848. High grade precision timepieces and chronometers were characteristic of this reputable firm's output.

TYPE – DESCRIPTION	Avg	Ex-Fn	Mint
Time only, gold, 40- 44mm, OF	$300	$385	$525
HC	400	485	650
Time only, gold, 45- 50mm, OF	400	485	650
HC	600	750	950
Chronograph, gold, 45-50mm, OF	700	750	950
HC	800	975	1,100
Split second chronograph, gold, 45-52mm, OF	1,000	1,300	1,700
HC	1,200	1,600	2,200
1/4 hr. repeater, gold, 46-52mm, OF	900	1,100	1,500
HC	1,100	1,300	1,700
Minute repeater, gold, 46-52mm, OF	1,500	1,900	2,500
OF w/split chrono.	3,500	4,200	5,000
OF w/cal. & moonphase	4,000	4,500	5,000
Perpetual moonphase calendar, gold, OF	7,000	8,000	10,000
Perp. moonphase cal. w/min. repeater, OF	25,000	29,000	35,000
HC	26,000	31,000	37,000
Perp. moonphase cal. w/min. rep. and chrono., OF	28,000	34,000	40,000
Clock Watch, Gold, OF	5,000	6,500	9,000
HC	7,000	8,500	12,000

HEBDOMAS
Swiss

The Hebdomas name is commonly found on imported Swiss novelty "8" day watches. Produced from the early 1900's to the 1960's, these popular timepieces featured fancy colored dials with an opening at the bottom of dial to expose the balance wheel and pallet-fork. This style watch is now being made by Arnex Time Corp. under the name of (Lucien Piccard) & other Co. names.

Hebdomas, 8 day (JOURS) 6 jewels, balance seen from the face of the watch, Ca.1920s. This style watch is now being made by Arnex Time Corp. (Lucien Piccard).

Hebdomas, 8 day (JOURS), 6 jewels, 1 adjustment, exposed balance, day date, center seconds, Ca.1920s

TYPE – DESCRIPTION	Avg	Ex-Fn	Mint
8 day, exposed balance, 7J, gun metal, 50mm, OF, C. 1920............	$150	$200	$300
8 day, exposed balance, 7J, base metal, fancy dial, 50mm, OF, C.1920	185	245	325
8 day, exposed balance, 7J, silver, 50mm, OF, C. 1920....................	200	255	350
8 day, exposed balance, 7J, silver, 50mm, HC, C. 1920's ....★	250	350	500
with fancy dial, silver, 55mm, OF, C. 1920's........................	350	450	650

🕐 Note: Some models and grades are not included. Their values can be determined by comparing with similar age, size, metal content, style, models and grades listed.

🕐 Watches listed in this book are priced at the collectable fair market **value** at the Trade Show level, as complete watches having an original case, an original white enamel dial, and with the entire original movement in good working order with no repairs needed, unless otherwise noted.

The Complete Price Guide to Watches goal is to stimulate the orderly exchange of **Watches** between *"buyers"* and *"sellers"*.

COMPARISON OF WATCH CASE SIZES

U. S. A.	EUROPEAN
10-12 SIZE	40—44 MM
16 SIZE	45—49 MM
18 SIZE	50—55 MM

HUGUENIN & CO.
Swiss
Founded by Adolphe Huguenin and the firm name registered in 1880. Purchased by Hamilton W. Co. in March of 1959.

Huguenin & Co., 2-Train 1/4 second jump watch, center sweep hand, enamel dial, 54mm, KW KS, 18K, Ca. 1880.

Huguenin & Co., 2-Train 1/4 second jump watch, 2 main barrels & 2 gear trains, 54mm, KW KS, Ca. 1880.

TYPE – DESCRIPTION	Avg	Ex-Fn	Mint
KW, cylinder, silver, 46- 48mm, OF, C. 1870s	$85	$95	$135
KW, silver, 46- 48mm, HC, C. 1870s	125	150	200
KW, cylinder escapement, **18K,** 48mm, OF, C.1870s	250	325	450
KW, fancy engraved, **18K,** 47mm, HC, C. 1870s	500	635	800
1/4 Sec. Jump, 2-train, **silver,** 50-54mm	1,500	1,900	2,500
1/4 Sec. Jump, 2-train, **gold,** 50-54mm	2,500	2,900	3,500
Chronograph, gold, 45-52mm, OF	800	1,000	1,200
HC	1,000	1,200	1,500
1/4 hr. repeater, gold, 46-52mm, OF	1,400	1,600	2,000
HC	1,500	1,800	2,400
Minute repeater, gold, 46-52mm, OF	1,800	2,200	2,800
HC	2,500	3,000	4,000
OF, w/ chrono.	2,200	2,500	3,000
OF, w/ split chrono.	4,500	5,200	6,000
HC, w/ split chrono.	5,000	5,700	7,000
HC, w/ chrono., cal. & moonphase	4,500	5,200	6,500
Minute Clock Watch, Gold, OF	5,000	6,200	8,000
HC	7,000	8,200	10,000

Huguenin & Co., Chronograph, enamel dial, 51mm, 18K, Hunting Case, Ca. 1890.

Huguenin & Co., Chronograph, 3/4 plate movement, 51mm, 18K, Hunting Case, Ca. 1890.

International Watch Co. (Swiss)

The founder of the prestigious Swiss International Watch Co. was an American engineer F.A. Jones from Boston and previously worked for E. Howard Watch & Clock Company. F.A. Jones and C. L. Kidder for 3 years worked together from about 1869 to 1872 building up a new firm which was the only North-eastern watch factory founded in Switzerland by **Americans** and machinery was made in America. Mr. C. L. Kidder returned to U.S.A. in 1872 and took on a position with Cornell Watch Co. as first Superintendent in the new Newark factory. Mr. Jones stayed to continue building up the factory which was completed in spring of 1875. F.A. Jones in December of 1875 filed for bankruptcy and soon returned to U.S.A. in 1876. The I.W.Co., factory started by F.A. Jones was short lived and produced about 5,000 watches. In 1877 the production of the factory (now called "Internationale Uhrenfabrik") was delegated to F.F. Seeland of New York. In 1879 Mr. Seeland was removed from his position by managing director Johann Rauschenbach. The company today is still making precision, hand crafted watches.

International W. Co., apertures for jump hr. & min. disc, 11-15J., enamel dial, **Pallweber** Caliber, Ca.1880-90.

International Watch Co., 54mm, 17 jewels, Adj., serial number 741,073.

TYPE – DESCRIPTION	Avg	Ex-Fn	Mint
Early, KW, Time only, Swiss bar, silver case	$150	$185	$265
Time only, gold, 40-44mm, OF	425	485	575
HC	625	700	900
Time only, gold, 45-50mm, OF	585	675	850
HC	850	1,000	1,500
Jones Caliber, 13-16J., grades H, D, S, R, B ★★	675	800	1,000
Jones Caliber, **20J., grade E**, GJS, 3/4, SW ★★★★	900	1,200	1,800
Caliber 71-72, 16J., GJS, OF ★★	625	775	1,000
Caliber 72-72, 16J., GJS, HC ★★	725	900	1,200
Pallweber, 11-15J., jump hr. & min. disc, enamel dial, **Niello**, HC	1,500	1,900	2,400
silver, HC	1,500	1,900	2,400
14K, HC	2,400	3,000	4,000
Chronograph, gold, 45-50mm, OF	1,800	2,000	2,500
HC	2,000	2,400	3,000
Split second chronograph, gold, 45-52mm, OF	3,000	3,400	4,000
HC	4,000	4,400	5,000
Minute repeater, gold, 46-52mm, OF	2,800	3,500	4,500
HC	3,300	4,500	6,000
OF, w/split chrono.	6,500	7,200	8,500
HC, w/split chrono	8,000	8,500	10,000
OF, w/cal. & moonphase	7,000	8,000	10,000
HC, w/chrono., cal. & moonphase	9,000	10,000	12,000
Detent chronometer, gold, 48-52mm, OF	7,000	7,500	9,000
World Time watch, gold, 48-52mm, OF	10,000	12,000	15,000
Perpetual moonphase calendar, gold, OF	7,000	7,500	9,000
Perpetual moonphase calendar, w/minute repeater, HC	30,000	40,000	60,000
Clock Watch, Gold, 48-52mm, OF	8,000	9,000	12,000
HC	10,000	12,000	15,000

A new numbering system was started with serial # 01 in **1884**. The old register can not be found and the new uninterrupted serial numbers list started on the 9th of January 1885 with serial number 6,501. The highest known serial number for the "JONES" Caliber is 42,327, & the lowest "SEELAND" Caliber serial number is 26,211, the highest number for "SEELAND" Caliber is 60,014.

PRODUCTION TOTALS

OLD DATE – SERIAL #	DATE – SERIAL #	DATE – SERIAL #	DATE – SERIAL #
1875 — 7,000	1901 - 253,500	1926 - 845,000	1951 - 1,253,000
1877 — 25,000	1902 - 276,500	1927 - 866,000	1952 - 1,291,000
1879 — 50,000	1903 - 298,500	1928 - 890,500	1953 - 1,316,000
1881 — 80,000	1904 - 321,000	1929 - 919,500	1954 - 1,335,000
1883 — 100,000	1905 - 349,500	1930 - 929,000	1955 - 1,361,000
NEW	1906 - 377,500	1931 - 937,500	1956 - 1,399,000
DATE – SERIAL #	1907 - 406,000	1932 - 938,000	1957 - 1,436,000
1884 — 6,501	1908 - 435,000	1933 - 939,000	1958 - 1,480,000
1885 — 15,500	1909 - 463,500	1934 - 940,000	1959 - 1,513,000
1886 — 23,500	1910 - 492,000	1935 - 945,000	1960 - 1,553,000
1887 — 29,500	1911 - 521,000	1936 - 955,500	1961 - 1,612,000
1888 — 37,500	1912 - 557,000	1937 - 979,000	1962 - 1,666,000
1889 — 49,000	1913 - 594,000	1938 - 1,000,000	1963 - 1,733,000
1890 — 63,000	1914 - 620,500	1939 - 1,013,000	1964 - 1,778,000
1891 — 75,500	1915 - 635,000	1940 - 1,019,000	1965 - 1,796,000
1892 — 87,500	1916 - 657,000	1941 - 1,039,000	1966 - 1,820,000
1893 — 103,000	1917 - 684,000	1942 - 1,062,000	1967 - 1,889,000
1894 — 117,000	1918 - 714,000	1943 - 1,078,000	1968 - 1,905,000
1895 — 133,000	1919 - 742,000	1944 - 1,092,000	1969 - 1,970,000
1896 — 151,500	1920 - 765,000	1945 - 1,106,000	1970 - 2,026,000
1897 — 170,500	1921 - 780,000	1946 - 1,131,000	1971 - 2,113,000
1898 — 194,000	1922 - 783,500	1947 - 1,153,000	1972 - 2,218,000
1899 — 212,000	1923 - 793,500	1948 - 1,177,000	1973 - 2,230,000
1900 — 231,000	1924 - 807,000	1949 - 1,205,000	1974 - 2,265,000
	1925 - 827,500	1950 - 1,222,000	1975 - 2,275,000

The above list is provided for determining the APPROXIMATE age of your watch. Match serial number with date. Watches were not necessarily sold in the exact order of manufactured date.

OLD STYLE MOVEMENTS

NOTE: **"Jones"** Caliber, had 6 different grades, the highest grade was **E** = 20J, SW, 3/4 plate in nickel, 3 sets of screwed gold settings; next w grade **H** =16-18J, SW, 3/4 plate in nickel; grade **D** =16J, SW, 3/4 plate in nickel; grade **S** = 15J, SW, 3/4 plate in nickel; grade **R** = 15J, 3/4 plate; grade **B** = 13J, 3/4 plate. The **"Jones"** model used a stem- wind & set, a long index regulator & exposed winding gears. The *key- wind* models did not have exposed winding gears but used long index regulator. **"SEELAND"** Caliber, usually were full or 3/4 plate, with short index regulator, and lever or pin set.

"Jones" Caliber, grade "E", <u>HC</u>, 20J., long index regulator, exposed wolf tooth wind gears, gold train, 3 sets of screwed in gold jewel settings, SW, 3/4 plate, overcoil hair-spring, (may have a pat. date on movement of Sept. 15th, 1868) about 16 size 43mm, Ca. 1876.

"71" Caliber, 16J., OF, 4 sets of screw style gold jewel settings, 300 made in 1904 & 300 in 1917, also HC Caliber **"72"**, 300 made in 1904 & 300 in 1917, 71 & 72 total=1,200.

⊕ Some models and grades are not included. Their values can be determined by comparing with similar age, size, metal content, style, models and grades listed.

⊕ The year a watch was **sold** may differ from the year it was **produced**.

Ca.1873

Right: Exact
copy and
size of small
catalog, 23
pages with
16 different
movements
& 3 dials.
On the Cover:
**International
Watch Company
F.H. Mathez
Gen'l Agent
F. A. Jones
Managing
Director.
New York,
No. 5
Maiden Lane.**
Note: Patented
Feb. 2d 1869,
also Note:
6 pairs hole jewels,
3 pairs endstones
& 2 ruby pallets
total = 20 jewels.

Illustrated Catalogue of Movements
MANUFACTURED BY THE
International Watch Co.
OF NEW YORK.

GENERAL AGENCY, NO. 5, MAIDEN LANE.

Illustrations exact size of
movements. 16 Size.
19 Lignes or 43 Millimetres.

Millimetres.

Pattern N.
STEM-WINDER.
Automatic Hand Setting Attachment.
Nickel Movement.

Six pairs genuine Ruby jewels, and three pairs extra-
fine Ruby endstones; exposed Ruby pallets; Unique Double
Regulator; Elson Attachment; Isochronal Hair Spring;
Chronometer Balance (gold rim) accurately adjusted to heat,
cold, isochronism and position; named

Schaffhausen.

**Hunting
Case**

Without Patent Regulator,
if desired.

Pattern H, No.1, stem winder, automatic hand setting attachment, nickel movement, six pairs genuine ruby jewels
and three pair extra fine ruby endstones, exposed ruby
pallets, unique double regulator, Elson attachment, isochronal hairspring, chronometer balance (gold rim), adjusted.

Pattern B, Stem Winder, Nickel movement, Hunting Case,
5 pairs Rubies, and upper center jeweled, with Elson Attachment if desired. Special note: In Preparation an Open Face
Stem Winder, will be ready in a few months.

INTERNATIONAL WATCH CO SCHAFFHAUSEN
Fabrique d'Horlogerie de Précision fondée en 1868

Left, Cal. 57, OF
18 lig., 41mm

Right, Cal. 58, HC
19 lig., 43.15mm

Left, Cal. 52, OF
1st in 1893
18 lig., 41mm
19 lig., 43.15mm

Right, Cal. 53, HC
18 lig., 41mm
19 lig., 43.15mm

Left, Cal. 71, OF
19 lig., 43.15mm

Right, Cal. 72, HC
19 lig., 43.15mm

Center
Cal., Seeland
19 Lignes
3/4 Plate

Right: Cal. Pallweber, type III, 19 Lignes,
digital time indicator , 1st in 1885.

Left: Cal., Seeland, 18 Lignes, full plate Quality C.

INTERNATIONAL WATCH CO SCHAFFHAUSEN

Fabrique d'Horlogerie de Précision fondée en 1868

Cal. 65

Left, Cal. 65, OF
19 lig., 43.15mm

Right, Cal. 66, HC
19 lig., 43.15mm

Lépine

Left, Cal. 73, OF
17 lig., 38mm

Right, Cal. 74, HC
17 lig., 38mm

dessus

Left, Cal. 77, OF
17 lig., 38mm

Right, Cal. 95 & 97
HC,17 lig., 37.8mm

Left, Cal. 67, OF
18 lig., 41mm

Right, Cal. 68, HC
18 lig., 41mm

INVICTA (Swiss)

Founded by R. Picard in 1837. Invicta trade-mark was registered on May 18, 1896 by Files de R. Picard, of La Chaux-de-Fonds. Other names used Seeland Watch Co. and Eno Watch Co.

TYPE – DESCRIPTION	Avg	Ex-Fn	Mint
Time only, gold, 25-38mm, OF	$175	$225	$325
Time only, gold, 40–44mm, 10-12 size, OF	200	250	350
HC	225	300	400
Time only, gold, 45- 50mm, OF	225	300	450
Gold, HC	250	325	500
Time only, gold & **enamel**, 45- 50mm, OF	425	625	950
HC	475	685	1,100
1/4 hr. repeater, gun metal ,48mm, OF, C. 1900s	425	475	550
1/4 hr. repeater, silver, 48mm, OF, C. 1900s	500	600	775
1/4 hr. repeater, silver, 50mm, HC, C. 1900s	700	800	975
1/4 hr. repeater, **gold,** 58mm, HC, C. 1900s	800	1,100	1,500
with chronograph	1,200	1,500	2,000
Min. repeater, gun metal, 52mm, HC, C. 1900s	750	950	1,300
silver, HC	800	1,100	1,500
gold, HC	1,200	1,400	2,200
W/chronograph, gold, HC	1,500	2,100	2,800

INVICTA, 1/4 hour repeater with chronograph, 18 jewels, Hunting Case about 58MM, Ca. 1895.

JACOT, HENRI (PARIS)

Henri Jacot settled in Paris in 1820 and developed the carriage clock industry. He also invented and improved watchmaking and clock making tools. Henri Jacot died July 31, 1867.

TYPE – DESCRIPTION	Avg	Ex-Fn	Mint
KW, cylinder, silver, 46mm, OF	$85	$95	$125
HC	125	150	195
KW, LADIES, **18K**, 40-44mm, OF	225	285	385
HC	300	350	450
KW, GENTS, **18K**, 48mm, OF	400	465	600
HC	500	575	700
1/4 hr. repeater, SILVER, 50mm, OF	800	950	1,200
1/4 hr. repeater, GOLD, 50mm, OF	1,500	1,700	2,000

CHARLES E. JACOT
New York & Swiss

In 1837 Charles worked with his uncle, Louis Matthey in New York City. During the 20 year period of working in the U.S.A. he was sold a interest in the firm and the name was changed to Jacot, Courvoisier & Co. Charles E. Jacot had a patent for a star duplex escapement on Apr. 30, 1840 and July 20, 1852. He had about 12 or more watch patents.

In 1857 he returned to Switzerland he forms a company of Jacot & Saltzman. 1876 the name of the firm was Charles E. Jacot. He remained in close contact with his New York connections and in 1897 he died. In 1925 the firm Chas.E. Jacot was listed in Le Locle.

TYPE – DESCRIPTION	Avg	Ex-Fn	Mint
Early, KW, Time only, silver case	$165	$225	$300
Early, KW, Time only, gold case	200	265	450
Time only, gold, 40-44mm, OF	300	425	600
HC	400	550	800
Time only, gold, 45-50mm, OF	400	550	800
HC	700	800	1,000
Time only, 30J., independent 1/4 seconds, 2 train, gold, OF	1,200	1,700	2,500
HC	1,500	2,300	3,500
3 or 4 star duplex, Patented July 1852, gold case ★★★★	2,500	3,600	5,000

Cha's E. Jacot, Patents, Sept. 64, Nov. 67, Apr, 70; 50mm, lever escapement, SW, HC, Ca. 1871, S# 8133.

Cha's E. Jacot, on movement "Chaux de Fonds, Indep't Quarter Seconds Lever Escapement 28 Ruby Jewels Compensated Balance. Isochronal Vibrations. Patented June, 1858, S# 7715", 2 train, KW & KS from back.

Cha's E. Jacot, on movement "Chaux de Fonds, Improved Straight Line Lever, full jeweled in Ruby & Sapphire, Pat. Sept. 1859, S# 1637", KW & KS.

Cha's E. Jacot, on movement, " Pat, Oct. 1867, N=25338", KW & KS from back, 15 jewels, 40mm.

RIGHT: Cha's E. Jacot's STAR DUPLEX escapement with 3 pointed star, escapement with 4 pointed star Pat. # 1,570 on Apr. 30, 1840 also JULY 20, 1852.

JOSEPH JOHNSON
LIVERPOOL, (1810-1850)

Josh. Johnson of Liverpool started his firm in the early 1800's and lasted till mid 1800's. The Johnson firm supplied the U.S. market with low to medium cost key-wind watches.

TYPE – DESCRIPTION	Avg	Ex-Fn	Mint
KW, 7-15J, fusee, silver, 47mm, OF	$125	$200	$325
KW,7- 15J, fusee, silver, 47mm, HC	150	250	375
KW,7-15J, swiss, **gilt dial**, fancy case, **18K**, 48mm,OF	275	335	500
KW, lever, fusee, **gold dial**, **Heavy 18K**, 52mm, HC	800	950	1,200
KW, **rack lever** escapement, **Silver**, 56mm, OF	300	365	535
HC	400	450	650
KW, **rack lever** escapement, **Gold**, 56mm, OF	700	850	1,100
HC	1,100	1,200	1,500
KW, verge fusee, **multi-color gold dial & THIN case,** 52mm, OF	400	575	900
HC	700	850	1,000
KW, **15 sec. dial**, detached lever, fusee,			
multi-color gold dial & case, 50mm, OF	800	1,100	1,500

Signed on movement *Josh. Johnson Liverpool Detached Patent*, Key wind Key Set, diamond end stone, Massey style side lever, the escape wheel coverts the second hand to rotate once every 15-seconds rather than the normal 60-seconds. Multi-color gold case and dial with carved decorations on the back of case and outer rim of the case, S # 5563, 50mm open face case, Ca. 1850.

Jos. Johnson Escapement: Right: 30 tooth escape wheel with right angle lever. Left: Layout of movement the fusee has 60 teeth it engages with 10 leaf pinion on center wheel, center wheel has 90 teeth which engages 6 leaves on pinion of third wheel which has 88 teeth it engages with a pinion of 6 leaves on the escape wheel. (slow beat of 3 2/3 seconds)

JULES JURGENSEN (Swiss)

The firm of Jules Jurgensen was an extension of the earlier firm of Urban Jurgensen & Sons, which was located, at various times, in Copenhagen and Le Locle. Jules ultimately established his firm in Le Locle after his father's death in the early 1830's. From that time forward the company produced, generally speaking, very fine watches that were high grade and complicated. It appears that by 1850 the company had already established a strong market in America, offering beautiful heavy 18K gold watches of exemplary quality. Until around 1885, most stem-winding watches exhibited the **bow-setting feature.** After 1885, as the firm started to buy movements from other companies, we begin to see variations in Jurgensen watches. By 1930, Jurgensen watches barely resembled the quality and aesthetics of the early period, and they are not as desirable to the collector.

The Jules Jurgensen famous **bow-setting** feature, was Patented in 1867.

Jules Jurgensen, 1923 MODEL

Jules Jurgensen, movement signed on center bridge & case, counter poised lever, 18K hunting case numbered 14709, 20 jewels, wolf tooth winding, early stem wind, uncommon **pin** set for a J, Jurgensen, 45mm, Ca. 1865.

Jules Jurgensen, movement signed on barrel bridge "Jules Jurgensen Copenhagen No.6319", 18K Hunting Case, 17 jewels, with gold escape wheel & chronometer pivoted detent escapement, KWKS, Ca. 1860.

Almost any collectible Jurgensen watch will be fully signed on the dial and movement, with an impressively embossed "JJ" stamping on all covers of the case. Watches not so marked should be examined carefully; and untypical or inelegant stamping should be viewed suspiciously, as there have been some forgeries of these fine watches. Frequently one finds the original box and papers accompanying the watch, which enhances the value.

JULES JURGENSEN, 46mm, 21J., hands set by inclination of pendant ring (**Bow Set**), serial # 14,492, ca.1880.

JULES JURGENSEN, 46-52mm, Minute repeater, 32 jewels, Ca.1890.

TYPE – DESCRIPTION	Avg	Ex-Fn	Mint
Time only, gold, 35- 44mm, Ca. 1930, OF	$600	$750	$1,000
HC	800	900	1,200
Time only, gold, 45- 55mm, OF	900	1,100	1,500
HC	1,000	1,400	2,000
Time only, gold, 45- 55mm, **Pin Set**, OF ★	2,000	2,600	3,500
HC	3,000	3,400	4,000
Time only, gold, 45- 55mm, **Bow Set**, OF	2,000	2,600	3,500
HC	3,000	3,400	4,000
Wind Indicator, Enamel dial, 46-52mm, Gold OF ★★★	5,000	8,000	12,000
HC ★★★	7,000	12,000	20,000
Flat digital watch, 18J., gold, 40-44mm, OF, Ca. 1930	4,000	4,400	5,000
1/5 jump sec., with, 27J., 2 main barrels & 2 gear trains, 18K OF ..	3,500	4,700	6,500
Chronograph, gold, 45-50mm, OF	3,000	3,700	5,000
HC	4,000	4,600	6,000
HC w/register	4,500	5,500	7,500
Split second chronograph, gold, 45-52mm, OF	5,500	6,000	7,200
HC	6,500	7,000	8,200
5 minute repeater, gold, 46-52mm, OF	4,000	4,900	7,000
HC	5,000	5,900	8,000
Minute repeater, gold, 46-52mm, OF	5,000	6,200	8,000
HC	6,000	7,500	11,000
OF, w/ chrono.	6,500	7,200	8,500
HC, w/ chrono.	8,000	10,000	13,000
OF, w/split chrono.	10,000	13,000	18,000
HC, w/split chrono.	11,000	14,000	20,000
Detent chronometer, gold, 48-52mm, OF	6,500	8,000	10,000
HC	7,000	9,000	12,000
Perpetual moonphase calendar, gold, OF	20,000	24,000	30,000
HC	25,000	29,000	35,000
Perp. moonphase cal. w/min. repeater, OF	45,000	55,000	70,000
HC	50,000	60,000	75,000
Tourbillon ★★★★★	100,000	185,000	300,000
Clock Watch, OF	10,000	14,000	20,000
HC	12,000	17,000	25,000

EDWARD KOEHN

Swiss

Koehn was an innovative watchmaker and a specialist in the design of thin calibre watches. Formerly associated with Patek Phillipe and H. R. Ekegren, he produced watches under his own name from 1891-1930.

TYPE – DESCRIPTION	Avg	Ex-Fn	Mint
Time only, gold, 40- 44mm, OF	$400	$450	$575
HC	550	665	825
Time only, gold, 45- 50mm, OF	800	885	1,000
HC	1,000	1,200	1,500
Chronograph, gold, 45-50mm, OF	1,200	1,400	1,800
HC	1,400	1,600	2,000
Split second chronograph,gold, 45-52mm, OF	1,800	2,000	2,500
HC	2,500	2,900	3,500
5 minute repeater, gold, 45-52mm, OF	3,000	3,400	4,000
HC	3,500	3,900	4,500
Minute repeater, gold, 46-52mm, OF	2,200	2,700	3,500
HC	2,800	3,200	4,000
OF, w/split chrono.	4,000	4,500	5,500
HC, w/split chrono.	6,000	6,700	7,500

E. Koehn, of Geneve, 46mm, 18 jewels, note: **free standing barrel,** lever escapement, Ca. 1900.

🕐 Note: Some models and grades are not included. Their values can be determined by comparing with similar age, size, metal content, style, models and grades listed.

🕐 Watches listed in this book are priced at the collectable fair market **value** at the trade show level, as complete watches having an original case, an original white enamel dial, and with the entire original movement in good working order with no repairs needed, unless otherwise noted.

COMPARISON OF WATCH CASE SIZES

U. S. A.	EUROPEAN
10-12 SIZE	40—44 MM
16 SIZE	45—49 MM
18 SIZE	50—55 MM

The Complete Price Guide to Watches goal is to stimulate the orderly exchange of **Watches** between *"buyers"* and *"sellers"*.

A. LANGE & SOHNE

A. Lange & Sohne was established with the aid of the German government at Glashutte, Germany in 1845. Lange typically produced 3/4 plate lever watches in gilt finish for the domestic market, and in nickel for the export market. High grade and very practical, these watches had a banking system for the pallet that was later used briefly by E. Howard in America. Lange complicated watches are scarce and very desirable. On May 8, 1945 Russian bombers destroy workshops. All A. Lange & Sohne must be **triple signed** (Dial, Case, Movement) to bring top prices.

PRODUCTION TOTALS

single banking pin

DATE– SERIAL #	DATE– SERIAL #	DATE– SERIAL #
1870— 3,500	1895— 35,000	1920— 75,000
1875— 10,000	1900— 40,000	1925— 80,000
1880— 15,000	1905— 50,000	1930— 85,000
1885— 20,000	1910— 60,000	1935— 90,000
1890— 30,000	1915— 70,000	1940—100,000

TYPE – DESCRIPTION	Avg	Ex-Fn	Mint
Time only, **A.L.S.** first quality , GJS, **18k gold**, 45- 52mm, OF	$4,000	$5,500	$8,000
HC	5,500	7,000	9,000
Time only, **D.U.F.** grade, pressed jewels, **14k gold**, 45- 52mm, OF	1,500	2,000	3,000
HC	2,000	2,600	3,500
Time only, **O.L.I.W.** grade, pressed jewels, not adjusted...............	475	575	750
World War II model, wind indicator, 52mm, OF (before 1945)......	1,500	1,900	2,500
Chronograph, gold, 45-50mm, OF	9,000	13,000	18,000
HC	10,000	14,000	20,000
Split second chronograph, gold, 45-52mm, OF	15,000	22,000	30,000
HC	17,000	24,000	32,000
1/4 hr. repeater, gold, 45-52mm, OF	10,000	14,000	20,000
HC	12,000	18,000	25,000
Minute repeater, gold, 45-52mm, OF...	17,000	23,000	30,000
HC	18,000	28,000	40,000
OF, w/split chrono.	20,000	35,000	50,000
HC, w/split chrono.	23,000	37,000	55,000
Anker chronometer, gold, 48-52mm, OF..	8,000	9,500	13,000
HC (**Anker** = German for lever escapement)	10,000	14,000	20,000
Detent chronometer, gold, 48-52mm, OF	20,000	26,000	35,000
Karrusel, 14J., 60 min. carriage driven by **center wheel**, 18K ..... ★★★	50,000	65,000	90,000

Right: To identify a Glashutte movement note balance cock, and single banking pin .

A. LANGE & SOHNE, 52mm, serial number 87250, hunting case. The A.L.S. top grade watches had gold jewel settings & screwed to the plates, diamond end stone, gold lever & gold escape wheel, Adj. to 5 positions. Second A.L.S. grade the gold settings are not screwed into plates, and most had no diamond end stone, in 18K cases.

D. U. F. grade by Lange, 50mm, 3/4 plate, engraved on movement **"Deutsche Uhren Fabrikation Glashutte,"** serial number 58,398. The **D. U. F.** grade had pressed jewels, brass & nickel balance, adjusted to 3 positions, the D.U. F. grades came in 14K cases and introduced in about 1885 with lower production cost to compete with other Co.'s.

TYPE – DESCRIPTION	Avg	Ex-Fn	Mint
Perpetual moonphase calendar, gold, OF	$30,000	$42,000	$60,000
Perp. moonphase cal. w/min. repeater, OF	45,000	80,000	125,000
Perp. moonphase cal. w/min. rep. and chronograph, HC ....★	100,000	135,000	175,000
Perp. moonphase cal. w/min. rep., leap year indicator, 30 minutes recorder			
2 button split chronograph, 60mm, HC ....★★★★	185,000	200,000	275,000

A. Lange & Sohne, 60mm Hunter Cased Minute Repeating instantaneous Perpetual calendar with day, date, month and leap year indicator, full split second chronograph operated by two buttons with minute recorder and the phases of the moon. The white enamel dial has Arabic numbers, pierced gold hands, four subsidiary dials indicating day, date and the month is combined with leap year indicator and 30 minutes recorder, and the moon phases is combined constant seconds.

A. Lange & Sohne, the movement made in the typical Glashutte 3/4 plate style with a nickel finish, gold lever escapement with convex entry pallet & concave exit pallet, compensation balance, diamond endstone, gold escape wheel, gold lever, repeating on two gongs. This type of watches have 40 to 60 jewels, 75 wheels, over 300 screws and 24 bridges. The movement was supplied by Audemars Piguet in 1908-1909 & may be one of fourteen with a two button chronograph finished & cased by A. Lange & Sohne. Audemars Piguet supplied about 35 watches of this type to the Glashutte market.

LE COULTRE & CO.

Swiss

Antoine Le Coultre in 1833 formed a company to make ebauches. He created a machine to cut pinions from solid steel as well as other machines for manufacturing clocks and watches. By 1900 they were making flat or thin watches. 1936 Jaeger & Le Coultre officially merge. The signed watches with Jaeger - Le Coultre logo may fetch more money, but have the same quality grade movement as the signed Le Coultre dial & movement. They make movements & parts for Vacheron & Constantin, P. P. & Co., Omega, Longines & many more.

TYPE – DESCRIPTION	Avg	Ex-Fn	Mint
Early, KW, Time only, Swiss bar, Pre. 1870, silver case........	$75	$125	$200
Time only, gold, 40- 44mm, OF......................	200	275	425
HC..............................	250	375	550
Time only, gold, 45- 52mm, OF......................	225	300	450
HC..............................	385	465	600
8 day, 15J, wind indicator, 45mm, **18K**, OF............	600	750	1,100
8 day, 14K, OF..........................	500	650	900
8 day, S.S., OF..........................	300	435	600
Roulette wheel style bezel, gold, 40mm, OF............	500	750	1,100
World time watch, gold, 48-52mm, OF................	4,000	5,200	7,000
Chronograph, gold, 45-50mm, OF....................	700	865	1,100
HC...............................	800	1,000	1,300
OF, w/register........................	750	900	1,200
Split second chronograph,gold, 45-52mm, OF............	1,000	1,200	1,500
HC..............................	1,400	1,600	2,000

Le Coultre & Co., 52mm, 32J., minute repeater, exposed winding gears, high grade movement, 14K HC.

Le Coultre & Co., Min. repeater, 17 jewels, note the repeater **governor**, signed under the repeater hammer "L.C. & Co.", Ca. 1930.

TYPE – DESCRIPTION	Avg	Ex-Fn	Mint
1/4 hr. repeater, gold, 46-52mm, OF................	$1,000	$1,300	$1,800
HC w/chrono., cal. & moonphase............	2,400	3,500	5,000
Minute repeater, gold, 46-52mm, OF............	2,200	2,600	3,400
HC............................	2,300	2,800	3,600
OF, w/chrono. & register............	2,400	2,800	3,600
HC, w/chrono. & register............	2,600	3,200	4,000
HC, w/split chrono..............	3,500	4,000	5,500
HC w/chrono., cal. & moonphase............	5,000	6,200	8,000
Perpetual moonphase calendar, gold, OF............	7,000	8,200	10,000
HC..............................	7,500	8,700	11,000
Perp. moonphase cal. w/min. repeater, OF............	15,000	19,000	25,000
HC..............................	17,000	22,000	30,000
Perpetual moonphase cal. w/ min. rep. & chrono., OF........	18,000	23,000	30,000
HC..............................	20,000	26,000	35,000
Clock Watch, gold, 46-52mm, OF............	6,000	7,500	10,000
HC..............................	8,000	9,500	12,000

Note: Ebauche movements look under hammers for initials *L.C. & Co.*(not on all movements)

Caliber 30   Caliber 31   Caliber 46

Caliber 33 & 45   Caliber 32 & 44   Caliber 48

Caliber 43 A   Caliber 43 B HC

Caliber 49

LE PHARE
Swiss

Le Phare specialized in the production of repeater ebauches from 1890-1940. They were the first to mass produce or manufacture inexpensive repeaters with interchangeable parts. Le Phare *patented* a **centrifugal force governor**.

TYPE – DESCRIPTION	Avg	Ex-Fn	Mint
Chronograph, gold, 45-50mm, OF	$600	$765	$1,000
HC	700	865	1,100
Split second chronograph, gold, 45-52mm, OF	1,100	1,300	1,600
HC	1,200	1,400	1,800
1/4 hr. repeater, gold, 46-52mm, OF	900	1,000	1,300
HC	1,000	1,200	1,500
HC w/chrono., cal. & moonphase	2,200	2,800	3,500
Minute repeater, gold, 46-56mm, OF	1,500	1,800	2,200
high grade min. repeater with **helical** balance spring	2,600	3,000	4,000
HC	1,800	2,200	2,800
OF w/chrono. & register	1,800	2,200	3,000
HC w/chrono.	1,900	2,400	3,200
HC w/chrono., full cal. & moonphase	2,800	3,200	4,800

Le Phare, 56mm, minute repeater, chronograph and calendar with moon phases, Note the governor at 6 O'clock..

Le Phare, high grade min. repeater with **helical** balance spring, 5mm, Ca. 1910.

Below: Centrifugal style governor for the repeating mechanism.

Le Phare, Min. repeater, 54mm, HC, 17J., 3/4 plate, push button, Ca. 1895, Note centrifugal force governor at 6 o'clock.

Caliber OV   Caliber LV   Caliber OF

Caliber E   Caliber 115 V   Caliber EV

Caliber D   Caliber DV   Caliber J

Caliber 110 M   Caliber ZM   Caliber 105

L'Epine or Lepine
Paris France (1720 - 1814)

Jean-Antoine L'Epine more than any other one man, revolutionized the **form** of the watch. He developed and first used the following list of improvements in 1770 to 1790, bar bridges, suspended use of the fusee, free-standing **going** barrel, new style virgule, cylinder and lever escapements, stylized arabic numbers, center seconds, moon style hands, wolf's teeth gearing, gongs for repeaters, much thinner watches about 12-13mm, concealed case hinge, cuvette dust cover, engine turned cases, back wind & back set of the hands, pump or pull wind (1790), and open faced style case which is called L'Epine calibre by the Swiss watch makers. The House of Lepine was sold in 1914.

George Washington was the owner of a L'Epine *Gold Watch*. Governor Morris was commissioned to acquire for his friend, the President, a reliable watch while on a business trip to Paris, France. On April 23, 1789, Governor Morris selected a Lepine large gold watch with Virgule escapement as the best. Thomas Jefferson was asked to deliver the watch due to the fact the Governor had a delay in Paris. The watch is on exhibit in the Museum of the Historical Society of Pennsylvania, Pittsburgh, Pa.

TYPE – DESCRIPTION	Avg	Ex-Fn	Mint
Time only, **Silver,** KW, verge or cylinder escap., 46-52mm OF	$200	$335	$600
Time only, **Silver,** KW, virgule escap., 46-52mm OF	600	735	1,000
Time only, **Gold,** KW, verge or cylinder escap, , plain, 50mm, OF	500	665	900
Time only, **Gold,** KW, virgule escap., enamel & scene, 50mm, OF	2,000	2,600	3,800
Time only, **Gold,** KW, *lever with 40 tooth gold escape wheel,* Ca. 1778-1790, 50mm, OF .... ★★★	2,500	3,500	5,000
1/4 repeater, **SILVER,** 52mm, OF	800	1,100	1,500
1/4 repeater, **GOLD,** 54mm, OF	1,100	1,500	2,000
Minute Pump Repeater, Gold .... ★★★	6,000	8,500	12,000

Signed *L'Epine a Paris* on dial, virgule escapement, open face, free standing going barrel, concealed hinged cuvette, KW/KS from back, **number 1 in an oval**, Ca. 1790-95.

Lepine, virgule escapement, note horse-shoe shaped center bridge used for center seconds, free standing going barrel, Ca. 1790-95.

LE ROY ET CIE
Paris

Le Roy et Cie was the final product of a dynasty of great watchmakers, starting with Julien Le Roy and his son Pierre, whose credits are numerous in the development of horology in the 18th century. There is, however, much confusion and hoopla over "Le Roy" watches. Frequently, you will see watches signed "Le Roy" that have nothing to do with the original family. These watches are unimportant. You have to distinguish between the works of Julien, of Pierre, of Charles, and of their contemporary namesakes. The modern firm, Le Roy et Cie., established in the late 19th century, contracted and finished some very fine and, in some cases, extremely important complicated watches, using imported Swiss ebauches.

TYPE – DESCRIPTION	Avg	Ex-Fn	Mint
Verge, KW, paircase, silver, 49-50mm, C. 1775	$325	$400	$525
Verge, fusee, Enamel w/scene, **18K**, 38- 40mm, C. 1760	2,400	3,000	3,800
Miniature, 22mm, diamonds & pearls on enamel, OF	800	1,100	1,500
Time only, gold, 45- 50mm, OF	600	750	1,000
Digital Jump hour, extra thin, gold, Ca. 1930's	650	800	1,100
1/4 hr. repeater, gold, 46-52mm, OF	1,200	1,800	2,400
Min. repeater, two train, tandem winding wheels, fully jeweled jump center seconds, gold, 50mm	6,000	7,000	9,000

Le Roy, 50mm, minute repeater, two train, tandem winding wheels, jump center seconds.

Le Roy, 22mm, miniature watch with enamel, pearls, with Diamonds on the pin, 18K, OF, Ca. 1910.

🕐 This book endeavours to be a GUIDE or helpful manual and offers a wealth of material to be used as a tool not as a absolute document. Price Guides are like watches the worst may be better than none at all, but at best cannot be expected to be 100% accurate.

🕐 Characteristics of watches differ for the same age of both case and movement, because these features vary it may not be accurate to date a watch by one single influence. Example: the second hand was not commonly found on watches before 1750, but common about 1800. The first second hand appeared in 1665 and another in 1690. Therefore statements are broad rather than accurate.

🕐 A collector should expect to pay modestly higher prices at local shops.

The Complete Price Guide to Watches goal is to stimulate the orderly exchange of **Watches** between *"buyers"* and *"sellers"*.

LONGINES
Swiss

The beautiful Fabrique des Longines is situated in St. Imier, Switzerland. The company was founded by Ernest Francillon in 1866. They manufactured all grades of watches. Winged hour-glass trademark registered in May 1890.

PRODUCTION TOTALS

DATE-SERIAL #	DATE-SERIAL #	DATE-SERIAL #
1867 — 1	1911 - 2,500,000	1937 - 5,500,000
1870 — 20,000	1912 - 2,750,000	1938 - 5,750,000
1875 — 100,000	1913 - 3,000,000 - Aug.	1940 - 6,000,000 - June
1882 — 250,000	1915 - 3,250,000	1945 - 7,000,000 - July
1888 — 500,000	1917 - 3,500,000	1950 - 8,000,000 - May
1893 — 750,000	1919 - 3,750,000	1953 - 9,000,000 - July
1899 - 1,000,000 - Feb.	1922 - 4,000,000 - Oct.	1956-10,000,000 - May
1901 - 1,250,000	1925 - 4,250,000	1959-11,000,000 - April
1904 - 1,500,000	1926 - 4,500,000	1962-12,000,000 - May
1905 - 1,750,000	1928 - 4,750,000	1966-13,000,000 - June
1907 - 2,000,000 - July	1929 - 5,000,000 - Oct.	1967-14,000,000 - Feb.
1909 - 2,250,000	1934 - 5,250,000	1969-15,000,000 - Feb.

Right: Early KW or SW, cal.# L20B, Ca. 1870-85.

LONGINES, 44mm, 21 jewels, U.S. Army AC, adjusted to temp. & 5 positions, World War II model, cal. 2129.

LONGINES, 59mm, 21 jewels, Railroad Model , gold filled open face case, Ca. 1920-1935.

TYPE – DESCRIPTION	Avg	Ex-Fn	Mint
Early KW or SW, cal.# L20B, silver case, Ca. 1870-85	$125	$150	$200
15 -17J, silver, 48- 50mm, HC, Ca. 1890	100	125	175
KW, for Turkish market, .800 silver, HC, Ca. 1900	100	125	175
15-17J, for Tiffany, Sterling, 45- 50mm OF, Ca. 1905	135	155	200
Time only, **gold**, 40- 44mm, OF	250	325	450
HC	350	400	550
Time only, **gold**, 45- 50mm, OF	300	375	535
HC	450	550	850
15 -17J, GF, 40- 52mm, OF, Ca. 1930	60	75	95
21J, GF, 40- 50mm, OF, Ca. 1930	135	175	275
17J, "Express Leader", Adj., LS, **GF**, 48- 50mm, OF	150	200	325
19J, "Express Leader", Adj., LS, **GF**, 48- 50mm, OF	175	225	350
19J, "Express Monarch", Adj., LS, **GF**, 48- 50mm, OF	175	225	350
21J, "Express Monarch", Adj., LS, **GF**, 48- 50mm, OF	225	300	500
23J, "Express Monarch", Adj., LS, **GF**, 48- 50mm, OF	300	400	600
24J, "Express Monarch", Adj., LS, **GF**, 48- 50mm, OF	375	500	750
21J, Trans-Continental Express, Adj., LS, **GF**, 48- 50mm, OF	200	275	400
23J, Trans-Continental Express,Adj., LS, **GF**, 48- 50mm, OF	225	285	500
U.S. Army AC, World War II, 21J., silver, 44mm, **WI**., OF	600	975	1,500
U.S. Army, World War II, 17-21J., silver, 44mm, OF	350	475	600

Longines, open face minute repeater movement

Longines, 46mm, Min. repeater, 24 jewels, 3/4 plate design, open face, Ca. 1915.

TYPE – DESCRIPTION	Avg	Ex-Fn	Mint
World time watch, gold, 48-52mm, OF	$4,000	$5,200	$7,000
8 day watch with wind-indicator, **14K OF**	1,200	1,600	2,200
Chronograph w/register, silver, OF, 48- 50mm, C. 1905	250	300	425
Chronograph, gold, 45-50mm, OF	450	525	735
HC	700	800	1,000
Split second chronograph, gold, 45-52mm, OF	1,000	1,200	1,600
HC	1,200	1,400	1,800
Chronograph, Lugrin's Pat., fly back, silver OF case	375	425	525
1/4 hr. repeater, gold, 46-52mm, OF	1,200	1,400	1,800
HC	1,500	1,700	2,000
HC w/chrono., cal. & moonphase	3,500	4,500	6,000
Minute repeater, gold, 46-52mm, OF	2,000	2,600	3,500
HC	2,500	3,100	4,000
OF w/chrono.	2,500	3,100	4,000
HC w/chrono.	3,000	3,600	4,500
OF w/split chrono.	3,500	4,100	5,000
HC w/split chrono.	4,500	5,200	7,000
HC w/cal. & moon- phase	5,000	6,100	7,500
Perpetual moonphase calendar, gold, OF	6,000	8,200	10,000
Perp. moonphase cal. w/min.repeater & chrono., OF	15,000	19,000	25,000
HC	18,000	22,000	30,000
Clock Watch, gold, 46-52mm, OF	6,000	7,400	10,000
HC	8,000	9,500	12,000

Longines, Chronograph, H.A. Lugrin's Pat. June 13, Oct. **3, 1876, Start, Stop, Fly Back.**

Longines, 8 day with wind-indicator, Ca. 1930.

524

MARKWICK, MARKHAM
LONDON (1725-1825)

They enjoyed selling clocks and watches to the Turkish Market. Watches can be found with his name & that of another maker added, Example: Markwick, Markham "Perigal", or "Recordon". Also watches with the names "Story" Ca.1780, "Borrel" Ca.1813 and "Perigal" Ca.1825 are known.

TYPE – DESCRIPTION	Avg	Ex-Fn	Mint
Pair case, verge, silver plain, 50mm, OF	$300	$385	$535
GOLD	800	1,000	1,300
Pair case, verge, silver w/ **repousee**, 50mm, OF	450	650	1,000
GOLD	1,100	1,400	1,800
Triple cased, verge, silver & **Tortoise shell** outer case,	850	1,100	1,500
Triple cased, verge, Painted enamel on first & second case, for Turkish Market, 18K gold cases, Ca. 1800	7,500	8,500	10,000
Four cases, verge fusee, Silver Gilt and Tortoise, KW/KS, for Turkish Market, 45mm, Ca. 1820	1,500	2,000	2,800
1/4 hr. repeater, SILVER, 54mm, OF	750	900	1,200
GOLD	1,100	1,300	1,600
Pair case, verge, **20K Gold repousee**, 50mm, OF	6,000	7,200	9,000

Markwick, Markham, Triple cased , 18K gold cases, Painted enamel on first & second case, made for Turkish Market, Ca. 1800.

Markwick, London, 20K pair case, both cases hand pierced, 1/4 hour repeating on a bell, 55MM, Ca. 1720

MATHEY – TISSOT
Swiss

Firm founded in June 1886 by Edmond Mathey-Tissot. Makers of complicated and simple watches of good quality.

TYPE – DESCRIPTION	Avg	Ex-Fn	Mint
Early, KW, Time only, Swiss bar, Pre 1870, silver	$100	$135	$200
Time only, gold, 40- 44mm, OF	285	365	450
HC	425	525	600
Time only, gold, 45- 50mm, OF	435	545	650
HC	600	735	875
1/4 hr. repeater, gold, 46-52mm, OF	1,200	1,300	1,600
HC	1,500	1,700	2,000
OF w/chrono., cal. & moonphase	2,200	2,500	3,000
HC w/chrono., cal. & moonphase	2,500	2,900	3,500

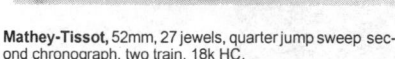

Mathey-Tissot, 52mm, 27 jewels, quarter jump sweep second chronograph, two train, 18k HC.

Mathey-Tissot, min. repeater with chronograph, day date month & moon phases, HC.

TYPE – DESCRIPTION	Avg	Ex-Fn	Mint
Minute repeater, gold, 46-52mm, OF	$1,800	$2,200	$2,800
HC	2,000	2,400	3,000
OF w/chrono. & register	2,000	2,400	3,000
HC w/chrono. & register	2,200	2,700	3,400
HC w/chrono. & moon ph,. day date month,	4,000	4,800	6,500
OF w/split chrono.	4,200	4,600	5,500
HC w/split chrono.	4,700	5,200	6,000
OF w/cal. & moonphase	3,800	4,300	5,000
HC w/cal. & moonphase	4,000	4,800	6,000
World time watch, gold, 48-52mm, OF	4,000	4,800	6,000
Perpetual moonphase calendar, gold, OF	6,000	7,200	9,000
Perp. moonphase cal. w/min. repeater, OF	15,000	19,000	25,000
HC	20,000	24,000	30,000
Perp. moonphase cal. w/min. rep. and chrono., OF	20,000	23,000	28,000
HC	22,000	26,000	32,000
Clock Watch, Gold, 48-52mm, OF	6,000	7,500	10,000
HC	8,000	9,000	12,000

☉ Note: Some models and grades are not included. Their values can be determined by comparing with **similar** age, size, metal content, style, models and grades listed.

☉ A collector should expect to pay modestly higher prices at local shops.

☉ Pricing in this Guide are fair market price for **COMPLETE** watches which are reflected from the "**NAWCC**" National and regional shows.

526

McCabe
London

William McCabe of Ireland was a clock & watch-maker who moved to London. This long lived firm has a good reputation for making watches. The son of William, James McCabe became the owner in about 1822. The business was carried on by nephew, Robert Jeremy till about 1883.

TYPE – DESCRIPTION	Avg	Ex-Fn	Mint
Time only, Verge escapement, KW, Silver, 58mm, OF	$200	$285	$400
HC	225	335	475
Time only, DUPLEX escapement, KW, Silver, 58mm, OF	225	325	500
HC	250	350	550
Time only, DUPLEX escapement, KW, GOLD, 58mm, OF	700	900	1,200
HC	800	1,000	1,400
Enamel, Time only, DUPLEX escap., KW, Silver, 58mm, OF	900	1,100	1,500
HC	1,000	1,300	1,700
Gold &Enamel, Time only, Duplex escap., KW, 55- 58mm, OF	5,000	6,500	9,000
HC	6,000	8,500	12,000
Time only, Lever escapment, gold, 45- 50mm, OF	600	775	1,000
HC	800	950	1,200
1/4 hr. repeater, gold, 46-52mm, OF	1,800	2,100	2,500
HC	2,500	2,800	3,200
Detent Chronometer, gold, 48-52mm, OF	4,000	5,200	7,000
HC	5,000	6,000	7,500

Ja. McCabe, "Royal Exchange London", key-wind with fusee, diamond stone, three arm gold balance, right angle lever, Ca. 1835.

🕐 A collector should expect to pay modestly higher prices at local shops.

🕐 Pricing in this Guide are fair market price for **COMPLETE** watches which are reflected from the "**NAWCC**" National and regional shows.

The Complete Price Guide to Watches goal is to stimulate the orderly exchange of **Watches** between *"buyers"* and *"sellers"*.

MEYLAN WATCH CO. (Swiss)

Meylan Watch Co., founded by C.H. Meylan in 1880, manufactured fine watches, with complications, in Le Brassus, Switzerland.

Right:
C.H. Meylan, movement
21 J., 7 Adj., Ca.1926.
Left:
Minute Repeater

C. H. Meylan, 42mm, 21 jewels, straight line lever escapement, 18K case with enamel on bezel.

C. H. Meylan, Minute Repeater, split second Chronograph, minute register, 18K gold OF case, Ca. 1895

TYPE – DESCRIPTION	Avg	Ex-Fn	Mint
Time only, gold, 40- 44mm, OF	$350	$450	$600
HC	450	575	700
Time only, **platinum**, + diamonds, 40- 44mm, OF	900	1,300	2,000
Time only, gold, 40- 44mm, 18K case & **enamel on bezel**, OF	1,200	1,500	2,000
Time only, gold, 45- 50mm, OF	500	565	725
HC	850	950	1,100
Chronograph, gold, 45-50mm, OF	600	725	950
HC	800	985	1,200
Split second chronograph, gold, 45-52mm, OF	1,000	1,200	1,600
HC	1,500	1,700	2,200
5 minute repeater, gold, 46-52mm, OF	1,700	2,000	2,400
HC	1,900	2,200	2,600
Minute repeater, gold, OF	2,400	2,700	3,200
HC	2,600	2,900	3,500
OF w/chrono.	2,600	2,900	3,500
HC w/chrono.	2,700	3,000	3,500
OF w/split chrono.	3,800	4,500	5,500
HC w/split chrono.	4,000	4,800	6,000
OF w/cal. & moonphase	4,000	4,800	6,000
HC w/cal. & moonphase	5,000	5,500	7,000
HC w/chrono., cal. & moonphase	5,500	6,200	7,500
Tourbillion, gold, 48-55mm, OF	25,000	32,000	40,000
Detent chronometer, gold, 48-52mm, OF	3,000	3,600	5,000
World time watch, gold, 48-52mm, OF	4,000	4,500	5,000
Perpetual moonphase calendar, gold, OF	7,000	8,200	10,000
HC	8,000	9,200	12,000
Perp. moonphase cal. w/min. rep. and chrono., OF	16,000	18,000	22,000
HC	20,000	22,000	25,000
Clock Watch, gold, 48-52mm, OF	6,000	7,500	10,000
HC	8,000	9,500	12,000

MORICAND, CH.
GENEVA

Firm specialized in making verge watches with cases highly decorated with stones and enameled portraits. Associates with brother Benjamin and Francois Colladon from 1752 to 1755, with a firm name of Colladon & Moricand. Later, with Jean Delisle then later in 1780 as Moricand.

Delisle & Moricand, 36MM, 1/4 hour repeater pendant activated, two-footed balance bridge, Ca.1775.

Ch. Moricand, 46mm, gilt and enamel with two ladies in a floral garden, KW KS, Ca.1800.

TYPE – DESCRIPTION	Avg	Ex-Fn	Mint
Verge, KW, paircase, **silver**, 50mm, OF	$250	$375	$500
Verge, enamel w/ portrait, **silver/ gilt**, 49-52mm, OF	900	1,500	2,000
Verge, KW, **gold**, 50-54mm, OF	800	950	1,200
Verge, KW, **gold** w/ enamel, 52mm, OF	1,800	3,000	4,000
1/4 hr. repeater, **silver**, 54mm, OF	600	825	1,200
1/4 hr. repeater, **gold**, 50-54mm, OF	1,000	1,300	2,000
1/4 hr. repeater, **gold** w/ enamel, 54mm, OF	2,500	3,700	5,000

C. MONTANDON
Swiss

This 19th century maker was associated with Perret & Company as well as other Le Locle and Chaux-de-Fonds factories. Montandon specialized in low cost keywind watches for the American market.

TYPE – DESCRIPTION	Avg	Ex-Fn	Mint
KW, cylinder escap., silver, 46mm, OF, C. 1870	$80	$90	$135
KW, silver, 46-48mm, HC, C. 1875	95	110	165
KW, 15J, lady's , **18K**, 40-44mm, OF, C. 1870	150	200	300
HC, C. 1870	200	285	425
KW, 15J, gent's, **18K**, 48mm, OF, C. 1875	275	345	450
Chronograph, gold, 45-50mm, OF	500	675	900
HC	700	800	1,000
1/4 hr. repeater, gold, 46-52mm, OF	800	900	1,200
HC	900	1,100	1,500
Minute repeater, gold, 46-52mm, OF	2,200	2,400	2,800
HC	2,600	2,900	3,400
Minute repeater, w/cal. & moonphase, OF	3,500	3,800	5,000
HC	4,500	5,000	6,000
Minute repeater, **w/chrono.**, cal. & moonphase, HC	5,000	5,300	6,500

MOVADO (Swiss)

L. A. I. Ditesheim & Freres (L.A.I. the initials of the 3 Ditesheim brothers) formed their company in 1881. The name Movado ("always in motion") was adopted in 1905. The Swiss company invented a system of watch making which they called "Polyplan." This was an arrangement of three different angles to the watch movement which produced a curve effect to the case so as to fit the curvature of the arm. Another unusual watch produced by this company in 1926-27 was the "Ermeto." This watch was designed to be protected while inside a purse or pocket and each time the cover was opened to view the time, the watch was partially wound. L., A. & I. Ditesheim (before Movado) used trade names as Ralco, Tanit, Ultra, Apogee, Record, Talma, Noblesse, Salud, Negus, Bonne, Belgravia, Surete and Mintral in about 1895.

Above: Movado, Automatic RACK-WINDING mechanism, a single opening provides winding for about 4 hours.

Top: **Movado,** Purse watch, **Sting Ray** leather, 17 jewels.
Bottom: **Movado,** Purse watch, **silver** case, 17 jewels.

TYPE – DESCRIPTION	Avg	Ex-Fn	Mint
SW, 17J, LS, Silver, 43mm, OF, C. 1920	$125	$150	$200
SW, 15J, LS, Silver, 47mm, HC, C. 1920	150	175	225
Time only, gold, 40-44mm, OF	225	265	350
HC	350	425	550
Time only, gold, 45-50mm, OF	425	525	650
HC	625	725	900
Purse watch, black leather, 50 x 33mm, C. 1930's	200	265	350
Alarm	275	350	500
silver	250	325	450
Sting Ray leather	265	350	475
18K	800	1,100	1,500
leather, **moonph. & calendar**	800	950	1,200
Coin form, 17J, St. Christopher coin, **18K**, closed case, 29mm	600	725	900
Chronograph, gold, 45-50mm, OF	800	950	1,200
Minute repeater, gold, 46-52mm, OF	2,200	2,700	3,200
HC	2,500	3,000	3,600
HC w/split chrono. & register	5,000	5,600	7,000

Movado, Purse watch with moonph. & calendar, auto-wind by opening & closing case, leather.

ULYSSE NARDIN
Swiss

Ulysse Nardin was born in 1823. The company he started in 1846 produced many fine timepieces and chronometers, as well as repeaters and more complicated watches. This firm, as did Assmann, found a strong market in South America as well as other countries. Ulysse's son, Paul David Nardin, succeeded him, as did Paul David's sons after him.

Ulysse Nardin, Key wind, 18 jewels, pivoted detent, bridge movement, 48mm, Ca. 1860.

Ulysse Nardin, pocket chronometer with date, 19J. pivoted detent, gold jewel settings, Ca.1890.

TYPE – DESCRIPTION	Avg	Ex-Fn	Mint
Early KW, 18J., **pivoted detent**, bar style mvt., gold, HC, C.1860	$1,200	$1,500	$2,000
Time only, gold, 40-44mm, OF	300	365	525
HC	450	525	675
Time only, gold, 45- 50mm, OF	600	700	750
HC	750	800	900
Chronograph, gold, 45-50mm, OF	800	1,000	1,300
HC	1,000	1,200	1,500
Deck chronometer **w/box**, detent chronometer, C. 1905	1,400	1,600	2,000
Pocket chronometer, lever escape., 21J., GJS, **18K**, HC, C.1910	900	1,100	1,400
Pocket chronometer, **pivoted detent, with date**, gold, 57mm	4,000	4,700	5,500
World time watch, gold, 48-52mm, OF	4,000	4,400	5,000
Karrusel, 52 Min. karrusel, free sprung balance, silver case	4,000	6,000	8,500

Ulysse Nardin, 53mm, 52 minute karrusel, free sprung balance, ca. 1905.

Ulysse Nardin, pocket chronometer, lever escapement, 21 jewels, gold jewel settings, Ca. 1910

TYPE – DESCRIPTION	Avg	Ex-Fn	Mint
1/4 hr. repeater, gold, 46-52mm, OF	$1,400	$1,700	$2,300
OF w/chrono., cal. moonphase	2,200	2,700	3,400
HC	1,600	2,100	2,700
HC w/chrono., cal. & moonphase	2,600	3,100	3,800
Minute repeater, gold, 46-52mm, OF	2,800	3,300	4,000
HC	3,200	3,700	4,500
OF w/split chrono.	3,800	4,600	5,500
HC w/split chrono.	4,200	4,900	6,000
OF w/cal. & moonphase	7,000	9,200	12,000
HC w/cal. & moonphase	7,500	9,400	12,500
HC w/chrono., cal. & moonphase	8,500	10,500	14,000
Perpetual moonphase calendar, gold, OF	9,000	10,000	12,000
HC	10,000	13,000	14,000
Perp. moonphase cal. w/min . repeater, OF	22,000	27,000	35,000
HC	24,000	31,000	38,000
Perp. moonphase cal. w/min. rep. and chrono. , OF	23,000	29,000	37,000
HC	25,000	32,000	40,000
Clock Watch, gold, 46-52mm, OF	6,000	7,500	10,000
HC	8,000	9,500	12,000

NICOLE, NIELSEN & CO.
14 Soho Square,   London

Adolphe Nicole in 1840 came to London from Switzerland and joined Henry Capt. By 1858 they had moved to **14 Soho Square**, London. In 1876 Emil Nielsen became a partner in the firm. The company was purchased by S. Smith & Sons in 1904. Tourbillons were made by V. Kullberg and Nicole, Nielsen for the England market. Last watches made Ca. 1933-34. In 1910 the wholesale price for a 1st quality Min. repeater with a chronograph was 95 Lb.,a Min. repeater was 55Lb., 1st quality Extra Flat watch was 32 Lb.
(Made ebauche for Dent, Frodsham, and Smith)

Nicole, Nielsen, 50mm, chronograph, 15 jewels, 3/4 plate, gilded movement, Ca. 1890.

Nicole, Nielsen, 64mm, min. repeater, split-second chronograph, tourbillon, free sprung escapement , most were made for **Frodsham.**

TYPE – DESCRIPTION	Avg	Ex-Fn	Mint
Time only, gold, 45- 50mm, OF	$600	$850	$1,200
HC	700	950	1,300
Chronograph, gold, 45-50mm, HC	1,200	1,400	1,800
Minute repeater, gold, 46-52mm, OF	2,700	3,200	4,000
HC	3,000	3,800	5,000
OF w/chrono. & register	3,500	4,400	6,000
HC w/chrono. & register	4,000	4,800	6,500

TYPE – DESCRIPTION	Avg	Ex-Fn	Mint
Minute repeater, **tourbillon**, split-second chronograph,			
free sprung escapement, gold, 64mm, ...	$100,000	$140,000	$200,000
Tourbillon, gold, 48-55mm, OF	50,000	70,000	95,000
Karrusel, gold, 48-55mm, OF..	6,000	7,500	10,000
Perpetual moon phase calendar, gold, OF......................................	12,000	14,500	18,000
HC	14,000	17,000	22,000
Perp. moonphase cal. w/min.rep. and chrono., OF..........................	24,000	29,000	35,000
HC	26,000	33,000	40,000
Clock Watch, gold, 48-55mm, OF	10,000	12,000	15,000
HC	12,000	15,000	20,000

NON–MAGNETIC WATCH CO.
Swiss
(NOT MARKED PAILLARD'S PATENT)

TYPE – DESCRIPTION	Avg	Ex-Fn	Mint
Time only, gold, 45- 50mm, OF...	$275	$335	$425
HC	350	400	525
Chronograph, gold, 45-50mm, OF	500	650	850
HC	600	750	1,100
Split second chronograph, gold, 45-52mm, OF	750	875	1,200
HC	850	975	1,300
1/4 hr. repeater, gold, 46-52mm, OF...	1,100	1,300	1,500
HC	1,300	1,600	2,000
Minute repeater, gold, 46-52mm, OF...	2,200	2,400	2,800
HC	2,400	2,700	3,200
OF w/split chrono.	4,000	4,500	5,500
HC w/split chrono.	4,500	5,200	6,000
HC w/chrono., cal. & moonphase	5,000	5,700	6,500

Non–magnetic W.Co., min. repeater, jeweled through the hammers, 50mm.

Omega pocket watch movement, 45-48mm, 15 jewels, serial number 9,888,934.

🕐 Watches listed in this book are priced at the collectable fair market **value** at the Trade Show level, as complete watches having an original case, an original white enamel dial, and with the entire original movement in good working order with no repairs needed, unless otherwise noted.

The Complete Price Guide to Watches goal is to stimulate the orderly exchange of **Watches** between *"buyers"* and *"sellers"*.

OMEGA WATCH CO.
Swiss

Omega Watch Co. was founded by Louis Brandt in 1848. They produced watches of different grades. In 1930, they began to produce different lines with Tissot under the name Societe Sussie pour l'Industrie Horlogere. Omega is now part of the SMH (Societe Suisse de Microelectronique et d' Horlogerie).

PRODUCTION TOTALS

DATE-SERIAL #	DATE-SERIAL #	DATE-SERIAL #	DATE-SERIAL #
1895 –1,000,000	1935 - 8,000,000	1956-15,000,000	1965-22,000,000
1902 - 2,000,000	1939- 9,000,000	1958-16,000,000	1966-23,000,000
1908 - 3,000,000	1944-10,000,000	1960-17,000,000	1967-25,000,000
1912 - 4,000,000	1947-11,000,000	1961-18,000,000	1968-26,000,000
1916 - 5,000,000	1950-12,000,000	1962-19,000,000	1969-28,000,000
1923 - 6,000,000	1952-13,500,000	1963-20,000,000	1970-29,000,000
1929 - 7,000,000	1954-14,000,000	1964-21,000,000	

The above list is provided for determining the APPROXIMATE age of your watch. Match serial number with date. Watches were not necessarily sold in the exact order of manufactured date.

Note: By 1980 ETA Calibers were being used by Omega.

TYPE – DESCRIPTION	Avg	Ex-Fn	Mint
15J, SW, gilt, silver, 48mm, OF, C.1900	$80	$95	$150
15J, SW, gilt, silver, 48mm, HC, C.1900	100	135	200
Time only, gold, 45- 48mm, OF	400	485	625
HC	500	585	735
Chronograph, gold, 45-50mm, OF	700	900	1,200
HC	800	1,000	1,300
Pulsation (Doctor Watch), gold HC	900	1,100	1,500
Chronograph, gold, 45-50mm, **Double-Dial**, OF	2,200	3,000	4,000
Minute repeater, gold, 46-52mm, OF	2,000	2,500	3,200
HC	2,200	2,800	3,500
OF w/split chrono.	4,000	4,600	6,000
HC w/split chrono.	4,200	4,800	6,500
HC w/chrono., cal. & moonphase	5,000	6,200	8,000

Omega, Chronograph, gold, 45-50mm, **Double-Dial**, open face, Multi-color enamel dials.

In 1894 the creation of the Omega "19" caliber, remarkable for the perfection of its construction, the ingenuity of certain mechanisms (time-setting) and its modest price, owing to new manufacturing methods. The 19 caliber resulted from the **FIRST** introduction in Switzerland of the ***DIVIDED ASSEMBLY SYSTEM*** based on the interchange-ability of standard parts, a system which would be adopted progressively by the entire Swiss watch industry. This was also the year when Omega chronometers began receiving official rating certificates from the Neuchatel, Geneva and Kew/Teddington (London) observatories. That year the owners of the company registered the word **Omega** as the new trademark.

The source of information from the book OMEGA The History of a Great Brand.

Omega 19 Grade DDR, 23 jewels with 2 diamond end stones, jeweled barrel arbor, **18** screwed gold jewel settings, a swan-neck regulator with graduated snail. Signed ***Ls Brandt & frere SA***, grade DDR, 23 jewels, Adjusted to 5 positions and movement serial number is 2584692.

TYPE – DESCRIPTION	Avg	Ex-Fn	Mint
23J, grade **DDR** = RR grade, **18** GJS, 2 diamond end stones, **GF** OF ★	$500	$750	$1,200
19J, grade **DR** = RR grade, **15** GJS, **GF** OF	325	475	700
23J, grade **CCCR** = RR grade, **15** GJS, **GF** OF	350	450	800
19J, grade **CCR** = RR grade, **10** GJS, **GF** OF	300	425	625

Omega 19 Grade CCCR, 16-18 size, 23 jewels, signed Omega Watch Co. Swiss, 15 gold settings, S# 3,658,546.

16 size Movement

Omega 19 caliber, basic MOVEMENT open face 16 size, & 20 caliber = 18 size. (used for official chronometers)

CHARLES OUDIN
PARIS

Oudin was a pupil of Breguet and became a talented maker from 1807-1830. He produced quality timepieces and invented an early "keyless" watch. He signed some of his Watches "Eleve de Breguet" = Student of Breguet.

Charles Oudin, Dial & Movement, 51mm, 32J., Minute repeater with Chronograph, Ca.1910.

TYPE – DESCRIPTION	Avg	Ex-Fn	Mint
Verge, KW, silver single case, 45mm, OF, C. 1865	$300	$365	$500
Early, KW, Time only, Swiss bar, silver , OF	75	85	125
GOLD, OF	300	425	625
Split sec. chrono., 29J, w/ register,**18K**, 51mm, HC, C. 1900	800	1,000	1,300
Minute repeater, gold, 46-52mm, OF	2,000	2,400	3,000
HC	2,200	2,700	3,500
OF w/chrono. & register	2,200	2,700	3,500
HC w/chrono. & register	3,000	3,400	4,000

"CHs. OUDIN, Paris," engraved on movement, Key Wind, cylinder escapement, Swiss bar, Ca. 1865.

PATEK, PHILIPPE & CIE.
Swiss

Patek, Philippe & Cie. has produced some of the world's most desirable factory-made watches. Antoine Norbert de Patek began contracting and selling watches in the late 1830's, later became partners with Francois Czapek and generally produced lovely decorative watches for a high class of clientele. In 1845 Adrien Philippe, inventor of the modern stem-winding system, joined the firm of Patek & Cie., and in 1851, the firm established its present name. Between Philippe's talent as a watchmaker and Patek's talent as a businessman with a taste for the impeccable, the firm rapidly established an international reputation which lasts to this day. Early Patek, Philippe & Cie. watches are generally signed only on the dust cover, but some are signed on the dial and cuvette. It was not until the 1880's that the practice began of fully signing the dial, movement and case-perhaps in response to some contemporary forgery but more likely a necessity to conform to customs' regulations for their growing international market. Many early and totally original Patek watches have suffered from the misconception that all products of the company are fully signed. Never the less, collectors find such pieces more desirable. It requires more experience, however, to determine the originality of the earlier pieces. As with many Swiss watches they were originally cased in U.S.A., but this may lower their value.

PRODUCTION TOTALS

DATE— SERIAL #	DATE— SERIAL #	DATE— SERIAL #	EARLIER KEY WIND
1840— 100	1950—700,000	1940— 900,100	NOTE: Watches signed *PATEK & CIE.* usually
1845— 1,200	1955—725,000	1945— 915,200	have serial numbers from about 1,129 to 3,729,
1850— 3,000	1960—750,000	1950— 930,300	Ca. 1845 to 1850. Usually signed on cuvette with
1855— 8,000	1965—775,000	1955— 940,400	serial number & Patek & Cie., and not on the
1860— 15,000	1970—795,000	1960— 960,500	movement. *"Patek et Czapek"* found signed on
1865— 22,000		1965— 975,600	cuvette for earlier <u>KEY WIND</u> watches.
1870— 35,000	DATE— SERIAL #	1970— 995,700	
1875— 45,000	1920— 801,000		
1880— 55,000	1925— 802,000	DATE— SERIAL #	Important note: From about 1880 forward all
1885— 70,000	1930— 823,000	1960—1,100,800	watches were signed on dial, case & movement .
1890— 85,000	1935— 824,000	1965—1,130,900	
1895—100,000	1940— 835,000	1970—1,250,000	
1900—110,000	1945— 856,000	1975—1,350,000	1854 Tiffany & Co. became a official customer of
1905—125,000	1950— 867,000	1980—1,450,000	the Patek firm.
1910—150,000	1955— 878,000	1985—1,600,000	
1915—175,000	1960— 889,000	1990—1,850,000	
1920—190,000	1965— 890,000		Patented their **Stem Wind** system in
1925—200,200	1970— 895,000		**1861**.

The above list is provided for determining the APPROXIMATE age of your watch. Match serial number with date. Watches were not necessarily sold in the exact order of manufactured date.

Patek, Philippe & Cie., 15-17J., KWKS, gilt movement, lever escapement ("moustache lever"), **signed on 18K cuvette**, 47mm, Ca. 1865-69.

Patek, Philippe & Co., signed on 18K cuvette, early Stem Wind, **moustache lever**, wolf tooth winding, 18J. gilt movement, S# 45,483, 49mm, Ca. 1875.

Patek, Philippe & Cie., 18 jewels, engraved gold dial with enamel center, 18K, 43mm, Ca. 1920's.

Patek, Philippe & Cie. 43mm, time only, 18K, open face.

Patek, Philippe & Co., Perpetual calendar, moonphase, min. repeater & split second chronograph, 18K, OF.

P.P.& Co. signed **"Chronometro Gondolo"**, 24 hr. dial, 19-20J, moustache lever , gold train, 55mm, Ca. 1908.

Patek, Philippe & Co., dial & movement, min. repeater, 29J, perpetual calendar, day, date, month, moon-phases, 18K.

TYPE – DESCRIPTION	Avg	Ex-Fn	Mint
EARLY Time only, KWKS, gilt mvt., lever or cylinder escapement			
pre 1865, signed on gold case, 40-45mm, ...	$1,200	$1,500	$2,000
EARLY Time only, 18J., SW, gilt mvt., moustache lever, Ca. 1870-75			
wolf tooth winding, signed on gold case, 45-52mm, ...	1,500	1,900	2,500
Time only, gold, 25- 30mm, ladies, OF	700	850	1,100
HC	1,000	1,300	1,800
Time only, gold, 32- 44mm, OF...	1,800	2,100	2,500
HC	2,500	2,900	3,500
Time only, **Platinum**, 32- 44mm, OF..	2,500	3,200	4,000
Time only, **enameled bezel**, gold, 32- 44mm, OF	2,700	3,200	4,000
Time only, gold, 45- 55mm, OF...	2,500	2,900	3,500
HC	3,000	3,400	4,000
Time only, with **Wind Indicator**, gold, 45- 50mm, OF	4,000	5,200	7,000
Military, Silver deck Watch with Wind Indicator...........................	6,500	8,200	12,000
Time only, Chronometro **Gondolo**, gold, 38mm, OF	2,000	2,800	4,000
Time only, Chronometro **Gondolo**, gold, 50-55mm, OF	2,500	3,400	5,000
Time only, Chronometro **Gondolo**, gold, **24** Hr. dial, 52mm, OF ★	2,900	3,800	5,500

Patek, Philippe & Co., enameled bezel, 18K OF, 42mm

Patek, Philippe & Co., perpetual calendar & moon phases, signed, 18 jewels, 49mm, Ca. 1949

TYPE – DESCRIPTION	Avg	Ex-Fn	Mint
Chronograph, gold, 45-50mm, OF	$3,200	$3,500	$4,500
HC	4,000	4,400	5,000
OF w/register	3,600	4,200	5,500
HC w/register..	4,200	5,000	6,000
Split second chronograph, gold, 45-52mm, OF	5,200	6,200	8,000
HC	6,000	7,000	10,000
OF w/register	6,000	7,500	10,000
HC w/register..	7,500	10,000	15,000
1/4 hr. repeater, **Niello** Silver & Gold case, 45-50mm, OF.............	4,500	6,200	8,500
1/4 hr. repeater, gold, 46-52mm, OF..★	4,500	6,000	8,000
HC ....★	6,000	7,500	10,000
5 minute repeater, gold, 46-52mm, OF	3,500	4,800	7,000
HC	4,000	5,500	8,000
OF w/split chrono.	8,000	9,500	12,000
HC w/split chrono..	9,000	11,000	15,000
Minute repeater, gold, 46-52mm, OF..	6,000	8,000	11,000
HC	10,000	13,000	18,000
OF w/chrono.	10,000	12,000	16,000
HC w/chrono.	12,000	16,000	22,000
OF w/chrono. & register...	11,000	14,000	19,000
HC w/chrono. & register	14,000	18,000	24,000
Minute repeater, **2 train**, self contained, 18K, OF	18,000	25,000	35,000

TYPE – DESCRIPTION	Avg	Ex-Fn	Mint
Minute repeater, w/split chrono., gold, 46-52mm, OF	$15,000	$19,000	$25,000
HC w/split chrono.	16,000	22,000	30,000
OF w/split chrono. & register	16,000	24,000	30,000
HC w/split chrono. & register	20,000	27,000	35,000
Perpetual moonphase calendar, gold, OF	25,000	30,000	35,000
HC	27,000	32,000	40,000
Perp. moonphase cal. w/min. repeater, OF	40,000	55,000	75,000
HC	50,000	60,000	80,000
Perpetual moonphase cal. w/ min. rep. & chrono. , OF	50,000	80,000	120,000
HC	65,000	85,000	125,000
Perpetual moonphase cal. w/ min. rep. & split sec. chrono. , OF	75,000	125,000	175,000
HC	95,000	150,000	200,000
Clock Watch, gold, 48-52mm, OF	25,000	30,000	40,000
HC	28,000	35,000	50,000

Patek, Philippe & Co., Digital Jump Hour, with minute hand & second hand, 18 jewels, 45mm, 18K.

Patek, Philippe & Co., gold coin watch, 100 pesetas, secret push-piece opens lid to disclose dial, 35mm, Ca.1928.

TYPE – DESCRIPTION	Avg	Ex-Fn	Mint
Lady's pendant watch w/ brooch,18K & small diamonds, 27mm	$2,400	$3,200	$5,500
Gold Coin, 100 pesetas 18K, 18J., coin opens to disclose dial	4,000	4,900	6,000
Digital Jump Hour, W/minute hand & sec. hand, 45mm, 18K	30,000	38,000	50,000
Karrusel, gold, 48-55mm, OF	85,000	95,000	100,000
Tourbillon, gold, 48-55mm, OF ★★★★	125,000	200,000	250,000
HC ★★★★	185,000	250,000	300,000
Detent chronometer, gold, 48-52mm, OF	25,000	30,000	40,000
HC	30,000	36,000	50,000
World time watch, gold, 48-52mm, OF	25,000	30,000	40,000
World time watch, Cloisonne map of America, pink gold case	95,000	150,000	200,000

World time watch, gold, 48-52mm, OF

PICARD, JAMES
GENEVA

Watch dealer and finisher in the latter part of the 19th Century. Known for his complicated watches and pocket chronometers of high quality.

TYPE – DESCRIPTION	Avg	Ex-Fn	Mint
Time only, gold, 45- 50mm, OF	$450	$565	$725
HC	600	725	875
Chronograph, gold, 45-50mm, OF	750	875	1,100
Split sec. chronograph, 27J., independent jumping 1/5 seconds,			
Tandem wind, 2 gear train, 56mm, 18K , OF	2,200	2,800	3,500
Split second chronograph, gold, 45-52mm, OF	1,500	1,700	2,000
HC w/register	2,200	2,500	3,000
5 minute repeater, gold, 45-52mm, OF	3,000	3,400	4,000
HC	3,500	3,800	4,500
Minute repeater, gold, 45-52mm, OF	3,500	3,800	4,500
HC	3,700	4,100	4,700
OF w/split chrono.	4,800	5,300	6,000
HC w/split chrono.	7,000	7,500	8,200
OF w/cal. & moonphase	9,000	9,600	11,000
HC w/chrono., cal. & moonphase	10,000	11,000	13,000
Tourbillon, gold, 48-55mm, OF	30,000	36,000	45,000
Detent chronometer, gold, 48-52mm , OF	4,000	4,600	6,000
HC	5,000	5,600	7,000
Perp. moonphase cal. w/min.rep. and chrono, OF	20,000	26,000	35,000
HC	25,000	32,000	45,000
Clock Watch, gold, 48-52mm, OF	6,000	7,500	10,000
HC	8,000	9,500	12,000

James Picard, 27J, Split sec. chronograph, independent jumping 1/5 seconds, 2 gear train, 56mm, **Tandem wind,** Ca. 1885.

🕐 A collector should expect to pay modestly higher prices at local shops.

The Complete Price Guide to Watches goal is to stimulate the orderly exchange of **Watches** between *"buyers"* and *"sellers"*.

ALBERT H. POTTER & CO.

(Note: For further information on Potter timepieces, see U.S. Watch Section.)

Albert Potter was born in Saratoga county, New York. He started his apprenticeship in 1852 with Wood & Foley Albany (N.Y.). When this was completed he moved to New York to take up watchmaking on his own. He made about 35 watches in USA that sold for $225 to $350. Some were chronometers, some were lever escapements, key wind, gilded and movements, some were fusee driven, both bridge and 3/4 plate. Potter was a contemporary of Charles Fasoldt and John Mulford, both horological inventors from Albany, N. Y. Potter moved to Cuba in 1861 but returned to New York in 1868. In 1872 he worked in Chicago and formed the Potter Brothers Company with his brother William. He moved to Geneva about 1876. His Geneva ultra high grade ebauches timepieces may have been made by the maker Charles Ami LeCoultre of Le Sentier, Le Brassus area. In 1896 the firm failed with about 600 watches being made.

TYPE – DESCRIPTION	Avg	Ex-Fn	Mint
Time only, gold, 45- 48mm, OF	$4,000	$5,200	$7,000
HC	4,500	5,800	7,500
Pocket chronometer, pivoted detent ,free-spring balance, porcelain dial, bridge mvt., 58mm, **18K** case, C.1875	12,000	15,000	20,000
Calendar, nickel, offset seconds and days of week dials, SW, **18K**, 50mm, OF, C.1800	8,000	9,500	12,000
Regulator dial (center minute hand, offset hours, offset seconds), half moon- shaped nickel mvt., **18K**, 50mm, OF, C.1880	10,000	13,000	20,000
Minute repeater, gold, 46-52mm, OF	15,000	18,000	22,000
HC	20,000	22,000	26,000
Detent chronometer, gold, 48-52mm, OF	15,000	20,000	28,000
HC	18,000	22,000	30,000
Perp. moonphase cal. w/min. repeater, HC	30,000	38,000	50,000
Perp. moonphase cal. w/min. rep. & chrono.,HC	32,000	40,000	55,000
4 SIZE, 21J., hour repeater, **original 18K** HC ★★	4,000	5,200	7,000

Below trade mark found on some cases.

Albert Potter, 22 jewels, hunting case, helical hair spring, Free sprung, detent escapement. Note: The style bridge used for his pocket Chronometer, 58mm, Ca. 1880.

Albert Potter, 21 jewels, Note kidney-form bridge, Serial # 22, Ca. 1880. Note: A. H. Potter used a unique patented style of stem-wind & stem-set for his Geneva watches.

PRIOR, GEORGE & EDWARD PRIOR
LONDON

George Prior born in 1793 and died in 1830. He was a recipient of two prestigious awards and well known for his pieces for the turkish market. He also produced tortoise shell and triple-case watches with the outer case featuring wood with silver inlay. He made gold watches with Oriental chased cases, watches with pierced outer cases and triple-cased enamel engraved and repeaters.

Edward Prior born in 1800 and died in 1868.

TYPE – DESCRIPTION	Avg	Ex-Fn	Mint
Verge, pair case, plain silver, 50mm, OF	$450	$500	$625
Verge, pair case w/ repousee, silver, 50mm, OF	1,000	1,200	1,500
Verge, **Triple** case w/Shagreen outer case, Gilded case, 57mm	1,200	1,400	1,800
Verge, **Triple** case w/ **tortoise shell**, silver, 56mm, OF	1,500	1,800	2,200
Verge, **Quadruple** cases w/ **tortoise shell**, silver, 56mm, OF	2,000	2,400	3,000
Verge, pair case, GOLD, 48-52mm, OF	2,000	2,300	2,800
Verge, pair case, GOLD & enamel, 48-54mm, OF	2,800	3,100	3,500
1/4 hr. repeater, pair case, GOLD & enamel, 50mm, OF	6,000	6,700	7,500

Left: **Edward Prior**, 57mm, Triple Shagreen case, white enamel signed dial, verge with fusee, KW KS, Ca. 1820.

Right: **George Prior, Quadruple** case with third case made of **tortoise** shell, fourth outer case of embossed silver, the first two cases made of silver, verge escapement, note the stag beetle hour hand and poker minute hand, Ca. 1810.

ROLEX WATCH CO.
Swiss

Rolex was founded by Hans Wilsdorf in 1905 & in <u>1908</u> the trade-mark **"Rolex"** was officially registered. In 1926, they made the first real waterproof wrist watch and called it the **"Oyster."** In 1931, Rolex introduced a self-wind movement which they called **"Perpetual"**. In 1945, they introduced the **"Date-Just"** which showed the day of the month. The **"Submariner"** was introduced in 1953 and in 1954 the **"GMT Master"** model. In 1956, a "Day-Date" model was released which indicates the day of the month (in numbers) and the day of the week (in letters.)

Rolex, SPORTING PRINCE, 17 jewels, Adjusted to six positions, silver & leather case.

Rolex, 42-43mm, 17 jewels, three adjustments, cam regulator, exposed winding gears.

IMPORTANT:
The following is a *guide* to help determine the age of your Rolex watches. However on **some** Oyster style watches Rolex added **inside** the case a Roman number (I,II,III,IV) to denote first, second, third, or fourth quarter + "53", "54", "55", "56" to denote the year of production. Example outside Oyster case # 955454 inside case IV-53 which = last quarter of 1953. Example outside Oyster case # 282621 inside case III-55 which = third quarter of 1955. Rolex went back to 100,000 in 1954 on some cases.

ROLEX ESTIMATED PRODUCTION DATES

DATE–SERIAL #	DATE–SERIAL #	DATE–SERIAL #	DATE–SERIAL #	DATE–SERIAL #	DATE–SERIAL #	DATE–SERIAL #
1925 - 25,000	1937- 99,000	1949 - 608,000	1961-1,480,000	1973-3,741,000	1985 — 8,815,000	1992 1/4-C000,001
1926 - 28,500	1938-118,000	1950 - 673,500	1962-1,557,000	1974-4,002,000	1986 — 9,292,000	1993 3/4-S000,001
1927 - 30,500	1939-136,000	1951 - 738,500	1963-1,635,000	1975-4,266,000	1987 — 9,765,000	1995 — W000,001
1928 - 33,000	1940-165,000	1952 - 804,000	1964-1,713,000	1976-4,538,000	1987 1/2-R999,999	1996 — T000,001
1929 - 35,500	1941-194,000	1953 - 950,000	1965-1,792,000	1977-5,005,000	1987 3/4-R000,001	1997 3/4-U000,001
1930 - 38,000	1942-224,000	1954 - 999,999	1966-1,870,000	1978-5,481,000	1988 — R999,999	1999 — A000,001
1931 - 40,000	1943-253,000	1955 - 200,000	1967-2,164,000	1979-5,965,000	1989 — L000,001	2000 — P000,001
1932 - 43,000	1944-285,000	1956 - 400,000	1968-2,426,000	1980-6,432,000	1990 — L999,999	2001 — K000,001
1933 - 47,000	1945-348,000	1957 - 600,000	1969-2,689,000	1981-6,910,000	1990 1/2-E000,001	2002 — Y000,001
1934 - 55,000	1946-413,000	1958 - 800,000	1970-2,952,000	1982-7,385,000	1991 1/2-E999,999	
1935 - 68,000	1947-478,000	1959-1,100,000	1971-3,215,000	1983-7,860,000	1991 1/2-X000,001	
1936 - 81,000	1948-543,000	1960-1,401,000	1972-3,478,000	1984-8,338,000	1991 3/4-N000,001	

The above list is provided for determining the APPROXIMATE age of your watch. Match serial number with date. Watches were not necessarily sold in the exact order of manufactured date.The above list was furnished with the help of TOM ENGLE.

Hans Wilsdorf started in 1905 with his brother-in-law using the name of Wilsdorf & Davis. They used movement supplier **Aegler** in Bienne and bought cases in London. In 1919 Wilsdorf started the "Manufacture des Montres Rolex", the movements were manufactured in Bienne but finished in Geneva. 1950 the **Turn-o-graph** was used, the forerunner of the **SUBMARINER.**

ROLEX, split seconds Chronograph, register, S.S. case.   ROLEX, Masonic watch, mother of pearl dial, 15J.

TYPE – DESCRIPTION	Avg	Ex-Fn	Mint
17J, silver, 45mm, OF, C. 1920's	$400	$550	$800
17J, 3 adj., CAM regulator, **14K**, 43mm, OF, C. 1920	600	850	1,200
1/4 Century Club, 17J, **14K**, 41mm, OF, C. 1940	700	850	1,200
Thin line, 17J, **18K**, 42mm, OF, C. 1940	700	850	1,200
Time only, gold, 40-44mm, **18K**, OF	700	850	1,200
HC	800	1,000	1,500
Time only, gold, 45-50mm, **18K**, OF	1,000	1,300	1,800
HC	1,200	1,500	2,000
Rolex, **SPORTING PRINCE**, 17J, Adj. 6P ★★	3,000	3,600	4,500
Duo dial, fancy-shaped, 17J, **18K/WG**, OF, 41mm, C. 1930	2,000	2,600	3,500
$20 dollar coin watch in closed case, triple signed, C.1950	2,500	3,100	4,000
World time watch, gold, 45-52mm	9,000	10,000	12,000
Chronograph, split seconds, register, S.S. case, 50mm	3,000	4,200	6,000
Masonic, mother of pearl dial, silver case, Ca.1930s ★★★	4,000	4,700	6,000

Romilly, Gold , verge, pair case with polychrome enamel & scene, 52mm, OF, Ca.1730.

ROMILLY, JEAN
PARIS

Became a master Watchmaker in 1752 after studying in Geneva and Paris. In 1755, he completed a repeater with beating seconds and a large balance (at one oscillation per second). He also made watches with a 8 day power reserve. Also known for his very ornate paintings on enamel.

TYPE – DESCRIPTION	Avg	Ex-Fn	Mint
Time only, KW, verge, silver, 46-52mm OF	$700	$900	$1,200
Time & Calendar, verge, silver, 50mm, OF	1,500	1,600	1,800
Gold , verge, pair case, plain, 48mm, OF	2,000	2,100	2,300
Gold , verge, pair case w/ enamel & scene, Ca.1730, 52mm, OF	4,000	4,300	4,800
1/4 repeater, **SILVER**, 52mm, OF	2,500	2,900	3,500
1/4 repeater, **GOLD**, 54mm, OF	3,500	3,900	4,500

ROBERT ROSKELL
Liverpool

Roskell was active from 1798-1830 and worked in both Liverpool and London. He made fine rack lever fusees and gold dial watches. Other family members also produced watches for many years in Liverpool.

R. Roskell, 47mm, bar style movement, cylinder escapement, Ca. 1850. (Swiss ebauche)

Roskell, Monochrome Scene, Hour & Min. Hand removed to show scene, KW KS, Ca. 1810-20.

TYPE – DESCRIPTION	Avg	Ex-Fn	Mint
KW, (Swiss ebauche) 15J, silver, 48mm, OF, C. 1830-70	$75	$85	$125
KW, (Swiss) 15J, silver, 46-48mm, HC, C. 1830-70	100	110	150
KW, 13J, dust cover, fancy gold dial, **18K,** 47mm, OF, C.1830-70	275	365	500
KW, Tortoise shell case	525	700	950

Roskell, 48mm, lever escapement, KW KS, Ca.1830.   Roskell, 55mm, Rack & pinion lever fusee, KW KS, Ca. 1825

TYPE – DESCRIPTION	Avg	Ex-Fn	Mint
Rack & pinion lever fusee, porcelain dial, **silver**, about 1800-25, OF	$350	$425	$600
Rack & pinion lever fusee, gold dial, **Gold**, about 1800-25, OF	500	650	900
2 day marine chronometer fusee, spring detent escapement, helical hairspring, 54 hr. wind ind., gimbal & box	1,800	2,000	2,500
Debaufre escapement, KW KS, silver, 55mm, OF .... ★★	3,000	3,400	4,000

Debaufre escapement,
D-shaped & inclined pallet.

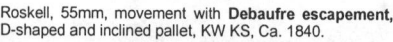

Roskell, 55mm, movement with **Debaufre escapement**, D-shaped and inclined pallet, KW KS, Ca. 1840.

Robert Roskell, 52mm, London, fusee, spring detent escapement, helical hairspring, 54 hr. wind ind., KW KS.

ROSKOPF (Swiss)

Maker of pin lever, early low cost stem wind watches, often found with fancy dials. A **true** Roskopf watch has only *3 wheels* in its train of gears.

Roskopf, multi-colored blue enamel dial, nail set.

Roskopf, 45mm, pin lever escapement, 3 wheel train.

TYPE – DESCRIPTION	Avg	Ex-Fn	Mint
4J, pin lever, **3 wheel train**, nail set, base metal, OF, Ca. 1885	$65	$75	$125
Fancy dial, oversize plain case, 55mm, OF, Ca. 1880	75	95	135
Fancy enamel dial, **fancy enamel case**, 55mm, OF, Ca. 1880	125	150	265

< Adjusting Screw
Depthing of
Pallets

Above: Pin Pallet Lever escapement note the <u>Lever</u> can be adjusted for **depth.**

Right: Roskopf, multi-colored enamel with blue & purple Butterflies & silver case, nail set.

THOMAS RUSSELL & SONS
London

Thomas Russell & Sons produced quality early keyless watches including Karrusels and chronometers. (Circa 1870-1910)

TYPE – DESCRIPTION	Avg	Ex-Fn	Mint
Time only, gold, 45-48mm, OF	$600	$750	$950
Chronograph, gold, 45-50mm, OF	1,200	1,350	1,600
Split second chronograph, gold, 45-52mm, OF	1,800	2,000	2,500
Minute repeater, gold, 46-52mm, OF	2,500	3,200	4,000
HC	3,000	3,600	4,500
Karrusel, 18K, 51mm, OF, C. 1890	4,000	4,400	5,000

Signed *Thomas Russell & Sons Liverpool,* KW KS, lever with a club foot escape wheel, Ca. 1905.   Sandoz, 52mm, KW, nickel bridge, gold train, Ca.1880.

SANDOZ & FILS
SWISS

Large family of watchmakers in the La Chaux-de-Fonds area. Known for repeating watches and pocket chronometers of fine quality.

TYPE – DESCRIPTION	Avg	Ex-Fn	Mint
Time only, gold, 40- 44mm, OF	$325	$385	$475
HC	400	445	525
Time only, gold, 45- 50mm, OF	500	545	635
HC	600	650	850
Chronograph, gold, 45-50mm, OF	700	765	850
Split second chronograph, gold, 45-52mm, OF	1,600	1,700	2,000
HC w/register	2,250	2,450	2,750
5 minute repeater, gold, 45-52mm, OF	2,000	2,400	3,000
HC	2,200	3,000	4,000
Minute repeater, gold, 45-52mm, OF	2,000	2,700	3,500
HC	2,500	3,200	4,500
OF w/split chrono.	4,000	4,800	6,000
HC w/split chrono.	6,000	7,000	8,500
OF w/cal. & moonphase	7,000	8,200	10,000
HC w/chrono., cal. & moonphase	8,000	9,500	12,000
Tourbillion, gold, 48-55mm, OF	20,000	25,000	35,000
Detent chronometer, gold, 48-52mm , OF	4,000	4,600	6,000
HC	5,000	5,600	6,500
World time watch, gold, 48-52mm, OF	5,000	6,200	8,000
Perp. moonphase cal. w/min.rep. and chrono, OF	20,000	24,000	30,000
HC	24,000	27,000	32,000

TAVANNES
Swiss

Created watches in 1895, other names used Dvina, La Tavannes, Obi, Lena Azow, and Kawa.

TYPE – DESCRIPTION	Avg	Ex-Fn	Mint
15J, GF, 35mm, HC, C. 1910	$85	$95	$135
15J, **14K**, 35mm, HC, C. 1910	200	235	285
17J, **14K**, 45mm, OF, C. 1915	225	265	325
21J, **14K**, 45mm, OF, C. 1920	250	285	350
Enamel Bezel & gold, **14K**, 40mm, OF	400	500	675
Enamel **Scene** & gold, **18K**, 45mm, OF, C. 1925	4,000	5,500	7,000

Non-Magnet Watch Co. occupied the old Tiffany plant in 1889.

TAVANNES, Enamel Scene, 45mm, 18K, OF, C. 1925.   Tiffany & Co. 21J., HC, manufactured by Tiffany, Ca. 1875.

TIFFANY & CO.

In 1837 Charles Lewis Tiffany opened a store with John P. Young. They enlarged this operation in 1841, with the help of J.L. Ellis, and imported fine jewelry, watches and clocks from Europe. They incorporated as Tiffany & Co. in 1853. Tiffany made clocks, on special order, in New York around the mid-1800's. In 1874 Tiffany & Co. started a **watch** factory in Geneva, which lasted about 4 years (low production). Patek, Philippe & Co. assumed the management of their Geneva watch business. The watch machinery was returned to America. Tiffany, Young & Ellis had been a client of Patek, Philippe & Co. since 1849. Tiffany & Co. introduced Patek, Philippe to the American market in 1885. Audemars, Piguet and International Watch Co. also made watches for this esteemed company. Tiffany & Co. sells watches of simple elegance as well as watches with complications such as chronographs, moon phases, repeaters, etc.

Engraved on cuvette **"Tiffany, Young & Ellis,** by Jules Jurgensen, fully jeweled, S # 5526, Ca. 1850s.

Tiffany & Co. 21J., **manufactured** by Tiffany, open face, note: the lever has a screw at pallet, S # 13,596.

Tiffany & Co.,21J., manufactured by Tiffany, HC, S# 1516, some models engraved on balance cock **Wilmot** patent.

TYPE – DESCRIPTION	Avg	Ex-Fn	Mint
Tiffany, Young & Ellis, KW KS, gold, 48MM, OF	$1,500	$1,700	$2,000
Tiffany 21J., **manufactured** by Tiffany, gold, 50-55MM, OF....★	400	535	700
Tiffany 21J., **manufactured** by Tiffany, gold, 50-55MM, HC ....★	500	650	900
Time only, gold, 40- 44mm, OF	300	385	525
HC	450	525	735
Time only, gold, 40-44mm, (P.P.Co.), **18K, enamel on bezel**, OF.	1,000	1,400	2,000
Time only, gold, 45- 55mm, OF	600	765	975
HC	700	900	1,200
Chronograph, gold, 45-50mm, OF	1,000	1,300	1,800
HC	1,500	1,800	2,200
OF w/register	1,200	1,600	2,200
Split second chronograph, gold, 45-52mm, OF	2,400	2,800	3,400
HC	2,800	3,400	5,000
5 minute repeater, gold, 46-52mm, OF	2,500	3,200	4,500
HC	3,000	3,500	5,000
OF w/split chrono.	4,000	5,000	7,000
HC w/split chrono.	5,000	6,000	7,500
Minute repeater, gold, 46-52mm, OF	2,500	3,100	4,000
HC	3,500	5,000	7,000
by **P. P. & Co.**, flat, 29J., gold, 45mm, OF, C.1912	8,000	9,500	12,000
OF w/split chrono. & register	6,000	7,500	10,000
HC w/split chrono. & register	7,000	9,500	12,000
HC w/chrono., cal. & moonphase	9,000	12,000	16,000
World time watch, gold, 48-52mm, OF	10,000	12,500	16,000
8 day watch with wind indicator, enamel dial, gold OF	995	1,100	1,300
Moonphase, full calendar, gold, OF	3,500	4,000	5,500
Perpetual moonphase calendar, gold, OF	8,000	9,500	12,000
Perp. moonphase cal. w/**min. rep**. and chrono, OF	30,000	38,000	50,000
HC	35,000	48,000	60,000

Tiffany & Co., 50mm, 25J., split-second chronograph. Tiffany & Co., flat min. repeater, 29J., signed P.P & Co., ca. 1911.

TIMING & REPEATING WATCH CO.
Geneva

Timing & Repeating W. Co. watches were based on American Waltham model designs and look similar to American Waltham model. They used H. A. Lugrin's patented chronograph mechanism, patented June 12 and October 3, 1876 also July 6 and September 28, 1880. Mr. Lugrin was a foreman for E. Eugene Robert Co. in New York from about 1870 to 1880s. Lugrin used his modular construction and fitted them to American Waltham, Longines and other companies to form a chronograph. E. Eugene Robert Co. in 1890 became A Wittnauer Co. In the mid 1890s the Timing & Repeating W. Co. was formed.

American Waltham W. Co., Chronograph movement, Min. register, Patented Sept. 28, 1880 - Eng. Pat. # 3224.　**Timing & Repeating W. Co.**, Chronograph movement, Min. register, Patented Sept. 28, 1880 - Eng. Pat. # 3224.

TYPE – DESCRIPTION	Avg	Ex-Fn	Mint
Chronograph, 17J, GF, 45mm, OF, C. 1900	$150	$165	$185
Chronograph w/register, 17J, GF, 45mm, OF, C. 1900	185	200	250
Chronograph, 17J, gilt mvt., silver, 45mm, HC, C. 1900	200	225	275
Chronograph w/register & split sec., 17J, GF, 45mm, OF, C. 1900	250	300	375
5 Min. Repeater, 15 jewels, gold jewel settings, **14K** Gold case	$2,500	$3,000	$4,000

5 Min. Repeater, 15 jewels, gold jewel settings, signed "Patd. Aug.23.87, April 30.89 + 894 Swiss made, S# 49420.

TISSOT
Swiss

The firm of Chs. Tissot & Fils was founded in 1853 in Le Locle by Charles Tissot. This skilled watchmaker worked from his home and in 1907 a factory was started. In 1971 the worlds first plastic wrist watch was made.

TYPE – DESCRIPTION	Avg	Ex-Fn	Mint
Early, KW, Time only, Swiss bar, Pre. 1870, silver case...............	$75	$110	$185
Time only, gold, 40- 44mm, OF...	350	400	525
HC	450	500	645
Time only, gold, 45- 50mm, OF...	500	575	750
HC	600	700	885
2-Train 1/4 second jump watch, silver, 50mm, ...	700	800	1,000
2-Train 1/4 second jump watch, **gold,** 50mm, ...	1,700	2,200	3,000
Chronograph, gold, 45-50mm, OF	800	865	950
Split second chronograph, gold, 45-52mm, OF	1,600	2,000	3,000
HC w/register..	2,500	3,000	3,500
5 minute repeater, gold, 45-52mm, OF	2,200	2,800	3,300
HC	2,500	3,200	4,000
Minute repeater, gold, 45-52mm, OF............................	2,500	2,900	3,500
HC	3,000	3,400	4,000
OF w/split chrono.	3,500	4,200	5,000
HC w/split chrono.	4,000	5,000	6,500
OF w/cal. & **moonphase**...	6,200	6,500	7,000
Tourbillon, gold, 48-55mm, OF	38,000	42,000	55,000
Detent chronometer, gold, 48-52mm , OF	4,000	5,200	7,000
HC	5,000	6,000	7,500
World time watch, gold, 48-52mm, OF	8,000	9,500	12,000
Moonphase, full calendar, gold, OF..............................	2,500	2,900	3,500
HC	3,200	3,600	4,500
Moonphase, full calendar, **chronoghaph**, gold, OF.......	4,700	5,000	5,500
HC	5,200	5,500	6,000
Moonphase, full calendar, **min. repeater, chronoghaph**, gold, OF	6,000	6,600	7,500
HC	6,500	7,200	8,000
Perp. moonphase cal. w/min.rep. and chrono, OF	20,000	25,000	35,000
HC	25,000	30,000	40,000
Clock Watch, gold, 48-52mm, OF	6,000	7,000	10,000
HC	8,000	9,500	12,000

Tissot, 2-Train 1/4 second jump watch, center sweep hand, enamel dial, 28 J., gold train, 54mm, KW KS, 18K, Ca. 1880.

Tissot, Minute repeater, with chronograph, day date month, moonphase, 27 jewels, 18K, HC, Ca. 1910.

The Complete Price Guide to Watches goal is to stimulate the orderly exchange of **Watches** between *"buyers"* and *"sellers"*.

M. I. TOBIAS & CO.

The M. I. Tobias firm started in Liverpool, about 1805. The Tobias <u>family</u> did not manufacture watches and specialized in exporting watches to U.S.A.. Watches signed *M.J. Tobias* are swiss made. The Tobias family activity extends from about 1805 to 1868. (As with most firms they had several different grades.)

M. I. Tobias & Co., Lord Street, Liverpool, 2 train independent sec., Pat.21 Feb, 1848, 52mm, right angle lever.

M. I. Tobias, 18K multi-color gold dial & gold case, KW/KS, fusee, diamond end stone, Ca. 1845, 52mm.

TYPE – DESCRIPTION	Avg	Ex-Fn	Mint
KW, 7-15J, 47-52mm, **Swiss**, silver, OF	$75	$95	$135
HC	100	125	175
KW, 7-15J, 47-52mm, **English**, silver, OF	100	135	200
HC	125	150	225
KW, 7-15J, lever or verge fusee, fancy **gold** case, 48mm,OF	250	300	385
KW, lever or verge fusee, **gold dial, Heavy 18K**, 52mm, HC	700	900	1,200
KW, **2 train** independent sec., **Silver**, 56mm, OF	350	425	500
KW, verge fusee, **multi-color gold dial & case**, 52mm, OF	700	900	1,200
HC	800	1,100	1,500
KW, **rack lever** escapement, **Silver**, 56mm, OF	350	425	500
HC	400	475	600
KW, **rack** lever escapement, **Gold**, 56mm, OF	700	845	1,000
HC	900	1,000	1,200
Captain's watch, center sec., sub-sec., gold dial, **18K,** 51mm, OF..	1,300	1,700	2,200
18K, 51mm, HC	1,500	1,800	2,500

Tobias, (Liverpool), 51mm, 18K, OF, Captain's watch, center & sub-seconds, gold dial.

554

TOUCHON & CO.
Swiss

Touchon & Co. started using this name as a trade mark in 1907. They manufactured complex and simple watches. In 1921 they associated with the firm of Wittnauer & Co.

Touchon & Co., 47mm, 29 jewels, minute repeater, open face, jeweled through hammers.

Touchon & Co., 47mm, 29 jewels, split-second chronograph and minute repeater, ca. 1910.

TYPE – DESCRIPTION	Avg	Ex-Fn	Mint
Time only, gold, 45- 50mm, OF	$450	$500	$625
HC	550	600	775
1/4 hr. repeater, gold, 46-52mm, OF	800	900	1,100
HC	900	1,100	1,500
OF w/chrono.	900	1,100	1,500
HC w/chrono.	1,100	1,500	2,200
OF w/chrono., cal. & moonphase	2,200	2,700	3,500
HC w/chrono., cal. & moonphase	2,400	2,900	3,700
5 minute repeater, gold, 46-52mm, OF	1,800	2,200	3,000
HC	2,000	2,400	3,200
Minute repeater, gold, 46-52mm, OF	2,500	3,100	4,000
HC	2,700	3,200	4,200
OF w/chrono. & register	2,700	3,200	4,200
HC w/chrono. & register	2,900	3,400	4,400
OF w/split chrono.	4,500	5,000	6,000
HC w/split chrono. & register	4,800	5,500	7,000
HC w/chrono., cal. & moonphase	5,500	6,200	7,500
HC, **Perp.** moonphase cal.	22,000	24,000	28,000
HC, **Perp.** moonphase cal. and chrono.	25,000	28,000	32,000
World time watch, gold, 48-52mm, OF	4,500	5,000	6,500
Perpetual moonphase calendar, gold, OF	7,000	8,200	10,000
Clock Watch, gold, 46-52mm, OF	6,000	7,500	10,000
HC	8,000	9,500	12,000

COMPARISON OF WATCH CASE SIZES

U. S. A.	EUROPEAN
10-12 SIZE	40—44 MM
16 SIZE	45—49 MM
18 SIZE	50—55 MM

VACHERON & CONSTANTIN
Swiss

The oldest Swiss factory, founded by Jean-Marc Vacheron, in 1775. The firm of Vacheron & the firm of Constantin were in business about the same date 1785, but the association bearing the name today did not come into being until 1819. In these early periods, different grades of watches produced by Vacheron & Constantin bore different names.

The association with Leschot, around 1840, catapulted the firm into its position as a top quality manufacturer. Before that time, their watches were typical of Genevese production. Vacheron & Constantin exported many movements to the United States to firms such as Bigelow, Kennard & Co., which were cased domestically, typically in the period 1900-1935. In its early period the firm produced some lovely ladies' enameled watches, later it produced high grade timepieces and complicated watches, and to this day produces fine watches.

ESTIMATED PRODUCTION DATES

DATE–SERIAL #	DATE–SERIAL #	DATE–SERIAL #
1830 - 30,000	1880-170,000	1925-400,000
1835 - 40,000	1885-180,000	1930-410,000
1840 - 50,000	1890-190,000	1935-420,000
1845 - 60,000	1895-223,000	1940-440,000
1850 - 75,000	1900-256,000	1945-464,000
1855 - 95,000	1905-289,000	1950-488,000
1860-110,000	1910-322,000	1955-512,000
1865-125,000	1915-355,000	1960-536,000
1870-140,000	1920-385,000	1965-560,000
1875-155,000		1970-585,000

The above list is provided for determining the APPROXIMATE age of your watch. Match serial number with date. Watches were not necessarily sold in the exact order of manufactured date.

🕐 The date a watch **sold** is not an indication of the date it was **produced**.

Early movements manufactured with the machines invented by George-Auguste Leschot. The machines were built in the Vacheron Constantin factory Ca. 1839 to 1840. In about 1863 to 1865 V. & C. manufactured a inexpensive watch using the names Abraham Vacheron or Abm. Vacheron also the name of Chossat & Cie.

Vacheron & Constantin, 44mm, 18 jewels, enamel bezel, 18K, Ca. 1930.

Early Vacheron & Constantin's With Different Names

1755 - Jean-Marc Vacheron
1785 - Abraham Vacheron
1786 - Abraham Vacheron - Girod
1810 -Vacheron - Chossat & Cie.
1819 - Vacheron & Constantin

1857 - C'esar Vacheron
1869 - Charles Vacheron & Cie
1870 - Veuve C'esar Vacheron & Cie
1887 - Ancienne Fabrique Vacheron & Constantin SA
1896 - Vacheron & Constantin SA

Signed **"VACHERON & CONSTANTIN"**
13-15 jewels, gilt movement, Ca.1925.

TYPE – DESCRIPTION	Avg	Ex-Fn	Mint
Early bar movement, lever escap., **signed Vacheron & Constantin**			
time only, KW KS, silver case, 30-39mm, OF	$135	$185	$300
(same as above) 40-44mm, OF	185	265	400
(same as above) 45-48mm, OF	200	275	400
(same as above) 45-48mm, **HC**	250	350	500
Early Le-Pine bar movement, duplex escap., GOLD & ENAMEL			
KW KS, **signed Vacheron & Constantin**, 49mm, OF	4,500	5,500	7,000
Time only, 18K gold & **enamel bezel**, 40-44mm, OF	1,200	1,500	2,000

Vacheron & Constantin, 49mm, Early Lepine bar style movement, duplex escapement, GOLD & ENAMEL, KW KS, **signed Vacheron & Constantin**, 49mm, OF, Ca. 1840.

Vacheron & Constantin, Gold coin 50 pesos 900 fine, coin hollowed out to receive watch, LEFT view shows dial & movement.

TYPE – DESCRIPTION	Avg	Ex-Fn	Mint
Time only, **18K** gold, 40-44mm, OF..	$600	$800	$1,200
HC	900	1,100	1,500
Time only, gold, 45-50mm, OF...	1,000	1,300	1,800
HC	1,600	1,900	2,400
X-thin, 17J., **Aluminum,** weight =20 grains, OF, C. 1940.....	1,400	2,000	3,000
Desk chronometer, wooden box, 21J., silver, 60mm,OF, C.1943 ...	2,000	2,600	3,500
Gold coin 50 pesos 900 fine, coin hollowed out to receive watch...	2,500	3,200	4,000

V. & C., Chronograph, for the corps of engineers USA, 20 jewels, enamel dial, nail set, 50mm, 3,000 made, Ca.1917.

V. & C., Astronomic with moon phases, perpetual calendar, minute repeater, split-second chronograph, 1905.

TYPE – DESCRIPTION	Avg	Ex-Fn	Mint
Chronograph, 20J, corps of engineers USA, **Silver**, 45-50mm, OF	$1,000	$1,300	$1,800
Chronograph, gold, 45-50mm, **V& C case**, OF	2,200	2,500	3,000
HC	2,500	2,900	3,500
OF w/register	2,500	2,900	3,500
HC w/register...	3,200	3,500	4,000

V. & C., 40mm, wolf tooth winding, open face.

V. & C., 40mm, 31J., Min. repeater, slide activated, OF.

TYPE – DESCRIPTION	Avg	Ex-Fn	Mint
Split second chronograph, gold, 45-52mm, OF	$4,500	$5,200	$6,500
HC	5,500	6,200	7,500
OF w/register	5,000	5,800	7,000
HC w/register	7,000	7,300	8,500
Minute repeater, gold, 46-52mm, OF	5,000	6,200	8,000
HC	6,000	8,000	11,000
OF w/chrono.	6,000	7,500	10,000
HC w/chrono.	9,000	12,000	17,000
OF w/chrono. & register	6,000	8,000	11,000
HC w/chrono. & register	10,000	12,000	18,000
OF w/split chrono.	8,000	9,500	13,000
HC w/split chrono.	10,000	14,000	20,000
OF w/split chrono. & register	8,000	10,000	15,000
HC w/split chrono. & register	12,000	16,000	22,000
OF w/chrono., cal. & moonphase	12,000	16,000	22,000
Tourbillon, gold, 48-55mm, OF	45,000	70,000	100,000
World time watch, gold, 48-52mm, OF	20,000	25,000	35,000
Perp. moonphase cal. w/min. repeater, OF	40,000	50,000	65,000
HC	45,000	55,000	70,000
Perp. moonphase cal. w/min. rep. and split sec. chrono., OF	50,000	65,000	90,000
Perp. moonphase cal. w/min. rep. and split sec. chrono., HC	60,000	75,000	100,000
Clock Watch, gold, 46-52mm, OF	15,000	18,000	25,000
HC	20,000	24,000	30,000

V. & C., extra thin and light weight **Aluminum,** (20 grains), about 12 size, 44mm, OF, 17 jewels, Ca. 1940.

V. & C., World time, revolving 24 hour dial, 31 citys of the world, 18 jewels, 45mm, Ca. 1945

VINER (LONDON)

Charles Viner apprenticed in about 1802 and in records till 1840. The company continued after his death as Viner & Co. Viner also made clocks.

TYPE – DESCRIPTION	Avg	Ex-Fn	Mint
VINER, Verge Fusee / Alarm, 50MM, Silver, OF, Ca.1835	$1,000	$1,400	$2,000
Pull Wind, winds by pulling knob in pendant, 40-50mm, Silver	1,200	1,600	2,200

VINER, Verge Fusee with Alarm, marked on cuvette for the two arbors *"wind up"* & the other marked *"warning"*, under sprung hairspring, 50MM, Silver Open Face Case, Ca. 1835.

WINDMILL
LONDON

Joseph and his son Thomas made clocks and watches and at one time employed 10 workers. Started in business in 1671 and lasted till about 1732.

TYPE – DESCRIPTION	Avg	Ex-Fn	Mint
Tho. WINDMILL,1/4 hr. repeater, 55MM, silver, OF, Ca.1675-90	$5,500	$8,000	$12,000
Tho. WINDMILL,1/4 hr. repeater, 55MM, **gold**, OF, Ca.1675-90 .	7,000	12,000	20,000

Tho. WINDMILL, 1/4 hour repeater activated by pendant and sounds on inner bell, champleve dial, note D shaped foot on balance bridge, silver Open Face, 55MM, Ca. 1675-90.

ZENITH
Le Locle Swiss

Founded in 1865 by Georges Favre- Jacot. The name *Zenith* was registered
in 1897 & by 1920 they had made 2,000,000 watches.

ZENITH, alarm watch, enamel dial, 17J., 50mm, Ca. 1930   ZENITH, Military Deck Watch, 51mm, nickel case, Ca.1940.

TYPE – DESCRIPTION	Avg	Ex-Fn	Mint
Time only, gold, 40-44mm, OF	$250	$300	$425
HC	400	450	525
Time only, gold, 40-44mm, with **enamel** on bezel, **18K**, OF	600	700	900
Time only, gold, 45-52mm, OF	450	500	650
HC	550	600	750
RR Extra, 21J., **Grade 56**, (16 size), **Gold Filled** OF	185	235	385
Military Deck Watch, 51mm, nickel case, Ca.1940	250	300	425
Alarm watch, 17J., nail set, **two barrels**, gold, 50mm, C.1930	1,200	1,400	1,800
Chronograph, gold, 45-50mm, OF	800	900	1,100
HC	900	1,000	1,200
Minute repeater, gold, 46-52mm, OF	2,500	2,900	3,500
HC	3,200	3,500	4,000
OF w/split chrono.	4,000	4,500	5,200
HC w/split chrono.	4,500	5,200	6,500
OF w/chrono., cal. & moonphase	5,000	5,500	7,000
HC w/chrono., cal. & moonphase	6,000	6,500	8,000
Perp. moonphase cal. w/min. rep. and chrono., OF	20,000	24,000	30,000
HC	22,000	27,000	35,000

ZENITH, 42mm, 18K, enamel on case,
open face, 17J., signed ZENITH, Ca. 1930's.

PRE-1850 REPEATERS

Swiss or French 1/4 hr. repeater, verge or cylinder, silver, 55mm, Ca. 1820, OF. Note: Parachute (illo.1)

Swiss or French 1/4 hr. rep., pump, verge or cylinder, 18K, 52mm, OF, Ca.1800s. (illo.2)

TYPE – DESCRIPTION	Avg	Ex-Fn	Mint
Swiss or French 1/4 hr. rep., verge, silver, 55mm, OF (illo.1).........	$1,200	$1,400	$1,800
Swiss or French 1/4 hr. rep., cylinder, silver, 55mm, OF (illo.1)	1,000	1,200	1,500
Swiss 1/4 hr. rep., **pump**, verge, 18K, 52mm, OF, C.1800s (illo.2)	2,000	2,700	3,500
Swiss 1/4 hr. rep., **pump**, cylinder,18K, 52mm, OF, C.1800s (illo.2)	1,500	2,100	3,000
Swiss 1/4 hr., **automaton** on dial (2 figures), gilt, verge, KW, 55mm, OF, early 1800s	2,500	3,100	4,000
Swiss 1/4 hr. repeater, 32-35mm, KW KS, **gold**, Ca. 1850 (illo.3) .	1,800	2,200	2,800
<u>English</u>, **striking** device with repetition for hours & 1/4 hour (illo.A)	4,500	5,500	7,000
French 1/4 hr. musical repeater **disc-driven**, KW KS, cylinder,**18K**, 57mm, OF, C. 1825 (illo.B).............................	4,000	4,800	6,000

Swiss or French 1/4 hr. repeater,
cylinder escapement,
Swiss bar movement,
32-35mm, KW KS,
gold, Ca. 1850, **(illo.3)**

English gold watch with a striking device with repetition for hours & 1/4 hour, Verge, gold dial, 48mm Ca. 1730.(illo.A)

French 1/4 hr. musical repeater disc-driven, cylinder, KW KS, 18k, 57mm, OF, C. 1825, **(illo.B)**

French, 1/4 hr. repeater, gold and enamel superior quality, enameled scene, outer case with pearls, verge, 20K, 52mm, OF, C.1785. **(illo.5)**

1/4 hr. repeater, Virgule escap., KW, 18K, 46mm, OF, Ca. 1840. **(illo.6)**

TYPE – DESCRIPTION	Avg	Ex-Fn	Mint
Skeletonized 1/4 hr., cylinder, Swiss, 18K, 58mm, OF, C.1810......	$3,200	$3,600	$4,500
French 1/4 hr. repeater, **20K** gold and enamel, verge, enameled scene, superior quality, outer pearls, 52mm, OF, C.1785 (illo.5)	5,000	6,000	7,500
1/4 hr. repeater, Virgule escap., KW, 18K, 46mm, OF (illo.6)........	2,500	3,000	3,600
1/4 hr. rep., erotic scene (concealed in cuvette), automated, multi-color gold figures, verge, pump 1/4 hr., 18K, 54mm, OF, C.1800...	3,500	4,500	6,000
French or Swiss pump 1/4 hr. repeater, free standing barrel, **Thin gold** case, cylinder escape., tapered bridges , Ca.1790-1835 (illo.7)	2,000	2,500	3,200
Early 1/4 hr. rep., Paris (Clouzier) gilt dial w/ enamel hour cartouches, verge, gilt & shagreen case, 58mm, OF, C.1700	5,500	7,000	9,000
1/4 hr. repeater, London, gilt & shagreen paircase, verge, extremely fine, 56mm, OF, C.1700s	5,000	6,000	8,000

French or Swiss pump 1/4 hr. repeater, free standing barrel, cylinder escapement, tapered bridges, **Thin** gold engine turned case, Ca. 1790-1835. **(illo.7)**

1/4 hour verge repeater, 49mm, 22K gold repousse pair case, repeating on an inner bell, repeat mechanism is activated from the pendant, ca. 1700-1750, (illo.8)

1/4 hour repeater, musical, 25 musical tines, cylinder, center seconds, KW, 18K, 58mm, OF, Ca.1820, (illo.9)

1/4 hour repeater, verge (London, Dutch), pierced inner case, repousse outer case, gold, 49mm, C.1700, (illo.10)

1/4 Hr. repeating coach watch, with alarm, about 120 MM, verge fusee, silver repousse case, ca.1700-40. (illo. 11)

TYPE – DESCRIPTION	Avg	Ex-Fn	Mint
1/4 hr. repeater, repousse pair case, verge, **22K**, 49mm (illo.8)	$4,500	$5,200	$6,500
1/4 hr. repeater, musical, **25 musical tines**, cylinder, center seconds, KW, 18K, 58mm,OF, C. 1820 (illo.9)	5,000	6,000	7,500
1/4 hr. rep., verge (London, Dutch), pierced inner case, repousse outer case, gold, 49mm, C.1700 (illo.10)	5,000	6,700	9,000
1/4 hr. repeating coach watch w/alarm, verge, fusee, silver repousse case, large, C. 1700-40 (illo. 11).....................	7,500	9,000	11,000
1/4 hr. repeater with automaton dial, verge, Swiss, KW, 3 automated figures on dial and carillon chimes, silver, 52mm, OF, C. 1790.	2,000	2,700	3,500
Gold & enamel, 1/4 hr. repeater, London, cylinder, Fusee, paircase, enamel on outer case, 18K, 48mm, C. 1790	3,500	4,300	5,500
Swiss, 1/4 hr. pump repeater, w/ automaton, verge, 18K, 54mm, OF, C. 1800	3,500	4,600	6,000
Virgule escapement, 1/4 hr. repeater, fancy gold & multi-dial, London, KW, 18K, OF, C. 1840	2,200	2,800	3,500

REPEATERS

RIGHT: (illo.A)
1/2 - 1/4 Repeater,
back wind and back set by
folding **button** system,
17J., diamond end stone,
18K HC, Ca.1863.

Watkin's Patent
Ca. Apr. 1870
Folding Button
can be attached
to any key watch

1/4 hour repeater, 17 jewels, nail set, gun metal case, 49mm, C. 1910. (illo.12)

1/4 hour repeater with chronograph, gun metal base-metal or gold filled, 49-50mm, (illo.13)

TYPE – DESCRIPTION	Avg	Ex-Fn	Mint
1/4 hr. repeater, 17J, gun metal, 49-52mm, C. 1910 (illo.12)	$450	$525	$625
1/4 hr. repeater, 17J, silver, 49-52mm, OF, C. 1910	550	625	725
1/4 hr. repeater, 17J, silver, 49-52mm, HC, C. 1910.......................	600	650	850
1/4 hr. rep. w/**chrono**.,17J, base metal, gun metal or GF, **OF** 49-50mm, C.1910 (illo.13)...	650	735	850
1/4 hr. rep. w/**chrono**.,17J, base metal, gun metal or GF, **HC** 49-50mm, C.1910	750	850	1,000
1/2 - 1/4 repeater, back wind & set button, **18K** HC, Ca.1863 (illo.A)	1,800	2,300	3,000

1/4 hr. repeater with Calendar, 17J, gold filled, 3/4 plate, open face, 50mm, C. 1910 (illo.14)

1/4 hour repeater, 55mm, 2 Jacquemarts, gilt case, Ca. 1820. (illo.15)

TYPE – DESCRIPTION	Avg	Ex-Fn	Mint
1/4 hr. repeater with Calendar, 17J, gun metal or gold filled, 3/4 plate, OF, 49-50mm, C. 1910 (illo.14)	$700	$900	$1,200
Swiss 1/4 hr. repeater w/moonphase & calendar, 17J, 18K, 53mm, HC, C. 1900	3,000	3,400	4,000
55mm, 1/4 repeater, 2 Jacquemarts, gilt case, Ca. 1820 (illo.15) ...	2,200	2,800	3,500
Swiss, 1/4 repeater, **musical**, pinned cylinder & comb, 18K, 50-55mm, Ca. 1800. (illo.16)	5,000	5,700	6,500
Swiss 1/4 hr. repeater, **Erotic Scene,** 14K, HC, 50-54mm, ALL ORIGINAL, (note: beware of fakes) (illo.16A)	7,500	10,000	15,000

Swiss 18K, 1/4 repeater, **musical**, pinned cylinder & comb, 50-55 mm, Ca. 1800. (illo.16)

Swiss 1/4 hour repeater, Erotic Scene with automaton action dial, 14K, HC, 50-54mm, (illo.16A) This watch has CONVERSION not original (note: beware of fakes)

A bit of musical history in 1796, Antoine Favre of Geneva invented a comb with **vibrating strips**. This innovation lead to the production of the musical pocket watch.

COMPARISON OF WATCH CASE SIZES

U. S. A.	EUROPEAN
10-12 SIZE	40—44 MM
16 SIZE	45—49 MM
18 SIZE	50—55 MM

Minute Repeater, 48 jewels, 2 train Independent seconds TANDEM wind, 55mm, Ca. 1890, 18K HC. (illo.17)

Swiss minute repeater, 54mm, jeweled through hammers, 14k case. (illo.18)

TYPE – DESCRIPTION	Avg	Ex-Fn	Mint
Min. rep., 20J, Swiss, gilt mvt., gun metal, 52mm, **OF**, 1910	$700	$900	$1,200
Min. rep., 48 jewels, 2 train Independent seconds **TANDEM** wind, 55mm, Ca. 1890, 18K HC. (illo.17)......................................	6,000	7,200	9,000
Min. rep., 17J, Swiss, gilt, 18K, 52mm, HC, C. 1910	2,500	2,900	3,500
Min. rep., 32 J, Swiss, gilt, 18K, 54mm, HC, C. 1910	2,700	3,200	4,000
Min. rep., 32 J, Swiss, NI, porc. dial, 14K, OF, C. 1905 (illo.18) ...	2,200	2,800	3,500
Min. rep., 32 J, Swiss, NI, porc. dial, 18K, OF, C. 1905 (illo.19) ...	2,500	3,100	3,800
Min. repeater, 25J, Self contained, (activated from button on crown) 14K, OF, C. 1915	3,500	4,400	5,000
Min. repeater, Swiss, ultra thin, 32J, 18K, OF, C. 1930..................	4,000	4,700	6,000
18K, 54mm (illo.20)	5,000	6,600	8,500

Minute Repeater, 32 jewels., Swiss, enamel dial, wolf tooth winding, 18K, Ca. 1905, (illo.19)

Father & Baby Time, automated min. repeater, 54mm, note father and baby striking bell, 18K. (illo.20)

Minute repeating **Clock Watch,** 3/4 plate, a on or off strike activated mechanism, three gongs, tandem-winding barrels, 18K, 48-50mm, HC, Ca.1900 (illo.21)

Minute repeater, split second chronograph, Swiss, 18K, 47-50mm, OF, Ca.1900 . (illo.22)

TYPE – DESCRIPTION	Avg	Ex-Fn	Mint
Min. repeating Clock Watch, 18K, 48-50mm, HC, Ca.1900 (illo.21)	$8,000	$9,500	$12,000
Min.rep. w/ chrono, Swiss ,SW, 18K, large 58mm, OF, C.1900	2,000	2,400	3,000
Min. repeater w/chrono. register, 32J, nickel, very high quality, 18K, 50mm, OF, C. 1900	3,500	4,200	5,000
Min. rep.w/chrono, 30 min. register, Swiss, 36J, 18K ,HC, C.1895	3,500	4,200	5,000
Min. rep., split sec. chrono, Swiss, 18K, 47-50mm, OF, C.1900 (illo.22)	5,000	5,800	7,000
Min. rep., split sec. chrono, Swiss, 18K, 47-50mm, HC,C.1900	6,000	6,900	8,000
Swiss min. repeater, chrono, moonphase and calendar, 30J or more, 18K, 60mm, HC, C. 1895	5,500	6,300	7,500
Swiss min. repeater, moonphase and **perpetual calendar,** 30J or more, 18K, 60mm, HC, C. 1895 (illo.23)	★14,000	18,000	25,000
Swiss min. rep., **4 hammers & Westminster carillon** on gongs, 32J, 18K, 53mm, HC, C. 1910 (illo.24)	8,500	13,000	20,000

Swiss minute repeater, moonphase and **perpetual calendar,** 30J or more, 18K, 60mm, HC, C. 1895. (illo.23)

Swiss min. rep., 4 hammers & Westminster carillon on gongs, 32J, 18K, 53mm, HC, C. 1910. (illo.24)

PRE–1850 ALARMS

TYPE – DESCRIPTION	Avg	Ex-Fn	Mint
Alarm, (**Blois, France**), double silver case pierced and engraved, gilt mvt., cut gut cord fusee, 2 wheel train + verge escape. w/foliot, silver balance cock, 44mm, Ca. 1640 (illo.25)	$13,000	$19,000	$25,000
Alarm, 2 cases pierced, 3 wheel train, Egyptian pierced pillars, verge & foliot, 51mm, Ca. 1665 (illo.26)	9,000	14,000	20,000

ALARM, **from BLOIS**, FRANCE, double silver case pierced and engraved, silver crown dial with roman numbers, alarm center dial with arabic numbers, gilt movement, cut gut cord fusee, 2 wheel train plus verge escapement with foliot, silver balance cock, 44mm, Ca. 1640. It is believed French watch-making started in the town of **Blois, France.** (illo.25)

ALARM, 2 cases pierced & engraved, roman outer dial, alarm center dial, blued hands , 3 wheel train, Egyptian pierced pillars, verge & foliot, endless screw adjustment, Paris, 51mm, Ca. 1665. (illo.26)

In 1675 when the spiral hairspring was invented, the method of regulating a watch changed. Before 1675 a watch was regulated by winding up, or letting down, the mainspring by means of a endless screw driving wheel. The endless screw was fixed to the back-plate. At one end of the endless screw which was squared to take a small key. The power of the mainspring is evened out over a period of time by means of the fusee, however the variation in the strength of the mainspring when regulated would alter the rate of the watch.

ALARM, strikes on bell, pair cased, verge, C. 1650. (illo.27)

Alarm, pair cased, first case pique nailed skin, second case pierced, 4 wheel train, verge, amphora pillers, 56mm, Ca. 1680. (illo.28)

TYPE – DESCRIPTION	Avg	Ex-Fn	Mint
Alarm, strikes on bell, pair cased, verge, C. 1650 (illo.27)	$7,000	$10,000	$15,000
Alarm, pair cased, first case pique nailed skin, 4 wheel train, verge, 56mm, Ca. 1680 (illo.28)	9,000	14,000	20,000
Alarm, Rotterdam, silver pierced case, gilt, tulip pillars, verge, fusee, 48mm, Ca. 1685 (illo.29)	7,000	10,000	14,000
Alarm, "oignon", verge, fusee, large pierced bal. bridge (illo.30)	6,500	8,500	12,000

ALARM, Rotterdam, silver pierced case, gilt, tulip pillars, verge, fusee, 48mm, Ca. 1685. (illo.29)

ALARM, "oignon", verge, fusee, large pierced balance bridge, French. Ca. 1675-80. (illo.30)

The term Oignon is the **nickname** of large domed bulb shaped watches, they start to appear after 1675 & having some uniform construction features point to a source of specialized workshops, (ebauches) thus becoming reasonably priced & improved time keeping due to the **Spiral** hair-spring. **French** Oignon watches wind from the front dial side and the balance bridge cock has two screws & usually have domed shaped dials. **English** Oignon watches generally wind from back & the balance cock use a single screw & foot & the dials have a flat appearance. (Ca. 1680 the minute hand starts to appear.)

ALARM, nailed pique shagreen skin, second case pierced silver, balance cock has short feet, 4 wheel train verge, 60mm, London, Ca. 1675-80. (illo.31)

Alarm-Oignon, nailed pique shagreen **Sting-Ray** skin, triple cases, entirely pierced throughout, richly decorated, 4 wheel train, verge, fusee, English, Ca. 1690. (illo.32) **Sting-Ray** skin note the enamel caps arranged in a mosaic pattern.

TYPE – DESCRIPTION	Avg	Ex-Fn	Mint
Alarm, nailed pique shagreen skin, second case pierced silver, 4 wheel train verge, 60mm, London, Ca. 1670 (illo.31)	$6,500	$8,000	$10,000
Alarm-Oignon, nailed pique shagreen (**Sting-Ray**) skin, English-Swiss, verge, fusee, Ca.1690s, (illo.32)	6,500	8,000	10,000
Oignon alarm, verge, French, silver and animal skin cover, movement wound from center arbor on dial, silver champleve dial, 60mm, OF, C. 1710	6,500	8,000	10,000

OIGNON

The invention of the regulatory spiral hairspring (1675), did for watches what the pendulum did for clocks. The two inventions revolutionized watch and clock making. The precision that was achieved by the introduction of the spiral hairspring had a immediate effect on the shape and larger dimension of the watch. This new hairspring could not be very finely shaped, so the watchmakers had to use larger balances. This led them to make a watch with greater diameter thus the so called "OIGNON". Now that watches were more accurate the watch was soon fitted with a minute hand.

ALARMS

The most common Swiss and German alarms are usually in base metal or gun metal cases. Early makes with porcelain dials are more desirable than later (post 1920's) metal dial alarms.

TYPE – DESCRIPTION	Avg	Ex-Fn	Mint
Swiss alarm sounding on bell,7J, base metal, 49mm,OF, C.1915 ...	$100	$125	$165
Swiss alarm sounding on gongs, 15J, tandem wind, gun metal, 50mm, OF, C. 1900	175	200	275
Cricket alarm, w/cricket design, Swiss , SW, silver case, 48mm, OF, C.1890	500	600	725

TIMERS & CHRONOGRAPHS

Timer, 1/5 sec., 7J, register, base metal, 48mm, OF.   Timer, **split second,** register, base metal, 56mm, Ca. 1970

TYPE – DESCRIPTION	Avg	Ex-Fn	Mint
Timer, 1/5 sec., register,7J, base metal, 48mm, OF, C. 1940	$35	$45	$70
Timer, 1/5 sec. register, **17J,** base metal, 48mm, OF, C. 1940	40	60	95
Timer, **split sec.,** register, base metal, 46mm, OF, C. 1940	55	85	150
Timer,15-17J, **split sec.**, register, base metal, 56mm, OF, C. 1970.	55	85	150
Timer and Watch, **silver,** 48mm, **HC,** 1925	125	150	185
Chronograph, **7J, GF or silver,** 48mm, OF, C. 1905......................	130	155	200
HC	155	175	225
Chronograph, **15-17J, porcelain** dial, GF or silver, 50mm, OF, ...	200	235	325
HC, ...	250	285	365
Chronograph, **20J, 18K,** 52mm, OF, C. 1895	500	635	775
HC	600	725	875

Timer and Watch, **silver,** 48mm, HC.   Chronograph, 7-17J, GF, 48mm, OF, C. 1905.

Chronograph, w/register, porc. dial, **20J**, **14K**, 52mm, HC, Ca. 1890. (illo.A)

Chronograph, Split Seconds, w/register, porc. dial, **20J**, **18K**, 52mm, OF, Ca. 1910. (illo.B)

TYPE – DESCRIPTION	Avg	Ex-Fn	Mint
Chronog. w/register, porc. dial, **15J, silver,** 52mm, OF, C. 1890....	$250	$300	$400
HC (illo.A)	300	365	475
Chronog. w/register, porc. dial, **20J, 14K,** 52mm, OF, C. 1890......	400	465	575
HC	500	565	675
Chronog. w/register, porc. dial, **20J, 18K,** 52mm, OF, C. 1890......	600	665	750
HC	800	885	1,100
Split sec. chronograph, 15-17J, **.800 silver,** 52mm, OF, C. 1900..	300	350	425
Split sec. chronograph, 19-32J, **18K,** 52mm, OF, C. 1900	800	975	1,200
HC (illo.B)	1,000	1,200	1,500
Double dial (time on front, chrono. on back), Swiss , 17J,			
14K display case , 51mm, OF, Ca. 1885 (illo.C)	800	1,200	1,800
1/4 second jump watch, 26J, two gear train, SW , **18K,**			
HC, C.1880 (illo.D)	2,200	2,700	3,500

Double dial (time on front, Chronograph on back), Swiss, 17J, 14K display case, 51mm, OF, Ca. 1885. (illo.C)

1/4 second jump watch, 26J, two gear train, two main spring barrels, KW , 18K, 53mm, HC, C.1880. (illo.D)

POCKET CHRONOMETER

JOHN ARNOLD, chronometer, KWKS, spring detent, Z balance with adjustable weights, helical hair spring, 18K case, serial # 14, upright escape wheel, "INV ET FECT" engraved on movement (made by), his chronometer factory was located in Chigwell (London), #36 pocket chronometers sold for about $500.00 in 1776. (illo.33)

Right: John Arnold spring detent escapement.

TYPE – DESCRIPTION	Avg	Ex-Fn	Mint
Chronometer, KWKS, spring detent, Z bal., helical hair-spring, "JOHN ARNOLD", 18K case, C. 1776 (illo.33)	$20,000	$30,000	$45,000
French pocket chronometer, gilt bar movement, pivoted detent, free sprung, KW/KS, 58mm, Ca. 1850 (illo.34)	5,000	6,500	10,000
Chronometer, KW/KS, spring detent, Z bal., helical hair-spring, "J. R. ARNOLD", 18K case, C. 1805 (illo.35)	12,000	20,000	35,000

French pocket chronometer, gilt bar movement, pivoted detent escapement, free sprung helical balance spring, KW/KS, 58mm, Ca. 1850. (illo.34)

J. R. ARNOLD, chronometer, KWKS, spring detent, Z balance with screw counterpoise on terminal curves, helical hair-spring, 18K case, 58mm, C. 1805. (illo.35)

JOHANNES KESSELS "ALTON", deck chronometer, KWKS, spring detent, fusee, silver case, C. 1830 . (illo.36)

Detent chronometer, Helical hairspring, Swiss, SW, 18K, wolf teeth winding, 56mm, HC, C. 1900. (illo.37)

TYPE – DESCRIPTION	Avg	Ex-Fn	Mint
Chronometer, KWKS, spring detent, Z bal., helical hair-spring,			
"KESSELS", silver case, C. 1830 (illo.36)	$2,200	$3,300	$5,000
Chronometer, KW, spring detent, coin, OF, C. 1875	600	725	900
Detent chronometer, Swiss, SW, 18K, 56mm, HC, Ca.1900 (ill0.37)	1,500	1,900	2,500
Detent chronometer, English, w/ wind indicator, 18K, 48mm, OF .	3,500	4,800	6,500
Chronometer, pivoted detent, helical hairspring, (French),			
SW, silver, 56mm, OF (illo.38)	300	400	550
Pocket chronometer, Swiss, 20 jewel, fancy case, silver and gilt dial,			
detent, w/ helical spring, 18K, 49mm, HC, C. 1890 (illo.38A)	2,600	3,600	4,500

Engraved on movement "*Chronome'tre*" (French), 16 jewels, pivoted detent, helical hairspring, stem wind, manufactured by LIP in Besancon France, silver, 56mm, OF, Ca. 1910-30. (illo.38)

Detent chronometer, English, w/ fusee, helical hairspring, note: Trapezoidal weights on balance. (illo.38A)

🕐 Note: Some models and grades are not included. Their values can be determined by comparing with similar age, size, metal content, style, models and grades listed.

🕐 Note: Watches listed in this book are priced at the collectable trade show level, as complete watches having an original case, an original dial, and with the entire original movement in good working order with no repairs needed.

TOURBILLON, KARRUSEL, RARE & UNUSUAL MOVEMENTS

One minute so called "Poor Man's Tourbillon", center seconds silver watch with centered dial & visible Tourbillon carriage from back of watch. Swiss, 54mm. (illo.39)

Signed **Mobilis**,Visible Tourbillon, 53mm, 13 to 15 jewels, tourbillon carriage is visible from dial side, Pat. No. 30754 (made by Courvoisier Freres), ca. 1905. (illo.40)

TYPE – DESCRIPTION	Avg	Ex-Fn	Mint
Tourbillon, Swiss, center sec., base metal, 54mm, OF (illo.39) ...★	$1,500	$2,400	$3,500
Tourbillon, 53mm, 13J, **Mobilis**, Ca. 1905 (illo.40) ....★	2,000	2,900	4,000
Tourbillon, **4 min.**, 15J, enamel dial, silver, C.1910 (illo.41).......★	2,800	3,600	5,000
Karrusel, **52 min.**, English, 3/4, gilt, 16J, SW,			
silver case, 56mm, OF, C.1885 (illo.42)	2,500	3,300	4,600
18K case, (illo.42)...	3,500	5,000	8,000

signed **TOURBILLON**, one complete turn in 4-5 minutes, 15 jewels, enamel dial, silver case, Ca.1930. (illo.41)
Note: On dial *"BREVET"* translation Patented.

52 minute **KARRUSEL**, 57mm, 14J., English, silver case, Ca.1885. (illo.42)

NOTE:

The Tourbillon **Mobilis** is signed "Mobilis Pat. no. 30754" the Pat. date was June 11,1904 and was Patented by Paul Loichet of Charquemont, France, Tourbillon movement was made by Courvoisier Freres of La Chaux de Fonds Switzerland from 1905 to about 1910.

Helicoil Mainspring, 51mm, 15J., rare winding system, cylindrical spring replaces standard mainspring. (illo.43)

Lever with Fusee, KW KS, (Liverpool), hallmarked, silver, **undersprung**, 46mm, OF, Ca. 1850-70.(illo.44)

EARLY PRE–1850 NON—GOLD

TYPE – DESCRIPTION		Avg	Ex-Fn	Mint
Helicoil mainspring, Swiss, 15J , cylinder esc., base metal, 51mm, OF, C. 1910 (illo.43)	★★	$2,000	$2,800	$4,000
Lever, Fusee, (Liverpool), silver, 46mm, OF, Ca. 1850-70 (illo.44)		135	185	275
Lever or cylinder, BAR, KW KS, silver, 46-52mm, OF (illo.45)		95	125	165
Lever or cylinder, **engraved** BAR, KW KS, silver, 46-52mm, OF, Ca. 1840-85 (illo.46)		135	150	200
Lever or cylinder, **Le-PINE**, KW KS, silver, 46-52mm (illo.47)		135	150	200
Rack & pinion escap., KW KS, silver, 46-52mm, OF (illo.48)		250	325	475

Lever, KW KS, bar style movement, note **curved barrel bridge,** silver, 46-52mm, OF, C. 1830-50. (illo.45)

Lever, **Lepine style bar, engraved,** KW KS, silver, 46-52mm, OF, Ca. 1840-85. (illo.46)

Lever, **Lepine style tapered bar movement,** KW KS, silver, 46-52mm, OF, Ca. 1820-35. (illo.47)

Rack & pinion escapement, KW KS, silver, 46-52mm, Ca. 1830. (illo.48)

Verge, chain driven fusee, (English) paircase, 52mm, OF, C.1800- 40. (illo.49)

Verge, fusee, (English) paircase, hallmarked, KW, 52mm, OF, Ca. 1780-90. (illo.50)

TYPE – DESCRIPTION	Avg	Ex-Fn	Mint
Verge, Fusee (Swiss), KW, (unmarked) single case, silver, 49mm, OF, C. 1810-40	$250	$300	$400
Verge (English) paircase, 52mm, OF, C.1800- 40 (illo.49)	250	325	450
Painted "farmer's dial," verge, Swiss / London, silver, 52-55m, OF	500	635	850
Cylinder, Fusee, silver, 48-52mm, OF, C. 1830s	250	300	400
Verge, Fusee (Swiss), KW, silver single case, 49mm OF, C. 1810-1840	250	300	400
Verge (English) paircase, hallmarked, KW, 52mm, OF, C. 1780-90 (illo.50)	275	345	500
Miniature, verge, lady's, plain, porcelain dial, hallmarked silver, 24mm, OF, C. 1810	700	850	1,100
Gilt & enamel, verge, Swiss or French, 46mm, OF, C. 1800	800	1,100	1,500
Skeletonized, verge, Swiss, double case, hand-carved movement, case silver & horn, 53mm,OF, C. 1800	700	900	1.200
Repousse paircase, fancy dial, verge, London, hallmarked silver, 49mm, OF, C. 1800 (illo.51)	800	1,100	1,600
Erotic Repousse paircase, Swan & Lady, verge, London (illo.52)	1,000	1,400	2,000

Repousse paircase, fancy dial, verge, English hallmarked silver case, 49mm, OF, C. 1800. (illo.51)

Erotic Repousse silver paircase, Swan & Lady, verge, Fusee, London. (illo.52)

OIGNON watch with mock pendulum, 58mm, Ca. 1700-1720. (illo.53)

Lady & mock pendulum, mock pendulum can be seen at top of Lady's head , 58mm, Ca. 1690 (illo.54)

TYPE – DESCRIPTION	Avg	Ex-Fn	Mint
Oignon watch with mock pendulum, 58mm, ca. 1700-20 (illo.53) .	$2,800	$4,000	$6,000
Lady & mock pendulum, enamel Lady, 58mm, Ca. 1690 (illo.54) .	3,200	4,600	6,500
Verge w/ calendar, repousse paircase, London hallmarked, silver, 51mm, OF, C. 1690	2,500	3,200	4,000
Dublin, early verge, silver paircase, champleve silver dial (signed), 54mm, OF, C. 1720	1,800	2,200	2,800
Early verge, large winged cock, signed silver dial, London, Egyptian pillars, silver, 55mm, OF, C. 1700 (illo.55)	2,000	2,400	3,000
Viennese enamel on gilt, verge, fusee, multi-scenes on case, KW, 55mm, HC, C. 1780	2,200	2,600	3,500
English, verge w/ calendar, signed champleve dial, silver & horn, 54mm OF, C. 1680	2,500	3,200	4,000

Early verge, large D shaped foot on the cock, London, signed silver dial, Egyptian pillars, silver, 55mm, OF, C. 1700 . (illo.55)

Oignon bulb shaped appearance start to appear after 1675 & having some uniform construction features point to a source of specialized workshops (ebauches) thus becoming reasonable priced & improved time keeping. **French** Oignon watches wind from the front dial side and the balance bridge cock has two screws & usually have domed shaped dials. **English** Oignon watches generally wind from back & the balance cock use a single screw & foot & the dials have a flat appearance.

Tortoise shell case, verge with chain driven fusee, calendar, D shaped foot balance cock, C. 1700, (illo.56)

English, verge, hand pierced cock, fusee, silver, note face on balance cock, C. 1720, (illo.57)

TYPE – DESCRIPTION	Avg	Ex-Fn	Mint
Tortoise shell, verge, calendar, Ca. 1700 (illo.56)	$1,900	$2,900	$5,000
English, verge, hand pierced cock, fusee, silver, Ca. 1720, (illo.57)	1,200	1,700	2,500
Pumpkin Form Case, verge, silver, 40mm, Ca. 1775 (illo.58)	1,800	2,600	4,000
Garooned Case, verge, fusee, 44mm, silver, Ca. 1650 (illo.59)	8,000	12,000	18,000
Painted scene on horn, verge, gilt, 57mm, OF, Ca. 1780 (illo.60)	1,800	2,600	3,500
(Amsterdam) verge fusee, 2 footed cock, 57mm , Ca.1685 (illo.60A)	5,000	7,000	10,000

Pumpkin Form Case, verge, silver, Ca. 1775. (illo.58)

Garooned Case, verge, fusee, 44mm, Ca. 1650. (illo.59)

Painted horn (full scene in color) London, verge, gilt, 57mm, OF, C. 1780. (illo.60)

(Amsterdam) verge fusee with mock pendulum, 2 footed cock, 57mm silver & Shagreen pair case, Ca.1685. (illo.60A)

EARLY NON—GOLD

Early Astronomic watch with day date month calendar, lunar calendar, 57mm, Ca. 1680. (illo.61)

TYPE – DESCRIPTION	Avg	Ex-Fn	Mint
Early Astronomic watch with day date month calendar, lunar calendar, 57mm, Ca. 1680 (illo.61)	$12,000	$20,000	$30,000
Early Astronomic watch with moon phases and triple date, fusee with cut-gut cord, 3 gear train, foliot, Ca.1660 (illo.62)	20,000	28,000	40,000

Early Astronomic watch with moon phases and triple date, fusee with cut-gut cord, 3 gear train, 6 armed foliot, Ca.1660. (illo.62)

Early German made silver watch, verge and foliot, silver pierced dial, "Hamburg", Ca. 1660. (illo.63)

TYPE – DESCRIPTION	Avg	Ex-Fn	Mint
Early German made silver watch, verge and foliot, silver pierced dial, "Hamburg", Ca. 1660 (illo.63)	$6,000	$8,500	$12,500
Early silver watch, blued steel hand, cut-gut fusee, foliot, rosette for adj., 53mm, Ca.1660 (illo.64)	12,000	15,000	20,000

Early silver watch, silver dial with blued steel hand, cut gut fusee, 3 wheel train, foliot, rosette (endless screw) for adjustment of the motor-spring tension(endless screw), 53mm, Ca.1660. (illo.64)

Pair cased, first case silver covered with nailed skin, verge, cut-gut cord fusee, 3 wheel train, foliot, pierced cock, endless screw adjustment for main spring tension, 45mm, Ca. 1660. (illo.65)

Early French watch movement with hour and minute hand, striking bell each hour, hand pierced case & gilt brass movement, cut-gut fusee, c. 1600s. (illo.66)

TYPE – DESCRIPTION	Avg	Ex-Fn	Mint
Pair cased, first case silver & nailed skin, verge, fusee, 3 wheel train, foliot, pierced cock, 45mm, Ca. 1660 (illo.65)	$7,000	$9,500	$13,000
Early Sun and Moon, verge escapement, Ca. 1680-1700	$4,000	$5,500	$8,000
Early French watch hour and minute hand, striking on bell, cut-gut fusee, c. 1600s (illo.66)	12,000	17,000	25,000
Early Drum Clock, iron plates, 4 wheel train, brass fusee on a steel great wheel, steel contrate wheel with brass teeth, steel verge and foliot balance w/ T-shaped ends, 34mm high (illo.67)	30,000	40,000	55,000

Early Drum style portable time-piece, Clock, iron plates, 4 wheel train, brass fusee on a steel great wheel, steel contrate wheel with brass teeth, steel verge and foliot balance with T-shaped ends . The cylindrical gilt brass case is finely engraved and is about 34mm high, Ca. 1550 - 1560. (illo.67)

🕐 Pricing in this Guide are fair market price for **COMPLETE** watches which are reflected from the "**NAWCC**" National and regional shows.

PRE–1850 *GOLD*

Lever or verge, Fusee, (Liverpool), 18K, multi-colored gold dial, 52mm, OF, C.1820-75. (illo.68).

Lever or cylinder, BAR style movement, GOLD, 45-52mm, OF, 1840-1865. (illo.69)

TYPE – DESCRIPTION	Avg	Ex-Fn	Mint
Lever, (Liverpool), **18K**, 52mm, OF, C.1820-75 (illo.68)	$300	$365	$500
Verge, (Liverpool), **18K**, 52mm, HC, C. 1820-75	400	525	700
Lever or cylinder, BAR, GOLD, 45-52mm, OF(illo.69)	250	300	425
(same as above) w / skeletonized movement,**18K** (illo.70)	375	465	600
Lever or cylinder, Le-Pine style, GOLD, 45-52mm, OF (illo.71)	250	300	425
Cylinder Fusee, paircase, London, plain case, porcelain dial,**18K**, 48mm, OF, C. 1880	1,100	1,400	1,900
Verge, multi-color case, Swiss/ French, porcelain dial, **18K**, 42mm,OF, Ca. 1770-1800	1,200	1,500	2,000
Verge, French, gold & enamel patterns on case, KWKS, OF, C. 1805	1,400	1,700	2,200
Verge, (Swiss), **18K**, 52-54mm, plain case, OF, C. 1790-1820	550	750	1,000
Verge, Swiss, gold scene, high quality, **18K**, 50mm, OF, C.1790	1,200	1,600	2,200

Lever or cylinder, skeletonized & engraved bar movement, Swiss, 45-52mm, OF,18K. (illo.70)

Lever or cylinder escapement, Lepine style movement, Ca. 1820-1835, GOLD, 45-52mm, OF. (illo.71)

Verge, repousse paircase, 20K gold case, 43mm, Open Face, Ca.1720 to 1750, (illo.72)

Early verge, D shaped balance cock, signed dial, London, Egyptian pillars, gold, 55mm, OF, Ca. 1690 to 1720. (illo.73)

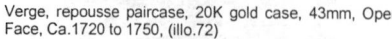

TYPE – DESCRIPTION	Avg	Ex-Fn	Mint
Verge, repousse paircase, 20K, 43mm, OF, C.1730 (illo.72)	$1,800	$2,500	$3,500
Early verge, large winged cock, signed dial, London,Egyptian pillars, gold, 55mm, OF, C. 1700 (illo.73).............................	2,000	2,400	3,000
Virgule, Fusee, Swiss or French, **18K,** 50-55mm, OF, C. 1790	1,200	1,400	1,800
Fusee, made in HOLLAND, Ca. 1720-50, silver case (illo.74)......	800	1,200	2,000
Skeletonized French, diamonds on bezel, 39mm, C.1780 (illo.75) .	1,400	1,900	2,500
Rack & Pinion lever escapement, **18K,** OF, Ca. 1830 (illo.75A)....	600	775	1,000

Fusee, movement made in **HOLLAND**, silver case, note the 2 footed bridge style, 55-60mm, OF, Ca. 1720 (illo.74)

Skeletonized French watch, diamonds on bezel, 39mm, C.1780 (illo.75)

Rack and Pinion Lever Escapement, 18K, OF, Ca. 1830 (illo.75A)

CHATELAINE, verge, fusee, 22k pair case, 45mm, (illo.76)

TYPE – DESCRIPTION	Avg	Ex-Fn	Mint
Chatelaine, verge, fusee, 22k pair case (illo.76)	$3,200	$4,200	$5,500
Early gold & nailed double case watch, foliot, C.1650-60 (illo.77)	20,000	24,000	30,000

Early gold & nailed double case watch, Champleve gold dial, 3 wheel train, verge, foliot, rosette adjustment and endless screw, 50mm, C.1670 (illo.77)

GOLD KEYS, the tops are all gold and the bottom key shaft is base metal, PRICES= **$90 to $175** each.

MISC. MEN'S GF / SILVER / BASE METAL

Dollar watch **German**, base metal ,OF, C.1895. (illo.78)

German, with camera, back wind, **waterproof style model,** base metal, OF, C.1885. (illo.79)

TYPE – DESCRIPTION	Avg	Ex-Fn	Mint
Dollar watch **German**, base metal ,OF, C.1895 (illo.78)	$40	$50	$75
German, back wind, **waterproof**, OF, C.1885 (illo.79)	250	285	350
Base metal, 7-17J, SW, 43-48mm, OF, C. 1900-1930	40	50	75
GF or silver, 7-17J, SW, 43-48mm, OF, C. 1895-1940	60	70	100
GF or silver, 7-17J, SW, 43-52mm, **HC**, C. 1895-1940.................	85	100	150
Swiss Fakes , 7J, KW, base metal, OF, 52mm, C. 1870-90............	65	75	100
Non-magnetic, pat.# 7546/780, **Moeris**, base metal (illo.80)	95	125	165
Cylinder, (Liverpool), 1/2 plate design (illo.81)...........................	85	100	125

Non-magnetic, pat.#7546-780, **Moeris**, base metal, thumb-nail set, SW, OF. (illo.80)

Cylinder escapement, (Liverpool), 1/2 plate design, marked 4 hole jeweled=8 jewels. (illo.81)

COMPARISON OF WATCH CASE SIZES

U. S. A.	EUROPEAN
10-12 SIZE	40—44 MM
16 SIZE	45—49 MM
18 SIZE	50—55 MM

KW KS, **Chinese Duplex** escapement, 3/4 plate design, note **BAT** style weights on balance, OF. (illo.82)

KW KS, with a **Compass** on movement, lever escapement, Ca. 1855. (illo.83)

TYPE – DESCRIPTION	Avg	Ex-Fn	Mint
KWKS, **Chinese Duplex**, 3/4 plate design, OF (illo.82)	$250	$300	$400
KWKS, **Compass** on movement, lever escap., (illo.83)	100	125	175
KWKS, 6-15J, silver, 45-52mm, OF, C. 1860-85	65	75	100
KWKS, 8-17J, silver, 45-52mm, HC, C. 1860-85	75	90	130
Engraved movement, KWKS, 15J, silver, 46mm, HC, C.1870	90	100	150
KWKS, marked railway, pin lever, Swiss (illo.84)	45	55	90
21J, RR type, GF, 48mm, OF, C. 1910-30	80	100	150
25J, Waltham (Swiss made), GF, 48mm, OF, C. 1950	100	125	175
Enamel & **embossed** hunting scene on **base metal** case, enamel dial, 3/4 plate, made in **Beaucourt France**, OF (illo.85)	100	125	175

KWKS, marked railway, pin lever, Swiss, Ca. 1889. (illo.84)

Niello enamel & embossed hunting scene on case, enamel dial, 3/4 plate, made in Beaucourt France, made by Japy Freres et Cie, OF, Ca. 1890. (illo.85)

1/4 repeater early rim activated, Swiss or French, silver, OF, Ca.1820. (illo.86)

Automaton, **Adam & Eve**, note snake circles Adam & Eve, hand painted enamel dial, KW KS, OF. (illo. 87)

TYPE – DESCRIPTION	Avg	Ex-Fn	Mint
1/4 repeater early rim activated, silver, OF, Ca.1820 (illo.86).........	$900	$1,200	$1,800
Automaton, **Adam & Eve**, w/ snake, KW KS, OF (illo. 87)...........	3,800	4,500	5,500
Spring detent chronometer w/**Tandem** wind, fusee, 56mm, Ca.1875 (illo.88)...	700	850	1,200
Gamblers playing cards on dial porcelain, Swiss, silver, OF (illo.89)	300	400	600

Spring Detent chronometer with **Tandem** wind, chain driven fusee, Helical hair spring, 56mm, Ca.1875. (illo.88)

Gamblers playing cards on porcelain dial, Swiss, silver, OF. (illo.89)

Exposed Skeletonized Balance from dial, enamel painted dial, verge, fusee, KW KS, large advance-retard index, Ca.1790. (illo.90)

TYPE – DESCRIPTION	Avg	Ex-Fn	Mint
Exposed Balance from dial, enamel painted dial, Ca.1790 (illo.90)	$1,600	$2,000	$2,600
Wandering Digital Jump Hour Hand, 45mm, Ca. 1880 (illo.91)....	3,500	4,800	7,000
Jump Digital Hour, W/ Date at 6, sec. hand at 3, Ca. 1820 (illo.92)	1,200	1,600	2,200

Wandering Digital Jump Hour Hand, Fusee, Cylinder Escapement, 45mm, silver, OF, Ca. 1880, (illo.91)

Jump Digital Hour, W/ Date at 6, sec. hand at 3, silver, engine turned dial, OF, Ca. 1820 (illo.92)

COMPARISON OF WATCH CASE SIZES

U. S. A.	EUROPEAN
10-12 SIZE	40—44 MM
16 SIZE	45—49 MM
18 SIZE	50—55 MM

Day, date, moon phases, Swiss, fancy dial, lever set at rim of case, GF, 46mm (illo.93)

Day, date, Swiss, fancy dial, **base metal**, 46mm. (illo.94)

TYPE – DESCRIPTION	Avg	Ex-Fn	Mint
Day, date, moon phases, Swiss, fancy dial, **GF**, 46mm (illo.93).....	$200	$275	$375
Day, date, moon phases, Swiss, fancy dial, **gun metal**, 46mm	150	235	350
Day, date, Swiss, fancy dial, **base metal**, 46mm (illo.94)	85	110	175
Self winding, (Von Loehr patent), KW, set from back (illo.95).....	400	525	700
Mock pendulum (dial side), **all original**, duplex escap. (illo.96) ..	350	425	500

Self winding, (Von Loehr patent), KW, set from back. (illo.95)

Mock pendulum (seen from face side), duplex escap. Multi-color dial. **FAKES** SEEN (illo.96)

MISC. MEN'S *GOLD, PLATINUM*

TYPE – DESCRIPTION	Avg	Ex-Fn	Mint
SW, 17J, **14K**, 43-46mm, OF, C. 1910-1940	$200	$225	$285
SW, 17J-19J, **18K**, 43-46mm, OF, C. 1910-1940	250	300	375
SW, 17J, **14K**, 48mm, HC, C. 1910-1940	375	400	525
SW, 17J, **Platinum**, 42mm, OF, C. 1940's	500	650	850
KWKS, 15J, lever, fancy ,gilt dial, **18K**, 45mm, C. 1870...............	275	335	425
KWKS, 15-20J, lever **18K**, 49-53mm, C. 1870-1885	400	500	685
Lever, Fusee, (Liverpool), 15J, porcelain dial, **18K**, 52mm, C.1860	450	550	750

UNUSUAL NON—GOLD

Skull (miniature) form watch, fusee, cylinder escapement, 25mm. Reproduction Ca. 1950 w/ early movement. (illo.97)

Silver Compass Watch, a small compass set into the movement can be seen through a hole in cuvette, (illo.98)

TYPE – DESCRIPTION	Avg	Ex-Fn	Mint
Skull (miniature) form, fusee, cylinder escape., 25mm, (illo.97)	$350	$565	$900
Silver Compass Watch, a small compass set into the móvement can be seen through a hole in cuvette, 43mm, OF (illo.98)	300	365	450
Blinking Eyes, pin set animated eyes, 46mm, (illo.99)....................	250	295	375
8 day, exposed balance, 7J, gun metal, 50mm, C. 1920s (illo.100).	125	185	275
8 day, exposed balance, 7J, Swiss, **DAY & DATE,** gun metal, 50mm, C. 1920s	200	275	400

Blinking Eyes, pin set animated eyes, 46mm. (illo.99)

8 day, exposed balance, 7J, by Hebdomas but with other name, gun metal, 50mm, C. 1920s. (illo.100)

🕐 Note: Some models and grades are not included. Their values can be determined by comparing with **similar** age, size, metal content, style, models and grades listed.

🕐 Note: Watches listed in this book are priced at the collectable trade show level, as **complete** watches having an original case, an original dial, and with the entire original movement in good working order with no repairs needed.

CHINESE DUPLEX
or CRAB LEG DUPLEX

BAT style weights
on balance

Chinese market, KWKS, duplex esc. silver, 58mm, OF,
note **BAT** style weights on balance, C.1870. (illo.101)

Chinese market, KW, duplex esc. silver, 58mm,
OF, C.1870. (illo.102)

TYPE – DESCRIPTION	Avg	Ex-Fn	Mint
For Chinese market, lever esc., 12J, KWKS, silver,			
BAT style weights on balance, 55mm, OF, C. 1880	$175	$235	$325
Chinese market, KW, duplex esc. silver, 58mm, OF, C.1870 (illo.101)	200	265	350
Chinese market, KW, duplex esc. silver, 58mm, OF, C.1870 (illo.102)	200	265	350
same as above with a **GOLD CASE**	450	565	700
same as above with a **GOLD CASE** + pearls	500	700	1,000
Chinese market, KW, duplex esc. silver, carved movement,			
58mm, OF, C.1870 (illo.103)	250	325	450
Carved movement, lever escap., KWKS, silver, 58mm, OF(illo.104)	95	125	200
KW, for Turkish market, 15J, .800 silver, 47mm, HC, C. 1880	100	150	225

Chinese market, KW, duplex esc. silver, carved movement,
58mm, OF, Ca.1850-70. (illo.103)

Carved movement, lever escap., KW KS, silver, 58mm, OF,
Ca.1850-70. (illo.104)

Oversize, moon phase & calendar, silver, 65-70mm, Ca.1900. (illo.105)

Moonphase triple cal., Swiss, gun metal, 50mm, OF, Ca. 1905. (illo.106)

TYPE – DESCRIPTION	Avg	Ex-Fn	Mint
Oversize PW, 15J, base metal, 65-70mm, C. 1900-1915	$125	$185	$250
Oversize, moon ph. & calendar, silver,65-70mm, Ca.1900 (illo.105)	700	1,000	1,500
Moonphase triple cal., Swiss, gun metal , 50mm, OF, C.1905(illo.106)	300	365	500
Moonphase triple cal., Swiss, silver or GF, 50mm, OF, C.1905	350	450	575
Moonphase triple cal., Swiss, silver, 52-54mm, **HC**, C. 1905	550	725	1,000
Moonphase calendar, sterling, , oversize 65mm, OF, C. 1895	700	975	1,400
Verge (Swiss) skeletonized KW movement, silver & horn pair-case, 61mm, C. 1800	650	785	1,000
Captain's watch, 2 hour dials, 1 train, KW KS, center second, silver, 50mm, HC, C. 1870 (illo.107)	325	465	700
Digital enamel dial, 15J, SW, Swiss, jump hr. & min. discs, silver, HC, Ca. 1900 (illo.108)	350	485	700
Above with gun metal case	250	350	500

Captain's watch, 2 hour dials, 1 train, KW KS, center second, silver, 50mm, HC, C. 1870. (illo.107)

Digital dial (porcelain), 15J, SW, Swiss, jump hr. & min. discs, silver,HC, C. 1900. (illo.108)

Swiss Pocket Watch with **BAROMETER,** Left: White enamel dial and outer Barometer chapter is signed "Made in France, Watch Barometer Patent", Right: Barometer is attached to movement, 7 jewels, Cylinder escapement, 54MM, Gun Metal, Ca. 1890. (illo.108A)

TYPE – DESCRIPTION	Avg	Ex-Fn	Mint
Swiss Pocket Watch with **BAROMETER,** Made in France, 54MM, Gun Metal, Ca. 1890. (illo.108A)	$900	$1,300	$2,000
Oversized 1/4 Hour Repeater, 3-1/4" diameter Gun Metal Watch Case, leather box, Ca. 1890. (illo.108B)	500	800	1,200

Oversized 1/4 Hour Repeater, 3-1/4" diameter Gun Metal Case, 29 jewels, 3/4 plate gilt movement, large white enamel dial, velvet-lined leather box , Ca. 1890. (illo.108B)

Ivory Case with matching ivory chain, verge movement, digital dial, key wind and key set, Ca. 1800. (illo.109)

Masonic triangular watch, Swiss ,17J, **mother of pearl** masonic dial, sterling, C. 1920's. (illo.110)

TYPE – DESCRIPTION	Avg	Ex-Fn	Mint
Ivory Case with matching ivory chain, verge movement, digital dial, key wind and key set, Ca. 1800. (illo.109)	$5,000	$6,300	$8,000
Automated w/moving windmill on dial, Swiss, colored scene, exposed balance, 8 day , base metal, OF, C.1910	400	500	625
Masonic triangular watch, Swiss ,17J, **mother of pearl** masonic dial, sterling, C. 1920's (illo.110)	1,100	1,700	2,500
Masonic, as above, with blue stone in crown, 1905	1,500	2,200	3,000
World time w/ 6 zones, Swiss, **Gun Metal**, OF, C. 1900 (illo.111)	500	650	800
Swiss, **Niello** scene on back of case	800	925	1,200
Swiss, **silver**, 52mm, OF, C. 1900	750	850	1,100
World time, 24 Cities, w/ coded color rotating dial, **18K GOLD**, 61mm (illo.112)	2,500	4,000	6,500

World time, with 6 zones, Swiss, GUN METAL, 52mm, OF, Ca.1900. (illo.111)

World time, 24 Cities, with coded color rotating dial, Ca. 1895, 61mm. (illo.112)

TYPE – DESCRIPTION	Avg	Ex-Fn	Mint
Mysterieuse watch, Swiss, see-through dial, hidden movement			
silver, 52mm, OF, Ca. 1895 (illo.113-114)............................	$1,000	$1,900	$3,000
GOLD, 52mm, OF, Ca. 1895 (illo.113-114).................... ★★	2,000	2,600	3,500
Wooden works, wooden wheels, wooden case, (illo.115)...... ★★	2,800	3,700	5,000
above w/ wooden **chain** and wooden storage style box ★★★	4,500	5,800	8,000
Sector watch, fan-shaped, fly back hour & min. hands, 17J,			
"Record Watch Co.," silver, 49x34mm, Ca. 1900 (illo.116)...	1,800	2,800	4,500
Musical, play's 2 tunes, silver, HC, 50mm, Ca. 1900 (illo.117)......	2,400	3,100	4,200

Mysterieuse watch, Swiss, see-through dial, showing dial side of watch, 52mm, OF, Ca. 1895. (illo.113)

Mysterieuse watch, Swiss, see-through dial, showing the hidden movement, 52mm, OF, Ca. 1895. (illo.114)

Wooden works, wooden wheels, wooden case, all wooden watch, 50mm, made in **Russia**, Ca. 1860. (illo.115)

Sector watch, fan-shaped, fly back hour & min. hands, 17J, "Record Watch Co.," silver, 49x34mm, Ca. 1900. (illo.116)

Musical, play's 2 tunes, silver, 30 Tines, HC, 50mm, 1900. (illo.117)

Wandering hour hands, 12 hands appear one at a time and move across minute sector, the 12 hands are on 3 star wheels, pin lever escapement, **gun metal** case, Ca. 1900. (illo.M1)

TYPE – DESCRIPTION		Avg	Ex-Fn	Mint
Wandering hour hands, 12 hands are on 3 star wheel, **gun metal** , pin lever escapement, Ca. 1900. (illo.M1)	★★	$1,000	$1,700	$2,500
Wandering hour hands and **1/4 repeater**, 12 hands are on 3 star wheel, cylinder escapement, **18K gold**, Ca. 1800. (illo.M2)	★★★	6,000	8,500	12,000

Wandering hour hands and **1/4 repeater**, 12 hands appear one at a time and move across minute sector, the 12 hands are on 3 star wheels, cylinder escapement, **18K** gold case. Ca. 1800. (illo.M2)

Pouzait style escape wheel, with 15 upright teeth (see"T" on escapement illo.), the center seconds hand jumps (dead seconds), silver 60 MM hunting case, Ca. 1885.(illo. M3)

TYPE – DESCRIPTION		Avg	Ex-Fn	Mint
Pouzait style escape wheel, with 15 upright teeth, dead seconds, **silver**, 60 MM, hunting case, Ca. 1885 (illo. M3)..............★		$1,400	$2,500	$4,000
Pouzait, 15 upright teeth on the escape wheel, large 5 arm balance, by Du Bois et Fils, **gold**, 57MM, Ca. 1800 (illo. M4).....★★		8,000	9,500	12,000

Pouzait style lever with 15 upright teeth on the escape wheel, each swing of the large 5 arm balance is one second, J.M. Pouzait lever escapement was introduced in 1786, the escape wheel with upright teeth are seen in 15 and 30 teeth, escapement seen through plate, many watches of this style were signed and made by Du Bois et Fils, also seen signed Breguet et Fils, Ca. 1800 (illo. M4)

Constant Force escapement, has a system for a force of transmission to the escapement, by a superimposed double wheel maintained in constant force by a calibrated impulse spring. The case is 18K hunter case, enamel dial signed Hess & Metford Geneve Chronometer Constant Force, key wind, 19 jewels, 50mm, Ca.1850. (illo. E1)

TYPE – DESCRIPTION

TYPE – DESCRIPTION	Avg	Ex-Fn	Mint
Constant Force escapement, 19J, 55mm, 18K, HC (illo. E1)	$6,000	$7,500	$10,000
Robin detent lever escapement, 20J, 52mm, 18K, HC (illo. E2)	$6,000	$7,500	$10,000

Robin type detent lever escapement, the lever with its two locks, is in straight line with the balance and the escape wheel, but behind the latter. Nickel movement, 20 jewels, in gold screwed settings, 52mm, HC, Ca.1800.(illo.E2)

Thomas Prest patented a devise for winding a watch by the pendant or knob. On October of **1820** he received his UK patent No. 4501. This system had no provision for setting the hands. The first stem-winding and setting of the hands system was invented by Louis Audemars of La Brassus in the Valley de Joux in the year of 1838. In 1842 Jean Adrien Philippe made a watch which could be wound and set by means of the crown. In **1844** Adolphe Nicole took out 2 patent's for winding and setting, one for fusee & chain, one for going barrel, UK patent No. 10348 which looks similar to the Prest with his improvements. In **1845** Philippe receives his patent No. 1317 for his modern winding system. The most successful design by Charles Antoine LeCoultre of Le Sentier in about **1847**.

Above: Left, movement signed "Brinkman London No. 4321", (may be Prest design winding system), Ca. 1850.
Right: "Nicole Nilson & Co. 14 Soho Square London," Ca. 1857-70s. Also seen signed J.Dent. (See **Dent** listing)

TYPE – DESCRIPTION	Avg	Ex-Fn	Mint
Early Wind, Ca. 1820-1870, Gold case	$2,000	$2,600	$3,500

Unique winding design (Each time the hunting case style watch is opened to view the time, the mainspring is partially wound) Patented in 1873 by B. Haas. (illo.A)

TYPE – DESCRIPTION	Avg	Ex-Fn	Mint
Unique winding design, 42mm, **gold HC**, (A)	$2,200	$2,700	$3,500
Endless screw winding system, 42mm, **silver HC** (B)	400	600	1,000
Automaton & Musical **Carillon a <u>nest</u>** of 5 bells,18K,HC (C)	40,000	60,000	90,000

Peculiar Endless screw winding system, stem wind, pin set, 15 jewels, pat. by Lehmann, Pat. # 56,683 Ca. 1868, Serial number 85,290. (illo. B)

Musical Carillon with a **nest** of 5 bells & 5 hammers, enamel painted ship scene on back in the manner of Richter, enamel dial with center seconds, Automaton scene, 63mm, Ca 1790. (illo. C)

A. Roulette wheel style dial, press a lever & the center pointer spins to a red or black number.
B. Roulette wheel style dial, press a button & the center pointer spins to a red or black number.
C. Horse Race dial, twist the crown & a tiny ball spins & falls into a indentation at one of 9 horses.

TYPE – DESCRIPTION	Avg	Ex-Fn	Mint
A. Roulette wheel style dial, press a lever & the center pointer spins to a red or black number.	$125	$225	$400
B. Roulette wheel style dial, press a button & the center pointer spins to a red or black number.	125	225	400
C. Horse Race dial, twist the crown & a tiny ball spins & falls into a indentation at one of 9 horses.	200	325	500
D. Roulette wheel style dial, press a button & the center pointer spins to a red or black number.	125	225	400
E. Horse Race dial, push the crown & 8 horses rotate , the winner appears in an aperture (window).	200	325	500
F. Dice Game, press a lever & the platform spins causing 5 dice to roll and come up randomly.	125	225	400
G. Calendar watch key Day, Date & Moon Phase, Ca. 1800-1820	300	400	650

D. Roulette wheel style dial, press a button & the center pointer spins to a red or black number.
E. Horse Race dial, push the crown & 8 horses rotate , the winner appears in an aperture (window).
F. Dice Game, press a lever & the platform spins causing 5 dice to roll and come up randomly.

G. Calendar watch key with DAY, DATE & MOON PHASE, Ca. 1800-1820.

NIELLO WATCH CASES

Niello (nye-el-oh) is a black or dark blue composition of lead, silver, copper, sulfur and ammonium chloride. The mixture is fused onto an engraved or cut out metal base by firing the mix in a process similar to **champleve** enameling. Silver was the most often used metal for Niello cases. Rose gold inlay is also seen in combination with Niello. Niello cases appeared in the early 1900s about the same time Art Nouveau and Art Deco was popular. Huegenin Brothers of Le Locle, Favre of Le Locle, Duchene of Geneva, Rene Lalique of Paris and Longines of St. Imier played prominent roles in the design and marketing of Niello cases. Niello cases were never made in quantity by the American case factories.

Above: (A)
signed
Huegenin.

(A) Niello, silver only, floral motif, signed, 46mm OF, Ca.1905. (B) Niello, silver & rose gold, floral motif, 40mm HC, Ca.1910.

TYPE – DESCRIPTION	Avg	Ex-Fn	Mint
(A) Niello, silver only, floral motif, signed, 46mm OF	$300	$525	$850
HC	400	625	950
(B) Niello, silver & rose **gold**, floral motif, Ca. 1910, 40mm OF	200	335	575
HC	250	425	650
(C) Niello, silver only, Floral motif, signed, 46mm OF	325	575	825
HC	400	625	950
(D) Niello, silver only, Floral motif, **NOT** signed, OF	225	385	700
HC	300	475	800

(C) Niello, silver only, floral motif, signed, 46mm HC.   (D) Niello, silver only, floral motif, **NOT** signed, HC.

(E) Niello, silver only, portrait motif (**Lady Liberty**), 50mm HC.   (F) Niello, silver & gold, portrait+floral+scene, 47mm HC.

TYPE – DESCRIPTION	Avg	Ex-Fn	Mint
(E) Niello, silver only, portrait Lady Liberty, 50mm OF	$400	$700	$1,200
HC	500	850	1,300
(F) Niello, silver & gold, portrait+floral+scene, 47mm OF	400	685	1,100
HC	500	850	1,300
(G) Niello, silver & gold, with a portrait, (Omega), 47mm OF	400	750	1,200
HC	500	850	1,300
(H) Niello, silver, **equestrian** motif, 47mm OF	325	575	875
HC	400	625	1,000

(G) Niello, silver & gold, portrait motif, (Omega), 47mm HC.   (H) Niello, silver, **equestrian** motif, 47mm HC.

Art Nouveau: A style of art decoration popular from about 1890 to 1910, depicted as curves & flowing intertwining floral designs, Gazelles & female with long hair. Designs by Tiffany & Coco Channel.
Art Deco: Derived from the discovery of King Tut's tomb in 1922. A style of art decoration using Cubism, Egyptian, Aztec & Mayan themes. The angle was in & curves were out.

(J) Niello, silver & rose gold, hunting Motif, 47mm HC.   (K) Niello, silver & gold, hunting motif, 47mm HC.

TYPE – DESCRIPTION	Avg	Ex-Fn	Mint
(J) Niello, silver & **rose** gold, hunting scene, 47 mm OF	$350	$500	$875
HC	400	650	950
(K) Niello, silver & **gold**, hunting scene, 47mm OF	450	700	1,100
HC	550	850	1,300
(L) Niello, silver, **owl**, animal motif, 47mm OF	300	450	800
HC	400	600	950
(M) Niello, silver & **rose** gold, **tiger**, animal motif, 48mm OF	425	725	1,000
HC	500	775	1,100

(L) Niello, silver, owl, animal motif, 47mm HC.   (M) Niello, silver & rose gold, **tiger**, animal motif, 48mm HC.

Art Nouveau: A style of art decoration popular from about 1890 to 1910, depicted as curves & flowing intertwining floral designs, Gazelles & female with long hair. Designs by Tiffany & Coco Channel.
Art Deco: Derived from the discovery of King Tut's tomb in 1922. A style of art decoration using Cubism, Egyptian, Aztec & Mayan themes. The angle was in & curves were out.

(N) Niello, silver & gold, automobile motif, 47mm HC.

(P) Niello, silver, **signed** pattern motif, 47mm HC.

TYPE – DESCRIPTION	Avg	Ex-Fn	Mint
(N) Niello, silver & gold, automobile motif, 47mm OF	$400	$650	$1,000
HC	500	750	1,100
(P) Niello, silver, **signed** pattern motif, 47mm OF	100	285	475
HC	185	300	550
(R) 1/4 hour repeater, silver & gold, 50MM, Ca.1905, OF	1,500	1,700	2,000
HC	1,800	2,000	2,400
(S) **Minute** repeater, silver & rose gold, 54MM, Ca.1900 OF	1,900	2,100	2,500
HC	2,200	2,500	3,000

(R) 1/4 hr. repeater, Niello silver & gold OF, gold crest and with swirling leafs & roses, 50MM, Ca.1905.

(S) Min. slide activated repeater, Niello silver & rose gold, 38J., wolfs tooth winding, 54MM, Ca.1900.

Rock crystal & enamel, star shape case, champleve enameled dial, verge, gilt & crystal case, 57x27mm, original French form Ca. 1600-1660, **Shown** Viennese form Ca. 1780-1800. (illo.118)

TYPE – DESCRIPTION	Avg	Ex-Fn	Mint
Rock crystal & enamel, star shape case, champleve dial, **Shown** Viennese verge, gilt & crystal case, 57x27mm, C.1800 (illo.118)	$4,000	$4,600	$7,000
Crucifix form 1/4 hr. repeater & musical, crystal & silver form case, **Shown** Viennese (illo.119)...	6,500	9,500	15,000

Crucifix form 1/4 hr. repeater & musical, crystal & silver form case, original French form Ca. 1600-1660, **Shown** Viennese form Ca. 1780-1800. (illo.119)

Early Cross Watch, the Cross form pierced silver case depicts the Christ Crucifixion scene. Side view of movement. The Crucifix form fusee movement has a T shaped foliot style balance made of steel and the balance is supported by a hand pierced free form silver cock, a pre-hairspring balance, verge escapement with a gut style fusee, Ca.1640.

TYPE – DESCRIPTION	Avg	Ex-Fn	Mint
Early Cross form Watch,	$9,000	$11,000	$14,000
Early Octagon Crystal Watch,	8,000	9,500	13,000

Early Octagon Crystal Watch, the movement has a T shaped foliot style balance made of brass and the balance is supported by a hand pierced free form silver cock, a pre-hairspring balance, verge escapement with a gut style fusee, Ca.1650.

Above note thin watch.
Extra flat watch, **1.5mm thick,** Swiss, 18K, HC,__ACTUAL SIZE__,50mm. (illo.120)

TYPE – DESCRIPTION	Avg	Ex-Fn	Mint
Extra flat watch, 1.5mm thick, Swiss, **18K**, HC, 50mm (illo.120)..	$2,000	$2,700	$3,500
Jump 1/4 seconds, 2 train, 30J, KW, nickel, (Swiss), **18K**, 56mm, HC, C. 1870-90	2,000	2,700	3,500
Captain's watch, enameled portraits on case, Maharaja & Queen Victoria, KW, lever movement, **18K**, 44mm, HC, C.1870	2,500	3,100	4,000
Captain's watch, KW, 15J, engraved case & enamel dial, **2 train, 18K**, 52-58mm, OF, C. 1870 (illo.121)	1,000	1,900	3,000
1776-1876 centennial watch, Henry O. Stauffer, bridges in 1776 form, 17J, **18K**, 53mm, HC, C. 1876 (illo.122)	1,500	2,400	3,500
Above not marked Henry Stauffer, base metal	400	525	750

Captain's watch, KW, 15J, engraved case & enamel dial, **2 train,**18K, 52-58mm, OF, Ca. 1870. (illo.121)

1776-1876 Centennial watch, H.O. Stauffer, bridges in 1776 form, 17J, 18K, 53mm, HC, Ca. 1876. Made by Georges Favre- Jacot of le Locle later became *Zenith* (illo.122)

Above: Hour and Minute hands **CONTRACTED.**

Extremely RARE oval watches with hands that **EXPAND** and **CONTRACT**. The hands work much like a pantograph or scissors that follow cams to expand and contract the hands. Eight day going movement , 60 seconds auxiliary dial, also a 1/4 seconds dial. The case has 60 pearls and the watch is thought to be made by **William Anthony** of London, Ca. 1795. William Anthony was famous for his verge watches and watches set in pearls and diamonds, with many of his watches being made for the Chinese market. There is a good example of this type watch and may be seen in Lisbon, Portugal at the Casa Museum "Foundation Medeiros e Almeida.

TYPE – DESCRIPTION

		Avg	Ex-Fn	Mint
Oval watch with hands that **EXPAND** and **CONTRACT**				
eight day, 60 sec. & 1/4 sec. dials, Gold case........	★★★★★	$90,000	$125,000	$175,000
above with 60 pearls	★★★★★	95,000	150,000	200,000

Above: Hour and Minute hands **EXPANDED.**

Above: The Expanding and Contracting hour and minute follow an oval or egg shaped lead and follow cam, at the center of the dial. Thus while rotating around the cam, they lengthen & shorten according to the axis of the dial or cam. This system is similar to Pantograph or much like scissors in action.

Moonphase, double dial, calendar, Swiss, 17J, back lid opens to reveal cal. dial, 14K, HC, C.1890. (illo.123)

TYPE – DESCRIPTION	Avg	Ex-Fn	Mint
Captain's watch, KW KS, 15J, ornate case, Swiss, single train, **18K**, 52mm, HC, C. 1870	$800	$1,200	$1,800
Digital dial, hrs. & min. on digital jump discs, Swiss, 15J, SW, **18K**, 51mm, HC, C. 1905	1,000	1,300	1,800
Moonphase, double dial, full calendar, Swiss, 17J, Moonphase, back lid opens to reveal cal. dial, **14K**, HC, C.1890 (illo.123)	2,300	2,800	3,500
Moonphase, full calendar, gold, OF	2,000	2,400	3,000
Two train, center independent sec.,2 going barrels, lever escap., KW KS, GOLD, 42mm, Ca. 1880, HC (illo. 124)	1,000	1,300	1,800
Art Deco dial, Swiss, **18K**, 45mm,OF (illo.125)	600	850	1,200

Two train, center independent sec.,2 going barrels, lever escap.,KW KS, GOLD, 42mm, Ca. 1880, HC. (illo. 124)

Art Deco style with **exaggerated** numbers on dial, Swiss, 18K, 45mm,OF. (illo.125)

TYPE – DESCRIPTION	Avg	Ex-Fn	Mint
Double dials, world time & moon ph. triple date,**18K** (illo.126)	$4,500	$5,700	$8,000
Perpetual calendar with moonphase and chrono., Swiss , 20J, porcelain dial, 3/4 plate, 18K, 51mm, OF, C.1890-1900	5,500	7,200	9,000
Rare verge, w/ automaton "Serpent, Adam & Eve" on dial with moving serpent, verge, French , 18K, OF, C. 1800	4,500	5,300	7,000
Musical, two train of gears, pin cylinder & 24 blades, one tune, 18K (illo.127)	2,500	3,300	5,500
Waterproof watch w/wind ind. 17J., C.1885 (illo.128)	1,000	1,400	2,000
Cigarette lighter & Swiss watch, Dunhill, Silver, C.1926 (illo.129)	300	450	700
9K case	900	1,100	1,400
14K case	1,200	1,400	1,700
$20.00 U.S. gold coin, 17J, mvt. in coin, 35mm, Ca.1920's (illo.130)	1,200	1,500	2,000

Double dials, world time & moon ph. triple date,18K. (illo.126)

Musical, two train of gears, pin cylinder & 24 blades, one tune, 18K. (illo.127)

Waterproof watch w/wind ind. 17J., C.1885. (illo.128)

Cigarette lighter & Swiss watch, Dunhill, Silver, Ca.1926. (illo.129)

$20.00 U.S. gold coin, 17J, Swiss mvt. in coin, 35mm, Ca.1920's. (illo.130)

Skeletonized Verge & Fusee *(French)*, Multi-color 18K Case & rose cut diamonds, horseshoe shaped plate, balance end stone is a large Cabochon Ruby,45MM, KW KS, Ca. 1785.(illo.130A)

TYPE – DESCRIPTION	Avg	Ex-Fn	Mint
Skeletonized Verge & Fusee movement, 45MM, KWKS with Multi-color 18K Case, Ca. 1785 (illo.130A)	$2,800	$3,300	$4,000
Lorgnette Form Watch, 3/8" x 7/8 x 3-1/4", *18K Closed Case,* KWKS, Ca. 1850. (illo.130B)	3,700	4,800	6,500

Lorgnette Form Watch, 3/8" x 7/8 x 3-1/4", *18K Closed Case,* the case is chased with leaf patterns and arabesque, signed "Echappement a Cylindre Huit Trous en Rubis", the looking frames are rose gold and flip out with a push button, KWKS, Ca. 1850. (illo.130B)

MISC. SWISS LADY'S Ca. 1850–1950 SILVER or GOLD FILLED

TYPE – DESCRIPTION	Avg	Ex-Fn	Mint
GF or silver, 7-17J, SW, 35mm, OF, C. 1900-1930	$45	$55	$85
GF or silver, 10-15J, SW, 35mm, fancy dial, OF, C. 1910	65	75	125
GF or silver, 7-17J, SW, 35- 40mm, HC, C. 1890-1930	75	95	135
Enamel or silver, cylinder, pinset, 35mm, OF, C. 1910	65	75	125
KWKS, silver, 40- 45mm, OF, C. 1865-1885	75	95	125
KWKS, silver, 37- 45mm, **HC**, C. 1865-1885	100	125	175
Ball shaped, 17J, 35mm, SW, GF or silver with chain	125	165	200

MISC. LADYS Ca. 1850–1950 *GOLD* (NO ENAMEL)

TYPE – DESCRIPTION	Avg	Ex-Fn	Mint
SW, 7-15J, 14K, 35- 40mm, OF, C. 1910-1930	$100	$135	$200
SW, 7-15J, 14K, 35- 40mm, HC, C. 1910-1930	200	250	325
KWKS, 10J, cylinder, 18K, 34- 40mm, OF, C.1865-90	150	200	275
KWKS, 10J, cylinder, 18K, 38- 43mm, HC, C. 1865-85	200	265	400
Fusee, lever, fancy dial, 18K, 38- 43mm, OF, C. 1845-75	300	385	500
Fusee, lever, fancy dial, 18K, 38- 43mm, HC, C. 1850s	400	485	600
Ball shaped w/pin, 10J, 14K, 25mm, OF, C. 1890	500	575	650

MISC. LADYS Ca. 1850–1950 ENAMEL ON *GOLD*

TYPE – DESCRIPTION	Avg	Ex-Fn	Mint
KW, enamel (black outlines) 18K, 40- 42mm HC, C. 1860	$250	$350	$475
KW, enamel & dia., Swiss, 10J, 18K, OF, C. 1860	350	465	650
Pattern enamel & demi-hunter, 15J, 18K , 35mm, HC, C.1885	400	550	800
Portrait enamel, KWKS, Swiss, 14K, 34- 42mm, HC, C. 1870	425	600	900
Enamel , with pearls and/ or dia., 10-17J, w/ matching pin, 18K, 23-26mm, OF	700	1,000	1,400
Enamel, w/dia. or pearls, w/ pin, 18K, 26-30mm, HC, C. 1895	900	1,300	1,800
Miniature verge, gold & enamel w/ pearls, superior enamel, Swiss, KW, gold case, 27mm, OF, C. 1770	2,500	3,600	5,000
Miniature HC enamel & dia., 17J, Swiss, with orig. pin, 18K, 23mm, HC, C. 1890	1,200	1,800	2,500
Ball-shaped (Duchene) Geneva, verge, KW, enamel and gold, 25mm, C. 1800	1,200	1,800	2,500

⊕ Note: Some models and grades are not included. Their values can be determined by comparing with similar age, size, metal content, style, models and grades listed.

⊕ Note: Watches listed in this book are priced at the collectable Trade Show level, as complete watches having an original case, an original dial, and with the entire original movement in good working order with no repairs needed.

COMPARISON OF WATCH CASE SIZES

U. S. A.	EUROPEAN
10-12 SIZE	40—44 MM
16 SIZE	45—49 MM
18 SIZE	50—55 MM

LADY'S UNUSUAL *GOLD* & ENAMEL

LEFT; Ball-shaped, bezel wind, 18K, enamel & diamonds, Swiss, 16mm, OF, C. 1920. (illo.131) CENTER: Ring watch w/enamel & dia., Swiss, 18K, 18mm, C.1910. (illo.132) RIGHT: Padlock form enamel and gold, Swiss, KW. (illo.133)

TYPE – DESCRIPTION	Avg	Ex-Fn	Mint
Ball-shaped, bezel wind, Swiss, enamel & diamonds on **18K** case, size of a marble, 16mm, OF, C. 1920 (illo.131)	$900	$1,400	$2,000
Above in gold plated case	500	625	800
Ring watch w/enamel & dia., Swiss, 18K, 18mm, C.1910 (illo.132)	750	1,100	1,500
Cherry form enamel & 18K, 17J, closed case, bezel wind, Swiss, 22mm,	1,500	2,300	3,500
Flower basket form, enamel and 18K, Swiss, KWKS, with heart form movement, 10J, 18K, 30x24mm, HC, C. 1860	2,500	3,500	5,000
Padlock form enamel and gold, Swiss, KW (illo.133)	900	1,500	2,500
Padlock form enamel and gold (cover over dial,) Swiss, KW, diamonds on case, heart shaped mvt.,18K, 28x51mm, HC, C.1870	1,200	1,900	3,000
Form watch in shape of **leaf**, gold & enamel, Bar mvt. (illo.134)	1,200	1,900	3,000

Form watch in shape of **leaf**, gold & enamel, cylinder escapement, Bar movement., KW KS, Ca.1865. (illo.134)

🕐 Pricing in this Guide are fair market price for **COMPLETE** watches which are reflected from the "**NAWCC**" National and regional shows. The Complete Price Guide to Watches goal is to stimulate the orderly exchange of **Watches** between *"buyers"* and *"sellers"*.

Scarab form gold & enamel, 10J, cylinder, diamonds, closed case w/wings that open, 18K, 54x23mm, C.1885. (illo.135)

Rare enamel & gold harps, matched pair w/ music, verge, diamonds, lapis and enameled scenes, 3 3/4" high, C.1830. (illo.136)

TYPE – DESCRIPTION	Avg	Ex-Fn	Mint
Scarab form gold & enamel, 10J, cylinder, diamonds, closed case w/wings that open, 18K, 54x23mm, C.1885 (illo.135)	$4,000	$5,400	$7,500
Lorgnette with enamel & gold, KW, 10J, Swiss, 3 1/4" x 1" cover ornamented w/dia., 18K	3,500	4,500	6,000
Rare enamel &gold harps, matched pair w/ music, verge, diamonds, lapis and enameled scenes, 3 3/4" high, C.1830 (illo.136)	20,000	30,000	45,000
Rock crystal case, silver dial, **Viennese** made, C. 1830 (illo.137)	4,000	6,000	10,000

Rock crystal case, silver dial, Viennese made, C. 1830. (illo.137)

ENAMEL WATCHES

Floral enamel watch. Bouquet of flowers within a champleve border of scrolls enclosing panels of flowers. (illo.E-2)

Floral enamel watch. Finely painted floral enamel panel within border of seed pearls. (illo.E-1)

SIZE AND DESCRIPTION	Avg	Ex-Fn	Mint
55mm, finely painted floral, seed pearls, (Bovet also Ilbery),18K (illo.E.1)	$8,000	$11,000	$15,000
47mm, gold enamel repeater, with chatelaine of pierced gold links & enamel plaques with enamel key & fob seals (illo.E.2)	5,000	6,500	9,000
Enamel & pearls, hunting scene of lion, for China market, silver gilt duplex escapement, 62mm, Ca. 1845 (illo.E-3)	4,000	5,500	8,000
Enamel and 18K case, automated horseman and windmill also fountain, horse drinks water (illo.E-4)	25,000	32,000	45,000
Enamel floral scene, enamel and pearls on gold case, finely painted floral bouquet, 55mm (illo.E-5)	20,000	28,000	40,000
Enamel and 18K case, MINUTE- REPEATER, HC, surrounded with pearls, 55mm, (illo.E-5A)	12,000	15,000	20,000
VIENNESE enamel watch, the front cover shows a lady and gentleman in a scene, the back cover pictures three boys in a scene, 55mm (illo.E-6 & E-6A)	1,500	1,900	2,500
54mm, 29J., 1/4 repeater, pearls & enamel, silver case (illo.E-8)	1,800	2,300	3,000
VIENNESE Lapis Lazuli enamel watch, verge fusee, top and bottom covers are finely cut solid lapis stone, champleve enamel dial, Ca. 1830 (illo.E-9)	2,800	4,200	6,000

⊕ French watch-making believed to have started in town of Blois, France. French Enamel Watches also believed to have started in Blois, in early 1600's.

Enamel & pearls, hunting scene of lion, for China market, duplex escapement, 62mm, Ca. 1845. (illo.E-3)

Enamel and 18K case, automated horseman and windmill also fountain, horse drinks water. (illo.E-4)

Enamel floral scene, enamel and pearls on gold case, finely painted floral bouquet, 55mm (illo.E-5)

Enamel and 18K case, MINUTE- REPEATER, Hunting Case, surrounded with pearls, 55mm, Ca.1890. (illo.E-5A)

VIENNESE enamel watch, the front cover shows a lady and gentleman in a scene, the back cover pictures three boys in a scene, 55mm. see movement below. (illo.E-6)

VIENNESE enamel watch, same watch as above, two-footed balance bridge, the inner lids are decorated with polychrome enamelled scenes. (illo.E-6A)

54mm, 29J, 1/4 hour repeater, Pearls and enamel on a silver case, ca. 1885. (illo.E-8)

VIENNESE Lapis Lazuli enamel watch, verge fusee, top and bottom covers are finely cut solid lapis stone, champleve enamel dial, Viennese made, Ca. 1830 (illo.E-9)

Floral enamel watch, 57mm, bouquet of flowers within a gold case set with split pearls. (illo.E-10)

Enamel scene watch, 58mm, finely painted scene of ships in harbor. (illo.E-11)

SIZE AND DESCRIPTION	Avg	Ex-Fn	Mint
57mm, floral enamel, duplex, (Bovet), pearls, 18K, (illo.E-10)	$6,500	$8,000	$10,000
58mm, harbor scene enamel, duplex, 18k, Ca. 1790 (illo.E-11)	18,000	25,000	35,000
43mm, basket form champleve enamel, 18k, Ca.1800 (illo.E.12) ...	2,800	4,000	6,000
42mm, champleve border, finely painted flowers, (Le Roy), gold case & chain..	2,500	2,900	3,500
37mm, rose gold guilloche enamel demi-hunter..............................	350	475	600
36mm, gold enamel & champleve enamel, verge, Ca. 1800	1,500	2,200	3,000
35mm, gold champleve enamel, (L'Epine), cylinder	700	900	1,200
35mm, gold enamel & seed pearls, rose cut diamonds	300	425	600
34mm, gold egg-shaped form enamel, verge, (Austrian)	1,200	2,000	3,500
30mm, gold miniature enamel, verge, seed pearls, Ca. 1800	800	900	1,200
27mm, gold enamel lapel brooch with seed pearls & rose cut diamonds, Ca. 1890	550	700	900
27mm, gold fine enamel lapel brooch with cut diamonds by C. H. Meylan (illo.E.13)	1,500	1,900	2,500

Enamel form tapered oval basket with rising rope handle, enhanced with panels of flowers, 18K case. (illo.E-12)

A chased enamel gold lady's pendant watch. Enamel portrait of a lady. (illo.E-13)

(ILLO. A)   (ILLO. B)   (ILLO. D)

Size and Description	Avg	Ex-Fn	Mint
27mm, Art Noveau design, multi-colored flowers gold & diamond pendant watch & pin, 18K, OF, Ca.1890 (illo. A)	$800	$1,200	$1,800
25mm, Enamel & pearls & diamonds, star shaped gold settings , pendant and pen, 18K, OF, Ca. 1890 (illo. B)	700	900	1,200
25mm, enamel pendant with pin, golden frame of vines around a scene of a lady , 14K, OF, Ca. 1900	900	1,300	1,800
24mm, pearl pendant watch with pin, seed pearls also on classic fleur-de-lis designed pin, 14K OF, Ca.1885 (illo. C)	800	1,100	1,500
24mm, enamel and gold pendant watch with a starburst gold and pearl pin, 10 J, cylinder movement, 18K, OF, Ca.1900 (illo. D)	800	1,100	1,500
22mm, ball-shaped enamel & pearl pendant watch, exposed balance, lever escapement can be seen back crystal (illo. E)	1,400	1,700	2,200
20mm, 17J, three-finger bridge miniature movement, Adj.5P, by Didsheim platinum OF case, Ca.1930s (illo. F)	1,100	1,400	1,800

(ILLO. C)   (ILLO. E)   (ILLO. F)

Am. Waltham W. Co.

Date	Serial #
1852 –	50
1853 –	400
1854 –	1,000
1855 –	2,500
1856 –	4,000
1857 –	6,000
1858 –	10,000
1859 –	15,000
1860 –	20,000
1861 –	30,000
1862 –	45,000
1863 –	65,000
1864 –	110,000
1865 –	180,000
1866 –	260,000
1867 –	330,000
1868 –	410,000
1869 –	460,000
1870 –	500,000
1871 –	540,000
1872 –	590,000
1873 –	680,000
1874 –	730,000
1875 –	810,000
1876 –	910,000
1877 –	1,000,000
1878 –	1,150,000
1879 –	1,350,000
1880 –	1,500,000
1881 –	1,670,000
1882 –	1,835,000
1883 –	2,000,000
1884 –	2,350,000
1885 –	2,650,000
1886 –	3,000,000
1887 –	3,400,000
1888 –	3,800,000
1889 –	4,200,000
1890 –	4,700,000
1891 –	5,200,000
1892 –	5,800,000
1893 –	6,300,000
1894 –	6,700,000
1895 –	7,100,000
1896 –	7,450,000
1897 –	8,100,000
1898 –	8,400,000
1899 –	9,000,000
1900 –	9,500,000
1901 –	10,200,000
1902 –	11,100,000
1903 –	12,100,000
1904 –	13,500,000
1905 –	14,300,000
1906 –	14,700,000
1907 –	15,500,000
1908 –	16,400,000
1909 –	17,600,000
1910 –	17,900,000
1911 –	18,100,000
1912 –	18,200,000
1913 –	18,900,000
1914 –	19,500,000
1915 –	20,000,000
1916 –	20,500,000
1917 –	20,900,000
1918 –	21,800,000
1919 –	22,500,000
1920 –	23,400,000
1921 –	23,900,000
1922 –	24,100,000
1923 –	24,300,000
1924 –	24,550,000
1925 –	24,800,000
1926 –	25,200,000
1927 –	26,100,000
1928 –	26,400,000
1929 –	26,900,000
1930 –	27,100,000
1931 –	27,300,000
1932 –	27,550,000
1933 –	27,750,000
1934 –	28,100,000
1935 –	28,600,000
1936 –	29,100,000
1937 –	29,400,000
1938 –	29,750,000
1939 –	30,050,000
1940 –	30,250,000
1941 –	30,400,000
1942 –	31,000,000
1943 –	31,400,000
1944 –	31,700,000
1945 –	32,100,000
1946 –	32,350,000
1947 –	32,750,000
1948 –	33,100,000
1949 –	33,500,000
1950 –	33,560,000
1951 –	33,600,000
1952 –	33,700,000
1953 –	33,800,000
1954 –	34,100,000
1955 –	34,450,000
1956 –	34,700,000
1957 –	35,000,000

AURORA W. Co.

Date	Serial #
1884 –	10,001
1885 –	60,000
1886 –	100,000
1887 –	160,000
1888 –	200,000
1889 –	215,000
1891 –	230,901

COLUMBUS W. Co.

Date	Serial #
1875 –	1,000
1876 –	3,000
1877 –	6,000
1878 –	9,000
1879 –	12,000
1880 –	15,000
1881 –	18,000
1882 –	21,000
1883 –	25,000
1887 –	75,000
1888 –	97,000
1889 –	119,000
1891 –	163,000
1892 –	185,000
1894 –	207,000
1894 –	209,000
1895 –	251,000
1897 –	295,000
1898 –	317,000
1899 –	339,000
1900 –	361,000
1901 –	383,000

SPECIAL BLOCK OF SERIAL NOS.

Date	Serial #
1894 –	500,001
1896 –	501,500
1898 –	503,000
1900 –	504,500
1902 –	506,000

ELGIN WATCH Co.

Date	Serial #
1867 –	10,000
1868 –	25,001 Nov,20th
1869 –	40,001 May, 20th
1870 –	50,001 Aug. 24th
1871 –	185,101 Sep. 8th
1872 –	201,001 Dec. 20th
1873 –	325,001
1874 –	400,001 Aug.28th
1875 –	430,000
1876 –	480,000
1877 –	520,000
1878 –	550,000
1879 –	625,001 Feb.8th
1880 –	750,000
1881 –	900,000
1882 –	1,000,000 March,9th
1883 –	1,250,000
1884 –	1,500,000
1885 –	1,855,001 May,28th
1886 –	2,000,000 Aug.4th
1887 –	2,500,000
1888 –	3,000,000 June 20th
1889 –	3,500,000
1890 –	4,000,000 Aug.16th
1891 –	4,449,001 Mar.26th
1892 –	4,600,000
1893 –	5,000,000 July 1st
1894 –	5,500,000
1895 –	6,000,000 Nov.26th
1896 –	6,500,000
1897 –	7,000,000 Oct. 28th.
1898 –	7,494,001 May,14th
1899 –	8,000,000 Jan.18th
1900 –	9,000,000 Nov.14th
1901 –	9,300,000
1902 –	9,600,000
1903 –	10,000,000 May 15th
1904 –	11,000,000 April 4th
1905 –	12,000,000 Oct.6th
1906 –	12,500,000
1907 –	13,000,000 April 4th
1908 –	13,500,000
1909 –	14,000,000 Feb.9th
1910 –	15,000,000 April 2nd
1911 –	16,000,000 July 11th
1912 –	17,000,000 Nov.6th
1913 –	17,339,001 Apr.14th
1914 –	18,000,000
1915 –	18,877,001 Feb.11th
1916 –	19,000,000
1917 –	20,031,001 June,27th
1918 –	21,000,000
1919 –	22,000,000
1920 –	23,000,000
1921 –	24,521,001 July,6th
1922 –	25,100,000
1923 –	26,050,000
1924 –	27,000,000
1925 –	28,421,001 July,14th
1926 –	29,100,000
1927 –	30,050,000
1928 –	31,500,000
1929 –	32,000,000
1930 –	32,599,001 July
1931 –	33,000,000
1932 –	33,700,000
1933 –	34,558,001 July,24th
1934 –	35,000,000
1935 –	35,650,000
1936 –	36,200,000
1937 –	36,978,001 July,24th
1938 –	37,900,000
1939 –	38,200,000
1940 –	39,100,000
1941 –	40,200,000
1942 –	41,100,000
1943 –	42,200,000
1944 –	43,200,000
1945 –	43,200,000
1946 –	44,000,000
1947 –	45,000,000
1948 –	46,000,000
1949 –	47,000,000
1950 –	48,000,000
1951 –	50,000,000 Sept. 7th
1952 –	52,000,000
1953 –	53,500,000
1954 –	50,000
1955 –	54,500,000
1956 –	55,000,000

HAMILTON WATCH Co.

Date–Serial No.	
1893 —	1-2,000
1894 —	5,000
1895 —	11,500
1896 —	16,000
1897 —	27,000
1898 —	50,000
1899 —	74,000
1900 —	104,000
1901 —	143,000
1902 —	196,000
1903 —	260,000
1904 —	340,000
1905 —	435,000
1906 —	500,000
1907 —	588,000
1908 —	680,000
1909 —	750,000
1910 —	790,000
1911 —	860,000
1912 —	940,000
1913 —	1,000,000
1914 —	1,100,000
1915 —	1,200,000
1916 —	1,300,000
1917 —	1,400,000
1918 —	1,500,000
1919 —	1,600,000
1920 —	1,700,000
1921 —	1,800,000
1922 —	1,900,000
1923 —	1,950,000
1924 —	2,500,000
1925 —	2,150,000
1926 —	2,250,000
1927 —	2,200,000
1928 —	2,250,000
1929 —	2,300,000
1930 —	2,350,000
1931 —	2,400,000
1932 —	2,480,000
1933 —	2,520,000
1934 —	2,560,000
1935 —	2,600,000
1936 —	2,600,000
1937 —	2,900,000
1938 —	3,200,000
1939 —	3,400,000
1940 —	4,000,000
1941 —	4,250,000
1942 —	4,500,000

DATE LETTERS

2B on 950B=1941-43
C on 992B=1944-69
S on 950B=1941-65
4C On 4992B=1941-68
3992B=1943-45

HAMPDEN W. Co.

Date	Serial #
1877 —	59,000
1878 —	70,000
1879 —	100,000
1880 —	140,000
1881 —	180,000
1882 —	215,000
1883 —	250,000
1884 —	300,000
1885 —	350,000
1886 —	400,000
1887 —	480,000
1888 —	560,000
1889 —	640,000
1890 —	740,000
1891 —	805,500
1892 —	835,000
1893 —	865,000
1894 —	900,000
1895 —	930,000
1896 —	970,000
1897 —	1,000,000
1898 —	1,120,000
1899 —	1,255,000
1900 —	1,384,000
1901 —	1,512,000
1902 —	1,642,000
1903 —	1,768,000
1904 —	1,896,000
1905 —	2,024,000
1906 —	2,152,000
1907 —	2,280,000
1908 —	2,400,000
1909 —	2,520,000
1910 —	2,650,000
1911 —	2,700,000
1912 —	2,760,000
1913 —	2,850,000
1914 —	2,920,000
1915 —	3,000,000
1916 —	3,100,000
1917 —	3,240,000
1918 —	3,390,000
1919 —	3,500,000
1920 —	3,600,000
1921 —	3,700,000
1922 —	3,750,000
1923 —	3,800,000
1924 —	3,850,000
1925 —	3,900,000
1926 —	3,950,000
1927 —	3,980,000

E. HOWARD & Co.

Date	Serial #
1858(60)	113-1,800
1860-61)	1,801-3,000
1861)	3,001-3,100
1861)	3,101-3,300
1861)	3,401- 3,500
1861-71)	3,501-28,000
1868-83)	30,001-50,000
1869-99)	50,001-71,500
1869-90)	100,001-105,500
1880-99)	200,001-227,500
1895)	228,001-231,000
1884-99)	301,001-309,000
1895)	309,301-310,000
1890-95)	400,001-405,000
1890-99)	500,001-501,500
1896-1903)	600,001-601,500
1896-1903)	700,001-701,500

HOWARD WATCH Co. (KEYSTONE)

Date	Serial #
1902 —	850,000
1903 —	900,000
1909 —	980,000
1912 —	1,100,000
1915 —	1,285,000
1917 —	1,340,000
1929 —	1,400,000
1930 —	1,500,000

ILLINOIS WATCH Co.

Date	Serial #
1872 —	5,000
1873 —	20,000
1874 —	50,000
1875 —	75,000
1876 —	100,000
1877 —	145,000
1878 —	210,000
1879 —	250,000
1880 —	300,000
1881 —	350,000
1882 —	400,000
1883 —	450,000
1884 —	500,000
1885 —	550,000
1886 —	600,000
1887 —	700,000
1888 —	800,000
1889 —	900,000
1890 —	1,000,000
1891 —	1,040,000
1892 —	1,080,000
1893 —	1,120,000
1894 —	1,160,000
1895 —	1,220,000
1896 —	1,250,000
1897 —	1,290,000
1898 —	1,330,000
1899 —	1,370,000
1900 —	1,410,000
1901 —	1,450,000
1902 —	1,500,000
1903 —	1,550,000
1904 —	1,600,000
1905 —	1,800,000
1906 —	1,840,000
1907 —	1,900,000
1908 —	2,100,000
1909 —	2,150,000
1910 —	2,200,000
1911 —	2,300,000
1912 —	2,400,000
1913 —	2,600,000
1914 —	2,600,000
1915 —	2,700,000
1916 —	2,800,000
1917 —	3,000,000
1918 —	3,100,000
1919 —	3,400,000
1920 —	3,600,000
1921 —	3,750,000
1922 —	3,900,000
1923 —	4,000,000
1924 —	4,600,000
1925 —	4,800,000
1927 —	5,000,000
(Sold to Hamilton)	
1928 —	5,100,000
1929 —	5,200,000
1931 —	5,400,000
1938 —	5,500,000
1948 —	5,600,000

ROCKFORD W.Co.

Date	Serial #
1876 —	1,200
1877 —	22,600
1878 —	43,000
1879 —	64,000
1880 —	95,000
1881 —	136,000
1882 —	167,000
1883 —	200,000
1884 —	226,000
1885 —	247,000
1886 —	267,000
1887 —	287,500
1888 —	308,500
1889 —	328,500
1890 —	347,000
1891 —	369,500
1892 —	390,000
1893 —	410,000
1894 —	430,000
1895 —	450,000
1896 —	470,000
1897 —	490,000
1898 —	510,000
1899 —	530,000
1900 —	550,000
1901 —	570,000
1902 —	590,000
1903 —	610,000
1904 —	630,000
1905 —	650,000
1906 —	670,000
1907 —	690,000
1908 —	734,000
1909 —	790,000
1910 —	824,000
1911 —	880,000
1912 —	936,000
1913 —	958,000
1914 —	980,000
1915–1,000,000	

SOUTH BEND W. Co.

Date	Serial #
1903 —	380,501
1904 —	390,000
1905 —	405,000
1906 —	425,000
1907 —	460,000
1908 —	500,000
1909 —	550,000
1910 —	600,000
1911 —	660,000
1912 —	715,000
1913 —	765,000
1914 —	800,000
1915 —	720,000
1916 —	840,000
1917 —	860,000
1918 —	880,000
1919 —	905,000
1920 —	935,000
1921 —	975,000
1922 —	1,000,000
1923 —	1,035,000
1924 —	1,070,000
1925 —	1,105,000
1926 —	1,140,000
1927 —	1,275,000
1928 —	1,210,000
1929 —	1,240,000

SETH THOMAS W. Co.

Date	Serial #
1885 —	5,000
1886 —	20,000
1887 —	40,000
1888 —	80,000
1889 —	150,000
1890 —	235,000
1891 —	310,000
1892 —	420,000
1893 —	510,000
1894 —	600,000
1895 —	690,000
1896 —	780,000
1897 —	870,000
1898 —	960,000
1899 —	1,050,000
1900 —	1,140,000
1901 —	1,230,000
1902 —	1,320,000
1903 —	1,410,000
1904 —	1,500,000
1905 —	1,700,000
1906 —	1,900,000
1907 —	2,100,000
1908 —	2,300,000
1909 —	2,500,000
1910 —	2,725,000
1911 —	2,950,000
1912 —	3,175,000
1913 —	3,490,000
1914 —	3,600,000

BALL WATCH Co. (Hamilton)

Date	Serial #
1895 -	13,000
1897 -	20,500
1900 -	42,200
1902-170,000	
1905- 462,000	
1910-116,000	
1915-603,000	
1920-610,000	
1925-620,000	
1930-637,000	
1935-641,000	
1939-650,000	
1940-651,000	
1941-652,000	
1942-654,000	
Ball-(Waltham)	
1900-700,000	
1905-202,000	
1910-216,000	
1915-250,000	
1920-260,000	
1925-270,000	
Ball-(Illinois)	
1929-800,000	
1930-801,000	
1931-803,000	
1932-804,000	
Ball-(Elgin) 1904-1906	
S # range	
11,853,000-12,282,000	
Ball- (E. Howard & C0.)	
1893-1895	
S # range	
226,000-308,000	
Ball-(Hampden)	
1890-1892	
S # range	
626,750-657,960-759,720	

Audemars Piguet

DATE–SERIAL #	
1882 –	2,000
1890 –	4,000
1895 –	5,350
1900 –	6,500
1905 –	9,500
1910 –	13,400
1915 -	17,000
1920 -	25,000
1925 -	33,000
1930 -	40,000
1935 -	42,200
1940 -	44,000
1945 -	48,000
1950 -	55,000
1955 -	65,000
1960 -	75,000
1965 -	90,000
1970-115,000	
1975-160,000	
1980-225,000	

International W.Co. (Schaffhausen)

DATE – SERIAL #	
1884 —	6,501
1886 —	23,500
1888 —	37,500
1890 —	63,000
1892 —	87,500
1894 —	117,000
1896 —	151,500
1898 —	194,000
1900 -	231,000
1902 -	276,500
1904 -	321,000
1906 -	377,500
1908 -	435,000
1910 -	492,000
1912 -	557,000
1914 -	620,500
1916 -	657,000
1918 -	714,000
1920 -	765,000
1922 -	783,500
1924 -	807,000
1926 -	845,000
1928 -	890,500
1930 -	929,000
1932 -	938,000
1934 -	940,000
1936 -	955,500
1938 -	1,000,000
1940 -	1,019,000
1942 -	1,062,000
1944 -	1,092,000
1946 -	1,131,000
1948 -	1,177,000
1950 -	1,222,000
1952 -	1,291,000
1954 -	1,335,000
1956 -	1,399,000
1958 -	1,480,000
1960 -	1,553,000
1962 -	1,666,000
1964 -	1,778,000
1966 -	1,820,000
1968 -	1,905,000
1970 -	2,026,000
1972 -	2,218,000
1974 -	2,265,000
1975 -	2,275,000

A. Lange & Sohne

DATE–SERIAL #	
1870 —	3,500
1875 —	10,000
1880 —	15,000
1885 —	20,000
1890 —	30,000
1895 —	35,000
1900 —	40,000
1905 —	50,000
1910 —	60,000
1915 —	70,000
1920 —	75,000
1925 —	80,000
1930 —	85,000
1935 —	90,000
1940 —	100,000

LONGINES

DATE–SERIAL #	
1867 —	1
1870 —	20,000
1875 —	100,000
1880 —	250,000
1888 —	500,000
1893 —	750,000
1899 -1,000,000-Feb.	
1901-1,250,000	
1904 -1,500,000	
1905 -1,750,000	
1907 -2,000,000-July	
1909 -2,250,000	
1911 -2,500,000	
1912 -2,750,000	
1913 -3,000,000-Aug	
1917 -3,250,000	
1919 -3,750,000	
1922 -4,000,000-Oct.	
1925 -4,250,000	
1926 -4,500,000	
1928 -4,750,000	
1929 -5,000,000-Oct.	
1934 -5,250,000	
1937 -5,500,000	
1938 -5,750,000	
1940 -6,000,000-July	
1945 -7,000,000-June	
1950 -8,000,000-May	
1953 -9,000,000-July	
1956 -10,000,000-May	
1959-11,000,000Apr.	
1962-12,000,000May	
1966-13,000,000June	
1967-14,000,000-Feb	
1969-15,000,000-Feb	

OMEGA

DATE– SERIAL #	
1895 -1,000,000	
1902 -2,000,000	
1908 -3,000,000	
1912 -4,000,000	
1916 -5,000,000	
1923 -6,000,000	
1929 -7,000,000	
1935 -8,000,000	
1939-10,000,000	
1944-10,000,000	
1947-11,000,000	
1950-12,000,000	
1956-15,000,000	
1961-18,000,000	
1963-20,000,000	
1965-22,000,000	
1967-25,000,000	
1968-26,000,000	
1969-29,000,000	

PATEK PHILIPPE & Co.

DATE–SERIAL #.	
1840 —	100
1845 —	1,200
1850 —	3,000
1855 —	8,000
1860 —	15,000
1865 —	22,000
1870 —	35,000
1875 —	45,000
1880 —	55,000
1885 —	70,000
1890 —	85,000
1895 —	100,000
1900 —	110,000
1905 —	125,000
1910 —	150,000
1915 —	175,000
1920 —	190,100
1925 —	200,200
1950 —	700,300
1955 —	725,400
1960 —	750,500
1965 —	775,600
1970 —	795,700
1920 —	800,800
1925 —	805,900
1930 —	820,000
1935 —	821,000
1940 —	832,000
1945 —	853,000
1950 —	864,000
1955 —	875,000
1960 —	886,000
1965 —	897,000
1970 —	898,000
1940 —	909,000
1945 —	915,000
1950 —	930,000
1955 —	940,000
1960 —	960,000
1965 —	975,000
1970 —	995,000
1960--1,100,000	
1965--1,130,000	
1970--1,250,000	
1975--1,350,000	
1980--1,450,000	
1985--1,600,000	
1990--1,850,000	

ROLEX (Case S #)

DATE–SERIAL #	
1925 —	25,000
1926 —	28,500
1927 —	30,500
1928 —	33,000
1929 —	35,500
1930 —	38,000
1931 —	40,000
1932 —	43,000
1933 —	47,000
1934 —	55,000
1935 —	68,000
1936 —	81,000
1937 —	99,000
1938 —	110,000
1939 —	136,000
1940 —	165,000
1941 —	194,000
1942 —	224,000
1943 —	253,000
1944 —	285,000
1945 —	348,000
1946 —	413,000
1947 —	478,000
1948 —	543,000
1949 —	608,000
1950 —	673,500
1951 —	738,500
1952 —	804,000
1953 —	950,000
1954 —	999,999
1955 —	*200,000
1956 —	*400,000
1957 —	*600,000
1958 —	*800,000
1959 —	1,100,000
1960 —	1,401,000
1961 —	1,480,000
1962 —	1,557,000
1963 —	1,635,000
1964 —	1,713,000
1965 —	1,792,000
1966 —	1,870,000
1967 —	2,164,000
1968 —	2,426,000
1969 —	2,680,000
1970 —	2,952,000
1971 —	3,215,000
1972 —	3,478,000
1973 —	3,741,000
1974 —	4,002,000
1975 —	4,266,000
1976 —	4,538,000
1977 —	5,005,000
1978 —	5,481,000
1979 —	5,965,000
1980 —	6,432,000
1981 —	6,910,000
1982 —	7,385,000
1983 —	7,860,000
1984 —	8,338,000
1985 —	8,815,000
1986 —	9,292,000
1987 —	9,765,000
1987 1/2-9,999,999	
1988 1/2-R,999,999	
1989 —	R,999,999
1989 —	L,000,001
1990 —	L,999,999
1991 —	N,000,001
1991 1/2-N,999,999	
1991 1/2-X,000,001	

VACHERON

DATE–SERIAL #	
1830 —	30,000
1835 —	40,000
1840 —	50,000
1845 —	60,000
1850 —	75,000
1855 —	95,000
1860 —	110,000
1865 —	125,000
1870 —	140,000
1875 —	155,000
1880 —	170,000
1885 —	180,000
1890 —	190,000
1895 —	223,000
1900 —	256,000
1905 —	289,000
1910 —	322,000
1915 —	355,000
1920 —	388,000
1925 —	400,000
1930 —	410,000
1935 —	420,000
1940 —	432,000
1945 —	464,000
1950 —	508,000
1955 —	512,000
1960 —	536,000
1965 —	560,000
1970 —	585,000

The above list is provided for determining the **approximate** age of your watch. Match serial number with date. Watches were not necessarily sold in the exact order of manufactured date.

A BIT OF WRIST WATCH HISTORY

While no one is sure who invented the first wrist watch or when the first wrist watch was ever worn. Watch-bracelets were created by great makers for ladies of great wealth. Queen Elizabeth I had a small jewel-studded watch that was made to fasten on the arm (about **1575**). David Rosseau made a watch which was about 18mm in diameter (the size of a dime) in the **late 1600s**. In **1810** Breguet made his first ladies wrist watch & **1868** for Patek Philippe & Co.

Early BRACELET that holds a small pendant-watch, with a lid that opens on this 18K & enamel case to view the watch, Ca.1840.

Girard-Perregaux said they produced wrist watches which were to be used by officers of the German Navy about **1880**. The 1,000 watches used a protective mesh guard.

Wrist watches were at first thought to be too small and delicate to be practical for men to wear. However, during World War I a German officer was said to have strapped a small pocket watch to his wrist with a leather webbed cup. This arrangement freed both hands and proved to be most useful. After the war, the wrist watch gained in popularity. **Girard - Perregaux** factory **said** they made wrist watches around **1880** and were designed to be used by officers of the German Navy. In **1892 Omega** makes the first minute repeating wrist watch in the world, they used a movement by Audmars Piguet. In **1898** the Omega small Caliber 42.86 was manufactured & by **1902** were being sold as wrist watches. Herman Aegler of Bienne, Switzerland in **1902** manufacture wrist watch movements, the **Aegler** manufacture became the largest supplier of movements for **Rolex**. A **Omega** ad in **1904** states 12 wrist watches being used by military in the Boer War (1899-1902). **Cartier** created the famous **Santos** wrist watch in **1904**. **1905** the Ditisheim brothers named their **Movado**, meaning "always in movement". In **1908** Gruen W. Co. are now selling wrist watches and the Rolex trade mark is registered. **1909** Cartier patented the deployment wrist watch buckle. Wrist watch movements were basically derived from the ladies pocket or pendant watch. About **1910-15** American Watch Co. and Elgin Watch Co. were offering wrist watches for sale. **1910** a wrist stop watch was advertised by Fritz Moeri of Saint-Imier of Switzerland. Eterna in **1912** developed the first alarm wrist watch. In **1912** Movado produced the Polyplan movement. (below)

624

In **1912** Omega in collaboration with Movado and Ulysse Nardin, **Omega** creates the 18 P CHRO caliber chronograph, specially made for aviation.

Left: Longines ad, **1909**.   Right: **1913** ad for Omega chronograph.

1913 a 8 day wrist watch by "Hebdomas". In **1918** the American Armed Forces buys 5,000 wrist watches from Omega. In **1919-20** Elinvar, was invented and the Cartier "Tank" wrist watch arrives. These early round wrist watch used enamel dials and for other shapes wrist watches metal dials were preferred. **1920**s Hamilton, Illinois and others begin producing wrist watches.

Miniaturization was a great challenge to many of the famous watch makers including Louis Jaquet, Paul Ditisheim, John Arnold and Henri Capt. The smallest watch in semi-mass production was 12mm by 5mm. In early **1930**, the American Waltham Watch Co. made a 9mm by 20mm Model 400 watch.

Miniaturized wrist watch by Waltham model # 400.   Oscillating weight for   HARWOOD self-winding wrist watch,
Note size comparison to dime.   self winding Wrist Watch.   RIM SET, Ca.**1928**.

By **1920** the round styles were being replaced with square, rectangular and tonneau shapes and decorated with gems. By **1928** wrist watches were outselling pocket watches, and, by **1935**, over 85 percent of the watches being produced were wrist watches.

Self-wind pocket watches were first developed by Abraham Louis Perrelet in 1770 and by Abraham Louis Breguet about 1777. Louis Recordon made improvements in 1780, but is was not until **1923-4** that the principle of self-winding was adapted to the wrist watch by John Harwood, an Englishman who set up factories to make his patented self-wind wrist watches in Switzerland, London, France, and the United States. His watches first reached the market about **1929**. The firm A. Schild manufactured about 15,000 watches in Switzerland. Mr. Harwood's watch company removed the traditional stem or crown to wind the mainspring, but in order to set the hands it was necessary to turn the bezel. The Harwood Watch Co. failed around **1931** and the patent expired.

1924 Plexiglas was first used for crystals. **1926** Rolex patented "Oyster" cases. Rolex patented and invented the screw down crown. **1929** Omega makes a superior anti-shock wrist watch "Armure" and the same year Rolex launches the Prince wrist watch RF# 971 which was used for six years. **1929** LeCoultre made a caliber 101, which was the smallest movement in the world and still is. **1930** Lip makes the first wrist watch with a Tourbillon.

Snap on protector for Wrist Watches, Ca.**1920**s.

Gruen Curvex wrist watch AD 1st appearance in **1935**.

In **1931** the Rolex Watch Co. introduced the Rolex Oyster Perpetual, the first waterproof & self-winding wrist watch. **1932** LeCoultre creates the Duoplan movement and Longines introduced the Lindbergh type wrist watch. In **1933** the first "Incabloc" shock protection device was used. **1933** the first appearance of the "Nivarox" hairspring. In the **mid** to late **1930**s the wrist watches became more technical advanced with a higher jewel count (21 jewels) and two button chronographs which stop, start and return to zero functions. Split second chronographs, perpetual calendars, world timers and more. Different metals are used stainless steel, platinum, painted dials made of metal and wrist watches were being made thinner. In **1935** the Glucidur (berrylium-bronze) balance made it's first appearance. Gruen produces and patented the Curvex wrist watch in **1935**. By **1940** wrist watches came in all shapes and types including complicated chronographs, calendars, and repeaters. Novelties, digital jump hour and multidial were very popular, as well. In **1942** Felsa invented a bi-directional rotor for a self-winding movement. The lugs became part of the case design and the lugs appear in different fancy shapes as tear drops and flared cases.

Right: Gruen flared case with Crown-guard, Ca.**1931**

Rolex Oyster Perpetual, BUBBLE BACK, Ca. **1940**.

1945 Rolex launches the "Date Just", the first automatic water-resistant wrist chronometer with a visible date through a dial aperture. 1947 Vulcain creates the "Cricket" which has a alarm. 1948 Eterna introduced the ball-bearing rotor style watch. 1949 Patek Philippe patents their "Gyromax" balance Wheel.

Right: Patek Philippe, "Gyromax" balance wheel.   Breitling launches the "Navitimer", Ca. 1952.

1950 Rolex creates the "turn-o-Graph", RF# 6202. 1950 U. S. Time Corp. introduced the **"Timex"** watch. 1952 Omega produces the renowned chronometer "Constellation". 1952 Breitling launches the "Navitimer", the wrist watch was designed for pilots. 1953 Rolex produces the first automatic diver's wrist watch water resistant to 100 meters, the "Submariner", RF.# 6204. Professional wrist watches are being made for electrical engineers such as the "Milgaus", the "Submariner", for the swimmers and divers, GMT models for the travelers, the rolex RF.# 6036 called the "Jean-Claude Killy" and the Daytona chronograph RF.# 6034. 1954 Buren introduced the Micro-rotor self wind watch. A **dramatic change** occurred in 1957 when the Hamilton Watch Co. eliminated the mainspring and replaced it with a small battery that lasted well over one year. In 1960 the balance wheel was removed in the "Accutron" by Bulova and replaced by a tuning fork with miniature pawls.

Above: **"Ventura"**, by Hamilton W. Co., the "Van Horn" and "Ventura" were both introduced in 1957.   Accutron by Bulova, "Alpha" Spaceview, Ca. 1960.

1960 Movado introduces the "Museum Watch". 1962 Rado makes the first scratch proof wrist watch. 1965 the "Speedmaster Professional" which Omega supplied the wrist watch that was worn on the outside of the space suit the first space walk. The Omega "Speedmaster" was one of the most successful watch in the history of watchmaking. About this time occurred the start of a period of watch manufacturing that is herald as the most difficult crisis ever experienced by the Swiss watch industry. However the watch makers continued to produce mechanical marvels and hard times was experienced for the next decade or so.

1969 Seiko, with the Quartz Watch, remolds the watch industry with the "Astron" model. In **1970** Tissot had a transparent **idea** with it's "Idea 2001", the first plastic watch, a synthetic movement and case made of transparent plastic. In **1978** Dr. George Daniels makes a Gold-cased one-minute tourbillon with his **co-axial** escapement (not requiring oil). In the period <u>1980 to 1996</u> Daniels used Swiss made wrist watches and converted them to his coaxial escapement, he used Omega, Zenith, Rolex and Patek Philippe watches. Overriding all was George Daniels 25 year quest for a lower friction escapement, his success and then the years long battle to gain a reluctant Swiss acceptance culminating in the Omega model. Omega introduced a limited edition of 6,000 watches featuring the co-axial escapement in **1998**. They sold for about $6,600.00.

Tissot: "Idea 2001 Synthetic" **1st.** watch made of plastic.   Diagram of George Daniels, Co-Axial escapement

1981 Swatch christened their new baby **Swatch**. In August of **1982** ETA supplied 4,000 Swatches in 25 different models, and by March of **1983** launched their campaign to the public. **1986** Citizen is now the number one producer of Quartz type watches replacing Seiko. **1990** Jurghan launches their radio controlled wrist watch which receives a signal from an atomic clock. **2002** a World Time Platinum wrist sold for a record price **$4,026,524.00**, a RF# 1415 by P.P& Co.

Swatch: Early Design wrist watch by Swatch, Ca. **1982**.

1. Case number.   2. Movement serial number.   3. Caliber number.   4. Caliber number.

NOTE: Some wrist watches have a grade, reference or caliber number engraved on the case, or movement. For example, Patek, Phillipe & Co. has a caliber number 27-460Q. The '27' stands for 27mm; the '460Q' is the grade; the 'Q' designates Quantieme (Perpetual calendar and moon phases).

AUTOMATIC WINDING

The self-winding watch uses the movements of the body in order to wind up the mainspring slowly and nearly continuously. The first pocket self-winding watches were executed by a watchmaker from Le Locle, Abraham-Louis Perrelet, around 1770.

Early self wind pocket watch by Breguet Ca. 1785.

ETERNA-MATIC automatic winding mechanism with rotor oscillating on *5 ball bearings 1st introduced in 1949*. 1.–Oscillating weight. 2. –Oscillating gear. 3. –Upper wheel of auxiliary pawl-wheel. 4. –Lower wheel of auxiliary pawl-wheel. 5. –Pawl-wheel with pinion. 6. –Lower wheel of pawl wheel with pinion. 7. –Transmission-wheel with pinion. 8. –Crown-wheel yoke. 9. –Winding pinion. 10. –Crown-wheel. 11. –Ratchet-wheel. 12. –Barrel. 13. –Driving runner for ratchet-wheel. 14. –Winding stem. 15. –Winding button.

They were improved soon after by Abraham-Louis Breguet. In the case of the pocket watch, the movements causing the winding of the watch were essentially the result of walking. This system of winding was never widely adopted. The watch was a fancy model and not a really useful one. Herman von der Heydt was the only maker in America to work with the self-winding pocket watch. However, inventors always kept the idea of the self-winding watch in mind.

In 1923, the British firm Harwood took up once again the solution of the problem of automatic winding, for wrist watches. This was the spark which rapidly resulted in research to improve and simplify this type of mechanism. A company was formed in London to manufacture Harwood's watch, and before long over 500 jewelers in the United Kingdom were selling his automatic watch. A second company was formed in France, and a third in the United States. The business flourished about two and one-half years. Then, in 1931, these companies were liquidated.

Early self-winding wrist watch by FREY W. Co., Ca. 1930's. NOTE: The pendulum style weight for self-winding.

Early self-winding wrist watch by AUTORIST W. Co. Ca.1930's. Winding by moving flexible lugs.

CHRONOGRAPH

The term chronograph is derived from the Greek words chronos which means "time" and grapho which means "to write." The first recording of intervals of time was around 1821 by the inventor Rieussec. His chronograph (*Time-Writer*) made dots of ink on a dial as a measure of time. Around 1862 Adolph Nicole introduced the first chronograph with a hand that returned to zero. The split second chronograph made its appearance around 1879. Today a chronograph can be described as a timepiece that starts at will, stops at will, and can return to zero at will. A mechanical chronograph had a sweep or center second hand that will start, stop, and fly back to zero. The term chronometer should not be confused with chronograph. A chronometer is a timepiece that has superior time keeping qualities at the time it is made. The CHRONOGRAPH **1 button** wrist watch was 1st. advertised in 1910 & a 2 **button** CHRONOGRAPH in 1939 by Breitling.

A. Day window. **B.** Split second hand. **C.** Calendar pusher. **D.** Register for seconds. **E.** Calendar pusher. **F.** Date hand. **G.** Register for total hours. **H.** Sweep center second hand. **I.** Month window. **J.** Start/stop pusher. **K.** Register for total minutes. **L.** Return pusher. **M.** Date of month.

TRADE MARK   MANUFACTURER   TRADE MARK   MANUFACTURER

 VALJOUX
Now part of the **ETA** group

 LANDERON

 VENUS

 FONTAINEMELON

CHRONOGRAPH MECHANISM
NUMBERS & NAMES USED IN THE EBAUCHE BOOK
" TECHNOLOGICAL DICTIONARY OF WATCH PARTS " Ca. 1953

8000 = Chronograph central wheel, w/ finger.
8020 = Minute-recording wheel, register.
8060 = Driving wheel.
8070 = Pillar or Crown wheel, 3 functions.
8080 = Coupling clutch w/ transmission wheel, 2 functions.
8100 = Sliding or star gear, 2 functions.
8140 = Operating or starting lever, 2 functions.
8180 = Fly-back lever, reset to zero.
8200 = Blocking lever, 2 functions.
8220 = Hammer or heart piece striker, 2 functions.
8270 = Minute-recording jumper spring.
8290 = Friction spring , for chronograph central wheel.
8320 = Coupling clutch spring.
8325 = Sliding gear spring, 2 functions.
8335 = Operating or starting lever spring.
8345 = Blocking lever spring.
8350 = Hammer or heartpiece lever spring, 2 functions.
8355 = Pillar or crown wheel jumper or block.
8500 = Chronograph bridge, for center & min. recording wheels.

ABOVE: Illustration of a
Modular construction or
a chronograph Attachment.

The chronograph is a fitted attachment to a time only watch movement, with a additional function that can be used independently of the time indication. The chronograph ebauche factories who make 80% of the raw chronograph attachments (about 10 ebauche manufacturers), are rarely known by the public. The chronograph modular or attachment are made to be fitted or added to a time only movement. The same is true of repeaters. Companies as Patek Philippe, Audemars Piguet, Rolex and many more are fitted with ebauche chronograph attachments to their <u>own</u> time only movement. Watch Companies as Breitling, Heuer, Eberhard and many more are finished with ebauche chronograph attachments fitted to raw movements made by other wrist-watch ebauche factories.

LEFT: CHRONOGRAPH with 1 push piece & **CENTER** 2 push pieces. **RIGHT**: CHRONOGRAPH module or attachment

Chronograph with two push pieces:

Action and movement of hands : <u>The pusher No .1</u> sets the hands in action and second action stops the same hands.

<u>Pusher No. 2</u> brings the hands back to zero. During their movement this pusher is a fixture, thus preventing the accidental return of the hands to zero. The double pusher chronograph permits an interruption in the reading, the hands are set going again from the position they stopped, thus indispensable for any time lost during a control of any description.

HOW TO READ THE TACHOMETER-TELEMETER DIAL

The **TACHOMETER** may have a spiral scale around center of dial, this indicates miles per hour, based on a trial over one mile. It indicates speeds from 400 to 20 miles per hour on three turns. Each turn of spiral corresponds to one minute (scale for first 8 seconds being omitted), the outer turn from 400 to 60 (0 to 1 minute) and the center turn from 30 to 20 miles per hour (2 to 3 minutes).

When passing the first marker of mile zone, start chronograph hand by pressing push piece. When passing following mile marker, press push piece again. The chronograph hand now indicates the speed in miles per hour on the spiral. If a mile has been made in less than one minute the speed will be indicated on outside turn of spiral; from 1 to 2 minutes on middle turn and 2 to 3 minutes on center turn.

EXAMPLE: If a mile has been made in 1 minute and 15 seconds the chronograph hand indicates 48 miles per hour on middle turn of spiral.

The **TELEMETER** scale around margin of dial is based on the speed of sound compared with the speed of light. Each small division is 100 meters. The scale is read in kilometers & hundreds of meters. Approximately 16 divisions equal 1 mile.

To determine the distance of a storm: When you see the flash of lightning press push piece of chronograph. When hearing thunder press again, the chronograph hand will indicate on the Telemeter scale the distance in kilometers and hundreds of meters. One kilometer equals 5/8 of a mile.

NOTE: The chronograph is a fitted attachment to a time only watch movement, with a additional function that can be used independently of the time indication. The chronograph ebauche factories who make 80% of the raw chronograph attachments (about 10 ebauche manufacturers), are rarely known by the public. The chronograph module or attachment are made to be fitted or added to a time only movement. The same is true of repeaters. Companies as Patek Philippe, Rolex, Audemars Piguet and many more are fitted with ebauche chronograph attachments to their <u>own</u> time only movement. Watch Companies as Breitling, Heuer, Eberhard and many more are finished with ebauche chronograph attachments fitted to raw movements made by other wrist-watch ebauche factories.

Dial No. 1 is a simple stop watch and chronograph dial. Graduated into fifths of seconds.

Dial No. 2 is used to time a car over a quarter-mile track and read the numbers of miles per hour directly from dial.

Dial No. 3 is used to measure speed in kilometers per hour over a course of one fifth of a kilometer.

Dial No. 4 used by physicians to count the pulse beats of a patient.

Dial No. 5 is used by artillery officers for determining distance by means of sound in kilometers.

Dial No. 6 shows a tachometer: many watches are made with several scales on the same dial in order to cover a greater range of functions. The figures are sometimes grouped in a spiral form or in several circles, thus the hand may make more than one complete revolution.

Tachy-télémètre.

Tachy-télémètre.

Tachy-télémètre.

Pulsomètre.

WRIST WATCH CASE AND DIAL STYLES

Barrel

Maxine

Square

Round

Square Cut Corner

Cushion

Rectangle

Flared

Curved or Curvex

Round
(Ladies style; converts to lapel or wrist)

Rectangle Cut Corner

Tonneau

Baguette

Oval

< LEFT
EXAGGERATED
NUMBERS

RIGHT >
ART DECO

Coded number

Caliber number

Coded symbol

Company name

MERCEDES

TRYLON

BATON (RECTILINE)

BATON

MOON

REGATE

POINTEX

LEAF

HOUR and MINUTE HANDS

ALPHA

INDEX

DAUPHINE

MODERN

DAUPHINE PITCHED

FUSEAUX

DIAMOND

LANCE

FILS

RADIUM DAUPHINE

RADIUM

SECOND HANDS

ALPHA   DAUPHINE   INDEX   MODERN

FILS   (REGULAR)

SPRING BAR

LEFT: Watch has SOLDERED lugs. **RIGHT**: Watch has SOLID lugs or ONE PIECE lug.

Between the years of 1880 & 1927 over 8,000 trademarks & brand names were registered in Switzerland. Some Swiss watches have three initials on the balance bridge. These initials are not model identification but are for house identification. Following is a list of import initials with the name of the firm. The Code is found on Balance Cock.

AOC–Roamer
AOG--Ch. Aerni S.A.
AOH--Hamilton
AOL–Adolph Schwarcz & Son
AOX–Alstater W. Co.
AXA–Wittnauer
AXJ--A.R.Je Meylan stopwatchCo.
AXP--Aristo Import Co. Inc.
AXR--Mural W. Co.
AZZ–Benrus
AYP–Audemars Piguet
AZO--AD Allemann & Son Ltd.
BOL–Lemania
BOM--Berman W. Co. Inc.
BOP--Robert Ronnel
BXC–Ball, Avia, Garland
BXD--Leonidas W. Fy.
BXJ–Midland
BXL–Lion
BXN–Benrus
BXP–Imperial, Bayer,
    Pretzfelder & Mills
BXP--Ulysse Nardin
BXU--Eickmann & Co.,
    E.Baumann, Aristo Imports Inc.
BXW–Bulova
BYM--Michael Z. Berger
BZK--Berci Inc.
BZM--J.C.Penny, Towncraft
COC–Crawford
COR--Cornell, Orloff
COW–Croton
COY--Cyma
CXC–Concord
CXD–Cypres
CXH--Avia W. Fy., Clinton
CXJ--Central
CXL--Leonidas W. Fy.
CXM--Clinton, Wolbrook,
    Circle W. Corp.
CXV--Cort
CXW--Central; Benrus
CXY--Croydon
CYW--Chesterfield
CZA--Canoe
DOB--Dreffa W. Co.
DOW–Deauville
DWQ--Langendorf, Lanco
DXO--Minerva
DYR--Den-Ro, Bernard Vuille
EOE–Elrex, Pierpont W.Co.
EOM--EMO W.Co.
EON–Avalon, Calvert
EOP–Harvel, Rensie
EOT–Lavina
EOY--Compass Instrument &
    Optical Co. Inc.
EXA–ETERNA
EXC–Everbrite
EXO--Empire
EXM--Savoy, Milos
EXW--Empire W. Co.
EZR--Enicar
FWR--Amko W. Co.
FXE–Provis
FXF--Fairfax, Rytime
FXN--W. Rosch
FXU–Louis Aisenstein & Bros.
    Roamer W. Co.
FXW–Louis
FYG–Eloga W. Co.
FYL--Dreffa W. Co.
GOC--Crawford, Rexton
GOG–Greygor, Hoga
GXC–Gruen, Onsa
GXI–Gotham (Ollendorff)
GXM–Girard-Perregaux
GXR--Crysler, Grant,
    Heyworth W. Co.
GXT--Silvana
GXW–Gothic
GYH–Hilton
GYP–Global W. Co.
GZR--Grensler Lee
HOB--Jackson W.Co. Wakmann
HOM–Homis
HON--A. Hirsch, Tissot,
    Universal Geneve
HOP--Hall
HOR--Lanco; Langendorf
HOU–Oris
HXF–Harman

HXH--Harvel
HXL--Easton
HXM–R. H. Macy & Co.
HXN–Harvel
HXO–Harold K. Oleet
HXL--Easton
HXW–Helbros
HXW--Jos.Boillat fils, Louis
HYL--Hamilton
HYO–Hilton W Co.
HYQ--Hilton
HYW--Harper W.Co.
HZE--Hetega
IXK--Pilgrim Electronic Corp.
JXE--Normandie
JXJ–Alprosa, Jules Jurgensen
JXL--Sultana W. Co.
JXR--Gallet, Jules Racine Co.
KBH--Endura
KOT–Landau
KXA--Astin W. Co.
KXB--Ernest Borel
KXF--Clebar W.Co. Zodiac
KXJ--Wm. J. Kappel
KXV--Louis
KXZ–Kelton, Benrus, Central
KZX--Rutex,J.Weber, Sellita
LBA--Ollech & Wajs
LOA–Emil Langer, Selza
LOD–Latham
LOE–Delbana, Hydepark,
    Emil Leichter, Packard
LON--Lorna W. Co.
LOT--Lathin
LOV--Levrette, Robbin
LOY--Lathin
LXA--Elbon, Laco, Nassu,
    Tremont, Winton,
LXE–Evkob
LXJ--Jaegar-LeCoultre
LXM--Accro Bond, Accro W.Co.
LXW--Longines
LYE--Aureole
LZF--Joseph Laufer
LZL--Henry Gireaux W. Co.
MOG--Mead & Co.; Boulevard
MOK--Montauk W. Co.
MOU--Buttes W. Co.,Delbana,
    Leonidas, Tower
MOV--Marvin
MWS--Lebur Time Co.
MXE–Monarch
MXF--Harman
MXH–Seeland
MXI–Movado
MXT–Mathey-Tissot
MXU--Zimet W. Co.
NGH--Universal Geneve
NJD--Nastrix
NOA–U.Nardin
NOG--Enicar, Kuper W. Co.
NOH--Heyworty, A, Hirsch
NOK--Pilot, Ralco
NOS--Defender, Heritage, Nova
NOU--Louvic W. Co., Vulcain
NXJ–National Jewelers Co.
NXO–Oris
NXS--Popper W. Co.
NYN--Conoseur W. Co.
OWT--Carvelle
OXG–Omega
OXL–Wyler
OXY--Artis
OYM--Cromwell
OYT–Shriro (Sandoz)
POB--General, Helvetia
POF--Alexora, Delaware, Eloga,
    Gorgerat, Grenar, Nuhall,
    Rogers, Rosieres, Sellita
POH--Perfine W. Co.
POX--Lucerne, Wega
PWY--Spera
POY--Camy; Copley
PXA–Pierce
PXP--Patek, Philippe
PXT–Paul Breguette
PXW--Monarch, Parker, Renise
PYC--Pedre
PYS–Langel
PYS--Guyora
QXL--Emerson, Lauret
QXO--Kelbert

QXY--Acme, Lyceum
ROC–Raleigh
ROD--Regent
ROH--Calvert
ROL–Ribaux
ROM--Avia,Belvu, Reyco,
    E.W. Reynolds Co.
ROP–Rodania
ROP--Zone-x W. Fy.
ROR–Audemars Piguet
ROW–Rolex
RXE--Brenet
RXG--Olympic, Zodiac
RXM–Galmor
RXV--Juvenia
RXW–Parker, Rima
RXY–Liengme
RYW– Ritex
RXZ--Benrus
SOA–Felca
SOE–Semca
SOL--Stuart
SON--Defender
SOW–Seeland, Sussex
SOX–Cortebert
SOX--Orvin, Sears, Serco,
    Sears Roebuck & Co.,Tradition
SWU--Alben Semag
SXE–Savoy, Banner
SXK--Cardnial, Rosieres, Royce
SXK–S. Kocher & Co.
SXS–Franco
SXU--Segud W. Co.
TOB--Pronto
TOC--Capt & Co.,E.Schlup-Abrecht
TOH--Banner, Rivera
TXJ--Latham
TXW--Tavannes
TYW--Elgin, Seth Thomas
TYX--Trebex
UOA–Actua
UOB–Aero, Enicar, Heloisa W. Co.
UOR–RADO
UOW–Universal
UWP--Palmer Sales Co.
UXM–Medana, Meyer & Studeli
UXN–Marsh
UXO–Wega
UYW–Stanley W. Co.
VCS--Britix
VOB--Certina
VOS– Eloga, Sheffield Merchandise
VXB--Chase, Hamlin, Louis
VXN--LeCoultre & Co.
VXN–V & C & LeCoultre
VXO–Transit
VXT–Hilton, Kingston
VXX--Libela
VYE--Benrus
WOA–Tower
WOB–Wyler
WOG–Breitling, Wakmann
WOR–Creston
WXC–Buren, Legant,
    Montgomery Ward
WXE–Welsbro
WXO–Waltham
WXW–Benrus Wadsworth
WXW–Westfield
WYX Continental, Harvester
XOU–Pronto W. Co.
XOV–Alstate, Marcel
XXZ–Kelton
XYG–Westclox
XYH–Alpha
YOA–Perfecta W. Co
YOU–Hallmark
YXD–Crysler, Lucerne
YXV–Hampden
YXY–Elgin
ZBH Mondaine
ZFX–Zenith W.Co.
ZOA--Baylor
ZOB–Belvior, Evans
ZOK–Telda
ZOV--Titus W. Co.
ZXW–Benrus, Watches Inc.
ZYB–Hawthorne W. Co.
ZYV–Hampden (new company)

Like many industries consolidation of the major market brands increase vendors market share and higher volume to increase profitability. Many of the famous names of the past are no longer independent, but owned by a larger company. Concentration is bad when boarders between various brands become indistinct; it lessons their unique character. Interesting to note is that Swatch Group owns 90% of movements. Below are some of the conglomerates and a list of the watch brands under their control.

OWNER	BRAND NAME	OWNER	BRAND NAME
Artime	Philip Watch	Richemont Group	Alfred Dunhill
	Sector No Limits		A. Lange & Sohne
Audemars,Piguet	Audemars Piguet	(Cartier family)	Baume & Mercier
Bottinelli Families	Jaeger Le Coultre 40%		Cartier
+ shareholders	Renaud, Papi		IWC (International W. Co.)
Chung Nam Group	ISA		Jaeger Le Coultre
	Roamer		Montblanc, Piaget
Citizen	Citizen		Officine Panerai
	Miyota	Dials by	Stern Group
Desco	Maurice Lacroix		Vacheron Constantin
Diehl family	Junghans		Van Cleef & Arpels 80%
Dixi Paul Castella	Mondia		Yves Saint Laurent
Egana	Benetton	SAB	St. John
	Caravelles	(Swiss Army Brands)	Swiss Air Force
	Chromachron		Swiss Army Watches
	Dugena 70%		Victorinox
	Esprit		Wenger
	Morellato	Scheufele	Chopard
	Pierre Cardin	Schneider Family	Breitling
	ZenRa		Kelek
Eterna SA	Eterna	Seiko	Alba, Credor
	Porche Design		Lassale Lorus
Fossil Inc.	Fossil, Diesel, Zodiac		Pulsar
	DKNY, Relic		Seiko Spoon
Frey family	Minerva	Stern family	Patek Philippe
Bvlgari	Bvlgari, Daniel Roth	P. P. & Co.	Cases by Calame & Cie.
	Gerald Genta, Sector	P. P. & Co.	Parts by Ergas Sarl
Gerd-R. Lang	Chronoswiss	Swatch Group	Blancpain, Breguet
Sowind SA	Daniel Jean Richard		Calvin Kline (CK)
	Girard-Perregaux		Certina, Endura
			ETA (movements)
LVMH	Chaumet, Christian Dior	case maker by	Favre & Perret
(Louis Vuitton,	Ebel, Fred, Joallier		Flick Flak
Moet, Hennessy)	Favre-Leuba		Glashutte Original
	Fendi, Givenchy		Hamilton, Leon Hatot
	Gucci 20%		Jaquet-Droz, Lanco
	Tag Heuer		Lemania (movements)
	Zenith		Longines, Mido
Maddox AG	Bernini	springs & escapements by	Nivarox - Far
	BWC		Omega, Pierre Balmain
	Cerutti	Hi grade movements by	Frederic Piguet
NAWC (North	Concord, Coach Watch		Rado, Record
American W. Co.)	ESQ, Movado		Renata (movements)
Renley W. Co.	Le Phare-Jean d'Eve		Swatch
	Sultana		Tissot, Union
Timex Corp.	Humvee, Indigo		Unitas (movements)
	Ironman, Timex	watch hands by	Universo

Poljot Watch Factory of Moscow Russia
Poljot = Flight

ETA (Named after the 7th letter of the Greek alphabet).

Valjoux (movement)

Wilsdorf Foundation Rolex, Cellini, Tudor
dials by Beyeler & Cie, crowns by Boninchi SA
Bracelets by Gay Freres

The table below list the brand name alphabetically and the owner of the company.

Brand Name .... Owners	Brand Name .... Owners
A. Lange & Sohne — Richemont Group	Lorus — Seiko Watch Corp.
Alfred Dunhill — Richemont Group (Cartier Family)	Marvin — Revue-Thommen
Audemars Piguet — Audemars, Piguet, Bottinelli families, + Shareholders	Maurice Lacroix — Desco von Schulthess, Bodmer family
Baume & Mercier — Richemont Group (Cartier Family)	Mido — Swatch Group
Benetton — Egana	Minerva — A. & J.J. Frey
Bernini — Maddox AG	Miyota — Citizen
Blancpain — Swatch Group	Mondia — Dixi Paul Castella
Bovet — Thierry Oulevay & Roger Guye	Montblanc — Richemont Group (Cartier Family)
Breguet — Swatch Group	Morellato (49%) — Egana
Breitling — Schneider Family - Kelek	Movado — NAWC (North American Watch Co.)
Bvlgari — Bvlgari Group	Muhle Glashutte — Nautische Instrument
BWC — Maddox AG	Officine Panerai — Richemont Group (Cartier Family)
Calvin Kline (CK) — Swatch Group	Omega — Swatch Group
Caravelles — Egana	Parmigiani — Parmigiani Fleurier - Sandoz family
Cartier — Richemont Group (Cartier Family)	Patek Philippe — Stern family
Certina — Swatch Group	Philip Watch — Artime
Cerutti — Maddox AG	Piaget — Richemont Group (Cartier Family)
Chaumet — LVMH (Louis Vuitton, Moet, Hennessy)	Pierre Balmain — Swatch Group
Chopard — Scheufele Family	Pierre Cardin — Egana
Christan Dior — LVMH (Louis Vuitton, Moet, Hennessy)	Frederic Piguet (mvm't) — Swatch Group
Chromachron — Egana	Porche Design — Eterna SA
Chronoswiss — Gerd-Rudiger Lang	Pulsar — Seiko Watch Corp.
Citizen — Miyota	Rado — Swatch Group
Concord — NAWC (North American Watch Co.)	Raymond Weil — Seville Watch Corp.
Corum — Jean-Rene Bannwart 10% Severin Wundermann 90%	Renata (mvm't) — Swatch Group
Daniel Roth — Bvlgari Group	RGM — Roland Murphy
Dunhill — Richemont Group (Cartier Family)	Roamer — Chuung Nam Group
Ebel — LVMH (Louis Vuitton, Moet, Hennessy)	Rolex — Wilsdorf Foundation
Endura — Swatch Group	Sector No Limits — Artime
ETA (mvm't) — Swatch Group	Speidel — Hisch
Eterna — Eterna SA	Spoon — Seiko Watch Corp.
Favre-Leuba — Benedom SA	St. John — SAB (Swiss Army Brands)
Flik Flak — Swaych Group	Sultana — Renley Watch Co.
Fortis — Rolf Voght family; Prince Ernst August von Hannover	Swatch — Swatch Group
Franck Muller — Franck Muller Group	Swiss Air Force — SAB (Swiss Army Brands)
Genta — Bvlgari Group	Swiss Army Watches — SAB (Swiss Army Brands)
Girard-Perregaux — Sowind Group SA	Tag Heuer — LVMH (Louis Vuitton, Moet, Hennessy)
Givenchy — LVMH (Louis Vuitton, Moet, Hennessy)	Timex — Timex Corp.
Glashutte Original — Swatch Group	Tissot — Swatch Group
Gucci Watches - Gucci, LVMH, PPR	Tutima — Tutima Uhrenfabik
Hamilton — Swatch Group	Ulysse Nardin — Rolf W. Schnyder
Hermes — Hermes family	Union — Swatch Group
IWC Schaffhausen — Richemont Group	Unitas (mvm't) — Swatch Group
Jaeger-LeColture — Richemont Group 60%	Universal Geneve — Stelux Holdings
Jaquet-Droz — Swatch Group	Vacheron Constantin — Richemont Group (Cartier Family)
Jughans — Diehl family	Valjoux (mvm't) — Swatch Group
Kelek — Schneider family	Van Cleef & Arpels — Richemont Group 80% (Cartier Family)
Lanco — Swatch Group	Ventura — Ventura Design on time SA
Lassale — Seiko Watch Corp.	Victornox — SAB (Swiss Army Brands)
Le Phare- Jean d'Eve — Renley Watch Co.	Wenger — SAB (Swiss Army Brands)
Lemania (mvm't) — Swatch Group	Xemex — Xemex Swiss watch
Limes — Ickler Gmbh	Yves Saint Laurent — Richemont Group (Cartier Family)
Longines — Swatch Group	Zeneth — LVMH (Louis Vuitton Moet, Hennessy)
	Zenta Ra — Egana

Above: October, 1940 **AD**

WRIST WATCH LISTINGS
Priced At The Collectable Fair Market Trade Show Level
(Complete Watches Only)

Unless otherwise noted, wrist watches listed in this section are priced at the *collectable* fair market **TRADE SHOW** level (What a **collector** may expect to pay for a watch from a watch dealer) and as **complete** watches having an original gold-filled case and stainless steel back, also with original dial, and the entire original movement in good working order with no repairs needed. They are also priced as having a watch band made of **leather** except where a bracelet is described. Watches listed as 14k and 18k are solid gold cases. Coin or base-metal and stainless steel cases will be listed as such. Low cost production watches, are listed as having a base metal type case and a composition dial.

Many of the watch manufacturers were commissioned to put jewelers' or jobbers' **names** on their movements in place of their own. Because of this practice, the true manufacturers of these movements are difficult to identify. Between the years 1880 & 1927 over 8,000 trade-mark titles were registered in Switzerland, such as Alpha, Bulova, Camy, Jaeger, Reverso, Submariner, Valjoux, Zodiac, etc. Warning: There are currently fake wrist watches being sold on the worldwide market.

The prices shown were averaged from dealers' trade show display's just prior to publication and are an indication of the trade show level or what collectors will pay. **Prices** are provided in three categories: **average condition, extra fine, and mint condition,** and are shown in whole dollar amounts only. The values listed are a guide for the *collectable* trade show level and are provided for your information only. **Dealers** will not necessarily pay **full** trade show price. Prices listed are for watches with **original** cases, movement and dials and in good running order. With today's use of computers, web pages and inernet auctions, we have reached a world wide market. Some of the prices in this book, for **mint condition, new in the box** are bringing much higher prices, than prices reflected in this Guide, as much as 50% to 100%. Signed gold cases by important case makers, as "**Schwob & Wuischpard**", are bringing higher prices than prices listed in this Guide.

Important Notice. All of the information, including valuations, in this book has been compiled from the most reliable sources, and every effort has been made to eliminate errors and questionable data. Nevertheless, the possibility of error, in a work of such immense scope, always exists. The publisher or authors will not be held responsible for losses which may occur in the purchase, sale, statements of its advertisers, or other transaction of items, because of information contained herein. Readers who feel they have discovered errors are invited to write and inform us, so they may be corrected in subsequent editions.

⊕ Wrist Watch terminology or communication in this book has evolved over the years, in search of better & more precise language with a effort to improve, purify, adjust itself & make it easier to understand.

INFORMATION NEEDED — The authors are interested in any facts and information you might have that should possibly be considered for future editions. Documented facts are needed, so please send photo or sources of information. I will respect & appreciate positive sound reliable comments, corrections, improvements or remarks but reserve the right to accept the statement or keep my own observations & views. Send information to:

COOKSEY SHUGART
P.O. BOX 3147
CLEVELAND, TN. 37320-3147

When **CORRESPONDING**, Please send a 🖃 self addressed, stamped **ENVELOPE**.

ABERCROMBIE & FITCH, 17J., chronog.by Valj.,3 reg.
14K..$700 $900 $1,300
s.steel $250 $375 $600

Abercrombie & Fitch, 17J., **Seafarer,** chronog., waterproof
18k $900 $1,300 $1,700
s. steel $300 $450 $700

Abercrombie & Fitch, 17J., chronog.by Valj.,3 reg., Ca.1950
s.steel $275 $365 $575

ABRA, 17J., step case, c.1930s
base metal $35 $45 $85

⏱ Pricing in this Guide are trade show fair market price for
COMPLETE watches which are reflected from the "**NAWCC**"
National and regional shows.

DIALS FOR MINT PRICES MUST BE ALL **ORIGINAL**.

ABRA,17J., carved case, c.1930s
base metal $35 $45 $85

ABRA, 17J., engraved case
base metal $35 $45 $85

ABRA,15J., curved case, c.1930s
base metal $35 $45 $85

ABRA, 17J., **jump hour**
s. steel $150 $195 $265

ACE, 17 jewels, Ca. 1936
gold filled $55 $70 $110

DIALS FOR MINT PRICES MUST BE ALL <u>ORIGINAL</u>.

ACRO, W. Co., 17 jewels, **Hinged Back**, Ca. 1930s
18k $185 $225 $300

ADMES, 17 jewels, self wind, waterproof, center sec.,
14K..$100 $135 $185
gold filled................................ $50 $60 $100

AGASSIZ, 17 jewels, **World Time**
18k .... ★$3,500 $4,000 $5,200

AGASSIZ, 17 jewels, fancy bezel,
18k $400 $500 $750

AGASSIZ, 18 jewels, for Tiffany & Co., 48mm, oversize
18k $700 $850 $1,100

AGASSIZ,17J., C. 1940s
18K(W).................................. $400 $550 $750

AGASSIZ, 18 jewels, barrel shaped dial, 40mm,
18k $300 $400 $600

AGASSIZ, 17 jewels, for Tiffany & Co., 45mm
18k $650 $800 $1,000

ALAVENTE, 7J., "Mystery", **simulated** jewels, ca.1965
base metal $75 $125 $200

ALPHA, 17J., chrono. 2 reg., cal.48, c.1950s
14K $325 $425 $550
s.steel $200 $275 $375

ALPHA, 17J, autowind, c.1950s
18K..$195 $235 $300

ALPINA, 17 jewels, automatic, ca. 1950
18k $185 $225 $295

ALPINA, 17 jewels, automatic, Ca. 1950
14K..$150 $175 $225

ALPINA, 17J., chronograph, ca. 1940
14k $325 $400 $525

ALPINA, 17 jewels, automatic, water proof, aux. sec.
18k $195 $235 $300

ALSTA, 17J., chronograph, **3 reg.**
14K $385 $500 $725
base metal $200 $300 $500

ALSTA, 17 jewels, **wrist alarm**
gold filled $95 $125 $185

ALTERNO, 15J., **Reverso**, Ca.1935
s. steel $750 $900 $1,250

ALTUS, 17 jewels, ref. 827
18k $160 $195 $275

AM. WALTHAM, 21J., "Adair", ca.1941
gold filled..................................$60 $85 $160

AM. WALTHAM, 21J., "Albright", ca.1940
14k $125 $165 $250

AM. WALTHAM, 17J., "Allen", ca.1940
gold filled..................................$60 $80 $135

AM. WALTHAM, 21J., "Bonus", sold for $75.00 in 1937
case signed "Schwob & Wuischpard" 14K gold
14K..$175 $225 $325

AM. WALTHAM, 21J., "Boxford", gold numbers, ca.1941
18k yellow $175 $225 $300
18K red $200 $250 $375

AM. WALTHAM, 17J., "Braintree", **Side Wrist**, ca.1940
gold filled..................................$85 $110 $200

AM. WALTHAM, 21J., "Cadet", sold for $77.50 in 1937
14K $135 $185 $275

AM. WALTHAM, 17J., "Camden", ca.1941
gold plate $50 $70 $100

AM. WALTHAM, 21J., "Campton", **note** bezel, c.1940
14k $185 $225 $300

AM. WALTHAM, 17J., "Canton", gold numbers, ca.1941
gold filled $60 $85 $150

AM. WALTHAM, 10J., "Chandler", sweep sec., ca.1941
gold plate $45 $55 $80

AM. WALTHAM, 17J., "Charlton", ca.1940
gold plate $45 $55 $95

AM. WALTHAM, 9J., "Conway", ca.1941
gold plate $45 $55 $95

AM. WALTHAM, 17J., "Creston", ca.1941
gold filled..............................$70 $85 $145

AM. WALTHAM, 17J., "Cronwell", ca.1940
gold filled..............................$65 $85 $145

AM. WALTHAM, 17J., "Danbury", coin edge, ca.1941
gold filled..............................$65 $85 $155

AM. WALTHAM, 17J., "Dighton", thin model, ca.1941
gold filled yellow or red..........$80 $100 $175

AM. WALTHAM, 9J., "Duxbury", ca.1941
gold plate $50 $65 $90

AM. WALTHAM, 17J., "Escort", sold for $47.50 in 1937
gold filled..............................$75 $100 $165

🕐 Pricing in this Guide are trade show fair market price for
COMPLETE watches which are reflected from the "**NAWCC**"
National and regional shows.

AM. WALTHAM, 17J., "Fairmont", ca.1940
gold filled $65 $85 $160

AM. WALTHAM, 17J., "Fremont", gold numbers, ca.1941
14k $155 $195 $275

AM. WALTHAM, 21J., "Gardner", gold numbers, ca.1940
gold filled $65 $85 $160

AM. WALTHAM, 17J., "Goodwin", ca.1941
gold filled $65 $85 $160

AM. WALTHAM, 17J., "Granby", gold numbers, ca.1941
14k $155 $195 $275

AM. WALTHAM, 17J., "Heath", ca.1941
gold filled $65 $85 $160

AM. WALTHAM, 21J., "Hingham", gold numbers, ca.1941
14k $175 $195 $295

AM. WALTHAM, 17J., "Hollis", applied numbers, ca.1941
14k $155 $200 $295

AM. WALTHAM, 21J., "Hubbard", 13 rubies or sapphires
set in gold on dial, ca.1941
14k yellow $130 $155 $210
14k red $180 $210 $285

AM. WALTHAM, 17J., "Jeffery", ca.1941
gold filled................................. $65 $85 $165

AM. WALTHAM, 17J., "Lebanon", ca.1941
gold filled................................. $65 $85 $160

AM. WALTHAM, 17J., "Mendon", ca.1941
gold filled................................. $65 $85 $160

AM. WALTHAM, 17J., "Norton", ca.1941
gold filled................................. $65 $85 $160

AM. WALTHAM, 17J., "Oberlin", ca.1941
gold filled $65 $85 $160

AM. WALTHAM, 17J., "Pacer", Sec. hand, ca.1941
gold filled $65 $85 $160

AM. WALTHAM, 21J., "Pacer", no sec. hand, Ca. 1937
case signed "Schwob & Wuischpard" 14K gold
14K $150 $200 $300

AM. WALTHAM, 21J., "Paddock", sold for $75.00 in 1937
14K $125 $150 $225

AM. WALTHAM, 17J., "Patriot", sold for $45.00 in 1937
gold filled $65 $85 $160

AM. WALTHAM, 17J., "Patten", hidden lugs, ca.1941
14k yellow $135 $155 $225
14K red $185 $225 $300

AM. WALTHAM, 17J., "Paxton", ca.1941
gold plate $50 $60 $95

AM. WALTHAM, 17J., "Peabody", ca.1941
gold plate $50 $60 $95

AM. WALTHAM, 17J., "Penton", ca.1941
gold filled................................. $65 $85 $160

AM. WALTHAM, 17J., "Preston", ca.1941
gold filled yellow $65 $85 $160
gold filled red $80 $100 $195

AM. WALTHAM, 17J., "Quincy", ca.1941
gold filled................................. $65 $85 $160

AM. WALTHAM, 17J., "Reading", ca.1941
gold filled................................. $65 $85 $160

AM. WALTHAM, 17J., "Regal", ca.1941
gold plate $45 $55 $100

AM. WALTHAM, 17J., "Reward", sold for $70.00 in 1937
14K.. $135 $155 $225

AM. WALTHAM, 17J., "Richford", ca.1941
gold filled $65 $85 $160

AM. WALTHAM, 17J., "Rowe", ca.1941
gold filled $65 $85 $160

AM. WALTHAM, 21J., "Sheraton", ca.1941
14k $135 $165 $250

AM. WALTHAM, 17J., "Side-wrist", ca.1941
gold filled $125 $150 $235

AM. WALTHAM, 17J., "Stan Hope", ca.1941
gold filled $65 $85 $160

AM. WALTHAM, 9-17J., "Submarine", ca.1941
gold filled=17J $65 $85 $160
Chrome=9J $35 $45 $80

AM. WALTHAM, 17J., "Swagger", sold for $45.00 in 1937
gold filled $65 $85 $160

AM. WALTHAM, 17J., "Townsend", ca.1941
gold plate yellow $45 $60 $100
gold plate red $60 $70 $150

AM. WALTHAM, 21J., "Traveler", ca.1941
gold filled...................................$65 $85 $160

AM. WALTHAM, 17J., "Tulane", ca.1941
gold filled...................................$65 $85 $160

AM. WALTHAM, 18J., "Upton", ca.1941
gold filled...................................$65 $85 $160

AM. WALTHAM, 18J., "Upton", **pulse computing dial**
gold filled...................................$80 $110 $175

AM. WALTHAM, 21J., "Wachusett", gold numbers, ca.1941
gold filled...................................$65 $85 $160

AM. WALTHAM, 17J., "Wesley", ca.1941
gold plate red...........................$50 $65 $100

AM. WALTHAM, 17J., "Windfield", ca.1941
gold filled...................................$65 $85 $160

AM. WALTHAM, 9J., "Wollaston", ca.1941
gold plate yellow or red $50 $65 $110

AM. WALTHAM, 21J., "Woodland", gold numbers, ca.1941
14k $150 $175 $265

AM. WALTHAM, 17J., "Wyman", ca.1941
gold filled $65 $85 $160

AM. WALTHAM, 7-15J., "Generic", ca.1929
gold filled $65 $85 $160

AM. WALTHAM, 7-15J., "Generic", ca.1929
gold filled $65 $85 $160

AM. WALTHAM, 7-15J., "Generic", ca.1929
gold filled..................................$65 $85 $160

AM. WALTHAM, 7-15J., "Generic", ca.1929
gold filled..................................$65 $85 $160

AM. WALTHAM, 7-15J., "Generic", ca.1929
gold filled..................................$65 $85 $160

AM. WALTHAM, 7-15J., "Generic", ca.1929
gold filled..................................$65 $85 $160

AM. WALTHAM, 15J.,"Harley-Davidson", c.1935
gold filled..................................$85 $100 $185

AM. WALTHAM, 17J., curved, Ca.1930s
14k $150 $185 $325

🕐 Some grades are not included. Their values can be
determined by comparing with **similar** age, size, metal
content, style, grades, or models such as **time only**,
chronograph, repeater etc. listed.

AM. WALTHAM, 17J., Driver style, Ca. 1935
gold filled $65 $85 $160

AM. WALTHAM, 21J., cal.750B, GJS, c.1950s
14k $125 $165 $265

AM. WALTHAM, 17J., cal.750B, c.1951
gold filled $65 $85 $165

AM. WALTHAM, 15J., "Masonic" model, c.1925
14k (original dial)..................$165 $235 $365

AM. WALTHAM, 15-17J, **solid lugs,** c.1920s
sterling silver..........................$175 $200 $300

AM. WALTHAM, 15-17J, "Ruby", enamel dial, c.1920s
gold filled................................$125 $155 $250

AM. WALTHAM, 17 J, barrel shaped dial, c. 1920
14k $150 $175 $250

AM. WALTHAM, 17 J, Premier, diamond dial, Ca. 1938
14K (rose)..............................$500 $600 $800

AM. WALTHAM, 15J., enamel dial, wire lugs, Ca. 1915
silver $150 $200 $300

AM. WALTHAM, 17J., enamel dial, for Tiffany & Co.
14k $200 $265 $425

AM.WALTHAM, 19J., enamel dial, C. 1905
silver $135 $175 $265

AM. WALTHAM, 17 jewels, enamel dial, wire lugs
14k $250 $365 $500

AM. WALTHAM, 21J, stepped case, curved back
14k $175 $195 $300

AM. WALTHAM, 7-15 jewels, wandering sec., c. 1930
gold filled $100 $150 $250

AM. WALTHAM, 17 jewels, wandering sec., c. 1930
gold filled $100 $150 $250

AM. WALTHAM, wandering min., **jumping hour.**, c. 1933
gold filled...............................$375 $500 $750

AM. WALTHAM, 17J., center sec.
gold filled...................................$60 $80 $150

AM. WALTHAM, 17 jewels, center sec.
gold filled...................................$60 $80 $150

AM. WALTHAM, 15 jewels, **winds at 12**, wire lugs, c. 1916
silver & enamel dial $250 $325 $500

AM. WALTHAM, 15 J., case by **Rolland Fischer**
silver $500 $600 $800

AM. WALTHAM, 15J., **enamel dial, center lugs**, c.1915
silver $200 $275 $450

AM. WALTHAM, 17J., **multi-color enamel dial**, c.1910s
gold filled $150 $200 $325

AM. WALTHAM, 15J, **multi-color enamel dial**, Ca. 1920
silver $150 $200 $325

AM. WALTHAM, 7-15J., **pulsations**, solid lugs, c.1925
silver $300 $375 $525

AM. WALTHAM, 17J.,"Riverside", GJS, c.1918
silver $400 $500 $650

AM. WALTHAM, 15 jewels, c. 1930
gold filled................................$60 $80 $150

AM. WALTHAM, 7J., **oxidized bezel**, c.1930s
gold filled................................$60 $80 $150

AM. WALTHAM, 7-15J., **cut corner dial**, c.1930s
gold filled................................$60 $80 $150

AM. WALTHAM, 15 jewels,
gold filled................................$60 $80 $150

AM. WALTHAM, 15J., **engraved oxidized bezel**,c.1930s
gold filled $60 $80 $150

AM. WALTHAM, 15J.,**engraved case**
gold filled $60 $80 $150

AM. WALTHAM, 17 jewels, 18K applied #s
silver $125 $165 $225

AM. WALTHAM, 7-15 jewels, **engraved case**
gold filled $60 $80 $150

AM. WALTHAM, 7-15 jewels, **carved** case
gold filled $60 $80 $150

AM. WALTHAM, 15 jewels, **curved back**
14k $150 $185 $250

AM. WALTHAM, 7-15 jewels, engraved case
gold filled.................................$60 $80 $150

AM. WALTHAM, 17 jewels, **18K applied #s**
14kw $175 $225 $300

AM. WALTHAM, 15-17 jewels,
gold filled.................................$60 $80 $150

AM. WALTHAM, 7-15 jewels,
gold filled.................................$60 $75 $125

AM. WALTHAM, 15J., case by Rolland Fischer,
silver $400 $500 $850

AM. WALTHAM, 15 jewels, "Depollier," **early water
proof, (Canteen style)**, c. 1917
silver.......................................$350 $475 $900

AM. WALTHAM, 15 jewels, protective grill, c. 1907
gold filled..............................$250 $300 $435
14k..$650 $775 $900

AM. WALTHAM, 15 jewels, protective grill, c. 1907
silver.......................................$250 $325 $475

AM. WALTHAM, 17 jewels, military with **hack setting**
s. steel.....................................$85 $125 $200

AM. WALTHAM, 9J., luminous dial, military, Ca. 1943
s. steel $85 $100 $150

AM. WALTHAM, 17 jewels, **WINDS at 12,** wire lugs
gold filled...............................$175 $225 $350

AM. WALTHAM, 17 jewels, **center lugs**
14k $175 $200 $275

AM. WALTHAM, 17 jewels, **curvex, 42mm**
14k $300 $375 $550

AM. WALTHAM, 17 jewels, **curvex, 52mm**
14k $400 $550 $800

AM. WALTHAM, 17 jewels, **curvex, 42mm**
gold filled.................................$75 $100 $175

AM. WALTHAM, 15 jewels, **enamel bezel,** Ca. 1927
14K(W) $600 $700 $850

AM. WALTHAM, 17 jewels, curved, aux. sec.
gold filled.................................$60 $80 $150

AM. WALTHAM, 17 jewels, curved
gold filled.................................$60 $80 $150

AM. WALTHAM, 21 jewels, C.1938
14K...$150 $195 $300

AM. WALTHAM, 17 jewels, curved
gold filled.................................$60 $80 $150

AM. WALTHAM, 17 jewels, curved
gold filled...............................$60 $80 $150

AM. WALTHAM, 15J., note bow swings, screw back case,
solid lugs, enamel dial, early water proof , c. 1920s
14K...................★★★★★$1,000 $1,200 $1,500

AM. WALTHAM, 17 jewels, enamel bezel
14k $550 $750 $950
14k (w)...................................$500 $700 $800
gold filled...............................$150 $225 $375

AM. WALTHAM,21J., enamel bezel,"Ruby" model,c.1928
14k(w)..................................... $450 $575 $800

AM. WALTHAM,7J., enamel bezel, Ca. 1920
Nickel.....................................$150 $200 $295

AM. WALTHAM, 15 jewels, square, 1929
gold filled...............................$60 $80 $150

AM. WALTHAM, 7-15 jewels, cut corner, ca. 1929
gold filled................................$60 $80 $150

AM. WALTHAM, 17J., triangular, masonic symbols
fancy hands, mother of pearl dial, Ca. 1950
gold filled..............................$700 $900 $1,300

AM. WALTHAM, 7-15J., luminous dial, c.1928
base metal................................$45 $55 $85

AM. WALTHAM, 7-15J., cushion case, c.1928
gold filled................................$60 $80 $150

AM. WALTHAM, 7-15J., tonneau case, c. 1928
gold filled................................$60 $80 $150

AM. WALTHAM, 7J., luminous dial, c.1928
base metal $45 $55 $85

AM. WALTHAM, 7J., **radial**, luminous, c. 1928
gold filled $60 $80 $150

AM. WALTHAM, 17J., luminous dial, c.1929
gold filled $60 $80 $150
14k(w) $150 $185 $265

AM. WALTHAM, 17J., aux. sec., c. 1928
14k(w) $125 $155 $235

AM. WALTHAM, 7-15J., **lugless case**, c.1928
gold filled $60 $80 $150

AM. WALTHAM, 15J., generic, luminous dial, c.1928
14k $150 $200 $300

AM. WALTHAM, 15J., generic style brush finish, c.1928
14k $150 $200 $300

AM. WALTHAM, 7J., luminous dial, c.1928
gold plate $60 $80 $150

AM. WALTHAM, 17J., GJS, ca.1940
14K $125 $165 $235

AM. WALTHAM, 7-15J., cut corner case, c.1929
gold filled $60 $80 $150

AM. WALTHAM, 15J., **fluted case for men**, GJS, c.1925
14k(w)+enamel $150 $175 $265

AM. WALTHAM,7-15J., **Butler finish** = (smooth), c.1928
gold filled.................................$50 $65 $110

AM. WALTHAM, 7-15J., GJS, Ca.1927
14K(w)...................................$150 $175 $200

AM. WALTHAM,7-15J., engraved case, etched dial, c.1929
14k(w)......................................$50 $70 $100
gold filled................................$20 $40 $70

AM. WALTHAM,15J., engraved case, etched dial, c.1928
14K(W) $95 $125 $175
gold filled................................$20 $40 $65

AM. WALTHAM,7-15J., enamel case, c. 1928
14k(w) $70 $100 $150

AM. WALTHAM,15J., enamel case, c.1929
gold filled (w) $45 $75 $125

AM. WALTHAM,15-17J., enamel bezel, c.1929
14K (Y) $550 $750 $950
14K (W) $500 $700 $800

AM. WALTHAM,15-17J., enamel decoration on case, c.1929
14K...$70 $100 $150

AM. WALTHAM,15-17J., c.1929
14K...$70 $100 $150

AM. WALTHAM,15-17J., 6½ Ligne, c.1929
14K...$70 $100 $150

AM. WALTHAM,15-17J., 6½ Ligne, c.1929
14K...$70 $100 $150

AM. WALTHAM,15J., 6½ Ligne, c.1929
gold filled.................................$50 $60 $75

AMERICAN WALTHAM WATCH CO. IDENTIFICATION BY MOVEMENT

Model 1900, 0 size

Model 1907, 0 size

Jewel Series

Model 1900, 0/3 size,
open face

Model 1907, 0/3 size,
hunting

Model 1898 & 1912,
0/6 size, hunting

Model 1898 & 1912,
0/6 size, open face

10½ ligne

10 ligne

7½ ligne

5¼ ligne

Model 400

Model 450

Model 650

Model 675

Model 750

AMERICUS, 17 jewels, **"8 day"** movement, c. 1933

18k	★★★★$700	$825	$1,000
gold filled	★★$200	$325	$500
s. steel	★★$200	$325	$500

AMERICUS, 7 jewels, curved, c.1935

gold filled	$55	$75	$125

ANGELUS, 17 jewels, chronograph, 2 reg., c. 1943

18k	$450	$565	$800
14k	$300	$425	$650
gold filled	$150	$185	$265

ANGELUS, 17J., chronograph, **triple date**, C. 1949

s. steel	$300	$400	$500
14k	$600	$750	$1,000
18k	$1,000	$1,250	$1,700

ANGELUS, 17J., day, date, moon ph.,C. 1949

s. steel	$300	$425	$650

ANGELUS, 17 jewels, chronograph, 2 reg., water proof

14k	$450	$650	$850
18k	$550	$875	$1,100
s. steel	$225	$300	$450

ANGELUS, 17J., **date and alarm**, c.1955

s. steel	$85	$100	$225

ANGELUS, 27 jewels, **1/4 hour repeater**

s. steel	$2,000	$2,400	$3,200

ARAMIS, 15 jewels, **early self wind, lug action winding by back & forth motion of watch case**, c. 1933
s. steel .... ★ ★ $500 $650 $900

ARCTOS, 17J., "PARAT", world map on dial, c.1955
base metal..................................$90 $125 $200

ARBU, 17 jewels, triple date, **moon phase**
18k $500 $650 $900
s. steel $180 $200 $300

ARDATH, 17J., chronograph, triple date, c.1947
s. steel....................................$200 $300 $450

ARBU, 17 jewels, chronograph, 3 reg., day-date-month
18k $500 $650 $900
s. steel $250 $300 $450

ARISTO, 17 jewels, chronog., water proof
14k..$400 $500 $750
s. steel....................................$125 $175 $235

ARBU, 17 jewels, **split second chronograph**
18k $2,500 $3,300 $4,500

ARISTO, 17J., chronog., 3 reg., **triple date, moonphase**
14k..$800 $900 $1,200
s. steel....................................$250 $350 $600

ARISTO, 17 jewels, day-date-month, **moon phase**
s. steel $200 $300 $450

ASPREY, 16 jewels, **curved hinged back**
9k..$125 $150 $250

ARSA, 17 jewels, chronog., day-date-month, Ca. 1950
18k $600 $800 $1,200

ASPREY, 17J., **date**, ca. 1930s
14k..$300 $400 $600
gold filled...............................$125 $150 $200

ARSA, 17 jewels, day-date-month, **moon phase**
18k $600 $800 $1,100
s. steel $200 $325 $450

ASPREY, 15 jewels, **duo dial**
18k...$900 $1,100 $1,600

ASPREY, 17 jewels, **enamel dial, center lugs**
9k..$125 $150 $250

ARSA, 15 jewels, day-date-month, **moon phase**
18k $600 $750 $1,000
s. steel $200 $275 $400

AUDAX, 15J., Ca.1938
9k..$95 $125 $200

🕐 Some grades are not included. Their values can be determined by comparing with **similar** age, size, metal content, style, grades, or models such as **time only**, chronograph, repeater etc. listed.

AUDEMARS PIGUET, 33J., **minute** repeater, gold train, platinum & 18K with **40** diamond bezel, diamond dial & diamonds on band
18K & platinum................$60,000 $70,000 $90,000

AUDEMARS PIGUET, Royal Oak Offshore, auto wind, Chronograph, 10 atmospheres
s. steel..................................$6,000 $6,500 $7,500

AUDEMARS PIGUET, 29 J., **minute repeater**, c. 1917
18k $55,000 $65,000 $80,000

AUDEMARS PIGUET, 33J., day date, moon ph., c.1989
18k..$2,500 $2,800 $3,500

AUDEMARS PIGUET, 29 J., **minute repeater**, c. 1925
platinum $65,000 $75,000 $100,000

AUDEMARS PIGUET, day date, moon ph., C. 1980s
18k..$2,200 $2,400 $3,000

AUDEMARS PIGUET, 19 J., **tourbillon,** self-winding tourbillon can be seen from dial side
18k $6,000 $7,000 $9,000

AUDEMARS PIGUET, chronograph, triple date, moon ph., tear drop lugs, Ca. 1940s
18k..$16,000 $18,000 $22,000

AUDEMARS PIGUET, 36 jewels, gold rotor, day-date
month, moon phase, perpetual
18 k C&B.............................$9,000 $10,000 $11,500

AUDEMARS PIGUET, skeletonized, triple date,
moon phase, perpetual , C. 1980s
platinum.............................$16,000 $18,000 $22,000

AUDEMARS PIGUET, 17 J., chronog., 3 reg., c. 1945
s.steel $8,000 $9,000 $11,000
18k $12,000 $13,000 $15,000

AUDEMARS PIGUET, 18 J., ''Le Brassus,'' **chronog.**
skeletonized
18k C&B.............................$6,000 $7,000 $9,000

AUDEMARS PIGUET, 22 jewels, chronog., 2 reg.,
s.steel $7,000 $8,000 $10,000
18k $14,000 $15,000 $16,000

AUDEMARS PIGUET, 18 jewels, skeletonized
18k $3,500 $4,000 $5,500

AUDEMARS PIGUET, 18 J., triple date, moonphase
18k $3,500 $4,000 $5,000

AUDEMARS PIGUET, **Star Wheel**, showing the passing of
time on Sapphire discs bearing the hours and moving over a
concentric circular aperture showing the minutes
18k $3,500 $4,500 $6,000

AUDEMARS PIGUET, 36 jewels, skeletonized
18k $4,000 $5,000 $7,000

AUDEMARS PIGUET, 17 J., center lugs, skeletonized
18k $3,500 $4,500 $6,500

AUDEMARS PIGUET, 17J., Dodecagonal, black dial
18k $1,200 $1,300 $1,600

AUDEMARS PIGUET, 17J., diamond dial, c. 1970
18k $1,500 $1,600 $1,900

AUDEMARS PIGUET, 12 diamond dial c.1960
platinum $2,000 $2,200 $2,500

AUDEMARS PIGUET, 11 diamond dial
18k $1,400 $1,600 $2,000

AUDEMARS PIGUET, 12 sapphire dial, c.1950
18k $2,000 $2,200 $2,600

AUDEMARS PIGUET, 17 jewels, 12 diamond dial
18k (w) $2,200 $2,400 $2,800

AUDEMARS PIGUET, 36 jewels, self-winding
18k $1,200 $1,400 $1,700

AUDEMARS PIGUET, 17 jewels, adj. to 5 positions
18k C&B..............................$1,400 $1,600 $2,000

AUDEMARS PIGUET, 17 jewels, rope style bezel
18k C&B $1,500 $1,700 $2,000

AUDEMARS PIGUET, 36 jewels, self-winding
18k $1,500 $1,700 $2,000

AUDEMARS PIGUET, 17J., diamond bezel, center lugs
18k $1,800 $2,000 $2,400

AUDEMARS PIGUET, 36 jewels, lazuli dial
18k C&B.............................. $2,000 $2,200 $2,600

AUDEMARS PIGUET, 20J., rope style bezel, c. 1980s
18k case, 14k band $1,000 $1,100 $1,300

AUDEMARS PIGUET, 17 jewels, thin style
18k C&B.............................. $2,000 $2,200 $2,600

AUDEMARS PIGUET, 20J., "Le Brassus", Ca. 1970
18k C&B..............................$1,800 $2,200 $2,400

AUDEMARS PIGUET, 17J, RF# 8326, fancy bezel, c.1950
18k $1,900 $2,200 $2,800

AUDEMARS PIGUET, fancy shaped, c.1960s
18k $4,000 $4,500 $6,000

AUDEMARS PIGUET, 17J., "Philosopher", hour hand only
18k $2,800 $3,200 $3,800

DIALS FOR MINT PRICES MUST BE ALL **ORIGINAL**.

AUDEMARS PIGUET, 20 jewels, thin model
18k $800 $1,000 $1,300

AUDEMARS PIGUET, 17J., engraved bezel, c. 1963
18k $1,200 $1,400 $1,800

AUDEMARS PIGUET, 17J., wide bezel, thin model
14k C&B $1,200 $1,400 $1,800

AUDEMARS PIGUET, 21J., auto wind, center sec.
18k $1,600 $1,800 $2,200

🕐 Pricing in this Guide are fair market price for **COMPLETE** watches which are reflected from the "**NAWCC**" National and regional shows.

🕐 A collector should expect to pay modestly higher prices at local shops.

AUDEMARS PIGUET, **painted world time**, fancy lugs
s. steel $7,000 $8,000 $10,000

AUDEMARS PIGUET, **painted world time** , c. 1940s
14k $8,000 $9,000 $10,000

AUDEMARS PIGUET, 18 jewels, gold train
18k $2,500 $2,800 $3,500

AUDEMARS PIGUET, 18J., **hidden lugs**, Ca. 1950
18k $1,800 $2,000 $2,400

AUDEMARS PIGUET, 18 jewels, aux. sec. c. 1940
18k $1,400 $1,700 $2,200

AUDEMARS PIGUET, 17 jewels, for Tiffany & Co.
18k C&B $2,000 $2,200 $2,600

AUDEMARS PIGUET, 18 jewels, aux. sec.
18k $1,600 $1,800 $2,200

AUDEMARS PIGUET, 18 jewels, black dial, Ca. 1960
18k (w)................................$1,400 $1,600 $1,900

AUDEMARS PIGUET, 18 jewels, hooded lugs
18k $1,900 $2,200 $2,600

AUDEMARS PIGUET, 17J., engraved bezel, c.1966
18k $900 $1,000 $1,200

AUDEMARS PIGUET, 18J., date, auto wind, Ca.1990
18k $900 $1,200 $1,600

AUDEMARS PIGUET, 18 jewels, center sec., c. 1950
18k $1,400 $1,500 $1,800

AUDEMARS PIGUET,18J., straight line lever escape.
18k $1,000 $1,200 $1,500

AUDEMARS PIGUET, 17 jewels, mid-size
18k $600 $700 $900

AUDEMARS PIGUET, 18J., mid size, **flat bezel**, Ca. 1969
18k $900 $1,000 $1,300

AUDEMARS PIGUET, gold textured dial, c.1960s
18k $900 $1,000 $1,200

AUDEMARS PIGUET, 19J., center sec.
18k $1,400 $1,600 $2,000

AUDEMARS PIGUET,18J., aux. sec., c. 1950s
18k $1,000 $1,200 $1,500

AUDEMARS PIGUET, 18J., Manual wind, waterproof
18k $1,500 $1,700 $2,000

AUDEMARS PIGUET, 18J., auto wind, waterproof
18k $1,600 $1,800 $2,200

AUDEMARS PIGUET, 17 jewels, gold train
18k $1,000 $1,200 $1,500

AUDEMARS PIGUET, 18 jewels, **painted dial**, Ca. 1970
18k $900 $1,000 $1,200

AUDEMARS PIGUET, **triple date, moon ph.**, dial & mvt.
Signed "A L'Emeraude, Lausanne" Cal.# GHSM, Ca.1926
18k $12,000 $14,000 $18,000

AUDEMARS PIGUET, 18 J.," **top hat**", aux. sec., c. 1950
platinum................................$3,200 $3,500 $4,500
Wrist Watches listed in this section are priced at the collectable
fair market **Trade Show** level as **complete** watches having an
original gold-filled case and stainless steel back, also with
original dial, leather watch band, and the entire original movement in good working order with no repairs needed.

AUDEMARS PIGUET, 21J, sweep sec., automatic -18k rotor
18k $1,700 $1,900 $2,300

AUDEMARS PIGUET, 17J., gold train, 2 tone case in
platinum & gold
18k (w) C&B $2,500 $2,700 $3,000

AUDEMARS PIGUET, engraved bezel, c.1950s
18k $1,500 $1,800 $2,500

AUDEMARS PIGUET, 17 jewels, gold train
14k C&B $1,200 $1,400 $2,000

AUDEMARS PIGUET, 18 J., textured bezel, c. 1950
18k $1,200 $1,400 $1,800

AUDEMARS PIGUET, 2 tone dial, c.1930s
18k $2,500 $3,000 $4,000

🕐 Some grades are not included. Their values can be
determined by comparing with **similar** age, size, metal
content, style, grades, or models such as **time only**,
chronograph, repeater etc. listed.

AUDEMARS PIGUET, 18J, curvex, large bezel, c. 1950
18k $1,500 $1,700 $2,000

AUDEMARS PIGUET, 18 jewels, Sq. lugs, c. 1950's
18k $1,500 $1,700 $2,000

AUDEMARS PIGUET, Royal Oak, **date,** auto wind, c.1973

18K & s. steel $2,500	$2,800	$4,000
18K C&B.............................$5,000	$5,500	$7,000
18K C&B,day/date/moonphase.$6,000	$6,500	$8,000
18K C&B,perpetual/moonph. $12,000	$13,000	$15,000
s. steel, auto wind...............$2,000	$2,500	$3,000
s. steel, LARGE, auto wind $2,200	$2,600	$3,220
2-tone, LARGE, auto wind. $2,500	$2,800	$3,400
Ladies, 18K, C&B $2,500	$3,000	$4,000
Ladies 18K C&B,day/date/ auto $3,500	$4,000	$5,500

Note: Add 20% for new style button release clasp.

AUDEMARS PIGUET, quartz, 12 diamonds, c. 1981
s. steel $1,200 $1,300 $1,600

AUDEMARS PIGUET, Ladies, 72 small diamonds, C. 1930's
plat. case & band $1,800 $2,000 $2,500

AUDEMARS PIGUET, ladys, 36 diamonds, c.1930s
plat.case $1,500 $1,700 $2,000

AUTOMATIQUE, 17J., cal.F699, c. 1955
s. steel $45 $55 $85

AUTORIST, 15 jewels, **lug action wind**, enamel dial
s. steel $400 $500 $700

AUTORIST, 15 jewels, **lug action wind**, c. 1930
s. steel $350 $450 $600

AUTORIST, 15 jewels, **lug action wind**, movement.

AUTORIST, 15 jewels, **lug action wind**, c. 1930
gold filled $400 $485 $600

AUTORIST, 15 jewels, **lug action wind**, (lady's)
s. steel $175 $225 $350

AVALON,17J., aux.sec.
gold filled $60 $80 $125

AVIA,15J., center sec., Ca. 1953
9K rose $120 $140 $175

BALL W. CO., 25 jewels, "Trainmaster", auto wind,
adj. to 5 pos., E.T.A.
10k $295 $400 $550

BALL W. CO., 25 jewels, "Trainmaster"auto wind,
adj. to 5 pos., E.T.A.
gold filled................................$150 $200 $325

BAUME & MERCIER, 17J., chronog., 2 reg.,c.1950s
18k $500 $650 $850

BALL W. CO., 25 jewels, "Trainmaster"auto wind,
adj. to 5 pos., E.T.A.
s. steel (auto wind) $150 $200 $325
s. steel (manual wind)............$150 $175 $300

BAUME & MERCIER, 18J., chronog., 3 reg. & dates
s. steel $350 $400 $550

BAUME & MERCIER, 18J., triple date, moon phase
s. steel $400 $495 $700

BAUME & MERCIER, 18 J., chronog., 3 reg. & dates
18k $900 $1,000 $1,200

BAUME & MERCIER, 17J., chronog., 2 reg., c.1949
gold filled................................$250 $325 $450

BAUME & MERCIER, 18 jewels, tachymeter, c. 1940
s. steel, original black dial..... $500 $600 $800

BAUME & MERCIER, 17J., triple date, chronog.
moon ph., c.1950s
18k $1,000 $1,100 $1,400

BAUME & MERCIER, 18 J., chronog., fancy lugs
18k $1,500 $1,800 $2,300

BAUME & MERCIER, 17J., chronog., triple date
18k $800 $900 $1,200

BAUME & MERCIER, 18J., triple date, moon phase
18k $600 $750 $1,000

BAUME & MERCIER, 17J., 2 dials, **2 time zones &
2 movements**
18k $400 $525 $750

BAUME & MERCIER, 18 jewels, gold dial, date
14k C&B................................ $400 $525 $750

BAUME & MERCIER, 18 jewels, thin model
14k C&B................................ $400 $475 $600

BAUME & MERCIER, 17 jewels, center sec., c. 1956
14k $200 $250 $350

BAUME & MERCIER, 17J, fancy lugs, aux. sec., c. 1955
14k $250 $300 $400

BAUME & MERCIER,17J., auto-w., Wind ind., Ca.1950s
base metal $100 $130 $200

BAUME & MERCIER, 17J., RF#49300, c. 1965
14k $150 $185 $235

BAUME & MERCIER, 17J.,diam. mystery dial, c.1950s
14k(W)...................................$500 $625 $800

BAUME & MERCIER, 18 J., "Riviera", date, c. 1980s
18k & s. steel $400 $450 $525

BAYLOR, 17J., hidden lugs
gold filled $50 $70 $125
14k $120 $150 $200

BAUME & MERCIER, **quartz**, enamel dial, Ca.1990s
14k $300 $350 $550

BAYLOR, 17J., diamonds on bezel & dial, c.1948
14k $175 $200 $265

BAUME & MERCIER, 30J, "Baumatic", Ca. 1976
18K(W) $350 $465 $650

BAYLOR, 25J., auto-wind, wind-ind., Ca. 1958
14k $135 $165 $250

BEMONTOIR, 15J., enamel dial, c.1920
14k $95 $120 $150

BENRUS,17J., day date
base metal $30 $35 $65

BENRUS, 18J., **mystery**-diamond dial
18k $225 $275 $350
gold filled................................$75 $110 $175

BENRUS, 15 jewels, day, date, c. 1948
s. steel $50 $60 $95

🕐 Pricing in this Guide are fair market price for **COMPLETE** watches which are reflected from the "**NAWCC**" National and regional shows.

🕐 A collector should expect to pay modestly higher prices at local shops

BENRUS, 15 jewels, quick change date
gold filled $70 $85 $150

BENRUS,17J.,"Sky Chief", chronog., 3-reg., c.1945
s. steel $225 $300 $450

BENRUS,17J., "Sky Chief",**triple date**,chronog.,3-reg, c.1940s
s. steel $250 $325 $500

BENRUS,17J.,Wrist Alarm c.1945
base metal $100 $125 $175

DIALS FOR MINT PRICES MUST BE ALL **ORIGINAL**.

BENRUS, 15 jewels, calendar, auto wind, fancy lugs, c.1950
14k ....$100   - $135 $200
gold filled................................$60 $85 $150

BENRUS, 15 jewels, jumping hour, wandering min.
gold filled (**Chevron style case**) . $150 $185 $250
gold filled $150 $185 $250
s. steel $100 $125 $225

BENRUS, 15J., auto wind, fancy bezel, by ETA, c. 1950
gold filled................................$40 $55 $100
14k $100 $135 $185

BENRUS,17J., fancy lugs
gold filled $50 $75 $125

BENRUS,17J., auto wind with **wind indicator**, Ca. 1955
gold filled................................$60 $85 $135

BENRUS,17J., fancy lugs
gold filled $50 $60 $95

BENRUS,17J., dial-0-rama, direct read, c. 1958
gold filled................................$150 $195 $300
Wrist Watches listed in this section are priced at the collectable
fair market **Trade Show** level as **complete** watches having an
original gold-filled case and stainless steel back, also with
original dial, leather watch band, and the entire original movement in good working order with no repairs needed.

BENRUS,21J., Diamond Dial, Ca. 1956
14K $100 $135 $225
⊕ Some grades are not included. Their values can be
determined by comparing with **similar** age, size, metal
content, style, grades, or models such as **time only**,
chronograph, repeater etc. listed.

674 / BENRUS (continued)

BENRUS, 15 jewels, fancy lugs, **recased**, c. 1948
14k $75 $100 $150
gold filled................................$55 $65 $95

BENRUS, 15J., auto-wind, **water-proof**
gold filled................................$50 $60 $100

BENRUS, 15 jewels, fancy bezel, cal. BB14
14k $150 $185 $275
gold filled................................$75 $100 $150

BENRUS, 21J., aux. sec., c. 1950s
14k $90 $125 $185

🕐 Pricing in this Guide are fair market price for **COMPLETE**
watches which are reflected from the "<u>NAWCC</u>" National and
regional shows.

🕐 Some grades are not included. Their values can be
determined by comparing with **similar** age, size, metal
content, style, grades, or models such as **time only**,
chronograph, repeater etc. listed.

BENRUS, 17J., 3 diam. dial, one diam. on each hand, c.1955
14K $125 $150 $225

BENRUS, 21J., aux. sec., fancy lugs, c.1950
gold filled $55 $70 $100

BENRUS, 17J., hidden lugs
14K $100 $125 $175

BENRUS, 17J., cadillac logo, c.1950s
gold plate $40 $50 $80

BENRUS, 17J., movement by ETA, c.1955
gold filled $45 $60 $100

BENRUS, 15J., engraved bezel, c.1935
14k $100 $135 $200

BENRUS,17J., **flared case**, cal.180, c. 1951
gold filled $60 $85 $150

BENRUS, 17J., rhinestone dial, c. 1945
gold filled.................................$60 $75 $125

BENRUS, 7J., rhinestone dial, fancy lugs, c. 1948
base metal $35 $45 $75

BENRUS, 17J., date, fancy lugs, c.1950
gold filled.................................$65 $95 $165

BENRUS,17J., rhinestone dial, cal. bb1, c. 1945
gold plate $35 $45 $75

BENRUS, 17J., aux. sec., c.1940
14k $100 $125 $175

BENRUS, 7J., Ford Logo, Ca. 1950
gold filled $45 $55 $95

BENRUS, 15J.,aux sec.
gold filled.................................$55 $70 $125

Pricing in this Guide are fair market price for **COMPLETE** watches which are reflected from the "**NAWCC**" National and regional shows.

BENRUS, 15J.,fancy lugs
14K $125 $150 $200

BENRUS, 17J., hidden lugs, cal.11ax, Ca.1951
14k $125 $165 $250

BENRUS, 15J., fancy hooded lugs, cal#ax11, Ca.1946
14K...$125 $165 $250

BENRUS, 15J., **enamel bezel**, c. 1930
14k (w)...................................$200 $300 $450

BENRUS, 17 jewels, Flared case, Ca. 1955
14k $125 $165 $250

BENRUS,17J., aux sec., Ca.1935
gold filled................................$45 $60 $100

BENRUS, 15 jewels, **flip-up case**, c. 1940
gold filled $250 $285 $375

BENRUS,17J., hooded lugs, c.1948
14k $125 $135 $175

BENRUS,17J., hooded lugs, cal.AX11, c. 1950
14k $135 $165 $200

BENRUS, 15 jewels, hooded lugs
gold filled $60 $70 $100

BENRUS, 15 jewels, cal. AX, 3 small diam. dial, c. 1950
14k $135 $165 $225

Wrist Watches listed in this section are priced at the collectable
fair market **Trade Show** level as **complete** watches having an
original gold-filled case and stainless steel back, also with
original dial, leather watch band, and the entire original movement in good working order with no repairs needed.

BENRUS, 17 jewels, curved, hooded lugs, Ca. 1950s
14k $150 $185 $275

BENSON J.W., 15 jewels, , curved back, c. 1942
9K.. $150 $200 $300

BENSON J.W., 15-16J., made in England, aux sec. Ca.1955
9k .... ★$400 $500 $750

BENSON J.W., 15J., of London, Ca.1938
9k $150 $200 $300

BENSON J.W., 15 jewels, enamel dial, London
9k $150 $200 $300

BENSON J.W., 15J., enamel dial, hunter case, Ca. 1920
Silver...................................... $295 $350 $475

BENSON J.W., 15 jewels, enamel dial, 2-tone flared case
9k $275 $325 $425

BLANCPAIN, 17J., **"Aqua Lung"**, auto-wind, date, 1000 Ft. revolving bezel, 37mm, Ca.1960
S. S $500 $600 $800

BLANCPAIN, 23J, day-date-month, perpetual, auto-wind
s. steel- perpetual................. $2,500 $3,000 $4,000
18K - perpetual.................... $4,000 $4,500 $5,500

BLANCPAIN, 17J.,hooded lugs, c.1945
14k $200 $250 $350

DIALS FOR MINT PRICES MUST BE ALL <u>ORIGINAL</u>.

BLANCPAIN, 16J., fancy lugs, Ca.1958
14K...$150 $200 $275

E. BOREL, 17J., cocktail dial, date, c. 1969
base metal $55 $65 $100

BOILLAT FRERES, 17 jewels, ''Blita,'' waterproof
s. steel $40 $50 $70

E. BOREL, 15J., *"Regulator Dial"*, hour dial, minute dial,
with center sec., c.1940
s. steel $350 $400 $500

E. BOREL, 17 jewels, chronometer, aux. sec.
18k $175 $225 $300
gold filled...............................$45 $55 $85

E. BOREL, 17 jewels, auto wind, date
gold filled $65 $75 $125

E. BOREL, 17J., cocktail style, c.1960s
gold filled...............................$55 $75 $125
s. steel $55 $75 $125

BOUCHERON, 17J., c.1930s
18k $400 $450 $650

🕐 A collector should expect to pay modestly higher prices
at local shops.

🕐 Some grades are not included. Their values can be
determined by comparing with **similar** age, size, metal
content, style, grades, or models such as **time only**,
chronograph, repeater etc. listed.

Wrist Watches listed in this section are priced at the collectable
fair market Trade Show **retail** level as **complete** watches having
an original gold-filled case and stainless steel back, also with
original dial, leather watch band, and the entire original movement in good working order with no repairs needed.

🕐 Pricing in this Guide are fair market price for **COM-
PLETE** watches which are reflected from the "**NAWCC**" National and regional shows.

DIALS FOR MINT PRICES MUST BE ALL **ORIGINAL**.

BOULEVARD, 17J., "STOP", c.1950s
s. steel $75 $110 $200

BREGUET, 17J., chronog., triple date, Ca.1950
s. steel $6,000 $7,000 $9,000

BOVET, 17 jewels, chronog., 2 reg., c. 1940
s. steel $150 $175 $250

BREGUET, auto-w., triple date, moon ph., perpetual
18k $13,500 $14,500 $18,000

BOVET, 17 jewels, chronog., triple date & 3 reg.
14k $700 $800 $1,000
gold filled...............................$375 $425 $500

BREGUET, jump hour, c.1980s, **total made =50**
18k ....★$9,000 $10,000 $12,000

BREGUET, 21 jewels, skeletonized
18k C&B $5,000 $6,000 $8,000

BREGUET,37J., auto-w.,date, moon ph.,45 hr.wind ind.
18k $11,000 $12,000 $14,000

BREGUET, 17 jewels, silver dial, thin model
18k $1,400 $1,600 $2,000

BREGUET, 17 jewels, curvex
platinum $3,000 $3,500 $5,000

P. BREGUETTE, 17J., gold jewel settings, Ca.1948
14k $110 $150 $200

P. BREGUETTE, 17J., gold jewel settings, flared case
14k $175 $200 $250

P. BREGUETTE, 17 jewels, **top hat**, diamond dial, c. 1940
14k $500 $600 $750

Add up to **150%** over mint for new old stock (N.O.S.)

P. BREGUETTE, 17J., triple date, c.1960s
gold filled $125 $200
s. steel $125 $135 $185

Breitling, 17 J., Precision, red & blue Tacky.-rings, Ca. 1940
s. steel $1,500 $1,700 $2,500

Breitling, 17 J., "Chronomat," slide rule bezel
18k $2,000 $2,200 $2,500
gold filled $900 $1,000 $1,200
s. steel $800 $900 $1,100

Breitling, 17 J., **Navitimer**, date, slide rule bezel, RF 7806
s. steel $1,100 $1,200 $1,400

Add up to **150%** over mint for new old stock (N.O.S.)

BREITLING, 17J., **Chronomat.**, RF 808, c.1950
gold filled...............................$900 $1,000 $1,200

BREITLING, 18J., date, moon ph., split chronog. Ca. 1950's
18k $6,000 $7,000 $9,500

BREITLING, 17J., chronog., RF#1199, sq. button, c.1958
s. steel $400 $450 $550

BREITLING, 17 J, chronog., "Navitimer," RF 806

18K C&B............................	$5,000	$5,500	$6,000
18K case only	$4,000	$4,500	$5,500
gold filled	$1,100	$1,200	$1,500
s. steel	$1,000	$1,100	$1,400

BREITLING, 17J., chronog., "Cosmonaute", **24 hour,** 3 reg.
18k $4,500 $5,000 $6,500
s. steel $1,200 $1,400 $1,800

BREITLING, 17 J., chronog., "Navitimer," **AOPA** logo, Ca. 1952
s. steel $1,300 $1,400 $1,600

AOPA logo ☞ ⇢⟨⟩

A.O.P.A., the initials of Aircraft Owners & Pilots Association, This logo first appeared in 1952 on the "*Navitimer*", a word derived from <u>Navi</u>gation, **Navi** + the word Timer. The AOPA logo and other logos are being collected such as Blue Angles (*U.S.Navy*), Red Arrow (*Royal Air Force*), Frecce Tricolori (*Aeronautica Militare Italiana*), Patrouille Suisse (*Escadre de Surveillance*), Thunderbirds (*U.S. Air Force*), Blue Impulse (*Japan Self Defense Force*), Team 60 (*Swedish Air Force*) Patrouille de France (*French Air Force*) and others.

BREITLING, 17 jewels, split sec. chronog., 2 reg.
s. steel $4,000 $5,000 $6,500

Add up to **150%** over mint for new old stock (N.O.S.)

BREITLING, 17 J., chronog., ''Chronomat,'' 3 reg.
s. steel $600 $700 $900

BREITLING, 17 jewels, chronog., pulsations
s. steel $650 $750 $950

BREITLING, 17 J., telemeter, 1 button, hinged lugs
s. steel- 44mm.........................$850 $950 $1,150

BREITLING, 17 jewels, chronog., 2 reg.
s. steel $1,000 $1,100 $1,300

BREITLING, 17 J., 1 button, Chronograph, Ca. 1930
s. steel $800 $900 $1,100

BREITLING, 17 jewels, tachymeter, center hinged lugs
s. steel - 35mm $800 $900 $1,200

BREITLING, 17 jewels, tachymeter, Ca.1930
s. steel $1,200 $1,500 $2,000

BREITLING, 17J., chronog., RF#765, c.1960
14k $1,400 $1,600 $2,000
s. steel $700 $900 $1,200

BREITLING (continued)

683

Add up to **150%** over mint for new old stock (N.O.S.)

BREITLING, 17 jewels, chronog., Toptime, 24 HR.
s. steel $425 $550 $800

BREITLING, 17 jewels, chronog., "Premier," 3 reg.
s. steel $500 $600 $800

BREITLING, 17 jewels, chronog., 2 reg. RF#790
18K refinished dial...............$800 $900 $1,100
18K original dial.................$1,200 $1,400 $1,700

BREITLING, 17 J., chronog., day-date-month, 3 reg.
18k $2,000 $2,200 $2,500
s. steel $800 $900 $1,100

BREITLING, 17J., chronog., 2 reg., "Premier", RF#790
18k $1,600 $1,800 $2,200

BREITLING, 17 jewels, chronog., 2 reg. RF # 178
s. steel $375 $450 $550

BREITLING, 17J., chronog., 3 reg., RF#787, c.1942
14k C&B $1,200 $1,400 $1,800

BREITLING, 17 jewels, chronog., 2 reg. RF # 769
18k $1,200 $1,500 $2,000
s. steel $335 $500 $700

BREITLING, 17 J., **split sec.** chronog., "Duograph", C.1945
18k $6,000 $7,000 $9,000
s. steel $4,000 $5,000 $7,000

BREITLING, 17J., chronog., 3 reg., RF#815, c.1968
gold filled.............................. $600 $700 $900

BREITLING, 17J., **AOPA** logo , Toptime, RF#810, c.1968
s. steel $650 $750 $950

BREITLING, 17J., **Tour de France**, c. 1945
18K... $1,200 $1,400 $1,700

BREITLING, 17J., **Super Ocean**, RF # 2005, c.1960
s. steel $1,000 $1,200 $1,500

BREITLING, 17J., chronog., RF#2110, c.1970
s. steel $400 $450 $600

BREITLING, 17J., chronog., RF#2009-33, c. 1975
s. steel $325 $350 $400

BREITLING, 17J., **Co-Pilot**, enamel bezel, RF # 765, c. 1960
s. steel $1,300 $1,500 $2,000

Add up to **150%** over mint for new old stock (N.O.S.)

BREITLING, 17J., **Cosmonaute II**, 24 hr., Ca.1990
s.steel C&B $1,200 $1,400 $1,800

BREITLING,17J., "Blue Angel 92", **total production 1,000**
s. steel & gold bezel $1,800 $2,000 $2,400

BREITLING, 17J., **Old Navitimer II**, gold bezel, Ca.1990
s.steel & G-Bezel $900 $1,000 $1,200

BREITLING, 17J., **Corono QP**, day date moon ph., Ca.1990
18K C&B $6,000 $7,000 $9,000

BREITLING, 17J., **Navitimer 92**, self-wind, Ca.1992
s.steel case $1,200 $1,300 $1,500
18K case $3,500 $4,000 $4,800

BREITLING, 17J., **Corono 1461**, day date moon ph., c.1990
s.steel C&B $2,100 $2,300 $2,600

BREITLING, 17J., **Chronomat**, date, self-wind, Ca.1990
s.steel $900 $1,100 $1,400
18K & s.steel C&B $1,800 $2,000 $2,400

BREITLING, 17J., **Chrono Longitude**, date, Ca.1990
s.steel & gold C&B $1,500 $1,600 $1,800

BREITLING, 17J., **Chronomat Yachting**, date, Ca.1990
s.steel C&B $1,200 $1,300 $1,600

BREITLING, 17J., **Navitimer Airborne**, date, Ca.1990
s.steel case $1,100 $1,200 $1,500

BREITLING, 17J., **Chrono Cockpit**, date, Ca.1990
18K & s.steel C&B $1,300 $1,400 $1,600

BREITLING, 17J., **Navitimer AVI**, date, Ca.1990
s.steel case $700 $800 $1,000

BREITLING, "Golden Knights", only 50 made, **only 20 made available to general public**, to bring top price watch should have a factory letter, papers & 2 boxes. **(U.S. Army)**
s. steel $1,500 $1,600 $2,000

BREITLING, "Blue Angels Limited Edition", only 100 made, **only 25 made available to general public**, to bring top price watch should have a factory letter, papers & 2 boxes. **Sonic Minute Repeater   (U.S. Navy)**
Titanium.............................$2,500 $2,900 $3,800

BREITLING, "Top Gun", Limited Edition, 1,000 made
s. steel & gold bezel $1,250 $1,400 $1,800

BREITLING, "Blue Angels Limited Edition 96", Montbrillant
18K..$3,700 $4,400 $5,500

UTC (Universal Time Coordinated), small Quartz that is
fitted between lugs & used for second time zone = **$300 to $450**

BREITLING, "Team 60", Limited Edition, 1,000 made,
Pluton model, Ca. 1995
s. steel $450 $550 $800

Add up to **150%** over mint for new old stock (N.O.S.)

BUCHERER,17 jewels, **note: day date in lugs**
18k $350 $450 $600

BREITLING, 17J., chronog., RF#1450, 3 reg., c.1970
s. steel $300 $350 $450

BREITLING, 17J., day date month,
18k $300 $350 $465

BUCHERER,17 jewels, chronog., 2 reg.
18k $450 $500 $600

BREITLING, 21J., "UNITIME", date, 24 hour, c.1958
gold filled............................... $900 $1,100 $1,500
18k $1,800 $2,000 $2,500

BUCHERER, 17J., chronog., 2 reg., C.1959
18k $400 $450 $600
s. steel $250 $300 $375

BREITLING, 21J., auto-wind, rf#2528, c.1959
s. steel $50 $75 $125

BUCHERER, 25 J., triple date moon ph., cal.693, c.1950
18k $700 $800 $1,000

BUCHERER, 21J., 3 dates, moon ph., diamond dial
18k $2,000 $2,200 $2,600

BUCHERER, 15 jewels, **8 day** movement
18k $700 $800 $1,000
gold filled...............................$300 $350 $500

BUECHE-GIROD, 17 J., day-date-month, **moon ph**.
s. steel $325 $375 $500

BUECHE-GIROD, 17J., by Piguet, cal.99, c.1975
18k $250 $300 $400

🕐 Some grades are not included. Their values can be
determined by comparing with **similar** age, size, metal
content, style, grades, or models such as **time only**,
chronograph, repeater etc. listed.

Wrist Watches listed in this section are priced at the collectable
fair market **Trade Show** level as **complete** watches having an
original gold-filled case and stainless steel back, also with
original dial, leather watch band, and the entire original movement in good working order with no repairs needed.

BUECHE-GIROD, 17J., dual time movements,
18k $500 $625 $800

BUECHE-GIROD, 17 jewels, Sq. lugs
18k $450 $525 $650

BUECHE-GIROD, 17 jewels
18k C&B..............................$500 $550 $650

P. BUHRE, 17 jewels, aux. sec.
gold filled $60 $70 $125

P. BUHRE, 17J., alarm, C.1956
s. steel $50 $75 $125

BULOVA WATCH CO.

In 1875 Joseph Bulova starts a wholesale jewelry business. Basically, it was always a Swiss-USA company & in 1930 Bulova sets up to make bridges and plates at Woodside, NY. By 1934 the company manufactured watches by the millions, using ebauches manufactured in its own Swiss plant. The New York Plant by now was making escapements, dials, plates and other parts and also cased and assembled the watches. About 1940 or sooner they were able to make complete watches. By the early 1950s they produced over a million watches a year of which over half were imported movements & the remaining were domestic. The *Accutron* was introduced on October 25, 1960, it was the **first** electronic watch made. The watch used a tuning fork that vibrated 360 times a second using a transistorized electronic circuit and a battery which would last for about a year. Micro-miniaturization of components was a technical achievement. The tuning fork vibrates, a jewel-tipped (pawl spring) index finger advancing the index wheel. The index wheel is only 0.0945 inches in diameter ● (about the size of a pin head) yet it has 320 ratchet teeth. The coil is less than a 1/4 inch long but contains 8,000 turns of wire that is 0.0006 inches in diameter. The original **214** model, (identified by absence of a crown) was produced until about 1966 and about a 2,000,000 were made. The newer **218** model has a crown at the 4 0'clock position. By 1975- 76 the Accutron production ended and about 5,000,000 were sold.

The **"Spaceview"** so named due to the conventional dial was left off so the **tuning fork** can be viewed from the top using a transparent crystal. With the conventional dial missing it had to be replaced with a dial spacer. The **"Spaceview Alpha"**, as delivered from factory, used a transparent crystal with **dots** and a dial spacer only. The **"Spaceview H"** used a crystal and a dial reflector (chapter ring) not a dial spacer. There are many different **original factory** combinations of the **"Spaceview"** crystals with many different styles of hands. **Spaceviews** came in both 214 & 218 models.

"Spaceview Alpha" with **dots** on crystal & dial spacer   "Spaceview H" with chapter ring & dial reflector

Different Spaceview transparent dot crystals   Above: Different Hands

Different Hands - tuning fork (white-red-gold) seconds hands - also orange second hand

Spaceview "Alpha", was the 1st model, Ca 1960
1963 ad Alpha model sold for $200

BULOVA, Accutron, "Spaceview Alpha" Ca. 1960
Accutron the first transistorized watch was sold Oct. 25, 1960.
14k $600 $800 $1,100

Accutron tuning fork vibration-to-rotary motion conversion the
indexing mechanism. Magnified view of index wheel with 2
jewels, a rachet & pawl system advancing the wheel.

BULOVA, Accutron, "Spaceview B", yellow dots & hands,
sold for $150 in 1964.
s.steel $295 $350 $500

BULOVA, Accutron, "Spaceview H"
gold filled..............................$275 $325 $425

Note: model 214 = back set & model 218 = crown at 4.

BULOVA, Accutron, "Spaceview T", clearview dial,
orange second hand, sold for $135.00 in 1967.
s. steel $250 $325 $450

BULOVA, Accutron, RF # 202, RR approved,
sold for $125.00 in 1964.
s. steel $150 $200 $300
gold filled $175 $225 $325

BULOVA, Accutron, RF # 210, gold bezel & s.steel case
s.steel & 14k...........................$250 $300 $400

BULOVA, Accutron, RF # 213, sold for $125.00 in 1964.
s.steel $150 $175 $250

BULOVA, Accutron, RF # 214
s.steel $150 $175 $250

BULOVA, Accutron, RF # 216, sold for $175.00 in 1964.
s.steel $150 $175 $250

BULOVA, Accutron, RF # 218, **bow tie** lugs
s.steel $200 $250 $325

BULOVA, Accutron, RF # 223
s.steel $200 $250 $325
14k $450 $525 $650

BULOVA, Accutron, RF # 241, **bow tie** lugs,
sold for $125.00 in 1967.
s.steel $200 $250 $350

BULOVA, Accutron, RF # 252, red second hand,
sold for $110.00 in 1967.
s. steel $150 $175 $250

BULOVA, Accutron, RF # 254, red second hand,
sold for $125.00 in 1967.
s. steel $100 $125 $200

BULOVA, Accutron, RF # 301, basketweave band,
sold $150.00 in 1967.
gold filled $150 $175 $250

BULOVA, Accutron, RF # 400
gold filled $150 $175 $250

BULOVA, Accutron, RF # 401, sold for $150.00 in 1964.
s.steel $150 $175 $250

BULOVA, Accutron, RF # 403, sold for $175.00 in 1964.
gold filled $150 $175 $250

BULOVA, Accutron, RF # 411
gold filled $150 $175 $250

BULOVA, Accutron, RF # 412 gold filled bezel & s.steel
gold filled & s.steel case $150 $175 $250

BULOVA, Accutron, RF # 500, center lugs,
sold for $300.00 in 1964.
14k $500 $550 $750

BULOVA, Accutron, RF # 413, GF bezel & s. steel case
gold filled & s.steel case $100 $125 $225

BULOVA, Accutron, RF # 505, Ca. 1960
14k yellow or white............... $525 $575 $750

BULOVA, Accutron, RF # 417
gold filled.............................. $175 $225 $275

BULOVA, Accutron, RF # 513
14k $350 $400 $550

BULOVA, Accutron, RF # 420
gold filled.............................. $200 $225 $275

BULOVA, Accutron, RF # 514, Florentine engraved case
14k $400 $450 $600

BULOVA, Milady's Accutron, RF # 430,
sold for $185.00 in 1967.
gold filled................................. $85 $100 $150

Note: model **214** = back set & model **218** = crown at 4.

BULOVA, Accutron, RF # D515, 20 diamonds on case,
sold for $750.00 in 1967.
14K (w) C&B $400 $450 $600

 NOTE: Some Bulova cases are stamped with a year date
code letter & number . **L** = 1950s, **M** = 1960s, **N** = 1970s,
P = 1980s, **T** = 1990s.
example: L3=1953, M4=1964, N5=1975, P6=1986, T7=1997.

BULOVA, Accutron, RF # 560
14k $350 $400 $600

BULOVA, Accutron, RF # 602
18k $700 $750 $900

BULOVA, Accutron, RF # AK, Day & Date,
sold for $200.00 in 1967.
gold filled...............................$150 $185 $275

BULOVA, Accutron, RF # AG, Day at 12 & Date at 6,
sold for $185.00 in 1967.
s. steel $150 $185 $275

BULOVA, Accutron, RF # CK, date at 6,
sold for $135.00 in 1967.
s. steel $185 $265 $375

Note: A small **predictable** position error can be taken into
consideration in the daily regulation of your Accutron. In the 12
- down **vertical** position the rate is about 5 seconds per day faster
conversely in the 6-down **vertical** position a rate of 5 seconds
per day slower. You can take advantage of this, if slow place it
in the 12-down <u>vertical</u> position at night and it will gain back
lost time, if fast use the 6-down <u>vertical</u> position to slow it down.

BULOVA, Accutron, RF # CL, tortoise-toned dial,
sold for $250.00 in 1967.
14K $350 $400 $525

BULOVA, Accutron, ''Mickey'' day & date, **RARE** (218)
s. steel(214) $400 $500 $700
14k C&B(original dial) ★ ★ ★$700 $850 $1,200

BULOVA, Accutron, date, "M 8" on back - Ca. 1968
14k $350 $400 $575

BULOVA, Accutron, Ca. 1969-70.
14K $500 $600 $800

Note Below: Bulova Accutron regulator, to regulate use a
tooth pick and move regulator up or down. (Tuning Fork)

12 O'CLOCK   SLOWER

FASTER 6 O'CLOCK

🕐 NOTE: Some Bulova cases are stamped with a year date
code letter & number . **L** = 1950s, **M** = 1960s, **N** = 1970s
P =1980s, **T** = 1990s.
example: L3=1953, M4=1964, N5=1975, P6=1986, T7=1997.

Note: model **214** = back set & model **218** = crown set at 4.

BULOVA, Accutron, "Spaceview"
s. steel $250 $300 $450

BULOVA, Accutron, "Spaceview"
s. steel $250 $300 $400

BULOVA, Accutron, **"Not Factory"**, cal. 214, c.1963
gold filled................................. $75 $100 $150

BULOVA, Accutron, "Spaceview"
18k $800 $900 $1,200
14k $500 $600 $750
s. steel $250 $300 $400

BULOVA, Accutron, cal. 214, c. 1963
s. steel $225 $275 $400

BULOVA, Accutron, "Spaceview," Accutron second hand
gold filled $200 $250 $400

BULOVA, Accutron, "Spaceview," c. 1960
18K.. $750 $850 $1,200
14k $600 $650 $850
gold filled................................. $250 $275 $400
s. steel $250 $275 $400

BULOVA, Accutron, "Spaceview," c. 1961
gold filled $225 $250 $350

DIALS FOR MINT PRICES MUST BE ALL **ORIGINAL**.

BULOVA, Accutron, "Spaceview," c. 1967
gold filled.............................$250 $275 $425
s. steel $250 $275 $425
14k $450 $500 $675

BULOVA, Accutron, "Spaceview," center lugs
14k C & B..............................$700 $800 $1,200

BULOVA, Accutron, **Not Factory,** Alpha, waterproof
14k $200 $225 $275

BULOVA, Accutron, **Not Factory** dial, date, cal.218
14k 2 tone $200 $225 $250

BULOVA, Accutron, "Spaceview," **Bowtie** lugs
gold filled...............................$300 $350 $450

BULOVA, Accutron, Skeletonized, date, cal.218, Ca.1967
14k $550 $600 $750

BULOVA, Accutron, center lugs
s. steel $275 $300 $375
gold filled...............................$275 $300 $375

BULOVA, Accutron, day, date, sold for $135.00 in 1976
gold filled $100 $150 $250

Accutron the **first** electronic watch was sold Oct. 25, 1960.
**By 1966 Accutron had sold over 1 1/2 million,
and by 1976, 5 million watches.**

🕐 Some grades are not included. Their values can be determined by comparing with **similar** age, size, metal content, style, grades, or models such as **time only,** chronograph, repeater etc. listed.

🕐 A collector should expect to pay modestly higher prices at local shops.

BULOVA, Accutron, "Spaceview," **Not Factory**
s. steel $100 $125 $175

BULOVA, Accutron, "Spaceview," RED second hand.
s. steel $275 $325 $475

BULOVA, Accutron, 2 tone, Ca. 1967
gold filled...............................$275 $300 $450

BULOVA, Accutron, "Spaceview," gold bezel
14k $450 $500 $650
gold bezel & s. steel case $300 $325 $425

BULOVA, Accutron, oval, "Spaceview" Ca. 1962
18K............................... $600 $700 $950
14K............................... $350 $400 $525
gold filled................................$225 $250 $325
s. steel $225 $250 $325

BULOVA, Accutron, M# 214, **railroad** approved, Ca. 1962
gold filled $175 $200 $300
s. steel $175 $200 $300

BULOVA, Accutron, "Spaceview,"
s. steel $225 $250 $350

BULOVA, Accutron, M# 218, RR approved, **red 24 hr.** #s,
sold for $125.00 in 1976
gold filled $175 $200 $300

DIALS FOR MINT PRICES MUST BE ALL **ORIGINAL**.

BULOVA, Accutron, RR approved
gold filled..............................$175 $200 $300

BULOVA, Accutron, RR approved
s. steel $175 $225 $325

BULOVA, Accutron,**" Mark IV" / RR approved,** date
Crown at 2 sets the hour hand, Crown at 4 sets Time & Date
two hour hands for two time zones
s. steel $275 $350 $500

BULOVA, Accutron, cal. 214," Pulsation", c. 1966
gold filled..............................$250 $335 $500
14k .... ★$700 $800 $950

BULOVA, Accutron, cal. 214," Pulsation", c. 1966
14k .... ★$700 $800 $950

BULOVA, Accutron, "Alpha", model 214, 6 diamond dial
14k $650 $700 $900
18K .... ★$1,000 $1,200 $1,500

BULOVA, Accutron, sweep sec. hand
gold filled $150 $210 $325

BULOVA, Accutron, masonic dial (all original dial)
NOTE: This dial can be printed for about $35.00.
14k $350 $375 $475

BULOVA, Accutron, asymmetric
14k $550 $575 $750

BULOVA, Accutron, asymmetric, 2- tone dial, Ca.1963
14k $600 $650 $750

BULOVA, Accutron, "ASTRONAUT A", 24 hour dial,
the s. steel case & band sold for $175.00 in 1964.
18kC&B $1,500 $1,600 $2,100
14k $800 $1,000 $1,400
gold filled...............................$350 $475 $700
s. steel $300 $365 $600

BULOVA, Accutron, "ASTRONAUT B", rotating bezel
s. steel $300 $375 $525

BULOVA, Accutron, "ASTRONAUT C", 18k case & band,
sold for $1,000.00 in 1964.
18k C & B $1,400 $1,600 $2,100
also made with a gold filled case & 14K bezel
GF case & 14K bezel $500 $600 $850

BULOVA, Accutron, "Astronaut Mark II", time zone, window
at six o'clock, date at 12, note: on back N2 = 1972
14k $450 $500 $650
s. steel $225 $265 $400

BULOVA, Accutron, "Astronaut Mark II", time zone, original sales price was $275.00 in S. Steel.
14k $450 $500 $650
gold filled $250 $325 $450
s. steel $250 $325 $450

BULOVA, Accutron, "Astronaut Mark II", auxiliary time
zone window at 6-o'clock & date at 12-o'clock.
14k $500 $550 $700

BULOVA, Accutron, "Astronaut Mark II", time zone with a extra red hour hand, date at 3 o'clock, on back M9 = 1969 gold filled................................$265 $325 $450

BULOVA, Accutron, "Spaceview"
gold filled $250 $275 $375

BULOVA, Accutron,"Astronaut Mark II **E**", travel time zone sold for $185.00 in 1967, orange sec. hand & hour markers s. steel $250 $300 $400

BULOVA, Accutron, **4 diamond** dial, Ca. 1967
gold filled $225 $275 $400

BULOVA, Accutron, Ca. 1966
gold filled...............................$150 $200 $275

BULOVA, Accutron, "spaceview", sold for $180.00 in 1976
gold filled $200 $275 $400

BULOVA, Accutron, date, gold filled bezel
s. steel $100 $125 $175

BULOVA, Accutron, fancy lugs
gold filled...............................$150 $175 $250

BULOVA, day, date, sold for $150.00 in 1976
gold filled $100 $135 $225

BULOVA, Accutron, date, **Tiffany & Co.** M7=1967,
note: accutron **tuning fork** second hand.
14K $450 $525 $650

BULOVA, Accutron, day, date, sold for $185.00 in 1976,
gold filled $125 $150 $225

BULOVA, Accutron, date
18K $450 $550 $700
gold filled $150 $175 $250

BULOVA, Accutron, date, Ca.1972
base metal $75 $100 $150

*Note the design of case (shaped like a Accutron tuning fork).
BULOVA, Accutron, **Spaceview Anniversary**, model 214
gold filled & s. steel $500 $525 $675
s. steel (large case) $500 $525 $675

BULOVA, Accutron, gold filled bezel, day date
gold filled $125 $165 $250

BULOVA, Accutron, red second hand, Ca. 1970
s. steel $275 $325 $450

BULOVA, day date
s. steel $100 $125 $175
14k diamond bezel $350 $400 $450

BULOVA, Accutron, **wood bezel**, day date
gold filled $100 $125 $175

BULOVA, Accutron, day date
gold filled $125 $150 $200

BULOVA, Accutron, red dial, date
gold filled $125 $150 $225

BULOVA, Accutron, day date, Ca. 1972
gold filled $100 $125 $175

BULOVA, Accutron, numbered bezel, day date
14k $350 $400 $575

BULOVA, Accutron, date
gold plate $100 $125 $175

BULOVA, Accu**quartz**, note band with **accutron symbol**
18k C&B $700 $800 $1,000

BULOVA, Accutron, day date, c. 1970
14K... $300 $350 $450
s. steel $125 $150 $200

BULOVA, Accutron, model 2186, direct read
gold filled................................ $200 $250 $350

BULOVA, Accutron, **Accutron 14k Gold Band**, Ca.1972
14k C & B.............................. $600 $650 $800

BULOVA, Accutron, **DEEP SEA**, 666 ft.depth, day date, 12
& 24 hr.dial, crown at 2 rotates outside dial to locate city.
s. steel $375 $450 $600

BULOVA, Accutron, **DEEP SEA "A"**, 666 feet, day date,
crown at 2 rotates elapsed for REMAINING time dial,
sold for $195.00 in 1967.
SNORKEL model similar to above but in a square case.
s. steel $275 $365 $500

BULOVA, Accutron, **DEEP SEA**, 666 feet, date
rotating enamel bezel for REMAINING time.
s. steel $275 $365 $500

BULOVA, Accutron, day date, note <u>Accutron style sec. hand</u>
s. steel $200 $285 $450

BULOVA, Accutron, date, Ca. 1968
gold filled $100 $125 $175

BULOVA, Accutron, day, date, sold for $125.00 in 1976
gold filled..............................$125 $150 $225

BULOVA, Accutron, day, date, sold for $450.00 in 1976
14k $300 $365 $525

BULOVA, Accutron, "Spaceview", Bowtie lugs
18K..$800 $1,000 $1,300

BULOVA, Accutron, cal. #221, textured bezel
sterling & 14k........................$100 $125 $175

BULOVA, Accutron, model "AO", asymmetrical,
Sold for $225.00 in 1971.
gold filled..............................$100 $125 $175

BULOVA, Accutron, day, date, sold for $125.00 in 1976
gold filled $100 $150 $225

704 / BULOVA (continued)

🕐 NOTE: Some Bulova cases are stamped with a year date **code letter & number**. L = 1950s, M = 1960s, N = 1970s P =1980s, T = 1990s.
example: L3=1953, M4=1964, N5=1975, P6=1986, T7=1997.

BULOVA, digital,
s. steel $125 $165 $275

BULOVA, 17J., chronog., "660 feet" dive watch, c.1972
s. steel $100 $165 $250

BULOVA, enamel bezel
s. steel $100 $150 $250

BULOVA, 16 jewels, military style
s. steel $250 $325 $400

BULOVA, 15J., one button chronog.,1/5 sec.,C.1946
14k $400 $500 $650
gold filled...............................$250 $300 $400

BULOVA, 17J., **Alarm**, cal.11aerc, c.1967
s. steel $100 $175 $275

BULOVA, 17J., one button chronog., cal.10BK, c.1947
gold filled...............................$250 $300 $400

BULOVA, self winding, c. 1960
14k $150 $185 $250
gold filled $75 $100 $200

BULOVA, 17J., fancy lugs, aux. sec., Ca. 1951
gold filled.................................$75 $100 $175

BULOVA, 23 jewels, waterproof
14k $125 $135 $225

BULOVA, 23 jewels, **date, 6 adj.,** c. 1951
gold filled.................................$95 $135 $225

BULOVA, 17J., cal.11 af, ca.1959
gold filled.................................$60 $85 $150
14K...$100 $135 $225

BULOVA, 17jewels, fancy long lugs, c. 1954
gold filled $65 $95 $165

BULOVA, 17J., center sec., auto wind, Ca.1951
gold filled $65 $90 $165

BULOVA, 21J., fancy lugs, c.1950
gold filled $65 $90 $165

BULOVA, 23J., Mystery dial, center sec., c.1959
14K $150 $200 $275

BULOVA, 15J., military style, c.1940
s. steel $50 $65 $135

BULOVA, cal. 700, **canteen** style, c. 1946
s. steel .... ★ ★ ★ $400 $535 $800

BULOVA, 15J., military style, cal.10 bnch, c.1940
s. steel $75 $100 $150

BULOVA, 17J., U.S.A. military, c.1945
s. steel $75 $100 $150

BULOVA, 17J., 20 diamond dial
14k(w)....................................$185 $250 $375

BULOVA, 23J., 12 diamond dial, c. 1959
14k(w)....................................$185 $250 $375

BULOVA, 30J., diam. dial, cal#10B2AC, C.1960s
14k(w)....................................$185 $250 $375

BULOVA, diamond dial, c. 1939
platinum..................................$600 $750 $1,000
14k (w) $400 $500 $850

BULOVA, 21 jewels, hidden lugs, diamond dial, c. 1935
14k $400 $500 $850

BULOVA, **hidden lugs**, diamond dial, c. 1945
14k $350 $450 $700

BULOVA, 21 jewels, diamond dial, long lugs, c. 1941
14k (w)...................................$250 $350 $475

BULOVA, 17J., 3 diamond dial, cal.8ae, c.1949
14k $150 $185 $275

BULOVA, **early auto wind** movement (see below)

BULOVA, **early auto wind, "Champ"**, c. 1930
some may be signed on dial **"Aster"**
gold filled...................... ★★★$400 $495 $725

BULOVA, 17 jewels, curved, cal. 7AP, c. 1939
14k $250 $300 $400

BULOVA, 17J., drivers watch, c.1935
gold filled $250 $300 $400

BULOVA, 17J., engraved, Ca. 1928
gold filled $50 $75 $125

BULOVA, 17J., 5th ave., cal.6am, engraved bezel, c.1935
gold filled $60 $85 $150

BULOVA, 21J., stepped bezel, curved,
gold filled $60 $85 $150

BULOVA, 21J., plain bezel, curved,
gold filled $60 $85 $150

BULOVA, 17J., cal. 7ap, c.1937
gold filled $60 $85 $150

BULOVA, 17J., **curved**, cal.7ap, c.1936
gold filled...............................$65 $95 $175

BULOVA, 17J., cal.13al,c.1935
14k $125 $165 $250

BULOVA, 17J., cal.9af, c.1929
s. steel $45 $60 $100

BULOVA, 17J., cal.7ap, c.1934
gold filled...............................$60 $85 $150

BULOVA, 15J., cal.10ae, c.1938
gold filled...............................$60 $85 $150

BULOVA, 17 jewels, curved, c. 1939
gold filled...............................$60 $85 $150

BULOVA, 21 jewels, curved, c. 1939
gold filled $65 $95 $175

BULOVA, 21J., cal# 6AE,
14k $125 $155 $265

BULOVA, 17 jewels, duo dial, c. 1935
gold filled(S.S.back) $175 $235 $500
s. steel $175 $225 $450

BULOVA, 17 jewels, **2 tone**, duo dial
gold filled(S.S.back) $175 $235 $500
s. steel $175 $225 $450

BULOVA, 17 jewels, 2 tone dial, **flexible lugs,** fancy bezel
s. steel $75 $120 $185
Wrist Watches listed in this section are priced at the collectable
fair market Trade Show level as **complete** watches having an
original gold-filled case and stainless steel back, also with
original dial, leather watch band, and the entire original movement in good working order with no repairs needed.

DIALS FOR MINT PRICES MUST BE ALL **ORIGINAL**.

BULOVA, 21 J., **President, wandering sec.**, c. 1932
gold filled..............................$125 $150 $225
gold filled (**32 jewels**) $135 $165 $250

BULOVA, 17J., cal.8ad, fancy lugs, c.1939
gold plate $40 $50 $85

BULOVA, 17 jewels, cal. 10GM, fancy lugs, c. 1953
gold filled.................................$75 $95 $175
14k $150 $185 $275

BULOVA, 21J., cal. 7ak, c.1945
gold filled $75 $100 $175

BULOVA, 15J., fancy lugs, c.1952
gold filled................................$60 $80 $165

BULOVA, 21J., c.1950s
14K $125 $165 $250
gold filled $60 $80 $150

BULOVA, 21J., fancy lugs, c.1952
14k $150 $175 $265
gold filled................................$60 $80 $165

BULOVA, 21J., scalloped case, c.1950s
gold filled $75 $100 $175

BULOVA, 17J., fancy lugs, cal.8an, c.1951
14k $200 $250 $400
gold filled................................$85 $125 $200

BULOVA, 7J., c.1945
gold filled $60 $80 $150

🕐 Pricing in this Guide are fair market price for **COMPLETE** watches which are reflected from the "**NAWCC**" National and regional shows.

BULOVA, 17J., fancy lugs, Ca. 1941
14K...$175 $225 $300
gold filled.................................$75 $100 $175

BULOVA, 17J., Ca.1953
gold filled.................................$75 $100 $175

BULOVA, 21J., **curved case,** c.1948
14k $150 $200 $300

BULOVA, 21J., cal.7ak, c.1945
gold filled.................................$75 $100 $175

BULOVA, 17J., cal.8ae, fancy hidden lugs, c.1941
gold filled.................................$60 $80 $150

BULOVA, 21J., c.1945
gold filled $75 $100 $165

BULOVA, 17 jewels, cal. 7AK, c. 1930
gold filled $85 $135 $185

BULOVA, 17 jewels, fancy long lugs, c. 1942
14k $125 $175 $275

BULOVA, 17 jewels, cal. 10BM, Ca. 1954
gold filled $60 $85 $165

BULOVA, 17J., cal. 8AC, **flip up, photo watch,** c. 1940
gold filled $250 $325 $450
14k $350 $450 $650

🕐 Some grades are not included. Their values can be determined by comparing with **similar** age, size, metal content, style, models and grades listed.

DIALS FOR MINT PRICES MUST BE ALL **ORIGINAL**.

BULOVA, 15 jewels, wandering hr. min. sec., c. 1928
s. steel $150 $225 $325

BULOVA, 17J., rite angle, cal. 8AZ, c. 1938
gold filled................................ $150 $175 $300
14k $250 $325 $500

BULOVA, 17 jewels, aux. sec.
14k $125 $160 $235

BULOVA, 17 jewels, fancy bezel
gold filled................................ $100 $135 $200

BULOVA, 17 jewels, bell shaped lugs
14k $150 $225 $325

BULOVA, 17J., rite angle case
gold filled $150 $185 $250

BULOVA, 17J., center sec., cal.10bac, c.1935
gold filled $65 $85 $165

BULOVA, 17J., cal.8ac, fancy lugs, c.1940
gold plate $45 $55 $85

BULOVA, 17J., flared top of case & sides,
gold filled $75 $100 $175

BULOVA, 21J., hidden lugs, c.1961
gold filled $75 $100 $175

BULOVA, 21J., hidden lugs, c.1950s
14k $150 $200 $300

BULOVA, 17J., engraved bezel only
base metal $40 $50 $75

BULOVA, 21J., hidden lugs, c.1945
gold filled................................$75 $100 $175

BULOVA, 15J., cal.11ac, c.1958
gold filled $75 $100 $150

BULOVA, 17J., BMW- logo, c.1957
gold filled................................$70 $95 $165

BULOVA, 15J., cal.10ae, c.1935
gold filled $70 $95 $165

BULOVA, 17J., FORD logo, c.1947
base metal $40 $50 $85

BULOVA, 7J., cal.10bc, c.1949
gold filled $60 $80 $150

BULOVA, 17J., engraved lugs & bezel, cal.10an,c.1928
s. steel $45 $60 $100

BULOVA, **Masonic** dial, Ca. 1944
gold filled $100 $135 $225

BULOVA, 15 jewels, **Senator**,
gold filled.................................$75 $100 $175

BULOVA, 15 jewels, **Ambassador**,
gold filled $60 $80 $150

BULOVA, 17 jewels, **Oakley**,
gold filled.................................$60 $80 $150

BULOVA, 17 jewels, **Argyle**,
14K $125 $165 $250

BULOVA, 17 jewels, **LONE EAGLE**, stepped style case
gold filled $75 $100 $175

BULOVA, 15 jewels, **Norman**,
gold filled $60 $80 $150

BULOVA, 15 jewels, **LONE EAGLE**, tonneau style case
gold filled $60 $80 $150

BULOVA, 15 jewels, **Spencer**,
gold filled $60 $80 $150

BULOVA, 17J., **LONE EAGLE**, radium & cut corner dial
gold filled $60 $80 $150

BULOVA, 17 jewels, **Wellington**,
14K $125 $165 $235

DIALS FOR MINT PRICES MUST BE ALL **ORIGINAL**.

BULOVA, 17 jewels, fancy lugs
14k $150 $185 $275

BUREN, 17 jewels, day-date-month, moon phase
s. steel $195 $250 $350

BULOVA, 17 jewels, ''The Ambassador''
gold filled.................................$60 $80 $150

BUREN, 17 jewels, long lugs
14k (rose)...............................$135 $175 $250

BULOVA, 17 jewels, "The Curtis,"
gold filled.................................$60 $80 $150

BUREN, 17 jewels, center lugs, c.1940
9k $95 $125 $175

BULOVA, 15 jewels, "The Athelet"
gold filled.................................$75 $100 $175

BUTEX, 17J., triple date, moon ph.
gold filled $150 $200 $300

BULOVA, 17 jewels, ''The Governor,''
14K...$135 $165 $250

CARLTON, 15 jewels, **"Rite angle"** case, c. 1939
gold filled $125 $175 $250
14k $250 $300 $400

CARTIER, "Pasha", automatic, 300ft, **recent**
18k C & B............................$6,500 $7,000 $8,000
18k leather $3,000 $3,500 $4,500

CARTIER, "Golf", **Quartz**, 100 ft., **4 counters**, **recent**
18k C & B.........................$14,500 $15,000 $16,500
18k leather $9,500 $10,000 $12,000

CARTIER, "Pasha", automatic, 300 ft., rotating bezel, **recent**
18k C & B.........................$7,000 $7,500 $8,500
18k leather $2,200 $3,600 $4,500

CARTIER, "Diabolo", automatic, 100ft, **tourbillon**, **recent**
18k leather $35,000 $38,000 $42,000

CARTIER, "Pasha", automatic, 300ft, W/grill, **recent**
18k C & B..........................$7,000 $9,000 $11,000
18k leather $4,000 $4,500 $5,500

CARTIER, "Diabolo", manual wind, **Min. Repeater, recent**
18k leather $40,000 $45,000 $55,000

CARTIER, "Tank Francaise", automatic, date, 100 ft., **large**
18k C & B.......................$6,500 $7,500 $9,000
18k leather $3,000 $3,300 $4,000

CARTIER, "Pasha", automatic, rotating bezel, 100 ft., **recent**
18k C & B.......................$11,000 $13,000 $15,000
18k leather $9,000 $9,500 $11,000

CARTIER, "Tank Americaine", automatic, date, **recent**
18k C & B.......................$6,500 $7,500 $9,000
18k leather $3,500 $3,800 $4,500

CARTIER, "Pasha", automatic, moon phases, 100 ft., **recent**
18k C & B.......................$11,000 $12,000 $14,000
18k leather $7,500 $8,000 $10,000

CARTIER, "Cloche", manual wind, **recent**
18k leather $3,000 $3,500 $4,500

CARTIER, "Pasha", **Min. Repeater**, moon phases, **recent**
18k C & B.......................$60,000 $68,000 $75,000
18k leather $55,000 $62,000 $70,000

🕐 Pricing in this Guide are fair market price for **COMPLETE** watches which are reflected from the "**NAWCC**" National and regional shows.

CARTIER, "Santos Ronde", automatic, rotating bezel,100 ft., **recent**
18k C & B.......................$3,000 $4,000 $5,500

CARTIER, 18 J., **8 day** Mvt., tank style, by E. W. Co.
18k .... ★$22,000 $24,000 $29,000

CARTIER, 18 J., sapphire crown & bezel, c. 1970
18k $3,000 $3,500 $4,500

CARTIER, 18 jewels, curved, tank style, Ca.1970's
18k $6,000 $6,500 $8,000

CARTIER, 18 jewels, curved, signed E. W. Co., c.1930s
18k $5,000 $5,500 $6,500

CARTIER, 18 J., tank style, platinum case & band
platinum C&B.....................$9,000 $11,000 $14,000

NOTE: With original Cartier 18K Deployment clasp
ADD $400 to $600.

CARTIER, 18 jewels, tank style case, c. 1970s
18k $1,600 $1,900 $2,500

CARTIER, 20 jewels, tank style case, c. 1950
18k $2,200 $2,600 $3,200

CARTIER, Must de, **quartz,** tank style case, c.1980s
Vermeil =(gold over sterling)
G.P. vermeil...........................$200 $250 $400
SAME STYLE CASE AS ABOVE
CARTIER, Must de, **Mechanical,** tank style case, c.1980s
Vermeil =(gold over sterling)
G.P. vermeil...........................$200 $250 $400

CARTIER, 18 jewels, tank style, European W. Co.
platinum.............................$7,000 $8,000 $10,000

CARTIER, 18 jewels, by Movado
14k $950 $1,100 $1,400

CARTIER, 18 jewels, **duo plan**, European W. Co.
18k C&B $2,000 $2,200 $2,600

CARTIER, 18J., by Le Coultre, long lugs
18k $1,000 $1,200 $1,600

CARTIER, 18 jewels, curved, hidden lugs
18k $2,500 $2,800 $3,500

CARTIER, 18 jewels, by Universal, c. 1960
18k $750 $900 $1,200

CARTIER, 18 jewels, center lugs, c. 1930
18k $2,000 $2,300 $2,800

CARTIER, 18 J., Prince, by Le Coultre, C.1930
18k $12,000 $14,000 $18,000

CARTIER, 18 J., **reversible** to view 2nd **time zone**
18k $16,000 $18,000 $22,000

CARTIER, 18 jewels, Gents, by European W. Co. c. 1927
18k $3,000 $3,500 $4,500

CARTIER, 18 J., early E.W.Co., C. 1928
18k $2,500 $3,000 $4,000

CARTIER, 18 J., lady's watch by European W. Co.
18k C&B $2,000 $2,300 $2,900

CARTIER, 18 J., sovonnette (hunter case style), C. 1928
18k $5,000 $5,500 $6,500

CARTIER, 18 J., E.W.Co., Tank Normale, Ca. 1925
18k $3,000 $3,500 $4,500

CARTIER,18 J., guichet tank, jump hr. & min. by E.W.Co.
18k $25,000 $30,000 $36,000

CARTIER, 18 jewels, "Santos," octagonal, date
18k & s. steel C&B $700 $800 $1,000

CARTIER, 18 J., jump hr. & min., E. W. Co. c. 1930
platinum $30,000 $33,000 $40,000

CARTIER, Panthere, date, water resistant, Medium size

s. steel band	$900	$1,000	$1,300
1 stripe of gold, quartz	$800	$900	$1,200
2 stripes of gold, quartz.......	$1,000	$1,200	$1,600
3 stripes of gold, quartz.......	$1,800	$2,100	$2,600
18k **reg**. C & B...................	$4,500	$5,000	$6,000
18k **large** C & B..................	$5,000	$5,500	$6,500
lady's, s. steel band	$600	$800	$1,200
lady's, 1 stripe of gold, ...	$700	$900	$1,100
lady's, 2 stripe of gold, ...	$1,200	$1,400	$1,800
lady's, 3 stripe of gold, ...	$1,400	$1,600	$2,000
lady's, 18k C & B	$4,500	$5,000	$6,000

CARTIER, 18 J.,"Santos", mechanical, cal.21
mens18k.............................. $2,500 $2,800 $3,500
ladies 18k............................ $2,000 $2,200 $2,700

CARTIER, 18 J., "Santos," 18k & s. steel case, band, **Lady's**
platinum & 18k C&B $6,000 $7,000 $9,000
18k & s. steel C&B................ $800 $900 $1,200

CARTIER, 25 jewels, chronog., European W. Co.
18k $60,000 $65,000 $80,000

CARTIER, 18 jewels, "Santos," date, Gents, Ca. 1980's
18k & s. steel C&B................ $950 $1,100 $1,400

CARTIER, 29 jewels, min. repeater, c. 1925
18k $90,000 $110,000 $140,000

CARTIER, 18 jewels, c. 1925
18k $2,500 $2,800 $3,500

CARTIER, 18 jewels, asymmetric, E. W. Co., c. 1928
18k $6,000 $7,000 $9,000

CARTIER, 18 J., oval maxi, C. 1968
18k $6,500 $7,500 $10,000

CARTIER, 18 jewels, by Le Coultre
18k $1,700 $2,100 $3,000

CARTIER, 18 J., bamboo style bezel, Gents, C.1970s
18k $3,000 $3,500 $4,500

NOTE: With original Cartier 18K Deployment clasp
ADD $400 to $600.

CARTIER, 18 J., large cut corner bezel, C.1970s
18k $2,000 $2,200 $2,800

CARTIER, 18 J., "Helm", single lug, C. 1950s
18k $8,000 $9,000 $12,000
platinum............................$16,000 $18,000 $22,000

CARTIER, 18 J.,by E.W.CO., single lug, C. 1949
18k $5,000 $6,000 $8,000

CARTIER, 29 J., min. repeater, by Le Coultre, c. 1930
platinum............................$70,000 $75,000 $85,000

CARTIER, 18 J., **triple date, moon ph**., tear-drop lugs,
marked European Watch & Clock Co., Ca.1945
s. steel $4,000 $4,500 $5,500
18K.. $6,000 $6,500 $7,500

CARTIER, 18 J., **Ca. 1985**
18K.. $1,500 $1,700 $2,000

CARTIER, 18J, day of week & date chapter, by Le Coultre
14k $1,000 $1,200 $1,500

CARTIER, Quartz, 296 diamonds on bezel & 18k Band
18k $18,000 $19,000 $22,000

CARTIER, 18 J., lady's, back wind, E.W.CO., c.1940s
18k $1,200 $1,800 $2,800

CARTIER, 18J., tonneau, Ca. 1920
platinum............................... $3,500 $4,000 $5,000

CARTIER, 18 J., lady's, E.W.Co., C.1949
14k(w) C&B $500 $600 $800

CERTINA, 17J., "NEWART", auto-wind, date, c.1965
14k $100 $125 $165

CENTRAL, 7J., cal.39, c.1937
gold filled $55 $75 $125

CHEVROLET, 6J., in form of car radiator, C. 1927
silver $500 $750 $1,100

CHOPARD, 18 J., 2 dial , 2 time zones, diam.bezel
18k C&B $1,500 $1,800 $2,400

CHOPARD, 18 J., skeletonized, diamonds on case & hands
18k $2,000 $2,200 $3,000

CHOPARD, 28J., triple date moon ph., cal.900, c.1980
18k $900 $1,000 $1,200

CHOPARD, 20 J., RF#2113, c.1978
18k $325 $350 $400

CHOPARD, 17J., RF#2134, c.1978
18k $285 $335 $375

CLEBAR, 17 jewels, chronog., 2 reg., cal.2248, c.1952
gold filled $125 $250 $325
base metal $100 $150 $275

CLEBAR, 17 jewels, chronog., 3 reg. c.1950s
gold filled $200 $275 $400
s. steel $250 $325 $450

CLEBAR, 17J., chronog.,triple date, moon ph.
gold filled $450 $600 $800
s. steel $450 $600 $800

CLEBAR, 17 jewels, center lugs, chronog., c. 1938
s. steel $300 $365 $525

CONCORD, 17J., aux. sec., ca. 1947
14k $100 $135 $200

CONCORD, 17 jewels, center sec.
14k $100 $135 $200

CONCORD, 17 jewels, chronog. 2 reg., c.1940s
s. steel $175 $225 $300

CONDAL,15J. **hunter style**, flip top, C.1928
silver $250 $365 $500

CONTINENTAL, 17J., 3 diamond dial
14k $120 $135 $225

CORNAVIN, 17J., day date, c. 1960
gold filled $60 $75 $125

CORNAVIN, 17J., date, auto, RF#1243, C.1963
gold filled $40 $50 $100
s. steel $40 $50 $100

CORONET, 17J., chronog.
s. steel $175 $200 $250

CORTEBERT, 17 jewels, "Chronometre", Ca. 1945
18K $200 $250 $350

CORTEBERT, 17 J., "Sport," triple date, moon phase
18k $400 $525 $700
gold filled................................ $100 $125 $275

CORTEBERT, 17 jewels, center sec.
s. steel $45 $55 $75

CORTEBERT, quartz, U.K. military, (CWC)
s. steel $50 $75 $100

CORTEBERT, (CWC), chronog., by Valjoux, c.1971
s. steel $185 $225 $295

CORUM, 17 J., twenty dollar gold piece= 22K
22k leather band (quartz) $1,800 $2,400 $3,200
22k, leather band (M. wind) $2,000 $2,600 $3,500
22k, gold band, (M. wind) . $3,000 $3,500 $5,000

CORUM, 24k gold ingot, 15 Grams, manual wind
24k $1,100 $1,300 $1,600

CORUM, 17 J., in form of Rolls-Royce car Grill
18k (reg.) $2,000 $2,300 $3,000
18k (large) $2,600 $3,000 $4,000

CORUM, 17 jewels, "Golden Bridge", in line train, recent
18k $2,200 $2,600 $3,500

CORUM, 17 jewels, rope style bezel
18k C&B................................ $800 $1,000 $1,300

CORUM, 17 jewels, peacock feather dial
18k $650 $800 $1,000

CORUM, 21 jewels, "Pave" diamond dial, c.1990
18k C&B $2,200 $2,500 $3,000

CORUM, 21 jewels, gold dial
18k $250 $300 $375

CORUM, 17J., "Graff", 2 time zones, Ca. 1965
18K $700 $800 $1,000

CRAWFORD, 17J., chronog.engraved bezel
base metal $125 $150 $200

CRAWFORD, 17J., hooded lugs, c. 1940
14k $100 $110 $165

CRAWFORD, 17J., pendant watch
base metal $45 $55 $85

CROTON, 17 jewels, day date
gold filled $40 $50 $75

CROTON, 17 jewels, diamond bezel & dial
14k (w) $175 $225 $300

CROTON, 17 jewels, chronog., c. 1948
s. steel $185 $235 $375

CROTON, 17 jewels, chronog., c. 1946
s. steel $200 $265 $350

CROTON, 17 jewels, cal.630, c.1943
gold filled $65 $80 $100

CROTON, 17 jewels, Ca.1937
14k $100 $135 $200

CROTON, 17 jewels, fancy lugs
14k $150 $195 $285

CROTON, 7J., drivers style, winds at 12 o'clock, c.1938
gold filled $100 $165 $250

CROTON, 17 jewels, swinging lugs, cal.f3x, c.1940
14k $100 $135 $185

CROWN, 7J., luminous dial
base metal $40 $50 $65

CROWN, 7J., luminous dial
gold filled $50 $65 $85

CYMA, 15J., aux. sec., ca. 1935
nickel $40 $50 $75

CYMA, 7J., enamel dial, wire lugs, (signal corp.USA), c.1928
silver $250 $295 $375

CYMA, 17 jewels, aux. sec.

18k	$175	$210	$275
14k	$100	$120	$150
gold filled	$35	$50	$75

CYMA, 15J., Ca. 1930
gold filled................................$65 $80 $125

CYMA, 15J., military style, cal.234, Ca.1945
s. steel $100 $135 $175

CYMA, 15J.,
base metal $30 $40 $75

🕐 Some grades are not included. Their values can be determined by comparing with **similar** age, size, metal content, style, models and grades listed.

🕐 A collector should expect to pay modestly higher prices at local shops

CYMA, 15J., engraved case
chromium..............................$30 $40 $75

CYMA, 15J., engraved case
chromium..............................$30 $40 $75

CYMA, 15J., 2-tone case
chromium..............................$30 $40 $75

CYMA, 15J., engraved case
chromium..............................$30 $40 $75

CYMA, 15J.,
chromium..............................$30 $40 $75

🕐 Pricing in this Guide are fair market price for **COMPLETE** watches which are reflected from the "**NAWCC**" National and regional shows.

CYMA, 15J., engraved case
chromium.................................$30 $40 $75

DAU, 15J., wire lugs, c.1915
14k $75 $90 $135

DAYNITE, 7J., **8 day movement by Hebdomas**, Ca. 1920
s. steel $250 $325 $450

DELBANA, 17J., fancy hooded lugs, c.1951
14k $100 $135 $185

DIDISHEIM, 15J., "Winton", enamel art deco bezel, c.1927
14k(w)...................................$235 $275 $350

P. DITISHEIM, 16 J., "Solvil,"fancy bezel, c. 1935
18k $300 $350 $425

P. DITISHEIM, 17 J., "Solvil," diamond dial, c. 1947
18K $285 $325 $400

P. DITISHEIM, 17 J., "Solvil," diamond dial, c. 1948
platinum..................................$600 $685 $800

P. DITISHEIM, 17 J., "Solvil," curved, diamond dial
platinum...........................$1,000 $1,200 $1,500

P. DITISHEIM, 17 jewels, diamond dial, curved
platinum...........................$1,000 $1,200 $1,500

P. DITISHEIM, 17 J., baguette diamonds, fancy bezel
platinum $1,200 $1,400 $1,700

P. DITISHEIM, 17 jewels, hinged lugs, enameled bezel
14k $700 $785 $900

DOME, 25 jewels, triple dates, moon ph., auto wind
18k $400 $485 $575

DORIC, 17J., fancy lugs, two tone case, c.1935
gold filled.................................$55 $70 $135

DOXA, 17 jewels, aux sec.
gold filled.................................$50 $65 $125

DOXA, 17 jewels, center sec., fancy lugs
14k $125 $165 $225

DOXA, 17 jewels, chronog., fluted lugs
14k $350 $400 $475

DOXA, 17J., chronog., date, 3 reg., by Valjoux
gold filled $300 $345 $435
14k $500 $565 $675

DOXA, 17 jewels, chronog., triple dates, **moon phase**
14k $900 $1,100 $1,400

DOXA, 17 jewels, chronog., 2 reg., c. 1942
gold filled...............................$300 $425 $600

DOXA, 17 jewels, chronog., cal. 1220, c. 1940
gold filled...............................$175 $200 $300
s. steel $175 $200 $300

DOXA, 17 jewels, center sec
s. steel $50 $65 $95

DOXA, 17 jewels, center sec., c. 1949
gold filled...............................$50 $65 $125

DOXA, 17J., "Grafic" date,
14k $100 $135 $225

DOXA, 17J., cal. 1361, c.1948
14k $100 $135 $225

DRIVA, 15 jewels, repeater, repeats on gong, **1/4 repeater**
activated by bolt above hand, c. 1930
s. steel $3,000 $3,400 $4,000

DRIVA, 15 jewels, 5 min. **repeater**, activated by bolt
14k $2,000 $2,400 $3,200

DRIVA, 17 jewels, double teardrop lugs, c.1945
14k $125 $150 $200

DUGENA, 17J., cal.985, c.1960
14k $100 $125 $185

DUNHILL, 17J., date, auto w., alarm by Le Coultre, c. 1965
s. steel $900 $1,100 $1,500

DUNHILL, 15J., by Bulwark W.Co., engraved bezel,c.1930
gold filled.................................$45 $55 $75

DUODIAL, 15 jewels, c. 1934
9k $400 $525 $700

EBEL, 21 jewels, chronog., self winding, perpetual cal.
18k $6,000 $7,000 $9,000

EBEL, 18 jewels, Ca.1959
18k $175 $200 $300

EBEL, 18 jewels, applied gold numbers, c. 1950
18k $250 $300 $375

EBEL, 18 jewels, Ca. 1958
14k $150 $175 $225

EBEL, 17 jewels, slide open to wind
leather $200 $250 $325

EBEL, 17 jewels, chronog., 2 reg., enamel dial
s. steel $200 $250 $325

EBEL, 17 jewels, chronog., c. 1955
14k $350 $400 $500
gold filled $200 $250 $325

EBEL, 17 jewels, chronog., "pulsation", c. 1943
s. steel $350 $400 $500

EBEL, 17 jewels, chronog., 3 reg., c. 1941
14k $500 $575 $700
s. steel $300 $365 $500

EBEL, 17J., "Sport", c.1949
gold filled $60 $80 $135

EBEL, 17J., cal.119, auto-wind, c.1950
s. steel $60 $80 $135

EBEL, 17J., cal.93, auto-wind, center sec., c.1950
18k $200 $250 $325

EBERHARD, 15 jewels, Protective Guard, Ca.1920
Silver $300 $375 $500

EBERHARD, 18 jewels, split sec. chronog., 3 reg.
18k $4,500 $5,000 $6,200

🕐 Pricing in this Guide are fair market price for **COMPLETE** watches which are reflected from the "**NAWCC**" National and regional shows.

EBERHARD, 17 J., tele-tachymeter, enamel dial, c. 1930
18k $1,600 $1,800 $2,200

EBERHARD, 17J., water proof, auto wind, triple date, moon phases
18k rose $900 $1,000 $1,600

EBERHARD, 17 jewels, "Extra Fort", chronog., 2 reg.,
note: Button at 4 slides to **lock** chronograph action.
18k $1,500 $1,800 $2,200

EKEGREN, 18 jewels, **jumping hr.**, c. 1920
platinum...............................$4,000 $4,500 $6,000
18k $2,000 $2,500 $3,500

EBERHARD, 17 J., chronog., center lugs, 1 button, enamel dial
s. steel $750 $850 $1,100

ELECTRA W. Co., 17J, chronog., 1 button, hinged back, enamel dial
silver $450 $585 $800

EBERHARD, 17 J., wire lugs, enamel dial, c.1928
watch fits inside of early waterproof case
silver $400 $465 $550

ELECTRA W. Co., 17J, chronog., 1 button, hinged back, wire lugs, enamel dial
silver $650 $785 $1,000

ELGIN, 17J., Fancy hidden lugs, Ca. 1950
gold filled.............................$100 $135 $225

LORD ELGIN, 21J., extended lugs, Ca.1955
14k $100 $150 $275

LORD ELGIN, 21J., extended lugs,
gold filled.............................$100 $135 $225

LORD ELGIN, 21J., hooded bezel, Ca. 1953
14K.............................$100 $165 $275

ELGIN, 19J., fancy bezel, c.1950s
gold filled.............................$100 $145 $225

ELGIN, 17J., hidden lugs, 7 diamonds & 8 baguettes
14K $300 $365 $550

LORD ELGIN, 21J., hinged lugs
gold filled $75 $110 $175

ELGIN, 15-17J., hooded lugs, gold jewel settings, Ca. 1925
gold filled $125 $165 $225
14k(w).............................$300 $375 $550

LORD ELGIN, 21J., Ca. 1948
14K $100 $165 $250

LORD ELGIN, 21J., 3 diamonds, cal.626, c.1950
14k(w).............................$150 $185 $250

ELGIN, 21J., cal.626, 3 diamonds, Ca.1950's
14k $150 $185 $250

ELGIN, 17J., stepped hooded lugs, c.1925
gold filled $75 $110 $185

ELGIN, 17J., stepped case, Ca. 1935
gold filled................................$75 $110 $175

ELGIN, 17J., side lugs, Ca. 1958
gold filled $100 $165 $275

ELGIN, 15J., cal. 554, Ca. 1950's
gold filled................................$75 $110 $175

ELGIN, 7-15J., stepped case, sold for $25.00 in 1936
gold filled $75 $110 $175

ELGIN, 15J., Sq. lugs, embossed dial, Ca.1929
gold filled................................$75 $110 $175

ELGIN, 21J., Lord Elgin, Ca. 1945
14k $100 $165 $275

ELGIN, 15J., Crown Guard, Ca.1929
gold filled................................$110 $175

ELGIN, 17J., **Dollar markers** on dial, Ca. 1955
gold filled $75 $110 $175

ELGIN, 19J., cal. 626, Ca. 1946
14k $100 $165 $275

ELGIN, engraved case, Ca. 1924
14k $100 $150 $275

ELGIN, 17J., embossed dial, sold for $35.00 in 1936,
gold filled................................. $75 $110 $175

LORD ELGIN, 21J., cal.625, c.1950
14k $100 $175 $275

LORD ELGIN, 21J., **11 diamonds**, Ca. 1946
14K.. $200 $265 $350

LORD ELGIN, 21J., cal. 713, GJS, c.1958
14k $125 $185 $285

LORD ELGIN, 21J.,
gold filled................................. $75 $110 $175

ELGIN, 17J., deluxe, Ca. 1955
gold filled $75 $110 $175

ELGIN, 15J., Legionnaire, Ca. 1929
gold filled................................. $75 $110 $185

LORD ELGIN, 21J., cal.559, c.1942
gold filled $75 $110 $175

Wrist Watches listed in this section are priced at the collectable
fair market Trade Show level as **complete** watches having an
original gold-filled case and stainless steel back, also with
original dial, leather watch band, and the entire original movement in good working order with no repairs needed.

LORD ELGIN, 21J., GJS, c. 1936
14k $125 $175 $285

LORD ELGIN, 21J., GJS, cal.626, c.1940
14k $125 $175 $285

ELGIN, 17J., **Adonis**, engraved, Ca. 1929
gold filled................................$75 $110 $175

ELGIN, 17J., "Dura Power" mainspring LOGO,
gold plate $35 $50 $95

ELGIN, 7J., **hinged case**, engraved case, c.1920s
gold filled................................$75 $110 $175

ELGIN,17J., embossed dial, sold for $25.00 in 1936
gold filled $75 $110 $175

ELGIN, 17 jewels, raised numbers
14k $125 $175 $275

LORD ELGIN, 21 jewels, curved, raised numbers
14k $125 $175 $275

ELGIN, 17 jewels, embossed dial
14k $125 $175 $275

LORD ELGIN, 21 jewels, curved
gold filled $75 $110 $175

ELGIN, 17 jewels, curved, "Streamlined"
gold filled $75 $110 $175

Some grades are not included. Their values can be determined by comparing with **similar** age, size, metal content, style, grades, or models such as **time only**, chronograph, repeater etc. listed.

ELGIN, 17 jewels, raised numbers
gold filled..................................$75 $110 $175

ELGIN, 15 jewels, curved, fancy bezel
gold filled..................................$75 $110 $175

LORD ELGIN, 21 jewels, curved
platinum................................$275 $350 $500

LORD ELGIN, 21 jewels, curved
14k..$125 $175 $275

ELGIN, 15 jewels, Ca. 1929
Sterling..................................$100 $145 $225

ELGIN, 17 jewels, curved
gold filled..................................$75 $110 $175

Wrist Watches listed in this section are priced at the collectable
fair market **Trade Show** level as **complete** watches having an
original gold-filled case and stainless steel back, also with
original dial, leather watch band, and the entire original movement in good working order with no repairs needed.

🕐 A collector should expect to pay modestly higher prices
at local shops

ELGIN, 15 jewels, drivers style, winds at 12 O'clock
gold filled..............................$150 $200 $325

ELGIN, 17 jewels, "Ristflo" winds at 12 O'clock
gold filled..............................$135 $185 $275

ELGIN, 17 jewels, crown guard
gold filled................................$75 $110 $175

ELGIN, 17 jewels, hidden lugs
gold filled................................$75 $110 $175

ELGIN, 17 jewels, embossed dial, thin model
gold filled................................$75 $110 $175

🕐 Pricing in this Guide are fair market price for **COMPLETE**
watches which are reflected from the "**NAWCC**" National and
regional shows.

ELGIN, 17 jewels, curved, thin model
gold filled................................$75 $110 $175

ELGIN, 17 jewels, stepped case
gold filled................................$65 $80 $125

ELGIN, 17J., center sec., cal.11553, c.1928
gold filled................................$75 $110 $175

ELGIN, 15 jewels, "William Osler" recess crown
gold filled................................$75 $125 $195

ELGIN, 7 jewels, center sec., recess crown
gold filled................................$75 $125 $195

ELGIN, 17J., engraved case, c.1928
gold filled................................$75 $110 $175

ELGIN, 17J., sold for $47.50 in 1936
gold filled................................$75 $110 $175

ELGIN,7-15J., engraved case, c. 1928
14K $125 $175 $275
gold filled................................$75 $110 $175

ELGIN, 15J., engraved **Mermaid** design case, c.1928
gold filled $200 $285 $395

ELGIN, 15J., engraved case, c. 1928
gold filled $75 $110 $175

ELGIN, 15J., curved engraved case, c. 1928
gold filled $75 $110 $175

ELGIN, 7J., Ca. 1925
nickel......................................$60 $75 $95

ELGIN, 17 jewels, "Crusade"
gold filled $75 $110 $175

ELGIN, 15 jewels, center lugs
gold filled................................$75 $110 $185

ELGIN, 7 jewels
gold filled $75 $110 $175

ELGIN, 7 jewels, fancy bezel
nickel......................................$65 $85 $135

ELGIN, 7 jewels, stepped bezel
s. steel $65 $85 $125

ELGIN, 7 jewels, fancy bezel
gold filled................................$75 $110 $175

ELGIN, 15J., wire lugs, stem at "12", c.1920s
silver $100 $185 $300

ELGIN, 15J.,combination lighter and Elgin Watch
Sterling....................................$200 $285 $400

ELGIN, 15J., cut-corner case, Art Deco numbers, Ca. 1925
gold filled $75 $110 $175

ELGIN, 15J., (note the **radial**), engraved case, c.1925
gold filled..................................$75 $110 $175

LORD ELGIN, 21J., stepped case, c.1930
gold filled..................................$75 $110 $175

LORD ELGIN, 21J., stepped case, c.1930
gold filled..................................$75 $110 $175

ELGIN, 7J., stepped case, c.1925
gold filled..................................$75 $110 $175

ELGIN, 17J., **BMW** logo, Ca.1955
gold filled..................................$75 $110 $175

LORD ELGIN, 21J., GJS, c.1937
14k $125 $175 $275

ELGIN, 17J., stepped case, c.1930
gold filled $75 $110 $175

ELGIN, 17J., curved, stepped case, c.1927
gold filled $75 $110 $175

ELGIN, 17 jewels, raised numbers
gold filled $75 $110 $175

ELGIN, 17 jewels, c. 1927
14k $125 $175 $275

🕐 A collector should expect to pay modestly higher prices at local shops

🕐 Some grades are not included. Their values can be determined by comparing with **similar** age, size, metal content, style, models and grades listed.

LORD ELGIN, 21 jewels, diamond dial
14k (w)..................................$150 $225 $325

ELGIN, 19 jewels, flared case
14k $200 $265 $375

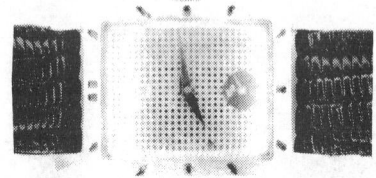

ELGIN, 19 jewels, c. 1947
14k $135 $185 $300
gold filled................................$85 $125 $185

ELGIN, 19 jewels, flared case, fancy lugs
14k $200 $250 $335

LORD ELGIN, 21 jewels, diamond dial
14k (w)..................................$150 $200 $350

ELGIN, 7-15J., **Star dial**, Military, manual wind
gold filled $75 $125 $185

LORD ELGIN, 21 jewels, aux. sec., fancy lugs
14k $150 $200 $350

ELGIN, 7-15J., cushion case, c.1930
chromium..................................$50 $65 $100

LORD ELGIN, 21J., cal.670, c.1948
gold filled...............................$100 $185 $225
14k $200 $265 $375

Wrist Watches listed in this section are priced at the collectable fair market **Trade Show** level as **complete** watches having an original gold-filled case and stainless steel back, also with original dial, leather watch band, and the entire original movement in good working order with no repairs needed.

ELGIN, 7-15J., **star** dial, solid lugs, Ca. 1925
s. steel $75 $125 $185

ELGIN, 15J., **pierced** shield, **star** dial, wire lugs, c.1918
silver $300 $365 $450

ELGIN, 15J., **pierced** shield, c.1918
silver $300 $365 $450

ELGIN, 15J., **canteen** style case, **star** dial, wire lugs, c.1919
nickel...............................★★$400 $475 $550

ELGIN, 16J., **canteen** style case, U.S.N.234C, c.1930s
s. steel ....★★★$400 $550 $750

ELGIN, 15J., U.S.GOV'T grade II, c.1960s
s. steel $75 $100 $165

ELGIN, 15J., military style, 24 hr. dial, c.1942
s. steel $85 $100 $165

ELGIN, 15J., military style, cal.539, c.1940
s. steel $75 $100 $165

ELGIN, 15 jewels, "Official Boy Scout" model
s. steel $125 $150 $250

🕐 A collector should expect to pay modestly higher prices at local shops

🕐 Some grades are not included. Their values can be determined by comparing with **similar** age, size, metal content, style, grades, or models such as **time only**, chronograph, repeater etc. listed.

ELGIN, 7 jewels, "Official Boy Scout" model
s. steel $60 $75 $135

ELGIN, 15 jewels, enamel dial, wire lugs, c. 1915
silver $100 $175 $275

ELGIN, 15 jewels, enamel dial, wire lugs, c. 1915
silver $175 $225 $300

ELGIN, 15 jewels, center lugs
gold filled.................................$100 $150 $225

ELGIN, 15 jewels, center lugs, c. 1922
silver $125 $185 $300

ELGIN, 15J., case by **Rolland Fischer,** c. 1928
silver $400 $500 $700

ELGIN, 7J., center sec., sold for $27.50 in 1936
gold filled $100 $125 $175

ELGIN, 21 jewels, "Black / Golden Knight"
gold filled $100 $150 $235
14k $200 $285 $450

ELGIN, 7 jewels, "Avigo ", Ca. 1929
base metal $85 $125 $185

Wrist Watches listed in this section are priced at the collectable
fair market Trade Show level as **complete** watches having an
original gold-filled case and stainless steel back, also with
original dial, leather watch band, and the entire original movement in good working order with no repairs needed.

ELGIN, 21J., center sec., wire lugs, cal. 680, c.1952
gold filled.................................$75 $110 $175

Elgin the **only** American Co. to **manufacture** a self-winding
movement. The 760 & 761 also used a Free Sprung Balance.
ELGIN, 27-30J., auto-wind, grade 760-761
gold filled $75 $110 $175

ELGIN, 17 jewels, **Alarm**, Ca. 1960
gold filled..............................$100 $135 $200

ELGIN, 19J.,cal.681 , c.1959
gold filled $75 $110 $175

ELGIN, 21J., water-proof, c.1952
s. steel $55 $70 $125

LORD ELGIN, 21J., **enamel bezel**, cal.688, c.1948
gold filled $100 $165 $250

LORD ELGIN, 21J., **shockmaster,** aux. sec., ca. 1955
14K..$125 $165 $275

ELGIN, 23 J., "B. W. Raymond," R.R. approved
14k $300 $385 $550
gold filled $150 $200 $300
s. steel $150 $200 $300

⊕ Some grades are not included. Their values can be
determined by comparing with **similar** age, size, metal
content, style, grades, or models such as **time only,**
chronograph, repeater etc. listed.

DIALS FOR MINT PRICES MUST BE ALL **ORIGINAL**.

LORD ELGIN, 21J., "Oxford", sold for $100.00 in1954
gold filled...............................$100 $125 $200

ELGIN, 17J., "Sinclair", sold for $39.75 in1954
gold filled $75 $100 $175

LORD ELGIN, 21J., "Thornton", sold for $71.50 in1954
gold filled...............................$100 $125 $200

ELGIN, 19J., "Gulfport", sold for $69.55 in1954
gold filled $75 $100 $175

ELGIN, 19J., "Garfield", sold for $69.50 in1954
gold filled...............................$75 $100 $175

ELGIN, 17J., "Edgewater", sold for $62.55 in1954
gold filled $75 $100 $175

ELGIN, 17J., "Milburn", sold for $59.50 in1954
gold filled...............................$75 $100 $175

ELGIN, 17J., "Windsor", auto-wind, sold for $95.00 in1954
gold filled $75 $110 $185

LORD ELGIN, 21J., "Wakefield", sold for $71.50 in1954
gold filled...............................$75 $100 $175

ELGIN, 17J., "Dante", auto-wind, sold for $71.50 in1954
s. steel $75 $110 $185

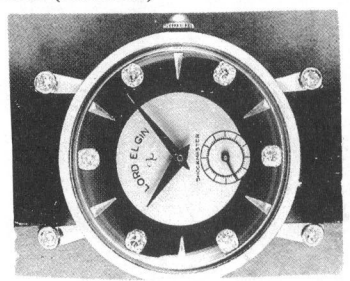

LORD ELGIN, 21J., diamond on lugs not factory, c. 1958
14k (w)....................................$200 $225 $275

LORD ELGIN, 21 jewels, mystery dial, c. 1957
14k (w)....................................$150 $200 $300

LORD ELGIN, 21J., direct reading, Chevron style, Ca.1957
gold filled...............................$225 $300 $400

ELGIN, 17 J., in form of golf ball, rotating hr. & min.
gold filled...............................$225 $300 $400

LORD ELGIN, 21 jewels, applied numbers, c. 1946
14k $125 $175 $275

LORD ELGIN, 21 jewels, curved, applied numbers
14k $150 $195 $285

LORD ELGIN, 21 jewels, diamond dial, faceted crystal
14k $150 $195 $285

ELGIN, 17 jewels, hinged back
14k (w) $125 $175 $275

ELGIN, 17 jewels, enamel bezel, Ca. 1930
14k (w) $200 $285 $400

ELGIN, 15 jewels, Art Deco bezel, c. 1935
gold filled $100 $125 $185

🕐 A collector should expect to pay modestly higher prices
at local shops

🕐 Some grades are not included. Their values can be
determined by comparing with **similar** age, size, metal
content, style, grades, or models such as **time only**,
chronograph, repeater etc. listed.

ELGIN, 15 jewels, 2 tone case, c. 1930
gold filled 2 tone case............ $100 $135 $195

ELGIN, 15 jewels, enamel bezel, c. 1920
14k (w)..................................... $300 $425 $600

ELGIN, 17 jewels, raised numbers
gold filled................................. $75 $100 $175

ELGIN, 15-21J., enamel bezel, 2 tone, in 1929 sold for
$24.00
14k $350 $425 $500
 gold filled.............................. $150 $185 $250

ELGIN, 7 jewels, engraved bezel
s. steel $50 $65 $125

ELGIN, 17 jewels, aux. sec., curved
gold filled $75 $110 $175

ELGIN, 17 jewels, curved
gold filled $75 $110 $175

ELGIN, 17 jewels, curved
gold filled $75 $110 $175

ELGIN, 21 jewels, blue enamel bezel, c. 1920
14k(yellow gold) $1,200 $1,500 $2,200

ELGIN, 15J., Luminous hands, sold for $27.50 in 1929
gold filled (Y or W)................ $75 $110 $175

ELGIN, 15 jewels, enamel bezel
14k $1,000 $1,300 $2,000

LORD ELGIN, 21J, grade 670, large lugs, anniversary of 50 million watches made serial # 50,000,000 to 50,000,999, gold plated movement, Ca. 1951
18k ....★★★$1,000 $1,300 $2,000

LORD ELGIN, 21J., Jump Hr. & Wandering Min., curved
gold filled................................$350 $475 $700

ELGIN, 17 jewels, double dial
gold filled................................$350 $450 $600

LORD ELGIN, 21 jewels, hooded lugs, c. 1952
14k $200 $250 $375

LORD ELGIN, 21 jewels, curved, c. 1957
14k $200 $265 $350

LORD ELGIN, 21 jewels, hooded lugs, c. 1950s
14k $150 $185 $265

ELGIN, 15 jewels, waterproof
s. steel $40 $55 $95

ELGIN, 15 jewels, center sec.
gold filled $50 $75 $125

ELGIN, 7 jewels, aux. sec.
gold filled $50 $75 $125

LORD ELGIN, 21 jewels, stepped case
18k $250 $295 $395

LORD ELGIN, 21 jewels, stepped case, curved
14k $125 $175 $275

ELGIN, 17 jewels, stepped case
14k $125 $175 $275

LORD ELGIN, 21 jewels, curved
gold filled.................................$75 $110 $175

ELGIN, 17 jewels, curved, fancy bezel
gold filled.................................$75 $110 $175

ELGIN, 17 jewels, curved, stepped case
gold filled.................................$75 $110 $175

ELGIN, 17 jewels, curved, stepped case
gold filled.................................$75 $110 $175

ELGIN, 17 jewels, curved
gold filled $75 $110 $175

ELGIN, 19 jewels, stepped case
gold filled $75 $110 $175

ELGIN, 15 jewels
gold filled $75 $110 $175

ELGIN, 7 jewels, fancy bezel
base metal $45 $55 $85

ELGIN, 7 jewels, fancy bezel
gold filled $75 $110 $175

LORD ELGIN, 21 jewels, curved, c. 1938
14k $150 $185 $275

ELGIN, 15 jewels, fancy bezel
gold filled...................................$75 $100 $175

ELGIN, 21 jewels, curved
gold filled...................................$75 $110 $175

LORD ELGIN, 21 jewels, raised numbers
14k $125 $175 $275

LORD ELGIN, 21 jewels, curved
14k $125 $175 $275

LORD ELGIN, 21 jewels, curved
14k $150 $185 $285

LORD ELGIN, 21 jewels, aux. sec.
gold filled...................................$75 $110 $175

LORD ELGIN, 21 jewels, curved
14k $150 $185 $275

ELGIN, 17 jewels, curved
gold filled...................................$75 $110 $175

ELGIN, 17 Jewels, raised numbers
14k...$150 $185 $275

LORD ELGIN, 15 jewels, **electric**, 6 adj., Ca. 1962, (sold
for $89.50, July of 1962), grade 725, in <u>good running order</u>
gold filled.........................★★$200 $265 $350

**Elgin pioneering effort in electric watches
started in 1955.**

LORD ELGIN, 15 jewels, **electric**, c. 1962
(back–set)
s. steel .... ★★$200 $265 $350

LORD ELGIN, 15 jewels, **electric**, c.1962
(grade 725, 6 adj.)
gold filled........................ ★★$200 $265 $350

ELGIN, 17 Jewels, Lady Elgin, flared case, cal. 650, c.1950
14k $100 $125 $175

ELGIN, 15 Jewels, art deco, c.1925
gold filled...................................$40 $50 $80

ELGIN, 15 Jewels, art deco, c.1928
14k $90 $125 $165

ELGIN, 17 Jewels, art deco, c.1928
18k(w)....................................$125 $150 $225

ELGIN, 15J., art deco, Tiger & Lady, Ca. 1929
14K(W) $100 $125 $185

ELGIN, 15 jewels, art deco, Ca. 1928
gold filled................................$50 $75 $125

ELGIN, 15 jewels, art deco, Ca. 1928
gold filled................................$25 $30 $50

ELGIN, 15 jewels, art deco, Ca. 1928
gold filled................................$25 $30 $50

ELGIN, 15 jewels, sports model, Ca. 1928
14k...$75 $85 $135

ELGIN, 17J., 20 diamonds, art deco, Ca. 1928
18k...$225 $275 $365

ELGIN, 15 jewels, 2 diamonds, art deco, Ca. 1928
gold filled.................................$75 $95 $150

Model 3, 3-0 size, three-quarter plate, open face, pendant set, first serial number 18,179,001, Grade 414, March, 1915.

Model 1, 5-0 size, three-quarter plate, hunting, pendant set, first serial number 14,699,001, Grade 380, Feb., 1910.

Model 2, 5-0 size, three-quarter plate, open face, pendant set, first serial number 17,890,001, Grade 399, Feb., 1914.

Model 2, 8-0 size, Grade 532, 539, sweep second.

Model 7, 8-0 size, Grades 554, 555,

Model 20, 8-0 size, Grades 681, 682.

Model 1, 10-0 size, three-quarter plate, open face

Model 2, 15-0 size, Grades 623, 624, 626.

15-0 Size, movement, Grades 670, 672, 673.

15-0 size, movement. Grade 674.

15-0 size, movement, Grades 557, 558, 559.

Model 2, 21-0 size, Grade 541, 533, 535.

Model 3, 21-0 size, Grade 547, sweep second.

Model 4, 21-0 size, Grades 617, 617L, 619, 619L.

Model 9, 21-0 size, Grades 650, 651.

Model 9, 21-0 size, Grades 655, 656.

GRADE 725, 15 jewels,"electric" model movement

"ELECTRIC", case showing back—set

Grade 607, self wind. **Grade 630,** sweep second. **Grade 641, 642** **Grade 643,** self wind.

Grades 644, 645, self wind. **Grade 647,** sweep second. **Grade 661** **Grade 666,** sweep second.

Grade 668, sweep second. **Grade 685** **Grade 687** **Grade 700**

GRADE 710 & 719
719 = DIRECT READ TRAIN SIDE **719 = DIAL SIDE OF MOVEMENT** **Grade 716**

1925 AD

Elgin strap watches for men, in gold and gold-filled cases of yellow, white or green; also silver and nickel. Prices ranging from $20 to $75.

ELOGA, triple calendar,
gold filled bezel $75 $110 $175

EMERSON, 17J., hooded lugs,
gold filled...................................$60 $80 $135

ENICAR, 17 jewels, auto- wind, center sec.
gold filled...................................$60 $80 $135
18k $175 $250 $350

ENICAR, 17J., chronograph, 2 reg. Ca. 1955
s. steel $175 $225 $300

ENICAR, 17 jewels, center sec.
s. steel.......................................$50 $70 $100

ENICAR, 17 jewels, triple date, moon phase
gold filled................................$200 $250 $335

ENICAR, 15 jewels, egg shaped with compass, c. 1918
silver..$275 $325 $450

ENICAR, 17J., auto-w., date, 24 hour dial, C.1970
s. steel.....................................$100 $135 $200

ESKA, 17J.,chronog., triple date, moon phase
14k...$1,200 $1,400 $1,700

ESKA, 17 jewels, chronog., 2 reg., C. 1950s
s. steel $200 $250 $350

ESKA, 17 jewels, chronog., 2 reg., c. 1940
s. steel $900 $1,000 $1,200

ESKA, 17 jewels, multi-colored enamel dial
18k $1,800 $2,100 $2,600

ETERNA, quartz, date, by ETA, cal#954, C.1975
s. steel $45 $65 $95

Ⓛ Pricing in this Guide are fair market price for COM-
PLETE watches which are reflected from the "NAWCC" National and regional shows.

ETERNA, "Sonic", double tuning fork (for position errors), Ca. 1937
s. steel $100 $135 $200

ETERNA, 17 jewels, chronog., triple date, 3 reg.
s.steel $400 $550 $750
18k $700 $800 $1,000

ETERNA, 21 jewels, date, auto-w., cal. # 14390, c.1960
" Eternamatic" (5 ball-bearing rotor)
18k $150 $225 $325

ETERNA, 19 jewels, c.1944
14k $100 $150 $225

ETERNA, 16 jewels, aux. sec., c.1945
gold filled..................................$60 $75 $110

ETERNA, 19 jewels, c.1938
gold filled..................................$60 $75 $125

ETERNA, 17 jewels, gold jewel settings, c.1935
14k $100 $135 $195

EVANS, 17 jewels, rhinestones on bezel & dial, c. 1948
gold plate $55 $65 $95

EVANS, 17 jewels, chronog., 2 reg., c. 1940
18k $300 $350 $450

EXACTUS, 17 J., chronog.,triple-date, moon ph.
s. steel....................................$450 $500 $650

EXCELSIOR, 17 jewels, chronog., 2 reg.
14k...$300 $350 $450
gold filled..............................$150 $185 $250

EXCELSIOR, 17 jewels, chronog.
gold filled..............................$150 $185 $250
s. steel....................................$150 $185 $250

EXCELSIOR PARK, 17 jewels, chronog.
s. steel....................................$185 $225 $300

FAIRFAX, 6J, engraved case, c.1929
base metal $40 $50 $75

FAIRFAX, 6J, engraved case, c.1929
base metal $40 $50 $75

FAIRFAX, 6J, butler finish case, c.1929
base metal $40 $50 $75

FAITH, 17J, **flip top case** HC style, by Hyde Park, c.1950
gold filled................................$200 $235 $300

FAVRE LEUBA,17J., triple date, cal.Valj.89, c.1948
s. steel $125 $140 $175

🕀 A collector should expect to pay modestly higher prices
at local shops

🕀 Some grades are not included. Their values can be determined by comparing with **similar** age, size, metal content,
style, grades, or models such as **time only**, chronograph,
repeater etc. listed.

FAVRE LEUBA,17J., "Bivouac", altimeter with aneroid cap-
sule transmitting variations of atmospheric pressure to the baro-
metric mechanism, revolving bezel, Ca. 1968.
s. steel....................................$275 $335 $450

FAVRE LEUBA,17J., "Bathy 50", depth reading to about 165
feet, waterproof to 470 feet, Ca. 1968.
s. steel....................................$275 $335 $450

FERRARI, **quartz**, chronog., c.1988
base metal................................$100 $125 $200

FELCA, 17 jewels, auto wind
gold filled................................$60 $75 $125
14k...$100 $145 $225
18k...$175 $225 $335

FONTAINEMELON, S. A., 17 J., gold train, digital
14k $1,100 $1,200 $1,500

FRAMONT, 17J, timer, date, cal. 290, c.1970
s. steel $75 $85 $125

FREY, 25J., rotating outside chapter, c.1970
s. steel $50 $60 $85

FREY,15J., Early auto- wind, with a pendulum type weight,
Ca.1930's
gold filled.........................★★$400 $475 $600

FREY,15J., engraved case, c.1933
base metal................................$40 $50 $70

FREY,15J., engraved stepped case, c.1933
base metal................................$40 $50 $70

FREY,15J., engraved case, c.1933
base metal................................$40 $50 $70

FRIEDLI, 17 jewels, auto wind, center sec.
gold filled.................................$60 $75 $125
18k..$175 $200 $250

FRODSHAM, 17J., Ca. 1935
18k(w) $350 $450 $600

GALLET, 15 jewels, wire lugs, Ca. 1925
silver $75 $100 $150

GALLET, 15 jewels, waterproof, auto wind
s. steel $60 $75 $135

GALLET, 17 jewels, chronog., single button, c. 1950
s. steel $200 $300 $500

GALLET, 17J., chronog., by Racine, US air force, c. 1978
s. steel $175 $250 $400

🕐 Pricing in this Guide are fair market price for **COM-PLETE** watches which are reflected from the **"NAWCC"** National and regional shows.

GALLET, 17 jewels, chronog., 3 reg., c. 1945
s. steel....................................$250 $300 $425

GALLET, 17 jewels, chronog., 3 reg., c. 1942
gold filled...............................$250 $300 $425

GALLET, 17J., chronog., 2 reg.,single button, C.1925,
silver"small size" $600 $750 $950

GALLET, 17J., chronog., 3 reg., triple date, moon ph.
18k......................................$1,300 $1,500 $2,000

GALLET, 17J., chronog., 3 reg., triple **date**
14k $750 $850 $1,100
s. steel $400 $500 $750

GALLET, 17 jewels, chronog., 3 reg., c. 1955
s. steel $275 $335 $500

GALLET, 17 jewels, 2 reg., Ca. 1958
s. steel $175 $200 $300

GALLET, 17 jewels, chronog., 2 reg.
14k $300 $350 $525
s. steel $175 $200 $275

GALLET, 17 jewels, chronog., mid size, c. 1940
s. steel $250 $300 $400

GALLET, 17-23J., chronog., "Flying Officer", Ca. 1958
s. steel $350 $465 $675

GALLET, 17 jewels, chronog., waterproof
s. steel $275 $350 $500

GALLET, 17 jewels, chronog., 2 reg.
s. steel $200 $225 $300

🕐 Some grades are not included. Their values can be determined by comparing with **similar** age, size, metal content, style, grades, or models such as **time only**, chronograph, repeater etc. listed.

GALLET, 17 jewels, chronog., 2 reg.
s.steel $325 $400 $575

GALLET, 17 jewels, **regulator** dial, chronog.
s. steel....................................$300 $350 $450

GALLET, 17 jewels, chronog., 2 reg.
gold filled..............................$200 $225 $275

P. GARNIER, 17 jewels, minu-stop, c. 1965
s. steel....................................$75 $110 $175

GALLET, 17 jewels, chronog., 2 reg.
s. steel $175 $200 $250

P. GARNIER, 17 jewels, world time, c. 1968
s. steel.................................. $150 $185 $250

GALLET, 17 jewels, chronog., 2 reg., c. 1939
s. steel $200 $250 $375

GARLAND, 17J., center sec., water-proof.
s. steel....................................$45 $55 $85

Wrist Watches listed in this section are priced at the collectable fair market Trade Show level as **complete** watches having an original gold-filled case and stainless steel back, also with original dial, leather watch band, and the entire original movement in good working order with no repairs needed.

Pricing in this Guide are fair market price for **COMPLETE** watches which are reflected from the "**NAWCC**" National and regional shows.

GENEVE, 15 jewels, doctors watch, c. 1939
s. steel $350 $450 $600

GENEVE, 15 jewels, doctors watch, c. 1937
s. steel $350 $450 $600

GENEVE, 17 jewels, curly lugs, c.1950
14k $150 $200 $300

GERMINAL, 17 J., center sec.
s. steel $60 $70 $95
14k $100 $125 $225

GERMINAL, 15 J., **early auto wind, case action**, c. 1933
s. steel ....★ ★ ★ $550 $650 $750

GIRARD-PERREGAUX, Tourbillon with golden bridge,
a hand is attached to the one minute tourbillon for seconds,
wind indicator at 12, manual wind.(Limited edition)
18K.....................................$12,000 $16,000 $22,000

GIRARD-PERREGAUX, 17J., auto wind, C.1951
s. steel $75 $100 $175

GIRARD-PERREGAUX, 17J., alarm, c.1960
gold filled................................$125 $150 $250

GIRARD-PERREGAUX, 39J., center sec. c.1955
14k...$150 $200 $300

🕐 Some grades are not included. Their values can be
determined by comparing with **similar** age, size, metal
content, style, grades, or models such as time only,
chronograph, repeater etc. listed.

GIRARD-PERREGAUX, 17J., auto w., center sec., c.1948
18k ....$250 $275   `$325

GIRARD-PERREGAUX, 17J., aux. sec., c.1958
gold filled.............................$100 $125 $165

GIRARD-PERREGAUX, 17J., Gyromatic, center sec., c.1960
s. steel $75 $95 $135

GIRARD-PERREGAUX, 17J., "Sea Hawk", aux. sec., c.1950
s. steel.....................................$100 $125 $175

GIRARD-PERREGAUX, 17J., Gyromatic, cal.47ae, c.1953
14k $150 $185 $235

GIRARD-PERREGAUX, 17J., Gyromatic, date, c.1960
gold filled.............................$100 $125 $165

GIRARD-PERREGAUX, 17J., Sea Hawk., c.1960
gold filled.............................$100 $125 $165

GIRARD-PERREGAUX, 39J., Gyromatic, "HF", date, c.1960
18k...$225 $275 $350

⊕ Some grades are not included. Their values can be
determined by comparing with **similar** age, size, metal
content, style, grades, or models such as **time only**,
chronograph, repeater etc. listed.

GIRARD-PERREGAUX, 39J., chronometer "HF", c.1970
s. steel $100 $125 $165

GIRARD-PERREGAUX, 17 jewels, triple date, aux. sec.
s.steel....................................$150 $175 $235

GIRARD-PERREGAUX,17J.,"Gyromatic",date
gold filled..............................$100 $125 $165

GIRARD-PERREGAUX, 17J., chronog., 2 reg., waterproof
s. steel....................................$275 $325 $425

GIRARD-PERREGAUX, 39J.,"Gyromatic",date, Ca. 1960
18k $200 $250 $350

GIRARD-PERREGAUX, 17J., by Valjoux cal.72, c.1955
s. steel....................................$400 $475 $650

GIRARD-PERREGAUX, 17J., triple date, autow.
s. steel $150 $175 $250

GIRARD-PERREGAUX, 17J., chronog cal.285, c.1940
gold filled...............................$200 $265 $375

GIRARD-PERREGAUX, 17J., pulsations, c.1948
14k $400 $450 $550

GIRARD-PERREGAUX, 17 J., chronog., 3 reg., c. 1952
s. steel $400 $450 $600

GIRARD-PERREGAUX, 17J, chronog., triple date, **moon phase**
18k $1,400 $1,700 $2,300

GIRARD-PERREGAUX, 39 J., Ca. 1955
14k $125 $150 $225
18k $150 $225 $325

GIRARD-PERREGAUX, 17J., hooded lugs, Ca.1960
14k $150 $175 $250

GIRARD-PERREGAUX, 17J., "gyromatic", cnter sec.
14k $150 $175 $250

GIRARD-PERREGAUX, 17J., RF#2459, c.1970
14k $150 $165 $225

GIRARD-PERREGAUX, 17J., cal.a6 3606, GJS, c.1955
14k $150 $175 $250

GIRARD-PERREGAUX, 17J., recess crown, GJS, c.1954
14k $175 $225 $300

GIRARD-PERREGAUX, 17J., cal.86, GJS, Ca.1948
14k $125 $175 $275

GIRARD-PERREGAUX, 17J., recess crown, GJS, c.1947
gold filled..................................$75 $100 $175

GIRARD-PERREGAUX, 17J., cal.86ae, GJS, c.1940
s. steel $60 $90 $150

GIRARD-PERREGAUX, 17J., "1791", GJS, c.1942
s. steel.....................................$75 $100 $175

GIRARD-PERREGAUX, 17J., two tone case, GJS, Ca.1942
14k $200 $230 $300

GIRARD-PERREGAUX, 17J., cal.91ae220, GJS, c.1948
gold filled..................................$75 $100 $175

GIRARD-PERREGAUX, 17J., GJS, c.1953
14k $125 $175 $275

GIRARD-PERREGAUX, 17J., GJS, c.1936
gold filled..................................$75 $100 $175

GIRARD-PERREGAUX, 17J., cal. 86ae, GJS, c.1942
s. steel $75 $100 $150

GIRARD-PERREGAUX, 17J., cal.86ae, GJS, c.1942
14k...$125 $175 $275

Wrist Watches listed in this section are priced at the collectable
fair market **Trade Show** level as **complete** watches having an
original gold-filled case and stainless steel back, also with
original dial, leather watch band, and the entire original movement in good working order with no repairs needed.

🕐 A collector should expect to pay modestly higher prices
at local shops

GIRARD-PERREGAUX, 39 jewels, center sec.
14k $125 $175 $275

GIRARD-PERREGAUX, 17 jewels, aux. sec.
gold filled...................................$75 $110 $175

GIRARD-PERREGAUX, 17 jewels,Ca. 1948
14k $125 $175 $275

GIRARD-PERREGAUX, 17 J., C. 1948
14k $125 $175 $275

GIRARD-PERREGAUX, 17 J., date, stepped case,
18k $500 $575 $700
14k $300 $375 $500

GLASHUTTE, 17J., 2 reg., fluted bezel, c.1942
s. steel...................................$900 $1,100 $1,400

GLASHUTTE, 17J., signed Uhrenfabrik Glashutte, c.1935
18k...$500 $575 $700

GLASHUTTE, 15J., signed "GUB", Ca.1950's
gold filled...............................$200 $265 $350

GLYCINE, 17J., **Airman** ,auto-wind, 24hr., date, c.1970
s. steel...................................$200 $250 $350

GLYCINE, 17J., 15 diamond dial, cal.4645, c.1945
14k...$450 $575 $700

GLYCINE the first modular self-winding works patented in 1931 by E. Meylan of La Chaux-de-Fonds.

GLYCINE, 17 J., **Airman**, 24 hr. dial, autow, date, C.1960s
s. steel $175 $275 $450

GLYCINE, 17 jewels, **curved**, c. 1938
18k $200 $265 $350

GLYCINE, 17 jewels, aux. sec., c. 1934
14k (w)....................................$135 $175 $250

GLYCINE, 18 jewels, faceted crystal & bezel
gold filled..............................$75 $100 $150

GOERING W. Co., jump hr., wandering sec.,C.1935
14k $1,100 $1,300 $1,700

GOERING W. Co., **jump hr.**, wandering sec.,C.1935
chrome....................................$200 $250 $350

GOERING W. Co., 15J., center sec., C.1935
base metal................................$30 $45 $65

GOERING W. Co., 15J., engraved case, C.1935
gold filled................................$40 $55 $85

GOERING W. Co., 15J., engraved case, C.1935
gold filled................................$40 $55 $85

GOERING W. Co., 15J., engraved case, C.1935
gold filled................................$40 $55 $85

DIALS FOR MINT PRICES MUST BE ALL **ORIGINAL**.

GOERING W. Co., 15J., rectangular, C.1935
gold filled.................................$60 $80 $125

GOERING W. Co., 15J., **ladies** engraved case, C.1935
gold filled.................................$40 $55 $85

GOLAY, 18 jewels, aux. sec., c. 1928
18k & platinum...................$1,200 $1,400 $1,800

GOLAY, 32 jewels, **min.** repeater, adj. to 5 positions
(pocket watch movement)
18k $12,000 $14,000 $18,000

GRANA, 16J., **Masonic dial**, original dial, GJS, ca. 1948
14k $175 $200 $275

GRUEN, 17J., curved, precision, cal. 330, Ca. 1937
platinum..........................★$1,500 $1,800 $2,400

GRUEN, 15J., enamel dial, wire lugs, c. 1915
silver $150 $200 $300

GRUEN, 17J., **driver's** watch, winds at **12**, cal.400, c.1938
gold filled $200 $285 $400

GRUEN,17J., curved, drivers, cal.401, RF#352, c.1932
gold filled $450 $585 $850

GRUEN, 17J., extremely curved, drivers, c. 1932 , and
 side view of watch
gold filled $650 $800 $1,000

GRUEN, 17 J., extremely curved, driver's watch
gold filled................................$650 $800 $1,000

GRUEN, 17J., driver's watch , flexible long lugs , RF # 641
gold filled................................$700 $900 $1,200

GRUEN, 17 jewels, curvex, c. 1949
gold filled................................$150 $250 $375

GRUEN, 17 jewels, curvex, 35mm long
gold filled................................$200 $275 $400

GRUEN, 17J, curvex Majesty, 52mm long, C.1937
gold filled..........................$1,200 $1,400 $1,800
14k ....★ ★ ★$2,500 $3,000 $4,000

GRUEN, 17J.,curvex, precision, C. 1936
14k $400 $450 $550

GRUEN, 17 jewels, curvex, c. 1937
gold filled................................$175 $250 $350

GRUEN, 17 jewels, curvex, RF# 228, c. 1935
gold filled $175 $250 $350

GRUEN, 17 jewels, curvex, 50mm long, c. 1937
gold filled $500 $675 $850

GRUEN, 17 jewels, curvex, c. 1937
s. steel $300 $350 $500

GRUEN, 15-17 jewels, curvex, 46mm lug to lug, Ca 1940s.
gold filled $250 $300 $450

GRUEN, 17J., note bezel, curvex, ca.1936
gold filled $200 $285 $400

GRUEN, 17 jewels, curvex, RF# 334, Ca. 1939
gold filled $175 $200 $300

🕐 First CURVEX was introduced on October 26, 1935, it was
series # 311, the 2nd series was #330 in 1939, and in 1940 series
440 was issued.

GRUEN, 17 jewels, Precision, **2 Tone** case, Ca. 1933
18K **2 tone**..............................$500 $700 $900

GRUEN, 17J., Precision, "Antique" sold for $100 in 1930
14K...$275 $350 $450

GRUEN, 17J., Precision, "Antique" & inlaid black enamel
18K(W) $275 $350 $450

GRUEN, 15J., curvex, RF#226, c. 1936
gold filled.............................. $150 $185 $275

GRUEN, 15J., curvex, stepped case, RF#278, c. 1936
gold filled.............................. $150 $225 $335

GRUEN, 15J., curvex, RF#255, cal.500, c. 1936
gold filled.............................. $150 $185 $250

GRUEN, 17J., curvex, RF#266, cal.165, c. 1935
gold filled $150 $200 $275

GRUEN, 17J., curvex, RF#280, cal.330, c. 1936
gold filled $150 $200 $275

GRUEN, 17J., curvex, stepped case, RF#280, c. 1937
14k $300 $350 $500
gold filled $150 $200 $275

GRUEN, 17J., curvex, precision, RF#292, cal.330, c. 1937
gold filled $225 $300 $400

GRUEN, 15J., curvex, RF#202, cal.500, c. 1936
gold filled $225 $300 $400

GRUEN, 17J., curvex, RF#308, cal.330, c. 1936
14k $350 $400 $500
gold filled $200 $235 $325

"Curved to fit the wrist"

GRUEN, 17J., curved, aux. sec., curved crystal, precision,
sold for $135.00 in 1931
14k (w) $125 $165 $250

GRUEN, 17J., curvex, cal#440, hooded lugs, ca.1943
14k $175 $200 $300

GRUEN, 17 jewels, curvex, fancy lugs
14k $150 $200 $300

GRUEN, 17 jewels, curvex, long lugs
14k $200 $225 $300

GRUEN, 15-17 jewels, **tu-tone case**, doctors watch, c. 1937
14k W & Y $3,000 $3,500 $4,500

GRUEN, 15-17 jewels, **jumping hr.**, double dial
s. steel $4,000 $5,000 $6,500
14k $5,000 $6,000 $8,000

GRUEN, 15-17 jewels, doctors watch
gold filled $900 $1,100 $1,600

GRUEN, 15-17 jewels, curved, c.1930s
gold filled $250 $275 $350

GRUEN, 15-17 jewels, doctors watch, curved, c. 1938
gold filled $900 $1,100 $1,600

GRUEN, 15-17 jewels, doctors watch
gold filled $900 $1,100 $1,500

GRUEN, 15-17 jewels, doctors watch, c. 1932
gold filled $900 $1,100 $1,600

GRUEN, 15-17 jewels, doctors watch, sold for $75 in 1931
gold filled
14K(W).............................$2,200 $2,500 $3,000

GRUEN, 15-17 jewels, doctors watch, sold for $67.00 in 1929
gold filled.............................$900 $1,100 $1,600

GRUEN, 15-17 jewels, doctors watch, sold for $60 in 1929
gold filled.............................$900 $1,100 $1,600

GRUEN, 15-17 jewels, doctors watch, sold for $67.50 in 1929
gold filled.............................$900 $1,100 $1,600

GRUEN, 15-17 jewels, doctors watch, sold for $75.00 in 1931
gold filled.............................$900 $1,100 $1,600
14K.......................................$2,200 $2,500 $3,000

GRUEN, 15-17 jewels, doctors watch, sold for $55.00 in 1931
base metal $800 $1,000 $1,400

GRUEN, 15-17J., doctors watch, sold for $115.00 in 1931
2 TONE 14K case...............$2,800 $3,100 $3,800
14K(W or Y) $2,200 $2,500 $3,000

GRUEN, 15-17J., doctors watch, sold for $115.00 in 1931
2 TONE 14K case...............$3,000 $3,500 $4,500
14K(W or Y) $2,200 $2,500 $3,000

GRUEN, 15-17 jewels, doctors watch, sold for $85.00 in 1931
14K(W)...............................$2,500 $3,000 $3,500

GRUEN, 15-17 jewels, doctors watch, sold for $85.00 in 1931
14K(W)...............................$2,500 $3,000 $3,500

Gruen Doctors watch movement by Aegler (Swiss)

GRUEN, 15 jewels, in form of car radiator, curved
nickel......................................$700 $900 $1,200

GRUEN, 17J., RF# 615, curvex, diamond dial, faceted crystal
14k $250 $300 $400

GRUEN, 17J., **diamond** dial & bezel, RF # 568, Ca. 1946
14k $250 $300 $400

GRUEN, 17 jewels, veri-thin model, fancy lugs
14k $200 $225 $300

GRUEN, 17J., curvex, 3 diam., RF#568, cal.440, c. 1945
14k(w).....................................$200 $265 $350

GRUEN, 17 jewels, auto wind, cal. 840, c. 1952
18k $250 $300 $400

GRUEN, 17J., "Antique", sold for $65 in 1930
gold filled...............................$150 $200 $300

GRUEN, 17 jewels, curvex, fancy lugs
gold filled $75 $110 $175

GRUEN, 17J., "Antique" & inlaid enamel, large second hand
18K(w)....................................$225 $300 $450

GRUEN, 21J, RF#798, curvex, diamond dial, fancy lugs
14k (w) $200 $250 $350

* Signed on dial **Gruen 21** = 21Jewels & **American** Made.

GRUEN, **21** jewels, diamond dial, fancy center lugs, Ca. 1944
14k $225 $285 $400

GRUEN, **21** jewels, fancy lugs, Ca. 1944
14k $250 $275 $350

GRUEN, 17 jewels, curvex, fancy lugs, c. 1943
gold filled..................................$75 $100 $150
14k $150 $185 $250

GRUEN, 17 jewels, curvex, diamond dial, Ca. 1947
14k $200 $235 $300

GRUEN, **21J.**, **flared**, diamond dial, Ca. 1945
14k(w)....................................$300 $335 $400

GRUEN, **21** jewels, Precision, RF# 558, cal.335, Ca.1944
  Flexible long lugs
gold filled $75 $100 $175

GRUEN, 17 jewels, curvex, diamond dial, c. 1951
14k(w)**C&B**.........................$300 $400 $450

GRUEN, 17J., so called **50th Anniversary**, with a engraved
quadron precision extra **mvt. G# 119**, Adj., also used **G# 123.**
14k(w)............................. ★★$800 $950 $1,200

GRUEN, 17 jewels, "Constellation", curvex, c.1951
14k $300 $375 $500

GRUEN, 17 jewels, curvex, "Belmont"
14k $200 $275 $400

GRUEN, 17J., Hunter style case, "Veri-Thin", Ca. 1940s
gold filled...............................$800 $1,000 $1,400

GRUEN, 17J., Precision Quadron, crown guard, Ca. 1931
14K(W)................................. $165 $200 $300

GRUEN, 15J., RF#93, cal.179, c. 1925
gold filled................................ $70 $90 $125

GRUEN, 17J., curvex, RF#498, cal.440, c. 1945
gold filled $70 $90 $125

GRUEN, 17J., curvex, stepped lugs, RF#449, cal.440, c.1945
gold filled................................ $70 $90 $125

GRUEN, 17J., curvex, RF#498, cal.440, c. 1945
gold filled $100 $125 $175

GRUEN, 17J., curvex, large lugs, RF#449, cal.440, c. 1945
gold filled................................ $125 $150 $200

GRUEN, 17J., curvex, RF#530, c. 1948
gold filled $70 $90 $125

GRUEN, 17J., curvex, RF#449, cal.440, c. 1943
gold filled................................ $75 $90 $150

GRUEN, 17J., veri-thin, RF#530, cal.430, c. 1945
14k $125 $150 $200

🕐 A collector should expect to pay modestly higher prices
at local shops

GRUEN, 17J., curvex, RF#544, cal.440, c. 1942
gold filled................................. $75 $90 $150

GRUEN, 17J., fancy lugs, curvex, RF#610, c. 1945
14k $250 $325 $450

GRUEN, 17J., veri-thin **3 diam**., RF#558, c. 1945
14k(w)................................. $150 $185 $265

GRUEN, 17J., curvex, RF#610, cal.370, c. 1945
14k $200 $250 $425

GRUEN, 17J., curvex, RF#576, cal.440, c. 1942
gold filled.................................$70 $90 $125
14k $150 $185 $235

GRUEN, 17J., 3 diam., curvex, RF#615, cal.370, c. 1945
14k $150 $185 $265

GRUEN, 17J., precision, sold for $125. in 1930
18K(W) $250 $300 $400

GRUEN, 17J., curvex, RF#642, "Marshall", c. 1945
gold filled $75 $100 $150

GRUEN, 17J., curvex, RF#607, "Citadel", c. 1943
gold filled................................. $75 $100 $150

GRUEN, 15J., Precision, Antique finish, sold for $55 in 1930
gold filled(W)....................... $100 $135 $200

Pricing in this Guide are fair market price for **COMPLETE** watches which are reflected from the "**NAWCC**" National and regional shows.

GRUEN advertising campaign in 1908, ("**The first to introduce wrist watches in U.S.A.**")

* Signed on dial **Gruen 21** = 21Jewels & **American** Made.

GRUEN, **21J.**, twisted bezel, RF#657, cal.335, c. 1944
gold filled.............................. $125 $165 $235

GRUEN, **21J.**, precision, RF#674, cal.430, c. 1944
gold filled................................$75 $100 $150

GRUEN, **21J.**, precision, RF#738, cal.335, c. 1944
14k $150 $185 $250

GRUEN, 17J., curvex, RF#750, cal.370, c. 1940
gold filled................................ $75 $100 $150

GRUEN, 17J., curvex, RF#773, cal.370, c. 1945
gold filled................................$75 $100 $150

GRUEN, 17J., curvex, faceted crystal, cal.440, c. 1947
14k $175 $200 $285

GRUEN, **21J.**, precision, RF#801, cal. 335., c. 1944
14k $175 $200 $285

GRUEN, 17J., "Collegian", curvex - precision, Ca. 1944
gold filled $100 $165 $250

GRUEN, 17J., RF # 578, Curvex Precision, Ca. 1943
gold filled $75 $100 $150

GRUEN, 17J., RF# 755, stepped bezel, **Auto wind,** Ca. 1950
gold filled $100 $125 $175

GRUEN, 19 jewels, precision, c. 1920
14k $200 $235 $300

GRUEN, 17 jewels, curvex
14k $200 $235 $300

GRUEN, 17J., RF # 575, Curvex Precision, Ca.1945
gold filled.................................$70 $90 $125

GRUEN, 17 jewels, RF# 650, curvex, c. 1950
14k $175 $235 $300

GRUEN, 15-17, Radium dial, center & no sec., Ca. 1925
14k $150 $185 $275

🕐 Some grades are not included. Their values can be
determined by comparing with **similar** age, size, metal
content, style, grades, or models such as **time only**,
chronograph, repeater etc. listed.

GRUEN, 17 jewels, Curvex, RF#610, 3 diam.dial, Ca.1945
14k(w) 6 diam.case $250 $300 $400

* Signed on dial **Gruen 21** = 21Jewels & **American** Made.
GRUEN, **21J**., "Precision", RF#709, cal.335, Ca.1945
gold filled $70 $90 $125

GRUEN, 15 jewels, RF#8w, cal.157, Ca. 1929
gold filled $70 $90 $125

GRUEN, 15 jewels, 3 Adj., sold for $25.00 in 1930
nickel $55 $70 $100

GRUEN, 17J., veri-thin, cal.405, c. 1946
gold filled $60 $80 $100

GRUEN, 17J., curvex, RF#450, cal.440, c. 1938
gold filled.............................. $75 $100 $150

GRUEN, 17J., curvex, RF#448, cal.440, c. 1941
gold filled $75 $100 $150
14K $150 $200 $300

GRUEN, 17J., curvex, RF#450, cal.440, c. 1938
14k $200 $235 $300

GRUEN, 17J., curvex, RF#448, cal.440, c. 1944
gold filled $75 $110 $150
14k $150 $200 $300

GRUEN, 17J., curvex, RF#450, cal.440, c. 1942
14k ....$ 200 $235 $300

GRUEN, 17J., curvex, RF#879, cal.370, c. 1942
14k $150 $200 $300

GRUEN, 17J., curvex, RF#364, cal.440, c. 1935
gold filled.............................. $75 $100 $150

GRUEN, 17J., curvex, RF#293, cal.330, c. 1940
gold filled $75 $100 $150

GRUEN, 17J., precision, RF#271, cal., c. 1936
gold filled.............................. $100 $165 $250

Note:Different dial styles were used on same RF# and Caliber.

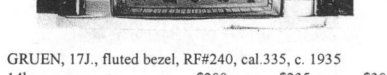

GRUEN, 17J., fluted bezel, RF#240, cal.335, c. 1935
14k $200 $235 $300

GRUEN advertising campaign in 1908 was the first to introduce wrist watches in U.S.A.

Gruen Quadron rectangular movement

GRUEN, 15J., enamel on nickel case, mvt# 158, Ca. 1927
nickel $100 $135 $200

GRUEN, 17J., crown-guard, quadron mvt# 59, Ca. 1927
18K........................$250 $285 $350

GRUEN, 15-17J., enamel Art Deco, Ca. 1927
gold filled $125 $175 $250

GRUEN, 15-17J., inlaid enamel case, quadron mvt, Ca. 1927
gold filled.................................$70 $90 $125

GRUEN, 15J., aux. sec., radium dial, sold for $55. in 1927
14K(W)...................................$150 $175 $250

GRUEN, 15-17J., engraved case, quadron mvt# 47, Ca. 1927
gold filled.................................$70 $90 $125

GRUEN, 15-17J., engraved case, radium dial,, Ca. 1927
nickel $75 $95 $125

GRUEN, 17J., crown-guard, quadron mvt, Ca. 1927
14K..$150 $200 $325

GRUEN, 15-17J., crown-guard, Ca. 1927
14K $150 $185 $250

GRUEN, 17J., crown-guard, quadron mvt, Ca. 1927
gold filled.................................$70 $90 $125

GRUEN, 15-17J., engraved case, mvt # 13, Ca. 1927
14K $150 $185 $250

GRUEN, 17J., crown-guard, sold for $135 in 1931
14K(W) $150 $185 $250

GRUEN, 15J., antique finished, sold for $45 in 1930
gold filled(W) $70 $90 $135

GRUEN, 17J., crown-guard, sold for $160 in 1931
14K(W) $150 $185 $250

GRUEN, 15J., crown-guard, sold for $45 in 1930
gold filled..................................$70 $90 $135

GRUEN, 17J., "Centurion" , sold for $85 in 1930
14K(W) $185 $235 $285

GRUEN, 15J., antique finished, sold for $35 in 1930
gold filled..................................$70 $90 $135

GRUEN, 15J., inlaid green enamel, sold for $47.50 in 1930
gold filled (W) $70 $90 $135

GRUEN, 15J., Quadron movement, sold for $50 in 1931
gold filled..................................$70 $90 $135

GRUEN,15J., inlaid red & black enamel, sold for $55 in 1931
gold filled..................................$70 $90 $135

GRUEN, 17J., Precision movement, sold for $100 in 1930
14K..$150 $185 $250

GRUEN, 15J., antique finished, sold for $55 in 1930
gold filled..................................$70 $90 $135

GRUEN, 17J., Precision movement, sold for $100 in 1930
14K..$150 $185 $250

GRUEN, 17J., curvex, RF#602, cal.370, c. 1943
14k $200 $250 $350

GRUEN, 17J., curvex, RF#449, cal.440, c. 1945
14k $125 $165 $250

GRUEN, 17J., Curvex Precision, RF # 601, Ca. 1949
gold filled................................ $85 $125 $185

GRUEN, 17 jewels, curvex, RF # 271, c. 1936
gold filled................................$200 $235 $300

GRUEN, 17 jewels, precision, fancy lugs
14k $200 $245 $325

⊕ Some grades are not included. Their values can be
determined by comparing with **similar** age, size, metal
content, style, grades, or models such as **time only**,
chronograph, repeater etc. listed.

GRUEN, 17jewels, Precision, Ca. 1928
14k(W) $175 $200 $285

GRUEN, 17J., Curvex Precision, RF # 600, Ca.1945
gold filled...............................$100 $125 $185

GRUEN, 17 jewels, curvex, fancy lugs
14k..$150 $175 $250

GRUEN, 17 jewels, curvex, c. 1939
14k..$200 $265 $350
gold filled...............................$100 $150 $250

GRUEN, 17 jewels, "Eagle", curvex, fancy lugs, c. 1951
14k..$300 $400 $600

The *Adjutant* features a case
and crystal curved to fit the
wrist

GRUEN, 15J., "Adjutant", curved case,1931 sold @ $57.50
gold filled................................$70 $90 $125

GRUEN, 17J., "Annapolis", Quadron mvt., 1931 @ $90.00
gold filled................................$70 $90 $125

GRUEN,"Arlington or Fleetwood" cal.325=17J., sold @$67.50
in 1931 & "Carlton" cal.3251= **21J.**, 1931 sold @ $92.50, all 3
use Quadron style movement. Note: Quadron mvt. # 3251 =
21J. & has capped escape wheel + center jeweled & pallet fork
capped also used a different balance staff & pallet arbor.
gold filled (W) **21J**.................$100 $125 $200
gold filled(W) 17J....................$75 $100 $150

GRUEN, 17J., "Ascot", 1931sold for $55.00
gold filled................................$100 $125 $175

GRUEN, 15J., "Aviator", 1931 sold for $42.50
gold filled(W) $135 $150 $175

GRUEN, 15J., "Chief or Courier", 1931 sold for $27.50
nickel..$55 $65 $95

GRUEN, 15J., "Commander", 1931 sold for $50.00
gold filled (W) $75 $100 $150

GRUEN, 15J., "Courier or Chief", 1931 sold for $27.50
nickel..$55 $65 $95

GRUEN, 15J., "Culver", 1931 sold for $57.50
gold filled................................$60 $80 $125

GRUEN, 17J., "Dartmouth", Quadron mvt.,1931@ $85.00
gold filled................................$75 $100 $150

GRUEN, 17J., "Kensington", 1931 sold for $45.00
gold filled................................$75 $100 $150

GRUEN, 15J., "Lakehurst", 1931 sold for $47.50
gold filled..................................$60 $80 $125

GRUEN, **21J.**, "Longacre", Quadron mvt., <u>1931</u> @ $100.00
Note: Quadron mvt. # 3251 = **21 jewels**, Ca. **1931**.
14K(Y) $150 $185 $275
14K(W) $150 $185 $275

GRUEN, 17J., "Marcus", 1931 sold for $47.50
gold filled..................................$75 $100 $150

GRUEN, 15J., "Rutgers", 1931 sold for $35.00
gold filled..................................$70 $90 $125

GRUEN, 15J., "Scout or Trooper", 1931 sold for $25.00
nickel...$55 $65 $95

GRUEN, 15J., "Stadium", 1931 sold for $42.50
gold filled (**2 tone**)...................$85 $110 $175

GRUEN, 15J., "Stanford", 1931 sold for $35.00
gold filled..................................$60 $80 $125

GRUEN, 15-17J., "Varsity", 1931 15J@ $55.00, 17J@$60.00
gold filled..................................$75 $100 $150

GRUEN, 15J., "Wesleyan", 1931 sold for $37.50
gold filled(W) $75 $100 $150

GRUEN, 15J., "West Point", 1931 sold for $52.50
gold filled (**2 tone**)...................$85 $110 $175

GRUEN, 17J., "Whitehall", Quadron mvt.1931 @ $75.00
gold filled..................................$75 $100 $150

GRUEN, 17J, physicians 1 button chronog., screw back
s. steel $300 $425 $600

GRUEN, 17J., triple date, cal.415, c. 1953
s. steel.................................. $100 $135 $200
gold filled.............................. $100 $135 $200

GRUEN, 17J, physicians 1 button chronog., screw back
18k $1,000 $1,200 $1,600

GRUEN, 17 jewels, rope style bezel with diamonds
14k...$200 $235 $300

GRUEN, 17J., jump 24 hour, c. 1970
s. steel $175 $250 $350

GRUEN, 17J., "Day-Night", cal.n510, waterproof, Ca. 1960
The "Day-night" markers have a self-powered illumination system.
base metal.......................... ★ $150 $185 $275

GRUEN, 17J., alarm, date, c. 1964
s. steel $100 $125 $175

GRUEN, 17J., **"Airflight"**, jumping hours, c. 1960
base metal..............................$225 $265 $350

GRUEN, 17 jewels, 17 diamonds, RF# 744, Ca. 1955
14k(w).....................................$250 $300 $400

GRUEN, 17J., mystery dial, Ca. 1950
14k(w)....................................$400 $475 $600

GRUEN, 17 jewels, veri-thin model, fancy lugs
14k $150 $175 $225

GRUEN, 15J., sold for $32.50 in 1928
gold filled $70 $90 $135

GRUEN, 17J., mystery dial, cal#215, ca.1965
gold filled................................$100 $135 $200

GRUEN, 15-17J., barrel shaped, Ca. 1939
gold filled................................ $75 $95 $150

GRUEN, 17J., veri-thin model, fancy lugs, 24 hr. dial
14k $150 $200 $300

GRUEN, 17J., veri-thin, fancy bezel, Ca. 1948
gold filled............................. $100 $135 $185

GRUEN, 15-17J., **curvex**, RF# 544, Ca. 1949
gold filled................................$75 $100 $150

GRUEN, 17J., fluted center lugs, cal.343, c. 1936
gold filled.................................$70 $90 $125

GRUEN, 17J., nurse style double dial, ca.1937
s. steel $150 $200 $300

E. GUBELIN, 29 jewels, min. repeater
18k C&B $25,000 $29,000 $35,000

E. GUBELIN, 17 jewels, chronog. 3 reg., Valj.72, c. 1950
18k (waterproof).................$1,000 $1,100 $1,500

E. GUBELIN, 25J., ipso-matic, triple date, moon ph.
14k & steel back $1,000 $1,200 $1,500
18k.......................................$1,800 $2,200 $2,800

E. GUBELIN, 19 jewels, chronog., day-date-month
18k $1,300 $1,500 $1,900

E. GUBELIN, 15J., triple date, c.1945
s. steel....................................$250 $300 $400

E. GUBELIN, 19J., chronog.by Valjoux, waterpf, 3 reg.
18k $1,000 $1,100 $1,500

E. GUBELIN, 19 jewels, 18k case, 14k band
18k & **14k C&B** $400 $500 $650

E. GUBELIN, 17J., ca. 1970s
18k $200 $235 $300

E. GUBELIN, 17-25J., alarm, autow., ipso-vox, c.1960
18k......................................$1,200 $1,400 $1,800

E. GUBELIN,25J., cal#F690, autow., center sec., ca. 1950s
18k $250 $275 $400
s. steel $125 $165 $250

E. GUBELIN, 17-25J., ipso-vox, date, autow., alarm, c.1960
s. steel....................................$500 $650 $950

E. GUBELIN, 17J., autow., ca. 1952
s. steel $250 $300 $400

E. GUBELIN, 17J., carved lugs, center sec., c.1944
18k... $300 $375 $500

E. GUBELIN, 17J., 3 baguettes, 8 diamonds, autow., c.1948
platinum $650 $785 $1,000

E. GUBELIN, 25J., ipso-matic, c.1955
14k $250 $300 $400

E. GUBELIN, 15J., **back wind duoplan**, c.1935
s. steel....................................$250 $325 $450

E. GUBELIN (continued)

791

E. GUBELIN, 15J., ca. 1935
18k(W).................................$700 $785 $900

E. GUBELIN, 19 J., hunter style pop-up lid, c. 1930
18k (w)................................$2,500 $2,800 $3,500

E. GUBELIN, 17 jewels, jumping hr., c. 1924
14k $5,500 $6,000 $7,000

E. GUBELIN, 25J., triple date, moon phase, autow., c. 1950
18k $3,200 $3,500 $4,500

E. GUBELIN, triple date & moon ph., by Audemars-Piguet,
Ca. 1930
18k $11,000 $14,000 $18,000

E. GUBELIN, 25J., milled bezel, autow., center sec., c. 1955
18k..$350 $425 $550

E. GUBELIN, 19 jewels, fancy hooded lugs
18k..$700 $800 $1,000

E. GUBELIN, 19 jewels, curvex, 2 tone
18k..$800 $900 $1,100

E. GUBELIN, 19J., center sec., flared case, c. 1950
18k..$350 $425 $600

E. GUBELIN, 17-21J., milled bezel, center sec., Ca. 1958
18k..$250 $300 $400

E. GUBELIN, 17 jewels, by Vacheron & Constantin
18k $1,800 $2,200 $2,800

E. GUBELIN, 18 jewels, curved, stepped case, c. 1940
18k $600 $750 $1,000

GUINAND, 17J., chronog., day-date-month, 3 reg.
18k $600 $700 $900
s. steel $250 $300 $400

GUINAND, 17 J., chronog., triple date, moon phase
18k $1,000 $1,100 $1,400
s. steel $500 $600 $750

HAFIS, 15J., center sec., cushion style
gold plate $35 $40 $55

HAFIS, 15J., luminous dial
gold plate..................................$35 $40 $55

HAFIS, 15J., engraved case
gold plate..................................$40 $50 $75
14k..$125 $135 $175

HAFIS, 15J., engraved case
gold plate..................................$40 $50 $70

HAFIS, 17J., "Queen Druga", 52 diamonds
Platinum $300 $350 $450

HALLMARK, 17 jewels, day-date-month, autowind
gold filled.................................$75 $100 $165

HAMILTON WATCH CO.

Hamilton made their first ladies **bracelet** watch in 1912. During the Art Deco period they were very successful with the "Coronado", "Piping Rock" and "Spur" model wrist watches using a enamel bezel. A **dramatic change** occurred for the watch industry in April, 1957 when the Hamilton Watch Co. eliminated the mainspring and replaced it with a small battery that lasted well over one year. The "Ventura" and "Van Horn" model 500 goes on sale and the Hamilton Watch Co. won the race to introduce the worlds' **first electric** Wrist Watch, also the first watch with no moving parts, the revolutionary *"Pulsar"* on May 10, 1970.

A very brief review of the 500 series moving coil and contact control system. The coil is fixed on the balance and a electric current flows in the magnetic field, producing a electromagnetic force. At the moment the magnetic field reaches the right and left side of the coil, the contact spring are closed by a small pin on the balance. Thus electric current through the coil will receive an impulse from the electromagnetic force and give the balance one impulse each swing. The basic principle is the same for electric motors.

Below Left: **500** balance & coil.   Center: **501** balance & coil.   Right: **505** balance & coil.

Above Left: **500** movement.   Center: **501** movement.   Right: **505** movement.

PROFILE OF BALANCE WHEEL MOTOR

DIALS FOR MINT PRICES MUST BE ALL **ORIGINAL**.

Prices for electric watch to be in **good running order**.

HAMILTON, electric, "Altair", Ca. 1962
gold filled...................... ★★$1,500 $2,000 $3,000

HAMILTON, electric, "Converta I", Ca.1958
18k bezel & s.s. case............. $200 $325 $475

HAMILTON, electric, "Aquatel", Ca. 1961
gold filled................................$100 $165 $250

HAMILTON, electric, "Converta II", Ca.1958
14k bezel & s.s. case............. $125 $200 $350

HAMILTON, electric, "Aquatel B", Ca. 1962
gold filled................................$100 $165 $250

HAMILTON, electric, "Converta III", Ca.1958
GF bezel & s.s. case.............. $125 $175 $285

HAMILTON, electric, "Atlantis", Ca. 1958
gold filled................................$100 $165 $250

HAMILTON, electric, "Converta IV", Ca.1958
S.S. bezel & case................. $100 $165 $250

HAMILTON, electric, "Centaur", Ca. 1965
gold filled................................$100 $165 $250

HAMILTON, electric, "Everest", Ca.1958
gold filled $250 $365 $550

HAMILTON, electric, "Clearview" **display back**,
sold for $100.00 in 1965
s.steel case & GF bezel ... ★★$300 $400 $650

HAMILTON, electric, "EverestII", sold for $99.50 in 1964
gold filled $125 $185 $285

Prices for electric watch to be in **good running order.**

HAMILTON, electric, "Gemini" Ca.1962
gold filled..............................$100 $165 $250

HAMILTON, electric, "Gemini II", sold for $125.00 in 1964
gold filled..............................$100 $165 $250

HAMILTON, electric, "Lord Lancaster E" , Ca.1963
14k, 12 diamonds $400 $500 $675

HAMILTON, electric, "Lord Lancaster J" , Ca.1965
gold filled, 8 diamonds...........$275 $375 $575

HAMILTON, electric, "Meteor," c. 1960
gold filled........................... ★$400 $500 $700

HAMILTON, electric, "Nautilus" 200, single lugs, Ca.1962
14k $150 $235 $375

HAMILTON, electric, "Nautilus" 201, Ca.1964
14k $150 $225 $375

HAMILTON, electric,"Nautilus" 202, sold for $160.00 in 1964
14k $125 $200 $325

HAMILTON, electric, "Nautilus" 400, Ca.1962
gold filled $75 $110 $175

HAMILTON, electric, "Nautilus" 401, Ca.1964
gold filled $75 $110 $175

HAMILTON, electric, "Nautilus" 402, Ca.1963
gold filled $75 $110 $175

HAMILTON, electric, "Nautilus" 403, pocket watch, Ca.1965
gold filled .... ★★$400 $500 $800

DIALS FOR MINT PRICES MUST BE ALL **ORIGINAL**.

HAMILTON, electric, "Nautilus" 404, Ca.1964
gold filled.................................$75 $110 $175

HAMILTON, electric, "Nautilus" 503, Ca.1964
s. steel $75 $110 $175

HAMILTON, electric, "Nautilus" 405, Ca.1966
gold filled.................................$75 $110 $175

HAMILTON, electric, "Nautilus" 506, Ca.1965
s. steel $75 $110 $175

HAMILTON, electric, "Nautilus" 450, Ca.1963
gold filled bezel $75 $110 $175

HAMILTON, electric, "Nautilus" 507, Ca.1966
s. steel $75 $110 $175

HAMILTON, electric, "Nautilus" 500, Ca.1962
s. steel $75 $110 $175

HAMILTON, electric, "Nautilus" 508, Ca.1962
s. steel $75 $110 $175

HAMILTON, electric, "Nautilus" 501, Ca.1962
s. steel $75 $110 $175

HAMILTON, electric, "Nautilus" 509, Ca.1966
s. steel $75 $110 $175

HAMILTON, electric, "Nautilus" 502, Ca.1963
s. steel $75 $110 $175

HAMILTON, electric, "Nautilus" 600, Ca.1963
rolled gold................................$60 $80 $125

HAMILTON (continued)

Prices for electric watch to be in **good running order**.

HAMILTON, electric, "Nautilus" 601, Ca. 1963
rolled gold..............................$60 $80 $125

HAMILTON, electric, "Nautilus" 602, Ca. 1965
rolled gold..............................$60 $80 $125

HAMILTON, electric, "Nautilus" 604, Ca. 1965
rolled gold..............................$60 $80 $125

HAMILTON, electric, "Nautilus" 605, Ca. 1965
rolled gold..............................$60 $80 $125

HAMILTON, electric, "Pacer," 2 tone , Ca. 1957
14k ....★★★$1,500 $1,800 $2,200
gold filled..............................$300 $365 $500
gold filled (black dial)...........$325 $435 $600

Wrist Watches listed in this section are priced at the collectable fair market **Trade Show** level as **complete** watches having an original gold-filled case and stainless steel back, also with original dial, leather watch band, and the entire original movement in good working order with no repairs needed.

HAMILTON, electric, "Pegasus", engraved bezel, sold for $125.00 in 1965
gold filled $275 $345 $450

HAMILTON, electric, "Polaris", Ca. 1960
14k **Y**.....................................$300 $400 $650
14k **W**....................................$400 $550 $800

HAMILTON, electric,"Polaris II", Ca. 1965
14k $275 $335 $450

HAMILTON, electric, "Regulus" , Ca. 1958
s. steel $450 $565 $700

HAMILTON, electric, "Regulus" II, Ca. 1962
s. steel $75 $110 $175

A collector should expect to pay modestly higher prices at local shops

DIALS FOR MINT PRICES MUST BE ALL **ORIGINAL**.

HAMILTON, electric, "R. R. Special", Ca. 1962
model#52 = all 10k GF $150 $200 $325
model#51 = GF bezel only $150 $200 $325
model#50 = all s. steel............$150 $200 $325

HAMILTON, electric, "Sea-Lectric II" , Ca. 1962
s. steel $100 $135 $200

HAMILTON, electric, "Saturn", Ca. 1960
gold filled........................... ★$350 $425 $575

HAMILTON, electric, "Skip Jack" , Ca. 1961
s. steel $75 $110 $175

HAMILTON, electric, "Savitar", Ca. 1961
14k .... ★$425 $535 $675

HAMILTON, electric, "Spectra" , Ca. 1957
18k **Rose gold** .... ★★★★$1,200 $1,500 $1,900
18k .... ★★★$700 $900 $1,200
14k .... ★$550 $650 $800
gold filled .... ★★$250 $350 $500

HAMILTON, electric, "Savitar 11", Ca.1965
gold filled...............................$250 $350 $500

HAMILTON, electric, "Spectra" II, Ca. 1963
gold filled $100 $165 $250

HAMILTON, electric, "Sea-Lectric I", GF bezel, Ca. 1965
s. steel $125 $165 $275

HAMILTON, electric, "Summit" , Ca. 1961
14k $200 $250 $325

Prices for electric watch to be in **good running order.**

HAMILTON, electric, "Summit" II, Ca. 1964
gold filled............................ ★$200 $235 $325

HAMILTON, electric, "Titan IV-B" , Ca. 1966
14kC&B................... ★ ★ ★ ★$600 $750 $1,000

HAMILTON, electric, "Taurus" , Ca. 1962
gold filled.................................$75 $110 $175

HAMILTON, electric, "Uranus" , Ca. 1959
gold filled $150 $225 $350

HAMILTON, electric, "Titan", Ca. 1958
gold filled...............................$150 $235 $325

HAMILTON, electric, "Van Horn", Ca.1957
14k $250 $325 $475
14k +diam. dial......................$400 $500 $650

HAMILTON, electric, "Titan II" , Ca. 1961
gold filled...............................$150 $235 $325

HAMILTON, electric, Vantage , ca.1958
gold filled $135 $185 $275

HAMILTON, electric, "Titan III" , Ca. 1964
gold filled...............................$175 $235 $325

HAMILTON, electric, "Vega" , Ca. 1961
gold filled .... ★$500 $650 $800

DIALS FOR MINT PRICES MUST BE ALL <u>ORIGINAL</u>.

HAMILTON, electric, "Vela" , sold for $115.00 in 1966
gold filled................................$150 $185 $250

HAMILTON, 19 jewels, "Adrian", ca. 1953
gold filled $100 $135 $200

HAMILTON electric, "Ventura",
14k sold for $200.00 in 1957,
18k rose................. ★ ★ ★ ★ $2,600 $3,000 $3,500
18k .... ★ ★ ★ $1,600 $1,800 $2,300
14k(w)........................... ★ ★ $1,800 $2,000 $2,500
14k(Y)............................$1,200 $1,400 $1,800

HAMILTON, 17 jewels, "Alan", ca.1942
gold filled $100 $135 $200

HAMILTON, 22 jewels, " Aldrich", Ca. 1958
14k $150 $200 $300

HAMILTON electric, "Ventura, **6 diamond dial**, Ca. 1957
14K......................................$1,500 $1,800 $2,200

HAMILTON, 19 jewels, "Allison" , Ca. 1937
14k $165 $225 $350

HAMILTON, electric,"Victor", ca.1957
gold filled................................$175 $250 $400

HAMILTON,17J., " Amherst", 14k markers , Ca. 1956
gold filled $100 $135 $200

Hamilton, electric, "Victor II" , Ca. 1961
gold filled................................$250 $350 $475

HAMILTON, 19 jewels, "Andrews", ca.1930
14k(y & w) .... ★ $250 $300 $425

HAMILTON, 22J., " Ansley " , 14k markers, Ca. 1960
gold filled................................$100 $125 $175

HAMILTON, 17J., "Aqualine ", 14k markers, Ca. 1957
gold filled................................$75 $85 $125

HAMILTON, 19J., " Ardmore", Ca. 1935
14k $350 $400 $500

HAMILTON, 17J., " Arnold", Ca. 1957
rolled gold...............................$50 $60 $100

HAMILTON, 19J., " Ashley", grade 982, Ca. 1948
gold filled................................$100 $135 $200

HAMILTON, 22J., "Attache", 14k markers, c.1961
gold filled................................$175 $235 $335

HAMILTON, 17J.," Austin ", Ca. 1949
gold filled $100 $125 $175

HAMILTON, 17J, ''Bagley,'' applied numbers, Ca. 1939
gold filled $100 $135 $200

HAMILTON, 19J.," Bailey ", c.1949
gold filled $100 $125 $175

HAMILTON, 22J., " Barbizon", diam. bezel, Ca.1957
18k(w)............... ★ ★ ★ ★ ★$3,000 $4,000 $5,500

HAMILTON, 22J., " Baron ", 5 diam. dial, BIG lugs, c.1960
14k $185 $250 $350

HAMILTON, 22J., " Baron II" , 5 diamond dial, ca. 1961
14k $185 $250 $350

HAMILTON, 22J., "Barry", sterling silver dial, ca.1957
gold filled................................$100 $125 $175

HAMILTON, 17J.," Bartley", Ca.1936
gold filled...............................$135 $175 $250

HAMILTON, 19J.,"Barton", tu tone dial, c.1948
14k $175 $225 $300

HAMILTON, 22J., "Baton", 14k markers, ca.1958
14k $135 $175 $250

HAMILTON, 17J., "Baxter", sterling silver dial, ca.1957
gold filled................................$100 $135 $200

HAMILTON,17J.,"Beldon", 2 tone dial, sealed case, c.1949
gold filled................................$100 $135 $200

HAMILTON, 22J., " Bentley", 14k markers, ca. 1961
gold filled $100 $125 $175

HAMILTON, 19J., " Bentley", 14k markers, Ca. 1937
14k $700 $850 $1,000

HAMILTON, 17-19J., "Benton" , 14k markers, c. 1952
14k $250 $325 $450

HAMILTON, 17J., "Berkshire" , 14k markers, Ca. 1953
14k $200 $250 $375

HAMILTON, 22J.,"Blade", asymmetrical, note lugs, Ca.1962
gold filled ....★ $250 $350 $500

HAMILTON, 22J.," Blair ", sterling silver dial, c.1957
gold filled $100 $135 $200

HAMILTON, 17-21J.," Blake", c.1949
gold filled $100 $135 $200

HAMILTON, 17J., " Boatswain" , center sec., c. 1958
rolled gold...............................$50 $65 $100

HAMILTON, 17J., " Boatswain II" , c. 1961
rolled gold...............................$50 $65 $100

HAMILTON, 17J.," Boone ", Curved, Ca.1936
gold filled...............................$100 $165 $250

HAMILTON, 19 jewels, "Boulton", Ca. 1941
gold filled...............................$125 $165 $225

HAMILTON, 22J., " Boulton II", 14k markers, c. 1961
gold filled...............................$100 $125 $175

HAMILTON, 17J.,"Bowman", c.1939
gold filled...............................$175 $225 $300

HAMILTON, 17J.,"Boyd", c.1949
gold filled $100 $125 $175

HAMILTON, 22J., "Bradford ", 14k markers, c. 1954
14k $125 $175 $275

HAMILTON, 22J., "Bradford B" , **11 diam. dial,** c. 1954
14k $175 $225 $335

HAMILTON, 17J., "Brandon", swing lugs, ca. 1946
gold filled $100 $135 $200

HAMILTON, 17 jewels, "Brandon", Ca. 1948
gold filled $100 $125 $175

HAMILTON, 19J.,"Brent" **faceted** crystal, c.1949
gold filled $100 $125 $175

HAMILTON, 22J.," Brewster ", sterling silver dial, Ca.1957
gold filled................................$100 $125 $175

HAMILTON, 17J.,"Cabot", cal.960, Ca. 1938
gold filled $100 $125 $175

HAMILTON, 19 jewels, ''Brock'' , c. 1939
14k(coral)....................★★★$300 $365 $550
14k(yellow).........................$175 $225 $325

HAMILTON, 17J.,"Cabot", luminous, Ca. 1957
s.steel $55 $65 $100

HAMILTON, 19 jewels, " Brockton", c. 1952
10k $100 $135 $200

HAMILTON, 17J.,"Cadet", Ca. 1957
rolled gold................................$50 $60 $100

HAMILTON, 17J., ''Calvin'', applied gold numbers, ca.1936
gold filled $100 $125 $175

HAMILTON, 19J.," Brooke ", Curved, Ca.1938
gold filled............................ ★$400 $500 $700

HAMILTON, 17J.,"Cambridge", ca.1930
14k(w)........................★★★$900 $1,000 $1,200
14k(y) ....★★★$900 $1,000 $1,200

HAMILTON, 19 jewels, ''Byrd'' ca.1930
18k ....★★★★$2,500 $2,800 $3,500
14k(W)........................★★$1,500 $1,800 $2,500
14k(Y)........................★★$1,200 $1,500 $2,000

HAMILTON, 19J.," Cambridge ", c.1949
HAMILTON signed case
platinum............................★$700 $800 $1,000

HAMILTON, 19 jewels, "Cameron" , c. 1937
14k $185 $250 $350

HAMILTON, 17J.,"Captain Rice", Ca. 1930
14k(w or y) .... ★★★$600 $685 $850

HAMILTON, 17J.," Carl ", Ca.1953
gold filled................................ $100 $135 $200

HAMILTON, 17J.," Carlisle ", 44mm, cal. 937, Ca.1937
gold filled................................ $175 $225 $335

HAMILTON, 17J.," Carson ", Ca.1935
gold filled................................ $100 $135 $200

HAMILTON, 17J., " Carson ", c. 1961
rolled gold................................ $50 $60 $80

HAMILTON, 17J.," Carlton ", c.1949
gold filled $100 $125 $175

HAMILTON, 17J., " Carlyle " , c. 1958
rolled gold................................ $45 $55 $85

HAMILTON, 17J., " Carteret" 14k markers, Ca. 1958
14k $125 $175 $250

HAMILTON, 17J.,"Casino", 5 diamond, Ca. 1957
14kYorW $185 $250 $350

HAMILTON, 19J.," Cedric ", c.1949
gold filled $100 $125 $175

Wrist Watches listed in this section are priced at the collectable fair market **Trade Show** level as **complete** watches having an original gold-filled case and stainless steel back, also with original dial, leather watch band, and the entire original movement in good working order with no repairs needed.

🕐 A collector should expect to pay modestly higher prices at local shops

HAMILTON, 22J., "Chadwick ", 14k markers, c. 1959
14k $135 $175 $250

HAMILTON, 18J., "Clearview" , left = 1958, right = 1961
14k (1958) $165 $200 $300
14k (1961) $135 $175 $275

HAMILTON,17J.,"Chanticleer", **alarm & power reserve**, c.1957
gold filled................................$125 $165 $250

HAMILTON, 17J.," Clinton ", c.1949
s. steel $60 $75 $125

HAMILTON, 22J., "Chapman", 14k markers, Ca. 1958
gold filled................................$100 $125 $175

HAMILTON, 17J.," Clyde ", c.1950
gold filled $100 $125 $175

HAMILTON, 17-19J., "Chatham", Ca. 1953
14k $400 $500 $650

HAMILTON, 17J., "Clark", Ca. 1936
gold filled.................................$135 $165 $235

HAMILTON, 17J., "Coburn ", c. 1958
rolled gold...............................$45 $60 $90

HAMILTON, 17-18J., "Clark", sterling silver dial, Ca. 1957
gold filled.................................$125 $165 $250

HAMILTON, 17J., "Colby ", c. 1957
rolled gold................................$55 $75 $100

HAMILTON, 17J.,"Contour", Drivers, Crown at 12, c. 1938
gold filled..............................$385 $500 $700

HAMILTON, 17J., "Conway ", c. 1961
rolled gold..............................$50 $65 $95

HAMILTON, 17J., " Cordell", Ca. 1961
14k C&B..............................$250 $300 $400

HAMILTON,17J., "Coronado ", black enamel bezel, ca.1928
14k(w or y) $1,200 $1,400 $1,800

HAMILTON, 22J., "Corvet ", 14k markers, c. 1961
gold filled..............................$100 $125 $165

HAMILTON, 17J., "Courtney ", 14k markers, c. 1958
14k $135 $175 $250

HAMILTON, 22J., "Courtney ", 6 diamond dial, c. 1958
14k $200 $235 $300

HAMILTON, 17J.," Craig ", c.1949
gold filled $100 $125 $175

HAMILTON, 19J., "Cranston ", gold markers, c. 1952
gold filled $100 $125 $175

HAMILTON, 22J., "Crispin", sterling silver dial, c. 1957
14k $135 $175 $250

Wrist Watches listed in this section are priced at the collectable
fair market **Trade Show** level as **complete** watches having an
original gold-filled case and stainless steel back, also with
original dial, leather watch band, and the entire original movement in good working order with no repairs needed.

5 Time Zones, Introduced Jan. 6th, 1956, the G hand = Greenwich
Pacific - Mountain - Central - Eastern

HAMILTON, 17J., "Cross Country", 5 time zones, ca. 1956
* Marked Illinois W. Co. on movement, (sold for $75.00)
gold filled..............................$250 $350 $450

HAMILTON, 18J.,"Cross Country II", 5 time zones,
sold for $85.00 in 1957
gold filled..............................$250 $350 $450

HAMILTON, 18J., "Croydon", sweep seconds, ca.1953
s.steel $45 $60 $95

HAMILTON, 22J., " Cullen" , 14k markers, c. 1957
gold filled..............................$100 $125 $175

HAMILTON, 22J., " Curtiss", hinged lugs, Ca. 1953
14k $200 $265 $400

HAMILTON, 19J., " Custer", Ca. 1936
14k $225 $275 $375

HAMILTON, 17J., "Cyril", Ca. 1957
gold filled $100 $125 $175

HAMILTON, 17J., "Darrell", cal#747, c. 1951
gold filled $100 $125 $175

HAMILTON, 17J., "Dawson ", c. 1959
gold filled $100 $125 $175

HAMILTON, 17J., "Dean ", c. 1957
gold filled $100 $125 $175

HAMILTON, 17J., "Deauville ", c. 1962
rolled gold..............................$45 $55 $90

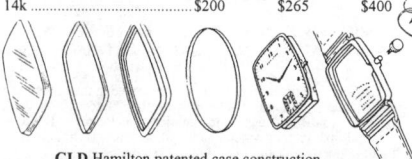

CLD Hamilton patented case construction.
DIALS FOR MINT PRICES MUST BE ALL **ORIGINAL**.

HAMILTON, 17J.," Dennis", Ca.1961
14k $125 $165 $250

HAMILTON, 17J.," Dennis ", Ca.1948
gold filled.............................$100 $125 $175

HAMILTON, 17J.," Dewitt ", c.1950
gold filled.............................$100 $125 $175

HAMILTON, 17J., " Dexter", c. 1959
rolled gold................................$50 $60 $90

HAMILTON, 17J.," Dexter ", c.1950
gold filled.............................$100 $125 $175

HAMILTON, 17J.,"Dixon", left = Ca.1936, right = Ca. 1953
gold filled = 1936..................$100 $125 $175
gold filled = 1953..................$100 $125 $175

HAMILTON, 17 jewels, "Dodson" , c. 1939
gold filled $100 $135 $200

HAMILTON, 19J.," Donald ", c.1941
note: Turner 10K (look-a-like)
14k $200 $265 $365

HAMILTON, 19J.," Donavan ", center lugs, Ca. 1935
14k $600 $725 $950

HAMILTON, 22J.,"Donavan II", **6 diamonds**, Ca.1956
14k $185 $250 $375

HAMILTON, 22J.," Donavan II", Ca.1955
14k $150 $200 $300

HAMILTON, 17J.," Dickens ", 44MM long, Ca.1937
Note: Also see **Gilman** = 14k (**look-a-like**)
gold filled.............................$150 $200 $300

DIALS FOR MINT PRICES MUST BE ALL **ORIGINAL**.

HAMILTON, 17J.," Dorsey ", Ca.1936
14k $175 $225 $300

HAMILTON, 17J.," Doublet ", Ca.1962
14k $165 $200 $275

HAMILTON, 17J.," Drake ", Ca.1951
14k $175 $225 $325

HAMILTON, 17J.," Drake ", Ca.1935
gold filled...............................$100 $150 $225

HAMILTON, 17J.,"Drew", Ca.1957
rolled gold.................................$40 $50 $95

HAMILTON, 17J., "Drummond ", 14k markers, c. 1959
gold filled................................$100 $125 $175

HAMILTON, 17J.," Dunham ", c.1951
gold filled $100 $125 $175

HAMILTON, 19 jewels, "Dunkirk", c. 1937
14k $400 $450 $550

HAMILTON, 17J., "Dwight", gold numbers, ca. 1948
gold filled $100 $135 $200

HAMILTON, 17 jewels, "Dyson", c. 1951
gold filled $100 $125 $175

HAMILTON, 17J., Eaton ", c.1948
gold filled $100 $125 $175

HAMILTON, 22J.,"Edgemere B", sterling silver dial, c.1957
gold filled $75 $85 $125

DIALS FOR MINT PRICES MUST BE ALL **ORIGINAL**.

HAMILTON, 17J.," Eliott ", Cal.980, Ca. 1936
gold filled...............................$100 $135 $200

HAMILTON, 17J.," Emery ", c.1949
gold filled...............................$100 $125 $175

HAMILTON, 17 jewels, "Eric" , c. 1948
gold filled...............................$100 $135 $200

HAMILTON, 17 jewels, "Ericsson" , Ca. 1930
18k ....★★★★$1,800 $2,200 $2,800
14k Y or W .... ★★★$800 $900 $1,100

HAMILTON, 17 jewels, "Emerson" , c. 1941
gold filled...............................$100 $125 $175

Wrist Watches listed in this section are priced at the collectable
fair market **Trade Show** level as **complete** watches having an
original gold-filled case and stainless steel back, also with
original dial, leather watch band, and the entire original movement in good working order with no repairs needed.

🕐 A collector should expect to pay modestly higher prices
at local shops.

HAMILTON, 17 jewels, "Endicott" , c. 1941
gold filled yellow $100 $135 $200
gold filled **coral**........ ★★★★$600 $800 $1,000

HAMILTON, 17J., "Errol", 2-tone sterling silver dial, c.1957
gold filled $100 $125 $175

HAMILTON, 17 jewels, "Essex" , c. 1941
gold filled yellow $100 $135 $200
gold filled coral ....★$200 $275 $375

HAMILTON, 17J., "Essex", c.1957
rolled gold................................$40 $50 $95

HAMILTON, 17J., "Farrell", 14k # s, c.1959
rolled gold................................$40 $50 $95

HAMILTON, 17J., " First Mate", c.1960
rolled gold..................................$40 $50 $90

HAMILTON, 19 jewels, "Foster" , c. 1939
14k $250 $300 $450

HAMILTON, 18J.,"Fleetwood ", c.1949
14k $125 $175 $250

HAMILTON, 17J., "Franklin", c.1949
gold filled $100 $125 $175

HAMILTON, 22J., "Flight I", 14k **marks** & # 12, ca. 1960
14k case ....★ ★$2,500 $3,200 $4,000

HAMILTON, 17J., "Fulton", sterling silver dial, c.1957
gold filled $100 $125 $175

HAMILTON, 22J.,"Flight II",14k **dots** & #s 12,3,6,9, c.1961
gold filled case................★$1,200 $1,400 $1,800

HAMILTON, 17J., " Gardner", c.1961
rolled gold...............................$50 $55 $90

HAMILTON, 17J.," Gary ", c.1949
gold filled $100 $125 $175

HAMILTON, "Flint Ridge", flip top is lug activated,
Grade 987=17J, Grade 979=19J, Ca. 1930
14k (w or y) ....★ ★$2,500 $2,900 $3,500

HAMILTON, 19J.," Gilbert ", c.1941
14k $150 $200 $275

HAMILTON, 19 jewels, "Gilman" , 44mm long, c. 1937
Note: Also see **Dickens** = *Gold Filled* (**look-a-like**)
14k .... ★ $350 $450 $600

HAMILTON, 17J.,"Gladstone", cal.981, c.1931
gold filled **W**...........................$125 $185 $275
gold filled **Y**............................$125 $185 $275

HAMILTON, 19J.," Glendale ", engraved case, Ca. 1928
14k **W** .... ★★★$2,200 $2,500 $3,200
14K **Y**.................. ★★★★$2,200 $2,500 $3,200

HAMILTON, 17J., " Glendon", c.1961
rolled gold..................................$40 $45 $90

HAMILTON, 17J.," Glenn ", c.1948
14k $150 $200 $275

HAMILTON, 19 jewels, "Glenn Curtis", Ca.1931
14k(Y or W) .... ★★$325 $400 $550

HAMILTON, 18J., "Golden Tempus", c.1957
14k regular style dial.............$300 $350 $450
14k **time zones** dial...............$500 $575 $800

HAMILTON, 18J., "Diamond Tempus", (masterpiece),
NOTE: **Both with 11 diamond** dial, c.1957
14k regular style dial.............$600 $700 $1,000
14k time zones dial................$700 $900 $1,200

HAMILTON, 18J., " Golden Tempus II", 14k #s, c.1959
gold filled $100 $125 $175

HAMILTON, 19J.," Gordon ", c.1941
platinum..............................$1,000 $1,400 $1,800
18k $350 $425 $550

HAMILTON, 22J., '' Gramercy'', 14k #s, c.1958
gold filled...............................$100 $125 $175

HAMILTON, 17 jewels, ''Grant'', Ca. 1933
sterling $250 $325 $450
gold filled $150 $225 $350

HAMILTON, 17 jewels, ''Grant'', Ca. 1957
rolled gold...............................$55 $65 $100

HAMILTON, 17 jewels, ''Greenwich'' Ca. 1931
gold filled (Y or W)...............$100 $135 $200

HAMILTON, 18J.,''Grenadier I'', sterling silver dial, c.1957
gold filled................................$75 $100 $150

HAMILTON, 18J.,''Grenadier II'', sterling silver dial, c.1957
gold filled................................$75 $100 $150

DIALS FOR MINT PRICES MUST BE ALL **ORIGINAL**.

HAMILTON, 17J.,''Grover'', c.1949
gold filled $100 $125 $175

HAMILTON, 18J.,''Guardsman I'', sterling silver dial, c.1957
gold filled $100 $125 $165

HAMILTON, 17J.,''Guardsman II'', c.1957
gold filled $100 $125 $165

HAMILTON, 17J., ''Haddon'', sold for $69.50 in 1952
gold filled $100 $135 $200

HAMILTON, 17J.,''Halesworth B'', sterling silver dial, c.1957
gold filled $100 $125 $175

HAMILTON, 17J.,'' Harris '', Ca.1937
gold filled $100 $125 $175

HAMILTON, 18J., "Hartman", **hinged lugs**, Ca.1953
18k, sold for $225.00 .. ★★★$300 $350 $450
14k, sold for $175.00 ...... ★★$250 $300 $385

HAMILTON, 17J.,"Hastings", **14k** sold for $75.00 in 1928
14k (Y or W) $200 $250 $350
gold filled (Y or W)...............$100 $125 $175

HAMILTON, 19J.," Hayden ", c.1948
gold filled...............................$100 $135 $200

HAMILTON, 17J., "Heyward", sold for $37.50 in 1936
gold filled...............................$100 $150 $225

HAMILTON, 18J.,"Holden", ca.1961
gold filled...............................$100 $110 $150

HAMILTON, 17J.," Huntley ", Ca.1961
14k $150 $200 $275

HAMILTON, 17J., "**Howard**", on dial & movement, c.1939
gold filled .... ★★$325 $400 $500

HAMILTON, 17J.,"Jason", sold for $55.00 in1957
s.steel $40 $50 $95

HAMILTON, 17J.," Jeffrey ", c.1949
gold filled $100 $150 $225

HAMILTON, 19 jewels, "Judson" Ca. 1935
gold filled $100 $125 $175

HAMILTON, 17J., " Keane ", c.1958
rolled gold................................$50 $65 $100

HAMILTON, 19J.," Keith ", c.1949
14k $150 $200 $275
18k $275 $350 $500

HAMILTON, 17J.," Kirk ", c.1949
14k $150 $175 $250

HAMILTON, 22J.,"Kevin", **swivel lugs**, sterling silver dial,
14k mumbers, Ca.1954
18k .... ★ $400 $500 $650

HAMILTON, 17J., '' Lakeland'', c.1959
s. steel $40 $50 $90

HAMILTON, 17J., '' Khyber'', 14k #s, c.1959
gold filled................................$225 $250 $300

HAMILTON, 17J.,"Lambert ", c.1950
gold filled $100 $125 $175

HAMILTON, 17J.," Kinematic I ", Ca.1957
rolled gold................................$40 $50 $90

HAMILTON, 22J.,"Lance I", sterling silver dial, Ca.1957
14k Y or W...........................$125 $150 $225

HAMILTON, 17J.," Kinematic II ", Ca.1960
rolled gold................................$40 $50 $90

HAMILTON, 22J.,"Lance II", sterling silver dial, Ca.1957
14k Y or W...........................$125 $150 $225

HAMILTON, 19J.," Kirby ", c.1949
gold filled................................$100 $125 $175

HAMILTON, 22J.,"Lance II", (masterpiece), 12 diamonds
sterling silver dial, Ca.1957
14k W....................................$150 $225 $325

HAMILTON, 22J.,"Landon", Ca.1957
rolled gold................................$50 $60 $90

HAMILTON, 17J,(Lange is =14k), Langdon is =G. filled
Ca. 1949
14k $125 $150 $225
gold filled................................$75 $90 $125

HAMILTON, 17J.," Langford ", Ca.1937
14k $185 $225 $300

HAMILTON, 17J, "Langley", **14k** sold for $100.00 in1933
14k $300 $385 $500
18k ....★★★★$1,000 $1,200 $1,500

Wrist Watches listed in this section are priced at the collectable
fair market **Trade Show** level as **complete** watches having an
original gold-filled case and stainless steel back, also with
original dial, leather watch band, and the entire original movement in good working order with no repairs needed.

HAMILTON, 17J.," Lawrence ", Ca.1936
gold filled $125 $185 $250

HAMILTON, 17 jewels, "Lee" Ca. 1934
gold filled (w).............. ★★★$300 $375 $500
gold filled (y).........................$200 $250 $325

HAMILTON, 19J., "Lester", gold numbers, ca. 1941
gold filled $100 $125 $175

HAMILTON, 18J.,"Lincrest", Ca.1957
gold filled $75 $100 $150

HAMILTON, 17J., "Lindsay", sold for $65.00 in 1952
gold filled $100 $125 $175

HAMILTON, 17 & 19 jewels, "Linwood" Ca. 1937
gold filled......................... ★$175 $250 $350

HAMILTON, 19 jewels, "Livingston", Ca. 1930
gold filled (Y).................... ★$275 $350 $450
gold filled (W) .... ★★$300 $400 $550

HAMILTON, 19J., " Lowell", Ca.1935
14k $175 $250 $350

HAMILTON, 17J., " Lowell", Ca.1961
rolled gold................................$40 $45 $90

HAMILTON, 18J., "Lyle B", sterling silver dial, Ca.1957
14k $175 $235 $350

HAMILTON, 18J., "Lyndon", sold for $71.50 in 1952
gold filled................................$100 $135 $200

DIALS FOR MINT PRICES MUST BE ALL **ORIGINAL**.

HAMILTON, 22J., "Malcom", sterling silver dial, Ca.1955
14k $175 $225 $300

HAMILTON, 17 jewels, "Martin" Ca. 1941
gold filled coral .... ★$125 $165 $250
gold filled **Y** $100 $125 $175

HAMILTON,17J., "Martin", Ca. 1966
gold plate $50 $65 $90

HAMILTON, 17J.,"Mason", sold for $40.00 in 1935
gold filled (w or y) .... ★★$125 $175 $275

HAMILTON, 19J.,"Meadowbrook", right = **radial**, Ca. 1927
14k $250 $350 $500
18k .... ★★★$750 $875 $1,100
Platinum................. ★★★★$2,500 $3,200 $4,000

HAMILTON, 19J., "Medford", sold for $71.50 in 1952
gold filled $100 $125 $175

HAMILTON, 17J., " Merritt", Ca.1937
gold filled...............................$100 $150 $225

HAMILTON, 19 jewels, "Midas," hidden lugs , c. 1941
14k yellow $200 $250 $350
14k (coral)........................... ★$225 $285 $400

HAMILTON, 19J.," Milton ", c.1948
gold filled...............................$100 $125 $175

HAMILTON, 17J., " Montclair", 14k #s, c.1961
14k $100 $150 $225

HAMILTON, 17J.," Morley ", c.1936
gold filled...............................$100 $150 $225

HAMILTON, 22J., "Morton", sterling silver dial, c.1957
gold filled...............................$100 $135 $200

HAMILTON, 17J., " Mount Vernon", Ca.1932
gold filled ....★$225 $325 $450

HAMILTON, 17J.,"Murray", sterling silver dial, c.1957
gold filled $100 $125 $175

HAMILTON, 17J.," Myron ", c.1941
gold filled $100 $125 $175

HAMILTON, 22J., " Newlin", 14k #s, c.1958
gold filled $75 $95 $125

HAMILTON, 17J.," Neil ", c.1948
gold filled $100 $110 $150

DIALS FOR MINT PRICES MUST BE ALL <u>ORIGINAL</u>.

HAMILTON, 17J., "Nelson", Ca.1936
gold filled...............................$150 $195 $250

HAMILTON, 17J., "Newton", cal.747, Ca.1954
gold filled...............................$100 $135 $200

HAMILTON, 17J, <u>Norde is 14k</u>, Nordon,18J, is <u>gold filled</u>
Ca. 1949
14k $125 $175 $250
gold filled.................................$75 $95 $135

HAMILTON, 19 jewels, "Norman", c. 1949
gold filled...............................$100 $125 $175

HAMILTON, 17J., "Norman", 14k #s, c.1958
gold filled.................................$75 $95 $125

🕐 A collector should expect to pay modestly higher prices
at local shops

HAMILTON, 17 jewels, "Norfolk", Ca. 1936
gold filled $100 $125 $175

HAMILTON, 22J., "Norton", 14k #s, c.1961
14k $125 $165 $250

HAMILTON, 19 jewels, "Oakmont"
14k (y) ....★$700 $800 $1,000
14k (w) $700 $800 $1,000

HAMILTON, 17J., "Orson ", c.1961
gold filled $75 $95 $125

HAMILTON, 19J., "Otis", reversible, sold for $67.50 in1938
14k ....★★★★$5,000 $6,500 $9,000
gold filled ....★$1,200 $1,700 $2,400

HAMILTON,17J., "Pacermatic", **automatic** on dial, cal. 667
swiss movement, tu-tone case, Ca. 1961, beware of **FAKES**
gold filled.................. ★★★$1,000 $1,200 $1,600

HAMILTON, 17 jewels, "Perry" , Ca. 1933
gold filled **Y** $135 $200 $300
gold filled **W** .... ★★$175 $275 $400

HAMILTON, 19 jewels, "Paige" , c. 1941
gold filled................................$100 $125 $175

HAMILTON, 19J.," Perry ", c.1948
gold filled $100 $125 $175

HAMILTON, 22 jewels, "Paige", sterling silver dial, c. 1957
14k $150 $200 $275

HAMILTON, 22J., "Peyton ", c.1959
gold filled $75 $95 $125

HAMILTON, 22J., " Parker B", 14k #s, anti-magnetic,
sold for $95.00 in 1957
10k $100 $150 $225

HAMILTON, 19 jewels, "Pierre" Ca. 1936
14k $500 $600 $750

HAMILTON, 17 jewels, "Paxton", c. 1957
rolled gold................................$40 $50 $90

HAMILTON, 17J., "Pinehurst", note **radial**, CA. 1930
14k (y) .... ★★★$2,200 $2,400 $2,800
14k (w) .... ★★★$2,200 $2,400 $2,800

HAMILTON, 19J.,"Piping Rock", enamel bezel, ca.1928
14k (y) $900 $1,100 $1,400
14k (w) $1,000 $1,200 $1,500
See Ca. 1948 Piping Rock next page

HAMILTON, 17J.,"Piping Rock", grade 747, ca.1948
14k Y \$900   \$1,000   \$1,200
14k W ....★★★\$1,200   \$1,300   \$1,500

HAMILTON, 17J.,"Powell", ca.1957
gold filled...................................\$75   \$95   \$125

HAMILTON, 17J., " Prentice'', c.1959
rolled gold.................................\$70   \$85   \$125

HAMILTON, 17J., ''Prescott '', sold for \$45.00 in 1936
gold filled..............................\$100   \$125   \$175

HAMILTON, 22J., "Prescott B", sterling silver dial, Ca. 1957
14k \$125   \$150   \$225

HAMILTON, 17J, "Putnam", sold for \$50.00 in 1932
gold filled (w or y) \$150   \$200   \$300

HAMILTON, 22J., '' Radburn'', 14k #s, c.1959
14k \$125   \$165   \$250

HAMILTON, 17J.," Raleigh ", Plain, ca.1931
gold filled Y \$175   \$250   \$350
gold filled W \$175   \$250   \$350

HAMILTON, 17J.,"Raleigh", Engraved, ca.1931
gold filled Y \$185   \$265   \$375
gold filled W \$185   \$265   \$375

HAMILTON, 19J.,"Raleigh", gold numbers, ca.1953
gold filled \$100   \$125   \$175

HAMILTON, 17J., '' Ramsey'', c.1961
rolled gold..................................\$40   \$50   \$90

HAMILTON, 17J., "Randolph", c. 1935
14k $125 $165 $225

HAMILTON, 18J., " Randolph", 14k #s, c.1958
14k $125 $165 $225

HAMILTON, 17J., "Raymon", ca.1950
s.steel $75 $95 $135

HAMILTON, 17 jewels, "Reagan", c. 1937
gold filled.................................$100 $125 $175

HAMILTON, 17J., "Reardon", ca.1949
14k $125 $175 $250

HAMILTON, 19J., " Richmond", curved, Ca.1933
18k Y $400 $500 $600
18k W ....★★$600 $750 $900

HAMILTON, 17J., Robert=gents & Roberta= ladies, Ca.1953
14k $300 $450 $600

HAMILTON, 18J., " Rodney", 14k #s, Ca.1953
Masonic dial $100 $125 $175
gold filled $75 $100 $125

HAMILTON, 19J., "Rodney", ca.1941
14 k coral ....★$250 $300 $400
14k Y $150 $200 $275

HAMILTON, 17J., "Roland", Ca.1937
gold filled $100 $125 $175

HAMILTON, 17J., "Roland", sterling silver dial, Ca.1955
14k $500 $600 $750

HAMILTON, 22J., " Romanesque M", c.1960
14k $135 $185 $275

DIALS FOR MINT PRICES MUST BE ALL **ORIGINAL**.

HAMILTON, 17J., "Romanesque N", c.1960
gold filled..........................$75 $85 $125

HAMILTON, 17 jewels, "Russell", c. 1957
gold filled $100 $135 $200

HAMILTON, 22J., " Romanesque R", c.1960
gold filled..........................$75 $85 $125

HAMILTON, 19 jewels, "Rutledge", c. 1935
platinum...........................$1,000 $1,200 $1,600

HAMILTON, 22J., "Romanesque S ", c.1960
gold filled..........................$75 $100 $135

HAMILTON, 17J., "Ryan", sold for $65.00 in 1952
gold filled $100 $125 $175

HAMILTON, 17J., " Romanesque T", c.1960
rolled gold..............................$50 $60 $90

HAMILTON, 17 jewels, "Samson", c. 1957
gold filled $75 $95 $135

HAMILTON, 19 jewels, "Ross" , c. 1939
gold filled yellow...................$100 $125 $175
gold filled Coral................ ★$150 $200 $300

HAMILTON, 17J., " Sawyer", 14k #s, c.1955
gold filled $100 $125 $175

HAMILTON, 17 jewels, "Russell", hinged lugs , c. 1941
gold filled..............................$100 $125 $175

HAMILTON,17J., "Scott", sold for 79.50 in 1966
gold filled $75 $100 $165

HAMILTON, 17J.," Scott ", GJS, Ca..1935
gold filled **Y**..........................$100 $125 $175
gold filled **W**.....................★$125 $175 $275

HAMILTON, 19J.," Scott ", GJS, 982, Ca.1949
14k $300 $375 $500

HAMILTON, 17J., " Sea Breeze", c.1961
rolled gold................................$35 $40 $75

HAMILTON, 17J., " Seabrook", c.1961
rolled gold................................$35 $40 $75

HAMILTON, 17J., " Sea-cap ", c.1961
rolled gold................................$35 $40 $75

HAMILTON, 22J., " Sea Cliff ", 14k #s, c.1961
gold filled $50 $75 $125

HAMILTON, 17J., " Sea - crest", c.1961
s. steel $35 $45 $90

HAMILTON, 17J., " Sea- glo ", c.1961
s. steel $35 $45 $90

HAMILTON, 17J., " Sea - guard", c.1962
s. steel $35 $45 $90

HAMILTON, 17J., " Sea - mate", c.1961
rolled gold................................$50 $75 $125

HAMILTON, 22J., " Sea Ranger" , 14K #s, c.1961
gold filled $75 $100 $150

HAMILTON, 17J., " Sea Rover B", c.1961
s. steel $40 $55 $90

HAMILTON, 17J., " Sea- scape ", c.1961
gold plate $35 $40 $90

HAMILTON, 17J., " Sea- scout B ", c.1961
s. steel $40 $45 $90

HAMILTON, 17J., " Sea - skip", c.1962
s. steel $35 $45 $90

HAMILTON, 17J., " Seaview", 14k #s, c.1961
14k $125 $150 $225

DIALS FOR MINT PRICES MUST BE ALL **ORIGINAL**.

HAMILTON, 17J.,"Seckron", dual dial, grade 980, c.1935
gold filled $750 $900 $1,200

HAMILTON, 17J.,"Seckron", grade 980B, dual dial, c.1940
gold filled $750 $900 $1,200

HAMILTON, 17J., "Sectometer", sweep sec., ca.1945
gold filled (hack).....................$75 $100 $165

HAMILTON, 18J.,"Sectometer B", sweep sec., ca.1948
gold filled (hack).....................$75 $100 $165

HAMILTON, 18J.,"Sectometer C", sweep sec., ca.1951
14k (hack)............................$135 $185 $225

Wrist Watches listed in this section are priced at the collectable
fair market **Trade Show** level as **complete** watches having an
original gold-filled case and stainless steel back, also with
original dial, leather watch band, and the entire original movement in good working order with no repairs needed.

HAMILTON, 18J., '' Sedgman'', Ca. 1952
14k $150 $185 $250

HAMILTON, 17 jewels, ''Sentinel,'', Ca. 1941
gold filled (hack) $75 $100 $165

HAMILTON, 18J., "Seville", c.1958
gold filled.................................$75 $95 $125

HAMILTON, 19J., "Sheldon", sold for $89.50 in 1953
gold filled.................................$100 $125 $175

HAMILTON, 19J., "Sherwood", (also - Seneca), Ca.1935
14k $200 $250 $350

HAMILTON, 22J., '' Sherwood M'', 14k #s, wood dial,
American walnut wood dial, c.1961
14k .... ★$700 $1,000 $1,500

HAMILTON, 17J., "Sherwood N"', 14k #s, auto-wind, wood
dial, **Mexican Mahogany wood dial,** c.1961
14k .... ★$600 $900 $1,400

HAMILTON, 22J., "Sherwood R", dial is made of wood,
(dial is American walnut) c.1961
14k .... ★$600 $850 $1,300

HAMILTON, 19J.," Sherwood, c.1949
gold filled $125 $150 $225

HAMILTON, 17J.,"Sheryll", matched styling to the
Sherwood for men, Sheryll = ladies watch, Ca. 1949
gold filled $75 $95 $125

HAMILTON, 22 jewels, "Sinclair" , c. 1957
14k $135 $175 $250

HAMILTON, 17 jewels, ''Sidney'' , c. 1937
gold filled $125 $150 $225

HAMILTON, 22J., " Sir Echo" ,14K #s, 6 diamond, c.1957
14k (W) $150 $200 $275

HAMILTON, 22J., " Sir Echo", 2 diamonds, 14K #s, c.1957
14k (W) $135 $165 $225

HAMILTON, 22J., " Sir Echo" , 14K #s, c.1957
14k (W) $125 $150 $200

HAMILTON, 17J., "Sloane " , c.1959
rolled gold............................... $45 $55 $95

HAMILTON, 17J.,"Spencer", gold numbers, ca.1951
10k,With Masonic symbols... $150 $185 $250
10k $100 $135 $200

⊕ A collector should expect to pay modestly higher prices
at local shops

HAMILTON, 19J., "Spur", enamel bezel, ca.1928
14k (y) .... ★ ★ ★$2,000 $2,400 $3,000
14k(w)...................... ★ ★ ★$2,000 $2,400 $3,000
14k(w) box & papers . ★ ★ ★ ★$2,500 $3,500 $5,500

HAMILTON, 22J., " Stafford" , 14K #s, c.1952
14k $150 $200 $275

HAMILTON, 18 jewels, "Steeldon" , c. 1949
s. steel $50 $70 $100

HAMILTON, 17 jewels, "Stanford" , c. 1940
gold filled $100 $125 $175

HAMILTON, 19 jewels, "Stanley" Ca. 1930
gold filled $150 $225 $325

HAMILTON, 22 jewels, "Staunton", c. 1957
14 k $135 $165 $225

DIALS FOR MINT PRICES MUST BE ALL **ORIGINAL**.

HAMILTON, 18J., "Stormking V", sterling silver dial, c.1957
s.steel $50 $75 $135

HAMILTON, 18J., "Stormking I", sterling silver dial, c.1957
18K..$200 $300 $450

HAMILTON, 18J., " Stormking VI", c.1955
gold filled $50 $75 $135

HAMILTON, 18J., "Stormking II", sterling silver dial, c.1957
14k $135 $175 $250

HAMILTON, 18J., " Stormking VII" , c.1961
gold filled $50 $75 $135

HAMILTON, 18J.,"Stormking III", sterling silver dial, c.1957
14k $135 $175 $250

HAMILTON, 18J., " Stormking VIII" , 14K #s, c.1961
10k $100 $135 $185

HAMILTON,18J.,"Stormking IV ", 14K#, c.1957
gold filled.................................$75 $100 $150

HAMILTON, 17J., " Stormking IX" , 14K #s, c.1961
14k $125 $175 $250

HAMILTON, 18J., "Stormking IV Military", c.1957
s.steel **24 hour** $200 $265 $350

HAMILTON, 19J.," Stuart ", c.1949
gold filled $100 $125 $175

HAMILTON, 17J., "Surf", c.1957
s.steel $50 $75 $125

HAMILTON, 17-19 jewels, "Sutton", Ca. 1936
gold filled................................ $175 $200 $250

HAMILTON, 22 jewels, "Sutton ", Ca. 1957
14k $185 $225 $275

HAMILTON, 17J., " Talbot ", Ca.1937
gold filled................................ $100 $125 $175

HAMILTON, 17J., " Talbot " , c.1961
gold filled................................ $75 $100 $150

HAMILTON, 17J., " Taylor", hinged lugs, Ca.1935
gold filled................................ $150 $185 $265

HAMILTON, 22J., " Thor" , 14K #s, c.1959
gold filled $225 $300 $450

HAMILTON, 19J., "Tildon", sold for $225.00 in 1953
14k $450 $500 $600

HAMILTON, 18J.," Todd ", c.1951
gold filled $75 $90 $150

HAMILTON, 19 jewels, "Touraine" , c. 1935
14k $150 $200 $300

HAMILTON, 17J, "Transcontinental A", Time Zone, Ca.1957
gold filled $250 $300 $450
Transcontinental B next page

HAMILTON, 17J, "Transcontinental B", Time Zone, Ca.1957
14k $600 $700 $900

HAMILTON, 22J., " Tuxedo II" , 44 diamonds,14K #s,
Ca. 1961
14k(w)...................................$250 $300 $400

HAMILTON, 22J., " Trent" , sterling silver dial, c.1955
gold filled...............................$100 $125 $175

HAMILTON, 17J, "Tyrone", 14k markers, Ca.1957
gold filled $100 $125 $175

HAMILTON, 17J, "Turner", Ca.1936
gold filled Y...........................$100 $135 $200
gold filled W.................. ★ ★$125 $200 $300

HAMILTON, 17J.," Vardon ", sealed. c.1949
s. steel $50 $75 $125

HAMILTON, 19J., "Turner", sold for $100.00 in 1953
(look-a-like) Donald, 14k
10k(w or y) $135 $175 $275

HAMILTON, 22J., " Valiant" , 14K #s, c.1959
gold filled $250 $300 $400

HAMILTON,22J., "Tuxedo B " , 44 diamonds,14K #s,
Ca. 1956
14k(w)................................... $250 $300 $400

HAMILTON, 17J, "Vernon", sterling silver dial, Ca.1957
10 k $100 $135 $200

Wrist Watches listed in this section are priced at the collectable
fair market **Trade Show** level as **complete** watches having an
original gold-filled case and stainless steel back, also with
original dial, leather watch band, and the entire original movement in good working order with no repairs needed.

🕐 A collector should expect to pay modestly higher prices
at local shops

HAMILTON, 17J., " Viking" , c.1961
rolled gold.................... $50 $75 $100

HAMILTON, 17J., " Viking II" , c.1961
rolled gold.................... $50 $75 $100

HAMILTON, 17 jewels, "Vincent" , c. 1941
gold filled...................$100 $125 $250

HAMILTON, 22J., "Viscount", sterling silver dial, ca.1955
14k .... ★★$400 $500 $650

HAMILTON, 17J., "Ward", ca.1957
gold filled...................$100 $125 $175

HAMILTON, 18J., "Warwick", sold for $150.00 in 1953
gold filled...................$100 $125 $175

DIALS FOR MINT PRICES MUST BE ALL **ORIGINAL**.

HAMILTON, 17 jewels, "Watson", Ca. 1930
gold filled plain $100 $135 $200
gold filled engraved .... ★★★$200 $265 $400

HAMILTON, 19 jewels, "Wayne", Ca. 1935
14k $250 $300 $425

HAMILTON, 17 jewels, "Webster", Ca. 1932
14k W .... ★★★★$500 $600 $800
gold filled $100 $135 $200

HAMILTON, 19J.," Wesley ", c.1941
14k $200 $250 $400

HAMILTON, 17 jewels, "Whitford", Ca. 1960
14k $100 $150 $225

🕐 A collector should expect to pay modestly higher prices
at local shops

HAMILTON, 17 jewels, "Whitman" , c. 1940
gold filled..............................$100 $125 $175

HAMILTON, 17 jewels, "Wilson", **flared**, Ca. 1954
gold filled $100 $125 $175

HAMILTON, 17J, "Whitman", sterling silver dial, Ca. 1957
gold filled................................$75 $100 $150
gold filled Masonic dial............$85 $125 $175

HAMILTON, 19J., "Windsor", sold for $87.50 in1953
gold filled $100 $125 $175

HAMILTON, 18 jewels, "Winfield", Ca. 1957
14k $125 $165 $225

HAMILTON, 17 jewels, "Whitney" , Ca. 1932
gold filled(w or y)........ ★ ★ $250 $300 $400

HAMILTON, 19 jewels, "Winthrop" , c. 1939
gold filled $100 $125 $175

HAMILTON, 19 jewels, "Wilkinson", Ca. 1930
14k (w or y) .... ★ ★ ★ ★$2,000 $2,200 $2,500

HAMILTON, 17 jewels, "Yorktown" , c. 1940
gold filled $125 $165 $250

HAMILTON, 19 jewels, "Wilshire", hinged lugs, c. 1941
gold filled yellow...................$175 $200 $250
gold filled coral.................. ★$200 $235 $300

HAMILTON, 17 jewels,"Yeoman II", Ca. 1965
gold filled $50 $65 $100

DIALS FOR MINT PRICES MUST BE ALL **ORIGINAL**.

HAMILTON, 17 jewels, "Accumatic II" , c. 1957
rolled gold..............................$45 $55 $90

HAMILTON, 17 jewels, "Accumatic **X**"
s. steel $45 $55 $90

HAMILTON, 17 jewels, "Accumatic **XI**"
s. steel $45 $55 $90

HAMILTON, 17J, "Accumatic **A-201**", Ca. 1968
shaped like a early TV screen dial.
14k $150 $175 $250

HAMILTON, 17 jewels, "Accumatic **A-575**", date
s. steel $45 $55 $90

HAMILTON, 17 jewels, "Accumatic **A-650**"
rolled gold $45 $55 $90

HAMILTON, 17 jewels, "Accumatic **A-651**"
gold plate $45 $55 $90

HAMILTON, 17 jewels, "Automatic **K-203**"
14k $100 $125 $175

HAMILTON, 17 jewels, "Automatic **K-303**"
10k $75 $95 $125

HAMILTON, 17 jewels, "Automatic **K-304**"
10k $75 $95 $125

Note: Hamilton acquired the Buren Watch
Factory of Switzerland in 1966 and
adapted a ultra thin self-winding movement for the **Thin-o-matic**.
(Bruen closed in 1972.)

HAMILTON, 17 jewels, "Automatic **K-414**"
gold filled.................................$60 $70 $100

HAMILTON, 17 jewels, "Automatic **K-417**"
gold filled $60 $70 $100

HAMILTON, 17 jewels, "Accumatic **VII**"
rolled gold................................$40 $50 $80

HAMILTON, 17 jewels, "Automatic **K-418**"
gold filled $60 $70 $100

HAMILTON, 17 jewels, "Automatic **K-415**"
gold filled................................$60 $70 $100

HAMILTON, 17 jewels, "Automatic **K-419**"
gold filled $60 $70 $100

HAMILTON, 17 jewels, "Automatic **K-416**"
gold filled................................$60 $70 $100

HAMILTON, 17 jewels, "Automatic **K-420**"
gold filled $60 $70 $100

HAMILTON, 17 jewels, "**Kinematic II**"
rolled gold................................$40 $50 $75

HAMILTON, 17 jewels, "Automatic **K-458**"
gold filled $60 $70 $100

Pricing in this Guide are fair market price for **COMPLETE** watches which are reflected from the "**NAWCC**" National and regional shows.

Some grades are not included. Their values can be determined by comparing with **similar** age, size, metal content, style, grades, or models such as **time only**, chronograph, repeater etc. listed.

HAMILTON, 17 jewels, "Automatic **K-459**"
gold filled..............................$60 $70 $100

HAMILTON, 17 jewels, "Automatic **K-460**"
gold filled..............................$60 $70 $100

HAMILTON, 17J, "Automatic **K-475**", with date,
Swiss movement, sold for $100.00 in 1960
gold filled.................★★★ $1,400 $1,600 $2,000

HAMILTON, 17 jewels, "Automatic **K-503**" Ca.1962
s. steel $50 $60 $100

HAMILTON, 17 jewels, "Automatic **K-507**"
s. steel $50 $60 $100

HAMILTON, 17 jewels, "Automatic **K-650**"
gold plate $40 $50 $75

HAMILTON, 18 jewels, "Thincraft **II**"
gold filled $50 $60 $100

HAMILTON, 17 jewels, "Thinline **2000**"
14k $100 $125 $175

HAMILTON, 17 jewels, "Thinline **2001**"
14k $100 $125 $175

HAMILTON, 17 jewels, "Thinline **3000**"
10k $75 $95 $125

HAMILTON, 17 jewels, "Thinline **4000**"
gold filled..................................\$50   \$60   \$100

HAMILTON, 17 jewels, "Thinline **4001**"
gold filled..................................\$50   \$60   \$100

HAMILTON, 17 jewels, "Thin-o-matic", **date**
rolled gold..................................\$50   \$60   \$85

HAMILTON, 17 jewels, "Thin-o-matic", **Masterpiece**
14k \$100   \$135   \$200

HAMILTON, 17 jewels, "Thin-o-matic **T-200**"
14k \$100   \$135   \$200

HAMILTON, 17 jewels, "Thin-o-matic **T-201**", **6- diamonds**
14k \$150   \$185   \$250

HAMILTON, 17 jewels, "Thin-o-matic **T-201**"
14k \$100   \$135   \$200

HAMILTON, 17 jewels, "Thin-o-matic **T-202**"
14k \$100   \$135   \$200

HAMILTON, 17 jewels, "Thin-o-matic **T-300**"
10k \$85   \$110   \$150

HAMILTON, 17 jewels, "Thin-o-matic **T-400**"
gold filled \$40   \$50   \$100

🕐 Pricing in this Guide are fair market price for **COMPLETE** watches which are reflected from the "**NAWCC**" National and regional shows.

HAMILTON, 17 jewels, ''Thin-o-matic **T-401**''
gold filled..................................$70 $80 $100

HAMILTON, 17 jewels, ''Thin-o-matic **T-402**''
gold filled..................................$40 $60 $100

HAMILTON, 17J, "Thin-o-matic **T-403**", Swiss movement
Ca. 1960
rolled gold (with date). ★ ★ ★$500 $650 $850
gold filled **W**...................★ ★$450 $525 $650
gold filled **Y**.......................★ $350 $425 $550

HAMILTON, 17 jewels, ''Thin-o-matic **T-404**''
gold filled..................................$40 $60 $100

HAMILTON, 17 jewels, ''Thin-o-matic **T-405**''
gold filled..................................$40 $60 $100

HAMILTON, 17 jewels, ''Thin-o-matic **T-450**''
gold filled $40 $60 $100

HAMILTON, 17 jewels, ''Thin-o-matic **T-451**''
gold filled $40 $60 $100

HAMILTON, 17 jewels, ''Thin-o-matic **T-475**''
gold filled $40 $50 $100

HAMILTON, 17 jewels, ''Thin-o-matic **T-476**'', date
gold filled $40 $50 $100

HAMILTON, 17 jewels, ''Thin-o-matic **T-500**''
s. steel $40 $50 $100

Wrist Watches listed in this section are priced at the collectable fair market **Trade Show** level as **complete** watches having an original gold-filled case and stainless steel back, also
with original dial, leather watch band, and the entire original
movement in good working order with no repairs needed.

🕐 Some grades are not included. Their values can be
determined by comparing with **similar** age, size, metal
content, style, grades, or models such as **time only**,
chronograph, repeater etc. listed.

HAMILTON, 17 jewels, "Thin-o-matic **T-501**"
s. steel $40 $50 $100

HAMILTON, 17 jewels, "Thin-o-matic **T-502**"
s. steel $40 $50 $100

HAMILTON, 17 jewels, "Thin-o-matic **T-575**" date
s. steel $40 $50 $100

HAMILTON, 17 jewels, "Thin-o-matic **T-650**"
rolled gold................................$40 $50 $90

HAMILTON, 17 jewels, "Thinline **5000**"
s. steel $40 $50 $100

HAMILTON, 17 jewels, "Cushion ", **(round)**, grade 987,
ca.1927
gold filled $75 $100 $175

HAMILTON, 17 jewels, "Cushion", plain, grade 987,
ca.1927
14k $200 $250 $325
gold filled $75 $100 $175

HAMILTON, 17J.,"Cushion " , no sec., grade 986, c.1923
gold filled $75 $100 $165

HAMILTON, 17 jewels, "Cushion", **engraved**, grade 987,
note **radial**, ca.1927
14k $200 $265 $350
gold filled $100 $125 $175

HAMILTON, 17 jewels, tonneau engraved
14k $225 $300 $400
gold filled $100 $125 $185

HAMILTON, 17J.,"Tonneau" plain
14k $200 $235 $325
gold filled................................$75 $100 $165

HAMILTON, 17J., "Square", cut corner, no sec., ca.1927
gold filled................................$75 $100 $165
14k $100 $135 $250

HAMILTON, 17J., "Square B", cut corner, with sec., ca.1927
gold filled................................$75 $100 $165
14k $125 $185 $300

HAMILTON, 17J., "Square", cut corner, enameled, ca.1927
gold filled................................$85 $125 $175
14k $135 $200 $350

HAMILTON, 17J., Square cut corner, **engraved LUGS**
gold filled................................$75 $100 $165

HAMILTON, 17J., "Square B", engraved, ca.1931
gold filled $75 $100 $165
14k $100 $150 $235

HAMILTON, 17 jewels, "Raleigh", engraved fancy, Ca.1930
gold filled $100 $150 $250

HAMILTON, 17J., "Barrel", Plain bezel, ca.1928
gold filled $75 $100 $165
14k $100 $135 $225

HAMILTON, 17J., "Barrel", engraved, ca.1927
gold filled $75 $100 $165
14k $125 $150 $250

HAMILTON, 17J., grade 987, w/ gold or Platinum buckle,
note **Radial**, sold for $485.00 in 1927
Platinum.................... ★ ★ ★$2,200 $2,500 $3,000

HAMILTON, 17J., cal.987, **enamel** on case, c.1930
14K..$700 $800 $1,000

HAMILTON, 17 jewels, engraved bezel, hinged back
Note **Radial**
14k(w)....................................$700 $800 $1,000

HAMILTON, 17J., "Oval", plain or engraved, grade 987,
sold for in1927 $70.00 Gold Filled & $105.50 14K.
gold filled........................... ★$900 $1,100 $1,500
14K(White - Green).. ★★★$1,900 $2,100 $2,500

HAMILTON, 17 jewels, engraved bezel, c. 1920
14k $150 $185 $300

HAMILTON, 17J, *Hamilton Illinois* on dial, sold by Hamilton & Illinois marked on case with Illinois mvt. (**crossover**).
gold filled $100 $135 $175

HAMILTON, 19 jewels
platinum C&B $1,000 $1,200 $1,500

HAMILTON,17- 19J.,"bomb timer", c.1943
gold filled $400 $500 $700

HAMILTON, 17-19J.,"bomb timer", c.1943
base metal $250 $325 $550

HAMILTON, 15 J., military frogman style, waterproof
(USN BU SHIPS on dial), canteen style.
base metal $450 $650 $900

HAMILTON, 17 J., military issue, **hack** setting, c.1960s
base metal $100 $125 $175

HAMILTON, 17 J., British issue note broad arrow symbol,
Grade 649, swiss movement
base metal $100 $125 $175

HAMILTON, 7 J., military issue, hack setting, note "H3" for
Hydrogen 3 and radioactive symbol, c.1970s
base metal $75 $100 $150

HAMILTON, 17J., "Aqua-date", autow, waterproof - 600 feet
elapsed time indicator, sold for $115.00 in 1966
s. steel $100 $125 $175

HAMILTON, 17J., chronomatic "A", auto wind, Ca.1975
s. steel $400 $465 $550

HAMILTON, 17J., chronomatic "B", auto wind, Ca.1975
s. steel $225 $275 $385

HAMILTON, chronomatic "C", auto wind, Ca.1975
s. steel $200 $250 $350

Hamilton, 17J., Chrono Diver, stem wind, Ca.1975
s. steel $200 $250 $350

HAMILTON, **ELECTRONIC** railroad approved, Ca.1975
s. steel $100 $150 $250

HAMILTON, 17-19 jewels, diamond dial, hooded lugs
14k $800 $900 $1,100

HAMILTON, 17-19 jewels, diamond dial
14k(w)....................................$800 $900 $1,100

HAMILTON, 17-19 jewels, diamond dial , curved
platinum $1,000 $1,100 $1,300
14k $800 $900 $1,100

HAMILTON, 17-19J., **Top Hat,** diamond dial, c. 1940
14k $800 $900 $1,100

HAMILTON, 17-19 jewels, diamond dial
14k $500 $600 $900

HAMILTON, 17-19 jewels, diamond dial, hooded lugs
14k $600 $750 $1,000

HAMILTON, 17-19 jewels,diamond dial
14k $600 $750 $1,000

HAMILTON, 17-19 jewels, diam. dial, c.1948, **TOP HAT**
platinum..............................$1,200 $1,500 $2,000
14k (w) $900 $1,000 $1,200

HAMILTON, 17-19 jewels, diamond dial
14k (w) $600 $700 $900

HAMILTON, 17-19 jewels, diamond dial, hooded lugs
platinum..............................$1,200 $1,500 $2,000

HAMILTON, 17-19 jewels, diamond dial
platinum..............................$1,200 $1,500 $2,000
14k (w) $900 $1,000 $1,200

Wrist Watches listed in this section are priced at the collectable
fair market **Trade Show** level as **complete** watches having an
original gold-filled case and stainless steel back, also with
original dial, leather watch band, and the entire original movement in good working order with no repairs needed.

HAMILTON, 17-19J., mystery dial with diamonds & **bezel**
Swiss made
18k $550 $650 $800
14k $450 $550 $650

HAMILTON, 17J. "Lord Lancaster **B**", sold for $89.50 in 1966
gold plate $125 $150 $200

HAMILTON, 17J. "Lord Lancaster **C**", sold for $125.00 in 1966
gold filled...............................$150 $175 $250

HAMILTON, 17J. "Lord Lancaster **H**", sold for $115.00 in 1966
gold plate $125 $150 $200

HAMILTON, 17J. "Lord Lancaster **K**", sold for $89.50 in 1966
gold plate $125 $150 $200

HAMILTON, 17J. "Lord Lancaster **L**", 24 diamonds, Ca. 1966
14K(W) $175 $235 $350

HAMILTON, 17J. "Lord Lancaster **M**", 40 diamonds, Ca. 1966
14K(W) $175 $235 $350

HAMILTON, 17J. "Lord Lancaster **N**", 36 diamonds, Ca. 1966
14K(W) $175 $235 $350

HAMILTON, 17J. "Lord Lancaster **R**", sold for $210.00 in 1966
14K(W) $175 $235 $350

HAMILTON, 17J. "Lord Lancaster **T**", sold for $275.00 in 1966
14K(W) $175 $235 $350

HAMILTON, 17J.,Chronograph,Valjoux, cal# 7733, Ca.1971
s. steel $200 $235 $350

HAMILTON, 17J., Date, chronog. Valjoux cal#7733,Ca.1971
s. steel $225 $275 $385

HAMILTON17J., Chronograph, Screw Back
s. steel $200 $235 $350

HAMILTON,17J., 40 diamond bezel, Ca. 1955
18k (w)...................................$300 $365 $475

HAMILTON,17J., "Bianca", diamond & sapphire, c.1933
18k(w)....................................$150 $175 $250

HAMILTON,17J., " Bryn Mawr ", c.1933
14k..$60 $70 $100

HAMILTON,17J., " Briarcliffe ", c.1933
gold filled.................................$30 $35 $50

HAMILTON,17J., " Caroline ", cal.995, c.1933
gold filled.................................$20 $25 $35

HAMILTON,17J., " Cedarcrest ", cal.995, c.1933
14k..$50 $60 $80

HAMILTON,17J., " Chevy Chase A ", c.1933
14k(w).....................................$60 $70 $90

HAMILTON,17J., " Chevy Chase B ", cal.989 , c.1933
14k $70 $80 $100

HAMILTON,17J., " Chevy Chase C ", cal. , c.1933
14k(w)..............................$60 $70 $90

HAMILTON,17J., " Chevy Chase E ", c.1933
14k(w)..............................$70 $80 $100

HAMILTON,17J., " Diane ", c.1933
14k $60 $70 $90

HAMILTON,17J., " Drexel ", cal.955 , c.1933
14k $70 $75 $90

HAMILTON,17J., " Edgewood ", c.1933
gold filled..............................$30 $35 $45

HAMILTON,17J., " Eugenie ", 44 diamonds, c.1933
platinum..............................$250 $275 $350

HAMILTON,17J., " Glenwood ", cal.955, c.1933
gold filled..............................$30 $35 $50

HAMILTON,17J., " Linden Hall ", c.1933
gold filled..............................$30 $35 $50

HAMILTON,17J.," Maritza ", 6 diamonds, cal.955 , c.1933
18k(w)..............................$80 $90 $120

HAMILTON,17J., " Mayfield ", cal.955 , c.1933
gold filled..............................$30 $35 $50

HAMILTON,17J., " Newcomb ", cal.989, c.1933
gold filled..............................$30 $35 $50

HAMILTON,17J., " Nightingale ", 40 diamonds, c.1933
18k(w)..............................$200 $225 $300

HAMILTON,17J., " Portia ", 8 diamonds, c.1933
18k(w)..............................$200 $225 $300

HAMILTON,17J., " Trudy ", c.1948
14k..............................$50 $60 $80

Grade 986A, 6/0 size
Open face, ¾ plate movt., 17 jewels, double roller

Grade 987, 6/0 size
Hunting, ¾ plate movt., 17 jewels, double roller

Grade 987A, 6/0 size
Open face, ¾ plate movt., 17 jewels, double roller

Grade 987S, 6/0 size
Hunting, ¾ plate movt., 17 jewels, double roller

Grade 747, 8/0 size
Open face, ¾ plate movt., 17 jewels, double roller

Grade 980, 14/0 size
Open face, ¾ plate movt., 17 jewels, double roller

Grade 982, 14/0 size
Open face, ¾ plate movt., 19 jewels, double roller

Grade 982M, 14/0 size
Open face, ¾ plate movt., 19 jewels, double roller

Grade 989, 18/0 size
Open face, ¾ plate movt., 17 jewels, double roller

Grade 997, 20/0 size
Open face, ¾ plate movt., 17 jewels, double roller

Grade 721, 21/0 size
Open face, ¾ plate movt., 17 jewels, double roller

Grade 995, 21/0 size
Open face, ¾ plate movt., 17 jewels, double roller

Grade 911, 22/0 size
Open face, ¾ plate movt., 17 jewels, double roller

Grade 911M, 22/0 size
Open face, ¾ plate movt., 17 jewels, double roller

Grade 780, 21/0 size
17 jewels

Grade 770, 12/0 size
22 jewels

Grade 761, 21/0 size
22 jewels

Grade 757, 21/0 size
22 jewels

Grade 753, 12/0 size, 19 jewels
Grade 752, 12/0 size, 17 jewels

Grade 754, 12/0 size, 19 jewels
Grade 770, 12/0 size, 17 jewels

Grade 750 & 751, 21/0 size
17 jewels

Grade 748, 8/0 size
18 jewels

Grade 747, 8/0 size
17 jewels

22 m/m 20 m/m 19 m/m 18 m/m 16 m/m 14 m/m 13 m/m 12 m/m 11 m/m 10 m/m 8 m/m

7/8" 13/16" 3/4" 11/16" 5/8" 9/16" 1/2" 7/16" 3/8" 5/16"

To determine your wrist watch band size use the above gauge and measure between the lugs. The band sizes are listed on each side of the gauge.

Grade 735, 8/0 size
18 jewels

Grade 730, 8/0 size
17 jewels

Grade 679, 17 jewels
Grade 692, 694 - calendar

Grade 666 & 663, 17 jewels
Grade 668 - calendar

Grade 658, 661, 667, 17 jewels
Grade 665, 23J, **Grade 664**, 25J
Grade 662, 690 - calendar, 17J

Grade 623 & 624, 17 jewels

Grade 500
Electric

Grade 505, electric, 11 jewels

Cell Clamp for
500A or 501

THE SPUR

**1930
AD**

A Hamilton the true Sportsman will
love. In either 14K yellow or white
gold with numerals of gold in a black
enamel circlet on the outside of the
case—19 jewel movement, $125

HAMPDEN,15J., **old stock, all original**, engraved case, c.1925
Note the **radial**
gold filled..................................$75 $100 $185

HAMPDEN, 17 jewels., c. 1936
14k $125 $165 $250

HAMPDEN, 17J., by Lonville W. Co., c. 1936
gold filled.................................$50 $75 $125

HAMPDEN, 17 jewels, regulator dial, c. 1938
gold filled.................................$350 $400 $500

HAMPDEN, 15J, **old stock, all original**, c. 1928
14k $125 $165 $250
gold filled.................................$100 $125 $165

⊕ Some grades are not included. Their values can be
determined by comparing with **similar** age, size, metal
content, style, grades, or models such as **time only**,
chronograph, repeater etc. listed.

HAMPDEN,11=15J., "LEVER SET" , 3/0 size, **old stock, all
original**, c.1928
silver.......................................$125 $165 $250

HAMPDEN, 15J, **old stock, all original**, c. 1928
14k...$125 $165 $225
gold filled.................................$75 $100 $150

HAMPDEN, 11J., Molly Stark, **old stock, all original**, c. 1928
base metal................................$40 $50 $75

HAMPDEN, 7J., tonneau shaped, **old stock, all original**, c. 1928
gold filled.................................$75 $85 $135

HARMAN,7J.,doctor style doctors watch
gold filled.................................$250 $300 $450

HARMAN, 17J., **one button** chronog., mid size, c.1940s
s. steel $250 $275 $325

HARVEL, 17 jewels, date-o-graph
s. steel.....................................$75 $95 $150

HARMAN, 17J., **two button** chronog., mid size, c.1945
gold filled................................$200 $265 $375

HARWOOD, 15 jewels, early self winding, c. 1928
18k (w)...................................$700 $850 $1,200
14k...$600 $700 $900
gold filled..............................$200 $300 $500
s. steel...................................$250 $350 $550

HARVARD, 17 jewels, chronog., tach-telemeter
s. steel $200 $265 $350

HARWOOD, 15 J., rim set by turning bezel clockwise
9k...$350 $425 $625

HARVARD, 17 jewels, 1/5 sec. chronog.
s. steel $200 $265 $375

HARWOOD, 15 jewels, back set, c. 1925
18k...$450 $550 $750

Wrist Watches listed in this section are priced at the collectable
fair market **Trade Show** level as **complete** watches having an
original gold-filled case and stainless steel back, also with
original dial, leather watch band, and the entire original movement in good working order with no repairs needed.

🕐 Pricing in this Guide are fair market price for **COM-
PLETE** watches which are reflected from the "**NAWCC**" National and regional shows.

HASTE, 17J., triple calendar moon ph.
gold filled...............................$250 $300 $400

HAYDEN, 7J., by Solomax W.Co., hinged case
gold filled..................................$60 $75 $110

HEBDOMAS, 7-15 J., visible escapement, **8 day** movement
s. steel $400 $500 $650

HEBDOMAS, 7-15 J., **8 day** movement, Ca. 1915
s. steel $200 $250 $325

HELBROS, 17 jewels, aux.sec., alarm
gold filled..................................$75 $100 $135

HELBROS, 7 jewels, "Fairfax", Ca 1928
gold filled..................................$50 $60 $90

HELBROS, 17 jewels, aux. sec.
gold filled..................................$40 $50 $80

HELBROS, 17 jewels,
14k................................$95 $125 $175

HELBROS, 7J., "Federal", c. 1929
base metal..................................$25 $35 $75

HELBROS,17J., **24** hour dial
base metal..................................$40 $50 $95

HENDA, 15J., direct read, c. 1930
nickel..$75 $110 $175

Pricing in this Guide are fair market price for **COM-PLETE** watches which are reflected from the "**NAWCC**" National and regional shows.

HERMES, 17J., big wire lugs, enamel dial
14k $100 $125 $200

HELVETIA, 15 jewels, Ca. 1935
9k $75 $100 $135

HELVETIA, 21 jewels, auto wind
gold filled................................$30 $45 $80

HEUER, 15 jewels, chronog., 2 reg., one button,
14k $1,100 $1,300 $1,600

🕐 Some grades are not included. Their values can be
determined by comparing with **similar** age, size, metal
content, style, grades, or models such as **time only**,
chronograph, repeater etc. listed.

🕐 Pricing in this Guide are fair market price for **COMPLETE** watches which are reflected from the "**NAWCC**" National and regional shows.

HEUER, 17J., chronog., 3 reg., 3 dates, moon phase
18k.................................$1,800 $2,000 $2,500
s. steel.............................$1,000 $1,200 $1,600

HEUER, 17 J., chronog., 3 reg., "Carrera", c.1960
s. steel................................$700 $950 $1,300

HEUER, 17 jewels, chronog., 3 dates, 3 reg. c.1948
14k.................................$800 $1,000 $1,400
s. steel...............................$600 $725 $900

HEUER, 17 jewels, "Carrera," chronog., 2 reg., c.1960s
14k.................................$1,000 $1,200 $1,600
s. steel...............................$600 $800 $1,200

HEUER,17J., "Carrera", RF# 2547, day date month, Ca. 1970
14k $1,200 $1,400 $1,800
s. steel $900 $1,000 $1,200

HEUER,17J., "Monaco", date, c. 1974
base metal...........................$1,000 $1,200 $1,600

HEUER,17J., "Camaro", by Valjoux #7730, c. 1965
14k $700 $850 $1,100
s. steel $400 $500 $700

HEUER,17J., TAG, split sec., date, 600 ft., gold & s. steel,
sold new for $1,895.00 in Ca.1991
gold tone $200 $250 $350
s. steel & gold tone $200 $250 $350

HEUER,17J., "Autavia", cal.72, micro rotor, c. 1972
s. steel $350 $450 $600

HEUER, 17 jewels, day-date-month, **moon phase**
s. steel...................................$350 $465 $700

Wrist Watches listed in this section are priced at the collectable
fair market **Trade Show** level as **complete** watches having an
original gold-filled case and stainless steel back, also with
original dial, leather watch band, and the entire original movement in good working order with no repairs needed.

A collector should expect to pay modestly higher prices
at local shops

Some grades are not included. Their values can be
determined by comparing with **similar** age, size, metal
content, style, grades, or models such as **time only**,
chronograph, repeater etc. listed.

HEUER, 17 jewels, day-date-month
14k...$300 $350 $465
s. steel...................................$150 $225 $365

E. HUGUENIN, 17J., "Black Star", Ca. 1940
14k $250 $300 $400

ILLINOIS, 17J., GJS, 207 on Mvt., model 250 on case
14K .... ★★★★★$1,300 $1,500 $1,800

ILLINOIS, 15-17J., gold center wheel, Ca.1925
silver(Grill protection)............ $300 $375 $550

ILLINOIS, 17J., **direct read**, Aluminum, case & band, c.1925
Chrome,case & band $225 $265 $350
Aluminum case & Aluminum band
.... ★★★★★ $2,000 $2,300 $2,700

ILLINOIS, 17J., "Art Deco", grade # 207, Ca.1925
same case style as <u>Chesterfield</u>
gold filled................................ $400 $465 $550

ILLINOIS, 17J., "Andover", Ca. 1929
gold filled $175 $200 $285

ILLINOIS, 15J., "Arlington also Hawthorne", Ca. 1929
gold filled $175 $200 $285

ILLINOIS, 17J., case # 196, "Art Deco", cal.207, c.1925
same case style as <u>Chesterfield</u>
gold filled................................ $250 $300 $400

ILLINOIS, 17J., "Ardsley", Ca. 1929
gold filled $150 $185 $275

🕐 Some grades are not included. Their values can be
determined by comparing with **similar** age, size, metal
content, style, grades, or models such as **time only**,
chronograph, repeater etc. listed.

ILLINOIS, 17 jewels, "Aviator"
gold filled..............................$200 $265 $350

ILLINOIS, 17-21J.= Beau Monde=14k, Beau Gest =WGF
14k $400 $500 $650
gold filled **W** $200 $250 $350

ILLINOIS, 21J., " BARONET ", GJS, cal.601, c.1925
14k $500 $625 $800
gold filled..............................$200 $265 $350

ILLINOIS, 15J., "Beau Royal "
gold filled $200 $265 $350

ILLINOIS, 19J., " Beau Brummel"
14k $700 $800 $1,000

ILLINOIS, 17J., " Blackstone"
gold filled $150 $200 $300

ILLINOIS, 17-19 jewels, "Beau Brummel",
19J. sold for $60. & 15J. for $50. in 1929
gold filled................................$275 $335 $450

ILLINOIS, 15J., showing as advertised the "Bostonian" with
metal band also look a like "Commodore" came in leather.
gold filled $150 $185 $250

ILLINOIS, 17J., "Beau Brummel", also aux.sec @ 6,Ca.1929
gold filled..............................$275 $335 $450

ILLINOIS, 17J., " Cavalier "
gold filled $165 $210 $300

DIALS FOR MINT PRICES MUST BE ALL **ORIGINAL**.

ILLINOIS, 15 jewels, "Champion"
gold filled..............................$150 $185 $250

ILLINOIS, 19-21 jewels, "Consul"
14k $600 $700 $800

ILLINOIS, 15 jewels, "Chatham"
gold filled..............................$150 $225 $325

ILLINOIS, 19-21J., "Consul", 21J.sold for $90. in 1929
14k .... ★$650 $750 $900
14k smooth bezel......... ★★★$750 $900 $1,200

ILLINOIS, 17J., " The Chief's", chased bezel, note radial
gold filled (w).......................$150 $200 $300

ILLINOIS, 17J., " Derby also Pimlico"
gold filled $150 $225 $375

ILLINOIS, 15-17J., "Chieftain", 15J. sold for $40. in 1929
gold filled..............................$400 $500 $675

ILLINOIS, 15-17J., "Ensign", aux.sec.at 6, sold for $40. in 1929
gold filled plain bezel............$225 $275 $385
gold filled engraved bezel......$250 $300 $425

ILLINOIS, 15-17J., showing as advertised the "Commodore"
with leather band also look a like "Bostonian" came in metal.
gold filled..............................$150 $185 $250

ILLINOIS, 15-17J., "Ensign" engraved bezel, aux. sec. at 9
gold filled $250 $300 $425

ILLINOIS, 17J., " Frontenac "
gold filled...............................$175 $210 $275

ILLINOIS, 17J., " Finalist also Chesterfield"
gold filled...............................$300 $365 $450

ILLINOIS, 17J., " Futura ", rect. mvt., sold for $60. in 1929
gold filled...............................$200 $265 $350

ILLINOIS, 17J., " Guardsman ", plain, rotor second dial
gold filled...............................$350 $400 $475

ILLINOIS, 17J., ''Guardsman '', engraved, cal.307, c.1929
gold filled...............................$350 $400 $500
Note: Many Illinois look the same but with two names old ads
show same **style case** but with different bands. Example in 1931
a advertisement for a New Yorker with leather band grade
607,17J., priced at $50.00 & Manhattan with metal band grade
607,17J., priced at $55.00. The same 1931 ad a New Yorker
with leather band grade 601, 21J., priced at $75.00 & Manhattan
with metal band grade 601, 21J., priced at $85.00. Larchmont
leather & Vernon metal, Commodore leather Bostonian metal
and others with same **style case** & different bands.

ILLINOIS, 17 jewels, "Hudson"
gold filled $175 $210 $285

ILLINOIS, 17J., "Jolly Roger", engraved bezel, Ca.1929
gold filled (smooth bezel) $450 $565 $800
gold filled (green, engraved).. $500 $750 $1,100
gold filled (White, engraved). $350 $465 $600

ILLINOIS, 17J., " Kenilworth " also "Gallahad"
gold filled $225 $285 $450

ILLINOIS, 17 jewels, "Larchmont also Vernon",
gold filled $175 $210 $275

ILLINOIS, 17J, "Major", engraved bevel & plain lugs
gold filled plain lugs $250 $300 $400
gold filled engraved lugs........$250 $300 $400
gold filled plain bezel............$250 $300 $400
note right dial= **radial**, & sold for $42.50 in 1929

ILLINOIS,17-21J., "Manhattan or New Yorker", aux. sec. at 9
14k $385 $500 $700

ILLINOIS, 17-19J., "Marquis", plain,19J.sold for $60 in 1929
gold filled $250 $300 $400

ILLINOIS, 17-21J., **"Yorktown** or New Yorker", with smooth
bezel & aux. sec. at 9, also came with aux. sec. at 6
gold filled................................$200 $265 $375

ILLINOIS, 17J., "Mate", engraved, sold for $42.50 in 1929
gold filled $175 $225 $300

ILLINOIS, 17-21J., "Manhattan", aux. sec. at 6, metal band
14k $385 $500 $700

ILLINOIS, 17J., "Mate" , plain
gold filled $150 $195 $275

ILLINOIS, 17-21J, "New Yorker", aux. sec. at 6, leather band
gold filled................................$200 $265 $350

ILLINOIS, 17J., engraved case in "Maxine", plain, ladies
gold filled $125 $150 $200

ILLINOIS, 17-19 jewels, "Marquis", engraved, curved case
gold filled................................$250 $300 $400

ILLINOIS, 17 jewels, "Maxine", wire lugs, ladies
14k $175 $200 $250

ILLINOIS, 17J., "Medalist also Wembley", rect. mvt. c.1929
sold for $60. in 1929
gold filled.............................$150 $200 $300

ILLINOIS, 17 jewels, "Piccadilly" in white or yellow G.F.
came with Luminous or Modern as a option
sold for $45. in 1929
gold filled plain.......................$800 $1,000 $1,400
gold filled engraved...............$900 $1,100 $1,500

ILLINOIS, 17 jewels, "Pilot"
gold filled..............................$200 $235 $300

ILLINOIS, 17 jewels, "Prince"
gold filled..............................$200 $235 $300

ILLINOIS, 17J., "Ritz", white bezel & yellow center case
also called "Valedictorian"
gold filled..............................$400 $500 $800

ILLINOIS, 15 jewels, "Rockingham also Potomac"
gold filled $200 $265 $350

ILLINOIS, 17J., " Rockliffe ", cal.805, c.1925
14k $350 $400 $500

ILLINOIS, 15 jewels, "Sangamo"
gold filled $200 $285 $450

ILLINOIS, 17J., " Skyway ", engraved case, G#307
gold filled .... ★★★$1,400 $1,600 $2,000

ILLINOIS, 17J., "Special", plain bezel, ca.1929
nickel $250 $325 $450

Note: Auxiliary seconds = (aux. sec.), aux. sec. at 6 o'clock
position is a hunting model, aux. sec. at 9 is a open face
model.

DIALS FOR MINT PRICES MUST BE ALL **ORIGINAL**.

ILLINOIS, 17J., "Special", engraved bezel, ca.1929
nickel......................................$250 $300 $450

ILLINOIS, 17J., "Trophy also Westchester"
gold filled $125 $185 $275

ILLINOIS, 17J., "Speedway", sold for $42.50 in 1929
gold filled..............................$250 $325 $500

ILLINOIS, 17J., "Tuxedo", 2 tone, sold for $75. in 1929
14k $500 $650 $1,000

ILLINOIS, 15 jewels, "Standish"
gold filled..............................$175 $235 $350

ILLINOIS, 17J., "Viking", sold for $42.50 in 1929
gold filled $250 $300 $450

ILLINOIS, 17J., " Sterling ", direct read, c.1929
sterling silver $235 $295 $400

ILLINOIS, 17 jewels, "Off Duty", stars on bezel, Ca. 1927
gold filled .... ★★★$1,100 $1,300 $1,600

ILLINOIS, 15-17J., left "Townsman" carved case
right "Metropolitan", **2-tone** carved case
gold filled Townsman.............$250 $300 $450
gold filled Metropolitan ..... ★$400 $550 $885

ILLINOIS, 15J., "Urbana",
gold filled $175 $225 $350

Note: Auxiliary seconds = (aux. sec.), aux. sec. at 6 o'clock
position is a hunting model, aux. sec. at 9 is a open face model.

ILLINOIS, 17J., Debonair model "A", ca.1953
base metal $50 $75 $125

ILLINOIS, 17J., Debonair model "B", ca.1953
base metal $50 $75 $125

ILLINOIS, 17J., Debonair model "C", ca.1953
base metal $50 $75 $125

ILLINOIS, 17J., Debonair model "D", ca.1953
base metal $50 $65 $100

ILLINOIS, 17J., Debonair model "E", ca.1953
base metal $50 $75 $125

ILLINOIS, 17J., Debonair model "F", ca.1953
base metal $50 $75 $125

ILLINOIS, 17J., Topper model "A", ca.1953
base metal $50 $75 $125

ILLINOIS, 17J., Topper model "B", ca.1953
base metal $50 $75 $125

ILLINOIS, 17J., Automatic model "A", ca.1953
gold filled $50 $65 $85

ILLINOIS, 17J., Automatic model "B", ca.1953
base metal $40 $50 $70

ILLINOIS, 17J., Automatic **Signamatic / wind ind.**, ca.1953
base metal $50 $65 $85

ILLINOIS, 17J., Automatic Nautilus "A", ca.1953
waterproof anti-magnetic
s. steel $50 $60 $75

ILLINOIS, 15-17J., Generic, Telephone Dial, **enamel dial**
14k $700 $850 $1,100

ILLINOIS, 15-17J., Generic, Admiral Evans, **enamel dial**
sterling $500 $625 $800

ILLINOIS, 15J., Generic, seconds at "9" c.1929
gold filled............................... $125 $185 $275

ILLINOIS, 15-17-19J., Generic, Square cut corner **plain**
gold filled............................... $125 $185 $275

ILLINOIS, 15-17-19J., Generic, Square cut corner **engraved**
gold filled............................... $125 $185 $275

ILLINOIS, 17J., Generic Cushion Form, round dial
gold filled $150 $200 $300

ILLINOIS, 19J., Generic Cushion Form, plain, sec. at 6
gold filled $150 $200 $300

ILLINOIS, 19J., Generic Cushion Form, engraved, sec. at 9
gold filled $150 $200 $300

ILLINOIS, 19J., Generic Cushion Form, plain, sec. at 9
gold filled $150 $200 $300
14k (enamel dial).................. $200 $325 $500

ILLINOIS, 15-17J., Generic, Ca.1926
sterling silver........................ $300 $385 $650

Note: *Generic* period about 1915 to about 1927 is a period
ILLINOIS advertised "Only delivered fitted in cases supplied
by jobbers". July 1st 1924 ad **retail** selling price "Movement
only NO. 907, 19 jewels at $35.00, & NO. 903, 15 jewels
$26.50". Jewelers **cost** "Movement only NO. 907, $20.00 &
NO. 903, $14.50". After about 1934 Illinois wrist watch ads fade
away and not seen again till about 1953, ads state cased & timed
by Hamilton. See July 1926 Illinois ad and jobbers ad this book.

ILLINOIS, 17J., Generic, Cushion round, engraved, c.1926
gold filled.............................$150 $200 $300

ILLINOIS, 17J., GENERIC, tonneau style, hand engraved,
14k (W).................................$150 $200 $300

ILLINOIS, 17J., Generic, Cushion round, plain, c.1926
nickel.......................................$100 $125 $200

ILLINOIS, 15-19J., GENERIC, square, c.1925
gold filled $125 $185 $275

ILLINOIS, 17J., Barrel & side of case engraved, Ca.1928
S# 5,091,926, G# 24, 3/0 size, M# 4 HC, gold gilded train.
base metal $85 $100 $150

ILLINOIS, 17J., black or blue **enamel** bezel, Ca.1929
base metal $250 $300 $400

ILLINOIS, 17J., Generic, Barrel engraved, sec at 9, ca. 1926
gold filled..............................$125 $185 $275

ILLINOIS, 15J., GENERIC, c.1926
gold filled $100 $150 $225

ILLINOIS, 17 jewels, GENERIC, hand engraved, wire lugs
14k (W)..................................$150 $200 $300

ILLINOIS, 17J., GENERIC, engraved case
silver $135 $175 $250

ILLINOIS, 15J., GENERIC, engraved bezel, GJS, c.1926
14k (w)..................................$150 $185 $250

ILLINOIS, 15J., **GENERIC, winds at 12:00 o'clock**
silver $200 $265 $350

ILLINOIS, 17J., Golden Treasure "A", ca.1953
14k $65 $75 $95

ILLINOIS, 17J., Golden Treasure "B", ca.1953
14k $65 $75 $110

ILLINOIS, 17J., Kimberly "A", 8 diamonds, ca.1953
gold filled..............................$75 $95 $150

ILLINOIS, 17J., Kimberly "B", 2 diamonds, ca.1953
gold filled..............................$70 $80 $110

ILLINOIS, 15-17J., lady's watch, black enamel on bezel
14k $100 $125 $175
gold filled..............................$30 $40 $60

ILLINOIS, 17J., " Eliza ", c.1929
gold filled.................................$65 $75 $95

ILLINOIS, 17J., " Long Beach ", c.1929
gold filled.................................$55 $65 $85

ILLINOIS, 17J., " Lynette ", c.1929
gold filled.................................$50 $60 $80

ILLINOIS, 17J., " Mariette ", c.1929
gold filled.................................$50 $60 $80

ILLINOIS, 17J., " Marionette ", c.1929
gold filled.................................$50 $60 $80

ILLINOIS, 17J., " Marlette ", c.1929
gold filled.................................$50 $60 $80

ILLINOIS, 16J., " Mary Todd ", c.1929
18k(w)....................................$150 $200 $250

ILLINOIS, 16J., " Mary Todd ", black enamel bezel, c.1929
18k(w)....................................$150 $200 $250

ILLINOIS, 16J., " Mary Todd ", c.1929
18k...$150 $200 $250

ILLINOIS, 17J., " Mateel ", c.1929
14k(w)....................................$90 $100 $140

ILLINOIS, 17J., " Miami ", c.1929
gold filled $55 $65 $85

ILLINOIS, 17J., " Narragansett ", c.1929
14k $85 $100 $125

ILLINOIS, 17J., " Newport ", engraved case, c.1929
gold filled $55 $65 $85

ILLINOIS, 16J., " Queen Wilhelmina ", 22 diamonds and
8 synthetic sapphires
18k(w)....................................$200 $275 $350

ILLINOIS, rectangular, Grade 207,17 jewels

ILLINOIS, rectangular, 1st, 2nd & 3rd model

ILLINOIS, Model #4, 3/0 size, bridge, hunting,movement.

IMPERIAL,17J.,fancy lugs
14k(W).....................................$135 $150 $175

IMPERIAL, 7J., enamel dial, wire lugs, Ca. 1915
silver $100 $135 $225

⊕ Some grades are not included. Their values can be determined by comparing with **similar** age, size, metal content, style, grades, or models such as **time only**, chronograph, repeater etc. listed.

INGERSOLL, 2 J.," Rist-Arch", stepped case
base metal $20 $25 $45

INGERSOLL, "Swagger",
base metal $20 $25 $45

INGERSOLL, 7 jewels
base metal $20 $30 $45

INGERSOLL, 7 jewels, radiolite dial wire lugs
W/ original band $30 $40 $65
base metal $20 $30 $45

INGERSOLL, 7 J., military style, **protective grill cover wire lugs, all original band and cover**
base metal $85 $100 $150

INTERNATIONAL W. CO., 17J., Ca. 1926
18k $650 $800 $1,000

INTERNATIONAL W. CO., 17 jewels, c. 1925
18k $600 $700 $900

INTERNATIONAL W. CO., 16J., **enamel dial**, c. 1920
silver $450 $600 $800

INTERNATIONAL W. CO., 17 jewels
14k $400 $500 $700

INTERNATIONAL W. CO., 16J., **enamel dial**, 12 in **red**
cal. 53, Ca. 1920
18k $650 $800 $1,000

INTERNATIONAL W. CO., 21 J., **auto-w**, center sec.,
Ca. 1940
18k $950 $1,100 $1,400

INTERNATIONAL W. CO., 17 jewels, c. 1920
18k $600 $700 $900

INTERNATIONAL W. CO., 17J., "Art Deco", Ca. 1925
TU-TONE case w/ enamel on bezel
18k $1,400 $1,700 $2,200

INTERNATIONAL W. CO., 17 jewels, **curved**
14k $700 $900 $1,300

INTERNATIONAL W. CO., 17 jewels
14k C&B $600 $700 $900

INTERNATIONAL W. CO., 17 jewels, c. 1940
18k $400 $500 $700

INTERNATIONAL W. CO., 17J., RF # 1160, auto wind,
Ca. 1964
18k $500 $600 $800

INTERNATIONAL W. CO., 17J., c. 1945
14k $300 $400 $600

INTERNATIONAL W. CO., 17 jewels, Ca. 1937
18k $500 $600 $800

INTERNATIONAL W. CO., 17J., Tiffany on dial, c. 1942
14k $350 $450 $650

INTERNATIONAL W. CO., 17J., c. 1926
s. steel $300 $400 $550

INTERNATIONAL W. CO., 17 jewels, hidden lugs
14k $400 $500 $700

INTERNATIONAL W. CO., 17J., aux. sec.
14k $300 $400 $600

Wrist Watches listed in this section are priced at the collectable
fair market Trade Show level as **complete** watches having an
original gold-filled case and stainless steel back, also with
original dial, leather watch band, and the entire original movement in good working order with no repairs needed.

INTERNATIONAL W. CO., 17 J., on dial "Yard"
18k $800 $900 $1,200

INTERNATIONAL W. CO., 17 J., curved, on dial "Yard"
platinum.............................$1,400 $1,600 $2,000

INTERNATIONAL W. CO., 17 jewels, **hinged back**
14k $400 $500 $700

INTERNATIONAL W. CO., 17 jewels, curved
14k $600 $850 $1,200

INTERNATIONAL W. CO., 17J, date, auto-wind,
waterproof
18k $1,200 $1,400 $1,800

INTERNATIONAL W. CO., 17 jewels, center sec.
18k... $550 $725 $900

INTERNATIONAL W. CO., 17J., cen. sec., auto-w., date
platinum $1,900 $2,100 $2,500

INTERNATIONAL W. CO.,17J., RF# 802a, cal.8541, auto
wind, Ca.1960
s. steel.................................... $550 $665 $900

INTERNATIONAL W. CO., 21 jewels, auto wind, date
18k $1,000 $1,200 $1,500

INTERNATIONAL W. CO., 17 jewels, center sec.
18k $600 $750 $975

INTERNATIONAL W. CO., 21J., **"Ingeneur"**, date, c.1976
18k **non-magnetic** .... ★ ★ $2,200 $2,600 $3,200
s. steel **non-magnetic** ...... ★ $1,400 $1,600 $2,000

🕐 Some grades are not included. Their values can be
determined by comparing with **similar** age, size, metal
content, style, grades, or models such as **time only**,
chronograph, repeater etc. listed.

DIALS FOR MINT PRICES MUST BE ALL **ORIGINAL**.

INTERNATIONAL W. CO., 21J., date, auto wind, c. 1960
18k $1,000 $1,200 $1,500

INTERNATIONAL W. CO., 17J., center sec.cal.89, c.1957
18k..$650 $750 $900

INTERNATIONAL W. CO., 21J., cal.853, auto wind,
Ca. 1961
18k $800 $900 $1,200

INTERNATIONAL W. CO., 17J., wide lugs, c. 1960
18k..$700 $800 $1,000

INTERNATIONAL W. CO.,17J., **Bombe'** lugs,
cal. C89, Ca.1952
18k $800 $900 $1,100

INTERNATIONAL W. CO., 21J., cal.C852, auto wind,
Ca. 1952
18k..$700 $800 $1,000

INTERNATIONAL W. CO., 21J., cal.853, auto wind,
Ca. 1958
18k $800 $900 $1,100

INTERNATIONAL W. CO., 17J., cal.89, c. 1962
s. steel......................................$400 $500 $700

INTERNATIONAL W. CO., 17J., ca.1960s
18k C & B $800 $900 $1,100

INTERNATIONAL W. CO., 17J., auto wind, Ca. 1960
18k.......................................$700 $750 $900

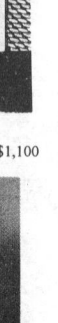

INTERNATIONAL W. CO., 17J., center sec., **Bombe'** lugs
18k $700 $900 $1,000

INTERNATIONAL W. CO., 17 jewels, center sec.
18k.......................................$500 $550 $675

INTERNATIONAL W. CO., 17J., fancy lugs, cen. sec.
18k $600 $700 $900

INTERNATIONAL W. CO., 17 jewels, center sec., cal.402
18k.......................................$500 $550 $675

INTERNATIONAL W. Co., 18 jewels, center sec.
18k $650 $750 $950

INTERNATIONAL W. CO., 17 jewels, center sec., cal. 89
18k.......................................$500 $550 $675

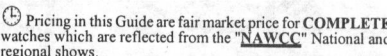

Pricing in this Guide are fair market price for **COMPLETE** watches which are reflected from the "**NAWCC**" National and regional shows.

Wrist Watches listed in this section are priced at the collectable fair market **Trade Show** level as **complete** watches having an original gold-filled case and stainless steel back, also with original dial, leather watch band, and the entire original movement in good working order with no repairs needed.

DIALS FOR MINT PRICES MUST BE ALL **ORIGINAL**.

INTERNATIONAL W. CO., 17 jewels, center sec., cal. 89
18k $600 $700 $900

INTERNATIONAL W. CO., 17J, for Royal Navy, ca. 1950
s. steel....................................$800 $1,000 $1,300

INTERNATIONAL W. CO., 36J., "Da Vinci," chronog.
auto wind, triple date, moon ph., center lugs
18k C & B............................$8,000 $8,500 $10,000
18k $6,000 $6,500 $8,000

INTERNATIONAL W. CO., 17J., winds at 12 o'clock
s. steel....................................$600 $725 $950

INTERNATIONAL W. CO., 17 jewels, Autowind, Ca. 1958
s. steel....................................$400 $435 $500

INTERNATIONAL W. CO., 17J., anti-magnet, Ca. 1942
s. steel....................................$200 $250 $325

INTERNATIONAL W. CO., "Porsche Design", date, auto-
wind, compass, sapphire mirror, RF#3510-LMW, Ca. 1988
Titanium..................................$800 $950 $1,300
base metal $400 $475 $650

🕐 A collector should expect to pay modestly higher prices
at local shops

INTERNATIONAL W. CO., 17 jewels, c. 1948
18k $600 $735 $950

INTERNATIONAL W. CO., 17J.,date, 30 ATM=1,000 ft.
s. steel $450 $550 $750

INTERNATIONAL W. CO., 17J., aux sec., cal.83, c.1938
14k $500 $565 $650

INTERNATIONAL W. CO., 17J., **Bombe'** lugs, Ca.1952
18k $800 $950 $1,200

INTERNATIONAL W. CO., 17J., aux. sec., cal., c.1948
s. steel $500 $600 $800

INTERNATIONAL W. CO., 15J., cal. 83, ca.1945
14k.. $500 $635 $800

INTERNATIONAL W. CO., 17J., cal.461, c.1962
18k $500 $635 $800

INTERNATIONAL W. CO., 17J., mid-size, Ca.1945
s. steel...................................... $400 $500 $700

INTERNATIONAL W. CO., 17J., 36 small diamonds
platinum $450 $550 $700

INTERNATIONAL WATCH CO.
MOVEMENT IDENTIFICATION

Caliber 51N

Caliber 51

Caliber 41

Caliber 93, Baguette

Caliber 92

Caliber 431

Caliber 91

Caliber 90

Caliber 96

Caliber 94

Caliber 84

Caliber 44

Caliber 85

Caliber 852
Calendar - 8521

Caliber 853
Calendar - 8531

Caliber 401

Caliber 60   Caliber 62   Caliber 61   Caliber 86

Caliber 75 & 76   Caliber 87   Caliber 89

Caliber 88   Caliber 70   Caliber 83

Caliber 64   Caliber 63   Caliber 64

MILLIMETERS 10 20 30 40 50 60

LIGNES 4 6 8 10 12 14 16 18 20
5 7 9 11 13 15 17 19

INVICTA, 15 jewels, chronograph, min. reg. at 6 o'clock,
decimal aperture for sec. at 12 o'clock
18k $1,500 $1,800 $2,400

INVICTA, 17 jewels, date, center sec.
18k $200 $275 $425
s. steel $65 $75 $125

INVICTA, 17 jewels, day-date, waterproof
18k $150 $200 $300
s. steel $60 $75 $125

INVICTA, 17 jewels, day-date-month
18k $200 $250 $325
s. steel $75 $100 $150

⊕ Some grades are not included. Their values can be
determined by comparing with **similar** age, size, metal
content, style, grades, or models such as **time only**,
chronograph, repeater etc. listed.

⊕ A collector should expect to pay modestly higher prices
at local shops

INVICTA, 17 jewels, day-date-month, moon phase
18k..$400 $535 $750
s. steel.....................................$200 $265 $375

INVICTA, 17 jewels, waterproof
18k..$125 $165 $225
s. steel.....................................$40 $50 $75

INVICTA, 17 jewels, auto wind, waterproof
18k..$125 $165 $225
s. steel.....................................$50 $60 $75

JAEGER W. CO., 17J., RF#5184, chronog., Ca.1942
s.steel......................................$250 $300 $400
18k..$500 $565 $650

⊕ Pricing in this Guide are fair market price for **COMPLETE**
watches which are reflected from the "**NAWCC**" National and
regional shows.

JAEGER W. CO., 15J., **duoplan, backwind**, c.1935
s steel $300 $375 $550

JARDUR W. CO., 17J., RF#29840, c.1950
s. steel $250 $325 $425

JEAN LOUIS, 17 jewels, double dial, c. 1930
14k $200 $265 $350

J. E. Watch Co., 17J., c.1950
gold plate $40 $50 $70

JEWEL, 15 jewels, dual dial, c. 1938
gold filled................................$250 $325 $450

JOHNSON-MATTHEY, 15 J., 5-10-15 gram ingot 24k gold
24k 5 gram $200 $250 $350
24k 10 gram $400 $500 $650
24k 15 gram $700 $800 $950

JUNGHANS, 16J., chronometer, c.1965
14k..$100 $125 $175

JUNGHANS, electronic "Ato Chron" , C.1978
14k..$100 $125 $175

JUNGHANS , 17J., cal.J88, c.1980
s. steel....................................$200 $250 $350

Wrist Watches listed in this section are priced at the collectable fair market **Trade Show** level as **complete** watches having an original gold-filled case and stainless steel back, also with original dial, leather watch band, and the entire original movement in good working order with no repairs needed.

DIALS FOR MINT PRICES MUST BE ALL **ORIGINAL**.

J. JURGENSEN, 31J, 5 min. repeater, **recased**, c.1906
18k $6,000 $6,500 $7,500

J. JURGENSEN, 15J, jumping hr., revolving min., c.1930s
18k $2,000 $2,500 $3,500

J. JURGENSEN,17J., large lugs, recess crown, c.1950
14k $150 $200 $275

J. JURGENSEN,17J., long lugs, c.1948
18k $175 $225 $300

J. JURGENSEN,17J., recess crown, fancy lugs, c.1952
14k $150 $200 $275

J. JURGENSEN,17J., 2 tone, center lugs, c.1940
14k $250 $300 $400

J. JURGENSEN, 17 jewels, fancy lugs, ca.1949
14k $300 $350 $425

J. JURGENSEN, 17 jewels, fancy lugs
14k $300 $350 $425

J. JURGENSEN, 17 jewels, extra fancy lugs, c. 1946
18k $500 $565 $650

J. JURGENSEN, 17 jewels, c. 1950
18k $175 $225 $350

🕐 Pricing in this Guide are fair market price for **COMPLETE** watches which are reflected from the **"NAWCC"** National and regional shows.

J. JURGENSEN, 17 jewels
18k $165 $200 $265

J. JURGENSEN,17J., center sec., c.1946
14k $100 $150 $225

J. JURGENSEN,17J., aux. sec., c.1948
14k $100 $150 $225

J. JURGENSEN,17J., aux. sec., c.1940
14k $100 $150 $225

J. JURGENSEN,17J., textured bezel, c.1960
14k $100 $150 $225

J. JURGENSEN,17J., hidden lugs, c.1948
14k $165 $200 $275

J. JURGENSEN,17J., hidden lugs, c.1940
14k...$150 $175 $250

J. JURGENSEN,17J., hidden lugs, c.1952
14k...$300 $365 $465

J. JURGENSEN,17J., hidden lugs, c.1950
14k...$300 $350 $450

J. JURGENSEN,17J., hidden lugs, c.1948
14k...$150 $175 $235

J. JURGENSEN, 17 J., flared case, Ca. 1954
14k...$175 $235 $325

🕐 Some grades are not included. Their values can be determined by comparing with **similar** age, size, metal content, style, grades, or models such as **time only**, chronograph, repeater etc. listed.

J. JURGENSEN,17J., by Valjoux, 30mm, cal. 69, c.1944
14K.................................$400 $525 $700
s. steel $250 $300 $400

J. JURGENSEN, 17 J., auto-w., cen. sec., ca. 1954
14k $150 $175 $265

J. JURGENSEN,17J., cal.8273, extended lugs, c.1958
14k $175 $195 $265

J. JURGENSEN,17J., aux. sec., c.1968
14k $125 $165 $200

Wrist Watches listed in this section are priced at the collectable fair market **Trade Show** level as **complete** watches having an original gold-filled case and stainless steel back, also with original dial, leather watch band, and the entire original movement in good working order with no repairs needed.

J. JURGENSEN,17J., extended bezel, c.1950
14k...$300 $325 $400

J. JURGENSEN,17J., cal.1139, c.1950
18k...$225 $265 $325

J. JURGENSEN,17J., center sec., date, c.1960
14k...$150 $185 $225

J. JURGENSEN,17J., center sec., mid size, c.1940
14k...$150 $185 $225

🕐 Some grades are not included. Their values can be determined by comparing with **similar** age, size, metal content, style, grades, or models such as **time only**, chronograph, repeater etc. listed.

J. JURGENSEN,17J., 3 diamond dial, date, c.1960
14k(w)....................................$150 $185 $225

JUVENIA, 21 jewels, **gold movement**
18k...$200 $250 $350

J. JURGENSEN,17J., 40 diamond bezel, c.1960
14k(w)....................................$300 $365 $450

JUVENIA, 17J.,
s. steel....................................$30 $35 $65

J. JURGENSEN, 17 J., 12 diamond dial, ca. 1960s
14k(W)....................................$150 $185 $225

JUVENIA, 17J.,
s. steel....................................$30 $40 $65

JUVENIA,17J.,3 dates, moon ph., screw on back c. 1950s
18k $400 $525 $700

Wrist Watches listed in this section are priced at the collectable
fair market **Trade Show** level as **complete** watches having an
original gold-filled case and stainless steel back, also with
original dial, leather watch band, and the entire original movement in good working order with no repairs needed.

JUVENIA, 17J.,
s. steel....................................$30 $40 $65

⏱ Some grades are not included. Their values can be
determined by comparing with **similar** age, size, metal
content, style, grades, or models such as **time only**,
chronograph, repeater etc. listed.

JUVENIA, 17J.,
s. steel $40 $50 $85

JUVENIA, 17J.
s. steel $40 $50 $85

JUVENIA, 17J., "Arithmo", Ca. 1955
s. steel $100 $125 $175

KELBERT, 17J., triple date, moon ph., ca.1945
gold filled.............................. $200 $250 $350
s. steel $250 $300 $400

KELBERT, 17 jewels, fancy lugs, c. 1949
gold filled.............................. $50 $65 $100

KELEK,17J., tachymeter, auto-wind, c.1970
s. steel $85 $100 $150

Kelton, 7 jewels, curved, stepped case
gold filled $30 $40 $65

KELTON, 7 jewels, "Drake"
gold filled $30 $40 $65

KENT W. CO.,17J., Continental W.Co.(French), chronog.
s. steel $250 $300 $400

KINGSTON, 17 jewels, day-date-month, moon phase
gold filled $250 $285 $375

DIALS FOR MINT PRICES MUST BE ALL **ORIGINAL**.

KINGSTON,17J., cal.G10, hidden lugs, c.1943
gold filled.................................$50 $65 $95

KORD, day date month, moon ph., auto wind
s. steel $150 $200 $275

KURTH, 17 jewels, "Certina"
gold filled.................................$30 $35 $75

LACO, 17J., center sec., c.1955
gold plate $20 $30 $60

⏲ Some grades are not included. Their values can be
determined by comparing with **similar** age, size, metal
content, style, grades, or models such as **time only**,
chronograph, repeater etc. listed.

⏲ Pricing in this Guide are fair market price for **COM-PLETE** watches which are reflected from the "**NAWCC**" National and regional shows.

LANCEL (Paris),17J., **one** button chronog. by Nicolet, c.1960
gold filled $225 $250 $300

A.LANGE & SOHNE,17J., 55mm., c.1940
s. steel $1,500 $1,800 $2,200

A.LANGE & SOHNE, 17J, (Glashutte), c.1936
14k $700 $800 $950

LANGE "UHR" (Glashutte),15J., c.1936
14k $800 $850 $950

LANGE "UHR" (Glashutte),17J., c.1937
s. steel $500 $600 $800

LANGE, 17J, (Glashutte), date, auto wind, waterproof
18k $600 $665 $750

LAVINA, 17J., ca.1937
9K...$100 $125 $175

LE COULTRE, 15 jewels, wire lugs, c. 1919
silver $175 $200 $265

LE COULTRE, 18J., skeletonized,
18k $1,400 $1,600 $2,000

LE COULTRE, 19 jewels, alarm
18k $800 $950 $1,300
14k $600 $750 $1,000
gold filled................................$200 $300 $450
s. steel $200 $300 $450

LE COULTRE, 19 jewels, alarm, sold for $99.00 with gold
filled case & $235.00 with 18K case in1950
18k $700 $850 $1,200
14k $500 $650 $950
gold filled $200 $300 $450
s. steel $200 $300 $450

LE COULTRE, 17J., auto-wind, alarm, cal.815, c.1960
gold filled $200 $300 $450

LE COULTRE, 17J., **ruby** dial, alarm, auto wind, c.1960
gold filled $400 $500 $700

LE COULTRE, 17J.,cal.814, memovox, alarm, c.1960
14k $700 $800 $1,000
gold filled $200 $300 $450

LE COULTRE, 17J., cal.p815, alarm, c.1960
gold filled...............................$200 $300 $450

LE COULTRE, 17J.,memovox , alarm, auto wind,c.1973
14k & s.s.................................. $600 $700 $850

LE COULTRE, 17J., RF#3025, wrist-alarm, c.1948
gold filled...............................$200 $300 $450

LE COULTRE, 17J., RF#2676, date, memovox, c.1960
gold filled $200 $300 $450

LE COULTRE, 17J., wrist alarm, Ca.1949
gold filled...............................$200 $300 $450

LE COULTRE, 17J., date, auto-w., memovox, c.1975
s. steel $200 $300 $450

LE COULTRE, 17J., "Polaris", memovox, underwater alarm
tested to 600 feet, date, Ca. 1968, s.s. band by Le Coultre.
s. steel $1,400 $1,600 $2,000

LE COULTRE, 17J., auto wind, **date**, memovox, c.1976
gold filled $400 $450 $550

LE COULTRE, 19J., date, Memovox, ca. 1959
18k $750 $800 $1,000
gold filled..............................$200 $300 $500
s. steel $200 $300 $500

LE COULTRE, 19J., alarm, date, autowind
14k $900 $1,000 $1,200

LE COULTRE, 19 jewels, alarm, date, autowind, ca. 1950
18k $1,000 $1,100 $1,400
gold filled..............................$500 $600 $800
s. steel $600 $700 $900

LE COULTRE, 17-19J., **World Time,** Memovox, ca. 1956
s. steel $700 $900 $1,200

LE COULTRE, 17J., Powermatic Nautilus "S", wind-ind.,
auto-w., sold for $85.00 with gold filled case in 1950
gold filled $225 $250 $350

LE COULTRE, 17J., cal. 481, wind-ind., auto-w., c.1954
the cal. 481,up & down wind-ind. has **Differential Gearing**
gold filled $225 $250 $350

LE COULTRE, 17J., auto wind, wind indicator, sold for
$150.00 with a 14K case in 1951
14k $550 $600 $750

LE COULTRE, 17 jewels, auto wind, screw back
18k $200 $285 $375

LE COULTRE, 17J., "Master Mariner, auto wind, c.1960
14k $250 $300 $400

LE COULTRE, 17J., "Master Mariner", autow., date, Ca.1960
gold filled $125 $150 $225

LE COULTRE, 17J., cal.p478, center sec.c.1947
s. steel $100 $150 $225

LE COULTRE, 17J., auto-wind, cal.p812, c.1955
gold filled $125 $150 $225

LE COULTRE, 17J., "Master Mariner", auto wind, c.1952
14k $250 $325 $450

LE COULTRE, 17J., RF#.480-C-380, autow., Ca.1955
14k $150 $195 $285

LE COULTRE, 17J., "Master Mariner", auto-wind, c.1960
s. steel $125 $150 $225

LE COULTRE, 17J., RF#555-149, Ca.1955
14k $150 $195 $285

🕐 A collector should expect to pay modestly higher prices at local shops

Wrist Watches listed in this section are priced at the collectable fair market **Trade Show** level as **complete** watches having an original gold-filled case and stainless steel back, also with original dial, leather watch band, and the entire original movement in good working order with no repairs needed.

DIALS FOR MINT PRICES MUST BE ALL **ORIGINAL**.

LE COULTRE, 17J., cal. 812, auto-wind, c.1952
s. steel $125 $150 $225

LE COULTRE, 17J., RF#7534, c.1960
14k $200 $285 $400

LE COULTRE, 17J.,"Coronet", cal.480cw, c.1951
gold filled...............................$225 $275 $350

LE COULTRE, 17J., 11 diamond dial, RF#197, c.1955
14k(w)....................................$200 $285 $400

LE COULTRE, 17J., cal.480, wide bezel, c.1958
gold filled...............................$125 $150 $225

LE COULTRE, 17 jewels, center lugs, c. 1960
18k $500 $600 $750

LE COULTRE, 17J., cal.480, c.1955
14k $150 $185 $325

LE COULTRE, 17 jewels, "Pershing", fancy lugs, c. 1950
14k $200 $300 $450

🕐 Pricing in this Guide are fair market price for **COM-PLETE** watches which are reflected from the "**NAWCC**" National and regional shows.

🕐 Some grades are not included. Their values can be determined by comparing with **similar** age, size, metal content, style, grades, or models such as **time only**, chronograph, repeater etc. listed.

LE COULTRE, 17J., fancy lugs
14k $200 $300 $450

LE COULTRE, 17J., fancy lugs, ca. 1950s
18k $300 $375 $500

LE COULTRE, 17 jewels, fancy lugs, c. 1952
14k $300 $335 $400

LE COULTRE, 17 jewels, fancy bezel & lugs
14k $600 $750 $950

LE COULTRE, 17 jewels, fancy bezel & lugs, Ca.1953
14k $325 $385 $500

LE COULTRE, 17J., fancy bezel, Ca.1952
gold filled $125 $150 $225

LE COULTRE, 17J., auto wind, textured bezel, c. 1950
18k $250 $325 $450

LE COULTRE, 17 jewels, center sec., c. 1949
18k $500 $600 $800
s. steel $250 $300 $450

LE COULTRE, 17J., cen. sec., 24 hr dial, c. 1940
s. steel $200 $275 $400

This book endeavours to be a GUIDE or helpful manual and offers a wealth of material to be used as a tool not as a absolute document. Price Guides are like watches the worst may be better than none at all, but at best cannot be expected to be 100% accurate.

LE COULTRE, 17J., "Quartermaster", 24 hr dial, auto-w.,
RF#114
s.steel $400 $475 $600

LE COULTRE, 17J., auto-w., cal.813, RF#388-870, Ca.1959
gold filled..............................$125 $150 $225

LE COULTRE, 17J., center sec., cal.468/ACa.1940
s.steel $125 $150 $225

LE COULTRE, 17J., center sec., ca. 1930s
silver $250 $300 $375

LE COULTRE, 17J., alarm, auto-w., date, ca.1964
s. steel $200 $275 $400

LE COULTRE, 17J., **quartz**, cal.352, c.1970
gold filled $55 $65 $95

LE COULTRE, 17J., date alarm, auto-w., c.1975
gold filled $150 $200 $300

LE COULTRE, 17 jewels, alarm, date, auto wind
s.steel $185 $250 $350

LE COULTRE, 17J., chronog., 2 reg.
14k $700 $800 $1,000
s. steel $350 $450 $600

LE COULTRE, 17 jewels, chronog., 3 reg.
18k $2,200 $2,500 $3,000

LE COULTRE, 17J., chronog., cal.281, c.1940
s. steel $350 $450 $600

LE COULTRE, 17 jewels, mystery dial, c. 1955
14k yellow $400 $485 $600

LE COULTRE, 17J., chronog., FR#2644, blue dial,
s. steel $600 $675 $800

LE COULTRE, 17J., 15 diamond mystery dial, RF # 182
14k(W) $650 $750 $900

LE COULTRE, 17J., 2 diamond mystery dial, RF # 182
14k(W)...................................$400 $450 $600

LE COULTRE, 17J., chronog. 3 reg., ca. 1958
14k $1,500 $1,800 $2,500
s. steel $700 $900 $1,200

LE COULTRE, 17J., 36 diamond mystery dial, waterproof,
auto wind, **"Vacheron Galaxy"**
14k(w).................................$1,200 $1,400 $1,800

LE COULTRE, 15 jewels, triple-date, c. 1945
s. steel $400 $475 $600
14k $700 $800 $1,000
18k $900 $1,100 $1,400

LE COULTRE, 17J, diamond dial, textured bezel, c. 1960s
14k (w)....................................$150 $225 $335

LE COULTRE, 17J, triple date, moon ph., c. 1940s
18k $1,500 $1,700 $2,000
gold filled $500 $625 $700

LE COULTRE, 17J., **date**, cal.810, c.1952
14k $300 $365 $450

LE COULTRE, 17J., triple date, moon ph., fancy lugs
14k $1,800 $2,100 $2,600

LE COULTRE, 17J., date, center sec., c.1950
14k $325 $375 $465

🕐 Some grades are not included. Their values can be
determined by comparing with **similar** age, size, metal
content, style, grades, or models such as **time only**,
chronograph, repeater etc. listed.

LE COULTRE, 17J., auto-w., Memovox, world time, c.1960
Beware of **FAKES** /|\
14k $1,500 $1,700 $2,000

DIALS FOR MINT PRICES MUST BE ALL **ORIGINAL**.

LE COULTRE, 17J., weems style, cal.450, c.1942
s. steel $600 $675 $800

LE COULTRE, 17J, ''Futurematic'', auto- w., W. Ind.
sold for $95.00 with s. steel case in 1950
18k $550 $675 $900
gold filled $300 $425 $600
s. steel ....★ $400 $535 $700

LE COULTRE, 17J., Memovox, world time, **date**, Ca.1968
14k $1,500 $1,700 $2,000

LE COULTRE, 23 J., auto-w., date cen. sec.
14k $150 $200 $285

LE COULTRE, 17J., ''Futurematic'', cal.817, c.1952
gold filled...............................$400 $500 $750
14k $600 $750 $950

LE COULTRE, 17J., Master Mariner, auto-w., date
gold filled $125 $150 $225
14k $150 $200 $285

LE COULTRE, 17 jewels, ''Futurematic'' power-reserve
18k $700 $750 $850
14k $550 $600 $700

LE COULTRE, 17J., day date, mid size, ca. 1940s
gold filled $125 $150 $225

Wrist Watches listed in this section are priced at the collectable
fair market **Trade Show** level as **complete** watches having an
original gold-filled case and stainless steel back, also with
original dial, leather watch band, and the entire original movement in good working order with no repairs needed.

LE COULTRE, 17J., fancy lugs, aux. sec., ca. 1948
14k $500 $600 $800

LE COULTRE, 17 jewels, fancy wide bezel, ca.1955
14k (W)....................................$125 $165 $250

LE COULTRE, 17J., auto-w., ca. 1950s
14k $150 $200 $285

LE COULTRE, 17J., alarm, date,
14k $500 $625 $775

LE COULTRE, 17J., fancy lugs
14k $300 $350 $500

LE COULTRE, 15J., drivers style wind at 12, c.1960s
s. steel $250 $300 $385

LE COULTRE,17J.,drivers style crown at 6, RF#9041
s. steel $250 $300 $385

LE COULTRE, 17J., aux. sec. ca.1950s
14k $150 $200 $285

LE COULTRE, 17J., RF#9041, cal.818, crown at 6, c.1960s
18k $400 $450 $600

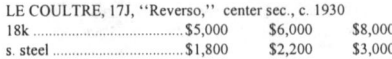

LE COULTRE, 17J, "Reverso," center sec., c. 1930
18k \$5,000   \$6,000   \$8,000
s. steel \$1,800   \$2,200   \$3,000

LE COULTRE, 17J., "Reverso," c. 1940s
18k \$4,000   \$5,000   \$7,000
s. steel \$1,500   \$1,800   \$2,500

LE COULTRE, 17 jewels, fancy hooded lugs, c. 1952
14k \$250   \$300   \$400

LE COULTRE, 17 jewels, fancy lugs
14k \$225   \$250   \$300

LE COULTRE, 17 jewels, large fancy lugs
14k \$450   \$500   \$600

LE COULTRE, 17J., curvex,
14k \$200   \$250   \$350

LE COULTRE, 17J., curvex, ca. 1940s
14k \$200   \$250   \$350

LE COULTRE, 17J., stepped lugs, ca. 1944
gold filled \$125   \$150   \$200

LE COULTRE, 17J., aux. sec., ca. 1940s
gold filled \$125   \$150   \$200

LE COULTRE, 17J., square lugs, ca. 1948
14k \$300   \$375   \$500

LE COULTRE, 17J., extended lugs, c.1938
gold filled...............................$125 $150 $200

LE COULTRE, 17J., aux. sec., c.1940
14k $150 $175 $275

LE COULTRE, 17J., tu tone dial, c.1940
gold filled...............................$125 $150 $200

LE COULTRE, 17J., large lugs, c.1938
gold filled...............................$125 $150 $200

LE COULTRE, 17J.,hidden lugs, c.1942
14k $175 $225 $325
gold filled...............................$125 $150 $225

LE COULTRE, 17J., hooded lugs, ca. 1940s
14k $250 $300 $400

LE COULTRE, 17J., fluted bezel, Ca. 1949
gold filled $125 $150 $200

LE COULTRE, 17J., fancy bezel, ca. 1940s
14k $300 $350 $500

LE COULTRE, 17J., RF # 2406, 15 diamonds, Ca. 1957
14k $350 $375 $450

LE COULTRE, 17J., Asymmetric, cal.438.4cw, Ca.1957
gold filled $150 $175 $225

LE COULTRE, 17J., Asymmetric, diamond dial, RF#2406, Ca.1960
14k $300 $335 $400

LE COULTRE, 15J., **Duoplan, back-wind,** c. 1930
18k $700 $800 $1,000

LE COULTRE, 17 jewels, **uniplan,** c. 1938
14k (w)...................................$400 $465 $550

LE COULTRE, 15J., **Duoplan, back-wind,** c. 1930
14k(G&S) $900 $1,000 $1,200

LE COULTRE, 17 jewels, fancy lugs, c. 1948
14k $500 $600 $750

LE COULTRE, 17J., fancy lugs, cal.438-4cw, c.1951
18k $750 $900 $1,100

LE COULTRE, 17 jewels, fancy lugs
14k $700 $800 $1,000

LE COULTRE, 17 jewels, diamond dial, fancy lugs
14k $800 $900 $1,200

LE COULTRE, 17J., diamond dial, ca. 1940s
14k $250 $325 $475

LE COULTRE, 17J., 12 diamond dial, cal.4870cw, c.1958
14k(w)...................................$150 $200 $300

LE COULTRE, 17J., 15 diamond mystery dial ca.1940s
14k $1,000 $1,200 $1,500

LE COULTRE, 15J., hinged case, c.1920
14k $400 $465 $550

Pricing in this Guide are fair market price for **COM-
PLETE** watches which are reflected from the **"NAWCC"** National and regional shows.

LE COULTRE, 17J., stepped case & lugs, cal., c.1950
gold filled................................$125 $150 $225

LE COULTRE, 17J., aux. sec., c.1940
14k $150 $185 $285

LE COULTRE, 17J., cal.493, **auto wind**, c.1955
14k $250 $275 $375

LE COULTRE, 17J., cal.438-4cw, wide bezel, c.1950
14k $250 $275 $375

LE COULTRE, 17J., textured bezel, c.1952
14k $250 $275 $375

🕐 Pricing in this Guide are fair market price for **COM-
PLETE** watches which are reflected from the "**NAWCC**" National and regional shows.

LE COULTRE, 17J., textured bezel, c.1950
14k $250 $275 $375

LE COULTRE, 17J., RF#7540,enamel bezel, cal., c.1960
14k $250 $350 $600

LE COULTRE, 17J., auto wind, cal.p812, c.1948
gold filled $125 $150 $225

LE COULTRE, 17 jewels, Ca.1958
18k $450 $500 $600

LE COULTRE, 17J., textured bezel, cen. sec.
18k $350 $400 $500

LE COULTRE, 17J., aux. sec., auto wind, ca. 1940s
14k $300 $365 $500

LE COULTRE, 17J, triple date, moon ph., fancy bezel
sold for $99.50 with gold filled case in 1951
18k ....★ ★ $3,200 $3,700 $4,500
14k $2,400 $2,800 $3,500
gold filled...........................$1,600 $1,800 $2,200

LE COULTRE, 17 jewels, c. 1945
18k $200 $275 $375

LE COULTRE, 17 jewels, fancy lugs, c. 1948
14k $250 $300 $450

LE COULTRE, 17 jewels, Ca. 1940
14k(rose) $150 $200 $275

LE COULTRE, 17 jewels, center lugs, c. 1945
14k $150 $200 $275

LE COULTRE, 17 jewels, c. 1950s
14k $150 $200 $275

LE COULTRE, 17 jewels, 18k case & band
18k C&B..............................$700 $750 $850

LE COULTRE, 17 jewels, date cal. 810, c. 1952
14k $300 $375 $500

LE COULTRE, 17 jewels, two tone **dial**
14k $150 $225 $335
18k $250 $285 $475

🕐 Some grades are not included. Their values can be
determined by comparing with **similar** age, size, metal
content, style, grades, or models such as **time only**,
chronograph, repeater etc. listed.

LE COULTRE, 15 jewels, by Blancpain, c.1925
gold filled...............................$125 $150 $200

LE COULTRE, quartz, date, waterproof, c. 1960s
18k $175 $200 $300

LE COULTRE, electric, digital calendar (good running order)
silver & gold filled $150 $175 $225

LE COULTRE, 17J, "Aristocrat", sold for $71.50 with gold
filled case either Gents or Ladies model in 1951
gold filled................................$400 $450 $550

LE COULTRE, 17 jewels, small, "Aristocrat", c. 1953
gold filled................................$300 $365 $450

LE COULTRE, 15J., lady's
14k(W)......................................$95 $125 $165

LE COULTRE, 15J., lady's art deco, by Blancpain, c.1925
silver $200 $250 $350

LE COULTRE, 15J., lady's REVERSO, c.1940
s. steel $700 $800 $950

LE COULTRE, 15J., **Duoplan, back-wind**, c. 1930
silver $550 $600 $700

LE COULTRE, 17J., lady's MYSTERY dial, c.1959
gold filled $95 $125 $175

LE COULTRE, 17J., photo-watch, winds at 12, Ca. 1950
14k $450 $500 $600

LEMANIA, 17 jewels, auto wind
s. steel $50 $75 $125

LEMANIA, 17 jewels, chronog., military, ca.1970s
s. steel $400 $450 $600

LEMANIA,17J., chronog., 3 reg., c.1946
14k $550 $625 $750

LEONIDAS,17J., chronog., triple date, c.1945
gold filled $300 $350 $450

LEMANIA, 17 jewels, chronog., 2 reg., auto wind, c. 1950
18k $500 $600 $750

LEONIDAS, 17 jewels, triple date, 3 reg.
18k $700 $800 $950
s. steel $400 $500 $600

LEMANIA, 17 jewels, chronog., waterproof
s. steel $350 $450 $600

LEONIDAS, 17 jewels, auto wind, triple date, moon phase
s. steel $300 $365 $450

LEONIDAS, 17 jewels, chronog., 2 reg.
s. steel $100 $135 $200

LEVRETTE,17J., chronog., (fly back), center lugs, c.1935
18k(1 button)......................$1,000 $1,100 $1,300

LE PHARE, 17J, chronog., triple date, 3 reg., antimagnetic
14k $500 $575 $700

LIBELA,7J., direct read, c.1952
base metal $50 $75 $125

LE PHARE, 17 jewels, chronog., 2 reg., antimagnetic
18k $375 $435 $550
14k $275 $335 $450
s. steel $135 $175 $250

LIP,15J., chronog., tu-tone, center lugs, (French), c.1940
gold filled & s.steel. $550 $650 $800

LIP, electric, bulbous crown, (French)
s. steel $200 $235 $300

Wrist Watches listed in this section are priced at the collectable fair market Trade Show level as **complete** watches having an original gold-filled case and stainless steel back, also with original dial, leather watch band, and the entire original movement in good working order with no repairs needed.

LE PHARE, 17J., triple date, moon ph., waterproof, autow.
18k $400 $500 $700
gold filled...............................$200 $265 $400

LONGINES, 15J., center lugs, enamel dial, ca.1923
silver $250 $300 $400

LONGINES,15J., enamel dial, exaggerated #s, Ca.1923
18K...$800 $900 $1,200

LONGINES,15J., metal dial, GJS, c.1925
14k $150 $185 $275

LONGINES, 18J.,wire lugs, ca.1928
14k $300 $335 $400

🕐 Some grades are not included. Their values can be determined by comparing with **similar** age, size, metal content, style, grades, or models such as **time only**, chronograph, repeater etc. listed.

LONGINES, 15J., wire lugs, enamel dial, c.1927
silver $200 $225 $275

LONGINES, 15J., wire lugs, ca. 1930s
silver $250 $275 $350

LONGINES,17J., tu-tone, GJS, c.1936
14k & s.s.............................$200 $225 $300

LONGINES,17J., double dial, cal.932, c.1937
s. steel $900 $1,100 $1,500

LONGINES,17J., large & curved, GJS, exaggerated numbers
gold filled $250 $300 $400

LONGINES, 15J., GJS, c.1922
silver $225 $275 $400

LONGINES, 17J., GJS, cal.940, c.1931
18k $450 $500 $600

LONGINES, 17J., GJS, cal.1086, c.1928
14k $400 $500 $700

LONGINES, 15-17J., enamel dial, Ca.1920s
14k $800 $900 $1,200

LONGINES, 17J., large Lindberg model 47mm., movable
center dial (weem's second setting), Ca. 1930s
18k .... ★★★ $10,000 $12,000 $15,000
silver $4,000 $4,800 $6,500
nickel.................................... $3,000 $3,500 $5,000

LONGINES, 17J., small Lindberg model, original retail price
for gold filled $97.50, movable center dial, Ca. 1930s
18k .... ★★ $5,000 $5,500 $6,500
14k $3,000 $3,500 $4,500
gold filled $900 $1,000 $1,200
s. steel $1,200 $1,400 $1,800

LONGINES, 17J., Weems U.S. Patent 2008734 on dial
gold filled $300 $425 $650
s. steel $450 $550 $750
14k $750 $900 $1,100

LONGINES, 17J., "Weems", revolving bezel, Ca. 1940s
gold filled $325 $425 $650
s. steel $475 $550 $750

LONGINES, 17J., "Weems", revolving bezel, Ca. 1940s
gold filled $350 $450 $650
s. steel $500 $650 $850

LONGINES, 17J., fly back hand, center recording, c.1945
s. steel(1 button) $900 $1,100 $1,500

LONGINES, 17 jewels, chronog., 1 button, 2 reg., c. 1923
silver $1,600 $1,800 $2,200

LONGINES,17J., 1 button chronog., 2 reg., c.1946
14k $1,900 $2,200 $2,600

LONGINES, 17J., chronog., one button
gold filled $600 $700 $900
14k $1,400 $1,700 $2,000

LONGINES,17J., 1 button, fly back hand, center recording,
RF# 5034, Ca. 1940
s. steel $900 $1,100 $1,500

LONGINES, 17J. chronog., ref. 1333, enamel dial, Ca. 1925
silver(1 button) $1,400 $1,600 $1,900

LONGINES, 17J., one button chronog., 2 reg., Ca. 1928
18k $2,300 $2,500 $3,000

LONGINES, 17J., chronog. 2 reg., tach.
14k $2,200 $2,400 $3,000

LONGINES,17J., chronog., c.1942
s. steel $1,400 $1,600 $1,900

LONGINES,17J., RF#6474, c.1955
s. steel $1,600 $1,800 $2,200

LONGINES, 17 jewels, chronog., 2 reg., Telemeter
Anti Magnetic, Ca. 1940s
18k $2,500 $2,800 $3,500

LONGINES, 17 jewels, chronog., 2 reg.
14k $2,000 $2,200 $2,600
s. steel $1,500 $1,700 $2,000

LONGINES, 17J., 1 button, chronog., ca. 1945
gold filled $300 $375 $500

LONGINES, 17 jewels, chronog. 1 button
14k $1,000 $1,200 $1,500

LONGINES,17J., chronog., cal.539, c.1969
s steel $185 $225 $275

LONGINES,17J., Valjoux 726, cal.332, c.1972
s. steel $225 $275 $350

LONGINES, 16J., military issue, waterpr., ca. 1940s
s. steel $500 $600 $750

LONGINES,17J., GJS, c.1965
18k $200 $250 $325

LONGINES,17J., GJS, cal.23z, c.1958
gold filled...................................$75 $100 $165

LONGINES, 17J., GJS, cal.194, c.1963
gold filled.................................$75 $100 $165

🕐 A collector should expect to pay modestly higher prices
at local shops

LONGINES,17J., GJS, cal.352, auto wind, c.1960
14k $125 $165 $250

LONGINES,17J., GJS, cal., c.1960
14k $125 $165 $250

LONGINES,17J., aux. seconds, Ca. 1960
gold filled $75 $100 $165

LONGINES,17J., Aux. seconds, gold jewel settings,
automatic, Ca. 1957
14k $125 $165 $250

🕐 Some grades are not included. Their values can be
determined by comparing with **similar** age, size, metal
content, style, grades, or models such as **time only**,
chronograph, repeater etc. listed.

LONGINES,17J., RF#2033p, GJS, cal., c.1958
14k $125 $165 $250

LONGINES,17J., RF#2021, GJS, cal.23z, c.1955
14k $200 $250 $325

LONGINES,17J., GJS, cal.23z, c.1955
14k $125 $165 $250

LONGINES,17J., large fluted lugs, GJS, c.1940
14k $300 $350 $450

LONGINES,17J., large lugs, GJS, c.1952
18k $300 $350 $425

LONGINES,17J., GJS, cal.18LN, c.1952
14k $225 $275 $350

LONGINES,17J., one lug at 11 & one at 5, GJS, 1955
14k $250 $285 $350

LONGINES,17J., GJS, cal.22a, auto-wind, c.1958
14k $225 $275 $350

Wrist Watches listed in this section are priced at the collectable
fair market **Trade Show** level as **complete** watches having an
original gold-filled case and stainless steel back, also with
original dial, leather watch band, and the entire original movement in good working order with no repairs needed.

A collector should expect to pay modestly higher prices
at local shops

Pricing in this Guide are fair market price for **COM-
PLETE** watches which are reflected from the "**NAWCC**" National and regional shows.

LONGINES,17J., GJS, cal.10L, c.1952
14k $125 $165 $250

LONGINES, 17 jewels, fancy lugs, c. 1954
14k $300 $375 $500

LONGINES,17J., GJS, cal.23z, c.1954
18k $275 $325 $400

LONGINES, 17 jewels, fancy lugs, c. 1949
14k $300 $350 $450

LONGINES, 15 jewels, c. 1940s
18k $225 $265 $350
14k $150 $185 $250
s. steel $125 $165 $175

LONGINES, 19J.,"Conquest", auto-wind,
14k $400 $475 $650

LONGINES, 17J., fancy lugs, diamond dial,
14k $325 $375 $500

LONGINES,17J., GJS, cal.22ls, c.1950
14k $200 $235 $285

⊕ Some grades are not included. Their values can be
determined by comparing with **similar** age, size, metal
content, style, grades, or models such as **time only**,
chronograph, repeater etc. listed.

LONGINES,17J., "Flagship", GJS, cal.340, autow., c.1960
18k $200 $250 $350

LONGINES,17J., center sec., GJS, c.1948
14k $150 $185 $250

LONGINES,17J., GJS, cal.19as, autow., c.1955
gold filled..................................$75 $100 $165

LONGINES,17J., "Admiral", GJS, cal.340, autow., c.1960
14k $125 $165 $250

LONGINES,17J., RF#3759, GJS, cal.22as, autow., c.1949
14k $225 $250 $325

LONGINES,17J., GJS, center sec., Ca.1951
gold filled $125 $150 $200

LONGINES,17J., center sec., GJS, cal., c.1940
14k $150 $185 $250

LONGINES,17J., GJS, center sec., c.1943
14k $125 $165 $250

Wrist Watches listed in this section are priced at the collectable fair market Trade Show level as **complete** watches having an original gold-filled case and stainless steel back, also with original dial, leather watch band, and the entire original movement in good working order with no repairs needed.

Pricing in this Guide are fair market price for **COMPLETE** watches which are reflected from the "**NAWCC**" National and regional shows.

LONGINES, 17J., military, Ca.1942
s. steel $300 $400 $550

LONGINES,17J., GJS, "Flagship", date, autow., c.1964
gold filled..................................$75 $100 $165

LONGINES,17J., 36,000 (beat), auto-wind, "Ultra-Chron"
14k $200 $225 $265

LONGINES,17J., Date, GJS, " 5 Star Admiral", autowind,
Cal. 501, Ca.1968
gold filled..............................$100 $125 $185

LONGINES,17J., a-wind, "5 star Admiral", date, Ca.1963
gold filled $75 $100 $165

LONGINES,17J., "5 star Admiral", cal.506, autow., c.1965
14k $125 $150 $225

LONGINES,17J., high frequency, date, autow., c.1972
s. steel $75 $100 $165

LONGINES, 17 jewels, ''Flagship'' autowind
14k $125 $165 $250

LONGINES, 17 jewels, gold jewel settings, Ca. 1950
s. steel $75 $100 $150

LONGINES, 17J., "Grand Prize", auto-w., date, Ca. 1950
gold filled $75 $100 $175
14k $250 $300 $350

LONGINES, 17 jewels, center seconds
14k $175 $200 $250

LONGINES, 17J., aux. seconds, large lugs
14k $150 $200 $250

LONGINES, 17J., "Conquest", auto-w., date, w.-indicator
s. steel $375 $425 $500

LONGINES, 17J., auto wind
14k $125 $165 $250

LONGINES, 17J., date, ca. 1940s
14k $275 $300 $350

LONGINES, 19J., "Conquest", auto-w., date, ca.1962
s. steel $400 $450 $600

LONGINES,17J., mystery dial, cal.232 c.1960
gold filled $200 $250 $350

LONGINES,17J., mystery dial,
gold filled..............................$200　　$250　　$325

LONGINES, 17 jewels, mystery hand, ca.1962
gold filled..............................$200　　$250　　$325

LONGINES, 17 jewels, mystery hand, autowind
14k ....$300　　$375　　$500

LONGINES, 17 jewels, diamond dial, center lugs
14k ....$400　　$425　　$500

LONGINES, 17J., "Ultra Chron," diamond dial, autow.
14k ....$195　　$250　　$350

LONGINES, 17 jewels, "Ultra Chron," date, autow., c.1949
14k ....$125　　$175　　$250

LONGINES, 17 jewels, mystery hand, 12 diamond dial
14k ....$500　　$550　　$700

LONGINES,17J., mystery 39 diamond dial, RF#1017
14k(w)....................................$750　　$850　　$1,000

LONGINES, 17J., auto-w., aux. sec.
14k ....$125　　$165　　$250

🕐 Some grades are not included. Their values can be
determined by comparing with **similar** age, size, metal
content, style, grades, or models such as **time only**,
chronograph, repeater etc. listed.

LONGINES, 17J., auto-w., aux. sec.
14k $175 $200 $250

LONGINES, 17J., aux sec.
14k $150 $185 $250

LONGINES, 17J., diamond dial
14k(W)....................................$200 $250 $350

LONGINES, 17J., diamond bezel
gold filled................................$175 $200 $275

LONGINES, 17J.,3 diamond dial
gold filled $100 $125 $200

LONGINES, 17J., diamond dial,
14k(W)..................................$150 $200 $300

LONGINES, 17 jewels, cocktail style, 36 diamond dial
14k(W)..................................$275 $300 $385

LONGINES, 17J., 12 diamond dial, textured case
14k (w) $175 $225 $325

LONGINES,17J., GJS, 34 diamond dial, date, autow., c.1962
14k $300 $325 $385

LONGINES,17J., 44 diamond bezel, GJS, cal.22L, c.1952
18k(w).............................$450 $500 $600

LONGINES, 17J., 14 diamond dial, Ca. 1960
14k $150 $185 $285

LONGINES,17J., 14 diamonds,GJS, cal.370, c.1960
14k $150 $200 $300

LONGINES,17J., "Admiral", GJS, auto-wind, Ca. 1960
14k $275 $300 $400

LONGINES,17J., 4 diamonds, cal.194, c.1958
gold filled...............................$100 $125 $185

LONGINES, 17J., GJS, Ca. 1935-
14k (rose)...............................$300 $350 $450

LONGINES,17J., 37 diamonds on bezel 24 on dial, c.1958
14k(w)......................................$350 $400 $500

LONGINES, 17J., GJS, faceted crystal, Ca.1951
gold filled $75 $100 $165

LONGINES, 17J., GJS, cal.9L, Ca.1939
gold filled $75 $100 $185

LONGINES, 17J., 4 diamonds, GJS, cal.23z, c.1948
14k $125 $165 $250

LONGINES, 17J., 3 diamonds, hidden lugs, GJS, c.1943
gold filled $75 $100 $165

LONGINES, 17J., 5 diamonds, GJS, cal.8ln, c.1940
14k(w)....................................$125 $165 $250

LONGINES, 17J., 17 diamonds, GJS, c.1951
14k $250 $300 $400

LONGINES, 17J., 8 diamonds, GJS, cal.22L, c.1958
14k $125 $165 $250

LONGINES, 17J., 15 diamonds, GJS, cal.9L, c.1945
platinum...................................$750 $850 $1,100
14k $300 $375 $500

LONGINES,17J.,4 diamonds, textured bezel,cal.194, c.1955
gold filled................................$75 $100 $165

LONGINES, 17J., 18 diamonds, RF#176, GJS, c.1950
14k(w)................................ $300 $350 $500

LONGINES, 17J., 8 diamonds, GJS
14k $125 $165 $250

LONGINES, 17J., 16 diamonds, cal.9LT, c.1958
14k(w)....................................$225 $275 $375

LONGINES, 17J., 4 diamonds, GJS, cal.L8474, c.1960
gold filled.................................$75 $100 $185

LONGINES, 17J., 6 diamonds, RF#2763, GJS, c.1955
14k $175 $225 $325

LONGINES, 17J., 8 diamonds, GJS, cal.9LT, c.1958
14k(w)....................................$175 $225 $325

LONGINES, 17J., 5 diamonds, GJS, c.1945
14k C&B $450 $500 $550

LONGINES, 17J., 5 diamonds, GJS, cal.9L, c.1952
14k $250 $275 $350

LONGINES, 17 jewels, 17 diamond dial, c. 1951
14k(w)....................................$300 $350 $425

LONGINES, 17 jewels, diamond dial, hidden lugs, c. 1938
s. steel $125 $200 $300

LONGINES, 17 jewels, fancy hidden lugs, diamond dial
14k (w) $400 $500 $700

LONGINES, 17 jewels, diamond dial, c. 1944
14k $300 $350 $450

LONGINES, 17 jewels, 17 diamond dial, c. 1951
14k $200 $250 $350

LONGINES, 17 jewels, diamond dial, c. 1935
platinum.............................. $1,100 $1,200 $1,500
14k $750 $800 $950

LONGINES, 17 jewels, 18 diamond dial
14k (w) $150 $200 $325

LONGINES, 17 jewels, flared, 6 diamond dial
14k $600 $650 $750

LONGINES, 17 jewels, 4 diamond dial
14k $175 $225 $300

LONGINES, 17 jewels, 12 diamond dial
s.steel $150 $175 $225

LONGINES, 17 jewels, stepped case, Ca. 1951
14k $175 $225 $300

LONGINES, 17 jewels, c. 1923
gold filled..................................$75 $100 $175

LONGINES, 17 jewels, flared, c. 1959
14k $600 $650 $750

LONGINES, 17 jewels, flared
14k C&B................................$750 $850 $1,000

LONGINES, 17 jewels, fancy lugs, c. 1943
14k $300 $350 $450

LONGINES, 17 jewels, torpedo shaped numbers
14k $150 $175 $275

LONGINES, 17 jewels, curved, fancy lugs, c. 1939
14k $300 $350 $450

LONGINES, 17 jewels, center lugs, c. 1955
14k $175 $200 $275

LONGINES, 17 jewels, hooded lugs, diamond dial
14k(w)...................................$700 $800 $950

LONGINES, 17 jewels, hooded lugs
14k $200 $225 $300

LONGINES, 17J., 2 diamonds & 1 baguette, Ca. 1944
14K $500 $600 $800

LONGINES, 17 jewels, diamond dial, fancy lugs
14k $450 $500 $600

LONGINES, 17 jewels, diamond dial
14k(W) $250 $300 $375

LONGINES, 17 jewels, diamond dial, c. 1944
14k $175 $200 $275

LONGINES, 17J., curved,
14k $150 $200 $300

LONGINES, 17 jewels, fancy lugs
14k $175 $200 $275

LONGINES, 17J., stepped case,
14k $300 $325 $400

LONGINES, 17 jewels, c. 1930
18k $700 $775 $900
14k $500 $550 $700
gold filled $175 $200 $275

LONGINES, 17J., curvex, 52mm, ca. 1930
gold filled $400 $450 $600

DIALS FOR MINT PRICES MUST BE ALL **ORIGINAL**.

LONGINES, 15J., tonneau, GJS, c.1925
silver $300 $350 $450

LONGINES, 17J., carved bezel, GJS, cal.9LT, c.1950
gold filled $75 $100 $165

LONGINES, 17J., stepped case, GJS, cal.9L, c.1939
14k $250 $275 $325

LONGINES, 17J., butler finish, GJS, cal., c.1951
gold filled $75 $100 $165

LONGINES, 17J., extended lugs, GJS, cal.9L, c.1942
14k $175 $200 $300

LONGINES, 17J., beveled bezel, GJS, cal., c.1935
gold filled $75 $100 $175

LONGINES, 17J., cut corner, cal.94w, c.1929
gold filled.................................$75 $100 $175

LONGINES, 17J., aux. sec., GJS, cal.9L, c.1948
gold filled $75 $100 $175

LONGINES, 17J., tonneau, cal.9L, c.1948
gold filled..............................$125 $150 $225

Wrist Watches listed in this section are priced at the collectable
fair market **Trade Show** level as **complete** watches having an
original gold-filled case and stainless steel back, also with
original dial, leather watch band, and the entire original movement in good working order with no repairs needed.

LONGINES, 17J., carved case, GJS, cal.9LT, c.1950s
14k $200 $225 $275

🕐 A collector should expect to pay modestly higher prices
at local shops

🕐 Some grades are not included. Their values can be
determined by comparing with **similar** age, size, metal
content, style, grades, or models such as **time only**,
chronograph, repeater etc. listed.

DIALS FOR MINT PRICES MUST BE ALL **ORIGINAL**.

LONGINES, 17J., butler finish, GJS, cal.9LT, c.1957
14k $150 $185 $250

LONGINES, 17J., fluted lugs, GJS, cal.9L, c.1949
gold filled $75 $100 $175

LONGINES, 15-17J., butler finish, c.1926
gold filled................................$75 $100 $165

LONGINES, 17J., carved case, GJS, cal.9LT, c.1959
gold filled $75 $100 $175

LONGINES, 17J., stepped case, GJS, cal.9LT, c.1958
14k $200 $250 $350

LONGINES, 17J., spur lugs, GJS, cal., c.1948
gold filled $75 $100 $175

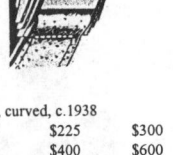

LONGINES, 17J., right angle, GJS, curved, c.1938
gold filled................................$175 $225 $300
s. steel $350 $400 $600
14k $500 $600 $900

LONGINES, 17J., extended lugs, GJS, cal.9LT, c.1955
14k $200 $250 $325

LONGINES, 17J., fancy lugs, GJS, cal.9LT, c.1957
14k $175 $200 $265

LONGINES, 17J., fancy bezel, GJS, Ca. 1950
14k $175 $200 $275

LONGINES, 17J., fluted sides, GJS, cal.9LT, c.1950
gold filled.................................$100 $125 $185

LONGINES, 17J., carved case, GJS, cal.9LT, c.1955
14k $300 $350 $450

LONGINES, 17J., flared case, GJS, Ca. 1956
14K..$200 $265 $350

LONGINES, 17J., gold jewel settings, Ca. 1951
gold filled.................................$75 $100 $165
14k (w)....................................$175 $195 $250

LONGINES, 17J., RF#8475, GJS, cal.10L, c.1948
14k $175 $200 $250

LONGINES,17J., GJS, c.1958
14k $175 $200 $250

LONGINES, 17J., RF#3327, GJS, cal.10L c.1948
gold filled $75 $100 $165

LONGINES, 17J., extended lugs, GJS, cal.9LT, c.1951
14k $225 $265 $325

LONGINES, 17J., aux. sec., GJS, Ca.1951
14k $125 $165 $250

LONGINES, 17J., butler finish, GJS, cal.9L, c.1955
14k $125 $150 $225

⊕ Some grades are not included. Their values can be
determined by comparing with **similar** age, size, metal
content, style, grades, or models such as **time only**,
chronograph, repeater etc. listed.

LONGINES, 17J., aux. sec., GJS, cal.9LT, c.1950
14k $150 $185 $275

LONGINES, 17J., fancy lugs, GJS, cal.10L, c.1951
gold filled $75 $100 $165

LONGINES, 17J., butler finish, GJS, cal.8LN, c.1942
14k $125 $165 $250

LONGINES, 17J., GJS, cal. 23Z, Ca. 1950
gold filled $75 $100 $165

LONGINES, 17J., beveled lugs, GJS, cal.8LN, c.1947
14k $125 $165 $250

LONGINES, 17J., beveled case, GJS, cal.9LT, c.1955
gold filled $75 $100 $165

LONGINES, 17J., wide bezel, GJS, cal.23z, c.1950
gold filled.................................$75 $100 $165

LONGINES, 17J., curly lugs, GJS, cal.23z, c.1950
gold filled $75 $100 $165

LONGINES, 17J., GJS, cal.23z, c.1957
14k $150 $185 $250

🕐 Pricing in this Guide are fair market price for **COMPLETE**
watches which are reflected from the "**NAWCC**" National and
regional shows.

LONGINES, 17J., checked dial, GJS, cal.22L, c.1957
14k $125 $175 $250

DIALS FOR MINT PRICES MUST BE ALL **ORIGINAL**.

LONGINES, 17J., RF#1050, mystery dial, cal.23z, c.1960
14k $300 $350 $425

LONGINES, 17J., center seconds, GJS, hidden lugs, Ca.1942
14k (rose)................................$150 $175 $265

LONGINES, 17J., textured bezel, GJS, cal.22L, c.1950
14k $225 $250 $350

LONGINES, 17J., stepped case, GJS, cal.23z, c.1955
14k $125 $165 $250
gold filled................................$75 $100 $165

LONGINES, 17J., carved case, GJS,
gold filled................................$75 $100 $165

LONGINES, 17J., hooded lugs, GJS, cal.8LN, c.1942
gold filled $75 $100 $175

LONGINES, 17J., RF#2288, hidden lugs, GJS, c.1955
14k $250 $285 $375

LONGINES, 17J., hidden lugs
14k (rose)................................$400 $450 $600

LONGINES, 17J., **contract** case or recent case,
14k $75 $100 $175

LONGINES, 17 jewels, 42mm
14k (w) $300 $350 $500

Wrist Watches listed in this section are priced at the collectable
fair market **Trade Show** level as **complete** watches having an
original gold-filled case and stainless steel back, also with
original dial, leather watch band, and the entire original movement in good working order with no repairs needed.

🕑 A collector should expect to pay modestly higher prices
at local shops

LONGINES, 17 jewels, **hinged** lugs
14k $200 $265 $375

LONGINES, 17 jewels, Ca. 1939
14k $250 $325 $475

LONGINES, 17 jewels, curvex, slanted lugs
14k (w)......................................$150 $175 $250

LONGINES, 17 jewels, fancy lugs, c. 1942
14k $250 $275 $350

LONGINES, 17 jewels, fancy U shaped lugs, c. 1947
14k $250 $285 $375

LONGINES, 17 jewels, curved, flared
14k $150 $185 $250

LONGINES, 15 jewels, chased bezel
14k $600 $700 $850

LONGINES, 15 jewels, engraved bezel, c. 1928
14k (w) $600 $700 $850

LONGINES, 17J., faceted crystal, center seconds
14k $125 $175 $250

LONGINES, 17J., fancy lugs & diamond bezel
14k(W)......................................$400 $475 $600

LONGINES, 17J., curved case, Ca. 1930s
14k $300 $350 $450

🕐 Pricing in this Guide are fair market price for **COMPLETE** watches which are reflected from the "**NAWCC**" National and regional shows.

LONGINES, 17J., fancy lugs
14k $275 $300 $375

LONGINES, 17J., cal#10L, center sec.,
14k ...., $175 $200 $285

LONGINES, 17J., fancy lugs,
14k $275 $300 $375

LONGINES, 17J., center sec., fancy lugs, ca.1946
14k $175 $200 $285

LONGINES, 17J., cal#232, ca. 1948
14k $125 $165 $265

LONGINES, 17J., fancy lugs, cal#10L
14k $150 $200 $285

LONGINES, 17J., aux. sec.
14k $200 $235 $300

LONGINES, 17J., aux. sec.
14k $125 $175 $250

LONGINES, 17J., ca. 1952
14k $175 $200 $275

🕀 Some grades are not included. Their values can be determined by comparing with **similar** age, size, metal content, style, grades, or models such as **time only**, chronograph, repeater etc. listed.

LONGINES, 17J., offset lugs
14k $400 $450 $600

🕀 A collector should expect to pay modestly higher prices at local shops

LONGINES, 17J., fancy lugs, ca. 1951
14k $175 $200 $275

LONGINES, 17J., hidden lugs, Ca. 1940
14k(rose)................................ $400 $435 $500

LONGINES, 17J., fancy bezel
14k $125 $165 $250

LONGINES, 17 jewels, **enameled** bezel, c. 1928
14k $400 $435 $500

LONGINES, 17J., flared case, GJS, c.1955
gold filled............................... $175 $200 $275

LONGINES, 17 jewels, formed case
14k $200 $275 $400

LONGINES, 17J., flared case, GJS, cal.9LT, c.1950
gold filled............................... $150 $200 $275

LONGINES, 17J., flared case, textured dial
14k $450 $500 $600

LONGINES, 17J., antimagnetic, military
s. steel $400 $500 $700

Wrist Watches listed in this section are priced at the collectable fair market **Trade Show** level as **complete** watches having an original gold-filled case and stainless steel back, also with original dial, leather watch band, and the entire original movement in good working order with no repairs needed.

🕐 Some grades are not included. Their values can be determined by comparing with **similar** age, size, metal content, style, grades, or models such as **time only**, chronograph, repeater etc. listed.

LONGINES MOVEMENT IDENTIFICATION

Cal. No. 4.21, Ca.1930

Cal. No. 5.16, Ca.1922

Cal. No. 6.22, Ca.1932

Cal. No. 7.45, Ca.1916

Cal. No. 7.48, Ca.1925

Cal. No. 8.23, Ca.1931

Cal. No. 8.47, Ca.1916

Cal. No. 9.32, Ca.1932

Cal. No. 9.47, Ca.1922

Cal. No. 12.19, Ca.1934

Cal. No. 13.15, Ca.1936

Cal. No. 25.17, Ca.1935

PRODUCTION TOTALS
LONGINES DATE OF MOVEMENT MANUFACTURE

DATE– SERIAL #	DATE– SERIAL #	DATE– SERIAL #
1867 — 1	1911 - 2,500,000	1937 - 5,500,000
1870 — 20,000	1912 - 2,750,000	1938 - 5,750,000
1875 — 100,000	1913 - 3,000,000 - Aug.	1940 - 6,000,000 - June
1882 — 250,000	1915 - 3,250,000	1945 - 7,000,000 - July
1888 — 500,000	1917 - 3,500,000	1950 - 8,000,000 - May
1893 — 750,000	1919 - 3,750,000	1953 - 9,000,000 - July
1899 - 1,000,000 - Feb.	1922 - 4,000,000 - Oct.	1956-10,000,000 - May
1901 - 1,250,000	1925 - 4,250,000	1959-11,000,000 - April
1904 - 1,500,000	1926 - 4,500,000	1962-12,000,000 - May
1905 - 1,750,000	1928 - 4,750,000	1966-13,000,000 - June
1907 - 2,000,000 - July	1929 - 5,000,000 - Oct.	1967-14,000,000 - Feb.
1909 - 2,250,000	1934 - 5,250,000	1969-15,000,000 - Feb.

The above list is provided for determining the APPROXIMATE age of your watch. Match serial number with date. Watches were not necessarily sold in the exact order of manufactured date.
LONGINES date of movement manufacture

Caliber number

Caliber number

Movement number

Reference number

Cal. No. 10.68, Ca.1932   Cal. No. 10.68, Lindburg   Cal. No. 12.68, Ca.1938   Cal. No. 12.68 Z, Ca.1939

Cal. No. 14.16, Ca.1951   Cal. No. 14.16 S, Ca.1954   Cal. No. 14.17, Ca.1952   Cal. No. 15.18, Ca.1941

Cal. No. 19 A, Ca.1952   Cal. No. 19.4, Ca.1953   Cal. No. 19.4 S, Ca.1953   Cal. No. 22 A, Ca.1945

Cal. No. 22 L, Ca.1946   Cal. No. 23 Z, Ca.1948   Cal. No. 23 ZD, Ca.1954   Cal. No. 25.17, Ca.1935

Cal. No. RR 280, Ca.1963   Cal. No. 290, Ca.1958   Cal. No. 310   Cal. No. 312

Cal. No. 380

Cal. No. 420

Cal. No. 430, Ca.1967

Cal. No. 320

Cal. No. 450

Cal. No. 460

Cal. No. 470

Cal. No. 30 CH, Ca.1947

Cal. No. 30 ZN

Cal. No. 330

To determine your Wrist watch **band** size use the ABOVE GAUGE and measure between the lugs.

LONGINES, 17J., "COMET", cal.702, c.1972
s. steel $75 $100 $175

LONGINES, 17J., lady's style, center lugs, c.1948
14k C&B.................................$175 $200 $275

LONGINES, 15J., lady's style,
14k C&B.................................$175 $200 $275

LONGINES, 15-17J., **ring watch** lady's style, Ca. 1949
14k $175 $200 $300

LORTON, 17 jewels, chronog., c. 1950
s. steel $150 $200 $275

LOUVIC, 17J., mystery dial, long triangular case, c.1950
base metal $60 $85 $100

LOUVIC, 17J., hunter style case, ca. 1965
s. steel $75 $100 $165

LOUVIC, 17J., **mystery** diamond dial, ca.1960
s. steel $200 $225 $275

LUCERNE, 17 jewels, 14k case & band , 3 diamonds
14k C&B............................... $200 $225 $275

LUCIEN PICCARD, 17J., movement by Ditisheim
14k $100 $125 $175

LUCIEN PICCARD, 17 jewels, gem set bezel
14k $200 $225 $300

LUCIEN PICCARD, 17 jewels, "Seahawk," auto wind
18k C&B................................$300 $335 $400

LUCIEN PICCARD, 17J., auto wind, wind indicator, c. 1958
s. steel $75 $100 $150

LUCIEN PICCARD, 17 jewels, skeletonized
18k $300 $350 $450

🕐 Some grades are not included. Their values can be
determined by comparing with **similar** age, size, metal
content, style, grades, or models such as **time only**,
chronograph, repeater etc. listed.

LUSINA, 17 jewels, aux. sec., fancy lugs
gold filled $60 $85 $125

LYCEUM, 17J., beveled case, aux. sec.
14k $100 $135 $200

MAPPIN, 15 jewels, duo dial, c. 1930
9k $500 $575 $700

MARLYS, 15J., G.J.S., c.1935
14k $125 $135 $175

MARS, 17J, "Dateur," date on lugs, hinged back, c. 1934
gold filled $250 $275 $350

MARVIN, 17J., center sec., cal.520s, c.1943
14k $100 $125 $200

MARVIN, 17J., non magnetic,
gold filled..................................$50 $65 $95

MARVIN, 17J., c.1943
base metal $50 $60 $90

MASTER, 17J., tonneau case, c.1943
gold plate $30 $40 $65

MASTER, 17J., stepped case, c.1943
gold plate $30 $40 $65

⊕ Pricing in this Guide are fair market price for **COMPLETE**
watches which are reflected from the "**NAWCC**" National and
regional shows.

C.H. MEYLAN, 17 jewels, c. 1940s
18k $200 $250 $350

C.H. MEYLAN, 18 jewels, **jump** hr., c. 1920
18k $3,000 $3,500 $4,500

C.H. MEYLAN, 16 jewels, wire lugs
14k $225 $250 $325

C.H. MEYLAN, 27J, 1 button chronog., 2 reg., enamel dial
18k $2,500 $2,900 $3,700

C.H. MEYLAN, 18J., ladies , Octagon case, c.1917
platinum.................................$300 $325 $400

J.E. MEYLAN, 17J., chronograph, 2 reg., ca. 1937
14k $500 $600 $800
s. steel $250 $300 $400

J.E. MEYLAN,17J., stop watch,
s. steel $175 $225 $350

MIDO, 15J., **"KAR"**, in form of car radiator, Ca. 1930s
Note: winds at 12
silver $2,000 $2,200 $2,800

MIDO, 17 jewels, chronog., "Multi-centerchrono", c. 1952
s. steel $400 $500 $700

MIDO, 17 jewels, chronog., "Multi-centerchrono"
s. steel $500 $600 $800
with telemeter dial $600 $700 $900

MIDO, 17J., choronog., Pulsations, cal.1300, c.1954
gold filled $500 $600 $800
14k $700 $800 $1,000
18k $800 $900 $1,200

MIDO, 15J., "DIRECT-TIME", **jump** hour, Ca. 1932
14k (w) $500 $550 $800
18k (w) $600 $700 $1,000
s. steel $350 $400 $550

MIDO, 17J., carved case, cal.2m, c.1947
14k $150 $185 $250

DIALS FOR MINT PRICES MUST BE ALL **ORIGINAL**.

MIDO, 17 jewels, diamond dial

s. steel	$100	$135	$200
14k	$175	$200	$275
platinum	$300	$400	$650

MIDO, 17J., RF#7204, cal.d917b, autow., c.1958
s. steel $60 $70 $95

MIDO, 17J., **"Radiotime"**, to correct time push button on crown advances minutes & seconds hand, Ca. 1939
gold filled......................★ ★ $400 $500 $700

MIDO, 17J., RF#228, **mid size** case, autow., c.1943
s. steel $40 $55 $85

MIDO, 17 jewels, fancy lugs, c. 1945
14k $150 $185 $250

MIDO, 17J., autowind, Ca. 1958
s. steel $65 $75 $95

MIDO, 15 jewels, mystery dial, c. 1935
s. steel $500 $600 $800

MIDO, 17J., multifort grand luxe, autow., date, ca. 1950s
18k C&B $300 $400 $650

MIDO, 17J., **mid size** case, cal.917r, autow., c.1949
s. steel $40 $55 $85

🕐 Some grades are not included. Their values can be determined by comparing with **similar** age, size, metal content, style, grades, or models such as **time only**, chronograph, repeater etc. listed.

MIDO, 17J., super auto-wind, muiltfort extra,
14k $100 $135 $235
s. steel $50 $65 $95

MIDO, 17J., "Power Wind", c.1955
s. steel $50 $65 $95

MIDO, 17J., rotating bezel, autow., c.1960
s. steel $150 $195 $300

MIDO, 17J., multifort grand luxe, extra-flat
s. steel $50 $60 $95

MILDIA, 17 jewels
s. steel $30 $45 $85

MIMO, 15 jewels, date
gold filled $75 $100 $150

MIMO, 17J., "De Frece", date, c.1935
14k(w) $125 $150 $200

MIMO, 17 jewels, **jumping** hr., wandering min. & sec.
gold filled $300 $350 $450

MIMO, 17 jewels, **8 day**, 6 gear train, c. 1950s
gold filled $400 $500 $650

MIMO, 17 jewels, duo dial, doctors watch
s. steel $325 $385 $500

MINERVA, 15 jewels, one button chronog., 2 reg.,
enamel dial, Ca.1920
gold $500 $600 $800

MIMO, 15 jewels, engraved bezel
gold filled................................... $35 $45 $75

MINERVA, 17 jewels, waterproof, chronog., c. 1950s
14k $400 $450 $700
s. steel $250 $300 $400

MIMO, 15 jewels, "Mimomatic," c. 1932
s. steel $60 $75 $100

MINERVA, 17J., 3 reg. chronog., Valjoux cal.723, c.1955
14k $750 $850 $1,100
s. steel $500 $550 $750

MINERVA, 29J., **min. repeater**, repeats on **2** gongs
18k $12,000 $14,000 $18,000

MINERVA, 17 jewels, chronog., 2 reg. telemeter km
18k $700 $900 $1,400
s. steel $275 $350 $500

MINERVA, 19 jewels, chronog., 3 reg.
s. steel $300 $350 $500

MINERVA, 17 jewels, one button chronog., c. 1942
s. steel $300 $350 $450

MINERVA, 17J., chronog., day-date-month, 3 reg.
18k $900 $1,000 $1,200

MINERVA, 17 jewels, center sec., auto wind
gold filled................................. $50 $65 $95

MISC. SWISS, 15J., hunter style, wire lugs, ca. 1926
silver $450 $500 $600
Watches listed in this BOOK as Misc. Swiss are just a few
examples of miscellaneous jobbers, distributors & jewelry
firms. Example Abc Watch Co., to Zuma Watch Co., etc. with
the name xxxx out.

Watches listed in this BOOK as Misc. Swiss are just a few
examples of miscellaneous jobbers, distributors & jewelry
firms. Example Abc Watch Co., to Zuma Watch Co., etc. with
the name xxxx out.

MISC. SWISS, 15J., shield cover, enamel dial, ca. 1927
silver $600 $650 $750

MISC. SWISS,15J., **rim wind,** wire lugs, cal., c.1920
s. steel .... ★$250 $300 $400

MISC. SWISS,15J., mother of pearl dial, c.1925
s. steel $150 $200 $275

MISC. SWISS,15J., wire lugs, exaggerated no.s, c.1925
silver $200 $265 $375

🕐 Some grades are not included. Their values can be
determined by comparing with **similar** age, size, metal
content, style, grades, or models such as **time only**,
chronograph, repeater etc. listed.

MISC. SWISS, 15J., wire lugs, Ca. 1918
silver $100 $125 $165

MISC. SWISS, 15J., wire lugs, Ca. 1917
silver $85 $100 $125

MISC. SWISS, 15J., wire lugs, Ca. 1918
silver $100 $135 $175

MISC. SWISS, 15J., wire lugs, Ca. 1917
silver $100 $125 $165

MISC. SWISS, 15J., wire lugs, Ca. 1917
base metal $55 $65 $90

MISC. SWISS, 15J., wire lugs, Ca. 1917
silver $100 $125 $165

MISC. SWISS, 15J., wire lugs, Ca. 1917
silver $100 $125 $175

MISC. SWISS, 15J., **protective grill**, wire lugs, Ca. 1917
silver $250 $300 $400

MISC. SWISS, 15J., wire lugs, Ca. 1917
base metal $65 $75 $90

Watches listed in this BOOK as Misc. Swiss are just a few
examples of miscellaneous jobbers, distributors & jewelry
firms. Example Abc Watch Co., to Zuma Watch Co., etc. with
the name xxxx out.

MISC. SWISS, 15J., wire lugs, **Demi** Hunter style, Ca. 1919
base metal $55 $65 $75

Watches listed in this BOOK as Misc. Swiss are just a few examples of miscellaneous jobbers, distributors & jewelry firms. Example Abc Watch Co., to Zuma Watch Co., etc. with the name xxxx out.

MISC. SWISS, 15J., wire lugs, Ca. 1917
silver $75 $100 $125

MISC. SWISS, 15J., wire lugs, Ca. 1917
14K...$100 $110 $150

MISC. SWISS, 15J., wire lugs, Ca. 1917
14K...$125 $150 $200

MISC. SWISS, 15J., wire lugs, Ca. 1917
14K...$100 $125 $165

MISC. SWISS, 15J., wire lugs, Ca. 1917
14K...$100 $125 $165

MISC. SWISS, 15J., wire lugs, Ca. 1917
14K...$100 $125 $165

MISC. SWISS, 15J., wire lugs, Ca. 1917
14k $100 $125 $165

MISC. SWISS, 15J., wire lugs, Ca. 1917
14K $100 $125 $165

MISC. SWISS, 15J., horseshoe style, Ca. 1935
base metal $100 $135 $200

MISC. SWISS, 17J., nail set, 31 X 52mm, exaggerated no.s, ca.1915
18k $1,200 $1,400 $2,000

MISC. SWISS, 15J., exaggerated no.s, 42mm, ca.1916
silver $600 $650 $850

MISC. SWISS, 15J., exaggerated no.s, 40mm. Ca.1916
18K..$1,100 $1,300 $1,600

MISC. SWISS, 15J., exaggerated no.s, 35mm. Ca.1916
18K $450 $575 $800

MISC. SWISS, 15J., exaggerated no.s, 40mm. Ca.1916
18K..$1,100 $1,300 $1,600

MISC. SWISS, 15J., exaggerated no.s, 40mm. Ca.1916
18K $1,600 $1,800 $2,200

MISC. SWISS, 15J., exaggerated no.s, 35mm. Ca.1920
14K..$300 $450 $650

MISC. SWISS, 15J., exaggerated no.s, wire lugs, Ca.1916
silver $125 $175 $250

MISC. SWISS, 15J., exaggerated no.s, 40mm. Ca.1916
18K....................................$1,100 $1,300 $1,600

MISC. SWISS, 15J., exaggerated no.s, wire lugs, Ca.1916
silver $125 $175 $250

MISC. SWISS, 15J., exaggerated no.s, 28mm. Ca.1916
silver $85 $110 $165

MISC. SWISS, 15J., exaggerated no.s, wire lugs, Ca.1916
14K..$200 $250 $400

Watches listed in this BOOK as Misc. Swiss are just a few examples of miscellaneous jobbers, distributors & jewelry
firms. Example Abc Watch Co., to Zuma Watch Co., etc.
with the name xxxx out.

MISC. SWISS, 15J., wire lugs, Ca.1917
silver $70 $85 $135

MISC. SWISS, 15J., wire lugs, Ca.1917
silver $135 $165 $225

MISC. SWISS, 15J., wire lugs, Ca.1917
silver $135 $165 $225

MISC. SWISS, 15J., wire lugs, Ca.1917
14k $135 $165 $225

MISC. SWISS, 15J., Ca.1925
14K...$135 $165 $225

MISC. SWISS, 15J., Ca.1925
14K...$135 $165 $225

MISC. SWISS, 15J., Ca.1925
14K $135 $165 $225

MISC. SWISS, 15J., Ca.1925
14K $135 $165 $225

MISC. SWISS, 15J., Ca.1925
14K $135 $165 $225

MISC. SWISS, 15J., Ca.1925
14K $135 $165 $225

MISC. SWISS, 15J., Ca.1925
14K $135 $165 $225

⏱ A collector should expect to pay modestly higher prices
at local shops

Wrist Watches listed in this section are priced at the collectable
fair market **Trade Show** level as **complete** watches having an
original gold-filled case and stainless steel back, also with
original dial, leather watch band, and the entire original movement in good working order with no repairs needed.

Watches listed in this BOOK as Misc. Swiss are just a few examples of miscellaneous jobbers, distributors & jewelry firms. Example Abc Watch Co., to Zuma Watch Co., etc. with the name xxxx out.

MISC. SWISS, 15J., Ca.1925
14K...$150 $175 $250

MISC. SWISS, 15J., Ca.1925
14K...$135 $165 $225

MISC. SWISS, 15J., Ca.1930
14K...$200 $250 $325

MISC. SWISS, 15J., Ca.1930
18K...$250 $300 $375

MISC. SWISS, 15J., Ca.1930
18K...$250 $300 $375

MISC. SWISS, 15J., Ca.1930
18K...$250 $300 $375

MISC. SWISS, 15J., Ca.1930
18K...$250 $300 $375

MISC. SWISS, 15J., Ca.1930
14K...$150 $175 $225

MISC. SWISS, 15J., Ca.1930
18K...$250 $300 $375

MISC. SWISS, 15J., Ca.1930
18K...$175 $200 $250

MISC. SWISS, 15J., flex lugs, Ca.1930
18K...$250 $300 $375

MISC. SWISS, 15J., aux. sec., ca. 1930s
gold filled $75 $100 $175

🕐 Some grades are not included. Their values can be determined by comparing with **similar** age, size, metal content, style, grades, or models such as **time only**, chronograph, repeater etc. listed.

MISC. SWISS, 15J., enamel dial, wire lugs, ca. 1925
silver $150 $200 $300

MISC. SWISS, 15J., wire lugs, nail set, ca.1925
silver $125 $165 $250

MISC. SWISS, 17 jewels, hunter, "Flip up"
gold filled................................ $300 $350 $450

MISC. SWISS, 15 jewels, "Flip open" Ca.1930
gold filled................................ $300 $350 $450

MISC.SWISS, 17J, Flip Top **winds by opening lid**, Ca.1932
gold filled................................ $600 $700 $900
base metal $400 $500 $700

MISC. SWISS, 17J., case flips up to view photo, c.1950
gold filled $200 $250 $335

MISC. SWISS, 17J., day date month moon phase, Ca. 1955
gold filled $500 $600 $850
14K $1,200 $1,400 $1,800

MISC. SWISS, 17J., jump hr., wandering min., c. 1930
9k $350 $400 $500
14k $500 $600 $750

MISC. SWISS, 17J., wandering min., hr. by red mark
s. steel $150 $200 $300

MISC. SWISS, 17 jewels, fancy bezel
14k $125 $150 $200
18k $175 $200 $250

MISC. SWISS, 17 jewels, masonic symbols, c. 1950s
s. steel & gold filled $900 $1,000 $1,200

MISC. SWISS, 17 jewels, digital hr., min.& sec.
s. steel $250 $300 $375
gold filled $275 $325 $400
s. steel (8 day)................... ★$400 $450 $600

MISC. SWISS, 17 jewels, masonic symbols, c. 1975
base metal $300 $350 $425

MISC. SWISS, 15 jewels, double dial, c.1935
9K $375 $475 $650

MISC. SWISS, 15 jewels, early auto wind, c. 1930s
s. steel $400 $500 $650

MISC. SWISS, 15 jewels, center lugs, c.1936
9K $100 $125 $175

(note tandem wind)
(see watch below for prices)
MISC. SWISS, 15J, 2 barrels, 8 day movement , (8 JOURS)

MISC. SWISS, 17J, drivers style winds at 12, Ca. 1930
gold filled $150 $200 $300

MISC. SWISS, 15 jewels, 2 barrels, 8 day watch, Ca. 1935
base metal $225 $250 $350
s. steel $275 $325 $400
silver $350 $550 $650

MISC. SWISS, 7J, "Corvette or Mercedes Benz", c.1970
base metal $60 $80 $125

Watches listed in this BOOK as Misc. Swiss are just a few examples of miscellaneous jobbers, distributors & jewelry firms. Example Abc Watch Co., to Zuma Watch Co., etc. with the name xxxx out.

MISC. SWISS, 29J, repeater, 2 jacquemart, **all original**
18k $3,000 $3,500 $4,500

MISC. SWISS, 17J., jump hour at 12:00, Ca. 1930
14k $1,000 $1,200 $1,500
18K $1,200 $1,400 $1,800

MISC. SWISS, 17J., silver coin, Ca. 1960
silver $100 $125 $175

MISC. SWISS,15J., one button chronog. wind and sets at 12, center hinged lugs, enamel dial, c.1920s
silver $1,400 $1,600 $2,000

MISC. SWISS, 17J., world time, date, Ca. 1965
s. steel $75 $90 $125

MISC. SWISS,15J., 1 button chronog., enamel dial, wire lugs, Ca.1923
silver $500 $600 $900

MISC. SWISS, 27J., perpetual calendar, Ca. 1970
base metal $50 $70 $110

MISC. SWISS, 15-17J, enamel dial, **one button** chronog.
s. steel $800 $900 $1,200

MISC. SWISS, 17J.,early 1 button chronog., ca.1929
18k $1,200 $1,400 $1,800

MISC. SWISS, 17J., 2 reg., chronograph
s. steel $175 $200 $275

MISC. SWISS, 15J., one button chronog., ca. 1925
silver $600 $700 $900

MISC. SWISS, 17J, chronog., 2 reg.
gold filled $175 $200 $275

MISC. SWISS,15-17J, enamel dial, 1 button chronog., 2 reg.
s. steel $500 $600 $800

MISC. SWISS,17J., "chronographe" on dial, c.1940
base metal $125 $150 $200

MISC. SWISS, 17J., one button, chronog., ca. 1950
gold filled..............................$250 $300 $450

MISC. SWISS,17J., by Venus
s. steel $125 $150 $200
14k $225 $250 $300
18K $275 $300 $350

Watches listed in this BOOK as Misc. Swiss are just a few examples of miscellaneous jobbers, distributors & jewelry
firms. Example Abc Watch Co., to Zuma Watch Co., etc.
with the name xxxx out.

MISC. SWISS, 17J., triple date, chronog., 2 reg., c.1955
s. steel $350 $400 $500

MISC. SWISS, 17J., chronog., triple date, moon ph., c. 1945
14k $800 $900 $1,100
s. steel $500 $600 $800

MISC. SWISS, 17 jewels, **split sec.** chronog., 2 reg.
18k $3,000 $3,500 $4,500
s. steel $2,000 $2,200 $2,600

MISC. SWISS, 18 jewels, Jaeger, chronog., c. 1930s
18k $600 $700 $900

MISC. SWISS, 17J., triple date, moon ph., ca. 1967
gold filled $250 $325 $450

MISC. SWISS, 17 jewels, **early auto wind**, Ca. 1930
14k $300 $350 $500

MISC. SWISS, 17J., diamond dial, Ca. 1945
14K $200 $225 $275

MISC. SWISS, 17J., diamond dial, **top hat**, Ca. 1945
platinum..................................$900 $1,000 $1,200

MISC. SWISS, 17J., mystery diamond dial, Ca. 1960
gold filled $175 $200 $275

MISC. SWISS, 17J., Rhinestone dial & bezel, Ca. 1950
gold filled................................$60 $75 $100

MISC. SWISS, 17J., Rhinestone dial & bezel, Ca. 1950
gold filled................................$60 $75 $100

MISC. SWISS, 17J., hidden lugs, Ca. 1934
gold filled................................$50 $65 $90

MISC. SWISS, 17J., fancy lugs, Ca. 1945
14k $150 $185 $250
18K...$185 $235 $350

MISC. SWISS, 17J., fancy lugs, Ca. 1940
gold filled................................$40 $50 $75

Watches listed in this BOOK as Misc. Swiss are just a few examples of miscellaneous jobbers, distributors & jewelry
firms. Example Abc Watch Co., to Zuma Watch Co., etc.
with the name xxxx out.

MISC. SWISS, 17J., fancy bezel, Ca. 1938
14K $125 $150 $200

MISC. SWISS, 17J., fancy bezel, Ca. 1947
gold filled $70 $85 $125
14K $125 $165 $225

MISC. SWISS, 17J., fancy bezel, Ca. 1930
18K (W)..................................$175 $225 $300

MISC. SWISS, 7J., stepped case, Ca. 1935
gold filled $40 $50 $80

MISC. SWISS, 17J., wandering minute & hour, Ca. 1938
base metal $150 $200 $300

MISC. SWISS, 15J., Ca. 1938
14K...$125 $150 $200

MISC. SWISS, 15J., Ca. 1925
silver $70 $85 $125

MISC. SWISS, 21J., curved, Ca. 1938
gold filled..............................$125 $165 $200

MISC. SWISS, 17J., Fancy lugs, Chronometer, Ca. 1950
14K...$150 $185 $225

MISC. SWISS, 17J., Fancy lugs & bezel, Ca. 1950
gold filled................................$75 $100 $125

Pricing in this Guide are fair market price for **COMPLETE** watches which are reflected from the "**NAWCC**" National and regional shows.

Watches listed in this BOOK as Misc. Swiss are just a few examples of miscellaneous jobbers, distributors & jewelry firms. Example Abc Watch Co., to Zuma Watch Co., etc. with the name xxxx out.

MISC. SWISS, 17J., Fancy lugs, Ca. 1950
gold filled $100 $135 $175

MISC. SWISS, 17J., Fancy lugs, Ca. 1950
14K $150 $185 $225

MISC. SWISS, 21J., Fancy lugs, Ca. 1955
18K $185 $225 $275

MISC. SWISS, 17J., Fancy lugs, Ca. 1948
gold filled $75 $100 $150

Some grades are not included. Their values can be determined by comparing with **similar** age, size, metal content, style, grades, or models such as **time only**, chronograph, repeater etc. listed.

MISC. SWISS, 22J., Military, Ca. 1941
base metal $400 $500 $700

MISC. SWISS, 15J., Military, Ca. 1942
s. steel $75 $100 $125

MISC. SWISS, 16J., Military, Ca. 1940
base metal $60 $75 $110

Watches listed in this BOOK as Misc. Swiss are just a few examples of miscellaneous jobbers, distributors & jewelry
firms. Example Abc Watch Co., to Zuma Watch Co., etc.
with the name xxxx out.

MISC. SWISS, 17J., enamel & gold bezel, pin set, c.1925
18k $175 $185 $225

MISC. SWISS, 15J., wire lugs, Ca. 1930
14K rose $75 $95 $125

MISC. SWISS, 15J., Ruby on case, Ca. 1950
14K $75 $95 $125

MISC. SWISS, 15J., Ca. 1930
14K case & band..................$195 $225 $275

MISC. SWISS, 15J., **Ring watch**, Ca. 1955
14K $85 $100 $150

MISC. SWISS, 21J., horseshoe shaped, Ca. 1939
gold filled $100 $125 $175

MONARCH, 7 jewels, stepped case
gold filled.................................$60 $75 $100

MONARCH, 7 jewels,
gold filled.................................$60 $75 $100

MONARCH, 7 jewels, engraved bezel, curved
gold filled.................................$70 $80 $110

MONARCH, 7 jewels , curved
14k $150 $200 $275
gold filled.................................$75 $100 $150

MONTBRILLANT, 15J., one button chronog. Ca 1915-20
MONTBRILLANT = early **BREITLING**
18k $1,500 $1,800 $2,500

MONTE, 16J., "Ancre", ca.1938
14k $125 $150 $200

MORIVA,17J., auto-w. with wind indicator,
s. steel $75 $100 $150

HY. MOSER & CIE., 14J., "Signal Corps USA", ctr. lugs
silver $375 $450 $600

HY. MOSER & CIE., 14-18J., one button chronograph, wind
and set at 12, center lugs, 2 reg. Ca. 1920s
silver $1,400 $1,700 $2,000

MOVADO, 15J., polyplan, winds at 12 o'clock, 46mm, curved, c. 1910
18k $5,000 $5,500 $6,500

MOVADO, 15J., polyplan, winds at 12 o'clock,
14k $3,500 $4,000 $4,800

MOVADO, 15J., polyplan, winds at 12 o'clock,
silver $2,200 $2,500 $3,000

Movado, Purse Watches See P.W. section Movado

ABOVE: **Polyplan**
MOVADO, side view of movement with three inclined plans.

MOVADO, 15J., "Chronometre", c.1930
14k $175 $265 $335

MOVADO, 17J., day date month, "Sportsman"
14k $300 $350 $450

MOVADO, 17J., day date month, snap back
18k $500 $575 $735

MOVADO, 17J., triple date, snap back ," calendomatic"
18k $600 $650 $800

MOVADO, 28J., date, "Kingmatic", c.1959
s. steel $80 $100 $150
14k(w)....................................$225 $250 $300

MOVADO, 17J., month date, ca. 1950s
14k $250 $300 $375

MOVADO, 17J., 1 button chronog., c.1948
s. steel $450 $500 $600

MOVADO, 17 jewels, day-date-month, c. 1945
18k $500 $600 $800
14k $300 $400 $600
s. steel $200 $265 $375

MOVADO, 17J., chronog., 2 reg., c.1940
14k $800 $900 $1,200

MOVADO, 17J, triple date, moon phases, Ca. 1959
Rose GF & s.s. $1,000 $1,200 $1,500
s. steel $900 $1,100 $1,400

MOVADO, 17J., 3 reg. chronog.
s. steel $800 $900 $1,200

MOVADO, 17J., 3 reg. chronog.,
18k $2,000 $2,200 $2,600
14k $1,500 $1,700 $2,200
s. steel $800 $900 $1,200

MOVADO, 17J., "Tempograf, chronog., 2 reg., c.1935
s. steel $1,000 $1,200 $1,500

The Movado trademark M over flat V was Registered in 1958.

MOVADO, 17J., 3 reg. chronog., date, auto wind
18k $700 $800 $1,000
s. steel $300 $375 $550

MOVADO, 17J., cal # 246, Cabochon crown, Ca. 1955
18K $300 $400 $600

MOVADO, 17J., El Primero date at 5, auto wind, c.1972
s. steel $300 $375 $550

MOVADO, 17J., center sec., auto wind, c.1948
14k $200 $225 $275

MOVADO,17J., RF#2652, rotating chapter,cal.352, c.1958
s. steel $300 $375 $550

MOVADO, 17J., "Cronoplan", Ca. 1940s
s. steel $700 $900 $1,200

MOVADO, 15J., aux. sec., cal.75, c.1946
s. steel $100 $125 $175

MOVADO, 17J., center sec., cal.261, c.1948
18k $175 $225 $300

🕐 Some grades are not included. Their values can be
determined by comparing with **similar** age, size, metal
content, style, grades, or models such as **time only**,
chronograph, repeater etc. listed.

MOVADO, 17J., aux. sec., cal.135, c.1960
s. steel $100 $125 $175

MOVADO, 17J., auto-wind, cal.8577, c.1957
14k $125 $150 $225

MOVADO, 17J., Tiffany & Co. on dial, center sec.,
14k $250 $275 $350

MOVADO, 15J., **2 colors of gold**, tonneau, Ca. 1940
18k $400 $500 $700

The Movado trademark M over flat V was Registered in 1958.

MOVADO, 17J., "Kingmatic", center sec.
14k $235 $275 $350

MOVADO, 17J., center sec.
s. steel $100 $125 $175

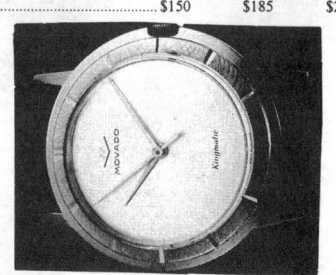

MOVADO, 20J., auto-wind,
14k $150 $185 $250

MOVADO, 28J., center sec.,"Kingmatic",
14k $150 $185 $250

In about 1895, L. A. & I. Ditesheim (before Movado) used trade names for pocket watches such as Ralco, Tanit, Ultra, Apogee, Record, Talma, Noblesse, Salud, Negus, Bonne, Belgravia, Surete and Mintral.

MOVADO, 17J., aux. sec.
18k $200 $250 $325

MOVADO, 15 jewels, aux. sec.
14k C&B............................... $400 $450 $550

MOVADO, 17J., auto-w., ca. 1949
14k $150 $200 $300

MOVADO, 17 jewels, aux. sec., center lugs
14k $200 $250 $325

MOVADO, 17J., nonmagnetic, RF # 11730, Ca. 1940
s. steel $100 $125 $175

MOVADO, 17J., cal.7025, GJS, c.1964
18k $200 $250 $325

MOVADO, 15 jewels, center lugs, c. 1930
18k $250 $285 $350

MOVADO, 17J., hidden lugs, **red** - 2-tone dial, c.1960
18k $300 $350 $425

MOVADO, 17J., textured 18k dial
18k $250 $285 $350

MOVADO, 17 jewels, "Museum", date at 12 o'clock
14k C&B................................. $400 $450 $600

MOVADO, 15 jewels, fancy lugs
18k $300 $325 $375

MOVADO, 17J., wide bezel, c.1958
gold filled..............................$100 $125 $175

MOVADO, 17J., diamond bezel,
18k $175 $225 $300

MOVADO, 17J., RF#621, c.1932
gold filled..............................$100 $125 $185

MOVADO, 17J., stepped case, "Curviplan", GJS, c.1942
14k $300 $350 $425

⊕ Pricing in this Guide are fair market price for **COMPLETE**
watches which are reflected from the "**NAWCC**" National and
regional shows.

MOVADO, 17J., aux. sec., c.1940
14k $150 $185 $250

MOVADO, 17J., extended lugs, c.1945
14k $150 $185 $250

MOVADO, 17J., aux. sec., c.1945
14k $150 $185 $275

MOVADO, 17J., extended lugs, GJS, c.1940
14k $150 $185 $275

MOVADO, 17J., tu-tone case, RF#13906, Ca.1948
14k $150 $185 $275

MOVADO, 17J., *Andy Warhol*,"**Times/5**", Ca.1988
Note: Total of **5** watches (only 3 watches shown)
Quartz (**250 made**)... ★★★$4,000 $4,500 $6,000

MOVADO, 15 jewels, curved, chronometre
14k $400 $450 $550

MOVADO, 15 jewels, exaggerated numbers, c. 1929
18k $400 $475 $600

MOVADO, 17J., cal#510, ca.1941
14k $300 $350 $425

MOVADO, 17 jewels
14k $100 $150 $225

MOVADO, 17J., curviplan,
gold filled.............................$150 $175 $250

MOVADO, 17 jewels, automatic, tank style
18k $300 $350 $425

MOVADO, 17J., curviplan, ca.1941
14k $400 $450 $525

MOVADO, 17 jewels, fancy lugs, c. 1947
14k $150 $200 $275

MOVADO, 17J., RF # 43872, ca.1945
14k $200 $250 $375

Wrist Watches listed in this section are priced at the collectable
fair market **Trade Show** level as **complete** watches having an
original gold-filled case and stainless steel back, also with
original dial, leather watch band, and the entire original movement in good working order with no repairs needed.

MOVADO, 17J., Ca. 1940s
14k $150 $175 $250

🕐 Pricing in this Guide are fair market price for **COMPLETE**
watches which are reflected from the "**NAWCC**" National and
regional shows.

MOVADO, 17 jewels
18k $300 $350 $425

MOVADO, 17 jewels, , Ca.1948
14k $300 $350 $425
18k $400 $450 $525

MOVADO, 17 jewels, hidden lugs, Ca.1940
14k $250 $300 $400

MOVADO,17 jewels, curviplan, , GJS, Ca.1937
14k $300 $350 $425

MOVADO, 17J., gold jewel settings, cal.510, Ca.1940
14k $175 $200 $250

MOVADO, 15 jewels, cal. 440, Ca. 1940
18k..$250 $300 $400

MOVADO, 15 jewels, gold jewel settings, Ca. 1930
18K(W) $250 $300 $400

MOVADO, 17 jewels, Ca. 1990s'
18K..$200 $225 $300

MOVADO, 17 jewels, gold jewel settings, Ca. 1940s'
14K..$175 $200 $250

MOVADO, 15J, hinged lugs, gold jewel settings, Ca. 1930s'
s. steel......................................$125 $150 $200

MOVADO, 17 jewels, ladies, alarm, Ca.1960
18k..$150 $185 $275

MOVADO MOVEMENT IDENTIFICATION

Caliber 35   Caliber 65   Caliber 575   Caliber25, 27-Sweep Second

Caliber 28   Caliber 575, Ermeto-Baby   Caliber 578, Ermeto Calendine   579, Calendoplan Baby

Caliber 5   Caliber 15   Caliber 50SP   Caliber 105, 107-Center Second

Caliber 190   Caliber 375, 377-Center Second   Caliber 440, 443-Center Second

Caliber 510   Caliber 260M, 261   Caliber 150MN, 157-Sweep Second

Polyplan
(first used in 1922)

Caliber 155, Calendermeto   Caliber 470, 477-Center Second   Caliber 473, 473SC-Calendar/Moon phase

Caliber 475, 475SC-Center Second   Caliber 225, 255M

Caliber 115   Caliber 118   Caliber 220, 220M

Caliber 221, 226   Caliber 223, 228   Caliber 224, 224A

Chronograph

Cal. 90M, 95M

12''' – 26,60 mm

U. NARDIN, 29 J., "Astrolabium," self wind, waterproof, local time, equinoctial time, months, signs of zodiac, elevation & azimuth of sun & moon, aspect in which sun & moon stand to each other. **recent**
18k $9,000 $10,000 $15,000

U. NARDIN, 17J., one button pulsations, ca. 1920
18k $1,800 $2,100 $2,600

U. NARDIN, 17J., one button, enamel dial, Pulsations, Ca. 1920
18k $2,000 $2,200 $3,000

🕑 Pricing in this Guide are fair market price for **COMPLETE** watches which are reflected from the "**NAWCC**" National and regional shows.

🕑 Some grades are not included. Their values can be determined by comparing with **similar** age, size, metal content, style, grades, or models such as **time only**, chronograph, repeater etc. listed.

U. NARDIN, 17 jewels, chronog., c. 1950s
18k..$1,500 $1,600 $1,900

U. NARDIN, 17 jewels, split sec. chronog., c. 1910
silver....................................$3,500 $4,000 $5,500

U. NARDIN, 17 jewels, chronog., 3 reg. c. 1940s
18k..$1,800 $2,000 $2,400

U. NARDIN, 25 jewels, date
14k..$175 $200 $275

U. NARDIN, 17 jewels, auto wind, c. 1952
14k $175 $200 $265

U. NARDIN,21J.,auto-wind
18k...$250 $275 $350

U. NARDIN, 17J., center sec., chronometer, c.1950
gold filled...................................$75 $100 $150

U. NARDIN, 17J., aux sec.
s. steel.....................................$100 $125 $175

U. NARDIN, 17J., center sec., auto-wind, c.1950
14k $175 $200 $265

U. NARDIN, 17J., aux. sec.
18k...$200 $225 $275

U. NARDIN, 17J., center sec., auto-wind, c.1950
18k $250 $275 $350

U. NARDIN, 17J., fancy lugs
18k...$250 $300 $425

A collector should expect to pay modestly higher prices at local shops

Pricing in this Guide are fair market price for **COMPLETE** watches which are reflected from the "**NAWCC**" National and regional shows.

U. NARDIN, 17J., aux. sec., carved lugs, c.1950
18k $200 $250 $350

U. NARDIN, 17J., aux. sec., chronometer, c.1964
gold plate.................................$65 $85 $125

U. NARDIN, 17J., aux. sec., chronometer, c.1950
14k $125 $150 $200

U. NARDIN, 17J., aux. sec., chronometer, c.1948
gold filled.................................$75 $100 $150

U. NARDIN, 17J., aux. sec., chronometer, c.1947
18k $200 $250 $350

U. NARDIN, 17J., fancy lugs
14k...$200 $250 $350

U. NARDIN, 17J., aux. sec., chronometer, C.1951
14k $150 $175 $225

Wrist Watches listed in this section are priced at the collectable
fair market Trade Show level as **complete** watches having an
original gold-filled case and stainless steel back, also with
original dial, leather watch band, and the entire original movement in good working order with no repairs needed.

U. NARDIN, 25J., chronometer, auto-w., date, c.1975
s. steel....................................$125 $150 $225

Some grades are not included. Their values can be
determined by comparing with **similar** age, size, metal
content, style, grades, or models such as **time only**,
chronograph, repeater etc. listed.

U. NARDIN, 17J., fluted case, chronometer
14k $150 $175 $225

U. NARDIN, 17J., aux. sec., chronometer, c.1949
14k $125 $150 $225

U. NARDIN, 17J., aux. sec., chronometer, c.1950
18k $175 $200 $250

U. NARDIN, 17J., extended side lugs, chronometer, c.1951
14k $150 $175 $250

U. NARDIN, 17 jewels, faceted crystal & bezel
s. steel $125 $135 $175

⌚ Some grades are not included. Their values can be
determined by comparing with **similar** age, size, metal
content, style, grades, or models such as **time only**,
chronograph, repeater etc. listed.

U. NARDIN, 17 jewels, chronometer, c. 1935
18k...$275 $300 $375

U. NARDIN, 17 jewels, WW I military style
s. steel....................................$450 $500 $600

U. NARDIN, 15 jewels, c. 1925
gold filled (w) $95 $125 $175

U. NARDIN, 15J., enamel dial, Ca. 1925
silver.......................................$450 $500 $600

U. NARDIN, 17J., lady's chronometer, c.1947
14k C&B ....$375 . $400 $500

NATIONAL W. Co., 16 J., 1 button Chronog., red & black color enamel dial, Ca. 1925
silver $700 $800 $1,100

NATIONAL W. Co., 15J., day-date-month,
gold filled..................................$75 $100 $165

NEW ENGLAND W. Co., 7J., Addison, Alden, Cavour, Hale, and other models, Ca.1915, colored dial add ($25)
14k $65 $75 $110
gold filled..................................$25 $30 $65

NEW HAVEN, 7 jewels, "Gem", engraved bezel
base metal $50 $55 $70

NEW HAVEN, 7 jewels
base metal..................................$50 $55 $70

NEW HAVEN,2 jewels, "Elf" ladies, etched case
base metal..................................$20 $25 $50

NEW HAVEN, 7 jewels, "Duchess" ladies, etched case
gold plate..................................$20 $25 $45

NEWMARK, 17J., military chronog., c.1979
s. steel....................................$250 $300 $400

NEW YORK STANDARD, 7 jewels, wire lugs
gold filled..................................$35 $45 $75
base metal..................................$20 $25 $50

NICE WATCH Co., 17J., one button chronog., c.1930
base metal $200 $225 $300

NICOLET W. CO., 17J., one button chronog., Ca. 1960
gold filled...............................$200 $250 $350

CHARLES NICOLET, 17J., chronog., ca. 1945
18k $250 $300 $400

MARC NICOLET, 17J., aux. seconds
14k $100 $125 $175

NITON, 18J., jump hr., (showing dial and movement)
(also made ebauche for P.P.&CO.)
18k(W) $3,000 $3,500 $4,500

NIVADA, 21J., center sec., c.1960
base metal................................$35 $45 $75

NIVADA, 21J., center sec., date, auto-w, c.1965
s. steel......................................$45 $50 $85

NIVADA, 25J., waterproof, triple date, moon ph., c. 1940
14k...$400 $450 $550
gold filled...............................$150 $175 $235

🕐 Pricing in this Guide are fair market price for **COMPLETE**
watches which are reflected from the "**NAWCC**" National and
regional shows.

NORMANDIE, 17 jewels, compass, c. 1945
s. steel $100 $125 $175

NORMANDIE, 17J., gold train, hidden lugs, cal.4873
14k $100 $125 $175

OCTO, 17J., fluted lugs, signed Octo on movement
Tiffany & Co. on dial
14k $100 $150 $275

OGIVAL, 17 jewels, auto wind
gold filled $45 $50 $75

OLLENDORFF, 17 jewels, fancy lugs
14k $125 $150 $225

OLLENDORFF, 17 jewels, movement plates made of **gold**
14k $175 $200 $250

OLLENDORFF, 7J., direct read, stepped case, c.1930
base metal $100 $125 $175

OLMA, 17J., **early** auto-wind, by Wyler, c.1928
s. steel $150 $200 $325

OFAIR, 17J., chronog., cal. Valjoux 72c, c.1948
gold filled $250 $300 $400
14k $450 $500 $650
18k $600 $650 $800

Wrist Watches listed in this section are priced at the collectable
fair market Trade Show level as **complete** watches having an
original gold-filled case and stainless steel back, also with
original dial, leather watch band, and the entire original movement in good working order with no repairs needed.

🕐 Some grades are not included. Their values can be
determined by comparing with **similar** age, size, metal
content, style, grades, or models such as **time only**,
chronograph, repeater etc. listed.

OMEGA-DANIELS CO-AXIAL ESCAPEMENT

OMEGA, 15J., center lugs, enamel dial, Ca. 1930
18k......................................$300 $425 $650

OMEGA, 27J., "DeVille", limited edition, Co-axial, auto-
wind, water resistant to 5 atm, RF# 5921, Ca. 1999
limited to 1,000 each for Yellow, Pink, White & 100 in Platinum
18K(Y-P-W) $2,500 $3,000 $4,500

OMEGA, 15J., wire lugs, **enamel dial**, Ca. 1925
silver......................................$185 $250 $375

OMEGA, 27J., Co-axial, auto-wind, RF#4832, Cal. 2500
s. steel $2,600 $2,700 $3,000

OMEGA, 15J., wire lugs, ca. 1930s
18k..$700 $800 $1,200

OMEGA,27J., Co-axial, **wind-indicator**, auto-wind, RF#4532, cal. 2627
s. steel $2,600 $2,700 $3,000

OMEGA, 15J., wire lugs,
14k..$600 $750 $1,000

OMEGA, 27J., Co-axial, auto-wind, GMT, Cal. 2628
s. steel $2,600 $2,700 $3,000

OMEGA, 17 jewels, one button chronog., c. 1935
18k..$2,500 $2,800 $3,500

OMEGA, 17J., 2 reg. chronog., ca. 1940s
s. steel $400 $600
14k $700 $750 $900
18k $1,000 $1,100 $1,400

OMEGA, 17J., "Speedmaster", chronog., c. 1950
s. steel....................................$600 $700 $900

OMEGA, 17J., 2 reg., chronog., c. 1958
18k $1,000 $1,200 $1,600

OMEGA, 17J., "Speedmaster Pro.", chronog., c. 1969
"the first watch worn on the **moon**" on back of watch
18k C&B $3,500 $4,000 $5,500
s. steel....................................$700 $900 $1,200

OMEGA, 17 jewels, chronog., "Seamaster," c. 1963
14k $1,500 $1,600 $1,900
s. steel $700 $800 $1,000

OMEGA, 17J., "Speedmaster Pro. Mark II", auto-w, c.1975
s. steel....................................$300 $375 $500

🕐 Some grades are not included. Their values can be
determined by comparing with **similar** age, size, metal
content, style, grades, or models such as **time only**,
chronograph, repeater etc. listed.

🕐 Pricing in this Guide are fair market price for **COMPLETE**
watches which are reflected from the "**NAWCC**" National and
regional shows.

OMEGA, 17J., "Seamaster", chronog., cal.321, c. 1962
s. steel $600 $700 $900
14k $1,500 $1,600 $1,900
18k $1,700 $1,800 $2,100

OMEGA, 22J., "Seamaster", date, 2 reg., auto-wind, c.1975
s. steel $400 $450 $600

OMEGA, 17J., "Seamaster", chronostop, auto-w., c.1965
s. steel......................................$300 $350 $500

OMEGA, 17J., Speedmaster Pro. MarkIII, auto-w, c.1978
s. steel $500 $550 $700

OMEGA, 17J., "Seamaster", chronostop., rotating bezel,
auto-w
s. steel...................................$400 $450 $550

OMEGA, 17J., Speedmaster, auto-wind, chronog., c.1975
s. steel $500 $575 $700

Wrist Watches listed in this section are priced at the collectable
fair market Trade Show level as **complete** watches having an
original gold-filled case and stainless steel back, also with
original dial, leather watch band, and the entire original movement in good working order with no repairs needed.

🕐 Some grades are not included. Their values can be
determined by comparing with **similar** age, size, metal
content, style, grades, or models such as **time only**,
chronograph, repeater etc. listed.

OMEGA, 17J., "Seamaster", chronog., cal.321, c.1970
s. steel...................................$400 $450 $575

🕐 A collector should expect to pay modestly higher prices
at local shops

🕐 Pricing in this Guide are fair market price for **COMPLETE**
watches which are reflected from the "**NAWCC**" National and
regional shows.

OMEGA, 17 jewels, chronog., "Seamaster", 3 reg., auto-w
14k $600 $700 $900

OMEGA, 17 jewels, chronog., "Flightmaster", 3 reg., auto-w
18kC&B.............................$2,800 $3,400 $4,500
s. steel $400 $585 $850

OMEGA, 17 jewels, day-date-month, moon phase
18k $1,400 $1,600 $2,000
14k $1,200 $1,400 $1,800

OMEGA, 17J., day-date-month, moon phase, c. 1940
s. steel $1,000 $1,100 $1,400
14k $1,200 $1,400 $1,800

OMEGA, 17J., day-date-month, moon phase, c. 1950s
14k......................................$2,500 $3,000 $4,000
18k......................................$3,500 $4,000 $5,000

OMEGA, 24J.,date, "Constellation", auto wind, chronometer
18k..$600 $700 $900
14k..$400 $500 $650
2 tone case................................$275 $325 $400

OMEGA, 24J., "Constellation", auto-wind, c.1960
14k..$600 $700 $900
2 tone case................................$300 $350 $450
s. steel.....................................$300 $350 $450

OMEGA, 24J., "Constellation", auto-wind, c.1968
gold filled...............................$300 $350 $425

OMEGA, 24J., "Constellation", auto-wind, c.1969
s. steel $200 $250 $325

OMEGA, 24 jewels, "Constellation," auto wind, date
18k............................ ★★★$2,000 $2,400 $3,000

OMEGA, 7J., "Constellation", **quartz**, cal.1342, c.1970
18k & s. s. $350 $400 $525

OMEGA, 24J., "Constellation," auto-w., date, c. 1959
18k..$600 $700 $850

OMEGA, 17-24J., Chronometre, auto-w.,
14k $600 $700 $850

OMEGA, 17 jewels, "Seamaster", date, auto-w., waterproof
18k..$450 $500 $575

OMEGA, electronic, "F300," c. 1950s
18k C&B...............................$700 $750 $900

OMEGA, 24J., "Seamaster", auto-w, date, Ca. 1963
18k (rose) $500 $550 $700

OMEGA, 24J., "Seamaster", auto-wind, c.1962
14k $300 $350 $450
s. steel $150 $195 $300

OMEGA, 17 jewels, "Seamaster," auto wind
14k $350 $400 $500

OMEGA, 24J., "Seamaster", auto-wind, cal.562, c.1962
gold filled $100 $125 $175

OMEGA, 17J.,"Seamaster",chronometer, auto wind
18k $550 $650 $800

OMEGA, 23J.,"Seamaster", auto-wind, cal.1022, c.1978
s. steel $100 $125 $175

OMEGA, 17J., "Seamaster", auto wind, c.1953
gold filled $100 $125 $175

OMEGA, 17J., "Seamaster Deluxe", auto-wind
18k $450 $550 $700

OMEGA, 17 jewels, automatic, date at 6
14k $450 $550 $750

OMEGA, 20J., "Seamaster", auto-wind, cal.501, c.1957
s. steel $150 $200 $300

OMEGA, 24J., "Constellation", auto-wind, cal.551, c.1962
2 tone case...........................$225 $250 $400
14k..$750 $800 $900

OMEGA, 17J., "Seamaster", auto-wind, cal.1570, c.1955
gold filled..............................$100 $125 $175

OMEGA, 16-18J., gold train, center seconds, auto wind
s. steel....................................$150 $200 $300

OMEGA, 24J., "Constellation", chronometer, auto-wind
2 tone case...........................$300 $325 $400
18k $700 $800 $1,000

OMEGA, 16J., center sec., c.1940
s. steel....................................$225 $250 $300

OMEGA, 24J., "Constellation", auto-wind, cal.505, c.1958
18k $750 $850 $1,200

OMEGA, 16J., **U.S. Army**, cal., c.1948
s. steel....................................$250 $275 $350

OMEGA, 16J., center sec., c.1948
s. steel $200 $250 $350

OMEGA, 15J., Military, large, c.1930
s. steel....................................$400 $500 $700

OMEGA, 15J., Military (**England**), c.1946
s. steel $400 $500 $700

OMEGA, 17J., "Seamaster", diamond dial, cal.563,
auto wind, Ca.1955
14K...$400 $450 $550
s. steel....................................$300 $350 $450

OMEGA, 17J , "Railmaster", center sec.
s. steel $300 $350 $450

OMEGA, 17J., 12 diamond dial, center sec.
14k(W) $400 $450 $550

OMEGA, 15-17J., 24 hour marked, Ca. 1930
s. steel $350 $400 $500

OMEGA, 17J., fancy lugs, ca.1948
14k...$400 $450 $600

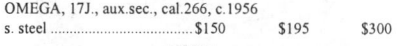

OMEGA, 17J., aux.sec., cal.266, c.1956
s. steel $150 $195 $300

OMEGA, 17J., aux. sec., cal.266, c.1945
14k $300 $350 $450

OMEGA, 17J., auto-wind, c.1952
18k $500 $600 $800

OMEGA, 17J., auto-wind, c.1949
18k $500 $600 $800

OMEGA, 17J., aux. sec., cal.360, c.1950
14k..$200 $250 $350

OMEGA, 17J., auto-wind, c.1949
18k..$300 $350 $500

OMEGA, 17J., auto-wind, cal.342, c.1955
gold filled...............................$100 $125 $175

OMEGA, 17J., "Seamaster", auto-wind
s. steel.....................................$200 $250 $350

Pricing in this Guide are fair market price for **COMPLETE** watches which are reflected from the "**NAWCC**" National and regional shows.

OMEGA, 17J., aux. sec., cal.302, c.1948
gold filled..............................$100 $125 $165

OMEGA, 15J., small lugs, c.1937
s. steel..................................$125 $150 $225

OMEGA, 15J., extended lugs, c.1939
14k $325 $350 $400
gold filled..............................$100 $125 $165

OMEGA, 17J., fancy lugs, ca. 1950s
14k...$150 $185 $250

OMEGA, 15J., aux. sec., c.1937
s. steel $125 $150 $225

OMEGA, 17J., faceted crystal,
14k(W) $150 $185 $250

OMEGA, 15J., small lugs, c.1935
gold filled..............................$125 $150 $200

OMEGA, 17J., fancy lugs, ca. 1948
14k...$150 $200 $275

OMEGA, 17J., bevelled case, c.1936
s. steel $125 $150 $225

Wrist Watches listed in this section are priced at the collectable
fair market **Trade Show** level as **complete** watches having an
original gold-filled case and stainless steel back, also with
original dial, leather watch band, and the entire original movement in good working order with no repairs needed.

OMEGA, 17J., 9 diamond dial, ca. 1955
14k(W) $175 $200 $275

OMEGA, 17 jewels, aux. sec.
14k **C&B** $600 $650 $750

OMEGA, 17 jewels, curved center lugs, auto wind
14k...$250 $300 $375

OMEGA, 17J., flared & extended lugs, cal.301, c.1948
14k $300 $350 $425

OMEGA, 17J., flared & sculptured lugs, cal.302, c.1953
14k $300 $325 $400

OMEGA, 17 jewels, sculptured lugs
14k...$400 $465 $600

OMEGA, 17 jewels, c. 1948
14k...$225 $285 $350

OMEGA, 17J., flared & hidden lugs, c.1947
14k $175 $200 $265

OMEGA, 17 jewels, hidden lugs, asymmetric
14k $600 $700 $900

⏱ A collector should expect to pay modestly higher prices
at local shops

OMEGA, 17 jewels, c. 1938
14k...$175 $200 $275

OMEGA, 15 jewels, large, c. 1935
14k...$300 $350 $450

OMEGA, 17J., wide bezel, center sec., auto-w., c.1955
14k $250 $275 $350

OMEGA, 17J., RF#347sc, cal.471, auto wind, c.1956
18k $300 $325 $400

OMEGA, 17J., wide bezel & lugs, cal.369, auto wind, c.1947
platinum .... ★★$1,800 $2,200 $3,000

OMEGA, 17J., "De Ville",
18k $275 $300 $350

OMEGA, 17J., cal.620, c.1960
14k $125 $165 $250

OMEGA, 17 jewels, aux. sec.
18k..$225 $265 $350

OMEGA, 17 jewels, c. 1937
s. steel....................................$175 $200 $275

OMEGA, 17 jewels, aux.sec.,
14k..$200 $300 $450

OMEGA, 15J., sliding case, winds at 12, Ca.1930s
"Marine" model
18k..$1,800 $2,200 $3,000

OMEGA, 15 jewels, hidden winding stem, c. 1930
"Marine" model, wire lugs
14k..$1,200 $1,400 $1,700
s. steel....................................$1,000 $1,200 $1,500

🕐 Some grades are not included. Their values can be
determined by comparing with **similar** age, size, metal
content, style, grades, or models such as **time only**,
chronograph, repeater etc. listed.

OMEGA, 15J., engraved case, c.1925
14k $275 $300 $400

OMEGA, 15J., ladies, wire lugs, c.1925
silver.. $50 $65 $100

OMEGA, 19J., alarm,"Memomatic", c.1975
s. steel $300 $350 $450

OMEGA, 17J., ladies center sec., c.1938
silver.................................... $100 $125 $175

OMEGA, 17J., ladies flip open, 16 diamonds, c.1955
14k C&B $700 $800 $1,000

OMEGA, "Chrono-quartz, cal.1611, c.1975
s. steel $450 $500 $650

OMEGA, 15J., ladies, non-magnetic, c.1945
s. steel...................................... $50 $60 $85

OMEGA, quartz, marine chronometer
s. steel $600 $700 $900

OMEGA, 17J., ladies, sapphire stones on lugs, c.1950
14k C&B $400 $500 $650

🕐 Pricing in this Guide are fair market price for **COMPLETE** watches which are reflected from the "**NAWCC**" National and regional shows.

OMEGA, 17J., ladies, RF#8065, c.1965
18k C&B $400 $450 $600

OMEGA BASIC CALIBRE IDENTIFICATION

Cal. No. 100, Ca.1943   Cal. No. 210, Ca.1946   Cal. No. 220, Ca.1941   Cal. No. 230, center seconds

Cal. No. 240, Ca.1939 Cal. No. 250, center seconds Cal. No. 260, Ca.1943   Cal. No. 280, center seconds

Cal. No. 300, Ca.1944   Cal. No. 310, center seconds   Cal. No. 330, Ca.1943   Cal. No. 360, Ca.1944

Cal. No. 440

Cal. No. 372, jumping seconds Cal. No. 410, Ca.1951 Cal. No. 420, center seconds   Cal. No. 455, Ca.1955

PRODUCTION TOTALS

DATE– SERIAL #	DATE– SERIAL #	DATE– SERIAL #
1895 –1,000,000	1944-10,000,000	1962-19,000,000
1902 - 2,000,000	1947-11,000,000	1963-20,000,000
1908 - 3,000,000	1950-12,000,000	1964-21,000,000
1912 - 4,000,000	1952-13,500,000	1965-22,000,000
1916 - 5,000,000	1954-14,000,000	1966-23,000,000
1923 - 6,000,000	1956-15,000,000	1967-25,000,000
1929 - 7,000,000	1958-16,000,000	1968-26,000,000
1935 - 8,000,000	1960-17,000,000	1969-28,000,000
1939- 9,000,000	1961-18,000,000	1970-29,000,000

Note: By 1980 ETA Calibers were being used by Omega.
The above list is provided for determining the APPROXIMATE age of your watch. Match serial number with date. Watches were not necessarily sold in the exact order of manufactured date.

Cal. No. 470, Ca.1955   Cal. No. 480, Ca.1955   Cal. No. 490, Ca.1956   Cal. No. 500, Ca.1956

Cal. No. 510, Ca.1956   Cal. No. 520, center seconds   Cal. No. 540, Ca.1957   Cal. No. 550, Ca.1959

Cal. No. 570, Ca.1959   Cal. No. 590, Ca.1960   Cal. No. 600, Ca.1960   Cal. No. 620, Ca.1961

Cal. No. 580, Ca. 1959

Cal. No. 660, Ca.1963   Cal. No. 670, Ca.1963   Cal. No. 690, Ca.1962   Cal. No. 700, Ca.1964

Cal. No. 711, Ca.1966   Cal. No. 730, Ca.1967   Cal. No. 980, Ca.1969   Cal. No. 1040, Ca. 1971

Cal. No. 320, Chronograph   Cal. No. 321, Chronograph

Cal. No. 1010, Ca.1973

Cal. No. 1250-1260,
Ca.1970

To determine your wrist watch band size use the **ABOVE GAUGE** and measure between the lugs. The band sizes are listed on each side of the gauge.

When performing any underwater activity, the dynamic pressure generated through movement is greater than the static pressure. Below a ranking of water resistance for most watches.

    1 **meter** = 3.28 ft.,   330 ft. =about 100 **meters**.   33.89 ft. =1 **atmosphere,**   100 ft. = about 3 **atmospheres**.

               30M/100Ft/3ATM/3Bar = sweat-resistant
               50M/160Ft/5ATM/5Bar = shower only, rain
               100M/300Ft/10ATM/10Bar = swimming (**no diving**)
               200M/660Ft/20ATM/20Bar = snorkeling, skin diving
                  1000M =scuba diving -3,300 ft.

DIALS FOR MINT PRICES MUST BE ALL **ORIGINAL**.

OPEL, 21 jewels, waterproof
gold filled..................................$45 $55 $80

ORATOR, 17 jewels, auto wind
s. steel $45 $55 $80

ORFINA, 17 jewels, triple date, moon phase, **bombe' lugs**
gold filled..............................$200 $250 $325

ORFINA, 17 jewels, triple date, moon phase, **carved lugs**
gold filled..............................$200 $250 $325

ORFINA, 17 jewels, day-date-month
gold filled $75 $95 $135

ORIS, 27J., date, auto wind, Ca. 1996
s. steel $125 $135 $175

ORVIN, 17 jewels, day-date, c. 1945
s. steel $45 $55 $80

PABRO, 17J., ladies 76 diamond watch, c.1930
platinum..................................$350 $450 $600

PARKER, 17J., 2 reg. chronog.,ca.1948
s. steel $150 $175 $225

PATEK, PHILIPPE & CIE.
Swiss

Patek, Philippe & Cie. has produced some of the world's most desirable factory-made watches. Antoine Norbert de Patek began contracting and selling watches in the 1830's, later became partners with Francois Czapek and generally produced lovely decorative watches for a high class of clientele. In 1845 Adrien Philippe, inventor of the modern stem-winding system, joined the firm of Patek & Cie., and in 1851, the firm established its present name. Between Philippe's talent as a watchmaker and Patek's talent as a businessman with a taste for the impeccable, the firm rapidly established an international reputation which lasts to this day. A *classic* wrist watch the **"Calatrava"** model 96 was 1st used in 1932. The case and dial was designed at a time of transition from pocket watches to wrist watches. The coin was used as a perfect geometric shape to design a wrist watch case that has harmony and balance. Many variations from the classic model 96 have been used, but to most collectors the **classic** model 96 is known as the **Calatrava** model. The original 96 Calatrava model used a flat bezel, 31mm one piece case (lugs are not soldered on), manual wind, white dial, barrette-shaped hour markers, dauphine hands and aux. seconds chapter with a inside and outside circle and long 5 sec. markers. A black dial was added in 1937. The recent classic style Calatrava case is RF # 3796. To date there are many P.P. & Co. wrist watches named Calatrava.

PRODUCTION TOTALS

DATE—SERIAL #	DATE—SERIAL #	DATE—SERIAL #	DATE—SERIAL #
1840— 100	1915—175,000	1945— 850,000	1960—1,100,000
1845— 1,200	1920—190,000	1950— 860,000	1965—1,130,000
1850— 3,000	1925—200,000	1955— 870,000	1970—1,250,000
1855— 8,000	1950—700,000	1960— 880,000	1975—1,350,000
1860— 15,000	1955—725,000	1965— 890,000	1980—1,450,000
1865— 22,000	1960—750,000	1970— 895,000	1985—1,600,000
1870— 35,000	1965—775,000	1940— 900,000	1990—1,850,000
1875— 45,000	1970—795,000	1945— 915,000	
1880— 55,000		1950— 930,000	
1885— 70,000		1955— 940,000	
1890— 85,000	**DATE—SERIAL #**	1960— 960,000	
1895—100,000	1920— 800,000	1965— 975,000	
1900—110,000	1925— 805,000	1970— 995,000	
1905—125,000	1930— 820,000		
1910—150,000	1935— 824,000		
	1940— 835,000		

The above list is provided for determining the APPROXIMATE age of your watch. Match serial number with date. Watches were not necessarily sold in the exact order of manufactured date.

Patek, Philippe & Cie. REFERENCE # INDEX

REF # PAGE	REF # PAGE	REF # PAGE	REF # PAGE	REF # PAGE	REF # PAGE
96 —1009	1432 —1000	1571 —1010	2461 — 991	2526 —1012	3497 — 990
96 —1009	1433 —1013	1574 —1002	2466 —1016	2530-1-1002	3509 —1019
96 —1012	1436 —1006	1575 —1001	2468 — 997	2531 — 991	3514 —1008
96 —1013	1438 — 993	1578 —1016	2468 — 998	2533 —1016	3514-1-1008
96 —1014	1442 — 995	1579 —1006	2469 —1005	2536 —1011	3519 —1001
130 —1006	1444 — 991	1580 — 996	2471 — 994	2537 —1012	3541 —1018
130 —1007	1450 — 997	1584 —1015	2472 — 993	2540 —1002	3555 —1000
137 — 990	1461 —1010	1585 —1023	2474 —1003	2541 —1017	3558 —1018
139 — 989	1463 —1006	1588 — 991	2476 — 995	2545 —1015	3569 —1019
244 —1003	1480 — 996	1589 —1018	2477 — 992	2548 —1023	3574 —1019
404 — 991	1481 —1003	1590 —1014	2479 —1002	2549 —1015	3588 —1022
406 — 994	1482 — 994	1592 —1003	2480 — 997	2550 —1015	3601 —1008
409 — 991	1486 —1000	1593 — 977	2481 —1005	2553 —1001	3604 —1009
420 — 995	1486 — 992	1595 —1018	2481 —1016	2554 — 998	3606 —1019
422 — 995	1487 — 993	2066 — 996	2482 —1016	2557 —1014	3633 —1001
425 — 997	1491 —1015	2334 — 992	2484 —1011	2568-1-1018	3700 —1021
425 — 998	1491 —1017	2403 — 996	2486 —1002	2573 —1019	3727 — 999
426 — 989	1493 — 995	2404 — 992	2488 —1003	2574 —1002	3738 —1023
430 — 993	1505 —1009	2404 — 996	2491 —1000	2577 —1012	3745 —1023
433 — 991	1506 —1007	2406 —1015	2493 — 999	2588 —1020	3796 —1012
448 —1010	1509 —1011	2414 — 994	2494 —1014	2589 —1019	3800 —1020
462 — 994	1513 —1013	2423 — 999	2496 —1000	2592 —1019	" "-103-1021
490 — 992	1516 —1013	2424 — 999	2496 —1001	2597 —1005	" "-105-1021
491 — 992	1517 —1014	2429 —1012	2497 —1009	2597 —1006	" "-108-1021
497 —1020	1518 —1007	2434 — 995	2499 —1007	3025 —1016	3834 — 989
497 —1024	1526 —1010	2437 —1000	2499 —1008	3404 —1001	3878 —1022
504 — 989	1530 — 995	2438 —1009	2500 —1013	3405 —1000	3884 —1022
513 — 992	1531 — 995	2440 —1003	2503 — 995	3406 —1000	3885 —1021
513-1 — 993	1532 — 993	2441 — 998	2506-1- 1011	3410 —1018	3885 —1022
515 —1005	1535 — 995	2442 — 998	2508 —1017	3411 —1017	3886 —1022
530 —1006	1543 —1013	2443 — 996	2509 —1014	3412 — 990	3900-1-1020
534 —1011	1557 —1000	2445 —1013	2513 —1001	3413 — 990	3900-3-1020
556 —1002	1559 — 992	2447 — 999	2514-1-1003	3424 — 990	3900-5-1020
565 —1016	1559 — 991	2451— 1018	2515 —1013	3429 —1012	" "-101-1020
570 —1014	1560 — 991	2452 —1011	2516 —1002	3445 —1009	" "-103-1020
591 —1006	1564 — 991	2456 — 997	2517 — 990	3448 —1009	" "-105-1021
655 — 994	1564 — 992	2456 — 998	2518 — 993	3450 —1009	3960 —1010
1402 — 993	1566 —1001	2456 — 999	2520 — 994	3465 —1003	3969 —1005
1408 —1002	1567 —1006	2457 —1017	2523 —1005	3467 —1001	3970-E-1007
1415 —1005	1568 — 995	2459 —1011	2524 — 989	3473 —1018	3974 — 989
1431 — 999	1570 — 994	2460 —1017	2525-1- 1011	3495 —1017	

Note: Most Stainless Steel Pateks **usually** bring higher prices than 18K due to small production.

"**PATEK PHILIPPE**" watches should be signed on the case, dial & movement to bring the prices listed in this book.
(triple signed P.P.CO.)

DIALS FOR MINT PRICES MUST BE ALL **ORIGINAL**.

PATEK PHILIPPE, 29 jewels, min. repeater, c. 1920
platinum $400,000 $500,000 $700,000

PATEK PHILIPPE, 29 jewels, min. repeater, six watches finished by E. Gublin, 18k case & band, triple signed
18k C&B......................... $250,000 $300,000 $375,000

PATEK PHILIPPE, 29J., min. repeater, 30 x 34mm
18k $325,000 $400,000 $600,000

PATEK PHILIPPE, 50 sec. tourbillon, 57 hr. power reserve 5 gear train, 28 x 38mm, RF#3834
18k $225,000 $250,000 $300,000

PATEK PHILIPPE, 39J., auto-wind, min. repeater, perpetual day date month calendars, moon ph., 24 hr. ind., leap year ind., RF#3974, Ca.1989
18K................................. $300,000 $325,000 $400,000

PATEK PHILIPPE,18J., horizontal case, RF#504, 2 tone
18k $7,000 $8,000 $10,000

PATEK PHILIPPE,18 J., horizontal case, RF#139 &426
18k $5,000 $6,000 $8,000

PATEK PHILIPPE, 29 jewels, min. repeater, RF#2524
18k $150,000 $185,000 $225,000

"**PATEK PHILIPPE**" watches should be signed on the case, dial & movement to bring the prices listed in this book.
(triple signed P.P.CO.)

PATEK PHILIPPE, 18J., designed by Gilbert Albert,
RF#3412, c. 1958
18k $25,000 $30,000 $40,000

PATEK PHILIPPE, 18J., asymmetric case designed by
Gilbert Albert, RF#3413, c. 1958
18k $22,000 $26,000 $30,000

PATEK PHILIPPE,18J., fluted hooded lugs, RF#2517
18k $5,500 $6,500 $8,000

PATEK PHILIPPE, 18 J., RF#3497, diamond set case
platinum C&B...................$16,000 $19,000 $25,000

🕐 Pricing in this Guide are fair market price for **COMPLETE**
watches which are reflected from the "**NAWCC**" National and
regional shows.

PATEK PHILIPPE, 18J., RF#3424, asymmetric, c. 1960
18k $16,000 $20,000 $25,000

PATEK PHILIPPE, 18J., RF # 3424, asymmetric, diamond
set on bezel, Ca. 1960
platinum............................$21,000 $25,000 $30,000

PATEK PHILIPPE, 18 J., **hinged back**, Ca. 1920s
note: **auxiliary seconds**
18k $8,000 $9,000 $11,000

PATEK PHILIPPE, 18 J., **hinged back**, c.1920s
note: **NO seconds**
18k $7,500 $8,500 $10,500

PATEK PHILIPPE, 18 jewels, RF # 137, curved, Ca. 1931
18k - 44mm $4,000 $5,000 $6,000

PATEK PHILIPPE, 18J., RF # 1444, Cal.# 9, c. 1940s
18k $4,000 $5,500 $7,000

PATEK PHILIPPE, 18 jewels, RF # 2461, Cal.. 9, c. 1950s
18k $4,000 $4,500 $6,500

PATEK PHILIPPE,18J., cal.990, c.1936
18K..............................$4,000 $4,500 $6,500

PATEK PHILIPPE,18J., RF# 409, Ca.1934
18K..............................$3,500 $3,800 $4,500

PATEK PHILIPPE, 18 J., RF # 433, stepped case, c. 1940s
18k $4,500 $5,500 $7,000

PATEK PHILIPPE, 18 jewels, RF # 2531, c. 1950s
18k $3,500 $4,000 $5,000

PATEK PHILIPPE, 18 jewels, RF # 1564, Cal.# 9
18k $4,000 $4,500 $5,500

PATEK PHILIPPE, 18 jewels, RF# 1560
18k $3,000 $3,500 $4,500

PATEK PHILIPPE, 18 jewels, RF # 1560, c. 1940s
18k $4,000 $4,500 $5,500

PATEK PHILIPPE, 18 jewels, RF # 1559, c. 1943
18k $4,000 $4,500 $5,500

PATEK PHILIPPE, 18 jewels, RF # 404, c. 1930s
18k $3,000 $3,500 $4,500

PATEK PHILIPPE, 18J., RF # 1588, beveled crystal, c. 1945
18k $6,000 $6,500 $8,000

PATEK PHILIPPE, 18 jewels
18k $4,000 $4,500 $5,500

PATEK PHILIPPE, 18 jewels, RF # 2477, Cal.# 9, c. 1953
18k $4,500 $5,000 $6,000

PATEK PHILIPPE, 18 J., RF # 490 & 491, curved, cal. # 9
18k $8,000 $9,000 $11,000

PATEK PHILIPPE, 18J., decorated enamel case, c. 1920s
18k $10,000 $12,000 $15,000

PATEK PHILIPPE,18J., RF # 2334
18K......................................$4,500 $5,000 $6,000

DIALS FOR MINT PRICES MUST BE ALL **ORIGINAL**.

PATEK PHILIPPE,18J., diamonds on dial & case
18K C&B............................ $3,000 $3,500 $4,500

PATEK PHILIPPE, 18 J., RF # 1486, hidden lugs, c. 1930s
18k $3,000 $3,500 $4,500

PATEK PHILIPPE, 18 jewels, RF # 1564, c. 1940s
18k $3,500 $4,000 $5,000

PATEK PHILIPPE, 18 J., RF # 1559, hinged back, c. 1920s
18k $4,500 $5,000 $6,500

PATEK PHILIPPE, 18 J., RF # 2404, applied gold numbers
18K $8,000 $9,000 $11,000

PATEK PHILIPPE,18J., RF # 513, extended lugs, two tone case, cal. 885, c.1943
18K..$5,000 $5,500 $8,000

" PATEK PHILIPPE" watches should be signed on the case, dial & movement to bring the prices listed in this book.
(triple signed P.P.CO.)

DIALS FOR MINT PRICES MUST BE ALL **ORIGINAL**.

PATEK PHILIPPE, 18J., RF # 1487, Cal.#9, fancy lugs
18k $7,000 $8,000 $10,000

PATEK PHILIPPE, 18J., RF # 1402, hooded satin lugs
18k asymmetric $10,000 $12,000 $16,000

PATEK PHILIPPE, 18J., RF # 430, "Staybrite," curved case
s. steel $7,500 $8,500 $10,000

PATEK PHILIPPE, 18 J., RF # 1438, Cal.# 9, hooded lugs
18k $3,000 $3,300 $4,000

PATEK PHILIPPE, 18 jewels, RF # 513-1, curved
18k $4,000 $4,500 $5,500

⊕ Pricing in this Guide are fair market price for **COMPLETE**
watches which are reflected from the "**NAWCC**" National and
regional shows.

DIALS FOR MINT PRICES MUST BE ALL **ORIGINAL**.

PATEK PHILIPPE,18J., engraved bezel,hinged back,c.1920
18k $8,000 $9,000 $11,000

PATEK PHILIPPE, 18J., RF # 2472, ribbed case & fancy lugs
18k $3,000 $3,500 $4,500

PATEK PHILIPPE, 18 J., RF # 2518, large lugs, c. 1960s
18k $6,000 $7,000 $9,000

PATEK PHILIPPE, 18 J., RF # 1532, Ca.1940s
18k $4,000 $4,500 $5,500

PATEK PHILIPPE, 18 jewels, c. 1930s
18k $3,000 $3,500 $4,500

PATEK PHILIPPE, 18J., fluted bezel, RF# 462, Ca.1937
18k $3,500 $4,000 $5,000

PATEK PHILIPPE, 18 jewels, RF # 655, c. 1940s
18k $4,000 $4,500 $5,500

PATEK PHILIPPE, 18J., triple lugs, RF#2471, ca.1951
18k $18,000 $20,000 $25,000

PATEK PHILIPPE, 18 jewels, triple lugs, RF#1482
18k $9,000 $11,000 $15,000

PATEK PHILIPPE, 18 jewels, curved, c. 1940s
18k $4,000 $4,500 $6,000

PATEK PHILIPPE, 18 jewels, RF # 1570, Cal.# 9, c. 1940s
18k $4,500 $5,200 $6,500

PATEK PHILIPPE, 18 jewels, RF # 406, curved, c. 1940s
18k $5,000 $5,500 $7,000

PATEK PHILIPPE, 18 jewels, hinged back, c. 1920s
18k $3,500 $4,000 $5,000

PATEK PHILIPPE, 18J., hinged back, stepped case
18k $5,000 $5,500 $6,500

PATEK PHILIPPE, 18J., RF#2520, cal. # 9, extended lugs
18k C&B...........................$10,000 $12,000 $15,000

PATEK PHILIPPE, 18J., RF # 2414, fancy lugs, ca.1949
18k $10,000 $12,000 $15,000

PATEK PHILIPPE 18J., RF# 2503, fancy lugs, ca. 1950s
18k ....$12,000　　$14,000　　$18,000

PATEK PHILIPPE 18J., RF# 1493, ca. 1940s
18k ....$5,000　　$5,500　　$6,500

PATEK PHILIPPE 18J., RF# 1530, fancy lugs, ca. 1940s
18k ....$5,000　　$5,500　　$7,000

PATEK PHILIPPE 18J., RF# 1442, ca. 1940s
18k ....$3,500　　$4,000　　$5,000

PATEK PHILIPPE 18J., RF# 1568, fancy lugs, ca. 1940s
18k ....$5,000　　$5,500　　$7,000

PATEK PHILIPPE 18J., RF# 2434, ca. 1950s
18k ....$4,500　　$5,000　　$6,000

PATEK PHILIPPE 18J., RF# 1535, fancy lugs, ca. 1940
18k ....$3,500　　$4,000　　$5,000

PATEK PHILIPPE 18J., RF# 420, ca. 1930s
18k ....$3,000　　$3,500　　$4,500

PATEK PHILIPPE 18J., RF# 1531, fancy lugs, ca. 1940s
18k ....$4,000　　$4,500　　$5,500

PATEK PHILIPPE 18J., RF# 2476, curved, ca. 1950s
18k ....$4,500　　$5,000　　$6,000

PATEK PHILIPPE 18J., RF# 422, ca. 1950s
18k ....$3,000　　$3,500　　$4,500

🕐 Pricing in this Guide are fair market price for **COMPLETE** watches which are reflected from the "**NAWCC**" National and regional shows.

PATEK PHILIPPE, 18 J., RF # 1580, Cal.# 9, concave lugs
18k $7,000 $8,000 $10,000

PATEK PHILIPPE, 18 jewels, RF # 2404, fancy lugs
18k $6,500 $7,500 $9,000

PATEK PHILIPPE, 18 J., Cal.#9, aux. sec., Ca.1940
18k $4,000 $4,500 $6,000

PATEK PHILIPPE, 18J., stylized hooded lugs
18k $8,000 $9,000 $11,000

PATEK PHILIPPE, 18 jewels, RF # 2066, moveable lugs
18K...$6,000 $7,000 $9,000

PATEK PHILIPPE, 18 jewels, RF # 2443, Cal.# 9, c. 1940s
18k $5,000 $6,000 $7,500

PATEK PHILIPPE, 18 jewels, RF # 2403, lapidated lugs
18k $6,500 $7,500 $9,000

PATEK PHILIPPE, 18J., **2 tone**, hooded & stepped lugs
18k $10,000 $12,000 $16,000

PATEK PHILIPPE, 18 jewels, fancy lugs, RF#1480
18k $6,000 $7,000 $10,000

PATEK PHILIPPE, 18 jewels, "Reverso"
18k $20,000 $25,000 $35,000
s. steel .... ★★$25,000 $30,000 $40,000

PATEK PHILIPPE, 18J., RF # 1450, top hat style, c. 1940s
18k $5,000 $6,000 $6,800
platinum $10,000 $12,000 $15,000

PATEK PHILIPPE, 18 jewels, RF # 1450, top hat style
18k **C&B** $7,000 $7,500 $9,000

PATEK PHILIPPE, 18 J., RF # 2480, top hat, diamond dial
platinum $11,000 $13,000 $16,000

PATEK PHILIPPE, 18 jewels, M# 9, curved style
18k $7,000 $8,500 $10,000

PATEK PHILIPPE, 18J., inclined & curved case, Ca.1940s
18k $16,000 $19,000 $25,000

PATEK PHILIPPE, 18 jewels, RF # 425, Adj. to 8 positions
18k $4,500 $5,000 $6,000

PATEK PHILIPPE, 18 jewels, RF # 425, curved, c. 1940s
18k $5,000 $5,500 $6,500

PATEK PHILIPPE, 18 J., converted to jump hr., **(recased)**
18k $2,500 $3,000 $3,500

PATEK PHILIPPE, 18 J., RF # 2468, flared case, c. 1940s
18k $8,000 $9,000 $11,000

PATEK PHILIPPE, 18 jewels, RF # 1593, Cal.# 9, c. 1950s
platinum $14,000 $16,000 $22,000

PATEK PHILIPPE, 18J., RF # 2456, flared case, Ca. 1950s
18k $7,000 $8,000 $10,000

PATEK PHILIPPE, 18 J., RF # 2442, massive flared case
18k $22,000 $24,000 $30,000
platinum $35,000 $39,000 $48,000

PATEK PHILIPPE, 18J., RF#2441, Eiffel tower, c. 1945
18k $28,000 $33,000 $44,000

PATEK PHILIPPE,18J., RF#2441, Eiffel tower, c. 1945
18k $28,000 $33,000 $44,000

PATEK PHILIPPE, 18 jewels, RF # 2456, flared case
18k $6,500 $7,500 $9,000

PATEK PHILIPPE, 18J., RF # 2468, flared case, c. 1950s
18k (dial not original) $4,500 $5,000 $6,000

PATEK PHILIPPE, 18 jewels, RF # 2554, c. 1950s
18k $8,000 $9,000 $11,000

PATEK PHILIPPE, 18J., 16 diamond bezel, ca.1960
18k C&B $7,000 $8,000 $10,000

PATEK PHILIPPE, 18 J., RF # 425, diamond dial, c. 1945
18K $5,500 $6,500 $8,000
platinum...............................$8,000 $9,000 $11,000

PATEK PHILIPPE, 18 jewels, RF # 425, diamond dial
platinum(dial not original) $7,000 $7,500 $9,000

PATEK PHILIPPE, 18J., RF # 425, diamond dial, c. 1935
platinum...............................$8,500 $10,500 $13,000

PATEK PHILIPPE, 18 J., RF # 425, diamond dial & bezel
platinum...............................$9,000 $11,000 $13,500

DIALS FOR MINT PRICES MUST BE ALL **ORIGINAL**.

PATEK PHILIPPE, 18J., hinged back, diamond bezel
18k $7,000 $8,000 $10,000

PATEK PHILIPPE,18J., RF#2493, c.1953
18K $3,500 $4,000 $5,000

PATEK PHILIPPE, 18 jewels, Ca. 1940s
18k $4,500 $5,000 $6,000

PATEK PHILIPPE,18J., RF#1431, cal., c.1940
18K $2,500 $3,000 $4,000

PATEK PHILIPPE, 18J., RF # 2456, diamond dial, flared
18k $9,000 $10,000 $13,000

PATEK PHILIPPE,18J., RF#2447, c.1950
18K $2,500 $3,000 $4,000

PATEK PHILIPPE, 18J, Hooded Lugs
s. steel $6,000 $7,000 $8,500

PATEK PHILIPPE,18J., carved lugs, RF#2423, c.1946
18K $4,500 $5,000 $6,000

PATEK PHILIPPE, 18J., RF# 3727, **Lapis & 54 Diamonds**,
Ca.1974
18k $4,000 $4,500 $5,500

PATEK PHILIPPE,18J., RF#2424, c.1951
18K $4,500 $5,000 $6,000

PATEK PHILIPPE,18J., RF # 2437, stepped lugs, c.1940
18K $4,000 $4,500 $5,500

PATEK PHILIPPE, 18 J., RF # 1486, Ca. 1950s
18k C&B $4,000 $4,500 $5,500

PATEK PHILIPPE, 18J., RF # 2496, textured bezel, c. 1940s
18k $3,000 $3,500 $4,500

PATEK PHILIPPE, 18J., RF # 2491, fancy off set lugs
18k $3,000 $3,500 $4,500

PATEK PHILIPPE, 18 jewels, RF # 1567, Ca. 1940s
18k $4,000 $4,500 $5,500

PATEK PHILIPPE, 18 jewels, RF # 3405, cal. # 9, c. 1963
18k $2,500 $2,800 $3,500

PATEK PHILIPPE, 18 jewels, RF # 1432, Ca. 1940s
18k $2,500 $2,800 $3,500

PATEK PHILIPPE, 18 jewels, RF # 3406, c. 1960s
18k $2,200 $2,400 $3,000

PATEK PHILIPPE, 18 jewels, RF # 1557, oval lugs
18k $4,000 $4,500 $5,500

PATEK PHILIPPE, 18 jewels, RF # 3555
18k $2,200 $2,400 $3,000

🕐 Pricing in this Guide are fair market price for **COMPLETE** watches which are reflected from the "**NAWCC**" National and regional shows.

PATEK PHILIPPE, 18 J., RF # 2553, Cal.# 9-90, Ca. 1955
18k $4,500 $5,000 $6,000

PATEK PHILIPPE, 18 J., RF # 2496, diamond bezel
platinum $8,000 $9,000 $12,000

PATEK PHILIPPE, 18 J., RF # 3519, Ca. 1967
18k(w)..................................$2,500 $2,800 $3,300

PATEK PHILIPPE,18J., hidden dial, 18k & plat. c.**1930's**
"Cabriolet", remade in 2001 & list for $13,900 in 2001
18k & platinum (ca.1930's)...$30,000 $35,000 $45,000

PATEK PHILIPPE, 18 jewels, RF # 3633, Cal.# 9, c. 1980s
18k C&B.............................$3,000 $3,500 $4,500

PATEK PHILIPPE, 18 jewels, RF # 1575, Ca. 1940s
18k $2,500 $2,800 $3,300

PATEK PHILIPPE, 18 jewels, RF # 1566, Ca. 1940s
18k $3,000 $3,500 $4,500

PATEK PHILIPPE, 18 jewels, RF # 3404
18k C&B.............................$2,500 $2,800 $3,300

PATEK PHILIPPE, 18 J., RF # 3467, textured dial & bezel
18k $3,000 $3,500 $4,500

PATEK PHILIPPE, 18 jewels, RF # 2513, c. 1950s
18k $3,500 $4,000 $5,000

Some grades are not included. Their values can be
determined by comparing with **similar** age, size, metal
content, style, grades, or models such as **time only**,
chronograph, repeater etc. listed.

DIALS FOR MINT PRICES MUST BE ALL <u>**ORIGINAL**</u>.

PATEK PHILIPPE, 18 J., RF # 2574, center sec., c. 1960s
18k C&B $4,500 $5,000 $6,000

PATEK PHILIPPE, 18 jewels, RF # 2516, Ca. 1950s
18k $3,000 $3,500 $4,500

PATEK PHILIPPE, 18 J., RF#2530-1, Ca. 1959
18k C&B $4,500 $5,000 $6,000

PATEK PHILIPPE, 18 jewels, RF # 2540, Ca. 1960s
18k $4,000 $4,500 $5,500

PATEK PHILIPPE, 18J., Cal.# 9, c. early 1910s
18k C&B $4,500 $5,000 $6,000

PATEK PHILIPPE, 18 J., RF # 2479, guilloche bezel
18k $3,500 $4,000 $5,500

PATEK PHILIPPE, 18 jewels, RF # 1408, Ca. 1940s
18k $2,500 $2,800 $3,300

PATEK PHILIPPE, 18 J., RF # 1574, hidden lugs, c. 1945
18k $3,000 $3,500 $4,000

PATEK PHILIPPE, 18 jewels, RF # 2486, Ca. 1950s
18k $3,000 $3,500 $4,500

PATEK PHILIPPE, 18J., RF # 556, fluted cylindrical lugs
18k $6,500 $7,500 $9,500

PATEK PHILIPPE, 18 jewels, RF # 1592, hidden lugs
18k $3,000 $3,500 $4,000

PATEK PHILIPPE, 18 jewels, RF # 2474, Ca. 1940s
18k $3,500 $4,000 $5,000

PATEK PHILIPPE, 18 J., RF # 2514-1, Ca. 1940s
18k $3,500 $4,000 $5,000

PATEK PHILIPPE, 18 jewels, RF # 244, large bezel
18k $2,800 $3,000 $3,600

PATEK PHILIPPE, 18 J., RF # 3465, blue sapphire bezel
platinum $8,000 $9,000 $12,000

PATEK PHILIPPE, 18 jewels, RF # 2488, Ca. 1940s
18k $2,800 $3,000 $3,600

PATEK PHILIPPE, 18 jewels, RF # 1481, overhanging lugs
18k $7,000 $8,000 $10,000

PATEK PHILIPPE, 15J.,for Baily,Banks & Biddle, ca.1920
18k $4,000 $4,500 $5,500

PATEK PHILIPPE, 18 J., RF # 2440, fluted dropped lugs
18k $4,500 $5,000 $6,500

Wrist Watches listed in this section are priced at the collectable fair market **Trade Show** level as **complete** watches having an original gold-filled case and stainless steel back, also with original dial, leather watch band, and the entire original movement in good working order with no repairs needed.

PATEK PHILIPPE, 16J., ca.1923
18k $4,500 $5,500 $6,500

PATEK PHILIPPE, 18 jewels, note **radial**, Ca. 1910
18k ....$3,000 $3,500   · $4,500

PATEK PHILIPPE, 18 jewels, c. 1920s
18k $4,000 $4,500 $5,500

PATEK PHILIPPE, 18 jewels, c. 1920s
18k $3,000 $3,500 $4,500

PATEK PHILIPPE, 18J, **recased** & wrong dial, c. 1920s
18k $1,000 $1,200 $1,500

PATEK PHILIPPE, 18 jewels, Cal.# 9, c. 1910
platinum $9,000 $10,000 $13,000

DIALS FOR MINT PRICES MUST BE ALL **ORIGINAL**.

PATEK PHILIPPE, 18 jewels, c. 1930s
18k $3,500 $4,000 $5,000

PATEK PHILIPPE, 18 jewels, c. 1930s
18k $4,000 $4,500 $5,500

PATEK PHILIPPE, 18 jewels, **contract case, not signed**
18k (w) $1,200 $1,400 $1,700

PATEK PHILIPPE, 18 jewels, Cal.# 9, c. 1925
18k $5,000 $5,500 $6,500

PATEK PHILIPPE, 18 jewels, M# 9, c. 1920s
18k $6,000 $6,500 $8,000

🕒 Pricing in this Guide are fair market price for **COMPLETE**
watches which are reflected from the "**NAWCC**" National and
regional shows.

PATEK PHILIPPE, 18J, **Jump Hour**, RF # 3969, Ca. 1989
18k $30,000 $35,000 $45,000

PATEK PHILIPPE, 18 jewels, RF#2523, ''World Time,''
cloisonne polychrome enamel map on dial, **41 cities**
18k .... ★ ★ ★$450,000 $550,000 $750,000

PATEK PHILIPPE, 18 jewels
18k $2,500 $3,000 $4,000

PATEK PHILIPPE,18J.,''World Time,'' **41 cities**, RF#1415
At auction sold for over **$4,000,000.00**, in <u>platinum</u>, Ca.2002
18K $50,000 $55,000 $65,000
platinum...........................$150,000 $200,000 $300,000

PATEK PHILIPPE, 18 J., RF # 2469, made for E. Gublin
18k $5,500 $6,000 $7,000

PATEK PHILIPPE, 18J, RF # 2481, landscape cloisonne
polychrome enamel dial, at auction for $129,000.00, Ca.2002
18k $90,000 $100,000 $120,000

PATEK PHILIPPE, 18 jewels, ''Chronometro Gondolo''
18k $8,000 $9,000 $11,000

PATEK PHILIPPE,18jewels, RF#515, world time zone,
24 hr. rotating outside chapter, **tu-tone** case and band
18K C&B........................$400,000 $500,000 $700,000

PATEK PHILIPPE, 18 J., RF # 2597, **2 hr. hands,**
2 time zones
18k $35,000 $40,000 $50,000
18k **(PINK)** $100,000 $125,000 $200,000

PATEK PHILIPPE, 18J., RF # 2597, **time zone**, hour hand can be stepped forward or backward 1 hour at a time
18k $35,000 $40,000 $55,000

PATEK PHILIPPE,18J.,chronog., RF#1579, fancy lugs
18k $25,000 $28,000 $35,000

PATEK PHILIPPE, 18J., RF # 1436, **split sec.** chronog., Ca. 1940-50
Platinum...........................$200,000 $250,000 $350,000
18k $100,000 $125,000 $150,000

PATEK PHILIPPE,18J., chronog., RF# 591, 2 reg., c.1943
18k **(black dial)** $50,000 $60,000 $75,000

PATEK PHILIPPE, 18J., RF#530, chronog.
18k $28,000 $32,000 $42,000

PATEK PHILIPPE,18J., RF# 130, chronog., **black dial**
18k & s. steel **(case)**.......... $50,000 $60,000 $75,000

PATEK PHILIPPE, 18J., RF # 1463, 2-tone dial, Ca.1940s
18k $40,000 $45,000 $60,000

PATEK PHILIPPE, 32J., **split sec.** chronog.
18k $500,000 $600,000 $750,000

DIALS FOR MINT PRICES MUST BE ALL <u>**ORIGINAL**</u>.

PATEK PHILIPPE, 26J., **split sec**. chronog. **one button**, for
Cartier, Sq. button for Rattrapante hand, crown for start stop
functions, RF#130, 8 adj., **Breguet dial**, ca.1938
18k $250,000 $300,000 $400,000

PATEK PHILIPPE,18J., RF#130, chronog., Ca.1940s
18k $28,000 $32,000 $42,000

PATEK PHILIPPE,18J., RF# 1506, chronog., **waterproof**
18k $50,000 $60,000 $80,000

PATEK PHILIPPE, 18J., chronog., pulsometer, c. 1965
18k $70,000 $80,000 $100,000

🕓 Pricing in this Guide are fair market price for **COM-
PLETE** watches which are reflected from the "**NAWCC**" National and regional shows.

PATEK PHILIPPE, 18J., RF#3970E, chronog,triple date
moon ph., 24 hr. indicator, leap year indicator
18k $45,000 $50,000 $60,000

PATEK PHILIPPE, 23 jewels, chronog., day-date month,
moon phase, made for E. Gueblin
18k C&B.............................$100,000 $120,000 $150,000

PATEK PHILIPPE, 23J., chronog., triple date, moon ph.
perpetual calendar,RF# 1518, Calatrava case, Ca.1941-54
18k ....★★ $100,000 $120,000 $160,000

PATEK PHILIPPE, 23 J., chronog., triple date, moon ph. perpetual calendar, arabic dial, ref.2499 (1 series) square button
note: At auction with **black dial** for $700,000.00, in 2002
18K $120,000 $140,000 $180,000

" PATEK PHILIPPE" watches should be signed on the case, dial & movement to bring the prices listed in this book.
(triple signed P.P.CO.)

DIALS FOR MINT PRICES MUST BE ALL **ORIGINAL**.

PATEK PHILIPPE, 23 J., chronog., triple date, moon ph. perpetual calendar, RF#2499 (2 series)
18K.......................................$90,000 $100,000 $140,000

PATEK PHILIPPE, 23J., chronog., triple date, moon ph. perpetual calendar, RF#2499 (4 series)sapphire crystal
18k $75,000 $85,000 $100,000

PATEK PHILIPPE, 23J., chronog., triple date, moon ph. perpetual calendar, RF#2499 (3 series)glass crystal
18k $80,000 $90,000 $120,000

PATEK PHILIPPE, 37jewels, RF # 3514, date, auto wind
platinum............................$24,000 $26,000 $32,000

PATEK PHILIPPE, 18 J., RF # 3601, auto wind, date, Ca. 1970s
18k C&B.............................$4,000 $4,500 $5,500

PATEK PHILIPPE, 23J., chronog., triple date, moon ph. perpetual calendar, RF#2499 (3 series)only 2 in platinum
platinum $350,000 $400,000 $500,000

Wrist Watches listed in this section are priced at the collectable fair market **Trade Show** level as **complete** watches having an original gold-filled case and stainless steel back, also with original dial, leather watch band, and the entire original movement in good working order with no repairs needed.

PATEK PHILIPPE,37J., Auto-wind, RF#3514/1, date, c.1967
18K C&B.............................$4,500 $5,000 $6,000

DIALS FOR MINT PRICES MUST BE ALL **ORIGINAL**.

PATEK PHILIPPE,37J., date, RF#3445, auto-wind, c.1961
18K..................................$4,500 $5,000 $6,000

PATEK PHILIPPE,18J., date, RF#3604, textured dial, c.1977
18K(w)...............................$2,500 $2,800 $3,300

PATEK PHILIPPE,18J., RF # 96 or 1505 (**day, date, month, at 9-12-3**), Calatrava, manual wind, Ca.1934-38
18K................ ★ ★ ★ ★ ★ $600,000 $650,000 $750,000

PATEK PHILIPPE, 18J., RF#96, Calatrava, triple date note moon phases at 12, Ca.1936
In 1996 a similar watch sold for $1.7 million US dollars
18K..................................$500,000 $550,000 $700,000
platinum $600,000 $650,000 $800,000

PATEK PHILIPPE, 37J., RF#3450, day-date-month, moon phase, waterproof, **perpetual date at 3**, Ca. 1985
18k $35,000 $40,000 $50,000

PATEK PHILIPPE, 37J,RF#3448, triple date moon ph, c.1968
platinum................. ★ ★ ★ $70,000 $90,000 $120,000
18K $30,000 $35,000 $45,000

PATEK PHILIPPE, 37J., Perpetual, triple date, moon ph.
RF # 2497
18k $60,000 $70,000 $90,000

PATEK PHILIPPE,18J., triple date, moon ph., RF#2438, Ca.1962. (at auction for $200,000.00, in 2002)
18k $75,000 $100,000 $150,000

DIALS FOR MINT PRICES MUST BE ALL **ORIGINAL**.

PATEK PHILIPPE, 18J, Perpetual, Moon Ph., RF# 1526, Ca.1940
18k (rare dial) $60,000 $75,000 $100,000

PATEK PHILIPPE,18J., "Officer", RF#3960, c.1992
18k 2,000 made, 18k(w) 150 made, platinum 50 made
18K....................................$14,000 $16,000 $19,000
18k(w)...............................$16,000 $18,000 $21,000
platinum $26,000 $29,000 $33,000

PATEK PHILIPPE, 15J., enamel dial, c. 1910
18k $8,000 $9,000 $12,000

PATEK PHILIPPE, 18 jewels, RF#1461
18k $3,000 $3,300 $4,000

PATEK PHILIPPE, 18 jewels, RF # 1571, Ca. 1940s
18k $3,500 $3,800 $4,800

PATEK PHILIPPE, 18 jewels, RF # 1461, aux. sec.
18k $3,000 $3,300 $4,000

PATEK PHILIPPE, 18J., *Amagnetic* on dial, ca. 1960
18k $6,000 $7,000 $9,000

PATEK PHILIPPE, 18J.,RF # 448,"Calatrava", aux. sec., Ca. 1950s
18k $3,500 $3,800 $4,500

⊕ Pricing in this Guide are fair market price for **COMPLETE** watches which are reflected from the "**NAWCC**" National and regional shows.

DIALS FOR MINT PRICES MUST BE ALL <u>ORIGINAL</u>.

PATEK PHILIPPE, 18 jewels, RF # 2536, Ca. 1950s
18k $4,500 $5,000 $6,000

PATEK PHILIPPE, 18 jewels, RF # 2452, Ca. 1950s
18k $4,000 $4,500 $5,500

PATEK PHILIPPE, 18 jewels, RF # 2459, Ca. 1950s
18k $3,500 $4,000 $5,000

PATEK PHILIPPE, 18 jewels, RF # 1509, Ca. 1940s
18k $3,000 $3,300 $3,800

PATEK PHILIPPE, 18 jewels, RF # 2525 / 1, Ca. 1950s
18k $2,800 $3,200 $4,000

PATEK PHILIPPE, 18 jewels, RF # 2484, Ca. 1950s
18k $3,000 $3,300 $3,800

PATEK PHILIPPE, 18 jewels, RF # 2506 / 1, Ca. 1950s
18k $3,000 $3,300 $3,800

PATEK PHILIPPE, 18 jewels, RF # 534, Ca. 1940s
18k(**2-tone dial**) $3,000 $3,400 $4,000

⊕ Pricing in this Guide are fair market price for **COMPLETE** watches which are reflected from the "<u>**NAWCC**</u>" National and regional shows.

PATEK PHILIPPE, 18 jewels, RF # 2577, Ca. 1955
18k $3,000 $3,300 $4,000

PATEK PHILIPPE, 37J., RF#3429, auto-wind, Ca.1960's
18k $5,000 $5,500 $6,500

PATEK PHILIPPE, 18J., **Calatrava**, RF# 3796, Rose only
18k (**Rose**) $3,500 $4,000 $5,000

PATEK PHILIPPE, 30J., auto-w, screw back, RF#2526,
18K PINK............... ★ ★ ★$20,000 $25,000 $35,000
18K .... ★ ★$15,000 $18,000 $25,000
Rare black enamel dial, with 100% MINT
10 made .... ★ ★ ★ ★ ★$70,000 $80,000 $100,000

PATEK PHILIPPE, 18 jewels, RF# 2429, Ca. 1950s
18k $3,300 $3,500 $4,000

PATEK PHILIPPE,18J., <u>**CLASSIC**</u> **Calatrava**, RF# 96

18k	$3,500	$4,000	$5,000
18k Rose	$4,000	$4,500	$5,500
s. steel	$4,000	$4,500	$5,500
platinum	$10,000	$12,000	$15,000
platinum + diam. dial	$11,500	$13,000	$16,000

The **above <u>CLASSIC</u>** Calatrava case and dial model **96** was 1st used in 1932. It was designed at a time of transition from pocket watches to wrist watches. The coin was used as a perfect geometric shape to design a wrist watch case that has harmony and balance. Many variations from the classic model **96** have been used, but to most collectors the **CLASSIC** model 96 is known as the <u>**Calatrava**</u> model. The original 96 Calatrava model used a flat bezel, 31mm one piece case (lugs are not soldered on), <u>manual</u> wind, white dial, barrette-shaped hour markers, dauphine hands and aux. seconds chapter with a inside and outside circle and long 5 sec. markers. A black dial was added in 1937. The recent classic style Calatrava case is RF # 3796. To date there are many Calatrava styles and models.

PATEK PHILIPPE, 18 jewels, RF # 2537, aux. sec., c. 1950s
18k $3,000 $3,300 $4,000

DIALS FOR MINT PRICES MUST BE ALL **ORIGINAL**.

PATEK PHILIPPE, 18J., RF# 2500, Ca. 1950s
18k $2,500 $2,800 $3,200

PATEK PHILIPPE,18J., RF # 1513, aux. sec., Ca.1943
18K $2,500 $2,800 $3,200

PATEK PHILIPPE, 18 J., RF # 2515, Ca.1950s
18k $2,500 $2,800 $3,200

PATEK PHILIPPE,18J., RF# 1433, Ca.1940s
18K $2,500 $2,800 $3,200

PATEK PHILIPPE,18J., manual w., RF#1516, c.1950
18K..$3,000 $3,300 $4,000

PATEK PHILIPPE,18J., aux. sec., RF#96, cal.12-20, c.1937
18K $3,500 $4,000 $5,000

PATEK PHILIPPE,18J., aux. sec., RF#2445,
18K..$2,500 $2,800 $3,200

PATEK PHILIPPE,18J., RF#1543, c.1947
18K $3,000 $3,300 $4,000

Wrist Watches listed in this section are priced at the collectable fair market **Trade Show** level as **complete** watches having an original gold-filled case and stainless steel back, also with original dial, leather watch band, and the entire original movement in good working order with no repairs needed.

Some grades are not included. Their values can be determined by comparing with **similar** age, size, metal content, style, grades, or models such as **time only**, chronograph, repeater etc. listed.

DIALS FOR MINT PRICES MUST BE ALL <u>**ORIGINAL**</u>.

PATEK PHILIPPE,18J., RF# 1590, c.1951
18K......................................$3,000 $3,300 $4,000

PATEK PHILIPPE, 18 jewels, RF # 2509, Ca. 1950s
18k $3,200 $3,600 $4,400

PATEK PHILIPPE, 18J., RF # 2494, extra long lugs, c. 1950
18k $2,800 $3,100 $3,700

PATEK PHILIPPE, 18J., RF # 2557, Ca. 1950s
18k $2,800 $3,100 $3,700

PATEK PHILIPPE, 18 jewels, RF # 570, aux. sec., Ca. 1950s
18k $3,500 $4,200 $5,500

PATEK PHILIPPE, 30J.,"Calatrava", auto wind, gold rotor
18k $6,000 $7,000 $10,000

PATEK PHILIPPE, 18 jewels, RF # 1517, aux. sec.
18k $2,800 $3,200 $3,800

PATEK PHILIPPE,18J.,"Calatrava", RF # 96, <u>**enamel dial**</u>,
Breguet style numbers, Ca.1940s
Platinum.....................★★$15,000 $17,000 $22,000
18k ....★ $10,000 $12,000 $15,000

DIALS FOR MINT PRICES MUST BE ALL **ORIGINAL**.

PATEK PHILIPPE, 18J.,waterproof, "Calatrava", RF# 2545
18k $4,000 $4,500 $5,500

PATEK PHILIPPE, 18 jewels, RF # 2406, Ca. 1950s
18k $3,500 $4,000 $5,000

PATEK PHILIPPE, 18J., RF# 1584, **extended lugs,** aux. sec.
18k $4,000 $4,500 $6,000

PATEK PHILIPPE, 18J., fancy lugs, c. 1940s
18k $5,000 $5,500 $6,500

🕐 A collector should expect to pay modestly higher prices
at local shops

PATEK PHILIPPE, 18J., fancy lugs, ca. 1948
18k $7,000 $8,000 $10,000

PATEK PHILIPPE, 18 jewels, curled lugs, RF# 1491
* Add **$2,000** for sweep seconds
18K Yellow $8,000 $9,000 $11,000
18K Pink............................$9,000 $10,000 $12,000

PATEK PHILIPPE, 18 jewels, RF # 2549, Ca. 1950s
18k ....★★$15,000 $19,000 $26,000

PATEK PHILIPPE, 18 jewels, RF # 2550, Ca. 1950s
18k $10,000 $12,000 $18,000

PATEK PHILIPPE, 18J., RF# 2533, screw back,
manual wind, Ca. 1950s
18k $3,000 $3,500 $4,500

PATEK PHILIPPE, 21J., RF # 3025, "Calatrava", Ca.1950s
note: <u>center seconds</u> and **Breguet dial**
18k $3,500 $4,000 $5,000

PATEK PHILIPPE, 18J., center sec., RF#2466, ca.1949
18k $3,800 $4,200 $4,800

PATEK PHILIPPE, 18J., RF# 1578, center sec., c. 1950s
18k $3,200 $3,500 $4,200

PATEK PHILIPPE, 18 jewels, RF # 2482, Ca. 1950s
18k $3,500 $3,800 $4,500

PATEK PHILIPPE, 18 jewels, RF # 565, Ca. 1940s
18k $3,000 $3,300 $4,000

PATEK PHILIPPE, 18 jewels, conical lugs, center sec.
18k $3,500 $4,000 $5,500

PATEK PHILIPPE, 18 jewels, RF # 2481, center sec.
18k $4,000 $4,500 $5,500

DIALS FOR MINT PRICES MUST BE ALL **ORIGINAL**.

PATEK PHILIPPE, 18J., RF# 1491, **Curled lugs**, Ca. 1940
* <u>Center Seconds</u> add $2,000.
18k $8,000 $9,000 $11,000

PATEK PHILIPPE,18J., center sec., RF#3411, c.1960
18K $2,500 $2,800 $3,300

PATEK PHILIPPE, 18 J., RF # 2508, center sec., c. 1950s
18k $3,500 $4,000 $5,000

PATEK PHILIPPE, 18J., RF # 2457, center sec., c. 1950s
18k $2,500 $3,800 $4,500

PATEK PHILIPPE, 18 jewels, center sec., waterproof
18k ....,.....$4,000 $4,500 $5,500

PATEK PHILIPPE,18J., RF#3495, cal.27sc, c.1969
18K $2,400 $2,700 $3,200

PATEK PHILIPPE, 18 jewels, RF # 2460, center sec.
18k $3,400 $3,700 $4,400

PATEK PHILIPPE, 18 jewels, RF# 2541, Ca. 1940s
18k $3,500 $3,800 $4,500

PATEK PHILIPPE,18J., RF# 3541, auto wind, Ca. 1966
18K.......................................$4,500 $5,200 $6,000

PATEK PHILIPPE,18J., RF# 3410, Ca. 1971
18K C&B...........................$3,500 $3,800 $4,500

PATEK PHILIPPE,18J., RF# 3558, auto wind, Ca. 1968
18K.......................................$4,500 $5,200 $6,000

PATEK PHILIPPE,18J., RF# 3473, Ca. 1962
18K $3,000 $3,300 $3,800

PATEK PHILIPPE,18J., RF# 2451, "Calatrava", Ca. 1952
18K.......................................$3,400 $3,800 $4,500

PATEK PHILIPPE,18J., RF# 2568-1, Ca. 1957
18K $2,500 $2,800 $3,300

PATEK PHILIPPE,18J., RF# 1595, Ca. 1949
18K(rose)............................$3,800 $4,200 $5,200

PATEK PHILIPPE,18J., RF# 1589, Ca. 1955
18K(rose)............................$3,000 $3,300 $3,800

PATEK PHILIPPE, 18 J., RF # 3569, auto wind, **back set**
18k (fancy bezel).................$4,000 $4,500 $5,500

PATEK PHILIPPE, 18 jewels RF # 3606
18k C&B...........................$3,000 $3,500 $4,500

PATEK PHILIPPE, 18 jewels, RF # 3509
18k $2,500 $2,800 $3,300

PATEK PHILIPPE,18J., RF# 2573, c.1954
18K $2,500 $2,800 $3,400

PATEK PHILIPPE, 18 J., small "Calatrava," c. 1940s
18k $3,200 $3,600 $4,200

PATEK PHILIPPE,18J., RF#2592, c.1956
18K(center lugs)................$3,000 $3,500 $4,500

PATEK PHILIPPE, 18 jewels, RF # 2589, Ca. 1970s
18k $2,800 $3,000 $3,500

PATEK PHILIPPE,18J., RF#3574, c.1960
s. steel $3,500 $4,000 $4,500

DIALS FOR MINT PRICES MUST BE ALL **ORIGINAL**.

PATEK PHILIPPE, 18J., "Calatrava", RF# 2588, Ca.1940s
18k $3,500 $3,800 $4,400

PATEK PHILIPPE, 18 J., RF # 497, unusual shape lugs,
CA. 1940s
18k $8,000 $9,000 $11,000

PATEK PHILIPPE, 36J., RF # 3800, "Nautilus", gold & steel
* Full Size
18K...$9,000 $9,500 $11,000
18k & s. steel $4,500 $5,000 $6,000
s. steel $4,500 $5,000 $6,000

PATEK PHILIPPE, **mid size, QUARTZ,** rf#3900/1, date
s. steel $2,000 $2,200 $2,700

PATEK PHILIPPE, quartz, rf#3900/101, date
pave diamonds=.50ct., ruby hour markers
18k $6,000 $7,500 $10,000

PATEK PHILIPPE, quartz, rf#3900/5, date, dia-
monds=2.27ct.
18k C&B.............................. $9,000 $10,000 $13,000

PATEK PHILIPPE, quartz, rf#3900/3, date, Carran dial
diamonds=.68ct.
platinum............................. $12,000 $14,000 $17,000

PATEK PHILIPPE, quartz, rf#3900/103, date
diamonds=.68ct, pave diamonds=.50, ruby markers
18k $7,000 $8,500 $11,000

DIALS FOR MINT PRICES MUST BE ALL **ORIGINAL**.

PATEK PHILIPPE, quartz, rf#3900/105, date,
diamonds=2.27ct., pave diamonds=.50, ruby markers
18k C&B............................$10,000 $11,000 $14,000

PATEK PHILIPPE, auto wind, rf#3800/108, date,
diamonds=7.46ct.,pave diam.=1.50ct.,sapphire markers
18k C&B............................$30,000 $33,000 $40,000

PATEK PHILIPPE, auto wind, rf#3800/103, date
diamonds=.91ct., pave diamonds=63ct., ruby markers
18kC&B............................$17,000 $19,000 $23,000

PATEK PHILIPPE, 36J., RF # 3700, "Nautilus," **large size**
s. steel $4,500 $5,000 $6,000
s. steel (RF# 3710) $6,500 $7,000 $8,000

PATEK PHILIPPE, auto wind, rf#3800/105, date
diamonds=2.40ct., pave diam.=.63ct., ruby markers
18kC&B............................$20,000 $22,000 $26,000

PATEK PHILIPPE, 36 J. ''Nautilus,'' diamond bezel
18k $11,000 $12,000 $14,000

" PATEK PHILIPPE" watches should be signed on the case,
dial & movement to bring the prices listed in this book.
(triple signed P.P.CO.)

⊕ Some grades are not included. Their values can be
determined by comparing with **similar** age, size, metal
content, style, grades, or models such as **time only**,
chronograph, repeater etc. listed.

PATEK PHILIPPE, skeleton, RF# 3885
18k $7,500 $8,000 $9,000

PATEK PHILIPPE, skeleton, rf# 3878, auto wind
18k $8,500 $9,500 $11,500

PATEK PHILIPPE, 36 J., RF # 3588, diamond dial & bezel
18k C&B............................$5,500 $6,500 $8,000

PATEK PHILIPPE, skeleton, rf# 3886
18k $7,500 $8,500 $10,500

PATEK PHILIPPE, 18J., diamond dial, Contract case, c. 1952
platinum..............................$3,500 $3,800 $4,500

PATEK PHILIPPE, skeleton, diamonds=.62ct., rf# 3885
18k $8,500 $9,500 $11,500

PATEK PHILIPPE, 18J., **diamond dial** "Calatrava", RF#96
platinum............................$10,000 $12,000 $15,000

PATEK PHILIPPE, skeleton, diamonds=.85ct., rf# 3884
manual wind
18k $9,500 $10,500 $12,500

PATEK PHILIPPE, 18J., ''Calatrava,'' mid size, **dia. dial**
platinum............................$10,000 $12,000 $15,000

Wrist Watches listed in this section are priced at the collectable
fair market **Trade Show** level as **complete** watches having an
original gold-filled case and stainless steel back, also with
original dial, leather watch band, and the entire original movement in good working order with no repairs needed.

PATEK PHILIPPE, 18 jewels, c. 1980s
18k C&B............................$3,000 $3,500 $4,000

PATEK PHILIPPE, **quartz**, c. 1980s
18k C&B............................$2,700 $3,000 $3,600

PATEK PHILIPPE, 23J., "Ellipse", RF # 3738, c. 1960s
18k C&B............................$3,500 $4,000 $5,000

PATEK PHILIPPE, 18 jewels, RF # 3745, c. 1980s
18k C&B............................$3,000 $3,500 $4,000

PATEK PHILIPPE, 18 jewels, RF # 2548, massive lugs
18k.......................................$6,500 $7,200 $8,500

PATEK PHILIPPE, 18 J., RF # 1585, concave & hooded
lugs
18k.......................................$5,000 $5,500 $6,500

PATEK PHILIPPE, 18 jewels,hooded lugs, c.1930s
18K.......................................$5,000 $5,500 $6,500

PATEK PHILIPPE, 18 jewels, mid-sized, 2 tone
note: **winds at 12**
18k (y & w).........................$7,000 $8,000 $10,000

Wrist Watches listed in this section are priced at the collectable
fair market **Trade Show** level as **complete** watches having an
original gold-filled case and stainless steel back, also with
original dial, leather watch band, and the entire original movement in good working order with no repairs needed.

⊕ Pricing in this Guide are fair market price for **COMPLETE**
watches which are reflected from the "**NAWCC**" National and
regional shows.

⊕ Some grades are not included. Their values can be
determined by comparing with **similar** age, size, metal
content, style, grades, or models such as **time only**,
chronograph, repeater etc. listed.

DIALS FOR MINT PRICES MUST BE ALL **ORIGINAL**.

PATEK PHILIPPE, 18 J., extended lugs, 2 tone, RF#497
18k (y & w) $10,000 $12,000 $14,000

PATEK PHILIPPE, 18 jewels, lady's watch, c. 1940s
18k C&B $2,500 $3,000 $4,000

PATEK PHILIPPE, 18 jewels, lady's watch
18k $1,200 $1,400 $1,800

PATEK PHILIPPE, 18J., lady's watch, min. repeater
18k $65,000 $75,000 $95,000

PATEK PHILIPPE, 18 J., lady's, hinged lid set in diamonds
18k $8,000 $9,000 $11,000

PATEK PHILIPPE, 18 jewels, lady's watch, c. 1950s
18k $1,400 $1,800 $2,500

PATEK PHILIPPE, 18 jewels, lady's watch
18k C&B $2,500 $3,000 $4,000

PATEK PHILIPPE, 18 jewels, lady's watch, c. 1940s
18k $1,000 $1,200 $1,500

PATEK PHILIPPE, 18 J., lady's watch, diamond bezel
platinum $3,000 $3,500 $4,500

PATEK PHILIPPE, 18 jewels, lady's watch, c. 1940s
18k $1,400 $1,600 $1,900

PATEK PHILIPPE, 18 jewels, lady's watch, c. 1950s
18k $2,500 $3,000 $4,000

PATEK PHILIPPE, 18 jewels, lady's watch, c. 1950s
18k $900 $1,100 $1,400

PATEK, PHILIPPE
MOVEMENT IDENTIFICATION

Caliber 6¾, no. 60
S.no. 865000-869999
(1940-1955)

Caliber 7, no. 70
S.no. 943300-949999
(1940-1960)
S.no. 940000-949999

Caliber 8, no. 80
S.no. 840000-849999
(1935-1960)

Caliber 8, no. 85
S.no. 850000-859999
(1935-1968)

Caliber 9, no. 90
S.no. 833150-839999
S.no. 970000-979999
(1940-1950)

Caliber 9, no. 90a
830000-833149
(1940-1950)

Caliber 10, no. 105
S.no. 900000-909999
(1940-1945)

Caliber 10, no. 110
S.no. 910000-919999
(1940-1950)

Caliber 10, no. 200
S.no. 740000-759999
(1952-1965)
S.no. 950000-959999
(1945-1955)

Caliber 23, no. 300
S.no. 780000-799999
(1955-1965)

Caliber 12, no. 600AT
S.no. 760000-779999
(1952-1960)

Caliber 12, no. 400
S.no. 720000-739999
(1950-1965)

Caliber 12, no. 120
826900-829999 (1935-1940)

Caliber 12, no. 120A
92000-929999 (1940-1950)
960000-969999 (1946-1952)
938000-939999 (1952-1954)

Caliber 12 , center seconds

Caliber 13, no. 130A

Caliber 13, no. 130B

Caliber 13, no. 130C

Chronograph, no. 862000-863995 (1940-1950); no. 867000-869999 (1950-1970)

Caliber 12-600 AT, S.no. 760,000-779,999 (1960-1970)

GYROMAX BALANCE WHEEL

DIALS FOR MINT PRICES MUST BE ALL **ORIGINAL**.

PATRIA, 7 jewels, enamel dial, **compass**, Ca. 1920
s. steel .... ★$250 $325 $450

PATRIA, 7 jewels, enamel dial,
silver $75 $90 $135

PERFINE, 17 jewels, chronog., 2 reg.
gold filled...............................$150 $175 $225
s. steel $100 $125 $175

PERPETUAL W. CO., 15 jewels, rim wind & set,
original retail price in 1933 was $31.50
14k...$700 $800 $1,000
gold filled.............................$350 $375 $450
s. steel $250 $275 $350
base metal $200 $235 $300

PERPETUAL W. CO., 15 jewels, c. 1930s
14k..$700 $800 $1,100
gold filled..............................$450 $550 $600

PERPETUAL W. CO., 15J., fluted bezel, and sold for
$37.50 in 1933
base metal...............................$300 $350 $450

PERPETUAL W. CO., 15 jewels, fluted bezel
gold filled...............................$400 $450 $550

PERPETUAL W. CO., 15 J., diamond bezel, c. 1930s
platinum $550 $600 $700

PHILLIPE W. CO., 17J., RF#2501, chronog., c.1950
s. steel.....................................$200 $250 $325

1,028 / PIAGET

PIAGET,18J., cal.9p2 , c.1980
18k(w)......................................$500 $575 $700

PIAGET, 18 jewels, 2 movements, 2 dials,
18k..$600 $700 $850

PIAGET,18J., center sec., RF#1176, cal.f1560, c.1952
18k $400 $475 $600

PIAGET, 18 jewels, black dial
18k..$500 $575 $700

PIAGET,18J., center sec., c.1950
18k $450 $500 $650

PIAGET, 18 jewels, center sec., auto wind
18k..$600 $700 $850

PIAGET, 18 jewels, 1904 $20 dollar gold piece, flip top
22k $900 $1,100 $1,400

⏰ Some grades are not included. Their values can be determined by comparing with **similar** age, size, metal content, style, grades, or models such as **time only**, chronograph, repeater etc. listed.

PIAGET, 18 jewels, ref. #8177, auto wind
18k..$600 $700 $850

DIALS FOR MINT PRICES MUST BE ALL **ORIGINAL**.

PIAGET, 18 jewels
18k $600 $700 $900

PIAGET, 18 jewels, oval style
18k C&B $500 $600 $750

PIAGET, 30 jewels, auto wind, gold rotor
18k $600 $700 $900

PIAGET, 18 jewels, oval style
18k...$300 $375 $500

PIAGET, 18 jewels, 18k case, 14k band
18k & 14k C&B.....................$800 $900 $1,100

PIAGET, 18 jewels, textured bezel
18k...$700 $775 $900

PIAGET, 18J., for Van Cleef, center lugs, thin model
18k $600 $700 $900

PIAGET, 18J, 2 time zones & 2 movements
18k...$800 $900 $1,200

PIAGET,18J., RF#9821 , c.1975
18k C&B $800 $900 $1,100

PIAGET, 30 jewels, auto-wind, textured bezel
18k...$600 $700 $1,000

PIAGET, 18J., RF#9298, c. 1970
18k $700 $800 $950

PIAGET, 18 jewels,
18k $700 $800 $1,000

PIAGET, 18 jewels, "Emperor", RF#7131C516
18k plain dial $3,000 $3,300 $4,000
18k pave dial.......................$3,500 $3,800 $4,500

PIAGET, "Polo", RF#7131C701, quartz
18kC&B $3,800 $4,000 $5,000

PIAGET, "Polo", RF#15562C701, quartz
18k $3,000 $3,500 $4,500
NOTE: PIAGET identification # the first 3 to 5 = case design, a letter as A, B, C, =bracelet design. All models beginning with 7, 8,15 may be worn while swimming.

PIAGET, "Polo", RF#15562C701, quartz
18kC&B $2,500 $3,000 $4,000

PIAGET,   RF#8065D4
18kC&B $1,500 $1,700 $2,100

PIAGET, 17 jewels, Ca. 1957
18k...$500 $550 $700

PIERCE,7J., Doctors style, Ca. 1930
base metal...............................$100 $150 $275

Wrist Watches listed in this section are priced at the collectable
fair market Trade Show level as complete watches having an
original gold-filled case and stainless steel back, also with
original dial, leather watch band, and the entire original movement in good working order with no repairs needed.

DIALS FOR MINT PRICES MUST BE ALL **ORIGINAL**.

PIERCE, 17J., early auto wind, **"Parashock,"** Ca. 1930s
weight moves from 12 to 6 0'clock
s. steel \$300   \$350   \$450

PIERCE, 17J., triple date, moon ph.
gold filled \$250   \$300   \$425

PIERCE, 21 jewels, "Duofon", **Alarm**, Ca. 1955
s. steel \$95   \$125   \$165

POBEDA, 15J., tonneau, Ca. 1930s
14k pink.................................\$200   \$225   \$275

PIERCE, 17 jewels, chronog. one button
s. steel \$225   \$250   \$300

POLJOT, 25J, "Selena", limited, made in Moscow, Moon Ph.
Russian chronograph, date, M-wind, Ca. 2002
s. steel \$225   \$265   \$325

PIERCE, 17 jewels, chronog., c. 1940s
s. steel \$150   \$175   \$225
14k \$350   \$385   \$450
18k \$425   \$465   \$525

PONTIFA, 17 jewels, chronog. day-date-month, 3 reg.
14k \$400   \$485   \$650
s. steel \$250   \$325   \$425

PRAESENT, 17J., triple date, moon ph., mid size, c.1948
gold filled................................$150 $175 $225

PULSAR, L.E.D. (light emitting diode), **working,** ca.1975
14k..$300 $335 $425
gold filled $95 $150 $250

PROVITA, 17J., cal.1525, c.1973
18k $150 $175 $250

PULSAR, L.E.D. (light emitting diode), **working,**
18k $400 $450 $550
14k $300 $350 $425
gold filled $95 $150 $250
s. steel $95 $150 $250

PRONTO, 17 jewels, triple date, auto wind, waterproof
s. steel $75 $95 $135

RADO, 7J., doctors style double dial, c.1938
gold filled $200 $235 $300

PULSAR, L.E.D. (light emitting diode), **working,** ca.1975
18k $400 $435 $550
14k $300 $335 $425
gold filled................................$95 $150 $250
s. steel $95 $150 $250

RADO, 17J., date, ca.1960
gold plate $30 $40 $75

RAPID, 17J., on mvt. PATHE W. CO.
gold filled.................................. $40 $50 $85

RECORD, 17J., split sec. chronog., date, moon phase
18k $4,500 $5,000 $6,000

RECORD, 17 jewels, split sec. chronog.
18k $3,500 $4,000 $5,000
s. steel $2,000 $2,200 $2,800

RECORD, 17 J., triple date, moon ph., auto wind ,
2 reg. chronograph,
18k $1,200 $1,400 $1,800

RECORD, 17 jewels, triple date, moon phase, c. 1940s
18k $700 $800 $1,000

RECORD, 17 jewels, day-date-month, moon phase
s. steel $300 $375 $500

RECORD, 17 J., triple date, moon phase, auto wind
18k $650 $750 $950

REGINA, enamel dial, center lugs, c.1929
silver $135 $185 $250

🕐 Some grades are not included. Their values can be
determined by comparing with **similar** age, size, metal
content, style, grades, or models such as **time only**,
chronograph, repeater etc. listed.

REMBRANT, 17J., chronog., c.1942
18k $350 $400 $500
s. steel $150 $175 $250

REVUE, 17J., beveled case, cal.54, c.1940
nickel..$35 $45 $75

RIMA, 17J., aux. sec.,
14k $100 $125 $165

ROAMER, 17 jewels, date, auto wind
gold filled...................................$50 $65 $100

ROAMER, 17 jewels, hidden lugs
gold filled $40 $50 $85

ROCKFORD,7J., **enaml dial** with red 5 min., wire lugs,
S#701,960, G# 180, 0 size, HC, M# 1, Ca.1910
nickel $150 $185 $250

ROCKFORD,15J., "Winona", made in USA, S#761074
gold filled $275 $325 $475
base metal $175 $200 $275

ROCKFORD, 17J., "Iroquois", gold train
gold filled $275 $325 $475

ROLEX WATCH CO.

Swiss

Rolex was founded by Hall Hans Wilsdorf in 1905, with his brother-in-law using the name of Wilsdorf & Davis and used movement supplier **Aegler** of Bienne, Switzerland, and bought cases from London. First wrist chronometer in 1910. In *1908* the trade-mark **"Rolex"** was officially registered, and by 1919, Wilsdorf started the *"Manufacture des Montres Rolex"* and the movements were manufactured in Bienne, but finished and cased in Geneva. In 1926, they made the first real waterproof wrist watch and called it the *"Oyster"*. Rolex introduced a self-winding movement they called *"Perpetual"* in 1931. In 1945, they introduced the *"Date-Just,"* which showed the day of the month. In 1950 the *"Turn-o-graph"* was used, the forerunner of the Submariner & in 1953 the *"Submariner"* was introduced and in 1954 the *"GMT Master"* model. In 1956, a *"Day-Date"* model was released which indicates the day of the month (in numbers) and the day of the week (in letters).

IMPORTANT:
The following is a *guide* to help determine the age of your Rolex watches. However on **some** Oyster style watches Rolex added **inside** the case a Roman number (I,II,III,IV) to denote first, second, third, or fourth quarter + "53", "54", "55", "56" to denote the year of production. Example outside Oyster case # 955454 inside case IV-53 which = last quarter of 1953. Example outside Oyster case # 282621 inside case III-55 which = third quarter of 1955. Rolex went back to 100,000 in 1954 on some cases.

ROLEX ESTIMATED PRODUCTION DATES

DATE–SERIAL #	DATE–SERIAL #	DATE–SERIAL #	DATE–SERIAL #	DATE–SERIAL #	DATE–SERIAL #	DATE–SERIAL #
1925 - 25,000	1937- 99,000	1949 - 608,000	1961-1,480,000	1973-3,741,000	1985 — 8,815,000	1992 1/4-C000,001
1926 - 28,500	1938-118,000	1950 - 673,500	1962-1,557,000	1974-4,002,000	1986 — 9,292,000	1993 3/4-S000,001
1927 - 30,500	1939-136,000	1951 - 738,500	1963-1,635,000	1975-4,266,000	1987 — 9,765,000	1995 — W000,001
1928 - 33,000	1940-165,000	1952 - 804,000	1964-1,713,000	1976-4,538,000	1987 1/2-R999,999	1996 — T000,001
1929 - 35,500	1941-194,000	1953 - 950,000	1965-1,792,000	1977-5,005,000	1987 3/4-R000,001	1997 3/4-U000,001
1930 - 38,000	1942-224,000	1954 - 999,999	1966-1,870,000	1978-5,481,000	1988 — R999,999	1999 — A000,001
1931 - 40,000	1943-253,000	1955 - 200,000	1967-2,164,000	1979-5,965,000	1989 — L000,001	2000 — P000,001
1932 - 43,000	1944-285,000	1956 - 400,000	1968-2,426,000	1980-6,432,000	1990 — L999,999	2001 — K000,001
1933 - 47,000	1945-348,000	1957 - 600,000	1969-2,689,000	1981-6,910,000	1990 1/2-E000,001	2002 — Y000,001
1934 - 55,000	1946-413,000	1958 - 800,000	1970-2,952,000	1982-7,385,000	1991 1/4-E999,999	2003 — H000,001
1935 - 68,000	1947-478,000	1959-1,100,000	1971-3,215,000	1983-7,860,000	1991 1/2-X000,001	
1936 - 81,000	1948-543,000	1960-1,401,000	1972-3,478,000	1984-8,338,000	1991 3/4-N000,001	

The above list is provided for determining the APPROXIMATE age of your watch. Match serial number with date. Watches were not necessarily sold in the exact order of manufactured date. The above list was furnished with the help of Jeffrey P. Hess. Jeff and James M. Dowling authored a book *"The Best of Time"* a unauthorized history of the Rolex Watch Co.

ROLEX W. CO. REFERENCE # INDEX

Original Box & Papers bring higher Prices.

ROLEX
BIENNE

Above: **Aegler, S.A. Montres**. Rolex Watch Co. used the movement supplier **Aegler** of Bienne, Switzerland.
* Below abbreviations used in Rolex section.
BB = bubble back
Chg. or chronog. = Chronograph
Chr = Chronometer
m.wind = manual wind
Pet. = perpetual or automatic winding - self-winding & etc.
Prs. = precision
Oy. = Oyster case (water-proof)
Q. = Quick set for calendar
RF# = reference number or case style

ROLEX,15 jewels, enamel dial, ca.1920
silver $800 $1,000 $1,400

ROLEX, 15 jewels, enamel dial, flip top, c. 1918
silver $1,000 $1,200 $1,600

ROLEX,15 jewels, enamel bezel, Ca.1935
9K $1,200 $1,400 $2,000

ROLEX, 17J., RF# 2940, screw on back is flat & tin can shaped case, which used a non-magnetic metal ???
non-magnetic... ★ ★ ★ ★ ★ $2,500 $2,800 $3,300

ROLEX,15 jewels, enamel dial, demi- hunter style, ca.1920
silver $1,200 $1,500 $1,800

ROLEX, 26J., **Milgauss** 1st registered in 1954, RF#1019,
Oy., Pet., Chr., withstands mag. fields to 1,000 Gauss Oersted, Ca.1988
s.steel $8,000 $9,000 $12,000

DIALS FOR MINT PRICES MUST BE ALL **ORIGINAL**.

ROLEX, 17J, **Milgauss** in red, oyster, perpetual, RF# 6541
Lighting bolt sec. hand, Milgauss 1st registered in 1954
s. steel $18,000 $25,000 $32,000

ROLEX, 17J., "Precision"
s. steel $350 $450 $600

ROLEX, 17 jewels,"1/4 Century Club", **BOMBE'**, c. 1960s
18k $1,500 $1,700 $2,200
14k $1,300 $1,500 $2,000

ROLEX,17J., center sec., RF#9829, cal.1210
s. steel $350 $450 $600

ROLEX, 17 jewels, "Precision," center sec., Roman bezel
18k $850 $1,000 $1,200

ROLEX, 17J., Oy., Chr., RF#6512 , Ca.1961
14k $700 $800 $1,100

ROLEX, 26J., **jumping** center sec., RF # 6556, cal.# 1040,
Tru-beat on dial, also RF # 6558 & RF # 1020, Ca. 1960
Note: Jumping center sec. must be working to bring prices listed.
s. steel .... ★ $4,000 $5,000 $7,000
14K............................... ★ ★ $6,000 $7,000 $9,000
18K.................... ★ ★ ★ ★ $7,000 $8,000 $10,000

ROLEX,17J., center sec., RF#9659, c.1960
14k $600 $700 $900

🕐 A collector should expect to pay modestly higher prices
at local shops

ROLEX,17J., "Chronometer", RF# 4222, Ca.1945
18k $1,000 $1,200 $1,500

ROLEX, 19J., RF # 8443 , c.1965
14k $600 $700 $900

ROLEX, 17J., "Precision", fancy lugs,
9k $800 $900 $1,100

ROLEX, 17 jewels, ''Precision''
18k $1,000 $1,100 $1,400

Wrist Watches listed in this section are priced at the collectable
fair market **Trade Show** level as **complete** watches having an
original gold-filled case and stainless steel back, also with
original dial, leather watch band, and the entire original movement in good working order with no repairs needed.

◷ Some grades are not included. Their values can be
determined by comparing with **similar** age, size, metal
content, style, grades, or models such as **time only**,
chronograph, repeater etc. listed.

ROLEX, 17 jewels, RF # 9659 , Ca 1960s
14k C&B...............................$1,200 $1,300 $1,600

ROLEX, 15 jewels, enamel dial, wire lugs
9k $1,000 $1,200 $1,500

ROLEX, 15j, early waterproof,"Tropical", (case within a case)
18k $2,400 $2,700 $3,500
silver $1,500 $1,700 $2,200

ROLEX, 17 jewels, RF# 2416, M.wind, Oy., Ca.1936
s.steel $500 $650 $850

ROLEX,15J., wire lugs, c.1925
silver $500 $600 $800

Oyster case was patented in 1926.

ROLEX, 15J., oyster, royal, 2 tone dial, c. 1930s
9k $1,200 $1,400 $1,700

ROLEX,15J.,"Aqua", RF # 2136, c.1928
s. steel $400 $500 $700

ROLEX, 15J., RF # 1071, oyster, ca. 1930
silver $800 $900 $1,100

ROLEX,15J., Oyster, RF # 6071, c.1927
s. steel $500 $600 $900

ROLEX, 15 jewels, oyster, center sec., enamel dial
18k $3,000 $3,300 $4,000
14k $2,000 $2,500 $3,200
9k $1,400 $1,600 $2,000
silver $1,000 $1,200 $1,500
s. steel $600 $700 $1,000

ROLEX,15J., by "Oyster W. Co". on movement, c. 1927
s. steel $500 $600 $800

ROLEX, 17 jewels, RF # 678, oyster, enamel dial, c. 1934
18k $2,800 $3,100 $3,800
14k $1,800 $2,200 $2,800
9k $1,200 $1,400 $1,800
silver $700 $900 $1,200
s. steel $600 $750 $1,000

ROLEX, 15 jewels, oyster, center sec, Ca. 1930
9K $1,500 $1,700 $2,500
14K $2,000 $2,400 $3,200

DIALS FOR MINT PRICES MUST BE ALL **ORIGINAL**.

ROLEX, 17 jewels, **not** oyster case, center sec.

18k	$1,000	$1,200	$1,500
14k	$800	$1,000	$1,300
9k	$600	$800	$1,100
s. steel	$500	$650	$900

ROLEX, 17 jewels, index bezel, **Oyster case**, c. 1928
silver $900 $1,100 $1,400

ROLEX, 18J., note dial top half & bottom, RF # 3139
Oyster case,
s. steel $1,200 $1,400 $1,700

ROLEX,17J., marked "Army", RF # 4647, c.1948
s. steel $1,300 $1,500 $1,800

Original Box & Papers bring higher Prices.

ROLEX, 18J., "Viceroy", center sec. Oyster case, ca. 1937
s. steel $600 $700 $1,000

ROLEX,17J., marked "Army", RF # 4647, 2 tone dial, Oyster
case, c.1943
s. steel $1,200 $1,300 $1,700

ROLEX,17J., RF # 3665, enamel dial, Ca.1930
s. steel $600 $800 $1,200

ROLEX, 17 jewels, oyster, RF # 4547
s. steel $500 $600 $800

⏱ Pricing in this Guide are fair market price for **COMPLETE**
watches which are reflected from the "**NAWCC**" National and
regional shows.

DIALS FOR MINT PRICES MUST BE ALL **ORIGINAL**.

ROLEX, 17 jewels, oyster, metal dial, c. 1930s
18k $2,800 $3,000 $3,600
14k $2,200 $2,400 $2,800

ROLEX, 17J., "Viceroy', Oy., RF # 3359, c.1943
14k (pink)...........................$1,700 $2,000 $3,000
14k & s. steel.....................$1,000 $1,200 $1,500

ROLEX,17J., "Observatory", Oy., RF # 3386, c.1940
gold filled.............................$700 $800 $1,000

ROLEX, 17 jewels, oyster, extra prima "Viceroy"
18k $1,800 $2,300 $3,000

ROLEX,17J., "Viceroy", Oy., RF # 3116, c.1942
14k (pink)...........................$1,700 $2,000 $3,000
14k $1,600 $1,900 $2,800

ROLEX, 26 jewels, "Viceroy", Oy., center sec.
9k (2-tone) $700 $800 $1,000

ROLEX, 17 jewels, oyster, cushion, 2 tone, c. 1943
14k & s. steel $1,400 $1,600 $2,000

🕐 Pricing in this Guide are fair market price for COMPLETE watches which are reflected from the "NAWCC" National and regional shows.

DIALS FOR MINT PRICES MUST BE ALL ORIGINAL.

ROLEX,17J., "Skyrocket", Ca.1944
gold filled $500 $600 $800

DIALS FOR MINT PRICES MUST BE ALL ORIGINAL.
Original Box & Papers bring higher Prices.

🕐 Some grades are not included. Their values can be determined by comparing with similar age, size, metal content, style, grades, or models such as time only, chronograph, repeater etc. listed.

ROLEX,17J., 28mm, small one button chronog., RF # 2303

9k ....★★★$10,000 $11,000 $14,000

ROLEX,17J., Chronograph, triple date & **moon-phases**, * <u>ALL FAKE</u>, Valjoux cal. 72C,

ROLEX,17J., split second chronog., RF # 4113, **15 examples**, large 43mm, Valjoux caliber 55 VBR, Ca.1943

s. steel ....★★★★$45,000 $60,000 $80,000

ROLEX, 17 J., chronog., 70-made, flat, tachometer, "Gabus", RF # 8206,c.1940s

18k ....★★★$20,000 $25,000 $35,000

ROLEX, 17J., RF# 3834, one button chronog. 2 reg., Antimagnetic, Ca. 1940's

18k ....★★★★$90,000 $100,000 $120,000

ROLEX, 17 J., chronog., center lugs, RF#3233, c. 1940s

18k	$8,000	$9,000	$11,000
14k	$6,000	$6,500	$7,500
9k	$3,500	$4,000	$5,000
s. steel	$4,000	$4,500	$6,000

🕐 **Note: Rolex chronographs must have original dial, deduct 30% for refinished dial.**

ROLEX,17J., RF # 3055 , Antimagnetic, 200 made, c.1956

18k $12,000 $16,000 $24,000

ROLEX, 17J., chronog., mid-sized, Antimagnetic, Ca. 1950s

18k	$9,000	$10,000	$12,000
14k	$8,000	$9,000	$11,000

ROLEX, 17J., Oy., chronog., 2 reg., RF # 3525, Ca.1942
s. steel $3,500 $4,500 $6,000

ROLEX, 17 jewels, chronog., 2 reg., RF # 3529, Ca.1942
s. steel $18,000 $20,000 $24,000

ROLEX, 17 jewels, chronog., 2 reg., RF # 3233, Ca.1942
s. steel $3,200 $3,700 $5,000

ROLEX, 17 jewels, chronog., 2 reg., RF # 4313, Ca.1950
s. steel $7,000 $8,000 $10,000

ROLEX, 17 jewels, chronog., 2 reg., RF # 3284, Ca.1942
s. steel $3,200 $3,700 $5,000

ROLEX, 17 jewels, chronog., 2 reg., RF # 3335, Ca.1942
s. steel $3,300 $3,800 $5,000

ROLEX, 31 jewels, tachometer, 3 reg., RF # 1652, Oy.330Ft.
S.Chr., Pet., triplock crown, screw-down push buttons, Ca.1991
18k $9,000 $10,000 $12,000

ROLEX,17J.,Valjoux cal.23, RF# 4062, Antimagnetic, c.1956
18k $8,000 $9,000 $10,000

ROLEX, 17 jewels, chronog., 3 reg. oyster, RF # 6238
s. steel $8,000 $9,000 $12,000

ROLEX, 17J., chronog., 3 reg., RF # 6234, Valjoux 72bc
s. steel, Antimagnetic $8,500 $9,500 $13,000
14k, Antimagnetic $11,000 $13,000 $18,000

ROLEX,17J., **triple date**, RF# 4767 & 5063, c.1948
Antimagnetic, Beware of **FAKES**
s. steel ....★ ★$24,000 $26,000 $32,000

ROLEX, 17J., chronog., triple-date, diamond style chapter,
RF # 6036, about 175 made in Y. gold , 144 made pink gold
18k, Antimagnetic $26,000 $28,000 $36,000
14k, Antimagnetic $24,000 $26,000 $32,000
s. steel, Antimagnetic $22,000 $24,000 $30,000

ROLEX, 17J., **pulsation**, 3 reg., RF # 6234, Ca. 1960
s. steel, Antimagnetic $8,500 $9,500 $13,000

ROLEX,17J., Antimagnetic chronog., 3 reg., RF # 6034,
very few produced, Ca.1950s
18k .... ★ ★ ★$14,000 $15,000 $19,000

Wrist Watches listed in this section are priced at the collectable
fair market **Trade Show** level as **complete** watches having an
original gold-filled case and stainless steel back, also with
original dial, leather watch band, and the entire original movement in good working order with no repairs needed.

ROLEX, 17J., RF # 6238, 3 reg., c. 1950s, rect. markers
18k $12,000 $14,000 $18,000

ROLEX,17J., exotic dial, RF#6239, Valjoux 727, c.1965
"PAUL NEWMAN", *(beware of reproduction dials)*
18k no band $20,000 $24,000 $30,000
s. steel $15,000 $17,000 $20,000

ROLEX, 17J., RF # 4768, 3 reg., date, tear drop lugs, 1950s
18k $13,000 $15,000 $19,000
14k $11,000 $13,000 $17,000
s. steel $10,000 $12,000 $16,000

ROLEX,17J., "Daytona", Oy., RF#6263, Ca.1978
s. steel $9,000 $10,000 $12,000

ROLEX,17J., triple-date,3 reg., Antimagnetic, RF# 6036
"Jean Claude Killy"= 50m.=165ft in red over Antimagnetic
s. steel .... ★ ★ ★ $25,000 $30,000 $40,000

ROLEX,17J., Oy. screw down pusher 1st used 1976, RF#6265,
s. steel $9,000 $10,000 $12,000

ROLEX, 17J., RF# 6241, Daytona, red outside chapter exotic
dial, **"PAUL NEWMAN"** (Beware of reproduction dials)
s. steel $16,000 $18,000 $22,000
18k & 18k oyster band $22,000 $26,000 $32,000

ROLEX, 17 jewels, RF # 3997, chronog., Ca. 1940
s . steel $3,500 $4,000 $5,000

ROLEX, 17 J., tachometer, 3 reg., RF # 6239, c.1960s
18k	$14,000	$16,000	$20,000
14k	$12,000	$14,000	$18,000
s. steel	$9,000	$10,000	$12,000

ROLEX,19J., day-date-month, moon ph., RF # 6062,c.1945
s. steel	$28,000	$33,000	$42,000
18k	★ ★ ★ $30,000	$35,000	$45,000

ROLEX, 17 J., "Daytona", 3 reg., RF # 6241, Ca.1972
s. steel	$9,000	$10,000	$12,000

ROLEX, 15J., jumping hr., duo dial, RF # 4402 &
RF # 1491, Ca. 1930s
platinum	$14,000	$16,000	$20,000
18k	$12,000	$14,000	$17,000
14k	$10,000	$11,000	$14,000
9k	$7,000	$8,000	$11,000
silver	$6,000	$7,000	$10,000
gold filled	$4,000	$5,000	$8,000
s. steel	$5,000	$6,000	$9,000

ROLEX,17J., triple-date, moon ph., RF # 8171, **1,000 made**
18k	★ ★ ★ $25,000	$35,000	$50,000
14k	★ ★ ★ $20,000	$30,000	$40,000
s. steel	★ ★ ★ $15,000	$20,000	$30,000

ROLEX,17J..jump hr., duo dial, stepped case, RF# 4376
18k 2 tone	$15,000	$18,000	$22,000
18k	$12,000	$13,000	$16,000
14k	$9,000	$10,000	$13,000
9k	$7,000	$8,000	$11,000
s. steel	$6,000	$7,000	$9,000

ROLEX,19J., STARS on dial, triple date, RF # 6062, Ca.1945
also seen in a very few black dials
18k Pink Gold	★ ★ ★ ★ $40,000	$50,000	$65,000
18k	★ ★ ★ ★ $30,000	$40,000	$55,000

ROLEX, 17 jewels, ''Prince,'' duo dial, RF#1490
18k C&B	$5,000	$6,000	$8,000

🕐 Pricing in this Guide are fair market price for **COMPLETE** watches which are reflected from the "**NAWCC**" National and regional shows.

DIALS FOR MINT PRICES MUST BE ALL **ORIGINAL**.

ROLEX, 17 jewels, RF # 1490, flared, duo dial, c. 1930s
9k \$4,500   \$5,000   \$6,000

ROLEX, 17J., RF # 2245 & RF # 1768, 2 tone case,
        beware of **FAKES**
18k \$10,000   \$12,000   \$18,000

ROLEX, 17 jewels, "Prince," duo dial, stepped case
18k \$6,500   \$7,500   \$9,500
14k \$5,500   \$6,500   \$8,000
9k \$4,500   \$5,000   \$6,500
silver \$4,000   \$4,500   \$5,500
s. steel \$3,500   \$4,000   \$5,000
gold filled............\$2,500   \$2,800   \$3,500

ROLEX, 17J., RF # 971, 2 tone stripes, Adj. to 6 pos.
        beware of **FAKES**
18k \$10,000   \$12,000   \$16,000
14k \$7,000   \$9,000   \$13,000
9k \$5,000   \$7,000   \$10,000

ROLEX, 15 jewels, RF # 971, flared, duo dial, Adj. to 6 pos.
silver \$4,000   \$4,500   \$6,000
9k \$4,500   \$5,000   \$6,000

ROLEX, 15 jewels, RF # 971, "Prince," duo dial, c. 1930s
s. steel \$4,000   \$4,500   \$5,500

ROLEX, 15 J., RF # 1862, chronometer, duo dial, c. 1930s
s. steel \$3,500   \$4,000   \$5,000

ROLEX, 15 J., RF # 1527, "Railway," stepped case,   1930s
18k 2 tone \$9,000   \$10,000   \$13,000
18k \$7,000   \$8,000   \$10,000
14k 2 tone \$6,000   \$7,500   \$10,000
14k \$5,500   \$6,500   \$8,500
9k 2 tone \$5,500   \$6,500   \$8,500
9k \$4,000   \$5,000   \$6,000
s. steel \$3,500   \$4,000   \$5,000

ROLEX, 15 J., RF # 3361, "Prince," center sec., c. 1940s
18k \$8,000   \$9,000   \$12,000

ROLEX, 15 jewels, 1/4 century club, RF # 2541
14k \$4,500   \$5,200   \$6,500

🕐 Pricing in this Guide are fair market price for **COMPLETE** watches which are reflected from the "**NAWCC**" National and regional shows.

DIALS FOR MINT PRICES MUST BE ALL **ORIGINAL**.

ROLEX, 15 jewels, RF # 3937, 1/4 century club,
18k $4,500 $5,000 $6,000

ROLEX, 15 jewels, "Prince," RF # 1343, c. 1935
platinum $12,000 $14,000 $20,000
18k $6,000 $7,000 $9,000
14k $5,000 $5,500 $6,500
gold filled............................$2,200 $2,800 $3,500

ROLEX, 17J., RF # 1615, "Observatory", c.1938
gold filled............................$1,800 $2,200 $2,800

ROLEX, 15 jewels, stepped case, RF # 1527
18k $6,500 $7,500 $9,500

ROLEX, 17J., Oy., date, mid size,
s. steel $600 $700 $900

ROLEX, 25J., Oy., Pet., RF # 6604 , date, c.1958
s. steel $600 $700 $900

ROLEX, 30J., Oy, Pet., Chr., RF # 1500 , date, Ca.1961
s. steel $600 $700 $900

ROLEX, 17J., RF # 6694 , m.wind, Oy., date, c.1971
s. steel $600 $700 $900

ROLEX, 17J., RF # 6094 , Oy., Prs., date, Ca.1951
s. steel $500 $550 $700

ROLEX, 26J., Oy., Pet., index bezel, RF # 1501 , c.1961
s. steel $650 $750 $900

ROLEX,25J., date, **index gold bezel**, 2 tone case, RF#6305
s. steel/gold bezel $900 $1,100 $1,600

ROLEX, 17J., date, RF # 6964, ca.1953
s. steel $500 $600 $800

ROLEX, 30J., Q.date just, Oy., Pet., Chr., RF# 1601, Ca.1972
s. steel & gold $1,000 $1,200 $1,500

Note: "Ovettone" = Big Bubble Back

ROLEX, 18J., RF# 6074, Oy., Pet., Chr., date, ca.1950s
14k $2,000 $2,200 $2,800

ROLEX, 25J., **"Ovettone"**, RF # 6105, auto wind, oyster,
note thin milled bezel, **Ovettone** = Big Bubble Back, Ca.1953
14k Pink.....................★ ★$3,500 $4,000 $5,000
14k ....★ ★$3,000 $3,500 $4,500

ROLEX, 25J., oyster, perpetual, date, **"Ovettone"**,
note thin milled bezel, RF # 4467, Ca. 1950s
18k Pink.....................★ ★$4,000 $4,500 $5,500
18k ....★ ★$3,500 $4,000 $5,000

ROLEX, 19J., **"Ovettone"**, RF # 6031, 6 positions, Ca. 1953
Note: Extra section between lugs.
18k ....★ ★$3,500 $4,000 $5,000

ROLEX, 17-18J., index bezel, RF# 4325 or 4327, Ca.1951
18k $900 $1,000 $1,400
14k $800 $900 $1,300

ROLEX, 19-25J., RF # 6634, center sec.,gold & s. steel 2 tone case, Ca. 1952
Gold & steel...........................$600 $700 $900

ROLEX, 18J., RF # 6075, 2 tone, index bezel, Ca. 1951
s. steel & 14k $700 $900 $1,200

ROLEX, 17J., RF # 6029, index bezel, rose gold, c.1950s
18k $1,400 $1,600 $2,000

ROLEX, 17J., RF # 6582, marked bezel 2 tone, Ca. 1955
similar RF#1008 & 1009, no lugs=RF#9522 aux. sec. & RF#9919 no sec.
gold & s. steel........................$550 $700 $900

ROLEX, 17J., RF # 6223, oyster, index bezel, Ca. 1954
18k $1,000 $1,200 $1,500
14k $900 $1,100 $1,400
9k $550 $700 $1,000
gold filled..............................$400 $450 $600
s. steel $400 $450 $600

ROLEX, 26J., Oy., Pet., Chr., RF# 1003, index bezel, Ca.1961
18k $1,400 $1,600 $2,000
14k $1,100 $1,300 $1,700
s. steel $500 $600 $800

ROLEX, 17J., Prs., center sec., refinished dial, RF # 6422
s. steel $400 $450 $600

ROLEX, 26J., Oy.330 Ft., Pet., RF # 1002, c.1988
14K.......................................$1,200 $1,300 $1,600

ROLEX, 25J., Oy., Pet., RF # 5502 , Ca. 1955
s. steel $500 $600 $800

ROLEX, 17J., Oy., Pet., RF # 6085, index bezel, Ca. 1951
14k $1,200 $1,300 $1,600

ROLEX, 16J., Oy., RF # 6082 , c.1950
s. steel $400 $500 $700

ROLEX, 25J., Oy., Pet., RF # 6565 , c.1958
s. steel $600 $700 $900

ROLEX, 25J., Oy., Pet., Chr., RF # 1025, c.1964
note the triangles on bezel
14k $1,200 $1,400 $1,700

ROLEX, 25J., Oy., RF # 6024 , c.1953
s. steel $400 $500 $700

ROLEX, 17J., Oy., Prs., RF # 6424 , Ca.1965
s. steel $500 $600 $800

ROLEX, 17J., RF # 2010 , Ca. 1960
s. steel $400 $500 $700

ROLEX, 27J., RF# 1423, Oy., Pet., Chr., Ca.1991
s. steel $800 $900 $1,200

ROLEX, 17J., Oy., Pet.Chr., RF # 6284 , c.1955
18k $1,400 $1,600 $2,000

ROLEX, 25J., Oy., Pet., RF # 6098 , **star dial**, c.1956
18k rose .... ★ ★ ★$3,000 $3,500 $4,500

ROLEX, 17J., Oyster precision, RF # 6024 , c.1952
s. steel $400 $500 $700

ROLEX, 17-25J., "Air King", Oy., Pet., RF#5500, Ca.1971
s. steel $600 $700 $1,000

ROLEX, 26J., Oy., Pet., Chr., RF # 1005 , c.1961
14k & S.S...............................$700 $900 $1,400

ROLEX, 25J., "Air King",Oy., Pet., RF # 5501, c.1961
s. steel & gold bezel $700 $800 $1,100

🕐 A collector should expect to pay modestly higher prices
at local shops

ROLEX, 17J., RF#6084, Oy., Pet., Chr., Ca.1951
14k $1,000 $1,300 $1,600

ROLEX, 25J., Oy., Pet., Chr., RF#6568, c.1956
s. steel $500 $550 $700

ROLEX, 25J., Oy., Pet., Chr., RF#6084, textured <u>dial,</u> c.1953
14k $1,400 $1,600 $2,000

ROLEX, 18J., Oy., Pet., Chr., RF#8405, c.1950
18k $1,000 $1,200 $1,500

ROLEX, 25J., Oy., Pet., Chr., RF#6564, c.1955
s. steel $500 $600 $800

ROLEX, 25J., Oy., Pet., Chr., RF# 6567, center sec., Ca. 1960
14k $900 $1,100 $1,400

ROLEX, 25J., index bezel, Oy., Pet., Chr., RF#6581, c.1954
14k $1,200 $1,500 $2,000

🕐 Pricing in this Guide are fair market price for **COMPLETE**
watches which are reflected from the "**<u>NAWCC</u>**" National and
regional shows.

DIALS FOR MINT PRICES MUST BE ALL **<u>ORIGINAL</u>**.

ROLEX, 18J., Chr., RF# 8952, center sec., Ca. 1950s
14k index bezel $1,000 $1,200 $1,500

ROLEX,17J., Prs., RF # 4478, 9 diamonds, Ca.1948
18k $1,300 $1,500 $2,000

ROLEX, 25J., Oy. Pet., Bombe', 12 diamond dial, RF # 1030
s. steel .... ★★ $1,500 $1,800 $2,500

ROLEX, 17J., Oy. Pet., Linz 1877, Bombe' lugs, c. 1950s
18k RF#5018 .... $1,500 $1,800 $2,500

ROLEX, 26J. Bombe' lugs, Oy., Pet., RF # 6590, c. 1950
14k $1,400 $1,600 $2,000

Note: **Bombe'** = style of lug which are Convexed.

ROLEX, 25J., Bombe' lugs, Oy. Pet., RF # 6102, c.1953
14k $1,500 $1,700 $2,200

ROLEX, 26J., Bombe' lugs, Oy. Pet., RF # 6102, c. 1950
18k $1,500 $1,700 $2,200

ROLEX, 19 J., Oy., Pet., RF # 6092, Bombe' lugs, c. 1950s
18k	$1,500	$1,800	$2,200
18k Pink	$1,900	$2,200	$2,800
14k	$1,400	$1,600	$2,000
14k Pink	$1,800	$2,000	$2,400
9k	$1,000	$1,200	$1,400
s. steel	$1,500	$1,800	$2,200

ROLEX, 26J., Oy., Pet., RF # 1011, Bombe' lugs, Ca. 1960
14k $1,400 $1,600 $2,000

ROLEX,17J., RF # 4365, Ca.1920s
s.steel (redone dial) $400 $500 $700

ROLEX,15J., Oy., RF # 2495, "Extra-Prima", Ca.1937
9k enamel dial $600 $800 $1,100
9k $400 $500 $700

ROLEX,17J., Oy. Chr., RF # 5020, 2 tone, Ca.1943
14k & s. steel (redone dial) .. $600 $700 $850

ROLEX,17J., Oy. Prs., RF # 6694, Date, "Honey Comb" textured dial, Ca.1952
s. steel $700 $800 $1,000

ROLEX,15J., RF # 4377, Oy. Chr., refinished dial, Ca.1944
s. steel $400 $500 $700

ROLEX,17J., Oy. Prs., RF # 6266, Date, Ca.1957
s. steel $500 $600 $800

ROLEX,17J., Oy. Chr. Pet., RF # 4392, Observatory,Ca.1948
s. steel $800 $1,000 $1,400

ROLEX,25J., Oy. Chr. Pet., RF # 1550, rare dial (crown at 3-
6-9) , Ca.1960
s. steel .... ★★$1,500 $1,800 $2,500

ROLEX,17J., RF # 3745, Precision, Ca.1949
18k $800 $900 $1,400

ROLEX,28J., RF # 6627, Oy. Chr. Pet., date, mid size,
Ca.1971
18k $1,200 $1,400 $1,800

ROLEX,18J., RF # 4891, Chronometer, Ca.1957
18k $1,200 $1,400 $1,800

ROLEX,28J., RF # 6800, Oy. Chr. Pet., date-just, Ca.1982
s. steel $900 $1,000 $1,200

ROLEX,25J., Oy. Chr. Pet., RF # 6611, day date, Ca.1956
Note: **First President** model **no band**
18k $2,500 $3,000 $3,800

ROLEX, 30J., RF # 1603, Oy. Chr. Pet., Q.date-just, Ca.1987
s. steel $1,000 $1,200 $1,500

ROLEX,25J., RF # 6552, Oyster, Perpetual, Ca.1972
s. steel $600 $700 $1,000

ROLEX,17J., RF # 9083, Precision, Ca.1955
s. steel $350 $450 $600

DIALS FOR MINT PRICES MUST BE ALL **ORIGINAL**.

ROLEX, 15J., RF # 3655, aux. sec. Ca. 1945
s. steel $500 $600 $800

ROLEX, 26J., bubble back, hooded lugs, RF#3595, Ca.1942

18k	$7,000	$8,000	$11,000
14k	$5,000	$5,500	$7,000
9k	$3,000	$3,500	$4,500
s. steel & gold	$3,000	$3,300	$4,000
s. steel	★★★$10,000	$11,000	$14,000

ROLEX, 18J., Oy. Prs., RF # 6427, center sec. Ca. 1964
s. steel $450 $550 $750

ROLEX, 17J., Pall Mall, manual wind, Ca. 1949

s. steel	★★★$1,200	$1,500	$1,700
14k	$600	$700	$900

ROLEX, 17J., Oyster, RF# 5004, plain bezel, Ca.1950s
Mid size or ladies
s. steel $400 $500 $700

ROLEX, 17J., "Royal Observatory", RF#3121, c.1937
s. steel $400 $500 $700

ROLEX, 17J., Oyster Pet., RF# 5003, index bezel, Ca.1950s
Mid size or ladies
18k $2,200 $2,400 $2,800

ROLEX, 17J., Oyster Co., "Record", manual wind, c.1940
s. steel $300 $350 $550

⊕ Pricing in this Guide are fair market price for **COMPLETE** watches which are reflected from the "**NAWCC**" National and regional shows.

ROLEX, 17J., "Neptune", mid-size, manual wind, c.1939
gold filled.............................$200 $250 $400

ROLEX, 17J., Oy.Pet.Prs., RF # 6421, "Speedking", Ca.1960
s. steel $500 $600 $750

ROLEX, 17J., RF # 4302, index bezel, 2 tone, Ca. 1944
gold filled & s. steel $600 $700 $900

ROLEX, 26J., Oy. Pet., bubble back, hooded lugs, 2 tone
18k & s. steel $7,000 $8,000 $11,000

ROLEX, 26J, BB, 2 tone dial, hooded scalloped lugs
s. steel .... ★ $8,000 $9,000 $11,000
18k & s. steel $7,500 $8,500 $11,500

ROLEX, 17J., Oyster, RF # 2280, manual wind, c.1951
s. steel $400 $450 $600

ROLEX, 17J., Speedking, Oyster, Precision, RF # 6021,
c.1953 index on bezel
s. steel $400 $450 $600

ROLEX, 18J., RF # 3767, mid size, Ca.1940
s. steel $600 $700 $900

ROLEX, 17J., mid size, Oy. Pet.Prs., RF # 3478, c.1940
gold filled $300 $350 $500
s. steel $400 $450 $600

🕐 Some grades are not included. Their values can be
determined by comparing with **similar** age, size, metal
content, style, grades, or models such as **time only**,
chronograph, repeater etc. listed.

ROLEX, 17J., "Speed King", Oy. Chr. Pet., RF#4220, c.1945
s. steel $400 $450 $600

ROLEX, 18J., "Royal", Oyster, mid size, aux. sec.
s. steel $400 $450 $600

ROLEX, 17J., "Speed King", Oy. Chr. Pet., RF#6056, c.1952
s. steel $400 $450 $600

ROLEX, 18J., "Speed King", Oyster, mid size, center sec.
s. steel $400 $450 $600

ROLEX, 17J., mid size, Oy. Prs., RF#6066, date, c.1951
s. steel $450 $550 $700

ROLEX, 18J., Oy. Chr. Pet., RF # 3065, B.B., hooded 2 tone
yellow gold
14k Gold & steel $4,000 $4,500 $5,500

ROLEX, 17J., mid size, Oy., Prs., m.wind, RF#6466, c.1957
s. steel $450 $550 $700

Wrist Watches listed in this section are priced at the collectable
fair market Trade Show level as **complete** watches having an
original gold-filled case and stainless steel back, also with
original dial, leather watch band, and the entire original movement in good working order with no repairs needed.

🕒 Pricing in this Guide are fair market price for **COMPLETE**
watches which are reflected from the "**NAWCC**" National and
regional shows.

DIALS FOR MINT PRICES MUST BE ALL **ORIGINAL**.

ROLEX, 18J., Oy. Chr. Pet., RF # 2319, B.B., hooded 2 tone
rose gold
14k Gold & steel $4,000 $4,500 $5,500

🕒 A collector should expect to pay modestly higher prices
at local shops

🕒 Some grades are not included. Their values can be
determined by comparing with **similar** age, size, metal
content, style, grades, or models such as **time only**,
chronograph, repeater etc. listed.

ROLEX, 18J., B.B., Oy., Pet., center sec.
s. steel $900 $1,100 $1,600

ROLEX, 18J., RF # 2764, Oy., Pet., B.B., index bezel
18k $2,500 $3,000 $4,000

ROLEX, 18J., B.B., Oy., Pet., **not** 2 tone, RF # 3131
14k $2,400 $2,900 $3,600

ROLEX, 18J., B.B., Oy., Pet., chronometer, RF # 3131,
14k $1,800 $2,200 $2,800
s. steel $900 $1,100 $1,600

ROLEX, 18J., RF # 3696, B.B., oyster perpetual, Ca. 1948
9K..$1,200 $1,400 $2,000

ROLEX, 18J., B.B., Oy., Pet., cal. # 600, aux. sec., ca. 1945
s. steel $900 $1,100 $1,600

ROLEX, 25J., Oy. Chr. Pet., RF # 2764, B.B., index bezel,
2 tone, c.1945
14k & s.steel. $1,100 $1,300 $1,900

ROLEX, 18J., B.B., Oy. Pet., self winding on dial
14k $3,300 $3,800 $4,600

*   Bubble-Back was introduced in **1934**.

ROLEX, 17J., BB, Oy., Pet., RF # 6011, c.1948
14k $1,800 $2,200 $2,800

ROLEX, 25J., Oy., Pet., RF # 6585, index on bezel, c.1958
14k $1,000 $1,200 $1,900

ROLEX, 17J., BB, Oy., Pet., RF # 3133, **tu-tone**, c.1940
14k & s.steel. $1,200 $1,400 $2,000

ROLEX, 26J., RF # 1007, Chronometer Oyster Perpetual,
index on bezel, c.1965
14k $1,000 $1,200 $1,800

ROLEX, 18J., BB, RF # 5050, Oy., Pet., c.1945
9k $1,100 $1,300 $1,900

ROLEX, 17J., RF # 5015, Oy., Pet., BB, index bezel, c.1949
18k (pink) $2,700 $3,000 $3,500
s. steel $900 $1,100 $1,600

ROLEX, 17J., center sec, cal.1530, c.1955
gold filled............................... $300 $400 $600

🕐 Pricing in this Guide are fair market price for **COMPLETE**
watches which are reflected from the "**NAWCC**" National and
regional shows.
DIALS FOR MINT PRICES MUST BE ALL **ORIGINAL**.

ROLEX, 18J., Oy., Pet., RF# 2595, center sec. Ca.1938
18k $2,500 $2,800 $3,500

ROLEX, 18J., Oy., Pet., RF # 3130, B.B., aux. sec., ca. 1945
14k $1,800 $2,200 $2,800

ROLEX, 26 J., Oy., Pet., BB, aux. sec., RF # 3458, Ca. 1940s

18k	$2,200	$2,400	$3,000
14k	$1,800	$2,200	$2,800
9k	$1,000	$1,300	$1,900
gold filled	$700	$900	$1,300
s. steel	$900	$1,100	$1,600

ROLEX, 18J., Oy., Chr., RF# 2574, BB, aux. sec., Ca.1938
18k $2,200 $2,400 $3,000

ROLEX, 26 J., Oy., Pet., BB, RF# 2940, center sec., c. 1940s

18k	$2,200	$2,400	$3,000
14k	$1,800	$2,200	$2,800
9k	$1,000	$1,300	$1,900
gold filled	$700	$900	$1,300
s. steel	$900	$1,100	$1,600

ROLEX, 18 jewels, RF# 2518, Oy., aux. sec., Ca.1938
s. steel $1,500 $1,800 $2,300

ROLEX, 26 J., Oy., Pet., BB, mercedes hands, c. 1940s
2 tone dial

18k	$2,400	$2,600	$3,200
14k	$2,000	$2,400	$3,000
9k	$1,200	$1,500	$2,100
gold filled	$900	$1,100	$1,500
s. steel	$1,100	$1,300	$1,800

⊕ A collector should expect to pay modestly higher prices at local shops

⊕ Some grades are not included. Their values can be determined by comparing with **similar** age, size, metal content, style, grades, or models such as **time only**, chronograph, repeater etc. listed.

ROLEX, 18 jewels, Oy., RF# 3039, aux. sec., Ca.1938
s. steel $700 $800 $1,000

Wrist Watches listed in this section are priced at the collectable fair market Trade Show level as **complete** watches having an original gold-filled case and stainless steel back, also with original dial, leather watch band, and the entire original movement in good working order with no repairs needed.

ROLEX, 18J., RF# 3372, OY., Pet., index bezel, Ca. 1940
18k	$2,400	$2,600	$3,200
14k	$2,000	$2,400	$3,000
9k	$1,200	$1,500	$2,100
gold filled	$900	$1,100	$1,500
s. steel	$1,100	$1,300	$1,800

ROLEX, 18J, BB, RF#271, Oy., Pet., Chr., Ca. 1944
s. steel	$1,100	$1,300	$1,800

ROLEX, 19 jewels, Oy., Pet., BB, center sec., rf#1453
18k	$2,200	$2,400	$3,000
14k	$1,800	$2,200	$2,800
s. steel	$1,200	$1,400	$1,800

ROLEX, 18 jewels, RF#3132, OY., Pet., Ca. 1940
14k	$1,800	$2,200	$2,800

ROLEX, 18 jewels, RF# 3081, M.wind, Pre., Ca.1938
18k	$1,500	$1,800	$2,400
s. steel	$400	$500	$700

ROLEX, 25J., Oy., Pet., RF # 6050, BB, Ca. 1949
s. steel	$1,100	$1,300	$1,800

ROLEX, 18 jewels, RF# 2948, Chr., M.wind, Ca.1938
18k	$1,200	$1,400	$2,000

ROLEX, 18 jewels, RF# 2280, OY., M.wind, Ca.1938
s. steel	$500	$600	$800

ROLEX, 15-18J., Chr., RF# 2582, Ca. 1938

18k	$1,000	$1,200	$1,500
14k	$900	$1,000	$1,200
s. steel	$600	$700	$900

ROLEX, 18 J., RF # 4467, date, left hand winds at 9 o'clock

s. steel .... ★$2,500 $3,000 $4,000

Mint prices are for Tight bands in gold & steel.

ROLEX, 18 jewels, bubble back, RF # 2940, c. 1940s

s.steel (black dial)	$1,200	$1,400	$2,000
s. steel	$1,100	$1,300	$1,800

ROLEX, 30 jewels, "Presidential," 44 diamonds on dial & bezel, day-date, oyster, perpetual, RF # 1803

18k C&B (**non-Quick**) $5,000 $5,500 $6,500

ROLEX, 18 jewels, RF# 3716, Oy., Pet., Ca. 1941

18k	$1,200	$1,400	$1,800
14k	$1,100	$1,200	$1,600
s. steel	$600	$700	$900

ROLEX, 26 jewels, day-date, 10 diamond dial, **non quick** hidden clasp, RF # 1803

18k C&B	$3,500	$4,000	$5,000
18k C&B (pink)	★★ $4,500	$5,000	$6,000
18k C&B(w)	$5,000	$5,500	$6,500

ROLEX, 26 jewels, RF# 1018, Oyster, Pet., Chr., Ca. 1972

s. steel $500 $600 $800

ROLEX, 26 jewels, "Presidential," diamond dial, day-date, perpetual, oyster, RF # 1804, quick set

18k C&B $6,000 $6,500 $7,500

ROLEX, 30 jewels, "Presidential," (Tridor), oyster, daydate, diamond dial, perpetual, oyster,

18k (y & w) single quick.....	$6,000	$6,500	$7,500
18k (y & w) double quick ...	$7,000	$7,500	$9,000

ROLEX, 30 Jewels, "Presidential," day-date, Single Quick set model RF # 1803, double quick-set

18kC&B double quick-set...	$7,000	$7,500	$9,000
18k C&B single quick-set...	$5,500	$6,000	$7,000
18k Single Quick (head).....	$3,500	$4,000	$4,500
18k, new rf# 18238, Presid. band.	$8,000	$8,500	$10,000
18k, new rf# 18238, Oyster band.	$7,500	$8,000	$9,500

ROLEX, 30J., "Presidential," bark finish, RF # 1807, c.1971

18k C&B(non quick)..........	$3,500	$4,000	$5,000

ROLEX, 26-30J., "Presidential," day-date, perpetual, non quick, note textured dial, **Pink gold**, RF#1803 old model

18k C & B .... ★ ★	$5,000	$5,500	$6,500

ROLEX, 30 jewels, "Presidential," day-date, perpetual, oyster, diamond bezel, bark finish, RF # 1807

18k C&B(quick set)............	$6,000	$6,500	$7,500

ROLEX, 11J., quartz, RF # 1901 diamond dial & diamond bezel add $500-$900

18k	$4,500	$5,000	$6,000

⊕ Pricing in this Guide are fair market price for **COMPLETE** watches which are reflected from the "**NAWCC**" National and regional shows.

    Mint prices are for Tight bands in gold & steel.
DIALS FOR MINT PRICES MUST BE ALL **ORIGINAL**.

ROLEX, 30J., RF# 1503, Oy., Pet., Chr., , date, Ca. 1973

14k	$2,500	$2,800	$3,300

ROLEX, 26 J., **jubilee** band, 10 diamond dial, date just
  Later sapphire crystal models add about 25%.
18k C&B quick set	$4,000	$4,500	$5,500
14k C&B non quick	$2,200	$2,500	$3,200
18K & s. steel C&B quick	$1,800	$2,200	$2,800

ROLEX, 17 jewels, RF# 6466, date, oyster, mid-size, Ca.1961
s. steel C&B	$450	$600	$750

ROLEX, 25J., "Turn-o-graph", RF # 6202, Ca.1955
14k & s. steel	$2,500	$3,000	$4,000
s. steel	$3,000	$3,500	$4,500

ROLEX, 21J., RF # 6309, "Thunderbird", Ca.1965
14k gold bezel, s.steel case	$1,000	$1,100	$1,400

ROLEX, 26J., quick set, date, Oyster bracelet, c.1965
14k C&B	$2,400	$2,700	$3,200

ROLEX, 17J., RF#6426, manual wind, c.1961
s. steel	$350	$450	$650

ROLEX, 31 J., RF# 1521, Oy., Pet., sapphire crystal, Ca.1991
18k	$2,400	$2,500	$2,800
18k & s. steel	$1,600	$1,800	$2,200
s. steel	$900	$1,100	$1,600

ROLEX, 21 jewels, date just, center sec., c. 1965
18k non quick set	$2,800	$3,000	$3,500

ROLEX, 27J.,"Explorer I", RF#1427, Oy., Pet., Chr., Ca.1991
s. steel $1,800 $2,000 $2,400

ROLEX, 26J., Sea-Dweller, **Comex**, RF# 1665, date, Ca.1977
s. steel $6,000 $7,000 $9,500

ROLEX, 26-30J., "Thunderbird", Oy., Pet., Chr., RF#1625
18k & s. steel quick set $2,200 $2,700 $3,400
14k & s. steel C&B non Q. . $1,200 $1,500 $1,900

ROLEX, 25J.,, ''Explorer,'' RF # 5504, Ca. 1970
s. steel $1,200 $1,500 $2,000
s. steel & gold bezel $1,600 $1,900 $2,400

ROLEX, 25 J., early Submariner, RF# 6538, Ca.1957
Note:This style watch worn by **007** Sean Connery (rf# 6538)
s. steel $3,000 $3,500 $5,000

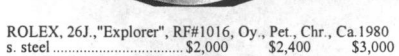

ROLEX, 26J.,"Explorer", RF#1016, Oy., Pet., Chr., Ca.1980
s. steel $2,000 $2,400 $3,000

ROLEX, "Submariner", RF# 5508, Ca.1958
s. steel $2,000 $2,500 $3,500

ROLEX, 17J., **Luminor Panerai,''** Italian military diving,
RF# 6151-1, Ca. **1940s,**   Note: Reproductions in 1992
s. steel (1940s)..................... $6,000 $7,000 $9,500

ROLEX, 26 jewels, "GMT-Master," perpetual, oyster, date
ruby & diamond dial, sapphire crystal
18k $5,000 $5,500 $6,500

ROLEX, 26 J., "Submariner" OY., Pet., Chr., RF # 5513
s. steel $1,500 $1,800 $2,200

ROLEX, 26 J., RF # 1671,"GMT-Master II," date
sapphire crystal, quick set
18k $5,500 $6,000 $7,000
s. steel $2,000 $2,500 $3,000

ROLEX, 26 J., "Submariner", perpetual, oyster, date
sapphire crystal, quick set
18k C&B.............................$8,500 $9,000 $11,500
18k & s. steel C&B $3,200 $3,600 $4,500
s. steel $2,000 $2,400 $2,900

ROLEX, 26 J., "GMT-Master", RF # 6542, c.1957
s. steel $2,000 $2,400 $3,000

ROLEX first used **HACK** system in Ca. 1972

ROLEX first used the Quick Set feature Ca. 1977

Sapphire crystals were added in U.S.A. Ca.1989

ROLEX, 26J., "SEA-DWELLER," RF # 1665, 2,000 ft, date
all with Fliplock Band.   RF#1660=4,000 & 31J.
s. steel plastic crystal..........$2,500 $2,800 $3,500
s. steel sapphire crystal $2,800 $3,200 $3,800
s.steel (Seadweller in red letters)$5,000 $5,600 $6,500
Note: Seadweller in red letters is rare.

🕐 Pricing in this Guide are fair market price for **COMPLETE**
watches which are reflected from the "**NAWCC**" National and
regional shows.

DIALS FOR MINT PRICES MUST BE ALL **ORIGINAL**.

ROLEX, 21J., ''SEA-DWELLER,'' up to 4,000 ft., RF # 1666, date, sapphire crystal, quick set
s. steel $2,200 $2,600 $3,000

ROLEX, 26J., ''Submariner'', RF # 6536,100M,c.1958
s. steel (no crown guard)... ★★ $1,800 $2,200 $3,800

ROLEX, 26 jewels, ''Explorer II,'' RF # 1655, date, Ca.1961
s. steel $3,500 $4,000 $5,500

ROLEX, 31J., "Explorer II", Oy., Pet., Chr., 24Hr. hand black dial add $100 to $200 more
s. steel $2,300 $2,500 $3,000

ROLEX, 26J., "Submariner", Oy., Pet., Chr., RF # 5512, s. steel (chronometer) $1,800 $2,200 $3,000

🕐 A collector should expect to pay modestly higher prices at local shops

Wrist Watches listed in this section are priced at the collectable fair market Trade Show level as **complete** watches having an original gold-filled case and stainless steel back, also with original dial, leather watch band, and the entire original movement in good working order with no repairs needed.

ROLEX, 31J., RF# 1626, "Thunderbird", Oy., Ca.1991 Turn-O-Graph Bezel, Pet., Chr.
s. steel $1,500 $1,800 $2,200
18K $2,500 $3,000 $3,800

🕐 Pricing in this Guide are fair market price for **COMPLETE** watches which are reflected from the "<u>NAWCC</u>" National and regional shows.

DIALS FOR MINT PRICES MUST BE ALL **ORIGINAL**.

ROLEX, 15J., ca. 1937
s. steel $600 $700 $900

ROLEX, 15J., engraved case, c.1930
s. steel $800 $900 $1,200

ROLEX, 15J., GJS, c.1935
9K..$1,000 $1,200 $1,500

ROLEX, 18J., RF # 4029, c.1945
18k $1,200 $1,600 $2,000

ROLEX, 17J., RF # 619, ROSE gold,c.1948
18k Pink $1,000 $1,200 $1,600

ROLEX, 18J., hidden lugs, RF # 2537,adj.6 pos. 2 tone,
Ca.1940s
gold & steel $1,600 $1,800 $2,500

ROLEX,15J., stepped case, c.1938
18k $1,200 $1,400 $1,800

ROLEX, 17J., 2 tone, center lug "Standard", c.1940
14k & s.s................................ $800 $1,000 $1,400

ROLEX, 17J., "Standard", c.1940 (no brass for mint)
gold filled $500 $600 $900

ROLEX, 15J., RF # 1878, beveled case, c.1927
s. steel $700 $800 $1,200

🕓 Some grades are not included. Their values can be
determined by comparing with **similar** age, size, metal
content, style, grades, or models such as **time only**,
chronograph, repeater etc. listed.

ROLEX, 17J., hidden lugs,
14k $1,600 $1,900 $2,400

ROLEX, 17J., "31 Victories",
18k $1,400 $1,600 $2,000

ROLEX, 18J., fluted bezel, RF # 3737
18k $1,400 $1,600 $2,000

ROLEX, 18J., RF # 8094, 3 diamond dial , ca. 1940s
18kC&B.............................$1,800 $2,200 $2,800

ROLEX, 18J., ca. 1940s
s. steel $600 $700 $1,000

ROLEX, 18J., round movement, ca. 1947
18k $1,000 $1,200 $1,500

ROLEX, 17 jewels, RF # 8126, "Precision", manual wind
18k $1,000 $1,200 $1,600

ROLEX, 17 jewels, curvex style
18k C&B.............................$3,000 $3,500 $4,500

ROLEX, 17 jewels, curved, c. 1940s
gold filled $300 $400 $600

ROLEX, 17 jewels, "Ultra Prima," gold train
18k $1,200 $1,400 $1,800

DIALS FOR MINT PRICES MUST BE ALL **ORIGINAL**.

ROLEX, 17 jewels, hooded lugs, 2 tone, **ladies**
Pink & White gold..............$1,000 $1,200 $1,600

ROLEX, 17 jewels, "Standard," c. 1939
gold filled................................$800 $900 $1,200
14k $2,200 $2,500 $3,200

ROLEX, 18J., RF# 4663, **small**, perpetual, chronometer,
24mm case, (auto wind), Ca. 1940s
18K..$2,200 $2,500 $3,000

ROLEX, 21 jewels, perpetual, **large**, c. 1945
18k $2,500 $3,000 $4,000

Wrist Watches listed in this section are priced at the collectable
fair market Trade Show level as **complete** watches having an
original gold-filled case and stainless steel back, also with
original dial, leather watch band, and the entire original movement in good working order with no repairs needed.

ROLEX, 17 jewels, "Precision," c. 1940s
18k $1,600 $1,800 $2,200
14k $1,000 $1,200 $1,700

ROLEX, 17 J. , "Precision," faceted bezel
18k $1,200 $1,500 $2,000

ROLEX, 17 jewels, extra flat, c. 1950s
18k $1,200 $1,500 $2,000

ROLEX, 17 J., RF # 9491, "Precision", Ca. 1958
18k $1,400 $1,600 $2,000

ROLEX, 17J., RF # 3893, hidden lugs, Ca. 1943
14k $900 $1,100 $1,500

ROLEX, 17J., "Victory", Tudor, mid size, Ca. 1940
s. steel $250 $300 $400

ROLEX,17J., "Tudor", auto-wind, RF # T7909, c.1955
s. steel $200 $250 $350

ROLEX, Quartz, RF # 1563-3, 2 tone, "Tudor", Ca. 1993
18k & s. steel $250 $300 $400

ROLEX, 25J., "Tudor", RF# T7016, submariner, by ETA, c.1970
s. steel $600 $700 $900

ROLEX, 17J., RF # T7928, "Tudor", ETA cal. 2438, Ca. 1968
s. steel $800 $900 $1,200

ROLEX, 25J., "Tudor", submariner, date, by ETA,
RF # T7610, Ca.1985
s. steel $700 $800 $1,000

ROLEX, "Tudor," (Prince)
s. steel $300 $350 $450

ROLEX, 25J., "Tudor", RF # T7809, auto-wind, c.1978
s. steel $200 $250 $300

ROLEX, 17J., "Tudor", auto-wind, c.1955
18k $500 $600 $750

ROLEX, "Tudor," chronog., date, RF # T9420,
Ca. 1970s
s. steel .... ★ $2,500 $3,000 $3,700

ROLEX, 17J., "Tudor", SOLAR, RF # T4463, c.1955
s. steel $225 $250 $300

ROLEX, 25J., Prince Oyster Ranger II, Ca.1973
s. steel $500 $600 $800

ROLEX, 17J., "Tudor", RF # T2765, TURTLE, Zell Bros
Gold filled..............................$175 $225 $300

ROLEX, quartz, "Tudor," date, Ca. 1992
s. steel & gold plate................$150 $200 $275

ROLEX, 17J., Drivers,Ca. 1935
gold filled $500 $600 $800

ROLEX, "Tudor," chronog., date, 165 ft., auto-wind
s. steel $1,200 $1,400 $1,800
Tiger Wood's model..........$1,000 $1,200 $1,600

ROLEX, 18J., lady's, Ca. 1948
18k...$250 $325 $450
14k...$200 $250 $400

ROLEX, 17J., ladies, "Oyster",
14k $1,000 $1,200 $1,500

ROLEX, 17J., ladies, "Oyster", RF # 3492
s. steel....................................$400 $500 $700

ROLEX, 29J., ladies, "Oyster", RF#6700-3
s. steel &14k,C&B..............$1,000 $1,100 $1,300

ROLEX, 17J., ladies, RF # 4593, c.1954
s. steel....................................$200 $250 $350

ROLEX, 17J., ladies, "Oyster", RF#4486, c.1957
14k & s.s.case.........................$400 $450 $600

ROLEX, 15J., 54 diamonds, 9k band 18k(w) case, c.1930
9k & 18k $1,600 $1,800 $2,500

ROLEX, 17J.,RF # 4554, "Precision", ladies, Ca. 1955
gold filled.............................$125 $150 $200

ROLEX, 17J., BB, ladies, "Oyster", c.1948
s. steel $400 $600 $900
s. steel & gold.........................$500 $700 $1,000

ROLEX, 15J., lady's, curved, ca.1925
9k...$250 $300 $400

ROLEX, 17J., RF # 1701, ladies, fancy lugs, Ca. 1950
14k $300 $400 $600

ROLEX, 15J., lady's, center lugs, ca.1925
9k enamel dial.........................$400 $500 $650

ROLEX, 18J., lady's, ca. 1930s
18k $400 $500 $650

ROLEX, 15J., lady's, Ca.1925
18k band.........................$400 $450 $600

ROLEX, 18J., wire lugs, diamond bezel, ca. 1940s
18k(W)................................$500 $550 $700

ROLEX, Oyster Perpetual Datejust, diamond dial &bezel
Sapphire Crystal, Quick Set
18k C&B $7,000 $7,500 $8,500

ROLEX, 18J., lady's,
14k $300 $350 $450

ROLEX, Oyster Perpetual Datejust, Plastic Crystal
18k C&B $3,000 $3,500 $4,500

ROLEX, 18J., lady's,
14k(W) C&B $350 $450 $650

ROLEX, 18J., lady's, bubble back
18k pink $1,200 $1,400 $1,800
18k $1,000 $1,200 $1,600

ROLEX, Oyster Perpetual Datejust, Sapphire Crystal,
Quick Set
18k & s. steel $1,700 $2,300 $2,800

Wrist Watches listed in this section are priced at the collectable
fair market Trade Show level as **complete** watches having an
original gold-filled case and stainless steel back, also with
original dial, leather watch band, and the entire original movement in good working order with no repairs needed.

ROLEX, Oyster Perpetual Sapphire Crystal, no date
18k & s. steel **no** date $1,200 $1,400 $1,800

Advertised as accurate timekeeper at a moderate price.
U = unicorn, **M** = Marcoin, **R** = Rolco.
Listed as **U., M., R.,** & 7 to 15 jewels, Ca. 1920s.

U. M. R., 7-15J., center sec. wire lugs, Ca. 1920s
base metal $300 $400 $600

U. M. R., 7-15J., aux. sec., Ca. 1920s
s. steel $195 $250 $350
9K..$300 $350 $450

U. M. R., 7-15J., tonneau, very flat, Ca. 1920s
s. steel $300 $350 $450
9K..$400 $450 $550

U. M. R., 7-15J., rect., aux. sec., Ca. 1920s
s. steel $450 $500 $650
9K..$400 $450 $550

U. M. R., 7-15J., hidden lugs, Ca. 1920s
base metal $150 $195 $300

U. M. R., 7-15J., black dial, Ca. 1920s
base metal...............................$150 $195 $300
s. steel...................................$400 $500 $700

U. M. R., 7-15J., square, Ca. 1920s
s. steel...................................$300 $350 $450
9K...$400 $450 $550

U. M. R., 7-15J., Ladies round, wire lugs, Ca. 1920s
base metal................................$50 $70 $100
9K...$95 $120 $150

U. M. R., 7-15J., Ladies, wire lugs, Ca. 1920s
base metal................................$50 $70 $95
9K...$95 $120 $150

U. M. R., 7-15J., Ladies, wire lugs, Ca. 1920s
base metal................................$50 $70 $95
9K...$95 $120 $150

6694

1705215

Reference number,
between the lugs

Serial number,
six or seven figures
engraved between the lugs

INSIDE OF BACK
Reference number
in four figures

NON-OYSTER CASE

OUTSIDE OF BACK
Serial number
in six or seven figures

On recent OYSTER models the number is engraved on the outside of the case between the lugs. Reference number of earlier models will be found engraved on the inside of the back of the case.

Reference number for NON-OYSTER models will be found engraved on the inside of the back of the case.

Above: Oyster style bracelet. **Below:** Presidential style band with hidden clasp. **Right:** Jubilee style bracelet.

New model Presidential bracelets use 8 screws for adjustment links.
Double quick set Presidential and Jubilee bracelets use 7 screws for adjustment links.
The older models **single quick** Presidential and Jubilee bracelets use 6 screw for adjustment links.

Note: Check Bracelet
for stretched links.

Stretched

NEW not Stretched

Triplock   Twinlock

ROLEX
MOVEMENT IDENTIFICATION

Ref. 90   Ref. 100   Ref. 150   Ref. 160   Ref. 161

(All without seconds)

Ref. 170   **Ref. 180**   **Ref. 200**   **Ref. 210**
without seconds   without seconds   without seconds   sweep seconds

Ref. 250   **Ref. 270**   **Ref. 300**
without seconds   without seconds   ordinary seconds

Ref. 310   **Ref. 350**   **Ref. 360**
sweep second   jump hour   ordinary second

Ref. 400   **Ref. 420**   **Ref. 420**   **Ref. 500**
ordinary seconds   ordinary seconds   rotor   ordinary seconds
Ca. 1941   **Ca. 1941**   **Ca. 1941**   **Ca. 1936**

When performing any underwater activity, the dynamic pressure generated through movement is greater than the static pressure. Below a ranking of water resistance for most watches.

1 **meter** = 3.28 ft., 330 ft. =about 100 **meters.** 33.89 ft. =1 **atmosphere,** 100 ft. = about 3 **atmospheres.**
30M/100Ft/3ATM/3Bar = sweat-resistant   50M/160Ft/5ATM/5Bar = shower only, rain
100M/300Ft/10ATM/10Bar = swimming (no diving)   200M/660Ft/20ATM/20Bar = snorkeling, skin diving
1000M =scuba diving -3,300 ft.

Ref. 510
sweep second
Ca. 1936

Ref. 520
sweep second
Ca. 1936

Ref. 520
rotor
Ca. 1936

Ref. 530
self wind, sweep sec.
Ca. 1936

Ref. 600   Ca. 1931
ordinary seconds

Ref. 620 Ca. 1931
ordinary seconds

Ref. 620 Ca. 1931
rotor

Ref. 630   Ca. 1931
self wind, sweep sec.

Ref. 700   Ca. 1940
ordinary seconds

Ref. 710   Ca. 1940
sweep seconds

Ref. 720 Ca. 1940
ordinary seconds

Ref. 720 Ca. 1940
rotor

Ref. 730   Ca. 1945
self wind, sweep sec.

Ref. 740 Ca. 1945
self wind, calendar, sweep sec.

Ref. 850
ordinary seconds

Ref. 72
chronograph, 3 registers

Ref. 23
chronograph, 2 registers

POSITIONS OF THE WINDING CROWN FOR CALENDAR MODELS

Pos. 1
Crown fully screwed down.
In this position the Rolex Oyster is warranted pressure-proof to a
depth of 330 feet/100 m.
The watch is ready to be worn.

Pos. 2
Crown unscrewed.
When the crown is free of the screw threads, the watch is in position
for handwinding, if necessary.
In quartz models, this is a neutral position.

Pos. 3
Crown pulled out to the first notch.
When turning the crown from three to six o'clock, the date will
change rapidly.
This position is used to correct the date when months have less
than 31 days.
The timing of the watch will not be altered.

Pos. 4
Crown pulled out to the last notch.
Position for setting the correct time, the date and the day.
The watch stops and enables adjustments to be made, for Day-Date
models, when the hands are turned counter-clockwise, the day of
the week changes while the date remains unchanged.
Change the day before correcting the date.

ROLLS, 15J., early auto wind, by Leon Hatot, movement inside case moves back & forth to wind, c. 1920s
s. steel .... ★★★$400 $550 $700

ROLLS, 15 jewels, early auto wind, c. 1920s
s. steel $400 $500 $700

ROLLS, 15 jewels, "ATO," flip top
s. steel $300 $450 $800

ROLLS, 15 jewels, ladies, "ATO," flip top, by Blancpain
18k $400 $450 $600

ROTARY, 15J., aux. sec., ca.1934
9k $100 $125 $165

ROXY, **8 day**, engraved case, ca. 1930s
s. steel .... ★$300 $350 $450

RUSSIAN Military Divers watch, 15J.,60mm, made in Russian factory using Hampden W. Co. parts, signed "Kamhem".
s. steel $400 $500 $750

SCHILD, 17J., "Aqua lung", tach.chronog., ca.1972
s. steel $150 $200 $300

SCHULTZ, 17J., diamond dial, c.1930
platinum C & B $1,500 $1,700 $2,000

J. SCHULTZ, 17J., enamel hunter style, ca. 1949
18k $1,000 $1,200 $1,800

SEELAND, 17J., "Quadramatic" auto-wind, c.1947
s. steel $35 $45 $75

SEELAND, 17J., manual wind, c.1947
chrome $35 $45 $75

SEIKO, 17J., Chronograph, day date, auto wind, Ca.1974
s. steel $100 $125 $175

SEIKO, 6J., wire lugs, on dial "LAUREL", ca.1925
Note: Looks like a Swiss Bar Mvt. but was made by the **Seiko Factory**.
s. steel .... ★$35 $45 $85

Wrist Watches listed in this section are priced at the collectable fair market **Trade Show** level as **complete** watches having an original gold-filled case and stainless steel back, also with original dial, leather watch band, and the entire original movement in good working order with no repairs needed.

SEIKO, quartz, rope style bezel
14k $95 $120 $150

SEMCA, 17J., day-date-month, moon phase, c. 1950s
18k $700 $800 $1,000

SEMCA, 17J., day-date-month, moon phase, c. 1950s
14k $500 $600 $900

SETH THOMAS, day date, moon phases, ca. 1949
s. steel $175 $200 $300

🕐 A collector should expect to pay modestly higher prices at local shops

🕐 Some grades are not included. Their values can be determined by comparing with **similar** age, size, metal content, style, grades, or models such as **time only**, chronograph, repeater etc. listed.

DIALS FOR MINT PRICES MUST BE ALL **ORIGINAL**.

SOUTH BEND,17J., **multi-color dial**, made U.S.A.
base metal .... ★$275 $325 $450

STANDARD,17J., 24 hr. dial, world time, c.1965
s. steel $95 $125 $175

SMITHS, on dial"Everest automatic 25 jewels", marked on
movement "Smith Imperial automatic 25 jewels made in England", note weight is mounted on ball-race, Ca.1965
9k $300 $450 $700

STOWA, 20-22J., Military watch, Ca. 1942
s. steel $500 $600 $800

SMITHS, 17J., military , Ca.1969
s. steel $95 $125 $150

SPERINA, 7 jewels, **day & date on lugs**
s. steel $65 $85 $135

TAVANNES, 15J., enamel dial, hunter, **flip top**, c.1915
silver $300 $350 $425

TAVANNES, 17J., chronog., c.1940
s. steel $200 $250 $325

TAVANNES, 17J., extended lugs, c.1955
gold filled.................................$65 $75 $110

TAVANNES,17J., 26 x 41mm., exaggerated #s, Ca.1920
18k $600 $700 $900

TAVANNES, 17J., GJS, cal.365k, c.1938
14k $100 $165 $275

TAVANNES, 17 jewels, hour glass dial, **curved**
14k $135 $185 $275

TAVANNES, 15 jewels, "334," c. 1939
14k (w) $175 $200 $250

TAVANNES, 17 jewels, aux. sec. ca. 1940s
s. steel $65 $75 $110

TAVANNES, 17 jewels, aux. sec.
14k $125 $165 $250

TECHNOS, 17J., "Sky Diver", auto-wind, 500m., c.1970
s. steel $55 $65 $135

Wrist Watches listed in this section are priced at the collectable
fair market **Trade Show** level as **complete** watches having an
original gold-filled case and stainless steel back, also with
original dial, leather watch band, and the entire original movement in good working order with no repairs needed.

🕐 Some grades are not included. Their values can be
determined by comparing with **similar** age, size, metal
content, style, grades, or models such as **time only**,
chronograph, repeater etc. listed.

TELDA, 17J., chronog.,3 reg, date, moon ph., c.1980s
s. steel $300 $325 $400

TELDA, 17J., center sec., c.1948
gold filled................................$35 $45 $65

NOTE: Examples of Tiffany made up watches are listed but were not sold by Tiffany & Co.. These off-brand watches will be listed but not priced as true Tiffany & Co. watches. EXAMPLES: *Kingston?, Emerson?, Banner?*, ETC. were not sold by Tiffany. (?)

TIFFANY & CO., 15-17J., enamel dial, Ca. 1905
18k $500 $600 $800

TIFFANY & CO.,17J., exaggerated numbers, Ca.1920
silver $600 $700 $1,000

TIFFANY & CO., 18J., by **P.P.& CO.**, exaggerated numbers, Ca. 1920s
18K $7,000 $8,000 $10,000

TIFFANY & CO., 17J., curved, mvt. by **P.P. & Co.**, c. 1910
18k $8,000 $9,000 $11,000

TIFFANY & CO.,17J., by Banner"?" , c.1926
18k $225 $250 $300

TIFFANY & CO.,17J., by Wheeler "?", c.1930
14k $150 $165 $200

TIFFANY & CO., 26 jewels, min. repeater, slide repeat, automaton, 40mm **(conversion)**
18k $2,500 $2,800 $3,500

TIFFANY & CO., 15J., wire lugs, ca. 1928
silver $200 $225 $300

TIFFANY & CO., 18J., by **P.P.& CO.**, Ca. 1930s
platinum............................ $10,000 $12,000 $15,000

TIFFANY & CO.,17J., by **P.P. & Co.**, wire lugs, c.1915
18k **(refinished dial)**...........$3,500 $4,000 $5,000

TIFFANY & CO., 15 jewels, Swiss, Ca. 1926
18k $400 $500 $700

TIFFANY & CO.,17J., by I.W.C., wire lugs, c.1918
14k $600 $685 $800

TIFFANY & CO.,17J., by Longines, c.1928
14k $200 $235 $300

TIFFANY & CO., 15J., enamel dial, ca. 1930s
silver $450 $525 $600

TIFFANY & CO.,17J., aux. sec., Swiss, c.1926
18k(w)....................................$500 $600 $800

TIFFANY & CO., 17J., Concord W. C0.
14k $600 $700 $900

TIFFANY & CO.,17J., by Fidea "?", c.1930
14k $125 $175 $275

TIFFANY & CO.,17J., GJS, by Movado, c.1940
14k $275 $300 $375

TIFFANY & CO.,17J., by Kingston "?", hidden lugs, c.1943
14k $125 $150 $200

TIFFANY & CO.,17J., by Charlin W. Co. "?", GJS, c.1940
14k $125 $150 $200

TIFFANY & CO.,17J., by Hampden "?", c.1949
14k $125 $150 $200

TIFFANY & CO.,17J., by I.W.C., c.1942
14k $375 $400 $500

TIFFANY & CO.,17J., by I.W.C., hidden lugs, c.1942
14k $375 $400 $500

TIFFANY & CO., 17J., top hat, by I. W. C.
14K $700 $800 $1,000

TIFFANY & CO., 30J., auto-wind, date, Ca.1955
18K $400 $465 $600

TIFFANY & CO.,15J., one button chronog., by Goering, Cal. 69 mvt., c.1925
silver $950 $1,100 $1,400

TIFFANY & CO.,17J., Valjoux cal.72c., c.1948
s. steel $550 $665 $850
14k $1,200 $1,300 $1,500
18k $1,400 $1,500 $1,700

🕐 Some grades are not included. Their values can be determined by comparing with **similar** age, size, metal content, style, grades, or models such as **time only**, chronograph, repeater etc. listed.

TIFFANY & CO.,17J., by Movado, c.1947
14k $1,000 $1,200 $1,500

TIFFANY & CO.,17J., by Bovet, c.1940
18k $800 $900 $1,100

TIFFANY & CO.,17J., by Tourneau , Valjoux 72c, c.1950
s. steel $800 $950 $1,200

TIFFANY & CO., 31J., chronog., triple date, moon ph. screw-
back, note window for date at 4 & 5
18k $2,200 $2,600 $3,200

TIFFANY & CO., 17J., chronog., day-date-month
14k $1,000 $1,200 $1,500

TIFFANY & CO., 21J., mvt. by **P.P. & Co.**, c. 1950
18k $3,500 $3,800 $4,800

TIFFANY & CO., 17J., curved , ca.1920s
platinum $1,200 $1,400 $1,800

TIFFANY & CO.,15J., engraved bezel, c.1919
18k $1,000 $1,100 $1,300

Wrist Watches listed in this section are priced at the collectable
fair market **Trade Show** level as **complete** watches having an
original gold-filled case and stainless steel back, also with
original dial, leather watch band, and the entire original movement in good working order with no repairs needed.

TIFFANY & CO., 15J., ca. 1920s
14k $200 $250 $350

TIFFANY & CO.,17J., by Zodiac , c.1942
14k $135 $175 $225

TIFFANY & CO.,17J., by Hampden "?", c.1945
gold filled.............................. $75 $100 $150
14k $125 $165 $225

TIFFANY & CO.,17J., by Glycine, c.1945
gold filled $85 $100 $125
14k $135 $165 $225

TIFFANY & CO.,17J., by Ollendorf, c.1945
14k $125 $165 $225

TIFFANY & CO.,17J., extended bezel, c.1942
14k $200 $225 $300

TIFFANY & CO.,17J., by Crawford "?", c.1947
14k $135 $150 $225

TIFFANY & CO.,17J., by Wyler, c.1950
gold filled $75 $90 $125

TIFFANY & CO.,17J., by Tissot, c.1948
14k $135 $175 $225

TIFFANY & CO., 17J., fancy lugs & bezel,ca.1950s
14k $200 $235 $325

TIFFANY & CO., 17J., applied numbers, ca. 1950s
14k ....$200　　$225　　$300

TIFFANY & CO., 17J., flared & stepped, ca.1950s
14k ....$235　　$275　　$350

TIFFANY & CO., 17 jewels, Swiss, c. 1935
18k ....$350　　$400　　$500

TIFFANY & CO., 17 jewels, fancy bezel, c. 1942
14k ....$250　　$300　　$400

TIFFANY & CO., 17 jewels, sculptured lugs, c. 1948
14k ....$500　　$600　　$800

TIFFANY & CO.,17J., 3 diamond dial, by Lathin "?",
14k(w).................................... $175　　$200　　$250

TIFFANY & CO.,15J., rhinestones "?", c.1948
base metal ....$35　　$45　　$70

TIFFANY & CO., 17J., "Movado", triple date, center sec.
s. steel ....$300　　$365　　$450

TIFFANY & CO.,17J., by Movado, triple date, c.1948
gold filled ....$325　　$400　　$550
14k & s.s..................................$400　　$450　　$600

🕐 A collector should expect to pay modestly higher prices
at local shops

TIFFANY & CO.,17J., by Tissot, triple date moon ph.,
14k $900 $1,000 $1,200

TIFFANY & CO.,17J., by Helvetia , c.1948
gold filled $95 $110 $150
14k $150 $175 $250

TIFFANY & CO., 17J., triple date, **moon ph**.
s. steel $400 $475 $650

TIFFANY & CO.,17J., "?", c.1940
gold filled $75 $85 $125

TIFFANY & CO.,17J., by Ardath "?", auto-wind, c.1950
14k $125 $150 $200

TIFFANY & CO.,17J., by Mepa "?", GJS, c.1949
gold filled $65 $75 $110
14k $100 $125 $175

TIFFANY & CO.,17J., by Nicolet, c.1955
gold filled..................................$75 $100 $150

TIFFANY & CO.,17J., by Zenith, c.1939
14k $135 $175 $225

TIFFANY & CO.,17J., c.1948
18k $300 $350 $475

TIFFANY & CO.,17J., carved lugs, c.1950
18k $250 $275 $350

TIFFANY & CO.,17J., ladies, by Longines, c.1920
18k $200 $225 $300

TIFFANY & CO.,17J., ladies, by I.W.C., c.1948
18k $100 $150 $225

TIFFANY & CO.,17J., ladies, I.W.C., c.1955
18k $135 $165 $255

TIFFANY & CO., 15J., 2 tone , ladies, ca. 1939
18k C&B...............................$300 $350 $400

TIFFANY & CO., 15J., early ladies, wire lugs ca.1925
14k $175 $195 $250

TIFFANY & CO., 17J., ladies, aux. sec., Ca.1940
gold filled $50 $65 $85

TIMECRAFT, 17 jewels, chronog., Ca. 1950
s. steel $125 $150 $200

TIMEX,**chronog.**, slide to start, stop & return to zero
base metal $65 $75 $125

TIMEX, "Ben Hogan", m/wind, Ca. 1961
base metal $50 $75 $125

TIMEX, engraved bezel, m/wind, Ca. 1970
base metal $5 $10 $35

TIMEX, checkerboard dial, m/wind, Ca. 1968
base metal $5 $10 $40

TIMEX, "Monroe", m/wind, wide bezel, Ca. 1961
base metal $5 $10 $35

TIMEX, "Mercury series", m/wind, Ca. 1969
base metal $5 $10 $35

TIMEX, military style, m/wind, Ca. 1966
base metal $15 $25 $50

TIMEX, "Fun Timer", m/wind, Ca. 1968
base metal $5 $10 $35

TIMEX, **Electric**, water-resistant, 14k sold for $125 in 1962
14k .... ★$75 $125 $250
base metal $5 $10 $35

TIMEX, **21jewels**, auto-wind, Ca. 1962
base metal $15 $20 $45

TIMEX, **Electric** calendar series, water-resistant, Ca. 1970
base metal $15 $20 $45

TIMEX, Skindiver or Sports series, 600 ft. depth, Ca. 1966
base metal (m/wind) $15 $20 $45

TIMEX, Skindiver or Sports series, 200 ft. depth, Ca. 1968
base metal(m/wind) $15 $20 $45

TISSOT, 17 jewels, 1898 USA 20 dollar gold piece
22K..$900 $1,000 $1,500

TISSOT,17J., one button chronog., Ca.1935
s. steel $300 $400 $550

TISSOT, 21 jewels, world time, 24 hr. dial, 24 cities, Ca.**1950**
gold filled................................$600 $700 $900
s. steel $1,200 $1,400 $1,800
18k $2,500 $2,700 $3,500

TISSOT,17J., Valjoux cal.726, c.1965
18k $800 $900 $1,100
14k $700 $750 $900

TISSOT, 21J, world time, 24 hr. dial, 24 cities, mid-size
18k (**1950**) $2,600 $2,800 $3,600

TISSOT,17J., auto-wind,"Navigator", date, c.1972
s. steel $150 $175 $225

TISSOT, 17J., "Stadium", tachymeter, c.1960
gold plate $150 $175 $225

TISSOT, 17 jewels, chronog., 3 reg., c. 1956
s. steel $325 $350 $450

TISSOT, 17 jewels, chronog., 3 reg.
gold filled................................$275 $300 $400
s. steel $275 $300 $400

TISSOT, 17 jewels, "Seastar", Cal.#782, Date, Ca. 1957
s. steel $100 $125 $200

TISSOT, 17 jewels, chronog., 3 reg.
18k $500 $600 $800
s. steel $250 $275 $350

TISSOT, 17J., "Visodate Camping", Date, Ca. 1955
s. steel $100 $125 $200

TISSOT, Worlds first transparent plastic watch, "Idea 2001",
with model "Synthic, Astrolon & Sytal", cal.2250, Ca. 1971
plastic(working) .... ★$400 $500 $700

TISSOT, 17J., "Mediostat", stop center second hand, Ca.1955
s. steel $125 $150 $200

TISSOT, 15J., Omega W. Co. & Tissot signatures, Ca.1938
14k $700 $500 $1,100

TISSOT, 17J., "Sonorous", Alarm, Cal# 780, Ca. 1960s
s. steel $100 $125 $200

TISSOT, 15J., 1st Tissot wrist model, "Banana", Ca. 1917
18K $900 $1,100 $1,400

TISSOT,17J., auto wind, aux. sec., c.1951
18k $175 $200 $265

TISSOT, 15 jewels, wire lugs, aux. sec., Ca. 1915
silver $250 $275 $375

TISSOT,17J., aux. sec., Ca.1950
14k $150 $165 $200

TISSOT,17J., aux. sec., c.1942
s. steel $35 $45 $85
14k $125 $150 $200
18k $175 $200 $250

TITUS, 17 jewels, chronog., 2 reg.
18k $300 $325 $400
14k $200 $225 $300
s. steel $100 $125 $200

TISSOT, 17 jewels, Masonic dial, Ca.1955
14k $125 $150 $225

TORNEK-RAYVILLE,17J., military, "SEAL", auto-wind,
water-proof, 150M or 490 ft., Ca. 1966
s. steel .... ★★$800 $900 $1,200

TISSOT, 17J., center sec., Ca. 1951
base metal $65 $75 $125

TOUCHON,17J., tonneau case, c.1928
18k(w)....................................$300 $350 $500

TOUCHON, 17J., jump hr., wandering min., c. 1930s
18k $2,000 $2,500 $3,000

TOURNEAU,17J, triple date, 3 reg., moon ph., c. 1952
s. steel $700 $750 $900

TOURNEAU,17J.,chronog. by Valjoux cal.886, c.1965
18k $800 $900 $1,100

TOURNEAU,17J., day date , c.1945
s. steel $175 $200 $275

🕐 Pricing in this Guide are fair market price for **COMPLETE**
watches which are reflected from the "**NAWCC**" National and
regional shows.

TOURNEAU,17J., beveled lugs, c.1945
14k $125 $150 $200

TOURIST, 17J., by MEPA, timer, c.1958
s. steel $35 $45 $75

TREBEX, 15 jewels,cut corner dial, c. 1940
gold filled $45 $50 $75

TREBEX, 15 jewels, c. 1940
gold filled $35 $40 $75

TREBEX, 15 jewels, c. 1940s
gold filled $35 $40 $75

TURLER, 15-17J., duo-dial, Ca.1930s
18k $1,000 $1,200 $1,500

UNITAS, 17 jewels, triple date, moon phase, c. 1948
s. steel $200 $250 $350

TURLER, 17 jewels, chronog., triple date, 3 reg.
18k $900 $1,000 $1,300

URANIA, 15 jewels, military style grill, c. 1915
silver $150 $195 $300

UHRENFABRIK GLASHUTTE, 17J., chronog., c. 1940s
s. steel $800 $1,000 $1,400

UNVER, 17J., triple date , moon ph., chronog.
14k $1,000 $1,200 $1,800

ULTIMOR, 17J., chronog., cal.51, c.1945
18k $250 $300 $400

UNIVERSAL,17J.,"medico compax", c.1949
18k $1,200 $1,400 $1,800

Wrist Watches listed in this section are priced at the collectable fair market **Trade Show** level as **complete** watches having an original gold-filled case and stainless steel back, also with original dial, leather watch band, and the entire original movement in good working order with no repairs needed.

UNIVERSAL,17J., "uni compax", c.1942
s. steel $400 $450 $600

UNIVERSAL,17J., tri-compax, day date moon ph.,c.1955
s. steel $1,000 $1,200 $1,800
14k $3,000 $3,500 $4,500

UNIVERSAL, 17J., chronog., triple date, moon phase
18k $1,200 $1,400 $2,000
14k $1,100 $1,300 $1,800

UNIVERSAL, 17J., chronog., aero compax, diff. meridian,
square pushers
14k $1,400 $1,600 $2,000

UNIVERSAL, 17J. chronog., tri-compax, day date moon ph.
s. steel $1,200 $1,400 $1,800

UNIVERSAL, 17J., chronog., aero compax, diff. meridian,
round pushers
18k $1,800 $2,000 $2,400

UNIVERSAL, 17J., chronog., tri-compax, moon phase
s. steel $1,000 $1,200 $1,500

UNIVERSAL, 17 jewels, chronog., M. #281, c. 1950s
18k $1,600 $1,800 $2,200

UNIVERSAL, 17J., chronog., compax, massive case
18k $2,200 $2,400 $3,000

UNIVERSAL, day-date-month, moon phase
18k $900 $1,200 $1,400

UNIVERSAL, 17J., chronog., dato-compax, c. 1950s
14k $1,200 $1,400 $1,800
s. steel $600 $700 $900

UNIVERSAL, 17 jewels, day-date-month
14k $600 $650 $800

UNIVERSAL,17J., compax, RF#885107, Valj.cal.72,c.1965
s. steel $600 $700 $900

UNIVERSAL,17J., "Polerouter Sub", date, auto-w., c.1960
14k $350 $400 $500
s. steel $150 $200 $300

UNIVERSAL, 17J. chronog., 10 ligne size,uni-compax
s. steel .... $ 700 $750 $900

🕐 Pricing in this Guide are fair market price for **COMPLETE**
watches which are reflected from the **"NAWCC"** National and
regional shows.

UNIVERSAL,28J.,"Polerouter Sub",rotating bezel, c.1980s
s. steel $225 $250 $325

UNIVERSAL, 17 jewels, "Polerouter", auto wind, day date
18k $300 $400 $550

UNIVERSAL, 23J., auto-wind, date, c.1965
14k $150 $175 $225

UNIVERSAL, 28J., center sec., date, auto-wind, c.1958
18k $200 $250 $325

UNIVERSAL,17J., cal. 138c, date, c.1952
18k $200 $235 $300

UNIVERSAL,17J., cal.52, date, c.1965
18k $200 $235 $300

UNIVERSAL, 17 jewels, Ca. 1952
14k $200 $225 $275

UNIVERSAL,17J., m#264, large lugs, c.1957
gold filled $100 $125 $175

UNIVERSAL,17J., Unisonic chronometer, date, c.1968
s. steel $100 $135 $200

🕐 Pricing in this Guide are fair market price for **COMPLETE** watches which are reflected from the "**NAWCC**" National and regional shows.

UNIVERSAL,17J., cal.267g, date, center sec. c.1948
18k $225 $275 $350

UNIVERSAL,17J., center sec., cal.263, c.1950
18k $200 $235 $300

UNIVERSAL, 16J., cal#230,ca. 1940s
s. steel $100 $135 $200

UNIVERSAL,17J., center sec., cal.138, c.1950
s. steel $100 $135 $185

UNIVERSAL, 17J., fancy lugs, Ca. 1948
14k $200 $225 $275

UNIVERSAL,17J., center sec., cal.236, c.1955
18k $175 $200 $300

UNIVERSAL, 17J., fancy lugs
14k $200 $225 $300

UNIVERSAL,17J., aux. sec., Ca.1955
s. steel $100 $125 $200

UNIVERSAL, 17 jewels, "Cabriolet," reverso, c. 1930s
s. steel $1,500 $1,800 $2,400

Wrist Watches listed in this section are priced at the collectable
fair market **Trade Show** level as **complete** watches having an
original gold-filled case and stainless steel back, also with
original dial, leather watch band, and the entire original movement in good working order with no repairs needed.

UNIVERSAL, 17 jewels, auto wind, c. 1955
14k $195 $225 $275
gold filled...............................$100 $125 $175

UNIVERSAL, quartz, day-date, center sec., c. 1960s
18k $175 $200 $250

UNIVERSAL, quartz, , c.1981
18k $175 $200 $250

UNIVERSAL, 17 jewels, auto wind
gold filled...............................$100 $110 $150

⏱ Some grades are not included. Their values can be determined by comparing with **similar** age, size, metal content, style, models and grades listed.

Wrist Watches listed in this section are priced at the collectable fair market Trade Show level as **complete** watches having an original gold-filled case and stainless steel back, also with original dial, leather watch band, and the entire original movement in good working order with no repairs needed.

VACHERON, 36J., skeletonized, triple date, moon phase, leap year, gold rotor
18k $14,000 $16,000 $20,000

VACHERON, 36J., diamond bezel, triple date, moon ph., leap year, gold rotor
18k C&B...........................$15,000 $17,000 $20,000

VACHERON, 17J., triple date, moon phase, c. 1947
18k $8,000 $9,000 $12,000

VACHERON, 17J., triple date, moon phase, c. 1945
18k $4,000 $5,000 $6,500

VACHERON, 17J., triple date, moon phase, c. 1950s
18k manual wind $5,000 $5,500 $7,000

VACHERON, 29 jewels, waterproof, auto-w, c. 1960s
18k $1,800 $2,100 $2,600

VACHERON,17J., triple date, fancy lugs, moon ph.,
c. 1940s
18k manual wind $6,000 $6,500 $8,000

VACHERON, 29 jewels, auto wind, c. 1960s
18k $1,900 $2,200 $2,500

VACHERON, 17J., triple date, fancy lugs, c. 1940s
18k $2,500 $2,800 $3,500

VACHERON, 17 jewels, RF # 6094, Ca. 1955
18k $1,000 $1,200 $1,600

VACHERON, 17 jewels, day-date-month, c. 1940s
18k $2,800 $3,200 $4,000

🕐 A collector should expect to pay modestly higher prices
at local shops

VACHERON, 29 jewels, center sec., auto wind, date
18k $1,800 $2,100 $2,600

VACHERON, 29 jewels, gold rotor, auto-wind, date
18k ....$2,000　　$2,200　　$2,800

VACHERON, 18J., chronog. 2 reg., ca.1942
s. steel ....$5,000　　$5,500　　$7,000

VACHERON, 33J., auto-wind 21k rotor, cal.1124 , c.1980s
18k & s.s................................$900　　$1,000　　$1,300

VACHERON, 17 jewels, chronog., 2 reg. Ca. 1934
18k & 14k band.................$18,000　　$20,000　　$25,000

VACHERON,17J., enamel dial,1 button chronog.,c. 1910s
18k ....$25,000　　$28,000　　$35,000

VACHERON, 19 jewels, chronog., 2 reg., c. 1950s
18k C&B..............................$6,500　　$7,000　　$8,500

VACHERON, 15J., early chronog.,2 reg.,one button,
ca. 1921, large in size
18k ....$20,000　　$22,000　　$26,000

VACHERON, 17 jewels, chronog., 2 reg., c. 1945
18k ....$5,000　　$5,500　　$7,000

VACHERON, 29J., min. repeater, slide repeat, c. 1950
18k $45,000 $55,000 $75,000

VACHERON, 29J., min. slide repeater, diamond dial
platinum $75,000 $85,000 $100,000

VACHERON, 29J., min. slide repeater, ca. 1950s
18k $50,000 $60,000 $75,000

VACHERON, 18J., diamond set case, skeletonized
18k(W)................................$4,500 $5,000 $6,000

VACHERON, 18J., skeletonized, diamond bezel
18k $4,500 $5,000 $6,000

VACHERON, 17 jewels, skeletonized
18k $2,500 $3,000 $4,000

VACHERON, 17 jewels, skeletonized, c. 1960s
18k $2,500 $3,000 $4,000

VACHERON, 17 jewels, mystery dial with diamonds
18k C&B.............................$1,800 $2,000 $2,400

VACHERON, 17 jewels, textured bezel
18k $800 $900 $1,100

DIALS FOR MINT PRICES MUST BE ALL <u>ORIGINAL</u>.

VACHERON, 18 jewels, center sec., c. 1940s
18k $1,200 $1,400 $1,700

VACHERON, 18J., fancy graduated bezel, c. 1950s
18k $4,500 $5,000 $6,000

VACHERON, 18 jewels, auto wind, center sec., Ca. 1945
18k $2,000 $2,300 $2,800

VACHERON, 18 jewels, center sec., Ca. 1945
18k $900 $1,000 $1,200

VACHERON, 18 jewels, center sec., Ca. 1945
s.steel $700 $800 $1,000

VACHERON, 18 jewels, center sec.
18k C&B.............................$1,500 $1,700 $2,000

VACHERON, 18 J., center sec., waterproof, c. 1950s
18k $1,700 $1,900 $2,200

VACHERON, 21J., auto wind, gold rotor, center sec.
18k $1,800 $2,000 $2,400

🕐 Pricing in this Guide are fair market price for **COMPLETE**
watches which are reflected from the "<u>NAWCC</u>" National and
regional shows.

VACHERON, 18J., center sec., ca.1940s
18k $1,200 $1,400 $1,800

VACHERON,17J., center sec., c.1940
s. steel $600 $700 $900

VACHERON, 18J., rf#6903, center sec., ca.1958
18k $800 $900 $1,100

VACHERON,17J., center sec., large lugs, c.1949
18k $2,000 $2,200 $2,500

VACHERON, 18J., center sec., ca.1953
18k $1,300 $1,800 $1,900

VACHERON,17J., center sec., c.1940
s. steel $600 $700 $900

VACHERON, 18J., textured dial center sec.
18k $1,200 $1,400 $1,700

VACHERON,17J., center sec., c.1940
18k $900 $1,000 $1,200

VACHERON, 18J., center sec.
s. steel $600 $700 $900

VACHERON, 18J., fancy large lugs, center sec., ca.1953
18k $1,600 $1,800 $2,200

VACHERON, 18J., center sec.
18k $900 $1,000 $1,200

VACHERON, 18J., rf#4730, fancy lugs, ca. 1950s
18k $1,600 $1,800 $2,300

VACHERON, 18J.,textured dial, center sec.,ca.1947
18k $2,200 $2,400 $3,000

VACHERON, 18J.,textured dial, fancy lugs
18k $1,800 $2,000 $2,400

VACHERON, 18J., rf#4824, ca.1950s
18k(W) $1,000 $1,100 $1,300

VACHERON, 18J., center sec., ca.1944
14k $800 $900 $1,100

🕐 A collector should expect to pay modestly higher prices
at local shops

VACHERON, 18J., royal chronometer, ca.1950s
18k $1,800 $2,000 $2,500

VACHERON, 29 jewels, textured dial, c. 1948
18k $1,800 $2,000 $2,500

VACHERON, 17J., center sec.auto-w., ca.1945
18k $1,800 $2,000 $2,500

VACHERON, 29 jewels, 2 tone dial, center sec.
18k $1,500 $1,700 $2,000

VACHERON, 29 jewels, center sec., center lugs,c. 1950s
18k $1,000 $1,200 $1,500

VACHERON, 29J., center sec., auto wind, c. 1950s
18k $1,800 $2,000 $2,500

VACHERON, 29 jewels, center sec.
18k $1,000 $1,100 $1,300

VACHERON, 29 jewels, center sec., auto wind, c. 1949
18k $1,800 $2,000 $2,500

VACHERON,17J., diamond dial, fancy lugs
platinum..............................$4,500 $5,000 $6,000

VACHERON,17J., aux. sec., c.1945
18k $1,200 $1,300 $1,500

VACHERON, 18J.,aux. sec., fancy lugs,ca. 1944
18k $1,400 $1,500 $1,800

VACHERON,17J., aux. sec., RF#4073, c.1942
s. steel $800 $900 $1,100

VACHERON, 18J., aux. sec.
18k $1,300 $1,400 $1,700

VACHERON,17J., aux. sec., tear drop lugs, c.1945
18k $1,400 $1,600 $2,000

VACHERON, 18J.,fancy lugs
18k $1,300 $1,400 $1,700

VACHERON,17J., aux. sec, fluted lugs, c.1950s
18k $2,200 $2,400 $2,800

Some grades are not included. Their values can be determined by comparing with **similar** age, size, metal content,
style, models and grades listed.

VACHERON, 18J., cal#p453/3b,aux.sec.
18k $2,200 $2,500 $3,000

VACHERON, 18J., aux. sec.,
s. steel $700 $800 $1,000

VACHERON, 18J., aux. sec., thin model
18k(W)................................$1,000 $1,200 $1,500

VACHERON, 18J., aux. sec., long lugs, ca.1942
18k $1,000 $1,100 $1,300

VACHERON, 18J., aux. sec., ca.1951
18k $1,000 $1,200 $1,500

⏱ Pricing in this Guide are fair market price for **COMPLETE**
watches which are reflected from the "**NAWCC**" National and
regional shows.

VACHERON, 18J., **winds at 12,** ca. 1928
18k $3,000 $3,200 $3,600

VACHERON, 15J., champagne dial, long lugs, ca.1935
18k $1,000 $1,100 $1,300

VACHERON, 17 jewels, aux. sec., fancy lugs
18k $1,500 $1,600 $1,800

VACHERON, 17 jewels, aux. sec., Ca. 1950
18k $1,100 $1,200 $1,400

VACHERON, 17 jewels, aux. sec., stepped lugs
18k $1,800 $2,100 $2,500

VACHERON, 17 jewels, 2 tone dial, aux. sec.
18k $1,400 $1,500 $1,800

VACHERON, 17 jewels, aux. sec., c. 1940s
18k $1,400 $1,500 $1,800

VACHERON, 17 jewels, aux. sec.
18k $1,400 $1,600 $2,000

VACHERON, 17 jewels, aux. sec., c. 1940s
18k $1,200 $1,300 $1,600

VACHERON, 17 jewels, aux. sec.
s. steel $500 $600 $800

VACHERON, 17 jewels, aux. sec., large lugs, c. 1950s
18k $2,000 $2,400 $3,000

VACHERON, 17 jewels, aux. sec.
14k C&B.............................$1,200 $1,400 $1,700

VACHERON, 17 jewels, aux. sec.
18k $1,600 $1,800 $2,500

VACHERON, 17 jewels, aux. sec., c. 1940s
18k $1,100 $1,200 $1,500

VACHERON, 17 jewels, aux. sec.
18k $1,300 $1,500 $1,800

VACHERON, 17 jewels
18k C&B..............................$2,000 $2,200 $2,500

VACHERON, 17J., RF# 6498, Ca. 1965
18k $1,000 $1,200 $1,500

VACHERON, 17 jewels
18k $1,000 $1,100 $1,300

VACHERON, 18J., no sec. hand,
18k $800 $900 $1,100

VACHERON,17J., RF#6099, cal.1003, c.1960
18k $800 $900 $1,100

VACHERON, 17J., 20 dollar gold piece, RF # 4928
18k $2,200 $2,500 $3,000

VACHERON, 16J., hidden lugs, Ca. 1945
14k $1,500 $1,700 $2,000

Wrist Watches listed in this section are priced at the collectable fair market **Trade Show** level as **complete** watches having an original gold-filled case and stainless steel back, also with original dial, leather watch band, and the entire original movement in good working order with no repairs needed.

🕐 Some grades are not included. Their values can be determined by comparing with **similar** age, size, metal content, style, models and grades listed.

VACHERON, 16J., wire lugs, silver dial, ca.1917
14k $2,500 $3,000 $3,500

VACHERON, 36 jewels, auto wind
18k C&B.............................$1,800 $2,000 $2,300

VACHERON, 18J., tonneau shaped, ca. 1930s
18k $2,500 $2,800 $3,500

VACHERON, 21 J., date, auto-w. ca. 1980s
s. steel $1,000 $1,100 $1,400

VACHERON, 15J., lady's with wire lugs,ca.1920
18k(W)....................................$400 $500 $650

VACHERON, 15J., shutters with center slide to view dial, 2
tone case, ca. 1933
18k $10,000 $11,000 $14,000

VACHERON, 15 jewels
18k C&B.............................$1,400 $1,600 $2,000

VACHERON, 17J, with shutters, crowns at 3 & 9
18k $12,000 $13,000 $16,000

🕐 Some grades are not included. Their values can be determined by comparing with **similar** age, size, metal content,
style, models and grades listed.

🕐 A collector should expect to pay modestly higher prices
at local shops

VACHERON, 17 jewels , 2 tone case yellow & white
18k $1,500 $1,600 $1,800

🕐 Pricing in this Guide are fair market price for **COMPLETE**
watches which are reflected from the "**NAWCC**" National and
regional shows.

VACHERON, 18J., heavy case, ca. 1930s
18k(W) $3,400 $3,600 $4,000

VACHERON, 18J., silver dial, ca. 1941
18k $1,700 $1,800 $2,000

VACHERON, 18J., applied numbers, ca. 1940
18k $1,700 $1,800 $2,000

VACHERON, 18J., black dial, aux. sec., ca. 1937
18k $1,800 $1,900 $2,100

VACHERON, 18J., silver dial, ca. 1942
18k $2,000 $2,200 $2,500

Wrist Watches listed in this section are priced at the collectable
fair market **Trade Show** level as **complete** watches having an
original gold-filled case and stainless steel back, also with
original dial, leather watch band, and the entire original movement in good working order with no repairs needed.

VACHERON, 18J., hidden lugs, ca. 1940s
18k $1,700 $1,800 $2,100

VACHERON, 18J., off set lugs,
18k $2,000 $2,200 $2,500

VACHERON, 18J., off set lugs,
18k $2,000 $2,200 $2,500

VACHERON, 18J., aux .sec.,
s. steel $1,200 $1,300 $1,600

VACHERON, 18J., textured dial, large lugs, ca. 1951
18k $4,000 $4,500 $6,000

VACHERON, 18J., fancy lugs,ca.1938
18k $2,800 $2,900 $3,200

VACHERON, 18J., textured bezel,ca.1950s
18k $1,800 $2,200 $2,400

VACHERON, 18 jewels, aux. sec., c. 1950s
18k $1,500 $1,600 $1,900

VACHERON, 18 jewels, aux. sec., c. 1940s
18k $1,500 $1,600 $1,900

VACHERON, 17J., applied gold numbers, c. 1940s
18k $1,400 $1,500 $1,800

VACHERON, 17 jewels, aux. sec., c. 1945
18k $1,000 $1,100 $1,400

VACHERON, 17 jewels, applied gold numbers
18k $900 $1,000 $1,200

VACHERON, 17 jewels, fancy lugs
18k $1,800 $1,900 $2,200

VACHERON, 17 jewels, c. 1950s
18k $1,500 $1,600 $1,900

VACHERON, 17 jewels, fancy lugs
14k $1,200 $1,400 $1,700

🕐 A collector should expect to pay modestly higher prices at local shops

VACHERON, 17 jewels, aux. sec., Ca. 1945
18k .... $1,600　　$1,700　　$1,900

VACHERON, 17 jewels, stepped bezel, fancy lugs, Ca. 1940
18k .... $2,700　　$2,900　　$3,400

VACHERON,17J., hidden barrel shaped lugs, c.1943
14k .... $1,200　　$1,400　　$1,700

VACHERON,17J., aux. sec., c.1947
18k .... $1,500　　$1,600　　$1,900

VACHERON,17J., aux. sec., c.1942
18k .... $1,300　　$1,400　　$1,700

VACHERON,17J., RF#6249, aux. sec., c.1963
18k .... $1,500　　$1,600　　$1,800

VACHERON,17J., aux. sec., c.1934
18k .... $1,500　　$1,600　　$1,800

VACHERON, 17 jewels, aux. sec., Ca. 1946
18k .... $1,500　　$1,600　　$1,800

VACHERON, 17 jewels, Art Deco bezel, c. 1925
18k .... $4,500　　$5,000　　$6,000

VACHERON, 15 jewels, exaggerated numbers, Ca. 1917
18k .... $2,200　　$2,500　　$3,000

🕐 Pricing in this Guide are fair market price for **COMPLETE**
watches which are reflected from the "**NAWCC**" National and
regional shows.

DIALS FOR MINT PRICES MUST BE ALL **ORIGINAL**.

VACHERON, 17 jewels, aux. sec.,
18k $2,200 $2,400 $2,800

VACHERON, 15J., hinged back, ca. 1930
18k $2,200 $2,400 $2,800

VACHERON, 18 jewels, aux. sec.
18k C&B $2,000 $2,100 $2,300

VACHERON, 18J., large 2 tone mans watch, ca.1928
18k $3,500 $4,000 $5,000

VACHERON, 15 jewels, heavy bezel, c.1925
18K C&B $3,500 $4,000 $5,000

VACHERON, 18J.,long curved case, ca.1929
platinum...............................$4,000 $4,500 $5,500

VACHERON, 17 jewels, fancy long lugs, Ca. 1940s
18k $2,000 $2,200 $2,600

VACHERON, 18J., ca. 1926
18k $1,600 $1,800 $2,200

VACHERON,15J., curvex,wire lugs,33mm long,ca.1923
18k $2,500 $2,700 $3,200

VACHERON, 18J., ca. 1950s
18k $900 $1,000 $1,200

DIALS FOR MINT PRICES MUST BE ALL **ORIGINAL**.

VACHERON, 15J., early movement, ca.1925
18k $1,300 $1,400 $1,800

VACHERON, 17 jewels, aux. sec.
14k $1,000 $1,200 $1,500

VACHERON, 15J.,2 tone case, ca. 1926
18k $1,400 $1,600 $2,000

VACHERON, 17 jewels, flat & thin model, c. 1960s
18k $800 $900 $1,200

VACHERON, 18J., tank style, ca.1960s
18k $1,200 $1,300 $1,500

VACHERON, 17 jewels
18k C&B............................$1,500 $1,700 $2,000

VACHERON, 17 jewels, hinged back
18k $1,000 $1,200 $1,500

VACHERON, 18 jewels, stepped case & beveled lugs
18k $1,600 $1,700 $2,000

VACHERON, 15J., wire lugs, enamel dial, Ca.1920s
18k $2,000 $2,200 $2,500

VACHERON, 15 jewels, c. 1920s
18k $900 $1,000 $1,200

VACHERON, 17 jewels, **star dial**, hidden lugs, c. 1943s
14k $1,300 $1,500 $1,800

VACHERON, 17 jewels, 68 diamond bezel
18k $2,200 $2,500 $2,800

VACHERON,17J., RF#7252, c.1962
18k $1,000 $1,200 $1,500

VACHERON, 17 jewels, flared, curvex, c. 1940s
18k $4,500 $5,000 $6,000

VACHERON, 17J., flared,**12 diam.dial**, aux. sec., c. 1948
platinum $5,500 $6,000 $7,000

VACHERON, 17 jewels, flared, c. 1948
18k $4,000 $4,200 $5,000

VACHERON, 17 jewels, flared, c. 1940s
18k $4,000 $4,200 $5,000

VACHERON, 17 jewels, "Chronoscope," jumping hr.,
revolving ruby min. indicator, c. 1930s
18k $20,000 $22,000 $26,000

VACHERON, 20 jewels, Adj. to 5 Pos., c. 1970s
18k $2,000 $2,200 $2,500

VACHERON, 22 jewels, lady's watch, c. 1970s
18k $800 $900 $1,200

🕐 Pricing in this Guide are fair market price for **COMPLETE**
watches which are reflected from the **"NAWCC"** National and
regional shows.

VACHERON, 17 jewels, aux. sec., ruby dial
18k $2,400 $2,600 $3,000

VACHERON,16J., black star & forrest, wire lugs, c.1919
18k ladies...............................$400 $450 $600

VACHERON, 21 jewels, center sec., auto wind, c. 1950s
18k $3,500 $4,000 $5,000

VACHERON, 17 jewels, heavy bezel
18k ladies.............................$1,200 $1,400 $1,700

VACHERON, 17 jewels, aux. sec., fancy lugs, c. 1947
18k $3,000 $3,500 $4,500

VACHERON,17J., ladies, c.1948
18k ladies...............................$800 $900 $1,100

VACHERON, 15 J., lady's, wire lugs, ca.1919
18k $400 $450 $600

VACHERON, 17 jewels , swinging lugs
14k $1,200 $1,400 $1,800

Wrist Watches listed in this section are priced at the collectable
fair market **Trade Show** level as **complete** watches having an
original gold-filled case and stainless steel back, also with
original dial, leather watch band, and the entire original movement in good working order with no repairs needed.

VACHERON, 17 jewels, lady's watch, c. 1960s
18k C&B.............................$1,200 $1,400 $1,800

VACHERON, 17J., cased & timed in U.S.A. by Vacheron &
Constantine , heavy 14k gold bracelet, ladies, Ca.1950s
14k heavy C&B...................$1,000 $1,100 $1,400

DIALS FOR MINT PRICES MUST BE ALL **ORIGINAL**.

VAN CLEEF & ARPELS,17J., center lugs, c.1970
18k $275 $350 $500

VULCAIN,17jewels, "Grand Prix", Ca. 1940
s. steel $35 $40 $75

VERNO, 15 jewels, chased bezel
gold filled (w) $45 $60 $85

VULCAIN,17J., "Cricket Alarm", c.1965
base metal $100 $125 $225

VULCAIN, 17 jewels, digital read out
base metal $45 $55 $75

VULCAIN,17J., "Cricket", alarm, c.1948
s. steel $125 $150 $250

VULCAIN, 17 jewels, "Cricket", alarm
14k $250 $300 $400
18k $300 $350 $450

VULCAIN,17J., "Cricket Calendar", Ca. 1965
18K $350 $400 $500

🕐 A collector should expect to pay modestly higher prices
at local shops

VULCAIN, 17 jewels, "Cricket," alarm
gold filled................................$125 $150 $235

WAKMANN,17J., "Gigandet" Valjoux cal.72, c.1955
18k $1,200 $1,400 $1,700

VULCAIN, 17 jewels, "Minstop"
s. steel $75 $85 $125

WAKMANN, 17J., chronog., 3 reg., triple date
14k $450 $550 $750

WAKMANN,17J., 24 hr. dial, c.1955
s. steel $75 $95 $125

WAKMANN,17J., chronog., 3 reg., triple date, sq.buttons
s. steel $250 $300 $400

WAKMANN, 17 jewels, chronog., 3 reg., c. 1958
s. steel $250 $300 $350

WAKMANN,17J., chronog., Valjoux cal.188, c.1960
s. steel $150 $200 $300

WAKMANN,17J., chronog., Valjoux cal.236, c.1968
s. steel $175 $195 $250

WAKMANN,17J., chronog., c.1955
18k $500 $550 $650
s. steel $175 $200 $250

WAKMANN,17J., chronog., c.1970s
s. steel $95 $150 $225

WARWICK, 6J., hinged back, 1930s
gold plate $45 $65 $95

WARWICK, 15J., 1930s
gold plate $45 $65 $95

WARWICK, 15J., 1930s
gold plate $45 $65 $95

WARWICK, 6-15J., 1930s
gold plate $45 $65 $95

WARWICK, 6-15J., 1930s
gold plate $45 $65 $95

WARWICK, 6-15J., 1930s
gold plate $45 $65 $95

WARWICK, 6-15J., 1930s
gold plate $45 $65 $95

WARWICK, 15J., 1930s
gold plate $45 $65 $95

WARWICK, 15J., 1930s
base metal $45 $65 $95

WATEX, 7J., fluted case, c.1940
gold filled................................ $100 $125 $185

WELDON,17J., aux. sec., large lugs c.1950s
gold filled................................ $75 $100 $150

WELSBRO ,17J., single button chronog., c.1940
s. steel $150 $195 $275

WELTALL W. Co., floral enamel on case, cylinder escp.
wire lugs, Ca. 1910
14k $100 $125 $175

WEST END, 17J., "Keepsake", (by Longines), Ca. 1925
silver $250 $350 $500

WEST END, 17 jewels, center lugs
18k $175 $195 $250

WESTFIELD, 17J., aux. sec., Ca. 1954
gold filled $55 $75 $125

WHITE STAR, 17J., triple date, moon phase, c. 1948
s. steel $400 $500 $650

WITTNAUER, 17 jewels, chronog., c. 1948
s. steel $250 $350 $425

WINTON, 17J., hooded lugs
14k $100 $125 $175

WITTNAUER,17J., "Professional", RF#6002, c.1955
18k $600 $655 $775
s. steel $275 $325 $400

WINTON, 16J., curvex, hinged back, c.1930s
silver $150 $175 $225

WITTNAUER, 17 jewels, fancy lugs
14k $125 $150 $200

WITTNAUER,17J., chronog., waterproof, c.1958
18k $400 $450 $550
s. steel $200 $250 $325

WITTNAUER, 17 jewels, chronog., day-date-month
s. steel $375 $450 $550

WITTNAUER,17J., chronog., by Venius, **Time Zone Bezel**,
Ca. 1955
s. steel $350 $400 $500

WITTNAUER,17J., chronog., by Valjoux, #72, cal.13w1
s. steel $250 $350 $500

WITTNAUER,7J., "Electronic", day date, c.1968
s. steel $25 $30 $50

WITTNAUER,7J., mid size , stop watch, c.1940
s. steel $125 $135 $150

WITTNAUER,17J., direct read, c.1970
s. steel $35 $45 $75

WITTNAUER, 17 J., day date, set year by button
s. steel $100 $135 $200

WITTNAUER,17J., Zircon on dial, direct read, c.1970
base metal $20 $35 $65

WITTNAUER,17J., perpetual calendar
base metal $65 $85 $100

WITTNAUER, 17 jewels, auto wind, sector, date
s. steel $150 $185 $275
gold filled $150 $185 $275

WITTNAUER, 17 jewels, fancy lugs, Ca. 1955
14k $100 $125 $200

WITTNAUER, 17 jewels, curved case, c.1950
14k $100 $125 $200

WITTNAUER,17J., aux. sec., c.1958
gold filled................................$65 $75 $95

WITTNAUER, 17 jewels, cal.9wn, fancy lugs, c.1954
gold filled $60 $75 $95

WITTNAUER,17J., aux. sec., c.1950
14k $100 $135 $225

WITTNAUER, 17 jewels, fancy lugs, GJS
14k $100 $125 $200

WITTNAUER,17J., aux. sec., GJS, c.1948
14k $100 $135 $225

WITTNAUER,17J., aux. sec., GJS, large lugs, c.1950
14k $100 $125 $225

WITTNAUER,17J., aux. sec., fancy lugs, c.1955
gold filled................................$65 $75 $95

WITTNAUER,17J., aux. sec., fancy case, c.1950
gold filled $75 $100 $150

WITTNAUER, 17J., aux. sec., flared case
14k $100 $125 $225

WITTNAUER, 17J., aux. sec.
gold filled................................. $70 $80 $125

WITTNAUER, 17 jewels, fancy lugs, c. 1950s
14k $100 $125 $235

WITTNAUER, 17J., aux. sec., GJS, c. 1955
14k $100 $125 $225

WITTNAUER, 17J., aux. sec., tu-tone dial, c. 1950
gold filled................................. $65 $75 $125

🕐 Pricing in this Guide are fair market price for **COMPLETE** watches which are reflected from the **"NAWCC"** National and regional shows.

WITTNAUER, 17J., aux. sec., c. 1950
gold filled $45 $60 $95

WITTNAUER, 15J., aux. sec., tonneau case, c.1945
gold plate $30 $40 $65

WITTNAUER, 17J., aux. sec.
gold filled $45 $55 $95

WITTNAUER, 15J., "Weems", rotating bezel, Ca. 1940
gold filled $250 $300 $450

WITTNAUER, 17J., flared case, Ca.1949
14k $100 $125 $225

🕐 Some grades are not included. Their values can be determined by comparing with **similar** age, size, metal content, style, models and grades listed.

WIG WAG, 15 jewels, **early auto wind**, c. 1932
s. steel .... ★ $500 $600 $800

WITTNAUER, 17J., RF#2067, c.1950
gold filled...........................$55 $65 $85

WYLER, 17 jewels, early auto wind, watch winds by using
the muscular movement of the wrist, back set
gold filled .... ★ $400 $450 $600

WITTNAUER, 17J., auto-wind, c.1960
base metal $35 $45 $65

WYLER, 17 jewels, early auto wind, back set
gold filled .... ★ $400 $450 $600

WITTNAUER, 17J., cal.7630, aux. sec., c.1955
14k $100 $125 $200

WYLER, 17 jewels, center sec., auto-wind
s. steel $55 $65 $100

WITTNAUER, 17J., "Alarm", c.1960
gold filled.................................$65 $75 $95

Wrist Watches listed in this section are priced at the collectable
fair market Trade Show level as **complete** watches having an
original gold-filled case and stainless steel back, also with
original dial, leather watch band, and the entire original movement in good working order with no repairs needed.

WYLER, 17 jewels, auto wind, center sec., Ca. 1950
gold filled $75 $85 $125

🕐 Some grades are not included. Their values can be determined by comparing with **similar** age, size, metal content,
style, models and grades listed.

WYLER, 17 jewels
s. steel $75 $95 $125

WYLER,17J., **early** auto-wind, c.1930
chrome $75 $100 $165

WYLER, 17 jewels, diamond dial, c. 1946
s. steel $55 $65 $100

WYLER,17J., day date month, c.1946
gold filled $95 $125 $175

WYLER,17J., center sec., c.1945
s. steel $45 $50 $75

WYLER,17J., center sec., waterproof, ca.1941
s. steel $45 $50 $75

WYLER, 17 jewels, chronog., c. 1940s
14k $250 $300 $385
s. steel $150 $175 $225

WYLER,17J., aux. sec., c.1938
s. steel $45 $50 $75

🕑 A collector should expect to pay modestly higher prices
at local shops

Wrist Watches listed in this section are priced at the collectable
fair market **Trade Show** level as **complete** watches having an
original gold-filled case and stainless steel back, also with
original dial, leather watch band, and the entire original movement in good working order with no repairs needed.

YALE, 15 jewels, calendar, c. 1939
14k $175 $200 $250
gold filled $75 $100 $125

🕑 Some grades are not included. Their values can be determined by comparing with **similar** age, size, metal content,
style, models and grades listed.

🕑 Pricing in this Guide are fair market price for **COMPLETE**
watches which are reflected from the "**NAWCC**" National and
regional shows.

ZENITH, 15 jewels, Engraved bezel, Ca. 1915
gold filled...............................$100 $135 $200

ZENITH, 19 jewels, **chronometer**, 33mm, c. 1950s
gold filled $75 $95 $135

ZENITH,15J., enamel dial, wire lugs, c. 1918
silver $275 $325 $400

ZENITH, 17 jewels, chronog., Ca. 1950
18k $500 $550 $650

ZENITH,15J., signal corps on enamel dial, center lug, 1918
silver $350 $400 $500

ZENITH, 36 jewels, chronog., auto wind, c. 1969
s. steel $500 $600 $800

ZENITH,17J., Chronog., Ca. 1930
18k $1,500 $1,700 $2,200

ZENITH,17J., Chronograph 3 reg., Ca.1965
14k $800 $900 $1,100
s. steel $400 $450 $600

ZENITH, 36J., "El Primero", RF#502,auto wind, c. 1970
18k $700 $800 $1,000

ZENITH, 36 jewels, "El Primero," chronog., triple date
moon phase, auto wind, c. 1970s
18k $1,600 $1,800 $2,400

ZENITH,36J., chronog., auto-wind, triple date, moon ph.
s. steel $700 $900 $1,200

ZENITH, 17 jewels, fancy bezel
18k $200 $225 $275

ZENITH, 17J., auto-wind, date at 5, Ca. 1959
18k $175 $200 $250

ZENTRA, 24 jewels, ladies,auto wind, c. 1958
14k $70 $85 $125

ZODIAC, 17J., chronog., 2 reg., fancy lugs, c.1948
gold filled $200 $225 $300
14k $400 $500 $700
18k $500 $600 $900

ZODIAC, 17J., chronog., auto-wind, date, c.1971
s. steel $100 $125 $200

⊕ A collector should expect to pay modestly higher prices
at local shops

ZODIAC, 17J., center sec., auto-wind, c.1959
s. steel $45 $55 $100

ZODIAC, 17J., day-date-month, moon phase, c. 1957
s. steel $300 $365 $450
14k $500 $575 $650

ZODIAC, 17 jewels, 24 hour dial
s. steel $65 $75 $125

ZODIAC, 17J., auto-wind, the power reserve has
differential gearing, c. 1959
14k $175 $200 $225
gold filled $75 $100 $150
s. steel $75 $100 $150

ZODIAC, 17 jewels, ref. #8088
14k $100 $125 $200

ZODIAC, 21J., date, "Olympos", date, auto-wind,c.1965
s. steel $50 $70 $100

ZODIAC, 17J., center sec., Ca.1948
s. steel $55 $75 $110

ZODIAC, 17J., by Valj. cal. 7733, Ca.1965
base metal $125 $150 $225

ADJUSTED-Derived from Latin *ad justus*, meaning just right. Adjusted to compensate for temperature, positions,and isochronism.

ALARM WATCH-A watch that will give an audible sound at a pre-set time.

ALL or NOTHING PIECE-A repeating watch mechanism which ensures that ALL the hour & minutes are struck or sounded or nothing is heard.

ANALOGUE-A term used to denote a watch dial with hands rather than digital display.

ANNEALING-Heating and cooling a metal slowly to relieve internal stress.

ANTI-MAGNETIC-Not affected by magnetic field.

ANTIQUARIAN-Of antiques or dealing in, also the study of old and out-of-date items.

ARBOR-The mechanical axle of a moving part; on the balance it is called the staff, on the lever it is called the arbor.

ASSAY-Analyzing a metal for its gold or silver content.

AUTOMATON-Automatic working figures moving in conjunction with the movement mechanism. Striking *Jacquemarts* or jacks which are figures (may be humans provided with hammers) striking bells to supply the sound for the hour & quarter hours. The hammers take the place of the bells clapper. *Automata* plural of **automaton.**

AUXILIARY COMPENSATION-For middle temperature errors found on marine chronometers.

AUXILIARY DIAL - Any extra dial for information.

AWI - American Watchmakers-Clockmakers Institute, 701 Enterprise Drive, Harrison, OH 45030. Tel # **(513) 367-9800**

BAGUETTE-A French term for oblong shape. A watch having it's length at least 3 times it's width. A long narrow diamond.

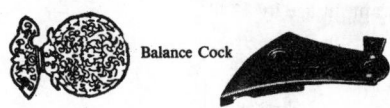

Balance Cock

BALANCE COCK-The bridge that holds the upper jewels and the balance and secured at one end only.

Balance Spring

BALANCE SPRING-Also called the hairspring; the spring governing the balance.

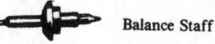

Balance Staff

BALANCE STAFF -The shaft of the balance wheel.

Balance Wheel

BALANCE WHEEL-A device shaped like a wheel that does for a watch what a pendulum does for a clock.

BANKING PINS-The two pins which limit the angular motion of the pallet.

Bar Movement

BAR MOVEMENT-A type of movement employing about six bridges to hold the train. In use by 1840.

Barrel

BARREL-Drum-shaped container that houses the mainspring.

BEAT-Refers to the tick or sound of a watch; about 1/5 of a second. The sound is produced by the escape wheel striking the pallets.

Beetle Hand

BEETLE HAND-Hour hand resembling a stag beetle; usually associated with the poker-type minute hand in 17th and 18th century watches.

BELL METAL-Four parts copper and one part tin used for metal laps to get a high polish on steel.

O S. Htg. Bezel,

BEZEL-The rim that covers the dial (face) & retains the crystal. Above snap on bezel.

Balance Wheel

BI-METALLIC BALANCE-A balance composed of brass and steel designed to compensate for temperature changes in the hairspring.

BLIND MAN'S WATCH- A Braille watch; also known as a tact watch.

BLUING or BUING-By heating polished steel to 540 degrees, the color will change to blue.

BOMBE'- Convex on one side.

Bow

BOW-The ring that is looped at the pendant to which a chain or fob is attached

BOX CHRONOMETER-A marine or other type chronometer in gimbals so the movement remains level at sea.

BOX JOINTED CASE-A heavy hinged decorative case with a simulated joint at the top under the pendant. (BOX CASE)

BREGUET KEY-A ratcheting watch key permitting winding in only one direction.

Overcoil Hairspring

BREGUET SPRING-A type of hairspring that improves time keeping also called overcoil hairspring.

BRIDGE-A metal bar which bear the pivot of wheels and is supported at both ends .(see cock.)

BUBBLE BACK-A Rolex wrist watch which were water proof (Oyster) and auto wind (Perpetual) Ca. 1930 to 1950's.

BULL'S EYE CRYSTAL-Used on old type watches; the center of the crystal was polished which achieved a bull's eye effect.

Top Side

BUFFER SPRING - Buffer spring is a stop spring for oscillating weight.

CABOCHON - An unfaceted cut stone of domed form or style. (on some crowns)

CALENDAR WATCH-A watch that shows the date, month and day.

CALIBRE or CALIBER-**Size** of a watch movement also to describe the model, style or shape of a watch movement.

CAP JEWEL-Also called the end stone, the flat jewel on which the staff rests.

CASE SCREW-A screw with part of the head cut away.

CENTER WHEEL-The second wheel; the arbor for the minute hand; this wheel makes one revolution per hour.

CHAIN (Fusee)-Looks like a miniature bicycle chain connecting the barrel and fusee.

CHAMFER-Sloping or beveled. Removing a sharp edge or edges of holes.

CHAMPLEVE-An area hollowed out and filled with enamel and then baked on.

CHAPTER-The hour, minute & seconds numbers on a dial. The chapter ring is the zone or circle that confines the numbers.

CHRONOGRAPH-A movement that can be started and stopped to measure short time intervals and return to zero. A stopwatch does not keep the time of day.

CHRONOMETER ESCAPEMENT - A detent escapement used in marine chronometers.

CIRCA-Approximately. (Ca.)

CLICK-A pawl that ratchets and permits the winding wheel to move in one direction; a clicking sound can be heard as the watch is wound.

CLOCK WATCH-A watch that strikes the hour but not on demand.

CLOISONNE-Enamel set between strips of metal and baked onto the dial.

CLUB TOOTH-Some escape wheels have a special design which increases the impulse plane; located at the tip of the tooth of the escape wheel.

COARSE TRAIN-16,000 beats per hour.

COCK -The metal bar which carries the bearing for the balance's upper pivot and is supported at one end.

COMPENSATION BALANCE-A balance wheel designed to correct for temperature.

COMPLICATED WATCH-A watch with complicated works;other than just telling time, it may have a perpetual calendar, moon phases, up and down dial, repeater, musical chimes or alarm.

CONTRATE WHEEL-A wheel with its teeth at a right angle to plane of the wheel.

CONVERTIBLE- Movement made by Elgin & other companies; a means of converting from a hunting case to a open-face watch or vice-versa.

CRAZE(crazing)-A minute crack in the glaze of enamel watch dials.

Railroad Style

Round Style   Antique Style
CROWN-A winding button.

Crown Wheel

CROWN WHEEL

CROWN WHEEL-The escape wheel of a verge escapement; looks like a crown. Also the lower illustration shows a crown wheel used in a stem winding pocket watch.

Curb Pin

CURB PINS-The two pins that change the rate of a watch; the two pins,in effect,change the length of the hairspring.

CUVETTE

CUVETTE-The inter dust cover of a pocket watch.

CYLINDER ESCAPEMENT-A type of escapement used on some watches.

DIAL-The face of a watch. Some are made of enamel.

DAMASKEENING-The art of producing a design, pattern, or wavy appearance on a metal. American idiom or terminology used in **all** American factory ads. The European terminology was Fausse Cotes or Geneva stripes.

DISCHARGE PALLET JEWEL-The right or 2nd jewel on lever. The 2nd of two pallet jewels with which a tooth of the escape wheel comes into engagement. Also called the **Exit** pallet.

DOUBLE ROLLER-A watch with one impulse roller table and a safety roller, thus two rollers.

DRAW-The angular position of the pallet jewels in the pallet frame which causes those jewels to be drawn deeper into the escape wheel under pressure of the escape wheel's tooth on the locking surface.

DROP-The space between a tooth of the escape wheel and the pallet from which it has just escaped.

DUMB –REPEATER-A repeating watch with hammers that strikes a block instead of bells or gongs.

DEMI-HUNTER-A hunting case with the center designed to allow the position of the hands to be seen without opening the case.

DETENT ESCAPEMENT-A detached escapement . The balance is impulsed in one direction; used on watches to provide greater accuracy. Detent a locking device.

DUPLEX ESCAPEMENT-An escape wheel with two sets of teeth, one for locking and one for impulse.

EBAUCHE(ay-boesh)-A movement not completely finished or in the rough; not detailed; a raw movement; a movement made up of two plates ,train, barrel & did not include a dial, case, or escapement.

ECCENTRIC-Not exactly circular, *Non-concentric*. A cam with a lobe or egg shape.

ENGINE TURNING-Engraving a watch case with a repetitive design by a machine.

ELECTRONIC WATCH-Newer type watch using quartz and electronics to produce a high degree of accuracy.

ELINVAR-A hairspring composed of a special alloy of nickel, steel, chromium, manganese and tungsten that does not vary at different temperatures. Elinvar was derived from the words elasticity invariable.

END SHAKE-The up and down play of an arbor between the plates and bridge or between the jewels.

END STONE-The jewel or cap at the end of the staff.

EPHEMEROUS TIME-The time calculated for the Earth to orbit around the sun.

ESCAPE WHEEL-The last wheel in a going train; works with the fork or lever and escapes one pulse at a time.

Fork

FORK-The part of the pallet lever that engages with the roller jewel.

FREE SPRUNG-A balance spring free from the influence of a regulator.

FULL PLATE -A plate (or disc) that covers the works and supports the wheels pivots. There is a top plate, a bottom plate, half, and 3/4 plate. The top plate has the balance resting on it.

ESCAPEMENT-The device in a watch by which the motion of the train is checked and the energy of the mainspring communicated to the balance. The escapement includes the escape wheel, lever, and balance complete with hairspring.

FARMER'S WATCH(OIGNON)-A large pocket watch with a verge escapement and a farm scene on the dial.

FECIT-A Latin word meaning"made by ".

FIVE-MINUTE REPEATER-A watch that denotes the time every five minutes, and on the hour and half hour, by operating a push piece.

FLINQUE-Enameling over hand engraving.

FLY BACK-The hand returns back to zero on a timer.

FOB-A decorative short strap or chain.

FUSEE-A spiral grooved, truncated cone used in some watches to equalize the power of the mainspring.

GRANDE SONNERIE-(**Grand strike**) a watch or clock that strikes the hour, 1/4 hours and minutes if minute repeater, a Petite Sonnerie strikes hour only.

GENEVA STOP WORK-A system used to stop the works preventing the barrel from being over wound.

GILT (or GILD)-To coat or plating with gold leaf or a gold color.

GOING BARREL-The barrel houses the mainspring; as the spring uncoils, the barrel turns, and the teeth on the outside of the barrel turn the train of gears as opposed to toothless fusee barrel.

Foliot

FOLIOT-A straight-armed balance with weights on each end used for regulation; found on the earliest clocks and watches.

GOLD-FILLED-Sandwich-type metal; a layer of gold, a layer of base metal in the middle, another layer of gold-then the layers of metals are soldered to each other to form a sandwich.

GOLD JEWEL SETTINGS-In high-grade watches the jewels were mounted in gold settings.

GREAT WHEEL-The main wheel of a fusee type watch.

GUILLOCHE - A decorative pattern of cross or interlaced lines. (engraving style)

HACK-WATCH-A watch with a balance that can be stopped to allow synchronization with another timepiece.

HAIRSPRING-The spring which vibrates the balance. Above flat style hairsprings. Also called balance spring

HAIRSPRING STUD-A hairspring stud is used to connect the hairspring to the balance cock.

HALLMARK-The silver or gold or platinum markings of many countries.

HEART CAM-PIECE-A heart-shaped cam which causes the hand on a chronograph to fly back to zero.

HELICAL HAIRSPRING-A cylindrical spring used in chronometers.

HOROLOGY (haw-rahl-uh-jee)-The study of time keeping.

HUNTER CASE-A pocket watch case with a covered face that must be opened to see the watch dial.

IMPULSE-The force transmitted by the escape wheel to the pallet by gliding over the angular or impulse face of the pallet jewel.

IMPULSE PIN(Ruby pin)(roller jewel)-A pin or jewel on the balance roller table which keeps the balance going.

INCABLOC-A patented shock absorbing device which permits the end stone of the balance to give when the watch is subjected to an impact or jolt. 1st. used in 1933.

INDEX-Another term for the racquet-shaped regulator which lengthens or shortens the effective length of the hairspring.

INDEPENDENT SECONDS-A seconds hand driven independently by a separate train but controlled by the time train.

ISOCHRONISM-"Isos" means equal; chronos means time-occurring at equal intervals of time. The balance and hairspring adjusted will allow the watch to run at the same rate regardless whether the watch is fully wound or almost run down.

JEWEL-A bearing made of a ruby or other type jewel; the four types of jewels include; cap jewel, hole jewel, roller jewel or ruby pin, pallet jewel or stone.

KARRUSEL-An invention of Bonniksen in 1894 which allows the entire escapement to revolve within the watch once in 52 1/2 minutes (in most karrusels), this unit is supported at one end only as opposed to the tourbillon which is supported at both ends and which most often revolves about once a minute.

KEY SET-Older watch that had to be set with a key.

LEAVES-The teeth of the pinion gears.

L'Epine' CALIBRE-Introduced by J.A. L'Epine about 1770. Swiss for **open face.**

LEVER ESCAPEMENT-Invented by Thomas Mudge in about 1759.

Lever

LEVER SETTING-The lever used to set some watches.

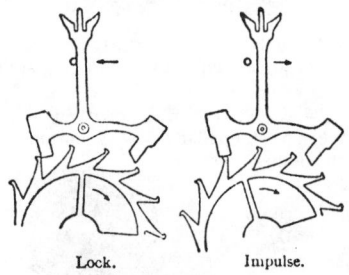

Lock. Impulse.

LOCKING-Arresting the advance of the escape wheel during the balance's free excursion.

LUGS-The metal extensions of a wrist watch case which the bracelet or band are attached usually with a spring bar.

MAIN SPRING-A flat spring coiled or wound to supply power to the watch. The non-magnetic mainspring, introduced 1947.

MAIN WHEEL-The first driving wheel, part of the barrel.

MALTESE CROSS-The part of the stop works preventing the barrel from being over wound.

MICROMETRIC REGULATOR-A regulator used on railroad grade watches to adjust for gain or loss in a very precise way.

MICRO-SECOND-A millionth of a second.

MINUTE REPEATER -A watch that strikes or sounds the hours , and minutes on demand.

MOVEMENT-The works of a mechanical watch without the case or dial. (quartz watches have modules)

MARINE CHRONOMETER- An accurate timepiece; may have a detent escapement and set in a box with gimbals which keep it in a right position.

MEAN TIME- Also equal hours; average mean solar time; the time shown by watches.

Meantime Screw

MUSICAL WATCH-A watch that plays a tune on demand or on the hour.

MULTI-GOLD-Different colors of gold-red, green, white, blue, pink, yellow and purple.

MEANTIME SCREWS-Balance screws used for timing,usually longer than other balance screws; when turned away from or toward the balance pin, they cause the balance vibrations to become faster or slower.

NANOSECOND-One billionth of a second.

N. A. W. C. C. - National Association of Watch and Clock Collectors 514 Poplar St. Columbia, Pa.   17512.

TEL. 1- 717- 684- 8261

NURENBURG EGG-Nickname for a German watch that was oval-shaped.

OVERCOIL-The raised up portion of the balance hairspring, not flat. Also called Breguet hairspring.

PATINA-Oxidation of any surface & change due to age. A natural staining or discoloration due to aging.

PAIR-CASE WATCH-An extra case around a watch-two cases,hence, a pair of cases. The outer case kept out the dust. The inner case could not be dustproof because it provided the access to the winding and setting keyholes in the watch case.

PALLADIUM-One of six platinum metals, used in watches in place of platinum, because it is harder, lighter and cheaper.

OIGNON-Large older (1675) style watch in the the shape of a onion or *in the shape of a bulb.*

OIL SINK-A small well around a pivot which retains oil.

PALLET-The part of the lever that works with the escape wheel-jeweled pallet jewels, entry and exit pallets.

OVERBANKED-A lever escapement error; the roller jewel passes to the wrong side of the lever notch, causing one side of the pallet to rest against the banking pin and the roller jewel to rest against the other side, thus locking the escapement and stopping the motion of the balance.

PARACHUTE-An early shock proofing system designed to fit as a spring on the end stone of balance.

PAVE'- A number of jewels or stone set close together. Paved in diamonds.

Pendant

PENDANT-The neck of the watch; attached to it is the bow (swing ring) and the crown.

PILLARS-The rods that hold the plates apart. In older watches they were fancy.

PINCHBECK-A metal similar in appearance to gold. Named after the inventor. Alloy of 4 parts copper &3 parts zinc.

PINION-The larger gear is called a wheel. The small solid gear is a pinion. The pinion is made of steel in some watches.

PLATE-A watch has a front and a back plate or top and bottom plate. The works are in between.

POISE-A term meaning in balance to equalize the weight around the balance.

PONTILLAGE(bull's eye crystal)-The grinding of the center of a crystal to form a concave or so called bull's eye crystal.

Stem UP   Stem Down

Stem Left   Stem Right

Dial Up   Dial Down

POSITION-As adjusted to five positions; a watch may differ in its time keeping accuracy as it lays in different positions . Due to the lack of poise, changes in the center of gravity, a watch can be adjusted to six positions: dial up, dial down, stem up, stem down, stem left, and stem right. Note: Adj. to 5 positions is also 8 adjustments.

QUICK TRAIN-A watch with five beats or more per second or 18,000 per hour.

RACK PINION

RACK & PINION LEVER ESCAPEMENT-Developed by Abbe de Huteville in 1722 and by Peter Litherhead in 1791; does not use a roller table, but a pinion.

Receiving Pallet

RECEIVING PALLET-Also called left or entrance jewel, the first of two pallet jewels with which a tooth of the escape wheel comes into engagement.

REPEATER WATCH-A complicated watch that repeats the time on demand with a sounding device.

REPOUSSE'-A watch with hammered, raised decoration on the case.

RIGHT ANGLE LEVER ESCAPEMENT Also called English escapement.

ROLLED GOLD- Thin layer of gold soldered to a base metal.

ROLLER JEWEL-The jewel mounted or seated in the roller table, which receives the impulse from the pallet fork.

ROLLER TABLE-The part of the balance in which the roller jewel is seated.

ROTOR-Oscillating weight for self-wind watches.

SAFETY PINION -A pinion in the center wheel designed to unscrew if the mainspring breaks; this protects the train from being stripped by the great force of the mainspring.

SAFETY ROLLER-The smaller of the two rollers in a double roller escapement.

SAPPHIRE CRYSTAL - Scratch resistant glass with a hardness of 9. Mineral glass has a hardness of 5.

SHAGREEN-The skin of a horse, shark, ray fish & other animal usually dyed *GREEN* or a *BLUE GREEN*. Then used as ornamental covers for older watch cases.

SIDEREAL DAY-The time of rotation of the Earth as measured from the stars. About 3 minutes 56 seconds shorter than the mean solar day.

SIDE-WINDER-A mismatched case and movement; a term used for a hunting movement that has been placed in an open face case and winds at 3 o'clock position. Open face winds at 12 o'clock.

SILVEROID-A type of case composed of alloys to simulate the appearance of silver.

SINGLE ROLLER-The safety roller and the roller jewel are one single table.

SIZE-System used to determine the size of the movement to the case.

SKELETON WATCH-A watch made so the viewer can see the works. Plates are pierced and very decorative.

SKULL WATCH-A antique pendant watch that that is hinged at jaw to reveal a watch.

SLOW TRAIN-A watch with four beats per second or 14,000 per hour.

SNAIL-A cam shaped much like a snail. The snail determines the # of blows to be struck by a repeater.(A count wheel)

SNAILING-Ornamentation of the surface of metals by means of a circle design; also called damaskeening.

SOLAR YEAR-365 days, 5 hours, 48 minutes, 49.7 seconds.

SOUSCRIPTION- The cheapest Breguet watch which he made with high quality made in batches or group lots in advance to lower the cost.(ebauches)

SPOTTING-Decoration used on a watch movement and barrel of movements.

SPRING BAR-The metal keeper that attaches the band to the lugs of a wrist watch & is spring loaded.

SPRING RING-A circular tube housing a coiled type spring.

STACKFREED-Curved spring and cam to equalize the uneven force of the mainspring on 16th century German movements.
STAFF-Name for the axle of the balance.

SUN DIAL-A device using a gnomon or style that cast a shadow over a graduated dial as the sun progresses, indicating solar time.

SWIVEL-A hinged spring catch with a loop of metal that may be opened to insert a watch bow.

TRANSITION WATCH - Watches sold with both key and stem-winding on same movement.

TOP PLATE-The metal plate that usually contains the name and serial #.

TORSION-A twisting force.

TRIPLE CASE WATCH-18th and 19th century verge escapement, fusee watches made for the Turkish market. A fourth case sometimes added is called Quadruple case.

TOURBILLON-(French for whirlwind) A watch that uses a escapement mounted in a carriage and pivoted at both ends and revolves 360 degrees at regular intervals of once a minute. The escape-pinion turns around the fixed fourth wheel. Design to eliminate position errors.

UP AND DOWN DIAL OR INDICATOR-A dial that shows how much of the mainspring is spent and how far up or down the mainspring is.

Contrate Wheel

— **Pallet**
— **Verge**
— **Pallet**
— **Crown**

TRAIN-A series of gears that form the works of a watch. The train is used for other functions such as chiming. The time train carries the power to the escapement.

VERGE ESCAPEMENT-Early type of escapement with wheel that is shaped like a crown.

VERMEIL-Gold plated over silver.

VIRGULE ESCAPEMENT-Early escapement introduced in the mid 1700s .

WATCH GLASS PROTECTOR- A snap on metal grill that covers the crystal .

WATCH PAPER-A disc of paper with the name of the watchmaker or repairman printed on it; used as a form of advertising and found in some pair-cased watches.

WIND INDICATOR-A watch that indicates how much of the mainspring is spent. The **illustration** shows a modified Geneva stop works. (see up and down dial)

WOLF TEETH-A winding wheel's teeth so named because of their shape.

Accutron — AC-kew-tron
Agassiz — A-guh-see
Antiquarian — an-tih-KWAIR-ee-un
Art Nouveau — art new-VO
Astrolabe — AS-trow-labe
Atelier — a-tea-lee-ay
Audemars, Piguet — oh-de-MAHR, p-GAY
Automaton — aw-TAW-muh-tahn
Baguette — bah-get
Bannatyne — BAN-uh-tyne
Basse-Taille— bus-tie
Basscine — bah-seen
Basel — BAH-zuhl
Baume & Mercier — bome-MAY & mair-cyay
Beaucourt— boe-koor
Benrus — BEN-rus
Bergeon — BEAR-juhn
Berne — bairn
Berthoud — bair-TWO
Besancon— buh-sahn-son or be-sahn-SON
Bezel — BEZ-EL
Biel — beel
Bienne — bee-en
Blancpain — blahnk-PAn
Blois — blu-wah
Bombe' — boom-bay
Bovet — boe-vay
Bras en L'Air— brah on lair
Breguet et Fils — bre-gay ay fee
Breitling — BRITE-ling
Brevet — bree-VET (or) bree-VTAY
Bucherer — boo-shay-er
Cadrature — kad-drah-TUER
Calibre(er) — KAL-ih-breh or kal-ie-ber
Capt — kapt
Carillon — kah-RIL-yon
Cartier — kar-t-yay
Cartouche — kar-toosh
Champleve — shamp-leh-VAY
Chatelaine — SHAT-e-lane
Chaton — sha-tawn or sha-ton
Chopard — sho-par
Chronograph — Kronn-oh-graff
Chronometer — kroe-NOM-meh-tur
Cie — see
Cloisonne' — kloy-zoe-NAY
Cortebert — coh-teh-ber
Courvoisier — koor-voh-ahs-yeh
Corum — Kore-um
Craze — krayze (or) crazing — krayze-ing
Cuvette — kue-vet
Cyma Travannes — SEE-mah trah-VUNN
Damaskeen — dam-us-KEEN
* damaskeen = A special terminology or American idiom
Detent — dee-TENT
Ditisheim — DEE-tis-heim
Doxa — docks-uh
Droz' — droze
Dauphine — dough-feen
Ebauche — AY-boesh or e-bosh
Ebel — AY-ble (sounds like **Abel)**
Elinvar — EL-in-var
Ermeto — air-MET-oh
Escapement — es-cape-ment
Escutcheon — es-KUHCH-un
et Fils — AY feece
ETA — EE-ta. (Named after the 7th letter of the Greek alphabet).
Fahys — fah-z
Fasoldt — fa-sole-dt
Favre Leuba — fahv-ruh lew-buh
Fecit — FEE-sit =(made by)
Fleur de lis — flur duh lee
Foliot — FOH-lee-oh
Fontainemelon — fone-ten-meh-loh
Francillon — fran-seel-yon
Freid — freed
Frodsham — FRAHD-shum
Fusee — few-ZEE or few-zayh
Gadroon —ga-drewn
Gallet — gah-lay
Girrard Perregaux — jir-ard per-ay-go
Glashutte — glass-huet-te
Glucydur — glu-sch-dor
Glycine — gly-seen
Grande sonnnerie — grawnd shon-uh-ree
Grenchen — GREN-chun
Gublin — goo-blin
Guilloche — gill-low-sha
Guinand — gwee-nahnd
Haute — AUT
Hebdomas — heb-DOM-us
Helical — HEL-ih-kul
Helvetia — hell-VEHT-sia
Henlein — HEN-line

Heuer — hoy-er (the watch Co.)
Heuer — oo-air also eu-air (French for time or hour)
Horology — haw-rahl-uh-gee
Huyghens — hi-guhnz
Illinois—ill-ih-NOY
Ingraham — ing-gram
Invar — in-VAR
Isochronism — i-SOCK-roe-nizm
Jacot— zha-koe
Jaeger — YAY-gur
Japy — zja-pee
Jaquet Droz — zha-KAY droze
Jura — yoo-rah (moutains on French & Swiss border)
Jurgensen — YUER-gen-sen
Karrusel — kare-us-sell
Kessels — kahr-rus-SEL
La Chaux de Fonds — lah show duh Fawn
A. Lange & Sohne — ah. lahn gee uhnd soehne
Landeron — lan-der-on
Lapis LAZULI — lah-pis lah-zoon-lee
Lavaliere — la-vahl-yare
Le Coultre — luh-kool-tray
Le Locle — luh LOKEl
Lemania — leh-mahn-yuh
Leonidas — lee-oh-NEE-dus
Le Phare — luh-fahr
Lepine — lay-peen
Le Roy — luh roy
Le Sentier — le san-tyay
Leschot—leh-show
Ligne — line or leen
Longines — long-djeen
Loupe—loop
Lucien Piccard (Arnex) — lew-see-en pee-kar (ar-nex)
Lyon — lee-OHn
Mathey — ma-tay
Mido — me-DOE
Mollineaux — MOLE-ih-noe
Montre — MON- tru (Swiss name for WATCH)
Moser, Henri & Cie—awn-ree mow-say eh see
Movado — moe-VAH-doe
Mozart — MOE-tsart
Nardin — nar din
Nivarox — niv-ah-rocks
Neuchatel — noo-sha-TELL
Nicole — nee-kol
Niello — nye-el-oh
Oignon — ohn-yoh
Omega — oh-me-guh
Ormoulu — or-muh-loo
Otay — oh-tay
Oudin — oo-dan as in (soon)
Paillard — pay-lar
Pallet — PAL-let
Parachute — PAR-ah-shoot
Patek, Philippe — Pa-tek fee-leep
Patina—pah-teen-ah
Pave' — pah-vay
Piaget — pee-uh-jaay
Piguet — pee-gay
Pique — pee-kay
Quare — kwair
Rado — rah-doe
Remontoire— rem-on-twor
Repousse' — reh-poo-say
Rococo — roe-ko-ko
Roskopf — ROSS-cawf
Sangamo — san-guh-moe
Schaffausen — shaf-HOW-zun
Schild — sheild or shuild
Shugart — sugar with a T, or Shug-gart
Sonnerie — shon-uh-ree
Souscription — sue-skrip-tshown
Stackfreed — stack-freed
St. Imier — sahnt-imm-yay
Tavannes — ta-vann
Tempus Fugit — TEM-pus FYOO-jit = (time flies)
Thuret, (Isaac) — Tur-ay
Tissot — tee-SOh
Tobias — toe-bye-us
Tompion, Thomas) — Tom-pih-un
Tonneau — tun-noe
Touchon — too-shahn
Tourbillon — toour-bee-yohn
Vacheron & Constantin — VASH-er-on , CON-stan-teen
Valjoux — val- zhoo or val-goo
Vallee de Joux — valley duh Zhoo
Verge — vurj
Veritas — VAIR-ih-tas
Vermeil — vair-may
Vertu — ver-too
Virgule — vir-guel
Wittnauer — Wit-nower
Woerd — verd

European Terminology — U. S. A. Terminology

ACIER	Steel or Gunmetal
AIGUILLES	Hour Hand
ALARUM	Alarm
ANCHOR, ANCRE (Fr.), ANKER (Ger.)	Lever Escapement
ATELIER	Small Workshop
BAGUETTE	Long & Narrow
BALANCIER	Balance
BOITE-DOUBLE	Pair-case
BOMBE'	Convex or Domed
BRAS EN L'AIR	Arms in the Air
BREVET	Patented
CADRATURE	Attachment (as repeater or chronograph)
CALIBRE	Model or caliber
CHASED	Embossing
CHATON	Jewel Setting
CHRONOMETRE	Chronometer
CIE	Company
COMPENSE	Compensating
CUVETTE or DOME	Inside Hinged Dust Cover
CUIVRE	Copper or Brass
DEPOSE	Registered Trademark
EBAUCHE	Raw Blank Movement
EMPIERRE	Jewelled
ECHAPPEMENT A' ANCRE	Lever escapement
FAUSSE COTES	Damaskeening
FILS	Sons
FLUTED	Grooved
GENEVE STRIPES	Damaskeening
GUILLOCHE	Engine Turned
HAUTE	High
INVENIT ET FECIT	Invented & Made By
JACQUE-MART	Figures That Strike Bells
JOURS	Days As In 8 Days
LEPINE	Open Face
LIGNE	Size
MONTRE (Swiss or French)	Watch
MONTRE A' TACT	Watch by Touch
MARQUE DEPOSE (M.D.)	Registered Trademark
OIGNON or TURNIP	Large Bulbous French Watch
ORMOULU	Gold Gilding
PARACHUTE	Shock Resisting
PAVE	Cover
PIQUE	Pin Work Decoration
PERPETUELLE	Self-Winding
POLYCHROME	Color
POUSSETTE	Push Piece
REPOUSSE	Embossing
RATTRAPANTE	Split Seconds
REFERENCE #	Case # & Style
REMONTOIRE	Constant Force also Keyless Winding
RESSORT DE CROCHEMENT	All-or-Nothing
RESSORT SPIRAL	Hairspring
ROSKOPH	Dollar Watch
RUBIS	Ruby Jewel
SAVONETTE	Hunting Case
SHAGREEN	Shark or Ray Fish Skins
SPIRAL BREGUET	Overcoil Hairspring
TANGENT SCREW	Endless Screw
TONNEAU	Barrel Shaped
TOUT-OU-RIEN	All-or-Nothing
UHR	Timepiece (German)

Vallee de Joux (Swiss - French cradle of watch making)

8 DAYS = 8 DIAS, 8 CIOANI, 8 JOURS, 8 TAGE

The following will explain the French days of the week abbreviations, Sunday =**DIM** (Dimanche), Monday = **LUN** (Lundi), Tuesday = **MAR** (Mardi), Wednesday = **MER** (Mercedi), Thursday = **JEU** (Jeudi), Friday = **VEN** (Vendredi), Saturday = **SAM** (Samedi).

Left: Rack & pinion lever escapement with a STRAIGHT HAIRSPRING **K**, main- wheel **A** has 30 teeth, center wheel **B** has 96 teeth, 3rd wheel **C** has 96 teeth, 4th wheel **M** is also the escape wheel. In 1722 Abbe' d' Hautefeuille patented this unique rack and pinion lever escapement.

Right: Litherland's type rack & pinion lever escapement, **A** fusee main-wheel drives pinion **B** of center wheel **C**, the third wheel **F** drives pinion **G**, **H** is the 4th or escape wheel. The adjustable sliding block **N** carry the pivot holes for the lever arbor **M** & depth of lever and escape wheel can be varied.

VARIOUS FORK ACTIONS

(1.) Savage 2 pin, **G** is for unlocking, the pin at **F** delivers impulse. (2.) **F** on the spring fork prevents breaking of the impulse jewel **G** when the impulse jewel travels a full circle. (3.) The interior of the fork is cylindrical shell of gold. (4, 5, & 6) Different forms of Louis Huguenin Patents.

Albert Potter's One Tooth Escape Wheel Lever (Ca.1887)

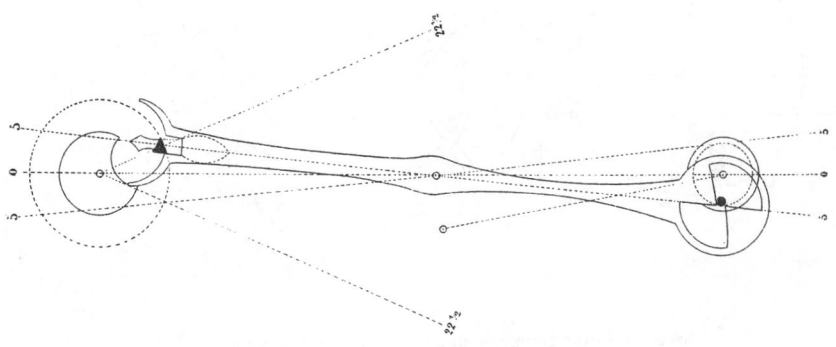

Escapement By MacDowall with one tooth escape Wheel (Ca.1851)

Important Note: I, Cooksey Shugart acquired the *Major Paul M. Chamberlain* original hand drawn mechanical drawings of escapements used in his BOOK **"Its About Time"**. A choice collection which fits in with my other drawings, horological images, illustrations and reference library of horology. I am **BUYING** and would be grateful to hear from anyone that may be considering the sale of antiquarian horological drawings, horological images, catalogs, illustrations and old books on horology.

One Jewel Pallet Lever By Edouard Bourquin (Ca. 1875)

Inverted Lever Escapement By Girard - Perregaux (Ca. 1886)

Note: Escapements may be classified into **2** categories **Frictional** & **Detached**. (**1**.) Frictional Rest Escapements example: Verge, Virgule, Duplex and Cylinder. (**2**.) Detached or Free Escapements example: Lever Escapements, Detent Escapements also combination of lever, Detent and Rotating Escapement as Karrusel and Tourbillon. *Frictional Escapements* the escape wheel is in contact with the balance staff or a part of it during the complete oscillation of the balance. *Detached or Free Escapements* have an arrangement where the escape teeth wheel are arrested for unlocking & impulse & then made free. Thus the Balance can rotate an arc of an oscillation with complete freedom.

C.V. Woerd patented Escapement. Note: Square Impulse Roller Jewel (L), Pat. in 1887.

Seconds Beating Watch Escapement by Joseph Jeunet of Pennsylvania, Pat. in 1858. Note: B is the escape wheel with 60 teeth, H is hairspring and D is balance wheel.

Important Note: I, Cooksey Shugart acquired the *Major Paul M. Chamberlain* original hand drawn mechanical drawings of escapements used in his BOOK **"Its About Time"**. A choice collection which fits in with my other drawings, horological images, illustrations and reference library of horology. I am **BUYING** and would be grateful to hear from anyone that may be considering the sale of antiquarian horological drawings, horological images, catalogs, illustrations and old books on horology.

Left is Example of **Detent** Escapement By Arnold, Chas. Frodsham.

Right is Example of a Pivoted or Bascule Escapement by James Nardin.

Note: Escapements may be classified into **2** categories **Frictional** & **Detached**. (**1**.) Frictional Rest Escapements example: Verge, Virgule, Duplex and Cylinder. (**2**.) Detached or Free Escapements example: Lever Escapements, Detent Escapements also combination of lever, Detent and Rotating Escapement as Karrusel and Tourbillon. *Frictional Escapements* the escape wheel is in contact with the balance staff or a part of it during the complete oscillation of the balance. *Detached or Free Escapements* have an arrangement where the escape teeth wheel are arrested for unlocking & impulse & then made free. Thus the Balance can rotate an arc of an oscillation with complete freedom.

Detent Escapement by George P. Reed Pat. April 1868. Note one spring performs the function of gold spring and locking spring.

English and engraved on movement "Patent Union Chronometer".

Left: Fleurier style Duplex Escapement.   Right: English style Duplex Escapement.
Below: Chinese style Duplex Escapement.

Pinion A drives escape wheels B and B′ through gears C and C′. The escape wheel B is locked on D. The locking point D is about to be unlocked by the balance through the ruby pin H and fork K. The tooth following B will deliver impulse to the balance through E, and the tooth B″ will lock on D. In the return of the balance, impulse will be delivered in opposite direction through F, acted on by tooth following B″.

Above: Breguets Ecsapement he called "NATUREL".

Breguet Hanging Ruby Cylinder (C), Parachute shock absorber (E) and Temperature device (F).

Breguet Lateral Lever Escapement.

Arnold Chronometer Detent Escapement, Pat. in 1782 and Helical balance spring (L), Pat. in 1776.

Right: Robin Escapement with Anti-overbanking,
note unusual form of fork with two springs E & F.

Left: Robin escapement with Duplex escape wheel.

Right: Typical Robin escapement.

Left: Robin escapement, requires over a full turn for locking &
unlocking.

Glashütter
Anker-Hemmung

Glashutter = Glashutte, Anker = Pallets and Lever, Hemmung = Escapement.
Note: The One Banking Pin in lever.

Échappement à force constante.

Above: Constant Force Escapement.

M. B. Pray cylinder escapement, the escape wheel is all in one plane.

Peto's Chronometer Escapement, C is similar to a Gold spring and E is similar to passing spring.

Two pin style Savage escapement.

One Banking Pin.

Above: Savage two pin style escapement and note it has one banking pin.

THE ART OF MICRO-MECHANICAL MARVELS

There is a breed of self employed independent watchmakers, the Breguet's of today who represent the ultimate in the micro-mechanical watchmaking art. They dare to be different and make watches totally from "scratch". I would ask you to reflect on just what it takes to make, from scratch, a simple watch component, as a screw, each screw has to be turned, the thread cut, the head slit, it must be hardened, tempered and polished. These watches take a wide range of skills and typically 2,000 to 4,000 + hours for one watch to be made. The product of these watchmakers are not widely advertised, they do not have a marketing or distribution organization. Not all of their watches are beyond the range of the true collector and should be the aim of some advanced collector, for good value in todays market as compared to "high end" luxury first tier elite brands. Who are some of these one of a kind watchmakers of today, George Daniels, Derek Pratt, Phillipe Dufour, Christopher Claret, and others. For those watch collectors who may want to focus more on these one of a kind watches, may see some of the watchmakers, who exhibit their watches at the AHI booth (Academy of Independent Horologist) at the Basel Fair each year in Switzerland.

NOTE: With some of the elite brands a ebauche movement is used, for their "limited editions" watches, even though they are highly finished and use high quality materials. These "high end" luxury first tier elite brands, "limited editions" watches do not reflect the cost saving that is usually achieved through manufacturing production.

Dr. George Daniels, the greatest living watchmaker and Abraham-Louis Breguet the greatest watchmaker of all time. George Daniels is really worth meeting, as I did, on May 29th, 1997, at his home on the Isle of Man. A group of us (The Time Trippers) talked with him about watches and visited with Mr. Daniels as we lunched in his garden verandah. He was gracious enough to show his workshop, also his stable of vintage cars and motorcycles. "Making watches came to me as naturally as music did to Mozart", observed George Daniels. At the early age of five he had taken his father's alarm clock apart to see how it worked. By the age of 10, he was repairing watches to earn a little pocket money. He was forced to leave school and earn his keep as a factory worker, he lasted about a week, then started to work as a grocery delivery boy. Pedaling his bicycle gave him such a feeling of freedom, he swore to never work again at something he hated

so much. He read every book he could lay his hands on regarding watchmaking while making a living at repairing all types of timepieces and also while in uniform. By the age of 22, he purchased a basic set of tools and set up a shop to repair and restore watches. After World War II, he studied horology in Clerkenwell, London along with related subjects such as math, physics, and geometry. Over the years he worked on a large number of original Breguets giving him a insider's look and knowledge of "The Art of Breguet" which he Authored and Published into a book. He grew tired of simply restoring old master timepieces so in 1967 he designed a watch and made each component and virtually every part of each first watch himself. How many watches has he made in well over a quarter of a century? Less than 80! In 1978 he makes a

George Daniels CO-AXIAL escapement wrist watch with every part individually hand finished and assembled.

Gold-cased one-minute tourbillon with his co-axial escapement (not requiring oil). In the period 1980 to 1996 he used swiss-made wrist watches and converted them to his co-axial escapement, he used Omega, Zenith, Rolex and Patek Philippe watches. Overriding all was Georges Daniels 25 year quest for a lower friction escapement, his success and the years long battle to gain a reluctant Swiss acceptance culminating in the Omega model. Omega introduced a limited edition of 6,000 watches featuring the co-axial escapement in 1998& sold for $6,600.00.

"The co-axial escapement is the first practical new watch escapement in the 250 years following the invention of the lever escapement by Thomas Mudge in the 18th century. It fulfills all the requirements of a precision watch escapement with the advantage of robust reliability and close precision rate for long term performance. In its present form the co-axial represents the culmination of 20 years of development of the watch escapement. It is intended to sustain the public affection for the mechanical watch during the 21st century". (**George Daniels**)

Dr. Daniels made a small number (about 50) of exquisite co-axial wrist watches at his shop on the Isle of Man with the help of Roger Smith. These wrist watches sold for over $50,000.00. The Time Trippers were again at the Daniels work shop (Aug. 7th, 1999) to see Mr. Smith at work on the co-axial wrist watches. On yet a another trip to London (Apr. 5th, 2000) at the Worshipful Company of Clock Makers we saw two lucky Time Trippers receive their co-axial wrist watch from George Danials. The George Daniels CO-AXIAL escapement wrist watch with every part individually hand finished and assembled. The Omega ebauche is specially prepared and supplied to Mr. Daniels. All other components are made by hand for each watch. The movement is self-winding with gilded plates and blued screws. The watch is fitted with Daniels Co-axail escapement and free sprung balance with adjusting screws. The 18K gold guilloche winding weight keeps the mainspring wound when in use. The dials are sterling silver and finished with three differing guilloche surfaces. The chapter and calendar rings are of 18K gold and hand engraved. The 18K gold hands are saw cut from raw material, filed to shape and hand finished. The case is 18K gold and fitted with a sapphire crystal to front and back. The hand setting crown is machined from 18K gold, as is, the hallmarked buckle.

Diagram of the Co-Axial escapement

The escapement is composed of an intermediary wheel A, a double Co-axial wheel B consisting of escapement pinion C and escapement wheel D, pallets E with 3 ruby pallet-stones F,G,H and a roller I carrying a ruby impulse stone J and a ruby impulse pin K. The roller is fitted to the sprung balance. The energy is transmitted to the oscillator in both clockwise and anti-clockwise vibrations. In the Co-axial escapement, the clockwise impulse is delivered to the oscillator directly by the escape wheel engaging the balance roller. The anti-clockwise pulse is delivered to the balance roller via the lever. After each impulse, the escape wheel is locked stationary by the lever locking pallets allowing the balance to complete its vibration undisturbed. (*"ALL IN GOOD TIME"* is Dr. George Daniels latest book, a Reflection of a Watchmaker). See George Daniels 8 page WEB site at WWW.DANIELS-LONDON.CO.UK.

Since the inception of wearable timepieces, watchmakers have been faced with the problem of gravity and its effect on the escapement and hence upon the time keeping quality of the watch itself. It must therefore be considered one of the most difficult horological compilation to overcome in watchmaking. A pocket watch was made by Derek Pratt and a wrist watch by Philippe Dufour, using two different approaches to the difficult escapement "error".

Derek Pratt a senior watchmaker of Urban Jurgensen & Sonner completed the pocket watch in 4,300 hours of work between 1981 and 1982. This example of a individual made pocket watch indicating full seconds (jumping seconds) with a carriage-mounted tourbillon incorporating a **one second remontoir** also a twin mainspring barrel and a state of wind indicator. The skeletonized variant of the tourbillon offers maximum visibility of the tourbillon carriage and the twin barrels. Mr. Pratt lives in Switzerland. The Author was privileged to have dinner meetings with Derek Pratt on several occasions.

Right: The carriage-mounted tourbillon incorporating a **one second remontoir**, which ensures that the optimum balance amplitude is maintained and inertia problems of accelerating and decelerating the carriage are fundamentally eliminated.

Above left: A view of **Derek Pratt's** one-minute tourbillon with a one-second remontoire mounted in the carriage and twin barrels also a Differential for the wind indication.

Above right: **Derek Pratt's one-second remontoire** incorporated into the one-minute tourbillon escapement, which ensures that the optimum balance amplitude is maintained and inertia problems of accelerating and decelerating the carriage are fundamentally eliminated.

Philippe Dufour's *"DUALITY"* a wrist watch with a <u>double escapement.</u> The technical aspect double escapement may be deceptive at first glance. A complicated **differential** system is essential for the operation of the two balances and the mutual compensation of the error, which reduces by half the errors caused by the escapement. The double escapement technical characteristics include 2 levers escapement, 2 Gulucydur balances with timing screws, 2 hairsprings and 40 jewels. Mr. Dufour was awarded a prize in 1992 at the Basel Watch Fair for his "Silence, Grand et Petite Sonnerier Minute Repeater" wrist watch and again with the worlds first double escapement wrist watch. Mr. Dufour is established in La Sentier Switzerland in the *"Vallee de Joux"*. The Author was privileged to have lunch with Mr. DuFour also meeting with him at the Basel Watch Fair.

Above right: The differential system and the two escape wheels. The average of 2 is always better than one.

Above: **Philippe Dufour's** *"DUALITY"* wrist watch with a double escapement. The movement has 40 jewels.

Left: The wrist watch movement, a Silence, Grand et Petite Sonnerier, Minute Repeater of Philippe Dufour (also referred to as a clock watch), about 32MM with 35 jewels, Strike reserve of 24 hours, Time reserve 38 hours.

The author first met **Mr.Christophe Claret** of La Chaux-de-Fonds, Switzerland in 1989. Christophe at the age of 16 embarked upon a 4 year training course at the Geneva watchmaking school. He soon began work with a "cabinotier" watchmaker learning many secrets of complicated watches. Christophe soon set up his own workshop and for six years, bought, restored and resold complicated watches. He went on to create his own company making Minute Repeaters and Tourbillon **modules** and his own manufacturing sector of high-level machinery which enables the company to produce mechanical parts and movements.

Below Left: Musical wrist watch movement with music on demand or in passing. The technical features of the musical wrist watch, 39-45 jewel, 20 tines or vibrating strips in the comb for the musical tune. The musical drum has about 150 pins which are set by hand. A musical "Power-Reserve" equivalent to **SIX** tunes of 15 seconds each. A detent, which insures each tune is played from beginning to end thus avoiding a tune from stopping in the middle of the piece. The governor is gold and is visible through the dial. A three position selecting slide making it possible to chose between music on the hour, on demand or opting for silence. The movement has two separate going - barrels, one for music and the other for time which has a 50 hour power reserve. The wrist watch has a three position crown, first position the music is rewound, the second the watch is rewound and the third is for setting the hands.

BRIDGE IN THE STYLE OF CHARLES X WATCHES

VISUAL ASPECT ENHANCED BY THE GEARS FOR THE HANDS FITTED ON THE DIAL SIDE

GOING BARREL WITH 110-HOUR POWER-RESERVE

PIVOTING ON RUBIES OR BLUE SPINELS MOUNTED IN GOLD BUSHINGS

ADJUSTED FIVE POSITIONS

CHRISTOPHE

39 JEWELS

HIDDEN WINDING AND ADJUSTING SYSTEM

BRIDGE AND BOTTOM-PLATE MADE OUT OF SAPPHIRE

1-MINUTE TOURBILLON

BALANCE 21600 VIBR./HOUR

WOLF-TOOTH GEAR-TRAINS WITH CURVED ARMS HAND-CHAMFERED ON BOTH SIDES

CHRISTOPHE CLARET SA La Chaux-de-Fonds

Above Right: One minute tourbillon with wolf-tooth gear-trains and curved arms hand-chamfered on both sides. The movement has a going barrel with a 110 hour power reserve. Christophe Claret, a builder of movements and supplier to prestigious brands, has chosen to work in the shadows. He creates and offers high-end complications and aesthetic viewpoints.

Steven Phillips the inventor of a new **self**-winding system and named it **Eternal Winding System**. I met with Mr. Phillips at the 2003 Basel Fair and we talked about his remarkable invention that will provide perpetual self-winding of a watch. He said that many people have used a thermostat many times but few have thought about now it works. The heart of a thermostat has a bi-metallic strip, and when the coiled strip is heated, the coil will expand and it tends to unwind. When it is cooled it contracts, and the coil tightens. He took this concept of a bi-metallic coil and created a version that fits in the case of a wrist watch. The coil is attached to a planetary gearing system and transfers rotation from the orbit gear that is driven by the outer end of the bi-metallic coil. The power module is attached to his own movement caliber to achieve the Remontoire effect. Mr. Phillips most challenging task was solving the mechanism to convert both clockwise and counterclockwise motion to wind the mainspring. His planetary gear system solved the transfer of motion that winds the mainspring (he called it a wig-wag system). The name of his company is Budapest Watch Co.in Guilford, Connecticut. He was born in Hungary and came to U.S.A. in 1956.

The invention utilizes a temperature sensitive bi-metallic coil, which is restrained from radial deflection and the free end moves to rotate the shaft in the self-winding mechanism and effects self-winging of the timepiece. The free end of the coil will move with change in temperature. The coil is anchored at its inner end and the other end is thereof, upon movement, will drive a driver member in the form of an orbit gear. The orbit gear will drive a plurality of planet gears, which drive a sun gear mounted to a shaft. The shaft of the sun gear then produces rotation of a cam which drives the bi-directional to uni-directional conversion mechanism.

Left: Planetary gearing system that transfers rotation from the temperature sensitive bi-metallic coil. Right: First experimental prototype of Planetary gearing system.

Above: Example of a temperature sensitive bi-metallic coil, left room temperature, right with heat.

ADVERTISE IN THE GUIDE

ATTENTION DEALERS: This book will receive world-wide <u>BOOKSTORE</u> distribution, reaching thousands of people buying & selling watches. It will also be sold directly to THE WATCH COLLECTOR'S MARKET as well. We will be offering limited advertising space in our next edition. Consider advertising in the Guide, as it is an annual publication, your ad will pull all year long or longer. Unlike monthly or quarterly publications, your ad will stay active for years at a *cost savings* to YOU.

PRINTED SIZES
FULL PAGE — 7 1/2 " LONG X 4 3/4" WIDE
HALF PAGE — 3 1/2" LONG X 4 3/4" WIDE
FOURTH PAGE — 1 7/8" LONG X 4 3/4" WIDE

<u>AD RATES</u> ARE SET IN THE LATE SUMMER PRIOR TO EACH EDITION'S RELEASE. CONTACT US FOR AD RATES BETWEEN **(AUGUST & SEPTEMBER)**.

NOTE: Submit your ad on white paper in a version of the actual printed size. We must ask that all ads be neatly & professionally finished, *camera ready.* **FULL PAYMENT** must be sent with all ads. Your ad will be run as received.

 TARGET YOUR MARKET

AD DEAD LINE NEXT EDITION IS - **OCTOBER 15**

This "GUIDE" is the PROFESSIONAL STANDARD and used by collector's and dealer's throughout the world. <u>Do not miss this opportunity to advertise in the guide.</u>

SEND YOUR AD TO:
COOKSEY SHUGART PUBLICATIONS
P. O. BOX 3147
CLEVELAND, TN. 37320-3147
Office: (423) 479-4813 — Fax: (423) 479-4813

WATCH & COLLECTIBLES SHOWS

Now you can attend more affordable Shows. We have several shows planned and need your support. If you're looking for less expensive, well-run, short shows with security, safes and showcases, these shows are for you. Because of the huge success of the past shows and the limited number of tables available, you should make your reservations today!! Send your reservations in advance and save over door prices. To assure the continued success of these shows, please pass the word along to your friends, ask them to meet you there!

We are having shows in:
Orlando, Florida - Oklahoma City, Oklahoma
with more shows planned.

For up-to-date show information please check our website at:
http://www.wwtshows.com
or call us at (810) 220-0011
Monday-Friday 10-5:30 or Saturday 10-5

World Wide Traders
4312 Ridge Rd. Pinckney, Michigan 48169
Email: info@wwtshows.com
Girard Sensoli and Sons
WWT Founder and a NAWCC Member since 1973

Join us at the NAWCC Local Chapter Meeting that never ends!

Enjoy all the features of an NAWCC Chapter Meeting in your own home.

NAWCC INTERNET HOROLOGY CHAPTER 185 provides all the comfort and support of a local chapter for every NAWCC Member. Especially those for whom geography, meeting times, health, or other circumstances have previously precluded involvement in the traditional land-based local chapter structure. Stop by and look us over! Register and take part in our family-friendly watch and clock discussions. Our Discussion Site is unlike anything else anywhere!

Join us on the Internet at our NAWCC Chapter Meeting that never ends!

nawcc-ihc.org

Lindell V. Riddle, Chapter 185 Founder and President

Call me directly (440) 461-0167 or eMail at: nawcc-ihc@adelphia.net

Internet Horology Chapter 185 co-hosts the NAWCC North-Coast Regional at Strongsville, in Northern Ohio near America's Progressive North-Coast in association with Lake Erie Chapter 28 and Ohio Valley Chapter 10

We all look forward to seeing you there in March!

TIME IS VALUABLE . . .
AND SO ARE THE BENEFITS
OF AWI MEMBERSHIP

The American Watchmakers-Clockmakers Institute (AWI) is the premier international organization dedicated to preserving and promoting the highest standards of workmanship in the horological crafts. It is the role of AWI to set the standard of excellence to be applied to the quality of instruction for both the restoration and repair practices that are taught worldwide.

Membership Benefits

- *Horological Times* monthly magazine
- Traveling Bench Courses
- Professional Certification Program
- Continuing Education Courses
- Home Study Course in Clock Repair
- Technial Support
- Yahoo Group *AWI Matters*

- Health & Benefits Insurance Program
- AWI Referral Directory
- Industry Advisory Board
- Henry B. Fried Lending Library
- Horological Books, DVDs & Videos
- Horological Museum
- AWI Affiliate & Theme Chapters

It's the ultimate time share.

Founded in 1943, the National Association of Watch and Clock Collectors, Inc. (NAWCC) is a nonprofit scientific organization that serves as a unique educational, cultural, and social resource for its membership and the public at large.

Members include hobbyists, students, educators, casual collectors, and professionals in related retail and manufacturing trades. The one common bond is a fascination with the art and science of timekeeping (horology).

514 Poplar St., Columbia, PA
Ph: 717-684-8261 • www.nawcc.org

The National
ASSOCIATION OF
WATCH & CLOCK
Collectors, Inc.

Don't waste another minute— join today!

Join the NAWCC now and receive these great benefits:

- Six issues a year of the NAWCC BULLETIN and the MART, plus admission to Assoc. "marts" nationwide.
- Local chapter activities, special meetings, seminars, and more.
- FREE NAWCC Library & Research Center access— on campus, via mail, or at www.nawcc.org .
- Complimentary admission to the National Watch and Clock Museum® in Columbia, PA.
- Plus much more!

Mail the Application below and start enjoying your NAWCC Membership benefits today!

Name

Address

City   State/Country   Zip

Phone *home* (   )   *work* (   )

Fax (   )   E-mail

Sponsor **Cooksey Shugart** Member # **23843**

Are you a former NAWCC member? Yes No   If yes, #

Charge my   ❏ MasterCard   ❏ VISA   ❏ Discover Card   ❏ American Express

Card #   Exp. (mo/yr)

Signature of Card Holder   Amt $

Enclose with remittance and send to:
NAWCC, Inc., 514 Poplar St., Columbia, PA 17512-2130
(717) 684-8261 • Fax: (717) 684-0878 • www.nawcc.org

New members: U.S. **$60.00** (First Year); International **$55.00**; U.S. Renewal **$50.00**. Additional membership for spouse/significant other or child under 18 (no publication subscriptions): **$10.00** per year. **Payment**: U.S. funds drawn on a U.S. bank, International Money Order, or VISA, MasterCard, Discover, or American Express.

PIERCE
BROSNAN'S CHOICE

SEAMASTER

Since 1948, the Omega Seamaster has been involved in many of man's most demanding adventures, earning itself a reputation for its precision, endurance and distinctive design. As a connoisseur of the finer things in life, Pierce Brosnan naturally relies on his Seamaster to accompany him wherever he dares to venture.

John D Huntley

313 B. South College Ave
College Station, TX 77840
(979) 846-8916

Since 1972

www.omegawatches.com